W9-DFY-147

DISCARDED
Goshen Public Library

GOSHEN PUBLIC LIBRARY
601 SOUTH FIFTH STREET
GOSHEN, IN 46526

FOURTH EDITION

New Guide *for* Occupational Exploration

LINKING INTERESTS, LEARNING, AND CAREERS

[MICHAEL FARR]   [LAURENCE SHATKIN, PH.D.]

GOSHEN PUBLIC LIBRARY
601 SOUTH FIFTH STREET
GOSHEN, IN 46526

Works
America's Career Publisher

New Guide for Occupational Exploration, Fourth Edition
Linking Interests, Learning, and Careers

© 2006 by JIST Publishing, Inc.

Previous edition was titled *Guide for Occupational Exploration,* Third Edition

Published by JIST Works, an imprint of JIST Publishing, Inc.
8902 Otis Avenue
Indianapolis, IN 46216-1033

Phone: 1-800-648-JIST   Fax: 1-800-JIST-FAX
E-mail: info@jist.com   Web site: www.jist.com

Quantity discounts are available for JIST products. Please call 1-800-648-JIST or visit www.jist.com for a free catalog and more information. Developers wanting to use the GOE structure should see the appendix for more information. Call 1-800-648-JIST for information about custom publishing using GOE content.

Visit www.jist.com for information on JIST, free job search information, book excerpts, and ordering information on our many products. For free information on 14,000 job titles, visit www.careeroink.com.

Acquisitions Editor: Susan Pines
Content Advisor: Eleanor Dietrich
Development Editor: Stephanie Koutek
Cover and Interior Designer: Aleata Howard
Interior Layout: Carolyn J. Newland
Indexer: Carolyn J. Newland

Printed in the United States of America

10 09 08 07 06 05   9 8 7 6 5 4 3 2 1

Library of Congress Cataloging-in-Publication Data

Farr, J. Michael.
    New guide for occupational exploration : linking interests, learning, and
    careers / Michael Farr, Laurence Shatkin.— 4th ed.
        p. cm.
    Previous ed. published as: Guide for occupational exploration. Indianapolis,
    IN : Jist Works, 2001.
    Includes bibliographical references and index.
    ISBN 1-59357-179-8 (softcover : alk. paper) — ISBN 1-59357-180-1 (hardcover
    : alk. paper)
    1. Occupations—United States. 2. Vocational interests—United States. 3.
    Vocational guidance—United States. I. Shatkin, Laurence. II. Guide for
    occupational exploration. III. Title.
    HF5382.5.U5F37 2006
    331.702'0973—dc22   2005017637

All rights reserved. No part of this book may be reproduced in any form or by any means, or stored in a database or retrieval system, without prior permission of the publisher except in the case of brief quotations embodied in articles or reviews. Making copies of any part of this book for any purpose other than your own personal use is a violation of United States copyright laws. For permission requests, please contact the Copyright Clearance Center at www.copyright.com or (978) 750-8400.

We have been careful to provide accurate information throughout this book, but it is possible that errors and omissions have been introduced. Please consider this in making any career plans or other important decisions. Trust your own judgment above all else and in all things.

Trademarks: All brand names and product names used in this book are trade names, service marks, trademarks, or registered trademarks of their respective owners.

ISBN 1-59357-179-8 Softcover
ISBN 1-59357-180-1 Hardcover

This Is a Big Book, But It's Easy to Use

Despite its size, this is an easy book to use. Through a unique format, it helps you uncover your career interests, match your interests to jobs, and plan your education and future.

In Part 1, you drill down to your most appealing job groups through questions that provide a feel for the work and whether it will interest you. Specific jobs are listed for each job group.

In Part 2, more than 900 job descriptions from the U.S. Department of Labor emphasize skills needed, related courses, education required, earnings, growth, and more, all for helpful career-path planning.

So, although this book contains a great deal of information, it's not meant to be read all the way through.

Here are three suggestions for quickly getting started with this book:

1. **Read the Quick Summary of Major Sections on page v.** It includes short descriptions of the major parts and tips on how to use them.

2. **Identify One or More Interest Areas.** This book organizes jobs into just 16 Interest Areas. The Interest Areas and the jobs are listed in the table of contents. Use the table of contents to quickly find job groups and specific jobs related to your interests. For example, do you have an interest in art? The table of contents will help you identify numerous job possibilities. Easy.

3. **Dig in as Deeply as You Want.** Part 1 asks you insightful questions for job groupings (called "Work Groups") so that you can determine your interest level in them. Part 2 provides information-packed descriptions for more than 900 jobs in each Work Group to help you explore career and related learning options.

This Edition Introduces a New Structure for the GOE

The original *Guide for Occupational Exploration* was developed in the 1970s by the U.S. Department of Labor to provide a user-friendly way to help people explore career options based on their interests.

History of Past Editions

The first-edition *GOE* was published in 1979. A second edition, which included major additional content, was released in 1984 by Thomas Harrington and Arthur O'Shea. Related books, titled *The Complete Guide for Occupational Exploration* and *The Enhanced Guide for Occupational Exploration,* improved on the first two editions of the *GOE.* These books, by Michael Farr, Marilyn Maze, and Donald Mayall, used the original GOE structure.

Then, in 2001, JIST published a third edition that reorganized the GOE's basic structure to reflect the many changes in jobs and our economy since the 1970s—for example, the growth of computer-related occupations. The third edition also broke new ground by using occupational information from the O*NET (Occupational Information Network) database of the U.S. Department of Labor.

Highlights of Changes in This Edition

With this *New Guide for Occupational Exploration,* Fourth Edition, we adopt a structure that combines the new with the tried and true. What is new is our use of 16 Interest Areas in place of the 14 that were used in the previous edition. But these 16 Interest Areas are actually tried and true in that they are based on the 16 career clusters that were developed by the U.S. Department of Education's Office of Vocational and Adult Education around 1999 and that are used by many states to organize their career-oriented programs and career information. So, this book closely links interests and careers to learning, which is an important foundation for success in the work world.

To simplify and speed career research, we use a two-tiered structure—Interest Areas and Work Groups—in place of the more confusing three-tiered structure of previous editions, which also included Subgroups. At the same time, some of the 117 Work Groups in this edition are carried over with minor changes from the third edition of the *GOE*. A new section in each Work Group lists careers available at different education and training levels.

As in the third edition, we include descriptions of every job in the GOE structure but have added information on projected number of job openings, education and training programs, and related courses. We put the job descriptions in alphabetical order within Work Groups rather than in O*NET number order for greater clarity.

A new crosswalk connects military occupations to GOE Work Groups, which helps veterans link military experience to jobs.

We think this edition builds on the strengths of previous editions and therefore is the most useful GOE ever. In fact, we added "new" to the book's title to emphasize these major changes and improvements.

If you have any suggestions for the next revision (which we will consider, once we recover from this one), please contact us through the publisher at info@jist.com or via mail to JIST's address on page ii.

We wish you well in your career and your life.

Mike Farr
Laurence Shatkin

To Occupational Systems Developers Who Want to Use the New GOE Structure

This edition introduces many changes to the GOE's original structure of Interest Areas and Work Groups. If you want to use this revised structure in your own publications or databases, we encourage you to do so and are making it easy for you to use. Please refer to the appendix for additional details.

© 2006 JIST Works

Quick Summary of Major Sections

Introduction. The introduction explains the major parts of the book and gives tips on how best to use it for exploring career options. *The introduction begins on page 1.*

Part 1. GOE Interest Areas and Work Groups: Essential Information for Exploring Career Options. Start with this part because it provides useful information for exploring career and learning options, including Interest Area and Work Group descriptions, kinds of work done, things about you that point to this work, skills and knowledge needed, and specific job titles along with levels of education and training. *Part 1 begins on page 27.*

Part 2. The Job Descriptions. Read brief, information-packed descriptions for the more than 900 jobs listed in Part 1. *Part 2 begins on page 225.*

Part 3. Crosswalks to Careers by Work Values, Leisure Activities, School Subjects, Work Settings, Skills, Abilities, Knowledges, and Military Occupations. These tables help you explore career options by work values, leisure activities, school subjects, work settings, skills, abilities, knowledges, and military occupations. Use these cross-references to find jobs that best suit your interests and past experiences. *Part 3 begins on page 467.*

Appendix. Information for Vocational Counselors and Other Professionals. The appendix contains information for developers who want to use the new GOE structure in their products, plus tips for career counselors using the GOE. *The appendix begins on page 537.*

Index. Use this alphabetic listing to locate the jobs, Interest Areas, and Work Groups described in this book. *The index begins on page 543.*

Table of Contents

This table of contents provides a quick way to identify Work Groups in Part 1 that are most likely to interest you. The 16 GOE Interest Areas are in large, bold letters preceded by a two-digit code number. Below each Interest Area are its related Work Groups. Work Groups have four-digit code numbers, with the first two numbers referring to the Interest Area. A listing of jobs in Part 2 (along with their O*NET numbers) by Interest Area and Work Group follows.

Part 1. GOE Interest Areas and Work Groups: Essential Information for Exploring Career Options 27

01 Agriculture and Natural Resources 29

01.01 Managerial Work in Agriculture and Natural Resources 30
01.02 Resource Science/Engineering for Plants, Animals, and the Environment.........................32
01.03 Resource Technologies for Plants, Animals, and the Environment 33
01.04 General Farming 35
01.05 Nursery, Groundskeeping, and Pest Control 36
01.06 Forestry and Logging 37
01.07 Hunting and Fishing................................38
01.08 Mining and Drilling 39

02 Architecture and Construction 42

02.01 Managerial Work in Architecture and Construction 43
02.02 Architectural Design 44
02.03 Architecture/Construction Engineering Technologies 45
02.04 Construction Crafts 47
02.05 Systems and Equipment Installation, Maintenance, and Repair 49
02.06 Construction Support/Labor 50

03 Arts and Communication 53

03.01 Managerial Work in Arts and Communication 54
03.02 Writing and Editing 55
03.03 News, Broadcasting, and Public Relations 57
03.04 Studio Art 58

03.05 Design 59
03.06 Drama 61
03.07 Music 62
03.08 Dance 63
03.09 Media Technology 65
03.10 Communications Technology 66
03.11 Musical Instrument Repair 67

04 Business and Administration 69

04.01 Managerial Work in General Business 70
04.02 Managerial Work in Business Detail 71
04.03 Human Resources Support 73
04.04 Secretarial Support 74
04.05 Accounting, Auditing, and Analytical Support 76
04.06 Mathematical Clerical Support 77
04.07 Records and Materials Processing ...79
04.08 Clerical Machine Operation 80

05 Education and Training 82

05.01 Managerial Work in Education 83
05.02 Preschool, Elementary, and Secondary Teaching and Instructing 84
05.03 Postsecondary and Adult Teaching and Instructing 86
05.04 Library Services 88
05.05 Archival and Museum Services 89
05.06 Counseling, Health, and Fitness Education 91

06 Finance and Insurance 93

06.01 Managerial Work in Finance and Insurance 94
06.02 Finance/Insurance Investigation and Analysis 95
06.03 Finance/Insurance Records Processing 97
06.04 Finance/Insurance Customer Service 98
06.05 Finance/Insurance Sales and Support 99

07 Government and Public Administration 101

07.01 Managerial Work in Government and Public Administration 102
07.02 Public Planning 103
07.03 Regulations Enforcement 104
07.04 Public Administration Clerical Support 106

08 Health Science 108

08.01 Managerial Work in Medical and Health Services 109
08.02 Medicine and Surgery 110
08.03 Dentistry 113
08.04 Health Specialties 114
08.05 Animal Care 116
08.06 Medical Technology 118
08.07 Medical Therapy 120
08.08 Patient Care and Assistance 121
08.09 Health Protection and Promotion 123

09 Hospitality, Tourism, and Recreation 125

09.01 Managerial Work in Hospitality and Tourism 126
09.02 Recreational Services 127
09.03 Hospitality and Travel Services 129
09.04 Food and Beverage Preparation 130
09.05 Food and Beverage Service 131
09.06 Sports 132
09.07 Barber and Beauty Services 134

10 Human Service 136

10.01 Counseling and Social Work 137
10.02 Religious Work 138
10.03 Child/Personal Care and Services ...140
10.04 Client Interviewing 141

11 Information Technology 143

11.01 Managerial Work in Information Technology 144
11.02 Information Technology Specialties ...145
11.03 Digital Equipment Repair 147

12 Law and Public Safety 149

12.01 Managerial Work in Law and Public Safety 150
12.02 Legal Practice and Justice Administration 151
12.03 Legal Support 153
12.04 Law Enforcement and Public Safety 154
12.05 Safety and Security 156
12.06 Emergency Responding 157
12.07 Military 158

© 2006 JIST Works

13 Manufacturing 160

13.01 Managerial Work in Manufacturing...............162
13.02 Machine Setup and Operation 163
13.03 Production Work, Assorted Materials
        Processing 165
13.04 Welding, Brazing, and Soldering 167
13.05 Production Machining Technology 168
13.06 Production Precision Work............................169
13.07 Production Quality Control 171
13.08 Graphic Arts Production 172
13.09 Hands-On Work, Assorted Materials...............174
13.10 Woodworking Technology 175
13.11 Apparel, Shoes, Leather, and Fabric Care 176
13.12 Electrical and Electronic Repair 177
13.13 Machinery Repair 179
13.14 Vehicle and Facility Mechanical Work............180
13.15 Medical and Technical Equipment Repair 182
13.16 Utility Operation and Energy Distribution....183
13.17 Loading, Moving, Hoisting, and Conveying ..185

14 Retail and Wholesale Sales
    and Service 187

14.01 Managerial Work in Retail/Wholesale
        Sales and Service 188
14.02 Technical Sales 189
14.03 General Sales 191
14.04 Personal Soliciting 192
14.05 Purchasing..194
14.06 Customer Service 195

15 Scientific Research, Engineering,
    and Mathematics 197

15.01 Managerial Work in Scientific Research,
        Engineering, and Mathematics 198
15.02 Physical Sciences 199
15.03 Life Sciences 201
15.04 Social Sciences 202
15.05 Physical Science Laboratory Technology........204
15.06 Mathematics and Data Analysis 205
15.07 Research and Design Engineering 207
15.08 Industrial and Safety Engineering.................209
15.09 Engineering Technology................................210

16 Transportation, Distribution,
    and Logistics...213

16.01 Managerial Work in Transportation 214
16.02 Air Vehicle Operation 215
16.03 Truck Driving 216
16.04 Rail Vehicle Operation 218
16.05 Water Vehicle Operation 219
16.06 Other Services Requiring Driving 220
16.07 Transportation Support Work 222

Part 2. The Job Descriptions.............225

01 Agriculture and Natural Resources 227

01.01 Managerial Work in Agriculture and
        Natural Resources 228
    *Agricultural Crop Farm Managers
    11-9011.02* 228
    Farmers and Ranchers 11-9012.00 228
    *First-Line Supervisors and Manager/
    Supervisors—Agricultural Crop Workers
    45-1011.01* 228
    *First-Line Supervisors and Manager/
    Supervisors—Animal Husbandry Workers
    45-1011.02* 229
    *First-Line Supervisors and Manager/
    Supervisors—Extractive Workers 47-1011.02* 229
    *First-Line Supervisors and Manager/
    Supervisors—Fishery Workers 45-1011.06* 229
    *First-Line Supervisors and Manager/
    Supervisors—Horticultural Workers
    45-1011.04* 229
    *First-Line Supervisors and Manager/
    Supervisors—Landscaping Workers
    37-1012.02* 230
    *First-Line Supervisors and Manager/
    Supervisors—Logging Workers 45-1011.05* 230
    Fish Hatchery Managers 11-9011.03 230
    Lawn Service Managers 37-1012.01 230
    *Nursery and Greenhouse Managers
    11-9011.01* 231
    Park Naturalists 19-1031.03 231
    *Purchasing Agents and Buyers, Farm Products
    13-1021.00* 231
01.02 Resource Science/Engineering for Plants,
        Animals, and the Environment.......................232
    Agricultural Engineers 17-2021.00 232
    Animal Scientists 19-1011.00 232
    Environmental Engineers 17-2081.00.................232

Foresters 19-1032.00 232

*Mining and Geological Engineers, Including
Mining Safety Engineers 17-2151.00* 233

Petroleum Engineers 17-2171.00 233

Plant Scientists 19-1013.01 233

Range Managers 19-1031.02 233

Soil Conservationists 19-1031.01 234

Soil Scientists 19-1013.02 234

*Zoologists and Wildlife Biologists
19-1023.00* 234

01.03 Resource Technologies for Plants,
Animals, and the Environment 234

Agricultural Technicians 19-4011.01 234

*Environmental Science and Protection
Technicians, Including Health 19-4091.00* 235

Food Science Technicians 19-4011.02 235

*Food Scientists and Technologists
19-1012.00* 235

Geological Data Technicians 19-4041.01 235

*Geological Sample Test Technicians
19-4041.02* 235

01.04 General Farming 236

*Agricultural Equipment Operators
45-2091.00* 236

*Farmworkers, Farm and Ranch Animals
45-2093.00* 236

General Farmworkers 45-2092.02 236

01.05 Nursery, Groundskeeping, and
Pest Control 237

*Landscaping and Groundskeeping Workers
37-3011.00* 237

Nursery Workers 45-2092.01 237

Pest Control Workers 37-2021.00 237

*Pesticide Handlers, Sprayers, and Applicators,
Vegetation 37-3012.00* 237

Tree Trimmers and Pruners 37-3013.00 237

01.06 Forestry and Logging 238

Fallers 45-4021.00 238

*Forest and Conservation Technicians
19-4093.00* 238

Forest and Conservation Workers 45-4011.00 238

Log Graders and Scalers 45-4023.00 238

Logging Tractor Operators 45-4022.01 239

01.07 Hunting and Fishing 239

*Fishers and Related Fishing Workers
45-3011.00* 239

Hunters and Trappers 45-3021.00 239

01.08 Mining and Drilling 239

Construction Drillers 47-5021.01 239

*Continuous Mining Machine Operators
47-5041.00* 239

Derrick Operators, Oil and Gas 47-5011.00 240

*Excavating and Loading Machine Operators
53-7032.01* 240

*Explosives Workers, Ordnance Handling
Experts, and Blasters 47-5031.00* 240

Helpers—Extraction Workers 47-5081.00 240

*Loading Machine Operators, Underground
Mining 53-7033.00* 240

*Mine Cutting and Channeling Machine
Operators 47-5042.00* 241

Rock Splitters, Quarry 47-5051.00 241

Roof Bolters, Mining 47-5061.00 241

*Rotary Drill Operators, Oil and Gas
47-5012.00* 241

Roustabouts, Oil and Gas 47-5071.00 241

*Service Unit Operators, Oil, Gas, and
Mining 47-5013.00* 242

Shuttle Car Operators 53-7111.00 242

Well and Core Drill Operators 47-5021.02 242

Wellhead Pumpers 53-7073.00 242

02 Architecture and Construction 243

02.01 Managerial Work in Architecture and
Construction 244

Construction Managers 11-9021.00 244

*First-Line Supervisors and Manager/
Supervisors—Construction Trades Workers
47-1011.01* 244

02.02 Architectural Design 244

*Architects, Except Landscape and Naval
17-1011.00* 244

Landscape Architects 17-1012.00 244

02.03 Architecture/Construction Engineering
Technologies 245

Architectural Drafters 17-3011.01 245

Civil Drafters 17-3011.02 245

*Construction and Building Inspectors
47-4011.00* 245

Electrical Drafters 17-3012.02 245

Surveyors 17-1022.00 246

02.04 Construction Crafts 246

Boat Builders and Shipwrights 47-2031.05 246

Boilermakers 47-2011.00 246

Brattice Builders 47-2031.06 246

© 2006 JIST Works

Brickmasons and Blockmasons 47-2021.00 247

Carpet Installers 47-2041.00 247

Ceiling Tile Installers 47-2081.01 247

Cement Masons and Concrete Finishers 47-2051.00 247

Commercial Divers 49-9092.00 248

Construction Carpenters 47-2031.01 248

Crane and Tower Operators 53-7021.00 248

Dragline Operators 53-7032.02 248

Drywall Installers 47-2081.02 248

Electricians 47-2111.00 249

Fence Erectors 47-4031.00 249

Floor Layers, Except Carpet, Wood, and Hard Tiles 47-2042.00 249

Floor Sanders and Finishers 47-2043.00 249

Glaziers 47-2121.00 249

Grader, Bulldozer, and Scraper Operators 47-2073.01 249

Hazardous Materials Removal Workers 47-4041.00 250

Insulation Workers, Floor, Ceiling, and Wall 47-2131.00 250

Insulation Workers, Mechanical 47-2132.00 250

Manufactured Building and Mobile Home Installers 49-9095.00 250

Operating Engineers 47-2073.02 250

Painters, Construction and Maintenance 47-2141.00 251

Paperhangers 47-2142.00 251

Paving, Surfacing, and Tamping Equipment Operators 47-2071.00 251

Pile-Driver Operators 47-2072.00 251

Pipe Fitters 47-2152.01 251

Pipelayers 47-2151.00 252

Pipelaying Fitters 47-2152.03 252

Plasterers and Stucco Masons 47-2161.00 252

Plumbers 47-2152.02 252

Rail-Track Laying and Maintenance Equipment Operators 47-4061.00 252

Refractory Materials Repairers, Except Brickmasons 49-9045.00 253

Reinforcing Iron and Rebar Workers 47-2171.00 253

Riggers 49-9096.00 253

Roofers 47-2181.00 253

Rough Carpenters 47-2031.02 253

Security and Fire Alarm Systems Installers 49-2098.00 254

Segmental Pavers 47-4091.00 254

Sheet Metal Workers 47-2211.00 254

Ship Carpenters and Joiners 47-2031.04 254

Stone Cutters and Carvers 51-9195.03 254

Stonemasons 47-2022.00 255

Structural Iron and Steel Workers 47-2221.00 255

Tapers 47-2082.00 255

Terrazzo Workers and Finishers 47-2053.00 255

Tile and Marble Setters 47-2044.00 255

02.05 Systems and Equipment Installation, Maintenance, and Repair 256

Central Office and PBX Installers and Repairers 49-2022.01 256

Communication Equipment Mechanics, Installers, and Repairers 49-2022.03 256

Electric Meter Installers and Repairers 49-9012.01 256

Electrical and Electronics Repairers, Powerhouse, Substation, and Relay 49-2095.00 256

Electrical Power-Line Installers and Repairers 49-9051.00 256

Elevator Installers and Repairers 47-4021.00 257

Frame Wirers, Central Office 49-2022.02 257

Heating and Air Conditioning Mechanics 49-9021.01 257

Home Appliance Installers 49-9031.01 257

Maintenance and Repair Workers, General 49-9042.00 258

Meter Mechanics 49-9012.03 258

Refrigeration Mechanics 49-9021.02 258

Station Installers and Repairers, Telephone 49-2022.05 258

Telecommunications Facility Examiners 49-2022.04 258

Telecommunications Line Installers and Repairers 49-9052.00 259

02.06 Construction Support/Labor 259

Carpenter Assemblers and Repairers 47-2031.03 259

Construction Laborers 47-2061.00 259

Grips and Set-Up Workers, Motion Picture Sets, Studios, and Stages 53-7062.02 259

Helpers—Brickmasons, Blockmasons, Stonemasons, and Tile and Marble Setters 47-3011.00 260

Helpers—Carpenters 47-3012.00 260

Helpers—Electricians 47-3013.00 260

Helpers—Installation, Maintenance, and
Repair Workers 49-9098.00 260

Helpers—Painters, Paperhangers, Plasterers,
and Stucco Masons 47-3014.00 260

Helpers—Pipelayers, Plumbers, Pipefitters,
and Steamfitters 47-3015.00 261

Highway Maintenance Workers 47-4051.00 261

Septic Tank Servicers and Sewer Pipe
Cleaners 47-4071.00 261

03 Arts and Communication 262

03.01 Managerial Work in Arts and
Communication 263

Agents and Business Managers of Artists,
Performers, and Athletes 13-1011.00 263

Art Directors 27-1011.00 263

Producers 27-2012.01 263

Program Directors 27-2012.03 263

Public Relations Managers 11-2031.00 264

Technical Directors/Managers 27-2012.05 264

03.02 Writing and Editing 264

Copy Writers 27-3043.04 264

Creative Writers 27-3043.02................................264

Editors 27-3041.00 265

Poets and Lyricists 27-3043.01 265

Technical Writers 27-3042.00 265

03.03 News, Broadcasting, and Public Relations 265

Broadcast News Analysts 27-3021.00 265

Caption Writers 27-3043.03................................265

Interpreters and Translators 27-3091.00 266

Public Relations Specialists 27-3031.00 266

Reporters and Correspondents 27-3022.00 266

03.04 Studio Art 267

Cartoonists 27-1013.03 267

Craft Artists 27-1012.00 267

Painters and Illustrators 27-1013.01 267

Potters 51-9195.05 267

Sculptors 27-1013.04...267

Sketch Artists 27-1013.02 268

03.05 Design 268

Commercial and Industrial Designers
27-1021.00 268

Exhibit Designers 27-1027.02 268

Fashion Designers 27-1022.00 268

Floral Designers 27-1023.00 269

Graphic Designers 27-1024.00 269

Interior Designers 27-1025.00.............................269

Merchandise Displayers and Window
Trimmers 27-1026.00 269

Set Designers 27-1027.01 269

03.06 Drama 270

Actors 27-2011.00 270

Costume Attendants 39-3092.00 270

Directors—Stage, Motion Pictures, Television,
and Radio 27-2012.02 270

Makeup Artists, Theatrical and Performance
39-5091.00 270

Public Address System and Other Announcers
27-3012.00 270

Radio and Television Announcers 27-3011.00....271

03.07 Music 271

Composers 27-2041.03 271

Music Arrangers and Orchestrators
27-2041.02 271

Music Directors 27-2041.01 271

Musicians, Instrumental 27-2042.02 271

Singers 27-2042.01 272

Talent Directors 27-2012.04 272

03.08 Dance 272

Choreographers 27-2032.00 272

Dancers 27-2031.00 272

03.09 Media Technology.......................................272

Audio and Video Equipment Technicians
27-4011.00 272

Broadcast Technicians 27-4012.00 273

Camera Operators, Television, Video, and
Motion Picture 27-4031.00 273

Film and Video Editors 27-4032.00 273

Multi-Media Artists and Animators
27-1014.00 273

Photographic Hand Developers 51-9131.03 274

Photographic Reproduction Technicians
51-9131.02 274

Photographic Retouchers and Restorers
51-9131.01 274

Professional Photographers 27-4021.01 274

Radio Operators 27-4013.00 274

Sound Engineering Technicians 27-4014.00 275

03.10 Communications Technology 275

Air Traffic Controllers 53-2021.00 275

Airfield Operations Specialists 53-2022.00........275

Central Office Operators 43-2021.02 275

Directory Assistance Operators 43-2021.01 275

Dispatchers, Except Police, Fire, and
Ambulance 43-5032.00 276

© 2006 JIST Works

Police, Fire, and Ambulance Dispatchers 43-5031.00 276

03.11 Musical Instrument Repair 276

Keyboard Instrument Repairers and Tuners 49-9063.01 276

Percussion Instrument Repairers and Tuners 49-9063.04 276

Reed or Wind Instrument Repairers and Tuners 49-9063.03 277

Stringed Instrument Repairers and Tuners 49-9063.02 277

04 Business and Administration 278

04.01 Managerial Work in General Business 279

Chief Executives 11-1011.00 279

Compensation and Benefits Managers 11-3041.00 279

General and Operations Managers 11-1021.00 279

Human Resources Managers 11-3040.00 279

Private Sector Executives 11-1011.02 279

Training and Development Managers 11-3042.00 280

04.02 Managerial Work in Business Detail 280

Administrative Services Managers 11-3011.00 280

First-Line Supervisors, Administrative Support 43-1011.02 280

First-Line Supervisors, Customer Service 43-1011.01 280

Housekeeping Supervisors 37-1011.01 281

Janitorial Supervisors 37-1011.02 281

Meeting and Convention Planners 13-1121.00 281

04.03 Human Resources Support 281

Compensation, Benefits, and Job Analysis Specialists 13-1072.00 281

Employment Interviewers, Private or Public Employment Service 13-1071.01 282

Personnel Recruiters 13-1071.02 282

Training and Development Specialists 13-1073.00 282

04.04 Secretarial Support 282

Executive Secretaries and Administrative Assistants 43-6011.00 282

Legal Secretaries 43-6012.00 283

Medical Secretaries 43-6013.00 283

Secretaries, Except Legal, Medical, and Executive 43-6014.00 283

04.05 Accounting, Auditing, and Analytical Support 283

Accountants 13-2011.01 283

Auditors 13-2011.02 284

Budget Analysts 13-2031.00 284

Industrial Engineering Technicians 17-3026.00 284

Logisticians 13-1081.00 284

Management Analysts 13-1111.00 285

Operations Research Analysts 15-2031.00 285

04.06 Mathematical Clerical Support 285

Billing, Cost, and Rate Clerks 43-3021.02 285

Bookkeeping, Accounting, and Auditing Clerks 43-3031.00 285

Brokerage Clerks 43-4011.00 286

Payroll and Timekeeping Clerks 43-3051.00 286

Statement Clerks 43-3021.01 286

Tax Preparers 13-2082.00 286

04.07 Records and Materials Processing 286

Correspondence Clerks 43-4021.00 286

File Clerks 43-4071.00 287

Human Resources Assistants, Except Payroll and Timekeeping 43-4161.00 287

Mail Clerks, Except Mail Machine Operators and Postal Service 43-9051.02 287

Marking Clerks 43-5081.02 287

Meter Readers, Utilities 43-5041.00 287

Office Clerks, General 43-9061.00 288

Order Fillers, Wholesale and Retail Sales 43-5081.04 288

Postal Service Clerks 43-5051.00 288

Postal Service Mail Sorters, Processors, and Processing Machine Operators 43-5053.00 288

Procurement Clerks 43-3061.00 288

Production, Planning, and Expediting Clerks 43-5061.00 289

Shipping, Receiving, and Traffic Clerks 43-5071.00 289

Stock Clerks, Sales Floor 43-5081.01 289

Stock Clerks—Stockroom, Warehouse, or Storage Yard 43-5081.03 289

Weighers, Measurers, Checkers, and Samplers, Recordkeeping 43-5111.00 290

04.08 Clerical Machine Operation 290

Billing, Posting, and Calculating Machine Operators 43-3021.03 290

Data Entry Keyers 43-9021.00 290

Duplicating Machine Operators 43-9071.01 290

Mail Machine Operators, Preparation and Handling 43-9051.01 291

Switchboard Operators, Including Answering Service 43-2011.00 291

Word Processors and Typists 43-9022.00 291

05 Education and Training 292

05.01 Managerial Work in Education 293

Education Administrators, Elementary and Secondary School 11-9032.00 293

Education Administrators, Postsecondary 11-9033.00 293

Education Administrators, Preschool and Child Care Center/Program 11-9031.00 293

Instructional Coordinators 25-9031.00 293

05.02 Preschool, Elementary, and Secondary Teaching and Instructing 294

Elementary School Teachers, Except Special Education 25-2021.00 294

Kindergarten Teachers, Except Special Education 25-2012.00 294

Middle School Teachers, Except Special and Vocational Education 25-2022.00 294

Preschool Teachers, Except Special Education 25-2011.00 294

Secondary School Teachers, Except Special and Vocational Education 25-2031.00 295

Special Education Teachers, Middle School 25-2042.00 295

Special Education Teachers, Preschool, Kindergarten, and Elementary School 25-2041.00 295

Special Education Teachers, Secondary School 25-2043.00 296

Teacher Assistants 25-9041.00 296

Vocational Education Teachers, Middle School 25-2023.00 296

Vocational Education Teachers, Secondary School 25-2032.00 296

05.03 Postsecondary and Adult Teaching and Instructing 296

Adult Literacy, Remedial Education, and GED Teachers and Instructors 25-3011.00 296

Agricultural Sciences Teachers, Postsecondary 25-1041.00 297

Anthropology and Archeology Teachers, Postsecondary 25-1061.00 297

Architecture Teachers, Postsecondary 25-1031.00 297

Area, Ethnic, and Cultural Studies Teachers, Postsecondary 25-1062.00 297

Art, Drama, and Music Teachers, Postsecondary 25-1121.00 298

Atmospheric, Earth, Marine, and Space Sciences Teachers, Postsecondary 25-1051.00 298

Biological Science Teachers, Postsecondary 25-1042.00 298

Business Teachers, Postsecondary 25-1011.00 299

Chemistry Teachers, Postsecondary 25-1052.00 299

Communications Teachers, Postsecondary 25-1122.00 299

Computer Science Teachers, Postsecondary 25-1021.00 299

Criminal Justice and Law Enforcement Teachers, Postsecondary 25-1111.00 300

Economics Teachers, Postsecondary 25-1063.00 300

Education Teachers, Postsecondary 25-1081.00 300

Engineering Teachers, Postsecondary 25-1032.00 300

English Language and Literature Teachers, Postsecondary 25-1123.00 301

Environmental Science Teachers, Postsecondary 25-1053.00 301

Farm and Home Management Advisors 25-9021.00 301

Foreign Language and Literature Teachers, Postsecondary 25-1124.00 301

Forestry and Conservation Science Teachers, Postsecondary 25-1043.00 302

Geography Teachers, Postsecondary 25-1064.00 302

Graduate Teaching Assistants 25-1191.00 302

Health Specialties Teachers, Postsecondary 25-1071.00 302

History Teachers, Postsecondary 25-1125.00 303

Home Economics Teachers, Postsecondary 25-1192.00 303

Law Teachers, Postsecondary 25-1112.00 303

Library Science Teachers, Postsecondary 25-1082.00 303

Mathematical Science Teachers, Postsecondary 25-1022.00 303

Nursing Instructors and Teachers, Postsecondary 25-1072.00 304

© 2006 JIST Works

Philosophy and Religion Teachers, Postsecondary 25-1126.00 ....*304*

Physics Teachers, Postsecondary 25-1054.00 ......*304*

Political Science Teachers, Postsecondary 25-1065.00 ....*304*

Psychology Teachers, Postsecondary 25-1066.00 ....*304*

Recreation and Fitness Studies Teachers, Postsecondary 25-1193.00 ....*305*

Self-Enrichment Education Teachers 25-3021.00 ....*305*

Social Work Teachers, Postsecondary 25-1113.00 ....*305*

Sociology Teachers, Postsecondary 25-1067.00 ....*305*

Vocational Education Teachers, Postsecondary 25-1194.00 ....*305*

05.04 Library Services 306

Librarians 25-4021.00 ....*306*

Library Assistants, Clerical 43-4121.00 ....*306*

Library Technicians 25-4031.00 ....*306*

05.05 Archival and Museum Services 306

Archivists 25-4011.00 ....*306*

Audio-Visual Collections Specialists 25-9011.00 ....*307*

Curators 25-4012.00 ....*307*

Museum Technicians and Conservators 25-4013.00 ....*307*

05.06 Counseling, Health, and Fitness Education 307

Educational, Vocational, and School Counselors 21-1012.00 ....*307*

Fitness Trainers and Aerobics Instructors 39-9031.00 ....*308*

Health Educators 21-1091.00 ....*308*

06 Finance and Insurance 309

06.01 Managerial Work in Finance and Insurance 310

Financial Managers, Branch or Department 11-3031.02 ....*310*

Treasurers, Controllers, and Chief Financial Officers 11-3031.01 ....*310*

06.02 Finance/Insurance Investigation and Analysis 310

Appraisers, Real Estate 13-2021.02 ....*310*

Assessors 13-2021.01 ....*310*

Claims Examiners, Property and Casualty Insurance 13-1031.01 ....*311*

Cost Estimators 13-1051.00 ....*311*

Credit Analysts 13-2041.00 ....*311*

Financial Analysts 13-2051.00 ....*311*

Insurance Adjusters, Examiners, and Investigators 13-1031.02 ....*311*

Insurance Appraisers, Auto Damage 13-1032.00 ....*312*

Insurance Underwriters 13-2053.00 ....*312*

Loan Counselors 13-2071.00 ....*312*

Loan Officers 13-2072.00 ....*312*

Market Research Analysts 19-3021.00 ....*313*

Survey Researchers 19-3022.00 ....*313*

06.03 Finance/Insurance Records Processing 313

Credit Authorizers 43-4041.01 ....*313*

Credit Checkers 43-4041.02 ....*313*

Insurance Claims Clerks 43-9041.01 ....*313*

Insurance Policy Processing Clerks 43-9041.02 ....*313*

Proofreaders and Copy Markers 43-9081.00 ......*314*

06.04 Finance/Insurance Customer Service 314

Bill and Account Collectors 43-3011.00 ....*314*

Loan Interviewers and Clerks 43-4131.00 ....*314*

New Accounts Clerks 43-4141.00 ....*314*

Tellers 43-3071.00 ....*315*

06.05 Finance/Insurance Sales and Support 315

Advertising Sales Agents 41-3011.00 ....*315*

Insurance Sales Agents 41-3021.00 ....*315*

Personal Financial Advisors 13-2052.00 ....*315*

Sales Agents, Financial Services 41-3031.02 ......*316*

Sales Agents, Securities and Commodities 41-3031.01 ....*316*

07 Government and Public Administration 317

07.01 Managerial Work in Government and Public Administration 318

Government Service Executives 11-1011.01 ....*318*

Social and Community Service Managers 11-9151.00 ....*318*

07.02 Public Planning 318

City Planning Aides 19-4061.01 ....*318*

Urban and Regional Planners 19-3051.00 ....*318*

07.03 Regulations Enforcement 319

Agricultural Inspectors 45-2011.00 ....*319*

Aviation Inspectors 53-6051.01 ....*319*

Child Support, Missing Persons, and Unemployment Insurance Fraud Investigators 33-3021.04 ....*319*

Environmental Compliance Inspectors 13-1041.01 319

Equal Opportunity Representatives and Officers 13-1041.03.........................319

Financial Examiners 13-2061.00 320

Fire Inspectors 33-2021.01 320

Fish and Game Wardens 33-3031.00 320

Forest Fire Inspectors and Prevention Specialists 33-2022.00 320

Government Property Inspectors and Investigators 13-1041.04...........................321

Immigration and Customs Inspectors 33-3021.05 321

Licensing Examiners and Inspectors 13-1041.02 321

Marine Cargo Inspectors 53-6051.03.................321

Mechanical Inspectors 51-9061.02 321

Motor Vehicle Inspectors 53-6051.05.................322

Nuclear Monitoring Technicians 19-4051.02 322

Occupational Health and Safety Specialists 29-9011.00 322

Pressure Vessel Inspectors 13-1041.05 322

Railroad Inspectors 53-6051.04........................322

Tax Examiners, Collectors, and Revenue Agents 13-2081.00 323

07.04 Public Administration Clerical Support..........323

Court Clerks 43-4031.01 323

Court Reporters 23-2091.00 323

License Clerks 43-4031.03................................323

Municipal Clerks 43-4031.02 323

08 Health Science....................................325

08.01 Managerial Work in Medical and Health Services 326

Coroners 13-1041.06..326

First-Line Supervisors and Manager/ Supervisors—Animal Care Workers, Except Livestock 45-1011.03...............................326

Medical and Health Services Managers 11-9111.00 326

08.02 Medicine and Surgery 326

Anesthesiologists 29-1061.00 326

Family and General Practitioners 29-1062.00..327

Internists, General 29-1063.00..........................327

Medical Assistants 31-9092.00 327

Medical Transcriptionists 31-9094.00 327

Obstetricians and Gynecologists 29-1064.00 328

Pediatricians, General 29-1065.00 328

Pharmacists 29-1051.00 328

Pharmacy Aides 31-9095.00 328

Pharmacy Technicians 29-2052.00.....................329

Physician Assistants 29-1071.00 329

Psychiatrists 29-1066.00 329

Registered Nurses 29-1111.00 329

Surgeons 29-1067.00...329

Surgical Technologists 29-2055.00 330

08.03 Dentistry 330

Dental Assistants 31-9091.00.............................330

Dental Hygienists 29-2021.00 330

Dentists, General 29-1021.00.............................330

Oral and Maxillofacial Surgeons 29-1022.00 331

Orthodontists 29-1023.00..................................331

Prosthodontists 29-1024.00 331

08.04 Health Specialties 331

Chiropractors 29-1011.00 331

Optometrists 29-1041.00 332

Podiatrists 29-1081.00 332

08.05 Animal Care...332

Animal Breeders 45-2021.00..............................332

Animal Trainers 39-2011.00 332

Nonfarm Animal Caretakers 39-2021.00 333

Veterinarians 29-1131.00 333

Veterinary Assistants and Laboratory Animal Caretakers 31-9096.00 333

Veterinary Technologists and Technicians 29-2056.00..333

08.06 Medical Technology 334

Biological Technicians 19-4021.00 334

Cardiovascular Technologists and Technicians 29-2031.00..334

Diagnostic Medical Sonographers 29-2032.00..334

Medical and Clinical Laboratory Technicians 29-2012.00..334

Medical and Clinical Laboratory Technologists 29-2011.00..335

Medical Equipment Preparers 31-9093.00..........335

Medical Records and Health Information Technicians 29-2071.00 335

Nuclear Medicine Technologists 29-2033.00......335

Opticians, Dispensing 29-2081.00 336

Orthotists and Prosthetists 29-2091.00 336

Radiologic Technicians 29-2034.02 336

Radiologic Technologists 29-2034.01 336

08.07 Medical Therapy 336
　　Audiologists 29-1121.00 336
　　Massage Therapists 31-9011.00...............337
　　Occupational Therapist Aides 31-2012.00 337
　　Occupational Therapist Assistants
　　_31-2011.00_ 337
　　Occupational Therapists 29-1122.00 337
　　Physical Therapist Aides 31-2022.00 337
　　Physical Therapist Assistants 31-2021.00..........338
　　Physical Therapists 29-1123.00 338
　　Radiation Therapists 29-1124.00 338
　　Recreational Therapists 29-1125.00 338
　　Respiratory Therapists 29-1126.00 339
　　Respiratory Therapy Technicians 29-2054.00....339
　　Speech-Language Pathologists 29-1127.00 339
08.08 Patient Care and Assistance 339
　　Home Health Aides 31-1011.00...................339
　　Licensed Practical and Licensed Vocational
　　Nurses 29-2061.00 340
　　Nursing Aides, Orderlies, and Attendants
　　_31-1012.00_ 340
　　Psychiatric Aides 31-1013.00 340
　　Psychiatric Technicians 29-2053.00..............340
08.09 Health Protection and Promotion 340
　　Athletic Trainers 29-9091.00 340
　　Dietetic Technicians 29-2051.00.................341
　　Dietitians and Nutritionists 29-1031.00 341
　　Embalmers 39-4011.00 341

09 Hospitality, Tourism, and Recreation ..342

09.01 Managerial Work in Hospitality
　　　　and Tourism 343
　　First-Line Supervisors/Managers of Food
　　Preparation and Serving Workers 35-1012.00....343
　　First-Line Supervisors/Managers of Personal
　　Service Workers 39-1021.00 343
　　Food Service Managers 11-9051.00...............343
　　Gaming Managers 11-9071.00 343
　　Gaming Supervisors 39-1011.00 344
　　Lodging Managers 11-9081.00 344
09.02 Recreational Services 344
　　Amusement and Recreation Attendants
　　_39-3091.00_....................................344
　　Gaming and Sports Book Writers and Runners
　　_39-3012.00_ 344
　　Gaming Dealers 39-3011.00 345
　　Locker Room, Coatroom, and Dressing Room
　　Attendants 39-3093.00.........................345

　　Motion Picture Projectionists 39-3021.00 345
　　Recreation Workers 39-9032.00 345
　　Slot Key Persons 39-1012.00 345
　　Ushers, Lobby Attendants, and Ticket Takers
　　_39-3031.00_ 346
09.03 Hospitality and Travel Services 346
　　Baggage Porters and Bellhops 39-6011.00 346
　　Concierges 39-6012.00 346
　　Flight Attendants 39-6031.00....................346
　　Hotel, Motel, and Resort Desk Clerks
　　_43-4081.00_ 346
　　Janitors and Cleaners, Except Maids and
　　Housekeeping Cleaners 37-2011.00 347
　　Maids and Housekeeping Cleaners
　　_37-2012.00_ 347
　　Reservation and Transportation Ticket Agents
　　_43-4181.02_ 347
　　Tour Guides and Escorts 39-6021.00 347
　　Transportation Attendants, Except Flight
　　Attendants and Baggage Porters 39-6032.00......348
　　Travel Agents 41-3041.00 348
　　Travel Clerks 43-4181.01 348
　　Travel Guides 39-6022.00.......................348
09.04 Food and Beverage Preparation 348
　　Bakers, Bread and Pastry 51-3011.01 348
　　Butchers and Meat Cutters 51-3021.00 349
　　Chefs and Head Cooks 35-1011.00 349
　　Cooks, Fast Food 35-2011.00 349
　　Cooks, Institution and Cafeteria 35-2012.00....349
　　Cooks, Restaurant 35-2014.00 349
　　Cooks, Short Order 35-2015.00...................350
　　Dishwashers 35-9021.00........................350
　　Food Preparation Workers 35-2021.00 350
09.05 Food and Beverage Service 350
　　Bartenders 35-3011.00 350
　　Combined Food Preparation and Serving
　　Workers, Including Fast Food 35-3021.00..........350
　　Counter Attendants, Cafeteria, Food
　　Concession, and Coffee Shop 35-3022.00 351
　　Dining Room and Cafeteria Attendants and
　　Bartender Helpers 35-9011.00....................351
　　Food Servers, Nonrestaurant 35-3041.00 351
　　Hosts and Hostesses, Restaurant, Lounge, and
　　Coffee Shop 35-9031.00 351
　　Waiters and Waitresses 35-3031.00 351
09.06 Sports...352
　　Athletes and Sports Competitors 27-2021.00 352
　　Coaches and Scouts 27-2022.00......................352

Umpires, Referees, and Other Sports Officials
27-2023.00 352

09.07 Barber and Beauty Services 352

Barbers 39-5011.00 352

Hairdressers, Hairstylists, and Cosmetologists
39-5012.00 353

Manicurists and Pedicurists 39-5092.00............353

Shampooers 39-5093.00 353

Skin Care Specialists 39-5094.00 353

10 Human Service 354

10.01 Counseling and Social Work 355

Child, Family, and School Social Workers
21-1021.00 355

Clinical Psychologists 19-3031.02 355

Counseling Psychologists 19-3031.03 355

Marriage and Family Therapists 21-1013.00 355

Medical and Public Health Social Workers
21-1022.00 355

Mental Health and Substance Abuse Social
Workers 21-1023.00 356

Mental Health Counselors 21-1014.00 356

Probation Officers and Correctional Treatment
Specialists 21-1092.00 356

Rehabilitation Counselors 21-1015.00................356

Residential Advisors 39-9041.00 357

Social and Human Service Assistants
21-1093.00 357

Substance Abuse and Behavioral Disorder
Counselors 21-1011.00 357

10.02 Religious Work 357

Clergy 21-2011.00...357

Directors, Religious Activities and Education
21-2021.00 358

10.03 Child/Personal Care and Services 358

Child Care Workers 39-9011.00 358

Funeral Attendants 39-4021.00 358

Nannies 39-9011.01 358

Personal and Home Care Aides 39-9021.00 358

10.04 Client Interviewing 359

Claims Takers, Unemployment Benefits
43-4061.01 359

Interviewers, Except Eligibility and Loan
43-4111.00 359

Welfare Eligibility Workers and Interviewers
43-4061.02 359

11 Information Technology 360

11.01 Managerial Work in Information
Technology 361

Computer and Information Systems
Managers 11-3021.00 361

Network and Computer Systems
Administrators 15-1071.00 361

11.02 Information Technology Specialties................361

Computer Operators 43-9011.00 361

Computer Programmers 15-1021.00 361

Computer Security Specialists 15-1071.01 362

Computer Software Engineers, Applications
15-1031.00 362

Computer Software Engineers, Systems
Software 15-1032.00.....................................362

Computer Support Specialists 15-1041.00..........363

Computer Systems Analysts 15-1051.00 363

Database Administrators 15-1061.00 363

Network Systems and Data Communications
Analysts 15-1081.00 363

11.03 Digital Equipment Repair..............................364

Automatic Teller Machine Servicers
49-2011.01 364

Coin, Vending, and Amusement Machine
Servicers and Repairers 49-9091.00 364

Data Processing Equipment Repairers
49-2011.02 364

Office Machine and Cash Register Servicers
49-2011.03 364

12 Law and Public Safety..........................365

12.01 Managerial Work in Law and Public Safety....366

Emergency Management Specialists
13-1061.00 366

First-Line Supervisors/Managers of
Correctional Officers 33-1011.00 366

First-Line Supervisors/Managers of Police
and Detectives 33-1012.00 366

Forest Fire Fighting and Prevention
Supervisors 33-1021.02..................................366

Municipal Fire Fighting and Prevention
Supervisors 33-1021.01 366

12.02 Legal Practice and Justice Administration 367

Administrative Law Judges, Adjudicators, and
Hearing Officers 23-1021.00............................367

Arbitrators, Mediators, and Conciliators
23-1022.00 367

© 2006 JIST Works

*Judges, Magistrate Judges, and Magistrates
23-1023.00* 367
Lawyers 23-1011.00................................367

12.03 Legal Support 368
Law Clerks 23-2092.00............................368
Paralegals and Legal Assistants 23-2011.00 368
Title Examiners and Abstractors 23-2093.02 368
Title Searchers 23-2093.01 368

12.04 Law Enforcement and Public Safety 369
Bailiffs 33-3011.00 369
Correctional Officers and Jailers 33-3012.00 369
*Criminal Investigators and Special Agents
33-3021.03* 369
Fire Investigators 33-2021.02 369
Forensic Science Technicians 19-4092.00 369
Highway Patrol Pilots 33-3051.02 370
Parking Enforcement Workers 33-3041.00 370
Police Detectives 33-3021.01 370
*Police Identification and Records Officers
33-3021.02* 370
Police Patrol Officers 33-3051.01 370
Sheriffs and Deputy Sheriffs 33-3051.03 371
Transit and Railroad Police 33-3052.00 371

12.05 Safety and Security 371
Animal Control Workers 33-9011.00...............371
Crossing Guards 33-9091.00.......................371
*Gaming Surveillance Officers and Gaming
Investigators 33-9031.00*...........................372
*Lifeguards, Ski Patrol, and Other Recreational
Protective Service Workers 33-9092.00* 372
*Private Detectives and Investigators
33-9021.00*..372
Security Guards 33-9032.00 372

12.06 Emergency Responding.........................372
*Emergency Medical Technicians and
Paramedics 29-2041.00*..............................372
Forest Fire Fighters 33-2011.02 373
Municipal Fire Fighters 33-2011.01 373

12.07 Military 373
Air Crew Members 55-3011.00 373
Air Crew Officers 55-1011.00 373
*Aircraft Launch and Recovery Officers
55-1012.00* 373
*Aircraft Launch and Recovery Specialists
55-3012.00* 374
*Armored Assault Vehicle Crew Members
55-3013.00* 374

Armored Assault Vehicle Officers 55-1013.00 374
*Artillery and Missile Crew Members
55-3014.00* 374
Artillery and Missile Officers 55-1014.00 374
*Command and Control Center Officers
55-1015.00* 374
*Command and Control Center Specialists
55-3015.00* 375
*First-Line Supervisors/Managers of Air Crew
Members 55-2011.00*................................375
*First-Line Supervisors/Managers of Weapons
Specialists/Crew Members 55-2012.00* 375
Infantry 55-3016.00 375
Infantry Officers 55-1016.00......................375
Radar and Sonar Technicians 55-3017.00.........375
Special Forces 55-3018.00 376
Special Forces Officers 55-1017.00..................376

13 Manufacturing **377**

13.01 Managerial Work in Manufacturing................378
*First-Line Supervisors/Managers of Helpers,
Laborers, and Material Movers, Hand
53-1021.00* 378
*First-Line Supervisors/Managers of Mechanics,
Installers, and Repairers 49-1011.00* 378
*First-Line Supervisors/Managers of Production
and Operating Workers 51-1011.00* 378
Industrial Production Managers 11-3051.00 378

13.02 Machine Set-Up and Operation 378
*Bindery Machine Setters and Set-Up Operators
51-5011.01*..378
*Buffing and Polishing Set-Up Operators
51-4033.02*..379
Casting Machine Set-Up Operators 51-4072.05 ..379
*Coating, Painting, and Spraying Machine
Setters and Set-Up Operators 51-9121.01* 379
*Combination Machine Tool Setters and Set-Up
Operators, Metal and Plastic 51-4081.01* 379
*Crushing, Grinding, and Polishing Machine
Setters, Operators, and Tenders 51-9021.00* 380
*Drilling and Boring Machine Tool Setters,
Operators, and Tenders, Metal and Plastic
51-4032.00* 380
*Electrolytic Plating and Coating Machine
Setters and Set-Up Operators, Metal and
Plastic 51-4193.01*...................................380
*Extruding and Drawing Machine Setters,
Operators, and Tenders, Metal and Plastic
51-4021.00* 380

Extruding and Forming Machine Setters, Operators, and Tenders, Synthetic and Glass Fibers 51-6091.00 380

Extruding, Forming, Pressing, and Compacting Machine Setters and Set-Up Operators 51-9041.01 381

Fiber Product Cutting Machine Setters and Set-Up Operators 51-9032.01 381

Forging Machine Setters, Operators, and Tenders, Metal and Plastic 51-4022.00 381

Glass Cutting Machine Setters and Set-Up Operators 51-9032.03 381

Grinding, Honing, Lapping, and Deburring Machine Set-Up Operators 51-4033.01 381

Heating Equipment Setters and Set-Up Operators, Metal and Plastic 51-4191.01 382

Lathe and Turning Machine Tool Setters, Operators, and Tenders, Metal and Plastic 51-4034.00 382

Metal Molding, Coremaking, and Casting Machine Operators and Tenders 51-4072.04 382

Metal Molding, Coremaking, and Casting Machine Setters and Set-Up Operators 51-4072.03 382

Milling and Planing Machine Setters, Operators, and Tenders, Metal and Plastic 51-4035.00 383

Multiple Machine Tool Setters, Operators, and Tenders, Metal and Plastic 51-4081.00 383

Nonelectrolytic Plating and Coating Machine Setters and Set-Up Operators, Metal and Plastic 51-4193.03 383

Paper Goods Machine Setters, Operators, and Tenders 51-9196.00 383

Plastic Molding and Casting Machine Setters and Set-Up Operators 51-4072.01 383

Press and Press Brake Machine Setters and Set-Up Operators, Metal and Plastic 51-4031.03 384

Punching Machine Setters and Set-Up Operators, Metal and Plastic 51-4031.02 384

Rolling Machine Setters, Operators, and Tenders, Metal and Plastic 51-4023.00 384

Sawing Machine Setters and Set-Up Operators 51-7041.01 384

Sawing Machine Tool Setters and Set-Up Operators, Metal and Plastic 51-4031.01 384

Screen Printing Machine Setters and Set-Up Operators 51-5023.06 385

Shear and Slitter Machine Setters and Set-Up Operators, Metal and Plastic 51-4031.04 385

Soldering and Brazing Machine Setters and Set-Up Operators 51-4122.03 385

Textile Cutting Machine Setters, Operators, and Tenders 51-6062.00 385

Textile Knitting and Weaving Machine Setters, Operators, and Tenders 51-6063.00 386

Textile Winding, Twisting, and Drawing Out Machine Setters, Operators, and Tenders 51-6064.00 386

Woodworking Machine Setters and Set-Up Operators, Except Sawing 51-7042.01 386

13.03 Production Work, Assorted Materials Processing 386

Bakers, Manufacturing 51-3011.02 386

Cementing and Gluing Machine Operators and Tenders 51-9191.00 387

Chemical Equipment Controllers and Operators 51-9011.01 387

Chemical Equipment Tenders 51-9011.02 387

Cleaning, Washing, and Metal Pickling Equipment Operators and Tenders 51-9192.00 387

Coating, Painting, and Spraying Machine Operators and Tenders 51-9121.02 387

Combination Machine Tool Operators and Tenders, Metal and Plastic 51-4081.02 388

Cooling and Freezing Equipment Operators and Tenders 51-9193.00 388

Cutting and Slicing Machine Operators and Tenders 51-9032.04 388

Electrolytic Plating and Coating Machine Operators and Tenders, Metal and Plastic 51-4193.02 388

Extruding and Forming Machine Operators and Tenders, Synthetic or Glass Fibers 51-6091.01 389

Extruding, Forming, Pressing, and Compacting Machine Operators and Tenders 51-9041.02 389

Food and Tobacco Roasting, Baking, and Drying Machine Operators and Tenders 51-3091.00 389

Food Batchmakers 51-3092.00 389

Food Cooking Machine Operators and Tenders 51-3093.00 389

Furnace, Kiln, Oven, Drier, and Kettle Operators and Tenders 51-9051.00 390

Heat Treating, Annealing, and Tempering Machine Operators and Tenders, Metal and Plastic 51-4191.02 390

Heaters, Metal and Plastic 51-4191.03 390

© 2006 JIST Works

Meat, Poultry, and Fish Cutters and Trimmers 51-3022.00 390

Metal-Refining Furnace Operators and Tenders 51-4051.00............................391

Mixing and Blending Machine Setters, Operators, and Tenders 51-9023.00 391

Nonelectrolytic Plating and Coating Machine Operators and Tenders, Metal and Plastic 51-4193.04 391

Packaging and Filling Machine Operators and Tenders 51-9111.00 391

Plastic Molding and Casting Machine Operators and Tenders 51-4072.02 391

Pourers and Casters, Metal 51-4052.00.............392

Pressing Machine Operators and Tenders—Textile, Garment, and Related Materials 51-6021.02 392

Production Helpers 51-9198.02 392

Production Laborers 51-9198.01 392

Sawing Machine Operators and Tenders 51-7041.02 392

Separating, Filtering, Clarifying, Precipitating, and Still Machine Setters, Operators, and Tenders 51-9012.00...........................393

Sewing Machine Operators, Garment 51-6031.01 393

Sewing Machine Operators, Non-Garment 51-6031.02 393

Shoe Machine Operators and Tenders 51-6042.00 393

Slaughterers and Meat Packers 51-3023.00 393

Stone Sawyers 51-9032.02.................................394

Team Assemblers 51-2092.00 394

Textile Bleaching and Dyeing Machine Operators and Tenders 51-6061.00 394

Tire Builders 51-9197.00 394

Woodworking Machine Operators and Tenders, Except Sawing 51-7042.02 394

13.04 Welding, Brazing, and Soldering 395

Brazers 51-4121.05 395

Fitters, Structural Metal—Precision 51-2041.02 395

Metal Fabricators, Structural Metal Products 51-2041.01 395

Solderers 51-4121.04 395

Soldering and Brazing Machine Operators and Tenders 51-4122.04 396

Welder-Fitters 51-4121.03 396

Welders and Cutters 51-4121.02 396

Welders, Production 51-4121.01 396

Welding Machine Operators and Tenders 51-4122.02 396

Welding Machine Setters and Set-Up Operators 51-4122.01 397

13.05 Production Machining Technology 397

Foundry Mold and Coremakers 51-4071.00........397

Lay-Out Workers, Metal and Plastic 51-4192.00 397

Machinists 51-4041.00 397

Model Makers, Metal and Plastic 51-4061.00....398

Numerical Control Machine Tool Operators and Tenders, Metal and Plastic 51-4011.01 398

Numerical Tool and Process Control Programmers 51-4012.00 398

Patternmakers, Metal and Plastic 51-4062.00 398

Tool and Die Makers 51-4111.00......................398

Tool Grinders, Filers, and Sharpeners 51-4194.00 399

13.06 Production Precision Work 399

Bench Workers, Jewelry 51-9071.04 399

Bookbinders 51-5012.00 399

Dental Laboratory Technicians 51-9081.00 399

Electrical and Electronic Equipment Assemblers 51-2022.00 400

Electromechanical Equipment Assemblers 51-2023.00..400

Engine and Other Machine Assemblers 51-2031.00..400

Gem and Diamond Workers 51-9071.06 400

Jewelers 51-9071.01 400

Medical Appliance Technicians 51-9082.00 401

Model and Mold Makers, Jewelry 51-9071.03 401

Optical Instrument Assemblers 51-9083.02 401

Pewter Casters and Finishers 51-9071.05............401

Precision Lens Grinders and Polishers 51-9083.01 401

Precision Mold and Pattern Casters, Except Nonferrous Metals 51-9195.01 402

Precision Pattern and Die Casters, Nonferrous Metals 51-9195.02 402

Semiconductor Processors 51-9141.00 402

Silversmiths 51-9071.02 402

Timing Device Assemblers, Adjusters, and Calibrators 51-2093.00................................402

13.07 Production Quality Control...........................403

Electrical and Electronic Inspectors and Testers 51-9061.04 403

Graders and Sorters, Agricultural Products
45-2041.00..403

Materials Inspectors 51-9061.01 403

Precision Devices Inspectors and Testers
51-9061.03..403

Production Inspectors, Testers, Graders,
Sorters, Samplers, Weighers 51-9061.05 404

13.08 Graphic Arts Production 404

Bindery Machine Operators and Tenders
51-5011.02..404

Camera Operators 51-5022.04 404

Design Printing Machine Setters and Set-Up
Operators 51-5023.04................................404

Desktop Publishers 43-9031.00....................404

Dot Etchers 51-5022.08 405

Electronic Masking System Operators
51-5022.09..405

Electrotypers and Stereotypers 51-5022.10.........405

Embossing Machine Set-Up Operators
51-5023.07..405

Engraver Set-Up Operators 51-5023.08 406

Engravers, Hand 51-9194.06 406

Engravers/Carvers 51-9194.02......................406

Etchers 51-9194.03 406

Etchers, Hand 51-9194.05 406

Film Laboratory Technicians 51-9131.04 406

Hand Compositors and Typesetters
51-5022.01..407

Job Printers 51-5021.00................................407

Letterpress Setters and Set-Up Operators
51-5023.03..407

Marking and Identification Printing Machine
Setters and Set-Up Operators 51-5023.05 407

Offset Lithographic Press Setters and Set-Up
Operators 51-5023.02................................408

Pantograph Engravers 51-9194.04....................408

Paste-Up Workers 51-5022.02 408

Photoengravers 51-5022.03 408

Photoengraving and Lithographing Machine
Operators and Tenders 51-5022.13 408

Photographic Processing Machine Operators
51-9132.00..409

Plate Finishers 51-5022.11 409

Platemakers 51-5022.07 409

Precision Etchers and Engravers, Hand or
Machine 51-9194.01 409

Precision Printing Workers 51-5023.01 410

Printing Press Machine Operators and
Tenders 51-5023.09................................410

Scanner Operators 51-5022.05 410

Strippers 51-5022.06................................410

Typesetting and Composing Machine
Operators and Tenders 51-5022.12 410

13.09 Hands-On Work, Assorted Materials................411

Coil Winders, Tapers, and Finishers
51-2021.00..411

Cutters and Trimmers, Hand 51-9031.00 411

Fabric and Apparel Patternmakers
51-6092.00..411

Glass Blowers, Molders, Benders, and Finishers
51-9195.04..411

Grinding and Polishing Workers, Hand
51-9022.00..411

Mold Makers, Hand 51-9195.06 412

Molding and Casting Workers 51-9195.07.........412

Painters, Transportation Equipment
51-9122.00..412

Painting, Coating, and Decorating Workers
51-9123.00..412

Sewers, Hand 51-6051.00 412

13.10 Woodworking Technology 413

Cabinetmakers and Bench Carpenters
51-7011.00..413

Furniture Finishers 51-7021.00 413

Model Makers, Wood 51-7031.00 413

Patternmakers, Wood 51-7032.00..................413

13.11 Apparel, Shoes, Leather, and Fabric Care 413

Custom Tailors 51-6052.02 413

Fabric Menders, Except Garment 49-9093.00 414

Laundry and Drycleaning Machine Operators
and Tenders, Except Pressing 51-6011.03...........414

Precision Dyers 51-6011.02 414

Pressers, Delicate Fabrics 51-6021.01..............414

Pressers, Hand 51-6021.03 414

Shoe and Leather Workers and Repairers
51-6041.00..415

Shop and Alteration Tailors 51-6052.01 415

Spotters, Dry Cleaning 51-6011.01 415

Upholsterers 51-6093.00 415

13.12 Electrical and Electronic Repair 415

Avionics Technicians 49-2091.00 415

Battery Repairers 49-2092.03 416

Electric Home Appliance and Power Tool
Repairers 49-2092.01................................416

© 2006 JIST Works

Electric Motor and Switch Assemblers and Repairers 49-2092.02............................416

Electrical and Electronics Installers and Repairers, Transportation Equipment 49-2093.00............................416

Electrical and Electronics Repairers, Commercial and Industrial Equipment 49-2094.00............................416

Electrical Parts Reconditioners 49-2092.05........417

Electronic Equipment Installers and Repairers, Motor Vehicles 49-2096.00 417

Electronic Home Entertainment Equipment Installers and Repairers 49-2097.00 417

Radio Mechanics 49-2021.00 417

Transformer Repairers 49-2092.04......................418

13.13 Machinery Repair 418

Bicycle Repairers 49-3091.00............................418

Gas Appliance Repairers 49-9031.02 418

Hand and Portable Power Tool Repairers 49-2092.06 418

Industrial Machinery Mechanics 49-9041.00 418

Locksmiths and Safe Repairers 49-9094.00 419

Maintenance Workers, Machinery 49-9043.00 419

Mechanical Door Repairers 49-9011.00 419

Millwrights 49-9044.00 419

Signal and Track Switch Repairers 49-9097.00 419

Valve and Regulator Repairers 49-9012.02 420

13.14 Vehicle and Facility Mechanical Work 420

Aircraft Body and Bonded Structure Repairers 49-3011.03 420

Aircraft Engine Specialists 49-3011.02 420

Aircraft Rigging Assemblers 51-2011.03 420

Aircraft Structure Assemblers, Precision 51-2011.01 421

Aircraft Systems Assemblers, Precision 51-2011.02 421

Airframe-and-Power-Plant Mechanics 49-3011.01 421

Automotive Body and Related Repairers 49-3021.00 421

Automotive Glass Installers and Repairers 49-3022.00 421

Automotive Master Mechanics 49-3023.01 422

Automotive Specialty Technicians 49-3023.02 422

Bus and Truck Mechanics and Diesel Engine Specialists 49-3031.00 422

Farm Equipment Mechanics 49-3041.00 422

Fiberglass Laminators and Fabricators 51-2091.00 423

Mobile Heavy Equipment Mechanics, Except Engines 49-3042.00 423

Motorboat Mechanics 49-3051.00....................423

Motorcycle Mechanics 49-3052.00 423

Outdoor Power Equipment and Other Small Engine Mechanics 49-3053.00 423

Rail Car Repairers 49-3043.00 424

Recreational Vehicle Service Technicians 49-3092.00 424

Tire Repairers and Changers 49-3093.00 424

13.15 Medical and Technical Equipment Repair......424

Camera and Photographic Equipment Repairers 49-9061.00 424

Medical Equipment Repairers 49-9062.00 424

Watch Repairers 49-9064.00 425

13.16 Utility Operation and Energy Distribution....425

Auxiliary Equipment Operators, Power 51-8013.02 425

Boiler Operators and Tenders, Low Pressure 51-8021.01 425

Chemical Plant and System Operators 51-8091.00 425

Gas Compressor Operators 53-7071.02 425

Gas Distribution Plant Operators 51-8092.02 426

Gas Processing Plant Operators 51-8092.01 426

Gas Pumping Station Operators 53-7071.01 426

Gaugers 51-8093.03 426

Nuclear Power Reactor Operators 51-8011.00 426

Petroleum Pump System Operators 51-8093.01 427

Petroleum Refinery and Control Panel Operators 51-8093.02 427

Power Distributors and Dispatchers 51-8012.00 427

Power Generating Plant Operators, Except Auxiliary Equipment Operators 51-8013.01 427

Ship Engineers 53-5031.00 427

Stationary Engineers 51-8021.02 428

Water and Liquid Waste Treatment Plant and System Operators 51-8031.00 428

13.17 Loading, Moving, Hoisting, and Conveying 428

Conveyor Operators and Tenders 53-7011.00 428

Freight, Stock, and Material Movers, Hand 53-7062.03 428

Hoist and Winch Operators 53-7041.00 429

Industrial Truck and Tractor Operators
53-7051.00 429

Irradiated-Fuel Handlers 47-4041.01 429

Machine Feeders and Offbearers 53-7063.00 429

Packers and Packagers, Hand 53-7064.00..........429

Pump Operators, Except Wellhead Pumpers
53-7072.00 430

Refuse and Recyclable Material Collectors
53-7081.00 430

Tank Car, Truck, and Ship Loaders
53-7121.00 430

14 Retail and Wholesale Sales and Service 431

14.01 Managerial Work in Retail/Wholesale Sales
and Service 432

Advertising and Promotions Managers
11-2011.00 432

First-Line Supervisors/Managers of Non-Retail
Sales Workers 41-1012.00 432

First-Line Supervisors/Managers of Retail Sales
Workers 41-1011.00....................................432

Funeral Directors 11-9061.00 432

Marketing Managers 11-2021.00......................433

Property, Real Estate, and Community
Association Managers 11-9141.00 433

Purchasing Managers 11-3061.00 433

Sales Managers 11-2022.00............................433

14.02 Technical Sales 434

Sales Engineers 41-9031.00.............................434

Sales Representatives, Agricultural
41-4011.01 434

Sales Representatives, Chemical and
Pharmaceutical 41-4011.02 434

Sales Representatives, Electrical/Electronic
41-4011.03 434

Sales Representatives, Instruments
41-4011.06 434

Sales Representatives, Mechanical Equipment
and Supplies 41-4011.04 435

Sales Representatives, Medical 41-4011.05 435

14.03 General Sales 435

Parts Salespersons 41-2022.00 435

Real Estate Brokers 41-9021.00......................435

Real Estate Sales Agents 41-9022.00................435

Retail Salespersons 41-2031.00 436

Sales Representatives, Wholesale and
Manufacturing, Except Technical and
Scientific Products 41-4012.00 436

Service Station Attendants 53-6031.00.............436

14.04 Personal Soliciting 436

Demonstrators and Product Promoters
41-9011.00 436

Door-To-Door Sales Workers, News and Street
Vendors, and Related Workers 41-9091.00 437

Models 41-9012.00 437

Telemarketers 41-9041.00 437

14.05 Purchasing 437

Purchasing Agents, Except Wholesale, Retail,
and Farm Products 13-1023.00 437

Wholesale and Retail Buyers, Except Farm
Products 13-1022.00....................................437

14.06 Customer Service 438

Adjustment Clerks 43-4051.01 438

Cashiers 41-2011.00 438

Counter and Rental Clerks 41-2021.00.............438

Customer Service Representatives, Utilities
43-4051.02 438

Gaming Change Persons and Booth Cashiers
41-2012.00 439

Order Clerks 43-4151.00 439

Receptionists and Information Clerks
43-4171.00 439

15 Scientific Research, Engineering, and Mathematics 440

15.01 Managerial Work in Scientific Research,
Engineering, and Mathematics......................441

Engineering Managers 11-9041.00 441

Natural Sciences Managers 11-9121.00.............441

15.02 Physical Sciences..442

Astronomers 19-2011.00 442

Atmospheric and Space Scientists
19-2021.00 442

Chemists 19-2031.00 442

Geographers 19-3092.00 442

Geologists 19-2042.01 443

Hydrologists 19-2043.00................................443

Materials Scientists 19-2032.00 443

Physicists 19-2012.00 443

15.03 Life Sciences 444

Biochemists 19-1021.01 444

Biologists 19-1020.01 444

Biophysicists 19-1021.02 444

© 2006 JIST Works

Environmental Scientists and Specialists, Including Health 19-2041.00 444

Epidemiologists 19-1041.00 444

Medical Scientists, Except Epidemiologists 19-1042.00 445

Microbiologists 19-1022.00............445

15.04 Social Sciences 445

Anthropologists 19-3091.01 445

Archeologists 19-3091.02 445

Economists 19-3011.00............446

Educational Psychologists 19-3031.01 446

Historians 19-3093.00 446

Industrial-Organizational Psychologists 19-3032.00............446

Political Scientists 19-3094.00 447

Sociologists 19-3041.00 447

15.05 Physical Science Laboratory Technology........447

Chemical Technicians 19-4031.00 447

Nuclear Equipment Operation Technicians 19-4051.01 447

Photographers, Scientific 27-4021.02 448

15.06 Mathematics and Data Analysis 448

Actuaries 15-2011.00 448

Mathematical Technicians 15-2091.00............448

Mathematicians 15-2021.00 448

Social Science Research Assistants 19-4061.00 449

Statistical Assistants 43-9111.00........449

Statisticians 15-2041.00........449

15.07 Research and Design Engineering 449

Aerospace Engineers 17-2011.00 449

Biomedical Engineers 17-2031.00 449

Chemical Engineers 17-2041.00 450

Civil Engineers 17-2051.00 450

Computer Hardware Engineers 17-2061.00 450

Electrical Engineers 17-2071.00 450

Electronics Engineers, Except Computer 17-2072.00 450

Marine Architects 17-2121.02 451

Marine Engineers 17-2121.01 451

Materials Engineers 17-2131.00 451

Mechanical Engineers 17-2141.00........451

Nuclear Engineers 17-2161.00............452

15.08 Industrial and Safety Engineering 452

Fire-Prevention and Protection Engineers 17-2111.02 452

Industrial Engineers 17-2112.00 452

Industrial Safety and Health Engineers 17-2111.01 452

Product Safety Engineers 17-2111.03........452

15.09 Engineering Technology............453

Aerospace Engineering and Operations Technicians 17-3021.00 453

Calibration and Instrumentation Technicians 17-3023.02 453

Cartographers and Photogrammetrists 17-1021.00 453

Civil Engineering Technicians 17-3022.00 453

Electrical Engineering Technicians 17-3023.03 454

Electro-Mechanical Technicians 17-3024.00......454

Electronic Drafters 17-3012.01 454

Electronics Engineering Technicians 17-3023.01 454

Environmental Engineering Technicians 17-3025.00 455

Mapping Technicians 17-3031.02 455

Mechanical Drafters 17-3013.00........455

Mechanical Engineering Technicians 17-3027.00 455

Surveying Technicians 17-3031.01 456

16 Transportation, Distribution, and Logistics 457

16.01 Managerial Work in Transportation............458

Aircraft Cargo Handling Supervisors 53-1011.00 458

First-Line Supervisors/Managers of Transportation and Material-Moving Machine and Vehicle Operators 53-1031.00 458

Postmasters and Mail Superintendents 11-9131.00 458

Railroad Conductors and Yardmasters 53-4031.00 458

Storage and Distribution Managers 11-3071.02 458

Transportation Managers 11-3071.01 459

16.02 Air Vehicle Operation 459

Airline Pilots, Copilots, and Flight Engineers 53-2011.00 459

Commercial Pilots 53-2012.00 459

16.03 Truck Driving 459

Tractor-Trailer Truck Drivers 53-3032.02 459

Truck Drivers, Heavy 53-3032.01 460

Truck Drivers, Light or Delivery Services 53-3033.00........460

16.04 Rail Vehicle Operation 460

    Locomotive Engineers 53-4011.00 460

    Locomotive Firers 53-4012.00 460

    Rail Yard Engineers, Dinkey Operators, and
    Hostlers 53-4013.00 461

    Subway and Streetcar Operators 53-4041.00 461

16.05 Water Vehicle Operation.................................461

    Able Seamen 53-5011.01 461

    Dredge Operators 53-7031.00 461

    Mates—Ship, Boat, and Barge 53-5021.02..........462

    Motorboat Operators 53-5022.00 462

    Ordinary Seamen and Marine Oilers
    53-5011.02 462

    Pilots, Ship 53-5021.03 462

    Ship and Boat Captains 53-5021.01 462

16.06 Other Services Requiring Driving 463

    Ambulance Drivers and Attendants, Except
    Emergency Medical Technicians 53-3011.00......463

    Bus Drivers, School 53-3022.00 463

    Bus Drivers, Transit and Intercity
    53-3021.00..463

    Couriers and Messengers 43-5021.00 463

    Driver/Sales Workers 53-3031.00 463

    Parking Lot Attendants 53-6021.00 464

    Postal Service Mail Carriers 43-5052.00............464

    Taxi Drivers and Chauffeurs 53-3041.00 464

16.07 Transportation Support Work 464

    Bridge and Lock Tenders 53-6011.00 464

    Cargo and Freight Agents 43-5011.00................464

    Cleaners of Vehicles and Equipment
    53-7061.00 465

    Freight Inspectors 53-6051.06............................465

    Public Transportation Inspectors 53-6051.02 465

    Railroad Yard Workers 53-4021.02 465

    Stevedores, Except Equipment Operators
    53-7062.01 465

    Traffic Technicians 53-6041.00 466

    Train Crew Members 53-4021.01 466

Part 3. Crosswalks to Careers by Work Values, Leisure Activities, School Subjects, Work Settings, Skills, Abilities, Knowledges, and Military Occupations......467

    Crosswalk A: Work Values with
    Corresponding Work Groups 469

    Crosswalk B: Leisure Activities with
    Corresponding Work Groups 473

    Crosswalk C: School Subjects with
    Corresponding Work Groups 483

    Crosswalk D: Work Settings with
    Corresponding Work Groups 496

    Crosswalk E: Skills with Corresponding
    Work Groups...502

    Crosswalk F: Abilities with Corresponding
    Work Groups 510

    Crosswalk G: Knowledges with
    Corresponding Work Groups 517

    Crosswalk H: Military Occupations with
    Corresponding Work Groups 524

Appendix: Information for Vocational Counselors and Other Professionals 537

Index...543

© 2006 JIST Works

Introduction

But First, a Few Words to People Who Do Not Read Introductions

We assume that most people will not read this entire introduction, so we worked hard to make the book easy to understand. Even so, we encourage you to skim the following material.

To avoid complexity, we decided not to address this introduction to technical users, such as labor market experts. Instead, it is written to someone using the book for career exploration, although we include some boring technical details. We use headings and bold type to help you skip information that doesn't interest you and more quickly identify information that does.

If you are a counselor or technical user, tips on using the book as a counseling tool are included in the appendix. So, without further ado, we present the introduction to this book and ask that you at least skim it for the information you need.

Overview

The GOE was originally developed by the U.S. Department of Labor to help people explore career and learning options based on their interests. It remains an important tool for students, career changers, job seekers, educators, counselors, and other career development professionals. The GOE has an extensive history that is rooted in research into how people can most effectively explore career options based on their interests. There is a lot of validity to this approach, and Part 1 is designed to help you explore career and education options based on your interests. Another major section, Part 2, provides descriptions for more than 900 jobs, covering well over 90 percent of the labor market. These features make the GOE a unique and valuable tool for exploring career, education, and other life options.

Exploring career and learning options based on interests makes sense, and it is something you have been doing most of your life. For example, when you were a child, you were probably asked, "What do you want to be when you grow up?" Children often respond to this question by mentioning careers of people who are easily recognized and understood, like a police officer, doctor, or teacher. Older children often change their responses to careers of heroes, such as astronaut, professional athlete, musician, or movie actor. These responses are based on what interests us at that time. As we mature, our career interests often change based on what we learn and as our personalities and interests develop.

Too often, however, people make career decisions based on interests, but without good information on the occupations or learning options that most closely match those interests. For example, a hotel management career would sound interesting to some people, but a decision to get a four-year college degree in that field (and there is such a degree) or to change careers to this field would best be made knowing that pay is often modest and that weekend and night work is the norm. Those details could make a big difference to you. You need to know as many facts as you can before making important decisions—and the GOE is one of the best places to start.

The GOE helps you quickly pinpoint jobs that match your interests by first asking you to choose from among 16 major Interest Areas. It then provides substantial information on groups of jobs within these 16 areas and cross-references more than 900 job descriptions.

While it sounds complicated, the GOE is very easy to use. The table of contents is the best place to start, because it offers a quick overview of the major sections as well as listing GOE Interest Areas, Work Groups, and specific job titles.

A Quick Review of the Acronyms Used in This Introduction

Government programs and vocational experts use a variety of systems to name, organize, and code occupations. Many of these systems can be cross-referenced so that information from one database can be used with another. For clarification, here are the systems we refer to most often in this introduction:

* **O*NET:** This is short for the Occupational Information Network, a database of information on occupations that was developed by the U.S. Department of Labor.

* **OES:** This refers to the Occupational Employment Statistics survey classification system.

* **SOC:** This refers to the Standard Occupational Classification, yet another system of organizing and coding jobs. The SOC provides a standard for naming and numbering all jobs that every other occupational system plans to use. The O*NET is organized by a numbering scheme adapted from this system.

* **DOT:** This refers to a book, the *Dictionary of Occupational Titles,* formerly published by the U.S. Department of Labor. The *DOT* used a system to organize and code occupations that has been replaced by the newer O*NET system.

* **GOE:** This refers to a book titled the *Guide for Occupational Exploration,* originally published by the U.S. Department of Labor. The *GOE* presents a way of organizing jobs within groupings based on interests.

* **CIP 2000:** This refers to the Classification of Instructional Programs Edition 2000, a scheme for organizing all postsecondary educational and training programs, developed by the U.S. Department of Education's National Center for Education Statistics (NCES).

Quick Tips on Using the *GOE* for Career Exploration

The *GOE* is a unique and valuable book for career exploration because it provides in one location the most popular information for all major jobs. If you need help in deciding what kind of work you should choose or switch to, you can use the *GOE* to help you plan your career, identify jobs you qualify for, or consider jobs requiring additional training or education. Your task is to find not just any job, but one you can do well and that will be satisfying to you.

To find the right kind of job, you need two types of information:

1. **Information about yourself.** You need to know the kind of work you would like to do and whether you are able to do such work. If you can't do it now, can you learn it through an educational or training program?

2. **Information about occupations that sound interesting to you.** What does the worker do on such jobs? What knowledge and skills must the worker have? What training is required?

The *GOE* helps you locate and learn about occupations that relate to your interests and abilities. When you use it properly, you will be better prepared to plan your career or seek employment. You will learn about many jobs, including some you never knew existed.

The *GOE* clusters occupations into major Interest Areas that are further divided into Work Groups. Specific jobs are then listed within each Work Group. Rather than making you explore the impossibly large world of job options, the *GOE* allows you to identify groups of similar jobs. It begins with broad areas of interest and then narrows down to job groupings that are most closely related to your interests, skills, values, education, training, and physical abilities. Following are some suggestions for how to use this book to explore career alternatives.

Step 1. Identify Your Interests

What kind of work would you most like to do? Did you know that all jobs have been organized into groups according to workers' interests? Some workers like to help others. Some would rather work with their hands or tools. Others prefer writing, selling, or clerical work. This new *GOE* edition is based on the occupational clustering scheme developed by the U.S. Department of Education, which organizes all jobs into 16 families that we refer to as Interest Areas, using the terminology of previous editions of the *GOE*. Each Interest Area has been given a name, a code number, and a brief description, and we will provide more details on them later in this introduction.

Step 2. Select One or More Work Groups to Explore

After you identify one or more major Interest Areas, your next task is to review Work Groups of jobs within the Interest Areas that appeal to you. To know what jobs to explore, you need to decide whether you would enjoy work activities required by the occupations within these groupings. The table of contents includes listings of GOE Interest Areas, Work Groups, and related job titles.

As you identify GOE Work Groups you would like to learn more about, note the page numbers listed next to each. Simply look for the narrative descriptions for each Work Group in Part 1. Within many Interest Areas are Work Groups and jobs that fit your interests and that you can do or can learn to do quickly. You will also likely find options that interest you but that may require knowledge and skills that you do not have or would have difficulty acquiring. Do not exclude these options too quickly. Depending on your interest level, you may want to consider getting the education or training you need to enter these jobs.

Part 3 provides helpful "crosswalks" for identifying job groupings related to your values, leisure activities, preferred work settings, military experience, and other characteristics. These cross-references may help you identify career options that you may otherwise overlook, so consider using them to discover Work Groups to explore in more detail.

Step 3. Explore the Work Groups You Selected

After you identify Work Groups that interest you, look up their descriptions in Part 1 and read them carefully. As you read about a group, you may discover that it is not what you thought it would be and that you are not interested in it. Or you may find that the training or other requirements are more difficult than you wish to undertake. As you discover more, you can drop some groups from consideration and go on to others.

Step 4: Read the Descriptions for Jobs That Interest You

The information on Work Groups found in Part 1 includes listings of specific job titles. After you have learned more about the Work Groups that most interest you, you can read the information in Part 2 on specific jobs within the Work Group.

Step 5. Create a Plan of Action

When you have identified job titles that interest you most, you need to decide what to do next. Perhaps you can obtain some of these jobs with your present qualifications, while other jobs will demand additional training, education, or experience. Your next step may be clear to you. If, however, you are still not sure about what you want to do, you can get career-planning help in a variety of ways.

Check for career-planning assistance often available to students and graduates at many schools. Also, most areas have government-funded programs that provide similar services, as do local colleges and universities. Call 1-877-US-2JOBS (a toll-free information source provided by the U.S. Department of Labor), look in the yellow pages under Vocational or Career Counseling, ask your librarian for help in locating these resources, or look at http://www.servicelocator.org/ (also provided by the Department of Labor) on the Web.

Because the descriptions in this book are brief, you may want additional information on one or more jobs before you make a decision on what to do. Many good books and Internet resources can help you in your career planning. A resource list appears at the end of this introduction.

A Brief History of the *Guide for Occupational Exploration*

The idea of exploring career options based on interests is surely thousands of years old. For example: "I'd rather work on making really good arrows than killing mastodons." Interests, you see, don't exist in isolation from those things we are good at—they are often one and the same.

So people have been making career decisions based on interests for a long, long time. But the GOE was the result of the first concerted "scientific" effort to create a systematic process using interests for exploring career, learning, and life options. The research for the GOE began in the 1950s and 1960s when researchers worked on coming up with a simple, intuitive way for people to explore careers. They did this under the direction of the U.S. Department of Labor in response to many requests from career counselors and others who wanted a more user-friendly system than the complex approach used in the *Dictionary of Occupational Titles (DOT)*.

In the mid-1970s, these researchers organized all 12,741 job titles in the *DOT* into 12 broad areas of interests. These original 12 "Interest Areas" were Artistic; Scientific; Plants and Animals; Protective; Mechanical; Industrial; Business Detail; Selling; Accommodating; Humanitarian; Leading-Influencing; and Physical Performing. Each Interest Area was further divided into increasingly specific Work Groups and Subgroups of related jobs. This arrangement made a complex system easy to understand and use.

The new arrangement was called the Guide for Occupational Exploration, and a book with this name was first published in 1979. That first edition presented substantial information on the 12 GOE Interest Areas and their groupings of related jobs, as well as listings of related jobs within each grouping. The original *GOE* was well received and widely used, and it became a standard career reference that was cross-referenced in most major career information systems. The major limitation of this 1979 edition was that you had to use the separate *DOT* to obtain descriptions for listed jobs, an awkward process.

Drs. Thomas Harrington and Arthur O'Shea released the first major revision of the *GOE* in 1984. This included the original GOE Interest Areas but added important content developed from research by the Labor Department. One of its important additions was the crosswalks that allowed you to look up jobs related to work values, leisure activities, home activities, school subjects, work settings, and military occupational specialties.

In 1991, a book titled *The Enhanced Guide for Occupational Exploration* by Marilyn Maze and Michael Farr was released. Its inclusion of descriptions of the 2,500 largest occupations made the *GOE* much easier to use. Another book followed in 1993 by Michael Farr that included many of the improvements from the Harrington and O'Shea edition. Titled *The Complete Guide for Occupational Exploration*, it added newer occupations from a revised *DOT* and other improvements. *The Enhanced Guide for Occupational Exploration* was revised in 1995 (by Marilyn Maze and Donald Mayall) and included newer data on occupations and other changes. JIST published all of these editions.

As the 21st century dawned, the GOE classification structure developed in the mid-1970s clearly needed revision to reflect the many changes in our economy. The concept of Interest Areas and more specific job groupings within them remained valid, but the original system did not handle the many changes that had occurred in America's transition from an industrial to an information- and service-based economy. So in 2001 the *Guide for Occupational Exploration*, Third Edition, was released, authored by Michael Farr, LaVerne L. Ludden, and Laurence Shatkin. This edition expanded the Interest Areas from 12 to 14 and renamed some of them to align better with the Standard Occupational Classification (SOC) scheme that the U.S. Department of Labor had adopted. This edition also based its occupational information on the new O*NET (Occupational Information Network) database instead of the obsolete DOT, and it distributed the O*NET occupations among the various Work Groups where they most made sense. Since the O*NET divides the world of work into only about 1,000 jobs, we were able to include descriptions for all O*NET jobs in the third edition—an enormous advantage over the original *GOE*, which had listings but no descriptions of 12,741 DOT job titles.

But even as the third edition of the *GOE* was coming out, the U.S. Department of Education was promoting still another way of structuring the world of work—into 16 easy-to-understand categories called career clusters. This clustering scheme was perceived as a good way to provide a common language for career education planners, career development professionals, career information providers, and education-minded representatives of industry to talk about education, work, and how the two are related. The long-term plan was to outline for each career cluster the academic and technical knowledge and skills that young people would need to acquire to succeed in the occupations that belonged to the cluster. Then high school programs would be developed by states and communities to meet those educational goals. Of course, a large number of career-oriented programs were already in place. So even though a standard set of educational outcomes had not yet been agreed on, for a couple of years the Department of Education required that state vocational-technical directors report on their Perkins-funded programs in terms of the 16 career clusters (a requirement that lapsed but may be reinstated).

This career cluster scheme was so successful that it became—and remains—the standard that is used by many state and local school career-oriented programs and that continues to be championed by the National Association of State Directors of Career Technical Education Consortium. CORD (formerly the Center for Occupational Research and Development), the National Association for Workforce Improvement, the Vocational Technical Education Consortium of States, and many state departments of education have also organized programs, resources, and conferences around this clustering scheme. As the new standard, it has often superseded, or at least been cross-referenced to, previous schemes for grouping educational programs, such as career pathways and Tech Prep clusters.

In addition, the 16 career clusters have been adopted as the framework for aligning secondary and postsecondary educational programs under the College and Career Transitions Initiative, a program launched in 2002 by the Department of Education in cooperation with the League for Innovation in the Community Colleges. The CCTI program is intended to extend the principles of the No Child Left Behind act from high school to postsecondary education, using the career cluster scheme as a common vocabulary for describing the goals and skill standards of educational programs at both levels. The hope is that when programs are more closely aligned, students will make the transition between levels in greater numbers and with greater success.

Therefore, when we felt it was time for JIST Publishing to develop a fourth edition of the *GOE*, the U.S. Department of Education's career cluster scheme was the obvious framework to use.

In turning the U.S. Department of Education's career clusters into our GOE Interest Areas, we made some minor modifications to the names of clusters. For example, we felt that Finance and Insurance better characterized the occupations in that Interest Area than the original title, which was simply Finance. Similarly we expanded Hospitality and Tourism to Hospitality, Tourism, and Recreation. Conversely, we cut back some titles that we thought contained redundancies—thus Law, Public Safety, and Security became Law and Public Safety in the *GOE*, and Business, Management, and Administration became Business and Administration.

We also departed from the practices of the Department of Education when we assigned occupations to Interest Areas. For example, had we followed the official crosswalk developed for the Department of Education career clusters, we would have divided the following occupations among three different Interest Areas:

O*NET Code, Occupation Name, and GOE Interest Area

49-2091.00 Avionics Technicians; 15 Scientific Research, Engineering, and Mathematics

49-2093.00 Electrical and Electronics Installers and Repairers, Transportation Equipment; 16 Transportation, Distribution, and Logistics

49-2094.00 Electrical and Electronics Repairers, Commercial and Industrial Equipment; 13 Manufacturing

However, in the third edition of the *GOE*, these occupations had been neighbors in the same Work Group, and the fact that their O*NET code numbers are extremely close reinforced our perception that they have a lot in common. Therefore, in the fourth edition of the *GOE*, we kept these occupations together, assigning all three to the Work Group 13.14 Electrical and Electronic Repair in the Manufacturing Interest Area.

In making all such decisions, we were guided by the same goal that guided the first edition of the *GOE*: to group occupations that share common characteristics so that people can explore careers more easily. In the book that you now hold in your hands, we believe that we have combined the best of the original GOE concept with the Department of Education's career cluster scheme.

This Edition Presents a Completely Revised Classification System

The following table compares the 12 old GOE Interest Areas with the 16 new ones used in this edition. The new arrangement of Work Groups within the Interest Areas is best seen in the table of contents.

The 12 Old Compared to the 16 New GOE Interest Areas

Original GOE Interest Structure	New GOE Interest Structure
01 Artistic	03 Arts and Communication
02 Scientific	15 Scientific Research, Engineering, and Mathematics
	08 Health Science
	11 Information Technology
03 Plants and Animals	01 Agriculture and Natural Resources
04 Protective	12 Law and Public Safety
05 Mechanical	13 Manufacturing
	16 Transportation, Distribution, and Logistics
	02 Architecture and Construction
06 Industrial	13 Manufacturing
07 Business Detail	04 Business and Administration
08 Selling	14 Retail and Wholesale Sales and Service
09 Accommodating	09 Hospitality, Tourism, and Recreation
10 Humanitarian	10 Human Service
	05 Education and Training
11 Leading-Influencing	07 Government and Public Administration
	06 Finance and Insurance
12 Physical Performing	03 Arts and Communication

Tips to Understand and Use the Major Parts of This Book

The Quick Summary of Major Sections in the table of contents provides brief descriptions for the book's main sections:

* **Part 1.** GOE Interest Areas and Work Groups: Essential Information for Exploring Career Options
* **Part 2.** The Job Descriptions
* **Part 3.** Crosswalks to Careers by Work Values, Leisure Activities, School Subjects, Work Settings, Skills, Abilities, Knowledges, and Military Occupations
* **Appendix.** Information for Vocational Counselors and Other Professionals

Following are more detailed descriptions of each section.

Part 1. GOE Interest Areas and Work Groups

This section is more interesting than it sounds. The GOE organizes jobs into 16 broad Interest Areas and more-specific Work Groups of related jobs. You can use the table of contents to identify Interest Areas and Work Groups that appeal to you and then turn to the appropriate pages in Part 1 to learn more about them. There you will identify specific jobs within the groupings. If you choose, you can then read the descriptions for these jobs in Part 2. Think of this process as a funnel that narrows your job choices until you are left with those that best match your interests. This process is illustrated in the following figure.

Occupational Choices

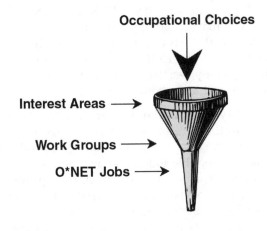

There is a lot of helpful information in Part 1, and it is easier to use than to describe, so please bear with us in this explanation.

Part 1 gives useful details for exploring career options based on interests. It presents information on the GOE's 16 Interest Areas and their related Work Groups so that you know what sorts of jobs they include, the skills required, and the typical education and training needed. It also provides you with information related to school courses, leisure activities, work environments, and other points that may support exploring jobs in certain groups more carefully.

The 16 GOE Interest Areas

Let's begin with the basis for the GOE, the 16 Interest Areas. Remember that the GOE, following the scheme developed by the U.S. Department of Education, organizes all jobs within one of these Interest Areas:

01 Agriculture and Natural Resources

02 Architecture and Construction

03 Arts and Communication

04 Business and Administration

05 Education and Training

06 Finance and Insurance

07 Government and Public Administration

08 Health Science

09 Hospitality, Tourism, and Recreation

10 Human Service

11 Information Technology

12 Law and Public Safety

13 Manufacturing

14 Retail and Wholesale Sales and Service

15 Scientific Research, Engineering, and Mathematics

16 Transportation, Distribution, and Logistics

Brief descriptions for each Interest Area follow. As you read them, try to identify the ones that appeal to you most. These are the ones you should explore in more detail in Part 1.

01 Agriculture and Natural Resources. An interest in working with plants, animals, forests, or mineral resources for agriculture, horticulture, conservation, extraction, and other purposes. You can satisfy this interest by working in farming, landscaping, forestry, fishing, mining, and related fields. You may like doing physical work outdoors, such as on a farm or ranch, in a forest, or on a drilling rig. If you have scientific curiosity, you could study plants and animals or analyze biological or rock samples in a lab. If you have management ability, you could own, operate, or manage a fish hatchery, a landscaping business, or a greenhouse.

02 Architecture and Construction. An interest in designing, assembling, and maintaining components of buildings and other structures. You may want to be part of the team of architects, drafters, and others who design buildings and render the plans. If construction interests you, you can find fulfillment in the many building projects that are being undertaken at all times. If you like to organize and plan, you can find careers in managing these projects. Or you can play a more direct role in putting up and finishing buildings by doing jobs such as plumbing, carpentry, masonry, painting, or roofing, either as a skilled craftsworker or as a helper. You can prepare the building site by operating heavy equipment or install, maintain, and repair vital building equipment and systems such as electricity and heating.

03 Arts and Communication. An interest in creatively expressing feelings or ideas, in communicating news or information, or in performing. You can satisfy this interest in creative, verbal, or performing activities. For example, if you enjoy literature, perhaps writing or editing would appeal to you. Journalism and public relations are other fields for people who like to use their writing or speaking skills. Do you prefer to work in the performing arts? If so, you could direct or perform in drama, music, or dance. If you especially enjoy the visual arts, you could create paintings, sculpture, or ceramics or design products or visual displays. A flair for technology might lead you to specialize in photography, broadcast production, or dispatching.

04 Business and Administration. An interest in making a business organization or function run smoothly. You can satisfy this interest by working in a position of leadership or by specializing in a function that contributes to the overall effort in a business, nonprofit organization, or government agency. If you especially enjoy working with people, you may find fulfillment from working in human resources. An interest in numbers may lead you to consider accounting, finance, budgeting, billing, or financial record-keeping. A job as an administrative assistant may interest you if you like a variety of work in a busy environment. If you are good with details and word processing, you may enjoy a job as a secretary or data entry keyer. Or perhaps you would do well as the manager of a business.

05 Education and Training. An interest in helping people learn. You can satisfy this interest by teaching students, who may be preschoolers, retirees, or any age in between. You may specialize in a particular academic field or work with learners of a particular age, with a particular interest, or with a particular learning problem. Working in a library or museum may give you an opportunity to expand people's understanding of the world.

06 Finance and Insurance. An interest in helping businesses and people be assured of a financially secure future. You can satisfy this interest by working in a financial or insurance business in a leadership or support role. If you like gathering and analyzing information, you may find fulfillment as an insurance adjuster or financial analyst. Or you may deal with information at the clerical level as a banking or insurance clerk or in person-to-person situations providing customer service. Another way to interact with people is to sell financial or insurance services that will meet their needs.

07 Government and Public Administration. An interest in helping a government agency serve the needs of the public. You can satisfy this interest by working in a position of leadership or by specializing in a function that contributes to the role of government. You may help protect the public by working as an inspector or

examiner to enforce standards. If you enjoy using clerical skills, you may work as a clerk in a law court or government office. Or perhaps you prefer the top-down perspective of a government executive or urban planner.

08 Health Science. An interest in helping people and animals be healthy. You can satisfy this interest by working in a health care team as a doctor, therapist, or nurse. You might specialize in one of the many different parts of the body (such as the teeth or eyes) or in one of the many different types of care. Or you may wish to be a generalist who deals with the whole patient. If you like technology, you might find satisfaction working with X rays or new methods of diagnosis. You might work with healthy people, helping them eat right. If you enjoy working with animals, you might care for them and keep them healthy.

09 Hospitality, Tourism, and Recreation. An interest in catering to the personal wishes and needs of others so that they may enjoy a clean environment, good food and drink, comfortable lodging away from home, and recreation. You can satisfy this interest by providing services for the convenience, care, and pampering of others in hotels, restaurants, airplanes, beauty parlors, and so on. You may wish to use your love of cooking as a chef. If you like working with people, you may wish to provide personal services by being a travel guide, a flight attendant, a concierge, a hairdresser, or a waiter. You may wish to work in cleaning and building services if you like a clean environment. If you enjoy sports or games, you may work for an athletic team or casino.

10 Human Service. An interest in improving people's social, mental, emotional, or spiritual well-being. You can satisfy this interest as a counselor, social worker, or religious worker who helps people sort out their complicated lives or solve personal problems. You may work as a caretaker for very young people or the elderly. Or you may interview people to help identify the social services they need.

11 Information Technology. An interest in designing, developing, managing, and supporting information systems. You can satisfy this interest by working with hardware, software, multimedia, or integrated systems. If you like to use your organizational skills, you might work as an administrator of a system or database. Or you can solve complex problems as a software engineer or systems analyst. If you enjoy getting your hands on the hardware, you might find work servicing computers, peripherals, and information-intense machines such as cash registers and ATMs.

12 Law and Public Safety. An interest in upholding people's rights or in protecting people and property by using authority, inspecting, or investigating. You can satisfy this interest by working in law, law enforcement, fire fighting, the military, and related fields. For example, if you enjoy mental challenge and intrigue, you could investigate crimes or fires for a living. If you enjoy working with verbal skills and research skills, you may want to defend citizens in court or research deeds, wills, and other legal documents. If you want to help people in critical situations, you may want to fight fires, work as a police officer, or become a paramedic. Or, if you want more routine work in public safety, perhaps a job in guarding, patrolling, or inspecting would appeal to you. If you have management ability, you could seek a leadership position in law enforcement and the protective services. Work in the military gives you a chance to use technical and leadership skills while serving your country.

13 Manufacturing. An interest in processing materials into intermediate or final products or maintaining and repairing products by using machines or hand tools. You can satisfy this interest by working in one of many industries that mass-produce goods or by working for a utility that distributes electric power or other resources. You may enjoy manual work, using your hands or hand tools in highly skilled jobs such as assembling engines or electronic equipment. If you enjoy making machines run efficiently or fixing them when they break down, you could seek a job installing or repairing such devices as copiers, aircraft engines, cars, or watches. Perhaps you prefer to set up or operate machines that are used to manufacture products made of food, glass, or paper. You may enjoy cutting and grinding metal and plastic parts to desired shapes and measurements. Or you may wish to operate equipment in systems that provide water and process wastewater. You may like inspecting, sorting, counting, or weighing products. Another option is to work with your hands and machinery to move boxes and freight in a warehouse. If leadership appeals to you, you could manage people engaged in production and repair.

14 Retail and Wholesale Sales and Service. An interest in bringing others to a particular point of view by personal persuasion and by sales and promotional techniques. You can satisfy this interest in a variety of jobs that involve persuasion and selling. If you like using your knowledge of science, you may enjoy selling pharmaceutical, medical, or electronic products or services. Real estate offers several kinds of sales jobs as well. If you like speaking on the phone, you could work as a telemarketer. Or you may enjoy selling apparel and other merchandise in a retail setting. If you prefer to help people, you may want a job in customer service.

15 Scientific Research, Engineering, and Mathematics. An interest in discovering, collecting, and analyzing information about the natural world; in applying scientific research findings to problems in medicine, the life sciences, human behavior, and the natural sciences; in imagining and manipulating quantitative data; and in applying technology to manufacturing, transportation, and other economic activities. You can satisfy this interest by working with the knowledge and processes of the sciences. You may enjoy researching and developing new knowledge in mathematics, or perhaps solving problems in the physical, life, or social sciences would appeal to you. You may wish to study engineering and help create new machines, processes, and structures. If you want to work with scientific equipment and procedures, you could seek a job in a research or testing laboratory.

16 Transportation, Distribution, and Logistics. An interest in operations that move people or materials. You can satisfy this interest by managing a transportation service, by helping vehicles keep on their assigned schedules and routes, or by driving or piloting a vehicle. If you enjoy taking responsibility, perhaps managing a rail line would appeal to you. If you work well with details and can take pressure on the job, you might consider being an air traffic controller. Or would you rather get out on the highway, on the water, or up in the air? If so, then you could drive a truck from state to state, be employed on a ship, or fly a crop duster over a cornfield. If you prefer to stay closer to home, you could drive a delivery van, taxi, or school bus. You can use your physical strength to load freight and arrange it so it gets to its destination in one piece.

Interest Areas Are Divided into More-Specific Work Groups

The 16 GOE Interest Areas are divided into more-specific Work Groups of related jobs. This process allows you to more clearly see the types of more-specific interests within each GOE Interest Area. For example, the Agriculture and Natural Resources Interest Area has the following Work Groups.

01.01   Managerial Work in Agriculture and Natural Resources

01.02   Resource Science/Engineering for Plants, Animals, and the Environment

01.03   Resource Technologies for Plants, Animals, and the Environment

01.04   General Farming

01.05   Nursery, Groundskeeping, and Pest Control

01.06   Forestry and Logging

01.07   Hunting and Fishing

01.08   Mining and Drilling

In reviewing this list, note that each Work Group has a four-digit identification number. The first two digits designate the GOE Interest Area (which is 01 for the Agriculture and Natural Resources Interest Area). The third and fourth digits provide a unique number for each Work Group within that Interest Area. For example, 01.05 is the Work Group titled Nursery, Groundskeeping, and Pest Control. A complete list of the GOE Work Groups is included in the table of contents.

Helpful Career Planning Information Is Provided for Each Work Group

Part 1 gives a substantial amount of information on each GOE Work Group. This material is carefully selected to help you determine if you are likely to be interested in or good at the jobs within that Work Group. The information is presented in an easy-to-use format that includes details to help you understand and evaluate the career opportunities within that group. Following are the details provided for each Work Group.

GOE number and Work Group name. As described previously, each Work Group is assigned a four-digit number. This number is listed before the name of the Work Group. For example, under the Agriculture and Natural Resources is the Work Group 01.01 Managerial Work in Agriculture and Natural Resources. (We will continue to use examples from this Work Group throughout this overview.)

Brief definition. This is a short statement that defines the Work Group, and it appears directly following the GOE Work Group number and name. The definition also provides examples of the types of jobs in the group and where they might occur. Here is the brief definition statement for 01.01 Managerial Work in Agriculture and Natural Resources:

Workers in this group manage and coordinate businesses or workers who tend plants and animals or who drill or dig for oil or minerals.

What kind of work would you do? This is a list of typical work activities people do in jobs related to the Work Group. Some of the tasks might be similar to

things that you have done in school, at another job, at home, in leisure activities, or as a volunteer. Take into consideration how attractive these activities are when evaluating your interest in this Work Group. Here are just three of the entries for our sample Work Group:

Your work activities would depend on your job. For example, you might

* Analyze and plan extraction process of geological materials.
* Assign workers to tasks, such as feeding and treating animals, cleaning quarters, transferring animals, and maintaining facilities.
* Conduct field trips to point out scientific, historic, and natural features of parks, forests, historic sites, or other attractions.

What things about you point to this kind of work? This portion of the Work Group description deals with personal preferences. Information is provided in response to five questions that are helpful to consider in exploring career and life options. Each of these questions is presented below, along with brief explanations and examples.

Is it important for you to...? This question is followed by items that deal with a person's temperament or style of behavior. Sometimes these are referred to as work values, meaning the satisfaction related to work that is most important to you. If you feel that most items listed are important to you, then this Work Group probably contains occupations that would be a good fit for you. For example:

Is it important for you to

* Give directions and instructions to others?
* Plan your work with little supervision?
* Make decisions on your own?

Have you enjoyed any of the following as a hobby or leisure-time activity? A list of hobbies, leisure activities, and extracurricular activities follows this question. Pastimes that you engage in as a hobby or leisure activity are an important measure of the appeal jobs in the Work Group might have for you. For example:

* Belonging to a 4-H club, a garden club, or Future Farmers of America
* Breeding animals
* Designing and landscaping a flower garden

Have you liked and done well in any of the following school subjects? A list of school subjects that are related to this work follows this question. If you like these school subjects, then you probably would do well in studying the knowledges and skills needed for entry into the jobs

© 2006 JIST Works

found in the Work Group. Some school subjects related to our example include the following:

Management · Dairy Science/Technology · Plant Pest Management/Pathology · Agriculture, Mechanized · Agronomy · Agribusiness

Are you able to...? This question is followed by a list of basic abilities. Abilities are mental, social, and physical traits used to accomplish tasks. Typically, abilities don't change over a long period of time. The more your abilities match those on the list, the more likely you are to do well in the related jobs. Some abilities listed for our example include the following:

* Listen to and understand information and ideas presented through spoken words and sentences?
* Add, subtract, multiply, or divide quickly and correctly?
* See objects in the presence of glare or bright lighting?

Would you work in places such as...? A list of workplaces follows this question. The place where people work is an important factor in how well they like the job. If you are not sure what some of the workplaces are like, you might want to visit them. Here are a few of the entries for our example:

Farms? · Fish hatcheries? · Forests? · Ships and boats? · Plant nurseries? · Golf courses and tennis courts?

What skills and knowledges do you need for this kind of work? This part of the Work Group's description has two items, skills and knowledges, which are covered separately. A brief explanation and examples follow.

For most of these jobs, you need these skills. Skills are what you need to perform a task, and we all have thousands of them. Some seem so simple that we take them for granted. For example, riding a bicycle is a skill, but it is so complicated that no one has been able to develop a robot that can perform this task. Each job has skills that are important to perform the work effectively. The skills you find in this section are ones important to the jobs in the Work Group. You should consider whether you have these skills or could acquire them to decide if the related jobs are a good match. Here are some skills listed for our example:

* Management of Personnel Resources—motivating, developing, and directing people as they work, identifying the best people for the job
* Management of Material Resources—obtaining and seeing to the appropriate use of equipment, facilities, and materials needed to do certain work

* Management of Financial Resources—determining how money will be spent to get the work done and accounting for these expenditures

These knowledges are important in most of these jobs. Knowledge about a job comes through education, experience, or training. The entries here often include topics that are presented as areas of learning, such as a high school course, a training program, or a college course or major. Some entries for our example include the following:

* Food Production—techniques and equipment for planting, growing, and harvesting food products (both plant and animal) for consumption, including storage/handling techniques
* Personnel and Human Resources—principles and procedures for personnel recruitment, selection, training, compensation and benefits, labor relations and negotiation, and personnel information systems

What else should you consider about this kind of work? This entry identifies other issues that are important to consider when choosing a career. This includes typical ways to enter the occupation, opportunities for promotions, competition for job openings, working conditions, and advantages or disadvantages to the occupation. Here is a partial entry for our example:

While some work in rural areas or woodlands, others find employment with commercial nurseries, landscaping firms, business services, or government agencies located in large and small communities all over the country.

It is hard for newcomers to start their own farming businesses. Openings are more plentiful for people who want to manage farms for others. Many large farms are owned by large companies that hire well-trained managers to take responsibility for day-to-day operations. Competition for jobs is increasing as these agricultural companies merge.

How can you prepare for jobs of this kind? This entry provides information on the type of training, education, or experience that is typically needed for entry into jobs within the Work Group. Because there are often many jobs within each Work Group, the information is general but helpful. Here is an excerpt from what it says for the example Work Group we have been using:

Occupations in this group usually require education and/or training ranging from one or two years to less than ten years. Several jobs in this group are open primarily to people with work experience in a related field.

Growing up on a farm is good initial preparation for many of these jobs. Formal training for management jobs is available at the high school and higher levels. For example, vocational agriculture courses are offered in many high schools to high school students during the day and to adults at night and on weekends.

How much education or training is required for the jobs in this Work Group? Following this question is an alphabetical listing of jobs in each Work Group by level of education and training. For example, under 01.01 Managerial Work in Agriculture and Natural Resources, these job titles are listed:

Long-term on-the-job training

* Farmers and Ranchers

Work experience in a related occupation

* Agricultural Crop Farm Managers
* First-Line Supervisors and Manager/Supervisors—Extractive Workers
* First-Line Supervisors and Manager/Supervisors—Landscaping Workers
* Fish Hatchery Managers
* Lawn Service Managers
* Nursery and Greenhouse Managers
* Purchasing Agents and Buyers, Farm Products

Associate degree

* First-Line Supervisors and Manager/Supervisors—Agricultural Crop Workers
* First-Line Supervisors and Manager/Supervisors—Animal Husbandry Workers
* First-Line Supervisors and Manager/Supervisors—Fishery Workers
* First-Line Supervisors and Manager/Supervisors—Horticultural Workers

Bachelor's degree

* First-Line Supervisors and Manager/Supervisors—Logging Workers
* Park Naturalists

Each and every job listed under the Work Groups has a description you can read in Part 2.

Part 2. The Job Descriptions

Part 2 provides job descriptions for all jobs listed in Part 1. More than 900 jobs are described in Part 2, including all that are listed in the current O*NET database maintained by the U.S. Department of Labor for which the O*NET provides more data than just a name and definition. The job descriptions are presented in Part 2 in alphabetical order within GOE Interest Areas and Work Groups.

How the Job Descriptions Are Derived from the Data

Technical and other users of this book will want to know the process we used to get to the information we include in the job descriptions, so we've provided a brief explanation here. The O*NET is a database that offers an enormous amount of data on hundreds of measures for each job. We set out to provide descriptions that were both brief and useful. To do this, we had to be flexible in the criteria we used. For example, numeric measures are used for many criteria, such as Occupational Values, Abilities, and Skills Required. Because it is impractical and boring to give you numerical values for such measures, we used some fancy database work to include more-useful information.

Following is a brief review of where the information in the descriptions comes from and the criteria we used to include or exclude information. If you want the specific numerical ratings on each measure for a specific job, you can find them in the O*NET database on the Internet at http://online.onetcenter.org.

The **O*NET titles, job descriptions, and code numbers** are derived directly from the newest O*NET database, Release 7.

Average Salary is derived from the OES wage database of the Bureau of Labor Statistics. The most recent OES database available provides 2003 earnings. It uses SOC (Standard Occupational Classification) codes to classify occupations, and although these are similar to O*NET codes, they are not always identical. For example, the O*NET has separate information for Accountants and for Auditors, but the SOC reports salary for a single occupation called Accountants and Auditors. In cases such as this, we needed to crosswalk a single SOC occupation to multiple O*NET occupations, so you may notice (to continue the present example) that the salary we report for Accountants ($49,770) is identical to the salary we report for Auditors. In reality there probably is a difference, but this is the best information that is available.

Projected Growth, Annual Openings, and the **Education** statement are derived from the Industry-Occupation Employment Matrix, which we also crosswalked from the SOC occupations to the O*NET occupations used in this book.

Job Zone is based on the Job Zone rating assigned to the job in the O*NET database. More information on Job Zone ratings appears later in the introduction.

The **Education/Training Programs** are derived from a crosswalk developed by the Department of Labor to connect O*NET occupations to programs in the Classification of Instructional Programs Edition 2000 (CIP 2000).

The **Related Knowledge/Courses** are based on the Knowledge table from the O*NET. We use a complicated formula to decide which knowledges best represent each occupation. First, for each of the 33 knowledges in the O*NET taxonomy, we compute the mean and the standard deviation for the ratings given to *all* occupations, using the scale for level of knowledge required. (The mean rating is never exactly equal to 3.5, the value that represents the midpoint of the rating scale.) We use the sum of the mean and standard deviation as our cutoff score for a "high" rating on that knowledge. Then, for each occupation, we list all the knowledges that are rated higher than their cutoff scores in descending order by the amounts by which they exceed the cutoff score. For some occupations, this would result in a large number of knowledges, so for the sake of brevity we limit this entry to the top six knowledges—although if the seventh- or eighth-highest knowledges have a score tied with the sixth, we include those, too. Conversely, for other occupations no knowledge exceeds its cutoff score. Since the knowledge used in an occupation tells something of the flavor of the occupation even when the knowledge is not used at a high level, in such cases we

include the two knowledges that come closest to their cutoff scores.

The **Personality Type** is based on the value for the field called "First Interest High-Point" in the Interest table from the O*NET. This is the highest rated of the six Holland personality types. We provide more information on the Holland system later in this introduction.

Occupational Values are determined by an approach similar to the one we used for knowledges, except that we limit the number of values listed to five (except in cases of tied scores, when there may be as many as eight), and if no value has a rating higher than its cutoff score, we state "None met the criteria."

Skills Required are determined by the same formula that we use for values, except that we present the highest eight, or in case of tied scores, as many as 10. A similar approach is also used for **Abilities** (the highest four, or as many as six in the event of a tie) and for the **Interacting with Others** tasks (the highest five, or six in the event of a tie). The latter consist of those generalized work tasks listed in the O*NET table called WorkActivity with an identity code beginning with 4.A.4.

The approach for Interacting with Others is also used for **Physical Work Conditions.** The features used are those provided in an O*NET database table called WorkContext with an identity code beginning with 4.C.2.

The job descriptions are brief but packed with useful information. We selected information that we think you will find most helpful. Note that if we included all information in the O*NET database, it would require about 20 pages for each job. The O*NET database includes data on hundreds of measures that would probably be of little interest to you. It was impossible to print a book of over 20,000 pages, and most people would not want all that information. Here is a sample job description from Part 2.

A Sample Job Description

This description is listed under

* GOE Interest Area: 01 Arts, Entertainment, and Media
* Work Group 01.01: Managerial Work in Arts, Entertainment, and Media

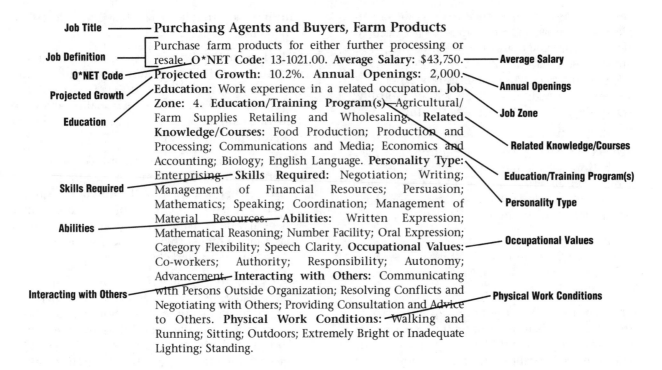

The elements of this job description are pointed out by name for illustration purposes. Each element is explained in detail in the next section.

What Each Job Description Includes

We wanted to include lots of useful information in each job description yet keep it short and easy to understand. To do this, we had to make some compromises, such as providing codes for the Job Zone information. The descriptions are pretty easy to understand, with the exception of Job Zone information. Here are descriptions of each component.

Job Title. This is the official title given to the job by the Department of Labor. Some organizations may use a different job title, but the tasks performed by workers in the job are quite similar.

Job Definition. This is a short one- or two-sentence statement that describes the job.

O*NET Code. Each job has a unique number assigned to it in the U.S. Department of Labor's O*NET database. This number can be used to look up a job in any system that uses the O*NET number.

Average Salary. The average salary is obtained from data collected by the Bureau of Labor Statistics. We used the most recently available data, which was based on information collected for 2003. While this may sound like old information, it takes a few years of analysis before it is released by the government, so this is as good as it gets. The salary is based on the median for all workers in this occupation. This means that half earn more and half less. Keep in mind that new workers usually make much less than the median when starting in an occupation. Wages also vary from one part of the United States to another. Workers in larger cities often make more than those in rural areas, and workers in larger organizations typically earn more than those in smaller ones.

Projected Growth. The projected growth rate is obtained from the Bureau of Labor Statistics and is estimated for the 2002 to 2012 time period. Again, due to delays in analysis and release, this is the most recent data available. The growth figure represents the percent of new jobs that are projected to be created during this 10-year period. This figure provides some indication of the demand for this occupation in the years to come. The average growth rate for all occupations during this time is projected to be 14.8%. One-quarter of the occupations have a growth projection of 4.7% or lower. Growth of 12.4% is the median, meaning that half of the occupations have more, half less. Only one-quarter of the occupations have growth projected at more than 19.4%.

Annual Openings. This is an estimate of the number of jobs in this occupation that the Bureau of Labor Statistics projects will open each year during the years between 2002 and 2012. This statistic provides a useful balance for the growth statistic in helping you to understand the demand for the occupation. For example, consider the occupation Makeup Artists, Theatrical and Performance. It has a projected growth rate of 18.2%, which sounds very promising until you notice that fewer than 500 job openings per year are projected. This occupation has a tiny workforce, so even though it is growing rapidly, it will need very few new workers. By contrast, consider Secretaries, Except Legal, Medical, and Executive, which actually has a negative growth rate (–2.9%), but which has such a large workforce that it will account for 254,000 job openings per year. Not bad for a shrinking occupation!

Education. While this section of the O*NET description is titled "Education" for simplicity, it includes information on the education, training, or experience typically required for entry into the job. Please note, however, that some (or many) who work in the job may have higher or lower levels than indicated. Certification or licensing also may be required for some jobs, but accurate information on these requirements was not available from the O*NET database and often varies from state to state. There are 11 levels of education used to classify the education, training, and experience needs of each job:

* *Short-term on-the-job training.* It is possible to work in these occupations and achieve an average level of performance within a few days or weeks through on-the-job training.

* *Moderate-term on-the-job training.* Occupations that require this type of training can be performed adequately after a 1- to 12-month period of combined on-the-job and informal training. Typically, untrained workers observe experienced workers performing tasks and are gradually moved into progressively more difficult assignments.

* *Long-term on-the-job training.* This type of training requires more than 12 months of on-the-job training or combined work experience and formal classroom instruction. This includes occupations that use formal apprenticeships for training workers that may take up to four years. It also includes intensive occupation-specific, employer-sponsored training like police academies. Furthermore, it includes occupations that require natural talent that must be developed over many years.

* *Work experience in a related occupation.* This type of job requires a worker to have experience in a related occupation. For example, police detectives are selected based on their experience as police patrol officers.

* *Postsecondary vocational training.* This requirement can vary in length; training usually lasts from a few months up to one year. In a few instances, there may be as many as four years of training.

* *Associate degree.* This degree usually requires two years of full-time academic work beyond high school.

* *Bachelor's degree.* This is a degree that requires approximately four to five years of full-time academic work beyond high school.

* *Work experience plus degree.* Jobs in this category are often management-related and require some experience in a related nonmanagerial position.

* *Master's degree.* Completion of a master's degree usually requires one to two years of full-time study beyond the bachelor's degree.

* *Doctoral degree.* This degree normally requires two or more years of full-time academic work beyond the bachelor's degree.

* *First professional degree.* This type of degree normally requires a minimum of two years of education beyond the bachelor's degree and frequently requires three years.

Job Zone. The concept of Job Zones takes a bit of explaining. In the descriptions, we use number codes for this because providing text to describe each one would take too much space, as you will soon see. This is the only coded item in the job descriptions, so please forgive us.

Job Zone information is included in the O*NET database, and we decided it was useful enough to include in the job descriptions. Job Zones provide information that is related to and expands on the Education entry in the description. In general, the higher the Job Zone number, the more education, training, or experience is required. Jobs within each Job Zone are similar in terms of the following:

* The overall experience needed to do the job
* The general range of education needed to do the job
* On-the-job training needed to do the job

Job Zone information includes a measure that represents the months or years of education, training, and experience needed to become fully competent in performing the job. This measure is called the Standard

Vocational Preparation or SVP. You will see the SVP measure used in the following sidebar.

Job Zone Definitions

Job Zone 1

Experience: Little or no preparation needed. No previous work-related skill, knowledge, or experience is needed for these occupations. For example, a person can become a general office clerk even if the person has never worked in an office before.

Education: These occupations may require a high school diploma or GED certificate. Some may require a formal training course to obtain a license.

Training: Employees in these occupations need anywhere from a few days to a few months of training. Usually, an experienced worker could show you how to do the job.

Examples: These occupations involve following instructions and helping others. Examples include bus drivers, forest and conservation workers, general office clerks, home health aides, and waiters/waitresses.

SVP Range: Below 4.0—less than six months.

Job Zone 2

Experience: Some preparation needed. Some previous work-related skill, knowledge, or experience may be helpful in these occupations but usually is not needed. For example, a drywall installer might benefit from experience installing drywall, but an inexperienced person could still learn to be an installer with little difficulty.

Education: These occupations usually require a high school diploma and may require some vocational training or job-related course work. In some cases, an associate or bachelor's degree could be needed.

Training: Employees in these occupations need anywhere from a few months to one year of working with experienced employees.

Examples: These occupations often involve using your knowledge and skills to help others. Examples include drywall installers, fire inspectors, flight attendants, pharmacy technicians, salespersons (retail), and tellers.

SVP Range: 4.00 to 5.99—six months to less than two years.

Job Zone 3

Experience: Medium preparation needed. Previous work-related skill, knowledge, or experience is required for these occupations. For example, an electrician must have completed three or four years of apprenticeship or several years of vocational training and often must have passed a licensing exam to perform the job.

Education: Most occupations in this zone require training in vocational schools, related on-the-job experience, or an associate degree. Some may require a bachelor's degree.

Training: Employees in these occupations usually need one or two years of training involving both on-the-job experience and informal training with experienced workers.

Examples: These occupations usually involve using communication and organizational skills to coordinate, supervise, manage, or train others to accomplish goals. Examples include dental assistants, electricians, fish and game wardens, legal secretaries, personnel recruiters, and recreation workers.

SVP Range: 6.0 to less than 7.0—more than one year and less than four years.

Job Zone 4

Experience: Considerable preparation needed. A minimum of two to four years of work-related skill, knowledge, or experience is needed for these occupations. For example, an accountant must complete four years of college and work for several years in accounting to be considered qualified.

Education: Most of these occupations require a four-year bachelor's degree, but some do not.

Training: Employees in these occupations usually need several years of work-related experience, on-the-job training, and/or vocational training.

Examples: Many of these occupations involve coordinating, supervising, managing, or training others. Examples include accountants, chefs and head cooks, computer programmers, historians, pharmacists, and police detectives.

SVP Range: 7.0 to less than 8.0—two years to less than ten years.

© 2006 JIST Works

Job Zone 5

Experience: Extensive preparation needed. Extensive skill, knowledge, and experience are needed for these occupations. Many require more than five years of experience. For example, surgeons must complete four years of college and an additional five to seven years of specialized medical training to be able to do their job.

Education: A bachelor's degree is the minimum formal education required for these occupations. However, many also require graduate school. For example, they may require a master's degree, and some require a Ph.D., M.D., or J.D. law degree.

Training: Employees may need some on-the-job training, but most of these occupations assume that the person will already have the required skills, knowledge, work-related experience, and/or training.

Examples: These occupations often involve coordinating, training, supervising, or managing the activities of others to accomplish goals. Very advanced communication and organizational skills are required. Examples include athletic trainers, lawyers, managing editors, physicists, social psychologists, and surgeons.

SVP Range: 8.0 and above—four years to more than ten years.

Education/Training Program(s). This list identifies the educational or training programs that the Department of Labor considers appropriate for the job. The names of the programs are taken from the Classification of Instructional Programs Edition 2000 (CIP 2000), developed by the U.S. Department of Education. The titles of the programs do not necessarily match the titles used at every educational institution, but they are usually close. For example, there may well not be any college that offers a major called Political Science and Government, General, but this is obviously the equivalent of a major called Political Science or one called Government. For jobs that require an advanced degree, the title of the program listed here usually reflects the highest course of study to be completed. So, for example, the occupation Librarian, which usually requires a master's degree, lists Library Science/Librarianship but does not mention that most graduate schools of library science prefer students to enter with a bachelor's degree in some *other* subject. If the program is primarily a training program for a particular job, the title may look like the name of that job. For example, for Teacher Assistants, one program listed is Teacher Assistant/Aide. This is simply an abbreviated way of saying "Teacher Assistant/Aide Training." The programs are listed alphabetically, and for the sake of space we did not let any list exceed about 2,000 characters.

Related Knowledge/Courses. This is a list of the most important types of knowledge that are used on the job in descending order of importance. It gives you an idea of what you might learn in the education/training programs listed in the previous topic and also what kinds of problems you may have to deal with on a day-to-day basis in the job.

Personality Type. This provides a cross-reference to a system used in a variety of career assessment tests and information systems. Called Holland codes, the system organizes all occupations into six personality types: Artistic, Conventional, Enterprising, Investigative, Realistic, and Social. The Self-Directed Search (SDS), a career interest inventory published by Psychological Assessment Resources, Inc., uses this system to help people explore occupations. The SDS and other instruments, like the Strong Campbell Interest Inventory and Armed Services Vocational Battery, identify interest areas using the Holland model. Many counselors and educators use these instruments, so you may have taken one. If so, you might recall your type and can use that information in identifying jobs that match. It is also possible to use this information even though you haven't taken one of the assessments. Simply read the personality's definition and determine the one that most closely describes jobs that would interest you. Following are brief descriptions of the six Holland groupings.

The Six Holland Personality Types

Artistic. These occupations frequently involve working with forms, designs, and patterns. They often require self-expression, and the work can be done without following a clear set of rules.

Conventional. These occupations frequently involve following set procedures and routines. These occupations can include working with data and details more than with ideas. Usually there is a clear line of authority to follow.

Enterprising. These occupations frequently involve starting up and carrying out projects. These occupations can involve leading people and making many decisions. They sometimes require risk taking and often deal with business.

Investigative. These occupations frequently involve working with ideas and require an extensive amount of thinking. These occupations can involve searching for facts and figuring out problems mentally.

Realistic. These occupations frequently involve work activities that include practical, hands-on problems and solutions. They often deal with plants, animals, and real-world materials like wood, tools, and machinery. Many of the occupations require working outside and do not involve a lot of paperwork or working closely with others.

Social. These occupations frequently involve working with, communicating with, and teaching people. These occupations often involve helping or providing service to others.

GOE Interest Areas Related to Holland Categories

The GOE Interest Areas are easily cross-referenced to Holland categories. Here is a table that shows this relationship.

GOE Interest Area	Holland Occupational Category
01 Agriculture and Natural Resources	Realistic, Investigative
02 Architecture and Construction	Realistic
03 Arts and Communication	Artistic
04 Business and Administration	Conventional, Enterprising
05 Education and Training	Social, Investigative
06 Finance and Insurance	Conventional, Enterprising
07 Government and Public Administration	Conventional, Realistic
08 Health Science	Social, Investigative
09 Hospitality, Tourism, and Recreation	Enterprising, Realistic
10 Human Service	Social
11 Information Technology	Investigative
12 Law and Public Safety	Enterprising
13 Manufacturing	Realistic
14 Retail and Wholesale Sales and Service	Enterprising
15 Scientific Research, Engineering, and Mathematics	Investigative
16 Transportation, Distribution, and Logistics	Realistic

Skills Required. A skill is a person's capacity to perform a task. Skills are typically developed through education, training, and experience, although they also interact with abilities. In developing the job descriptions, we had data from the O*NET database on 35 skills for each job. That was too much information to be useful, so we included only those skills with higher numerical ratings for each job. The skills that are included in a description are, therefore, those that are particularly important for that job. Descriptions for the 35 skills follow, organized into two major groupings.

The 35 Skills Used in the Job Descriptions

Basic Skills. These capacities facilitate the acquisition of new knowledge and skills.

Reading Comprehension. Understanding written sentences and paragraphs in work-related documents.

© 2006 JIST Works

Active Listening. Giving full attention to what other people are saying, taking time to understand the points being made, asking questions as appropriate, and not interrupting at inappropriate times.

Writing. Communicating effectively in writing as appropriate for the needs of the audience.

Speaking. Talking to others to convey information effectively.

Mathematics. Using mathematics to solve problems.

Science. Using scientific rules and methods to solve problems.

Critical Thinking. Using logic and reasoning to identify the strengths and weaknesses of alternative solutions, conclusions, or approaches to problems.

Active Learning. Understanding the implications of new information for both current and future problem solving and decision making.

Learning Strategies. Selecting and using training/instructional methods and procedures appropriate for the situation when learning or teaching new things.

Monitoring. Monitoring/assessing your performance or that of other individuals or organizations to make improvements or take corrective action.

Cross-Functional Skills. These skills facilitate performance in a variety of job settings.

Social Perceptiveness. Being aware of others' reactions and understanding why they react as they do.

Coordination. Adjusting actions in relation to others' actions.

Persuasion. Persuading others to change their minds or behavior.

Negotiation. Bringing others together and trying to reconcile differences.

Instructing. Teaching others how to do something.

Service Orientation. Actively looking for ways to help people.

Complex Problem Solving. Identifying complex problems and reviewing related information to develop and evaluate options and implement solutions.

Operations Analysis. Analyzing needs and product requirements to create a design.

Technology Design. Generating or adapting equipment and technology to serve user needs.

Equipment Selection. Determining the kind of tools and equipment needed to do a job.

Installation. Installing equipment, machines, wiring, or programs to meet specifications.

Programming. Writing computer programs for various purposes.

Operation Monitoring. Watching gauges, dials, or other indicators to make sure a machine is working properly.

Operation and Control. Controlling operations of equipment or systems.

Equipment Maintenance. Performing routine maintenance on equipment and determining when and what kind of maintenance is needed.

Troubleshooting. Determining causes of operating errors and deciding what to do about them.

Repairing. Repairing machines or systems, using the needed tools.

Quality Control Analysis. Conducting tests and inspections of products, services, or processes to evaluate quality or performance.

Judgment and Decision Making. Considering the relative costs and benefits of potential actions to choose the most appropriate one.

Systems Analysis. Determining how a system should work and how changes in conditions, operations, and the environment will affect outcomes.

Systems Evaluation. Identifying measures or indicators of system performance and the actions needed to improve or correct performance relative to the goals of the system.

Time Management. Managing one's own time and the time of others.

Management of Financial Resources. Determining how money will be spent to get the work done and accounting for these expenditures.

Management of Material Resources. Obtaining and seeing to the appropriate use of equipment, facilities, and materials needed to do certain work.

Management of Personnel Resources. Motivating, developing, and directing people as they work, identifying the best people for the job.

Abilities. Abilities are general traits we have or don't have that allow us to learn or do other things. When someone says you are "good at" or "talented in" something, this often refers to your basic abilities. An example is someone who has the ability to write well. Your basic abilities tend to be stable over time, although you can develop your basic abilities with learning and practice.

The descriptions include one or more abilities from a set of 52 used in the O*NET database. The O*NET provides numeric measures on all of them, but space limitations and common sense helped us decide to include only abilities that were rated highly for the job described. The 52 abilities are organized into four categories. Following are brief descriptions for each, organized within the categories.

The 52 Abilities Used in the Job Descriptions

Cognitive Abilities. These are mental processes that influence the acquisition and application of knowledge in problem solving.

Oral Comprehension. The ability to listen to and understand information and ideas presented through spoken words and sentences.

Written Comprehension. The ability to read and understand information and ideas presented in writing.

Oral Expression. The ability to communicate information and ideas in speaking so others will understand.

Written Expression. The ability to communicate information and ideas in writing so others will understand.

Fluency of Ideas. The ability to come up with a number of ideas about a given topic. It concerns the number of ideas produced and not the quality, correctness, or creativity of the ideas.

Originality. The ability to come up with unusual or clever ideas about a given topic or situation or to develop creative ways to solve a problem.

Problem Sensitivity. The ability to tell when something is wrong or is likely to go wrong. It does not involve solving the problem, only recognizing that there is a problem.

Deductive Reasoning. The ability to apply general rules to specific problems to come up with logical answers. It involves deciding if an answer makes sense or provides a logical explanation for why a series of seemingly unrelated events occur together.

Inductive Reasoning. The ability to combine separate pieces of information, or specific answers to problems, to form general rules or conclusions. It includes coming up with a logical explanation for why a series of seemingly unrelated events occur together.

Information Ordering. The ability to correctly follow a given rule or set of rules in order to arrange things or actions in a certain order. The things or actions can include numbers, letters, words, pictures, procedures, sentences, and mathematical or logical operations.

Category Flexibility. The ability to produce many rules so that each rule tells how to group (or combine) a set of things in a different way.

Mathematical Reasoning. The ability to understand and organize a problem and then to select a mathematical method or formula to solve the problem.

Number Facility. The ability to add, subtract, multiply, or divide quickly and correctly.

Memorization. The ability to remember information such as words, numbers, pictures, and procedures.

Speed of Closure. The ability to quickly make sense of information that seems to be without meaning or organization. It involves quickly combining and organizing different pieces of information into a meaningful pattern.

Flexibility of Closure. The ability to identify or detect a known pattern (a figure, object, word, or sound) that is hidden in other distracting material.

Perceptual Speed. The ability to quickly and accurately compare letters, numbers, objects, pictures, or patterns. The things to be compared may be presented at the same time or one after the other. This ability also includes comparing a presented object with a remembered object.

Spatial Orientation. The ability to know one's location in relation to the environment or to know where other objects are in relation to one's self.

Visualization. The ability to imagine how something will look after it is moved around or when its parts are moved or rearranged.

Selective Attention. The ability to concentrate and not be distracted while performing a task over a period of time.

Time Sharing. The ability to efficiently shift back and forth between two or more activities or sources of information (such as speech, sounds, touch, or other sources).

Psychomotor Abilities. These abilities influence the capacity to manipulate and control objects, primarily using fine motor skills.

Arm-Hand Steadiness. The ability to keep the hand and arm steady while making an arm movement or while holding the arm and hand in one position.

Manual Dexterity. The ability to quickly make coordinated movements of one hand, a hand together with its arm, or two hands to grasp, manipulate, or assemble objects.

Finger Dexterity. The ability to make precisely coordinated movements of the fingers of one or both hands to grasp, manipulate, or assemble very small objects.

Control Precision. The ability to quickly and repeatedly make precise adjustments in moving the controls of a machine or vehicle to exact positions.

Multilimb Coordination. The ability to coordinate movements of two or more limbs together (for example, two arms, two legs, or one leg and one arm) while sitting, standing, or lying down. It does not involve performing the activities while the body is in motion.

Response Orientation. The ability to choose quickly and correctly between two or more movements in response to two or more signals (lights, sounds, pictures, and so on). It includes the speed with which the correct response is started with the hand, foot, or other body parts.

Rate Control. The ability to time the adjustments of a movement or equipment control in anticipation of changes in the speed and/or direction of a continuously moving object or scene.

Reaction Time. The ability to quickly respond (with the hand, finger, or foot) to one signal (sound, light, picture, and so on) when it appears.

Wrist-Finger Speed. The ability to make fast, simple, repeated movements of the fingers, hands, and wrists.

Speed of Limb Movement. The ability to quickly move the arms or legs.

Physical Strength Abilities. These abilities influence strength, endurance, flexibility, balance, and coordination.

Static Strength. The ability to exert maximum muscle force to lift, push, pull, or carry objects.

Explosive Strength. The ability to use short bursts of muscle force to propel oneself (as in jumping or sprinting) or to throw an object.

Dynamic Strength. The ability to exert muscle force repeatedly or continuously over time. This involves muscular endurance and resistance to muscle fatigue.

Trunk Strength. The ability to use one's abdominal and lower back muscles to support part of the body repeatedly or continuously over time without giving out or fatiguing.

Stamina. The ability to exert one's self physically over long periods of time without getting winded or out of breath.

Extent Flexibility. The ability to bend, stretch, twist, or reach out with the body, arms, and/or legs.

Dynamic Flexibility. The ability to quickly and repeatedly bend, stretch, twist, or reach out with the body, arms, and/or legs.

Gross Body Coordination. The ability to coordinate the movement of the arms, legs, and torso together in activities where the whole body is in motion.

Gross Body Equilibrium. The ability to keep or regain one's body balance or stay upright when in an unstable position.

Sensory Abilities. These abilities influence visual, auditory, and speech perception.

Near Vision. The ability to see details of objects at a close range (within a few feet of the observer).

Far Vision. The ability to see details at a distance.

Visual Color Discrimination. The ability to match or detect differences between colors, including shades of color and brightness.

Night Vision. The ability to see under low light conditions.

Peripheral Vision. The ability to see objects or movement of objects to one's side when the eyes are focused forward.

Depth Perception. The ability to judge which of several objects is closer or farther away from the observer or to judge the distance between an object and the observer.

Glare Sensitivity. The ability to see objects in the presence of glare or bright lighting.

Hearing Sensitivity. The ability to detect or tell the difference between sounds that vary over broad ranges of pitch and loudness.

Auditory Attention. The ability to focus on a single source of auditory (hearing) information in the presence of other distracting sounds.

Sound Localization. The ability to tell the direction from which a sound originated.

Speech Recognition. The ability to identify and understand the speech of another person.

Speech Clarity. The ability to speak clearly so that it is understandable to a listener.

Occupational Values. Occupational (or work) values are things that can be very important to you. While there are hundreds of work values, the O*NET database includes 21 occupational values organized into six major categories. While the O*NET provides numeric measures for each value, we listed only those with higher measures for each job. We think this results in a more useful description.

All 21 occupational values are described in the list that follows. They are arranged within groups of related values. (For some groups, we modified the name used in the O*NET.) You may want to write down values that are of particular importance to you and look for jobs where these values exist.

The 21 Occupational Values Used in the Job Descriptions

Achievement. Occupations that satisfy these work values are results-oriented and allow employees to use their strongest abilities, giving them a feeling of accomplishment.

Ability Utilization. Workers on this job make use of their individual abilities.

Achievement. Workers on ths job get a feeling of accomplishment.**Comfort. Occupations that satisfy these work values offer job security and good working conditions.**

Activity. Workers on this job are busy all the time.

Independence. Workers on this job do their work alone.

Variety. Workers on this job have something different to do every day.

Compensation. Workers on this job are paid well in comparison with other workers.

Security. Workers on this job have steady employment.

Working Conditions. Workers on this job have good working conditions.

Status. Occupations that satisfy these work values offer advancement and potential for leadership and are often considered prestigious.

Advancement. Workers on this job have opportunities for advancement.

Recognition. Workers on this job receive recognition for the work they do.

Authority. Workers on this job give directions and instructions to others.

Social Status. Workers on this job are looked up to by others in their company and their community.

Altruism. Occupations that satisfy these work values allow employees to provide service to others and work with co-workers in a friendly, noncompetitive environment.

Co-workers. Workers on this job have co-workers who are easy to get along with.

Social Service. Workers on this job have work where they do things for other people.

Moral Values. Workers on this job are never pressured to do things that go against their sense of right and wrong.

Safety. Occupations that satisfy these work values offer supportive management that stands behind employees and provides a predictable and stable work environment.

Company Policies and Practices. Workers on this job are treated fairly by the company.

Supervision, Human Relations. Workers on this job have supervisors who back up their workers with management.

Supervision, Technical. Workers on this job have supervisors who train their workers well.

Autonomy. Occupations that satisfy this work value allow employees to work on their own and make decisions.

Creativity. Workers on this job try out their own ideas.

Responsibility. Workers on this job make decisions on their own.

Autonomy. Workers on this job plan their work with little supervision.

Interacting with Others. Almost all jobs require at least some interaction with others. The O*NET database provides data on 17 measures related to interacting with others, organized into three categories. As with abilities and skills, we include only those with higher ratings for each job. Following are brief descriptions for each measure.

The 17 Measures Used in the Job Descriptions for Interacting with Others

Communicating and Interacting

Interpreting Meaning of Information to Others. Translating or explaining what information means and how it can be understood or used to support responses or feedback to others.

Communicating with Other Workers. Providing information to supervisors, fellow workers, and subordinates. This information can be exchanged face-to-face, in writing, or via telephone/electronic transfer.

Communicating with Persons Outside. Communicating with persons outside the organization, representing the organization to customers, the public, government, the organization, and other external sources. This information can be exchanged face-to-face, in writing, or via telephone/electronic transfer.

Establishing and Maintaining Relationships. Developing constructive and cooperative working relationships with others.

Assisting and Caring for Others. Providing assistance or personal care to others.

Selling or Influencing Others. Convincing others to buy merchandise/goods or otherwise changing their minds or actions.

Resolving Conflict, Negotiating with Others. Handling complaints, arbitrating disputes, and resolving grievances or otherwise negotiating with others.

Performing for/Working with Public. Performing for people or dealing directly with the public, including serving persons in restaurants and stores and receiving clients or guests.

Coordinating, Developing, Managing, and Advising Others

Coordinating Work and Activities of Others. Coordinating members of a work group to accomplish tasks.

Developing and Building Teams. Encouraging and building mutual trust, respect, and cooperation among team members.

Teaching Others. Identifying educational needs, developing formal training programs or classes, and teaching or instructing others.

Guiding, Directing, and Motivating Subordinates. Providing guidance and direction to subordinates, including setting performance standards and monitoring subordinates.

Coaching and Developing Others. Identifying developmental needs of others and coaching or otherwise helping others to improve their knowledge or skills.

Providing Consultation and Advice to Others. Providing consultation and expert advice to management or other groups on technical, systems-related, or process-related topics.

Administering

Performing Administrative Activities. Approving requests, handling paperwork, and performing day-to-day administrative tasks.

Staffing Organizational Units. Recruiting, interviewing, selecting, hiring, and promoting persons for the organization.

Monitoring and Controlling Resources. Monitoring and controlling resources and overseeing the spending of money.

Physical Work Conditions. This category describes the work context as it relates to the interactions between the worker and the physical job environment. This includes work setting, environmental conditions, job hazards, body positioning, and work attire. The O*NET provides measures of 26 items that evaluate each occupation's physical work conditions. As with the other job characteristics, we included only those that were rated highest. Brief descriptions for each measure follow.

The 26 Physical Work Conditions Used in the Descriptions

Indoors. Job requires working mostly indoors.

Outdoors. Job requires working mostly outdoors.

Distracting Sounds and Noise Levels. Sounds and noise levels that are distracting and uncomfortable.

Very Hot or Cold. Very hot (above 90°F) or very cold (under 32°F) temperatures.

Extremely Bright or Inadequate Lighting. Extremely bright or inadequate lighting conditions.

Contaminants. Contaminants present, such as pollutants, gases, dust, odors, and so on.

Cramped Work Space, Awkward Positions. Cramped work space that requires getting into awkward positions.

Whole Body Vibration. For example, operating a jackhammer or earthmoving equipment.

Radiation. Potential exposure to radiation.

Diseases/Infections. Potential diseases/infections (for example, patient care, some laboratory work, and sanitation control).

High Places. For example, heights above eight feet on ladders, poles, scaffolding, and catwalks.

Hazardous Conditions. For example, high-voltage electricity, combustibles, explosives, chemicals; does not include hazardous equipment or situations.

Hazardous Equipment. For example, saws and machinery/mechanical parts. Includes exposure to vehicular traffic but not driving a vehicle.

Hazardous Situations. Situations involving likely cuts, bites, stings, or minor burns.

Sitting. Job requires long periods of sitting.

Standing. Job requires long periods of standing.

Climbing Ladders, Scaffolds, Poles, etc. Covers all climbing to elevated locations.

Walking or Running. Job requires a lot of walking or running.

Kneeling, Crouching, or Crawling. Job requires a lot of kneeling, stooping, crouching, or crawling.

Keeping or Regaining Balance. Job requires a lot of keeping or regaining balance.

Using Hands on Objects, Tools, Controls. Using hands to handle, control, or feel objects, tools, or controls.

Bending or Twisting the Body. Job requires a lot of bending or twisting the body.

Making Repetitive Motions. Need to make repetitive motions.

Special Uniform. Examples are that of a commercial pilot, nurse, police officer, or military personnel.

Common Protective or Safety Attire. Examples are safety shoes, glasses, gloves, hearing protection, hard hat, or personal flotation device.

Specialized Protective or Safety Attire. Examples are breathing apparatus, safety harness, full protection suit, or radiation protection.

Whew! You now should understand why, when we said the job descriptions were packed with information, we were not exaggerating. We hope you understand why we did not and could not include all available information. We tried our best to create useful and easily understood job descriptions, but doing so required some compromise.

Part 3. Crosswalks to Careers

Think of this section of the book as a series of career assessment inventories. It consists of eight tables, called "crosswalks" because they allow you to cross-reference jobs that are related to the things they list. They are very useful for exploring career options based on your interests, values, previous experiences, and other factors. You can use one or more of the eight tables to explore your career options in a variety of interesting ways.

Crosswalk A: Work Values with Corresponding
Work Groups

Crosswalk B: Leisure Activities with Corresponding
Work Groups

Crosswalk C: School Subjects with Corresponding
Work Groups

Crosswalk D: Work Settings with Corresponding
Work Groups

Crosswalk E: Skills with Corresponding Work Groups

Crosswalk F: Abilities with Corresponding Work
Groups

Crosswalk G: Knowledges with Corresponding Work
Groups

Crosswalk H: Military Occupations with
Corresponding Work Groups

These crosswalks were designed to help you identify possible career options based on interests and other factors. Using one or more of the crosswalks in this way is likely to help you discover career options you may not have previously considered. For example, if you like to cook for your friends or family, using the crosswalks would help you identify the possibility of becoming a chef even though you had not seriously considered that option before.

The first four crosswalks were originally developed by staff under the direction of the U.S. Department of Labor and first presented in the 1984 edition of the *GOE* by Thomas Harrington and Arthur O'Shea. We have updated them in a number of ways. We also added the last four crosswalks based on the data we have developed. All crosswalks now use the new GOE groupings and relate to the new O*NET occupations. This means that you can look up information on any of the listed GOE Work Groups in Part 1.

The Appendix and Index

We considered a variety of additional appendices but ended up with just one titled "Information for Vocational Counselors and Other Professionals." It includes information for developers interested in using the new GOE structure in their own products and tips for using the GOE to help others explore career options.

We also included an index that arranges all the job titles, Interest Areas, and Work Groups in this book in alphabetical order.

The Top Sources of Additional Information

If you have read the introduction thus far, you know that there is a ton (or, more accurately, pounds) of information in this book. This book is intended to help you identify career options, and we hope you will understand that you will need additional information before jumping into a new career or educational program.

Thousands of career resources are available in books, Internet sites, magazines, and more, providing endless information on careers, jobs, education, training, earnings, and many related topics. Many resources are not worth your time to read, and some Internet sites are hard to find when they change their location. So we decided that we would not try to provide you with a long list of printed and Internet resources but, rather, with a few that are particularly good or that can lead you to other resources. Here are our suggestions for places to begin your search for additional information.

The resources here are those that cross-reference the O*NET job titles we've included in the *GOE* or that we consider will be most useful as supplements to those who use the *GOE*. We admit that our selection is subjective and that we could not include many worthy resources, but we hope that the quality and usefulness of our listed resources will make up for the brevity of the list.

Occupational Outlook Handbook (OOH). Updated every two years by the U.S. Department of Labor, this book is the most widely used of all career references. It provides excellent descriptions for about 250 major jobs, covering about 85 percent of the workforce. It includes well-written information on skills required, working conditions, duties, qualifications, pay, and advancement. Very helpful for preparing for interviews by identifying key skills to emphasize. JIST publishes the *Enhanced Occupational Outlook Handbook,* which features over 8,000 job descriptions for serious career research.

O*NET Dictionary of Occupational Titles. This is the only book (besides this new *GOE*) to include descriptions for all jobs from the government's O*NET database. Its descriptions provide more details than we could include in the *GOE,* so it is a useful resource.

Best Jobs for the 21st Century. Provides lots of job lists, including fastest growing, highest pay, and many others by age, gender, education level, and other criteria. It also provides descriptions for the hundreds of jobs included in the various lists. There are also several variations of this book, including *200 Best Jobs for College Graduates, 300 Best Jobs Without a Four-Year Degree, 50 Best Jobs for Your Personality, 250 Best Jobs Through Apprenticeships,* and *40 Best Fields for Your Career.*

The Very Quick Job Search. If you need one job search book, this is the one to have. Very thorough and has won multiple awards.

People at Work!, Young Person's Occupational Outlook Handbook, Exploring Careers. These resources from JIST help young people learn more about jobs and the world of work.

JIST's Web site (www.jist.com). You can buy any book mentioned here at this site, review sample pages and tables of contents, purchase and take online career assessments, and more.

CareerOINK.com. For free information on 14,000 job titles, a brief career interest inventory, sample resumes, and "best jobs" lists, visit www.careeroink.com.

America's Career InfoNet. This Web site, at www.acinet.org, combines O*NET data with state-specific information about wages, job outlook, and education. This site also has links that let you explore related state-specific information about certification, licensing, and recent job openings.

Career Exploration Inventory. This best-selling assessment from JIST leads you from your interests to the 16 career Interest Areas described in this book.

People you already know or can come to know. If you want to know more about a particular job or place of employment, ask the people who do that kind of work or who work in that particular place. This is often the only source of information for small organizations.

You. That's right. We believe that your very best career exploration resource is yourself. So plan to spend more time on learning about yourself and your many strengths and options. As always, you are your own best resource.

PART 1

GOE Interest Areas and Work Groups: Essential Information for Exploring Career Options

This part provides helpful information on each GOE Interest Area and its related Work Groups. The introduction gives a good overview of the content, but here is a brief review.

Each of the GOE's 16 Interest Areas is divided into Work Groups of related jobs. Because the jobs within groupings are similar, this structure will help you quickly identify the major jobs that are most likely to meet your interests.

Each Interest Area is given a two-digit code number. For example, the Agriculture and Natural Resources Interest Area is given the code 01. Major groupings of jobs within each Interest Area are given a four-digit code number. For example 01.01 is for the jobs in the "Managerial Work in Agriculture and Natural Resources" area.

Part 1 provides a brief description of each Work Group, followed by questions that will help you decide whether the grouping is worthy of more exploration. The approach is simple to use and will help you quickly identify groups of jobs you should consider in more detail. Training and education usually needed for the jobs in each grouping are also listed. You can then go to Part 2 for more information on specific jobs. For more details on the contents of Part 1, please read this book's introduction.

The 16 GOE Interest Areas

Here are the 16 major Interest Areas covered in Part 1. Information is presented in numeric order by two-digit Interest Area code and four-digit Work Group code.

01—Agriculture and Natural Resources

02—Architecture and Construction

03—Arts and Communication

04—Business and Administration

05—Education and Training

06—Finance and Insurance

07—Government and Public Administration

08—Health Science

09—Hospitality, Tourism, and Recreation

10—Human Service

11—Information Technology

12—Law and Public Safety

13—Manufacturing

14—Retail and Wholesale Sales and Service

15—Scientific Research, Engineering, and Mathematics

16—Transportation, Distribution, and Logistics

© 2006 JIST Works

01 Agriculture and Natural Resources

An interest in working with plants, animals, forests, or mineral resources for agriculture, horticulture, conservation, extraction, and other purposes. You can satisfy this interest by working in farming, landscaping, forestry, fishing, mining, and related fields. You may like doing physical work outdoors, such as on a farm or ranch, in a forest, or on a drilling rig. If you have scientific curiosity, you could study plants and animals or analyze biological or rock samples in a lab. If you have management ability, you could own, operate, or manage a fish hatchery, a landscaping business, or a greenhouse.

01.01 Managerial Work in Agriculture and Natural Resources

01.02 Resource Science/Engineering for Plants, Animals, and the Environment

01.03 Resource Technologies for Plants, Animals, and the Environment

01.04 General Farming

01.05 Nursery, Groundskeeping, and Pest Control

01.06 Forestry and Logging

01.07 Hunting and Fishing

01.08 Mining and Drilling

01.01 Managerial Work in Agriculture and Natural Resources

Workers in this group manage and coordinate businesses or workers who tend plants and animals or who drill or dig for oil or minerals.

What kind of work would you do?

Your work activities would depend on your job. For example, you might

* Analyze and plan the extraction process of geological materials.
* Assign workers to tasks, such as feeding and treating animals, cleaning quarters, transferring animals, and maintaining facilities.
* Conduct field trips to point out scientific, historic, and natural features of parks, forests, historic sites, or other attractions.
* Hire, discharge, transfer, and promote workers.
* Inspect growing environment to maintain optimum growing or breeding conditions.
* Monitor workers to ensure that safety regulations are followed, warning or disciplining those who violate safety regulations.
* Observe ongoing work to ascertain whether work is being performed according to instructions and will be completed on time.
* Prepare reports required by state and federal laws.
* Record number and type of fish or shellfish reared and harvested.

What things about you point to this kind of work?

Is it important for you to

* Give directions and instructions to others?
* Plan your work with little supervision?
* Make decisions on your own?

Have you enjoyed any of the following as a hobby or leisure-time activity?

* Belonging to a 4-H club, a garden club, or Future Farmers of America
* Breeding animals
* Designing and landscaping a flower garden
* Raising vegetables in a home garden
* Raising or caring for animals
* Serving as president of a club or other organization
* Planting trees
* Reading farm magazines
* Collecting rocks or minerals

Have you liked and done well in any of the following school subjects?

* Management

* Dairy Science/Technology
* Plant Pest Management/Pathology
* Agriculture, Mechanized
* Agronomy
* Agribusiness
* Accounting
* Animal Science
* Farm and Ranch Management
* Personnel Management
* Foreign Languages

Are you able to

* Know your location in relation to the environment or know where other objects are in relation to you?
* Add, subtract, multiply, or divide quickly and correctly?
* See objects in the presence of glare or bright lighting?
* Arrange things or actions in a certain order or pattern according to a specific rule or set of rules?

Would you work in places such as

* Farms?
* Fish hatcheries?
* Forests?
* Ships and boats?
* Plant nurseries?
* Golf courses and tennis courts?
* Parks and campgrounds?
* Mines and quarries?
* Oil fields?

What skills and knowledges do you need for this kind of work?

For most of these jobs, you need these skills:

* Management of Personnel Resources—motivating, developing, and directing people as they work, identifying the best people for the job
* Management of Material Resources—obtaining and seeing to the appropriate use of equipment, facilities, and materials needed to do certain work
* Management of Financial Resources—determining how money will be spent to get the work done and accounting for these expenditures

These knowledges are important in most of these jobs:

* Food Production—techniques and equipment for planting, growing, and harvesting food products (both plant and animal) for consumption, including storage/handling techniques
* Personnel and Human Resources—principles and procedures for personnel recruitment, selection, training, compensation and benefits, labor relations and negotiation, and personnel information systems
* Biology—plant and animal organisms and their tissues, cells, functions, interdependencies, and interactions with each other and the environment

© 2006 JIST Works

✳ Administration and Management—business and management principles involved in strategic planning, resource allocation, human resources modeling, leadership techniques, production methods, and coordination of people and resources

What else should you consider about this kind of work?

Many workers in agriculture and fishing are in business for themselves. They run plant nurseries, plan and care for lawns and trees, have their own large or small farms, or own their own fishing boats. Many of these businesses are small, with few employees.

Others in this group work for someone else, managing a farm, ranch, stand of timber, fish hatchery, or quarry or providing services to help the owners with production or harvesting. Some jobs are available with state government agencies.

While some work in rural areas or woodlands, others find employment with commercial nurseries, landscaping firms, business services, or government agencies located in large and small communities all over the country.

It is hard for newcomers to start their own farming businesses. Openings are more plentiful for people who want to manage farms for others. Many large farms are owned by large companies that hire well-trained managers to take responsibility for day-to-day operations. Competition for jobs is increasing as these agricultural companies merge.

Job opportunities in the petroleum industry fluctuate sharply, although some mining industries are more stable. Management jobs in petroleum production and mining are available only where the natural resources are located, but because these sites are often scattered, these workers also may be moved frequently. In addition, both types of workers tend to be specialists who can transfer to another firm in the same or a related industry.

People who do this kind of work put in long hours. Whether they own or manage the business, doing all the work themselves or having many people work under them, most spend much more than eight hours a day on the job. Work in landscaping or other "city farming" is not likely to take as much time.

In most of these jobs, workers spend a lot of time outside in all kinds of weather. For some jobs, these managers have to be physically strong and active.

In addition to being experts in plants, animals, or natural resources, people who do well in this kind of work are knowledgeable about business and government regulations and skilled in marketing their products and managing their money.

How can you prepare for jobs of this kind?

Occupations in this group usually require education and/or training ranging from one or two years to less than ten years. Several jobs in this group are open primarily to people with work experience in a related field.

Growing up on a farm is good initial preparation for many of these jobs. Formal training for management jobs is available at the high school and higher levels. For example, vocational agriculture courses are offered in many high schools to high school students during the day and to adults at night and on weekends. Programs in agribusiness, agronomy, animal science, forest management, poultry science, dairy science, mechanized agriculture, and small business management are provided by colleges and technical schools. Each state has at least one college that offers four- or five-year programs in agricultural fields.

Courses in horticulture, gardening, and turf management provide preparation for jobs in nurseries, tree services, and landscaping firms.

Ability to communicate in Spanish often is useful to supervisors of farm workers.

Supervisors of extractive workers often rise from the ranks of mine or oil workers. They may take night classes or get training from their employers to learn managerial skills.

How much education or training is required for the jobs in this Work Group?

For descriptions of these jobs, see Part 2.

Long-term on-the-job training

✳ Farmers and Ranchers

Work experience in a related occupation

✳ Agricultural Crop Farm Managers
✳ First-Line Supervisors and Manager/Supervisors—Extractive Workers
✳ First-Line Supervisors and Manager/Supervisors—Landscaping Workers
✳ Fish Hatchery Managers
✳ Lawn Service Managers
✳ Nursery and Greenhouse Managers
✳ Purchasing Agents and Buyers, Farm Products

Associate degree

✳ First-Line Supervisors and Manager/Supervisors—Agricultural Crop Workers
✳ First-Line Supervisors and Manager/Supervisors—Animal Husbandry Workers
✳ First-Line Supervisors and Manager/Supervisors—Fishery Workers
✳ First-Line Supervisors and Manager/Supervisors—Horticultural Workers

Bachelor's degree

✳ First-Line Supervisors and Manager/Supervisors—Logging Workers
✳ Park Naturalists

01.02 Resource Science/Engineering for Plants, Animals, and the Environment

Workers in this group do research to find out more about plants, animals, and natural resources. Some plan, design, and direct the development of processes and techniques for extracting natural resources or making use of minerals and agricultural products. Some study methods of producing better species of plants or animals. Others work to find ways of preserving the natural balance in the environment.

What kind of work would you do?

Your work activities would depend on your job. For example, you might

* Assess costs and estimate the production capabilities and economic value of oil and gas wells in order to evaluate the economic viability of potential drilling sites.
* Design structures for crop storage, animal shelter and loading, and animal and crop processing.
* Determine generic composition of animal population and heritability of traits, utilizing principles of genetics.
* Establish short- and long-term plans for management of forest lands and forest resources.
* Inventory or estimate plant and wildlife populations.
* Study grazing patterns to determine number and kind of livestock that can be most profitably grazed and to determine the best grazing seasons.
* Survey property to mark locations and measurements, using surveying instruments.
* Write technical reports for engineering and management personnel.

What things about you point to this kind of work?

Is it important for you to

* Plan your work with little supervision?
* Try out your own ideas?
* Make decisions on your own?
* Make use of your individual abilities?

Have you enjoyed any of the following as a hobby or leisure-time activity?

* Performing experiments for a science fair
* Reading about technological developments, such as computer science or aerospace
* Belonging to a 4-H club, a garden club, or Future Farmers of America
* Raising vegetables in a home garden
* Raising or caring for animals
* Collecting rocks or minerals
* Studying plants in gardens, parks, or forests

Have you liked and done well in any of the following school subjects?

* Calculus
* Physics
* Computer Science
* Mechanics/Mechanics of Materials
* Physical Science
* Geology
* Agricultural Systems
* Biology
* Animal Science
* Zoology
* Soil Science

Are you able to

* Combine pieces of information to form general rules or conclusions?
* Communicate information and ideas in writing so others will understand?
* Apply general rules to specific problems to produce answers that make sense?
* Come up with unusual or clever ideas about a given topic or situation or develop creative ways to solve a problem?
* Generate or use different sets of rules for combining or grouping things in different ways?
* Come up with a number of ideas about a topic?
* Tell when something is wrong or is likely to go wrong?

Would you work in places such as

* Farms?
* Forests?
* Laboratories?
* Oil fields?
* Mines and quarries?
* Plant nurseries?
* Colleges and universities?
* Government offices?
* Parks and campgrounds?

What skills and knowledges do you need for this kind of work?

For most of these jobs, you need these skills:

* Science—using scientific rules and methods to solve problems
* Operations Analysis—analyzing needs and product requirements to create a design
* Complex Problem Solving—identifying complex problems and reviewing related information to develop and evaluate options and implement solutions
* Mathematics—using mathematics to solve problems
* Active Learning—understanding the implications of new information for both current and future problem solving and decision making
* Judgment and Decision Making—considering the relative costs and benefits of potential actions to choose the most appropriate one

✳ Systems Analysis—determining how a system should work and how changes in conditions, operations, and the environment will affect outcomes

These knowledges are important in most of these jobs:

✳ Biology—plant and animal organisms and their tissues, cells, functions, interdependencies, and interactions with each other and the environment

✳ Food Production—techniques and equipment for planting, growing, and harvesting food products (both plant and animal) for consumption, including storage/handling techniques

✳ Chemistry—the chemical composition, structure, and properties of substances and of the chemical processes and transformations that they undergo; this includes uses of chemicals and their danger signs, production techniques, and disposal methods

✳ Geography—principles and methods for describing the features of land, sea, and air masses, including their physical characteristics; locations; interrelationships; and distribution of plant, animal, and human life

✳ Mathematics—arithmetic, algebra, geometry, calculus, and statistics and their applications

✳ Physics—physical principles and laws and their interrelationships and applications to understanding fluid, material, and atmospheric dynamics and mechanical, electrical, atomic, and subatomic structures and processes

✳ Engineering and Technology—the practical application of engineering science and technology; this includes applying principles, techniques, procedures, and equipment to the design and production of various goods and services

What else should you consider about this kind of work?

Science and engineering jobs related to plants, animals, and the environment are found in large and small cities and in some small towns. A few are available only in places where there are forests, mines, quarries, or oil fields. The employers are government agencies; universities; and manufacturing, energy, and mining companies.

Some students and workers in this field must handle tissues and waste products of humans and animals.

Workers in this field must keep informed of scientific developments by attending seminars, reading professional books and magazines, and being active in professional organizations.

Chances of employment for scientists are believed to be better for those with a master's degree than with a doctorate. The outlook for environmental engineers is very good, and for mining and petroleum engineers, it is not as good.

How can you prepare for jobs of this kind?

Occupations in this group usually call for education and/or training ranging from four years to more than ten years.

For the scientific jobs, important academic courses include algebra, geometry, calculus, chemistry, and physics. Technical writing and composition courses are helpful. A bachelor's degree with a major in biology or another life science is generally required; graduate degrees are needed for most research work and college teaching.

For the engineering jobs, most workers entering the field have a bachelor's degree in engineering, and in many colleges, this program is expected to take five years. Course work typically is the same as for the scientists but also includes design graphics, computer programming, and mechanics. College graduates trained in one of the natural sciences or mathematics qualify for a few beginning jobs. Experienced technicians with some engineering education may advance to engineering jobs.

How much education or training is required for the jobs in this Work Group?

For descriptions of these jobs, see Part 2.

Bachelor's degree

✳ Agricultural Engineers
✳ Animal Scientists
✳ Environmental Engineers
✳ Foresters
✳ Mining and Geological Engineers, Including Mining Safety Engineers
✳ Petroleum Engineers
✳ Plant Scientists
✳ Range Managers
✳ Soil Conservationists
✳ Soil Scientists

Doctoral degree

✳ Zoologists and Wildlife Biologists

01.03 Resource Technologies for Plants, Animals, and the Environment

Workers in this group handle technical duties as part of a team doing research or engineering in the field of plants, animals, or natural resources. They use principles of science and math to solve problems in a laboratory; a manufacturing plant; or a field location such as a farm, forest, or oil exploration site.

What kind of work would you do?

Your work activities would depend on your job. For example, you might

✳ Collect samples of gases, soils, water, industrial wastewater, and asbestos products to conduct tests on pollutant levels and identify sources of pollution.

✳ Conduct standardized tests on food, beverages, additives, and preservatives in order to ensure compliance with standards and regulations regarding factors such as color, texture, and nutrients.

* Confer with process engineers, plant operators, flavor experts, and packaging and marketing specialists in order to resolve problems in product development.

* Evaluate and interpret core samples and cuttings and other geological data used in prospecting for oil or gas.

* Prepare notes, sketches, geological maps, and cross-sections.

* Record and compile test results and prepare graphs, charts, and reports.

* Set up laboratory or field equipment and prepare sites for testing.

What things about you point to this kind of work?

Is it important for you to

* Have opportunities for advancement?
* Have steady employment?

Have you enjoyed any of the following as a hobby or leisure-time activity?

* Performing experiments for a science fair
* Reading about technological developments, such as computer science or aerospace
* Installing and repairing home stereo equipment
* Belonging to a 4-H club, a garden club, or Future Farmers of America
* Raising or caring for animals
* Planting trees
* Raising vegetables in a home garden

Have you liked and done well in any of the following school subjects?

* Math Computing, Advanced/Special
* Drafting
* Mechanical Drawing
* Physical Science
* Soil Science
* Physics
* Animal Science
* Geology
* Biology
* Earth Science
* Food Science

Are you able to

* Choose the right mathematical methods or formulas to solve a problem?
* Add, subtract, multiply, or divide quickly and correctly?
* Generate or use different sets of rules for combining or grouping things in different ways?
* Combine pieces of information to form general rules or conclusions?

Would you work in places such as

* Farms?
* Forests?
* Laboratories?
* Oil fields?
* Mines and quarries?
* Plant nurseries?
* Fish hatcheries?
* Factories and plants?

What skills and knowledges do you need for this kind of work?

For most of these jobs, you need these skills:

* Science—using scientific rules and methods to solve problems
* Mathematics—using mathematics to solve problems
* Programming—writing computer programs for various purposes

These knowledges are important in most of these jobs:

* Chemistry—the chemical composition, structure, and properties of substances and of the chemical processes and transformations that they undergo; this includes uses of chemicals and their danger signs, production techniques, and disposal methods

* Biology—plant and animal organisms and their tissues, cells, functions, interdependencies, and interactions with each other and the environment

* Food Production—techniques and equipment for planting, growing, and harvesting food products (both plant and animal) for consumption, including storage/handling techniques

What else should you consider about this kind of work?

Government agencies, agribusiness companies, manufacturers, water treatment plants, energy companies, and universities employ these workers. Jobs may be located in cities or towns, although some are located only where there are farms, forests, or mine sites.

Occasional to frequent travel is required on jobs with oil producing and mining companies.

The outlook for environmental research technicians is considered better than for those working in food, agriculture, mining, or petroleum.

How can you prepare for jobs of this kind?

Occupations in this group usually require education and/or training ranging from one year to less than four years. Most of the jobs are entry positions requiring a two-year degree. Some workers move into laboratory or testing work from production areas. On-the-job training is sometimes available to applicants who have appropriate skills or work-related/military experience. Some jobs are offered to those who have taken scientific or technical courses in high school or a post–high school program. Courses in chemistry, physical science, math, and report writing are helpful.

How much education or training is required for the jobs in this Work Group?

For descriptions of these jobs, see Part 2.

Associate degree

* Agricultural Technicians
* Environmental Science and Protection Technicians, Including Health
* Food Science Technicians
* Geological Data Technicians
* Geological Sample Test Technicians

Bachelor's degree

* Food Scientists and Technologists

01.04 General Farming

Workers in this group raise plants or animals in a farm or ranch setting. They work with their hands, use tools and equipment, or operate machinery.

What kind of work would you do?

Your work activities would depend on your job. For example, you might

* Apply or administer medications and vaccinate animals.
* Attach farm implements, such as plow, disc, sprayer, or harvester, to tractor, using bolts and mechanic's hand tools.
* Dig and transplant seedlings by hand.
* Load agricultural products into trucks for transport.
* Milk farm animals, such as cows and goats, by hand or using milking machine.
* Spray fertilizer or pesticide solutions, using hand sprayer, to control insects, fungus and weed growth, and diseases.
* Weigh crop-filled containers and record weights and other identifying information.

What things about you point to this kind of work?

Is it important for you to

* Never be pressured to do things that go against your sense of right and wrong?
* Have something different to do every day?

Have you enjoyed any of the following as a hobby or leisure-time activity?

* Belonging to a 4-H club, a garden club, or Future Farmers of America
* Raising vegetables in a home garden
* Raising or caring for animals
* Breeding animals

Have you liked and done well in any of the following school subjects?

* Horticulture
* Vocational Agriculture
* Food and Fiber Crops
* Plant Pest Management/Pathology

* Agriculture, Mechanized
* Agribusiness
* Animal Science

Are you able to

* Exert maximum muscle force to lift, push, pull, or carry objects?
* Use short bursts of muscle force to propel yourself or to throw an object?
* Exert muscle force repeatedly or continuously over time?
* Coordinate two or more limbs while sitting, standing, or lying down?
* Use your abdominal and lower back muscles to support part of the body repeatedly or continuously over time without fatiguing?
* Time your movements or the movement of a piece of equipment in anticipation of changes in the speed and/or direction of a moving object or scene?
* Exert yourself physically over long periods of time without getting winded or out of breath?

Would you work in places such as

* Farms?
* Plant nurseries?

What skills and knowledges do you need for this kind of work?

For most of these jobs, you need these skills:

* Repairing—repairing machines or systems, using the needed tools
* Equipment Maintenance—performing routine maintenance on equipment and determining when and what kind of maintenance is needed
* Operation and Control—controlling operations of equipment or systems

These knowledges are important in most of these jobs:

* Food Production—techniques and equipment for planting, growing, and harvesting food products (both plant and animal) for consumption, including storage/handling techniques
* Chemistry—the chemical composition, structure, and properties of substances and of the chemical processes and transformations that they undergo; this includes uses of chemicals and their danger signs, production techniques, and disposal methods
* Biology—plant and animal organisms and their tissues, cells, functions, interdependencies, and interactions with each other and the environment

What else should you consider about this kind of work?

These workers are hired by farmers and ranchers. Many of these jobs are open to beginners, and some offer chances for advancement to supervisory work.

Much of this work is seasonal. If you live in a farming or ranching area, temporary work is available at certain times of the year.

This is active physical work. You have to be out in all kinds of weather and willing to put in a full day's work to succeed. Many of these jobs require long hours of hard work during planting or harvesting of crops. Persons wanting full-time work must look for other jobs in the "off" season.

The work also can be hazardous because it involves working closely with powerful machinery and sometimes with pesticides.

Consolidation of farms and increased use of technology are dampening job growth in this group, but many jobs will be available to replace workers who are retiring or finding work elsewhere.

How can you prepare for jobs of this kind?

Occupations in this group usually require education and/or training ranging from a short demonstration to less than six months. Agricultural equipment operators are the exception and may need to train for six months or more.

Prior training is not required for most jobs in this group. In some jobs, training is given by the employer when workers are hired or when their duties are changed. Most employers require job applicants to be in good physical condition.

Some vocational high schools offer courses in general farming, farm animal care, and equipment operation, and a few participate in work/study projects. This experience can be helpful in obtaining a job because employers prefer to hire workers who need less on-the-job training.

Many vocational schools and training programs offer courses in animal science, dairy science, and agricultural equipment operation.

Because many farm workers are Spanish speakers, knowledge of Spanish can be useful on the job.

How much education or training is required for the jobs in this Work Group?

For descriptions of these jobs, see Part 2.

Short-term on-the-job training

* Farmworkers, Farm and Ranch Animals
* General Farmworkers

Moderate-term on-the-job training

* Agricultural Equipment Operators

01.05 Nursery, Grounds-keeping, and Pest Control

Workers in this group care for trees, shrubs, and lawns or apply chemicals to control pests. They work with their hands, use tools and equipment, or operate machinery. They work on farms, tree nurseries, golf courses, parks, and residential properties; in greenhouses; and in and around buildings.

What kind of work would you do?

Your work activities would depend on your job. For example, you might

* Cut away dead and excess branches from trees, using handsaws, pruning hooks, shears, and clippers.
* Dig up and burn weeds or spray them with herbicides.
* Operate powered equipment such as mowers, tractors, twin-axle vehicles, snowblowers, chain saws, electric clippers, sod cutters, and pruning saws.
* Plant, spray, weed, and water plants, shrubs, and trees, using hand tools and gardening tools.
* Provide proper upkeep of sidewalks, driveways, parking lots, fountains, planters, burial sites, and other grounds features.
* Sow grass seed or plant plugs of grass and cut, roll, and stack sod.
* Spray livestock with pesticides.

What things about you point to this kind of work?

Is it important for you to

* Do your work alone?
* Never be pressured to do things that go against your sense of right and wrong?

Have you enjoyed any of the following as a hobby or leisure-time activity?

* Planting trees
* Mowing the lawn
* Belonging to a 4-H club, a garden club, or Future Farmers of America
* Trimming shrubs and hedges
* Gardening

Have you liked and done well in any of the following school subjects?

* Horticulture
* Landscaping
* Plant Pest Management/Pathology
* Turf Management
* Soil Science
* Biology
* Agronomy
* Agribusiness
* Vocational Agriculture
* Chemical Safety

Are you able to

* Quickly and repeatedly bend, stretch, twist, or reach out with your body, arms, and/or legs?
* Use short bursts of muscle force to propel yourself or to throw an object?
* Exert muscle force repeatedly or continuously over time?
* Exert yourself physically over long periods of time without getting winded or out of breath?

Would you work in places such as

* Farms?
* Plant nurseries?
* Parks and campgrounds?
* Private homes?

What skills and knowledges do you need for this kind of work?

For most of these jobs, you need these skills:

* Operation and Control—controlling operations of equipment or systems
* Equipment Maintenance—performing routine maintenance on equipment and determining when and what kind of maintenance is needed
* Equipment Selection—determining the kind of tools and equipment needed to do a job

These knowledges are important in most of these jobs:

* Chemistry—the chemical composition, structure, and properties of substances and of the chemical processes and transformations that they undergo; this includes uses of chemicals and their danger signs, production techniques, and disposal methods
* Biology—plant and animal organisms and their tissues, cells, functions, interdependencies, and interactions with each other and the environment
* Food Production—techniques and equipment for planting, growing, and harvesting food products (both plant and animal) for consumption, including storage/handling techniques

What else should you consider about this kind of work?

Workers in this group are hired by farmers, ranchers, lumber companies, and golf courses and for businesses that provide landscaping and pest control services to corporate campuses and private homes. A few of the jobs are with parks operated by state or local governments. Many of these jobs are open to beginners, and some offer chances for advancement to supervisory work.

Some of this work is seasonal. Farms, groundskeeping companies, and parks often hire extra workers in the spring and summer.

The work may be physically demanding and may require you to be outdoors in all kinds of weather. Those who handle pesticides are trained in safety procedures.

The job outlook for this group is good to excellent. During certain times of the year, the work hours may be long, whereas at other times you may need to find another temporary job.

How can you prepare for jobs of this kind?

Occupations in this group usually require education and/or training ranging from a short demonstration to less than two years. The training is almost always acquired on the job. One exception is workers responsible for use of pesticides, who often must take classes and pass an exam to prove their mastery of relevant federal and state regulations.

Most employers require job applicants to be in good physical condition. Applicants must pass civil service examinations to be eligible for jobs in local, state, or national parks or with other government agencies.

High school courses in math and chemistry are useful preparation for those who will handle pesticides, and biology is relevant to all the jobs in this group. Many vocational schools and training programs offer courses in landscaping.

How much education or training is required for the jobs in this Work Group?

For descriptions of these jobs, see Part 2.

Short-term on-the-job training

* Landscaping and Groundskeeping Workers
* Nursery Workers
* Tree Trimmers and Pruners

Moderate-term on-the-job training

* Pest Control Workers
* Pesticide Handlers, Sprayers, and Applicators, Vegetation

01.06 Forestry and Logging

Workers in this group maintain forests and extract wood from them. They work in forests, logging camps, and sawmills, and they use their hands, tools and equipment, or machinery. Some workers plant seedlings, spray pesticides, clear brush, and control erosion. Some fell trees with chainsaws, trim the branches, and use power equipment to drag and lift the logs onto trucks or unload them at sawmills and pulp mills. Others inspect the logs and record information about their value or marketable content.

What kind of work would you do?

Your work activities would depend on your job. For example, you might

* Appraise trees for certain characteristics, such as twist, rot, and heavy limb growth, and gauge amount and direction of lean in order to determine how to control the direction of a tree's fall with the least damage.
* Control equipment to load, unload, or stack logs; pull stumps; and clear brush.
* Drag cut trees from cutting areas and load trees onto trucks.
* Explain and enforce regulations regarding camping, vehicle use, fires, use of building, and sanitation.
* Measure felled logs or loads of pulpwood to calculate volume, weight, dimensions, and marketable value, using measuring devices and conversion tables.
* Saw felled trees into lengths.
* Select tree seedlings, prepare the ground, and plant the trees in reforestation areas, using manual planting tools.

* Split logs, using axes, wedges, and mauls, and stack wood in ricks or cord lots.
* Weigh log trucks before and after unloading and record load weights and supplier identities.

What things about you point to this kind of work?

Is it important for you to

* Never be pressured to do things that go against your sense of right and wrong?
* Have supervisors who train workers well?

Have you enjoyed any of the following as a hobby or leisure-time activity?

* Planting trees
* Doing strenuous activities, such as dancing, climbing, backpacking, running, swimming, and skiing
* Operating power tools for household projects

Have you liked and done well in any of the following school subjects?

* Forestry
* Biology
* Soil Science

Are you able to

* Use short bursts of muscle force to propel yourself or to throw an object?
* Exert maximum muscle force to lift, push, pull, or carry objects?
* Know your location in relation to the environment or know where other objects are in relation to you?
* Exert muscle force repeatedly or continuously over time?

Would you work in places such as

* Forests?

What skills and knowledges do you need for this kind of work?

For most of these jobs, you need these skills:

* Operation and Control—controlling operations of equipment or systems
* Equipment Selection—determining the kind of tools and equipment needed to do a job
* Programming—writing computer programs for various purposes

These knowledges are important in most of these jobs:

* Biology—plant and animal organisms and their tissues, cells, functions, interdependencies, and interactions with each other and the environment
* Food Production—techniques and equipment for planting, growing, and harvesting food products (both plant and animal) for consumption, including storage/handling techniques
* Foreign Language—the structure and content of a foreign (non-English) language, including the meaning and spelling of words, rules of composition and grammar, and pronunciation

What else should you consider about this kind of work?

Most of the workers in this group are hired by logging contractors, lumber companies, and parks operated by state or local governments. Many of these jobs are open to beginners and some offer chances for advancement to supervisory work.

The work is usually physically strenuous and often takes place in remote locations, with full or partial exposure to the weather. The work also can be hazardous, so workers need to wear appropriate safety gear and be on the lookout for falling trees and branches, as well as other hazards that may be encountered in the wild.

In some parts of the country the amount of work varies by season. Some tasks, such as planting seedlings, may be done intensively for only a short season.

The industry is facing competition from overseas, and many labor-intensive jobs are being replaced by mechanization. Job opportunities will be best for more-skilled workers.

How can you prepare for jobs of this kind?

Occupations in this group usually require education and/or training ranging from a short demonstration to less than two years. The jobs in this group requiring the most training are log graders and operators of heavy machinery. Most training is acquired on the job.

New hires are usually required to be in good physical condition. Jobs in local, state, or national parks or with other government agencies usually require applicants to pass civil service examinations.

Some vocational schools and training programs offer courses in forestry.

How much education or training is required for the jobs in this Work Group?

For descriptions of these jobs, see Part 2.

Moderate-term on-the-job training

* Fallers
* Forest and Conservation Workers
* Log Graders and Scalers
* Logging Tractor Operators

Associate degree

* Forest and Conservation Technicians

01.07 Hunting and Fishing

Workers in this group hunt, catch, trap, or gather various kinds of game animals or marine life for human consumption, animal feed, bait, fur, or pest control. They work outdoors in forests, in scrubland, in game preserves, onshore, or aboard commercial fishing boats.

© 2006 JIST Works

What kind of work would you do?

Your work activities would depend on your job. For example, you might

* Attach nets, slings, hooks, blades, and lifting devices to cables, booms, hoists, and dredges.
* Negotiate with buyers for sale of catch.
* Patrol trapline or nets to inspect settings, remove catch, and reset or relocate traps.
* Record date, harvest area, and yield in logbook.
* Remove catch from fishing equipment and use measuring equipment to ensure compliance with legal size.
* Select, bait, and set traps according to species, size, habits, and environs of bird or animal and reason for trapping.
* Train dogs for hunting.
* Wash and sort pelts according to species, color, and quality.

What things about you point to this kind of work?

Is it important for you to

* Do your work alone?
* Have something different to do every day?

Have you enjoyed any of the following as a hobby or leisure-time activity?

* Hunting or target shooting
* Fishing
* Doing strenuous activities, such as dancing, climbing, backpacking, running, swimming, and skiing

Have you liked and done well in any of the following school subjects?

* Biology
* Ecology/Environmental Science
* Water Safety

Are you able to

* Quickly move your arms and legs?
* Exert maximum muscle force to lift, push, pull, or carry objects?
* Exert muscle force repeatedly or continuously over time?
* Know your location in relation to the environment or know where other objects are in relation to you?
* See objects or movement of objects to your side when your eyes are looking ahead?
* See objects in the presence of glare or bright lighting?
* Use short bursts of muscle force to propel yourself or to throw an object?

Would you work in places such as

* Ships and boats?
* Forests?

What skills and knowledges do you need for this kind of work?

For most of these jobs, you need these skills:

* Equipment Maintenance—performing routine maintenance on equipment and determining when and what kind of maintenance is needed
* Repairing—repairing machines or systems, using the needed tools
* Equipment Selection—determining the kind of tools and equipment needed to do a job

These knowledges are important in most of these jobs:

* Food Production—techniques and equipment for planting, growing, and harvesting food products (both plant and animal) for consumption, including storage/handling techniques
* Transportation—principles and methods for moving people or goods by air, rail, sea, or road, including the relative costs and benefits
* Biology—plant and animal organisms and their tissues, cells, functions, interdependencies, and interactions with each other and the environment

What else should you consider about this kind of work?

About half of fishers are self-employed, and many of the other half work as crewmembers for small fishing businesses. Almost three-quarters of hunters and trappers are self-employed.

Some hunting and fishing work is seasonal. Most of it is strenuous and exposes you to the elements. Long hours may be required. Being out in the wild, and especially working out at sea, can be hazardous.

Stocks of fish in the wild are badly depleted (and in some cases polluted) now, costing many jobs, but in the long run there may be more opportunities.

How can you prepare for jobs of this kind?

Occupations in this group usually require education and/or training ranging from a short demonstration to less than two years. Most skills are learned on the job. Most employers require job applicants to be in good physical condition, and for jobs on fishing boats, commercial fisheries hire only persons who can swim.

Professional hunters and trappers typically learn their skills informally from recreational hunting or trapping.

How much education or training is required for the jobs in this Work Group?

For descriptions of these jobs, see Part 2.

Short-term on-the-job training

* Fishers and Related Fishing Workers

Moderate-term on-the-job training

* Hunters and Trappers

01.08 Mining and Drilling

Workers in this group operate drilling or other excavating and pumping equipment, usually in oil fields, quarries, or mines. They work where the resources are found, sometimes underground or on an offshore drilling platform.

What kind of work would you do?

Your work activities would depend on your job. For example, you might

* Dismantle extracting and boring equipment used for excavation, using hand tools.
* Drive machine into pile of material blasted from working face.
* Locate and recover lost or broken bits, casings, and drill pipes from wells, using special tools.
* Move pipes to and from trucks by hand or using truck winches and motorized lifts.
* Move, store, and maintain inventories of high explosives.
* Position jacks, timbers, or roof supports and install casings in order to prevent cave-ins.
* Record drilling progress and geological data.
* Repair gas and oil meters and gauges.
* Start pumps that circulate mud through drill pipes and boreholes to cool drill bits and flush out drill cuttings.

What things about you point to this kind of work?

Is it important for you to

* Have supervisors who train workers well?
* Never be pressured to do things that go against your sense of right and wrong?

Have you enjoyed any of the following as a hobby or leisure-time activity?

* Collecting rocks or minerals
* Operating power tools for household projects

Have you liked and done well in any of the following school subjects?

* Oilfield Practices
* Mining Practices
* Earth Science
* Heavy Equipment Operating
* Pump Operation

Are you able to

* Judge which of several objects is closer or farther away from you or judge the distance between you and an object?
* Exert maximum muscle force to lift, push, pull, or carry objects?
* See objects or movement of objects to your side when your eyes are looking ahead?
* Coordinate two or more limbs while sitting, standing, or lying down?
* Time your movements or the movement of a piece of equipment in anticipation of changes in the speed and/or direction of a moving object or scene?
* Choose quickly between two or more movements in response to two or more different signals?

* Use short bursts of muscle force to propel yourself or to throw an object?

Would you work in places such as

* Mines and quarries?
* Oil fields?
* Construction sites?

What skills and knowledges do you need for this kind of work?

For most of these jobs, you need these skills:

* Repairing—repairing machines or systems, using the needed tools
* Operation and Control—controlling operations of equipment or systems
* Equipment Maintenance—performing routine maintenance on equipment and determining when and what kind of maintenance is needed

These knowledges are important in most of these jobs:

* Mechanical Devices—machines and tools, including their designs, uses, repair, and maintenance
* Physics—physical principles and laws and their interrelationships and applications to understanding fluid, material, and atmospheric dynamics and mechanical, electrical, atomic, and subatomic structures and processes
* Transportation—principles and methods for moving people or goods by air, rail, sea, or road, including the relative costs and benefits

What else should you consider about this kind of work?

Workers in this group are mostly hired by small mining and drilling contractors or by the extraction departments of large mineral or petroleum companies.

Sites of rich deposits are scattered around the world, and not necessarily in the most comfortable climates or the most familiar cultures. As the resources are depleted or when the political and economic climates change, workers in this group often are relocated by their employers.

Working underground can sometimes be hazardous, and all the jobs involve heavy machinery that requires safety precautions.

The oil industry fluctuates greatly, but the long-term demand for petroleum is likely to continue, creating opportunities in this field over the long run. Many other mining industries are more stable, although some may experience boom or bust because of economic, political, or technological changes that affect supply and demand. Mining workers with good skills can often change industries in search of better opportunities.

How can you prepare for jobs of this kind?

Work in this group usually requires education and/or training ranging from six months to less than two years, although some jobs require more.

The skills are usually learned from on-the-job training programs offered by the employer. Explosives workers may acquire some skills in the military.

How much education or training is required for the jobs in this Work Group?

For descriptions of these jobs, see Part 2.

Short-term on-the-job training

* Helpers—Extraction Workers
* Roustabouts, Oil and Gas

Moderate-term on-the-job training

* Construction Drillers
* Continuous Mining Machine Operators
* Derrick Operators, Oil and Gas

* Excavating and Loading Machine Operators
* Explosives Workers, Ordnance Handling Experts, and Blasters
* Loading Machine Operators, Underground Mining
* Mine Cutting and Channeling Machine Operators
* Rock Splitters, Quarry
* Roof Bolters, Mining
* Rotary Drill Operators, Oil and Gas
* Service Unit Operators, Oil, Gas, and Mining
* Shuttle Car Operators
* Wellhead Pumpers

Long-term on-the-job training

* Well and Core Drill Operators

02 Architecture and Construction

An interest in designing, assembling, and maintaining components of buildings and other structures. You may want to be part of the team of architects, drafters, and others who design buildings and render the plans. If construction interests you, you can find fulfillment in the many building projects that are being undertaken at all times. If you like to organize and plan, you can find careers in managing these projects. Or you can play a more direct role in putting up and finishing buildings by doing jobs such as plumbing, carpentry, masonry, painting, or roofing, either as a skilled craftsworker or as a helper. You can prepare the building site by operating heavy equipment or install, maintain, and repair vital building equipment and systems such as electricity and heating.

02.01 **Managerial Work in Architecture and Construction**

02.02 **Architectural Design**

02.03 **Architecture/Construction Engineering Technologies**

02.04 **Construction Crafts**

02.05 **Systems and Equipment Installation, Maintenance, and Repair**

02.06 **Construction Support/Labor**

02.01 Managerial Work in Architecture and Construction

Workers in this group directly supervise and coordinate activities of the workers who construct buildings, roads, or other structures. They are responsible for setting and meeting goals and for bringing together the people and equipment needed to get the work done.

What kind of work would you do?

Your work activities would depend on your job. For example, you might

* Analyze and resolve worker problems and recommend motivational plans.
* Estimate material and worker requirements to complete jobs.
* Investigate damage, accidents, or delays at construction sites to ensure that proper procedures are being carried out.
* Study job specifications to determine appropriate construction methods.
* Suggest and initiate personnel actions, such as promotions, transfers, and hires.
* Supervise and coordinate activities of construction trades workers.
* Train workers in construction methods and operation of equipment.

What things about you point to this kind of work?

Is it important for you to

* Give directions and instructions to others?
* Have something different to do every day?
* Plan your work with little supervision?
* Make decisions on your own?

Have you enjoyed any of the following as a hobby or leisure-time activity?

* Building cabinets or furniture
* Constructing stage sets for school or other amateur theater
* Designing and building an addition or remodeling the interior of a home
* Serving as a leader of a scouting or other group
* Doing electrical wiring and repairs in the home
* Repairing plumbing in the home

Have you liked and done well in any of the following school subjects?

* Management
* Architectural History
* Business Computer Applications
* Business Writing
* Personnel Management
* Blueprint/Schematic Reading
* Construction Technology

Are you able to

* Arrange things or actions in a certain order or pattern according to a specific rule or set of rules?
* Imagine how something will look after it is moved around or when its parts are moved or rearranged?
* Come up with unusual or clever ideas about a given topic or situation or develop creative ways to solve a problem?

Would you work in places such as

* Business offices?
* Construction sites?

What skills and knowledges do you need for this kind of work?

For most of these jobs, you need these skills:

* Management of Material Resources—obtaining and seeing to the appropriate use of equipment, facilities, and materials needed to do certain work
* Installation—installing equipment, machines, wiring, or programs to meet specifications
* Management of Personnel Resources—motivating, developing, and directing people as they work, identifying the best people for the job
* Troubleshooting—determining causes of operating errors and deciding what to do about them
* Coordination—adjusting actions in relation to others' actions
* Management of Financial Resources—determining how money will be spent to get the work done and accounting for these expenditures
* Negotiation—bringing others together and trying to reconcile differences

These knowledges are important in most of these jobs:

* Building and Construction—the materials, methods, and tools involved in the construction or repair of houses; buildings; or other structures, such as highways and roads
* Design—design techniques, tools, and principles involved in production of precision technical plans, blueprints, drawings, and models
* Personnel and Human Resources—principles and procedures for personnel recruitment, selection, training, compensation and benefits, labor relations and negotiation, and personnel information systems
* Administration and Management—business and management principles involved in strategic planning, resource allocation, human resources modeling, leadership techniques, production methods, and coordination of people and resources
* Public Safety and Security—relevant equipment, policies, procedures, and strategies to promote effective local, state, or national security operations for the protection of people, data, property, and institutions
* Mechanical Devices—machines and tools, including their designs, uses, repair, and maintenance

✳ Engineering and Technology—the practical application of engineering science and technology; this includes applying principles, techniques, procedures, and equipment to the design and production of various goods and services

What else should you consider about this kind of work?

Construction managers work in all parts of the country. Some work for government agencies, such as the public works department. Others work for construction firms that may relocate workers frequently. They often specialize in one kind of construction (e.g., residential) and can transfer to another firm in the same or a related industry.

Most of these managers work a regular eight-hour day, but some have to work overtime without additional pay, especially to meet construction deadlines.

Workers divide their time between the office, where they do paperwork, and the work site, where they observe operations, monitor progress, detect possible problems, and give directions to workers.

Job opportunities are good for construction managers, although there is some sensitivity to the business cycle.

How can you prepare for jobs of this kind?

Work in this group usually requires education and/or training ranging from two to less than ten years. Generally, these workers must have college-level courses in management, business math, business writing, record-keeping, data processing, and industrial safety, plus technical competence in most or all of the jobs they supervise. The latter is acquired through college course work and training received while doing construction work. Many managers begin as craftsworkers, take on increasing levels of supervisory responsibility, and get training and eventually certification through an industry association.

How much education or training is required for the jobs in this Work Group?

For descriptions of these jobs, see Part 2.

Work experience in a related occupation

✳ First-Line Supervisors and Manager/Supervisors—Construction Trades Workers

Bachelor's degree

✳ Construction Managers

02.02 Architectural Design

Workers in this group plan and design buildings and landscapes and help supervise construction. They utilize artistic and scientific principles to design structures and environments that are functional, aesthetically appealing, and affordable. Workers may specialize in one or more kinds of design, such as residential or commercial buildings or golf courses. Most work for design firms, while

others find employment with federal, state, and local governments.

What kind of work would you do?

Your work activities would depend on your job. For example, you might

✳ Compile and analyze data on conditions such as location, drainage, and location of structures for environmental reports and landscaping plans.
✳ Consult with client to determine functional and spatial requirements of structure.
✳ Prepare information regarding design, structure specifications, materials, color, equipment, estimated costs, and construction time.
✳ Prepare scale drawings.
✳ Prepare site plans, specifications, and cost estimates for land development, coordinating arrangement of existing and proposed land features and structures.
✳ Represent client in obtaining bids and awarding construction contracts.

What things about you point to this kind of work?

Is it important for you to

✳ Try out your own ideas?
✳ Receive recognition for the work you do?
✳ Make use of your individual abilities?
✳ Be looked up to by others in your company and your community?
✳ Get a feeling of accomplishment?
✳ Be paid well in comparison with other workers?

Have you enjoyed any of the following as a hobby or leisure-time activity?

✳ Designing and building an addition or remodeling the interior of a home
✳ Constructing stage sets for school or other amateur theater
✳ Drawing posters for an organization or political campaign

Have you liked and done well in any of the following school subjects?

✳ Architectural Drafting
✳ Architectural History
✳ Art
✳ Mechanics/Mechanics of Materials
✳ Physics
✳ Computerized Drafting and Design
✳ Calculus
✳ Construction Technology
✳ Landscaping

Are you able to

✳ Imagine how something will look after it is moved around or when its parts are moved or rearranged?
✳ Come up with unusual or clever ideas about a given topic or situation or develop creative ways to solve a problem?

* Come up with a number of ideas about a topic?
* Generate or use different sets of rules for combining or grouping things in different ways?
* Apply general rules to specific problems to produce answers that make sense?
* See details at a distance?
* Arrange things or actions in a certain order or pattern according to a specific rule or set of rules?

Would you work in places such as

* Design studios?
* Construction sites?
* Business offices?
* Private homes?
* Golf courses and tennis courts?

What skills and knowledges do you need for this kind of work?

For most of these jobs, you need these skills:

* Operations Analysis—analyzing needs and product requirements to create a design
* Management of Financial Resources—determining how money will be spent to get the work done and accounting for these expenditures
* Coordination—adjusting actions in relation to others' actions
* Persuasion—persuading others to change their minds or behavior
* Complex Problem Solving—identifying complex problems and reviewing related information to develop and evaluate options and implement solutions
* Negotiation—bringing others together and trying to reconcile differences
* Management of Personnel Resources—motivating, developing, and directing people as they work, identifying the best people for the job

These knowledges are important in most of these jobs:

* Design—design techniques, tools, and principles involved in production of precision technical plans, blueprints, drawings, and models
* Building and Construction—the materials, methods, and tools involved in the construction or repair of houses; buildings; or other structures, such as highways and roads
* Engineering and Technology—the practical application of engineering science and technology; this includes applying principles, techniques, procedures, and equipment to the design and production of various goods and services
* Fine Arts—the theory and techniques required to compose, produce, and perform works of music, dance, visual arts, drama, and sculpture
* Geography—principles and methods for describing the features of land, sea, and air masses, including their physical characteristics; locations; interrelationships; and distribution of plant, animal, and human life

* Law and Government—laws, legal codes, court procedures, precedents, government regulations, executive orders, agency rules, and the democratic political process
* Sales and Marketing—principles and methods for showing, promoting, and selling products or services; this includes marketing strategy and tactics, product demonstrations, sales techniques, and sales control systems

What else should you consider about this kind of work?

Architectural design jobs are found in most cities and some towns. More than 20 percent of workers are self-employed.

Architects do most of their work in clean, quiet offices, but they spend some time outdoors at construction sites. At times they may need to put in overtime to meet project deadlines.

The job outlook is better for landscape architects than for other architects, but both kinds can expect keen competition for jobs at the most prestigious firms. You can gain an advantage by becoming skilled with computer-assisted design and by getting architecture-related work experience while still in school.

How can you prepare for jobs of this kind?

Work in this group usually requires education and/or training ranging from four years to more than ten years. Architects and landscape architects may prepare with a five-year first professional degree or by completing a master's degree in the field after a bachelor's in another (perhaps related) field. These degree programs include both technical and design courses. In architecture, the trend is toward an advanced degree.

All states require architects to pass an exam and other requirements for licensure, and several states require you to get continuing education to maintain licensure. Almost all states require landscape architects to be licensed.

How much education or training is required for the jobs in this Work Group?

For descriptions of these jobs, see Part 2.

Bachelor's degree

* Architects, Except Landscape and Naval
* Landscape Architects

02.03
Architecture/Construction Engineering Technologies

Workers in this group perform a variety of technical tasks. They make detailed drawings and work plans; measure and prepare maps of land and water areas; and inspect buildings for structural, mechanical, or electrical problems.

What kind of work would you do?

Your work activities would depend on your job. For example, you might

* Analyze technical implications of architect's design concept, calculating weights, volumes, and stress factors.
* Determine longitudes and latitudes of important features and boundaries in survey areas, using theodolites, transits, levels, and satellite-based global positioning systems (GPS).
* Draw maps, diagrams, and profiles, using cross-sections and surveys, to represent elevations, topographical contours, subsurface formations, and structures.
* Draw rough and detailed scale plans for foundations, buildings, and structures.
* Inspect and monitor construction sites to ensure adherence to safety standards, building codes, and specifications.
* Operate computer-aided drafting equipment or conventional drafting station to produce designs, working drawings, charts, forms, and records.
* Review completed construction drawings and cost estimates for accuracy and conformity to standards and regulations.
* Supervise and train other technologists, technicians, and drafters.

What things about you point to this kind of work?

Is it important for you to

* Have opportunities for advancement?
* Be paid well in comparison with other workers?

Have you enjoyed any of the following as a hobby or leisure-time activity?

* Drawing posters for an organization or political campaign
* Designing and building an addition or remodeling the interior of a home
* Reading about technological developments, such as computer science or aerospace

Have you liked and done well in any of the following school subjects?

* Architectural Drafting
* Drafting
* Surveying
* Blueprint/Schematic Reading
* Computerized Drafting and Design
* Calculus

Are you able to

* Imagine how something will look after it is moved around or when its parts are moved or rearranged?
* See details at a distance?
* Choose the right mathematical methods or formulas to solve a problem?

* Identify or detect a known pattern that is hidden in other distracting material?
* Add, subtract, multiply, or divide quickly and correctly?
* Quickly make sense of, combine, and organize information into meaningful patterns?
* Arrange things or actions in a certain order or pattern according to a specific rule or set of rules?

Would you work in places such as

* Construction sites?
* Design studios?
* Business offices?

What skills and knowledges do you need for this kind of work?

For most of these jobs, you need these skills:

* Mathematics—using mathematics to solve problems
* Operations Analysis—analyzing needs and product requirements to create a design
* Coordination—adjusting actions in relation to others' actions
* Time Management—managing one's own time and the time of others
* Technology Design—generating or adapting equipment and technology to serve user needs
* Active Listening—giving full attention to what other people are saying, taking time to understand the points being made, asking questions as appropriate, and not interrupting at inappropriate times
* Active Learning—understanding the implications of new information for both current and future problem solving and decision making

These knowledges are important in most of these jobs:

* Design—design techniques, tools, and principles involved in production of precision technical plans, blueprints, drawings, and models
* Building and Construction—the materials, methods, and tools involved in the construction or repair of houses; buildings; or other structures, such as highways and roads
* Engineering and Technology—the practical application of engineering science and technology; this includes applying principles, techniques, procedures, and equipment to the design and production of various goods and services
* Geography—principles and methods for describing the features of land, sea, and air masses, including their physical characteristics; locations; interrelationships; and distribution of plant, animal, and human life
* Mathematics—arithmetic, algebra, geometry, calculus, and statistics and their applications
* Computers and Electronics—circuit boards; processors; chips; electronic equipment; and computer hardware and software, including applications and programming
* Public Safety and Security—relevant equipment, policies, procedures, and strategies to promote effective

© 2006 JIST Works

local, state, or national security operations for the protection of people, data, property, and institutions

What else should you consider about this kind of work?

These workers are hired by architectural design firms; construction companies; firms offering specialized services (for example, surveying); and federal, state, and local governments.

Most workers have regular daytime hours, although overtime may be necessary to meet project deadlines.

Some of these jobs require frequent travel. You might have to spend time in a remote area with a surveying team, and construction inspectors spend part of their time on building sites. Drafters generally work in offices.

Construction work is sensitive to the business cycle. Opportunities will probably be best for those skilled at using computer applications. Civil service tests are required for most government jobs.

How can you prepare for jobs of this kind?

Work in this group usually requires education and/or training ranging from one year to less than ten years. The most common way to prepare for this kind of work is through related postsecondary courses, on-the-job training, and work experience.

For surveying jobs, an apprenticeship may offer this combination of training and experience. Also, many technical and vocational schools and two-year colleges offer programs in surveying. With some classroom instruction in surveying, beginners can start as instrument workers, but they will need a two- or possibly four-year degree to become licensed or registered. Advancement may be based on experience, additional education, and/or written examinations.

Basic preparation for jobs in drafting includes high school and two-year college courses in algebra, geometry, trigonometry, physical sciences, industrial arts, and mechanical drawing. Technical school or college courses in structural design, layout, and computer applications provide the knowledge and skills needed for advanced drafting jobs.

Surveyors and drafters usually begin work as trainees in routine jobs under close supervision of an experienced technician or engineer. With added training and experience, they may advance to supervisory or engineering positions.

Construction and building inspectors need a mix of technical knowledge, experience, and education, so employers favor applicants who have a degree and some experience in construction work. Some technical and community colleges offer two-year programs in building inspection.

How much education or training is required for the jobs in this Work Group?

For descriptions of these jobs, see Part 2.

Work experience in a related occupation

* Construction and Building Inspectors

Postsecondary vocational training

* Civil Drafters

Associate degree

* Architectural Drafters
* Electrical Drafters

Bachelor's degree

* Surveyors

02.04 Construction Crafts

Workers in this group perform tasks that contribute to the construction of buildings and other large structures. Usually they specialize in a particular craft, such as laying the foundations; putting up the framework, walls, floors, or roof; installing plumbing or electric conduits, windows, or insulation; or finishing interior surfaces with paint, paper, or carpeting. Outside, they may install driveways, parking lots, fences, or swimming pools. They may also apply their skills to servicing or refurbishing components of existing buildings.

What kind of work would you do?

Your work activities would depend on your job. For example, you might

* Assemble, install, test, and maintain electrical or electronic wiring, equipment, appliances, apparatus, and fixtures, using hand tools and power tools.
* Build or repair cabinets, doors, frameworks, floors, and other wooden fixtures used in buildings, using woodworking machines, carpenter's hand tools, and power tools.
* Clean and maintain equipment.
* Cut or saw boards, timbers, or plywood to required size, using handsaw, power saw, or woodworking machines.
* Interpret blueprints and drawings to determine specifications and to calculate the materials required.
* Lay and set mosaic tiles to create decorative wall, mural, and floor designs.
* Measure and mark pipes for cutting and threading.
* Move levers, depress foot pedals, and turn dials to operate cranes, cherry pickers, electromagnets, or other moving equipment for lifting, moving, and placing loads.
* Paint surfaces, using brushes, spray gun, or rollers.
* Spread, level, and smooth concrete, using rake, shovel, hand or power trowel, hand or power screed, and float.

What things about you point to this kind of work?

Is it important for you to

* Never be pressured to do things that go against your sense of right and wrong?
* Have supervisors who train workers well?

Have you enjoyed any of the following as a hobby or leisure-time activity?

* Doing electrical wiring and repairs in the home
* Repairing plumbing in the home
* Operating power tools for household projects
* Constructing stage sets for school or other amateur theater
* Painting the interior or exterior of a home

Have you liked and done well in any of the following school subjects?

* Construction Shop
* Construction Technology
* Electrical Circuits
* Shop Math
* Plumbing
* Masonry
* Carpentry
* Wood Shop/Woodworking
* Heavy Equipment Operating
* Blueprint/Schematic Reading
* Bricklaying
* Industrial Arts

Are you able to

* Exert muscle force repeatedly or continuously over time?
* Exert maximum muscle force to lift, push, pull, or carry objects?
* Keep or regain your body balance or stay upright when in an unstable position?
* Exert yourself physically over long periods of time without getting winded or out of breath?
* Bend, stretch, twist, or reach with your body, arms, and/or legs?

Would you work in places such as

* Construction sites?
* Private homes?

What skills and knowledges do you need for this kind of work?

For most of these jobs, you need these skills:

* Installation—installing equipment, machines, wiring, or programs to meet specifications
* Repairing—repairing machines or systems, using the needed tools
* Equipment Selection—determining the kind of tools and equipment needed to do a job

These knowledges are important in most of these jobs:

* Building and Construction—the materials, methods, and tools involved in the construction or repair of houses; buildings; or other structures, such as highways and roads
* Mechanical Devices—machines and tools, including their designs, uses, repair, and maintenance

* Design—design techniques, tools, and principles involved in production of precision technical plans, blueprints, drawings, and models

What else should you consider about this kind of work?

General construction companies and specialized installation and service firms employ these workers. Many construction workers have their own businesses, subcontracting for specialized work (for example, drywalling, roofing, or plumbing) within a larger construction project. Those who branch out on their own usually have gained experience working for someone else.

Almost all of these jobs are associated with craft unions, and in some regions you may have to join a union to be hired. For many jobs you must provide your own hand tools. Usually you are required to wear a hard hat and safety glasses and sometimes must also wear a safety strap and steel-toed shoes.

Regular working hours can be expected, with some overtime to meet construction deadlines. People who enjoy the outdoors often prefer construction work; however, the weather and seasons affect the availability of such work.

Construction jobs are affected by varying local labor market conditions and by periodic downturns in the business cycle, but over the long run many of the jobs in this group are in high demand in most locations. Skilled workers can usually find employment almost anywhere.

How can you prepare for jobs of this kind?

Work in this group usually requires education and/or training ranging from six months to six years.

The best way to acquire the skills required in the construction trades is a formal apprenticeship lasting three to four years and combining on-the-job training and classroom study. Apprentices generally must be at least 18 years old and in good physical condition. High school or vocational courses in mathematics (including computing fractions), mechanical drawing, carpentry, and electricity are helpful. Many people acquire construction skills by working as laborers and helpers and observing skilled workers.

How much education or training is required for the jobs in this Work Group?

For descriptions of these jobs, see Part 2.

Short-term on-the-job training

* Refractory Materials Repairers, Except Brickmasons
* Riggers

Moderate-term on-the-job training

* Brattice Builders
* Carpet Installers
* Ceiling Tile Installers
* Commercial Divers
* Crane and Tower Operators
* Dragline Operators
* Drywall Installers

* Fence Erectors
* Floor Layers, Except Carpet, Wood, and Hard Tiles
* Floor Sanders and Finishers
* Grader, Bulldozer, and Scraper Operators
* Hazardous Materials Removal Workers
* Insulation Workers, Floor, Ceiling, and Wall
* Insulation Workers, Mechanical
* Manufactured Building and Mobile Home Installers
* Operating Engineers
* Painters, Construction and Maintenance
* Paperhangers
* Paving, Surfacing, and Tamping Equipment Operators
* Pile-Driver Operators
* Pipelayers
* Pipelaying Fitters
* Rail-Track Laying and Maintenance Equipment Operators
* Roofers
* Rough Carpenters
* Segmental Pavers
* Sheet Metal Workers
* Ship Carpenters and Joiners
* Stone Cutters and Carvers
* Tapers

Long-term on-the-job training

* Boat Builders and Shipwrights
* Boilermakers
* Brickmasons and Blockmasons
* Cement Masons and Concrete Finishers
* Construction Carpenters
* Electricians
* Glaziers
* Pipe Fitters
* Plasterers and Stucco Masons
* Plumbers
* Reinforcing Iron and Rebar Workers
* Stonemasons
* Structural Iron and Steel Workers
* Terrazzo Workers and Finishers
* Tile and Marble Setters

Postsecondary vocational training

* Security and Fire Alarm Systems Installers

02.05 Systems and Equipment Installation, Maintenance, and Repair

Workers in this group repair and install electrical devices and systems that are important components of buildings and power transmission networks. They usually specialize in one type of equipment or system, such as motors, transformers, meters, appliances, heating and cooling systems, power lines, or components of telephone or data networks.

What kind of work would you do?

Your work activities would depend on your job. For example, you might

* Assemble, position, and mount heating or cooling equipment, following blueprints.
* Coordinate work assignment preparation and completion with other workers.
* Examine and test malfunctioning equipment to determine defects, using blueprints and electrical measuring instruments.
* Observe and test operation of appliances, such as refrigerators, washers, and dryers.
* Order parts, supplies, and equipment from catalogs and suppliers or obtain them from storerooms.
* Prepare and maintain records detailing tests, repairs, and maintenance.
* Splice cables, using hand tools, epoxy, or mechanical equipment.
* Supervise and instruct assistants.

What things about you point to this kind of work?

Is it important for you to

* Have supervisors who train workers well?
* Never be pressured to do things that go against your sense of right and wrong?

Have you enjoyed any of the following as a hobby or leisure-time activity?

* Repairing electrical household appliances
* Building or repairing radios or television sets
* Installing and repairing home stereo equipment
* Doing electrical wiring and repairs in the home

Have you liked and done well in any of the following school subjects?

* Construction Shop
* Construction Technology
* Electrical Circuits
* Shop Math
* Blueprint/Schematic Reading
* Industrial Arts

Are you able to

* Keep or regain your body balance or stay upright when in an unstable position?
* Exert muscle force repeatedly or continuously over time?
* Bend, stretch, twist, or reach with your body, arms, and/or legs?

Would you work in places such as

* Construction sites?
* Private homes?
* Office buildings?

What skills and knowledges do you need for this kind of work?

For most of these jobs, you need these skills:

✳ Installation—installing equipment, machines, wiring, or programs to meet specifications

✳ Repairing—repairing machines or systems, using the needed tools

✳ Troubleshooting—determining causes of operating errors and deciding what to do about them

✳ Equipment Maintenance—performing routine maintenance on equipment and determining when and what kind of maintenance is needed

These knowledges are important in most of these jobs:

✳ Telecommunications—transmission, broadcasting, switching, control, and operation of telecommunications systems

✳ Mechanical Devices—machines and tools, including their designs, uses, repair, and maintenance

✳ Engineering and Technology—the practical application of engineering science and technology; this includes applying principles, techniques, procedures, and equipment to the design and production of various goods and services

What else should you consider about this kind of work?

These workers are employed by construction companies, specialized subcontractors, manufacturers, utilities, and service companies. Since electrical and electronic equipment is used almost everywhere, many jobs in this group are found in almost every large and small city. Others are available only where certain industries are located. Some workers are self-employed, full-time or part-time.

Work schedules vary. Maintenance workers at factories, hospitals, and radio and TV studios, for instance, have rotating shifts.

Some jobs require climbing or crawling to reach wiring and components. Careful safety procedures must be observed on some jobs because of the chance of electric shock. Good color vision is usually needed, since electronic parts are often color-coded.

Best opportunities are in installation, service, and repair of equipment used for purposes other than manufacturing. Workers are especially needed for high-tech systems and equipment, such as telecommunication components. Because of miniaturization and better quality control, some products need fewer repairs and service calls, but new construction will continue to provide jobs, and new devices will cause continued growth of the field.

How can you prepare for jobs of this kind?

Work in this group usually requires education and/or training ranging from six months to less than ten years, depending on the type of systems or equipment. Colleges and technical schools offer two-year programs in electronics technology or electrical engineering technology. Courses in electricity, electronics, mathematics, and blueprint reading are especially helpful.

A few companies provide extensive training to prepare workers for repair jobs. Correspondence courses in such fields as electricity and electronics are often helpful. Apprenticeships are also available, and military experience can be a start.

Technology in this field is changing constantly, so workers need to take courses and get training to keep their skills current.

How much education or training is required for the jobs in this Work Group?

For descriptions of these jobs, see Part 2.

Moderate-term on-the-job training

✳ Electric Meter Installers and Repairers

✳ Meter Mechanics

Long-term on-the-job training

✳ Electrical Power-Line Installers and Repairers

✳ Elevator Installers and Repairers

✳ Heating and Air Conditioning Mechanics

✳ Home Appliance Installers

✳ Maintenance and Repair Workers, General

✳ Refrigeration Mechanics

✳ Telecommunications Facility Examiners

✳ Telecommunications Line Installers and Repairers

Postsecondary vocational training

✳ Central Office and PBX Installers and Repairers

✳ Communication Equipment Mechanics, Installers, and Repairers

✳ Electrical and Electronics Repairers, Powerhouse, Substation, and Relay

✳ Frame Wirers, Central Office

✳ Station Installers and Repairers, Telephone

02.06 Construction Support/Labor

Workers in this group perform a variety of tasks requiring little skill, such as moving construction materials, operating simple tools, and helping skilled workers. They work at construction sites and at buildings or other structures that are being repaired or maintained.

What kind of work would you do?

Your work activities would depend on your job. For example, you might

✳ Adjust, connect, or disconnect wiring, piping, tubing, and other parts, using hand tools or power tools.

✳ Apply grout between joints of bricks or tiles, using grouting trowel.

✳ Cut and install insulating or sound-absorbing material.

✳ Cut or drill holes in walls or floors to accommodate the passage of pipes.

* Haul and spread sand, gravel, and clay to fill washouts and repair road shoulders.
* Lay out and align materials on worktable or in assembly jig according to specified instructions.
* Prepare and keep records of actions taken, including maintenance and repair work.
* Trace out short circuits in wiring, using test meter.

What things about you point to this kind of work?

Is it important for you to

* Have opportunities for advancement?
* Have supervisors who train workers well?

Have you enjoyed any of the following as a hobby or leisure-time activity?

* Repairing plumbing in the home
* Constructing stage sets for school or other amateur theater
* Doing strenuous activities, such as dancing, climbing, backpacking, running, swimming, and skiing
* Painting the interior or exterior of a home

Have you liked and done well in any of the following school subjects?

* Industrial Arts
* Carpentry
* Bricklaying
* Plumbing
* Construction Shop

Are you able to

* Exert maximum muscle force to lift, push, pull, or carry objects?
* Exert muscle force repeatedly or continuously over time?
* Use your abdominal and lower back muscles to support part of the body repeatedly or continuously over time without fatiguing?
* Keep or regain your body balance or stay upright when in an unstable position?
* Bend, stretch, twist, or reach with your body, arms, and/or legs?
* Exert yourself physically over long periods of time without getting winded or out of breath?

Would you work in places such as

* Construction sites?
* Private homes?
* Movie studios?
* Theaters?

What skills and knowledges do you need for this kind of work?

For most of these jobs, you need these skills:

* Installation—installing equipment, machines, wiring, or programs to meet specifications
* Repairing—repairing machines or systems, using the needed tools

* Equipment Maintenance—performing routine maintenance on equipment and determining when and what kind of maintenance is needed

These knowledges are important in most of these jobs:

* Building and Construction—the materials, methods, and tools involved in the construction or repair of houses; buildings; or other structures, such as highways and roads
* Mechanical Devices—machines and tools, including their designs, uses, repair, and maintenance
* Design—design techniques, tools, and principles involved in production of precision technical plans, blueprints, drawings, and models

What else should you consider about this kind of work?

People in this group work for construction companies and subcontractors, a maintenance business, or the maintenance department of a large business. Grips and set-up workers are employed by theatrical and motion picture companies.

Evening or night shift jobs and overtime work are common in this group. Working conditions vary. Some jobs are hot or dirty; others are done mostly outdoors, in all kinds of weather.

You are likely to need to wear safety clothing as protection against common job hazards such as falling or flying objects. Your hiring may depend on your passing a physical exam that shows you can handle the physical labor required.

The job outlook is good, although the construction industry has some sensitivity to economic downturns. Many of the jobs are open to beginners. If you are in a job helping a skilled worker, you may be able to learn the trade from that person. Those with a high school education or its equal may qualify for apprenticeship programs leading to more skilled jobs.

How can you prepare for jobs of this kind?

Work in this group usually requires education and/or training ranging from a short demonstration or brief explanation to more than six months. The most important hiring consideration is usually the physical ability of the applicant. Some of these jobs are available through union hiring halls.

How much education or training is required for the jobs in this Work Group?

For descriptions of these jobs, see Part 2.

Short-term on-the-job training

* Grips and Set-Up Workers, Motion Picture Sets, Studios, and Stages
* Helpers—Brickmasons, Blockmasons, Stonemasons, and Tile and Marble Setters
* Helpers—Carpenters
* Helpers—Electricians
* Helpers—Installation, Maintenance, and Repair Workers

* Helpers—Painters, Paperhangers, Plasterers, and Stucco Masons
* Helpers—Pipelayers, Plumbers, Pipefitters, and Steamfitters

Moderate-term on-the-job training

* Carpenter Assemblers and Repairers
* Construction Laborers
* Highway Maintenance Workers
* Septic Tank Servicers and Sewer Pipe Cleaners

03 Arts and Communication

An interest in creatively expressing feelings or ideas, in communicating news or information, or in performing. You can satisfy this interest in creative, verbal, or performing activities. For example, if you enjoy literature, perhaps writing or editing would appeal to you. Journalism and public relations are other fields for people who like to use their writing or speaking skills. Do you prefer to work in the performing arts? If so, you could direct or perform in drama, music, or dance. If you especially enjoy the visual arts, you could create paintings, sculpture, or ceramics or design products or visual displays. A flair for technology might lead you to specialize in photography, broadcast production, or dispatching.

03.01 Managerial Work in Arts and Communication

03.02 Writing and Editing

03.03 News, Broadcasting, and Public Relations

03.04 Studio Art

03.05 Design

03.06 Drama

03.07 Music

03.08 Dance

03.09 Media Technology

03.10 Communications Technology

03.11 Musical Instrument Repair

03.01 Managerial Work in Arts and Communication

Workers in this group manage people who work in the arts and communication. They oversee performers and performances in the arts and sports.

What kind of work would you do?

Your work activities would depend on your job. For example, you might

* Develop ideas for programs and features that a station could produce.
* Manage business and financial affairs for clients, such as arranging travel and lodging, selling tickets, and directing marketing and advertising activities.
* Mark up, paste, and complete layouts and write typography instructions to prepare materials for typesetting or printing.
* Monitor and review programming in order to ensure that schedules are met, guidelines are adhered to, and performances are of adequate quality.
* Observe pictures through monitors and direct camera and video staff concerning shading and composition.
* Perform management activities such as budgeting, scheduling, planning, and marketing.
* Switch between video sources in a studio or on multi-camera remotes, using equipment such as switchers, video slide projectors, and video effects generators.

What things about you point to this kind of work?

Is it important for you to

* Give directions and instructions to others?
* Plan your work with little supervision?
* Try out your own ideas?
* Receive recognition for the work you do?
* Have something different to do every day?
* Make decisions on your own?
* Get a feeling of accomplishment?

Have you enjoyed any of the following as a hobby or leisure-time activity?

* Directing school or other amateur plays or musicals
* Drawing posters for an organization or political campaign
* Planning and arranging programs for school or community organizations
* Designing stage sets for school or community plays
* Making videos of family activities
* Writing articles, stories, or plays
* Editing or proofreading a school or organizational newspaper, yearbook, or magazine
* Designing your own greeting cards and writing original verses
* Developing publicity flyers for a school or community event

Have you liked and done well in any of the following school subjects?

* Management
* Accounting
* Editing
* Cinematography
* Theater Arts
* Contract Law
* Business Law
* Creative Writing
* Personnel Management
* Business Writing

Are you able to

* Come up with unusual or clever ideas about a given topic or situation or develop creative ways to solve a problem?
* Come up with a number of ideas about a topic?
* Identify and understand the speech of another person?
* Communicate information and ideas in writing so others will understand?

Would you work in places such as

* Business offices?
* Artists' studios and craft workshops?
* Movie studios?
* Theaters?
* Television and video studios?
* Music studios?
* Rehearsal halls?

What skills and knowledges do you need for this kind of work?

For most of these jobs, you need these skills:

* Time Management—managing one's own time and the time of others
* Management of Personnel Resources—motivating, developing, and directing people as they work, identifying the best people for the job
* Coordination—adjusting actions in relation to others' actions
* Negotiation—bringing others together and trying to reconcile differences
* Management of Financial Resources—determining how money will be spent to get the work done and accounting for these expenditures
* Monitoring—monitoring/assessing your own performance or that of other individuals or organizations to make improvements or take corrective action
* Persuasion—persuading others to change their minds or behavior

These knowledges are important in most of these jobs:

* Communications and Media—media production, communication, and dissemination techniques and methods; this includes alternative ways to inform and entertain via written, oral, and visual media
* Sales and Marketing—principles and methods for showing, promoting, and selling products or services; this includes marketing strategy and tactics, product demonstrations, sales techniques, and sales control systems
* Administration and Management—business and management principles involved in strategic planning, resource allocation, human resources modeling, leadership techniques, production methods, and coordination of people and resources
* Personnel and Human Resources—principles and procedures for personnel recruitment, selection, training, compensation and benefits, labor relations and negotiation, and personnel information systems
* Fine Arts—the theory and techniques required to compose, produce, and perform works of music, dance, visual arts, drama, and sculpture
* Economics and Accounting—economic and accounting principles and practices, the financial markets, banking, and the analysis and reporting of financial data

What else should you consider about this kind of work?

Managers of artists work for radio, television, and motion picture production companies and for artists and musicians. They feel some of the same competitive pressure as the artists themselves and must have creativity and the knowledge of what makes for artistic success.

Nevertheless, managers need to think just as much (or more) in terms of business success. As the media business is becoming more concentrated into large companies, opportunities to take artistic risks may be decreasing. This trend also tends to concentrate media jobs in larger cities.

How can you prepare for jobs of this kind?

Occupations in this group usually require education and training ranging from four to more than ten years. Typically, workers have a bachelor's degree plus experience working in arts or communication.

Generally it helps to have some mastery of the skill of the workers you will manage. At the very least, you need to know what makes the difference between good work and bad work.

For example, art directors need to know about art, layout design, and copy writing, probably from college courses in commercial art and writing, together with some experience working in this field.

Business managers of artists need some knowledge of an art form, which they may acquire either formally through education, possibly college-level, or informally through training and practice.

All jobs in this group require knowledge of business management. This is best learned through college courses in accounting, personnel management, and finance. Specialized courses and even majors in arts or media production and management are available at some colleges.

How much education or training is required for the jobs in this Work Group?

For descriptions of these jobs, see Part 2.

Long-term on-the-job training

* Technical Directors/Managers

Work experience plus degree

* Agents and Business Managers of Artists, Performers, and Athletes
* Art Directors
* Producers
* Program Directors
* Public Relations Managers

03.02 Writing and Editing

Workers in this group write or edit prose or poetry. Some use knowledge of a technical field to write manuals.

What kind of work would you do?

Your work activities would depend on your job. For example, you might

* Interview production and engineering personnel and read journals and other material to become familiar with product technologies and production methods.
* Plan the contents of publications according to the publication's style, editorial policy, and publishing requirements.
* Prepare, rewrite, and edit copy to improve readability or supervise others who do this work.
* Write advertising copy for use by publication, broadcast, or Internet media to promote the sale of goods and services.
* Write humorous material for publication or performance, such as comedy routines, gags, comedy shows, or scripts for entertainers.
* Write narrative, dramatic, lyric, or other types of poetry for publication.
* Write words to fit musical compositions, including lyrics for operas, musical plays, and choral works.
* Write play or script for moving pictures or television, based on original ideas or adapted from fictional, historical, or narrative sources.

What things about you point to this kind of work?

Is it important for you to

* Try out your own ideas?
* Receive recognition for the work you do?
* Make use of your individual abilities?
* Get a feeling of accomplishment?
* Plan your work with little supervision?
* Make decisions on your own?
* Have good working conditions?

Have you enjoyed any of the following as a hobby or leisure-time activity?

* Writing articles, stories, or plays
* Editing or proofreading a school or organizational newspaper, yearbook, or magazine
* Belonging to a literary or book club
* Designing your own greeting cards and writing original verses
* Doing crossword puzzles
* Doing desktop publishing for a school or community publication
* Planning advertisements for a school or community newspaper
* Keeping a journal or diary

Have you liked and done well in any of the following school subjects?

* Grammar
* Creative Writing
* Literature
* Technical Writing
* Psychology
* Abstract Writing
* Fiction Writing
* Editing
* Copy Writing
* Advertising

Are you able to

* Come up with unusual or clever ideas about a given topic or situation or develop creative ways to solve a problem?
* Communicate information and ideas in writing so others will understand?
* Come up with a number of ideas about a topic?

Would you work in places such as

* Business offices?
* Television and video studios?
* Movie studios?
* Theaters?

What skills and knowledges do you need for this kind of work?

For most of these jobs, you need these skills:

* Writing—communicating effectively in writing as appropriate for the needs of the audience
* Reading Comprehension—understanding written sentences and paragraphs in work-related documents
* Coordination—adjusting actions in relation to others' actions

These knowledges are important in most of these jobs:

* Communications and Media—media production, communication, and dissemination techniques and methods; this includes alternative ways to inform and entertain via written, oral, and visual media

* Fine Arts—the theory and techniques required to compose, produce, and perform works of music, dance, visual arts, drama, and sculpture
* English Language—the structure and content of the English language, including the meaning and spelling of words, rules of composition, and grammar

What else should you consider about this kind of work?

Most of these workers are employed by publishers, in radio and television studios, and in the theatre and motion picture industries. Some are self-employed and sell their stories and plays directly to publishers.

There is keen competition for most jobs in this group. Although some work is available in cities all over the country, most editing jobs are found in cities where large publishing companies have their headquarters. Editors also work for large and small newspapers throughout the country. Copy writers work for advertising agencies, mostly in cities.

Many creative writers are self-employed. They write stories, poetry, and other materials and submit them to publishers or producers for consideration. Many hire agents who help them sell their work. Well-known writers are asked to take assignments to write about specific subjects.

Technical writing jobs are not as competitive and may be found anywhere there are technology companies. They require a different kind of creativity in that they require you to translate complicated concepts and procedures into terms your readers can understand. Some technical writers freelance.

When applying for writing jobs, you should bring samples of your work with you.

How can you prepare for jobs of this kind?

Occupations in this group usually require four years of college education. All jobs in the group require spelling, grammar, punctuation, and composition skills, which are usually acquired in school and college courses in English, journalism, and creative writing.

Experience with minor publishers is helpful in getting positions with major publishers and advertising agencies.

For technical writing, a college degree or course work in a technical field such as computer programming or engineering is usually necessary.

How much education or training is required for the jobs in this Work Group?

For descriptions of these jobs, see Part 2.

Bachelor's degree

* Copy Writers
* Creative Writers
* Editors
* Poets and Lyricists
* Technical Writers

03.03 News, Broadcasting, and Public Relations

Workers in this group write, edit, translate, and report factual or persuasive information. They use their language skills and knowledge of special writing techniques to communicate facts or convince people of a point of view.

What kind of work would you do?

Your work activities would depend on your job. For example, you might

* Check translations of technical terms and terminology to ensure that they are accurate and remain consistent throughout translation revisions.
* Edit news material to ensure that it fits within available time or space.
* Edit translations for correctness of grammar, punctuation, and clarity of expression.
* Investigate breaking news developments such as disasters, crimes, and human interest stories.
* Operate computerized captioning system for movies or television productions for hearing-impaired and foreign language-speaking viewers.
* Photograph or videotape news events or request that a photographer be assigned to provide such coverage.
* Plan and direct development and communication of informational programs to maintain favorable public and stockholder perceptions of an organization's accomplishments and agenda.
* Proofread, edit, and revise translated materials.
* Travel with or guide tourists who speak another language.
* Write commentaries, columns, or scripts, using computers.

What things about you point to this kind of work?

Is it important for you to

* Receive recognition for the work you do?
* Make use of your individual abilities?
* Have opportunities for advancement?
* Have something different to do every day?

Have you enjoyed any of the following as a hobby or leisure-time activity?

* Planning advertisements for a school or community newspaper
* Announcing or emceeing a program
* Speaking on radio or television
* Developing publicity fliers for a school or community event
* Doing desktop publishing for a school or community publication
* Writing articles, stories, or plays
* Teaching immigrants or other individuals to speak, write, or read English

* Keeping a journal or diary

Have you liked and done well in any of the following school subjects?

* Grammar
* News Writing
* Abstract Writing
* Economics
* Journalism
* Public Speaking
* Editing
* Broadcast Journalism
* Newscasting

Are you able to

* Speak clearly so others can understand you?
* Identify and understand the speech of another person?
* Communicate information and ideas in writing so others will understand?
* Listen to and understand information and ideas presented through spoken words and sentences?
* Read and understand information and ideas presented in writing?

Would you work in places such as

* Business offices?
* Radio studios?
* Sports stadiums?
* Television and video studios?
* Courthouses?

What skills and knowledges do you need for this kind of work?

For most of these jobs, you need these skills:

* Writing—communicating effectively in writing as appropriate for the needs of the audience
* Active Listening—giving full attention to what other people are saying, taking time to understand the points being made, asking questions as appropriate, and not interrupting at inappropriate times
* Speaking—talking to others to convey information effectively
* Reading Comprehension—understanding written sentences and paragraphs in work-related documents

These knowledges are important in most of these jobs:

* Communications and Media—media production, communication, and dissemination techniques and methods; this includes alternative ways to inform and entertain via written, oral, and visual media
* Foreign Language—the structure and content of a foreign (non-English) language, including the meaning and spelling of words, rules of composition and grammar, and pronunciation
* English Language—the structure and content of the English language, including the meaning and spelling of words, rules of composition, and grammar

What else should you consider about this kind of work?

These workers are employed by radio and television stations, newspapers, publishing firms, and advertising agencies. Some interpreters travel with visiting foreign business people or diplomats; others work in courtrooms and law firms.

Competition is keen for jobs in journalism and public relations. An internship while you are in college can be very valuable for getting your first job. The trend in public relations is toward more work being done by public relations firms rather than by an in-house PR staff. Expect to start with a small PR firm or small city newspaper and advance your career by moving to larger employers as you gain experience and a portfolio of your work.

Broadcast news analysts must have a background in what they are writing about, such as politics, business, culture, or technology. They are hired by radio and television broadcasters.

The growth in international trade and immigration is increasing the need for interpreters and translators, but also the availability of multilingual people. The best opportunities are in languages not widely known in the U.S. Freelancers may find many opportunities.

When applying for writing jobs, you should bring samples of your work with you.

How can you prepare for jobs of this kind?

Most of these jobs require at least four years of education and/or training. You should have good skills with spelling, grammar, punctuation, and composition, usually acquired in school and college courses in English, journalism, and creative writing.

Experience with minor publications is helpful in getting positions with major publications and public relations agencies.

For interpreting or translating, experience living in a foreign country is very valuable, partly to hone your language skills and partly to improve your understanding of the culture.

How much education or training is required for the jobs in this Work Group?

For descriptions of these jobs, see Part 2.

Moderate-term on-the-job training

* Caption Writers

Long-term on-the-job training

* Interpreters and Translators

Bachelor's degree

* Broadcast News Analysts
* Public Relations Specialists
* Reporters and Correspondents

03.04 Studio Art

Workers in this group draw, paint, or sculpt works of art.

What kind of work would you do?

Your work activities would depend on your job. For example, you might

* Assemble, lead, and solder finished glass to fabricate stained glass articles.
* Carve objects from stone, concrete, plaster, wood, or other material, using abrasives and tools such as chisels, gouges, and malls.
* Draw sketch, profile, or likeness of posed subject or photograph, using pencil, charcoal, pastels, or other media.
* Etch, carve, paint, or draw artwork on material such as stone, glass, canvas, wood, or linoleum.
* Raise and shape clay into ware (such as vases and pitchers) on revolving wheel, using hands, fingers, and thumbs.
* Render drawings, illustrations, and sketches of buildings, manufactured products, or models.
* Sketch and submit cartoon or animation for approval.

What things about you point to this kind of work?

Is it important for you to

* Try out your own ideas?
* Do your work alone?
* Get a feeling of accomplishment?
* Make use of your individual abilities?
* Receive recognition for the work you do?
* Plan your work with little supervision?
* Have something different to do every day?

Have you enjoyed any of the following as a hobby or leisure-time activity?

* Drawing posters for an organization or political campaign
* Painting landscapes, seascapes, or portraits
* Illustrating the school yearbook
* Making ceramic objects
* Carving small wooden objects
* Doing crafts

Have you liked and done well in any of the following school subjects?

* Fine Arts
* Arts and Crafts
* Sculpture/Sculpting
* Fashion Illustration
* Ceramics
* Painting, Fine Arts and Applied

Are you able to

* Imagine how something will look after it is moved around or when its parts are moved or rearranged?

* Come up with unusual or clever ideas about a given topic or situation or develop creative ways to solve a problem?
* Keep your hand and arm steady while moving your arm or while holding your arm and hand in one position?

Would you work in places such as

* Artists' studios and craft workshops?
* Business offices?
* Movie studios?

What skills and knowledges do you need for this kind of work?

For most of these jobs, you need these skills:

* Operations Analysis—analyzing needs and product requirements to create a design
* Programming—writing computer programs for various purposes
* Management of Material Resources—obtaining and seeing to the appropriate use of equipment, facilities, and materials needed to do certain work

These knowledges are important in most of these jobs:

* Fine Arts—the theory and techniques required to compose, produce, and perform works of music, dance, visual arts, drama, and sculpture
* Design—design techniques, tools, and principles involved in production of precision technical plans, blueprints, drawings, and models
* History and Archeology—historical events and their causes, indicators, and effects on civilizations and cultures

What else should you consider about this kind of work?

These artists work for advertising agencies, printing and publishing firms, and television and motion picture studios. Many operate their own commercial art studios or do freelance work.

Art dealers and commercial art galleries exhibit and sell the work of artists, taking a commission on sales prices.

People who are just getting started in the field may have their work exhibited in community centers, hospitals, hotels, and other public places. They may show and sell their work at craft and community fairs.

Although the number of jobs is expected to grow, there will be keen competition for openings. Your chances for employment will be greater if you do many kinds of artwork rather than specializing in one or two.

When applying for either full-time or freelance work in this field, you should bring samples of your work to interviews.

How can you prepare for jobs of this kind?

Occupations in this group usually require education and training ranging from two to ten years. Some persons obtain a four-year degree with a major in fine art. Others earn an art institute certificate in two or three years.

Much learning in this field occurs on the job as artists tackle new problems and refine their skills.

Successful freelance visual artists must have established their reputations in their art form.

How much education or training is required for the jobs in this Work Group?

For descriptions of these jobs, see Part 2.

Long-term on-the-job training

* Cartoonists
* Painters and Illustrators
* Potters
* Sculptors
* Sketch Artists

Associate degree

* Craft Artists

03.05 Design

Workers in this group design consumer goods and interior spaces in which visual appeal is important.

What kind of work would you do?

Your work activities would depend on your job. For example, you might

* Advise clients on interior design factors, such as space planning, layout and utilization of furnishings and equipment, and color coordination.
* Confer with sales and management executives or with clients in order to discuss design ideas.
* Design custom clothing and accessories for individuals; retailers; or theatrical, television, or film productions.
* Design graphic material for use as ornamentation, illustration, or advertising on manufactured materials and packaging or containers.
* Design, draw, paint, or sketch backgrounds and fixtures for use in windows or interior displays.
* Draw and print charts, graphs, illustrations, and other artwork, using computer.
* Estimate costs of design materials and construction or rental of location or props.
* Plan and erect commercial displays to entice and appeal to customers.
* Select flora and foliage for arrangements, working with numerous combinations to synthesize and develop new creations.

What things about you point to this kind of work?

Is it important for you to

* Try out your own ideas?
* Make use of your individual abilities?
* Get a feeling of accomplishment?
* Receive recognition for the work you do?
* Have something different to do every day?

* Plan your work with little supervision?
* Have good working conditions?

Have you enjoyed any of the following as a hobby or leisure-time activity?

* Designing and making costumes for school plays, festivals, and other events
* Designing stage sets for school or community plays
* Developing publicity fliers for a school or community event
* Making tie-dyed clothes
* Mounting and framing pictures
* Creating Web pages

Have you liked and done well in any of the following school subjects?

* Fine Arts
* Fashion Illustration
* Design Media
* Design Graphics
* Theater Arts
* Marketing/Merchandising
* Drafting
* Advertising Art/Production
* Floral Arranging

Are you able to

* Match or detect differences between colors, including shades of color and brightness?
* Imagine how something will look after it is moved around or when its parts are moved or rearranged?
* Come up with unusual or clever ideas about a given topic or situation or develop creative ways to solve a problem?
* Come up with a number of ideas about a topic?

Would you work in places such as

* Design studios?
* Business offices?
* Private homes?
* Factories and plants?
* Stores and shopping malls?
* Theaters?
* Television and video studios?

What skills and knowledges do you need for this kind of work?

For most of these jobs, you need these skills:

* Management of Financial Resources—determining how money will be spent to get the work done and accounting for these expenditures
* Operations Analysis—analyzing needs and product requirements to create a design
* Persuasion—persuading others to change their minds or behavior
* Management of Material Resources—obtaining and seeing to the appropriate use of equipment, facilities, and materials needed to do certain work

* Negotiation—bringing others together and trying to reconcile differences

These knowledges are important in most of these jobs:

* Fine Arts—the theory and techniques required to compose, produce, and perform works of music, dance, visual arts, drama, and sculpture
* Design—design techniques, tools, and principles involved in production of precision technical plans, blueprints, drawings, and models
* Sales and Marketing—principles and methods for showing, promoting, and selling products or services; this includes marketing strategy and tactics, product demonstrations, sales techniques, and sales control systems

What else should you consider about this kind of work?

Designers work for manufacturers, retail and wholesale merchandisers, advertising agencies, printing and publishing firms, television and motion picture studios, and museums. Some do freelance work.

Competition is keen for jobs in design. Formal education, creativity, and perseverance can be advantages for job seekers.

The expansion of the World Wide Web and video-based forms of entertainment is expected to provide many job openings for graphic designers.

When applying for either full-time or freelance work in this field, you should bring samples of your work to interviews.

How can you prepare for jobs of this kind?

Occupations in this group usually require education and training ranging from one year to less than ten years. Most of these jobs require a bachelor's degree for entry-level work, and new hires get on-the-job training for several years. Floral and merchandise display designers are the exceptions; most of them are not expected to have a college degree and learn on the job over several months of training. Industrial designers often get a master's degree, and some other designers find it gives them an edge in competing for jobs.

Design majors are offered at many universities and art schools. Skill with computer-based design applications is becoming very important. High school courses in art and computer applications can be useful.

In some states, interior designers need to be licensed.

How much education or training is required for the jobs in this Work Group?

For descriptions of these jobs, see Part 2.

Moderate-term on-the-job training

* Floral Designers
* Merchandise Displayers and Window Trimmers

Bachelor's degree

* Commercial and Industrial Designers

* Exhibit Designers
* Fashion Designers
* Graphic Designers
* Interior Designers
* Set Designers

03.06 Drama

Workers in this group direct dramatic works, perform in them for the public, provide essential services for actors, or use their voices to make announcements. In addition to the time spent on stage, performers must spend a large portion of their time auditioning for parts and rehearsing their performances.

What kind of work would you do?

Your work activities would depend on your job. For example, you might

* Apply makeup to enhance and/or alter the appearance of people appearing in productions such as movies.
* Attend auditions and casting calls in order to audition for roles.
* Collaborate with film and sound editors during the post-production process as films are edited and soundtracks are added.
* Communicate to actors the approach, characterization, and movement needed for each scene in such a way that rehearsals and takes are minimized.
* Design and construct costumes or send them to tailors for construction, major repairs, or alterations.
* Perform humorous and serious interpretations of emotions, actions, and situations, using body movements, facial expressions, and gestures.
* Provide running commentaries of event activities, such as play-by-play descriptions, or explanations of official decisions.
* Read news flashes to inform audiences of important events.

What things about you point to this kind of work?

Is it important for you to

* Receive recognition for the work you do?
* Try out your own ideas?
* Have something different to do every day?

Have you enjoyed any of the following as a hobby or leisure-time activity?

* Acting in a play or amateur variety show
* Performing magic tricks for friends
* Announcing or emceeing a program
* Speaking on radio or television
* Applying makeup for amateur theater
* Doing impersonations
* Directing school or other amateur plays or musicals
* Entertaining at parties or other events

Have you liked and done well in any of the following school subjects?

* Theater Arts
* Acting Techniques
* Literature
* Public Speaking
* Costuming
* Directing
* Drama

Are you able to

* Come up with unusual or clever ideas about a given topic or situation or develop creative ways to solve a problem?
* Remember information such as words, numbers, pictures, and procedures?
* Speak clearly so others can understand you?

Would you work in places such as

* Theaters?
* Television and video studios?
* Movie studios?
* Radio studios?
* Bus and train stations?
* Rehearsal halls?

What skills and knowledges do you need for this kind of work?

For most of these jobs, you need these skills:

* Speaking—talking to others to convey information effectively
* Monitoring—monitoring/assessing your own performance or that of other individuals or organizations to make improvements or take corrective action
* Time Management—managing one's own time and the time of others

These knowledges are important in most of these jobs:

* Fine Arts—the theory and techniques required to compose, produce, and perform works of music, dance, visual arts, drama, and sculpture
* Communications and Media—media production, communication, and dissemination techniques and methods; this includes alternative ways to inform and entertain via written, oral, and visual media
* Telecommunications—transmission, broadcasting, switching, control, and operation of telecommunications systems

What else should you consider about this kind of work?

These workers are employed by motion picture, television, and radio studios and stock companies. Although many jobs in this field are found in large cities, people can find employment in smaller communities.

Performers are often required to meet demanding schedules with early and late hours for rehearsals and performances. Frequent travel may be necessary.

Competition for jobs is keen. Amateur performances can give you chances to improve your skills. It is to your advantage to gain as broad a background as possible in a variety of performing styles. The more versatile you are, the better your opportunities for full-time employment will be. Most performers are not permanently employed and must audition for roles.

How can you prepare for jobs of this kind?

Occupations in this group usually require education and/or training ranging from less than one year to more than ten years. Experience is also necessary to get a career started and is a vital part of the educational program.

For jobs in drama and announcing, initial training and experience are available in speech classes, debate classes, and school or community plays. Colleges and schools for the performing arts offer drama and communications programs with courses in speech, theater, pantomime, directing, and acting. Because acting careers are sometimes short and often never get beyond the amateur level, it helps to get an education that will also prepare you for another kind of work.

The usual career path in this group is to start a career in smaller venues—community theater or a local radio station—and, with talent, hard work, and luck, advance to a more prominent position.

How much education or training is required for the jobs in this Work Group?

For descriptions of these jobs, see Part 2.

Moderate-term on-the-job training

* Costume Attendants
* Radio and Television Announcers

Long-term on-the-job training

* Actors

Postsecondary vocational training

* Makeup Artists, Theatrical and Performance

Associate degree

* Public Address System and Other Announcers

Work experience plus degree

* Directors—Stage, Motion Pictures, Television, and Radio

03.07 Music

Workers in this group direct, compose, or perform instrumental or vocal music for the public. Performers are constantly auditioning for employers and rehearsing their performances. Similarly, composers and arrangers may have to devote time to promoting their work.

What kind of work would you do?

Your work activities would depend on your job. For example, you might

* Arrange for and/or design screen tests or auditions for prospective performers.
* Audition for orchestras, bands, or other musical groups.
* Create original musical form or write within circumscribed musical form, such as sonata, symphony, or opera.
* Play musical instruments as soloist or as member or guest artist of musical groups such as orchestras, ensembles, or bands.
* Practice singing exercises and study with vocal coaches in order to develop voice and skills and to rehearse for upcoming roles.
* Sing as a soloist or as a member of a vocal group.
* Study scores to learn the music in detail and to develop interpretations.
* Transpose music from one voice or instrument to another to accommodate particular musician in musical group.

What things about you point to this kind of work?

Is it important for you to

* Make use of your individual abilities?
* Try out your own ideas?
* Receive recognition for the work you do?
* Get a feeling of accomplishment?
* Plan your work with little supervision?
* Make decisions on your own?

Have you enjoyed any of the following as a hobby or leisure-time activity?

* Playing a musical instrument
* Singing in a choir or other group
* Writing songs for club socials or amateur performances
* Taking lessons in singing or in playing a musical instrument
* Entertaining at parties or other events

Have you liked and done well in any of the following school subjects?

* Music Composition/Arranging
* Music: Theory and History
* Band
* Choir/Chorus
* Voice
* Opera
* Orchestra

Are you able to

* Detect or tell the differences between sounds that vary in pitch and loudness?
* Tell the direction from which a sound originated?
* Focus on a single source of sound in the presence of other distracting sounds?
* Come up with unusual or clever ideas about a given topic or situation or develop creative ways to solve a problem?

* Remember information such as words, numbers, pictures, and procedures?

Would you work in places such as

* Theaters?
* Music studios?
* Radio studios?
* Television and video studios?
* Colleges and universities?
* Rehearsal halls?
* Nightclubs?

What skills and knowledges do you need for this kind of work?

For most of these jobs, you need these skills:

* Coordination—adjusting actions in relation to others' actions
* Management of Personnel Resources—motivating, developing, and directing people as they work, identifying the best people for the job
* Monitoring—monitoring/assessing your own performance or that of other individuals or organizations to make improvements or take corrective action

These knowledges are important in most of these jobs:

* Fine Arts—the theory and techniques required to compose, produce, and perform works of music, dance, visual arts, drama, and sculpture
* Foreign Language—the structure and content of a foreign (non-English) language, including the meaning and spelling of words, rules of composition and grammar, and pronunciation
* Communications and Media—media production, communication, and dissemination techniques and methods; this includes alternative ways to inform and entertain via written, oral, and visual media

What else should you consider about this kind of work?

These workers are employed by religious organizations and performance arts companies. Some work in nightclubs, on cruise ships, at weddings, or in recording studios. Composers and arrangers may work for music publishing and recording companies.

For all the occupations in this group, it helps to begin studying music at an early age and to gain experience as an amateur. Versatility is also useful, since skill with a variety of styles can make you more employable. The music industry is concentrated in large cities, but some jobs may be found in smaller communities.

Performers typically work when other people are relaxing, and they usually also have to devote a lot of time to rehearsals and auditions. They may have to travel to appear before different audiences. Some performers make career changes to teaching their art form or to composing, arranging, or directing.

Competition for jobs is keen, and many workers face periods of unemployment.

How can you prepare for jobs of this kind?

Occupations in this group usually require education and/or training ranging from one or two to more than ten years.

Although some persons with great natural talent may find work without formal instruction and even achieve great success as rock, country, or jazz singers or instrumental musicians, they are the rare exceptions. Professional instrumental musicians and singers usually begin their training while in elementary school and continue training throughout their working lives, with several hours of practice each day necessary for the development and maintenance of required skills. Courses in music theory and voice are offered in high schools, colleges, and music academies and by private instructors. Membership in a musical or singing group is valuable experience and preparation.

How much education or training is required for the jobs in this Work Group?

For descriptions of these jobs, see Part 2.

Long-term on-the-job training

* Musicians, Instrumental
* Singers
* Talent Directors

Bachelor's degree

* Music Arrangers and Orchestrators

Master's degree

* Composers
* Music Directors

03.08 Dance

Workers in this group plan or perform works of dance. Dancers spend considerable time in rehearsals, doing routines to stay in shape and maintain their skills, and auditioning for parts.

What kind of work would you do?

Your work activities would depend on your job. For example, you might

* Audition performers for one or more dance parts.
* Coordinate dancing with that of partners or dance ensembles.
* Create original dance routines for ballets, musicals, or other forms of entertainment.
* Instruct cast in dance movements at rehearsals to achieve desired effect.
* Perform in productions, singing or acting in addition to dancing, if required.
* Study and practice dance moves required in roles.
* Teach dance students.

What things about you point to this kind of work?

Is it important for you to

* Try out your own ideas?
* Receive recognition for the work you do?
* Make use of your individual abilities?
* Get a feeling of accomplishment?
* Never be pressured to do things that go against your sense of right and wrong?

Have you enjoyed any of the following as a hobby or leisure-time activity?

* Creating dance steps for school or other amateur musicals
* Taking ballet or other dance lessons
* Teaching dance as a volunteer in an after-school center

Have you liked and done well in any of the following school subjects?

* Dance
* Music: Theory and History
* Physical Education

Are you able to

* Coordinate the movement of your arms, legs, and torso together when the whole body is in motion?
* Quickly and repeatedly bend, stretch, twist, or reach out with your body, arms, and/or legs?
* Quickly move your arms and legs?
* Exert muscle force repeatedly or continuously over time?
* Exert yourself physically over long periods of time without getting winded or out of breath?
* Keep or regain your body balance or stay upright when in an unstable position?
* Use short bursts of muscle force to propel yourself or to throw an object?

Would you work in places such as

* Theaters?
* Music studios?
* Television and video studios?
* Colleges and universities?
* Rehearsal halls?
* Nightclubs?

What skills and knowledges do you need for this kind of work?

For most of these jobs, you need these skills:

* Instructing—teaching others how to do something
* Programming—writing computer programs for various purposes
* Coordination—adjusting actions in relation to others' actions

These knowledges are important in most of these jobs:

* Fine Arts—the theory and techniques required to compose, produce, and perform works of music, dance, visual arts, drama, and sculpture

* Communications and Media—media production, communication, and dissemination techniques and methods; this includes alternative ways to inform and entertain via written, oral, and visual media
* Philosophy and Theology—different philosophical systems and religions; this includes their basic principles, values, ethics, ways of thinking, customs, practices, and impact on human culture

What else should you consider about this kind of work?

These workers are employed by dance studios, educational institutions, performing arts organizations, and recreational venues such as cruise ships and amusement parks.

Amateur performances are a good way to improve your skills. You may also want to learn a variety of dance styles to increase your employability. Jobs are easier to find in large cities. Almost one-fifth of dancers and choreographers are self-employed.

Dance performances tend to take place in the evening, while the days are often devoted to rehearsals, so dancers may work long hours. They may also have to take their act on the road. Dancing is also strenuous work. Eating disorders are sometimes an occupational hazard. Most dancers stop performing by their late thirties, but they may continue to work in this field as dance teachers or choreographers.

As in all performing arts, competition for jobs is keen.

How can you prepare for jobs of this kind?

Occupations in this group usually require more than ten years of education and/or training.

Initial dance training is often found in elementary and high schools. However, instruction in a dance studio, beginning at a very early age and continuing while employed, is usually needed to develop and maintain skills. Daily practice is essential. Liberal arts colleges, community dance companies, ethnic culture societies, dance academies, and theater arts schools offer two- to four-year programs in dance techniques, interpretation, and the history of dance. Many of these organizations cooperate with professional ballet and interpretive dance companies to provide experience as well as instruction. Private dance teachers must be able to demonstrate the techniques of many different types of dance. Choreographers usually need to start as dancers and may take special college coursework in choreography.

How much education or training is required for the jobs in this Work Group?

For descriptions of these jobs, see Part 2.

Long-term on-the-job training

* Dancers

Work experience in a related occupation

* Choreographers

03.09 Media Technology

Workers in this group perform technical tasks associated with broadcasting and technological forms of art. They create the photographs, movies, and videos; radio and television broadcasts; and sound recordings that provide entertainment and information for all of us.

What kind of work would you do?

Your work activities would depend on your job. For example, you might

* Apply paint to retouch or enhance negatives or photographs, using airbrushes, pens, artist's brushes, cotton swabs, or gloved fingers.
* Focus camera and adjust settings based on lighting, subject material, distance, and film speed.
* Install, adjust, and operate electronic equipment used to record, edit, and transmit radio and television programs, cable programs, and motion pictures.
* Mix developing and processing solutions for use in developing, processing, and rinsing prints.
* Operate radio equipment in order to communicate with ships, aircraft, mining crews, offshore oil rigs, logging camps, and other remote operations.
* Operate television or motion picture cameras to record scenes for television broadcasts, advertising, or motion pictures.
* Organize and string together raw film footage into a continuous whole according to scripts and/or the instructions of directors and producers.
* Produce color photographs, negatives, and slides, using color reproduction processes.
* Record speech, music, and other sounds on recording media, using recording equipment.
* Regulate the fidelity, brightness, and contrast of video transmissions, using video console control panels.

What things about you point to this kind of work?

Is it important for you to

* Have good working conditions?
* Have something different to do every day?

Have you enjoyed any of the following as a hobby or leisure-time activity?

* Creating unusual lighting effects for school or other amateur plays
* Installing and repairing home stereo equipment
* Taking photographs
* Developing film
* Making videos of family activities

Have you liked and done well in any of the following school subjects?

* Photography
* Electricity/Electronics
* Art

* Computer Graphics
* Computer Concepts/Methods
* Radio/TV Operations
* Advertising Art/Production
* Acoustics
* Theater Arts
* Cinematography

Are you able to

* Match or detect differences between colors, including shades of color and brightness?
* Choose quickly between two or more movements in response to two or more different signals?
* Detect or tell the differences between sounds that vary in pitch and loudness?

Would you work in places such as

* Photographers' studios?
* Media workstation labs?
* Radio studios?
* Television and video studios?
* Movie studios?

What skills and knowledges do you need for this kind of work?

For most of these jobs, you need these skills:

* Operation and Control—controlling operations of equipment or systems
* Equipment Selection—determining the kind of tools and equipment needed to do a job
* Equipment Maintenance—performing routine maintenance on equipment and determining when and what kind of maintenance is needed

These knowledges are important in most of these jobs:

* Fine Arts—the theory and techniques required to compose, produce, and perform works of music, dance, visual arts, drama, and sculpture
* Telecommunications—transmission, broadcasting, switching, control, and operation of telecommunications systems
* Communications and Media—media production, communication, and dissemination techniques and methods; this includes alternative ways to inform and entertain via written, oral, and visual media

What else should you consider about this kind of work?

These workers are employed by local and network broadcasters, film studios and independent film or video production companies, recording studios, and photography studios.

Work associated with the arts and broadcasting is mostly found in cities. Photographers' studios are located in large and small communities throughout the country.

It may help for you to assemble a portfolio of amateur or student work to interest employers and thus gain entry to at least an apprenticeship, if not a first job.

The outlook for jobs in this group is mixed. Employment is generally expected to grow in technical jobs associated with the arts, but there will be a lot of competition from people interested in creative work. Growth of jobs in broadcasting may be limited because of media consolidation and the growth of satellite radio. The best opportunities will be in smaller cities.

How can you prepare for jobs of this kind?

Occupations in this group usually require education and/or training ranging from one year to less than ten years.

Photographers or camera operators may acquire their skills either through long-term on-the-job training or through an academic program at a technical or community college or art school. Either route takes several years.

Other photography workers, such as retouchers, get on-the-job training lasting a year or more, depending on the level of skill.

Technicians who work with electronics may get formal or informal training on the job, but the preferred route is to get a two-year degree in electronics or broadcasting at a technical or community college.

How much education or training is required for the jobs in this Work Group?

For descriptions of these jobs, see Part 2.

Moderate-term on-the-job training

* Camera Operators, Television, Video, and Motion Picture
* Photographic Hand Developers
* Photographic Reproduction Technicians
* Photographic Retouchers and Restorers

Long-term on-the-job training

* Audio and Video Equipment Technicians
* Professional Photographers
* Radio Operators

Postsecondary vocational training

* Broadcast Technicians
* Sound Engineering Technicians

Bachelor's degree

* Film and Video Editors
* Multi-Media Artists and Animators

03.10 Communications Technology

Workers in this group speak via radio or telephone to help connect people and services. Operators provide communications assistance to people who call in. Dispatchers use radio communications to coordinate service providers operating at a distance. Air traffic controllers keep airplanes at safe distances from each other.

What kind of work would you do?

Your work activities would depend on your job. For example, you might

* Calculate and quote charges on long-distance connections.
* Monitor aircraft within a specific airspace, using radar, computer equipment, and visual references.
* Monitor various radio frequencies such as those used by public works departments, school security, and civil defense in order to keep apprised of developing situations.
* Refer to alphabetical or geographical reels or directories to answer questions and provide telephone information.
* Schedule and dispatch workers, work crews, equipment, or service vehicles to appropriate locations according to customer requests, specifications, or needs, using radios or telephones.

What things about you point to this kind of work?

Is it important for you to

* Have supervisors who train workers well?
* Have supervisors who back up workers with management?

Have you enjoyed any of the following as a hobby or leisure-time activity?

* Talking on the phone
* Operating a CB or ham radio

Have you liked and done well in any of the following school subjects?

* Public Speaking
* Emergency Care/Rescue

Are you able to

* Identify and understand the speech of another person?
* Focus on a single source of sound in the presence of other distracting sounds?
* Quickly and accurately compare similarities and differences among sets of letters, numbers, objects, pictures, or patterns?

Would you work in places such as

* Police headquarters?
* Fire stations?
* Airports?
* Office buildings?

What skills and knowledges do you need for this kind of work?

For most of these jobs, you need these skills:

* Active Listening—giving full attention to what other people are saying, taking time to understand the points being made, asking questions as appropriate, and not interrupting at inappropriate times

* Operation and Control—controlling operations of equipment or systems
* Service Orientation—actively looking for ways to help people

These knowledges are important in most of these jobs:

* Telecommunications—transmission, broadcasting, switching, control, and operation of telecommunications systems
* Transportation—principles and methods for moving people or goods by air, rail, sea, or road, including the relative costs and benefits
* Geography—principles and methods for describing the features of land, sea, and air masses, including their physical characteristics; locations; interrelationships; and distribution of plant, animal, and human life

What else should you consider about this kind of work?

Dispatchers and operators are employed in offices, from which they communicate with the public or with other workers.

Most work for local agencies, such as fire and police departments, but others are with state and federal agencies. In cases of fires, crimes, or other emergencies, people's lives may depend on how fast and accurately information is transmitted.

Air traffic controllers work for the federal government at airports and in-flight control centers.

Airports, hospitals, hotels, and fire and police departments never close, so people who work there may have to work rotating shifts.

The outlook for jobs in this group is mixed. Telephone operators are being replaced by automation and will have fewer opportunities. Dispatchers will have more opportunities, although these will vary depending on the type of employer. Opportunities probably will be best for taxi and tow truck dispatchers.

How can you prepare for jobs of this kind?

Occupations in this group usually require education and/or training ranging from 30 days to four years or more.

Operators and dispatchers get most or all of their training on the job. For telephone operators, this training is brief, but dispatchers may need as much as two years. Jobs in the federal government usually require a civil service examination.

Air traffic controllers require several years of training. First, unless they have military experience, they must complete an FAA-approved training program and pass a test. Admission to these programs requires a combination of several years of prior education and work experience. After the program and test, plus a screening for medical conditions, drug use, and security risk, they may be hired as a controller. New hires undergo 12 weeks of training at the FAA school in Oklahoma City and continue to be trained on the job over several years. They are subject to periodic physical testing and drug screening.

How much education or training is required for the jobs in this Work Group?

For descriptions of these jobs, see Part 2.

Short-term on-the-job training

* Airfield Operations Specialists
* Central Office Operators
* Directory Assistance Operators

Moderate-term on-the-job training

* Dispatchers, Except Police, Fire, and Ambulance
* Police, Fire, and Ambulance Dispatchers

Long-term on-the-job training

* Air Traffic Controllers

03.11 Musical Instrument Repair

Workers in this group maintain and repair musical instruments. They usually specialize in one instrument or a family of instruments. They may specialize in a particular task, such as piano tuning.

What kind of work would you do?

Your work activities would depend on your job. For example, you might

* Adjust string tension to tune instruments, using hand tools and electronic tuning devices.
* Disassemble and reassemble instruments and parts to tune and repair, using hand tools and power tools.
* Inspect mechanical parts of instruments to determine defects.
* Play instruments to determine pitch.
* Polish instruments, using rags and polishing compounds, buffing wheels, or burnishing tools.
* Remove dents in tympani, using steel block and hammer.
* Repair cracks in wood or metal instruments, using wire, lathe, filler, clamps, or soldering iron.
* Solder or weld frames of mallet instruments and metal drum parts.

What things about you point to this kind of work?

Is it important for you to

* Do your work alone?
* Never be pressured to do things that go against your sense of right and wrong?

Have you enjoyed any of the following as a hobby or leisure-time activity?

* Playing a musical instrument
* Carving small wooden objects

Have you liked and done well in any of the following school subjects?

* Band
* Wood Machining
* Metal Forming and Fabrication/Technology
* Metal Shop
* Shop Math

Are you able to

* Detect or tell the differences between sounds that vary in pitch and loudness?
* Tell the direction from which a sound originated?
* Focus on a single source of sound in the presence of other distracting sounds?
* Quickly move your arms and legs?

Would you work in places such as

* Artists' studios and craft workshops?
* Theaters?

What skills and knowledges do you need for this kind of work?

For most of these jobs, you need these skills:

* Repairing—repairing machines or systems, using the needed tools
* Equipment Maintenance—performing routine maintenance on equipment and determining when and what kind of maintenance is needed
* Quality Control Analysis—conducting tests and inspections of products, services, or processes to evaluate quality or performance

These knowledges are important in most of these jobs:

* Fine Arts—the theory and techniques required to compose, produce, and perform works of music, dance, visual arts, drama, and sculpture
* Mechanical Devices—machines and tools, including their designs, uses, repair, and maintenance
* Foreign Language—the structure and content of a foreign (non-English) language, including the meaning and spelling of words, rules of composition and grammar, and pronunciation

What else should you consider about this kind of work?

Musical instrument repairers (often called technicians) combine a love of music with technical skills for working with metal, wood and its finishes, or mechanical devices. They work mostly for music shops and performing arts companies. Most work is done in workshops, although piano tuners typically make house calls and some technicians accompany touring performers.

About one-fifth are self-employed. The demand for workers and the supply of trained people is expected to be roughly equal.

How can you prepare for jobs of this kind?

Occupations in this group usually require education and/or training ranging from one year to less than four years, although those who work on band instruments typically require additional training.

A handful of colleges offer majors in this field. Some technicians learn at specialized vocational schools or through correspondence courses. Others learn through apprenticeship. On-the-job training is always a vital part of the preparation.

It is usually not necessary to have a lot of performance skill with the instrument, but some ability to play it is very useful.

How much education or training is required for the jobs in this Work Group?

For descriptions of these jobs, see Part 2.

Long-term on-the-job training

* Keyboard Instrument Repairers and Tuners
* Percussion Instrument Repairers and Tuners
* Reed or Wind Instrument Repairers and Tuners
* Stringed Instrument Repairers and Tuners

© 2006 JIST Works

04 Business and Administration

An interest in making a business organization or function run smoothly. You can satisfy this interest by working in a position of leadership or by specializing in a function that contributes to the overall effort in a business, a nonprofit organization, or a government agency. If you especially enjoy working with people, you may find fulfillment from working in human resources. An interest in numbers may lead you to consider accounting, finance, budgeting, billing, or financial record keeping. A job as an administrative assistant may interest you if you like a variety of work in a busy environment. If you are good with details and word processing, you may enjoy a job as a secretary or data entry keyer. Or perhaps you would do well as the manager of a business.

04.01   Managerial Work in General Business

04.02   Managerial Work in Business Detail

04.03   Human Resources Support

04.04   Secretarial Support

04.05   Accounting, Auditing, and Analytical Support

04.06   Mathematical Clerical Support

04.07   Records and Materials Processing

04.08   Clerical Machine Operation

04.01 Managerial Work in General Business

Workers in this group are top-level and middle-level administrators who direct all or part of the activities in business establishments. They set policies, make important decisions, and determine priorities. They use a variety of skills, including math, critical thinking, communications, insight into human nature, and computer applications. They have a good knowledge of how their industry operates and what laws and regulations they must follow.

What kind of work would you do?

Your work activities would depend on your job. For example, you might

* Advise management on such matters as equal employment opportunity, sexual harassment, and discrimination.
* Analyze compensation policies, government regulations, and prevailing wage rates to develop competitive compensation plan.
* Analyze training needs to develop new training programs or modify and improve existing programs.
* Assign or delegate responsibilities to subordinates.
* Conduct exit interviews to identify reasons for employee termination.
* Confer with board members, organization officials, and staff members to establish policies and formulate plans.
* Develop testing and evaluation procedures.
* Identify staff vacancies and recruit, interview, and select applicants.
* Negotiate or approve contracts with suppliers and distributors and with maintenance, janitorial, and security providers.
* Plan and conduct new employee orientations to foster positive attitude toward organizational objectives.

What things about you point to this kind of work?

Is it important for you to

* Give directions and instructions to others?
* Have good working conditions?
* Be busy all the time?
* Have something different to do every day?
* Plan your work with little supervision?

Have you enjoyed any of the following as a hobby or leisure-time activity?

* Balancing checkbooks for family members
* Budgeting the family income
* Helping run a school or community fair or carnival
* Planning and arranging programs for school or community organizations
* Reading business magazines and newspapers
* Serving as a leader of a scouting or other group
* Serving as president of a club or other organization
* Serving as treasurer of a club or other organization

Have you liked and done well in any of the following school subjects?

* Management
* Accounting
* Business Analysis
* Business Law
* Contract Law
* Personnel Management
* Business Writing
* Business Computer Applications
* Business Organization
* Marketing/Merchandising

Are you able to

* Speak clearly so others can understand you?
* Identify and understand the speech of another person?
* Come up with a number of ideas about a topic?
* Come up with unusual or clever ideas about a given topic or situation or develop creative ways to solve a problem?
* Generate or use different sets of rules for combining or grouping things in different ways?
* Choose the right mathematical methods or formulas to solve a problem?
* Remember information such as words, numbers, pictures, and procedures?

Would you work in places such as

* Business offices?
* Government offices?

What skills and knowledges do you need for this kind of work?

For most of these jobs, you need these skills:

* Management of Personnel Resources—motivating, developing, and directing people as they work, identifying the best people for the job
* Management of Financial Resources—determining how money will be spent to get the work done and accounting for these expenditures
* Negotiation—bringing others together and trying to reconcile differences
* Persuasion—persuading others to change their minds or behavior
* Time Management—managing one's own time and the time of others
* Monitoring—monitoring/assessing your own performance or that of other individuals or organizations to make improvements or take corrective action
* Management of Material Resources—obtaining and seeing to the appropriate use of equipment, facilities, and materials needed to do certain work

These knowledges are important in most of these jobs:

* Personnel and Human Resources—principles and procedures for personnel recruitment, selection, training, compensation and benefits, labor relations and negotiation, and personnel information systems
* Administration and Management—business and management principles involved in strategic planning, resource allocation, human resources modeling, leadership techniques, production methods, and coordination of people and resources
* Economics and Accounting—economic and accounting principles and practices, the financial markets, banking, and the analysis and reporting of financial data
* Sales and Marketing—principles and methods for showing, promoting, and selling products or services; this includes marketing strategy and tactics, product demonstrations, sales techniques, and sales control systems
* Law and Government—laws, legal codes, court procedures, precedents, government regulations, executive orders, agency rules, and the democratic political process
* Education and Training—principles and methods for curriculum and training design, teaching and instruction for individuals and groups, and the measurement of training effects
* Psychology—human behavior and performance; individual differences in ability, personality, and interests; learning and motivation; psychological research methods; and the assessment and treatment of behavioral and affective disorders

What else should you consider about this kind of work?

Many jobs in this group are found in large cities or in towns that are county seats, are state capitals, or have industrial parks. These workers play managerial roles within businesses and industries of all kinds.

In a few jobs, well-trained beginners are given consideration. This is more likely to happen in small businesses than in large ones. In most companies, people start out in lower-level positions and work their way up.

Workers in this group have heavy responsibilities. They may have to work long hours to meet specific situations or to solve problems such as shortages of materials or financial losses. They may have to travel to distant parts of the country or to foreign countries to attend meetings and conduct business. In order to move up the promotion ladder, these workers sometimes change employers and therefore must relocate.

The overall outlook for this group is for many opportunities (with ups and downs caused by economic trends) but keen competition. Job openings also vary, depending on the health of particular industries. Best opportunities will be for those with graduate degrees and those who are skilled with computers and verbal and written communication.

How can you prepare for jobs of this kind?

Occupations in this group usually require education and/or training ranging from two years to more than ten years.

Most jobs in this group call for experience in related positions, usually within the same industry or specialization. Degrees in business administration or law provide preparation for many jobs in this group. However, some administrative jobs require training and experience in such fields as engineering, chemistry, or sociology. Liberal arts graduates who take advantage of opportunities for management training or coursework sometimes parlay their communications and critical-thinking skills into a very successful career. College coursework in the following subjects is helpful: management, business law, business math, speech or public speaking, finance, accounting, economics, history, and English (especially writing).

Some businesses offer management-trainee programs to advance employees to administrative positions. Some employers accept inexperienced college graduates with business degrees and place them in these training programs.

How much education or training is required for the jobs in this Work Group?

For descriptions of these jobs, see Part 2.

Work experience plus degree

* Chief Executives
* Compensation and Benefits Managers
* General and Operations Managers
* Human Resources Managers
* Private Sector Executives
* Training and Development Managers

04.02 Managerial Work in Business Detail

Workers in this group supervise and coordinate certain high-level business activities: contracts for buying or selling goods and services, office support services, facilities planning and maintenance, customer service, and administrative support. Within the general policies and goals of their organization, they make plans, oversee financial and technical resources, and evaluate outcomes.

What kind of work would you do?

Your work activities would depend on your job. For example, you might

* Direct or coordinate the supportive services department of a business, agency, or organization.
* Establish standards and procedures for work of housekeeping staff.
* Evaluate records to forecast department personnel requirements.

* Negotiate contracts with such service providers and suppliers as hotels, convention centers, and speakers.
* Plan, prepare, and devise work schedules according to budgets and workloads.
* Set goals and deadlines for the department.
* Supervise and coordinate activities of workers engaged in clerical or administrative support activities.
* Supervise and coordinate activities of workers engaged in janitorial services.
* Supervise and coordinate activities of workers engaged in customer service activities.

What things about you point to this kind of work?

Is it important for you to

* Give directions and instructions to others?
* Have co-workers who are easy to get along with?
* Be busy all the time?

Have you enjoyed any of the following as a hobby or leisure-time activity?

* Addressing letters for an organization
* Balancing checkbooks for family members
* Budgeting the family income
* Conducting house-to-house or telephone surveys for a PTA or other organization
* Using a pocket calculator or spreadsheet to figure out income and expenses for an organization
* Helping run a school or community fair or carnival
* Serving as a leader of a scouting or other group

Have you liked and done well in any of the following school subjects?

* Management
* Accounting
* Business Law
* Contract Law
* Personnel Management
* Business Writing
* Business Computer Applications
* Marketing/Merchandising
* Property Management

Are you able to

* Remember information such as words, numbers, pictures, and procedures?
* Identify and understand the speech of another person?
* Shift back and forth between two or more activities or sources of information?

Would you work in places such as

* Business offices?
* Government offices?
* Hotels and motels?
* Stores and shopping malls?
* Convention and trade show centers?
* Factories and plants?

What skills and knowledges do you need for this kind of work?

For most of these jobs, you need these skills:

* Management of Personnel Resources—motivating, developing, and directing people as they work, identifying the best people for the job
* Management of Financial Resources—determining how money will be spent to get the work done and accounting for these expenditures
* Time Management—managing one's own time and the time of others
* Coordination—adjusting actions in relation to others' actions
* Management of Material Resources—obtaining and seeing to the appropriate use of equipment, facilities, and materials needed to do certain work
* Social Perceptiveness—being aware of others' reactions and understanding why they react as they do
* Service Orientation—actively looking for ways to help people

These knowledges are important in most of these jobs:

* Personnel and Human Resources—principles and procedures for personnel recruitment, selection, training, compensation and benefits, labor relations and negotiation, and personnel information systems
* Administration and Management—business and management principles involved in strategic planning, resource allocation, human resources modeling, leadership techniques, production methods, and coordination of people and resources
* Clerical Practices—administrative and clerical procedures and systems such as word processing, managing files and records, stenography and transcription, designing forms, and other office procedures and terminology
* Customer and Personal Service—principles and processes for providing customer and personal services; this includes customer needs assessment, meeting quality standards for services, and evaluation of customer satisfaction
* Economics and Accounting—economic and accounting principles and practices, the financial markets, banking, and the analysis and reporting of financial data

What else should you consider about this kind of work?

Workers in this group are employed in cities and towns throughout the United States. They work in the offices of every kind of business, government agency, or school. They put in a standard 40-hour week most of the time in offices that are clean, air conditioned, and well-lighted.

The outlook for these occupations is good—even though these managers are often the first workers to be let go when a business is downsizing and even though automation is cutting into certain routine parts of their work. They may not have secure employment in one business, but if they lose their position they can usually find one in

© 2006 JIST Works

another office, provided they keep their skills up to date (especially with computer productivity applications).

How can you prepare for jobs of this kind?

Work in this group requires education and/or training that lasts from two to less than ten years.

Some workers enter directly after getting a two- or four-year college degree in office supervision and management or perhaps in a specialization such as administrative support or customer service. Through experiences on the job, they learn the issues and procedures of their particular industry.

Workers with less formal education start by taking a job in administrative support or customer service and then may work their way up to management after gaining experience and taking courses in management.

Both kinds of workers benefit from high school classes in writing and math that go beyond the "business" level and in speech. It is also important to know how to work with computer applications such as word processing and spreadsheets. Continuous learning is the key to staying employable.

How much education or training is required for the jobs in this Work Group?

For descriptions of these jobs, see Part 2.

Work experience in a related occupation

* First-Line Supervisors, Administrative Support
* First-Line Supervisors, Customer Service
* Housekeeping Supervisors
* Janitorial Supervisors

Bachelor's degree

* Meeting and Convention Planners

Work experience plus degree

* Administrative Services Managers

04.03 Human Resources Support

Workers in this group help a business or government agency by identifying skills that the business needs, selecting the best job candidates, training and rewarding them appropriately, and evaluating their performance. They use interpersonal skills, computerized tools, and knowledge of industry practices and government regulations that apply to human resources. They supervise clerical staff that support them.

What kind of work would you do?

Your work activities would depend on your job. For example, you might

* Advise managers and employees on staffing policies and procedures.

* Assist in preparing and maintaining personnel records and handbooks.
* Conduct reference and background checks on applicants.
* Hire applicants and authorize paperwork assigning them to positions.
* Interview job applicants to match their qualifications with employers' needs, recording and evaluating applicant experience, education, training, and skills.
* Monitor, evaluate, and record training activities and program effectiveness.
* Offer specific training programs to help workers maintain or improve job skills.
* Prepare and maintain employment records.
* Prepare occupational classifications, job descriptions, and salary scales.
* Recruit applicants for open positions, arranging job fairs with college campus representatives.

What things about you point to this kind of work?

Is it important for you to

* Have good working conditions?
* Have co-workers who are easy to get along with?

Have you enjoyed any of the following as a hobby or leisure-time activity?

* Serving as a volunteer interviewer in a social service organization
* Reading business magazines and newspapers
* Balancing checkbooks for family members

Have you liked and done well in any of the following school subjects?

* Personnel Management
* Business Organization
* Business Law
* Accounting
* Contract Law
* Education

Are you able to

* Identify and understand the speech of another person?
* Speak clearly so others can understand you?
* Generate or use different sets of rules for combining or grouping things in different ways?

Would you work in places such as

* Business offices?
* Factories and plants?
* Government offices?

What skills and knowledges do you need for this kind of work?

For most of these jobs, you need these skills:

* Persuasion—persuading others to change their minds or behavior

* Service Orientation—actively looking for ways to help people
* Negotiation—bringing others together and trying to reconcile differences
* Time Management—managing one's own time and the time of others
* Social Perceptiveness—being aware of others' reactions and understanding why they react as they do
* Instructing—teaching others how to do something
* Active Listening—giving full attention to what other people are saying, taking time to understand the points being made, asking questions as appropriate, and not interrupting at inappropriate times

These knowledges are important in most of these jobs:

* Personnel and Human Resources—principles and procedures for personnel recruitment, selection, training, compensation and benefits, labor relations and negotiation, and personnel information systems
* Clerical Practices—administrative and clerical procedures and systems such as word processing, managing files and records, stenography and transcription, designing forms, and other office procedures and terminology
* Customer and Personal Service—principles and processes for providing customer and personal services; this includes customer needs assessment, meeting quality standards for services, and evaluation of customer satisfaction
* Education and Training—principles and methods for curriculum and training design, teaching and instruction for individuals and groups, and the measurement of training effects
* Administration and Management—business and management principles involved in strategic planning, resource allocation, human resources modeling, leadership techniques, production methods, and coordination of people and resources
* Foreign Language—the structure and content of a foreign (non-English) language, including the meaning and spelling of words, rules of composition and grammar, and pronunciation
* Sociology and Anthropology—group behavior and dynamics, societal trends and influences, human migrations, ethnicity, and cultures and their history and origins

What else should you consider about this kind of work?

These jobs are found in and around cities and large towns. All kinds of businesses and industries hire these workers. In some fields, such as training, it is common to work for several clients simultaneously or one after the other, either as a self-employed professional or as a contractor working for a consulting firm.

Many of the workers in government jobs must pass civil service tests.

The work is done in comfortable business offices and mostly occupies normal business hours. Trainers and recruiters sometimes need to work evening hours to meet their clients.

Most new workers start as trainees, but in many jobs they can advance rapidly. However, in many specializations, automation is allowing clerical and higher-level staff to handle some tasks that used to be assigned to middle managers. Therefore, keen competition may be expected in many of these specializations. Best opportunities will be for trainers and for those who have skills with computer-based applications, plus the interpersonal and communications skills required for advancement. Workers may not have long-term security with one company, but those with up-to-date skills and flexibility will remain employable.

How can you prepare for jobs of this kind?

Occupations in this group usually require education and/or training ranging from one year to less than ten years. For some jobs, two years of college may be acceptable but not preferable. Work experience is a major consideration in preparing for jobs in this group. Experience in related positions for the same employer is often required. However, courses in human resources, business law, writing, math, and computer applications are helpful. Some of these courses are available in high schools, but most are offered by business schools, colleges, and graduate schools of business.

How much education or training is required for the jobs in this Work Group?

For descriptions of these jobs, see Part 2.

Bachelor's degree

* Compensation, Benefits, and Job Analysis Specialists
* Employment Interviewers, Private or Public Employment Service
* Personnel Recruiters
* Training and Development Specialists

04.04 Secretarial Support

Workers in this group do high-level clerical work requiring special skills and knowledge, as well as some lower-level managerial work.

What kind of work would you do?

Your work activities would depend on your job. For example, you might

* Assist attorneys in collecting information such as employment, medical, and other records.
* Compile and record medical charts, reports, and correspondence, using typewriter or personal computer.
* Greet visitors, ascertain purpose of visit, and direct them to appropriate staff.
* Maintain scheduling and event calendars.
* Open, sort, and distribute incoming correspondence, including faxes and e-mail.

* Operate office equipment such as fax machines, copiers, and phone systems and use computers for spreadsheet, word-processing, database management, and other applications.
* Prepare agendas and make arrangements for committee, board, and other meetings.
* Prepare and process legal documents and papers, such as summonses, subpoenas, complaints, appeals, motions, and pretrial agreements.
* Schedule and make appointments.

What things about you point to this kind of work?

Is it important for you to

* Be busy all the time?
* Have good working conditions?

Have you enjoyed any of the following as a hobby or leisure-time activity?

* Keying in text for a school or community publication
* Keyboarding papers and letters for others
* Serving as secretary of a club or other organization

Have you liked and done well in any of the following school subjects?

* Spelling
* Clerical Practices/Office Practices
* Business Law
* Business Machine Operating
* Business Writing
* Accounting
* Record Keeping
* Medical Terminology
* Typing

Are you able to

* Identify and understand the speech of another person?
* See details at close range?
* Shift back and forth between two or more activities or sources of information?

Would you work in places such as

* Business offices?
* Government offices?
* Doctors' and dentists' offices and clinics?
* Hospitals and nursing homes?

What skills and knowledges do you need for this kind of work?

For most of these jobs, you need these skills:

* Time Management—managing one's own time and the time of others
* Active Listening—giving full attention to what other people are saying, taking time to understand the points being made, asking questions as appropriate, and not interrupting at inappropriate times
* Writing—communicating effectively in writing as appropriate for the needs of the audience

* Social Perceptiveness—being aware of others' reactions and understanding why they react as they do

These knowledges are important in most of these jobs:

* Clerical Practices—administrative and clerical procedures and systems such as word processing, managing files and records, stenography and transcription, designing forms, and other office procedures and terminology
* Customer and Personal Service—principles and processes for providing customer and personal services; this includes customer needs assessment, meeting quality standards for services, and evaluation of customer satisfaction
* English Language—the structure and content of the English language, including the meaning and spelling of words, rules of composition, and grammar
* Computers and Electronics—circuit boards; processors; chips; electronic equipment; and computer hardware and software, including applications and programming

What else should you consider about this kind of work?

These workers are employed in the offices of businesses, industries, and government agencies, as well as in medicine, law, and other professions.

Beginners with training are hired for many of the jobs in this group and gain responsibility as they gain experience. For government jobs with local, state, or federal agencies, a civil service test is often required.

Regular business hours apply in most of these jobs. If you work for a local government, you may have to attend meetings on weekends or at night.

Some positions require workers who can be trusted with confidential information. Workers in small offices often perform a variety of tasks. They may serve as bookkeeper, clerk, and receptionist. Working conditions are usually pleasant, often in a modern, well-lighted office building.

Job outlook is mixed, with better opportunities for legal, medical, and executive secretaries than for other kinds. Skill with office automation has become essential.

How can you prepare for jobs of this kind?

Occupations in this group usually require education and/or training ranging from six months to less than ten years.

People who have a good working knowledge of English, grammar, spelling, and basic math can qualify for beginning jobs in this group. These workers receive training on the job. Some must have special training, such as shorthand, stenotype, legal stenography, or medical terminology, which they may study at a business or community college.

Office automation requires constant retraining to learn new applications.

How much education or training is required for the jobs in this Work Group?

For descriptions of these jobs, see Part 2.

Moderate-term on-the-job training

* Executive Secretaries and Administrative Assistants
* Secretaries, Except Legal, Medical, and Executive

Postsecondary vocational training

* Legal Secretaries
* Medical Secretaries

04.05 Accounting, Auditing, and Analytical Support

Workers in this group use mathematics, logic, computerized tools, and knowledge of industry practices and government regulations to help businesses and government agencies make decisions. They supervise clerical and sometimes technical staff that support them.

What kind of work would you do?

Your work activities would depend on your job. For example, you might

* Confer with company officials about financial and regulatory matters.
* Develop and implement a records management program for filing, protection, and retrieval of records and assure compliance with the program.
* Direct the preparation of regular and special budget reports.
* Examine inventory to verify journal and ledger entries.
* Prepare, examine, and analyze accounting records, financial statements, and other financial reports to assess accuracy, completeness, and conformance to reporting and procedural standards.
* Report to management regarding the finances of establishment.
* Seek new ways to improve efficiency and increase profits.
* Select plans from competitive proposals that afford maximum probability of profit or effectiveness relating to cost or risk.
* Study time, motion, methods, and speed involved in maintenance, production, and other operations to establish standard production rates and improve efficiency.

What things about you point to this kind of work?

Is it important for you to

* Have opportunities for advancement?
* Be paid well in comparison with other workers?
* Have good working conditions?

Have you enjoyed any of the following as a hobby or leisure-time activity?

* Budgeting the family income
* Balancing checkbooks for family members
* Using a pocket calculator or spreadsheet to figure out income and expenses for an organization
* Preparing family income tax returns
* Reading business magazines and newspapers
* Serving as treasurer of a club or other organization

Have you liked and done well in any of the following school subjects?

* Accounting
* Business Analysis
* Business Organization
* Math Computing, Standard Formula
* Business Law
* Statistics
* Operations Research

Are you able to

* Add, subtract, multiply, or divide quickly and correctly?
* Choose the right mathematical methods or formulas to solve a problem?
* Apply general rules to specific problems to produce answers that make sense?
* Come up with a number of ideas about a topic?
* Tell when something is wrong or is likely to go wrong?
* See details at close range?
* Combine pieces of information to form general rules or conclusions?

Would you work in places such as

* Business offices?
* Government offices?
* Factories and plants?

What skills and knowledges do you need for this kind of work?

For most of these jobs, you need these skills:

* Management of Financial Resources—determining how money will be spent to get the work done and accounting for these expenditures
* Operations Analysis—analyzing needs and product requirements to create a design
* Monitoring—monitoring/assessing your own performance or that of other individuals or organizations to make improvements or take corrective action
* Judgment and Decision Making—considering the relative costs and benefits of potential actions to choose the most appropriate one
* Systems Analysis—determining how a system should work and how changes in conditions, operations, and the environment will affect outcomes
* Systems Evaluation—identifying measures or indicators of system performance and the actions needed to improve or correct performance relative to the goals of the system
* Complex Problem Solving—identifying complex problems and reviewing related information to develop and evaluate options and implement solutions

These knowledges are important in most of these jobs:

* Economics and Accounting—economic and accounting principles and practices, the financial markets, banking, and the analysis and reporting of financial data
* Mathematics—arithmetic, algebra, geometry, calculus, and statistics and their applications
* Personnel and Human Resources—principles and procedures for personnel recruitment, selection, training, compensation and benefits, labor relations and negotiation, and personnel information systems
* Administration and Management—business and management principles involved in strategic planning, resource allocation, human resources modeling, leadership techniques, production methods, and coordination of people and resources
* Clerical Practices—administrative and clerical procedures and systems such as word processing, managing files and records, stenography and transcription, designing forms, and other office procedures and terminology
* Computers and Electronics—circuit boards; processors; chips; electronic equipment; and computer hardware and software, including applications and programming
* Production and Processing—raw materials, production processes, quality control, costs, and other techniques for maximizing the effective manufacture and distribution of goods

What else should you consider about this kind of work?

The workers are hired by all kinds of businesses and industries in cities and towns. Some workers are self-employed professionals or contractors working for a consulting firm.

In some specialties, frequent travel or occasional overtime work (for example, when quarterly statements are due) is required.

In most of these fields, there are many openings for new workers when the economy is not on a downturn. However, automation is making it easier for clerical workers to perform some of the accounting and mathematical tasks that used to be handled by middle managers. Therefore, workers who find and advance in jobs will be those who have skills with computer-based applications and interpersonal communication. Government positions often require passing civil service tests.

How can you prepare for jobs of this kind?

Occupations in this group usually require education and/or training ranging from two years to less than ten years.

A bachelor's degree has become the standard qualification, although some talented workers with two-year degrees and work experience in related positions can advance to these jobs. Courses in accounting, human resources, business law, economics, investments, writing, math, government, and computer science are helpful. Some of these courses are available in high schools, but most are offered by business schools, colleges, and graduate schools of business.

How much education or training is required for the jobs in this Work Group?

For descriptions of these jobs, see Part 2.

Associate degree

* Industrial Engineering Technicians

Bachelor's degree

* Accountants
* Auditors
* Budget Analysts
* Logisticians

Work experience plus degree

* Management Analysts

Master's degree

* Operations Research Analysts

04.06 Mathematical Clerical Support

Workers in this group collect, organize, compute, and record the numerical information used in business and financial transactions. They use clerical and math skills, and some use machines.

What kind of work would you do?

Your work activities would depend on your job. For example, you might

* Compile employee time, production, and payroll data from timesheets and other records.
* Compute wages and deductions and enter data into computers.
* Encode and cancel checks, using bank machines.
* Furnish taxpayers with sufficient information and advice in order to ensure correct tax form completion.
* Interview clients to obtain additional information on taxable income and deductible expenses and allowances.
* Maintain files of canceled checks and customers' signatures.
* Monitor daily stock prices and compute fluctuations in order to determine the need for additional collateral to secure loans.
* Operate typing, adding, calculating, and billing machines.
* Reconcile or note and report discrepancies found in records.
* Verify signatures and required information on checks.

What things about you point to this kind of work?

Is it important for you to

* Have good working conditions?
* Have opportunities for advancement?

Have you enjoyed any of the following as a hobby or leisure-time activity?

* Helping friends and relatives with their tax reports
* Keying in text for a school or community publication
* Balancing checkbooks for family members
* Using a pocket calculator or spreadsheet to figure out income and expenses for an organization
* Operating a calculator or adding machine for an organization

Have you liked and done well in any of the following school subjects?

* Bookkeeping
* Accounting
* Auditing Procedures
* Math Computing, Standard Formula
* Business Computer Applications
* Statistics
* Clerical Practices/Office Practices
* Record Keeping
* Financial Information Systems
* Production/Inventory Control
* Data Entry

Are you able to

* Add, subtract, multiply, or divide quickly and correctly?
* Choose the right mathematical methods or formulas to solve a problem?
* See details at close range?

Would you work in places such as

* Business offices?
* Government offices?
* Factories and plants?

What skills and knowledges do you need for this kind of work?

For most of these jobs, you need these skills:

* Active Listening—giving full attention to what other people are saying, taking time to understand the points being made, asking questions as appropriate, and not interrupting at inappropriate times
* Mathematics—using mathematics to solve problems
* Service Orientation—actively looking for ways to help people

These knowledges are important in most of these jobs:

* Clerical Practices—administrative and clerical procedures and systems such as word processing, managing files and records, stenography and transcription, designing forms, and other office procedures and terminology
* Economics and Accounting—economic and accounting principles and practices, the financial markets, banking, and the analysis and reporting of financial data

* Mathematics—arithmetic, algebra, geometry, calculus, and statistics and their applications

What else should you consider about this kind of work?

Most jobs in this group are in business offices. Many of these people work for banks, savings and loan institutions, and insurance companies. Some have jobs with freight terminals, where they keep track of the costs of shipping by water, land, or air. Trained beginners are hired for many of these jobs.

Workers in small offices may do a variety of tasks. Some may keep all records for a business or agency. Usually experience is necessary for such positions.

In large offices, workers may have only certain tasks to do and may repeat these tasks every day. Most jobs of this nature are entry-level jobs requiring little or no experience.

Most of the work is done during regular daytime working hours. You may have to work the evening or night shift in freight terminals. Some jobs can lead to supervisory or management positions.

Automation is replacing many of the routine tasks handled by these workers. As a result, job opportunities in most of these occupations will primarily be found in replacing retiring workers. Workers in this group should make an effort to upgrade their skills so they can stay employable or move into a more managerial or technical role.

How can you prepare for jobs of this kind?

Occupations in this group usually require education and/or training ranging from six months to two years.

People with basic math skills can enter many of the jobs in this group. They receive on-the-job training for specific tasks. For entry to some jobs, training in bookkeeping or other business subjects such as word processing is required. Business training is offered by high schools, business schools, and two-year colleges.

How much education or training is required for the jobs in this Work Group?

For descriptions of these jobs, see Part 2.

Short-term on-the-job training

* Billing, Cost, and Rate Clerks
* Payroll and Timekeeping Clerks
* Statement Clerks

Moderate-term on-the-job training

* Bookkeeping, Accounting, and Auditing Clerks
* Brokerage Clerks
* Tax Preparers

04.07 Records and Materials Processing

Workers in this group prepare, review, file, and coordinate recorded information. Some check records and schedules for accuracy. Some schedule the activities of people or the use of equipment.

What kind of work would you do?

Your work activities would depend on your job. For example, you might

* Answer customers' questions about merchandise and advise customers on merchandise selection.
* Answer telephones, direct calls, and take messages.
* Check shipments when they arrive to ensure that orders have been filled correctly and that goods meet specifications.
* Compute prices of items or groups of items.
* Pack and unpack items to be stocked on shelves in stockrooms, warehouses, or storage yards.
* Place materials into storage receptacles, such as file cabinets, boxes, bins, or drawers, according to classification and identification information.
* Prepare documents, such as work orders, bills of lading, and shipping orders, to route materials.
* Put price information on tickets, marking by hand or using ticket-printing machine.
* Read electric, gas, water, or steam consumption meters and enter data in route books or hand-held computers.
* Read incoming correspondence to ascertain nature of writers' concerns and to determine disposition of correspondence.

What things about you point to this kind of work?

Is it important for you to

* Have supervisors who train workers well?
* Have supervisors who back up workers with management?

Have you enjoyed any of the following as a hobby or leisure-time activity?

* Keying in text for a school or community publication
* Keyboarding papers and letters for others
* Balancing checkbooks for family members
* Collecting and arranging stamps, coins, or other items

Have you liked and done well in any of the following school subjects?

* Bookkeeping
* Business Computer Applications
* Business Math
* Clerical Practices/Office Practices
* Record Keeping
* Production/Inventory Control
* Shipping Regulations
* Data Entry

Are you able to

* Quickly and accurately compare similarities and differences among sets of letters, numbers, objects, pictures, or patterns?
* See details at close range?
* Generate or use different sets of rules for combining or grouping things in different ways?

Would you work in places such as

* Business offices?
* Post offices?
* Government offices?
* Warehouses?
* Stores and shopping malls?
* Factories and plants?

What skills and knowledges do you need for this kind of work?

For most of these jobs, you need these skills:

* Service Orientation—actively looking for ways to help people
* Time Management—managing one's own time and the time of others
* Negotiation—bringing others together and trying to reconcile differences

These knowledges are important in most of these jobs:

* Clerical Practices—administrative and clerical procedures and systems such as word processing, managing files and records, stenography and transcription, designing forms, and other office procedures and terminology
* Foreign Language—the structure and content of a foreign (non-English) language, including the meaning and spelling of words, rules of composition and grammar, and pronunciation
* Transportation—principles and methods for moving people or goods by air, rail, sea, or road, including the relative costs and benefits

What else should you consider about this kind of work?

Many jobs in this group, such as file clerks, are found in almost every office and every locality. Others, such as order fillers, are available only in certain kinds of businesses. Workers entering federal government jobs generally are required to take civil service examinations.

Many of the jobs are open to newcomers. For some of them, your chances of finding work are improved if you type well. For others, employers look at your math and reading abilities. You can be promoted to higher-level jobs from many of these positions.

Most of this work is done during a regular eight-hour day. You might have to work evening or night shifts or weekends with establishments such as airlines, railroads, freight terminals, and shipping companies. Part-time or temporary work is usually available. Most of this work is done in a comfortable indoor setting and is considered "office work," although many jobs are done outside the office—for example, in a mail room or warehouse. In addition, some jobs with courier services are done at least partly outdoors.

Usually opportunities for promotion are good. As better jobs open up, many employers like to promote people who already work for them rather than hire from the outside. This is one reason why it is a good idea to take courses in bookkeeping, computer applications, or other office skills while you're in these jobs. When openings occur, you will be qualified.

The overall employment outlook for this group is mixed. Many clerical jobs formerly done by workers are being eliminated because automation can do them more cheaply. Yet some of these occupations employ so many workers that there will be many openings to replace retiring workers, even if the total number of jobs declines. In general, opportunities will be better in occupations where the work is non-routine, involves specialized knowledge or training, or brings the worker in contact with the public.

How can you prepare for jobs of this kind?

Occupations in this group usually require education and/or training ranging from less than six months to two years.

A high school education or its equivalent is generally required. It is helpful to have coursework in language skills such as punctuation, grammar, and spelling; in basic math; and in record-keeping. Some employers prefer workers who have completed general business or clerical courses. Many employers provide on-the-job training, ranging from a short demonstration to a one-year program. Sometimes applicants are tested to determine their ability to do or learn to do the tasks.

How much education or training is required for the jobs in this Work Group?

For descriptions of these jobs, see Part 2.

Short-term on-the-job training

* Correspondence Clerks
* File Clerks
* Human Resources Assistants, Except Payroll and Time-keeping
* Mail Clerks, Except Mail Machine Operators and Postal Service
* Marking Clerks
* Meter Readers, Utilities
* Office Clerks, General
* Postal Service Clerks
* Postal Service Mail Sorters, Processors, and Processing Machine Operators
* Procurement Clerks
* Production, Planning, and Expediting Clerks

* Shipping, Receiving, and Traffic Clerks
* Stock Clerks, Sales Floor
* Weighers, Measurers, Checkers, and Samplers, Record-keeping

Moderate-term on-the-job training

* Order Fillers, Wholesale and Retail Sales
* Stock Clerks—Stockroom, Warehouse, or Storage Yard

04.08 Clerical Machine Operation

Workers in this group use business machines to record or process data. They operate machines that type, print, sort, compute, send, or receive information.

What kind of work would you do?

Your work activities would depend on your job. For example, you might

* Affix postage to packages or letter by hand, or stamps with postage meter, and dispatch mail.
* Compile, sort, and verify the accuracy of data before it is entered.
* Load duplicating machine with blank paper or film and place paper roll in holding tray or rack of machine.
* Observe mail machine operation to detect evidence of malfunctions during production runs.
* Operate bookkeeping machines to copy and post data, make computations, and compile records of transactions.
* Operate communication systems, such as telephone, switchboard, intercom, two-way radio, or public address.
* Read source documents such as canceled checks, sales reports, or bills and enter data in specific data fields or onto tapes or disks for subsequent entry, using keyboards or scanners.
* Reformat documents, moving paragraphs and/or columns.
* Transcribe data from office records, using specified forms, billing machines, and transcribing machines.
* Type correspondence, reports, text, and other written material from rough drafts, corrected copies, voice recordings, dictation, or previous versions, using a computer, word processor, or typewriter.

What things about you point to this kind of work?

Is it important for you to

* Do your work alone?
* Have supervisors who back up workers with management?

Have you enjoyed any of the following as a hobby or leisure-time activity?

* Operating a calculator or adding machine for an organization

* Keying in text for a school or community publication
* Addressing letters for an organization

Have you liked and done well in any of the following school subjects?

* Bookkeeping
* Business Computer Applications
* Clerical Practices/Office Practices
* Record Keeping
* Data Entry
* Shipping Regulations

Are you able to

* Make fast, simple, repeated movements of your fingers, hands, and wrists?
* See details at close range?
* Concentrate on a task over a period of time without being distracted?

Would you work in places such as

* Business offices?
* Government offices?

What skills and knowledges do you need for this kind of work?

For most of these jobs, you need these skills:

* Programming—writing computer programs for various purposes
* Operation and Control—controlling operations of equipment or systems
* Operation Monitoring—watching gauges, dials, or other indicators to make sure a machine is working properly

These knowledges are important in most of these jobs:

* Clerical Practices—administrative and clerical procedures and systems such as word processing, managing files and records, stenography and transcription, designing forms, and other office procedures and terminology
* Foreign Language—the structure and content of a foreign (non-English) language, including the meaning and spelling of words, rules of composition and grammar, and pronunciation
* Computers and Electronics—circuit boards; processors; chips; electronic equipment; and computer hardware and software, including applications and programming

What else should you consider about this kind of work?

The jobs in this group can be found in almost every kind of business and industry, with the exception of automatic teller machine servicers.

Job opportunities are usually available for well-trained newcomers in this field. If you've been trained to operate many different kinds of equipment rather than just one, your chances of finding a job are better. However, advances in technology are causing declining demand for billing machine operators and data entry keyers.

In many places, these jobs can lead to higher-level work in the same field. However, you usually need more education to qualify for managerial or supervisory jobs. Workers in supervisory jobs should enjoy dealing with people because they often train new workers, interview job applicants, and assign workers to jobs.

Most of these jobs are done on a regular eight-hour daytime schedule in a comfortable office setting.

Because office equipment is constantly changing, you might have to learn to operate new machines from time to time. Some employers send you to training sessions given by equipment manufacturers to learn the new methods. In small firms, machine operators may also do a variety of other office tasks.

How can you prepare for jobs of this kind?

Occupations in this group usually require education and/or training ranging from less than six months to less than two years.

Most employers require that an applicant have a high school education or its equal. Courses in spelling, grammar, typing, and business machine operation are important preparation for jobs in this group. Basic arithmetic skills are required for some jobs.

Some employers provide machine instruction and on-the-job training. However, graduation from a business college can be an advantage.

How much education or training is required for the jobs in this Work Group?

For descriptions of these jobs, see Part 2.

Short-term on-the-job training

* Billing, Posting, and Calculating Machine Operators
* Duplicating Machine Operators
* Mail Machine Operators, Preparation and Handling
* Switchboard Operators, Including Answering Service

Moderate-term on-the-job training

* Data Entry Keyers
* Word Processors and Typists

05 Education and Training

An interest in helping people learn. You can satisfy this interest by teaching students, who may be preschoolers, retirees, or any age in between. You may specialize in a particular academic field or work with learners of a particular age, with a particular interest, or with a particular learning problem. Working in a library or museum may give you an opportunity to expand people's understanding of the world.

05.01   **Managerial Work in Education**

05.02   **Preschool, Elementary, and Secondary Teaching and Instructing**

05.03   **Postsecondary and Adult Teaching and Instructing**

05.04   **Library Services**

05.05   **Archival and Museum Services**

05.06   **Counseling, Health, and Fitness Education**

05.01 Managerial Work in Education

Workers in this group are responsible for planning, budgeting, evaluating results, and supervising workers at school districts and colleges. They need to balance their financial responsibilities against educational goals and sometimes must make trade-offs. They enjoy helping people achieve their learning goals, but they are content to do so behind the scenes.

What kind of work would you do?

Your work activities would depend on your job. For example, you might

* Confer with parents and staff to discuss educational activities, policies, and student behavioral or learning problems.
* Determine course schedules and coordinate teaching assignments and room assignments in order to ensure optimum use of buildings and equipment.
* Develop classroom-based and distance learning training courses, using needs assessments and skill level analyses.
* Develop instructional materials to be used by educators and instructors.
* Direct scholarship, fellowship, and loan programs, performing activities such as selecting recipients and distributing aid.
* Observe teaching methods and examine learning materials in order to evaluate and standardize curricula and teaching techniques and to determine areas where improvement is needed.
* Plan, direct, and monitor instructional methods and content of educational, vocational, or student activity programs.
* Recruit, hire, train, and evaluate primary and supplemental staff and recommend personnel actions for programs and services.
* Review registration statistics and consult with faculty officials to develop registration policies.
* Set educational standards and goals and help establish policies and procedures to carry them out.

What things about you point to this kind of work?

Is it important for you to

* Give directions and instructions to others?
* Be looked up to by others in your company and your community?
* Be busy all the time?
* Try out your own ideas?
* Receive recognition for the work you do?
* Have co-workers who are easy to get along with?
* Make use of your individual abilities?

Have you enjoyed any of the following as a hobby or leisure-time activity?

* Helping members of the family with their English lessons
* Instructing family members in observing traffic regulations
* Planning and arranging programs for school or community organizations
* Serving as a leader of a scouting or other group
* Teaching immigrants or other individuals to speak, write, or read English
* Teaching games to children as a volunteer aide in a nursery school

Have you liked and done well in any of the following school subjects?

* Management
* Education
* Psychology
* Business Law
* Contract Law
* Personnel Management
* Business Computer Applications
* Educational Psychology

Are you able to

* Communicate information and ideas in writing so others will understand?
* Remember information such as words, numbers, pictures, and procedures?
* Come up with a number of ideas about a topic?
* Speak clearly so others can understand you?
* Read and understand information and ideas presented in writing?
* Come up with unusual or clever ideas about a given topic or situation or develop creative ways to solve a problem?
* Communicate information and ideas in speaking so others will understand?

Would you work in places such as

* Elementary schools?
* High schools?
* Colleges and universities?
* Kindergartens and day care centers?
* Schools and homes for people with disabilities?

What skills and knowledges do you need for this kind of work?

For most of these jobs, you need these skills:

* Management of Financial Resources—determining how money will be spent to get the work done and accounting for these expenditures
* Management of Personnel Resources—motivating, developing, and directing people as they work, identifying the best people for the job
* Management of Material Resources—obtaining and seeing to the appropriate use of equipment, facilities, and materials needed to do certain work

* Systems Evaluation—identifying measures or indicators of system performance and the actions needed to improve or correct performance relative to the goals of the system
* Systems Analysis—determining how a system should work and how changes in conditions, operations, and the environment will affect outcomes
* Learning Strategies—selecting and using training/instructional methods and procedures appropriate for the situation when learning or teaching new things
* Coordination—adjusting actions in relation to others' actions

These knowledges are important in most of these jobs:

* Education and Training—principles and methods for curriculum and training design, teaching and instruction for individuals and groups, and the measurement of training effects
* Personnel and Human Resources—principles and procedures for personnel recruitment, selection, training, compensation and benefits, labor relations and negotiation, and personnel information systems
* Administration and Management—business and management principles involved in strategic planning, resource allocation, human resources modeling, leadership techniques, production methods, and coordination of people and resources
* Economics and Accounting—economic and accounting principles and practices, the financial markets, banking, and the analysis and reporting of financial data
* Sales and Marketing—principles and methods for showing, promoting, and selling products or services; this includes marketing strategy and tactics, product demonstrations, sales techniques, and sales control systems
* English Language—the structure and content of the English language, including the meaning and spelling of words, rules of composition, and grammar
* Psychology—human behavior and performance; individual differences in ability, personality, and interests; learning and motivation; psychological research methods; and the assessment and treatment of behavioral and affective disorders

What else should you consider about this kind of work?

Many of these workers are on the public payroll and therefore have to please several parties with possibly conflicting goals: students, parents, employers, employees, elected officials, governing boards, and taxpayers. Policy and personnel changes that an administrator makes may not show results for many years, yet there is often pressure to justify budgets.

Workdays often include evening hours for attending meetings. Some school administrators get long summer vacations, but others do not.

The overall outlook for educational managers is good, although competition can be intense in some fields, especially at the university level.

How can you prepare for jobs of this kind?

Occupations in this group require a minimum of four years of postsecondary education, and often six or more.

Workers typically hold at least the same degree as the people whom they are supervising—for example, a bachelor's or master's in education for those who supervise teachers, a master's for those who supervise social workers, and a doctorate for college and university administrators. Many hold a master's degree in administration or management in addition or instead. Usually they have teaching experience.

Like all managers, these must keep abreast of technological change to stay employable.

How much education or training is required for the jobs in this Work Group?

For descriptions of these jobs, see Part 2.

Work experience plus degree

* Education Administrators, Elementary and Secondary School
* Education Administrators, Postsecondary
* Education Administrators, Preschool and Child Care Center/Program

Master's degree

* Instructional Coordinators

05.02 Preschool, Elementary, and Secondary Teaching and Instructing

Workers in this group do general and specialized teaching in classrooms, working with young children or teenagers.

What kind of work would you do?

Your work activities would depend on your job. For example, you might

* Assign lessons and correct homework.
* Attend professional meetings, educational conferences, and teacher training workshops in order to maintain and improve professional competence.
* Attend staff meetings and serve on committees as required.
* Confer with parents or guardians, other teachers, counselors, and administrators in order to resolve students' behavioral and academic problems.
* Enforce all administration policies and rules governing students.
* Establish clear objectives for all lessons, units, and projects and communicate those objectives to students.
* Instruct students individually and in groups, using various teaching methods such as lectures, discussions, and demonstrations.

© 2006 JIST Works

* Modify the general education curriculum for special-needs students based upon a variety of instructional techniques and instructional technology.
* Plan and supervise class projects, field trips, visits by guests, or other experiential activities and guide students in learning from those activities.
* Prepare materials and classrooms for class activities.

What things about you point to this kind of work?

Is it important for you to

* Have work where you do things for other people?
* Give directions and instructions to others?
* Get a feeling of accomplishment?
* Try out your own ideas?
* Be busy all the time?
* Make decisions on your own?
* Have good working conditions?

Have you enjoyed any of the following as a hobby or leisure-time activity?

* Teaching games to children as a volunteer aide in a nursery school
* Tutoring pupils in school subjects
* Doing public speaking or debating
* Helping members of the family with their English lessons
* Instructing family members in observing traffic regulations

Have you liked and done well in any of the following school subjects?

* Education
* Educational Psychology
* Public Speaking
* Physical Education
* Biology
* Foreign Languages
* Human Growth and Development
* Child Development/Care
* Home/Consumer Economics

Are you able to

* Shift back and forth between two or more activities or sources of information?
* Remember information such as words, numbers, pictures, and procedures?
* Listen to and understand information and ideas presented through spoken words and sentences?

Would you work in places such as

* Kindergartens and day care centers?
* Elementary schools?
* High schools?
* Schools and homes for people with disabilities?

What skills and knowledges do you need for this kind of work?

For most of these jobs, you need these skills:

* Learning Strategies—selecting and using training/instructional methods and procedures appropriate for the situation when learning or teaching new things
* Social Perceptiveness—being aware of others' reactions and understanding why they react as they do
* Instructing—teaching others how to do something
* Speaking—talking to others to convey information effectively
* Monitoring—monitoring/assessing your own performance or that of other individuals or organizations to make improvements or take corrective action

These knowledges are important in most of these jobs:

* Education and Training—principles and methods for curriculum and training design, teaching and instruction for individuals and groups, and the measurement of training effects
* Therapy and Counseling—principles, methods, and procedures for diagnosis, treatment, and rehabilitation of physical and mental dysfunctions and for career counseling and guidance
* History and Archeology—historical events and their causes, indicators, and effects on civilizations and cultures
* Psychology—human behavior and performance; individual differences in ability, personality, and interests; learning and motivation; psychological research methods; and the assessment and treatment of behavioral and affective disorders
* Sociology and Anthropology—group behavior and dynamics, societal trends and influences, human migrations, ethnicity, and cultures and their history and origins
* Foreign Language—the structure and content of a foreign (non-English) language, including the meaning and spelling of words, rules of composition and grammar, and pronunciation
* Philosophy and Theology—different philosophical systems and religions; this includes their basic principles, values, ethics, ways of thinking, customs, practices, and impact on human culture

What else should you consider about this kind of work?

Almost all of these occupations offer opportunities for part-time or volunteer work. This is often a good way to get experience and decide whether you enjoy the work. Most of these workers take great satisfaction from improving people's lives by opening them up to new ideas and skills. These rewards offset the occasional feelings of burnout.

Teachers are employed by school districts and private and parochial schools. They teach in classrooms, lecture halls, labs, or simulated or real work situations (e.g., a garage or kitchen); meet in offices with fellow teachers, parents, students, and administrators; and often correct papers at home on evenings and weekends. Most teachers are hired for only nine months of each year, giving them time to further their education or find summer employment. Public school teachers who have achieved a graduate degree and a good record of teaching may be awarded tenure, which means they cannot be fired without due cause.

The outlook for teachers varies greatly, depending on specialty and location. Best opportunities will be in urban and rural areas and in special education, math, science, computers, and bilingual education.

Teacher assistants may help with instruction, often offering one-on-one help with remedial or special education, or they may be limited to non-instructional roles such as monitoring hallways, lunchrooms, and playgrounds; recording grades and attendance; and handling instructional equipment. Some workers do both. The outlook for jobs is very good, partly because of the large turnover in this occupation.

How can you prepare for jobs of this kind?

Occupations in this group usually require education and/or training ranging from four to six years. Teacher assistants need only one or two years.

Teachers in public schools qualify for their teacher's licenses by getting a bachelor's degree, most often with certain required coursework and with supervised classroom experience. (The same may not apply in some private or parochial schools, and in some states there are procedures by which experienced workers can begin teaching with only a college degree, provided they meet other requirements later.) A master's degree is often useful for beginning teachers, especially in some fields such as special education, and it may be a requirement for pay increases or tenure. Vocational teachers are often required to have extensive work experience in their teaching field. A good high school academic record is a helpful beginning for a teaching career, and some states require that teachers accumulate a certain minimum grade-point average while in college.

Requirements vary greatly for preschool teachers. In some states a Child Development Associate credential is helpful or required. To earn it, you need a mixture of training and experience working with children, and you are evaluated by a team of child-care professionals.

How much education or training is required for the jobs in this Work Group?

For descriptions of these jobs, see Part 2.

Short-term on-the-job training

* Teacher Assistants

Bachelor's degree

* Elementary School Teachers, Except Special Education
* Kindergarten Teachers, Except Special Education
* Middle School Teachers, Except Special and Vocational Education
* Preschool Teachers, Except Special Education
* Secondary School Teachers, Except Special and Vocational Education
* Special Education Teachers, Middle School
* Special Education Teachers, Preschool, Kindergarten, and Elementary School
* Special Education Teachers, Secondary School
* Vocational Education Teachers, Middle School
* Vocational Education Teachers, Secondary School

05.03 Postsecondary and Adult Teaching and Instructing

Workers in this group teach specialized subjects to adults.

What kind of work would you do?

Your work activities would depend on your job. For example, you might

* Act as adviser to student organizations.
* Advise farmers in matters such as feeding and health maintenance of livestock, cultivation, growing and harvesting practices, and budgeting.
* Advise students on academic and vocational curricula and on career issues.
* Assign and grade class work and homework.
* Assist faculty members or staff with student conferences.
* Compile bibliographies of specialized materials for outside reading assignments.
* Demonstrate patient care in clinical units of hospitals.
* Initiate, facilitate, and moderate classroom discussions.
* Maintain regularly scheduled office hours in order to advise and assist students.
* Maintain student attendance records, grades, and other required records.

What things about you point to this kind of work?

Is it important for you to

* Give directions and instructions to others?
* Have work where you do things for other people?
* Get a feeling of accomplishment?
* Try out your own ideas?
* Be looked up to by others in your company and your community?
* Have co-workers who are easy to get along with?
* Make use of your individual abilities?

Have you enjoyed any of the following as a hobby or leisure-time activity?

* Tutoring pupils in school subjects
* Doing public speaking or debating
* Teaching immigrants or other individuals to speak, write, or read English
* Helping members of the family with their English lessons
* Helping friends and others with math

Have you liked and done well in any of the following school subjects?

* Education
* Educational Psychology
* Public Speaking
* Physical Education
* Biology
* Foreign Languages
* Physics
* Chemistry
* Literature
* Math Computing, Advanced/Special
* Pathology

Are you able to

* Speak clearly so others can understand you?
* Communicate information and ideas in writing so others will understand?
* Communicate information and ideas in speaking so others will understand?
* Read and understand information and ideas presented in writing?
* Listen to and understand information and ideas presented through spoken words and sentences?
* Come up with a number of ideas about a topic?
* Choose the right mathematical methods or formulas to solve a problem?

Would you work in places such as

* Colleges and universities?

What skills and knowledges do you need for this kind of work?

For most of these jobs, you need these skills:

* Instructing—teaching others how to do something
* Learning Strategies—selecting and using training/ instructional methods and procedures appropriate for the situation when learning or teaching new things
* Reading Comprehension—understanding written sentences and paragraphs in work-related documents
* Writing—communicating effectively in writing as appropriate for the needs of the audience
* Speaking—talking to others to convey information effectively
* Active Learning—understanding the implications of new information for both current and future problem solving and decision making
* Programming—writing computer programs for various purposes

These knowledges are important in most of these jobs:

* Education and Training—principles and methods for curriculum and training design, teaching and instruction for individuals and groups, and the measurement of training effects

* English Language—the structure and content of the English language, including the meaning and spelling of words, rules of composition, and grammar
* Therapy and Counseling—principles, methods, and procedures for diagnosis, treatment, and rehabilitation of physical and mental dysfunctions and for career counseling and guidance
* History and Archeology—historical events and their causes, indicators, and effects on civilizations and cultures
* Sociology and Anthropology—group behavior and dynamics, societal trends and influences, human migrations, ethnicity, and cultures and their history and origins
* Psychology—human behavior and performance; individual differences in ability, personality, and interests; learning and motivation; psychological research methods; and the assessment and treatment of behavioral and affective disorders
* Communications and Media—media production, communication, and dissemination techniques and methods; this includes alternative ways to inform and entertain via written, oral, and visual media

What else should you consider about this kind of work?

These workers are employed by colleges, universities, school districts, and government extension agencies.

One special reward that many college faculty enjoy is tenure, which means they cannot be fired without due cause (this is designed to guarantee academic freedom). To qualify, they work under limited-term contracts for several years, during which they demonstrate their ability at teaching, research, and general contribution to the college. They are evaluated on these matters by a faculty committee, and if they are not granted tenure, they usually must find work elsewhere.

Adult education appears to be a growing area. The outlook for college faculty is gradually improving as many older faculty retire, but in certain disciplines many workers will continue to be hired only as temporary or part-time faculty. There tends to be less competition for college teaching when there are more job openings in industry.

How can you prepare for jobs of this kind?

Occupations in this group usually require education and/or training ranging from two years to more than ten years.

College faculty at four-year institutions need to have a doctoral degree in their field, except for temporary or part-time positions. At two-year colleges a master's degree is usually acceptable, but the pressure of competition makes a doctorate important in most fields.

Other adult educators need more than two years of education but less than ten years.

All types of educators must keep abreast of new developments in their fields.

How much education or training is required for the jobs in this Work Group?

For descriptions of these jobs, see Part 2.

Work experience in a related occupation

* Self-Enrichment Education Teachers
* Vocational Education Teachers, Postsecondary

Bachelor's degree

* Adult Literacy, Remedial Education, and GED Teachers and Instructors
* Farm and Home Management Advisors

Master's degree

* Agricultural Sciences Teachers, Postsecondary
* Anthropology and Archeology Teachers, Postsecondary
* Architecture Teachers, Postsecondary
* Area, Ethnic, and Cultural Studies Teachers, Postsecondary
* Art, Drama, and Music Teachers, Postsecondary
* Atmospheric, Earth, Marine, and Space Sciences Teachers, Postsecondary
* Biological Science Teachers, Postsecondary
* Business Teachers, Postsecondary
* Chemistry Teachers, Postsecondary
* Communications Teachers, Postsecondary
* Computer Science Teachers, Postsecondary
* Criminal Justice and Law Enforcement Teachers, Postsecondary
* Economics Teachers, Postsecondary
* Education Teachers, Postsecondary
* Engineering Teachers, Postsecondary
* English Language and Literature Teachers, Postsecondary
* Environmental Science Teachers, Postsecondary
* Foreign Language and Literature Teachers, Postsecondary
* Forestry and Conservation Science Teachers, Postsecondary
* Geography Teachers, Postsecondary
* Graduate Teaching Assistants
* Health Specialties Teachers, Postsecondary
* History Teachers, Postsecondary
* Home Economics Teachers, Postsecondary
* Library Science Teachers, Postsecondary
* Mathematical Science Teachers, Postsecondary
* Nursing Instructors and Teachers, Postsecondary
* Philosophy and Religion Teachers, Postsecondary
* Physics Teachers, Postsecondary
* Political Science Teachers, Postsecondary
* Psychology Teachers, Postsecondary
* Recreation and Fitness Studies Teachers, Postsecondary
* Social Work Teachers, Postsecondary
* Sociology Teachers, Postsecondary

First professional degree

* Law Teachers, Postsecondary

05.04 Library Services

Workers in this group provide library services that connect people with information.

What kind of work would you do?

Your work activities would depend on your job. For example, you might

* Check books in and out of the library.
* Conduct reference searches, using printed materials and in-house and online databases.
* Develop library policies and procedures.
* Enter and update patrons' records on computers.
* Inspect returned books for condition and due-date status and compute any applicable fines.
* Instruct patrons on how to use reference sources, card catalogs, and automated information systems.
* Locate unusual or unique information in response to specific requests.
* Organize collections of books, publications, documents, audiovisual aids, and other reference materials for convenient access.
* Take actions to halt disruption of library activities by problem patrons.

What things about you point to this kind of work?

Is it important for you to

* Have good working conditions?
* Have co-workers who are easy to get along with?
* Have work where you do things for other people?

Have you enjoyed any of the following as a hobby or leisure-time activity?

* Volunteering at the library
* Organizing your room, CDs, DVDs, tools, books, and other items
* Researching things that sound interesting to you

Have you liked and done well in any of the following school subjects?

* Education
* Record Keeping
* Business Computer Applications
* Clerical Practices/Office Practices
* Data Retrieval Techniques

Are you able to

* Generate or use different sets of rules for combining or grouping things in different ways?
* Identify or detect a known pattern that is hidden in other distracting material?
* See details at close range?

* Identify and understand the speech of another person?
* See details at a distance?

Would you work in places such as

* Libraries?
* Business offices?

What skills and knowledges do you need for this kind of work?

For most of these jobs, you need these skills:

* Service Orientation—actively looking for ways to help people
* Learning Strategies—selecting and using training/instructional methods and procedures appropriate for the situation when learning or teaching new things
* Instructing—teaching others how to do something
* Time Management—managing one's own time and the time of others
* Social Perceptiveness—being aware of others' reactions and understanding why they react as they do
* Active Listening—giving full attention to what other people are saying, taking time to understand the points being made, asking questions as appropriate, and not interrupting at inappropriate times
* Negotiation—bringing others together and trying to reconcile differences

These knowledges are important in most of these jobs:

* Clerical Practices—administrative and clerical procedures and systems such as word processing, managing files and records, stenography and transcription, designing forms, and other office procedures and terminology
* Customer and Personal Service—principles and processes for providing customer and personal services; this includes customer needs assessment, meeting quality standards for services, and evaluation of customer satisfaction
* History and Archeology—historical events and their causes, indicators, and effects on civilizations and cultures
* Computers and Electronics—circuit boards; processors; chips; electronic equipment; and computer hardware and software, including applications and programming
* Geography—principles and methods for describing the features of land, sea, and air masses, including their physical characteristics; locations; interrelationships; and distribution of plant, animal, and human life
* English Language—the structure and content of the English language, including the meaning and spelling of words, rules of composition, and grammar
* Philosophy and Theology—different philosophical systems and religions; this includes their basic principles, values, ethics, ways of thinking, customs, practices, and impact on human culture

What else should you consider about this kind of work?

These workers are employed by public and school libraries and also by corporations, nonprofit organizations, and consulting firms.

Part-time or volunteer work can be a good way to get experience and decide whether you enjoy this type of work. Librarians and library assistants may have to work evenings and/or weekends.

Automation is allowing library assistants to do much of the work formerly done by professional librarians. Nevertheless, the job outlook for professional librarians is good because a large number of retirements is expected. Computer skills are a must in this field.

How can you prepare for jobs of this kind?

Occupations in this group require education and/or training ranging from less than six months for clerical library assistants to less than ten years for professional librarians.

Professional librarians are usually required to have a master's, following a bachelor's in a subject other than library science. In university settings an additional master's in another field is very helpful.

A bachelor's degree with a broad background and computer training is probably good preparation for most library technician jobs. Library assistants may have only on-the-job training, but some postsecondary education is helpful, and knowledge of computer applications is becoming critical for any jobs other than clerical ones.

How much education or training is required for the jobs in this Work Group?

For descriptions of these jobs, see Part 2.

Short-term on-the-job training

* Library Assistants, Clerical
* Library Technicians

Master's degree

* Librarians

05.05 Archival and Museum Services

Workers in this group acquire and preserve items of lasting value for the benefit of researchers or the general public. They may catalogue, describe, or display the material they work with.

What kind of work would you do?

Your work activities would depend on your job. For example, you might

* Establish and administer policy guidelines concerning public access and use of materials.
* Install, arrange, assemble, and prepare artifacts for exhibition, ensuring the artifacts' safety, reporting their status and condition, and identifying and correcting any problems with the setup.

* Instruct users in the selection, use, and design of audio-visual materials and assist them in the preparation of instructional materials and the rehearsal of presentations.
* Negotiate and authorize purchase, sale, exchange, or loan of collections.
* Plan and organize the acquisition, storage, and exhibition of collections and related materials, including the selection of exhibition themes and designs.
* Present public programs and tours.
* Preserve records, documents, and objects, copying records to film, videotape, audiotape, disk, or computer formats as necessary.
* Research and record the origins and historical significance of archival materials.
* Set up, adjust, and operate audiovisual equipment such as cameras, film and slide projectors, and recording equipment for meetings, events, classes, seminars, and videoconferences.
* Supervise and work with volunteers.

What things about you point to this kind of work?

Is it important for you to

* Have good working conditions?
* Have co-workers who are easy to get along with?
* Give directions and instructions to others?

Have you enjoyed any of the following as a hobby or leisure-time activity?

* Organizing your room, CDs, DVDs, tools, books, and other items
* Visiting museums or historic sites
* Carving small wooden objects

Have you liked and done well in any of the following school subjects?

* History
* Arts and Crafts
* Biology
* Photography
* Archeology

Are you able to

* Generate or use different sets of rules for combining or grouping things in different ways?
* Speak clearly so others can understand you?
* Imagine how something will look after it is moved around or when its parts are moved or rearranged?

Would you work in places such as

* Museums?
* Libraries?
* Business offices?

What skills and knowledges do you need for this kind of work?

For most of these jobs, you need these skills:

* Time Management—managing one's own time and the time of others
* Management of Material Resources—obtaining and seeing to the appropriate use of equipment, facilities, and materials needed to do certain work
* Instructing—teaching others how to do something
* Operations Analysis—analyzing needs and product requirements to create a design
* Writing—communicating effectively in writing as appropriate for the needs of the audience
* Equipment Selection—determining the kind of tools and equipment needed to do a job
* Management of Personnel Resources—motivating, developing, and directing people as they work, identifying the best people for the job

These knowledges are important in most of these jobs:

* History and Archeology—historical events and their causes, indicators, and effects on civilizations and cultures
* Sociology and Anthropology—group behavior and dynamics, societal trends and influences, human migrations, ethnicity, and cultures and their history and origins
* Clerical Practices—administrative and clerical procedures and systems such as word processing, managing files and records, stenography and transcription, designing forms, and other office procedures and terminology
* Philosophy and Theology—different philosophical systems and religions; this includes their basic principles, values, ethics, ways of thinking, customs, practices, and impact on human culture
* Communications and Media—media production, communication, and dissemination techniques and methods; this includes alternative ways to inform and entertain via written, oral, and visual media
* Fine Arts—the theory and techniques required to compose, produce, and perform works of music, dance, visual arts, drama, and sculpture
* Education and Training—principles and methods for curriculum and training design, teaching and instruction for individuals and groups, and the measurement of training effects

What else should you consider about this kind of work?

Curators work for museums, zoos, botanical gardens, and historic sites.

Conservators and museum technicians usually have highly specialized skills for preserving and restoring exhibited items.

Many archivists work for corporations and federal and state governments. They generally work a 40-hour week in comfortable surroundings. For government positions, it may be necessary to pass a civil service exam.

Audio-visual collections specialists usually work for school districts, helping to prepare and show audiovisual resources as adjuncts to classroom teaching.

© 2006 JIST Works

Competition is expected to be keen for most of the jobs in this group. In museums and archives, the best opportunities will be for those with advanced degrees or dual specialties and those who are skilled with computer applications.

How can you prepare for jobs of this kind?

Occupations in this group usually require education and/or training ranging from one year to more than ten years.

Archivists and curators generally have a master's or doctorate. Conservators usually have a master's degree. Museum technicians generally have a master's degree or a bachelor's degree plus experience working in museums. Audio-visual collections specialists receive most of their training in a few months on the job.

How much education or training is required for the jobs in this Work Group?

For descriptions of these jobs, see Part 2.

Moderate-term on-the-job training

* Audio-Visual Collections Specialists

Master's degree

* Archivists
* Curators
* Museum Technicians and Conservators

05.06 Counseling, Health, and Fitness Education

Workers in this group help people lead healthy and well-directed lives. They educate and advise people to help them make educational choices, adopt healthier lifestyles, and get into better physical condition.

What kind of work would you do?

Your work activities would depend on your job. For example, you might

* Develop, conduct, or coordinate health needs assessments and other public health surveys.
* Develop, prepare, and coordinate grant applications and grant-related activities to obtain funding for health education programs and related work.
* Encourage students and/or parents to seek additional assistance from mental health professionals when necessary.
* Establish and supervise peer counseling and peer tutoring programs.
* Evaluate individuals' abilities, interests, and personality characteristics, using tests, records, interviews, and professional sources.
* Explain and enforce safety rules and regulations governing sports, recreational activities, and the use of exercise equipment.

* Instruct individuals in career development techniques such as job search and application strategies, resume writing, and interview skills.
* Plan exercise routines, choose appropriate music, and choose different movements for each set of muscles, depending on participants' capabilities and limitations.
* Plan physical education programs to promote development of participants' physical attributes and social skills.
* Prepare and distribute health education materials, including reports; bulletins; and visual aids such as films, videotapes, photographs, and posters.

What things about you point to this kind of work?

Is it important for you to

* Have work where you do things for other people?
* Give directions and instructions to others?
* Try out your own ideas?
* Get a feeling of accomplishment?
* Have something different to do every day?
* Make decisions on your own?

Have you enjoyed any of the following as a hobby or leisure-time activity?

* Coaching children or youth in sports activities
* Serving as a volunteer counselor at a youth camp or center
* Participating in gymnastics
* Doing strenuous activities, such as dancing, climbing, backpacking, running, swimming, and skiing
* Listening to friends and helping them with their personal problems

Have you liked and done well in any of the following school subjects?

* Counseling Techniques
* Guidance
* Psychology
* Child Development/Care
* Health
* Physical Education

Are you able to

* Speak clearly so others can understand you?
* Communicate information and ideas in speaking so others will understand?
* Listen to and understand information and ideas presented through spoken words and sentences?

Would you work in places such as

* High schools?
* Colleges and universities?
* Gymnasiums and health clubs?

What skills and knowledges do you need for this kind of work?

For most of these jobs, you need these skills:

* Service Orientation—actively looking for ways to help people
* Instructing—teaching others how to do something
* Social Perceptiveness—being aware of others' reactions and understanding why they react as they do
* Persuasion—persuading others to change their minds or behavior
* Speaking—talking to others to convey information effectively
* Coordination—adjusting actions in relation to others' actions
* Monitoring—monitoring/assessing your own performance or that of other individuals or organizations to make improvements or take corrective action

These knowledges are important in most of these jobs:

* Therapy and Counseling—principles, methods, and procedures for diagnosis, treatment, and rehabilitation of physical and mental dysfunctions and for career counseling and guidance
* Education and Training—principles and methods for curriculum and training design, teaching and instruction for individuals and groups, and the measurement of training effects
* Psychology—human behavior and performance; individual differences in ability, personality, and interests; learning and motivation; psychological research methods; and the assessment and treatment of behavioral and affective disorders
* Sociology and Anthropology—group behavior and dynamics, societal trends and influences, human migrations, ethnicity, and cultures and their history and origins

What else should you consider about this kind of work?

These occupations differ greatly in their hours and working environments. Educational, vocational, and school counselors work at educational institutions, generally during normal school hours, although some evening work is necessary to reach students and parents. Health educators may also work for schools, but many of them work for government agencies, community organizations, and corporations. They may need to travel or work many evenings to reach their students. Fitness and aerobics instructors work in gyms, fitness centers, and activity rooms in various settings. Many work part-time or evening hours.

The job outlook is expected to be good, especially in the health and fitness field.

How can you prepare for jobs of this kind?

Work in this group ranges from one to more than ten years of education and/or training.

Several organizations offer certification for fitness and aerobics instructors, and this credential is generally needed for employment. A bachelor's degree is also helpful.

School counselors are expected to be state-certified, which means they must have at least a bachelor's degree. Some states also require a teaching certificate and/or teaching experience.

Health educators and college-level counselors are expected to have a master's degree.

How much education or training is required for the jobs in this Work Group?

For descriptions of these jobs, see Part 2.

Postsecondary vocational training

* Fitness Trainers and Aerobics Instructors

Master's degree

* Educational, Vocational, and School Counselors
* Health Educators

06 Finance and Insurance

An interest in helping businesses and people be assured of a financially secure future. You can satisfy this interest by working in a financial or insurance business in a leadership or support role. If you like gathering and analyzing information, you may find fulfillment as an insurance adjuster or financial analyst. Or you may deal with information at the clerical level as a banking or insurance clerk or in person-to-person situations providing customer service. Another way to interact with people is to sell financial or insurance services that will meet their needs.

06.01   Managerial Work in Finance and Insurance

06.02   Finance/Insurance Investigation and Analysis

06.03   Finance/Insurance Records Processing

06.04   Finance/Insurance Customer Service

06.05   Finance/Insurance Sales and Support

06.01 Managerial Work in Finance and Insurance

Workers in this group manage an organization's financial forecasting and reporting, investments, and cash. They carry out their activities according to policies and procedures determined by owners, boards of directors, administrators, and other persons with higher authority.

What kind of work would you do?

Your work activities would depend on your job. For example, you might

* Communicate with stockholders and other investors to provide information and to raise capital.
* Compute, withhold, and account for all payroll deductions.
* Develop internal control policies, guidelines, and procedures for activities such as budget administration, cash and credit management, and accounting.
* Evaluate data pertaining to costs in order to plan budgets.
* Examine, evaluate, and process loan applications.
* Monitor financial activities and details such as reserve levels to ensure that all legal and regulatory requirements are met.
* Oversee the flow of cash and financial instruments.
* Perform tax planning work.
* Prepare and file annual tax returns or prepare financial information so that outside accountants can complete tax returns.
* Prepare or direct preparation of financial statements, business activity reports, financial position forecasts, annual budgets, and/or reports required by regulatory agencies.

What things about you point to this kind of work?

Is it important for you to

* Give directions and instructions to others?
* Have good working conditions?
* Have opportunities for advancement?
* Be busy all the time?
* Be treated fairly by the company?
* Be paid well in comparison with other workers?
* Have something different to do every day?

Have you enjoyed any of the following as a hobby or leisure-time activity?

* Serving as treasurer of a club or other organization
* Serving as a leader of a scouting or other group
* Reading business magazines and newspapers
* Helping run a school or community fair or carnival

Have you liked and done well in any of the following school subjects?

* Management
* Accounting
* Business Analysis
* Business Law
* Finance
* Personnel Management
* Business Writing
* Business Computer Applications
* Math Computing, Standard Formula
* Money and Banking

Are you able to

* Choose the right mathematical methods or formulas to solve a problem?
* Add, subtract, multiply, or divide quickly and correctly?
* Apply general rules to specific problems to produce answers that make sense?
* Quickly make sense of, combine, and organize information into meaningful patterns?
* Communicate information and ideas in writing so others will understand?
* Read and understand information and ideas presented in writing?
* Remember information such as words, numbers, pictures, and procedures?

Would you work in places such as

* Business offices?
* Government offices?

What skills and knowledges do you need for this kind of work?

For most of these jobs, you need these skills:

* Management of Financial Resources—determining how money will be spent to get the work done and accounting for these expenditures
* Systems Analysis—determining how a system should work and how changes in conditions, operations, and the environment will affect outcomes
* Systems Evaluation—identifying measures or indicators of system performance and the actions needed to improve or correct performance relative to the goals of the system
* Judgment and Decision Making—considering the relative costs and benefits of potential actions to choose the most appropriate one
* Management of Personnel Resources—motivating, developing, and directing people as they work, identifying the best people for the job
* Complex Problem Solving—identifying complex problems and reviewing related information to develop and evaluate options and implement solutions
* Monitoring—monitoring/assessing your own performance or that of other individuals or organizations to make improvements or take corrective action

© 2006 JIST Works

These knowledges are important in most of these jobs:

* Economics and Accounting—economic and accounting principles and practices, the financial markets, banking, and the analysis and reporting of financial data
* Administration and Management—business and management principles involved in strategic planning, resource allocation, human resources modeling, leadership techniques, production methods, and coordination of people and resources
* Law and Government—laws, legal codes, court procedures, precedents, government regulations, executive orders, agency rules, and the democratic political process
* Mathematics—arithmetic, algebra, geometry, calculus, and statistics and their applications
* Personnel and Human Resources—principles and procedures for personnel recruitment, selection, training, compensation and benefits, labor relations and negotiation, and personnel information systems
* History and Archeology—historical events and their causes, indicators, and effects on civilizations and cultures
* English Language—the structure and content of the English language, including the meaning and spelling of words, rules of composition, and grammar

What else should you consider about this kind of work?

These workers are employed by private businesses, non-profit organizations, and government agencies. Some of them work for consulting businesses that provide financial management services for companies that are too small to have their own financial officers.

They work in comfortable office settings, but many of them log longer hours than a typical office work week. They may also need to travel to meet clients and visit branch offices.

The outlook varies somewhat with the business cycle, and in the long term there is likely to be keen competition for jobs. Best opportunities will be for those with a master's degree, facility with computer applications, and good communications skills.

How can you prepare for jobs of this kind?

Occupations in this group require postsecondary education/training ranging from as little as two years for financial managers (although a bachelor's degree is normally required) to more than ten years for treasurers, controllers, and chief financial officers.

A bachelor's degree in finance, accounting, economics, or business administration is considered the minimum usually required for job entry in this field. Many more doors are open to those who hold a master's degree, which may be in finance or in a specialized subject such as risk management. Several professional organizations offer certification programs.

Like all managers, these workers must keep abreast of technological change to stay employable.

How much education or training is required for the jobs in this Work Group?

For descriptions of these jobs, see Part 2.

Work experience plus degree

* Financial Managers, Branch or Department
* Treasurers, Controllers, and Chief Financial Officers

06.02 Finance/Insurance Investigation and Analysis

Workers in this group analyze and evaluate financial information to help managers make decisions and plans regarding financial transactions, such as investments and insurance claims. They supervise clerical and sometimes technical staff who support them.

What kind of work would you do?

Your work activities would depend on your job. For example, you might

* Analyze blueprints and other documentation to prepare time, cost, materials, and labor estimates.
* Analyze loan applicants' financial status, credit, and property evaluations to determine feasibility of granting loans.
* Conduct research on consumer opinions and marketing strategies, collaborating with marketing professionals, statisticians, pollsters, and other professionals.
* Determine taxability and value of properties, using methods such as field inspection, structural measurement, calculation, sales analysis, market trend studies, and income and expense analysis.
* Examine damaged vehicle to determine extent of structural, body, mechanical, electrical, or interior damage.
* Explain to customers the different types of loans and credit options that are available, as well as the terms of those services.
* Inspect properties to evaluate construction, condition, special features, and functional design and to take property measurements.
* Investigate and assess damage to property.
* Investigate, evaluate, and settle insurance claims.
* Prepare reports that include the degree of risk involved in extending credit or lending money.

What things about you point to this kind of work?

Is it important for you to

* Have opportunities for advancement?
* Be treated fairly by the company?

Have you enjoyed any of the following as a hobby or leisure-time activity?

* Conducting house-to-house or telephone surveys for a PTA or other organization
* Reading business magazines and newspapers

* Using a pocket calculator or spreadsheet to figure out income and expenses for an organization

Have you liked and done well in any of the following school subjects?

* Finance
* Accounting
* Business Law
* Insurance
* Marketing/Merchandising
* Statistics
* Math Computing, Standard Formula
* Real Estate Laws/Regulations
* Consumer Behavior
* Criminal Investigating
* Money and Banking

Are you able to

* Add, subtract, multiply, or divide quickly and correctly?
* Choose the right mathematical methods or formulas to solve a problem?
* Apply general rules to specific problems to produce answers that make sense?

Would you work in places such as

* Business offices?
* Streets and highways?
* Stores and shopping malls?

What skills and knowledges do you need for this kind of work?

For most of these jobs, you need these skills:

* Negotiation—bringing others together and trying to reconcile differences
* Judgment and Decision Making—considering the relative costs and benefits of potential actions to choose the most appropriate one
* Mathematics—using mathematics to solve problems

These knowledges are important in most of these jobs:

* Economics and Accounting—economic and accounting principles and practices, the financial markets, banking, and the analysis and reporting of financial data
* Sales and Marketing—principles and methods for showing, promoting, and selling products or services; this includes marketing strategy and tactics, product demonstrations, sales techniques, and sales control systems
* Law and Government—laws, legal codes, court procedures, precedents, government regulations, executive orders, agency rules, and the democratic political process
* Mathematics—arithmetic, algebra, geometry, calculus, and statistics and their applications

What else should you consider about this kind of work?

Most of the jobs in this group are in businesses, such as banks and insurance agencies, that are part of the finance or insurance industry. However, some of these workers, such as financial analysts and market research analysts, may work in any kind of medium-sized to large business or organization.

The work setting is generally in a comfortable office, but insurance adjusters, assessors, and appraisers need to visit the sites of homes or automobile accidents to gather information. Insurance investigators may need to work nights to make calls and do surveillance. Market research analysts may need to travel to meet with clients and focus groups.

Most of these jobs are sensitive to downturns in the economy, and the overall outlook is mixed. Best opportunities are expected for market research analysts and, in other jobs, for people who know how to use the most up-to-date software.

How can you prepare for jobs of this kind?

Occupations in this group usually require education and/or training ranging from two years to less than ten years.

For most of these jobs, two years of college may be acceptable but not preferable. A bachelor's is often expected, and work experience in related positions for the same employer can be very helpful. Courses in accounting, business law, economics, investments, risk management, cash management, marketing writing, math, and computer science are helpful. Some of these courses are available in high schools, but most are offered by business schools, colleges, and graduate schools of business.

How much education or training is required for the jobs in this Work Group?

For descriptions of these jobs, see Part 2.

Long-term on-the-job training

* Claims Examiners, Property and Casualty Insurance
* Insurance Adjusters, Examiners, and Investigators
* Insurance Appraisers, Auto Damage

Postsecondary vocational training

* Appraisers, Real Estate
* Assessors

Bachelor's degree

* Cost Estimators
* Credit Analysts
* Financial Analysts
* Insurance Underwriters
* Loan Counselors
* Loan Officers
* Market Research Analysts
* Survey Researchers

06.03 Finance/Insurance Records Processing

Workers in this group verify, correct, file, and route recorded information. They need to be accurate with details and tolerant of repetitive work.

What kind of work would you do?

Your work activities would depend on your job. For example, you might

* Compare information or figures on one record against the same data on other records, or with original copy, to detect errors.
* Examine city directories and public records in order to verify residence property ownership, bankruptcies, liens, arrest record, or unpaid taxes of applicants.
* Interview credit applicants by telephone or in person in order to obtain personal and financial data needed to complete credit reports.
* Mark copy to indicate and correct errors in type, arrangement, grammar, punctuation, or spelling, using standard printers' marks.
* Prepare and review insurance-claim forms and related documents for completeness.
* Process and record new insurance policies and claims.
* Read corrected copies or proofs in order to ensure that all corrections have been made.
* Review and verify data, such as age, name, address, and principal sum and value of property, on insurance applications and policies.
* Review insurance policy to determine coverage.

What things about you point to this kind of work?

Is it important for you to

* Have good working conditions?
* Have supervisors who back up workers with management?

Have you enjoyed any of the following as a hobby or leisure-time activity?

* Operating a calculator or adding machine for an organization
* Using a pocket calculator or spreadsheet to figure out income and expenses for an organization
* Editing or proofreading a school or organizational newspaper, yearbook, or magazine

Have you liked and done well in any of the following school subjects?

* Insurance
* Clerical Practices/Office Practices
* Math Computing, Standard Formula
* Business Computer Applications
* Spelling
* Grammar
* Money and Banking

Are you able to

* See details at close range?
* Remember information such as words, numbers, pictures, and procedures?
* Add, subtract, multiply, or divide quickly and correctly?

Would you work in places such as

* Business offices?

What skills and knowledges do you need for this kind of work?

For most of these jobs, you need these skills:

* Reading Comprehension—understanding written sentences and paragraphs in work-related documents
* Active Listening—giving full attention to what other people are saying, taking time to understand the points being made, asking questions as appropriate, and not interrupting at inappropriate times
* Speaking—talking to others to convey information effectively

These knowledges are important in most of these jobs:

* Clerical Practices—administrative and clerical procedures and systems such as word processing, managing files and records, stenography and transcription, designing forms, and other office procedures and terminology
* Economics and Accounting—economic and accounting principles and practices, the financial markets, banking, and the analysis and reporting of financial data
* Telecommunications—transmission, broadcasting, switching, control, and operation of telecommunications systems

What else should you consider about this kind of work?

Workers who check credit information and authorize credit are mainly employed by the financial and insurance industries in businesses such as lending institutions and credit bureaus. Insurance brokerages and underwriting companies employ claims clerks and policy processing clerks. Proofreaders are employed by print shops and businesses that produce a lot of publications.

Almost all of this work is done in offices during a regular eight-hour day. Proofreaders for newspapers may need to work night shifts or weekends.

These jobs may serve as stepping-stones to more-skilled jobs with the same employer. For example, a proofreader may advance to editing, or a clerk may advance to bookkeeping.

Automation is causing a downturn in employment in these occupations. For example, much of the work of judging the creditworthiness of consumers is being taken over by software, so there will be fewer openings for credit authorizers. There will continue to be some openings to replace retiring workers, even if the total number of jobs declines.

How can you prepare for jobs of this kind?

Occupations in this group usually require education and/or training ranging from less than six months to two years.

A high school education or its equivalent is generally required. Proofreaders can benefit from coursework in language skills such as punctuation, grammar, and spelling; a bachelor's degree can be helpful. Clerks and authorizers can learn useful skills from courses in basic math and record keeping. Some employers prefer workers who have completed general business or clerical courses. Many employers provide on-the-job training.

How much education or training is required for the jobs in this Work Group?

For descriptions of these jobs, see Part 2.

Short-term on-the-job training

* Credit Authorizers
* Credit Checkers
* Proofreaders and Copy Markers

Moderate-term on-the-job training

* Insurance Claims Clerks
* Insurance Policy Processing Clerks

06.04 Finance/Insurance Customer Service

Workers in this group deal with people in person, often standing behind a window or in a booth. They may receive payment; collect information; give out change, cash, or merchandise; provide information in answer to questions; help customers fill out forms; or persuade debtors to settle their debts. Many keep written records of the information or money they receive or perform other clerical duties.

What kind of work would you do?

Your work activities would depend on your job. For example, you might

* Answer questions and advise customers regarding loans and transactions.
* Cash checks and pay out money after verifying that signatures are correct, that written and numerical amounts agree, and that accounts have sufficient funds.
* Inform customers of procedures for applying for services such as ATM cards, direct deposit of checks, and certificates of deposit.
* Interview loan applicants in order to obtain personal and financial data and to assist in completing applications.

* Locate and notify customers of delinquent accounts by mail, telephone, or personal visits in order to solicit payment.
* Persuade customers to pay amounts due on credit accounts, damage claims, or nonpayable checks or to return merchandise.
* Prepare and verify cashier's checks.
* Receive checks and cash for deposit, verify amounts, and check accuracy of deposit slips.
* Review customer accounts in order to determine whether payments are made on time and that other loan terms are being followed.
* Verify and examine information and accuracy of loan application and closing documents.

What things about you point to this kind of work?

Is it important for you to

* Have good working conditions?
* Have supervisors who back up workers with management?

Have you enjoyed any of the following as a hobby or leisure-time activity?

* Using a pocket calculator or spreadsheet to figure out income and expenses for an organization
* Serving as a volunteer interviewer in a social service organization
* Doing fundraising for school groups, teams, or community organizations

Have you liked and done well in any of the following school subjects?

* Public Speaking
* Business Math
* Business Machine Operating
* Clerical Practices/Office Practices
* Record Keeping

Are you able to

* See details at close range?
* Identify and understand the speech of another person?
* Quickly and accurately compare similarities and differences among sets of letters, numbers, objects, pictures, or patterns?

Would you work in places such as

* Business offices?

What skills and knowledges do you need for this kind of work?

For most of these jobs, you need these skills:

* Service Orientation—actively looking for ways to help people
* Active Listening—giving full attention to what other people are saying, taking time to understand the points being made, asking questions as appropriate, and not interrupting at inappropriate times

* Speaking—talking to others to convey information effectively

These knowledges are important in most of these jobs:

* Customer and Personal Service—principles and processes for providing customer and personal services; this includes customer needs assessment, meeting quality standards for services, and evaluation of customer satisfaction
* Clerical Practices—administrative and clerical procedures and systems such as word processing, managing files and records, stenography and transcription, designing forms, and other office procedures and terminology
* Economics and Accounting—economic and accounting principles and practices, the financial markets, banking, and the analysis and reporting of financial data
* Law and Government—laws, legal codes, court procedures, precedents, government regulations, executive orders, agency rules, and the democratic political process

What else should you consider about this kind of work?

The occupations in this group are found in a variety of places, such as banks, hospitals, retail stores, collection agencies, business offices, gambling casinos, and government agencies. Inexperienced people are hired for many of these jobs.

Most of these jobs are done during regular daytime hours. Some workers in this group have to ask strangers to pay overdue bills or divulge information that is considered personal or confidential and may encounter resistance.

The overall outlook for this group is only fair, with many of the openings serving to replace workers who retire or move on. Automation such as ATMs has replaced some workers and made others more efficient. Best opportunities will be for workers who have good math and people skills.

How can you prepare for jobs of this kind?

The occupations in this group require education and/or training ranging from six months to less than two years. Workers get most of their training on the job.

People who like contact with the public usually enter these jobs. Some jobs require data entry or other clerical skills. Many employers prefer workers with a high school education or its equal, with courses in speech, English, and math especially useful. Chances for promotion are improved with additional education and training.

How much education or training is required for the jobs in this Work Group?

For descriptions of these jobs, see Part 2.

Short-term on-the-job training

* Bill and Account Collectors
* Loan Interviewers and Clerks
* Tellers

Work experience in a related occupation

* New Accounts Clerks

06.05 Finance/Insurance Sales and Support

Workers in this group sell services such as investment counseling, insurance, and advertising. They advise customers of the capabilities, uses, and other important features of these services and help customers choose those best suited to their needs.

What kind of work would you do?

Your work activities would depend on your job. For example, you might

* Analyze market conditions in order to determine optimum times to execute securities transactions.
* Conduct seminars and workshops on financial planning topics such as retirement planning, estate planning, and the evaluation of severance packages.
* Customize insurance programs to suit individual customers, often covering a variety of risks.
* Determine customers' financial services needs and prepare proposals to sell services that address these needs.
* Draw up contracts for advertising work and collect payments due.
* Explain stock market terms and trading practices to clients.
* Monitor insurance claims to ensure they are settled equitably for both the client and the insurer.
* Prepare promotional plans, sales literature, media kits, and sales contracts, using computer.
* Read corporate reports and calculate ratios to determine best prospects for profit on stock purchases and to monitor client accounts.
* Recommend strategies clients can use to achieve their financial goals and objectives, including specific recommendations in such areas as cash management, insurance coverage, and investment planning.

What things about you point to this kind of work?

Is it important for you to

* Have good working conditions?
* Have opportunities for advancement?
* Be paid well in comparison with other workers?
* Receive recognition for the work you do?
* Be looked up to by others in your company and your community?

Have you enjoyed any of the following as a hobby or leisure-time activity?

* Selling advertising space for a school newspaper or yearbook
* Helping persuade people to sign petitions or support a cause

* Doing fundraising for school groups, teams, or community organizations
* Reading business magazines and newspapers

Have you liked and done well in any of the following school subjects?

* Finance
* Marketing/Merchandising
* Insurance
* Record Keeping
* Public Speaking
* Selling

Are you able to

* Identify and understand the speech of another person?
* Add, subtract, multiply, or divide quickly and correctly?
* Choose the right mathematical methods or formulas to solve a problem?
* See details at close range?

Would you work in places such as

* Business offices?
* Private homes?

What skills and knowledges do you need for this kind of work?

For most of these jobs, you need these skills:

* Management of Financial Resources—determining how money will be spent to get the work done and accounting for these expenditures
* Persuasion—persuading others to change their minds or behavior
* Negotiation—bringing others together and trying to reconcile differences
* Service Orientation—actively looking for ways to help people
* Judgment and Decision Making—considering the relative costs and benefits of potential actions to choose the most appropriate one
* Speaking—talking to others to convey information effectively
* Complex Problem Solving—identifying complex problems and reviewing related information to develop and evaluate options and implement solutions

These knowledges are important in most of these jobs:

* Economics and Accounting—economic and accounting principles and practices, the financial markets, banking, and the analysis and reporting of financial data
* Sales and Marketing—principles and methods for showing, promoting, and selling products or services; this includes marketing strategy and tactics, product demonstrations, sales techniques, and sales control systems
* Customer and Personal Service—principles and processes for providing customer and personal services; this includes customer needs assessment, meeting quality standards for services, and evaluation of customer satisfaction

What else should you consider about this kind of work?

These workers are employed by insurance companies, financial institutions, and media businesses. Some, particularly personal financial advisors, are self-employed.

Much of the work is done in offices, but workers may contact clients through a mixture of telephone conversations and personal visits. Advertising sales agents for specialized publications often need to travel to industry conferences. Personal financial advisors may need to meet clients in the evenings or on weekends, and they may teach evening classes to attract clients.

Some workers earn a commission based on volume of sales; others work for a salary and may get bonuses for high performance. Self-employed financial advisors may charge an hourly fee or one based on the complexity of the services being offered.

Jobs related to investments are sensitive to the ups and downs of the economy. Some jobs are being lost because the Internet is allowing consumers to do their own fact-finding and purchasing of securities and insurance policies. Competition for entry-level securities sales positions is expected to be keen, but trained workers should find continuing demand for their skills. The outlook for the other jobs in this group is better for beginners.

How can you prepare for jobs of this kind?

Occupations in this group usually require education and/or training ranging from one year to less than four years.

A common way to prepare is to obtain a four-year degree with a major in business administration, finance, risk management, economics, or a similar field.

Sales agents for insurance and securities need to be licensed, and financial advisors may want to be licensed so they can do some selling as part of their work. Some employers of securities sales workers prefer to hire persons who have work experience in another field.

New hires usually receive formal or informal training to learn company sales policies and procedures. Insurance companies and brokerage firms frequently send employees to training centers and universities for extensive training.

How much education or training is required for the jobs in this Work Group?

For descriptions of these jobs, see Part 2.

Moderate-term on-the-job training

* Advertising Sales Agents

Bachelor's degree

* Insurance Sales Agents
* Personal Financial Advisors
* Sales Agents, Financial Services
* Sales Agents, Securities and Commodities

07 Government and Public Administration

An interest in helping a government agency serve the needs of the public. You can satisfy this interest by working in a position of leadership or by specializing in a function that contributes to the role of government. You may help protect the public by working as an inspector or examiner to enforce standards. If you enjoy using clerical skills, you may work as a clerk in a law court or government office. Or perhaps you prefer the top-down perspective of a government executive or urban planner.

07.01 Managerial Work in Government and Public Administration

07.02 Public Planning

07.03 Regulations Enforcement

07.04 Public Administration Clerical Support

07.01 Managerial Work in Government and Public Administration

Workers in this group are top-level and middle-level administrators who direct all or part of the activities in government agencies or community outreach organizations.

What kind of work would you do?

Your work activities would depend on your job. For example, you might

* Conduct or direct investigations or hearings to resolve complaints and violations of laws.
* Direct activities of professional and technical staff members and volunteers.
* Direct, coordinate, and conduct activities between United States government and foreign entities to provide information to promote international interest and harmony.
* Prepare budgets and direct and monitor expenditures of department funds.
* Represent organizations in relations with governmental and media institutions.
* Research and analyze member or community needs in order to determine program directions and goals.
* Review and analyze legislation, laws, and public policy and recommend changes to promote and support interests of general population as well as special groups.
* Speak to community groups to explain and interpret agency purposes, programs, and policies.

What things about you point to this kind of work?

Is it important for you to

* Give directions and instructions to others?
* Be busy all the time?
* Have steady employment?
* Have something different to do every day?
* Be looked up to by others in your company and your community?
* Plan your work with little supervision?
* Be treated fairly by the company?

Have you enjoyed any of the following as a hobby or leisure-time activity?

* Helping run a school or community fair or carnival
* Serving as a leader of a scouting or other group
* Serving as president of a club or other organization
* Campaigning for political candidates or issues
* Belonging to a political science club

Have you liked and done well in any of the following school subjects?

* Management
* Accounting
* Government
* Business Law
* Finance
* Personnel Management
* Business Writing
* Business Computer Applications
* Public Speaking

Are you able to

* Speak clearly so others can understand you?
* Identify and understand the speech of another person?
* Choose the right mathematical methods or formulas to solve a problem?
* Remember information such as words, numbers, pictures, and procedures?
* Come up with unusual or clever ideas about a given topic or situation or develop creative ways to solve a problem?
* Come up with a number of ideas about a topic?
* Apply general rules to specific problems to produce answers that make sense?

Would you work in places such as

* Government offices?
* Business offices?

What skills and knowledges do you need for this kind of work?

For most of these jobs, you need these skills:

* Management of Financial Resources—determining how money will be spent to get the work done and accounting for these expenditures
* Management of Personnel Resources—motivating, developing, and directing people as they work, identifying the best people for the job
* Negotiation—bringing others together and trying to reconcile differences
* Systems Evaluation—identifying measures or indicators of system performance and the actions needed to improve or correct performance relative to the goals of the system
* Persuasion—persuading others to change their minds or behavior
* Monitoring—monitoring/assessing your own performance or that of other individuals or organizations to make improvements or take corrective action
* Social Perceptiveness—being aware of others' reactions and understanding why they react as they do

These knowledges are important in most of these jobs:

* Personnel and Human Resources—principles and procedures for personnel recruitment, selection, training, compensation and benefits, labor relations and negotiation, and personnel information systems

* Administration and Management—business and management principles involved in strategic planning, resource allocation, human resources modeling, leadership techniques, production methods, and coordination of people and resources

* Education and Training—principles and methods for curriculum and training design, teaching and instruction for individuals and groups, and the measurement of training effects

* Psychology—human behavior and performance; individual differences in ability, personality, and interests; learning and motivation; psychological research methods; and the assessment and treatment of behavioral and affective disorders

* Law and Government—laws, legal codes, court procedures, precedents, government regulations, executive orders, agency rules, and the democratic political process

* Sociology and Anthropology—group behavior and dynamics, societal trends and influences, human migrations, ethnicity, and cultures and their history and origins

* Economics and Accounting—economic and accounting principles and practices, the financial markets, banking, and the analysis and reporting of financial data

What else should you consider about this kind of work?

These workers are employed by local, state, and federal government agencies and by organizations that promote community health, education, and welfare. They find work in cities and towns, especially in larger communities and those that are county seats or state capitals. Government workers usually need to pass a civil service exam.

These jobs come with heavy responsibilities for dealing with community problems as they arise and for staying within (often restricted) budgets. Workers frequently experience pressure from the public and are expected to respond to the community's needs. They may have to put in evening hours to meet with constituencies.

The overall outlook for this group is for many opportunities, but keen competition in the public sector. Best opportunities will be for those with graduate degrees and those who are skilled with computers and verbal and written communication.

How can you prepare for jobs of this kind?

Occupations in this group usually require education and/or training ranging from two years to less than ten years.

Degrees in public administration or law provide preparation for many jobs in this group. However, some administrative jobs require training and experience in such fields as engineering, public health, or sociology. College coursework in the following subjects is helpful: management, business law, business math, speech or public speaking, government, finance, accounting, economics, history, and English (especially writing).

How much education or training is required for the jobs in this Work Group?

For descriptions of these jobs, see Part 2.

Bachelor's degree

* Social and Community Service Managers

Work experience plus degree

* Government Service Executives

07.02 Public Planning

Workers in this group plan the development or redevelopment of cities, towns, and rural areas or help the professionals who lead the planning projects. They conduct research, develop reports, and advise government officials on how to deal with economic, environmental, and social problems.

What kind of work would you do?

Your work activities would depend on your job. For example, you might

* Conduct interviews, surveys, and site inspections concerning factors that affect land usage, such as zoning, traffic flow, and housing.

* Create, prepare, or requisition graphic and narrative reports on land use data, including land area maps overlaid with geographic variables such as population density.

* Discuss with planning officials the purpose of land use projects such as transportation, conservation, residential, commercial, industrial, and community use.

* Hold public meetings and confer with government, social scientists, lawyers, developers, the public, and special interest groups to formulate and develop land use or community plans.

* Keep informed about economic and legal issues involved in zoning codes, building codes, and environmental regulations.

* Prepare reports, using statistics, charts, and graphs, to illustrate planning studies in areas such as population, land use, or zoning.

* Provide and process zoning and project permits and applications.

* Research, compile, analyze, and organize information from maps, reports, investigations, and books for use in reports and special projects.

What things about you point to this kind of work?

Is it important for you to

* Have opportunities for advancement?
* Have good working conditions?

Have you enjoyed any of the following as a hobby or leisure-time activity?

* Serving as a volunteer interviewer in a social service organization

* Helping to organize things at home, such as shopping lists and budgets
* Doing public speaking or debating

Have you liked and done well in any of the following school subjects?

* Sociology
* Geographic Information Systems
* Statistics
* Research Methods
* Architectural History
* Finance
* Public Speaking
* Government

Are you able to

* Communicate information and ideas in writing so others will understand?
* Listen to and understand information and ideas presented through spoken words and sentences?
* Read and understand information and ideas presented in writing?

Would you work in places such as

* Business offices?
* Government offices?
* Streets and highways?

What skills and knowledges do you need for this kind of work?

For most of these jobs, you need these skills:

* Writing—communicating effectively in writing as appropriate for the needs of the audience
* Speaking—talking to others to convey information effectively
* Mathematics—using mathematics to solve problems

These knowledges are important in most of these jobs:

* Geography—principles and methods for describing the features of land, sea, and air masses, including their physical characteristics; locations; interrelationships; and distribution of plant, animal, and human life
* Design—design techniques, tools, and principles involved in production of precision technical plans, blueprints, drawings, and models
* Clerical Practices—administrative and clerical procedures and systems such as word processing, managing files and records, stenography and transcription, designing forms, and other office procedures and terminology
* Law and Government—laws, legal codes, court procedures, precedents, government regulations, executive orders, agency rules, and the democratic political process
* History and Archeology—historical events and their causes, indicators, and effects on civilizations and cultures

* Mathematics—arithmetic, algebra, geometry, calculus, and statistics and their applications
* Building and Construction—the materials, methods, and tools involved in the construction or repair of houses; buildings; or other structures, such as highways and roads

What else should you consider about this kind of work?

Most of these workers are employed by local governments. Some work for state or federal government; others work for architectural or engineering firms or specialized consulting companies. Government employees usually need to pass a civil service exam.

Most of the work takes place in offices during normal business hours, but some field work is required for research, and workers may need to attend evening meetings with the public. Sometimes there is pressure to meet a deadline or from political opposition.

The job outlook is generally good, with better opportunities in private industry than in often-cash-strapped governments.

How can you prepare for jobs of this kind?

Occupations in this group usually require from one year (for aides) to less than ten years (for planners).

Although some resourceful aides may get into this field with only a few years of college, a bachelor's degree is usually expected. Courses in geography, economics, marketing, and statistics are helpful, and a degree from an accredited planning program is ideal. Skill with geographic information systems and other computer-based resources is growing in importance.

For planners, a master's degree from an accredited planning program is the usual credential, especially for government jobs. Course work in marketing, public relations, law, architecture, finance, and geographic information systems is helpful. Student internships are also valuable as a way to gain experience.

How much education or training is required for the jobs in this Work Group?

For descriptions of these jobs, see Part 2.

Associate degree

* City Planning Aides

Master's degree

* Urban and Regional Planners

07.03 Regulations Enforcement

Workers in this group protect the public by assuring that people are not exposed to unsafe products, facilities, or practices. They investigate business practices; examine records; and inspect materials, products, workplaces, utilities, and transportation equipment for compliance with government regulations or conformance to company policies.

What kind of work would you do?

Your work activities would depend on your job. For example, you might

* Collect samples of air, water, gases, and solids in order to determine radioactivity levels of contamination.
* Direct crews working on firelines during forest fires.
* Examine immigration applications, visas, and passports and interview persons in order to determine eligibility for admission, residence, and travel in the U.S.
* Examine vehicles for damage and drive vehicle to detect malfunctions.
* Inspect drawings, designs, and specifications for piping, boilers, and other vessels.
* Inspect government-owned equipment and materials in hands of private contractors to prevent waste, damage, theft, and other irregularities.
* Inspect horticultural products or livestock to detect harmful disease, infestation, or growth rate.
* Investigate air accidents and complaints to determine causes.
* Investigate complaints and suspected violations concerning illegal dumping, pollution, pesticides, product quality, or labeling laws.
* Meet with persons involved in equal opportunity complaints in order to verify case information and to arbitrate and settle disputes.

What things about you point to this kind of work?

Is it important for you to

* Have steady employment?
* Have supervisors who back up workers with management?

Have you enjoyed any of the following as a hobby or leisure-time activity?

* Reading detective stories; watching television detective shows
* Instructing family members in observing traffic regulations

Have you liked and done well in any of the following school subjects?

* Law Enforcement
* Public Health
* Biology
* Physical Science
* Government
* Bookkeeping
* Safety Regulations
* Criminal Investigating
* Customs Law

Are you able to

* Tell when something is wrong or is likely to go wrong?
* Identify or detect a known pattern that is hidden in other distracting material?
* Remember information such as words, numbers, pictures, and procedures?

Would you work in places such as

* Government offices?
* Business offices?
* Ships and boats?
* Ports and harbors?
* Forests?
* Waterworks and light and power plants?
* Factories and plants?
* Office buildings?
* Farms?
* Railroad tracks and yards?
* Hospitals and nursing homes?

What skills and knowledges do you need for this kind of work?

For most of these jobs, you need these skills:

* Systems Analysis—determining how a system should work and how changes in conditions, operations, and the environment will affect outcomes
* Systems Evaluation—identifying measures or indicators of system performance and the actions needed to improve or correct performance relative to the goals of the system
* Writing—communicating effectively in writing as appropriate for the needs of the audience

These knowledges are important in most of these jobs:

* Law and Government—laws, legal codes, court procedures, precedents, government regulations, executive orders, agency rules, and the democratic political process
* Public Safety and Security—relevant equipment, policies, procedures, and strategies to promote effective local, state, or national security operations for the protection of people, data, property, and institutions
* Food Production—techniques and equipment for planting, growing, and harvesting food products (both plant and animal) for consumption, including storage/handling techniques

What else should you consider about this kind of work?

Many jobs in this group are with local, state, and federal governments. For most government jobs you must pass civil service examinations. Some jobs are with private industry and nonprofit organizations.

Most jobs in the group have regular working hours, although some involve evening or night shift work. Some require travel, usually within the state or metropolitan area, to visit sites that need inspection.

Some work in an office all day; others must go from place to place to inspect licenses and determine compliance of beauty shop operators, food service workers, and so forth. Others are stationed at inspection locations, such as port-of-entry and border crossings.

Job outlook is mixed and is affected by changes in the balance between concern for safety and desire for smaller government. Jobs associated with homeland security may have a better outlook than others.

How can you prepare for jobs of this kind?

Occupations in this group usually require education and/or training ranging from six months to more than ten years.

Some jobs call for prior knowledge of the regulations to be enforced and the procedures to be used. Others demand special training, such as principles of insurance underwriting. Clerical and other workers within a company or government agency are sometimes promoted to positions in this group. Other jobs require skills and knowledge that may be acquired through a mixture of classes and work experience and are demonstrated by special tests. College-level course work in English (especially composition, reporting, and technical writing), government, and history may be useful.

Many of the jobs in this group are in government agencies and are filled by those who qualify through civil service examinations. Some jobs are filled through appointments made by governors, mayors, and other political leaders.

How much education or training is required for the jobs in this Work Group?

For descriptions of these jobs, see Part 2.

Moderate-term on-the-job training

* Fire Inspectors
* Forest Fire Inspectors and Prevention Specialists

Long-term on-the-job training

* Environmental Compliance Inspectors
* Equal Opportunity Representatives and Officers
* Fish and Game Wardens
* Government Property Inspectors and Investigators
* Licensing Examiners and Inspectors
* Mechanical Inspectors
* Pressure Vessel Inspectors

Work experience in a related occupation

* Agricultural Inspectors
* Aviation Inspectors
* Child Support, Missing Persons, and Unemployment Insurance Fraud Investigators
* Immigration and Customs Inspectors
* Marine Cargo Inspectors
* Motor Vehicle Inspectors
* Railroad Inspectors

Associate degree

* Nuclear Monitoring Technicians

Bachelor's degree

* Financial Examiners
* Tax Examiners, Collectors, and Revenue Agents

Master's degree

* Occupational Health and Safety Specialists

07.04 Public Administration Clerical Support

Workers in this group perform clerical tasks that contribute to the functioning of courts, city governments, and licensing bureaus. They schedule court dockets and meetings; obtain and record information from judges, attorneys, jurors, and license applicants; draft bylaws and agendas; answer inquiries from the public; issue licenses; and collect fees.

What kind of work would you do?

Your work activities would depend on your job. For example, you might

* Collect prescribed fees for licenses.
* Conduct and score oral, visual, written, or performance tests to determine applicant qualifications and notify applicants of their scores.
* Participate in the administration of municipal elections, including preparation and distribution of ballots, appointment and training of election officers, and tabulation and certification of results.
* Plan and direct the maintenance, filing, safekeeping, and computerization of all municipal documents.
* Record and edit the minutes of meetings; then distribute them to appropriate officials and staff members.
* Record case dispositions, court orders, and arrangements made for payment of court fees.
* Respond to requests for information from the public, other municipalities, state officials, and state and federal legislative offices.
* Search files and contact witnesses, attorneys, and litigants in order to obtain information for the court.

What things about you point to this kind of work?

Is it important for you to

* Have supervisors who back up workers with management?
* Be busy all the time?

Have you enjoyed any of the following as a hobby or leisure-time activity?

* Serving as secretary of a club or other organization
* Writing letters and e-mails to friends and family

Have you liked and done well in any of the following school subjects?

* Clerical Practices/Office Practices
* Legal Terminology
* Business Computer Applications
* Government

Are you able to

* See details at close range?
* Identify and understand the speech of another person?
* Communicate information and ideas in writing so others will understand?

Would you work in places such as

* Courthouses?
* Government offices?

What skills and knowledges do you need for this kind of work?

For most of these jobs, you need these skills:

* Service Orientation—actively looking for ways to help people
* Active Listening—giving full attention to what other people are saying, taking time to understand the points being made, asking questions as appropriate, and not interrupting at inappropriate times
* Social Perceptiveness—being aware of others' reactions and understanding why they react as they do

These knowledges are important in most of these jobs:

* Clerical Practices—administrative and clerical procedures and systems such as word processing, managing files and records, stenography and transcription, designing forms, and other office procedures and terminology
* Law and Government—laws, legal codes, court procedures, precedents, government regulations, executive orders, agency rules, and the democratic political process

* Foreign Language—the structure and content of a foreign (non-English) language, including the meaning and spelling of words, rules of composition and grammar, and pronunciation

What else should you consider about this kind of work?

These workers are employed by municipalities of all sizes. Generally the workers in smaller jurisdictions need to handle a greater variety of duties. Most of these workers need to pass a civil service exam.

The work is mostly done in comfortable offices during a 40-hour work week, although some must attend town meetings that are held in the evening.

The job outlook is generally good, in part because of the increase in court cases, although automation has eliminated some jobs.

How can you prepare for jobs of this kind?

Occupations in this group usually require education and/or training ranging from six months to less than four years.

A high school diploma or its equal is the usual requirement, although college course work in English, math, and government can be helpful. For some court clerk positions, a two-year degree from a business or college may be required. Most of the specific work tasks are learned on the job, but experience as a paralegal can be helpful in getting a job as a court clerk.

How much education or training is required for the jobs in this Work Group?

For descriptions of these jobs, see Part 2.

Short-term on-the-job training

* Court Clerks
* License Clerks
* Municipal Clerks

Postsecondary vocational training

* Court Reporters

08 Health Science

An interest in helping people and animals be healthy. You can satisfy this interest by working in a health care team as a doctor, therapist, or nurse. You might specialize in one of the many different parts of the body (such as the teeth or eyes) or in one of the many different types of care. Or you may wish to be a generalist who deals with the whole patient. If you like technology, you might find satisfaction working with X rays or new methods of diagnosis. You might work with healthy people, helping them eat right. If you enjoy working with animals, you might care for them and keep them healthy.

08.01 Managerial Work in Medical and Health Services

08.02 Medicine and Surgery

08.03 Dentistry

08.04 Health Specialties

08.05 Animal Care

08.06 Medical Technology

08.07 Medical Therapy

08.08 Patient Care and Assistance

08.09 Health Protection and Promotion

08.01 Managerial Work in Medical and Health Services

Workers in this group manage health care activities. Some primarily supervise doctors, nurses, therapists, and other health care workers. Others provide leadership for all aspects of a hospital or nursing home, including finance and physical facilities. Some make decisions about how an autopsy is to be conducted. Others supervise workers who care for animals in settings such as labs, race tracks, and animal shelters. They do planning, budgeting, staffing, and evaluation of outcomes.

What kind of work would you do?

Your work activities would depend on your job. For example, you might

* Direct investigations into circumstances of deaths to fix responsibility for accidental, violent, or unexplained death.
* Direct, supervise, and evaluate work activities of medical, nursing, technical, clerical, service, maintenance, and other personnel.
* Establish work schedules and assignments for staff according to workload, space, and equipment availability.
* Inspect facilities and recommend building or equipment modifications to ensure emergency readiness and compliance to access, safety, and sanitation regulations.
* Investigate complaints of animal neglect or cruelty and follow up on complaints appearing to justify prosecution.
* Monitor animal care, inspect facilities to identify problems, and discuss solutions with workers.
* Monitor the use of diagnostic services, inpatient beds, facilities, and staff to ensure effective use of resources and assess the need for additional staff, equipment, and services.
* Provide information concerning death circumstance to relatives of deceased.

What things about you point to this kind of work?

Is it important for you to

* Give directions and instructions to others?
* Have steady employment?
* Make decisions on your own?
* Plan your work with little supervision?

Have you enjoyed any of the following as a hobby or leisure-time activity?

* Serving as a leader of a scouting or other group
* Helping run a school or community fair or carnival
* Helping sick relatives, friends, and neighbors
* Nursing sick pets
* Serving as a volunteer in a hospital, nursing home, or retirement home

Have you liked and done well in any of the following school subjects?

* Management
* Accounting
* Health
* Business Law
* Finance
* Personnel Management
* Business Writing
* Biology
* Public Health
* Chemistry
* Laboratory Science

Are you able to

* Tell when something is wrong or is likely to go wrong?
* Combine pieces of information to form general rules or conclusions?
* Quickly make sense of, combine, and organize information into meaningful patterns?
* Identify or detect a known pattern that is hidden in other distracting material?
* Quickly and accurately compare similarities and differences among sets of letters, numbers, objects, pictures, or patterns?
* Apply general rules to specific problems to produce answers that make sense?
* Communicate information and ideas in writing so others will understand?

Would you work in places such as

* Hospitals and nursing homes?
* Animal hospitals, boarding kennels, and grooming parlors?
* Business offices?
* Zoos and aquariums?

What skills and knowledges do you need for this kind of work?

For most of these jobs, you need these skills:

* Management of Personnel Resources—motivating, developing, and directing people as they work, identifying the best people for the job
* Management of Financial Resources—determining how money will be spent to get the work done and accounting for these expenditures
* Science—using scientific rules and methods to solve problems
* Management of Material Resources—obtaining and seeing to the appropriate use of equipment, facilities, and materials needed to do certain work
* Speaking—talking to others to convey information effectively

* Systems Evaluation—identifying measures or indicators of system performance and the actions needed to improve or correct performance relative to the goals of the system
* Time Management—managing one's own time and the time of others

These knowledges are important in most of these jobs:

* Medicine and Dentistry—the information and techniques needed to diagnose and treat human injuries, diseases, and deformities; this includes symptoms, treatment alternatives, drug properties and interactions, and preventive health care measures
* Biology—plant and animal organisms and their tissues, cells, functions, interdependencies, and interactions with each other and the environment
* Administration and Management—business and management principles involved in strategic planning, resource allocation, human resources modeling, leadership techniques, production methods, and coordination of people and resources
* Chemistry—the chemical composition, structure, and properties of substances and of the chemical processes and transformations that they undergo; this includes uses of chemicals and their danger signs, production techniques, and disposal methods
* Personnel and Human Resources—principles and procedures for personnel recruitment, selection, training, compensation and benefits, labor relations and negotiation, and personnel information systems
* Philosophy and Theology—different philosophical systems and religions; this includes their basic principles, values, ethics, ways of thinking, customs, practices, and impact on human culture
* Therapy and Counseling—principles, methods, and procedures for diagnosis, treatment, and rehabilitation of physical and mental dysfunctions and for career counseling and guidance

What else should you consider about this kind of work?

These workers implement policies set by governing bodies and try to keep health care services excellent while containing costs. Sometimes they are under a lot of pressure from different parties—governing bodies, health care workers, patients, government officials—who have conflicting goals. Health care goes on around the clock, and these workers may be "on call" for emergency situations. The work can give great satisfaction because it contributes to health and even saves lives.

The overall outlook for these occupations is good. The growth of managed care and the development of expensive high-tech procedures such as organ transplantation have increased the need for good management. Although most of the jobs are in hospitals, consolidation and centralization of hospitals and the aging of the population will mean that the greatest growth will be in home health agencies and long-term care facilities.

Like any managers, these need to keep abreast of new management technologies, especially those using computer applications. In addition, the workers need to keep their medical knowledge and skills up to date.

How can you prepare for jobs of this kind?

Occupations in this group usually require education and/or training ranging from one year to less than ten years.

For most generalist jobs in health care management, standard preparation is a master's degree in health services administration, public health, public administration, or business management. The master's program may include supervised experience working in administration. Some workers get this managerial degree after getting a professional degree as a doctor, nurse, or therapist, but others do their undergraduate work in business or the liberal arts. Health service coordinators may begin with a bachelor's in health services administration or business management.

Managers of nursing care facilities must pass a specialized training program, pass a licensing exam, and get continuing education.

Animal care workers may advance to a supervisory position after some work experience and perhaps some courses in management.

High school courses in math, chemistry, biology, and writing are very useful.

How much education or training is required for the jobs in this Work Group?

For descriptions of these jobs, see Part 2.

Work experience in a related occupation

* Coroners

Associate degree

* First-Line Supervisors and Manager/Supervisors—Animal Care Workers, Except Livestock

Work experience plus degree

* Medical and Health Services Managers

08.02 Medicine and Surgery

Workers in this group diagnose and treat human diseases, disorders, and injuries. Some are professionals who make life-and-death decisions, perform invasive procedures, and prescribe drugs. They may specialize or work in general practice. Many are self-employed and have their own offices. Other workers in this group provide care under the supervision of professionals.

What kind of work would you do?

Your work activities would depend on your job. For example, you might

* Administer anesthetic or sedation during medical procedures, using local, intravenous, spinal, or caudal methods.
* Advise patients and community members concerning diet, activity, hygiene, and disease prevention.
* Analyze records, reports, test results, or examination information to diagnose medical condition of patient.
* Compound and dispense medications as prescribed by doctors and dentists by calculating, weighing, measuring, and mixing ingredients or oversee these activities.
* Counsel outpatients and other patients during office visits.
* Deliver babies.
* Direct and coordinate activities of nurses, assistants, specialists, residents, and other medical staff.
* Establish and maintain patient profiles, including lists of medications taken by individual patients.
* Explain treatment procedures, medications, diets, and physicians' instructions to patients.
* Interpret diagnostic test results for deviations from normal.

What things about you point to this kind of work?

Is it important for you to

* Have work where you do things for other people?
* Be looked up to by others in your company and your community?
* Have steady employment?
* Have co-workers who are easy to get along with?
* Get a feeling of accomplishment?
* Be paid well in comparison with other workers?
* Make use of your individual abilities?

Have you enjoyed any of the following as a hobby or leisure-time activity?

* Reading medical or scientific magazines
* Helping sick relatives, friends, and neighbors
* Experimenting with a chemistry set
* Serving as a volunteer in a hospital, nursing home, or retirement home

Have you liked and done well in any of the following school subjects?

* Biology
* Chemistry
* Health
* Biochemistry
* Anatomy
* Psychology
* Pharmacology
* Anesthesia
* Abnormal Psychology
* Laboratory Science
* Nursing Care
* Health Law

Are you able to

* Tell when something is wrong or is likely to go wrong?
* Combine pieces of information to form general rules or conclusions?
* Keep your hand and arm steady while moving your arm or while holding your arm and hand in one position?
* Quickly move your hand, your hand together with your arm, or your two hands to grasp, manipulate, or assemble objects?
* Communicate information and ideas in speaking so others will understand?
* Quickly make sense of, combine, and organize information into meaningful patterns?
* Make precisely coordinated movements of the fingers of one or both hands to grasp, manipulate, or assemble very small objects?

Would you work in places such as

* Doctors' and dentists' offices and clinics?
* Hospitals and nursing homes?
* Drug stores?

What skills and knowledges do you need for this kind of work?

For most of these jobs, you need these skills:

* Science—using scientific rules and methods to solve problems
* Active Learning—understanding the implications of new information for both current and future problem solving and decision making
* Service Orientation—actively looking for ways to help people
* Reading Comprehension—understanding written sentences and paragraphs in work-related documents
* Social Perceptiveness—being aware of others' reactions and understanding why they react as they do
* Instructing—teaching others how to do something
* Active Listening—giving full attention to what other people are saying, taking time to understand the points being made, asking questions as appropriate, and not interrupting at inappropriate times

These knowledges are important in most of these jobs:

* Medicine and Dentistry—the information and techniques needed to diagnose and treat human injuries, diseases, and deformities; this includes symptoms, treatment alternatives, drug properties and interactions, and preventive health care measures
* Biology—plant and animal organisms and their tissues, cells, functions, interdependencies, and interactions with each other and the environment
* Therapy and Counseling—principles, methods, and procedures for diagnosis, treatment, and rehabilitation of physical and mental dysfunctions and for career counseling and guidance
* Chemistry—the chemical composition, structure, and properties of substances and of the chemical processes

and transformations that they undergo; this includes uses of chemicals and their danger signs, production techniques, and disposal methods

* Psychology—human behavior and performance; individual differences in ability, personality, and interests; learning and motivation; psychological research methods; and the assessment and treatment of behavioral and affective disorders

* English Language—the structure and content of the English language, including the meaning and spelling of words, rules of composition, and grammar

* Customer and Personal Service—principles and processes for providing customer and personal services; this includes customer needs assessment, meeting quality standards for services, and evaluation of customer satisfaction

What else should you consider about this kind of work?

These workers are employed in such places as hospitals, clinics, health facilities, industrial plants, pharmacies, and government agencies.

People have medical needs at all hours of the day or night, so physicians, physician assistants, and surgical technologists are commonly "on call" for nights and weekends on a rotating basis. Registered nurses working in hospitals and long-term care facilities usually are expected to work evening, night, and weekend shifts. (In industrial and educational settings and doctors' offices, they usually have more conventional hours.) Many pharmacists and pharmacy technicians also do shift work.

All of the workers in this group need to take precautions in dealing with infectious agents and controlled substances. Most of them often deal with people who are in pain or dying. Despite the emotional drain, there is great satisfaction from relieving pain and helping people recover their health.

The educational and training program for physicians is extremely long, is highly stressful at times, and leaves most new physicians burdened with years of debt. Paperwork is increasing in all medical fields, and HMOs sometimes limit the therapies that physicians can apply. The outlook for physicians is mixed. Best opportunities will be in rural and low-income areas. The trend is for physicians to take salaried jobs in group practices and clinics.

Registered nurses often spend a lot of time standing and walking, and sometimes they must raise patients from bed. The job outlook is very good, especially in home health care and in nursing homes.

The outlook for physician assistants is very good because they are seen as a way of keeping down health care costs. The aging of the population and the development of new surgical procedures and drugs will cause a steady demand for surgical technologists, pharmacists, and pharmacy technicians. Best opportunities for pharmacists will be in long-term and home care settings and in research.

How can you prepare for jobs of this kind?

Education and/or training requirements for occupations in this group vary widely, from one year to more than ten years. These educational programs include supervised work with patients, especially toward the later parts of the curriculum.

Physicians typically complete a bachelor's degree plus four years of medical school plus three to seven years of internship and residency, depending on the specialty selected.

Some registered nurses take a two- or three-year associate degree program at a community college or technical school. Others get a bachelor of science in nursing in a four-year program. A small number enter through a two- to three-year diploma program at a hospital. Studies in all programs include biological, physical, and social sciences, as well as nursing theory and practice. Graduates of four-year baccalaureate programs qualify for general duty nursing, positions in public health agencies, or advancement to supervisory and administrative work.

Physician assistants prepare with a program that typically lasts two years. Usually they already have a previous two- or four-year degree, and many have experience working in the health care field.

Pharmacists obtain at least six years of education beyond high school to get their doctor of pharmacy degree. Most colleges of pharmacy require applicants to have two years of prior college education, with coursework in science, math, and other subjects. Those who are interested in research may pursue a master's or a PhD.

Pharmacy technicians are trained in programs that vary from six months to two years and may be given by an employer or in a more formal education setting.

Surgical technologists get nine months to two years of training, less if they have a background in nursing or military training.

Medical assistants may learn their skills several ways, including on-the-job training or a program at a technical school or community college lasting from one to two years.

For most jobs in this group, some useful high school courses are math concepts; English literature and composition; biological, social, and behavioral sciences; health; first aid; and cardiopulmonary resuscitation. Volunteer work in a hospital or health care facility is also recommended.

How much education or training is required for the jobs in this Work Group?

For descriptions of these jobs, see Part 2.

Moderate-term on-the-job training

* Medical Assistants
* Pharmacy Aides
* Pharmacy Technicians

Postsecondary vocational training

* Surgical Technologists

© 2006 JIST Works

Associate degree

* Medical Transcriptionists
* Registered Nurses

Bachelor's degree

* Physician Assistants

First professional degree

* Anesthesiologists
* Family and General Practitioners
* Internists, General
* Obstetricians and Gynecologists
* Pediatricians, General
* Pharmacists
* Psychiatrists
* Surgeons

08.03 Dentistry

Workers in this group provide health care for patients' teeth and mouth tissues. Most dentists are general practitioners, performing a variety of oral-care tasks. Others specialize: Orthodontists straighten teeth; prosthodontists make artificial teeth and dentures; oral and maxillofacial surgeons operate on the mouth and jaws. Dental hygienists clean teeth and teach people how to take care of their teeth. Dental assistants provide chairside help, get the patient and equipment ready, and keep records.

What kind of work would you do?

Your work activities would depend on your job. For example, you might

* Apply fluorides and other cavity-preventing agents to arrest dental decay.
* Bleach discolored teeth in order to brighten and whiten them.
* Clean calcareous deposits, accretions, and stains from teeth and beneath margins of gums, using dental instruments.
* Examine teeth, gums, and related tissues, using dental instruments, X rays, and other diagnostic equipment, to evaluate dental health, diagnose diseases or abnormalities, and plan appropriate treatments.
* Fit dental appliances in patients' mouths in order to alter the position and relationship of teeth and jaws and to realign teeth.
* Instruct patients in oral hygiene and plaque control programs.
* Perform surgery to prepare the mouth for dental implants.
* Place veneers onto teeth in order to conceal defects.
* Remove impacted, damaged, and non-restorable teeth.
* Take and record medical and dental histories and vital signs of patients.

What things about you point to this kind of work?

Is it important for you to

* Have work where you do things for other people?
* Be looked up to by others in your company and your community?
* Receive recognition for the work you do?
* Have steady employment?
* Get a feeling of accomplishment?
* Be paid well in comparison with other workers?
* Make use of your individual abilities?

Have you enjoyed any of the following as a hobby or leisure-time activity?

* Reading medical or scientific magazines
* Helping sick relatives, friends, and neighbors
* Performing experiments for a science fair
* Serving as a volunteer in a hospital, nursing home, or retirement home

Have you liked and done well in any of the following school subjects?

* Biology
* Chemistry
* Health
* Biochemistry
* Dental Anatomy
* Oral Anatomy
* Oral Development
* Oral Hygiene
* Pharmacology
* Laboratory Science

Are you able to

* Keep your hand and arm steady while moving your arm or while holding your arm and hand in one position?
* Make precisely coordinated movements of the fingers of one or both hands to grasp, manipulate, or assemble very small objects?
* Quickly and repeatedly adjust the controls of a machine or a vehicle to exact positions?

Would you work in places such as

* Doctors' and dentists' offices and clinics?

What skills and knowledges do you need for this kind of work?

For most of these jobs, you need these skills:

* Science—using scientific rules and methods to solve problems
* Reading Comprehension—understanding written sentences and paragraphs in work-related documents
* Service Orientation—actively looking for ways to help people
* Active Learning—understanding the implications of new information for both current and future problem solving and decision making

* Critical Thinking—using logic and reasoning to identify the strengths and weaknesses of alternative solutions, conclusions, or approaches to problems
* Equipment Selection—determining the kind of tools and equipment needed to do a job
* Technology Design—generating or adapting equipment and technology to serve user needs

These knowledges are important in most of these jobs:

* Medicine and Dentistry—the information and techniques needed to diagnose and treat human injuries, diseases, and deformities; this includes symptoms, treatment alternatives, drug properties and interactions, and preventive health care measures
* Biology—plant and animal organisms and their tissues, cells, functions, interdependencies, and interactions with each other and the environment
* Chemistry—the chemical composition, structure, and properties of substances and of the chemical processes and transformations that they undergo; this includes uses of chemicals and their danger signs, production techniques, and disposal methods

What else should you consider about this kind of work?

Some dentists work in hospitals and research, but most dentists are solo practitioners with a small staff of dental hygienists and assistants. They may work evenings or weekends to suit their patients' schedules. They may get considerably in debt to obtain their education and set up a practice. They need emotional stability to deal with patients who are in pain or discomfort. As an aging population will need more dental services, the job outlook for dentists is good, even though some routine and less-profitable tasks are likely to be given to hygienists and assistants.

Dentists and dental hygienists sometimes find chairside work physically demanding. Both need to take precautions to protect themselves from X rays and from communicable diseases.

Many dental hygienists' jobs are for only a few days a week, perhaps including weekends, so many workers hold jobs at more than one dental practice. Most work in private dental offices, but some are hired by school systems, HMOs, and long-term health care facilities. The employment outlook is excellent.

The dental assistant is sometimes called the dentist's "third hand." These workers often have a wide variety of duties, ranging from developing X rays to accepting payment for services. Job turnover will provide many openings in the occupation, and the outlook for employment is excellent.

How can you prepare for jobs of this kind?

Education and/or training requirements for occupations in this group vary widely, from one year to more than ten years. All the educational programs offer a mix of classroom study and supervised clinical practice.

Dentists qualify for their licenses by graduating from an accredited dental school and passing exams. Students usually get a bachelor's degree before being admitted to dental school, which takes about four years. It begins with classroom study and laboratory work and involves increasing amounts of supervised practice on patients. Specializing in orthodontics or some other field requires additional years of education and perhaps another licensing exam.

Dental hygienists are also licensed and must have an accredited education and pass an exam. Most dental hygiene programs take two years and grant an associate degree. Some prefer applicants to have a prior year of college. A bachelor's degree is usually needed for those who want to go into research, teaching, or clinical practice in an educational setting.

Most dental assistants learn on the job, but certification programs are available lasting a year or less.

For all of these occupations, high school courses in biology and chemistry are useful. Those planning to be dentists should also study math, and those planning to be dental assistants will be helped by learning office procedures either in class or through a part-time clerical job.

How much education or training is required for the jobs in this Work Group?

For descriptions of these jobs, see Part 2.

Moderate-term on-the-job training

* Dental Assistants

Associate degree

* Dental Hygienists

First professional degree

* Dentists, General
* Oral and Maxillofacial Surgeons
* Orthodontists
* Prosthodontists

08.04 Health Specialties

Workers in this group are health professionals who specialize in certain parts of the human body. Optometrists diagnose various diseases, disorders, and injuries of the eye. Podiatrists maintain the health of the feet and lower extremities. Chiropractors adjust the spinal column and other joints to prevent disease and correct abnormalities of the human body believed to be caused by interference with the nervous system.

What kind of work would you do?

Your work activities would depend on your job. For example, you might

* Counsel patients about nutrition, exercise, sleeping habits, stress management, and other matters.

* Diagnose diseases and deformities of the foot using medical histories, physical examinations, X rays, and laboratory test results.
* Examine eyes, using observation, instruments, and pharmaceutical agents, to determine visual acuity and perception, focus, and coordination and to diagnose diseases and other abnormalities such as glaucoma or color-blindness.
* Obtain and record patients' medical histories.
* Perform a series of manual adjustments to the spine or other articulations of the body in order to correct the musculoskeletal system.
* Prescribe medications, corrective devices, physical therapy, or surgery.
* Prescribe, supply, fit, and adjust eyeglasses, contact lenses, and other vision aids.
* Treat bone, muscle, and joint disorders affecting the feet.

What things about you point to this kind of work?

Is it important for you to

* Have work where you do things for other people?
* Receive recognition for the work you do?
* Make decisions on your own?
* Be looked up to by others in your company and your community?
* Be paid well in comparison with other workers?
* Plan your work with little supervision?
* Get a feeling of accomplishment?

Have you enjoyed any of the following as a hobby or leisure-time activity?

* Serving as a volunteer in a hospital, nursing home, or retirement home
* Reading medical or scientific magazines
* Helping sick relatives, friends, and neighbors

Have you liked and done well in any of the following school subjects?

* Biology
* Chemistry
* Health
* Biochemistry
* Anatomy, Specialized/Advanced
* Pharmacology
* Optics
* Psychology
* Laboratory Science

Are you able to

* Tell when something is wrong or is likely to go wrong?
* Make precisely coordinated movements of the fingers of one or both hands to grasp, manipulate, or assemble very small objects?
* Combine pieces of information to form general rules or conclusions?
* Quickly move your hand, your hand together with your arm, or your two hands to grasp, manipulate, or assemble objects?
* Quickly make sense of, combine, and organize information into meaningful patterns?
* Keep your hand and arm steady while moving your arm or while holding your arm and hand in one position?
* Quickly and repeatedly adjust the controls of a machine or a vehicle to exact positions?

Would you work in places such as

* Doctors' and dentists' offices and clinics?
* Hospitals and nursing homes?

What skills and knowledges do you need for this kind of work?

For most of these jobs, you need these skills:

* Judgment and Decision Making—considering the relative costs and benefits of potential actions to choose the most appropriate one
* Reading Comprehension—understanding written sentences and paragraphs in work-related documents
* Active Learning—understanding the implications of new information for both current and future problem solving and decision making
* Active Listening—giving full attention to what other people are saying, taking time to understand the points being made, asking questions as appropriate, and not interrupting at inappropriate times
* Science—using scientific rules and methods to solve problems
* Service Orientation—actively looking for ways to help people
* Complex Problem Solving—identifying complex problems and reviewing related information to develop and evaluate options and implement solutions

These knowledges are important in most of these jobs:

* Medicine and Dentistry—the information and techniques needed to diagnose and treat human injuries, diseases, and deformities; this includes symptoms, treatment alternatives, drug properties and interactions, and preventive health care measures
* Biology—plant and animal organisms and their tissues, cells, functions, interdependencies, and interactions with each other and the environment
* Therapy and Counseling—principles, methods, and procedures for diagnosis, treatment, and rehabilitation of physical and mental dysfunctions and for career counseling and guidance
* Chemistry—the chemical composition, structure, and properties of substances and of the chemical processes and transformations that they undergo; this includes uses of chemicals and their danger signs, production techniques, and disposal methods
* Psychology—human behavior and performance; individual differences in ability, personality, and interests;

learning and motivation; psychological research methods; and the assessment and treatment of behavioral and affective disorders

* Physics—physical principles and laws and their interrelationships and applications to understanding fluid, material, and atmospheric dynamics and mechanical, electrical, atomic, and subatomic structures and processes

* English Language—the structure and content of the English language, including the meaning and spelling of words, rules of composition, and grammar

What else should you consider about this kind of work?

These workers are employed in private practices, vision-care chains, hospitals, and long-term health care facilities.

The occupations in this group require a long education that can create considerable debt. To avoid the added expense of setting up a solo practice, an increasing number of new professionals go into partnerships or work as salaried employees of existing practices, HMOs, retail optical stores, etc. All workers in this group work in fairly comfortable surroundings, although they may have to spend some time on their feet. The work week is about 40 hours, but it may include evening and weekend hours for the convenience of patients.

Optometrists should not be confused with ophthalmologists, who are MDs who specialize in the eye and may do surgery. As the population ages, the employment outlook for optometrists is fairly good.

Podiatrists diagnose and treat a wide variety of foot problems, but some may specialize in surgery, orthopedics, or sports medicine. Most work in private practice and supervise a small staff. The outlook for jobs is fair, because although an aging and physically active population will need more care for their feet, the occupation has a low turnover. Another way of looking at this is that the work is satisfying and few workers retire early. Podiatrists often see results more quickly than other medical practitioners, and they are more likely to work fairly normal hours.

Chiropractors follow a holistic philosophy that treats the whole patient, emphasizes the body's ability to restore itself, and aims to encourage a healthful lifestyle. Some other therapeutic practices, such as naturopathy, share this outlook. As the baby boomer generation ages and needs more health care, their interest in alternative health therapies is going to mean a good job outlook for chiropractors.

How can you prepare for jobs of this kind?

All the occupations in this group require education and/or training that takes from eight to ten years.

Optometrists, podiatrists, and chiropractors all must complete a long educational and training process to qualify for their state licensing exam. First, they complete some undergraduate work that emphasizes biology, chemistry, math, and perhaps physics. For optometrists and podiatrists, this is usually a bachelor's degree; for chiropractors,

at least two years must be completed, and many states require a bachelor's. The professional program at a school of optometry, podiatric medicine, or chiropractic medicine takes about four years and is a combination of classroom and laboratory instruction, with supervised work with patients in the last two years. Most podiatrists also complete one to three years of a hospital residency program with extensive clinical work.

How much education or training is required for the jobs in this Work Group?

For descriptions of these jobs, see Part 2.

First professional degree

* Chiropractors
* Optometrists
* Podiatrists

08.05 Animal Care

Workers in this group care for and train animals of many kinds.

What kind of work would you do?

Your work activities would depend on your job. For example, you might

* Administer anesthetics during surgery and monitor the effects on animals.
* Anesthetize and inoculate animals according to instructions.
* Conduct postmortem studies and analyses to determine the causes of animals' deaths.
* Discuss with clients their pets' grooming needs.
* Examine and observe animals in order to detect signs of illness, disease, or injury.
* Feed and water animals and clean and disinfect pens, cages, yards, and hutches.
* Saddle and shoe animals.
* Select animals to be bred, and semen specimens to be used, according to knowledge of animals, genealogies, traits, and desired offspring characteristics.
* Train and rehearse animals according to scripts for motion picture, television, film, stage, or circus performances.
* Treat sick or injured animals by prescribing medication, setting bones, dressing wounds, or performing surgery.

What things about you point to this kind of work?

Is it important for you to

* Be busy all the time?
* Have something different to do every day?

Have you enjoyed any of the following as a hobby or leisure-time activity?

* Nursing sick pets
* Raising or caring for animals

* Reading medical or scientific magazines
* Training dogs or other animals to perform on command
* Breeding animals

Have you liked and done well in any of the following school subjects?

* Biology
* Chemistry
* Biochemistry
* Veterinary Sciences
* Animal Breeding
* Anatomy, Specialized/Advanced
* Pharmacology
* Animal Grooming
* Laboratory Science
* Animal Obedience Training
* Genetics

Are you able to

* Tell when something is wrong or is likely to go wrong?
* Coordinate the movement of your arms, legs, and torso together when the whole body is in motion?
* Bend, stretch, twist, or reach with your body, arms, and/or legs?

Would you work in places such as

* Animal hospitals, boarding kennels, and grooming parlors?
* Farms?
* Laboratories?
* Amusement parks, circuses, and carnivals?
* Zoos and aquariums?
* Fish hatcheries?

What skills and knowledges do you need for this kind of work?

For most of these jobs, you need these skills:

* Instructing—teaching others how to do something
* Science—using scientific rules and methods to solve problems
* Management of Material Resources—obtaining and seeing to the appropriate use of equipment, facilities, and materials needed to do certain work

These knowledges are important in most of these jobs:

* Biology—plant and animal organisms and their tissues, cells, functions, interdependencies, and interactions with each other and the environment
* Medicine and Dentistry—the information and techniques needed to diagnose and treat human injuries, diseases, and deformities; this includes symptoms, treatment alternatives, drug properties and interactions, and preventive health care measures
* Sales and Marketing—principles and methods for showing, promoting, and selling products or services; this includes marketing strategy and tactics, product demonstrations, sales techniques, and sales control systems

What else should you consider about this kind of work?

Some of these workers are employed by businesses that care for animals, such as pet shops, pet grooming parlors, testing laboratories, animal shelters, and veterinary offices. Some are employed by zoos, aquariums, circuses, and other places where animals are exhibited or used in entertainment acts. Still others work for animal training or obedience schools, stables, kennels, race tracks, or riding academies. A large number of these workers are self-employed, especially animal trainers, breeders, and groomers.

Most veterinarians work in private practice, but some work for farms taking care of livestock, while others work in research or meat inspection jobs.

Expansion in the testing of food and drugs by government agencies will increase the need for people to care for laboratory animals, and increasing numbers of household pets will create jobs for animal groomers, veterinary hospital helpers, and other pet caretakers. The outlook for veterinarians is very good, but competition for admittance to veterinary schools will be intense.

Many places hire beginners for the nonprofessional jobs in this group. Persons who have cared for animals at home or who have farm experience are more likely to be hired.

Most of this work is done at a fixed location on a regular schedule. Many jobs require cleaning up after animals. Jobs with carnivals or circuses require frequent travel.

Temporary work is sometimes available at race tracks and zoos and with traveling carnivals that hire people to help care for their animals in the towns where they perform.

Depending on the animals involved, physical requirements vary. Caring for guinea pigs in a testing laboratory takes much less strength and activity than caring for lions and tigers at a zoo.

How can you prepare for jobs of this kind?

Occupations in this group usually require education and/or training ranging from a short demonstration (e.g., for some animal caretaker jobs) to more than ten years (e.g., for a veterinarian).

Most beginning workers are given a few simple duties; more responsibility is added as these workers gain experience. Some high schools, vocational schools, and junior colleges have courses in animal care. These courses cover the housing and feeding of animals, basic zoology and anatomy, and methods of treating sick or injured animals. Also helpful are training in animal grooming and coursework in animal science and vocational agriculture.

Some of these jobs require special skills. For instance, workers who train or exercise horses must know how to ride, and those who work for aquariums must know how to swim. Zoos and aquariums may expect job applicants to have a bachelor's degree in a life science.

Animal groomers usually learn through an informal apprenticeship.

Veterinarians usually complete a four-year degree before getting four years of professional instruction in a veterinary college. A standardized test is required for admission, and experience working with animals is helpful. Before beginning practice, vets must pass a licensing exam, and they must get continuing education throughout their career.

How much education or training is required for the jobs in this Work Group?

For descriptions of these jobs, see Part 2.

Short-term on-the-job training

* Nonfarm Animal Caretakers
* Veterinary Assistants and Laboratory Animal Caretakers

Moderate-term on-the-job training

* Animal Trainers

Associate degree

* Animal Breeders
* Veterinary Technologists and Technicians

First professional degree

* Veterinarians

08.06 Medical Technology

Workers in this group use technology to detect signs of disease and to assist in treatment of patients. They perform tests requested by physicians and biological researchers, fabricate lenses or prosthetic devices, prepare laboratory or health care equipment, or maintain medical records.

What kind of work would you do?

Your work activities would depend on your job. For example, you might

* Administer radiopharmaceuticals or radiation to patients to detect or treat diseases, using radioisotope equipment, under the direction of a physician.
* Conduct chemical analyses of body fluids, such as blood and urine, using microscope or automatic analyzer to detect abnormalities or diseases, and enter findings into computer.
* Conduct electrocardiogram, phonocardiogram, echocardiogram, stress testing, and other cardiovascular tests to record patients' cardiac activity, using specialized electronic test equipment, recording devices, and laboratory instruments.
* Disinfect and sterilize equipment such as respirators, hospital beds, and oxygen and dialysis equipment, using sterilizers, aerators, and washers.
* Position X-ray equipment and adjust controls to set exposure factors, such as time and distance.

* Process patient admission and discharge documents.
* Repair, rebuild, and modify prosthetic and orthopedic appliances.
* Review and evaluate developed X rays, videotape, or computer-generated information to determine whether images are satisfactory for diagnostic purposes.
* Set up, adjust, calibrate, clean, maintain, and troubleshoot laboratory and field equipment.
* Show customers how to insert, remove, and care for their contact lenses.

What things about you point to this kind of work?

Is it important for you to

* Have steady employment?
* Have work where you do things for other people?

Have you enjoyed any of the following as a hobby or leisure-time activity?

* Experimenting with a chemistry set
* Helping sick relatives, friends, and neighbors
* Reading medical or scientific magazines
* Carving small wooden objects
* Serving as a volunteer in a hospital, nursing home, or retirement home

Have you liked and done well in any of the following school subjects?

* Biology
* Chemistry
* Biochemistry
* Health
* Medical Record Science
* Medical Terminology
* X-Ray Technology
* Hematology
* Physics
* Pathology
* Laboratory Science
* Genetics

Are you able to

* See details at close range?
* Quickly and accurately compare similarities and differences among sets of letters, numbers, objects, pictures, or patterns?
* Identify or detect a known pattern that is hidden in other distracting material?
* Tell when something is wrong or is likely to go wrong?
* Make precisely coordinated movements of the fingers of one or both hands to grasp, manipulate, or assemble very small objects?
* Generate or use different sets of rules for combining or grouping things in different ways?
* Keep your hand and arm steady while moving your arm or while holding your arm and hand in one position?

Would you work in places such as

* Laboratories?
* Hospitals and nursing homes?
* Doctors' and dentists' offices and clinics?
* Artists' studios and craft workshops?
* Fish hatcheries?

What skills and knowledges do you need for this kind of work?

For most of these jobs, you need these skills:

* Instructing—teaching others how to do something
* Service Orientation—actively looking for ways to help people
* Equipment Maintenance—performing routine maintenance on equipment and determining when and what kind of maintenance is needed
* Social Perceptiveness—being aware of others' reactions and understanding why they react as they do
* Learning Strategies—selecting and using training/ instructional methods and procedures appropriate for the situation when learning or teaching new things
* Science—using scientific rules and methods to solve problems
* Quality Control Analysis—conducting tests and inspections of products, services, or processes to evaluate quality or performance

These knowledges are important in most of these jobs:

* Medicine and Dentistry—the information and techniques needed to diagnose and treat human injuries, diseases, and deformities; this includes symptoms, treatment alternatives, drug properties and interactions, and preventive health care measures
* Biology—plant and animal organisms and their tissues, cells, functions, interdependencies, and interactions with each other and the environment
* Customer and Personal Service—principles and processes for providing customer and personal services; this includes customer needs assessment, meeting quality standards for services, and evaluation of customer satisfaction
* Chemistry—the chemical composition, structure, and properties of substances and of the chemical processes and transformations that they undergo; this includes uses of chemicals and their danger signs, production techniques, and disposal methods

What else should you consider about this kind of work?

These workers are employed by hospitals, long-term health care facilities, HMOs, vision care stores, physicians' offices, and specialized diagnostic laboratories and practices.

Like most health care workers, the workers in this group put in about a 40-hour week, with some availability on evenings and weekends to fit patients' schedules. The surroundings are generally pleasant, although some of them have to work with unpleasant chemicals or body fluids. Most of them need to take precautions to avoid exposing themselves or patients to infection or unintended radiation. They may deal with patients who are in pain or seriously ill. They find satisfaction in being part of the health care team that enables people to live longer and fuller lives.

The job outlook is generally good. As the American population grows older, the need for medical tests will increase. Some of the occupations have a large number of workers and therefore will create many jobs through turnover. Jobs are also being created as new technologies permit testing procedures for signs that previously were not detectable. On the other hand, technology is automating some routine laboratory procedures so that they can be done by robots or by fewer workers.

How can you prepare for jobs of this kind?

Occupations in this group usually require education and/or training ranging from six months to less than ten years.

The preparatory programs typically begin with classroom and laboratory work, and for those occupations that involve working directly with patients, there is supervised clinical work.

Clinical laboratory technologists usually prepare with a bachelor's degree in medical technology or a life science, whereas technicians usually have a two-year degree.

Radiologic technologists and technicians both get similar amounts of training—two to four years—but some radiologic technologists get extra training to specialize in ultrasound, CAT scanning, or other forms of noninvasive diagnosis.

Cardiovascular technologists (who test pulmonary and cardiovascular systems) usually get two or four years of education and training, whereas most cardiovascular technicians (who usually record only the heart) get a few months of on-the-job training.

Nuclear medicine technologists and diagnostic medical sonographers prepare with a two- or four-year program.

Many opticians learn through an apprenticeship or onthe-job training, but a two-year associate degree is becoming a requirement. Some obtain a bachelor's that combines study of opticianry and business management.

Prosthetists and orthotists usually get a bachelor's degree, which they may follow with a year of residency in order to earn certification.

High school courses in math, chemistry, biology, algebra, and health are very useful for all of these occupations. For those that involve nuclear or electronic technologies, a course in physics is also recommended.

How much education or training is required for the jobs in this Work Group?

For descriptions of these jobs, see Part 2.

Short-term on-the-job training

* Medical Equipment Preparers

Long-term on-the-job training

* Opticians, Dispensing

Associate degree

* Biological Technicians
* Cardiovascular Technologists and Technicians
* Diagnostic Medical Sonographers
* Medical and Clinical Laboratory Technicians
* Medical Records and Health Information Technicians
* Nuclear Medicine Technologists
* Radiologic Technicians
* Radiologic Technologists

Bachelor's degree

* Medical and Clinical Laboratory Technologists
* Orthotists and Prosthetists

08.07 Medical Therapy

Workers in this group care for, treat, or train people to improve their physical and emotional well-being. Most persons in this group work with people who are sick, injured, or disabled.

What kind of work would you do?

Your work activities would depend on your job. For example, you might

* Administer prescribed doses of radiation to specific body parts, using radiation therapy equipment according to established practices and standards.
* Counsel and encourage patients to develop leisure activities.
* Develop and implement treatment plans for problems such as stuttering, delayed language, swallowing disorders, and inappropriate pitch or harsh voice problems, based on own assessments and recommendations of physicians, psychologists, and social workers.
* Evaluate the living skills and capacities of physically, developmentally, or emotionally disabled clients.
* Fit and dispense assistive devices, such as hearing aids.
* Plan and conduct treatment programs for clients' hearing or speech problems, consulting with physicians, nurses, psychologists, and other health care personnel as necessary.
* Plan and implement programs and social activities to help patients learn work and school skills and adjust to handicaps.
* Plan, prepare, and carry out individually designed programs of physical treatment to maintain, improve, or restore physical functioning; alleviate pain; and prevent physical dysfunction in patients.
* Teach patients how to deal constructively with their emotions.
* Train patients in the use of orthopedic braces, prostheses, and supportive devices.

What things about you point to this kind of work?

Is it important for you to

* Have work where you do things for other people?
* Have co-workers who are easy to get along with?
* Get a feeling of accomplishment?

Have you enjoyed any of the following as a hobby or leisure-time activity?

* Helping conduct physical exercises for people with disabilities
* Helping sick relatives, friends, and neighbors
* Reading medical or scientific magazines
* Planning family recreational activities

Have you liked and done well in any of the following school subjects?

* Biology
* Chemistry
* Biochemistry
* Health
* Medical Terminology
* Psychology
* Anatomy
* Anatomy, Specialized/Advanced
* Recreation
* Auditory Development
* Physical Therapy

Are you able to

* Identify and understand the speech of another person?
* Tell when something is wrong or is likely to go wrong?
* Combine pieces of information to form general rules or conclusions?

Would you work in places such as

* Hospitals and nursing homes?
* Schools and homes for people with disabilities?
* Doctors' and dentists' offices and clinics?

What skills and knowledges do you need for this kind of work?

For most of these jobs, you need these skills:

* Social Perceptiveness—being aware of others' reactions and understanding why they react as they do
* Service Orientation—actively looking for ways to help people
* Instructing—teaching others how to do something
* Time Management—managing one's own time and the time of others
* Learning Strategies—selecting and using training/instructional methods and procedures appropriate for the situation when learning or teaching new things
* Technology Design—generating or adapting equipment and technology to serve user needs

© 2006 JIST Works

* Persuasion—persuading others to change their minds or behavior

These knowledges are important in most of these jobs:

* Therapy and Counseling—principles, methods, and procedures for diagnosis, treatment, and rehabilitation of physical and mental dysfunctions and for career counseling and guidance
* Psychology—human behavior and performance; individual differences in ability, personality, and interests; learning and motivation; psychological research methods; and the assessment and treatment of behavioral and affective disorders
* Medicine and Dentistry—the information and techniques needed to diagnose and treat human injuries, diseases, and deformities; this includes symptoms, treatment alternatives, drug properties and interactions, and preventive health care measures
* Philosophy and Theology—different philosophical systems and religions; this includes their basic principles, values, ethics, ways of thinking, customs, practices, and impact on human culture
* Customer and Personal Service—principles and processes for providing customer and personal services; this includes customer needs assessment, meeting quality standards for services, and evaluation of customer satisfaction
* Biology—plant and animal organisms and their tissues, cells, functions, interdependencies, and interactions with each other and the environment
* Sociology and Anthropology—group behavior and dynamics, societal trends and influences, human migrations, ethnicity, and cultures and their history and origins

What else should you consider about this kind of work?

Hospitals, nursing homes, and rehabilitation centers hire workers in this group, as do schools, industrial plants, doctors' offices, and sports organizations. Some of these workers are part-time employees, some are self-employed, and some open their own therapy facilities. The trend, however, is that large health care organizations are buying up practices and contracting their services to HMOs.

Many workers in this field have to do some evening or night-shift work and work on weekends. This is especially true for jobs in hospitals or other around-the-clock health care places. You may be on call or have to work overtime. Workers with seniority usually can be selective about the days and shifts they work.

The outlook for jobs in this group is generally good because an aging population needs more health care and these services cannot be performed by machines. However, there may be keen competition for jobs (or even for admission to training programs), and cost-control measures by HMOs and Medicare may limit growth.

How can you prepare for jobs of this kind?

Occupations in this group usually require education and/or training ranging from two to six years, although some jobs as aides require as little as six months of training.

Many of the therapist occupations are licensed, and workers qualify for the licensing exam by getting a college degree in the particular therapeutic field, sometimes as a specialization within a degree program in a field such as speech, music, recreation, art, or physical education. The program usually includes supervised work with patients. In some fields, many workers get a degree in another field, such as a life science, before taking the necessary academic and clinical courses in a master's program.

Therapy assistants usually need to get an associate degree in the particular type of therapy. Clinical experience is usually part of such a program. Therapy aides mostly receive on-the-job training.

How much education or training is required for the jobs in this Work Group?

For descriptions of these jobs, see Part 2.

Short-term on-the-job training

* Occupational Therapist Aides

Postsecondary vocational training

* Massage Therapists
* Respiratory Therapy Technicians

Associate degree

* Occupational Therapist Assistants
* Physical Therapist Aides
* Physical Therapist Assistants
* Radiation Therapists
* Respiratory Therapists

Bachelor's degree

* Occupational Therapists
* Recreational Therapists

Master's degree

* Audiologists
* Physical Therapists
* Speech-Language Pathologists

08.08 Patient Care and Assistance

Workers in this group are concerned with the physical needs and welfare of others. They may assist professional workers. These workers care for people who are very old, are very young, or have handicaps. Often they help people do the things they cannot do for themselves.

What kind of work would you do?

Your work activities would depend on your job. For example, you might

* Accompany clients to doctors' offices and on other trips outside the home, providing transportation, assistance, and companionship.
* Feed patients who are unable to feed themselves.
* Observe and influence patients' behavior, communicating and interacting with them and teaching, counseling, and befriending them.
* Prepare patients for examinations, tests, and treatments and explain procedures.
* Provide mentally impaired or emotionally disturbed patients with routine physical, emotional, psychological, or rehabilitation care under the direction of nursing and medical staff.

What things about you point to this kind of work?

Is it important for you to

* Have work where you do things for other people?
* Have co-workers who are easy to get along with?

Have you enjoyed any of the following as a hobby or leisure-time activity?

* Helping sick relatives, friends, and neighbors
* Serving as a volunteer in a hospital, nursing home, or retirement home
* Listening to friends and helping them with their personal problems

Have you liked and done well in any of the following school subjects?

* Biology
* Chemistry
* Health
* Medical Terminology
* Kinesiology
* Psychology
* Anatomy
* Diet and Therapy
* Nursing Care

Are you able to

* Identify and understand the speech of another person?
* Tell when something is wrong or is likely to go wrong?
* Shift back and forth between two or more activities or sources of information?

Would you work in places such as

* Hospitals and nursing homes?
* Doctors' and dentists' offices and clinics?
* Private homes?

What skills and knowledges do you need for this kind of work?

For most of these jobs, you need these skills:

* Social Perceptiveness—being aware of others' reactions and understanding why they react as they do
* Service Orientation—actively looking for ways to help people
* Persuasion—persuading others to change their minds or behavior
* Monitoring—monitoring/assessing your own performance or that of other individuals or organizations to make improvements or take corrective action
* Learning Strategies—selecting and using training/instructional methods and procedures appropriate for the situation when learning or teaching new things
* Active Listening—giving full attention to what other people are saying, taking time to understand the points being made, asking questions as appropriate, and not interrupting at inappropriate times
* Instructing—teaching others how to do something

These knowledges are important in most of these jobs:

* Psychology—human behavior and performance; individual differences in ability, personality, and interests; learning and motivation; psychological research methods; and the assessment and treatment of behavioral and affective disorders
* Therapy and Counseling—principles, methods, and procedures for diagnosis, treatment, and rehabilitation of physical and mental dysfunctions and for career counseling and guidance
* Medicine and Dentistry—the information and techniques needed to diagnose and treat human injuries, diseases, and deformities; this includes symptoms, treatment alternatives, drug properties and interactions, and preventive health care measures
* Customer and Personal Service—principles and processes for providing customer and personal services; this includes customer needs assessment, meeting quality standards for services, and evaluation of customer satisfaction
* Philosophy and Theology—different philosophical systems and religions; this includes their basic principles, values, ethics, ways of thinking, customs, practices, and impact on human culture
* Sociology and Anthropology—group behavior and dynamics, societal trends and influences, human migrations, ethnicity, and cultures and their history and origins

What else should you consider about this kind of work?

These workers are employed by hospitals, clinics, day care centers, nurseries, schools, private homes, and centers for disabled people. Some of them, such as practical nurses and home health aides, often work in temporary or part-time jobs.

If you take a job caring for someone in that person's home, you might have to be on duty 24 hours a day. People who work for places that provide around-the-clock patient care usually have to work evening or night shifts and weekends. An advantage of some of these jobs is that they include room and board as part of the wages. The job outlook for home health aides is excellent.

Some of these jobs involve close physical contact with people. Workers may have to help lift, bathe, groom, or feed people.

Additional schooling is necessary to advance to higher-level work.

There are usually many openings for well-trained newcomers in this field. Many of these jobs are with places operated by federal, state, or local governments. You may have to pass a civil service test to qualify for some of them. The outlook is mostly very good because of job turnover and the growing health care needs of a graying population.

How can you prepare for jobs of this kind?

Occupations in this group usually require education and/or training ranging from 30 days to a year. Employers usually require that applicants have a high school education or its equal. Course work in health, first aid, English grammar, and speech for interpersonal communication is useful. Hospitals, community agencies, colleges, and public vocational schools offer training courses for many of these jobs. LPNs need to pass a state licensing exam.

Hospitals and clinics provide on-the-job training for many of these jobs. This training usually includes classroom instruction, demonstration of skills and techniques, and practice. The length of training depends upon the job.

Interest and experience in home management, child care, or adult care provide good background for working with aged, blind, or very young people.

How much education or training is required for the jobs in this Work Group?

For descriptions of these jobs, see Part 2.

Short-term on-the-job training

* Home Health Aides
* Nursing Aides, Orderlies, and Attendants
* Psychiatric Aides

Postsecondary vocational training

* Licensed Practical and Licensed Vocational Nurses
* Psychiatric Technicians

08.09 Health Protection and Promotion

Workers in this group help people maintain good health. They help people eat well, prevent sports injuries, and prevent spread of disease from corpses.

What kind of work would you do?

Your work activities would depend on your job. For example, you might

* Analyze menus and recipes, standardize recipes, and test new products.

* Apply cosmetics to impart lifelike appearance to the deceased.
* Care for athletic injuries, using physical therapy equipment, techniques, and medication.
* Counsel individuals and groups on basic rules of good nutrition, healthy eating habits, and nutrition monitoring to improve their quality of life.
* Dress bodies and place them in caskets.
* Inspect meals served for conformance to prescribed diets and standards of palatability and appearance.
* Lead stretching exercises for team members prior to games and practices.
* Observe patient food intake and report progress and dietary problems to dietician.
* Wash and dry bodies, using germicidal soap and towels or hot-air dryers.

What things about you point to this kind of work?

Is it important for you to

* Have work where you do things for other people?
* Have something different to do every day?

Have you enjoyed any of the following as a hobby or leisure-time activity?

* Staying fit, eating right, and taking care of your health
* Reading medical or scientific magazines
* Applying makeup for amateur theater

Have you liked and done well in any of the following school subjects?

* Biology
* Chemistry
* Health
* Medical Terminology
* Psychology
* Anatomy
* Diet and Therapy
* Nutrition
* Kinesiology
* Physical Education

Are you able to

* Generate or use different sets of rules for combining or grouping things in different ways?
* Identify and understand the speech of another person?
* Speak clearly so others can understand you?

Would you work in places such as

* Hospitals and nursing homes?
* Gymnasiums and health clubs?
* Sports stadiums?
* Funeral homes?

What skills and knowledges do you need for this kind of work?

For most of these jobs, you need these skills:

* Social Perceptiveness—being aware of others' reactions and understanding why they react as they do
* Service Orientation—actively looking for ways to help people
* Time Management—managing one's own time and the time of others
* Instructing—teaching others how to do something
* Learning Strategies—selecting and using training/instructional methods and procedures appropriate for the situation when learning or teaching new things
* Persuasion—persuading others to change their minds or behavior
* Reading Comprehension—understanding written sentences and paragraphs in work-related documents

These knowledges are important in most of these jobs:

* Therapy and Counseling—principles, methods, and procedures for diagnosis, treatment, and rehabilitation of physical and mental dysfunctions and for career counseling and guidance
* Medicine and Dentistry—the information and techniques needed to diagnose and treat human injuries, diseases, and deformities; this includes symptoms, treatment alternatives, drug properties and interactions, and preventive health care measures
* Philosophy and Theology—different philosophical systems and religions; this includes their basic principles, values, ethics, ways of thinking, customs, practices, and impact on human culture
* Biology—plant and animal organisms and their tissues, cells, functions, interdependencies, and interactions with each other and the environment
* Sociology and Anthropology—group behavior and dynamics, societal trends and influences, human migrations, ethnicity, and cultures and their history and origins
* Psychology—human behavior and performance; individual differences in ability, personality, and interests; learning and motivation; psychological research methods; and the assessment and treatment of behavioral and affective disorders
* Customer and Personal Service—principles and processes for providing customer and personal services; this includes customer needs assessment, meeting quality standards for services, and evaluation of customer satisfaction

What else should you consider about this kind of work?

These jobs are unusual in the health care field because they may involve working with people who are not sick: Athletic trainers and nutrition specialists often work with healthy people, and embalmers work with bodies of people who have died.

Dietitians may practice clinical dietetics, working with individual patients in such settings as a hospital or nursing home; community dietetics, working to educate a large group or the public in such settings as a public health agency or HMO; management dietetics, planning meals for a food service; or consulting dietetics, contracting to offer their services to any of these employers or perhaps to individuals. Dietetic technicians work under the direction of dietitians in the same settings.

Athletic trainers help athletes maintain fitness and recover from injury. Most work with college athletic teams; others work for high schools, sports medicine clinics, and fitness centers.

Embalmers usually work for funeral parlors. They sometimes have to work with bodies that are disfigured, and they need to take precautions to avoid infections.

The job outlook for this group is generally good. Best opportunities for dietitians will be in commercial food services and the food industry. Athletic trainers will have increased opportunities because of the growth of professional sports and fear of lawsuits, but they also are likely to face keen competition for jobs with college and professional teams.

How can you prepare for jobs of this kind?

Occupations in this group usually require education and/or training ranging from two to less than ten years.

Dietitians usually get a bachelor's degree to enter the occupation and to be licensed in those states that require it. Programs accredited by the American Dietetics Association include some supervised clinical work. A master's is sometimes needed to go into management, public health, or teaching. Dietetic technicians may have less than a bachelor's.

Athletic trainers may have a bachelor's in athletic training, a program that includes supervised clinical experience. Some get a bachelor's in another field and complete an internship.

Embalmers complete a degree or certification program at a mortuary college and serve as an apprentice, usually for two years, before obtaining a license from the state.

For all of the occupations in this group, high school courses in biology, chemistry, health, and speech communication are useful. For those in dietetics, home economics may also be a good choice.

How much education or training is required for the jobs in this Work Group?

For descriptions of these jobs, see Part 2.

Moderate-term on-the-job training

* Dietetic Technicians

Postsecondary vocational training

* Embalmers

Bachelor's degree

* Athletic Trainers
* Dietitians and Nutritionists

09 Hospitality, Tourism, and Recreation

An interest in catering to the personal wishes and needs of others so that they may enjoy a clean environment, good food and drink, comfortable lodging away from home, and recreation. You can satisfy this interest by providing services for the convenience, care, and pampering of others in hotels, restaurants, airplanes, beauty parlors, and so on. You may wish to use your love of cooking as a chef. If you like working with people, you may wish to provide personal services by being a travel guide, a flight attendant, a concierge, a hairdresser, or a waiter. You may wish to work in cleaning and building services if you like a clean environment. If you enjoy sports or games, you may work for an athletic team or casino.

09.01 Managerial Work in Hospitality and Tourism

09.02 Recreational Services

09.03 Hospitality and Travel Services

09.04 Food and Beverage Preparation

09.05 Food and Beverage Service

09.06 Sports

09.07 Barber and Beauty Services

09.01 Managerial Work in Hospitality and Tourism

Workers in this group manage all or part of the activities in restaurants, hotels, resorts, and other places where people expect good personal service. Within the guidelines of their organization, they set goals, monitor resources, and evaluate the work of others.

What kind of work would you do?

Your work activities would depend on your job. For example, you might

* Circulate among gaming tables to ensure that operations are conducted properly, that dealers follow house rules, and that players are not cheating.
* Coordinate front-office activities of hotels or motels and resolve problems.
* Inspect guest rooms, public areas, and grounds for cleanliness and appearance.
* Maintain food and equipment inventories and keep inventory records.
* Monitor stations and games and move dealers from game to game to ensure adequate staffing.
* Recruit and hire staff members.
* Test cooked food by tasting and smelling it in order to ensure palatability and flavor conformity.
* Train workers in food preparation and in service, sanitation, and safety procedures.

What things about you point to this kind of work?

Is it important for you to

* Give directions and instructions to others?
* Make decisions on your own?

Have you enjoyed any of the following as a hobby or leisure-time activity?

* Cooking large quantities of food for community events
* Helping run a school or community fair or carnival
* Serving as a host or hostess for houseguests
* Serving as president of a club or other organization
* Helping to organize things at home, such as shopping lists and budgets
* Setting the table and serving family meals

Have you liked and done well in any of the following school subjects?

* Management
* Accounting
* Business Analysis
* Business Law
* Finance
* Personnel Management
* Business Writing
* Business Organization
* Hotel Administration
* Menu Planning

Are you able to

* Shift back and forth between two or more activities or sources of information?
* Concentrate on a task over a period of time without being distracted?
* Remember information such as words, numbers, pictures, and procedures?

Would you work in places such as

* Restaurants, cafeterias, and other eating places?
* Race tracks?
* Gambling casinos and card clubs?
* Hotels and motels?
* Barber shops and beauty salons?

What skills and knowledges do you need for this kind of work?

For most of these jobs, you need these skills:

* Management of Personnel Resources—motivating, developing, and directing people as they work, identifying the best people for the job
* Management of Financial Resources—determining how money will be spent to get the work done and accounting for these expenditures
* Time Management—managing one's own time and the time of others
* Service Orientation—actively looking for ways to help people
* Negotiation—bringing others together and trying to reconcile differences
* Monitoring—monitoring/assessing your own performance or that of other individuals or organizations to make improvements or take corrective action
* Management of Material Resources—obtaining and seeing to the appropriate use of equipment, facilities, and materials needed to do certain work

These knowledges are important in most of these jobs:

* Customer and Personal Service—principles and processes for providing customer and personal services; this includes customer needs assessment, meeting quality standards for services, and evaluation of customer satisfaction
* Personnel and Human Resources—principles and procedures for personnel recruitment, selection, training, compensation and benefits, labor relations and negotiation, and personnel information systems
* Administration and Management—business and management principles involved in strategic planning, resource allocation, human resources modeling, leadership techniques, production methods, and coordination of people and resources

* Economics and Accounting—economic and accounting principles and practices, the financial markets, banking, and the analysis and reporting of financial data
* Sales and Marketing—principles and methods for showing, promoting, and selling products or services; this includes marketing strategy and tactics, product demonstrations, sales techniques, and sales control systems
* Food Production—techniques and equipment for planting, growing, and harvesting food products (both plant and animal) for consumption, including storage/handling techniques

What else should you consider about this kind of work?

Workers in this group are employed by restaurants, hotels, casinos, resorts, and food service companies. Most of them work some evening and/or weekend hours. They may occasionally come under pressure because of an unexpected turnout of customers, a mechanical malfunction, or some other problem.

Opportunities in this field are generally very good, although the occupations have some sensitivity to the business cycle or to competition within the leisure industry. Dining out and travel for tourism, family vacations, and business conferences are all on the increase. As restaurants are increasingly owned by chains, owner-managers will increasingly be replaced by hired managers. In hotels, the trend is toward budget hotels with fewer services and thus a smaller staff of managers. In many settings, there is a trend toward outsourcing food service management to specialized service companies rather than keeping managers on staff, so many opportunities can be expected in those firms. The gaming industry continues to grow and offer management jobs, especially for people who hold a degree in management.

How can you prepare for jobs of this kind?

Work in this group mostly requires education and/or training that lasts from one year to less than four years. The one exception is food service management, which usually takes two to more than four years to learn.

Two- or four-year degrees in food service management, hotel management, or related subjects provide an entry route for some workers. Courses in bookkeeping, marketing, and personnel can be especially helpful.

Some workers begin by taking a job providing direct service to the public or support to management and then may work their way up to management after gaining experience and taking courses in management.

High school classes in business, math, and speech can be good background. Knowledge of computer applications such as word processing and spreadsheets is growing in importance. Continuous learning is the key to staying employable.

How much education or training is required for the jobs in this Work Group?

For descriptions of these jobs, see Part 2.

Work experience in a related occupation

* First-Line Supervisors/Managers of Food Preparation and Serving Workers
* First-Line Supervisors/Managers of Personal Service Workers
* Food Service Managers
* Lodging Managers

Postsecondary vocational training

* Gaming Supervisors

Work experience plus degree

* Gaming Managers

09.02 Recreational Services

Workers in this group provide services to help people enjoy their leisure activities. They may lead people in recreational activities such as exercise, crafts, music, or camping. Or they may help people engaged in recreation by performing such services as dealing cards, taking tickets, or operating thrill rides.

What kind of work would you do?

Your work activities would depend on your job. For example, you might

* Assign dressing room facilities, locker space, or clothing containers to patrons of athletic or bathing establishments.
* Collect bets in the form of cash or chips, verifying and recording amounts.
* Conduct gambling games such as dice, roulette, cards, or keno, following all applicable rules and regulations.
* Conduct gambling tables or games, such as dice, roulette, cards, or keno, and ensure that game rules are followed.
* Direct special activities or events such as aquatics, gymnastics, or performing arts.
* Operate equipment in order to show films in a number of theaters simultaneously.
* Organize, lead, and promote interest in recreational activities such as arts, crafts, sports, games, camping, and hobbies.
* Rent, sell, or issue sporting equipment and supplies such as bowling shoes, golf balls, swimming suits, and beach chairs.
* Sell and collect admission tickets and passes from patrons at entertainment events.
* Set up and adjust picture projectors and screens to achieve proper size, illumination, and focus of images and proper volume and tone of sound.

What things about you point to this kind of work?

Is it important for you to

* Have supervisors who train workers well?
* Have co-workers who are easy to get along with?

Have you enjoyed any of the following as a hobby or leisure-time activity?

* Helping run a school or community fair or carnival
* Planning family recreational activities
* Ushering for school or community events

Have you liked and done well in any of the following school subjects?

* Recreation
* Marketing/Merchandising
* Selling

Are you able to

* Focus on a single source of sound in the presence of other distracting sounds?
* See objects or movement of objects to your side when your eyes are looking ahead?
* Concentrate on a task over a period of time without being distracted?

Would you work in places such as

* Gambling casinos and card clubs?
* Theaters?
* Amusement parks, circuses, and carnivals?
* Bowling alleys?
* Recreation centers and playgrounds?
* Parks and campgrounds?
* Country clubs and resorts?

What skills and knowledges do you need for this kind of work?

For most of these jobs, you need these skills:

* Service Orientation—actively looking for ways to help people
* Social Perceptiveness—being aware of others' reactions and understanding why they react as they do
* Programming—writing computer programs for various purposes

These knowledges are important in most of these jobs:

* Sales and Marketing—principles and methods for showing, promoting, and selling products or services; this includes marketing strategy and tactics, product demonstrations, sales techniques, and sales control systems
* Customer and Personal Service—principles and processes for providing customer and personal services; this includes customer needs assessment, meeting quality standards for services, and evaluation of customer satisfaction
* Foreign Language—the structure and content of a foreign (non-English) language, including the meaning and spelling of words, rules of composition and grammar, and pronunciation

What else should you consider about this kind of work?

These workers are employed by resorts, cruise ships, casinos, theme parks, movie theaters, and municipal recreation departments throughout the United States. Some of them work part time. Weekend or evening work often is required.

As Americans increase their spending on leisure, these occupations will provide many job opportunities, although downturns in the economy may slow the demand for workers at times. Gaming service workers with formal training will have an advantage in the job market. Because the other jobs in this group require little specific education or training, there will be keen competition for jobs in some fields. Best opportunities will be for those who have gained some experience in the job, perhaps through part-time work while in school.

How can you prepare for jobs of this kind?

Most jobs in this group require education and/or training that lasts from a few weeks to less than two years. Recreation workers often have a bachelor's degree.

Some of these jobs (for example, taking tickets) can be learned from a brief demonstration. In general, a high school diploma or its equivalent is sometimes necessary, but for part-time work it may not be needed. Gaming dealers and motion picture projectionists receive training from their employers in situations that simulate work with the public.

Full-time recreation workers are generally expected to have a college degree. Although degrees in recreation are available, graduates seeking jobs as recreation workers do not need special course work as much as they need experience in part-time, volunteer, or temporary work.

How much education or training is required for the jobs in this Work Group?

For descriptions of these jobs, see Part 2.

Short-term on-the-job training

* Amusement and Recreation Attendants
* Locker Room, Coatroom, and Dressing Room Attendants
* Motion Picture Projectionists
* Slot Key Persons
* Ushers, Lobby Attendants, and Ticket Takers

Postsecondary vocational training

* Gaming and Sports Book Writers and Runners
* Gaming Dealers

Bachelor's degree

* Recreation Workers

09.03 Hospitality and Travel Services

Workers in this group help visitors, travelers, and customers plan trips and get acquainted with and feel at ease in an unfamiliar setting. They are charged with the safety, comfort, and edification of people who are traveling or vacationing. They may register travelers at hotels, book trips for passengers, guide tourists through a foreign city, vacuum and tidy up a room, or carry travelers' luggage.

What kind of work would you do?

Your work activities would depend on your job. For example, you might

* Arrange for tour or expedition details such as accommodations, transportation, equipment, and the availability of medical personnel.
* Book transportation and hotel reservations, using computer terminal or telephone.
* Clean rugs, carpets, upholstered furniture, and/or draperies, using vacuum cleaners and/or shampooers.
* Confer with customers by telephone, in writing, or in person to answer questions regarding services and determine travel preferences.
* Count and verify tickets and seat reservations and record number of passengers boarding and leaving mode of transportation.
* Escort individuals or groups on cruises; on sightseeing tours; or through places of interest such as industrial establishments, public buildings, and art galleries.
* Examine passenger tickets or passes to direct passengers to specified areas for loading.
* Greet, register, and assign rooms to guests of hotels or motels.
* Lead individuals or groups to tour site locations and describe points of interest.
* Receive and mark baggage by completing and attaching claim checks.

What things about you point to this kind of work?

Is it important for you to

* Have work where you do things for other people?
* Have supervisors who train workers well?

Have you enjoyed any of the following as a hobby or leisure-time activity?

* Serving as a host or hostess for houseguests
* Taking trips
* Organizing your room, CDs, DVDs, tools, books, and other items
* Planning parties and outings

Have you liked and done well in any of the following school subjects?

* Record Keeping
* Foreign Languages
* Selling

Are you able to

* Identify and understand the speech of another person?
* Use your abdominal and lower back muscles to support part of your body repeatedly or continuously over time without fatiguing?
* Shift back and forth between two or more activities or sources of information?

Would you work in places such as

* Hotels and motels?
* Bus and train stations?
* Travel agencies?
* Airplanes?
* Streets and highways?
* Office buildings?
* Private homes?

What skills and knowledges do you need for this kind of work?

For most of these jobs, you need these skills:

* Service Orientation—actively looking for ways to help people
* Social Perceptiveness—being aware of others' reactions and understanding why they react as they do
* Active Listening—giving full attention to what other people are saying, taking time to understand the points being made, asking questions as appropriate, and not interrupting at inappropriate times

These knowledges are important in most of these jobs:

* Transportation—principles and methods for moving people or goods by air, rail, sea, or road, including the relative costs and benefits
* Geography—principles and methods for describing the features of land, sea, and air masses, including their physical characteristics; locations; interrelationships; and distribution of plant, animal, and human life
* Customer and Personal Service—principles and processes for providing customer and personal services; this includes customer needs assessment, meeting quality standards for services, and evaluation of customer satisfaction

What else should you consider about this kind of work?

Workers in this group find employment with air, rail, and water transportation companies; hotels and restaurants; office complexes; and related establishments. They are employed throughout the country wherever travelers visit or pass through. Because travelers expect services around the clock, these workers sometimes work nights or weekends. Flight attendants and other transportation attendants have to spend nights away from home, but some enjoy the opportunities for free or low-cost travel. Travel and tour guides may spend weeks away from home.

Work associated with travel is partly sensitive to economic downturns, but in the long run travel seems to be increasing. These jobs also have fairly high turnover, so there are usually many job openings. Automation is likely to cut into the demand for some of the more routine clerical functions of ticket agents and desk clerks. Do-it-yourself Internet travel booking is also counteracting the demand for travel agents. On the other hand, flight attendants are required by federal law, and some of the other occupations will continue to be in demand because travelers expect personal service.

There should be many openings for jobs that involve cleaning buildings and homes.

How can you prepare for jobs of this kind?

Education and/or training requirements for this group vary from a few days to six months. Most training is done on the job.

However, travel agents often prepare by taking a specialized curriculum for several months at a proprietary school or community college.

Flight attendants, other travel attendants, desk clerks, and ticket agents are expected to have high school diplomas, and some college or experience working with the public is a plus. They are given from one to several weeks of intensive training by their employers. Flight attendants start with four to six weeks of training and need to take several hours of training in safety and other procedures each year. Ability to speak a foreign language can be very useful.

The other occupations require only a brief period of training on the job.

Travel and tour guides often will have an advantage if they speak a foreign language and are familiar with a foreign culture.

How much education or training is required for the jobs in this Work Group?

For descriptions of these jobs, see Part 2.

Short-term on-the-job training

* Baggage Porters and Bellhops
* Concierges
* Hotel, Motel, and Resort Desk Clerks
* Janitors and Cleaners, Except Maids and Housekeeping Cleaners
* Maids and Housekeeping Cleaners
* Reservation and Transportation Ticket Agents
* Tour Guides and Escorts
* Transportation Attendants, Except Flight Attendants and Baggage Porters
* Travel Clerks

Moderate-term on-the-job training

* Travel Guides

Long-term on-the-job training

* Flight Attendants

Postsecondary vocational training

* Travel Agents

09.04 Food and Beverage Preparation

Workers in this group prepare food or work where it is prepared. Some of them cook or do other tasks to prepare food in kitchens of restaurants or institutional cafeterias. Others aid in the preparation process by cutting meat, baking bread and pastries, decorating cakes, or cleaning the dishes.

What kind of work would you do?

Your work activities would depend on your job. For example, you might

* Cook the exact number of items ordered by each customer, working on several different orders simultaneously.
* Determine meal prices based on calculations of ingredient prices.
* Grill, cook, and fry foods such as french fries, eggs, and pancakes.
* Mix ingredients to form dough or batter by hand or using electric mixer.
* Portion and wrap the food or place it directly on plates for service to patrons.
* Prepare special cuts of meat ordered by customers.
* Supervise and coordinate activities of cooks and workers engaged in food preparation.
* Wash dishes, glassware, flatware, pots, and/or pans, using dishwashers or by hand.
* Wash, peel, cut, and seed fruits and vegetables to prepare them for consumption.

What things about you point to this kind of work?

Is it important for you to

* Never be pressured to do things that go against your sense of right and wrong?
* Have co-workers who are easy to get along with?

Have you enjoyed any of the following as a hobby or leisure-time activity?

* Cooking large quantities of food for community events
* Canning and preserving food
* Cooking and baking
* Baking and decorating cakes

Have you liked and done well in any of the following school subjects?

* Cookery, Quantity
* Food Preparation/Service
* Baking
* Cake Decorating

* Culinary Arts
* Menu Planning

Are you able to

* Make fast, simple, repeated movements of your fingers, hands, and wrists?
* Quickly move your hand, your hand together with your arm, or your two hands to grasp, manipulate, or assemble objects?
* Quickly and repeatedly bend, stretch, twist, or reach out with your body, arms, and/or legs?

Would you work in places such as

* Restaurants, cafeterias, and other eating places?

What skills and knowledges do you need for this kind of work?

For most of these jobs, you need these skills:

* Management of Material Resources—obtaining and seeing to the appropriate use of equipment, facilities, and materials needed to do certain work
* Management of Personnel Resources—motivating, developing, and directing people as they work, identifying the best people for the job
* Management of Financial Resources—determining how money will be spent to get the work done and accounting for these expenditures

These knowledges are important in most of these jobs:

* Food Production—techniques and equipment for planting, growing, and harvesting food products (both plant and animal) for consumption, including storage/handling techniques
* Foreign Language—the structure and content of a foreign (non-English) language, including the meaning and spelling of words, rules of composition and grammar, and pronunciation
* Production and Processing—raw materials, production processes, quality control, costs, and other techniques for maximizing the effective manufacture and distribution of goods

What else should you consider about this kind of work?

Restaurants, institutional cafeterias, and catering services employ these workers. Jobs may be found in cities and towns everywhere. Many workers are employed part-time.

Many of these jobs require work on evenings and weekends. Kitchen workers often have to stand for hours, endure a hot working environment, lift heavy pots, and take safety precautions against burns and cuts from sharp knives.

The increase in meals eaten out makes for a good outlook for most of these occupations, especially in family restaurants, meals-to-go settings, and specialty bakeries. Many jobs also will be created by turnover. Opportunities for custom meat cutters are declining because much of the work has shifted to industrial-scale production of meat cuts.

How can you prepare for jobs of this kind?

These occupations require education and/or training ranging from a few days to four years or more.

Chefs and head cooks typically learn through an apprenticeship program that takes several years. Many begin by studying in a culinary arts program at a vocational school, community college, or specialized culinary school. Restaurant cooks may go through a similar but somewhat shorter training program, but some simply start out as short-order or cafeteria cooks and improve their skills through on-the job training, sometimes provided in cooperation with the local school district. Butchers and bakers also apprentice for their jobs. A high school diploma or its equivalent is usually required for admission to an apprenticeship program. High school or community college coursework in business math and management can be especially useful, and it is very important to have experience in part-time and summer jobs in the food industry.

How much education or training is required for the jobs in this Work Group?

For descriptions of these jobs, see Part 2.

Short-term on-the-job training

* Cooks, Fast Food
* Cooks, Institution and Cafeteria
* Cooks, Short Order
* Dishwashers
* Food Preparation Workers

Long-term on-the-job training

* Bakers, Bread and Pastry
* Butchers and Meat Cutters
* Cooks, Restaurant

Postsecondary vocational training

* Chefs and Head Cooks

09.05 Food and Beverage Service

Workers in this group serve food and drink or work where they are served. Some wait on tables, serve diners at a counter, bring meals outside at drive-ins, or tend bar. Others play a supporting role by greeting diners as they enter a restaurant or by keeping the dining room set up with clean linens and silverware.

What kind of work would you do?

Your work activities would depend on your job. For example, you might

* Assign patrons to tables suitable for their needs.
* Mix ingredients, such as liquor, soda, water, sugar, and bitters, in order to prepare cocktails and other drinks.
* Prepare and serve cold drinks, frozen milk drinks, or desserts, using drink-dispensing, milkshake, or frozen custard machines.

* Present menus to patrons and answer questions about menu items, making recommendations upon request.
* Set tables with clean linens, condiments, and other supplies.
* Take food orders and relay orders to kitchens or serving counters so they can be filled.
* Take orders from patrons for food or beverages.

What things about you point to this kind of work?

Is it important for you to

* Have supervisors who train workers well?
* Have co-workers who are easy to get along with?

Have you enjoyed any of the following as a hobby or leisure-time activity?

* Mixing drinks for family or friends
* Setting tables for club or organizational functions
* Waiting on tables at club or organizational functions
* Setting the table and serving family meals

Have you liked and done well in any of the following school subjects?

* Food Preparation/Service
* Selling
* Cooking

Are you able to

* Exert yourself physically over long periods of time without getting winded or out of breath?
* Coordinate the movement of your arms, legs, and torso together when the whole body is in motion?
* Use your abdominal and lower back muscles to support part of the body repeatedly or continuously over time without fatiguing?

Would you work in places such as

* Restaurants, cafeterias, and other eating places?
* Country clubs and resorts?

What skills and knowledges do you need for this kind of work?

For most of these jobs, you need these skills:

* Service Orientation—actively looking for ways to help people
* Social Perceptiveness—being aware of others' reactions and understanding why they react as they do
* Programming—writing computer programs for various purposes

These knowledges are important in most of these jobs:

* Food Production—techniques and equipment for planting, growing, and harvesting food products (both plant and animal) for consumption, including storage/handling techniques
* Sales and Marketing—principles and methods for showing, promoting, and selling products or services; this includes marketing strategy and tactics, product demonstrations, sales techniques, and sales control systems
* Customer and Personal Service—principles and processes for providing customer and personal services; this includes customer needs assessment, meeting quality standards for services, and evaluation of customer satisfaction

What else should you consider about this kind of work?

These workers are employed by restaurants, institutional cafeterias, and catering services in cities and towns of all sizes. Part-time, evening, and weekend work is very common.

Most of these workers spend considerable time on their feet and can be under considerable pressure from a dining room full of hungry customers. Bartenders usually must be over 21, and employers often prefer to hire people over 25. They must have a knowledge of the laws applying to the sale of alcoholic beverages.

There is always a lot of turnover in these jobs, which creates a constant demand for workers. Because of the trend toward informal eateries and family restaurants, there will be keen competition for the highest-paying jobs in fancy restaurants.

How can you prepare for jobs of this kind?

These occupations require education and/or training ranging from a few days to several weeks.

Some bartenders learn their skills at a vocational or bartending school. The other occupations in this group require only a few days or weeks of training, usually provided by the employer.

Experience in part-time and summer jobs in the food service industry can be very helpful.

How much education or training is required for the jobs in this Work Group?

For descriptions of these jobs, see Part 2.

Short-term on-the-job training

* Bartenders
* Combined Food Preparation and Serving Workers, Including Fast Food
* Counter Attendants, Cafeteria, Food Concession, and Coffee Shop
* Dining Room and Cafeteria Attendants and Bartender Helpers
* Food Servers, Nonrestaurant
* Hosts and Hostesses, Restaurant, Lounge, and Coffee Shop
* Waiters and Waitresses

09.06 Sports

Workers in this group compete or officiate in athletic events or improve the athletic skills of teams and individual competitors.

What kind of work would you do?

Your work activities would depend on your job. For example, you might

* Analyze the strengths and weaknesses of opposing teams in order to develop game strategies.
* Identify and recruit potential athletes, arranging and offering incentives such as athletic scholarships.
* Judge performances in sporting competitions in order to award points, impose scoring penalties, and determine results.
* Maintain optimum physical fitness levels by training regularly, following nutrition plans, and consulting with health professionals.
* Officiate at sporting events, games, or competitions to maintain standards of play and to ensure that game rules are observed.
* Participate in athletic events and competitive sports according to established rules and regulations.
* Plan, organize, and conduct practice sessions.

What things about you point to this kind of work?

Is it important for you to

* Receive recognition for the work you do?
* Be paid well in comparison with other workers?
* Be looked up to by others in your company and your community?
* Have co-workers who are easy to get along with?
* Get a feeling of accomplishment?
* Make use of your individual abilities?

Have you enjoyed any of the following as a hobby or leisure-time activity?

* Coaching children or youth in sports activities
* Playing baseball, basketball, football, or other sports
* Keeping score for athletic events
* Handling equipment for a local athletic team
* Calculating sports statistics
* Umpiring or refereeing amateur sporting events

Have you liked and done well in any of the following school subjects?

* Coaching
* Physical Education
* Officiating

Are you able to

* Exert yourself physically over long periods of time without getting winded or out of breath?
* Coordinate the movement of your arms, legs, and torso together when the whole body is in motion?
* Exert muscle force repeatedly or continuously over time?

Would you work in places such as

* Sports stadiums?
* Colleges and universities?
* Business offices?
* Country clubs and resorts?

What skills and knowledges do you need for this kind of work?

For most of these jobs, you need these skills:

* Negotiation—bringing others together and trying to reconcile differences
* Social Perceptiveness—being aware of others' reactions and understanding why they react as they do
* Persuasion—persuading others to change their minds or behavior
* Monitoring—monitoring/assessing your own performance or that of other individuals or organizations to make improvements or take corrective action
* Coordination—adjusting actions in relation to others' actions
* Learning Strategies—selecting and using training/instructional methods and procedures appropriate for the situation when learning or teaching new things

These knowledges are important in most of these jobs:

* Psychology—human behavior and performance; individual differences in ability, personality, and interests; learning and motivation; psychological research methods; and the assessment and treatment of behavioral and affective disorders
* Sociology and Anthropology—group behavior and dynamics, societal trends and influences, human migrations, ethnicity, and cultures and their history and origins
* Therapy and Counseling—principles, methods, and procedures for diagnosis, treatment, and rehabilitation of physical and mental dysfunctions and for career counseling and guidance

What else should you consider about this kind of work?

These workers are employed at racetracks, golf courses, speedways, ballparks, and other places where people watch sports events. If you're interested in this kind of career, you should take part in as many school and amateur sports as possible and keep to a strict training schedule. Most coaches, scouts, instructors, and officials have some experience as players, at least at the amateur level.

Many of these jobs are seasonal. For example, most of the people who work at racetracks have other jobs when the tracks are not in session. Golf and tennis pros may do other work during the off-season, or they may contract to work at clubs in several parts of the country in order to work year-round.

A career in professional sports sounds like an exciting and glamorous way to earn a living, but there is a lot of hard work and constant competition. Frequent travel is common. The risk of physical injury is great, especially in the contact sports. Some injuries may shorten or end a player's sports career. Also, after reaching a certain age, many competitive players must find work in areas other than team play. For these reasons, expertise in a second area besides sports is desirable.

One possible career move is to instructing, officiating, coaching, or scouting. Because of the increase in professionalism and the role of women in sports such as soccer and basketball, there are more jobs in these fields, but competition remains keen. Best opportunities will be at the high school and amateur levels.

How can you prepare for jobs of this kind?

Occupations in this group usually require education and/or training ranging from six months to more than ten years.

Professional coaches and officials often obtain the necessary training and experience by working with high school and college athletic teams. Umpires in major league baseball usually receive training in special umpire schools and must have experience in the minor leagues. Officials in horse racing usually have some type of related work experience and receive on-the-job training.

Professional athletes often receive initial training while on high school or college teams. They are recruited by professional clubs or teams and work under a contract. Training continues as long as they remain in active competition.

How much education or training is required for the jobs in this Work Group?

For descriptions of these jobs, see Part 2.

Long-term on-the-job training

* Athletes and Sports Competitors
* Coaches and Scouts
* Umpires, Referees, and Other Sports Officials

09.07 Barber and Beauty Services

Workers in this group cut and style hair and provide a variety of other services to improve people's appearance or physical condition. They may specialize in one activity or perform many different duties.

What kind of work would you do?

Your work activities would depend on your job. For example, you might

* Apply undercoat and clear or colored polish onto nails with brush.
* Bleach, dye, or tint hair, using applicator or brush.
* Cut and trim hair according to clients' instructions and/or current hairstyles, using clippers, combs, hand-held blow driers, and scissors.
* Polish nails, using powdered polish and buffer.
* Shampoo, rinse, condition, and dry hair and scalp or hairpieces with water, liquid soap, or other solutions.
* Shape and smooth ends of nails, using scissors, files, and emery boards.

* Shape eyebrows and remove facial hair, using depilatory cream, tweezers, electrolysis, or wax.
* Update and maintain customer information records, such as beauty services provided.

What things about you point to this kind of work?

Is it important for you to

* Have work where you do things for other people?
* Never be pressured to do things that go against your sense of right and wrong?

Have you enjoyed any of the following as a hobby or leisure-time activity?

* Cutting and trimming hair for family and friends
* Doing makeup, hair, and nails for family and friends
* Creating or styling hairdos for friends
* Applying makeup for amateur theater

Have you liked and done well in any of the following school subjects?

* Cosmetology
* Consumer Behavior

Are you able to

* Keep your hand and arm steady while moving your arm or while holding your arm and hand in one position?
* Make precisely coordinated movements of the fingers of one or both hands to grasp, manipulate, or assemble very small objects?
* Match or detect differences between colors, including shades of color and brightness?

Would you work in places such as

* Barber shops and beauty salons?

What skills and knowledges do you need for this kind of work?

For most of these jobs, you need these skills:

* Service Orientation—actively looking for ways to help people
* Management of Material Resources—obtaining and seeing to the appropriate use of equipment, facilities, and materials needed to do certain work
* Management of Financial Resources—determining how money will be spent to get the work done and accounting for these expenditures

These knowledges are important in most of these jobs:

* Sales and Marketing—principles and methods for showing, promoting, and selling products or services; this includes marketing strategy and tactics, product demonstrations, sales techniques, and sales control systems
* Customer and Personal Service—principles and processes for providing customer and personal services; this includes customer needs assessment, meeting quality standards for services, and evaluation of customer satisfaction

✳ Chemistry—the chemical composition, structure, and properties of substances and of the chemical processes and transformations that they undergo; this includes uses of chemicals and their danger signs, production techniques, and disposal methods

What else should you consider about this kind of work?

Many people in this field are self-employed, either in their own shops, in their homes, or by renting space in someone else's shop. Most have had experience working for someone else. If you are considering this kind of work because you want your own business, you should realize that it's not done overnight. First you have to get regular customers and save enough money to buy your own equipment. Shops often hire well-trained beginners. Some schools help their graduates to find jobs.

Working hours depend on shop policy. You may have to work Saturdays, Sundays, and evenings.

In some jobs, you are on a salary. However, most employers set the prices for the services offered and share a percentage with the worker. The amount the worker is paid may vary and may depend on the supplies and tools provided by the employer. For example, some employers provide the needed towels, shampoo, or lotions and keep a larger share of the money collected. You usually receive tips from customers. You may be expected to join a union and pay membership dues.

In this kind of work, you stand and use your hands and arms all day. Some people are bothered by odors and fumes from the chemicals used in hair care.

In many of these jobs, you have to wear uniforms, which may or may not be furnished by the shop.

The outlook is generally good for these occupations. Demand is increasing over the long run, turnover produces a steady number of job openings, and automation is not likely to replace the human touch any time soon. Opportunities will be better at unisex hair salons than in traditional male barber shops. Competition for the highest-paying jobs is expected to be keen.

How can you prepare for jobs of this kind?

Occupations in this group usually require education and/or training ranging from six months to more than two years.

Both public and private vocational schools offer courses in cosmetology, barbering, electrolysis, and manicure. In a few areas, apprenticeships in cosmetology are available. Manufacturers of barbering and cosmetology equipment and materials offer training courses about the use of their products.

Formal training requirements vary according to the occupation and state. Studies usually include anatomy, bacteriology, dermatology, and physiology. Techniques such as hair cutting, permanent waving, electrolysis, and hair and scalp analysis are also included.

Students of cosmetology or barbering schools get supervised practical experience. Trainees and workers develop further expertise by attending seminars and participating in contests sponsored by schools, trade associations, and manufacturers. Changing hairstyles, new products, and new techniques make frequent attendance at training and demonstration classes necessary.

Workers need to have passed a state licensing exam.

How much education or training is required for the jobs in this Work Group?

For descriptions of these jobs, see Part 2.

Short-term on-the-job training

✳ Shampooers
✳ Skin Care Specialists

Postsecondary vocational training

✳ Barbers
✳ Hairdressers, Hairstylists, and Cosmetologists
✳ Manicurists and Pedicurists

10 Human Service

An interest in improving people's social, mental, emotional, or spiritual well-being. You can satisfy this interest as a counselor, social worker, or religious worker who helps people sort out their complicated lives or solve personal problems. You may work as a caretaker for very young people or the elderly. Or you may interview people to help identify the social services they need.

10.01 Counseling and Social Work

10.02 Religious Work

10.03 Child/Personal Care and Services

10.04 Client Interviewing

10.01 Counseling and Social Work

Workers in this group help people deal with their problems and major life events. They may work on a person-to-person basis or with groups of people. Workers sometimes specialize in problems that are personal, social, vocational, or physical in nature.

What kind of work would you do?

Your work activities would depend on your job. For example, you might

* Advise clients regarding food stamps, child care, food, money management, sanitation, and housekeeping.
* Conduct orientation sessions for chemical dependency programs.
* Consult with parents, teachers, and other school personnel to determine causes of problems such as truancy and misbehavior and to implement solutions.
* Counsel individuals, groups, or families to help them understand problems, define goals, and develop realistic action plans.
* Counsel students in the handling of issues such as family, financial, and educational problems.
* Develop rehabilitation programs for assigned offenders or inmates, establishing rules of conduct, goals, and objectives.
* Direct and participate in on- and off-campus recreational activities for residents of institutions, boarding schools, fraternities or sororities, children's homes, or similar establishments.
* Discuss with individual patients their plans for life after leaving therapy.
* Investigate child abuse or neglect cases and take authorized protective action when necessary.
* Plan and conduct programs to prevent substance abuse, to combat social problems, or to improve health and counseling services in community.

What things about you point to this kind of work?

Is it important for you to

* Have work where you do things for other people?
* Plan your work with little supervision?
* Try out your own ideas?
* Have something different to do every day?

Have you enjoyed any of the following as a hobby or leisure-time activity?

* Listening to friends and helping them with their personal problems
* Serving as a volunteer in a hospital, nursing home, or retirement home
* Helping people with disabilities take walks
* Serving as a leader of a scouting or other group
* Serving as a volunteer interviewer in a social service organization
* Serving as a volunteer counselor at a youth camp or center

Have you liked and done well in any of the following school subjects?

* Psychology
* Social Work
* Counseling Techniques
* Child Development/Care
* Abnormal Psychology
* Public Health
* Criminology

Are you able to

* Tell when something is wrong or is likely to go wrong?
* Identify and understand the speech of another person?
* Come up with unusual or clever ideas about a given topic or situation or develop creative ways to solve a problem?
* Combine pieces of information to form general rules or conclusions?

Would you work in places such as

* Business offices?
* Hospitals and nursing homes?
* High schools?
* Colleges and universities?
* Jails and reformatories?
* Government offices?

What skills and knowledges do you need for this kind of work?

For most of these jobs, you need these skills:

* Social Perceptiveness—being aware of others' reactions and understanding why they react as they do
* Service Orientation—actively looking for ways to help people
* Persuasion—persuading others to change their minds or behavior
* Negotiation—bringing others together and trying to reconcile differences
* Active Listening—giving full attention to what other people are saying, taking time to understand the points being made, asking questions as appropriate, and not interrupting at inappropriate times
* Learning Strategies—selecting and using training/instructional methods and procedures appropriate for the situation when learning or teaching new things
* Speaking—talking to others to convey information effectively

These knowledges are important in most of these jobs:

* Therapy and Counseling—principles, methods, and procedures for diagnosis, treatment, and rehabilitation of physical and mental dysfunctions and for career counseling and guidance

* Psychology—human behavior and performance; individual differences in ability, personality, and interests; learning and motivation; psychological research methods; and the assessment and treatment of behavioral and affective disorders
* Sociology and Anthropology—group behavior and dynamics, societal trends and influences, human migrations, ethnicity, and cultures and their history and origins
* Philosophy and Theology—different philosophical systems and religions; this includes their basic principles, values, ethics, ways of thinking, customs, practices, and impact on human culture
* Customer and Personal Service—principles and processes for providing customer and personal services; this includes customer needs assessment, meeting quality standards for services, and evaluation of customer satisfaction

What else should you consider about this kind of work?

These workers are employed by colleges, rehabilitation centers, mental health clinics, juvenile courts, and vocational rehabilitation programs.

Workers in this group want to make a difference in people's lives, and they often get many satisfactions of that kind, which can offset the occasional failures, bureaucratic roadblocks, people's natural resistance to change, emotionally draining situations, and (in some cases) low pay.

These occupations differ greatly in their hours and working environments, but most of them do not permit a regular 40-hour work week. Counseling psychologists and social workers in private practice may have office hours on some evenings for the convenience of their clients, but they usually can balance that by taking time off during the day. On the other hand, social workers on the public payroll, probation and parole officers, residential counselors, and human services workers often must see clients in the evening and/or on weekends and may often be "on call" or work extra hours.

Residential counselors often are short-term or part-time workers who are gaining experience and some income before or while they work on a higher degree in a counseling occupation.

In general, the employment outlook in this field is good. Probation and parole officers, despite tight budgets, will be needed to relieve prison overcrowding. Clinical and counseling psychologists will have mixed opportunities, depending on specialty; those with a doctorate will fare best. Private insurance is beginning to cover some services provided by social workers and human services workers; many new jobs will be created in the private sector, especially for those who work with elderly people.

How can you prepare for jobs of this kind?

Work in this group generally requires from two to six or more years of education and/or training.

Clinical and counseling psychologists need at least a master's in psychology, and in most cases a doctorate plus clinical training is advisable. Social workers generally need a bachelor's in the subject, plus a master's if they want to do counseling.

Probation and correctional treatment specialists can sometimes begin with a two-year degree, but a bachelor's is an advantage, and for jobs with the federal government it is necessary. Human services workers usually enter with a two-year degree.

How much education or training is required for the jobs in this Work Group?

For descriptions of these jobs, see Part 2.

Moderate-term on-the-job training

* Residential Advisors
* Social and Human Service Assistants

Bachelor's degree

* Child, Family, and School Social Workers
* Medical and Public Health Social Workers
* Probation Officers and Correctional Treatment Specialists
* Rehabilitation Counselors

Master's degree

* Clinical Psychologists
* Counseling Psychologists
* Marriage and Family Therapists
* Mental Health and Substance Abuse Social Workers
* Mental Health Counselors
* Substance Abuse and Behavioral Disorder Counselors

10.02 Religious Work

Workers in this group conduct worship services, help people deal with spiritual problems, and provide religious education.

What kind of work would you do?

Your work activities would depend on your job. For example, you might

* Analyze revenue and program cost data to determine budget priorities.
* Counsel individuals and groups concerning their spiritual, emotional, and personal needs.
* Organize and lead regular religious services.
* Participate in fundraising activities to support congregation activities and facilities.
* Schedule special events such as camps, conferences, meetings, seminars, and retreats.
* Select appropriate curricula and class structures for educational programs.
* Train and supervise religious education instructional staff.

© 2006 JIST Works

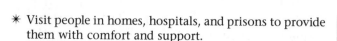

* Visit people in homes, hospitals, and prisons to provide them with comfort and support.

What things about you point to this kind of work?

Is it important for you to

* Have work where you do things for other people?
* Be looked up to by others in your company and your community?
* Get a feeling of accomplishment?
* Receive recognition for the work you do?
* Plan your work with little supervision?
* Have steady employment?
* Try out your own ideas?

Have you enjoyed any of the following as a hobby or leisure-time activity?

* Volunteering at a house of worship
* Teaching in a religious school
* Reading about religious issues
* Serving as a leader of a scouting or other group

Have you liked and done well in any of the following school subjects?

* Religion
* Counseling Techniques
* Education
* Child Development/Care
* Public Speaking
* Philosophy
* Social Problems

Are you able to

* Speak clearly so others can understand you?
* Communicate information and ideas in speaking so others will understand?
* Come up with a number of ideas about a topic?

Would you work in places such as

* Houses of worship?
* Elementary schools?
* High schools?

What skills and knowledges do you need for this kind of work?

For most of these jobs, you need these skills:

* Service Orientation—actively looking for ways to help people
* Social Perceptiveness—being aware of others' reactions and understanding why they react as they do
* Management of Financial Resources—determining how money will be spent to get the work done and accounting for these expenditures
* Speaking—talking to others to convey information effectively
* Writing—communicating effectively in writing as appropriate for the needs of the audience
* Active Listening—giving full attention to what other people are saying, taking time to understand the points being made, asking questions as appropriate, and not interrupting at inappropriate times
* Learning Strategies—selecting and using training/instructional methods and procedures appropriate for the situation when learning or teaching new things

These knowledges are important in most of these jobs:

* Philosophy and Theology—different philosophical systems and religions; this includes their basic principles, values, ethics, ways of thinking, customs, practices, and impact on human culture
* Therapy and Counseling—principles, methods, and procedures for diagnosis, treatment, and rehabilitation of physical and mental dysfunctions and for career counseling and guidance
* Education and Training—principles and methods for curriculum and training design, teaching and instruction for individuals and groups, and the measurement of training effects
* Psychology—human behavior and performance; individual differences in ability, personality, and interests; learning and motivation; psychological research methods; and the assessment and treatment of behavioral and affective disorders
* Sociology and Anthropology—group behavior and dynamics, societal trends and influences, human migrations, ethnicity, and cultures and their history and origins
* English Language—the structure and content of the English language, including the meaning and spelling of words, rules of composition, and grammar
* Communications and Media—media production, communication, and dissemination techniques and methods; this includes alternative ways to inform and entertain via written, oral, and visual media

What else should you consider about this kind of work?

These workers gain great satisfaction from helping people find spiritual meaning in their lives. Clergy take on not just a job but a way of life that gives them few hours off duty and that holds them up to constant scrutiny as a role model. Directors of religious education have more regular hours but usually must do some work on evenings and on weekends.

For clergy, there is a great need for Roman Catholic priests; opportunities in the other faiths are best outside of cities.

How can you prepare for jobs of this kind?

Work in this group generally requires more than ten years of education and/or training.

Most clergy need a bachelor's degree plus some education and training in seminary, but some denominations accept people with less formal education. Experience as a youth group leader or in missionary or volunteer work can be very helpful. Directors of religious education are usually expected to have a bachelor's degree, and a master's degree can be helpful in large congregations or religious organizations.

How much education or training is required for the jobs in this Work Group?

For descriptions of these jobs, see Part 2.

Bachelor's degree

* Directors, Religious Activities and Education

First professional degree

* Clergy

10.03 Child/Personal Care and Services

Workers in this group provide personal services to people who need a lot of attention: young children, people with chronic health problems, people in mourning, or very busy people. They provide such services as companionship, bathing and grooming, simple meal preparation, organizing the household, running errands, and basic emotional support.

What kind of work would you do?

Your work activities would depend on your job. For example, you might

* Administer bedside and personal care, such as ambulation and personal hygiene assistance.
* Care for children in institutional setting, such as group homes, nursery schools, private businesses, or schools for the handicapped.
* Direct or escort mourners to parlors or chapels in which wakes or funerals are being held.
* Help prepare and serve nutritionally balanced meals and snacks for children.
* Organize and participate in recreational activities, such as games.
* Perform a variety of tasks during funerals to assist funeral directors and to ensure that services run smoothly and as planned.
* Plan, shop for, and prepare meals, including special diets, and assist families in planning, shopping for, and preparing nutritious meals.
* Read to children and teach them simple painting, drawing, handicrafts, and songs.
* Regulate children's rest periods and nap schedules.
* Transport children to schools, social outings, and medical appointments.

What things about you point to this kind of work?

Is it important for you to

* Have work where you do things for other people?
* Have steady employment?

Have you enjoyed any of the following as a hobby or leisure-time activity?

* Teaching games to children as a volunteer aide in a nursery school
* Babysitting or caring for children
* Coaching children or youth in sports activities
* Planning and cooking meals
* Helping to organize things at home, such as shopping lists and budgets

Have you liked and done well in any of the following school subjects?

* Child Development/Care
* Home Management

Are you able to

* Identify and understand the speech of another person?
* Use your abdominal and lower back muscles to support part of your body repeatedly or continuously over time without fatiguing?
* Exert maximum muscle force to lift, push, pull, or carry objects?

Would you work in places such as

* Funeral homes?
* Kindergartens and day care centers?
* Private homes?
* Recreation centers and playgrounds?

What skills and knowledges do you need for this kind of work?

For most of these jobs, you need these skills:

* Social Perceptiveness—being aware of others' reactions and understanding why they react as they do
* Service Orientation—actively looking for ways to help people
* Persuasion—persuading others to change their minds or behavior
* Negotiation—bringing others together and trying to reconcile differences
* Time Management—managing one's own time and the time of others

These knowledges are important in most of these jobs:

* Philosophy and Theology—different philosophical systems and religions; this includes their basic principles, values, ethics, ways of thinking, customs, practices, and impact on human culture
* Customer and Personal Service—principles and processes for providing customer and personal services; this includes customer needs assessment, meeting quality standards for services, and evaluation of customer satisfaction
* Therapy and Counseling—principles, methods, and procedures for diagnosis, treatment, and rehabilitation of physical and mental dysfunctions and for career counseling and guidance

What else should you consider about this kind of work?

These workers are mostly employed by individuals or families. Funeral attendants work for funeral homes.

Many workers have a 40-hour week, but others work evenings or weekends, and live-in workers can expect longer hours. Some work part-time or for several clients. The working environment is usually pleasant, but work tasks can involve lifting, stooping, and a lot of time on your feet. Because the work usually requires close contact with people who may be very dependent, it can be emotionally draining. The people for whom you are responsible may be pleasant or difficult and demanding. These jobs offer few routes for advancement.

The outlook for jobs in this group is very good. Automation cannot supply the personal touch that these jobs require.

How can you prepare for jobs of this kind?

These jobs generally do not require formal education or training, but a few weeks of training will be helpful.

Because some jobs require workers to handle money, manage household budgets, or do simple meal preparation, basic arithmetic and/or home economics can be useful high school courses. Certification courses at community colleges and vocational schools are available for child monitors and home health care aides. Some workers receive training from organizations that recruit volunteers for this kind of work. Part-time babysitting jobs and care for your own family members can also be valuable experience.

How much education or training is required for the jobs in this Work Group?

For descriptions of these jobs, see Part 2.

Short-term on-the-job training

* Child Care Workers
* Funeral Attendants
* Nannies
* Personal and Home Care Aides

10.04 Client Interviewing

Workers in this group interview clients and business representatives to determine what services are appropriate for them. They often retrieve and maintain records about clients.

What kind of work would you do?

Your work activities would depend on your job. For example, you might

* Answer questions concerning registration for jobs or application for unemployment benefits.
* Assist applicants completing application forms for job referrals or unemployment compensation claims.
* Assist individuals in filling out applications or questionnaires.
* Compile, record, and code results and data from interview or survey, using computers or specified forms.
* Compute public housing rent in proportion to eligible tenant's income.
* Contact individuals to be interviewed at home, place of business, or field location by telephone, mail, or in person.
* Schedule unemployment insurance claimants for adjudication interviews when question of eligibility arises.
* Select and refer eligible applicants to public assistance or public housing agencies.

What things about you point to this kind of work?

Is it important for you to

* Have work where you do things for other people?
* Have supervisors who train workers well?

Have you enjoyed any of the following as a hobby or leisure-time activity?

* Serving as a volunteer interviewer in a social service organization
* Helping friends and relatives with their tax reports

Have you liked and done well in any of the following school subjects?

* Record Keeping
* Public Speaking

Are you able to

* Identify and understand the speech of another person?
* Communicate information and ideas in writing so others will understand?
* Listen to and understand information and ideas presented through spoken words and sentences?

Would you work in places such as

* Government offices?
* Business offices?

What skills and knowledges do you need for this kind of work?

For most of these jobs, you need these skills:

* Service Orientation—actively looking for ways to help people
* Speaking—talking to others to convey information effectively
* Active Listening—giving full attention to what other people are saying, taking time to understand the points being made, asking questions as appropriate, and not interrupting at inappropriate times

These knowledges are important in most of these jobs:

* Therapy and Counseling—principles, methods, and procedures for diagnosis, treatment, and rehabilitation of

physical and mental dysfunctions and for career counseling and guidance
* Personnel and Human Resources—principles and procedures for personnel recruitment, selection, training, compensation and benefits, labor relations and negotiation, and personnel information systems
* Foreign Language—the structure and content of a foreign (non-English) language, including the meaning and spelling of words, rules of composition and grammar, and pronunciation

What else should you consider about this kind of work?

These workers are employed by government agencies and by offices where medicine, law, and other professions are practiced. For government jobs with local, state, or federal agencies, a civil service test is often required.

Most of these jobs keep regular business hours, and they mostly take place in comfortable offices. Clients may sometimes be unpleasant because of delays and policies that are beyond the workers' control.

Some positions require workers who can be trusted with confidential information. Workers in small offices often perform a variety of tasks. They may also serve as bookkeepers, clerks, and receptionists.

Therefore, best opportunities are expected for workers who can handle a variety of office duties. The outlook is better for interviewers at medical and law offices than for welfare eligibility workers.

How can you prepare for jobs of this kind?

Occupations in this group usually require education and/or training ranging from a few weeks to six months. Workers receive their training on the job.

High school graduates who have a good working knowledge of English, grammar, spelling, and basic math can qualify for jobs in this group.

How much education or training is required for the jobs in this Work Group?

For descriptions of these jobs, see Part 2.

Short-term on-the-job training

* Interviewers, Except Eligibility and Loan

Moderate-term on-the-job training

* Claims Takers, Unemployment Benefits
* Welfare Eligibility Workers and Interviewers

© *2006 JIST Works*

11 Information Technology

An interest in designing, developing, managing, and supporting information systems. You can satisfy this interest by working with hardware, software, multimedia, or integrated systems. If you like to use your organizational skills, you might work as an administrator of a system or database. Or you can solve complex problems as a software engineer or systems analyst. If you enjoy getting your hands on the hardware, you might find work servicing computers, peripherals, and information-intense machines such as cash registers and ATMs.

11.01   Managerial Work in Information Technology

11.02   Information Technology Specialties

11.03   Digital Equipment Repair

11.01 Managerial Work in Information Technology

Workers in this group manage complex computer resources and the people who work with those resources. They have a combination of technical and supervisory skills.

What kind of work would you do?

Your work activities would depend on your job. For example, you might

* Assign and review the work of systems analysts, programmers, and other computer-related workers.
* Control operational budgets and expenditures.
* Evaluate data processing proposals to assess project feasibility and requirements.
* Manage backup, security, and user help systems.
* Recruit, hire, train, and supervise staff and/or participate in staffing decisions.
* Review project plans in order to plan and coordinate project activity.

What things about you point to this kind of work?

Is it important for you to

* Give directions and instructions to others?
* Have opportunities for advancement?
* Be paid well in comparison with other workers?
* Have good working conditions?
* Have co-workers who are easy to get along with?
* Have steady employment?
* Make decisions on your own?

Have you enjoyed any of the following as a hobby or leisure-time activity?

* Reading about technological developments, such as computer science or aerospace
* Writing computer programs
* Belonging to a computer club
* Serving as president of a club or other organization
* Serving as a leader of a scouting or other group

Have you liked and done well in any of the following school subjects?

* Management
* Accounting
* Computer Science
* Computer Network Management
* Personnel Management
* Technical Writing

Are you able to

* Apply general rules to specific problems to produce answers that make sense?

* Combine pieces of information to form general rules or conclusions?
* Come up with unusual or clever ideas about a given topic or situation or develop creative ways to solve a problem?
* Tell when something is wrong or is likely to go wrong?
* Identify or detect a known pattern that is hidden in other distracting material?
* Generate or use different sets of rules for combining or grouping things in different ways?
* Come up with a number of ideas about a topic?

Would you work in places such as

* Business offices?
* Government offices?
* Factories and plants?
* Hospitals and nursing homes?

What skills and knowledges do you need for this kind of work?

For most of these jobs, you need these skills:

* Programming—writing computer programs for various purposes
* Troubleshooting—determining causes of operating errors and deciding what to do about them
* Technology Design—generating or adapting equipment and technology to serve user needs
* Operations Analysis—analyzing needs and product requirements to create a design
* Installation—installing equipment, machines, wiring, or programs to meet specifications
* Systems Evaluation—identifying measures or indicators of system performance and the actions needed to improve or correct performance relative to the goals of the system
* Systems Analysis—determining how a system should work and how changes in conditions, operations, and the environment will affect outcomes

These knowledges are important in most of these jobs:

* Computers and Electronics—circuit boards; processors; chips; electronic equipment; and computer hardware and software, including applications and programming
* Telecommunications—transmission, broadcasting, switching, control, and operation of telecommunications systems
* Clerical Practices—administrative and clerical procedures and systems such as word processing, managing files and records, stenography and transcription, designing forms, and other office procedures and terminology
* Engineering and Technology—the practical application of engineering science and technology; this includes applying principles, techniques, procedures, and equipment to the design and production of various goods and services

* Administration and Management—business and management principles involved in strategic planning, resource allocation, human resources modeling, leadership techniques, production methods, and coordination of people and resources
* Design—design techniques, tools, and principles involved in production of precision technical plans, blueprints, drawings, and models
* Education and Training—principles and methods for curriculum and training design, teaching and instruction for individuals and groups, and the measurement of training effects

What else should you consider about this kind of work?

Information technology managers are employed by industry, government agencies, and educational institutions throughout the country.

They work most often in business offices, but they sometimes need to travel to visit clients or remote sites that are part of a computer network.

The outlook for these workers is good, especially for those who have a mixture of advanced technical know-how and managerial skills.

How can you prepare for jobs of this kind?

Computer and information systems managers usually need education and/or training ranging from four years to more than ten years.

The most common route to management is by first preparing to be a computer scientist, programmer, or engineer. After gaining experience and expertise in this kind of job, you might get formal or informal training in management that prepares you to deal with setting goals, measuring outcomes, accounting for financial resources, and managing human resources.

Another possible route is to obtain a master's degree in business administration with a concentration in technology or a bachelor's in management information systems with a good background in administration.

On this job, you need to keep your technical skills constantly up to date, but at the same time you need to take on greater managerial responsibilities so that your employer does not view you as simply an expensive programmer.

How much education or training is required for the jobs in this Work Group?

For descriptions of these jobs, see Part 2.

Bachelor's degree

* Network and Computer Systems Administrators

Work experience plus degree

* Computer and Information Systems Managers

11.02 Information Technology Specialties

Workers in this group use computer hardware and software to process information, solve problems, and conduct research. Many of these workers specialize in one aspect of computer systems, such as managing a database, keeping a system secure from hackers and virus attacks, or keeping the peripherals in working order.

What kind of work would you do?

Your work activities would depend on your job. For example, you might

* Analyze information processing or computation needs and plan and design computer systems, using techniques such as structured analysis, data modeling, and information engineering.
* Answer telephone calls to assist computer users encountering problems.
* Coordinate installation of software systems.
* Design and implement network configurations, network architecture, and systems.
* Design, develop, and modify software systems, using scientific analysis and mathematical models to predict and measure outcomes and consequences of designs.
* Develop plans to safeguard computer files against accidental or unauthorized modification, destruction, or disclosure and to meet emergency data processing needs.
* Modify existing databases and database management systems or direct programmers and analysts to make changes.
* Prepare evaluations of software or hardware and recommend improvements or upgrades.
* Write, update, and maintain computer programs or software packages to handle specific jobs, such as tracking inventory, storing or retrieving data, or controlling other equipment.

What things about you point to this kind of work?

Is it important for you to

* Be paid well in comparison with other workers?
* Have opportunities for advancement?
* Try out your own ideas?
* Have good working conditions?
* Have steady employment?
* Be treated fairly by the company?
* Make use of your individual abilities?

Have you enjoyed any of the following as a hobby or leisure-time activity?

* Writing computer programs
* Belonging to a computer club
* Playing chess or solving complex puzzles
* Creating Web pages

Have you liked and done well in any of the following school subjects?

* Computer Science
* Computer Programming
* Calculus
* Systems Analysis
* Database Theory/Design

Are you able to

* Arrange things or actions in a certain order or pattern according to a specific rule or set of rules?
* Apply general rules to specific problems to produce answers that make sense?
* Read and understand information and ideas presented in writing?
* Come up with unusual or clever ideas about a given topic or situation or develop creative ways to solve a problem?

Would you work in places such as

* Business offices?
* Government offices?
* Factories and plants?
* Hospitals and nursing homes?

What skills and knowledges do you need for this kind of work?

For most of these jobs, you need these skills:

* Programming—writing computer programs for various purposes
* Troubleshooting—determining causes of operating errors and deciding what to do about them
* Technology Design—generating or adapting equipment and technology to serve user needs
* Installation—installing equipment, machines, wiring, or programs to meet specifications
* Operations Analysis—analyzing needs and product requirements to create a design
* Systems Analysis—determining how a system should work and how changes in conditions, operations, and the environment will affect outcomes
* Complex Problem Solving—identifying complex problems and reviewing related information to develop and evaluate options and implement solutions

These knowledges are important in most of these jobs:

* Computers and Electronics—circuit boards; processors; chips; electronic equipment; and computer hardware and software, including applications and programming
* Telecommunications—transmission, broadcasting, switching, control, and operation of telecommunications systems
* Customer and Personal Service—principles and processes for providing customer and personal services; this includes customer needs assessment, meeting quality standards for services, and evaluation of customer satisfaction

* Design—design techniques, tools, and principles involved in production of precision technical plans, blueprints, drawings, and models
* Engineering and Technology—the practical application of engineering science and technology; this includes applying principles, techniques, procedures, and equipment to the design and production of various goods and services
* Mathematics—arithmetic, algebra, geometry, calculus, and statistics and their applications
* English Language—the structure and content of the English language, including the meaning and spelling of words, rules of composition, and grammar

What else should you consider about this kind of work?

Businesses and industries, colleges, research organizations, and government agencies hire these workers. Some specialists work as consultants on changing assignments. Those trained in financial analysis are most likely to have jobs with such places as banks, insurance companies, and government offices. Those trained in scientific analysis are most likely to work in colleges and in industrial research centers. People in government jobs usually must pass civil service tests.

The outlook for jobs in this group is mixed. There should be less demand for routine programming work and support specialists because sophisticated software makes it easy to perform many tasks and other tasks are being contracted out to offshore workers. Low-priced and easy-to-use peripherals and systems are cutting into the demand for computer operators. Specialists in computer security should be in demand. Best opportunities are for workers who combine the latest technical skills with an understanding of business and good communication skills.

How can you prepare for jobs of this kind?

Occupations in this group usually require education and/or training ranging from two years to more than ten years. Coursework in math concepts, statistics, technical writing, economics, computer science, programming languages, and accounting are useful for jobs in this group.

Beginners usually start as trainees even though they have the required education because the technology changes so fast that previous education or work may not be fully relevant to the new job. New hires are promoted to higher-level work after getting experience on the job.

Experience in banking, accounting, or a related field is helpful with some employers. Others prefer experience and training in a scientific or technical area.

Workers in this group are expected to keep up with developments and trends in their areas. They attend seminars and workshops, gain certifications from software vendors, or study for advanced degrees.

How much education or training is required for the jobs in this Work Group?

For descriptions of these jobs, see Part 2.

Moderate-term on-the-job training

✻ Computer Operators

Associate degree

✻ Computer Support Specialists

Bachelor's degree

✻ Computer Programmers
✻ Computer Security Specialists
✻ Computer Software Engineers, Applications
✻ Computer Software Engineers, Systems Software
✻ Computer Systems Analysts
✻ Database Administrators
✻ Network Systems and Data Communications Analysts

11.03 Digital Equipment Repair

Workers in this group repair and install digital electronic devices and systems such as computers, cash registers, printers, ATMs, and copiers.

What kind of work would you do?

Your work activities would depend on your job. For example, you might

✻ Adjust and repair vending machines and meters and replace defective mechanical and electrical parts.
✻ Align, adjust, and calibrate equipment according to specifications.
✻ Assemble and install machines according to specifications, using hand tools, power tools, and measuring devices.
✻ Instruct operators and servicers in operation, maintenance, and repair of machines.
✻ Keep records of machine maintenance and repair.
✻ Remove money canisters from ATMs and replenish machine supplies.
✻ Test electronic components and circuits to locate defects.

What things about you point to this kind of work?

Is it important for you to

✻ Do your work alone?
✻ Have supervisors who train workers well?

Have you enjoyed any of the following as a hobby or leisure-time activity?

✻ Upgrading hardware in personal computers
✻ Assembling radios, computers, and other devices from kits
✻ Taking apart or fixing mechanical and electronic devices
✻ Repairing electrical household appliances

Have you liked and done well in any of the following school subjects?

✻ Computer Concepts/Methods
✻ Electrical Circuits
✻ Electronic Devices
✻ Business Machine Repair

Are you able to

✻ Make precisely coordinated movements of the fingers of one or both hands to grasp, manipulate, or assemble very small objects?
✻ Match or detect differences between colors, including shades of color and brightness?
✻ Make fast, simple, repeated movements of the fingers, hands, and wrists?

Would you work in places such as

✻ Business offices?
✻ Government offices?
✻ Stores and shopping malls?

What skills and knowledges do you need for this kind of work?

For most of these jobs, you need these skills:

✻ Repairing—repairing machines or systems, using the needed tools
✻ Installation—installing equipment, machines, wiring, or programs to meet specifications
✻ Troubleshooting—determining causes of operating errors and deciding what to do about them
✻ Equipment Maintenance—performing routine maintenance on equipment and determining when and what kind of maintenance is needed

These knowledges are important in most of these jobs:

✻ Computers and Electronics—circuit boards; processors; chips; electronic equipment; and computer hardware and software, including applications and programming
✻ Telecommunications—transmission, broadcasting, switching, control, and operation of telecommunications systems
✻ Mechanical Devices—machines and tools, including their designs, uses, repair, and maintenance

What else should you consider about this kind of work?

Since digital equipment is used almost everywhere, the jobs in this group are found in almost every large and small city. Factories, service companies, and large companies with an in-house service staff hire many of these workers. Others are self-employed, working full-time or part-time. Work schedules vary.

Some equipment repairs or adjustments are made in a repair shop; others are made where the equipment is installed.

Best opportunities are for repairers who understand electronics and not just how to repair one product. Because of miniaturization and better quality control, some products need fewer repairs and service calls. Nevertheless, so many new digital devices are being created that the field as a whole is growing.

How can you prepare for jobs of this kind?

Work in this group usually requires education and/or training ranging from six months to less than two or three years, depending on the type of equipment. Regardless of prior education or training, most new hires receive on-the-job training to learn skills needed for particular machines.

Colleges and technical schools offer two-year programs in electronics technology or electrical engineering technology. Courses in electricity, electronics, mathematics, and blueprint reading are especially helpful.

Some workers learn about electricity and electronics through correspondence courses, apprenticeships, or military training.

Technology in this field is changing constantly, so workers need to take courses and get training to keep their skills current.

How much education or training is required for the jobs in this Work Group?

For descriptions of these jobs, see Part 2.

Moderate-term on-the-job training

* Coin, Vending, and Amusement Machine Servicers and Repairers

Long-term on-the-job training

* Automatic Teller Machine Servicers
* Office Machine and Cash Register Servicers

Postsecondary vocational training

* Data Processing Equipment Repairers

12 Law and Public Safety

An interest in upholding people's rights or in protecting people and property by using authority, inspecting, or investigating. You can satisfy this interest by working in law, law enforcement, fire fighting, the military, or related fields. For example, if you enjoy mental challenge and intrigue, you could investigate crimes or fires for a living. If you enjoy working with verbal skills and research skills, you may want to defend citizens in court or research deeds, wills, and other legal documents. If you want to help people in critical situations, you may want to fight fires, work as a police officer, or become a paramedic. Or, if you want more routine work in public safety, perhaps a job in guarding, patrolling, or inspecting would appeal to you. If you have management ability, you could seek a leadership position in law enforcement and the protective services. Work in the military gives you a chance to use technical and leadership skills while serving your country.

12.01 Managerial Work in Law and Public Safety

12.02 Legal Practice and Justice Administration

12.03 Legal Support

12.04 Law Enforcement and Public Safety

12.05 Safety and Security

12.06 Emergency Responding

12.07 Military

12.01 Managerial Work in Law and Public Safety

Workers in this group manage fire and police departments. They set goals and policies, oversee financial and human resources, evaluate outcomes, and represent their departments to the public and the governments of the jurisdictions they serve.

What kind of work would you do?

Your work activities would depend on your job. For example, you might

* Develop, implement, and revise departmental policies and procedures.
* Direct investigations of suspected arsons in wildfires, working closely with other investigating agencies.
* Discipline staff for violation of department rules and regulations.
* Educate the public about forest fire prevention by participating in activities such as exhibits and presentations and by distributing promotional materials.
* Evaluate the performance of assigned firefighting personnel.
* Write and submit proposals for repair, modification, or replacement of firefighting equipment.

What things about you point to this kind of work?

Is it important for you to

* Give directions and instructions to others?
* Be looked up to by others in your company and your community?
* Have co-workers who are easy to get along with?
* Get a feeling of accomplishment?
* Make decisions on your own?
* Have steady employment?
* Plan your work with little supervision?

Have you enjoyed any of the following as a hobby or leisure-time activity?

* Being a member of the school safety patrol
* Serving as a volunteer in a fire department or emergency rescue squad
* Applying first aid in emergencies as a volunteer
* Serving as president of a club or other organization
* Reading detective stories; watching television detective shows

Have you liked and done well in any of the following school subjects?

* Management
* Accounting
* Law Enforcement
* Fire Fighting
* Personnel Management
* Technical Writing

* Emergency Care/Rescue
* Penology
* Police Science
* Criminology

Are you able to

* See objects in the presence of glare or bright lighting?
* Respond quickly to a signal when it appears?
* Exert yourself physically over long periods of time without getting winded or out of breath?
* See under low light conditions?
* Know your location in relation to the environment or know where other objects are in relation to you?
* Choose quickly between two or more movements in response to two or more different signals?
* Keep or regain your body balance or stay upright when in an unstable position?

Would you work in places such as

* Jails and reformatories?
* Police headquarters?
* Fire stations?
* Government offices?
* Scenes of crimes or emergencies?

What skills and knowledges do you need for this kind of work?

For most of these jobs, you need these skills:

* Management of Personnel Resources—motivating, developing, and directing people as they work, identifying the best people for the job
* Service Orientation—actively looking for ways to help people
* Management of Material Resources—obtaining and seeing to the appropriate use of equipment, facilities, and materials needed to do certain work
* Coordination—adjusting actions in relation to others' actions
* Persuasion—persuading others to change their minds or behavior
* Judgment and Decision Making—considering the relative costs and benefits of potential actions to choose the most appropriate one
* Instructing—teaching others how to do something

These knowledges are important in most of these jobs:

* Public Safety and Security—relevant equipment, policies, procedures, and strategies to promote effective local, state, or national security operations for the protection of people, data, property, and institutions
* Education and Training—principles and methods for curriculum and training design, teaching and instruction for individuals and groups, and the measurement of training effects
* Personnel and Human Resources—principles and procedures for personnel recruitment, selection, training, compensation and benefits, labor relations and negotiation, and personnel information systems

* Telecommunications—transmission, broadcasting, switching, control, and operation of telecommunications systems
* Transportation—principles and methods for moving people or goods by air, rail, sea, or road, including the relative costs and benefits
* Law and Government—laws, legal codes, court procedures, precedents, government regulations, executive orders, agency rules, and the democratic political process
* Therapy and Counseling—principles, methods, and procedures for diagnosis, treatment, and rehabilitation of physical and mental dysfunctions and for career counseling and guidance

What else should you consider about this kind of work?

These workers are hired by police and fire departments in cities and towns throughout the U.S. They may have to take a civil service exam to qualify. Supervisors of forest fire fighters mostly work for the federal government.

These jobs carry considerable responsibility. Workers are responsible not only for budgets, facilities, equipment, and staff, but also for the safety and security of hundreds or maybe thousands of citizens. Because they are on the public payroll, the higher-level jobs are also political. They may be helped by an alliance with a popular political figure, but they may be threatened if that person loses power. They also require sensitivity to local neighborhood and ethnic interests.

Advancement proceeds up a series of ranks that vary from one jurisdiction to another. In addition to experience, some training or exams may be required for promotion. At the highest levels, many advance by taking a position in another town or city.

How can you prepare for jobs of this kind?

Occupations in this group usually require from four to six years of education and/or training. Less education is necessary initially, because almost all managers of police and firefighting agencies begin as police detectives or fire fighters and work up through the ranks. They may complete a two-year college major in fire science or a two- or four-year major in law enforcement and then get training to advance in rank.

Specialized training in an area such as juvenile crime or fire inspection helps early in the career; later, training in management is helpful to move up from the street to a managerial position.

How much education or training is required for the jobs in this Work Group?

For descriptions of these jobs, see Part 2.

Work experience in a related occupation

* Emergency Management Specialists
* First-Line Supervisors/Managers of Correctional Officers
* First-Line Supervisors/Managers of Police and Detectives

* Forest Fire Fighting and Prevention Supervisors
* Municipal Fire Fighting and Prevention Supervisors

12.02 Legal Practice and Justice Administration

Workers in this group provide legal advice and representation to clients, hear and make decisions on court cases, and help individuals and groups reach agreements. Although they specialize in many different fields, all of them apply knowledge of laws and regulations to the problems they must solve.

What kind of work would you do?

Your work activities would depend on your job. For example, you might

* Examine legal data to determine advisability of defending or prosecuting lawsuits.
* Monitor and direct the activities of trials and hearings to ensure that they are conducted fairly and that courts administer justice while safeguarding the legal rights of all involved parties.
* Prepare legal briefs and opinions and file appeals in state and federal courts of appeal.
* Sentence defendants in criminal cases on conviction by jury according to applicable government statutes.
* Use mediation techniques to facilitate communication between disputants, to further parties' understanding of different perspectives, and to guide parties toward mutual agreement.

What things about you point to this kind of work?

Is it important for you to

* Plan your work with little supervision?
* Make decisions on your own?
* Have steady employment?
* Have good working conditions?
* Be paid well in comparison with other workers?
* Receive recognition for the work you do?
* Be looked up to by others in your company and your community?

Have you enjoyed any of the following as a hobby or leisure-time activity?

* Doing public speaking or debating
* Writing articles, stories, or plays
* Playing chess or solving complex puzzles
* Being on the debate team

Have you liked and done well in any of the following school subjects?

* Law, Comprehensive
* Philosophy
* Arbitration/Negotiation
* Contract Law
* Business Law

Are you able to

* Remember information such as words, numbers, pictures, and procedures?
* Read and understand information and ideas presented in writing?
* Listen to and understand information and ideas presented through spoken words and sentences?
* Apply general rules to specific problems to produce answers that make sense?
* Speak clearly so others can understand you?
* Combine pieces of information to form general rules or conclusions?
* Communicate information and ideas in writing so others will understand?

Would you work in places such as

* Business offices?
* Courthouses?
* Government offices?

What skills and knowledges do you need for this kind of work?

For most of these jobs, you need these skills:

* Judgment and Decision Making—considering the relative costs and benefits of potential actions to choose the most appropriate one
* Active Listening—giving full attention to what other people are saying, taking time to understand the points being made, asking questions as appropriate, and not interrupting at inappropriate times
* Critical Thinking—using logic and reasoning to identify the strengths and weaknesses of alternative solutions, conclusions, or approaches to problems
* Negotiation—bringing others together and trying to reconcile differences
* Active Learning—understanding the implications of new information for both current and future problem solving and decision making
* Reading Comprehension—understanding written sentences and paragraphs in work-related documents
* Writing—communicating effectively in writing as appropriate for the needs of the audience

These knowledges are important in most of these jobs:

* Law and Government—laws, legal codes, court procedures, precedents, government regulations, executive orders, agency rules, and the democratic political process
* English Language—the structure and content of the English language, including the meaning and spelling of words, rules of composition, and grammar
* History and Archeology—historical events and their causes, indicators, and effects on civilizations and cultures
* Sociology and Anthropology—group behavior and dynamics, societal trends and influences, human migrations, ethnicity, and cultures and their history and origins

* Philosophy and Theology—different philosophical systems and religions; this includes their basic principles, values, ethics, ways of thinking, customs, practices, and impact on human culture
* Psychology—human behavior and performance; individual differences in ability, personality, and interests; learning and motivation; psychological research methods; and the assessment and treatment of behavioral and affective disorders

What else should you consider about this kind of work?

People in this group either work for others or set up private law practices. Many find work in private businesses or with government agencies. New lawyers and other workers in this group have better employment opportunities in large cities than in small communities.

Lawyers in small towns and cities conduct civil or criminal cases in court, draw up wills and other legal papers, and perform related activities. Those in large cities usually specialize in one kind of law, such as criminal, civil, tax, labor, or patent.

Some government workers in this group are elected or appointed to office. Others get jobs through civil service channels, which often requires passing an exam. Many of these jobs are in county seats or state capitals.

Most workers in this group have regular office hours, but many put in much more than the usual eight hours a day. They spend evenings and weekends doing things related to their work or get involved in social and community activities that will help their careers. Workers in private practice have to get and keep clients. Many of them try to get agreements with businesses and individuals to handle all their legal problems so they can be sure of a steady income.

The outlook for lawyers is mixed, with certain specializations (e.g., intellectual-property, environmental, and antitrust law) providing more job openings than others.

The outlook for judges is only fair because of budgetary pressures at all levels of government. The outlook is somewhat better for arbitrators, mediators, and conciliators.

How can you prepare for jobs of this kind?

Occupations in this group usually require more than ten years of education and/or training.

Lawyers must pass the bar exam to practice law. Educational requirements vary. In most states, proof of graduation from an approved law school is necessary. Some states accept a four-year college degree and completion of a program for law clerks or an apprenticeship with a licensed lawyer. Correspondence courses in law are accepted as preparation for the bar examination in a few states.

Competition for entry to law schools is keen. Most law schools require a four-year college degree. The major does not matter, so long as it prepares you with skills for logic, critical thinking, library research, writing, and speaking.

Law students take courses in constitutional law, legal procedures, criminal law, torts, wills and estates, real estate law, labor law, criminal versus civil procedure, and so forth.

Federal and state judges are usually required to be licensed lawyers, but some magistrates are not lawyers.

Some arbitrators, mediators, and conciliators have law degrees, but others get a master's degree in a field such as conflict resolution or get training and certification from a professional organization.

How much education or training is required for the jobs in this Work Group?

For descriptions of these jobs, see Part 2.

Work experience plus degree

* Administrative Law Judges, Adjudicators, and Hearing Officers
* Arbitrators, Mediators, and Conciliators
* Judges, Magistrate Judges, and Magistrates

First professional degree

* Lawyers

12.03 Legal Support

Workers in this group conduct investigations into legal matters and prepare drafts of legal documents. They handle many tasks that allow lawyers and judges to do their jobs more efficiently.

What kind of work would you do?

Your work activities would depend on your job. For example, you might

* Compare legal descriptions of property with legal descriptions contained in records and indices to verify such factors as deed ownership.
* Copy or summarize recorded documents, such as mortgages, trust deeds, and contracts, affecting title to property.
* Prepare legal documents, including briefs, pleadings, appeals, wills, contracts, and real estate closing statements.
* Search lot books, geographic and general indices, and assessor's rolls to compile lists of transactions pertaining to property.
* Search records to determine if delinquent taxes are due.

What things about you point to this kind of work?

Is it important for you to

* Have opportunities for advancement?
* Have good working conditions?

Have you enjoyed any of the following as a hobby or leisure-time activity?

* Researching things that sound interesting to you
* Learning to use new features of word-processing and other programs

Have you liked and done well in any of the following school subjects?

* Legal Terminology
* Business Writing
* Data Retrieval Techniques
* Business Computer Applications
* Business Machine Operating
* Business Law
* Contract Law

Are you able to

* See details at close range?
* Read and understand information and ideas presented in writing?
* Communicate information and ideas in writing so others will understand?

Would you work in places such as

* Business offices?
* Courthouses?
* Government offices?

What skills and knowledges do you need for this kind of work?

For most of these jobs, you need these skills:

* Writing—communicating effectively in writing as appropriate for the needs of the audience
* Active Listening—giving full attention to what other people are saying, taking time to understand the points being made, asking questions as appropriate, and not interrupting at inappropriate times
* Critical Thinking—using logic and reasoning to identify the strengths and weaknesses of alternative solutions, conclusions, or approaches to problems

These knowledges are important in most of these jobs:

* Law and Government—laws, legal codes, court procedures, precedents, government regulations, executive orders, agency rules, and the democratic political process
* Clerical Practices—administrative and clerical procedures and systems such as word processing, managing files and records, stenography and transcription, designing forms, and other office procedures and terminology
* English Language—the structure and content of the English language, including the meaning and spelling of words, rules of composition, and grammar
* Economics and Accounting—economic and accounting principles and practices, the financial markets, banking, and the analysis and reporting of financial data

What else should you consider about this kind of work?

People in this group work for law firms, legal departments of businesses, and government agencies.

In a large law firm or business, paralegals may specialize in one kind of law, such as criminal or tax, or one kind of responsibility, such as planning estates or drafting contracts.

Law clerks work for judges and large law firms. Most are recent law school graduates; some divide their time between work and law school.

Most of the work is done in comfortable offices during regular working hours, but sometimes late hours are required for the sake of a pressing court case, contract, or tax deadline.

The job outlook for paralegals is good, especially if they have formal training. Law clerks and title examiners, searchers, and abstractors have only a fair job outlook because automation has made workers more productive.

How can you prepare for jobs of this kind?

Occupations in this group usually require education and/or training ranging from six months to less than ten years.

Paralegals need legal knowledge but do not practice law. Many of them enter the field with a two- or four-year degree in paralegal studies; some get a certificate in paralegal studies after a degree in another field.

Law clerks generally hold a bachelor's degree or they have completed law school but have not yet passed the bar exam.

Title examiners, abstractors, and searchers receive on-the-job training for six months or more.

How much education or training is required for the jobs in this Work Group?

For descriptions of these jobs, see Part 2.

Moderate-term on-the-job training

* Title Searchers

Long-term on-the-job training

* Title Examiners and Abstractors

Associate degree

* Paralegals and Legal Assistants

Bachelor's degree

* Law Clerks

12.04 Law Enforcement and Public Safety

Workers in this group enforce laws and investigate suspicious persons and acts. They patrol an assigned territory to prevent crimes or investigate after crimes or fires to identify the causes or persons responsible and provide evidence for the courtroom.

What kind of work would you do?

Your work activities would depend on your job. For example, you might

* Examine fire sites and collect evidence such as glass, metal fragments, charred wood, and accelerant residue for use in determining the cause of a fire.
* Maintain order in courtroom during trials and guard juries from outside contact.
* Maintain surveillance of establishments to obtain identifying information on suspects.
* Patrol railroad yards, cars, stations, and other facilities in order to protect company property and shipments and to maintain order.
* Render aid to accident victims and other persons requiring first aid for physical injuries.
* Search for and collect evidence such as fingerprints, using investigative equipment.
* Search prisoners, cells, and vehicles for weapons, valuables, or drugs.
* Testify in court about investigative and analytical methods and findings.
* Transport or escort prisoners and defendants en route to courtrooms, prisons or jails, attorneys' offices, or medical facilities.
* Write warnings and citations for illegally parked vehicles.

What things about you point to this kind of work?

Is it important for you to

* Have steady employment?
* Have supervisors who back up workers with management?

Have you enjoyed any of the following as a hobby or leisure-time activity?

* Experimenting with a chemistry set
* Directing traffic at community events
* Reading detective stories; watching television detective shows
* Instructing family members in observing traffic regulations
* Researching things that sound interesting to you

Have you liked and done well in any of the following school subjects?

* Law Enforcement
* Laboratory Science
* Data Retrieval Techniques
* Record Keeping
* Police Science
* Criminal Investigating
* Criminology

Are you able to

* See under low light conditions?
* See objects in the presence of glare or bright lighting?

* Identify or detect a known pattern that is hidden in other distracting material?
* See details at a distance?
* Choose quickly between two or more movements in response to two or more different signals?
* See objects or movement of objects to your side when your eyes are looking ahead?
* Know your location in relation to the environment or know where other objects are in relation to you?

Would you work in places such as

* Police headquarters?
* Scenes of crimes or emergencies?
* Streets and highways?
* Bus and train stations?

What skills and knowledges do you need for this kind of work?

For most of these jobs, you need these skills:

* Social Perceptiveness—being aware of others' reactions and understanding why they react as they do
* Persuasion—persuading others to change their minds or behavior
* Active Listening—giving full attention to what other people are saying, taking time to understand the points being made, asking questions as appropriate, and not interrupting at inappropriate times
* Negotiation—bringing others together and trying to reconcile differences

These knowledges are important in most of these jobs:

* Public Safety and Security—relevant equipment, policies, procedures, and strategies to promote effective local, state, or national security operations for the protection of people, data, property, and institutions
* Law and Government—laws, legal codes, court procedures, precedents, government regulations, executive orders, agency rules, and the democratic political process
* Psychology—human behavior and performance; individual differences in ability, personality, and interests; learning and motivation; psychological research methods; and the assessment and treatment of behavioral and affective disorders
* Telecommunications—transmission, broadcasting, switching, control, and operation of telecommunications systems
* Philosophy and Theology—different philosophical systems and religions; this includes their basic principles, values, ethics, ways of thinking, customs, practices, and impact on human culture
* Sociology and Anthropology—group behavior and dynamics, societal trends and influences, human migrations, ethnicity, and cultures and their history and origins
* Transportation—principles and methods for moving people or goods by air, rail, sea, or road, including the relative costs and benefits

What else should you consider about this kind of work?

Most jobs in this group are with federal, state, and local government agencies. Some are hired by private businesses and operate in a variety of settings, such as stores, office buildings, airports, railroads, and industrial plants.

Government workers usually must pass civil service tests and meet certain physical and personal requirements to be hired. Applicants for jobs with government agencies can usually take the required tests at any time. The names of those who pass are kept on file for consideration when jobs open.

Shift work is standard, and sometimes overtime work is required. Most workers in these jobs are on call at all times to respond to emergencies.

Jobs in investigating can be physically demanding and dangerous, but the workers are trained to handle problems in the safest and most practical way possible. Crime scenes may be distressing, and workers there must take precautions to avoid infectious agents.

Keen competition is expected for higher-paying police jobs at the state and federal level, but opportunities will be good in local jurisdictions and high-crime areas. The outlook for correctional officers is excellent. Forensic science technicians with high-demand skills, such as DNA testing, will be in demand.

How can you prepare for jobs of this kind?

Occupations in this group usually require education and/or training ranging from less than six months to more than ten years.

Local civil service regulations usually control the selection of police officers. Workers must be U.S. citizens, and their height and weight must be within certain ranges. In addition, these workers may be required to take written, oral, and physical examinations. The physical examinations often include tests of strength and ability to move quickly and easily. To work in these jobs, persons should be in good physical condition to use firearms and work on dangerous missions. Background investigations are made of all applicants.

Many jobs in this group require knowledge of government, psychology, sociology, and law enforcement. Most police departments prefer to hire people with a high school education or its equal, and some require some college. Police and correctional officers get training at special academies lasting a few months plus additional training at the job site.

Forensic science technicians should hold a bachelor's degree. Many colleges offer a major or concentration in forensic science.

Jobs with federal law enforcement agencies usually require a college degree. For example, FBI special agents are required to have a degree in law or an accounting degree plus a year of related work experience. Promotions are usually based on written examinations and job performance, as specified by civil service laws.

How much education or training is required for the jobs in this Work Group?

For descriptions of these jobs, see Part 2.

Short-term on-the-job training

* Parking Enforcement Workers

Moderate-term on-the-job training

* Bailiffs
* Correctional Officers and Jailers

Long-term on-the-job training

* Highway Patrol Pilots
* Police Patrol Officers
* Sheriffs and Deputy Sheriffs
* Transit and Railroad Police

Work experience in a related occupation

* Criminal Investigators and Special Agents
* Police Detectives
* Police Identification and Records Officers

Associate degree

* Forensic Science Technicians

Bachelor's degree

* Fire Investigators

12.05 Safety and Security

Workers in this group protect people, animals, and property. They keep watch to make sure that safe and secure procedures are being followed. They may provide evidence in a court case involving damages, fraud, or divorce.

What kind of work would you do?

Your work activities would depend on your job. For example, you might

* Capture and remove stray, uncontrolled, or abused animals from undesirable conditions, using nets, nooses, or tranquilizer darts as necessary.
* Direct traffic movement or warn of hazards, using signs, flags, lanterns, and hand signals.
* Monitor and authorize entrance and departure of employees, visitors, and other persons to guard against theft and maintain security of premises.
* Patrol or monitor recreational areas such as trails, slopes, and swimming areas.
* Perform undercover operations such as evaluating the performance and honesty of employees by posing as customers or employees.

What things about you point to this kind of work?

Is it important for you to

* Give directions and instructions to others?

* Have work where you do things for other people?

Have you enjoyed any of the following as a hobby or leisure-time activity?

* Instructing family members in observing traffic regulations
* Reading detective stories; watching television detective shows
* Directing traffic at community events

Have you liked and done well in any of the following school subjects?

* Law Enforcement
* Safety Regulations
* Data Retrieval Techniques
* Criminal Investigating
* Emergency Care/Rescue
* First Aid

Are you able to

* See details at a distance?
* Tell the direction from which a sound originated?
* See under low light conditions?
* Exert yourself physically over long periods of time without getting winded or out of breath?
* See objects or movement of objects to your side when your eyes are looking ahead?
* Respond quickly to a signal when it appears?
* Use short bursts of muscle force to propel yourself or to throw an object?

Would you work in places such as

* Business offices?
* Office buildings?
* Factories and plants?
* Streets and highways?
* Stores and shopping malls?
* Gambling casinos and card clubs?
* Country clubs and resorts?
* Parks and campgrounds?

What skills and knowledges do you need for this kind of work?

For most of these jobs, you need these skills:

* Service Orientation—actively looking for ways to help people
* Social Perceptiveness—being aware of others' reactions and understanding why they react as they do
* Persuasion—persuading others to change their minds or behavior

These knowledges are important in most of these jobs:

* Public Safety and Security—relevant equipment, policies, procedures, and strategies to promote effective local, state, or national security operations for the protection of people, data, property, and institutions

* Telecommunications—transmission, broadcasting, switching, control, and operation of telecommunications systems
* Law and Government—laws, legal codes, court procedures, precedents, government regulations, executive orders, agency rules, and the democratic political process

What else should you consider about this kind of work?

Some of these workers are employed by federal, state, and local governments. Others are hired by private businesses, security services, or detective agencies. They operate in a variety of settings, such as stores, office buildings, streets, industrial plants, hotels, and resorts.

Some of these jobs can be dangerous, but workers are trained in how to avoid injury. Part-time or seasonal work is common in some of these occupations. Government workers usually must pass civil service tests.

The outlook for most of these jobs is good. Public concern for safety and security is resisting pressures to downsize governments, and in the private sector the wish to avoid theft, fraud, and lawsuits will create many jobs. About one-third of private detectives are self-employed.

How can you prepare for jobs of this kind?

Occupations in this group usually require education and/or training ranging from a few weeks to less than two years.

Employers provide on-the-job training for most of these jobs. Trainees learn safety procedures, relevant laws, and how to operate related equipment. Prior training in certain special skills may be helpful. For example, lifeguards are expected to be certified for their swimming and rescue skills, and some security guards need to be able to handle firearms. Many private detectives enter the field after experience in police work. Many of these jobs require job applicants to pass a test of physical condition or a background investigation.

How much education or training is required for the jobs in this Work Group?

For descriptions of these jobs, see Part 2.

Short-term on-the-job training

* Crossing Guards
* Lifeguards, Ski Patrol, and Other Recreational Protective Service Workers
* Security Guards

Moderate-term on-the-job training

* Animal Control Workers

Long-term on-the-job training

* Gaming Surveillance Officers and Gaming Investigators

Work experience in a related occupation

* Private Detectives and Investigators

12.06 Emergency Responding

Workers in this group protect the public by responding to emergencies. Working as fast as possible, they stabilize sick or injured people, put out fires, and evacuate people from buildings. Dealing with sudden crises requires them to have both technical skills and the ability keep a cool head.

What kind of work would you do?

Your work activities would depend on your job. For example, you might

* Administer first-aid treatment and life-support care to sick or injured persons in prehospital setting.
* Drive mobile intensive care unit to specified location, following instructions from emergency medical dispatcher.
* Extinguish flames and embers to suppress fires, using shovels or engine- or hand-driven water or chemical pumps.
* Fell trees, cut and clear brush, and dig trenches in order to create firelines, using axes, chainsaws, or shovels.
* Inform and educate the public about fire prevention.
* Participate in physical training activities in order to maintain a high level of physical fitness.
* Rescue victims from burning buildings and accident sites.
* Take action to contain hazardous chemicals that might catch fire, leak, or spill.

What things about you point to this kind of work?

Is it important for you to

* Have co-workers who are easy to get along with?
* Get a feeling of accomplishment?
* Have work where you do things for other people?
* Be looked up to by others in your company and your community?

Have you enjoyed any of the following as a hobby or leisure-time activity?

* Learning first aid and CPR
* Serving as a volunteer in a fire department or emergency rescue squad
* Applying first aid in emergencies as a volunteer
* Doing volunteer work for the Red Cross

Have you liked and done well in any of the following school subjects?

* Fire Fighting
* Emergency Care/Rescue
* Health
* First Aid

Are you able to

* Exert yourself physically over long periods of time without getting winded or out of breath?

* Exert maximum muscle force to lift, push, pull, or carry objects?
* Keep or regain your body balance or stay upright when in an unstable position?
* Exert muscle force repeatedly or continuously over time?
* See objects in the presence of glare or bright lighting?
* Quickly move your arms and legs?
* Time your movements or the movement of a piece of equipment in anticipation of changes in the speed and/or direction of a moving object or scene?

Would you work in places such as

* Fire stations?
* Scenes of crimes or emergencies?
* Forests?

What skills and knowledges do you need for this kind of work?

For most of these jobs, you need these skills:

* Equipment Maintenance—performing routine maintenance on equipment and determining when and what kind of maintenance is needed
* Service Orientation—actively looking for ways to help people
* Equipment Selection—determining the kind of tools and equipment needed to do a job
* Coordination—adjusting actions in relation to others' actions
* Social Perceptiveness—being aware of others' reactions and understanding why they react as they do
* Operation Monitoring—watching gauges, dials, or other indicators to make sure a machine is working properly
* Instructing—teaching others how to do something

These knowledges are important in most of these jobs:

* Customer and Personal Service—principles and processes for providing customer and personal services; this includes customer needs assessment, meeting quality standards for services, and evaluation of customer satisfaction
* Medicine and Dentistry—the information and techniques needed to diagnose and treat human injuries, diseases, and deformities; this includes symptoms, treatment alternatives, drug properties and interactions, and preventive health care measures
* Public Safety and Security—relevant equipment, policies, procedures, and strategies to promote effective local, state, or national security operations for the protection of people, data, property, and institutions
* Psychology—human behavior and performance; individual differences in ability, personality, and interests; learning and motivation; psychological research methods; and the assessment and treatment of behavioral and affective disorders
* Transportation—principles and methods for moving people or goods by air, rail, sea, or road, including the relative costs and benefits

* Chemistry—the chemical composition, structure, and properties of substances and of the chemical processes and transformations that they undergo; this includes uses of chemicals and their danger signs, production techniques, and disposal methods

What else should you consider about this kind of work?

Many jobs in this group are with local, state, and federal governments. For most government jobs, you must pass a civil service examination. Some jobs are with private industry, such as private ambulance services. Most jobs are in cities because in towns and rural communities most of this work is done by volunteers.

Emergencies can happen at any hour of the day or night, so these workers often put in some evening or night shift work. The work may be hazardous or expose workers to infectious agents.

The trend toward professionalizing is expected to improve the employment outlook for paramedics, with best opportunities expected in private ambulance services. Keen competition can be expected for firefighting jobs, however.

How can you prepare for jobs of this kind?

Occupations in this group usually require education and/or training ranging from six months to less than two years.

Emergency medical technicians take special classes at technical schools, community colleges, and propriety schools, perhaps as part of an apprenticeship. Some get training in the military. They must pass exams for certification and continue to recertify throughout their careers.

Fire fighters often qualify by scoring high on a series of tests that include physical stamina. Then they are trained at a local academy or training center. Prior academic training beyond high school is usually not required but is becoming more common. Some fire fighters learn their skills through an apprenticeship program that may take three or more years.

How much education or training is required for the jobs in this Work Group?

For descriptions of these jobs, see Part 2.

Long-term on-the-job training

* Forest Fire Fighters
* Municipal Fire Fighters

Postsecondary vocational training

* Emergency Medical Technicians and Paramedics

12.07 Military

Workers in this group serve in the armed forces of the United States: the Air Force, Army, Coast Guard, Marines, Navy, and National Guard. Although workers in the armed forces perform almost every occupation found in the

© 2006 JIST Works

civilian workforce, the occupations in this group are unique to the military and have no civilian counterparts. The purpose of workers in the military is to ensure peace and protect the nation in times of war. In unusual cases, the military must assist in national emergencies or to restore order in events of civil disobedience.

What things about you point to this kind of work?

Have you enjoyed any of the following as a hobby or leisure-time activity?

* Reading military stories; watching television shows and movies about the military
* Doing strenuous activities, such as dancing, climbing, backpacking, running, swimming, and skiing
* Hunting or target shooting
* Operating a motorboat or other pleasure boat

Would you work in places such as

* Military installations?
* Airplanes?
* Ships and boats?

What else should you consider about this kind of work?

You must pass physical and mental tests and be within certain age limits to qualify for military occupations. Women are excluded from jobs that involve direct exposure to combat. The jobs require a high degree of physical conditioning. Usually, workers are assigned for short periods and must move frequently. The work environment is highly structured, and you must be able to understand and follow orders. You are required to wear uniforms and obey some regulations not found in civilian life. The work schedule can vary a great deal. Military personnel who engage the enemy are under a great deal of physical and mental stress. Jobs can be highly dangerous, even during peacetime.

Although the military has done a lot of downsizing in recent years, there are many opportunities for new recruits. Military service can be a stepping stone to many good careers in civilian life.

How can you prepare for jobs of this kind?

Occupations in this group usually require a high school education. Officers and senior personnel are normally required to have a college education. Promotion to higher ranks in the officer corps usually requires graduate education. All jobs require several months to several years of specialized military training, including physical conditioning.

How much education or training is required for the jobs in this Work Group?

For descriptions of these jobs, see Part 2.

Moderate-term on-the-job training

* Air Crew Members
* Aircraft Launch and Recovery Specialists
* Armored Assault Vehicle Crew Members
* Artillery and Missile Crew Members
* Command and Control Center Specialists
* Infantry
* Radar and Sonar Technicians

Long-term on-the-job training

* Air Crew Officers
* Aircraft Launch and Recovery Officers
* Armored Assault Vehicle Officers
* Artillery and Missile Officers
* Command and Control Center Officers
* Infantry Officers
* Special Forces
* Special Forces Officers

Work experience in a related occupation

* First-Line Supervisors/Managers of Air Crew Members
* First-Line Supervisors/Managers of Weapons Specialists/Crew Members

13 Manufacturing

An interest in processing materials into intermediate or final products or maintaining and repairing products by using machines or hand tools. You can satisfy this interest by working in one of many industries that mass-produce goods or by working for a utility that distributes electric power or other resources. You may enjoy manual work, using your hands or hand tools in highly skilled jobs such as assembling engines or electronic equipment. If you enjoy making machines run efficiently or fixing them when they break down, you could seek a job installing or repairing such devices as copiers, aircraft engines, cars, or watches. Perhaps you prefer to set up or operate machines that are used to manufacture products made of food, glass, or paper. You may enjoy cutting and grinding metal and plastic parts to desired shapes and measurements. Or you may wish to operate equipment in systems that provide water and process wastewater. You may like inspecting, sorting, counting, or weighing products. Another option is to work with your hands and machinery to move boxes and freight in a warehouse. If leadership appeals to you, you could manage people engaged in production and repair.

13.01   Managerial Work in Manufacturing

13.02   Machine Setup and Operation

13.03   Production Work, Assorted Materials Processing

13.04   Welding, Brazing, and Soldering

13.05   Production Machining Technology

13.06   Production Precision Work

13.07   **Production Quality Control**

13.08   **Graphic Arts Production**

13.09   **Hands-On Work, Assorted Materials**

13.10   **Woodworking Technology**

13.11   **Apparel, Shoes, Leather, and Fabric Care**

13.12   **Electrical and Electronic Repair**

13.13   **Machinery Repair**

13.14   **Vehicle and Facility Mechanical Work**

13.15   **Medical and Technical Equipment Repair**

13.16   **Utility Operation and Energy Distribution**

13.17   **Loading, Moving, Hoisting, and Conveying**

13.01 Managerial Work in Manufacturing

Workers in this group manage manufacturing and repair processes. They make decisions about policy and operation in line with company policy and goals. They must have working knowledge of the equipment and methods for the activity that they direct.

What kind of work would you do?

Your work activities would depend on your job. For example, you might

* Coordinate and recommend procedures for maintaining or modifying facility and equipment.
* Develop and implement production tracking and quality control systems, analyzing production, quality control, maintenance, and other operational reports to detect production problems.
* Interpret specifications, blueprints, job orders, and company policies and procedures for workers.
* Monitor employees' work levels and review work performance.
* Transmit and explain work orders to laborers.

What things about you point to this kind of work?

Is it important for you to

* Give directions and instructions to others?
* Make decisions on your own?
* Have something different to do every day?
* Have co-workers who are easy to get along with?
* Plan your work with little supervision?
* Be busy all the time?
* Have opportunities for advancement?

Have you enjoyed any of the following as a hobby or leisure-time activity?

* Reading mechanical or automotive magazines
* Making sketches of machines or other mechanical equipment
* Building cabinets or furniture
* Serving as a leader of a scouting or other group
* Helping to organize things at home, such as shopping lists and budgets
* Repairing or assembling bicycles or tricycles

Have you liked and done well in any of the following school subjects?

* Management
* Accounting
* Personnel Management
* Industrial Organization
* Industrial Safety
* Manufacturing Processes
* Labor and Industry

* Shop Math
* Scheduling

Are you able to

* Focus on a single source of sound in the presence of other distracting sounds?
* Shift back and forth between two or more activities or sources of information?
* Choose the right mathematical methods or formulas to solve a problem?

Would you work in places such as

* Factories and plants?
* Business offices?

What skills and knowledges do you need for this kind of work?

For most of these jobs, you need these skills:

* Management of Personnel Resources—motivating, developing, and directing people as they work, identifying the best people for the job
* Management of Material Resources—obtaining and seeing to the appropriate use of equipment, facilities, and materials needed to do certain work
* Management of Financial Resources—determining how money will be spent to get the work done and accounting for these expenditures
* Time Management—managing one's own time and the time of others
* Systems Analysis—determining how a system should work and how changes in conditions, operations, and the environment will affect outcomes
* Systems Evaluation—identifying measures or indicators of system performance and the actions needed to improve or correct performance relative to the goals of the system
* Coordination—adjusting actions in relation to others' actions

These knowledges are important in most of these jobs:

* Production and Processing—raw materials, production processes, quality control, costs, and other techniques for maximizing the effective manufacture and distribution of goods
* Personnel and Human Resources—principles and procedures for personnel recruitment, selection, training, compensation and benefits, labor relations and negotiation, and personnel information systems
* Administration and Management—business and management principles involved in strategic planning, resource allocation, human resources modeling, leadership techniques, production methods, and coordination of people and resources
* Economics and Accounting—economic and accounting principles and practices, the financial markets, banking, and the analysis and reporting of financial data
* Education and Training—principles and methods for curriculum and training design, teaching and instruc-

© 2006 JIST Works

tion for individuals and groups, and the measurement of training effects

* Transportation—principles and methods for moving people or goods by air, rail, sea, or road, including the relative costs and benefits

* Psychology—human behavior and performance; individual differences in ability, personality, and interests; learning and motivation; psychological research methods; and the assessment and treatment of behavioral and affective disorders

What else should you consider about this kind of work?

Workers in this group are hired by manufacturing plants and utilities in cities and towns throughout the country.

Most of these managers work a regular eight-hour day, with occasional overtime. They divide their time between the office, where they do paperwork, and the work floor, where they observe production, monitor progress, detect possible problems, and give directions to workers. They also may spend a small amount of time doing the same work as the people whom they supervise. Industrial production work is increasingly being done outside of the United States, so demand for these occupations is growing only slightly or even shrinking. The ups and downs of the business cycle also affect job openings in this group. Nevertheless, there is a continuing need for workers to replace those who retire, and in a select few industries, jobs are being added. If an industry goes into decline, managers may be able to find work in a related or even very different industry, particularly if they have special skills that are portable, such as knowledge of computer applications.

How can you prepare for jobs of this kind?

Work in this group typically requires from one to less than ten years of education and/or training.

Some workers study industrial management in college and then learn the particular methods and materials of an industry mostly on the job. Others begin as production workers, learning their skills largely on the job, and move up into management by taking college-level classes, perhaps getting a degree.

How much education or training is required for the jobs in this Work Group?

For descriptions of these jobs, see Part 2.

Work experience in a related occupation

* First-Line Supervisors/Managers of Helpers, Laborers, and Material Movers, Hand
* First-Line Supervisors/Managers of Mechanics, Installers, and Repairers
* First-Line Supervisors/Managers of Production and Operating Workers

Bachelor's degree

* Industrial Production Managers

13.02 Machine Setup and Operation

Workers in this group set up the machines that perform industrial processes, such as grinding, drilling, molding, heat treating, or painting. They plan the machine operation according to blueprints or other instructions. They may adjust the speed of the machine, the feed rate, and other variables. They may measure the output against the specifications. Some of them also operate the machines.

What kind of work would you do?

Your work activities would depend on your job. For example, you might

* Adjust guide assemblies, forming bars, and folding mechanisms according to specifications, using hand tools.
* Instruct new workers in machine operation.
* Lubricate and clean machine.
* Maintain production records, such as quantity, type, and dimensions of materials produced.
* Maintain stock of machine parts and machining tools.
* Measure and inspect machined parts to ensure conformance to product specifications.
* Read production schedule to determine setup of equipment and machines.
* Replace defective blades or wheels, using hand tools.
* Select buffing or polishing tools and position and mount tools to machine tool, chuck, or jig, using hand tools.
* Sharpen knives, bits, and other cutting and shaping tools.

What things about you point to this kind of work?

Is it important for you to

* Never be pressured to do things that go against your sense of right and wrong?
* Do your work alone?

Have you enjoyed any of the following as a hobby or leisure-time activity?

* Operating power tools for household projects
* Taking apart or fixing mechanical and electronic devices
* Building model airplanes, automobiles, or boats
* Making sketches of machines or other mechanical equipment

Have you liked and done well in any of the following school subjects?

* Machine Operating
* Manufacturing Processes
* Industrial Materials
* Industrial Safety

* Metal Forming and Fabrication/Technology
* Shop Math
* Blueprint/Schematic Reading
* Chemical Safety
* Moldmaking

Are you able to

* Quickly and repeatedly adjust the controls of a machine or a vehicle to exact positions?
* Quickly and repeatedly bend, stretch, twist, or reach out with your body, arms, and/or legs?
* Use short bursts of muscle force to propel yourself or to throw an object?

Would you work in places such as

* Factories and plants?

What skills and knowledges do you need for this kind of work?

For most of these jobs, you need these skills:

* Operation Monitoring—watching gauges, dials, or other indicators to make sure a machine is working properly
* Operation and Control—controlling operations of equipment or systems
* Equipment Maintenance—performing routine maintenance on equipment and determining when and what kind of maintenance is needed

These knowledges are important in most of these jobs:

* Mechanical Devices—machines and tools, including their designs, uses, repair, and maintenance
* Production and Processing—raw materials, production processes, quality control, costs, and other techniques for maximizing the effective manufacture and distribution of goods
* Foreign Language—the structure and content of a foreign (non-English) language, including the meaning and spelling of words, rules of composition and grammar, and pronunciation

What else should you consider about this kind of work?

Workers in this group are hired by manufacturing plants in many different industries, mostly on assembly lines. Many of them are unionized.

The work can sometimes be noisy and expose workers to heat, fumes, sharp edges, or powerful machinery, but workers are trained in safety procedures to avoid injuries.

Manufacturing is generally in decline in the United States, so comparatively few new jobs are likely to open in these occupations. However, replacement workers are needed, and a few industries are exceptions and are growing.

How can you prepare for jobs of this kind?

Work in this group usually requires education and/or training ranging from a few weeks to a few years.

Some of the jobs involve fairly simple machinery or materials and can be learned through relatively rapid on-the-

job training. Other machines or materials are more complex, so workers get longer workplace training or may learn their skills at a vocational school or technical college.

For the jobs in this group, high school courses in blueprint reading, technical math, and mechanical drawing can be very useful.

As industrial technology advances, it is important to keep learning in order to stay employable.

How much education or training is required for the jobs in this Work Group?

For descriptions of these jobs, see Part 2.

Short-term on-the-job training

* Glass Cutting Machine Setters and Set-Up Operators
* Metal Molding, Coremaking, and Casting Machine Operators and Tenders

Moderate-term on-the-job training

* Bindery Machine Setters and Set-Up Operators
* Buffing and Polishing Set-Up Operators
* Coating, Painting, and Spraying Machine Setters and Set-Up Operators
* Combination Machine Tool Setters and Set-Up Operators, Metal and Plastic
* Crushing, Grinding, and Polishing Machine Setters, Operators, and Tenders
* Drilling and Boring Machine Tool Setters, Operators, and Tenders, Metal and Plastic
* Extruding and Drawing Machine Setters, Operators, and Tenders, Metal and Plastic
* Extruding and Forming Machine Setters, Operators, and Tenders, Synthetic and Glass Fibers
* Extruding, Forming, Pressing, and Compacting Machine Setters and Set-Up Operators
* Fiber Product Cutting Machine Setters and Set-Up Operators
* Forging Machine Setters, Operators, and Tenders, Metal and Plastic
* Grinding, Honing, Lapping, and Deburring Machine Set-Up Operators
* Lathe and Turning Machine Tool Setters, Operators, and Tenders, Metal and Plastic
* Metal Molding, Coremaking, and Casting Machine Setters and Set-Up Operators
* Milling and Planing Machine Setters, Operators, and Tenders, Metal and Plastic
* Paper Goods Machine Setters, Operators, and Tenders
* Plastic Molding and Casting Machine Setters and Set-Up Operators
* Press and Press Brake Machine Setters and Set-Up Operators, Metal and Plastic
* Punching Machine Setters and Set-Up Operators, Metal and Plastic
* Rolling Machine Setters, Operators, and Tenders, Metal and Plastic

* Sawing Machine Setters and Set-Up Operators
* Sawing Machine Tool Setters and Set-Up Operators, Metal and Plastic
* Screen Printing Machine Setters and Set-Up Operators
* Shear and Slitter Machine Setters and Set-Up Operators, Metal and Plastic
* Soldering and Brazing Machine Setters and Set-Up Operators
* Textile Cutting Machine Setters, Operators, and Tenders
* Textile Winding, Twisting, and Drawing Out Machine Setters, Operators, and Tenders
* Woodworking Machine Setters and Set-Up Operators, Except Sawing

Long-term on-the-job training

* Textile Knitting and Weaving Machine Setters, Operators, and Tenders

Postsecondary vocational training

* Casting Machine Set-Up Operators
* Electrolytic Plating and Coating Machine Setters and Set-Up Operators, Metal and Plastic
* Nonelectrolytic Plating and Coating Machine Setters and Set-Up Operators, Metal and Plastic
* Heating Equipment Setters and Set-Up Operators, Metal and Plastic
* Multiple Machine Tool Setters, Operators, and Tenders, Metal and Plastic

13.03 Production Work, Assorted Materials Processing

Workers in this group operate machines and equipment that perform industrial processes on various materials, including fabric, leather, wood, stone, metal, plastic, food, and fabrics. They may heat the materials, cool them, squeeze them, filter them, clean them, coat them, shape them, or move them around.

What kind of work would you do?

Your work activities would depend on your job. For example, you might

* Clean and maintain gluing and cementing machines, using solutions, lubricants, brushes, and scrapers.
* Cut and trim meat to prepare for packing.
* Decorate cakes.
* Follow recipes to produce food products of specified flavor, texture, clarity, bouquet, and/or color.
* Load and adjust materials into extruding and forming machines, using hand tools.
* Load specified amounts of chemicals into processing equipment.
* Make minor repairs and lubricate and maintain equipment, using hand tools.

* Observe machine operations, gauges, or thermometers and adjust controls to maintain specified conditions.
* Pack bottles into cartons or crates, using machines.
* Press materials, such as garments, drapes, and slipcovers, using hand iron.

What things about you point to this kind of work?

Is it important for you to

* Never be pressured to do things that go against your sense of right and wrong?
* Have supervisors who train workers well?

Have you enjoyed any of the following as a hobby or leisure-time activity?

* Cooking large quantities of food for community events
* Carving small wooden objects
* Operating power tools for household projects
* Canning and preserving food

Have you liked and done well in any of the following school subjects?

* Machine Operating
* Manufacturing Processes
* Industrial Materials
* Industrial Safety
* Metal Forming and Fabrication/Technology
* Shop Math
* Blueprint/Schematic Reading
* Chemical Safety
* Moldmaking
* Sewing

Are you able to

* Time your movements or the movement of a piece of equipment in anticipation of changes in the speed and/or direction of a moving object or scene?
* Quickly and repeatedly bend, stretch, twist, or reach out with your body, arms, and/or legs?
* Quickly and repeatedly adjust the controls of a machine or a vehicle to exact positions?

Would you work in places such as

* Factories and plants?

What skills and knowledges do you need for this kind of work?

For most of these jobs, you need these skills:

* Operation Monitoring—watching gauges, dials, or other indicators to make sure a machine is working properly
* Operation and Control—controlling operations of equipment or systems
* Equipment Maintenance—performing routine maintenance on equipment and determining when and what kind of maintenance is needed

These knowledges are important in most of these jobs:

* Production and Processing—raw materials, production processes, quality control, costs, and other techniques for maximizing the effective manufacture and distribution of goods
* Food Production—techniques and equipment for planting, growing, and harvesting food products (both plant and animal) for consumption, including storage/handling techniques
* Mechanical Devices—machines and tools, including their designs, uses, repair, and maintenance

What else should you consider about this kind of work?

Workers in this group mostly are employed in industrial settings, including manufacturing plants, bakeries, food processing plants, foundries, garment factories, and refineries. Many of the jobs are unionized. Some fabric workers and bulk bakers are self-employed.

The work environment may be hot, cold, noisy, or dusty, and workers may need to exercise caution because of hazardous equipment or materials. The pace of the work may be rapid and physically tiring. Workers in meat-packing plants have a high rate of injury and illness. In a plant that runs around the clock, some work is done on a night shift. Bakeries need to have fresh output ready by morning.

The employment outlook is mixed because some industries are growing, although manufacturing as a whole is shrinking in the United States. The growth of catalog and Internet shopping has created a demand for operators of packaging and filling machines. Food processing is a growing industry that continues to require human labor. Demand for production laborers and helpers is also growing.

How can you prepare for jobs of this kind?

Work in this group usually requires less than six months of education and/or training—sometimes only a few weeks—although a few of the occupations may require several years.

Most of these workers learn their jobs through short-term on-the-job training. For work that involves more complex or hazardous machines or materials, on-the-job training may take longer.

Advances in industrial technology are requiring workers to keep learning so their skills remain current.

How much education or training is required for the jobs in this Work Group?

For descriptions of these jobs, see Part 2.

Short-term on-the-job training

* Cutting and Slicing Machine Operators and Tenders
* Extruding, Forming, Pressing, and Compacting Machine Operators and Tenders
* Food and Tobacco Roasting, Baking, and Drying Machine Operators and Tenders
* Food Batchmakers

* Food Cooking Machine Operators and Tenders
* Meat, Poultry, and Fish Cutters and Trimmers
* Nonelectrolytic Plating and Coating Machine Operators and Tenders, Metal and Plastic
* Packaging and Filling Machine Operators and Tenders
* Plastic Molding and Casting Machine Operators and Tenders
* Pressing Machine Operators and Tenders—Textile, Garment, and Related Materials
* Production Helpers
* Production Laborers

Moderate-term on-the-job training

* Cementing and Gluing Machine Operators and Tenders
* Chemical Equipment Controllers and Operators
* Chemical Equipment Tenders
* Cleaning, Washing, and Metal Pickling Equipment Operators and Tenders
* Coating, Painting, and Spraying Machine Operators and Tenders
* Combination Machine Tool Operators and Tenders, Metal and Plastic
* Cooling and Freezing Equipment Operators and Tenders
* Electrolytic Plating and Coating Machine Operators and Tenders, Metal and Plastic
* Extruding and Forming Machine Operators and Tenders, Synthetic or Glass Fibers
* Furnace, Kiln, Oven, Drier, and Kettle Operators and Tenders
* Heat Treating, Annealing, and Tempering Machine Operators and Tenders, Metal and Plastic
* Heaters, Metal and Plastic
* Metal-Refining Furnace Operators and Tenders
* Mixing and Blending Machine Setters, Operators, and Tenders
* Pourers and Casters, Metal
* Sawing Machine Operators and Tenders
* Separating, Filtering, Clarifying, Precipitating, and Still Machine Setters, Operators, and Tenders
* Sewing Machine Operators, Garment
* Sewing Machine Operators, Non-Garment
* Shoe Machine Operators and Tenders
* Slaughterers and Meat Packers
* Stone Sawyers
* Team Assemblers
* Textile Bleaching and Dyeing Machine Operators and Tenders
* Tire Builders
* Woodworking Machine Operators and Tenders, Except Sawing

Long-term on-the-job training

* Bakers, Manufacturing

13.04 Welding, Brazing, and Soldering

Workers in this group join metal parts permanently. Fabricators and fitters cut and align metal parts that will be welded or riveted together. Welders join the parts by using melted metal of the same kind as the parts. Brazers and solderers use a metal with a lower melting temperature than that of the parts. Workers may control the work by hand or may operate a machine that controls the work.

What kind of work would you do?

Your work activities would depend on your job. For example, you might

* Clean workpieces, using chemical solution, file, wire brush, or grinder.
* Develop layout and plan sequence of operations for fabricating and assembling structural metal products, applying trigonometry and knowledge of metal.
* Develop templates and other work aids to hold and align parts.
* Examine workpieces for defects and measure workpieces with straightedge or template to ensure conformance with specifications.
* Heat-treat parts with acetylene torch.
* Observe meters, gauges, and machine to ensure solder or brazing process meets specifications.
* Read production schedule and specifications to ascertain product to be fabricated.
* Turn and press controls, such as cranks, knobs, and buttons, to adjust and activate welding process.
* Turn valves to start flow of gases, light flame, and adjust valves to obtain desired color and size of flame.
* Weld metal parts or components together, using brazing, gas, or arc welding equipment.

What things about you point to this kind of work?

Is it important for you to

* Never be pressured to do things that go against your sense of right and wrong?
* Be busy all the time?

Have you enjoyed any of the following as a hobby or leisure-time activity?

* Taking apart or fixing mechanical and electronic devices
* Making sketches of machines or other mechanical equipment
* Building model airplanes, automobiles, or boats

Have you liked and done well in any of the following school subjects?

* Welding
* Manufacturing Processes
* Machine Operating
* Industrial Materials
* Industrial Safety
* Metal Forming and Fabrication/Technology
* Shop Math
* Blueprint/Schematic Reading
* Metalsmithing

Are you able to

* Quickly and repeatedly bend, stretch, twist, or reach out with your body, arms, and/or legs?
* Keep your hand and arm steady while moving your arm or while holding your arm and hand in one position?
* Use short bursts of muscle force to propel yourself or to throw an object?

Would you work in places such as

* Factories and plants?
* Construction sites?

What skills and knowledges do you need for this kind of work?

For most of these jobs, you need these skills:

* Operation and Control—controlling operations of equipment or systems
* Operation Monitoring—watching gauges, dials, or other indicators to make sure a machine is working properly
* Equipment Selection—determining the kind of tools and equipment needed to do a job

These knowledges are important in most of these jobs:

* Building and Construction—the materials, methods, and tools involved in the construction or repair of houses; buildings; or other structures, such as highways and roads
* Production and Processing—raw materials, production processes, quality control, costs, and other techniques for maximizing the effective manufacture and distribution of goods
* Mechanical Devices—machines and tools, including their designs, uses, repair, and maintenance

What else should you consider about this kind of work?

These workers are employed by manufacturing plants of metal goods, construction companies erecting steel frameworks or assembling pipelines, shipyards, and auto body repair shops. Jobs may be found in cities and towns everywhere.

The work is noisy, and workers must take precautions and wear special gear when they work with high-voltage electricity, bright electric arcs, explosive and toxic gases, and hot metal parts. Hand welders may work outdoors, in cramped spaces or awkward positions, at heights, or even underwater. Machine operators work in a more controlled environment.

The employment outlook is excellent. Some low-skilled workers are being replaced by robots, and the field has some sensitivity to the business cycle, but many jobs for machine operators and hand workers are expected to open.

How can you prepare for jobs of this kind?

Work in this group usually requires education and/or training ranging from a few weeks to several years.

Most machine operators are trained on the job by experienced workers and learn their skills in a few months or less. Those who work with computer-controlled machines and robots may need a year or more of training at a technical college.

Many hand welders, as well as some fabricators and fitters, learn their trade through an apprenticeship that takes as much as four years of combined classroom learning and on-the-job training. Training is also available in the armed forces. Some welders gain certification by passing a performance test.

For the jobs in this group, high school courses in blueprint reading, technical math, mechanical drawing, and metal shop are very useful.

How much education or training is required for the jobs in this Work Group?

For descriptions of these jobs, see Part 2.

Short-term on-the-job training

* Brazers
* Solderers
* Soldering and Brazing Machine Operators and Tenders
* Welders, Production

Moderate-term on-the-job training

* Fitters, Structural Metal—Precision
* Metal Fabricators, Structural Metal Products
* Welding Machine Operators and Tenders

Long-term on-the-job training

* Welder-Fitters
* Welders and Cutters

Postsecondary vocational training

* Welding Machine Setters and Set-Up Operators

13.05 Production Machining Technology

Workers in this group fashion metal or plastic parts, often to precise tolerances. They operate machines that shave or grind away at a rough piece until it matches the specifications of a blueprint or layout. Some of them do the work as part of a production process; others create molds, dies, or other machine parts to be used in production. Some of them program computer-controlled machines.

What kind of work would you do?

Your work activities would depend on your job. For example, you might

* Fabricate metal or plastic parts, using hand tools.
* Inspect machined parts to verify conformance to specifications.
* Machine parts to specifications, using machine tools such as lathes, milling machines, shapers, or grinders.
* Pour molten metal into molds manually or by using crane ladles.
* Revise numerical control machine tape programs to eliminate instruction errors and omissions.
* Select metals to be used from a range of metals and alloys, based on properties such as hardness and heat tolerance.
* Study blueprint of pattern to be made, compute dimensions, and plan sequence of operations.
* Turn valves to direct flow of coolant against cutting wheels and workpieces during grinding.

What things about you point to this kind of work?

Is it important for you to

* Never be pressured to do things that go against your sense of right and wrong?
* Be treated fairly by the company?

Have you enjoyed any of the following as a hobby or leisure-time activity?

* Building model airplanes, automobiles, or boats
* Operating power tools for household projects
* Making sketches of machines or other mechanical equipment
* Taking apart or fixing mechanical and electronic devices

Have you liked and done well in any of the following school subjects?

* Machine Operating
* Manufacturing Processes
* Industrial Materials
* Industrial Safety
* Metal Forming and Fabrication/Technology
* Shop Math
* Blueprint/Schematic Reading
* Model Making
* Moldmaking
* Tool Design

Are you able to

* Make fast, simple, repeated movements of your fingers, hands, and wrists?
* Imagine how something will look after it is moved around or when its parts are moved or rearranged?
* Quickly and repeatedly adjust the controls of a machine or a vehicle to exact positions?

Would you work in places such as

* Factories and plants?

What skills and knowledges do you need for this kind of work?

For most of these jobs, you need these skills:

* Technology Design—generating or adapting equipment and technology to serve user needs
* Operation and Control—controlling operations of equipment or systems
* Quality Control Analysis—conducting tests and inspections of products, services, or processes to evaluate quality or performance
* Operation Monitoring—watching gauges, dials, or other indicators to make sure a machine is working properly

These knowledges are important in most of these jobs:

* Design—design techniques, tools, and principles involved in production of precision technical plans, blueprints, drawings, and models
* Production and Processing—raw materials, production processes, quality control, costs, and other techniques for maximizing the effective manufacture and distribution of goods
* Mechanical Devices—machines and tools, including their designs, uses, repair, and maintenance

What else should you consider about this kind of work?

These workers are employed by small machine shops and large plants that manufacture all kinds of products.

Some of the workers must take precautions against noise, flying bits of metal, and hazardous lubricants. Many workers need to stand for most of the workday, and some must lift heavy parts and equipment.

The employment outlook is mixed. The less skilled jobs in this group may have only a fair outlook because of automation and the offshore movement of manufacturing. For the highly skilled jobs, on the other hand, the outlook is excellent, even for the slower-growing occupations, because few young people are competing for the jobs of retiring workers.

How can you prepare for jobs of this kind?

Work in this group usually requires education and/or training ranging from six months to over four years.

In the less skilled jobs, workers receive on-the-job training, perhaps complemented by some classroom study. For somewhat more complex jobs, a certification program at a community or technical college may be helpful.

Most machinists and tool and die makers, plus some model makers, learn their trade through apprenticeships that typically require four years of combined classroom learning and on-the-job training. Some of them have prior work experience working with production machinery.

Computer-control programmers may complete either an apprenticeship lasting three or four years or a certification program at a technical or community college.

For the jobs in this group, high school courses in blueprint reading, technical math, mechanical drawing, and metal shop are very useful.

How much education or training is required for the jobs in this Work Group?

For descriptions of these jobs, see Part 2.

Moderate-term on-the-job training

* Foundry Mold and Coremakers
* Model Makers, Metal and Plastic
* Patternmakers, Metal and Plastic
* Tool Grinders, Filers, and Sharpeners

Long-term on-the-job training

* Machinists
* Numerical Control Machine Tool Operators and Tenders, Metal and Plastic
* Numerical Tool and Process Control Programmers
* Tool and Die Makers

Postsecondary vocational training

* Lay-Out Workers, Metal and Plastic

13.06 Production Precision Work

Workers in this group manufacture products with precise requirements for size, shape, color, freedom from contamination, or some other characteristic. These workers typically use some combination of machines and hand tools. They use good vision and precise measuring tools to verify that their output meets specifications.

What kind of work would you do?

Your work activities would depend on your job. For example, you might

* Assemble molds used to cast contact lenses.
* Assemble systems of gears by aligning and meshing gears in gearboxes.
* Brush, buff, clean, and polish metal items and jewelry pieces, using jeweler's tools, polishing wheel, and chemical bath.
* Clean parts, using cleaning solution, airhose, and cloth.
* Compute costs of labor and material to determine production costs of products and articles.
* Connect electrical wiring according to circuit diagram, using soldering iron.
* Cut and shape metal into jewelry pieces, using cutting and carving tools.
* Grind and polish optics, using hand tools and polishing cloths.
* Make orthotic/prosthetic devices, using materials such as thermoplastic and thermosetting materials, metal alloys and leather, and hand and power tools.
* Place semiconductor wafers in processing containers or equipment holders, using vacuum wand or tweezers.

What things about you point to this kind of work?

Is it important for you to

* Do your work alone?
* Never be pressured to do things that go against your sense of right and wrong?

Have you enjoyed any of the following as a hobby or leisure-time activity?

* Building robots or electronic devices
* Making jewelry or stringing beads
* Carving small wooden objects
* Building model airplanes, automobiles, or boats
* Taking apart or fixing mechanical and electronic devices
* Making ceramic objects
* Assembling toys, shelving, furniture, and other items around the house
* Doing crafts

Have you liked and done well in any of the following school subjects?

* Machine Operating
* Manufacturing Processes
* Industrial Materials
* Industrial Safety
* Jewelry
* Shop Math
* Bookbinding
* Laser Electronics/Optics
* Metalsmithing
* Moldmaking

Are you able to

* Make precisely coordinated movements of the fingers of one or both hands to grasp, manipulate, or assemble very small objects?
* Keep your hand and arm steady while moving your arm or while holding your arm and hand in one position?
* Quickly move your hand, your hand together with your arm, or your two hands to grasp, manipulate, or assemble objects?
* Make fast, simple, repeated movements of your fingers, hands, and wrists?

Would you work in places such as

* Factories and plants?

What skills and knowledges do you need for this kind of work?

For most of these jobs, you need these skills:

* Technology Design—generating or adapting equipment and technology to serve user needs
* Operation and Control—controlling operations of equipment or systems

* Quality Control Analysis—conducting tests and inspections of products, services, or processes to evaluate quality or performance

These knowledges are important in most of these jobs:

* Production and Processing—raw materials, production processes, quality control, costs, and other techniques for maximizing the effective manufacture and distribution of goods
* Mechanical Devices—machines and tools, including their designs, uses, repair, and maintenance
* Fine Arts—the theory and techniques required to compose, produce, and perform works of music, dance, visual arts, drama, and sculpture

What else should you consider about this kind of work?

Some of these workers are employed by manufacturers specializing in electronic equipment, engines, jewelry, silverware, optical equipment, and semiconductor chips. Others work at binderies and dental laboratories. A large number of those who work with jewelry, precious metals, dental prosthetics, medical appliances, and precision molds are self-employed.

The working conditions vary but usually contribute to the precision of the work. Lighting is usually very good. Some workers need to take precautions against noisy equipment or hazardous materials.

The job outlook is mixed. A few of these jobs are in small industries that employ few workers even in good economic times. Although automation and foreign manufacturers are reducing job openings in some industries, other industries require hand labor or local work. The more highly skilled jobs are having trouble attracting recruits, so there is little competition for openings.

How can you prepare for jobs of this kind?

Work in this group usually requires education and/or training ranging from a brief demonstration to over four years.

Most of these workers receive training on the job from experienced workers. For the more skilled occupations, such as those that work with jewelry, molds, and patterns, workers may train in apprenticeships that combine several years of on-the-job and classroom training.

Most semiconductor processors need some college-level study of science, and an associate degree is helpful. A small number of programs in dental lab technology, optical technology, and jewelry repair are available at technical and community colleges.

High school courses in shop math, blueprint reading, and mechanical drawing are useful preparation.

How much education or training is required for the jobs in this Work Group?

For descriptions of these jobs, see Part 2.

Short-term on-the-job training

* Electrical and Electronic Equipment Assemblers

* Electromechanical Equipment Assemblers
* Engine and Other Machine Assemblers

Moderate-term on-the-job training

* Bookbinders
* Gem and Diamond Workers
* Optical Instrument Assemblers
* Precision Lens Grinders and Polishers
* Precision Mold and Pattern Casters, Except Nonferrous Metals
* Timing Device Assemblers, Adjusters, and Calibrators

Long-term on-the-job training

* Bench Workers, Jewelry
* Dental Laboratory Technicians
* Medical Appliance Technicians
* Model and Mold Makers, Jewelry
* Precision Pattern and Die Casters, Nonferrous Metals
* Silversmiths

Postsecondary vocational training

* Jewelers
* Pewter Casters and Finishers

Associate degree

* Semiconductor Processors

13.07 Production Quality Control

Workers in this group make sure that products conform to specifications and perform as they should. Inspectors may use tools, equipment, or any of their five senses to judge the quality of a product. Some of them inspect the materials that go into a product. Testers subject a product to real-world conditions to see whether it holds up. These workers may work closely with production managers to pinpoint the cause of a defect or test failure and then help improve the manufacturing process.

What kind of work would you do?

Your work activities would depend on your job. For example, you might

* Collect samples for testing and compute findings.
* Disassemble defective parts and components.
* Discard or route defective products or contaminants for rework or reuse.
* Grade and sort products according to factors such as color, length, width, appearance, feel, and smell.
* Mark, affix, or stamp product or container to identify defects or denote grade or size information.
* Read dials and meters to verify functioning of equipment according to specifications.

What things about you point to this kind of work?

Is it important for you to

* Have supervisors who train workers well?
* Be busy all the time?

Have you enjoyed any of the following as a hobby or leisure-time activity?

* Taking apart or fixing mechanical and electronic devices
* Buying large quantities of food or other products for an organization
* Making sketches of machines or other mechanical equipment

Have you liked and done well in any of the following school subjects?

* Quality Control
* Manufacturing Processes
* Industrial Materials
* Industrial Safety
* Shop Math

Are you able to

* Quickly and accurately compare similarities and differences among sets of letters, numbers, objects, pictures, or patterns?
* Match or detect differences between colors, including shades of color and brightness?
* Concentrate on a task over a period of time without being distracted?
* Make precisely coordinated movements of the fingers of one or both hands to grasp, manipulate, or assemble very small objects?
* Tell the direction from which a sound originated?
* Detect or tell the differences between sounds that vary in pitch and loudness?
* Quickly and repeatedly adjust the controls of a machine or a vehicle to exact positions?

Would you work in places such as

* Factories and plants?
* Farms?

What skills and knowledges do you need for this kind of work?

For most of these jobs, you need these skills:

* Quality Control Analysis—conducting tests and inspections of products, services, or processes to evaluate quality or performance
* Operation Monitoring—watching gauges, dials, or other indicators to make sure a machine is working properly
* Troubleshooting—determining causes of operating errors and deciding what to do about them

These knowledges are important in most of these jobs:

* Production and Processing—raw materials, production processes, quality control, costs, and other techniques for maximizing the effective manufacture and distribution of goods

* Design—design techniques, tools, and principles involved in production of precision technical plans, blueprints, drawings, and models
* Telecommunications—transmission, broadcasting, switching, control, and operation of telecommunications systems

What else should you consider about this kind of work?

These workers are employed by all types of manufacturing companies in all parts of the country. Agricultural graders are employed by farms, grocery wholesalers and retailers, and food processing businesses.

Working conditions vary, depending on the industry. Some jobs are in hot, noisy, dirty places. Some require workers to spend much of the workday on their feet. Other jobs are in much more comfortable surroundings. Some workers inspect or test the same items throughout a work shift; others experience more variety.

The employment outlook is mixed. Although concern for product quality is growing, many inspection tasks are being automated or taken over by production workers. Job growth will probably be best in industries that require sensory tests that cannot be automated.

How can you prepare for jobs of this kind?

Work in this group usually requires education and/or training ranging from a brief demonstration to one or more years.

Most of the skills for these occupations are learned on the job. Workers who perform simple inspections or tests may need no prior training or experience. However, many employers prefer to recruit trainee inspectors and testers from production workers who are already familiar with the product and what can go wrong with it.

How much education or training is required for the jobs in this Work Group?

For descriptions of these jobs, see Part 2.

Short-term on-the-job training

* Production Inspectors, Testers, Graders, Sorters, Samplers, Weighers

Moderate-term on-the-job training

* Electrical and Electronic Inspectors and Testers
* Materials Inspectors
* Precision Devices Inspectors and Testers

Work experience in a related occupation

* Graders and Sorters, Agricultural Products

13.08 Graphic Arts Production

Workers in this group produce printed materials and photographic reproductions. Some specialize in text, some in pictures, and some in combining both. Some of them use precision engraving and etching equipment and use considerable manual dexterity. Others use computerized or photographic equipment and rely more on technical skills.

What kind of work would you do?

Your work activities would depend on your job. For example, you might

* Carve designs on workpieces, using electric hand tools.
* Clean ink rollers after runs are completed.
* Feed film into automatic film processor that develops, fixes, washes, and dries film.
* Fill reservoirs with ink or specified coloring agents.
* Insert spacers between words or units to balance and justify lines.
* Inspect etched work for uniformity, using calibrated microscope and gauge.
* Install printing plates, cylinders, or rollers on machine, using hand tools and gauges.
* Mix powdered ink pigments, using matching book and measuring and mixing tools.
* Monitor equipment operation to detect malfunctions.
* Operate automatic casting machine to produce electrotype or stereotype printing plates.

What things about you point to this kind of work?

Is it important for you to

* Do your work alone?
* Never be pressured to do things that go against your sense of right and wrong?

Have you enjoyed any of the following as a hobby or leisure-time activity?

* Doing desktop publishing for a school or community publication
* Learning to use new features of word-processing and other programs
* Making sketches of machines or other mechanical equipment
* Carving small wooden objects

Have you liked and done well in any of the following school subjects?

* Graphic Arts
* Print Shop/Printing
* Lithography
* Offset Printing
* Industrial Safety
* Shop Math
* Photography
* Printmaking

Are you able to

* Match or detect differences between colors, including shades of color and brightness?
* Keep your hand and arm steady while moving your arm or while holding your arm and hand in one position?

* Make fast, simple, repeated movements of your fingers, hands, and wrists?

Would you work in places such as

* Print shops?
* Laboratories?
* Business offices?
* Artists' studios and craft workshops?

What skills and knowledges do you need for this kind of work?

For most of these jobs, you need these skills:

* Operation and Control—controlling operations of equipment or systems
* Operation Monitoring—watching gauges, dials, or other indicators to make sure a machine is working properly
* Quality Control Analysis—conducting tests and inspections of products, services, or processes to evaluate quality or performance

These knowledges are important in most of these jobs:

* Fine Arts—the theory and techniques required to compose, produce, and perform works of music, dance, visual arts, drama, and sculpture
* Production and Processing—raw materials, production processes, quality control, costs, and other techniques for maximizing the effective manufacture and distribution of goods
* Foreign Language—the structure and content of a foreign (non-English) language, including the meaning and spelling of words, rules of composition and grammar, and pronunciation

What else should you consider about this kind of work?

These workers are employed by manufacturing firms, printing and publishing companies, and the publications departments in businesses of all kinds. Jobs are found in large and small communities all over the country.

The trend is toward replacing mechanical and photographic processes with computerized processes. This is reducing the noise and dirt of many of the worksites, but it is also making some jobs obsolete or less in need of workers while raising the training requirements of the jobs that are still in demand.

The job outlook is mixed. Prospects are good for workers who operate printing machines, especially if they have training from an apprenticeship or formal educational program. Among those who prepare materials for printing, desktop publishers will have better opportunities than workers using more traditional methods. Digital photography is decreasing the demand for photo developers.

How can you prepare for jobs of this kind?

Work in this group usually requires education and/or training ranging from a few weeks to four or more years.

Some of the less complex occupations can be learned quickly on the job from experienced workers. Employers prefer trainees who have studied graphics in high school and are familiar with computer technology. Courses in shop math are also useful.

The more complex jobs can be learned through two-year academic programs at technical and community colleges and through apprenticeships that last four years or more. Retraining is necessary as new technology emerges.

How much education or training is required for the jobs in this Work Group?

For descriptions of these jobs, see Part 2.

Short-term on-the-job training

* Bindery Machine Operators and Tenders
* Marking and Identification Printing Machine Setters and Set-Up Operators
* Photographic Processing Machine Operators
* Printing Press Machine Operators and Tenders

Moderate-term on-the-job training

* Etchers, Hand
* Film Laboratory Technicians
* Letterpress Setters and Set-Up Operators
* Pantograph Engravers
* Photoengraving and Lithographing Machine Operators and Tenders
* Precision Printing Workers
* Typesetting and Composing Machine Operators and Tenders

Long-term on-the-job training

* Camera Operators
* Dot Etchers
* Electronic Masking System Operators
* Electrotypers and Stereotypers
* Engraver Set-Up Operators
* Engravers, Hand
* Engravers/Carvers
* Etchers
* Hand Compositors and Typesetters
* Job Printers
* Offset Lithographic Press Setters and Set-Up Operators
* Paste-Up Workers
* Photoengravers
* Plate Finishers
* Platemakers
* Precision Etchers and Engravers, Hand or Machine
* Scanner Operators
* Strippers

Postsecondary vocational training

* Design Printing Machine Setters and Set-Up Operators
* Desktop Publishers
* Embossing Machine Set-Up Operators

13.09 Hands-On Work, Assorted Materials

Workers in this group perform manufacturing tasks mostly by hand, but with some use of tools and equipment.

What kind of work would you do?

Your work activities would depend on your job. For example, you might

* Apply coating, such as paint, ink, or lacquer, to protect or decorate workpiece surface, using spray gum, pen, or brush.
* Calculate dimensions and specifications from sales order and enter data on worksheet.
* Clean and maintain tools and equipment, using solvent, brushes, and rags.
* Construct molds used for casting metal, clay, or plaster objects, using plaster, fiberglass, rubber, casting machine, patterns and flasks.
* Cut materials, such as textiles, food, and metal, using hand tools, portable power tools, or bench-mounted tools.
* Develop sketch of glass product into blueprint specifications, applying knowledge of glass technology and glass blowing.
* Grind, sand, clean, or polish objects or parts, using hand tools or equipment.
* Operate or tend wire-coiling machine.
* Read work order or examine part to determine part or section of product to be produced.
* Select paint according to company requirements and match colors of paint following specified color charts.

What things about you point to this kind of work?

Is it important for you to

* Never be pressured to do things that go against your sense of right and wrong?
* Do your work alone?

Have you enjoyed any of the following as a hobby or leisure-time activity?

* Sewing, knitting, or doing needlework
* Making ceramic objects
* Painting, refinishing, or reupholstering furniture

Have you liked and done well in any of the following school subjects?

* Machine Operating
* Manufacturing Processes
* Industrial Materials
* Industrial Safety
* Crafts Shop
* Clothing
* Sewing

Are you able to

* Make fast, simple, repeated movements of the fingers, hands, and wrists?
* Keep your hand and arm steady while moving your arm or while holding your arm and hand in one position?
* Quickly and repeatedly bend, stretch, twist, or reach out with your body, arms, and/or legs?

Would you work in places such as

* Factories and plants?
* Artists' studios and craft workshops?

What skills and knowledges do you need for this kind of work?

For most of these jobs, you need these skills:

* Operation and Control—controlling operations of equipment or systems
* Repairing—repairing machines or systems, using the needed tools
* Equipment Maintenance—performing routine maintenance on equipment and determining when and what kind of maintenance is needed

These knowledges are important in most of these jobs:

* Production and Processing—raw materials, production processes, quality control, costs, and other techniques for maximizing the effective manufacture and distribution of goods
* Fine Arts—the theory and techniques required to compose, produce, and perform works of music, dance, visual arts, drama, and sculpture
* Foreign Language—the structure and content of a foreign (non-English) language, including the meaning and spelling of words, rules of composition and grammar, and pronunciation

What else should you consider about this kind of work?

These workers are employed by a wide variety of industries. Almost half the hand sewers are self-employed, and so are a significant number of painters.

Work that is done by hand can be physically tiring, but workers may take more pride in their output than machine operators do, and the work environment may be less noisy.

The employment outlook is mixed, but generally there are not a lot of openings for skilled hands-on production work. In addition, automation and low-paid foreign workers continue to make inroads on these jobs. Work that cannot be automated and must be done locally has the best outlook. For example, highly skilled transportation painters will be sought by many auto body shops.

How can you prepare for jobs of this kind?

Work in this group usually requires education and/or training ranging from a few weeks to less than two years.

All of these occupations are learned on the job from experienced workers. The amount of time required depends on

© 2006 JIST Works

the complexity of the task and the extent of the trainee's prior experience, if any, in a related job.

Apprenticeships are available in some areas for mold makers, glass blowers and benders, and transportation painters. They typically take three or four years and combine worksite training and classroom learning.

Because these jobs are found in very diverse industries, there is no shared set of high school courses that would help prepare for all of them, with the exception of shop math.

How much education or training is required for the jobs in this Work Group?

For descriptions of these jobs, see Part 2.

Short-term on-the-job training

* Coil Winders, Tapers, and Finishers
* Cutters and Trimmers, Hand
* Painting, Coating, and Decorating Workers
* Sewers, Hand

Moderate-term on-the-job training

* Grinding and Polishing Workers, Hand
* Mold Makers, Hand
* Molding and Casting Workers
* Painters, Transportation Equipment

Long-term on-the-job training

* Fabric and Apparel Patternmakers
* Glass Blowers, Molders, Benders, and Finishers

13.10 Woodworking Technology

Workers in this group follow specifications as they cut, shape, and finish wood products such as furniture and cabinets. Some create wooden models of products that will be mass-produced out of wood, metal, or plastic.

What kind of work would you do?

Your work activities would depend on your job. For example, you might

* Brush, spray, or hand-rub finishing ingredients onto and into grain of wood.
* Construct wooden models, templates, full-scale mock-up, and molds for parts of products.
* Fit, fasten, and assemble wood parts together to form pattern, model, or section, using glue, nails, dowels, bolts, and screws.
* Mix finish ingredients to obtain desired color or shade of existing finish.
* Shellac, lacquer, or wax finished pattern or model.
* Study blueprints, drawings, and written specifications of articles to be constructed or repaired and plan sequence of performing such operations.

* Trim, smooth, and shape surfaces and plane, shave, file, scrape, and sand models to attain specified shapes, using hand tools.

What things about you point to this kind of work?

Is it important for you to

* Never be pressured to do things that go against your sense of right and wrong?
* Do your work alone?

Have you enjoyed any of the following as a hobby or leisure-time activity?

* Carving small wooden objects
* Building cabinets or furniture
* Operating power tools for household projects
* Assembling toys, shelving, furniture, and other items around the house

Have you liked and done well in any of the following school subjects?

* Carpentry
* Cabinetmaking
* Manufacturing Processes
* Industrial Safety
* Shop Math
* Blueprint/Schematic Reading
* Model Making

Are you able to

* Quickly and repeatedly bend, stretch, twist, or reach out with your body, arms, and/or legs?
* Use short bursts of muscle force to propel yourself or to throw an object?
* Coordinate two or more limbs while sitting, standing, or lying down?

Would you work in places such as

* Factories and plants?
* Artists' studios and craft workshops?

What skills and knowledges do you need for this kind of work?

For most of these jobs, you need these skills:

* Equipment Selection—determining the kind of tools and equipment needed to do a job
* Installation—installing equipment, machines, wiring, or programs to meet specifications
* Operation and Control—controlling operations of equipment or systems

These knowledges are important in most of these jobs:

* Building and Construction—the materials, methods, and tools involved in the construction or repair of houses; buildings; or other structures, such as highways and roads

* Design—design techniques, tools, and principles involved in production of precision technical plans, blueprints, drawings, and models
* Engineering and Technology—the practical application of engineering science and technology; this includes applying principles, techniques, procedures, and equipment to the design and production of various goods and services

What else should you consider about this kind of work?

Workers in this group are employed by furniture manufacturers in various locations and by manufacturers of automobiles, boats, and other products that use wooden models as part of the design process. Many work for small or one-person businesses that custom-make cabinets, bookshelves, and other built-in kinds of furniture in clients' homes and offices.

These workers generally have a love of working with wood, although the amount of hand-work versus machine-work that they do varies from job to job. Work with power cutting tools and flammable finishes requires that workers use safety precautions. Some work is physically demanding.

Opportunities in the jobs are generally expected to be fair, with a need for replacement of older workers who are retiring. In manufacturing, workers who are skilled with computer-controlled woodworking equipment will have an edge. The work is sensitive to downturns in the economy.

How can you prepare for jobs of this kind?

Work in this group usually requires education and/or training ranging from two to four years.

Workers train in formal and informal apprenticeships, where they learn how to operate the various hand and machine tools, how to use various finishes, and the properties of various kinds of wood. These training programs are offered by manufacturers and by skilled self-employed workers who are interested in expanding their businesses. Manufacturers may prefer trainees who have learned some woodworking skills in vocational school or through work experience in a related job, such as construction carpentry. Some useful high school courses are blueprint reading, shop math, wood shop, computer applications, and mechanical drawing.

How much education or training is required for the jobs in this Work Group?

For descriptions of these jobs, see Part 2.

Long-term on-the-job training

* Cabinetmakers and Bench Carpenters
* Furniture Finishers
* Model Makers, Wood
* Patternmakers, Wood

13.11 Apparel, Shoes, Leather, and Fabric Care

Workers in this group clean, alter, restore, and repair clothing, shoes, or other items made from fabric or leather.

What kind of work would you do?

Your work activities would depend on your job. For example, you might

* Alter garments and join parts, using needle and thread or sewing machine, to form finished garments.
* Apply dye to articles, using spray gun, electrically rotated brush, or handbrush.
* Confer with customer to determine type of material and garment style desired.
* Finish fancy garments with hand iron to produce high-quality finishes that cannot be obtained on machine presses.
* Iron or press articles, fabrics, and furs, using hand iron or pressing machine.
* Maintain records of time required to perform each job.
* Mix and add detergents, dyes, bleach, starch, and other solutions and chemicals to clean, color, dry, or stiffen articles.
* Operate drycleaning machine.
* Repair and recondition products such as trunks, luggage, shoes, and saddles.
* Repair holes by weaving thread over them, using needle.

What things about you point to this kind of work?

Is it important for you to

* Never be pressured to do things that go against your sense of right and wrong?
* Do your work alone?

Have you enjoyed any of the following as a hobby or leisure-time activity?

* Painting, refinishing, or reupholstering furniture
* Making belts or other leather articles
* Sewing, knitting, or doing needlework
* Making tie-dyed clothes
* Weaving rugs or making quilts

Have you liked and done well in any of the following school subjects?

* Leathercraft
* Crafts Shop
* Machine Operating
* Industrial Materials
* Clothing

© 2006 JIST Works

Are you able to

* Match or detect differences between colors, including shades of color and brightness?
* Make fast, simple, repeated movements of your fingers, hands, and wrists?
* Keep your hand and arm steady while moving your arm or while holding your arm and hand in one position?

Would you work in places such as

* Laundries and dry cleaners?
* Stores and shopping malls?
* Factories and plants?

What skills and knowledges do you need for this kind of work?

For most of these jobs, you need these skills:

* Operation and Control—controlling operations of equipment or systems
* Programming—writing computer programs for various purposes
* Equipment Selection—determining the kind of tools and equipment needed to do a job

These knowledges are important in most of these jobs:

* Fine Arts—the theory and techniques required to compose, produce, and perform works of music, dance, visual arts, drama, and sculpture
* Production and Processing—raw materials, production processes, quality control, costs, and other techniques for maximizing the effective manufacture and distribution of goods
* Foreign Language—the structure and content of a foreign (non-English) language, including the meaning and spelling of words, rules of composition and grammar, and pronunciation

What else should you consider about this kind of work?

These workers are employed throughout the United States. Their jobs are found in clothing stores; manufacturing plants; and specialty cleaning, alteration, and repair shops. Most of them work a regular 40-hour week. Working conditions in some jobs are hot, noisy, or in the presence of bad-smelling chemicals.

The overall outlook for jobs in this group is only fair. Ready-made clothing and low-priced furniture are reducing the demand for tailoring services and reupholstering. Improved fabrics are also reducing the need for cleaning and pressing. Best opportunities will be for certain specialists, such as those who alter shoes for elderly wearers or who reupholster very valuable furniture.

How can you prepare for jobs of this kind?

These jobs require education and/or training ranging from a few days to four or more years.

Many of these trades are learned on the job. Workers begin as helpers and receive instruction from experienced workers, advancing to more skilled tasks over time. For-

mal apprenticeships are available for some of these trades, such as tailoring, upholstering, and custom shoe making. These combine classroom instruction with on-the-job training and take several years. A high school education is usually expected of new recruits. High school or vocational school classes in sewing are very helpful.

The dry cleaning occupations can generally be learned in only a few days or weeks.

How much education or training is required for the jobs in this Work Group?

For descriptions of these jobs, see Part 2.

Short-term on-the-job training

* Fabric Menders, Except Garment
* Pressers, Hand
* Spotters, Dry Cleaning

Moderate-term on-the-job training

* Laundry and Drycleaning Machine Operators and Tenders, Except Pressing
* Pressers, Delicate Fabrics

Long-term on-the-job training

* Shoe and Leather Workers and Repairers
* Upholsterers

Work experience in a related occupation

* Custom Tailors
* Shop and Alteration Tailors

Postsecondary vocational training

* Precision Dyers

13.12 Electrical and Electronic Repair

Workers in this group repair and install electrical devices and systems such as motors, transformers, appliances, and power lines and electronic devices and systems such as radios and aircraft navigational equipment.

What kind of work would you do?

Your work activities would depend on your job. For example, you might

* Clean and polish parts, using solvent and buffing wheel.
* Confer with customers to determine nature of malfunctions.
* Install electric fixtures, outlets, terminal boards, switches, and wall boxes, using hand tools.
* Install electrical and electronic components, assemblies, and systems in aircraft, using hand tools, power tools, and/or soldering irons.
* Keep records of maintenance and repair work.
* Maintain inventory of spare parts.

* Repair and rebuild defective mechanical parts in electric motors, generators, and related equipment, using hand tools and power tools.
* Repair battery-charging equipment.
* Replace worn and defective parts of electric home appliances, such as switches, bearings, transmissions, belts, gears, circuit boards, or defective wiring.
* Study blueprints, schematics, manuals, and other specifications to determine installation procedures.

What things about you point to this kind of work?

Is it important for you to

* Have supervisors who train workers well?
* Never be pressured to do things that go against your sense of right and wrong?

Have you enjoyed any of the following as a hobby or leisure-time activity?

* Building or repairing radios or television sets
* Assembling radios, computers, and other devices from kits
* Building robots or electronic devices
* Taking apart or fixing mechanical and electronic devices

Have you liked and done well in any of the following school subjects?

* Electric/Electronic Shop
* Electronic Devices
* Electrical Circuits
* Shop Math
* Industrial Safety
* Blueprint/Schematic Reading

Are you able to

* Make precisely coordinated movements of the fingers of one or both hands to grasp, manipulate, or assemble very small objects?
* Match or detect differences between colors, including shades of color and brightness?
* Bend, stretch, twist, or reach with your body, arms, and/or legs?

Would you work in places such as

* Factories and plants?
* Radio studios?
* Airplanes?
* Auto service stations and repair shops?

What skills and knowledges do you need for this kind of work?

For most of these jobs, you need these skills:

* Repairing—repairing machines or systems, using the needed tools
* Installation—installing equipment, machines, wiring, or programs to meet specifications

* Troubleshooting—determining causes of operating errors and deciding what to do about them
* Equipment Maintenance—performing routine maintenance on equipment and determining when and what kind of maintenance is needed

These knowledges are important in most of these jobs:

* Mechanical Devices—machines and tools, including their designs, uses, repair, and maintenance
* Computers and Electronics—circuit boards; processors; chips; electronic equipment; and computer hardware and software, including applications and programming
* Telecommunications—transmission, broadcasting, switching, control, and operation of telecommunications systems

What else should you consider about this kind of work?

Factories, service companies, and large companies with an in-house service staff hire many of these workers. Others are self-employed, working full-time or part-time. Since electrical and electronic equipment is used almost everywhere, these workers may be found in almost every large and small city. Some jobs are available only where certain industries are located.

Work schedules vary. Factories, hospitals, and radio and TV studios, for instance, have rotating shifts.

Some equipment repairs or adjustments are made in a repair shop; others are made in the customer's office or home. Some jobs require climbing or crawling to reach wiring and components.

Careful safety procedures must be observed for some jobs because of the chance of electric shock. Good color vision is usually needed, since electronic parts are often color-coded.

The employment outlook is lukewarm. Best opportunities are in installation, service, and repair of equipment used for purposes other than manufacturing, which is mostly happening in foreign countries. Because of miniaturization and better quality control, many products need fewer repairs and service calls.

How can you prepare for jobs of this kind?

Work in this group usually requires education and/or training ranging from six months to several years, depending on the type of equipment.

Colleges and technical schools offer two-year programs in electronics technology or electrical engineering technology. Courses in electricity, electronics, mathematics beyond the shop math level, and blueprint reading are especially helpful.

A few companies provide extensive training to prepare workers for repair jobs. Correspondence courses in such fields as electricity and electronics are often helpful. Apprenticeships are also available, and military experience can be a start.

 © 2006 JIST Works

Technology in this field is changing constantly, so workers need to take courses and get training to keep their skills current.

How much education or training is required for the jobs in this Work Group?

For descriptions of these jobs, see Part 2.

Moderate-term on-the-job training

* Battery Repairers
* Electrical Parts Reconditioners

Long-term on-the-job training

* Electric Home Appliance and Power Tool Repairers
* Electric Motor and Switch Assemblers and Repairers
* Transformer Repairers

Postsecondary vocational training

* Avionics Technicians
* Electrical and Electronics Installers and Repairers, Transportation Equipment
* Electrical and Electronics Repairers, Commercial and Industrial Equipment
* Electronic Equipment Installers and Repairers, Motor Vehicles
* Electronic Home Entertainment Equipment Installers and Repairers
* Radio Mechanics

13.13 Machinery Repair

Workers in this group install, service, and repair various kinds of machinery and equipment. Some are electromechanical devices, such as mechanical doors and industrial machinery; others are human-powered, such as locks and bicycles.

What kind of work would you do?

Your work activities would depend on your job. For example, you might

* Assemble machines and bolt, weld, rivet, or otherwise fasten them to foundations or other structures, using hand tools and power tools.
* Assemble new bicycles.
* Disassemble mechanical control devices or valves, such as regulators, thermostats, or hydrants, using power tools, hand tools, and cutting torch.
* Dismantle gas meters and regulators and replace defective pipes, thermocouples, thermostats, valves, and indicator spindles, using hand tools.
* Insert new or repaired tumblers into locks in order to change combinations.
* Lubricate moving parts on gate-crossing mechanisms and swinging signals.
* Move machinery and equipment, using hoists, dollies, rollers, and trucks.

* Read work orders and specifications to determine machines and equipment requiring repair or maintenance.
* Record repairs and maintenance performed.
* Repair or replace worn or broken door parts, using hand tools.

What things about you point to this kind of work?

Is it important for you to

* Never be pressured to do things that go against your sense of right and wrong?
* Do your work alone?

Have you enjoyed any of the following as a hobby or leisure-time activity?

* Repairing or assembling bicycles or tricycles
* Taking apart or fixing mechanical and electronic devices
* Assembling toys, shelving, furniture, and other items around the house
* Repairing electrical household appliances
* Repairing plumbing in the home

Have you liked and done well in any of the following school subjects?

* Electric/Electronic Shop
* Electrical Circuits
* Shop Math
* Blueprint/Schematic Reading
* Industrial Safety
* Locksmithing/Lock Repair

Are you able to

* Bend, stretch, twist, or reach with your body, arms, and/or legs?
* Make precisely coordinated movements of the fingers of one or both hands to grasp, manipulate, or assemble very small objects?
* Tell the direction from which a sound originated?

Would you work in places such as

* Factories and plants?
* Office buildings?
* Private homes?
* Railroad tracks and yards?
* Waterworks and light and power plants?

What skills and knowledges do you need for this kind of work?

For most of these jobs, you need these skills:

* Repairing—repairing machines or systems, using the needed tools
* Installation—installing equipment, machines, wiring, or programs to meet specifications
* Equipment Maintenance—performing routine maintenance on equipment and determining when and what kind of maintenance is needed

* Troubleshooting—determining causes of operating errors and deciding what to do about them

These knowledges are important in most of these jobs:

* Mechanical Devices—machines and tools, including their designs, uses, repair, and maintenance
* Engineering and Technology—the practical application of engineering science and technology; this includes applying principles, techniques, procedures, and equipment to the design and production of various goods and services
* Physics—physical principles and laws and their interrelationships and applications to understanding fluid, material, and atmospheric dynamics and mechanical, electrical, atomic, and subatomic structures and processes

What else should you consider about this kind of work?

Workers in this group do fabrication, installation, servicing, and repairs for manufacturers, merchandisers of appliances, specialized repair shops (such as bicycle shops), and service companies. Some are self-employed and market their skills directly to consumers or businesses.

As some devices become more electronic, cheaper, and more reliable, opportunities will decline in some specialties. On the other hand, the demand will continue or grow for some workers, such as gas appliance repairers, locksmiths, mechanical door repairers, and highly skilled millwrights and industrial machinery mechanics.

How can you prepare for jobs of this kind?

For work in this group, education and/or training requirements vary from six months to several years, depending on the sophistication of the machinery being worked on.

Some of these jobs (for example, bicycle repairers and locksmiths) are taught by a training program at the work site lasting six months to two years. Gas appliance repairers often are trained by the manufacturer in a program that can last several years. Millwrights and higher-skilled industrial machinery repairers learn their trade in an apprenticeship, combining on-the-job training and classroom learning over four years.

In almost all of the jobs, high school courses in blueprint reading and mechanical drawing are a good first step. Since keeping up with new technology is the key to continued employment and good income, high school courses should include physics or applied technology and mathematics beyond shop math.

How much education or training is required for the jobs in this Work Group?

For descriptions of these jobs, see Part 2.

Moderate-term on-the-job training

* Bicycle Repairers
* Hand and Portable Power Tool Repairers
* Locksmiths and Safe Repairers

* Mechanical Door Repairers
* Valve and Regulator Repairers

Long-term on-the-job training

* Gas Appliance Repairers
* Industrial Machinery Mechanics
* Maintenance Workers, Machinery
* Millwrights

Postsecondary vocational training

* Signal and Track Switch Repairers

13.14 Vehicle and Facility Mechanical Work

Workers in this group service and repair the bodies and engines of cars, trucks, buses, airplanes, boats, ships, and other motorized vehicles and equipment.

What kind of work would you do?

Your work activities would depend on your job. For example, you might

* Assemble and install parts, fittings, and assemblies on aircraft, using layout tools, hand tools, power tools, and fasteners.
* Confer with customers or read work orders to determine nature and extent of damage to units.
* Examine and inspect engines or other components for cracks, breaks, or leaks.
* Mix polyester resins and hardeners to be used in restoring damaged areas.
* Overhaul and test machines or equipment to ensure operating efficiency.
* Read and interpret blueprints, illustrations, and specifications to determine layout, sequence of operations, or identity and relationship of parts.
* Record repairs made, time spent, and parts used.
* Remove broken or damaged glass windshields or window glass from motor vehicles.
* Repair and replace defective ball joint suspensions, brakeshoes, and wheel bearings.
* Repair manual and automatic transmissions.

What things about you point to this kind of work?

Is it important for you to

* Never be pressured to do things that go against your sense of right and wrong?
* Be paid well in comparison with other workers?

Have you enjoyed any of the following as a hobby or leisure-time activity?

* Building model airplanes, automobiles, or boats
* Working on bicycles, minibikes, lawn mowers, or cars
* Reading mechanical or automotive magazines
* Repairing the family car

Have you liked and done well in any of the following school subjects?

* Auto Mechanics
* Aircraft Mechanics
* Shop Math
* Industrial Safety
* Electricity/Electronics
* Engine Mechanics
* Diesel Mechanics/Diesels
* Hydraulics/Hydraulic Shop

Are you able to

* Bend, stretch, twist, or reach with your body, arms, and/or legs?
* Detect or tell the differences between sounds that vary in pitch and loudness?
* Exert maximum muscle force to lift, push, pull, or carry objects?
* Coordinate two or more limbs while sitting, standing, or lying down?

Would you work in places such as

* Auto service stations and repair shops?
* Airplanes?
* Trains?
* Buses and trolleys?
* Farms?
* Ships and boats?
* Factories and plants?

What skills and knowledges do you need for this kind of work?

For most of these jobs, you need these skills:

* Repairing—repairing machines or systems, using the needed tools
* Installation—installing equipment, machines, wiring, or programs to meet specifications
* Equipment Maintenance—performing routine maintenance on equipment and determining when and what kind of maintenance is needed
* Troubleshooting—determining causes of operating errors and deciding what to do about them

These knowledges are important in most of these jobs:

* Mechanical Devices—machines and tools, including their designs, uses, repair, and maintenance
* Engineering and Technology—the practical application of engineering science and technology; this includes applying principles, techniques, procedures, and equipment to the design and production of various goods and services
* Building and Construction—the materials, methods, and tools involved in the construction or repair of houses; buildings; or other structures, such as highways and roads

What else should you consider about this kind of work?

These workers are employed by vehicle and engine manufacturers, dealerships, repair shops, and vehicle fleets. Many who repair automobiles, motorboats, motorcycles, and small engines are self-employed and run their own shops. Work of this kind may be found anywhere in the country, although certain specialties, such as snowmobile or motorboat repair, are limited geographically and may have seasonal ups and downs.

The work is often greasy and physically demanding. Workers need to take precautions to avoid hot or moving parts. Most of the work is done indoors in service bays or workshops.

Use of electronic equipment is growing, both in the vehicles and in diagnostic tools used by mechanics. However, automation is not replacing many jobs. In fact, the outlook in this field is mostly very good for workers with formal training who are willing to learn continuously to keep their skills up to date.

How can you prepare for jobs of this kind?

For work in this group, education and/or training requirements vary from six months to several years.

For some of these jobs, it is possible to learn informally on the job at a repair shop, perhaps after starting as a helper, lubrication worker, or gasoline station attendant. However, employers prefer workers who have completed formal training programs. These are available at vocational schools, at technical and community colleges, and in the form of apprenticeships. Three to four years of training is required to become a general automobile mechanic or body repairer. Less time is needed to train for repairing a particular automotive component, such as the brakes, cooling system, or glass, or for working on small engines.

For FAA certification in one specialization, aircraft mechanics must acquire at least 18 months of work experience; they need at least 30 months for combined aircraft-and-powerplant certification. Some of the work requirement can be offset by completion of an FAA-approved vocational program.

High school courses in auto shop, blueprint reading, mechanical drawing, and computer applications are helpful. Because keeping up with new technology is the key to continued employment and good income, high school courses should include physics and mathematics beyond shop math.

How much education or training is required for the jobs in this Work Group?

For descriptions of these jobs, see Part 2.

Short-term on-the-job training

* Tire Repairers and Changers

Moderate-term on-the-job training

* Fiberglass Laminators and Fabricators
* Outdoor Power Equipment and Other Small Engine Mechanics

Long-term on-the-job training

* Aircraft Rigging Assemblers
* Aircraft Structure Assemblers, Precision
* Aircraft Systems Assemblers, Precision
* Automotive Body and Related Repairers
* Automotive Glass Installers and Repairers
* Motorboat Mechanics
* Motorcycle Mechanics
* Rail Car Repairers
* Recreational Vehicle Service Technicians

Postsecondary vocational training

* Aircraft Body and Bonded Structure Repairers
* Aircraft Engine Specialists
* Airframe-and-Power-Plant Mechanics
* Automotive Master Mechanics
* Automotive Specialty Technicians
* Bus and Truck Mechanics and Diesel Engine Specialists
* Farm Equipment Mechanics
* Mobile Heavy Equipment Mechanics, Except Engines

13.15 Medical and Technical Equipment Repair

Workers in this group repair sophisticated equipment requiring great precision and attention to detail.

What kind of work would you do?

Your work activities would depend on your job. For example, you might

* Clean and lubricate cameras and polish camera lenses, using cleaning materials and work aids.
* Disassemble timepieces and inspect them for defective, worn, misaligned, or rusty parts, using loupes.
* Examine medical equipment and facility's structural environment and check for proper use of equipment.
* Inspect and test malfunctioning medical and related equipment, following manufacturers' specifications and using test and analysis instruments.
* Repair or replace broken, damaged, or worn parts on timepieces, using lathes, drill presses, and hand tools.

What things about you point to this kind of work?

Is it important for you to

* Do your work alone?
* Never be pressured to do things that go against your sense of right and wrong?

Have you enjoyed any of the following as a hobby or leisure-time activity?

* Taking apart or fixing mechanical and electronic devices
* Assembling radios, computers, and other devices from kits
* Building robots or electronic devices

Have you liked and done well in any of the following school subjects?

* Instrument Repair
* Electronic Devices
* Optics
* Watchmaking/Watch Repair Shop
* Blueprint/Schematic Reading

Are you able to

* Make precisely coordinated movements of the fingers of one or both hands to grasp, manipulate, or assemble very small objects?
* Keep your hand and arm steady while moving your arm or while holding your arm and hand in one position?
* See details at close range?
* Quickly and repeatedly adjust the controls of a machine or a vehicle to exact positions?

Would you work in places such as

* Factories and plants?
* Stores and shopping malls?

What skills and knowledges do you need for this kind of work?

For most of these jobs, you need these skills:

* Repairing—repairing machines or systems, using the needed tools
* Troubleshooting—determining causes of operating errors and deciding what to do about them
* Equipment Maintenance—performing routine maintenance on equipment and determining when and what kind of maintenance is needed
* Installation—installing equipment, machines, wiring, or programs to meet specifications
* Quality Control Analysis—conducting tests and inspections of products, services, or processes to evaluate quality or performance
* Technology Design—generating or adapting equipment and technology to serve user needs

These knowledges are important in most of these jobs:

* Mechanical Devices—machines and tools, including their designs, uses, repair, and maintenance
* Engineering and Technology—the practical application of engineering science and technology; this includes applying principles, techniques, procedures, and equipment to the design and production of various goods and services
* Physics—physical principles and laws and their interrelationships and applications to understanding fluid, material, and atmospheric dynamics and mechanical, electrical, atomic, and subatomic structures and processes

© 2006 JIST Works

What else should you consider about this kind of work?

These workers are employed by manufacturers, hospitals, and wholesale equipment suppliers. Some are self-employed and manage their own repair shops.

Most work is performed indoors in quiet repair shops during normal working hours, but those who repair hospital equipment may need to be on call to fix breakdowns that can occur at any hour. Most of the work is done with minimal supervision.

The employment outlook is mixed. Digital and disposable cameras are reducing the demand for camera repairers. Similar advances in technology have slowed the job growth for watch repairers, but this highly skilled trade is having trouble attracting recruits to replace workers who are retiring, so job opportunities should be good. Medical equipment repairers will have good prospects as the aging population requires more health care and new medical devices are constantly being developed.

How can you prepare for jobs of this kind?

For work in this group, education and/or training requirements vary from one year to several.

For most of these jobs, workers are trained on the job by experienced workers. Some employers prefer trainees who have had some postsecondary education in electronics. Highly skilled medical equipment repairers, such as those who work with CAT scanners and defibrillators, may need a college degree in medical technology or electronics engineering technology. In some areas, apprenticeships are available for these jobs, combining workplace learning and classroom study.

High school courses in electronics, mechanical drawing, and computer applications are helpful, plus physics and mathematics beyond the shop math level. Constant learning is the key to staying employable in these technical careers.

How much education or training is required for the jobs in this Work Group?

For descriptions of these jobs, see Part 2.

Moderate-term on-the-job training

* Camera and Photographic Equipment Repairers
* Medical Equipment Repairers

Long-term on-the-job training

* Watch Repairers

13.16 Utility Operation and Energy Distribution

Workers in this group operate and maintain equipment in systems that generate or distribute electricity, provide water or process wastewater, or pump oil or gas from storage facilities to consumers.

What kind of work would you do?

Your work activities would depend on your job. For example, you might

* Add chemicals, such as ammonia, chlorine, and lime, to disinfect and deodorize water and other liquids.
* Clean and maintain heating and steam boilers and equipment, using hand tools.
* Clean, lubricate, and adjust compressors, using hand tools.
* Control or operate chemical processes or systems of machines, using panelboards, control boards, or semi-automatic equipment.
* Control, monitor, or operate equipment that regulates or distributes electricity or steam, using data obtained from instruments or computers.
* Inspect pipelines, valves, and flanges to detect malfunctions, such as loose connections and leaks.
* Maintain and repair electrical power distribution machinery and equipment, using hand tools.
* Observe instruments, gauges, and meters to verify conformance to specified quality and quantity of product.
* Operate equipment to control transmission of natural gas through pipelines.
* Participate in nuclear fuel element handling activities such as preparation, transfer, loading, and unloading.

What things about you point to this kind of work?

Is it important for you to

* Have supervisors who train workers well?
* Have supervisors who back up workers with management?

Have you enjoyed any of the following as a hobby or leisure-time activity?

* Doing electrical wiring and repairs in the home
* Making sketches of machines or other mechanical equipment
* Reading about technological developments, such as computer science or aerospace
* Repairing electrical household appliances
* Repairing plumbing in the home

Have you liked and done well in any of the following school subjects?

* Nuclear Safety
* Wastewater/Water Treatment Processing
* Ship Systems
* Pump Operation
* Power Systems/Technology
* Blueprint/Schematic Reading

Are you able to

* Quickly and repeatedly adjust the controls of a machine or a vehicle to exact positions?
* Tell the direction from which a sound originated?
* Respond quickly to a signal when it appears?

Would you work in places such as

* Waterworks and light and power plants?
* Oil fields?
* Ships and boats?
* Office buildings?

What skills and knowledges do you need for this kind of work?

For most of these jobs, you need these skills:

* Operation Monitoring—watching gauges, dials, or other indicators to make sure a machine is working properly
* Operation and Control—controlling operations of equipment or systems
* Equipment Maintenance—performing routine maintenance on equipment and determining when and what kind of maintenance is needed
* Repairing—repairing machines or systems, using the needed tools

These knowledges are important in most of these jobs:

* Mechanical Devices—machines and tools, including their designs, uses, repair, and maintenance
* Physics—physical principles and laws and their interrelationships and applications to understanding fluid, material, and atmospheric dynamics and mechanical, electrical, atomic, and subatomic structures and processes
* Engineering and Technology—the practical application of engineering science and technology; this includes applying principles, techniques, procedures, and equipment to the design and production of various goods and services

What else should you consider about this kind of work?

Energy companies, utilities, city and county governments, industrial plants, farms, and shipping companies hire the workers in this group. Because energy and water are used around the clock, many of these occupations require shift work.

Many of the jobs in this group are with city and county governments, even large office and apartment complexes, that operate their own power plants or water processing systems. In most places you must pass a civil service examination to qualify for government jobs.

Many of these workers are surrounded by extremely hot, high-pressure, or explosive liquids and gases and must observe safety precautions. Wastewater treatment workers are exposed to unpleasant smells. Most of these workers have to be able to think and act quickly in case of emergencies. Some of them have to crawl inside boilers and work in cramped spaces to inspect, clean, or repair interiors.

The energy industry experiences periodic ups and downs caused by economic and political forces, but in general most jobs related to power generation and transmission are on a downward turn, largely because of increased competition among energy providers. Opportunities should be good for water and liquid waste treatment plant operators because of a shortage of recruits for the jobs.

How can you prepare for jobs of this kind?

Requirements for education and/or training in this group range from six months to several years.

High school and vocational school courses in machine shop, mechanical drawing, mathematics beyond the shop math level, and physics are helpful. Workers in nuclear-powered plants must have special training and be licensed by the government.

Apprenticeship programs lasting up to four years are available in some areas for many of these occupations, such as stationary engineer, water/wastewater treatment operator, and power plant operator. Some trainees learn more informally by working in a related job and getting instruction from experienced workers.

Operators of systems that transmit oil or natural gas usually start as helpers. Operators of generating or distributing systems for electricity usually start as manual workers, advancing with experience. One to four years of experience is usually required to develop the necessary knowledge and skills.

How much education or training is required for the jobs in this Work Group?

For descriptions of these jobs, see Part 2.

Moderate-term on-the-job training

* Boiler Operators and Tenders, Low Pressure
* Gas Compressor Operators
* Gas Pumping Station Operators

Long-term on-the-job training

* Auxiliary Equipment Operators, Power
* Chemical Plant and System Operators
* Gas Distribution Plant Operators
* Gas Processing Plant Operators
* Gaugers
* Nuclear Power Reactor Operators
* Petroleum Pump System Operators
* Petroleum Refinery and Control Panel Operators
* Power Distributors and Dispatchers
* Power Generating Plant Operators, Except Auxiliary Equipment Operators
* Stationary Engineers
* Water and Liquid Waste Treatment Plant and System Operators

Postsecondary vocational training

* Ship Engineers

13.17 Loading, Moving, Hoisting, and Conveying

Workers in this group use their hands, machinery, tools, and other equipment to package or move products or materials. They work in a variety of settings, including offices, mailrooms, manufacturing plants, water treatment plants, and construction sites. They may work with small packages or computer chips or with huge containers or structural components of buildings.

What kind of work would you do?

Your work activities would depend on your job. For example, you might

* Attach, fasten, and disconnect cables or lines to loads, materials, and equipment, using hand tools.
* Feed materials into machines and equipment to process and manufacture products.
* Follow prescribed safety procedures and comply with federal laws regulating waste disposal methods.
* Load, unload, or adjust materials or products on conveyors by hand; by using lifts, hoists, and scoops; or by opening gates, chutes, or hoppers.
* Measure, weigh, and count products and materials.
* Operate equipment that compresses collected refuse.
* Operate ship loading and unloading equipment, conveyors, hoists, and other specialized material handling equipment such as railroad tank car unloading equipment.
* Position lifting devices under, over, or around loaded pallets, skids, and boxes.
* Stack or pile materials, such as lumber, boards, or pallets.
* Turn valves and start pumps to start or regulate flows of substances such as gases, liquids, slurries, or powdered materials.

What things about you point to this kind of work?

Is it important for you to

* Have supervisors who train workers well?
* Have supervisors who back up workers with management?

Have you enjoyed any of the following as a hobby or leisure-time activity?

* Handling equipment for a local athletic team
* Operating a model train layout
* Reading mechanical or automotive magazines
* Building model airplanes, automobiles, or boats

Have you liked and done well in any of the following school subjects?

* Nuclear Safety
* Manufacturing Processes
* Industrial Safety
* Pump Operation

Are you able to

* Exert maximum muscle force to lift, push, pull, or carry objects?
* Time your movements or the movement of a piece of equipment in anticipation of changes in the speed and/or direction of a moving object or scene?
* Coordinate two or more limbs while sitting, standing, or lying down?

Would you work in places such as

* Waterworks and light and power plants?
* Warehouses?
* Factories and plants?
* Railroad tracks and yards?
* Ports and harbors?
* Bus and train stations?

What skills and knowledges do you need for this kind of work?

For most of these jobs, you need these skills:

* Operation and Control—controlling operations of equipment or systems
* Equipment Maintenance—performing routine maintenance on equipment and determining when and what kind of maintenance is needed
* Operation Monitoring—watching gauges, dials, or other indicators to make sure a machine is working properly

These knowledges are important in most of these jobs:

* Transportation—principles and methods for moving people or goods by air, rail, sea, or road, including the relative costs and benefits
* Production and Processing—raw materials, production processes, quality control, costs, and other techniques for maximizing the effective manufacture and distribution of goods
* Mechanical Devices—machines and tools, including their designs, uses, repair, and maintenance

What else should you consider about this kind of work?

A variety of different industries hire the workers in this group. Many manufacturers employ packers. Heavier industries and shipping companies need workers to move materials and large containers, and many machines used in manufacturing and processing need workers to feed in materials and take away the output.

Most of these jobs require a 40-hour work week, with some overtime or shift work. Some of the loading and moving jobs are noisy and/or dirty, some are physically demanding, and because of the presence of heavy machinery, they often require safety precautions.

Some industries are doing better than others, and as a result the outlook for jobs varies. In general, manufacturing is on the decline in the United States, and some material-moving jobs are being lost to automation and robotics. Nevertheless, this Work Group employs a large number of people, so there should be many job openings from replacement needs. Good opportunities are also expected in temporary help and warehousing businesses.

How can you prepare for jobs of this kind?

Most of these occupations require less than six months of education and/or training. A few require a year or more.

Often the tasks can be learned by observing experienced workers or through brief on-the-job training. Some of the more complex machines for moving and loading require a more involved training program. Irradiated-fuel handlers must have special training because of the hazardous materials they work with.

How much education or training is required for the jobs in this Work Group?

For descriptions of these jobs, see Part 2.

Short-term on-the-job training

* Conveyor Operators and Tenders
* Freight, Stock, and Material Movers, Hand
* Industrial Truck and Tractor Operators
* Machine Feeders and Offbearers
* Packers and Packagers, Hand
* Refuse and Recyclable Material Collectors

Moderate-term on-the-job training

* Hoist and Winch Operators
* Irradiated-Fuel Handlers
* Pump Operators, Except Wellhead Pumpers
* Tank Car, Truck, and Ship Loaders

© 2006 JIST Works

14 Retail and Wholesale Sales and Service

An interest in bringing others to a particular point of view by personal persuasion and by sales and promotional techniques. You can satisfy this interest in a variety of jobs that involve persuasion and selling. If you like using knowledge of science, you may enjoy selling pharmaceutical, medical, or electronic products or services. Real estate offers several kinds of sales jobs as well. If you like speaking on the phone, you could work as a telemarketer. Or you may enjoy selling apparel and other merchandise in a retail setting. If you prefer to help people, you may want a job in customer service.

14.01 Managerial Work in Retail/Wholesale Sales and Service

14.02 Technical Sales

14.03 General Sales

14.04 Personal Soliciting

14.05 Purchasing

14.06 Customer Service

14.01 Managerial Work in Retail/Wholesale Sales and Service

Workers in this group direct or manage various kinds of selling and/or advertising operations—either a department within a business or a specialized business firm that contracts to provide selling and/or advertising services. These workers usually carry out their activities according to policies and procedures determined by owners, boards of directors, administrators, and other persons with higher authority.

What kind of work would you do?

Your work activities would depend on your job. For example, you might

* Develop pricing strategies, balancing firm objectives and customer satisfaction.
* Gather and organize information to plan advertising campaigns.
* Instruct staff on how to handle difficult and complicated sales.
* Locate vendors of materials, equipment, or supplies and interview them in order to determine product availability and terms of sales.
* Market vacant space to prospective tenants through leasing agents, advertising, or other methods.
* Monitor sales staff performance to ensure that goals are met.
* Plan, schedule, and coordinate funerals, burials, and cremations, arranging such details as the time and place of services.
* Resolve customer complaints regarding sales and service.

What things about you point to this kind of work?

Is it important for you to

* Give directions and instructions to others?
* Plan your work with little supervision?
* Have opportunities for advancement?
* Have good working conditions?
* Be paid well in comparison with other workers?
* Have something different to do every day?

Have you enjoyed any of the following as a hobby or leisure-time activity?

* Conducting house-to-house or telephone surveys for a PTA or other organization
* Developing publicity fliers for a school or community event
* Helping persuade people to sign petitions or support a cause
* Planning advertisements for a school or community newspaper
* Reading business magazines and newspapers
* Selling advertising space for a school newspaper or yearbook
* Serving as a leader of a scouting or other group
* Soliciting funds for community organizations

Have you liked and done well in any of the following school subjects?

* Management
* Accounting
* Personnel Management
* Advertising
* Marketing/Merchandising
* Selling
* Business Law
* Consumer Behavior
* Retailing

Are you able to

* Identify and understand the speech of another person?
* Choose the right mathematical methods or formulas to solve a problem?
* Come up with a number of ideas about a topic?
* Add, subtract, multiply, or divide quickly and correctly?

Would you work in places such as

* Business offices?
* Stores and shopping malls?
* Funeral homes?
* Convention and trade show centers?

What skills and knowledges do you need for this kind of work?

For most of these jobs, you need these skills:

* Management of Financial Resources—determining how money will be spent to get the work done and accounting for these expenditures
* Negotiation—bringing others together and trying to reconcile differences
* Management of Personnel Resources—motivating, developing, and directing people as they work, identifying the best people for the job
* Time Management—managing one's own time and the time of others
* Service Orientation—actively looking for ways to help people
* Persuasion—persuading others to change their minds or behavior
* Coordination—adjusting actions in relation to others' actions

These knowledges are important in most of these jobs:

* Sales and Marketing—principles and methods for showing, promoting, and selling products or services; this includes marketing strategy and tactics, product demonstrations, sales techniques, and sales control systems

* Personnel and Human Resources—principles and procedures for personnel recruitment, selection, training, compensation and benefits, labor relations and negotiation, and personnel information systems
* Administration and Management—business and management principles involved in strategic planning, resource allocation, human resources modeling, leadership techniques, production methods, and coordination of people and resources
* Customer and Personal Service—principles and processes for providing customer and personal services; this includes customer needs assessment, meeting quality standards for services, and evaluation of customer satisfaction
* Economics and Accounting—economic and accounting principles and practices, the financial markets, banking, and the analysis and reporting of financial data
* Communications and Media—media production, communication, and dissemination techniques and methods; this includes alternative ways to inform and entertain via written, oral, and visual media
* Law and Government—laws, legal codes, court procedures, precedents, government regulations, executive orders, agency rules, and the democratic political process

What else should you consider about this kind of work?

Employment for workers in this group may be found in cities and towns throughout the United States. Self-employment is common in some of these specializations. The jobs are located in comfortable offices and usually require a standard 40-hour work week, with occasional late nights under the pressure of a marketing campaign.

People skills are very important in all of these jobs. Funeral directors need a dignified appearance and sometimes need to deal with bodies that are badly disfigured.

Competition for most of these jobs is likely to be keen. The best opportunities will be for college graduates with business experience, a high level of creativity, and good communications skills. Knowledge of how to work in new media such as the Internet can also be very valuable. Job openings related to service industries, including business services, funerals, and property management, will be more plentiful than those related to manufactured goods.

How can you prepare for jobs of this kind?

Work in this group generally requires four years of education and/or training. First-line supervisors and manager/supervisors may have fewer years.

A bachelor's degree in advertising or marketing is good preparation for most of these occupations. Courses in writing and speech communication can be very helpful. If you want to work in a particular industry (for example, high tech), you may want to take relevant coursework.

Workers with less formal education may start by taking a job selling advertising space or doing clerical work in support of marketing and then may be able to work their way

up to management after gaining experience and taking courses in management.

Funeral directors need to be licensed and usually prepare by studying for two to four years at a college of mortuary science. This study is sometimes combined with or followed by an apprenticeship lasting from one to three years. Opportunities are better for those who also learn embalming.

Advances in technology continue to have great impact on how marketing and advertising are done, so it is important to be learning new skills throughout a career in this field.

How much education or training is required for the jobs in this Work Group?

For descriptions of these jobs, see Part 2.

Work experience in a related occupation

* First-Line Supervisors/Managers of Non-Retail Sales Workers
* First-Line Supervisors/Managers of Retail Sales Workers

Associate degree

* Funeral Directors

Bachelor's degree

* Property, Real Estate, and Community Association Managers

Work experience plus degree

* Advertising and Promotions Managers
* Marketing Managers
* Purchasing Managers
* Sales Managers

14.02 Technical Sales

Workers in this group sell products such as industrial machinery, data processing equipment, and pharmaceuticals. They advise customers of the capabilities, uses, and other important features of these products and services and help customers choose those best suited to their needs.

What kind of work would you do?

Your work activities would depend on your job. For example, you might

* Attend sales and trade meetings and read related publications to obtain current market condition information, business trends, and industry developments.
* Demonstrate use of agricultural equipment or machines.
* Maintain sales forecasting reports.
* Negotiate terms of sale and services with customers.
* Promote and sell pharmaceutical and chemical products to potential customers.

* Research and identify potential customers for products or services.
* Sell weighing and other precision instruments, such as spring scales; dynamometers; and laboratory, navigational, and surveying instruments, to customers.
* Study data describing new products to recommend purchase of equipment and supplies accurately.

What things about you point to this kind of work?

Is it important for you to

* Receive recognition for the work you do?
* Be paid well in comparison with other workers?
* Have opportunities for advancement?
* Have something different to do every day?

Have you enjoyed any of the following as a hobby or leisure-time activity?

* Doing public speaking or debating
* Helping persuade people to sign petitions or support a cause
* Reading business magazines and newspapers
* Selling advertising space for a school newspaper or yearbook
* Conducting experiments involving plants
* Performing experiments for a science fair

Have you liked and done well in any of the following school subjects?

* Selling
* Electricity/Electronics
* Chemistry
* Agribusiness
* Marketing/Merchandising
* Record Keeping

Are you able to

* Communicate information and ideas in speaking so others will understand?
* Remember information such as words, numbers, pictures, and procedures?
* Add, subtract, multiply, or divide quickly and correctly?

Would you work in places such as

* Business offices?
* Factories and plants?
* Doctors' and dentists' offices and clinics?
* Hospitals and nursing homes?
* Waterworks and light and power plants?
* Convention and trade show centers?

What skills and knowledges do you need for this kind of work?

For most of these jobs, you need these skills:

* Persuasion—persuading others to change their minds or behavior

* Negotiation—bringing others together and trying to reconcile differences
* Operations Analysis—analyzing needs and product requirements to create a design

These knowledges are important in most of these jobs:

* Sales and Marketing—principles and methods for showing, promoting, and selling products or services; this includes marketing strategy and tactics, product demonstrations, sales techniques, and sales control systems
* Economics and Accounting—economic and accounting principles and practices, the financial markets, banking, and the analysis and reporting of financial data
* Telecommunications—transmission, broadcasting, switching, control, and operation of telecommunications systems

What else should you consider about this kind of work?

These workers are employed by manufacturers and wholesalers. Some are self-employed.

Many of the jobs in this group require frequent travel. Workers may be on the road, calling on customers in various communities, for as long as two or three weeks at a time. The "territories" of sales representatives may be as large as several states or as small as a single metropolitan area.

Sales representatives who cover a single metropolitan area use company (or sometimes their own) cars. Those whose territories include several states usually fly or use other public transportation.

Sales engineers often work with both the customers and the engineering departments of their employer to determine how to create products best suited to customers' needs.

Most of these jobs entail meeting new people and many require working under pressure, making decisions that affect sales involving large sums of money.

Some workers receive a salary; others work on a commission, usually a percentage of the selling price. Some workers receive a combination of salary and commission; some own their own businesses.

In many sales occupations, there is great competition at the beginning to establish a clientele, and many beginners drop out because they are not successful. On the other hand, those who can get past the first rung of this career will generally have good opportunities. In addition, the high turnover rate means that there will always be a large number of openings for beginners to try their luck and apply their skills.

Sales jobs in most fields are sensitive to the ups and downs of the economy. Automation is not likely to replace the person-to-person contact that is required for these jobs, but it may increase workers' productivity and thus reduce the overall number of jobs. Opportunities representing manufacturers will be better in fast-growing industries (such as medical equipment) than in some others.

How can you prepare for jobs of this kind?

Occupations in this group usually require education and/or training ranging from six months to more than ten years.

A common way to prepare is to obtain a two- or four-year degree with a major in business administration, marketing, or a similar field. Many jobs require a knowledge of accounting, psychology, composition, business law, speech, and economics. For jobs in technical sales, a degree in a field such as engineering, chemistry, or physics is helpful. Sometimes workers in other sales groups advance after obtaining related work experience.

Some employers prefer to hire persons who have sales experience and some technical or scientific education. The company then provides training, through classes or work in other jobs, to familiarize the employee with the products. All companies provide formal or informal training to explain company sales policies and procedures. Equipment manufacturers frequently send employees to training centers and universities for extensive training.

Most sales engineers have a bachelor's degree in engineering. Work experience as an engineer can be very helpful.

How much education or training is required for the jobs in this Work Group?

For descriptions of these jobs, see Part 2.

Moderate-term on-the-job training

* Sales Representatives, Agricultural
* Sales Representatives, Chemical and Pharmaceutical
* Sales Representatives, Electrical/Electronic
* Sales Representatives, Instruments
* Sales Representatives, Mechanical Equipment and Supplies
* Sales Representatives, Medical

Bachelor's degree

* Sales Engineers

14.03 General Sales

Workers in this group sell and solicit orders for products and services of many kinds. Some spend all their time in a single location, such as a department store or automobile agency. Others call on businesses or individuals to sell products or services or follow up on earlier sales.

What kind of work would you do?

Your work activities would depend on your job. For example, you might

* Activate fuel pumps and fill fuel tanks of vehicles with gasoline or diesel fuel to specified levels.
* Advise clients on market conditions, prices, mortgages, legal requirements, and related matters.
* Arrange and direct delivery and installation of products and equipment.
* Coordinate appointments to show homes to prospective buyers.
* Describe merchandise and explain use, operation, and care of merchandise to customers.
* Maintain records related to sales.
* Prepare sales slips or sales contracts.
* Provide customers with product samples and catalogs.
* Read catalogs, microfiche viewers, or computer displays in order to determine replacement part stock numbers and prices.

What things about you point to this kind of work?

Is it important for you to

* Have opportunities for advancement?
* Have co-workers who are easy to get along with?

Have you enjoyed any of the following as a hobby or leisure-time activity?

* Helping persuade people to sign petitions or support a cause
* Helping run a school or community fair or carnival
* Soliciting clothes, food, and other supplies for needy people
* Recruiting members for a club or other organization
* Using a pocket calculator or spreadsheet to figure out income and expenses for an organization
* Serving as a salesperson or clerk in a store run by a charity organization

Have you liked and done well in any of the following school subjects?

* Selling
* Marketing/Merchandising
* Record Keeping
* Real Estate Laws/Regulations
* Cashiering
* Consumer Behavior
* Retailing

Are you able to

* Identify and understand the speech of another person?
* See details at close range?
* Remember information such as words, numbers, pictures, and procedures?

Would you work in places such as

* Stores and shopping malls?
* Business offices?
* Private homes?
* Convention and trade show centers?

What skills and knowledges do you need for this kind of work?

For most of these jobs, you need these skills:

✳ Negotiation—bringing others together and trying to reconcile differences

✳ Service Orientation—actively looking for ways to help people

✳ Social Perceptiveness—being aware of others' reactions and understanding why they react as they do

These knowledges are important in most of these jobs:

✳ Sales and Marketing—principles and methods for showing, promoting, and selling products or services; this includes marketing strategy and tactics, product demonstrations, sales techniques, and sales control systems

✳ Customer and Personal Service—principles and processes for providing customer and personal services; this includes customer needs assessment, meeting quality standards for services, and evaluation of customer satisfaction

✳ Economics and Accounting—economic and accounting principles and practices, the financial markets, banking, and the analysis and reporting of financial data

What else should you consider about this kind of work?

These workers are hired by retail and wholesale firms, manufacturers and distributors, service businesses, and nonprofit organizations.

In many retail stores, part-time or temporary work is easier to get than a full-time job. Because so many stores are open nights and Sundays, they often hire part-time help for these hours. At Christmas and other busy shopping times, extra workers are hired.

Many of the people in this group earn the same salary no matter how much or how little they sell. Others get a base salary plus a commission on sales. A few depend only on commissions for their income.

Travel is necessary for many of these jobs. Some salespersons are away from home for weeks at a time, but others call on businesses only in the local area. Many of these jobs require use of a personal car.

The outlook for jobs in this group varies. In some occupations, such as real estate agents, many beginners drop out because they are not successful at building a clientele and closing sales, but the rewards are good for those with the skills and drive to overcome the early hurdles. The high turnover rate in most of these occupations will provide many openings for beginners, although there will sometimes be a lot of competition, especially for the jobs that require the least amount of education or training.

Sales jobs often are at risk when the economy slows down. Technology will limit job openings in some fields where buyers can use the Internet to view merchandise and make purchases directly from manufacturers and other sellers. Much of the work of service station attendants is now being done by self-service pumps that can read credit cards.

How can you prepare for jobs of this kind?

Occupations in this group usually require education and/or training ranging from a few weeks to less than two years.

Most employers require that applicants have a high school education or its equal. Course work in math computation, speech, English grammar, selling, and retailing is helpful. Many high schools, junior colleges, and community colleges offer courses and programs in this field. Some schools provide work-study programs in which students work part-time as well as attend classes. Sales experience during vacations is also helpful in preparing for this kind of work.

Employers usually provide on-the-job training to teach new workers about the company policies and the products or services to be sold. These training programs may last from one week to three months. Certain workers must have special skills, such as driving a truck or playing a musical instrument. Other workers are required to make minor repairs or adjustments on equipment they sell.

Real estate agents need a good background of knowledge about the communities where they show properties.

How much education or training is required for the jobs in this Work Group?

For descriptions of these jobs, see Part 2.

Short-term on-the-job training

✳ Retail Salespersons

✳ Service Station Attendants

Moderate-term on-the-job training

✳ Parts Salespersons

✳ Sales Representatives, Wholesale and Manufacturing, Except Technical and Scientific Products

Work experience in a related occupation

✳ Real Estate Brokers

Postsecondary vocational training

✳ Real Estate Sales Agents

14.04 Personal Soliciting

Workers in this group appeal to people directly and sell them merchandise or services. In most cases they do not build a long-term relationship with the buyer. They may sell products on the street, staying in one location or moving through business and residential areas. They may call potential buyers by telephone. They may demonstrate a product in a mall or other place with a lot of foot traffic.

What kind of work would you do?

Your work activities would depend on your job. For example, you might

✳ Apply makeup to face and style hair to enhance appearance, considering such factors as color, camera techniques, and facial features.

© 2006 JIST Works

* Contact businesses or private individuals by telephone in order to solicit sales for goods or services or to request donations for charitable causes.
* Contact customers by phone, by mail, or in person to offer or persuade them to purchase merchandise or services.
* Distribute product samples or literature that details products or services.
* Pose as directed or strike suitable interpretive poses for promoting and selling merchandise or fashions during photo sessions.
* Provide product information, using lectures, films, charts, and/or slide shows.
* Record names, addresses, purchases, and reactions of prospects contacted.
* Sell products being promoted and keep records of sales.

What things about you point to this kind of work?

Is it important for you to

* Do your work alone?
* Receive recognition for the work you do?

Have you enjoyed any of the following as a hobby or leisure-time activity?

* Soliciting clothes, food, and other supplies for needy people
* Soliciting funds for community organizations
* Campaigning for political candidates or issues
* Conducting house-to-house or telephone surveys for a PTA or other organization
* Doing public speaking or debating
* Posing for an artist or photographer
* Helping persuade people to sign petitions or support a cause
* Recruiting members for a club or other organization
* Modeling clothes for a fashion show

Have you liked and done well in any of the following school subjects?

* Selling
* Personal Grooming
* Public Speaking
* Cashiering
* Consumer Behavior
* Modeling, Personal

Are you able to

* Speak clearly so others can understand you?
* See objects in the presence of glare or bright lighting?
* Come up with unusual or clever ideas about a given topic or situation or develop creative ways to solve a problem?

Would you work in places such as

* Stores and shopping malls?
* Business offices?
* Private homes?
* Photographers' studios?
* Television and video studios?
* Convention and trade show centers?

What skills and knowledges do you need for this kind of work?

For most of these jobs, you need these skills:

* Persuasion—persuading others to change their minds or behavior
* Social Perceptiveness—being aware of others' reactions and understanding why they react as they do
* Speaking—talking to others to convey information effectively

These knowledges are important in most of these jobs:

* Sales and Marketing—principles and methods for showing, promoting, and selling products or services; this includes marketing strategy and tactics, product demonstrations, sales techniques, and sales control systems
* Communications and Media—media production, communication, and dissemination techniques and methods; this includes alternative ways to inform and entertain via written, oral, and visual media
* Fine Arts—the theory and techniques required to compose, produce, and perform works of music, dance, visual arts, drama, and sculpture

What else should you consider about this kind of work?

Workers in the sales occupations in this group are employed by a wide variety of businesses that need person-to-person selling. Telemarketers are employed by non-profit and charitable organizations for fundraising. Almost all models work through modeling agencies. People in these jobs feel comfortable talking with strangers, are persistent and persuasive, and do not take rejection personally.

Workers in these jobs may be paid a straight salary but often are paid at least in part based on the volume of sales. Occasionally workers may be under considerable pressure to close a lot of sales. Usually many part-time openings are available.

The general outlook for these occupations is good, although there is some sensitivity to the business cycle. Jobs are constantly being created because of turnover. Automation is not likely to diminish the need for motivated people who know how to appeal personally to others.

Models face keen competition and often face periods of unemployment. They must take very good care of their bodies. Because the demand is greatest for young models, careers in the field are likely to be short.

How can you prepare for jobs of this kind?

Occupations in this group usually require very little education and/or training. Employers give trainee workers a brief demonstration of the tasks and strategies.

Although it may not be required, a high school education or its equal is usually helpful. Course work in speech, selling, and retailing is particularly relevant. Sales experience during vacations is probably the best preparation for this kind of work.

Models are often hired because of their appearance or size and may get only part-time work until the quality of their work is recognized. Because modeling careers are often short, you may benefit from getting some education or training that will prepare you for other kinds of work.

How much education or training is required for the jobs in this Work Group?

For descriptions of these jobs, see Part 2.

Short-term on-the-job training

* Door-To-Door Sales Workers, News and Street Vendors, and Related Workers
* Telemarketers

Moderate-term on-the-job training

* Demonstrators and Product Promoters
* Models

14.05 Purchasing

These workers buy goods and services, either for a business to use or for resale. They need to stay well informed about the factors that make for good quality and good value and the economic forces that affect the marketplace.

What kind of work would you do?

Your work activities would depend on your job. For example, you might

* Analyze and monitor sales records, trends, and economic conditions to anticipate consumer buying patterns and determine what the company will sell and how much inventory is needed.
* Conduct staff meetings with sales personnel to introduce new merchandise.
* Consult with store or merchandise managers about budget and goods to be purchased.
* Negotiate, or renegotiate, and administer contracts with suppliers, vendors, and other representatives.
* Purchase the highest quality merchandise at the lowest possible price and in correct amounts.

What things about you point to this kind of work?

Is it important for you to

* Have opportunities for advancement?
* Have something different to do every day?

Have you enjoyed any of the following as a hobby or leisure-time activity?

* Buying large quantities of food or other products for an organization

* Reading business magazines and newspapers
* Researching things that sound interesting to you
* Serving as treasurer of a club or other organization

Have you liked and done well in any of the following school subjects?

* Marketing/Merchandising
* Agribusiness
* Business Analysis
* Data Retrieval Techniques
* Consumer Behavior

Are you able to

* Apply general rules to specific problems to produce answers that make sense?
* Generate or use different sets of rules for combining or grouping things in different ways?
* Identify and understand the speech of another person?
* Choose the right mathematical methods or formulas to solve a problem?
* Combine pieces of information to form general rules or conclusions?

Would you work in places such as

* Stores and shopping malls?
* Business offices?
* Factories and plants?
* Farms?
* Warehouses?
* Convention and trade show centers?

What skills and knowledges do you need for this kind of work?

For most of these jobs, you need these skills:

* Management of Financial Resources—determining how money will be spent to get the work done and accounting for these expenditures
* Negotiation—bringing others together and trying to reconcile differences
* Management of Material Resources—obtaining and seeing to the appropriate use of equipment, facilities, and materials needed to do certain work
* Time Management—managing one's own time and the time of others
* Operations Analysis—analyzing needs and product requirements to create a design
* Management of Personnel Resources—motivating, developing, and directing people as they work, identifying the best people for the job
* Persuasion—persuading others to change their minds or behavior

These knowledges are important in most of these jobs:

* Clerical Practices—administrative and clerical procedures and systems such as word processing, managing files and records, stenography and transcription, designing forms, and other office procedures and terminology

* Economics and Accounting—economic and accounting principles and practices, the financial markets, banking, and the analysis and reporting of financial data
* Sales and Marketing—principles and methods for showing, promoting, and selling products or services; this includes marketing strategy and tactics, product demonstrations, sales techniques, and sales control systems
* Administration and Management—business and management principles involved in strategic planning, resource allocation, human resources modeling, leadership techniques, production methods, and coordination of people and resources
* Transportation—principles and methods for moving people or goods by air, rail, sea, or road, including the relative costs and benefits
* Production and Processing—raw materials, production processes, quality control, costs, and other techniques for maximizing the effective manufacture and distribution of goods
* Mathematics—arithmetic, algebra, geometry, calculus, and statistics and their applications

What else should you consider about this kind of work?

Many of these workers are employed by wholesale businesses that resell merchandise to retailers. Another large fraction is employed by manufacturers that need to get the best deals on raw materials, machines, and components. Those who work for government agencies must be careful to follow strict regulations that promote fair bidding practices.

Computerization continues to have a major impact on these workers, facilitating the work of tracking inventories, measuring consumer behavior, researching products, and placing orders as late as possible. These increases in productivity are cutting into the demand for workers. Purchasing agents who buy complex machinery and agricultural products will have better opportunities than other workers in this group because these products are difficult to evaluate over the Internet.

How can you prepare for jobs of this kind?

Occupations in this group usually require education and/or training ranging from one year to less than ten years.

As a general rule, the larger the organization, the more formal education is preferred in job candidates. Smaller employers may promote someone who has a thorough knowledge of the business and some college education. Larger organizations are likely to expect job seekers to have a bachelor's or even a master's in business or economics. In some industries, a degree in engineering or science may be helpful.

Regardless of prior education, most new hires need to devote a few years to gaining an understanding of the business and the marketplace. They may learn by supervising sales staff or inventory, or they may work in the production planning department.

Part of the learning curve is gaining skill with computer-based applications. Throughout their careers, these workers need training to keep up with developments in these applications and in the impact of technology on the marketplace.

How much education or training is required for the jobs in this Work Group?

For descriptions of these jobs, see Part 2.

Bachelor's degree

* Purchasing Agents, Except Wholesale, Retail, and Farm Products
* Wholesale and Retail Buyers, Except Farm Products

14.06 Customer Service

Workers in this group deal directly with people to facilitate sales, provide routine information, or take orders for goods or services. Working at a booth or desk or over the telephone, they may accept payments, make change, greet visitors and direct them to an office, or make arrangements for merchandise or services to be delivered. Because they interact with the public, they need good people skills. They also need some clerical skills, because usually they record information about payments or other transactions they have engaged in.

What kind of work would you do?

Your work activities would depend on your job. For example, you might

* Answer telephones to provide information and receive orders.
* Check inventory records to determine availability of requested merchandise.
* Hear and resolve complaints from customers and the public.
* Issue receipts, refunds, credits, or change due to customers.
* Operate telephone switchboard to answer, screen, and forward calls, providing information, taking messages, and scheduling appointments.
* Order tests to detect product malfunction and determine whether defect resulted from faulty construction.
* Prepare invoices, shipping documents, and contracts.
* Receive payment by cash, check, credit cards, vouchers, or automatic debits.
* Solicit sale of new or additional utility services.

What things about you point to this kind of work?

Is it important for you to

* Have supervisors who train workers well?
* Have supervisors who back up workers with management?

Have you enjoyed any of the following as a hobby or leisure-time activity?

* Conducting house-to-house or telephone surveys for a PTA or other organization
* Volunteering at the library
* Serving as a salesperson or clerk in a store run by a charity organization
* Serving as a volunteer interviewer in a social service organization

Have you liked and done well in any of the following school subjects?

* Selling
* Business Machine Operating
* Cashiering
* Consumer Behavior

Are you able to

* Identify and understand the speech of another person?
* See details at close range?
* Speak clearly so others can understand you?

Would you work in places such as

* Stores and shopping malls?
* Gambling casinos and card clubs?
* Race tracks?
* Business offices?
* Government offices?
* Hospitals and nursing homes?
* Waterworks and light and power plants?

What skills and knowledges do you need for this kind of work?

For most of these jobs, you need these skills:

* Service Orientation—actively looking for ways to help people
* Active Listening—giving full attention to what other people are saying, taking time to understand the points being made, asking questions as appropriate, and not interrupting at inappropriate times
* Programming—writing computer programs for various purposes

These knowledges are important in most of these jobs:

* Sales and Marketing—principles and methods for showing, promoting, and selling products or services; this includes marketing strategy and tactics, product demonstrations, sales techniques, and sales control systems
* Customer and Personal Service—principles and processes for providing customer and personal services; this includes customer needs assessment, meeting quality standards for services, and evaluation of customer satisfaction

* Foreign Language—the structure and content of a foreign (non-English) language, including the meaning and spelling of words, rules of composition and grammar, and pronunciation

What else should you consider about this kind of work?

These workers are employed by retail stores, police departments, large business offices, utility companies, and government agencies. Government employees often need to pass a civil service exam. Some workers are hired for regular daytime hours; others work from noon until about eight or late into the night. A few have to be on the job on weekends and holidays. People who work for airports, hospitals, and fire and police departments may have to work rotating shifts.

Temporary jobs at state and national parks, sports stadiums, and amusement parks are available. If you're interested in this kind of work as a summer job, apply for it as early in the year as possible. Some places have all their summer hiring done by late winter.

The overall outlook for this group is good, even though much customer service is being automated or handled by offshore call centers.

How can you prepare for jobs of this kind?

About half the occupations in this group require less than six months of education and/or training; the other half require from six months to two years. Workers who need the higher level of training are those who handle more complex transactions, such as making adjustments to deal with consumer complaints or explaining rates and policies of a utility.

All of the training is done on the job, but some employers prefer candidates who have skill with computer entry or other clerical skills. For this reason, a high school education or its equal is often expected, particularly with courses in speech, English, and math.

How much education or training is required for the jobs in this Work Group?

For descriptions of these jobs, see Part 2.

Short-term on-the-job training

* Cashiers
* Counter and Rental Clerks
* Gaming Change Persons and Booth Cashiers
* Order Clerks
* Receptionists and Information Clerks

Moderate-term on-the-job training

* Adjustment Clerks
* Customer Service Representatives, Utilities

15 Scientific Research, Engineering, and Mathematics

An interest in discovering, collecting, and analyzing information about the natural world; in applying scientific research findings to problems in medicine, the life sciences, human behavior, and the natural sciences; in imagining and manipulating quantitative data; and in applying technology to manufacturing, transportation, and other economic activities. You can satisfy this interest by working with the knowledge and processes of the sciences. You may enjoy researching and developing new knowledge in mathematics, or perhaps solving problems in the physical, life, or social sciences would appeal to you. You may wish to study engineering and help create new machines, processes, and structures. If you want to work with scientific equipment and procedures, you could seek a job in a research or testing laboratory.

15.01 **Managerial Work in Scientific Research, Engineering, and Mathematics**

15.02 **Physical Sciences**

15.03 **Life Sciences**

15.04 **Social Sciences**

15.05 **Physical Science Laboratory Technology**

15.06 **Mathematics and Data Analysis**

15.07 **Research and Design Engineering**

15.08 **Industrial and Safety Engineering**

15.09 **Engineering Technology**

15.01 Managerial Work in Scientific Research, Engineering, and Mathematics

Workers in this group manage scientists who are doing research, engineers who are applying scientific principles to solve real-world problems, and workers who study and apply the principles of mathematics. They set goals, oversee financial and technical resources, and evaluate outcomes.

What kind of work would you do?

Your work activities would depend on your job. For example, you might

* Confer with management, production, and marketing staff to discuss project specifications and procedures.
* Develop and implement policies, standards, and procedures for the engineering and technical work performed in the department, service, laboratory, or firm.
* Develop innovative technology and train staff for its implementation.
* Make presentations at professional meetings to further knowledge in the field.
* Prepare budgets, bids, and contracts and direct the negotiation of research contracts.
* Prepare project proposals.
* Recruit personnel and oversee the development and maintenance of staff competence.

What things about you point to this kind of work?

Is it important for you to

* Give directions and instructions to others?
* Be paid well in comparison with other workers?
* Have good working conditions?
* Plan your work with little supervision?
* Have co-workers who are easy to get along with?
* Try out your own ideas?
* Be treated fairly by the company?

Have you enjoyed any of the following as a hobby or leisure-time activity?

* Conducting experiments involving plants
* Experimenting with a chemistry set
* Serving as president of a club or other organization
* Using a pocket calculator or spreadsheet to figure out income and expenses for an organization
* Budgeting the family income
* Helping run a school or community fair or carnival
* Reading about technological developments, such as computer science or aerospace

Have you liked and done well in any of the following school subjects?

* Management
* Accounting
* Personnel Management
* Calculus
* Biology

Are you able to

* Choose the right mathematical methods or formulas to solve a problem?
* Come up with a number of ideas about a topic?
* Read and understand information and ideas presented in writing?
* Come up with unusual or clever ideas about a given topic or situation or develop creative ways to solve a problem?
* Listen to and understand information and ideas presented through spoken words and sentences?
* Tell when something is wrong or is likely to go wrong?
* Apply general rules to specific problems to produce answers that make sense?

Would you work in places such as

* Business offices?
* Government offices?
* Colleges and universities?
* Factories and plants?
* Laboratories?
* Oil fields?
* Construction sites?

What skills and knowledges do you need for this kind of work?

For most of these jobs, you need these skills:

* Management of Financial Resources—determining how money will be spent to get the work done and accounting for these expenditures
* Science—using scientific rules and methods to solve problems
* Operations Analysis—analyzing needs and product requirements to create a design
* Technology Design—generating or adapting equipment and technology to serve user needs
* Time Management—managing one's own time and the time of others
* Management of Material Resources—obtaining and seeing to the appropriate use of equipment, facilities, and materials needed to do certain work
* Coordination—adjusting actions in relation to others' actions

These knowledges are important in most of these jobs:

* Chemistry—the chemical composition, structure, and properties of substances and of the chemical processes and transformations that they undergo; this includes uses of chemicals and their danger signs, production techniques, and disposal methods

* Engineering and Technology—the practical application of engineering science and technology; this includes applying principles, techniques, procedures, and equipment to the design and production of various goods and services
* Administration and Management—business and management principles involved in strategic planning, resource allocation, human resources modeling, leadership techniques, production methods, and coordination of people and resources
* Physics—physical principles and laws and their interrelationships and applications to understanding fluid, material, and atmospheric dynamics and mechanical, electrical, atomic, and subatomic structures and processes
* Mathematics—arithmetic, algebra, geometry, calculus, and statistics and their applications
* Economics and Accounting—economic and accounting principles and practices, the financial markets, banking, and the analysis and reporting of financial data
* Personnel and Human Resources—principles and procedures for personnel recruitment, selection, training, compensation and benefits, labor relations and negotiation, and personnel information systems

What else should you consider about this kind of work?

Engineering and science managers are employed by government agencies, industry, and colleges throughout the country.

Generally they work most often in business offices, classrooms, or research laboratories, but they sometimes need to visit such sites as the floor of a plant where manufacturing is being done, a remote natural setting where research is being conducted, or an urban neighborhood where surveying is being done.

The job outlook is generally good, but better in industries that are growing, such as biotechnology and computers, than in less dynamic industries, such as petroleum and manufacturing.

How can you prepare for jobs of this kind?

Occupations in engineering and science management usually require more than ten years of education and/or training.

The most common route to management is by first preparing to be a scientist, engineer, or some other worker in science, math, or engineering. After gaining experience and expertise in this kind of job, you might get formal or informal training in management that prepares you to deal with setting goals, measuring outcomes, accounting for financial resources, and managing human resources. Another possible route is to major in management in college with a minor or second degree in a field related to science, math, or engineering.

How much education or training is required for the jobs in this Work Group?

For descriptions of these jobs, see Part 2.

Work experience plus degree

* Engineering Managers
* Natural Sciences Managers

15.02 Physical Sciences

Workers in this group are concerned mostly with nonliving things, such as chemicals, rocks, metals, and movements of the earth and stars. They conduct scientific studies and perform other activities requiring a knowledge of math, physics, or chemistry. Some workers investigate, discover, and test new theories. Some develop new or improved materials or processes for use in production and construction. Some do research in such fields as geology, astronomy, oceanography, and meteorology. Workers base their conclusions on information that can be measured or proved.

What kind of work would you do?

Your work activities would depend on your job. For example, you might

* Analyze and interpret geological, geochemical, and geophysical information from sources such as survey data, well logs, boreholes, and aerial photos.
* Analyze organic and inorganic compounds to determine chemical and physical properties, composition, structure, relationships, and reactions, utilizing chromatography, spectroscopy, and spectrophotometry techniques.
* Develop and use weather forecasting tools such as mathematical and computer models.
* Study the history, structure, extent, and evolution of stars, stellar systems, and the universe.
* Study the economic, political, and cultural characteristics of a specific region's population.
* Study the nature, structure, and physical properties of metals and their alloys and their responses to applied forces.
* Study lakes, rivers, and wetlands to determine modes of water return to ocean and atmosphere.
* Teach physics to students.

What things about you point to this kind of work?

Is it important for you to

* Plan your work with little supervision?
* Try out your own ideas?
* Make use of your individual abilities?
* Make decisions on your own?
* Do your work alone?
* Receive recognition for the work you do?
* Be looked up to by others in your company and your community?

Have you enjoyed any of the following as a hobby or leisure-time activity?

* Experimenting with a chemistry set

✳ Performing experiments for a science fair
✳ Reading about technological developments, such as computer science or aerospace
✳ Reading medical or scientific magazines
✳ Belonging to a computer club
✳ Collecting rocks or minerals

Have you liked and done well in any of the following school subjects?

✳ Physics
✳ Calculus
✳ Astronomy
✳ Meteorology
✳ Earth Science
✳ Geography
✳ Geographic Information Systems
✳ Crystallography
✳ Metallurgy/Metal Properties

Are you able to

✳ Choose the right mathematical methods or formulas to solve a problem?
✳ Communicate information and ideas in writing so others will understand?
✳ Apply general rules to specific problems to produce answers that make sense?
✳ Read and understand information and ideas presented in writing?
✳ Combine pieces of information to form general rules or conclusions?
✳ Listen to and understand information and ideas presented through spoken words and sentences?
✳ Generate or use different sets of rules for combining or grouping things in different ways?

Would you work in places such as

✳ Colleges and universities?
✳ Factories and plants?
✳ Laboratories?
✳ Mines and quarries?
✳ Oil fields?
✳ Business offices?

What skills and knowledges do you need for this kind of work?

For most of these jobs, you need these skills:

✳ Science—using scientific rules and methods to solve problems
✳ Mathematics—using mathematics to solve problems
✳ Active Learning—understanding the implications of new information for both current and future problem solving and decision making
✳ Writing—communicating effectively in writing as appropriate for the needs of the audience
✳ Critical Thinking—using logic and reasoning to identify the strengths and weaknesses of alternative solutions, conclusions, or approaches to problems

✳ Reading Comprehension—understanding written sentences and paragraphs in work-related documents
✳ Operations Analysis—analyzing needs and product requirements to create a design

These knowledges are important in most of these jobs:

✳ Physics—physical principles and laws and their interrelationships and applications to understanding fluid, material, and atmospheric dynamics and mechanical, electrical, atomic, and subatomic structures and processes
✳ Mathematics—arithmetic, algebra, geometry, calculus, and statistics and their applications
✳ Geography—principles and methods for describing the features of land, sea, and air masses, including their physical characteristics; locations; interrelationships; and distribution of plant, animal, and human life
✳ Chemistry—the chemical composition, structure, and properties of substances and of the chemical processes and transformations that they undergo; this includes uses of chemicals and their danger signs, production techniques, and disposal methods
✳ Engineering and Technology—the practical application of engineering science and technology; this includes applying principles, techniques, procedures, and equipment to the design and production of various goods and services
✳ History and Archeology—historical events and their causes, indicators, and effects on civilizations and cultures
✳ Communications and Media—media production, communication, and dissemination techniques and methods; this includes alternative ways to inform and entertain via written, oral, and visual media

What else should you consider about this kind of work?

Workers in this group are employed by industry, government agencies, and universities in large and small communities across the country.

Some of the jobs require traveling to conduct field trips, during which workers must live without the usual domestic comforts. Physical scientists may be required to work long hours to meet research deadlines or to complete experiments. They must keep informed of the most recent developments in their fields by attending seminars, reading professional journals, and being active in professional organizations.

Job outlook is mixed, with some specializations in greater demand, especially those that have direct, practical applications other than defense, such as pharmaceuticals, biotechnology, and compliance with environmental regulations.

How can you prepare for jobs of this kind?

Occupations in the physical sciences usually require education and/or training ranging from four years to more than ten years.

A bachelor's degree with a major in mathematics or a specific physical science is the minimum requirement for entrance into this field. Graduate degrees are needed for most research work and college teaching. A master's degree may qualify an individual for work in laboratory teaching or applied research in a college, university, or industrial setting. Advanced studies or a Ph.D. is usually required for work in basic research. Important courses include advanced math, physics, and earth and space science. Chemistry and technical writing courses are helpful and in some cases required.

How much education or training is required for the jobs in this Work Group?

For descriptions of these jobs, see Part 2.

Bachelor's degree

* Atmospheric and Space Scientists
* Chemists
* Geographers
* Geologists
* Hydrologists
* Materials Scientists

Doctoral degree

* Astronomers
* Physicists

15.03 Life Sciences

Workers in this group do research and conduct experiments to find out more about plants, animals, and other living things. Some study methods of producing better species of plants or animals. Some work to find ways of preserving the natural balance in the environment. Others conduct research to improve medicine, health, and living conditions for human beings.

What kind of work would you do?

Your work activities would depend on your job. For example, you might

* Develop and test new drugs and medications used for commercial distribution.
* Evaluate effects of drugs, gases, pesticides, parasites, and microorganisms at various levels.
* Identify and analyze public health issues related to foodborne parasitic diseases and their impact on public policies or scientific studies or surveys.
* Isolate and make cultures of bacteria or other microorganisms in prescribed media, controlling moisture, aeration, temperature, and nutrition.
* Provide advice on proper standards and regulations and the development of policies, strategies, and codes of practice for environmental management.
* Study absorption of light by chlorophyll in photosynthesis.

* Study aquatic plants and animals and environmental conditions affecting them, such as radioactivity or pollution.
* Teach principles of medicine and medical and laboratory procedures to physicians, residents, students, and technicians.

What things about you point to this kind of work?

Is it important for you to

* Plan your work with little supervision?
* Try out your own ideas?
* Make use of your individual abilities?
* Be looked up to by others in your company and your community?
* Receive recognition for the work you do?
* Make decisions on your own?
* Have steady employment?

Have you enjoyed any of the following as a hobby or leisure-time activity?

* Studying the habits of wildlife
* Conducting experiments involving plants
* Experimenting with a chemistry set
* Nursing sick pets
* Performing experiments for a science fair
* Reading medical or scientific magazines
* Studying plants in gardens, parks, or forests

Have you liked and done well in any of the following school subjects?

* Biology
* Biochemistry
* Chemistry
* Calculus
* Public Health
* Microbiology
* Biostatistics and Epidemiology
* Botany
* Genetics
* Industrial Hygiene

Are you able to

* Combine pieces of information to form general rules or conclusions?
* Communicate information and ideas in writing so others will understand?
* Generate or use different sets of rules for combining or grouping things in different ways?
* Tell when something is wrong or is likely to go wrong?
* Read and understand information and ideas presented in writing?
* Listen to and understand information and ideas presented through spoken words and sentences?
* Choose the right mathematical methods or formulas to solve a problem?

Would you work in places such as

* Colleges and universities?
* Laboratories?
* Hospitals and nursing homes?
* Factories and plants?
* Government offices?

What skills and knowledges do you need for this kind of work?

For most of these jobs, you need these skills:

* Science—using scientific rules and methods to solve problems
* Active Learning—understanding the implications of new information for both current and future problem solving and decision making
* Reading Comprehension—understanding written sentences and paragraphs in work-related documents
* Writing—communicating effectively in writing as appropriate for the needs of the audience
* Complex Problem Solving—identifying complex problems and reviewing related information to develop and evaluate options and implement solutions
* Mathematics—using mathematics to solve problems
* Critical Thinking—using logic and reasoning to identify the strengths and weaknesses of alternative solutions, conclusions, or approaches to problems

These knowledges are important in most of these jobs:

* Biology—plant and animal organisms and their tissues, cells, functions, interdependencies, and interactions with each other and the environment
* Chemistry—the chemical composition, structure, and properties of substances and of the chemical processes and transformations that they undergo; this includes uses of chemicals and their danger signs, production techniques, and disposal methods
* Physics—physical principles and laws and their interrelationships and applications to understanding fluid, material, and atmospheric dynamics and mechanical, electrical, atomic, and subatomic structures and processes
* Mathematics—arithmetic, algebra, geometry, calculus, and statistics and their applications
* Medicine and Dentistry—the information and techniques needed to diagnose and treat human injuries, diseases, and deformities; this includes symptoms, treatment alternatives, drug properties and interactions, and preventive health care measures

What else should you consider about this kind of work?

These workers are employed by manufacturing plants, government agencies, universities, and hospitals.

Some students and workers in this field must handle tissues and waste products of humans and animals. Some work in remote areas such as forests and deserts. Sometimes there are long work hours to meet a research deadline.

Life scientists must keep informed of developments in their fields by attending seminars, reading professional books and magazines, and being active in professional organizations.

Chances of employment are best in high-growth fields such as biotechnology and environmental science.

How can you prepare for jobs of this kind?

Occupations in this group usually call for education and/or training ranging from four years to more than ten years.

Important academic courses include advanced math, chemistry, and physics. Technical writing and composition courses are helpful. A bachelor's degree with a major in biology or another life science is generally required; graduate degrees are needed for most research work and college teaching. A master's degree may qualify a person for laboratory teaching. Advanced studies or a Ph.D. is usually required for basic research positions.

How much education or training is required for the jobs in this Work Group?

For descriptions of these jobs, see Part 2.

Bachelor's degree

* Environmental Scientists and Specialists, Including Health

Doctoral degree

* Biochemists
* Biologists
* Biophysicists
* Epidemiologists
* Medical Scientists, Except Epidemiologists
* Microbiologists

15.04 Social Sciences

Workers in this group gather, study, and analyze information about individuals, groups, or entire societies. They conduct research into all aspects of human behavior, including abnormal behavior, language, work, politics, lifestyle, and cultural expression.

What kind of work would you do?

Your work activities would depend on your job. For example, you might

* Collect and analyze scientific data concerning social phenomena, such as community, associations, social institutions, ethnic minorities, and social change.
* Compare the customs, values, and social patterns of different cultures.
* Compile, analyze, and report data to explain economic phenomena and forecast market trends, applying mathematical models and statistical techniques.
* Conduct research into political philosophy and theories of political systems, such as governmental institutions, public laws, and international law.

* Develop interview techniques, rating scales, and psychological tests used to assess skills, abilities, and interests for the purpose of employee selection, placement, and promotion.
* Develop research designs on the basis of existing knowledge and evolving theory.
* Gather historical data from sources such as archives, court records, diaries, news files, and photographs.
* Promote an understanding of child development and its relationship to learning and behavior.
* Study objects and structures recovered by excavation to identify, date, and/or authenticate them and to interpret their significance.
* Supervise research projects and students' study projects.

What things about you point to this kind of work?

Is it important for you to

* Plan your work with little supervision?
* Try out your own ideas?
* Make decisions on your own?
* Make use of your individual abilities?
* Have good working conditions?
* Receive recognition for the work you do?
* Get a feeling of accomplishment?

Have you enjoyed any of the following as a hobby or leisure-time activity?

* Belonging to a political science club
* Campaigning for political candidates or issues
* Conducting house-to-house or telephone surveys for a PTA or other organization
* Reading business magazines and newspapers
* Visiting museums or historic sites
* Researching things that sound interesting to you

Have you liked and done well in any of the following school subjects?

* Economics
* Psychology
* Educational Psychology
* History
* Archeology
* Political Science
* Human Growth and Development
* Statistics
* Research Methods
* Social Anthropology

Are you able to

* Communicate information and ideas in writing so others will understand?
* Read and understand information and ideas presented in writing?
* Combine pieces of information to form general rules or conclusions?

* Listen to and understand information and ideas presented through spoken words and sentences?
* Apply general rules to specific problems to produce answers that make sense?
* Come up with a number of ideas about a topic?
* Communicate information and ideas in speaking so others will understand?

Would you work in places such as

* Colleges and universities?
* Business offices?
* Government offices?
* Factories and plants?
* Stores and shopping malls?
* Libraries?
* Museums?

What skills and knowledges do you need for this kind of work?

For most of these jobs, you need these skills:

* Systems Analysis—determining how a system should work and how changes in conditions, operations, and the environment will affect outcomes
* Writing—communicating effectively in writing as appropriate for the needs of the audience
* Complex Problem Solving—identifying complex problems and reviewing related information to develop and evaluate options and implement solutions
* Systems Evaluation—identifying measures or indicators of system performance and the actions needed to improve or correct performance relative to the goals of the system
* Active Learning—understanding the implications of new information for both current and future problem solving and decision making
* Social Perceptiveness—being aware of others' reactions and understanding why they react as they do
* Reading Comprehension—understanding written sentences and paragraphs in work-related documents

These knowledges are important in most of these jobs:

* History and Archeology—historical events and their causes, indicators, and effects on civilizations and cultures
* Sociology and Anthropology—group behavior and dynamics, societal trends and influences, human migrations, ethnicity, and cultures and their history and origins
* Philosophy and Theology—different philosophical systems and religions; this includes their basic principles, values, ethics, ways of thinking, customs, practices, and impact on human culture
* Foreign Language—the structure and content of a foreign (non-English) language, including the meaning and spelling of words, rules of composition and grammar, and pronunciation

* Geography—principles and methods for describing the features of land, sea, and air masses, including their physical characteristics; locations; interrelationships; and distribution of plant, animal, and human life
* Education and Training—principles and methods for curriculum and training design, teaching and instruction for individuals and groups, and the measurement of training effects
* English Language—the structure and content of the English language, including the meaning and spelling of words, rules of composition, and grammar

What else should you consider about this kind of work?

Many people in this group work for government agencies of one kind or another. Some work for private businesses and others for museums and other nonprofit institutions or for universities. You can apply directly for some of the government jobs, but for most you have to go through civil service channels.

Some of these workers are self-employed. They may get grants from the government or private groups to do research, or they may do special studies for business, industry, or government.

Most of this work is done during regular business hours. Archeologists and anthropologists make field trips to distant places in this country and abroad.

Employers expect workers in this group to keep up with developments and trends in their area. This is done by reading journals, attending seminars and workshops, and studying for advanced degrees.

The job outlook is mixed, with good opportunities for economists in the business world and for geographers who are skilled with geographic information systems. For the other social scientists, there will be keen competition for university jobs, so the challenge will be to find creative ways to use their skills in applied settings.

How can you prepare for jobs of this kind?

Almost all the occupations in this group require four or more years of college study in the social sciences.

For research and teaching jobs, a master's or doctorate is expected. Some jobs call for specialization in a particular field, such as government, sociology, history, economics, or psychology. Courses in computer science and statistics are important for use in designing research and interpreting data. Course work in English and math is also very helpful.

How much education or training is required for the jobs in this Work Group?

For descriptions of these jobs, see Part 2.

Bachelor's degree

* Anthropologists
* Archeologists
* Economists
* Historians

Master's degree

* Educational Psychologists
* Industrial-Organizational Psychologists
* Political Scientists
* Sociologists

15.05 Physical Science Laboratory Technology

Workers in this group use special laboratory techniques and equipment to perform tests in such fields as chemistry and physics; then they record information resulting from their experiments and tests. Some of them use photography to record scientifically interesting phenomena. Others use remote-control mechanisms to manipulate radioactive materials. The lab reports and photographs produced by these technicians are used by scientific researchers, engineers, and businesses.

What kind of work would you do?

Your work activities would depend on your job. For example, you might

* Compile and interpret results of tests and analyses.
* Install instrumentation leads in reactor cores in order to measure operating temperatures and pressures according to mockups, blueprints, and diagrams.
* Photograph subject material to illustrate or record scientific or medical data or phenomena.
* Prepare chemical solutions for products and processes, following standardized formulas, or create experimental formulas.
* Set up, mount, or install photographic equipment and cameras.

What things about you point to this kind of work?

Is it important for you to

* Be paid well in comparison with other workers?
* Have opportunities for advancement?

Have you enjoyed any of the following as a hobby or leisure-time activity?

* Performing experiments for a science fair
* Developing film
* Experimenting with a chemistry set
* Reading about technological developments, such as computer science or aerospace
* Reading medical or scientific magazines
* Taking photographs

Have you liked and done well in any of the following school subjects?

* Laboratory Science
* Chemical Safety
* Chemistry

© 2006 JIST Works

✳ Nuclear Safety
✳ Photography

Are you able to

✳ Arrange things or actions in a certain order or pattern according to a specific rule or set of rules?
✳ Match or detect differences between colors, including shades of color and brightness?
✳ Quickly and accurately compare similarities and differences among sets of letters, numbers, objects, pictures, or patterns?
✳ See details at close range?
✳ Shift back and forth between two or more activities or sources of information?
✳ Keep your hand and arm steady while moving your arm or while holding your arm and hand in one position?
✳ Generate or use different sets of rules for combining or grouping things in different ways?

Would you work in places such as

✳ Laboratories?
✳ Factories and plants?
✳ Waterworks and light and power plants?

What skills and knowledges do you need for this kind of work?

For most of these jobs, you need these skills:

✳ Science—using scientific rules and methods to solve problems
✳ Operation and Control—controlling operations of equipment or systems
✳ Operation Monitoring—watching gauges, dials, or other indicators to make sure a machine is working properly
✳ Equipment Selection—determining the kind of tools and equipment needed to do a job
✳ Installation—installing equipment, machines, wiring, or programs to meet specifications
✳ Quality Control Analysis—conducting tests and inspections of products, services, or processes to evaluate quality or performance

These knowledges are important in most of these jobs:

✳ Chemistry—the chemical composition, structure, and properties of substances and of the chemical processes and transformations that they undergo; this includes uses of chemicals and their danger signs, production techniques, and disposal methods
✳ Physics—physical principles and laws and their interrelationships and applications to understanding fluid, material, and atmospheric dynamics and mechanical, electrical, atomic, and subatomic structures and processes
✳ Engineering and Technology—the practical application of engineering science and technology; this includes applying principles, techniques, procedures, and equipment to the design and production of various goods and services

What else should you consider about this kind of work?

These workers are hired by commercial and industrial testing labs, university research labs, and water treatment and power distribution facilities.

Most of the work is done on a regular schedule. Occasional to frequent travel is required on jobs with oil-producing and mining companies. Some jobs involve hazardous materials and require workers to use safety precautions.

The job outlook is mixed, with best opportunities in the pharmaceutical and biotechnology industries and in environmental testing.

How can you prepare for jobs of this kind?

Occupations in this group usually require education and/or training ranging from one year to less than four years.

Most of the jobs are entry positions requiring a two- to four-year degree. Some workers move into laboratory or testing work from production areas. On-the-job training is sometimes available to applicants who have appropriate skills or work-related/military experience. A few jobs are offered to those who have taken scientific or technical courses in high school or a post–high school program. Courses in chemistry, physical science, math, and report writing are helpful.

How much education or training is required for the jobs in this Work Group?

For descriptions of these jobs, see Part 2.

Long-term on-the-job training

✳ Photographers, Scientific

Associate degree

✳ Chemical Technicians
✳ Nuclear Equipment Operation Technicians

15.06 Mathematics and Data Analysis

Workers in this group use advanced math, statistics, and computer programs to solve problems and conduct research. They analyze and interpret numerical data for planning and decision making.

What kind of work would you do?

Your work activities would depend on your job. For example, you might

✳ Analyze statistical information to estimate mortality, accident, sickness, disability, and retirement rates.
✳ Compile statistics from source materials, such as production and sales records, quality-control and test records, time sheets, and survey sheets.

* Design research projects that apply valid scientific techniques and utilize information obtained from baselines or historical data in order to structure uncompromised and efficient analyses.
* Design, analyze, and decipher encryption systems designed to transmit military, political, financial, or law-enforcement–related information in code.
* Organize paperwork such as survey forms and reports for distribution and for analysis.
* Supervise and provide instructions for workers collecting and tabulating data.
* Translate data into numbers, equations, flow charts, graphs, or other forms.

What things about you point to this kind of work?

Is it important for you to

* Do your work alone?
* Have good working conditions?
* Have opportunities for advancement?
* Plan your work with little supervision?

Have you enjoyed any of the following as a hobby or leisure-time activity?

* Calculating sports statistics
* Helping friends and others with math
* Using a pocket calculator or spreadsheet to figure out income and expenses for an organization
* Reading about technological developments, such as computer science or aerospace
* Writing computer programs
* Conducting house-to-house or telephone surveys for a PTA or other organization

Have you liked and done well in any of the following school subjects?

* Math Computing, Advanced/Special
* Statistics
* Research Methods
* Insurance

Are you able to

* Choose the right mathematical methods or formulas to solve a problem?
* Add, subtract, multiply, or divide quickly and correctly?
* Apply general rules to specific problems to produce answers that make sense?

Would you work in places such as

* Business offices?
* Colleges and universities?
* Government offices?

What skills and knowledges do you need for this kind of work?

For most of these jobs, you need these skills:

* Mathematics—using mathematics to solve problems
* Programming—writing computer programs for various purposes
* Active Learning—understanding the implications of new information for both current and future problem solving and decision making
* Complex Problem Solving—identifying complex problems and reviewing related information to develop and evaluate options and implement solutions

These knowledges are important in most of these jobs:

* Mathematics—arithmetic, algebra, geometry, calculus, and statistics and their applications
* Computers and Electronics—circuit boards; processors; chips; electronic equipment; and computer hardware and software, including applications and programming
* Economics and Accounting—economic and accounting principles and practices, the financial markets, banking, and the analysis and reporting of financial data

What else should you consider about this kind of work?

People who are hired for mathematical and data analysis work for all kinds of businesses and industries, government agencies, and service firms. Those trained in financial analysis are most likely to have jobs with such places as banks, insurance companies, and government offices. Those trained in scientific analysis are most likely to work in universities and in industrial research centers. People in government jobs are sometimes appointed but usually must pass civil service tests.

The job outlook is better for jobs in applied fields than in research and teaching. Therefore, opportunities will be better for those who have skill with computers or knowledge of business and industry.

How can you prepare for jobs of this kind?

Occupations in this group usually require education and/or training ranging from two years to more than ten years.

Statistical assistants may get no more than six months of education and/or training, but actuaries need considerable postgraduate training.

Courses in math concepts, technical writing, economics, computer science, programming languages, accounting, and finance are useful for jobs in this group. Most of the jobs call for four or more years of study in mathematics and statistics at the college level.

Workers in this group are expected to attend seminars and workshops to keep up with developments and trends in their areas.

Actuaries must continue to take tests after employment to upgrade their accreditation in the field. The tests are prepared by national professional organizations.

© 2006 JIST Works

How much education or training is required for the jobs in this Work Group?

For descriptions of these jobs, see Part 2.

Moderate-term on-the-job training

* Statistical Assistants

Associate degree

* Social Science Research Assistants

Bachelor's degree

* Mathematical Technicians

Work experience plus degree

* Actuaries

Master's degree

* Mathematicians
* Statisticians

15.07 Research and Design Engineering

Workers in this group plan, design, and direct the development and construction of buildings, bridges, roads, airports, dams, sewage systems, air conditioning systems, mining machinery, and other structures and equipment. They utilize scientific principles to develop processes and techniques for generating and transmitting electrical power and for manufacturing chemicals. Workers specialize in one or more kinds of engineering, such as civil, electrical, or mechanical.

What kind of work would you do?

Your work activities would depend on your job. For example, you might

* Confer with research personnel in order to clarify or resolve problems and to develop or modify designs.
* Design and develop computer hardware and support peripherals, including central processing units (CPUs), support logic, microprocessors, custom integrated circuits, and printers and disk drives.
* Design and oversee construction and operation of nuclear reactors and power plants and nuclear fuels reprocessing and reclamation systems.
* Formulate conceptual design of aeronautical or aerospace products or systems to meet customer requirements.
* Modify properties of metal alloys, using thermal and mechanical treatments.
* Operate computer-assisted engineering and design software and equipment to perform engineering tasks.
* Perform detailed calculations to compute and establish manufacturing, construction, and installation standards and specifications.
* Prepare estimate of chemical production costs for management.

* Provide feedback to design engineers on customer problems and needs.
* Teach in colleges and universities.

What things about you point to this kind of work?

Is it important for you to

* Try out your own ideas?
* Make use of your individual abilities?
* Be looked up to by others in your company and your community?
* Make decisions on your own?
* Plan your work with little supervision?
* Receive recognition for the work you do?
* Be paid well in comparison with other workers?

Have you enjoyed any of the following as a hobby or leisure-time activity?

* Belonging to a computer club
* Experimenting with a chemistry set
* Installing and repairing home stereo equipment
* Performing experiments for a science fair
* Reading about technological developments, such as computer science or aerospace
* Reading medical or scientific magazines
* Upgrading hardware in personal computers
* Designing and building an addition or remodeling the interior of a home

Have you liked and done well in any of the following school subjects?

* Physics
* Mechanics/Mechanics of Materials
* Calculus
* Naval Architecture
* Computer Concepts/Methods
* Electric/Electronic Theory
* Biochemistry
* Chemistry
* Construction Technology

Are you able to

* Choose the right mathematical methods or formulas to solve a problem?
* Come up with unusual or clever ideas about a given topic or situation or develop creative ways to solve a problem?
* Apply general rules to specific problems to produce answers that make sense?
* Imagine how something will look after it is moved around or when its parts are moved or rearranged?
* Arrange things or actions in a certain order or pattern according to a specific rule or set of rules?
* Read and understand information and ideas presented in writing?
* Combine pieces of information to form general rules or conclusions?

Would you work in places such as

* Colleges and universities?
* Business offices?
* Factories and plants?
* Laboratories?
* Oil fields?
* Mines and quarries?
* Government offices?
* Hospitals and nursing homes?
* Airplanes?
* Ships and boats?
* Waterworks and light and power plants?
* Construction sites?

What skills and knowledges do you need for this kind of work?

For most of these jobs, you need these skills:

* Science—using scientific rules and methods to solve problems
* Technology Design—generating or adapting equipment and technology to serve user needs
* Operations Analysis—analyzing needs and product requirements to create a design
* Mathematics—using mathematics to solve problems
* Systems Analysis—determining how a system should work and how changes in conditions, operations, and the environment will affect outcomes
* Judgment and Decision Making—considering the relative costs and benefits of potential actions to choose the most appropriate one
* Systems Evaluation—identifying measures or indicators of system performance and the actions needed to improve or correct performance relative to the goals of the system

These knowledges are important in most of these jobs:

* Engineering and Technology—the practical application of engineering science and technology; this includes applying principles, techniques, procedures, and equipment to the design and production of various goods and services
* Design—design techniques, tools, and principles involved in production of precision technical plans, blueprints, drawings, and models
* Physics—physical principles and laws and their interrelationships and applications to understanding fluid, material, and atmospheric dynamics and mechanical, electrical, atomic, and subatomic structures and processes
* Mathematics—arithmetic, algebra, geometry, calculus, and statistics and their applications
* Computers and Electronics—circuit boards; processors; chips; electronic equipment; and computer hardware and software, including applications and programming
* Administration and Management—business and management principles involved in strategic planning, resource allocation, human resources modeling, leadership techniques, production methods, and coordination of people and resources
* Production and Processing—raw materials, production processes, quality control, costs, and other techniques for maximizing the effective manufacture and distribution of goods

What else should you consider about this kind of work?

Most types of engineering jobs are found in every large city. Some workers are hired by industrial plants, research laboratories, and construction companies. Others find employment with federal, state, and local governments.

In most places, beginners work with more experienced engineers and later advance to higher-level work in research, design, or management. Many top executives and CEOs began as engineers.

Most engineers work in clean, quiet offices or laboratories. A few spend considerable time in factories or in production areas out-of-doors.

Cutbacks in defense spending and competition from offshore manufacturing have reduced openings in some fields and regions, but well-trained beginners can find openings in other regions and fields.

How can you prepare for jobs of this kind?

Work in this group usually requires education and/or training ranging from four years to more than ten years.

Most workers entering this field have a bachelor's degree in engineering, and in many colleges this program is expected to take five years. College graduates trained in one of the natural sciences or mathematics qualify for a few beginning jobs.

Course work for engineering includes English composition for technical writing skills, algebra, geometry, trigonometry, chemistry, physics, drafting or design graphics, computer programming, and social sciences (for example, government and economics). Most engineers study calculus, differential equations or numerical analysis, statics, dynamics, heat transfer, thermodynamics, and fluid dynamics or fluid mechanics. Specialized engineering courses are taken in the last two years of college.

Several engineering schools have agreements with liberal arts colleges to allow students to spend three years in the college and two years in the engineering school. A bachelor's degree is then granted by each school. Some engineering schools offer a five- or six-year cooperative work-study program in which the students alternate periods in school with employment in related jobs. These students earn part of their tuition costs and get on-the-job experience as they learn.

Engineers who offer their services directly to the public need to be licensed. To do so, they must meet requirements for education and work experience and pass an exam.

How much education or training is required for the jobs in this Work Group?

© 2006 JIST Works

For descriptions of these jobs, see Part 2.

Bachelor's degree

* Aerospace Engineers
* Biomedical Engineers
* Chemical Engineers
* Civil Engineers
* Computer Hardware Engineers
* Electrical Engineers
* Electronics Engineers, Except Computer
* Marine Architects
* Marine Engineers
* Materials Engineers
* Mechanical Engineers
* Nuclear Engineers

15.08 Industrial and Safety Engineering

Workers in this group utilize scientific principles to improve the functioning of a business or to make its processes and products safer.

What kind of work would you do?

Your work activities would depend on your job. For example, you might

* Analyze statistical data and product specifications to determine standards and establish quality and reliability objectives of finished product.
* Conduct research to evaluate safety levels for products.
* Conduct testing of air quality, noise, temperature, or radiation to verify compliance with health and safety regulations.
* Recommend methods for improving utilization of personnel, material, and utilities.
* Study buildings to evaluate fire prevention factors, resistance of construction, contents, water supply and delivery, and exits.

What things about you point to this kind of work?

Is it important for you to

* Try out your own ideas?
* Be looked up to by others in your company and your community?
* Give directions and instructions to others?
* Plan your work with little supervision?
* Make use of your individual abilities?
* Make decisions on your own?
* Be busy all the time?

Have you enjoyed any of the following as a hobby or leisure-time activity?

* Using a pocket calculator or spreadsheet to figure out income and expenses for an organization

* Organizing your room, CDs, DVDs, tools, books, and other items
* Belonging to a computer club
* Reading about technological developments, such as computer science or aerospace
* Reading business magazines and newspapers
* Helping run a school or community fair or carnival

Have you liked and done well in any of the following school subjects?

* Industrial Safety
* Physics
* Fire Safety
* Quality Control
* Calculus
* Industrial Organization

Are you able to

* Apply general rules to specific problems to produce answers that make sense?
* Combine pieces of information to form general rules or conclusions?
* Come up with a number of ideas about a topic?
* Choose the right mathematical methods or formulas to solve a problem?
* Communicate information and ideas in writing so others will understand?
* Generate or use different sets of rules for combining or grouping things in different ways?

Would you work in places such as

* Factories and plants?
* Business offices?
* Laboratories?
* Government offices?

What skills and knowledges do you need for this kind of work?

For most of these jobs, you need these skills:

* Technology Design—generating or adapting equipment and technology to serve user needs
* Operations Analysis—analyzing needs and product requirements to create a design
* Quality Control Analysis—conducting tests and inspections of products, services, or processes to evaluate quality or performance
* Mathematics—using mathematics to solve problems
* Science—using scientific rules and methods to solve problems
* Systems Evaluation—identifying measures or indicators of system performance and the actions needed to improve or correct performance relative to the goals of the system
* Complex Problem Solving—identifying complex problems and reviewing related information to develop and evaluate options and implement solutions

These knowledges are important in most of these jobs:

* Engineering and Technology—the practical application of engineering science and technology; this includes applying principles, techniques, procedures, and equipment to the design and production of various goods and services
* Design—design techniques, tools, and principles involved in production of precision technical plans, blueprints, drawings, and models
* Public Safety and Security—relevant equipment, policies, procedures, and strategies to promote effective local, state, or national security operations for the protection of people, data, property, and institutions
* Physics—physical principles and laws and their interrelationships and applications to understanding fluid, material, and atmospheric dynamics and mechanical, electrical, atomic, and subatomic structures and processes
* Chemistry—the chemical composition, structure, and properties of substances and of the chemical processes and transformations that they undergo; this includes uses of chemicals and their danger signs, production techniques, and disposal methods

What else should you consider about this kind of work?

These workers are employed by all kinds of businesses and organizations in all parts of the country. Some work for federal, state, or local government.

Much of the work is done in comfortable offices, but some work must be done where the business performs its work, and these surroundings may be noisier or dirtier. If a company has many branches, regular travel may be required.

Industrial and safety engineers study all parts of the production process and work closely with management, so they often advance to managerial positions.

Job outlook is fairly good, especially in service industries.

How can you prepare for jobs of this kind?

Work in this group usually requires education and/or training ranging from four years to more than ten years.

Most workers entering this field have a bachelor's degree in engineering, and in many colleges this program is expected to take five years. Course work for engineering includes English composition for technical writing skills, algebra, geometry, trigonometry, chemistry, physics, drafting or design graphics, computer programming, and social sciences (for example, government and economics). Most engineers study calculus, differential equations or numerical analysis, statics, dynamics, heat transfer, thermodynamics, and fluid dynamics or fluid mechanics. Industrial engineers also take courses in business-related subjects such as management theory and operations research. Specialized engineering courses are taken in the last two years of college.

Several engineering schools have agreements with liberal arts colleges to allow students to spend three years in the college and two years in the engineering school. A bachelor's degree is then granted by each school. Some engineering schools offer a five- or six-year cooperative work-study program in which the students alternate periods in school with employment in related jobs. These students earn part of their tuition costs and get on-the-job experience as they learn.

How much education or training is required for the jobs in this Work Group?

For descriptions of these jobs, see Part 2.

Bachelor's degree

* Fire-Prevention and Protection Engineers
* Industrial Engineers
* Industrial Safety and Health Engineers
* Product Safety Engineers

15.09 Engineering Technology

Workers in this group perform a variety of technical tasks. They make detailed drawings and work plans; measure and prepare maps of land and water areas; operate complex communications equipment; inspect buildings and equipment for structural, mechanical, or electrical problems; and schedule and control production and transportation operations.

What kind of work would you do?

Your work activities would depend on your job. For example, you might

* Adjust and replace defective or improperly functioning circuitry and electronics components, using hand tools and soldering iron.
* Build, calibrate, maintain, troubleshoot, and repair electrical instruments or testing equipment.
* Compile data required for map preparation, including aerial photographs, survey notes, records, reports, and original maps.
* Conduct surveys to ascertain the locations of natural features and human-made structures on the Earth's surface, using electronic distance-measuring equipment and other surveying instruments.
* Construct and maintain test facilities for aircraft parts and systems according to specifications.
* Design scale or full-size blueprints of specialty items, such as furniture and automobile body or chassis components.
* Devise, fabricate, and assemble new or modified mechanical components for products, such as industrial machinery or equipment and measuring instruments.
* Draft detail and assembly drawings of design components, circuitry, and printed circuit boards, using computer-assisted equipment or standard drafting techniques and devices.

© 2006 JIST Works

* Identify and compile database information in order to create maps in response to requests.
* Install electrical and electronic parts and hardware in housing or assembly, using soldering equipment and hand tools.

What things about you point to this kind of work?

Is it important for you to

* Have opportunities for advancement?
* Be busy all the time?

Have you enjoyed any of the following as a hobby or leisure-time activity?

* Building or repairing radios or television sets
* Doing electrical wiring and repairs in the home
* Installing and repairing home stereo equipment
* Operating a CB or ham radio
* Performing experiments for a science fair
* Reading about technological developments, such as computer science or aerospace
* Reading medical or scientific magazines
* Making sketches of machines or other mechanical equipment

Have you liked and done well in any of the following school subjects?

* Physics
* Mechanics/Mechanics of Materials
* Calculus
* Electricity/Electronics
* Drafting
* Surveying
* Geographic Information Systems
* Construction Technology

Are you able to

* Choose the right mathematical methods or formulas to solve a problem?
* Imagine how something will look after it is moved around or when its parts are moved or rearranged?
* Arrange things or actions in a certain order or pattern according to a specific rule or set of rules?

Would you work in places such as

* Business offices?
* Design studios?
* Construction sites?
* Factories and plants?
* Mines and quarries?
* Oil fields?
* Hospitals and nursing homes?
* Doctors' and dentists' offices and clinics?

What skills and knowledges do you need for this kind of work?

For most of these jobs, you need these skills:

* Technology Design—generating or adapting equipment and technology to serve user needs
* Mathematics—using mathematics to solve problems
* Programming—writing computer programs for various purposes
* Troubleshooting—determining causes of operating errors and deciding what to do about them
* Repairing—repairing machines or systems, using the needed tools
* Quality Control Analysis—conducting tests and inspections of products, services, or processes to evaluate quality or performance
* Installation—installing equipment, machines, wiring, or programs to meet specifications

These knowledges are important in most of these jobs:

* Design—design techniques, tools, and principles involved in production of precision technical plans, blueprints, drawings, and models
* Engineering and Technology—the practical application of engineering science and technology; this includes applying principles, techniques, procedures, and equipment to the design and production of various goods and services
* Computers and Electronics—circuit boards; processors; chips; electronic equipment; and computer hardware and software, including applications and programming
* Mathematics—arithmetic, algebra, geometry, calculus, and statistics and their applications
* Physics—physical principles and laws and their interrelationships and applications to understanding fluid, material, and atmospheric dynamics and mechanical, electrical, atomic, and subatomic structures and processes

What else should you consider about this kind of work?

Many industries and businesses hire engineering technologists. They work in industrial plants, research laboratories, and construction sites. They can also find jobs with federal, state, and local government agencies.

Most workers have regular daytime hours. Some of these jobs require frequent travel. Some workers spend time in remote areas with a surveying team. In quality control jobs, both with the government and private industry, workers may have to make regular visits to various work sites. Drafters generally work in offices and at times are under pressure to meet deadlines.

Some industrial jobs (e.g., with lasers or high-voltage electricity) require extra safety precautions.

Generally, there are many openings for newcomers with good training. Cutbacks on defense spending and outsourcing of manufacturing have reduced job openings in a few specialties and regions or have increased competition from out-of-work engineers. Civil service tests are required for most government jobs.

How can you prepare for jobs of this kind?

Work in this group usually requires education and/or training ranging from two years to more than ten years.

The most common way to prepare for this kind of work is through related post–high school courses, on-the-job training, and work experience. Academic programs vary widely in quality, so you should be careful to choose one that is respected by employers.

Many technical and vocational schools and two-year colleges offer programs in surveying. With some classroom instruction in surveying, beginners can start as instrument workers, but they will need a two- or possibly four-year degree to become licensed or registered. Advancement may be based on experience, additional education, and/or written examinations.

Basic preparation for jobs in drafting includes high school and two-year college courses in algebra, geometry, trigonometry, physical sciences, industrial arts, and mechanical drawing. Technical school courses in structural design and layout provide the knowledge and skills needed for advanced drafting jobs. A three- to four-year apprenticeship, combining classroom and workplace learning, is another method for entering drafting work.

Military training can be a way to begin many of these careers, but because the training there is very specialized, additional training is usually required to meet the needs of industry.

Technicians usually begin work as trainees in routine jobs under close supervision of an experienced technician or engineer. With added training and experience, they may advance to supervisory or engineering positions.

All of these jobs use high technology, such as global positioning systems and computerized drafting programs, so your education and training should cover these new tools, and you should seek training throughout your career to stay current with new developments.

How much education or training is required for the jobs in this Work Group?

For descriptions of these jobs, see Part 2.

Moderate-term on-the-job training

✳ Mapping Technicians

Long-term on-the-job training

✳ Surveying Technicians

Postsecondary vocational training

✳ Electronic Drafters
✳ Mechanical Drafters

Associate degree

✳ Aerospace Engineering and Operations Technicians
✳ Calibration and Instrumentation Technicians
✳ Civil Engineering Technicians
✳ Electrical Engineering Technicians
✳ Electro-Mechanical Technicians
✳ Electronics Engineering Technicians
✳ Environmental Engineering Technicians
✳ Mechanical Engineering Technicians

Bachelor's degree

✳ Cartographers and Photogrammetrists

© 2006 JIST Works

16 Transportation, Distribution, and Logistics

An interest in operations that move people or materials. You can satisfy this interest by managing a transportation service, by helping vehicles keep on their assigned schedules and routes, or by driving or piloting a vehicle. If you enjoy taking responsibility, perhaps managing a rail line would appeal to you. If you work well with details and can take pressure on the job, you might consider being an air traffic controller. Or would you rather get out on the highway, on the water, or up in the air? If so, then you could drive a truck from state to state, be employed on a ship, or fly a crop duster over a cornfield. If you prefer to stay closer to home, you could drive a delivery van, taxi, or school bus. You can use your physical strength to load freight and arrange it so it gets to its destination in one piece.

16.01   Managerial Work in Transportation

16.02   Air Vehicle Operation

16.03   Truck Driving

16.04   Rail Vehicle Operation

16.05   Water Vehicle Operation

16.06   Other Services Requiring Driving

16.07   Transportation Support Work

16.01 Managerial Work in Transportation

Workers in this group manage transportation services. They may be responsible for a whole airline, rail line, bus line, or subway system; they may oversee a fleet of trucks or cargo vessels; or they may coordinate the activities of the crew on one large train. They have a good knowledge of the transportation equipment for which they are responsible. They understand how to plan for and react to factors that might affect whether the vehicles complete their routes safely, on schedule, and within budget.

What kind of work would you do?

Your work activities would depend on your job. For example, you might

* Collect tickets, fares, or passes from passengers.
* Develop and document procedures for receiving, handling, storing, shipping, or salvaging products or materials.
* Direct activities related to dispatching, routing, and tracking transportation vehicles, such as aircraft and railroad cars.
* Direct investigations to verify and resolve customer or shipper complaints.
* Document and prepare reports of accidents, unscheduled stops, or delays.
* Interview, select, and train warehouse and supervisory personnel.
* Plan and establish transportation routes.
* Select and train postmasters and managers of associate postal units.

What things about you point to this kind of work?

Is it important for you to

* Give directions and instructions to others?
* Have steady employment?
* Be treated fairly by the company?
* Plan your work with little supervision?
* Be paid well in comparison with other workers?

Have you enjoyed any of the following as a hobby or leisure-time activity?

* Chauffeuring special groups, such as children, older people, or people with disabilities
* Serving as a leader of a scouting or other group
* Driving a bus as a volunteer for an organization
* Driving an ambulance as a volunteer
* Reading airplane or boat magazines
* Operating a model train layout
* Operating a motorboat or other pleasure boat

Have you liked and done well in any of the following school subjects?

* Management
* Accounting
* Personnel Management
* Industrial Distribution
* Traffic Control/Management
* Airport Safety
* Scheduling

Are you able to

* Identify and understand the speech of another person?
* Shift back and forth between two or more activities or sources of information?
* Speak clearly so others can understand you?

Would you work in places such as

* Business offices?
* Ports and harbors?
* Airports?
* Post offices?
* Warehouses?
* Railroad tracks and yards?
* Bus and train stations?
* Freight terminals?

What skills and knowledges do you need for this kind of work?

For most of these jobs, you need these skills:

* Management of Personnel Resources—motivating, developing, and directing people as they work, identifying the best people for the job
* Management of Material Resources—obtaining and seeing to the appropriate use of equipment, facilities, and materials needed to do certain work
* Management of Financial Resources—determining how money will be spent to get the work done and accounting for these expenditures
* Negotiation—bringing others together and trying to reconcile differences
* Coordination—adjusting actions in relation to others' actions
* Systems Analysis—determining how a system should work and how changes in conditions, operations, and the environment will affect outcomes
* Systems Evaluation—identifying measures or indicators of system performance and the actions needed to improve or correct performance relative to the goals of the system

These knowledges are important in most of these jobs:

* Transportation—principles and methods for moving people or goods by air, rail, sea, or road, including the relative costs and benefits
* Administration and Management—business and management principles involved in strategic planning, resource allocation, human resources modeling, leadership techniques, production methods, and coordination of people and resources

* Personnel and Human Resources—principles and procedures for personnel recruitment, selection, training, compensation and benefits, labor relations and negotiation, and personnel information systems
* Sales and Marketing—principles and methods for showing, promoting, and selling products or services; this includes marketing strategy and tactics, product demonstrations, sales techniques, and sales control systems
* Economics and Accounting—economic and accounting principles and practices, the financial markets, banking, and the analysis and reporting of financial data

What else should you consider about this kind of work?

Workers in this group are hired by transportation companies, such as airlines, bus lines, railroads, and trucking firms. They also manage the transportation services within large companies or government agencies that move around a lot of people, equipment, supplies, or products.

Success depends largely on getting vehicles to run on time, which means that the work can be stressful. Because government regulations on the industry are decreasing, some aspects of the job are becoming less complex, but competition among transportation service companies is also increasing. Among the high-level management jobs, the trend toward international trade and just-in-time inventory will create many opportunities, especially for those who have good computer skills. Among the lower-level supervisory jobs, increasing competition and consolidation among transportation providers are likely to limit growth of new jobs, but replacements will be needed as existing workers retire.

How can you prepare for jobs of this kind?

Work in this group usually requires education and/or training ranging from two to less than ten years.

Most workers learn from work experience in a related occupation, beginning in lower-level jobs and working their way up to management.

However, transportation managers can learn management skills and the practices of the industry in college majors such as logistics or aviation management.

Railroad conductors, yardmasters, and postal managers mostly learn their skills through employers' training programs and on the job, although some formal study of clerical skills in business college can be helpful.

How much education or training is required for the jobs in this Work Group?

For descriptions of these jobs, see Part 2.

Work experience in a related occupation

* Aircraft Cargo Handling Supervisors
* First-Line Supervisors/Managers of Transportation and Material-Moving Machine and Vehicle Operators
* Postmasters and Mail Superintendents
* Railroad Conductors and Yardmasters
* Storage and Distribution Managers
* Transportation Managers

16.02 Air Vehicle Operation

Workers in this group pilot airplanes or helicopters.

What kind of work would you do?

Your work activities would depend on your job. For example, you might

* Check aircraft prior to flights to ensure that the engines, controls, instruments, and other systems are functioning properly.
* Check baggage or cargo to ensure that it has been loaded correctly.
* Contact control towers for takeoff clearances, arrival instructions, and other information, using radio equipment.
* File instrument flight plans with air traffic control to ensure that flights are coordinated with other air traffic.
* Make announcements regarding flights, using public address systems.
* Pilot airplanes or helicopters over farmlands at low altitudes to dust or spray fields with fertilizers, fungicides, or pesticides.
* Request changes in altitudes or routes as circumstances dictate.
* Steer aircraft along planned routes with the assistance of autopilot and flight management computers.

What things about you point to this kind of work?

Is it important for you to

* Be paid well in comparison with other workers?
* Receive recognition for the work you do?
* Be treated fairly by the company?
* Have opportunities for advancement?
* Be looked up to by others in your company and your community?
* Give directions and instructions to others?
* Make use of your individual abilities?

Have you enjoyed any of the following as a hobby or leisure-time activity?

* Operating a CB or ham radio
* Racing midget or stock cars
* Reading airplane or boat magazines
* Building model airplanes, automobiles, or boats
* Operating flight or driving simulators on the computer

Have you liked and done well in any of the following school subjects?

* Flight Training/Pilot Training
* Flight Safety
* Navigation
* Aeronautical Charts

Are you able to

* See under low light conditions?
* See objects or movement of objects to your side when your eyes are looking ahead?
* Time your movements or the movement of a piece of equipment in anticipation of changes in the speed and/or direction of a moving object or scene?
* See details at a distance?
* Know your location in relation to the environment or know where other objects are in relation to you?
* See objects in the presence of glare or bright lighting?
* Choose quickly between two or more movements in response to two or more different signals?

Would you work in places such as

* Airplanes?
* Airports?

What skills and knowledges do you need for this kind of work?

For most of these jobs, you need these skills:

* Operation and Control—controlling operations of equipment or systems
* Operation Monitoring—watching gauges, dials, or other indicators to make sure a machine is working properly
* Instructing—teaching others how to do something
* Science—using scientific rules and methods to solve problems
* Coordination—adjusting actions in relation to others' actions
* Systems Evaluation—identifying measures or indicators of system performance and the actions needed to improve or correct performance relative to the goals of the system
* Systems Analysis—determining how a system should work and how changes in conditions, operations, and the environment will affect outcomes

These knowledges are important in most of these jobs:

* Transportation—principles and methods for moving people or goods by air, rail, sea, or road, including the relative costs and benefits
* Geography—principles and methods for describing the features of land, sea, and air masses, including their physical characteristics; locations; interrelationships; and distribution of plant, animal, and human life
* Public Safety and Security—relevant equipment, policies, procedures, and strategies to promote effective local, state, or national security operations for the protection of people, data, property, and institutions
* Education and Training—principles and methods for curriculum and training design, teaching and instruction for individuals and groups, and the measurement of training effects
* Telecommunications—transmission, broadcasting, switching, control, and operation of telecommunications systems

* Physics—physical principles and laws and their interrelationships and applications to understanding fluid, material, and atmospheric dynamics and mechanical, electrical, atomic, and subatomic structures and processes
* Mechanical Devices—machines and tools, including their designs, uses, repair, and maintenance

What else should you consider about this kind of work?

Most of these workers are hired by commercial airlines. Some find jobs piloting planes for private companies, such as package delivery services or crop-dusting services, or for individuals. Most of the jobs in flying are found in and around cities where there are major airports, although some are available in smaller towns. Crop dusters work in rural areas.

Airlines hire only pilots who have extensive experience. Pilots also get jobs with flying schools, private companies, and government agencies. Strong competition is expected for jobs with major airlines, and better opportunities will be found in regional airlines and business aviation.

For most of these jobs, work schedules change frequently. Pilots often work under mental stress and must always be alert and ready to make decisions quickly. They are given routine physical exams.

How can you prepare for jobs of this kind?

Work in this group usually requires education and/or training ranging from four to six years.

Flight training is available in the military and in civilian flight schools approved by the Federal Aviation Administration. A high school education or its equal is the minimum requirement for acceptance.

Most major airlines have their own programs to provide additional specialized training before assigning pilots to service. Some airlines require that a pilot have two years of college; many prefer college graduates. Employers require that pilots have a certain amount of accumulated flying time—1500 hours for airlines and helicopter services, less for crop dusting. One way to gain hours is by working as a flight instructor.

How much education or training is required for the jobs in this Work Group?

For descriptions of these jobs, see Part 2.

Postsecondary vocational training

* Commercial Pilots

Bachelor's degree

* Airline Pilots, Copilots, and Flight Engineers

16.03 Truck Driving

Workers in this group drive large trucks, small trucks, or delivery vans. They may cover long distances or a familiar local route.

What kind of work would you do?

Your work activities would depend on your job. For example, you might

* Drive tractor-trailer combination to transport and deliver products, livestock, or materials, usually over long distances.
* Drive vehicles with capacities under three tons in order to transport materials.
* Inspect and maintain vehicle supplies and equipment, such as gas, oil, water, tires, lights, and brakes, in order to ensure that vehicles are in proper working condition.
* Maintain driver log according to I.C.C. regulations.
* Maintain radio or telephone contact with base or supervisor to receive instructions or be dispatched to new location.
* Position blocks and tie rope around items to secure cargo for transport.

What things about you point to this kind of work?

Is it important for you to

* Be paid well in comparison with other workers?
* Do your work alone?

Have you enjoyed any of the following as a hobby or leisure-time activity?

* Driving a truck and tractor to harvest crops on a family farm
* Driving an ambulance as a volunteer
* Instructing family members in observing traffic regulations
* Racing midget or stock cars
* Repairing the family car
* Driving go-karts
* Operating flight or driving simulators on the computer

Have you liked and done well in any of the following school subjects?

* Truck Operating
* Driver Education

Are you able to

* Choose quickly between two or more movements in response to two or more different signals?
* Respond quickly to a signal when it appears?
* Exert maximum muscle force to lift, push, pull, or carry objects?
* Time your movements or the movement of a piece of equipment in anticipation of changes in the speed and/or direction of a moving object or scene?
* Know your location in relation to the environment or know where other objects are in relation to you?
* Use short bursts of muscle force to propel yourself or to throw an object?
* See objects or movement of objects to your side when your eyes are looking ahead?

Would you work in places such as

* Streets and highways?
* Freight terminals?
* Warehouses?

What skills and knowledges do you need for this kind of work?

For most of these jobs, you need these skills:

* Equipment Maintenance—performing routine maintenance on equipment and determining when and what kind of maintenance is needed
* Repairing—repairing machines or systems, using the needed tools
* Operation and Control—controlling operations of equipment or systems

These knowledges are important in most of these jobs:

* Transportation—principles and methods for moving people or goods by air, rail, sea, or road, including the relative costs and benefits
* Geography—principles and methods for describing the features of land, sea, and air masses, including their physical characteristics; locations; interrelationships; and distribution of plant, animal, and human life
* Telecommunications—transmission, broadcasting, switching, control, and operation of telecommunications systems

What else should you consider about this kind of work?

Most of these jobs are found with trucking companies or with wholesale and retail companies that do deliveries.

Beginners are more likely to be hired for local driving jobs than for long-distance operations. If you want to get into long-distance truck driving eventually, experience in local driving can be a big help. Many full-time drivers start by getting part-time and temporary work driving locally.

A regular eight-hour day is standard in some of the jobs, but for others you work evenings, nights, on call, weekends, or holidays, and you may often have to spend nights away from home.

Some truck drivers are self-employed. They do local or long-distance hauling or deliveries on their own, or they accept contracts to deliver mail for the Postal Service or merchandise for private businesses.

Some must load and unload their trucks. Many companies require that workers undergo a physical exam before they are hired and once each year after being hired.

Other forms of transportation are not likely to replace trucking for a long time, so job opportunities are expected to be good. However, there is some sensitivity to the business cycle, and self-employed truckers may be squeezed out of the business if demand slackens and the price of fuel rises at the same time.

How can you prepare for jobs of this kind?

Work in this group usually requires education and/or training ranging from a few days to more than a year.

Driver education courses offered by high schools and private schools are helpful. Truck driving courses are offered by some private vocational schools. Passing a driving test for a commercial license, and sometimes a physical, is required. A good driving record is also necessary.

Requirements for local drivers vary with the type of truck driven and the business of the employer. New workers may learn by riding with a veteran driver, but more training is given if a special type of truck is used. The requirements are similar for long-haul truckers. Some firms give classes on general duties, operating and loading procedures, and company rules and records.

The U.S. Department of Transportation sets standards for truckers driving from state to state. Long-distance truckers must pass a written test on the Motor Carrier Safety Regulations. They must also pass a driving test with the type of truck they will drive on the job. They may not have certain health problems, and they are tested for drugs and alcohol when hired and at random times afterward. Many firms have height and weight limits for their drivers. Others hire only those with several years of long-distance trucking experience.

How much education or training is required for the jobs in this Work Group?

For descriptions of these jobs, see Part 2.

Short-term on-the-job training

* Truck Drivers, Heavy
* Truck Drivers, Light or Delivery Services

Moderate-term on-the-job training

* Tractor-Trailer Truck Drivers

16.04 Rail Vehicle Operation

Workers in this group drive locomotives, subways, and streetcars.

What kind of work would you do?

Your work activities would depend on your job. For example, you might

* Check to see that trains are equipped with supplies such as fuel, water, and sand.
* Collect fares from passengers and issue change and transfers.
* Drive and control rail-guided public transportation, such as subways; elevated trains; and electric-powered streetcars, trams, or trolleys, in order to transport passengers.
* Drive engines within railroad yards or other establishments to couple, uncouple, or switch railroad cars.
* Greet passengers; provide information; and answer questions concerning fares, schedules, transfers, and routings.
* Inspect engines before and after use to ensure proper operation.

* Operate locomotives to transport freight or passengers between stations and to assemble and disassemble trains within rail yards.
* Receive signals from workers in rear of train and relay that information to engineers.
* Receive starting signals from conductors and then move controls such as throttles and air brakes to drive electric, diesel-electric, steam, or gas-turbine–electric locomotives.

What things about you point to this kind of work?

Is it important for you to

* Have supervisors who train workers well?
* Have supervisors who back up workers with management?

Have you enjoyed any of the following as a hobby or leisure-time activity?

* Driving a bus as a volunteer for an organization
* Driving an ambulance as a volunteer
* Operating a model train layout
* Reading mechanical or automotive magazines
* Driving go-karts
* Operating flight or driving simulators on the computer

Have you liked and done well in any of the following school subjects?

* Railroad Safety
* Locomotive Equipment/Operating

Are you able to

* See under low light conditions?
* Respond quickly to a signal when it appears?
* See objects or movement of objects to your side when your eyes are looking ahead?
* Choose quickly between two or more movements in response to two or more different signals?
* See objects in the presence of glare or bright lighting?
* Time your movements or the movement of a piece of equipment in anticipation of changes in the speed and/or direction of a moving object or scene?
* See details at a distance?

Would you work in places such as

* Trains?
* Railroad tracks and yards?

What skills and knowledges do you need for this kind of work?

For most of these jobs, you need these skills:

* Operation and Control—controlling operations of equipment or systems
* Operation Monitoring—watching gauges, dials, or other indicators to make sure a machine is working properly
* Equipment Maintenance—performing routine maintenance on equipment and determining when and what kind of maintenance is needed

These knowledges are important in most of these jobs:

* Transportation—principles and methods for moving people or goods by air, rail, sea, or road, including the relative costs and benefits
* Geography—principles and methods for describing the features of land, sea, and air masses, including their physical characteristics; locations; interrelationships; and distribution of plant, animal, and human life
* Telecommunications—transmission, broadcasting, switching, control, and operation of telecommunications systems

What else should you consider about this kind of work?

Workers in this group are hired by railroad lines that crisscross the nation or by subway lines in the largest cities.

Railroad jobs are usually filled through a seniority system: You have to start in a lower-level job and work your way up. Workers with less seniority are more likely to have to work evenings, nights, on call, weekends, or holidays. Frequent nights away from home may be required.

The job outlook is better for subway and light rail jobs than for intercity rail jobs.

How can you prepare for jobs of this kind?

Work in this group usually requires education and/or training ranging from six months to less than ten years.

Railroads prefer that engineer helpers have a high school education or its equal. Helpers are eligible for promotion when they pass tests on locomotive equipment and operation. They generally learn these skills on the job over several years and in specialized training programs.

Random drug and alcohol tests are conducted on all train crew members.

How much education or training is required for the jobs in this Work Group?

For descriptions of these jobs, see Part 2.

Moderate-term on-the-job training

* Subway and Streetcar Operators

Work experience in a related occupation

* Locomotive Engineers
* Rail Yard Engineers, Dinkey Operators, and Hostlers

Postsecondary vocational training

* Locomotive Firers

16.05 Water Vehicle Operation

Workers in this group operate ships, boats, and barges. They steer them, operate motor equipment, maintain the vessel, and see that passengers or cargo are handled well.

What kind of work would you do?

Your work activities would depend on your job. For example, you might

* Arrange repairs, fuel, and supplies for vessels.
* Determine geographical position of ship, using loran and azimuths of celestial bodies.
* Direct and coordinate activities of crew or workers, such as loading and unloading, operating signal devices, fishing, and repairing defective equipment.
* Interview, hire, and instruct crew and assign watches and living quarters.
* Load or unload material from vessels.
* Move levers to position dredge for excavation, engage hydraulic pump, raise and lower suction boom, and control rotation of cutterhead.
* Navigate ship to avoid reefs, outlying shoals, and other hazards, utilizing aids to navigation, such as lighthouses and buoys.
* Observe water from masthead and advise navigational direction.
* Service boat motors by performing tasks such as changing oil and lubricating parts.
* Stand watch from bow of ship or wing of bridge to look for obstructions in path of ship.

What things about you point to this kind of work?

Is it important for you to

* Have opportunities for advancement?
* Give directions and instructions to others?

Have you enjoyed any of the following as a hobby or leisure-time activity?

* Reading airplane or boat magazines
* Building model airplanes, automobiles, or boats
* Camping, hiking, or engaging in other outdoor activities
* Driving a bus as a volunteer for an organization
* Operating a CB or ham radio
* Operating a motorboat or other pleasure boat

Have you liked and done well in any of the following school subjects?

* Ship Systems
* Navigation

Are you able to

* See under low light conditions?
* See objects in the presence of glare or bright lighting?
* See details at a distance?
* Know your location in relation to the environment or know where other objects are in relation to you?
* See objects or movement of objects to your side when your eyes are looking ahead?
* Judge which of several objects is closer or farther away from you or judge the distance between you and an object?
* Tell the direction from which a sound originated?

Would you work in places such as

* Ships and boats?
* Ports and harbors?

What skills and knowledges do you need for this kind of work?

For most of these jobs, you need these skills:

* Operation and Control—controlling operations of equipment or systems
* Operation Monitoring—watching gauges, dials, or other indicators to make sure a machine is working properly
* Equipment Maintenance—performing routine maintenance on equipment and determining when and what kind of maintenance is needed

These knowledges are important in most of these jobs:

* Transportation—principles and methods for moving people or goods by air, rail, sea, or road, including the relative costs and benefits
* Geography—principles and methods for describing the features of land, sea, and air masses, including their physical characteristics; locations; interrelationships; and distribution of plant, animal, and human life
* Mechanical Devices—machines and tools, including their designs, uses, repair, and maintenance

What else should you consider about this kind of work?

People in water transportation work for barge lines, passenger ship lines, fishing fleets, and the government agencies in charge of port and harbor operation. The jobs are found in seaports, around the Great Lakes, and in cities along navigable rivers such as the Mississippi and the Ohio.

Ship officers are usually away from home for long periods and have to adjust to frequent changes in work schedules. In smaller and older vessels, workers are exposed to adverse weather and noise, and living quarters are cramped.

Because ship pilots and other workers in water transportation are promoted from lower-level work on the same kind of craft, there is strong competition for jobs. However, the outlook for merchant mariners and cruise ship crew members is improving.

How can you prepare for jobs of this kind?

Work in this group usually requires education and/or training ranging from six months to less than two years. For ship captains and pilots, however, as much as ten years may be required.

To qualify for a deck or engineering officer's license, workers need to meet certain physical requirements and be screened for drug use.

Ship captains advance through several officer ranks, beginning with third mate. Most third mate positions are earned by completing a four-year training course at a marine academy.

Some marine trade unions offer programs to train seamen (the term is used for both men and women) to become third mates. U.S. citizens who have been approved by the U.S. Public Health Service for vision and general health are eligible to become trainees. They must also pass Coast Guard tests on navigation, freight handling, and deck operations.

Many workers gain training and experience in the Navy or Coast Guard.

How much education or training is required for the jobs in this Work Group?

For descriptions of these jobs, see Part 2.

Short-term on-the-job training

* Able Seamen
* Ordinary Seamen and Marine Oilers

Moderate-term on-the-job training

* Dredge Operators
* Motorboat Operators

Long-term on-the-job training

* Ship and Boat Captains

Work experience in a related occupation

* Mates—Ship, Boat, and Barge

Work experience plus degree

* Pilots, Ship

16.06 Other Services Requiring Driving

Workers in this group drive ambulances, taxis, buses (city, intercity, or school), or other small vehicles, mostly to take people from place to place. Some drive a route to sell or deliver items, such as ice cream bars, take-out food, or newspapers. Some park cars in parking lots.

What kind of work would you do?

Your work activities would depend on your job. For example, you might

* Collect money from customers, make change, and record transactions on customer receipts.
* Deliver mail to residences and business establishments along specified routes by walking and/or driving, using a combination of satchels, carts, cars, and small trucks.
* Deliver messages and items, such as newspapers, documents, and packages, between establishment departments and to other establishments and private homes.
* Drive ambulances or assist ambulance drivers in transporting sick, injured, or convalescent persons.
* Drive gasoline, diesel, or electrically powered multi-passenger vehicles to transport students between neighborhoods, schools, and school activities.

* Drive taxicabs, limousines, company cars, or privately owned vehicles in order to transport passengers, either to destinations they request or over specified routes.
* Take numbered tags from customers, locate vehicles, and deliver vehicles or provide customers with instructions for locating vehicles.

What things about you point to this kind of work?

Is it important for you to

* Do your work alone?
* Have work where you do things for other people?

Have you enjoyed any of the following as a hobby or leisure-time activity?

* Chauffeuring special groups, such as children, older people, or people with disabilities
* Driving a bus as a volunteer for an organization
* Driving an ambulance as a volunteer
* Directing traffic at community events
* Instructing family members in observing traffic regulations
* Racing midget or stock cars
* Driving go-karts

Have you liked and done well in any of the following school subjects?

* Driver Education
* Truck Operating

Are you able to

* Choose quickly between two or more movements in response to two or more different signals?
* Know your location in relation to the environment or know where other objects are in relation to you?
* See objects or movement of objects to your side when your eyes are looking ahead?
* Tell the direction from which a sound originated?
* Respond quickly to a signal when it appears?
* Time your movements or the movement of a piece of equipment in anticipation of changes in the speed and/or direction of a moving object or scene?
* See under low light conditions?

Would you work in places such as

* Streets and highways?
* Bus and train stations?
* Buses and trolleys?
* Post offices?

What skills and knowledges do you need for this kind of work?

For most of these jobs, you need these skills:

* Service Orientation—actively looking for ways to help people
* Social Perceptiveness—being aware of others' reactions and understanding why they react as they do

* Equipment Maintenance—performing routine maintenance on equipment and determining when and what kind of maintenance is needed

These knowledges are important in most of these jobs:

* Transportation—principles and methods for moving people or goods by air, rail, sea, or road, including the relative costs and benefits
* Geography—principles and methods for describing the features of land, sea, and air masses, including their physical characteristics; locations; interrelationships; and distribution of plant, animal, and human life
* Public Safety and Security—relevant equipment, policies, procedures, and strategies to promote effective local, state, or national security operations for the protection of people, data, property, and institutions

What else should you consider about this kind of work?

These drivers work for bus, taxi, limousine, and ambulance services; school districts; restaurants; parts supply companies; the Postal Service; courier services; and parking lots.

Most of the jobs are for a standard eight-hour day, but some require evening or weekend work, and for others you must be on call. Usually workers with the least seniority must work the least desirable hours. Some jobs require you to wear a uniform. For most of these jobs, you need to deal with the public and show tact and politeness as well as good driving skills.

Some of the jobs are sensitive to the business cycle, but the outlook is generally good.

How can you prepare for jobs of this kind?

Work in this group sometimes requires only a brief demonstration of the tasks and rarely requires more than six months of training. In almost every case, you need to have a good driving record.

For jobs in which you drive passengers, you generally need a special driver's license. Bus and taxi companies often have in-house training programs for new hires. Bus drivers on interstate routes must meet certain health requirements and are tested for drugs and alcohol when hired and at random times afterward. Through some combination of classes and on-the-job training, taxi drivers and chauffeurs learn local geography, safe driving practices, and laws applying to their work.

How much education or training is required for the jobs in this Work Group?

For descriptions of these jobs, see Part 2.

Short-term on-the-job training

* Bus Drivers, School
* Couriers and Messengers
* Driver/Sales Workers
* Parking Lot Attendants
* Postal Service Mail Carriers
* Taxi Drivers and Chauffeurs

Moderate-term on-the-job training

* Ambulance Drivers and Attendants, Except Emergency Medical Technicians
* Bus Drivers, Transit and Intercity

16.07 Transportation Support Work

Workers in this group provide support for routine operations at airports, railroads, and docks. They load and unload cargo, secure cargo inside vehicles, track the movements of cargo and vehicles, and refuel and clean vehicles.

What kind of work would you do?

Your work activities would depend on your job. For example, you might

* Assist passengers to board and leave trains.
* Carry or move cargo by handtruck to wharfs and stack cargo on pallets to facilitate transfer to and from ships.
* Clean and polish vehicle windows.
* Clean, oil, grease, and make minor repairs and adjustments to equipment.
* Control machinery to open and close canal locks and dams, railroad or highway drawbridges, or horizontally or vertically adjustable bridges.
* Estimate freight or postal rates and record shipment costs and weights.
* Mix cleaning solutions, abrasive compositions, and other compounds according to formulas.
* Observe loading of freight to ensure that crews comply with procedures.
* Post warning signs on vehicles containing explosives or inflammatory or radioactive materials.
* Prepare manifests showing baggage, mail, and freight weights and number of passengers on airplanes and transmit data to destinations.

What things about you point to this kind of work?

Is it important for you to

* Have supervisors who train workers well?
* Have supervisors who back up workers with management?

Have you enjoyed any of the following as a hobby or leisure-time activity?

* Building model airplanes, automobiles, or boats
* Operating a CB or ham radio
* Operating a model train layout
* Reading airplane or boat magazines
* Repairing or assembling bicycles or tricycles
* Washing and waxing the family car

Have you liked and done well in any of the following school subjects?

* Shipping Regulations
* Traffic Control/Management

Are you able to

* See under low light conditions?
* Know your location in relation to the environment or know where other objects are in relation to you?
* See objects in the presence of glare or bright lighting?

Would you work in places such as

* Freight terminals?
* Ports and harbors?
* Railroad tracks and yards?
* Bus and train stations?
* Airports?
* Trains?

What skills and knowledges do you need for this kind of work?

For most of these jobs, you need these skills:

* Operation and Control—controlling operations of equipment or systems
* Troubleshooting—determining causes of operating errors and deciding what to do about them
* Equipment Maintenance—performing routine maintenance on equipment and determining when and what kind of maintenance is needed

These knowledges are important in most of these jobs:

* Transportation—principles and methods for moving people or goods by air, rail, sea, or road, including the relative costs and benefits
* Public Safety and Security—relevant equipment, policies, procedures, and strategies to promote effective local, state, or national security operations for the protection of people, data, property, and institutions
* Geography—principles and methods for describing the features of land, sea, and air masses, including their physical characteristics; locations; interrelationships; and distribution of plant, animal, and human life

What else should you consider about this kind of work?

Workers in this group are hired by railroad lines, airports, shipping lines, and government agencies.

Many of these jobs involve movement of large vehicles and loads of freight, and therefore safety precautions must be taken. Because vehicles arrive and depart at all hours, night or weekend work is sometimes required.

Job opportunities will be mixed and will fluctuate over time. The amount of traffic and the volume of goods being shipped depend on the health of the economy. Containerizing of cargo and mechanization of some routine tasks will eliminate certain jobs.

How can you prepare for jobs of this kind?

Work in this group usually requires only a few months of training or less. Usually no formal education beyond high school is required.

Some of the jobs are associated with unions. For most of them, you start with simpler tasks and learn more complex tasks by observing experienced workers on the job.

How much education or training is required for the jobs in this Work Group?

For descriptions of these jobs, see Part 2.

Short-term on-the-job training

* Bridge and Lock Tenders
* Cleaners of Vehicles and Equipment
* Stevedores, Except Equipment Operators
* Traffic Technicians

Moderate-term on-the-job training

* Cargo and Freight Agents

Work experience in a related occupation

* Freight Inspectors
* Public Transportation Inspectors
* Railroad Yard Workers
* Train Crew Members

PART 2

The Job Descriptions

The original edition of the *Guide for Occupational Exploration* cross-referenced so many job titles—more than 12,000—that their descriptions simply could not be included. The newest release of the U.S. Department of Labor's O*NET database, however, provides information on almost 1,000 job titles, a more manageable number.

We've included brief but information-packed descriptions for every job in the most recent O*NET database. The introduction gives additional details on how we created the descriptions, but we designed them to be easy to understand. The one exception is the coded Job Zone information. It is described in the introduction, so you'll have to refer to it to understand this one measure.

The jobs are arranged within Interest Areas and Work Groups in alphabetical order. The Interest Area and Work Group system is also explained in the introduction, but you can quickly see how it works by reviewing the table of contents. There you will see the GOE's system of Interest Areas followed by groupings of related jobs, or Work Groups. Simply use the table of contents to identify groups of jobs that sound interesting, learn more about the groups in Part 1, and then look up their job descriptions in Part 2. If you want more information than these job descriptions provide, the introduction lists print, Internet, and other resources.

01 Agriculture and Natural Resources

01.01 **Managerial Work in Agriculture and Natural Resources**

01.02 **Resource Science/Engineering for Plants, Animals, and the Environment**

01.03 **Resource Technologies for Plants, Animals, and the Environment**

01.04 **General Farming**

01.05 **Nursery, Groundskeeping, and Pest Control**

01.06 **Forestry and Logging**

01.07 **Hunting and Fishing**

01.08 **Mining and Drilling**

01.01 Managerial Work in Agriculture and Natural Resources

Agricultural Crop Farm Managers

Direct and coordinate, through subordinate supervisory personnel, activities of workers engaged in agricultural crop production for corporations, cooperatives, or other owners. **O*NET Code:** 11-9011.02. **Average Salary:** $47,680. **Projected Growth:** 5.1%. **Annual Openings:** 25,000. **Education:** Work experience in a related occupation. **Job Zone:** 4. **Education/Training Program(s)**—Agribusiness/Agricultural Business Operations; Agricultural Business and Management, General; Agricultural Business and Management, Other; Agricultural Production Operations, General; Agricultural Production Operations, Other; Agronomy and Crop Science; Crop Production; Dairy Husbandry and Production; Farm/Farm and Ranch Management; Greenhouse Operations and Management; Horticultural Science; Ornamental Horticulture; Plant Nursery Operations and Management; Plant Protection and Integrated Pest Management; Plant Sciences, General; Range Science and Management. **Related Knowledge/Courses:** Food Production; Economics and Accounting; Administration and Management; Production and Processing; Personnel and Human Resources; Mathematics. **Personality Type:** Enterprising. **Skills Required:** Management of Financial Resources; Negotiation; Management of Personnel Resources; Management of Material Resources; Coordination; Systems Analysis; Writing; Speaking; Instructing. **Abilities:** Mathematical Reasoning; Written Expression; Originality; Inductive Reasoning; Written Comprehension; Oral Expression. **Occupational Values:** Authority; Creativity; Autonomy; Responsibility; Variety. **Interacting with Others:** Communicating with Supervisors, Peers, or Subordinates; Communicating with Persons Outside Organization; Monitoring and Controlling Resources. **Physical Work Conditions:** Outdoors; Standing; Minor Burns, Cuts, Bites, or Stings; Hazardous Equipment; Contaminants.

Farmers and Ranchers

On an ownership or rental basis, operate farms, ranches, greenhouses, nurseries, timber tracts, or other agricultural production establishments that produce crops, horticultural specialties, livestock, poultry, finfish, shellfish, or animal specialties. May plant, cultivate, harvest, perform post-harvest activities for, and market crops and livestock; may hire, train, and supervise farm workers or supervise a farm labor contractor; may prepare cost, production, and other records. May maintain and operate machinery and perform physical work. **O*NET Code:** 11-9012.00. **Average Salary:** $72,180. **Projected Growth:** –20.6%. **Annual Openings:** 118,000. **Education:** Long-term on-the-job training. **Job Zone:** 3. **Education/Training Program(s)**—Agribusiness/Agricultural Business Operations; Agricultural Animal Breeding; Agricultural Business and Management, General; Agricultural Production Operations, General; Agricultural Production Operations, Other; Agronomy and Crop Science; Animal Nutrition; Animal Sciences, General; Animal/Livestock Husbandry and Production; Aquaculture; Crop Production; Dairy Husbandry and Production; Dairy Science; Farm/Farm and Ranch Management; Greenhouse Operations and Management; Horticultural Science; Livestock Management; Ornamental Horticulture; Plant Nursery Operations and Management; Plant Protection and Integrated Pest Management; Plant Sciences, General; Poultry Science; Range Science and Management. **Related Knowledge/Courses:** Food Production; Economics and Accounting; Personnel and Human Resources; Production and Processing; Sales and Marketing; Transportation. **Personality Type:** Realistic. **Skills Required:** Management of Financial Resources; Management of Personnel Resources; Installation; Management of Material Resources; Equipment Selection; Operation and Control; Equipment Maintenance; Repairing. **Abilities:** Stamina; Static Strength; Trunk Strength; Dynamic Strength; Control Precision. **Occupational Values:** Autonomy; Authority; Responsibility; Creativity; Variety. **Interacting with Others:** Monitoring and Controlling Resources; Communicating with Persons Outside Organization; Coordinating the Work and Activities of Others. **Physical Work Conditions:** Outdoors; Hazardous Equipment; Minor Burns, Cuts, Bites, or Stings; Standing; Using Hands on Objects, Tools, or Controls.

First-Line Supervisors and Manager/Supervisors—Agricultural Crop Workers

Directly supervise and coordinate activities of agricultural crop workers. Manager/Supervisors are generally found in smaller establishments, where they perform both supervisory and management functions, such as accounting, marketing, and personnel work, and may also engage in the same agricultural work as the workers they supervise. **O*NET Code:** 45-1011.01. **Average Salary:** $35,540. **Projected Growth:** 11.4%. **Annual Openings:** 6,000. **Education:** Associate degree. **Job Zone:** 3. **Education/Training Program(s)**—Agricultural Business and Management, Other; Agricultural Production Operations, General; Agricultural Production Operations, Other; Agriculture, Agriculture Operations, and Related Sciences, Other; Agronomy and Crop Science; Aquaculture; Crop Production; Farm/Farm and Ranch Management; Fishing and Fisheries Sciences and Management; Plant Sciences, General; Range Science and Management. **Related Knowledge/Courses:** Food Production; Personnel and Human Resources; Administration and Management; Biology; Mechanical; Transportation; Chemistry. **Personality Type:** Enterprising. **Skills Required:** Management of Personnel Resources; Management of Material Resources; Coordination; Equipment Maintenance; Time Management; Instructing; Management of Financial Resources; Repairing. **Abilities:** Multilimb Coordination; Control Precision; Static Strength; Number Facility; Extent Flexibility. **Occupational Values:** Authority; Responsibility; Autonomy; Variety; Achievement; Activity; Creativity. **Interacting with Others:** Communicating with Supervisors, Peers, or Subordinates; Coordinating the Work and Activities of Others; Guiding, Directing, and Motivating Subordinates.

© 2006, JIST Works

Physical Work Conditions: Outdoors; Hazardous Equipment; Standing; Minor Burns, Cuts, Bites, or Stings; Contaminants.

First-Line Supervisors and Manager/Supervisors—Animal Husbandry Workers

Directly supervise and coordinate activities of animal husbandry workers. Manager/Supervisors are generally found in smaller establishments, where they perform both supervisory and management functions, such as accounting, marketing, and personnel work, and may also engage in the same animal husbandry work as the workers they supervise. **O*NET Code:** 45-1011.02. **Average Salary:** $35,540. **Projected Growth:** 11.4%. **Annual Openings:** 6,000. **Education:** Associate degree. **Job Zone:** 3. **Education/Training Program(s)—** Agricultural Animal Breeding; Agricultural Business and Management, Other; Agricultural Production Operations, General; Agricultural Production Operations, Other; Agriculture, Agriculture Operations, and Related Sciences, Other; Animal Nutrition; Animal Sciences, General; Animal/Livestock Husbandry and Production; Aquaculture; Dairy Husbandry and Production; Dairy Science; Farm/Farm and Ranch Management; Fishing and Fisheries Sciences and Management; Horse Husbandry/Equine Science and Management; Livestock Management; Poultry Science; Range Science and Management. **Related Knowledge/Courses:** Food Production; Biology; Personnel and Human Resources; Administration and Management; Medicine and Dentistry; Transportation. **Personality Type:** Enterprising. **Skills Required:** Management of Personnel Resources; Management of Material Resources; Instructing; Systems Evaluation; Time Management; Coordination; Management of Financial Resources; Equipment Selection. **Abilities:** Perceptual Speed; Problem Sensitivity; Memorization; Spatial Orientation; Gross Body Coordination. **Occupational Values:** Authority; Responsibility; Autonomy; Variety; Achievement; Activity. **Interacting with Others:** Establishing and Maintaining Interpersonal Relationships; Staffing Organizational Units; Communicating with Supervisors, Peers, or Subordinates. **Physical Work Conditions:** Outdoors; Disease or Infections; Very Hot or Cold; Contaminants; Walking and Running.

First-Line Supervisors and Manager/Supervisors—Extractive Workers

Directly supervise and coordinate activities of extractive workers and their helpers. Manager/Supervisors are generally found in smaller establishments, where they perform both supervisory and management functions, such as accounting, marketing, and personnel work, and may also engage in the same extractive work as the workers they supervise. **O*NET Code:** 47-1011.02. **Average Salary:** $49,390. **Projected Growth:** 14.1%. **Annual Openings:** 67,000. **Education:** Work experience in a related occupation. **Job Zone:** 3. **Education/Training Program(s)—**Blasting/Blaster; Well Drilling/Driller. **Related Knowledge/Courses:** Personnel and Human Resources; Administration and Management; Engineering and Technology; Physics; Production and Processing; Mechanical; Education and Training. **Personality Type:** Enterprising. **Skills Required:** Management of Personnel Resources; Instructing; Management of Material Resources; Systems Evaluation; Coordination; Systems

Analysis; Time Management; Negotiation. **Abilities:** Visualization; Written Expression; Problem Sensitivity; Deductive Reasoning; Inductive Reasoning. **Occupational Values:** Authority; Responsibility; Variety; Autonomy; Coworkers. **Interacting with Others:** Communicating with Supervisors, Peers, or Subordinates; Coordinating the Work and Activities of Others; Establishing and Maintaining Interpersonal Relationships; Guiding, Directing, and Motivating Subordinates. **Physical Work Conditions:** Common Protective or Safety Equipment; Outdoors; Hazardous Equipment; Standing; Specialized Protective or Safety Equipment.

First-Line Supervisors and Manager/Supervisors—Fishery Workers

Directly supervise and coordinate activities of fishery workers. Manager/Supervisors are generally found in smaller establishments, where they perform both supervisory and management functions, such as accounting, marketing, and personnel work, and may also engage in the same fishery work as the workers they supervise. **O*NET Code:** 45-1011.06. **Average Salary:** $35,540. **Projected Growth:** 11.4%. **Annual Openings:** 6,000. **Education:** Associate degree. **Job Zone:** 3. **Education/Training Program(s)—**Agricultural Animal Breeding; Agricultural Business and Management, Other; Agricultural Production Operations, General; Agricultural Production Operations, Other; Agriculture, Agriculture Operations, and Related Sciences, Other; Animal Nutrition; Animal Sciences, General; Animal/Livestock Husbandry and Production; Farm/Farm and Ranch Management; Fishing and Fisheries Sciences and Management. **Related Knowledge/Courses:** Food Production; Biology; Personnel and Human Resources; Administration and Management; Production and Processing; Chemistry. **Personality Type:** Realistic. **Skills Required:** Management of Personnel Resources; Instructing; Time Management; Management of Material Resources; Coordination; Systems Analysis; Learning Strategies; Operations Analysis; Equipment Maintenance; Systems Evaluation. **Abilities:** Flexibility of Closure; Speed of Closure; Depth Perception; Category Flexibility; Wrist-Finger Speed; Far Vision. **Occupational Values:** Authority; Responsibility; Autonomy; Achievement; Creativity. **Interacting with Others:** Communicating with Supervisors, Peers, or Subordinates; Coordinating the Work and Activities of Others; Establishing and Maintaining Interpersonal Relationships. **Physical Work Conditions:** Outdoors; Walking and Running; Extremely Bright or Inadequate Lighting; Sitting; Disease or Infections; Standing.

First-Line Supervisors and Manager/Supervisors—Horticultural Workers

Directly supervise and coordinate activities of horticultural workers. Manager/Supervisors are generally found in smaller establishments, where they perform both supervisory and management functions, such as accounting, marketing, and personnel work, and may also engage in the same horticultural work as the workers they supervise. **O*NET Code:** 45-1011.04. **Average Salary:** $35,540. **Projected Growth:** 11.4%. **Annual Openings:** 6,000. **Education:** Associate degree. **Job Zone:** 3. **Education/Training Program(s)—**Agricultural Business and Management, Other; Agricultural Production

Operations, General; Agricultural Production Operations, Other; Agriculture, Agriculture Operations, and Related Sciences, Other; Agronomy and Crop Science; Crop Production; Farm/Farm and Ranch Management; Plant Sciences, General. **Related Knowledge/Courses:** Biology; Personnel and Human Resources; Administration and Management; Food Production; Chemistry; Clerical. **Personality Type:** Realistic. **Skills Required:** Management of Personnel Resources; Instructing; Management of Material Resources; Coordination; Time Management; Operation Monitoring; Troubleshooting; Repairing. **Abilities:** Multilimb Coordination; Control Precision; Static Strength; Visual Color Discrimination; Spatial Orientation. **Occupational Values:** Authority; Responsibility; Autonomy; Creativity; Variety. **Interacting with Others:** Communicating with Supervisors, Peers, or Subordinates; Establishing and Maintaining Interpersonal Relationships; Coordinating the Work and Activities of Others. **Physical Work Conditions:** Outdoors; Very Hot or Cold; Standing; Extremely Bright or Inadequate Lighting; Minor Burns, Cuts, Bites, or Stings.

First-Line Supervisors and Manager/Supervisors—Landscaping Workers

Directly supervise and coordinate activities of landscaping workers. Manager/Supervisors are generally found in smaller establishments, where they perform both supervisory and management functions, such as accounting, marketing, and personnel work, and may also engage in the same landscaping work as the workers they supervise. **O*NET Code:** 37-1012.02. **Average Salary:** $34,120. **Projected Growth:** 21.6%. **Annual Openings:** 18,000. **Education:** Work experience in a related occupation. **Job Zone:** 3. **Education/Training Program(s)—** Landscaping and Groundskeeping; Ornamental Horticulture; Turf and Turfgrass Management. **Related Knowledge/ Courses:** Personnel and Human Resources; Administration and Management; Chemistry; Mechanical; Biology; Building and Construction. **Personality Type:** Realistic. **Skills Required:** Management of Personnel Resources; Coordination; Management of Material Resources; Instructing; Systems Evaluation; Time Management; Systems Analysis; Speaking. **Abilities:** Static Strength; Spatial Orientation; Time Sharing; Information Ordering; Visual Color Discrimination. **Occupational Values:** Authority; Responsibility; Autonomy; Creativity; Activity. **Interacting with Others:** Communicating with Supervisors, Peers, or Subordinates; Establishing and Maintaining Interpersonal Relationships; Coordinating the Work and Activities of Others; Guiding, Directing, and Motivating Subordinates; Staffing Organizational Units. **Physical Work Conditions:** Outdoors; Standing; Contaminants; Walking and Running; Minor Burns, Cuts, Bites, or Stings.

First-Line Supervisors and Manager/Supervisors—Logging Workers

Directly supervise and coordinate activities of logging workers. Manager/Supervisors are generally found in smaller establishments, where they perform both supervisory and management functions, such as accounting, marketing, and personnel work, and may also engage in the same logging work as the workers they supervise. **O*NET Code:** 45-1011.05. **Average Salary:** $35,540. **Projected Growth:** 11.4%. **Annual**

Openings: 6,000. **Education:** Bachelor's degree. **Job Zone:** 4. **Education/Training Program(s)—**Agricultural Business and Management, Other; Agricultural Production Operations, General; Agricultural Production Operations, Other; Agriculture, Agriculture Operations, and Related Sciences, Other; Agronomy and Crop Science; Crop Production; Farm/Farm and Ranch Management; Plant Sciences, General. **Related Knowledge/Courses:** Administration and Management; Production and Processing; Personnel and Human Resources; Education and Training; Public Safety and Security; Transportation. **Personality Type:** Realistic. **Skills Required:** Management of Personnel Resources; Management of Material Resources; Instructing; Time Management; Coordination; Systems Analysis; Systems Evaluation; Operation and Control. **Abilities:** Auditory Attention; Far Vision; Rate Control; Static Strength; Multilimb Coordination. **Occupational Values:** Authority; Responsibility; Autonomy; Creativity; Activity. **Interacting with Others:** Communicating with Supervisors, Peers, or Subordinates; Communicating with Persons Outside Organization; Coordinating the Work and Activities of Others. **Physical Work Conditions:** Outdoors; Hazardous Equipment; Minor Burns, Cuts, Bites, or Stings; Standing; Very Hot or Cold.

Fish Hatchery Managers

Direct and coordinate, through subordinate supervisory personnel, activities of workers engaged in fish hatchery production for corporations, cooperatives, or other owners. **O*NET Code:** 11-9011.03. **Average Salary:** $47,680. **Projected Growth:** 5.1%. **Annual Openings:** 25,000. **Education:** Work experience in a related occupation. **Job Zone:** 4. **Education/Training Program(s)—**Agribusiness/Agricultural Business Operations; Agricultural Animal Breeding; Agricultural Business and Management, General; Agricultural Business and Management, Other; Agricultural Production Operations, General; Agricultural Production Operations, Other; Animal Nutrition; Animal Sciences, General; Animal/Livestock Husbandry and Production; Farm/Farm and Ranch Management; Livestock Management. **Related Knowledge/Courses:** Food Production; Administration and Management; Personnel and Human Resources; Economics and Accounting; Biology; Law and Government. **Personality Type:** Enterprising. **Skills Required:** Management of Financial Resources; Management of Personnel Resources; Management of Material Resources; Science; Time Management; Reading Comprehension; Writing; Critical Thinking; Coordination; Systems Analysis. **Abilities:** Number Facility; Flexibility of Closure; Far Vision; Written Expression; Spatial Orientation. **Occupational Values:** Authority; Creativity; Autonomy; Variety; Responsibility. **Interacting with Others:** Monitoring and Controlling Resources; Communicating with Supervisors, Peers, or Subordinates; Staffing Organizational Units. **Physical Work Conditions:** Outdoors; Contaminants; Extremely Bright or Inadequate Lighting; Minor Burns, Cuts, Bites, or Stings; Sitting.

Lawn Service Managers

Plan, direct, and coordinate activities of workers engaged in pruning trees and shrubs, cultivating lawns, and applying pesticides and other chemicals according to service contract specifications. **O*NET Code:** 37-1012.01. **Average Salary:** $34,120. **Projected Growth:** 21.6%. **Annual Openings:** 18,000. **Education:** Work experience in a related occupation. **Job Zone:** 4. **Education/Training Program(s)**—Landscaping and Groundskeeping; Ornamental Horticulture; Turf and Turfgrass Management. **Related Knowledge/Courses:** Administration and Management; Personnel and Human Resources; Customer and Personal Service; Economics and Accounting; Sales and Marketing; Geography. **Personality Type:** Enterprising. **Skills Required:** Management of Personnel Resources; Time Management; Management of Financial Resources; Coordination; Systems Evaluation; Management of Material Resources; Negotiation; Systems Analysis. **Abilities:** Number Facility; Oral Expression; Written Expression; Information Ordering; Oral Comprehension. **Occupational Values:** Authority; Autonomy; Responsibility; Social Service; Creativity. **Interacting with Others:** Communicating with Supervisors, Peers, or Subordinates; Communicating with Persons Outside Organization; Establishing and Maintaining Interpersonal Relationships; Coordinating the Work and Activities of Others; Guiding, Directing, and Motivating Subordinates. **Physical Work Conditions:** Outdoors; Very Hot or Cold; Extremely Bright or Inadequate Lighting; Minor Burns, Cuts, Bites, or Stings; Standing.

Nursery and Greenhouse Managers

Plan, organize, direct, control, and coordinate activities of workers engaged in propagating, cultivating, and harvesting horticultural specialties, such as trees, shrubs, flowers, mushrooms, and other plants. **O*NET Code:** 11-9011.01. **Average Salary:** $47,680. **Projected Growth:** 5.1%. **Annual Openings:** 25,000. **Education:** Work experience in a related occupation. **Job Zone:** 4. **Education/Training Program(s)**—Agribusiness/Agricultural Business Operations; Agricultural Business and Management, General; Agricultural Business and Management, Other; Agricultural Production Operations, General; Agricultural Production Operations, Other; Agronomy and Crop Science; Crop Production; Farm/Farm and Ranch Management; Greenhouse Operations and Management; Horticultural Science; Ornamental Horticulture; Plant Nursery Operations and Management; Plant Protection and Integrated Pest Management; Plant Sciences, General; Range Science and Management. **Related Knowledge/Courses:** Biology; Administration and Management; Personnel and Human Resources; Chemistry; Food Production; Production and Processing. **Personality Type:** Enterprising. **Skills Required:** Management of Personnel Resources; Management of Financial Resources; Management of Material Resources; Negotiation; Coordination; Time Management; Operations Analysis; Systems Analysis; Systems Evaluation. **Abilities:** Written Expression; Mathematical Reasoning; Number Facility; Originality; Oral Comprehension; Oral Expression. **Occupational Values:** Authority; Creativity; Autonomy; Ability Utilization; Responsibility. **Interacting with Others:** Monitoring and Controlling Resources; Communicating with Persons Outside Organization; Resolving Conflicts and Negotiating with Others. **Physical Work Conditions:** Kneeling, Crouching, Stooping, or Crawling; Outdoors; Very Hot or Cold; Minor Burns, Cuts, Bites, or Stings; Standing.

Park Naturalists

Plan, develop, and conduct programs to inform public of historical, natural, and scientific features of national, state, or local park. **O*NET Code:** 19-1031.03. **Average Salary:** $51,160. **Projected Growth:** 4.1%. **Annual Openings:** 1,000. **Education:** Bachelor's degree. **Job Zone:** 4. **Education/Training Program(s)**—Forest Management/Forest Resources Management; Forest Sciences and Biology; Forestry, General; Forestry, Other; Land Use Planning and Management/Development; Natural Resources and Conservation, Other; Natural Resources Management and Policy; Natural Resources Management and Policy, Other; Natural Resources/Conservation, General; Water, Wetlands, and Marine Resources Management; Wildlife and Wildlands Science and Management. **Related Knowledge/Courses:** Biology; Customer and Personal Service; History and Archeology; Geography; Sociology and Anthropology; Education and Training; Communications and Media. **Personality Type:** Social. **Skills Required:** Management of Personnel Resources; Management of Financial Resources; Service Orientation; Instructing; Persuasion; Writing; Learning Strategies; Coordination. **Abilities:** Spatial Orientation; Stamina; Visualization; Time Sharing; Dynamic Strength; Speech Clarity. **Occupational Values:** Autonomy; Creativity; Responsibility; Achievement; Variety; Recognition. **Interacting with Others:** Communicating with Persons Outside Organization; Performing for or Working Directly with the Public; Establishing and Maintaining Interpersonal Relationships. **Physical Work Conditions:** Indoors, Not Environmentally Controlled; Outdoors; In an Enclosed Vehicle or Equipment; Very Hot or Cold; Physical Proximity.

Purchasing Agents and Buyers, Farm Products

Purchase farm products for either further processing or resale. **O*NET Code:** 13-1021.00. **Average Salary:** $43,750. **Projected Growth:** 10.2%. **Annual Openings:** 2,000. **Education:** Work experience in a related occupation. **Job Zone:** 4. **Education/Training Program(s)**—Agricultural/Farm Supplies Retailing and Wholesaling. **Related Knowledge/Courses:** Food Production; Production and Processing; Communications and Media; Economics and Accounting; Biology; English Language. **Personality Type:** Enterprising. **Skills Required:** Negotiation; Writing; Management of Financial Resources; Persuasion; Mathematics; Speaking; Coordination; Management of Material Resources. **Abilities:** Written Expression; Mathematical Reasoning; Number Facility; Oral Expression; Category Flexibility; Speech Clarity. **Occupational Values:** Co-workers; Authority; Responsibility; Autonomy; Advancement. **Interacting with Others:** Communicating with Persons Outside Organization; Resolving Conflicts and Negotiating with Others; Providing Consultation and Advice to Others. **Physical Work Conditions:** Walking and Running; Sitting; Outdoors; Extremely Bright or Inadequate Lighting; Standing.

01.02 Resource Science/Engineering for Plants, Animals, and the Environment

Agricultural Engineers

Apply knowledge of engineering technology and biological science to agricultural problems concerned with power and machinery, electrification, structures, soil and water conservation, and processing of agricultural products. **O*NET Code:** 17-2021.00. **Average Salary:** $52,340. **Projected Growth:** 10.3%. **Annual Openings:** Fewer than 500. **Education:** Bachelor's degree. **Job Zone:** 5. **Education/Training Program(s)**—Agricultural/Biological Engineering and Bioengineering. **Related Knowledge/Courses:** Biology; Engineering and Technology; Food Production; Design; Physics; Communications and Media. **Personality Type:** Investigative. **Skills Required:** Technology Design; Science; Operations Analysis; Mathematics; Active Learning; Systems Analysis; Complex Problem Solving; Critical Thinking; Quality Control Analysis. **Abilities:** Originality; Visualization; Written Expression; Mathematical Reasoning; Deductive Reasoning. **Occupational Values:** Creativity; Ability Utilization; Responsibility; Autonomy; Social Status. **Interacting with Others:** Communicating with Supervisors, Peers, or Subordinates; Coordinating the Work and Activities of Others; Communicating with Persons Outside Organization. **Physical Work Conditions:** Hazardous Equipment; Extremely Bright or Inadequate Lighting; Outdoors; Sitting; Very Hot or Cold.

Animal Scientists

Conduct research in the genetics, nutrition, reproduction, growth, and development of domestic farm animals. **O*NET Code:** 19-1011.00. **Average Salary:** $49,610. **Projected Growth:** 9.1%. **Annual Openings:** 2,000. **Education:** Bachelor's degree. **Job Zone:** 5. **Education/Training Program(s)**—Agricultural Animal Breeding; Agriculture, General; Animal Health; Animal Nutrition; Animal Sciences, General; Animal Sciences, Other; Dairy Science; Poultry Science; Range Science and Management. **Related Knowledge/Courses:** Biology; Food Production; Medicine and Dentistry; Chemistry; English Language; History and Archeology. **Personality Type:** Investigative. **Skills Required:** Science; Operations Analysis; Active Learning; Critical Thinking; Complex Problem Solving; Quality Control Analysis; Reading Comprehension; Technology Design. **Abilities:** Written Expression; Inductive Reasoning; Oral Comprehension; Written Comprehension; Mathematical Reasoning. **Occupational Values:** Autonomy; Creativity; Responsibility; Independence; Ability Utilization; Achievement. **Interacting with Others:** Interpreting the Meaning of Information for Others; Providing Consultation and Advice to Others; Communicating with Supervisors, Peers, or Subordinates; Communicating with Persons Outside Organization. **Physical Work Conditions:** Minor Burns, Cuts, Bites, or Stings; Sitting; Disease or Infections; Specialized Protective or Safety Equipment; Kneeling, Crouching, Stooping, or Crawling.

Environmental Engineers

Design, plan, or perform engineering duties in the prevention, control, and remediation of environmental health hazards utilizing various engineering disciplines. Work may include waste treatment, site remediation, or pollution control technology. **O*NET Code:** 17-2081.00. **Average Salary:** $64,040. **Projected Growth:** 38.2%. **Annual Openings:** 6,000. **Education:** Bachelor's degree. **Job Zone:** 5. **Education/Training Program(s)**—Environmental/Environmental Health Engineering. **Related Knowledge/Courses:** Education and Training; Law and Government; Chemistry; Public Safety and Security; Engineering and Technology; Design. **Personality Type:** No data available. **Skills Required:** Science; Management of Financial Resources; Coordination; Writing; Persuasion; Negotiation; Mathematics; Technology Design. **Abilities:** Written Expression; Originality; Oral Comprehension; Oral Expression; Deductive Reasoning. **Occupational Values:** No data available. **Interacting with Others:** Communicating with Supervisors, Peers, or Subordinates; Communicating with Persons Outside Organization; Establishing and Maintaining Interpersonal Relationships. **Physical Work Conditions:** Sitting; Very Hot or Cold; Sounds, Noise Levels Are Distracting or Uncomfortable; Hazardous Conditions; Indoors, Not Environmentally Controlled; Physical Proximity.

Foresters

Manage forested lands for economic, recreational, and conservation purposes. May inventory the type, amount, and location of standing timber, appraise the timber's worth, negotiate the purchase, and draw up contracts for procurement. May determine how to conserve wildlife habitats, creek beds, water quality, and soil stability, and how best to comply with environmental regulations. May devise plans for planting and growing new trees, monitor trees for healthy growth, and determine the best time for harvesting. Develop forest management plans for public and privately-owned forested lands. **O*NET Code:** 19-1032.00. **Average Salary:** $47,070. **Projected Growth:** 4.7%. **Annual Openings:** 1,000. **Education:** Bachelor's degree. **Job Zone:** 4. **Education/Training Program(s)**—Forest Management/Forest Resources Management; Forest Resources Production and Management; Forest Sciences and Biology; Forestry, General; Forestry, Other; Natural Resources and Conservation, Other; Natural Resources Management and Policy; Natural Resources Management and Policy, Other; Natural Resources/Conservation, General; Urban Forestry; Wood Science and Wood Products/Pulp and Paper Technology. **Related Knowledge/Courses:** Geography; Biology; Mathematics; English Language; Computers and Electronics; Building and Construction. **Personality Type:** Realistic. **Skills Required:** Management of Financial Resources; Coordination; Science; Time Management; Operations Analysis; Mathematics; Quality Control Analysis; Programming. **Abilities:** Originality; Category Flexibility; Fluency of Ideas; Flexibility

© 2006, JIST Works

of Closure; Problem Sensitivity. **Occupational Values:** Autonomy; Responsibility; Creativity; Authority; Ability Utilization. **Interacting with Others:** Communicating with Supervisors, Peers, or Subordinates; Resolving Conflicts and Negotiating with Others; Performing for or Working Directly with the Public. **Physical Work Conditions:** In an Enclosed Vehicle or Equipment; Sitting; Sounds, Noise Levels Are Distracting or Uncomfortable; Outdoors; Very Hot or Cold.

Mining and Geological Engineers, Including Mining Safety Engineers

Determine the location and plan the extraction of coal, metallic ores, nonmetallic minerals, and building materials, such as stone and gravel. Work involves conducting preliminary surveys of deposits or undeveloped mines and planning their development; examining deposits or mines to determine whether they can be worked at a profit; making geological and topographical surveys; evolving methods of mining best suited to character, type, and size of deposits; and supervising mining operations. **O*NET Code:** 17-2151.00. **Average Salary:** $64,180. **Projected Growth:** -2.7%. **Annual Openings:** Fewer than 500. **Education:** Bachelor's degree. **Job Zone:** 4. **Education/Training Program(s)**—Mining and Mineral Engineering. **Related Knowledge/Courses:** Engineering and Technology; Design; Production and Processing; Chemistry; Computers and Electronics; Geography. **Personality Type:** Investigative. **Skills Required:** Operations Analysis; Management of Financial Resources; Science; Management of Material Resources; Mathematics; Persuasion; Programming; Negotiation. **Abilities:** Originality; Fluency of Ideas; Deductive Reasoning; Written Expression; Speed of Closure. **Occupational Values:** Authority; Responsibility; Social Status; Autonomy; Creativity. **Interacting with Others:** Communicating with Supervisors, Peers, or Subordinates; Establishing and Maintaining Interpersonal Relationships; Coordinating the Work and Activities of Others. **Physical Work Conditions:** Contaminants; Sitting; Very Hot or Cold; In an Enclosed Vehicle or Equipment; Hazardous Equipment.

Petroleum Engineers

Devise methods to improve oil and gas well production and determine the need for new or modified tool designs. Oversee drilling and offer technical advice to achieve economical and satisfactory progress. **O*NET Code:** 17-2171.00. **Average Salary:** $84,720. **Projected Growth:** -9.8%. **Annual Openings:** 1,000. **Education:** Bachelor's degree. **Job Zone:** 3. **Education/Training Program(s)**—Petroleum Engineering. **Related Knowledge/Courses:** Engineering and Technology; Physics; Geography; Mathematics; Administration and Management; Design; Chemistry. **Personality Type:** Realistic. **Skills Required:** Management of Financial Resources; Troubleshooting; Operations Analysis; Judgment and Decision Making; Science; Technology Design; Mathematics; Coordination. **Abilities:** Mathematical Reasoning; Originality; Number Facility; Deductive Reasoning; Written Expression. **Occupational Values:** Creativity; Authority; Social Status; Ability Utilization; Autonomy. **Interacting with Others:** Communicating with Supervisors, Peers, or Subordinates; Providing Consultation and Advice to Others; Monitoring and Controlling Resources. **Physical Work Conditions:** Sitting; Contaminants; Indoors; In an Enclosed Vehicle or Equipment; Sounds, Noise Levels Are Distracting or Uncomfortable.

Plant Scientists

Conduct research in breeding, production, and yield of plants or crops, and control of pests. **O*NET Code:** 19-1013.01. **Average Salary:** $49,610. **Projected Growth:** 9.1%. **Annual Openings:** 2,000. **Education:** Bachelor's degree. **Job Zone:** 5. **Education/Training Program(s)**—Agricultural and Horticultural Plant Breeding; Agriculture, General; Agronomy and Crop Science; Horticultural Science; Plant Protection and Integrated Pest Management; Plant Sciences, General; Plant Sciences, Other; Range Science and Management; Soil Chemistry and Physics; Soil Microbiology; Soil Science and Agronomy, General. **Related Knowledge/Courses:** Food Production; Biology; Chemistry; English Language; Communications and Media; Education and Training. **Personality Type:** Investigative. **Skills Required:** Science; Writing; Critical Thinking; Active Learning; Quality Control Analysis; Reading Comprehension; Complex Problem Solving; Operations Analysis. **Abilities:** Inductive Reasoning; Written Comprehension; Category Flexibility; Deductive Reasoning; Oral Comprehension; Mathematical Reasoning. **Occupational Values:** Autonomy; Creativity; Responsibility; Independence; Ability Utilization. **Interacting with Others:** Interpreting the Meaning of Information for Others; Providing Consultation and Advice to Others; Communicating with Persons Outside Organization. **Physical Work Conditions:** Outdoors; Minor Burns, Cuts, Bites, or Stings; Sitting; Very Hot or Cold; Specialized Protective or Safety Equipment.

Range Managers

Research or study range land management practices to provide sustained production of forage, livestock, and wildlife. **O*NET Code:** 19-1031.02. **Average Salary:** $51,160. **Projected Growth:** 4.1%. **Annual Openings:** 1,000. **Education:** Bachelor's degree. **Job Zone:** 5. **Education/Training Program(s)**—Forest Management/Forest Resources Management; Forest Sciences and Biology; Forestry, General; Forestry, Other; Land Use Planning and Management/Development; Natural Resources and Conservation, Other; Natural Resources Management and Policy; Natural Resources Management and Policy, Other; Natural Resources/Conservation, General; Water, Wetlands, and Marine Resources Management; Wildlife and Wildlands Science and Management. **Related Knowledge/Courses:** Food Production; Building and Construction; Biology; Administration and Management; Geography; Law and Government. **Personality Type:** Investigative. **Skills Required:** Operations Analysis; Judgment and Decision Making; Systems Evaluation; Systems Analysis; Science; Active Learning; Management of Personnel Resources; Complex Problem Solving. **Abilities:** Spatial Orientation; Flexibility of Closure; Far Vision; Peripheral Vision; Oral Expression. **Occupational Values:** Autonomy; Creativity; Independence; Responsibility; Ability Utilization. **Interacting with Others:** Providing Consultation and Advice to Others; Communicating with Supervisors, Peers, or Subordinates; Interpreting the Meaning of Information for Others. **Physical Work Conditions:** Outdoors; Walking and

Running; Minor Burns, Cuts, Bites, or Stings; Very Hot or Cold; Standing.

Soil Conservationists

Plan and develop coordinated practices for soil erosion control, soil and water conservation, and sound land use. **O*NET Code:** 19-1031.01. **Average Salary:** $51,160. **Projected Growth:** 4.1%. **Annual Openings:** 1,000. **Education:** Bachelor's degree. **Job Zone:** 4. **Education/Training Program(s)**—Forest Management/Forest Resources Management; Forest Sciences and Biology; Forestry, General; Forestry, Other; Land Use Planning and Management/Development; Natural Resources and Conservation, Other; Natural Resources Management and Policy; Natural Resources Management and Policy, Other; Natural Resources/Conservation, General; Water, Wetlands, and Marine Resources Management; Wildlife and Wildlands Science and Management. **Related Knowledge/Courses:** Biology; Food Production; Mathematics; Engineering and Technology; Chemistry; Physics. **Personality Type:** Investigative. **Skills Required:** Systems Analysis; Science; Systems Evaluation; Judgment and Decision Making; Complex Problem Solving; Mathematics; Monitoring; Active Learning. **Abilities:** Originality; Written Expression; Fluency of Ideas; Inductive Reasoning; Speed of Closure. **Occupational Values:** Autonomy; Creativity; Responsibility; Ability Utilization; Achievement; Independence; Variety. **Interacting with Others:** Communicating with Persons Outside Organization; Providing Consultation and Advice to Others; Interpreting the Meaning of Information for Others; Communicating with Supervisors, Peers, or Subordinates. **Physical Work Conditions:** Outdoors; Extremely Bright or Inadequate Lighting; Very Hot or Cold; Contaminants; Walking and Running.

Soil Scientists

Research or study soil characteristics, map soil types, and investigate responses of soils to known management practices to determine use capabilities of soils and effects of alternative practices on soil productivity. **O*NET Code:** 19-1013.02. **Average Salary:** $49,610. **Projected Growth:** 9.1%. **Annual Openings:** 2,000. **Education:** Bachelor's degree. **Job Zone:** 5. **Education/Training Program(s)**—Agricultural and Horticultural Plant Breeding; Agriculture, General; Agronomy and Crop Science; Horticultural Science; Plant Protection and Integrated Pest Management; Plant Sciences, General; Plant Sciences, Other; Range Science and Management; Soil Chemistry and Physics; Soil Microbiology; Soil Science and Agronomy, General. **Related Knowledge/Courses:** Food Production; Chemistry; Biology; Geography; Mathematics; Physics. **Personality Type:** Investigative. **Skills Required:** Science; Operations Analysis; Reading Comprehension; Active Learning; Writing; Critical Thinking; Mathematics; Systems Evaluation. **Abilities:** Mathematical Reasoning; Inductive Reasoning; Category Flexibility; Deductive Reasoning; Originality. **Occupational Values:** Creativity; Autonomy; Independence; Responsibility; Ability Utilization. **Interacting with Others:** Providing Consultation and Advice to Others; Interpreting the Meaning of Information for Others; Communicating with Persons Outside Organization. **Physical Work Conditions:** Outdoors; Minor Burns, Cuts, Bites, or Stings; Very Hot or Cold; Sitting; Extremely Bright or Inadequate Lighting.

Zoologists and Wildlife Biologists

Study the origins, behavior, diseases, genetics, and life processes of animals and wildlife. May specialize in wildlife research and management, including the collection and analysis of biological data to determine the environmental effects of present and potential use of land and water areas. **O*NET Code:** 19-1023.00. **Average Salary:** $49,320. **Projected Growth:** 7.7%. **Annual Openings:** 1,000. **Education:** Doctoral degree. **Job Zone:** 5. **Education/Training Program(s)**—Animal Behavior and Ethology; Animal Physiology; Cell/Cellular Biology and Anatomical Sciences, Other; Ecology; Entomology; Wildlife and Wildlands Science and Management; Wildlife Biology; Zoology/Animal Biology; Zoology/Animal Biology, Other. **Related Knowledge/Courses:** Biology; Geography; English Language; Law and Government; Administration and Management; Computers and Electronics. **Personality Type:** Investigative. **Skills Required:** Science; Management of Financial Resources; Coordination; Persuasion; Writing; Negotiation; Time Management; Management of Personnel Resources. **Abilities:** Written Expression; Inductive Reasoning; Category Flexibility; Problem Sensitivity; Oral Comprehension; Oral Expression. **Occupational Values:** Autonomy; Creativity; Achievement; Ability Utilization; Variety; Recognition; Responsibility. **Interacting with Others:** Communicating with Persons Outside Organization; Communicating with Supervisors, Peers, or Subordinates; Establishing and Maintaining Interpersonal Relationships. **Physical Work Conditions:** In an Enclosed Vehicle or Equipment; Outdoors; Very Hot or Cold; Sitting; Sounds, Noise Levels Are Distracting or Uncomfortable.

01.03 Resource Technologies for Plants, Animals, and the Environment

Agricultural Technicians

Set up and maintain laboratory and collect and record data to assist scientist in biology or related agricultural science experiments. **O*NET Code:** 19-4011.01. **Average Salary:** $29,170. **Projected Growth:** 9.3%. **Annual Openings:** 3,000. **Education:** Associate degree. **Job Zone:** 2. **Education/Training Program(s)**—Agricultural Animal Breeding; Agronomy and Crop Science; Animal Nutrition; Animal Sciences, General; Animal/Livestock Husbandry and Production; Crop Production; Dairy Science; Food Science. **Related Knowledge/Courses:** Biology; Food Production; Medicine and Dentistry. **Personality Type:** Realistic. **Skills Required:** Science. **Abilities:** Static Strength; Mathematical Reasoning; Dynamic Strength; Reaction Time; Dynamic

Flexibility; Sound Localization. **Occupational Values:** Supervision, Technical; Variety; Advancement. **Interacting with Others:** Communicating with Supervisors, Peers, or Subordinates; Establishing and Maintaining Interpersonal Relationships; Assisting and Caring for Others; Performing Administrative Activities. **Physical Work Conditions:** Disease or Infections; Kneeling, Crouching, Stooping, or Crawling; Outdoors; Walking and Running; Standing; Spend Time Bending or Twisting the Body.

Environmental Science and Protection Technicians, Including Health

Performs laboratory and field tests to monitor the environment and investigate sources of pollution, including those that affect health. Under direction of an environmental scientist or specialist, may collect samples of gases, soil, water, and other materials for testing and take corrective actions as assigned. **O*NET Code:** 19-4091.00. **Average Salary:** $35,790. **Projected Growth:** 36.8%. **Annual Openings:** 4,000. **Education:** Associate degree. **Job Zone:** 4. **Education/ Training Program(s)**—Environmental Science; Environmental Studies; Physical Science Technologies/Technicians, Other; Science Technologies/Technicians, Other. **Related Knowledge/Courses:** Biology; Engineering and Technology; Chemistry; Customer and Personal Service; Education and Training; Physics. **Personality Type:** Investigative. **Skills Required:** Science; Persuasion; Active Learning; Instructing; Critical Thinking; Reading Comprehension; Social Perceptiveness; Troubleshooting. **Abilities:** Inductive Reasoning; Written Expression; Mathematical Reasoning; Category Flexibility; Oral Expression; Flexibility of Closure. **Occupational Values:** Creativity; Recognition; Independence; Variety; Security; Advancement; Responsibility. **Interacting with Others:** Communicating with Supervisors, Peers, or Subordinates; Establishing and Maintaining Interpersonal Relationships; Resolving Conflicts and Negotiating with Others. **Physical Work Conditions:** Very Hot or Cold; In an Enclosed Vehicle or Equipment; Contaminants; Outdoors; Sounds, Noise Levels Are Distracting or Uncomfortable.

Food Science Technicians

Perform standardized qualitative and quantitative tests to determine physical or chemical properties of food or beverage products. **O*NET Code:** 19-4011.02. **Average Salary:** $29,170. **Projected Growth:** 9.3%. **Annual Openings:** 3,000. **Education:** Associate degree. **Job Zone:** 2. **Education/Training Program(s)**—Food Science. **Related Knowledge/Courses:** Chemistry; Biology; Food Production; Mathematics; English Language; Production and Processing. **Personality Type:** Realistic. **Skills Required:** Science; Mathematics; Quality Control Analysis; Active Learning; Writing; Operation Monitoring; Reading Comprehension; Critical Thinking. **Abilities:** Visual Color Discrimination; Number Facility; Category Flexibility; Mathematical Reasoning; Written Expression. **Occupational Values:** Security; Variety; Working Conditions; Advancement; Supervision, Human Relations. **Interacting with Others:** Interpreting the Meaning of Information for Others; Communicating with Supervisors, Peers, or Subordinates; Monitoring and Controlling Resources. **Physical Work Conditions:** Indoors; Common Protective or Safety Equipment; Sitting; Using Hands on Objects, Tools, or Controls; Standing.

Food Scientists and Technologists

Use chemistry, microbiology, engineering, and other sciences to study the principles underlying the processing and deterioration of foods; analyze food content to determine levels of vitamins, fat, sugar, and protein; discover new food sources; research ways to make processed foods safe, palatable, and healthful; and apply food science knowledge to determine best ways to process, package, preserve, store, and distribute food. **O*NET Code:** 19-1012.00. **Average Salary:** $49,610. **Projected Growth:** 9.1%. **Annual Openings:** 2,000. **Education:** Bachelor's degree. **Job Zone:** 4. **Education/ Training Program(s)**—Agriculture, General; Food Science; Food Technology and Processing; International Agriculture. **Related Knowledge/Courses:** Food Production; Production and Processing; Chemistry; Biology; Law and Government; Administration and Management. **Personality Type:** Investigative. **Skills Required:** Science; Active Learning; Operations Analysis; Quality Control Analysis; Critical Thinking; Judgment and Decision Making; Systems Evaluation; Systems Analysis. **Abilities:** Written Comprehension; Fluency of Ideas; Inductive Reasoning; Deductive Reasoning; Written Expression; Originality. **Occupational Values:** Autonomy; Creativity; Responsibility; Security; Ability Utilization. **Interacting with Others:** Interpreting the Meaning of Information for Others; Communicating with Supervisors, Peers, or Subordinates; Providing Consultation and Advice to Others. **Physical Work Conditions:** Indoors; Sitting; Minor Burns, Cuts, Bites, or Stings.

Geological Data Technicians

Measure, record, and evaluate geological data, using sonic, electronic, electrical, seismic, or gravity-measuring instruments to prospect for oil or gas. May collect and evaluate core samples and cuttings. **O*NET Code:** 19-4041.01. **Average Salary:** $40,770. **Projected Growth:** 1.3%. **Annual Openings:** 1,000. **Education:** Associate degree. **Job Zone:** 3. **Education/Training Program(s)**—Petroleum Technology/ Technician. **Related Knowledge/Courses:** Physics; Clerical; Engineering and Technology; Administration and Management; Mechanical; Production and Processing. **Personality Type:** Realistic. **Skills Required:** Science; Reading Comprehension; Mathematics; Speaking; Programming; Writing; Installation; Repairing. **Abilities:** Mathematical Reasoning; Speed of Closure; Control Precision; Fluency of Ideas; Written Comprehension; Number Facility. **Occupational Values:** Variety; Authority; Creativity; Compensation; Supervision, Technical. **Interacting with Others:** Communicating with Supervisors, Peers, or Subordinates; Coordinating the Work and Activities of Others; Communicating with Persons Outside Organization. **Physical Work Conditions:** Outdoors; Hazardous Equipment; Extremely Bright or Inadequate Lighting; Standing; Very Hot or Cold.

Geological Sample Test Technicians

Test and analyze geological samples, crude oil, or petroleum products to detect presence of petroleum, gas, or mineral deposits indicating potential for exploration and production or to determine physical and chemical properties to ensure that products meet quality standards. **O*NET Code:** 19-4041.02. **Average Salary:** $40,770. **Projected Growth:** 1.3%. **Annual Openings:** 1,000. **Education:** Associate degree. **Job Zone:** 3. **Education/Training Program(s)**—Petroleum Technology/Technician. **Related Knowledge/Courses:** Physics; Mechanical; Personnel and Human Resources; Engineering and Technology; Chemistry; Mathematics. **Personality Type:** Realistic. **Skills Required:** Science; Management of Personnel Resources; Equipment Maintenance; Quality Control Analysis; Repairing; Coordination; Troubleshooting; Mathematics. **Abilities:** Visual Color Discrimination; Mathematical Reasoning; Flexibility of Closure; Number Facility; Wrist-Finger Speed. **Occupational Values:** Advancement; Supervision, Technical; Authority; Co-workers; Company Policies and Practices. **Interacting with Others:** Communicating with Supervisors, Peers, or Subordinates; Establishing and Maintaining Interpersonal Relationships; Interpreting the Meaning of Information for Others. **Physical Work Conditions:** Outdoors; Minor Burns, Cuts, Bites, or Stings; Walking and Running; Common Protective or Safety Equipment; Extremely Bright or Inadequate Lighting.

01.04 General Farming

Agricultural Equipment Operators

Drive and control farm equipment to till soil and to plant, cultivate, and harvest crops. May perform tasks such as crop baling or hay bucking. May operate stationary equipment to perform post-harvest tasks such as husking, shelling, threshing, and ginning. **O*NET Code:** 45-2091.00. **Average Salary:** $18,300. **Projected Growth:** 7.3%. **Annual Openings:** 14,000. **Education:** Moderate-term on-the-job training. **Job Zone:** 2. **Education/Training Program(s)**—Agricultural Power Machinery Operation. **Related Knowledge/Courses:** Food Production; Mechanical; Chemistry; Physics; Transportation; Engineering and Technology; Biology; Foreign Language. **Personality Type:** Realistic. **Skills Required:** Repairing; Equipment Maintenance; Operation Monitoring; Operation and Control; Management of Personnel Resources; Technology Design; Management of Material Resources; Science; Systems Analysis. **Abilities:** Hearing Sensitivity; Static Strength; Multilimb Coordination; Stamina; Dynamic Strength. **Occupational Values:** Moral Values; Authority; Variety; Independence; Autonomy. **Interacting with Others:** Coordinating the Work and Activities of Others; Communicating with Supervisors, Peers, or Subordinates; Establishing and Maintaining Interpersonal Relationships. **Physical Work Conditions:** Hazardous Equipment; Outdoors; Minor Burns, Cuts, Bites, or Stings; Very Hot or Cold; Contaminants.

Farmworkers, Farm and Ranch Animals

Attend to live farm, ranch, or aquacultural animals that may include cattle, sheep, swine, goats, horses and other equines, poultry, finfish, shellfish, and bees. Attend to animals produced for animal products such as meat, fur, skins, feathers, eggs, milk, and honey. Duties may include feeding, watering, herding, grazing, castrating, branding, de-beaking, weighing, catching, and loading animals. May maintain records on animals; examine animals to detect diseases and injuries; assist in birth deliveries; and administer medications, vaccinations, or insecticides as appropriate. May clean and maintain animal housing areas. **O*NET Code:** 45-2093.00. **Average Salary:** $17,200. **Projected Growth:** 4.4%. **Annual Openings:** 12,000. **Education:** Short-term on-the-job training. **Job Zone:** 1. **Education/Training Program(s)**—Animal/Livestock Husbandry and Production; Aquaculture; Plant Nursery Operations and Management. **Related Knowledge/Courses:** Food Production; Biology; Medicine and Dentistry; Transportation; Building and Construction. **Personality Type:** Realistic. **Skills Required:** Repairing; Equipment Maintenance. **Abilities:** Static Strength; Multilimb Coordination; Trunk Strength; Dynamic Strength; Speed of Limb Movement; Explosive Strength. **Occupational Values:** Variety; Moral Values; Independence. **Interacting with Others:** Monitoring and Controlling Resources; Communicating with Supervisors, Peers, or Subordinates; Performing Administrative Activities. **Physical Work Conditions:** Minor Burns, Cuts, Bites, or Stings; Outdoors; Walking and Running; Kneeling, Crouching, Stooping, or Crawling; Spend Time Bending or Twisting the Body.

General Farmworkers

Apply pesticides, herbicides, and fertilizer to crops and livestock; plant, maintain, and harvest food crops; and tend livestock and poultry. Repair farm buildings and fences. Duties may include operating milking machines and other dairy processing equipment, supervising seasonal help, irrigating crops, and hauling livestock products to market. **O*NET Code:** 45-2092.02. **Average Salary:** $15,700. **Projected Growth:** 4.0%. **Annual Openings:** 142,000. **Education:** Short-term on-the-job training. **Job Zone:** 1. **Education/Training Program(s)**—Agricultural Production Operations, General; Crop Production. **Related Knowledge/Courses:** Food Production; Building and Construction; Mechanical; Chemistry; Transportation; Biology. **Personality Type:** Realistic. **Skills Required:** Repairing; Equipment Maintenance; Operation and Control; Operation Monitoring; Management of Personnel Resources; Installation; Management of Material Resources; Troubleshooting. **Abilities:** Static Strength; Extent Flexibility; Response Orientation; Explosive Strength; Multilimb Coordination; Dynamic Strength. **Occupational Values:** Variety; Moral Values; Independence. **Interacting with Others:** Coordinating the Work and Activities of Others; Monitoring and Controlling Resources; Communicating with Supervisors, Peers, or Subordinates; Establishing and Maintaining Interpersonal Relationships. **Physical Work Conditions:** Outdoors; Hazardous Equipment; Very Hot or Cold; Extremely Bright or Inadequate Lighting; Contaminants; Walking and Running.

01.05 Nursery, Groundskeeping, and Pest Control

Landscaping and Groundskeeping Workers

Landscape or maintain grounds of property, using hand or power tools or equipment. Workers typically perform a variety of tasks, which may include any combination of the following: sod laying, mowing, trimming, planting, watering, fertilizing, digging, raking, sprinkler installation, and installation of mortarless segmental concrete masonry wall units. **O*NET Code:** 37-3011.00. **Average Salary:** $20,170. **Projected Growth:** 22.0%. **Annual Openings:** 203,000. **Education:** Short-term on-the-job training. **Job Zone:** 1. **Education/Training Program(s)**—Landscaping and Groundskeeping; Turf and Turfgrass Management. **Related Knowledge/Courses:** Chemistry; Building and Construction; Mechanical; Biology. **Personality Type:** Realistic. **Skills Required:** Equipment Maintenance; Repairing; Operation and Control; Installation. **Abilities:** Stamina; Trunk Strength; Explosive Strength; Dynamic Strength; Static Strength. **Occupational Values:** Moral Values; Independence. **Interacting with Others:** Communicating with Supervisors, Peers, or Subordinates; Communicating with Persons Outside Organization; Establishing and Maintaining Interpersonal Relationships. **Physical Work Conditions:** Outdoors; Spend Time Bending or Twisting the Body; Walking and Running; Kneeling, Crouching, Stooping, or Crawling; Minor Burns, Cuts, Bites, or Stings.

Nursery Workers

Work in nursery facilities or at customer location planting, cultivating, harvesting, and transplanting trees, shrubs, or plants. **O*NET Code:** 45-2092.01. **Average Salary:** $15,700. **Projected Growth:** 4.0%. **Annual Openings:** 142,000. **Education:** Short-term on-the-job training. **Job Zone:** 1. **Education/Training Program(s)**—Agricultural Production Operations, General; Crop Production. **Related Knowledge/Courses:** Biology; Administration and Management. **Personality Type:** Realistic. **Skills Required:** Science. **Abilities:** Speed of Limb Movement; Dynamic Flexibility; Dynamic Strength; Extent Flexibility; Static Strength; Trunk Strength. **Occupational Values:** Moral Values; Supervision, Technical; Independence; Supervision, Human Relations. **Interacting with Others:** Communicating with Persons Outside Organization; Communicating with Supervisors, Peers, or Subordinates; Performing for or Working Directly with the Public. **Physical Work Conditions:** Outdoors; Standing; Minor Burns, Cuts, Bites, or Stings; Common Protective or Safety Equipment; Kneeling, Crouching, Stooping, or Crawling.

Pest Control Workers

Spray or release chemical solutions or toxic gases and set traps to kill pests and vermin, such as mice, termites, and roaches, that infest buildings and surrounding areas. **O*NET Code:** 37-2021.00. **Average Salary:** $25,750. **Projected Growth:** 17.0%. **Annual Openings:** 11,000. **Education:** Moderate-term on-the-job training. **Job Zone:** 2. **Education/Training Program(s)**—Agricultural/Farm Supplies Retailing and Wholesaling. **Related Knowledge/Courses:** Chemistry; Mechanical; Biology. **Personality Type:** Realistic. **Skills Required:** Mathematics; Operation and Control; Management of Personnel Resources; Judgment and Decision Making; Operation Monitoring; Equipment Selection. **Abilities:** Extent Flexibility; Trunk Strength; Gross Body Coordination; Depth Perception; Information Ordering. **Occupational Values:** Independence; Supervision, Technical; Social Service. **Interacting with Others:** Establishing and Maintaining Interpersonal Relationships; Communicating with Supervisors, Peers, or Subordinates; Communicating with Persons Outside Organization. **Physical Work Conditions:** Specialized Protective or Safety Equipment; Hazardous Conditions; Contaminants; Minor Burns, Cuts, Bites, or Stings; Kneeling, Crouching, Stooping, or Crawling.

Pesticide Handlers, Sprayers, and Applicators, Vegetation

Mix or apply pesticides, herbicides, fungicides, or insecticides through sprays, dusts, vapors, soil incorporation, or chemical application on trees, shrubs, lawns, or botanical crops. Usually requires specific training and state or federal certification. **O*NET Code:** 37-3012.00. **Average Salary:** $25,750. **Projected Growth:** 9.7%. **Annual Openings:** 5,000. **Education:** Moderate-term on-the-job training. **Job Zone:** 2. **Education/Training Program(s)**—Landscaping and Groundskeeping; Plant Nursery Operations and Management; Turf and Turfgrass Management. **Related Knowledge/Courses:** Chemistry; Mechanical; Engineering and Technology; Physics; Food Production. **Personality Type:** Realistic. **Skills Required:** Operation and Control; Equipment Maintenance; Repairing. **Abilities:** Dynamic Flexibility; Explosive Strength; Dynamic Strength; Stamina; Static Strength. **Occupational Values:** Independence; Supervision, Technical. **Interacting with Others:** Communicating with Supervisors, Peers, or Subordinates; Establishing and Maintaining Interpersonal Relationships; Communicating with Persons Outside Organization. **Physical Work Conditions:** Outdoors; Contaminants; Hazardous Conditions; Standing; Very Hot or Cold.

Tree Trimmers and Pruners

Cut away dead or excess branches from trees or shrubs to maintain right-of-way for roads, sidewalks, or utilities or to improve appearance, health, and value of tree. Prune or treat trees or shrubs, using handsaws, pruning hooks, sheers, and clippers. May use truck-mounted lifts and power pruners. May fill cavities in trees to promote healing and prevent deterioration. **O*NET Code:** 37-3013.00. **Average Salary:** $25,880. **Projected Growth:** 18.6%. **Annual Openings:** 11,000. **Education:** Short-term on-the-job training. **Job Zone:** 2. **Education/Training Program(s)**—Applied Horticulture/Horticultural Business Services, Other. **Related Knowledge/Courses:** Biology; Chemistry; Mechanical. **Personality Type:** Realistic. **Skills Required:** Operation and Control. **Abilities:** Explosive Strength; Multilimb

Coordination; Dynamic Strength; Extent Flexibility; Gross Body Coordination. **Occupational Values:** Moral Values; Independence. **Interacting with Others:** Communicating with Supervisors, Peers, or Subordinates; Communicating with Persons Outside Organization; Establishing and Maintaining Interpersonal Relationships. **Physical Work Conditions:** Outdoors; High Places; Minor Burns, Cuts, Bites, or Stings; Specialized Protective or Safety Equipment; Climbing Ladders, Scaffolds, or Poles.

01.06 Forestry and Logging

Fallers

Use axes or chainsaws to fell trees, using knowledge of tree characteristics and cutting techniques to control direction of fall and minimize tree damage. **O*NET Code:** 45-4021.00. **Average Salary:** $26,740. **Projected Growth:** -3.4%. **Annual Openings:** 3,000. **Education:** Moderate-term on-the-job training. **Job Zone:** 1. **Education/Training Program(s)**—Forest Resources Production and Management. **Related Knowledge/Courses:** Public Safety and Security; Mechanical. **Personality Type:** Realistic. **Skills Required:** Coordination; Equipment Selection; Operation and Control; Repairing. **Abilities:** Explosive Strength; Static Strength; Dynamic Strength; Stamina; Speed of Limb Movement. **Occupational Values:** Moral Values; Supervision, Technical; Activity. **Interacting with Others:** Communicating with Supervisors, Peers, or Subordinates; Establishing and Maintaining Interpersonal Relationships; Assisting and Caring for Others; Coordinating the Work and Activities of Others; Monitoring and Controlling Resources. **Physical Work Conditions:** Outdoors; Hazardous Equipment; Minor Burns, Cuts, Bites, or Stings; Exposed to Whole Body Vibration; Standing.

Forest and Conservation Technicians

Compile data pertaining to size, content, condition, and other characteristics of forest tracts under direction of foresters; train and lead forest workers in forest propagation and fire prevention and suppression. May assist conservation scientists in managing, improving, and protecting rangelands and wildlife habitats and help provide technical assistance regarding the conservation of soil, water, and related natural resources. **O*NET Code:** 19-4093.00. **Average Salary:** $31,980. **Projected Growth:** 4.0%. **Annual Openings:** 2,000. **Education:** Associate degree. **Job Zone:** No data available. **Education/Training Program(s)**—Forest Management/Forest Resources Management; Forest Resources Production and Management; Forest Sciences and Biology; Forest Technology/Technician; Forestry, General; Forestry, Other; Land Use Planning and Management/Development; Natural Resources and Conservation, Other; Natural Resources Management and Policy, Other; Natural Resources/Conservation, General; Urban Forestry; Water, Wetlands, and Marine Resources Management. **Related Knowledge/Courses:** No data available. **Personality Type:** No data available. **Skills Required:** No data available. **Abilities:** No data available.

Occupational Values: No data available. **Interacting with Others:** No data available. **Physical Work Conditions:** No data available.

Forest and Conservation Workers

Under supervision, perform manual labor necessary to develop, maintain, or protect forest, forested areas, and woodlands through such activities as raising and transporting tree seedlings; combating insects, pests, and diseases harmful to trees; and building structures to control water, erosion, and leaching of forest soil. Includes forester aides, seedling pullers, and tree planters. **O*NET Code:** 45-4011.00. **Average Salary:** $19,540. **Projected Growth:** 4.5%. **Annual Openings:** 3,000. **Education:** Moderate-term on-the-job training. **Job Zone:** 1. **Education/Training Program(s)**—Forest Management/Forest Resources Management; Forest Resources Production and Management; Forest Sciences and Biology; Forestry, General; Forestry, Other; Natural Resources and Conservation, Other; Natural Resources Management and Policy, Other; Natural Resources/Conservation, General; Urban Forestry; Wood Science and Wood Products/Pulp and Paper Technology. **Related Knowledge/Courses:** Biology; Chemistry; Public Safety and Security; Geography; Food Production; Physics. **Personality Type:** Realistic. **Skills Required:** Science; Systems Analysis. **Abilities:** Static Strength; Dynamic Strength; Spatial Orientation; Explosive Strength; Stamina. **Occupational Values:** Achievement; Independence; Variety; Moral Values; Co-workers; Responsibility; Autonomy. **Interacting with Others:** Communicating with Persons Outside Organization; Communicating with Supervisors, Peers, or Subordinates; Establishing and Maintaining Interpersonal Relationships. **Physical Work Conditions:** Outdoors; Minor Burns, Cuts, Bites, or Stings; Standing; Walking and Running; Common Protective or Safety Equipment.

Log Graders and Scalers

Grade logs or estimate the marketable content or value of logs or pulpwood in sorting yards, millpond, log deck, or similar locations. Inspect logs for defects or measure logs to determine volume. **O*NET Code:** 45-4023.00. **Average Salary:** $26,800. **Projected Growth:** -1.2%. **Annual Openings:** 2,000. **Education:** Moderate-term on-the-job training. **Job Zone:** 2. **Education/Training Program(s)**—Forest Resources Production and Management. **Related Knowledge/Courses:** Biology; Customer and Personal Service. **Personality Type:** Realistic. **Skills Required:** Mathematics; Quality Control Analysis. **Abilities:** Explosive Strength; Gross Body Coordination; Mathematical Reasoning; Number Facility; Reaction Time. **Occupational Values:** Independence; Moral Values; Supervision, Technical; Responsibility; Supervision, Human Relations. **Interacting with Others:** Communicating with Supervisors, Peers, or Subordinates; Communicating with Persons Outside Organization; Interpreting the Meaning of Information for Others; Establishing and Maintaining Interpersonal Relationships; Performing Administrative Activities. **Physical Work Conditions:** Outdoors; Standing; Common Protective or Safety Equipment; Very Hot or Cold; Spend Time Bending or Twisting the Body.

Logging Tractor Operators

Drive tractor equipped with one or more accessories, such as bulldozer blade, frontal hydraulic shear, grapple, logging arch, cable winches, hoisting rack, or crane boom, to fell tree; to skid, load and unload, or stack logs; or to pull stumps or clear brush. **O*NET Code:** 45-4022.01. **Average Salary:** $27,810. **Projected Growth:** –3.7%. **Annual Openings:** 9,000. **Education:** Moderate-term on-the-job training. **Job Zone:** 2. **Education/Training Program(s)**—Forest Resources Production and Management. **Related Knowledge/Courses:** Mechanical; Administration and Management. **Personality Type:** Realistic. **Skills Required:** Operation and Control; Operation Monitoring; Coordination. **Abilities:** Control Precision; Depth Perception; Reaction Time; Multilimb Coordination; Trunk Strength. **Occupational Values:** Moral Values; Co-workers; Supervision, Technical; Supervision, Human Relations. **Interacting with Others:** Communicating with Supervisors, Peers, or Subordinates; Establishing and Maintaining Interpersonal Relationships; Communicating with Persons Outside Organization; Assisting and Caring for Others; Coordinating the Work and Activities of Others; Monitoring and Controlling Resources. **Physical Work Conditions:** Outdoors; Exposed to Whole Body Vibration; Hazardous Equipment; Sitting; Minor Burns, Cuts, Bites, or Stings.

01.07 Hunting and Fishing

Fishers and Related Fishing Workers

Use nets, fishing rods, traps, or other equipment to catch and gather fish or other aquatic animals from rivers, lakes, or oceans for human consumption or other uses. May haul game onto ship. **O*NET Code:** 45-3011.00. **Average Salary:** $17,040. **Projected Growth:** –26.8%. **Annual Openings:** 6,000. **Education:** Short-term on-the-job training. **Job Zone:** 1. **Education/Training Program(s)**—Fishing and Fisheries Sciences and Management. **Related Knowledge/Courses:** Food Production; Transportation; Biology. **Personality Type:** Realistic. **Skills Required:** Equipment Maintenance; Repairing; Negotiation; Coordination; Equipment Selection; Operation and Control; Installation. **Abilities:** Static Strength; Glare Sensitivity; Dynamic Strength; Extent Flexibility; Far Vision. **Occupational Values:** None met the criteria. **Interacting with Others:** Selling or Influencing Others; Resolving Conflicts and Negotiating with Others; Communicating with Persons Outside Organization. **Physical Work Conditions:** Outdoors; Minor Burns, Cuts, Bites, or Stings; Standing; Contaminants; Using Hands on Objects, Tools, or Controls.

Hunters and Trappers

Hunt and trap wild animals for human consumption, fur, feed, bait, or other purposes. **O*NET Code:** 45-3021.00. **Average Salary:** $17,040. **Projected Growth:** 6.5%. **Annual Openings:** Fewer than 500. **Education:** Moderate-term on-the-job training. **Job Zone:** 2. **Education/Training Program(s)**—No data available. **Related Knowledge/Courses:** Public Safety and Security; Sales and Marketing. **Personality Type:** Realistic. **Skills Required:** Installation. **Abilities:** Speed of Limb Movement; Static Strength; Night Vision; Peripheral Vision; Explosive Strength. **Occupational Values:** Independence; Autonomy; Variety; Creativity. **Interacting with Others:** Monitoring and Controlling Resources; Communicating with Supervisors, Peers, or Subordinates; Communicating with Persons Outside Organization; Establishing and Maintaining Interpersonal Relationships. **Physical Work Conditions:** Outdoors; Minor Burns, Cuts, Bites, or Stings; Kneeling, Crouching, Stooping, or Crawling; Common Protective or Safety Equipment; Spend Time Bending or Twisting the Body.

01.08 Mining and Drilling

Construction Drillers

Operate machine to drill or bore through earth or rock. **O*NET Code:** 47-5021.01. **Average Salary:** $33,030. **Projected Growth:** 7.7%. **Annual Openings:** 3,000. **Education:** Moderate-term on-the-job training. **Job Zone:** 2. **Education/Training Program(s)**—Construction/Heavy Equipment/Earthmoving Equipment Operation; Well Drilling/Driller. **Related Knowledge/Courses:** Mechanical; Transportation; Engineering and Technology; Public Safety and Security; Physics; Geography. **Personality Type:** Realistic. **Skills Required:** Operation Monitoring; Operation and Control; Equipment Maintenance. **Abilities:** Static Strength; Response Orientation; Reaction Time; Depth Perception; Dynamic Strength. **Occupational Values:** Moral Values; Supervision, Technical. **Interacting with Others:** Communicating with Supervisors, Peers, or Subordinates; Establishing and Maintaining Interpersonal Relationships; Coordinating the Work and Activities of Others. **Physical Work Conditions:** Hazardous Equipment; Outdoors; Common Protective or Safety Equipment; Contaminants; Sounds, Noise Levels Are Distracting or Uncomfortable.

Continuous Mining Machine Operators

Operate self-propelled mining machines that rip coal, metal and nonmetal ores, rock, stone, or sand from the mine face and load it onto conveyors or into shuttle cars in a continuous operation. **O*NET Code:** 47-5041.00. **Average Salary:** $37,090. **Projected Growth:** –18.5%. **Annual Openings:** 1,000. **Education:** Moderate-term on-the-job training. **Job Zone:** 2. **Education/Training Program(s)**—Construction/Heavy Equipment/Earthmoving Equipment Operation. **Related Knowledge/Courses:** Mechanical; Engineering and Technology; Transportation; Building and Construction; Public Safety and Security; Physics. **Personality Type:** Realistic. **Skills Required:** Repairing; Operation and Control; Equipment Maintenance; Operation Monitoring; Coordination. **Abilities:** Depth Perception; Night Vision; Peripheral Vision; Multilimb Coordination; Static Strength. **Occupational Values:** Supervision, Technical; Supervision,

Human Relations; Moral Values. **Interacting with Others:** Communicating with Supervisors, Peers, or Subordinates; Establishing and Maintaining Interpersonal Relationships; Assisting and Caring for Others; Coordinating the Work and Activities of Others; Coaching and Developing Others. **Physical Work Conditions:** Outdoors; Hazardous Equipment; Common Protective or Safety Equipment; Sounds, Noise Levels Are Distracting or Uncomfortable; Extremely Bright or Inadequate Lighting.

Derrick Operators, Oil and Gas

Rig derrick equipment and operate pumps to circulate mud through drill hole. **O*NET Code:** 47-5011.00. **Average Salary:** $30,350. **Projected Growth:** 0.8%. **Annual Openings:** 2,000. **Education:** Moderate-term on-the-job training. **Job Zone:** 2. **Education/Training Program(s)—**Well Drilling/Driller. **Related Knowledge/Courses:** Mechanical; Physics; Building and Construction; Public Safety and Security; Geography; Engineering and Technology. **Personality Type:** Realistic. **Skills Required:** Repairing; Operation and Control; Equipment Maintenance; Troubleshooting; Operation Monitoring. **Abilities:** Static Strength; Extent Flexibility; Peripheral Vision; Explosive Strength; Trunk Strength; Depth Perception. **Occupational Values:** Moral Values; Supervision, Technical; Supervision, Human Relations. **Interacting with Others:** Communicating with Supervisors, Peers, or Subordinates; Establishing and Maintaining Interpersonal Relationships; Monitoring and Controlling Resources. **Physical Work Conditions:** Outdoors; Hazardous Equipment; Minor Burns, Cuts, Bites, or Stings; Sounds, Noise Levels Are Distracting or Uncomfortable; Contaminants.

Excavating and Loading Machine Operators

Operate machinery equipped with scoops, shovels, or buckets to excavate and load loose materials. **O*NET Code:** 53-7032.01. **Average Salary:** $31,810. **Projected Growth:** 8.9%. **Annual Openings:** 14,000. **Education:** Moderate-term on-the-job training. **Job Zone:** 2. **Education/Training Program(s)—**Construction/Heavy Equipment/Earthmoving Equipment Operation. **Related Knowledge/Courses:** Mechanical; Engineering and Technology; Physics. **Personality Type:** Realistic. **Skills Required:** Operation and Control; Operation Monitoring; Repairing; Equipment Maintenance; Management of Personnel Resources; Troubleshooting; Equipment Selection; Installation. **Abilities:** Multilimb Coordination; Depth Perception; Spatial Orientation; Reaction Time; Control Precision. **Occupational Values:** Authority; Supervision, Technical; Compensation; Moral Values; Advancement; Co-workers; Supervision, Human Relations. **Interacting with Others:** Communicating with Supervisors, Peers, or Subordinates; Coordinating the Work and Activities of Others; Establishing and Maintaining Interpersonal Relationships. **Physical Work Conditions:** Outdoors; Exposed to Whole Body Vibration; Hazardous Equipment; Very Hot or Cold; Sounds, Noise Levels Are Distracting or Uncomfortable.

Explosives Workers, Ordnance Handling Experts, and Blasters

Place and detonate explosives to demolish structures or to loosen, remove, or displace earth, rock, or other materials. May perform specialized handling, storage, and accounting procedures. Includes seismograph shooters. **O*NET Code:** 47-5031.00. **Average Salary:** $35,500. **Projected Growth:** 2.0%. **Annual Openings:** 1,000. **Education:** Moderate-term on-the-job training. **Job Zone:** 2. **Education/Training Program(s)—**Blasting/Blaster. **Related Knowledge/Courses:** Public Safety and Security; Physics; Engineering and Technology; Transportation; Telecommunications; Building and Construction. **Personality Type:** Realistic. **Skills Required:** Operation Monitoring; Operation and Control; Equipment Maintenance; Troubleshooting; Repairing; Installation; Equipment Selection; Technology Design; Management of Material Resources. **Abilities:** Extent Flexibility; Spatial Orientation; Reaction Time; Response Orientation; Depth Perception. **Occupational Values:** Supervision, Technical; Authority; Moral Values; Compensation. **Interacting with Others:** Communicating with Supervisors, Peers, or Subordinates; Establishing and Maintaining Interpersonal Relationships; Coordinating the Work and Activities of Others; Monitoring and Controlling Resources. **Physical Work Conditions:** Hazardous Conditions; Outdoors; Common Protective or Safety Equipment; Hazardous Equipment; Sounds, Noise Levels Are Distracting or Uncomfortable.

Helpers—Extraction Workers

Help extraction craft workers, such as earth drillers, blasters and explosives workers, derrick operators, and mining machine operators, by performing duties of lesser skill. Duties include supplying equipment or cleaning work area. **O*NET Code:** 47-5081.00. **Average Salary:** $26,380. **Projected Growth:** 3.9%. **Annual Openings:** 6,000. **Education:** Short-term on-the-job training. **Job Zone:** 1. **Education/Training Program(s)—**No data available. **Related Knowledge/Courses:** Physics; Mechanical; Transportation; Production and Processing; Engineering and Technology. **Personality Type:** Realistic. **Skills Required:** Equipment Maintenance; Repairing; Operation Monitoring; Technology Design; Operation and Control. **Abilities:** Static Strength; Explosive Strength; Stamina; Dynamic Strength; Extent Flexibility. **Occupational Values:** Supervision, Technical; Advancement; Moral Values; Co-workers; Supervision, Human Relations. **Interacting with Others:** Communicating with Supervisors, Peers, or Subordinates; Establishing and Maintaining Interpersonal Relationships; Assisting and Caring for Others. **Physical Work Conditions:** Outdoors; Exposed to Whole Body Vibration; Extremely Bright or Inadequate Lighting; Hazardous Equipment; Sounds, Noise Levels Are Distracting or Uncomfortable; Contaminants.

Loading Machine Operators, Underground Mining

Operate underground loading machine to load coal, ore, or rock into shuttle or mine car or onto conveyors. Loading equipment may include power shovels, hoisting engines equipped with cable-drawn scraper or scoop, or machines equipped with gathering arms and conveyor. **O*NET Code:** 53-7033.00. **Average Salary:** $32,840. **Projected Growth:** 8.9%. **Annual Openings:** 14,000. **Education:** Moderate-term on-the-job training. **Job Zone:** 2. **Education/Training Program(s)—**Ground Transportation, Other. **Related**

Knowledge/Courses: Mechanical; Engineering and Technology; Physics; Public Safety and Security; Transportation; Production and Processing. **Personality Type:** Realistic. **Skills Required:** Repairing; Equipment Maintenance; Operation and Control; Operation Monitoring. **Abilities:** Night Vision; Depth Perception; Peripheral Vision; Spatial Orientation; Static Strength; Sound Localization. **Occupational Values:** Supervision, Technical; Independence; Supervision, Human Relations; Moral Values; Advancement. **Interacting with Others:** Establishing and Maintaining Interpersonal Relationships; Communicating with Supervisors, Peers, or Subordinates; Assisting and Caring for Others; Monitoring and Controlling Resources. **Physical Work Conditions:** Hazardous Equipment; Outdoors; Common Protective or Safety Equipment; Extremely Bright or Inadequate Lighting; Minor Burns, Cuts, Bites, or Stings.

Mine Cutting and Channeling Machine Operators

Operate machinery—such as longwall shears, plows, and cutting machines—to cut or channel along the face or seams of coal mines, stone quarries, or other mining surfaces to facilitate blasting, separating, or removing minerals or materials from mines or from the earth's surface. **O*NET Code:** 47-5042.00. **Average Salary:** $37,000. **Projected Growth:** –18.5%. **Annual Openings:** 1,000. **Education:** Moderate-term on-the-job training. **Job Zone:** 2. **Education/Training Program(s)**—Construction/Heavy Equipment/Earthmoving Equipment Operation. **Related Knowledge/Courses:** Mechanical; Building and Construction; Engineering and Technology; Transportation; Public Safety and Security; Physics. **Personality Type:** Realistic. **Skills Required:** Operation and Control; Operation Monitoring; Repairing; Equipment Maintenance; Coordination; Troubleshooting. **Abilities:** Hearing Sensitivity; Depth Perception; Night Vision; Peripheral Vision; Multilimb Coordination. **Occupational Values:** Supervision, Technical; Moral Values; Co-workers; Supervision, Human Relations; Advancement. **Interacting with Others:** Communicating with Supervisors, Peers, or Subordinates; Coordinating the Work and Activities of Others; Establishing and Maintaining Interpersonal Relationships. **Physical Work Conditions:** Outdoors; Common Protective or Safety Equipment; Hazardous Conditions; Hazardous Equipment; Sounds, Noise Levels Are Distracting or Uncomfortable; Extremely Bright or Inadequate Lighting.

Rock Splitters, Quarry

Separate blocks of rough-dimension stone from quarry mass, using jackhammer and wedges. **O*NET Code:** 47-5051.00. **Average Salary:** $25,950. **Projected Growth:** 14.3%. **Annual Openings:** Fewer than 500. **Education:** Moderate-term on-the-job training. **Job Zone:** 2. **Education/Training Program(s)**—No data available. **Related Knowledge/Courses:** Mechanical; Physics; Public Safety and Security; Building and Construction; Engineering and Technology; Mathematics. **Personality Type:** Realistic. **Skills Required:** Operation and Control. **Abilities:** Static Strength; Explosive Strength; Dynamic Strength; Trunk Strength; Depth Perception. **Occupational Values:** Moral Values; Independence. **Interacting with Others:** Communicating with Supervisors,

Peers, or Subordinates; Coordinating the Work and Activities of Others; Establishing and Maintaining Interpersonal Relationships; Assisting and Caring for Others; Providing Consultation and Advice to Others. **Physical Work Conditions:** Outdoors; Common Protective or Safety Equipment; Hazardous Equipment; Sounds, Noise Levels Are Distracting or Uncomfortable; Exposed to Whole Body Vibration.

Roof Bolters, Mining

Operate machinery to install roof support bolts in underground mine. **O*NET Code:** 47-5061.00. **Average Salary:** $38,690. **Projected Growth:** –27.7%. **Annual Openings:** 1,000. **Education:** Moderate-term on-the-job training. **Job Zone:** 2. **Education/Training Program(s)**—No data available. **Related Knowledge/Courses:** Mechanical; Transportation; Education and Training; Public Safety and Security; Medicine and Dentistry; Law and Government. **Personality Type:** Realistic. **Skills Required:** Installation; Operation and Control; Equipment Maintenance; Repairing; Instructing; Equipment Selection; Troubleshooting; Technology Design. **Abilities:** Extent Flexibility; Manual Dexterity; Control Precision; Dynamic Strength; Explosive Strength; Gross Body Coordination. **Occupational Values:** Supervision, Technical; Moral Values; Supervision, Human Relations. **Interacting with Others:** Communicating with Supervisors, Peers, or Subordinates; Assisting and Caring for Others; Establishing and Maintaining Interpersonal Relationships; Training and Teaching Others. **Physical Work Conditions:** Sounds, Noise Levels Are Distracting or Uncomfortable; Contaminants; Hazardous Conditions; Extremely Bright or Inadequate Lighting; Hazardous Equipment.

Rotary Drill Operators, Oil and Gas

Set up or operate a variety of drills to remove petroleum products from the earth and to find and remove core samples for testing during oil and gas exploration. **O*NET Code:** 47-5012.00. **Average Salary:** $34,890. **Projected Growth:** 1.5%. **Annual Openings:** 2,000. **Education:** Moderate-term on-the-job training. **Job Zone:** 3. **Education/Training Program(s)**—Well Drilling/Driller. **Related Knowledge/Courses:** Mechanical; Physics; Engineering and Technology; Geography; Building and Construction; Transportation. **Personality Type:** Realistic. **Skills Required:** Repairing; Operation Monitoring; Operation and Control; Equipment Maintenance; Equipment Selection. **Abilities:** Depth Perception; Static Strength; Multilimb Coordination; Control Precision; Spatial Orientation. **Occupational Values:** Compensation; Supervision, Technical; Company Policies and Practices; Supervision, Human Relations; Advancement. **Interacting with Others:** Establishing and Maintaining Interpersonal Relationships; Communicating with Supervisors, Peers, or Subordinates; Performing Administrative Activities. **Physical Work Conditions:** Outdoors; Hazardous Equipment; Minor Burns, Cuts, Bites, or Stings; Hazardous Conditions; Contaminants.

Roustabouts, Oil and Gas

Assemble or repair oil field equipment, using hand and power tools. Perform other tasks as needed. **O*NET Code:** 47-5071.00. **Average Salary:** $21,890. **Projected Growth:** 6.4%.

Annual Openings: 5,000. **Education:** Short-term on-the-job training. **Job Zone:** 2. **Education/Training Program(s)—** Heavy/Industrial Equipment Maintenance Technologies, Other. **Related Knowledge/Courses:** Mechanical; Building and Construction; Engineering and Technology; Physics; Geography; Transportation. **Personality Type:** Realistic. **Skills Required:** Repairing; Installation; Troubleshooting; Equipment Maintenance. **Abilities:** Static Strength; Dynamic Strength; Explosive Strength; Stamina; Trunk Strength. **Occupational Values:** Moral Values; Supervision, Technical; Supervision, Human Relations. **Interacting with Others:** Establishing and Maintaining Interpersonal Relationships; Assisting and Caring for Others; Communicating with Supervisors, Peers, or Subordinates. **Physical Work Conditions:** Outdoors; Hazardous Equipment; Sounds, Noise Levels Are Distracting or Uncomfortable; Very Hot or Cold; Kneeling, Crouching, Stooping, or Crawling.

Service Unit Operators, Oil, Gas, and Mining

Operate equipment to increase oil flow from producing wells or to remove stuck pipe, casing, tools, or other obstructions from drilling wells. May also perform similar services in mining exploration operations. **O*NET Code:** 47-5013.00. **Average Salary:** $30,850. **Projected Growth:** -0.8%. **Annual Openings:** 2,000. **Education:** Moderate-term on-the-job training. **Job Zone:** 4. **Education/Training Program(s)—**Mining Technology/Technician. **Related Knowledge/Courses:** Mechanical; Physics; Engineering and Technology; Geography; Economics and Accounting; Public Safety and Security. **Personality Type:** Realistic. **Skills Required:** Operation Monitoring; Operation and Control; Equipment Selection; Management of Personnel Resources; Troubleshooting; Monitoring; Coordination; Judgment and Decision Making. **Abilities:** Depth Perception; Hearing Sensitivity; Auditory Attention; Sound Localization; Control Precision. **Occupational Values:** Authority; Supervision, Technical; Compensation; Supervision, Human Relations; Co-workers. **Interacting with Others:** Coordinating the Work and Activities of Others; Communicating with Supervisors, Peers, or Subordinates; Guiding, Directing, and Motivating Subordinates. **Physical Work Conditions:** Outdoors; Hazardous Equipment; Hazardous Conditions; Minor Burns, Cuts, Bites, or Stings; Extremely Bright or Inadequate Lighting.

Shuttle Car Operators

Operate diesel or electric-powered shuttle car in underground mine to transport materials from working face to mine cars or conveyor. **O*NET Code:** 53-7111.00. **Average Salary:** $38,810. **Projected Growth:** -31.3%. **Annual Openings:** 1,000. **Education:** Moderate-term on-the-job training. **Job Zone:** 2. **Education/Training Program(s)—**No data available. **Related Knowledge/Courses:** Mechanical; Transportation; Law and Government; Public Safety and Security; Chemistry; Psychology. **Personality Type:** Realistic. **Skills Required:** Operation and Control; Equipment Maintenance; Repairing; Coordination; Troubleshooting; Operation Monitoring; Instructing; Active Learning; Installation. **Abilities:** Depth Perception; Night Vision; Rate Control; Peripheral Vision; Multilimb Coordination. **Occupational Values:** Independence; Supervision, Technical; Supervision, Human Relations; Moral Values; Advancement. **Interacting with Others:** Establishing and Maintaining Interpersonal Relationships; Communicating with Supervisors, Peers, or Subordinates; Assisting and Caring for Others. **Physical Work Conditions:** Contaminants; Sounds, Noise Levels Are Distracting or Uncomfortable; Hazardous Conditions; Cramped Work Space, Awkward Positions; Extremely Bright or Inadequate Lighting; Exposed to Whole Body Vibration.

Well and Core Drill Operators

Operate machine to drill wells and take samples or cores for analysis of strata. **O*NET Code:** 47-5021.02. **Average Salary:** $33,030. **Projected Growth:** 7.7%. **Annual Openings:** 3,000. **Education:** Long-term on-the-job training. **Job Zone:** 3. **Education/Training Program(s)—**Construction/Heavy Equipment/Earthmoving Equipment Operation; Well Drilling/Driller. **Related Knowledge/Courses:** Mechanical; Physics; Transportation; Engineering and Technology; Geography; Public Safety and Security. **Personality Type:** Realistic. **Skills Required:** Operation Monitoring; Equipment Maintenance; Repairing; Operation and Control; Science; Equipment Selection; Installation; Management of Material Resources. **Abilities:** Response Orientation; Static Strength; Depth Perception; Control Precision; Reaction Time. **Occupational Values:** Moral Values; Advancement; Supervision, Technical. **Interacting with Others:** Communicating with Supervisors, Peers, or Subordinates; Establishing and Maintaining Interpersonal Relationships; Monitoring and Controlling Resources. **Physical Work Conditions:** Hazardous Equipment; Outdoors; Sounds, Noise Levels Are Distracting or Uncomfortable; Common Protective or Safety Equipment; Very Hot or Cold.

Wellhead Pumpers

Operate power pumps and auxiliary equipment to produce flow of oil or gas from wells in oil field. **O*NET Code:** 53-7073.00. **Average Salary:** $32,440. **Projected Growth:** -11.7%. **Annual Openings:** 1,000. **Education:** Moderate-term on-the-job training. **Job Zone:** 2. **Education/Training Program(s)—**No data available. **Related Knowledge/Courses:** Mechanical; Physics; Production and Processing; Engineering and Technology; Chemistry; Public Safety and Security. **Personality Type:** Realistic. **Skills Required:** Repairing; Equipment Maintenance; Operation Monitoring; Installation; Troubleshooting; Systems Analysis; Operation and Control; Technology Design. **Abilities:** Control Precision; Gross Body Coordination. **Occupational Values:** Independence; Supervision, Technical; Supervision, Human Relations; Moral Values. **Interacting with Others:** Communicating with Supervisors, Peers, or Subordinates; Establishing and Maintaining Interpersonal Relationships; Communicating with Persons Outside Organization. **Physical Work Conditions:** Very Hot or Cold; Contaminants; Hazardous Conditions; In an Enclosed Vehicle or Equipment; Outdoors.

© 2006, JIST Works

02 Architecture and Construction

02.01   **Managerial Work in Architecture and Construction**

02.02   **Architectural Design**

02.03   **Architecture/Construction Engineering Technologies**

02.04   **Construction Crafts**

02.05   **Systems and Equipment Installation, Maintenance, and Repair**

02.06   **Construction Support/Labor**

02.01 Managerial Work in Architecture and Construction

Construction Managers

Plan, direct, coordinate, or budget, usually through subordinate supervisory personnel, activities concerned with the construction and maintenance of structures, facilities, and systems. Participate in the conceptual development of a construction project and oversee its organization, scheduling, and implementation. **O*NET Code:** 11-9021.00. **Average Salary:** $67,620. **Projected Growth:** 12.0%. **Annual Openings:** 47,000. **Education:** Bachelor's degree. **Job Zone:** 3. **Education/Training Program(s)**—Business Administration and Management, General; Business/Commerce, General; Construction Engineering Technology/Technician; Operations Management and Supervision. **Related Knowledge/Courses:** Building and Construction; Design; Administration and Management; Public Safety and Security; Customer and Personal Service; Mechanical. **Personality Type:** Enterprising. **Skills Required:** Coordination; Negotiation; Troubleshooting; Installation; Repairing; Instructing; Management of Material Resources; Persuasion; Management of Financial Resources. **Abilities:** Written Expression; Written Comprehension; Oral Expression; Oral Comprehension; Speech Recognition. **Occupational Values:** Authority; Autonomy; Variety; Responsibility; Compensation. **Interacting with Others:** Coordinating the Work and Activities of Others; Resolving Conflicts and Negotiating with Others; Communicating with Persons Outside Organization; Establishing and Maintaining Interpersonal Relationships. **Physical Work Conditions:** In an Enclosed Vehicle or Equipment; Sounds, Noise Levels Are Distracting or Uncomfortable; Contaminants; Sitting; Very Hot or Cold.

First-Line Supervisors and Manager/Supervisors—Construction Trades Workers

Directly supervise and coordinate activities of construction trades workers and their helpers. Manager/Supervisors are generally found in smaller establishments, where they perform both supervisory and management functions, such as accounting, marketing, and personnel work, and may also engage in the same construction trades work as the workers they supervise. **O*NET Code:** 47-1011.01. **Average Salary:** $49,390. **Projected Growth:** 14.1%. **Annual Openings:** 67,000. **Education:** Work experience in a related occupation. **Job Zone:** 4. **Education/Training Program(s)**—Building/Construction Finishing, Management, and Inspection, Other; Building/Construction Site Management/Manager; Building/Home/Construction Inspection/Inspector; Building/Property Maintenance and Management; Carpentry/Carpenter; Concrete Finishing/Concrete Finisher; Construction Trades, Other; Drywall Installation/Drywaller; Electrical and Power Transmission Installation/Installer, General; Electrical and Power Transmission Installers, Other; Electrician; Glazier; Lineworker; Mason/Masonry; Painting/Painter and Wall Coverer; Plumbing Technology/Plumber; Roofer; Well Drilling/Driller. **Related Knowledge/Courses:** Building and Construction; Personnel and Human Resources; Administration and Management; Design; Engineering and Technology; Mechanical. **Personality Type:** Enterprising. **Skills Required:** Management of Personnel Resources; Management of Material Resources; Installation; Time Management; Coordination; Persuasion; Instructing; Quality Control Analysis; Systems Evaluation. **Abilities:** Spatial Orientation; Explosive Strength; Gross Body Equilibrium; Static Strength; Dynamic Strength; Extent Flexibility. **Occupational Values:** Authority; Responsibility; Autonomy; Variety; Co-workers. **Interacting with Others:** Communicating with Supervisors, Peers, or Subordinates; Coordinating the Work and Activities of Others; Establishing and Maintaining Interpersonal Relationships; Guiding, Directing, and Motivating Subordinates. **Physical Work Conditions:** Outdoors; Common Protective or Safety Equipment; Hazardous Equipment; High Places; Climbing Ladders, Scaffolds, or Poles.

02.02 Architectural Design

Architects, Except Landscape and Naval

Plan and design structures, such as private residences, office buildings, theaters, factories, and other structural property. **O*NET Code:** 17-1011.00. **Average Salary:** $58,630. **Projected Growth:** 17.3%. **Annual Openings:** 8,000. **Education:** Bachelor's degree. **Job Zone:** 5. **Education/Training Program(s)**—Architectural History and Criticism, General; Architecture (BArch, BA/BS, MArch, MA/MS, PhD); Architecture and Related Services, Other; Environmental Design/Architecture. **Related Knowledge/Courses:** Building and Construction; Design; Engineering and Technology; Law and Government; Public Safety and Security; Fine Arts. **Personality Type:** Artistic. **Skills Required:** Operations Analysis; Management of Financial Resources; Coordination; Management of Personnel Resources; Negotiation; Complex Problem Solving; Persuasion; Active Learning. **Abilities:** Originality; Visualization; Deductive Reasoning; Fluency of Ideas; Category Flexibility. **Occupational Values:** Creativity; Recognition; Ability Utilization; Social Status; Achievement. **Interacting with Others:** Coordinating the Work and Activities of Others; Establishing and Maintaining Interpersonal Relationships; Communicating with Persons Outside Organization. **Physical Work Conditions:** Sitting; Physical Proximity; Extremely Bright or Inadequate Lighting; In an Enclosed Vehicle or Equipment; Very Hot or Cold.

Landscape Architects

Plan and design land areas for such projects as parks and other recreational facilities; airports; highways; hospitals; schools; land subdivisions; and commercial, industrial, and residential sites. **O*NET Code:** 17-1012.00. **Average Salary:**

$50,780. **Projected Growth:** 22.2%. **Annual Openings:** 2,000. **Education:** Bachelor's degree. **Job Zone:** 4. **Education/Training Program(s)**—Environmental Design/ Architecture; Landscape Architecture (BS, BSLA, BLA, MSLA, MLA, PhD). **Related Knowledge/Courses:** Design; Building and Construction; Geography; Engineering and Technology; Biology; Sales and Marketing. **Personality Type:** Artistic. **Skills Required:** Coordination; Operations Analysis; Management of Financial Resources; Persuasion; Social Perceptiveness; Time Management; Instructing; Complex Problem Solving. **Abilities:** Originality; Fluency of Ideas; Visualization; Category Flexibility; Mathematical Reasoning; Far Vision. **Occupational Values:** Ability Utilization; Creativity; Social Status; Recognition; Achievement. **Interacting with Others:** Coordinating the Work and Activities of Others; Communicating with Persons Outside Organization; Communicating with Supervisors, Peers, or Subordinates; Establishing and Maintaining Interpersonal Relationships. **Physical Work Conditions:** Very Hot or Cold; In an Enclosed Vehicle or Equipment; Outdoors; Sitting; Extremely Bright or Inadequate Lighting.

02.03
Architecture/Construction Engineering Technologies

Architectural Drafters

Prepare detailed drawings of architectural designs and plans for buildings and structures according to specifications provided by architect. **O*NET Code:** 17-3011.01. **Average Salary:** $38,180. **Projected Growth:** 4.2%. **Annual Openings:** 14,000. **Education:** Associate degree. **Job Zone:** 3. **Education/Training Program(s)**—Architectural Drafting and Architectural CAD/CADD; Architectural Technology/ Technician; CAD/CADD Drafting and/or Design Technology/Technician; Civil Drafting and Civil Engineering CAD/CADD; Drafting and Design Technology/Technician, General. **Related Knowledge/Courses:** Design; Building and Construction; Computers and Electronics; Engineering and Technology; Mathematics; Customer and Personal Service; Public Safety and Security. **Personality Type:** Realistic. **Skills Required:** Coordination; Active Learning; Operations Analysis; Persuasion; Technology Design; Critical Thinking; Monitoring; Instructing; Service Orientation. **Abilities:** Visualization; Originality; Deductive Reasoning; Mathematical Reasoning; Visual Color Discrimination. **Occupational Values:** Working Conditions; Ability Utilization; Independence; Social Status; Compensation. **Interacting with Others:** Communicating with Persons Outside Organization; Establishing and Maintaining Interpersonal Relationships; Communicating with Supervisors, Peers, or Subordinates. **Physical Work Conditions:** Sitting; Sounds, Noise Levels Are Distracting or Uncomfortable; Physical Proximity; Indoors; Very Hot or Cold.

Civil Drafters

Prepare drawings and topographical and relief maps used in civil engineering projects, such as highways, bridges, pipelines, flood control projects, and water and sewerage control systems. **O*NET Code:** 17-3011.02. **Average Salary:** $38,180. **Projected Growth:** 4.2%. **Annual Openings:** 14,000. **Education:** Postsecondary vocational training. **Job Zone:** 3. **Education/Training Program(s)**—Architectural Drafting and Architectural CAD/CADD; Architectural Technology/Technician; CAD/CADD Drafting and/or Design Technology/Technician; Civil Drafting and Civil Engineering CAD/CADD; Drafting and Design Technology/Technician, General. **Related Knowledge/Courses:** Design; Engineering and Technology; Computers and Electronics; Geography; Mathematics; Law and Government. **Personality Type:** Realistic. **Skills Required:** Mathematics; Coordination; Instructing; Operations Analysis; Active Learning; Time Management; Technology Design; Active Listening. **Abilities:** Visualization; Mathematical Reasoning; Flexibility of Closure; Far Vision; Originality. **Occupational Values:** Ability Utilization; Working Conditions; Achievement; Advancement; Autonomy. **Interacting with Others:** Communicating with Supervisors, Peers, or Subordinates; Establishing and Maintaining Interpersonal Relationships; Communicating with Persons Outside Organization. **Physical Work Conditions:** Sitting; Physical Proximity; Sounds, Noise Levels Are Distracting or Uncomfortable; Indoors; Extremely Bright or Inadequate Lighting.

Construction and Building Inspectors

Inspect structures, using engineering skills, to determine structural soundness and compliance with specifications, building codes, and other regulations. Inspections may be general in nature or may be limited to a specific area, such as electrical systems or plumbing. **O*NET Code:** 47-4011.00. **Average Salary:** $43,100. **Projected Growth:** 13.8%. **Annual Openings:** 10,000. **Education:** Work experience in a related occupation. **Job Zone:** 3. **Education/Training Program(s)**— Building/Home/Construction Inspection/Inspector. **Related Knowledge/Courses:** Building and Construction; Design; Engineering and Technology; Public Safety and Security; Customer and Personal Service; Administration and Management; Computers and Electronics. **Personality Type:** Conventional. **Skills Required:** Persuasion; Time Management; Mathematics; Coordination; Active Learning; Instructing; Negotiation; Critical Thinking. **Abilities:** Problem Sensitivity; Auditory Attention; Gross Body Equilibrium; Deductive Reasoning; Speed of Closure. **Occupational Values:** Responsibility; Autonomy; Independence; Advancement; Supervision, Technical. **Interacting with Others:** Communicating with Supervisors, Peers, or Subordinates; Resolving Conflicts and Negotiating with Others; Establishing and Maintaining Interpersonal Relationships. **Physical Work Conditions:** Outdoors; In an Enclosed Vehicle or Equipment; Sounds, Noise Levels Are Distracting or Uncomfortable; Very Hot or Cold; Extremely Bright or Inadequate Lighting.

Electrical Drafters

Develop specifications and instructions for installation of voltage transformers, overhead or underground cables, and related electrical equipment used to conduct electrical energy from transmission lines or high-voltage distribution lines to consumers. **O*NET Code:** 17-3012.02. **Average Salary:** $42,620. **Projected Growth:** 0.7%. **Annual Openings:** 5,000. **Education:** Associate degree. **Job Zone:** 4. **Education/ Training Program(s)**—Electrical/Electronics Drafting and Electrical/Electronics CAD/CADD. **Related Knowledge/ Courses:** Design; Engineering and Technology; Building and Construction; Physics; Administration and Management; Economics and Accounting. **Personality Type:** Conventional. **Skills Required:** Operations Analysis; Management of Personnel Resources; Judgment and Decision Making; Management of Financial Resources; Systems Analysis; Management of Material Resources; Mathematics; Technology Design. **Abilities:** Originality; Speed of Closure; Spatial Orientation; Number Facility; Mathematical Reasoning; Visualization. **Occupational Values:** Authority; Ability Utilization; Autonomy; Achievement; Advancement; Creativity. **Interacting with Others:** Communicating with Supervisors, Peers, or Subordinates; Guiding, Directing, and Motivating Subordinates; Establishing and Maintaining Interpersonal Relationships; Coordinating the Work and Activities of Others; Providing Consultation and Advice to Others. **Physical Work Conditions:** Hazardous Conditions; Sitting; Exposed to Radiation; Hazardous Equipment; Extremely Bright or Inadequate Lighting.

Surveyors

Make exact measurements and determine property boundaries. Provide data relevant to the shape, contour, gravitation, location, elevation, or dimension of land or land features on or near the earth's surface for engineering, mapmaking, mining, land evaluation, construction, and other purposes. **O*NET Code:** 17-1022.00. **Average Salary:** $41,930. **Projected Growth:** 4.2%. **Annual Openings:** 6,000. **Education:** Bachelor's degree. **Job Zone:** 3. **Education/Training Program(s)**—Surveying Technology/Surveying. **Related Knowledge/Courses:** Building and Construction; Geography; Design; Mathematics; Engineering and Technology; Computers and Electronics. **Personality Type:** Investigative. **Skills Required:** Mathematics; Coordination; Management of Personnel Resources; Critical Thinking; Instructing; Time Management; Active Listening; Speaking; Equipment Selection; Troubleshooting. **Abilities:** Spatial Orientation; Mathematical Reasoning; Far Vision; Number Facility; Written Expression. **Occupational Values:** Achievement; Authority; Social Status; Variety; Autonomy. **Interacting with Others:** Guiding, Directing, and Motivating Subordinates; Resolving Conflicts and Negotiating with Others; Monitoring and Controlling Resources. **Physical Work Conditions:** Very Hot or Cold; Outdoors; Minor Burns, Cuts, Bites, or Stings; In an Enclosed Vehicle or Equipment; Extremely Bright or Inadequate Lighting.

02.04 Construction Crafts

Boat Builders and Shipwrights

Construct and repair ships or boats according to blueprints.

O*NET Code: 47-2031.05. **Average Salary:** $34,870. **Projected Growth:** 10.1%. **Annual Openings:** 193,000. **Education:** Long-term on-the-job training. **Job Zone:** 4. **Education/Training Program(s)**—Carpentry/Carpenter. **Related Knowledge/Courses:** Building and Construction; Design; Mechanical; Engineering and Technology; Production and Processing; Physics. **Personality Type:** Realistic. **Skills Required:** Installation; Repairing; Operations Analysis; Technology Design; Equipment Selection; Equipment Maintenance; Mathematics; Quality Control Analysis. **Abilities:** Visualization; Static Strength; Manual Dexterity; Dynamic Strength; Extent Flexibility. **Occupational Values:** Ability Utilization; Achievement; Variety; Supervision, Technical; Compensation; Recognition; Moral Values. **Interacting with Others:** Communicating with Supervisors, Peers, or Subordinates; Communicating with Persons Outside Organization; Establishing and Maintaining Interpersonal Relationships. **Physical Work Conditions:** Outdoors; Standing; Climbing Ladders, Scaffolds, or Poles; Hazardous Equipment; Using Hands on Objects, Tools, or Controls.

Boilermakers

Construct, assemble, maintain, and repair stationary steam boilers and boiler house auxiliaries. Align structures or plate sections to assemble boiler frame tanks or vats, following blueprints. Work involves use of hand and power tools, plumb bobs, levels, wedges, dogs, or turnbuckles. Assist in testing assembled vessels. Direct cleaning of boilers and boiler furnaces. Inspect and repair boiler fittings, such as safety valves, regulators, automatic-control mechanisms, water columns, and auxiliary machines. **O*NET Code:** 47-2011.00. **Average Salary:** $43,210. **Projected Growth:** 1.7%. **Annual Openings:** 2,000. **Education:** Long-term on-the-job training. **Job Zone:** 4. **Education/Training Program(s)**—Boilermaking/Boilermaker. **Related Knowledge/Courses:** Mechanical; Building and Construction; Engineering and Technology; Physics; Design; Public Safety and Security. **Personality Type:** Realistic. **Skills Required:** Installation; Repairing; Equipment Maintenance; Troubleshooting; Quality Control Analysis; Technology Design; Systems Analysis; Operation Monitoring. **Abilities:** Static Strength; Extent Flexibility; Manual Dexterity; Auditory Attention; Multilimb Coordination. **Occupational Values:** Supervision, Technical; Compensation; Supervision, Human Relations; Moral Values; Ability Utilization; Creativity. **Interacting with Others:** Communicating with Supervisors, Peers, or Subordinates; Establishing and Maintaining Interpersonal Relationships; Coordinating the Work and Activities of Others. **Physical Work Conditions:** Hazardous Equipment; Minor Burns, Cuts, Bites, or Stings; Common Protective or Safety Equipment; Using Hands on Objects, Tools, or Controls; Extremely Bright or Inadequate Lighting.

Brattice Builders

Build doors or brattices (ventilation walls or partitions) in underground passageways to control the proper circulation of air through the passageways and to the working places. **O*NET Code:** 47-2031.06. **Average Salary:** $34,870. **Projected Growth:** 10.1%. **Annual Openings:** 193,000. **Education:** Moderate-term on-the-job training. **Job Zone:** 2.

Education/Training Program(s)—Carpentry/Carpenter. **Related Knowledge/Courses:** Building and Construction; Physics; Engineering and Technology; Mechanical. **Personality Type:** Realistic. **Skills Required:** Installation; Technology Design; Operations Analysis; Equipment Selection; Quality Control Analysis. **Abilities:** Extent Flexibility; Dynamic Strength; Static Strength; Explosive Strength; Stamina. **Occupational Values:** Moral Values; Supervision, Technical; Supervision, Human Relations. **Interacting with Others:** Communicating with Supervisors, Peers, or Subordinates; Training and Teaching Others; Establishing and Maintaining Interpersonal Relationships; Coordinating the Work and Activities of Others; Coaching and Developing Others. **Physical Work Conditions:** Standing; Hazardous Conditions; Common Protective or Safety Equipment; Outdoors; Cramped Work Space, Awkward Positions; Specialized Protective or Safety Equipment.

Brickmasons and Blockmasons

Lay and bind building materials, such as brick, structural tile, concrete block, cinder block, glass block, and terra-cotta block, with mortar and other substances to construct or repair walls, partitions, arches, sewers, and other structures. **O*NET Code:** 47-2021.00. **Average Salary:** $42,070. **Projected Growth:** 14.2%. **Annual Openings:** 21,000. **Education:** Long-term on-the-job training. **Job Zone:** 2. **Education/Training Program(s)**—Mason/Masonry. **Related Knowledge/Courses:** Building and Construction; Design; Public Safety and Security; Mathematics; Production and Processing; Mechanical. **Personality Type:** Realistic. **Skills Required:** Equipment Maintenance; Mathematics; Instructing; Installation; Coordination; Social Perceptiveness; Management of Financial Resources; Technology Design. **Abilities:** Dynamic Strength; Extent Flexibility; Trunk Strength; Manual Dexterity; Static Strength. **Occupational Values:** Moral Values; Variety; Compensation; Independence; Ability Utilization; Achievement. **Interacting with Others:** Coordinating the Work and Activities of Others; Establishing and Maintaining Interpersonal Relationships; Coaching and Developing Others. **Physical Work Conditions:** Very Hot or Cold; Outdoors; Hazardous Equipment; Contaminants; Sounds, Noise Levels Are Distracting or Uncomfortable.

Carpet Installers

Lay and install carpet from rolls or blocks on floors. Install padding and trim flooring materials. **O*NET Code:** 47-2041.00. **Average Salary:** $32,840. **Projected Growth:** 16.8%. **Annual Openings:** 10,000. **Education:** Moderate-term on-the-job training. **Job Zone:** 1. **Education/Training Program(s)**—Construction Trades, Other. **Related Knowledge/Courses:** Public Safety and Security; Sales and Marketing; Transportation; Building and Construction; Customer and Personal Service; Personnel and Human Resources. **Personality Type:** Realistic. **Skills Required:** Installation; Equipment Selection; Repairing; Management of Personnel Resources; Coordination; Mathematics; Complex Problem Solving; Active Learning; Instructing. **Abilities:** Static Strength; Dynamic Strength; Extent Flexibility; Stamina; Trunk Strength. **Occupational Values:** Moral Values; Social Service. **Interacting with Others:** Communicating with Supervisors, Peers, or Subordinates;

Coaching and Developing Others; Establishing and Maintaining Interpersonal Relationships. **Physical Work Conditions:** Kneeling, Crouching, Stooping, or Crawling; Very Hot or Cold; Keeping or Regaining Balance; Minor Burns, Cuts, Bites, or Stings; Extremely Bright or Inadequate Lighting.

Ceiling Tile Installers

Apply or mount acoustical tiles or blocks, strips, or sheets of shock-absorbing materials to ceilings and walls of buildings to reduce or reflect sound. Materials may be of decorative quality. Includes lathers who fasten wooden, metal, or rock-board lath to walls, ceilings, or partitions of buildings to provide support base for plaster, fire-proofing, or acoustical material. **O*NET Code:** 47-2081.01. **Average Salary:** $34,040. **Projected Growth:** 21.4%. **Annual Openings:** 17,000. **Education:** Moderate-term on-the-job training. **Job Zone:** 4. **Education/Training Program(s)**—Drywall Installation/Drywaller. **Related Knowledge/Courses:** Building and Construction; Design; Mathematics; Physics. **Personality Type:** Realistic. **Skills Required:** None met the criteria. **Abilities:** Extent Flexibility; Gross Body Equilibrium; Dynamic Flexibility; Multilimb Coordination; Speed of Limb Movement; Explosive Strength. **Occupational Values:** Moral Values; Independence; Supervision, Human Relations; Compensation; Supervision, Technical. **Interacting with Others:** Establishing and Maintaining Interpersonal Relationships; Communicating with Supervisors, Peers, or Subordinates; Communicating with Persons Outside Organization; Monitoring and Controlling Resources. **Physical Work Conditions:** Minor Burns, Cuts, Bites, or Stings; Hazardous Equipment; Climbing Ladders, Scaffolds, or Poles; Common Protective or Safety Equipment; High Places.

Cement Masons and Concrete Finishers

Smooth and finish surfaces of poured concrete, such as floors, walks, sidewalks, roads, or curbs, using a variety of hand and power tools. Align forms for sidewalks, curbs, or gutters; patch voids; use saws to cut expansion joints. **O*NET Code:** 47-2051.00. **Average Salary:** $30,950. **Projected Growth:** 26.1%. **Annual Openings:** 24,000. **Education:** Long-term on-the-job training. **Job Zone:** 3. **Education/Training Program(s)**—Concrete Finishing/Concrete Finisher. **Related Knowledge/Courses:** Building and Construction; Engineering and Technology; Fine Arts; Design; Geography. **Personality Type:** Realistic. **Skills Required:** Technology Design; Repairing; Operations Analysis; Installation; Science. **Abilities:** Static Strength; Stamina; Trunk Strength; Manual Dexterity; Speed of Limb Movement. **Occupational Values:** Moral Values; Compensation; Co-workers; Ability Utilization; Supervision, Technical. **Interacting with Others:** Communicating with Supervisors, Peers, or Subordinates; Establishing and Maintaining Interpersonal Relationships; Communicating with Persons Outside Organization; Coordinating the Work and Activities of Others. **Physical Work Conditions:** Outdoors; Kneeling, Crouching, Stooping, or Crawling; Spend Time Bending or Twisting the Body; Standing; Very Hot or Cold.

Commercial Divers

Work below surface of water, using scuba gear to inspect, repair, remove, or install equipment and structures. May use a variety of power and hand tools, such as drills, sledgehammers, torches, and welding equipment. May conduct tests or experiments, rig explosives, or photograph structures or marine life. **O*NET Code:** 49-9092.00. **Average Salary:** $34,070. **Projected Growth:** 10.6%. **Annual Openings:** 1,000. **Education:** Moderate-term on-the-job training. **Job Zone:** 2. **Education/Training Program(s)**—Diver, Professional and Instructor. **Related Knowledge/Courses:** Building and Construction; Mechanical; Physics; Engineering and Technology; Fine Arts; Telecommunications. **Personality Type:** Realistic. **Skills Required:** Repairing; Installation; Equipment Maintenance; Technology Design; Operation and Control. **Abilities:** Gross Body Coordination; Spatial Orientation; Night Vision; Stamina; Dynamic Strength. **Occupational Values:** Variety; Ability Utilization; Responsibility; Achievement; Social Status; Co-workers. **Interacting with Others:** Communicating with Supervisors, Peers, or Subordinates; Establishing and Maintaining Interpersonal Relationships; Interpreting the Meaning of Information for Others; Communicating with Persons Outside Organization; Assisting and Caring for Others; Coordinating the Work and Activities of Others. **Physical Work Conditions:** Specialized Protective or Safety Equipment; Common Protective or Safety Equipment; Extremely Bright or Inadequate Lighting; Outdoors; Very Hot or Cold.

Construction Carpenters

Construct, erect, install, and repair structures and fixtures of wood, plywood, and wallboard, using carpenter's hand tools and power tools. **O*NET Code:** 47-2031.01. **Average Salary:** $34,870. **Projected Growth:** 10.1%. **Annual Openings:** 193,000. **Education:** Long-term on-the-job training. **Job Zone:** 3. **Education/Training Program(s)**—Carpentry/Carpenter. **Related Knowledge/Courses:** Building and Construction; Production and Processing; Engineering and Technology; Design; Public Safety and Security; Mechanical. **Personality Type:** Realistic. **Skills Required:** Management of Personnel Resources; Management of Financial Resources; Management of Material Resources; Equipment Maintenance; Repairing; Quality Control Analysis; Service Orientation; Speaking; Time Management. **Abilities:** Extent Flexibility; Gross Body Equilibrium; Static Strength; Stamina; Gross Body Coordination. **Occupational Values:** Variety; Compensation; Creativity; Moral Values; Ability Utilization. **Interacting with Others:** Coordinating the Work and Activities of Others; Training and Teaching Others; Communicating with Supervisors, Peers, or Subordinates; Guiding, Directing, and Motivating Subordinates. **Physical Work Conditions:** Sounds, Noise Levels Are Distracting or Uncomfortable; Hazardous Equipment; Very Hot or Cold; Contaminants; Outdoors.

Crane and Tower Operators

Operate mechanical boom and cable or tower and cable equipment to lift and move materials, machines, or products in many directions. **O*NET Code:** 53-7021.00. **Average Salary:** $36,710. **Projected Growth:** 10.8%. **Annual Openings:** 5,000. **Education:** Moderate-term on-the-job training. **Job Zone:** 2. **Education/Training Program(s)**—Construction/Heavy Equipment/Earthmoving Equipment Operation; Mobil Crane Operation/Operator. **Related Knowledge/Courses:** Mechanical; Transportation; Building and Construction. **Personality Type:** Realistic. **Skills Required:** Operation and Control; Repairing; Installation; Equipment Maintenance; Operation Monitoring; Equipment Selection. **Abilities:** Multilimb Coordination; Reaction Time; Depth Perception; Control Precision; Spatial Orientation. **Occupational Values:** Supervision, Technical; Moral Values; Authority; Supervision, Human Relations. **Interacting with Others:** Communicating with Supervisors, Peers, or Subordinates; Coordinating the Work and Activities of Others; Establishing and Maintaining Interpersonal Relationships. **Physical Work Conditions:** Outdoors; Hazardous Equipment; Climbing Ladders, Scaffolds, or Poles; Extremely Bright or Inadequate Lighting; Using Hands on Objects, Tools, or Controls.

Dragline Operators

Operate power-driven crane equipment with dragline bucket to excavate or move sand, gravel, mud, or other materials. **O*NET Code:** 53-7032.02. **Average Salary:** $31,810. **Projected Growth:** 8.9%. **Annual Openings:** 14,000. **Education:** Moderate-term on-the-job training. **Job Zone:** 2. **Education/Training Program(s)**—Construction/Heavy Equipment/Earthmoving Equipment Operation. **Related Knowledge/Courses:** Building and Construction; Transportation; Physics; Engineering and Technology; Mechanical; Public Safety and Security. **Personality Type:** Realistic. **Skills Required:** Operation and Control; Operation Monitoring. **Abilities:** Depth Perception; Multilimb Coordination; Control Precision; Rate Control; Response Orientation; Far Vision. **Occupational Values:** Authority; Supervision, Technical; Moral Values. **Interacting with Others:** Communicating with Supervisors, Peers, or Subordinates; Establishing and Maintaining Interpersonal Relationships; Coordinating the Work and Activities of Others. **Physical Work Conditions:** Outdoors; Hazardous Equipment; Exposed to Whole Body Vibration; Extremely Bright or Inadequate Lighting; Very Hot or Cold.

Drywall Installers

Apply plasterboard or other wallboard to ceilings and interior walls of buildings. **O*NET Code:** 47-2081.02. **Average Salary:** $34,040. **Projected Growth:** 21.4%. **Annual Openings:** 17,000. **Education:** Moderate-term on-the-job training. **Job Zone:** 2. **Education/Training Program(s)**—Drywall Installation/Drywaller. **Related Knowledge/Courses:** Building and Construction; Design; Engineering and Technology; Mechanical. **Personality Type:** Realistic. **Skills Required:** Installation; Equipment Selection. **Abilities:** Extent Flexibility; Explosive Strength; Gross Body Equilibrium; Control Precision; Static Strength; Trunk Strength. **Occupational Values:** Supervision, Technical; Moral Values; Supervision, Human Relations; Independence. **Interacting with Others:** Communicating with Supervisors, Peers, or Subordinates; Establishing and Maintaining Interpersonal Relationships; Communicating with Persons Outside Organization. **Physical Work Conditions:** Climbing Ladders, Scaffolds, or Poles; Hazardous Equipment; Minor Burns, Cuts,

Bites, or Stings; Using Hands on Objects, Tools, or Controls; Contaminants; Standing.

Electricians

Install, maintain, and repair electrical wiring, equipment, and fixtures. Ensure that work is in accordance with relevant codes. May install or service streetlights, intercom systems, or electrical control systems. **O*NET Code:** 47-2111.00. **Average Salary:** $41,940. **Projected Growth:** 23.4%. **Annual Openings:** 65,000. **Education:** Long-term on-the-job training. **Job Zone:** 3. **Education/Training Program(s)**—Electrician. **Related Knowledge/Courses:** Building and Construction; Mechanical; Design; Production and Processing; Customer and Personal Service; Physics. **Personality Type:** Realistic. **Skills Required:** Installation; Troubleshooting; Repairing; Equipment Maintenance; Technology Design; Management of Financial Resources; Equipment Selection; Operations Analysis. **Abilities:** Extent Flexibility; Gross Body Equilibrium; Dynamic Strength; Stamina; Static Strength. **Occupational Values:** Authority; Ability Utilization; Creativity; Variety; Compensation; Responsibility. **Interacting with Others:** Establishing and Maintaining Interpersonal Relationships; Coordinating the Work and Activities of Others; Communicating with Supervisors, Peers, or Subordinates. **Physical Work Conditions:** Very Hot or Cold; Indoors, Not Environmentally Controlled; Extremely Bright or Inadequate Lighting; Sounds, Noise Levels Are Distracting or Uncomfortable; Cramped Work Space, Awkward Positions.

Fence Erectors

Erect and repair metal and wooden fences and fence gates around highways, industrial establishments, residences, or farms, using hand and power tools. **O*NET Code:** 47-4031.00. **Average Salary:** $23,170. **Projected Growth:** 13.4%. **Annual Openings:** 4,000. **Education:** Moderate-term on-the-job training. **Job Zone:** 2. **Education/Training Program(s)**—Construction Trades, Other. **Related Knowledge/Courses:** Building and Construction; Geography; Design; Public Safety and Security; Engineering and Technology; Physics. **Personality Type:** Realistic. **Skills Required:** Repairing; Equipment Selection. **Abilities:** Static Strength; Depth Perception; Extent Flexibility; Trunk Strength; Glare Sensitivity. **Occupational Values:** Moral Values. **Interacting with Others:** Performing for or Working Directly with the Public; Communicating with Supervisors, Peers, or Subordinates; Communicating with Persons Outside Organization; Establishing and Maintaining Interpersonal Relationships. **Physical Work Conditions:** Outdoors; Standing; Minor Burns, Cuts, Bites, or Stings; Using Hands on Objects, Tools, or Controls; Very Hot or Cold.

Floor Layers, Except Carpet, Wood, and Hard Tiles

Apply blocks, strips, or sheets of shock-absorbing, sound-deadening, or decorative coverings to floors. **O*NET Code:** 47-2042.00. **Average Salary:** $32,890. **Projected Growth:** 13.4%. **Annual Openings:** 4,000. **Education:** Moderate-term on-the-job training. **Job Zone:** 3. **Education/Training Program(s)**—Construction Trades, Other. **Related Knowledge/Courses:** Building and Construction; Design.

Personality Type: Realistic. **Skills Required:** Installation; Repairing. **Abilities:** Extent Flexibility; Explosive Strength; Static Strength; Trunk Strength; Multilimb Coordination. **Occupational Values:** Moral Values. **Interacting with Others:** Communicating with Supervisors, Peers, or Subordinates; Communicating with Persons Outside Organization; Establishing and Maintaining Interpersonal Relationships; Monitoring and Controlling Resources. **Physical Work Conditions:** Kneeling, Crouching, Stooping, or Crawling; Spend Time Bending or Twisting the Body; Minor Burns, Cuts, Bites, or Stings; Indoors; Hazardous Equipment.

Floor Sanders and Finishers

Scrape and sand wooden floors to smooth surfaces, using floor scraper and floor sanding machine, and apply coats of finish. **O*NET Code:** 47-2043.00. **Average Salary:** $27,630. **Projected Growth:** 4.2%. **Annual Openings:** 2,000. **Education:** Moderate-term on-the-job training. **Job Zone:** 2. **Education/Training Program(s)**—Construction Trades, Other. **Related Knowledge/Courses:** Mechanical; Administration and Management. **Personality Type:** Realistic. **Skills Required:** Equipment Maintenance; Equipment Selection. **Abilities:** Stamina; Dynamic Strength; Static Strength; Dynamic Flexibility; Speed of Limb Movement. **Occupational Values:** Moral Values. **Interacting with Others:** Communicating with Supervisors, Peers, or Subordinates; Communicating with Persons Outside Organization; Performing for or Working Directly with the Public. **Physical Work Conditions:** Contaminants; Exposed to Whole Body Vibration; Walking and Running; Using Hands on Objects, Tools, or Controls; Spend Time Bending or Twisting the Body.

Glaziers

Install glass in windows, skylights, store fronts, and display cases or on surfaces such as building fronts, interior walls, ceilings, and tabletops. **O*NET Code:** 47-2121.00. **Average Salary:** $32,210. **Projected Growth:** 17.2%. **Annual Openings:** 7,000. **Education:** Long-term on-the-job training. **Job Zone:** 3. **Education/Training Program(s)**—Glazier. **Related Knowledge/Courses:** Building and Construction; Production and Processing; Design; Geography; Engineering and Technology; Transportation. **Personality Type:** Realistic. **Skills Required:** Installation; Technology Design; Repairing; Mathematics. **Abilities:** Static Strength; Gross Body Coordination; Extent Flexibility; Gross Body Equilibrium; Stamina. **Occupational Values:** Moral Values. **Interacting with Others:** Communicating with Persons Outside Organization; Establishing and Maintaining Interpersonal Relationships; Communicating with Supervisors, Peers, or Subordinates. **Physical Work Conditions:** Minor Burns, Cuts, Bites, or Stings; Climbing Ladders, Scaffolds, or Poles; Standing; Hazardous Equipment; Kneeling, Crouching, Stooping, or Crawling; Common Protective or Safety Equipment.

Grader, Bulldozer, and Scraper Operators

Operate machines or vehicles equipped with blades to remove, distribute, level, or grade earth. **O*NET Code:** 47-2073.01. **Average Salary:** $35,050. **Projected Growth:** 10.4%.

Annual Openings: 45,000. Education: Moderate-term on-the-job training. Job Zone: 2. Education/Training Program(s)—Construction/Heavy Equipment/Earthmoving Equipment Operation; Mobil Crane Operation/Operator. Related Knowledge/Courses: Mechanical; Transportation; Physics. Personality Type: Realistic. Skills Required: Operation and Control; Repairing; Operation Monitoring; Equipment Maintenance; Equipment Selection. Abilities: Control Precision; Reaction Time; Rate Control; Explosive Strength; Response Orientation; Dynamic Strength. Occupational Values: Moral Values; Independence; Supervision, Technical. Interacting with Others: Communicating with Supervisors, Peers, or Subordinates; Assisting and Caring for Others; Coordinating the Work and Activities of Others. Physical Work Conditions: Outdoors; Exposed to Whole Body Vibration; Hazardous Equipment; Very Hot or Cold; Sounds, Noise Levels Are Distracting or Uncomfortable.

Hazardous Materials Removal Workers

Identify, remove, pack, transport, or dispose of hazardous materials, including asbestos, lead-based paint, waste oil, fuel, transmission fluid, radioactive materials, contaminated soil, etc. Specialized training and certification in hazardous materials handling or a confined entry permit are generally required. May operate earthmoving equipment or trucks. O*NET Code: 47-4041.00. Average Salary: $33,080. Projected Growth: 43.1%. Annual Openings: 8,000. Education: Moderate-term on-the-job training. Job Zone: No data available. Education/Training Program(s)—Construction Trades, Other; Hazardous Materials Management and Waste Technology/Technician; Mechanic and Repair Technologies/Technicians, Other. Related Knowledge/Courses: No data available. Personality Type: No data available. Skills Required: No data available. Abilities: No data available. Occupational Values: No data available. Interacting with Others: No data available. Physical Work Conditions: No data available.

Insulation Workers, Floor, Ceiling, and Wall

Line and cover structures with insulating materials. May work with batt, roll, or blown insulation materials. O*NET Code: 47-2131.00. Average Salary: $30,310. Projected Growth: 15.8%. Annual Openings: 9,000. Education: Moderate-term on-the-job training. Job Zone: 3. Education/Training Program(s)—Construction Trades, Other. Related Knowledge/Courses: Building and Construction; Mechanical. Personality Type: Realistic. Skills Required: Installation. Abilities: Static Strength; Trunk Strength; Wrist-Finger Speed; Gross Body Coordination. Occupational Values: Moral Values; Independence. Interacting with Others: Communicating with Supervisors, Peers, or Subordinates; Monitoring and Controlling Resources; Establishing and Maintaining Interpersonal Relationships. Physical Work Conditions: Common Protective or Safety Equipment; Standing; Contaminants; Spend Time Bending or Twisting the Body; High Places.

Insulation Workers, Mechanical

Apply insulating materials to pipes, ductwork, or other mechanical systems in order to help control and maintain temperature. O*NET Code: 47-2132.00. Average Salary:

$30,310. Projected Growth: 15.8%. Annual Openings: 9,000. Education: Moderate-term on-the-job training. Job Zone: 3. Education/Training Program(s)—Construction Trades, Other. Related Knowledge/Courses: Building and Construction; Mechanical. Personality Type: Realistic. Skills Required: Installation. Abilities: Static Strength; Trunk Strength; Wrist-Finger Speed; Gross Body Coordination. Occupational Values: Moral Values; Independence. Interacting with Others: Communicating with Supervisors, Peers, or Subordinates; Monitoring and Controlling Resources; Establishing and Maintaining Interpersonal Relationships. Physical Work Conditions: Common Protective or Safety Equipment; Standing; Contaminants; Spend Time Bending or Twisting the Body; High Places.

Manufactured Building and Mobile Home Installers

Move or install mobile homes or prefabricated buildings. O*NET Code: 49-9095.00. Average Salary: $22,860. Projected Growth: 23.3%. Annual Openings: 2,000. Education: Moderate-term on-the-job training. Job Zone: 2. Education/Training Program(s)—Building/Construction Site Management/Manager. Related Knowledge/Courses: Building and Construction; Mechanical; Design; Engineering and Technology; Physics. Personality Type: Realistic. Skills Required: Installation; Repairing; Troubleshooting; Equipment Maintenance; Quality Control Analysis; Equipment Selection; Systems Evaluation; Technology Design; Management of Material Resources. Abilities: Extent Flexibility; Control Precision; Static Strength; Trunk Strength; Visualization. Occupational Values: Variety; Supervision, Technical; Moral Values; Supervision, Human Relations. Interacting with Others: Establishing and Maintaining Interpersonal Relationships; Communicating with Supervisors, Peers, or Subordinates; Communicating with Persons Outside Organization. Physical Work Conditions: Standing; Hazardous Conditions; Outdoors; Kneeling, Crouching, Stooping, or Crawling; Climbing Ladders, Scaffolds, or Poles.

Operating Engineers

Operate several types of power construction equipment, such as compressors, pumps, hoists, derricks, cranes, shovels, tractors, scrapers, or motor graders, to excavate, move, and grade earth; erect structures; or pour concrete or other hard-surface pavement. May repair and maintain equipment in addition to other duties. O*NET Code: 47-2073.02. Average Salary: $35,050. Projected Growth: 10.4%. Annual Openings: 45,000. Education: Moderate-term on-the-job training. Job Zone: 3. Education/Training Program(s)—Construction/Heavy Equipment/Earthmoving Equipment Operation; Mobil Crane Operation/Operator. Related Knowledge/Courses: Mechanical; Building and Construction; Sales and Marketing; Physics; Engineering and Technology; Public Safety and Security. Personality Type: Realistic. Skills Required: Repairing; Operation and Control; Equipment Maintenance; Operation Monitoring; Troubleshooting. Abilities: Multilimb Coordination; Response Orientation; Control Precision; Reaction Time; Static Strength; Explosive Strength. Occupational Values: Supervision, Technical; Moral Values; Independence. Interacting with Others: Communicating with Persons Outside Organization; Selling or Influencing Others; Communicating with Supervisors, Peers, or Subordinates; Coordinating the Work and Activities of Others. **Physical Work Conditions:** Hazardous Equipment; Exposed to Whole Body Vibration; Outdoors; Common Protective or Safety Equipment; Very Hot or Cold.

Painters, Construction and Maintenance

Paint walls, equipment, buildings, bridges, and other structural surfaces, using brushes, rollers, and spray guns. May remove old paint to prepare surface prior to painting. May mix colors or oils to obtain desired color or consistency. **O*NET Code:** 47-2141.00. **Average Salary:** $29,560. **Projected Growth:** 11.6%. **Annual Openings:** 69,000. **Education:** Moderate-term on-the-job training. **Job Zone:** 4. **Education/Training Program(s)**—Painting/Painter and Wall Coverer. **Related Knowledge/Courses:** Building and Construction; Fine Arts. **Personality Type:** Realistic. **Skills Required:** None met the criteria. **Abilities:** Visual Color Discrimination; Dynamic Strength; Wrist-Finger Speed; Stamina; Static Strength. **Occupational Values:** Moral Values; Independence; Supervision, Technical. **Interacting with Others:** Communicating with Supervisors, Peers, or Subordinates; Communicating with Persons Outside Organization; Performing for or Working Directly with the Public. **Physical Work Conditions:** Standing; High Places; Climbing Ladders, Scaffolds, or Poles; Spend Time Making Repetitive Motions; Contaminants.

Paperhangers

Cover interior walls and ceilings of rooms with decorative wallpaper or fabric or attach advertising posters on surfaces, such as walls and billboards. Duties include removing old materials from surface to be papered. **O*NET Code:** 47-2142.00. **Average Salary:** $32,800. **Projected Growth:** 5.9%. **Annual Openings:** 3,000. **Education:** Moderate-term on-the-job training. **Job Zone:** 2. **Education/Training Program(s)**—Painting/Painter and Wall Coverer. **Related Knowledge/Courses:** Building and Construction; Design. **Personality Type:** Realistic. **Skills Required:** Mathematics. **Abilities:** Extent Flexibility; Stamina; Multilimb Coordination; Gross Body Equilibrium; Dynamic Strength. **Occupational Values:** Moral Values; Supervision, Technical. **Interacting with Others:** Communicating with Supervisors, Peers, or Subordinates; Monitoring and Controlling Resources; Communicating with Persons Outside Organization. **Physical Work Conditions:** Climbing Ladders, Scaffolds, or Poles; Standing; Spend Time Making Repetitive Motions; High Places; Keeping or Regaining Balance; Spend Time Bending or Twisting the Body.

Paving, Surfacing, and Tamping Equipment Operators

Operate equipment used for applying concrete, asphalt, or other materials to road beds, parking lots, or airport runways and taxiways or equipment used for tamping gravel, dirt, or other materials. Includes concrete and asphalt paving machine operators, form tampers, tamping machine operators, and stone spreader operators. **O*NET Code:** 47-2071.00. **Average Salary:** $29,360. **Projected Growth:** 12.6%. **Annual Openings:** 8,000. **Education:** Moderate-term on-the-job train-ing. **Job Zone:** 2. **Education/Training Program(s)**—Construction/Heavy Equipment/Earthmoving Equipment Operation. **Related Knowledge/Courses:** Building and Construction; Transportation; Mechanical; Public Safety and Security; Engineering and Technology; Customer and Personal Service. **Personality Type:** Realistic. **Skills Required:** Equipment Maintenance; Operation Monitoring; Repairing; Instructing; Operation and Control; Troubleshooting; Equipment Selection; Installation. **Abilities:** Control Precision; Reaction Time; Depth Perception; Explosive Strength; Peripheral Vision. **Occupational Values:** Moral Values; Supervision, Technical; Independence. **Interacting with Others:** Communicating with Persons Outside Organization; Establishing and Maintaining Interpersonal Relationships; Communicating with Supervisors, Peers, or Subordinates; Coordinating the Work and Activities of Others. **Physical Work Conditions:** Very Hot or Cold; Contaminants; Outdoors; In an Open Vehicle or Equipment; Sounds, Noise Levels Are Distracting or Uncomfortable.

Pile-Driver Operators

Operate pile drivers mounted on skids, barges, crawler treads, or locomotive cranes to drive pilings for retaining walls, bulkheads, and foundations of structures such as buildings, bridges, and piers. **O*NET Code:** 47-2072.00. **Average Salary:** $48,700. **Projected Growth:** 8.2%. **Annual Openings:** 1,000. **Education:** Moderate-term on-the-job training. **Job Zone:** 2. **Education/Training Program(s)**—Construction/Heavy Equipment/Earthmoving Equipment Operation. **Related Knowledge/Courses:** Building and Construction; Engineering and Technology; Mechanical; Physics; Transportation; Public Safety and Security. **Personality Type:** Realistic. **Skills Required:** Operation and Control; Operation Monitoring. **Abilities:** Depth Perception; Multilimb Coordination; Control Precision; Far Vision; Peripheral Vision. **Occupational Values:** Moral Values; Independence. **Interacting with Others:** Communicating with Supervisors, Peers, or Subordinates; Establishing and Maintaining Interpersonal Relationships; Coordinating the Work and Activities of Others. **Physical Work Conditions:** Outdoors; Exposed to Whole Body Vibration; Hazardous Equipment; Sounds, Noise Levels Are Distracting or Uncomfortable; Extremely Bright or Inadequate Lighting.

Pipe Fitters

Lay out, assemble, install, and maintain pipe systems, pipe supports, and related hydraulic and pneumatic equipment for steam, hot water, heating, cooling, lubricating, sprinkling, and industrial production and processing systems. **O*NET Code:** 47-2152.01. **Average Salary:** $40,980. **Projected Growth:** 18.7%. **Annual Openings:** 56,000. **Education:** Long-term on-the-job training. **Job Zone:** 3. **Education/Training Program(s)**—Pipefitting/Pipefitter and Sprinkler Fitter; Plumbing and Related Water Supply Services, Other; Plumbing Technology/Plumber. **Related Knowledge/Courses:** Building and Construction; Design; Engineering and Technology; Mechanical; Economics and Accounting; Transportation. **Personality Type:** Realistic. **Skills Required:** Installation; Repairing; Management of Personnel Resources; Coordination; Persuasion; Service Orientation; Time Management; Equipment Maintenance; Systems Analysis.

Abilities: Static Strength; Extent Flexibility; Speed of Limb Movement; Visualization; Stamina. **Occupational Values:** Moral Values; Independence; Ability Utilization; Compensation; Responsibility. **Interacting with Others:** Coordinating the Work and Activities of Others; Performing for or Working Directly with the Public; Communicating with Supervisors, Peers, or Subordinates. **Physical Work Conditions:** Very Hot or Cold; Extremely Bright or Inadequate Lighting; Indoors, Not Environmentally Controlled; Outdoors; Hazardous Equipment.

Pipelayers

Lay pipe for storm or sanitation sewers, drains, and water mains. Perform any combination of the following tasks: grade trenches or culverts, position pipe, or seal joints. **O*NET Code:** 47-2151.00. **Average Salary:** $29,040. **Projected Growth:** 11.8%. **Annual Openings:** 6,000. **Education:** Moderate-term on-the-job training. **Job Zone:** 2. **Education/Training Program(s)—**Plumbing Technology/ Plumber. **Related Knowledge/Courses:** Building and Construction; Mechanical; Design; Physics; Engineering and Technology; Geography. **Personality Type:** Realistic. **Skills Required:** Installation; Equipment Maintenance; Equipment Selection; Operation and Control. **Abilities:** Trunk Strength; Dynamic Flexibility; Stamina; Dynamic Strength; Static Strength. **Occupational Values:** Moral Values; Supervision, Technical. **Interacting with Others:** Communicating with Supervisors, Peers, or Subordinates; Coordinating the Work and Activities of Others; Assisting and Caring for Others. **Physical Work Conditions:** Outdoors; Hazardous Equipment; Extremely Bright or Inadequate Lighting; Very Hot or Cold; Using Hands on Objects, Tools, or Controls.

Pipelaying Fitters

Align pipeline section in preparation of welding. Signal tractor driver for placement of pipeline sections in proper alignment. Insert steel spacer. **O*NET Code:** 47-2152.03. **Average Salary:** $40,980. **Projected Growth:** 18.7%. **Annual Openings:** 56,000. **Education:** Moderate-term on-the-job training. **Job Zone:** 2. **Education/Training Program(s)—**Pipefitting/Pipefitter and Sprinkler Fitter; Plumbing and Related Water Supply Services, Other; Plumbing Technology/Plumber. **Related Knowledge/Courses:** Mechanical; Building and Construction. **Personality Type:** Realistic. **Skills Required:** Installation; Equipment Maintenance; Repairing. **Abilities:** Explosive Strength; Gross Body Coordination; Speed of Limb Movement; Spatial Orientation; Dynamic Flexibility; Depth Perception. **Occupational Values:** Moral Values; Supervision, Technical; Advancement. **Interacting with Others:** Communicating with Supervisors, Peers, or Subordinates; Coordinating the Work and Activities of Others; Assisting and Caring for Others. **Physical Work Conditions:** Outdoors; Standing; Hazardous Equipment; Kneeling, Crouching, Stooping, or Crawling; Spend Time Bending or Twisting the Body.

Plasterers and Stucco Masons

Apply interior or exterior plaster, cement, stucco, or similar materials. May also set ornamental plaster. **O*NET Code:** 47-2161.00. **Average Salary:** $33,230. **Projected Growth:** 13.5%. **Annual Openings:** 8,000. **Education:** Long-term on-the-job

training. **Job Zone:** 4. **Education/Training Program(s)—**Construction Trades, Other. **Related Knowledge/Courses:** Building and Construction; Design; Engineering and Technology; Fine Arts. **Personality Type:** Realistic. **Skills Required:** Coordination; Installation; Management of Personnel Resources. **Abilities:** Dynamic Flexibility; Dynamic Strength; Gross Body Equilibrium; Manual Dexterity; Extent Flexibility. **Occupational Values:** Moral Values; Co-workers; Compensation; Supervision, Technical. **Interacting with Others:** Establishing and Maintaining Interpersonal Relationships; Coordinating the Work and Activities of Others; Communicating with Supervisors, Peers, or Subordinates; Communicating with Persons Outside Organization. **Physical Work Conditions:** Climbing Ladders, Scaffolds, or Poles; High Places; Contaminants; Spend Time Bending or Twisting the Body; Common Protective or Safety Equipment.

Plumbers

Assemble, install, and repair pipes, fittings, and fixtures of heating, water, and drainage systems according to specifications and plumbing codes. **O*NET Code:** 47-2152.02. **Average Salary:** $40,980. **Projected Growth:** 18.7%. **Annual Openings:** 56,000. **Education:** Long-term on-the-job training. **Job Zone:** 3. **Education/Training Program(s)—**Pipefitting/Pipefitter and Sprinkler Fitter; Plumbing and Related Water Supply Services, Other; Plumbing Technology/Plumber. **Related Knowledge/Courses:** Physics; Building and Construction; Mechanical; Chemistry; Sales and Marketing; Design. **Personality Type:** Realistic. **Skills Required:** Installation; Repairing; Troubleshooting; Management of Financial Resources; Management of Material Resources; Coordination; Equipment Selection; Management of Personnel Resources. **Abilities:** Extent Flexibility; Static Strength; Hearing Sensitivity; Visualization; Dynamic Strength. **Occupational Values:** Compensation; Authority; Responsibility; Social Service; Moral Values. **Interacting with Others:** Performing for or Working Directly with the Public; Establishing and Maintaining Interpersonal Relationships; Communicating with Supervisors, Peers, or Subordinates. **Physical Work Conditions:** Very Hot or Cold; Contaminants; Cramped Work Space, Awkward Positions; Minor Burns, Cuts, Bites, or Stings; Outdoors.

Rail-Track Laying and Maintenance Equipment Operators

Lay, repair, and maintain track for standard or narrow-gauge railroad equipment used in regular railroad service or in plant yards, quarries, sand and gravel pits, and mines. Includes ballast cleaning machine operators and road bed tamping machine operators. **O*NET Code:** 47-4061.00. **Average Salary:** $35,830. **Projected Growth:** –11.5%. **Annual Openings:** 1,000. **Education:** Moderate-term on-the-job training. **Job Zone:** 1. **Education/Training Program(s)—**Construction/Heavy Equipment/Earthmoving Equipment Operation. **Related Knowledge/Courses:** Building and Construction; Mechanical; Transportation; Engineering and Technology; Geography; Physics. **Personality Type:** Realistic. **Skills Required:** Operation and Control; Operation Monitoring; Equipment Maintenance; Repairing. **Abilities:** Depth Perception; Multilimb Coordination; Control

Precision; Peripheral Vision; Glare Sensitivity; Sound Localization. **Occupational Values:** Moral Values; Supervision, Human Relations; Supervision, Technical. **Interacting with Others:** Establishing and Maintaining Interpersonal Relationships; Communicating with Supervisors, Peers, or Subordinates; Coordinating the Work and Activities of Others; Coaching and Developing Others. **Physical Work Conditions:** Outdoors; Hazardous Equipment; Exposed to Whole Body Vibration; Minor Burns, Cuts, Bites, or Stings; Sounds, Noise Levels Are Distracting or Uncomfortable.

Refractory Materials Repairers, Except Brickmasons

Build or repair furnaces, kilns, cupolas, boilers, converters, ladles, soaking pits, ovens, etc., using refractory materials. O*NET Code: 49-9045.00. **Average Salary:** $37,480. **Projected Growth:** 16.3%. **Annual Openings:** 155,000. **Education:** Short-term on-the-job training. **Job Zone:** 1. **Education/Training Program(s)**—Industrial Mechanics and Maintenance Technology. **Related Knowledge/Courses:** Building and Construction; Mechanical; Production and Processing; Fine Arts; Engineering and Technology; Chemistry. **Personality Type:** Realistic. **Skills Required:** Repairing; Installation; Operation and Control; Equipment Maintenance; Troubleshooting; Science; Equipment Selection; Operation Monitoring. **Abilities:** Dynamic Strength; Extent Flexibility; Static Strength; Explosive Strength; Multilimb Coordination; Stamina. **Occupational Values:** Independence; Moral Values; Variety; Company Policies and Practices; Compensation; Supervision, Human Relations. **Interacting with Others:** Communicating with Supervisors, Peers, or Subordinates; Establishing and Maintaining Interpersonal Relationships; Coordinating the Work and Activities of Others; Providing Consultation and Advice to Others. **Physical Work Conditions:** Hazardous Equipment; Very Hot or Cold; Common Protective or Safety Equipment; Climbing Ladders, Scaffolds, or Poles; Extremely Bright or Inadequate Lighting.

Reinforcing Iron and Rebar Workers

Position and secure steel bars or mesh in concrete forms in order to reinforce concrete. Use a variety of fasteners, rod-bending machines, blowtorches, and hand tools. O*NET Code: 47-2171.00. **Average Salary:** $35,710. **Projected Growth:** 16.7%. **Annual Openings:** 2,000. **Education:** Long-term on-the-job training. **Job Zone:** 3. **Education/Training Program(s)**—Construction Trades, Other. **Related Knowledge/Courses:** Building and Construction; Physics; Design; Engineering and Technology. **Personality Type:** Realistic. **Skills Required:** None met the criteria. **Abilities:** Glare Sensitivity; Static Strength; Explosive Strength; Extent Flexibility; Dynamic Strength. **Occupational Values:** Moral Values; Supervision, Technical; Independence. **Interacting with Others:** Communicating with Supervisors, Peers, or Subordinates; Establishing and Maintaining Interpersonal Relationships; Monitoring and Controlling Resources. **Physical Work Conditions:** Minor Burns, Cuts, Bites, or Stings; Common Protective or Safety Equipment; Hazardous Equipment; Outdoors; Spend Time Bending or Twisting the Body.

Riggers

Set up or repair rigging for construction projects, manufacturing plants, logging yards, or ships and shipyards or for the entertainment industry. O*NET Code: 49-9096.00. **Average Salary:** $34,350. **Projected Growth:** 14.3%. **Annual Openings:** 3,000. **Education:** Short-term on-the-job training. **Job Zone:** 3. **Education/Training Program(s)**—Construction/Heavy Equipment/Earthmoving Equipment Operation. **Related Knowledge/Courses:** Public Safety and Security; Mechanical; Engineering and Technology; Building and Construction; Physics. **Personality Type:** Realistic. **Skills Required:** Technology Design; Repairing; Coordination; Science; Installation; Operation Monitoring; Management of Personnel Resources; Operation and Control; Management of Material Resources. **Abilities:** Gross Body Equilibrium; Extent Flexibility; Dynamic Strength; Stamina; Static Strength; Depth Perception. **Occupational Values:** Authority; Moral Values; Supervision, Technical; Co-workers; Responsibility. **Interacting with Others:** Coordinating the Work and Activities of Others; Communicating with Supervisors, Peers, or Subordinates; Establishing and Maintaining Interpersonal Relationships. **Physical Work Conditions:** Climbing Ladders, Scaffolds, or Poles; High Places; Outdoors; Hazardous Equipment; Keeping or Regaining Balance; Spend Time Bending or Twisting the Body.

Roofers

Cover roofs of structures with shingles, slate, asphalt, aluminum, wood, and related materials. May spray roofs, sidings, and walls with material to bind, seal, insulate, or soundproof sections of structures. O*NET Code: 47-2181.00. **Average Salary:** $30,430. **Projected Growth:** 18.6%. **Annual Openings:** 38,000. **Education:** Moderate-term on-the-job training. **Job Zone:** 3. **Education/Training Program(s)**—Roofer. **Related Knowledge/Courses:** Building and Construction; Mechanical. **Personality Type:** Realistic. **Skills Required:** Repairing; Installation; Coordination; Equipment Selection; Operation and Control. **Abilities:** Gross Body Equilibrium; Extent Flexibility; Static Strength; Stamina; Dynamic Strength. **Occupational Values:** None met the criteria. **Interacting with Others:** Communicating with Supervisors, Peers, or Subordinates; Establishing and Maintaining Interpersonal Relationships; Communicating with Persons Outside Organization. **Physical Work Conditions:** High Places; Outdoors; Kneeling, Crouching, Stooping, or Crawling; Very Hot or Cold; Climbing Ladders, Scaffolds, or Poles; Keeping or Regaining Balance.

Rough Carpenters

Build rough wooden structures, such as concrete forms; scaffolds; tunnel, bridge, or sewer supports; billboard signs; and temporary frame shelters, according to sketches, blueprints, or oral instructions. O*NET Code: 47-2031.02. **Average Salary:** $34,870. **Projected Growth:** 10.1%. **Annual Openings:** 193,000. **Education:** Moderate-term on-the-job training. **Job Zone:** 2. **Education/Training Program(s)**—Carpentry/Carpenter. **Related Knowledge/Courses:** Building and Construction; Design; Engineering and Technology; Mechanical; Production and Processing; Public Safety and Security. **Personality Type:** Realistic. **Skills Required:**

Repairing; Installation; Management of Personnel Resources; Equipment Selection; Coordination; Mathematics; Technology Design; Equipment Maintenance. **Abilities:** Static Strength; Manual Dexterity; Visualization; Trunk Strength; Speed of Limb Movement. **Occupational Values:** Variety; Moral Values; Creativity; Compensation; Recognition. **Interacting with Others:** Coordinating the Work and Activities of Others; Communicating with Supervisors, Peers, or Subordinates; Establishing and Maintaining Interpersonal Relationships. **Physical Work Conditions:** Very Hot or Cold; Extremely Bright or Inadequate Lighting; Sounds, Noise Levels Are Distracting or Uncomfortable; Contaminants; Outdoors.

Security and Fire Alarm Systems Installers

Install, program, maintain, and repair security and fire alarm wiring and equipment. Ensure that work is in accordance with relevant codes. **O*NET Code:** 49-2098.00. **Average Salary:** $34,080. **Projected Growth:** 30.2%. **Annual Openings:** 5,000. **Education:** Postsecondary vocational training. **Job Zone:** No data available. **Education/Training Program(s)**—Electrician; Security System Installation, Repair, and Inspection Technology/Technician. **Related Knowledge/Courses:** No data available. **Personality Type:** No data available. **Skills Required:** No data available. **Abilities:** No data available. **Occupational Values:** No data available. **Interacting with Others:** No data available. **Physical Work Conditions:** No data available.

Segmental Pavers

Lay out, cut, and paste segmental paving units. Includes installers of bedding and restraining materials for the paving units. **O*NET Code:** 47-4091.00. **Average Salary:** $26,970. **Projected Growth:** 16.5%. **Annual Openings:** Fewer than 500. **Education:** Moderate-term on-the-job training. **Job Zone:** No data available. **Education/Training Program(s)**—Concrete Finishing/Concrete Finisher. **Related Knowledge/Courses:** No data available. **Personality Type:** No data available. **Skills Required:** No data available. **Abilities:** No data available. **Occupational Values:** No data available. **Interacting with Others:** No data available. **Physical Work Conditions:** No data available.

Sheet Metal Workers

Fabricate, assemble, install, and repair sheet metal products and equipment, such as ducts, control boxes, drainpipes, and furnace casings. Work may involve any of the following: setting up and operating fabricating machines to cut, bend, and straighten sheet metal; shaping metal over anvils, blocks, or forms, using hammer; operating soldering and welding equipment to join sheet metal parts; inspecting, assembling, and smoothing seams and joints of burred surfaces. **O*NET Code:** 47-2211.00. **Average Salary:** $35,400. **Projected Growth:** 19.8%. **Annual Openings:** 30,000. **Education:** Moderate-term on-the-job training. **Job Zone:** 3. **Education/Training Program(s)**—Sheet Metal Technology/Sheetworking. **Related Knowledge/Courses:** Production and Processing; Building and Construction; Design; Mechanical; Computers and Electronics; Engineering and Technology. **Personality Type:** Realistic. **Skills Required:** Installation; Technology Design; Repairing; Equipment Selection; Quality

Control Analysis; Operation and Control; Operations Analysis; Mathematics. **Abilities:** Control Precision; Static Strength; Explosive Strength; Information Ordering; Trunk Strength. **Occupational Values:** Advancement; Moral Values; Supervision, Human Relations; Supervision, Technical; Compensation; Company Policies and Practices. **Interacting with Others:** Communicating with Supervisors, Peers, or Subordinates; Coordinating the Work and Activities of Others; Performing Administrative Activities; Monitoring and Controlling Resources. **Physical Work Conditions:** Hazardous Equipment; Common Protective or Safety Equipment; Sounds, Noise Levels Are Distracting or Uncomfortable; Standing; Indoors.

Ship Carpenters and Joiners

Fabricate, assemble, install, or repair wooden furnishings in ships or boats. **O*NET Code:** 47-2031.04. **Average Salary:** $34,870. **Projected Growth:** 10.1%. **Annual Openings:** 193,000. **Education:** Moderate-term on-the-job training. **Job Zone:** 3. **Education/Training Program(s)**—Carpentry/Carpenter. **Related Knowledge/Courses:** Building and Construction; Design; Engineering and Technology; Mechanical. **Personality Type:** Realistic. **Skills Required:** Installation; Repairing; Equipment Maintenance; Operations Analysis. **Abilities:** Dynamic Flexibility; Visualization; Manual Dexterity; Stamina; Speed of Limb Movement. **Occupational Values:** Independence; Variety; Activity; Compensation; Moral Values. **Interacting with Others:** Communicating with Supervisors, Peers, or Subordinates; Communicating with Persons Outside Organization; Establishing and Maintaining Interpersonal Relationships; Assisting and Caring for Others; Coordinating the Work and Activities of Others; Performing Administrative Activities. **Physical Work Conditions:** Hazardous Equipment; Standing; Climbing Ladders, Scaffolds, or Poles; Using Hands on Objects, Tools, or Controls; Minor Burns, Cuts, Bites, or Stings; Common Protective or Safety Equipment.

Stone Cutters and Carvers

Cut or carve stone according to diagrams and patterns. **O*NET Code:** 51-9195.03. **Average Salary:** $24,470. **Projected Growth:** 6.4%. **Annual Openings:** 6,000. **Education:** Moderate-term on-the-job training. **Job Zone:** 3. **Education/Training Program(s)**—No data available. **Related Knowledge/Courses:** Fine Arts; Design; Physics; Building and Construction; Engineering and Technology; Mechanical. **Personality Type:** Realistic. **Skills Required:** Operation and Control; Equipment Selection. **Abilities:** Arm-Hand Steadiness; Visualization; Depth Perception; Wrist-Finger Speed; Extent Flexibility. **Occupational Values:** Independence; Moral Values; Recognition; Achievement; Autonomy. **Interacting with Others:** Communicating with Supervisors, Peers, or Subordinates; Establishing and Maintaining Interpersonal Relationships; Assisting and Caring for Others; Coaching and Developing Others. **Physical Work Conditions:** Common Protective or Safety Equipment; Contaminants; Using Hands on Objects, Tools, or Controls; Sounds, Noise Levels Are Distracting or Uncomfortable; Standing.

Stonemasons

Build stone structures, such as piers, walls, and abutments. Lay walks, curbstones, or special types of masonry for vats, tanks, and floors. **O*NET Code:** 47-2022.00. **Average Salary:** $34,200. **Projected Growth:** 14.1%. **Annual Openings:** 2,000. **Education:** Long-term on-the-job training. **Job Zone:** 4. **Education/Training Program(s)**—Mason/Masonry. **Related Knowledge/Courses:** Building and Construction; Design. **Personality Type:** Realistic. **Skills Required:** Repairing; Technology Design; Operation and Control; Equipment Selection. **Abilities:** Static Strength; Dynamic Strength; Explosive Strength; Speed of Limb Movement; Wrist-Finger Speed. **Occupational Values:** Compensation; Moral Values; Achievement; Independence; Ability Utilization. **Interacting with Others:** Communicating with Supervisors, Peers, or Subordinates; Establishing and Maintaining Interpersonal Relationships; Assisting and Caring for Others. **Physical Work Conditions:** Outdoors; Kneeling, Crouching, Stooping, or Crawling; Spend Time Bending or Twisting the Body; Common Protective or Safety Equipment; Spend Time Making Repetitive Motions.

Structural Iron and Steel Workers

Raise, place, and unite iron or steel girders, columns, and other structural members to form completed structures or structural frameworks. May erect metal storage tanks and assemble prefabricated metal buildings. **O*NET Code:** 47-2221.00. **Average Salary:** $41,800. **Projected Growth:** 15.9%. **Annual Openings:** 9,000. **Education:** Long-term on-the-job training. **Job Zone:** 3. **Education/Training Program(s)**—Construction Trades, Other; Metal Building Assembly/Assembler. **Related Knowledge/Courses:** Building and Construction; Mechanical; Public Safety and Security; Engineering and Technology; Physics; Design. **Personality Type:** Realistic. **Skills Required:** Installation; Coordination; Repairing; Management of Material Resources; Equipment Selection; Operation and Control; Technology Design; Equipment Maintenance. **Abilities:** Gross Body Equilibrium; Static Strength; Dynamic Strength; Explosive Strength; Trunk Strength. **Occupational Values:** Moral Values; Co-workers; Supervision, Technical; Compensation; Advancement; Supervision, Human Relations. **Interacting with Others:** Communicating with Supervisors, Peers, or Subordinates; Coordinating the Work and Activities of Others; Establishing and Maintaining Interpersonal Relationships. **Physical Work Conditions:** Common Protective or Safety Equipment; Climbing Ladders, Scaffolds, or Poles; Outdoors; Very Hot or Cold; Extremely Bright or Inadequate Lighting.

Tapers

Seal joints between plasterboard or other wallboard to prepare wall surface for painting or papering. **O*NET Code:** 47-2082.00. **Average Salary:** $39,420. **Projected Growth:** 20.8%. **Annual Openings:** 5,000. **Education:** Moderate-term on-the-job training. **Job Zone:** 2. **Education/Training Program(s)**—Construction Trades, Other. **Related Knowledge/Courses:** Building and Construction; Sales and Marketing. **Personality Type:** Realistic. **Skills Required:** None met the criteria. **Abilities:** Depth Perception; Explosive Strength; Extent Flexibility; Gross Body Equilibrium; Manual Dexterity. **Occupational Values:** Moral Values; Supervision, Technical; Independence; Supervision, Human Relations. **Interacting with Others:** Communicating with Supervisors, Peers, or Subordinates; Establishing and Maintaining Interpersonal Relationships; Communicating with Persons Outside Organization; Assisting and Caring for Others. **Physical Work Conditions:** Climbing Ladders, Scaffolds, or Poles; Contaminants; Common Protective or Safety Equipment; Minor Burns, Cuts, Bites, or Stings; Standing; Spend Time Bending or Twisting the Body.

Terrazzo Workers and Finishers

Apply a mixture of cement, sand, pigment, or marble chips to floors, stairways, and cabinet fixtures to fashion durable and decorative surfaces. **O*NET Code:** 47-2053.00. **Average Salary:** $27,970. **Projected Growth:** 15.2%. **Annual Openings:** 1,000. **Education:** Long-term on-the-job training. **Job Zone:** 3. **Education/Training Program(s)**—Building/Construction Finishing, Management, and Inspection, Other. **Related Knowledge/Courses:** Building and Construction; Engineering and Technology; Fine Arts; Design; Geography. **Personality Type:** Realistic. **Skills Required:** Technology Design; Repairing; Operations Analysis; Installation; Science. **Abilities:** Static Strength; Stamina; Trunk Strength; Manual Dexterity; Speed of Limb Movement. **Occupational Values:** Moral Values; Compensation; Co-workers; Ability Utilization; Supervision, Technical. **Interacting with Others:** Communicating with Supervisors, Peers, or Subordinates; Establishing and Maintaining Interpersonal Relationships; Communicating with Persons Outside Organization; Coordinating the Work and Activities of Others. **Physical Work Conditions:** Outdoors; Kneeling, Crouching, Stooping, or Crawling; Spend Time Bending or Twisting the Body; Standing; Very Hot or Cold.

Tile and Marble Setters

Apply hard tile, marble, and wood tile to walls, floors, ceilings, and roof decks. **O*NET Code:** 47-2044.00. **Average Salary:** $35,530. **Projected Growth:** 26.5%. **Annual Openings:** 4,000. **Education:** Long-term on-the-job training. **Job Zone:** 2. **Education/Training Program(s)**—Building/Construction Finishing, Management, and Inspection, Other. **Related Knowledge/Courses:** Building and Construction; Administration and Management; Design; Production and Processing; Economics and Accounting; Transportation. **Personality Type:** Realistic. **Skills Required:** Installation; Management of Financial Resources; Social Perceptiveness; Instructing; Mathematics; Coordination; Critical Thinking; Negotiation. **Abilities:** Extent Flexibility; Dynamic Strength; Static Strength; Arm-Hand Steadiness; Multilimb Coordination. **Occupational Values:** Moral Values; Compensation; Independence; Achievement; Supervision, Technical. **Interacting with Others:** Establishing and Maintaining Interpersonal Relationships; Coordinating the Work and Activities of Others; Training and Teaching Others. **Physical Work Conditions:** Sounds, Noise Levels Are Distracting or Uncomfortable; Contaminants; Cramped Work Space, Awkward Positions; Physical Proximity; Kneeling, Crouching, Stooping, or Crawling.

02.05 Systems and Equipment Installation, Maintenance, and Repair

Central Office and PBX Installers and Repairers

Test, analyze, and repair telephone or telegraph circuits and equipment at a central office location, using test meters and hand tools. Analyze and repair defects in communications equipment on customers' premises, using circuit diagrams, polarity probes, meters, and a telephone test set. May install equipment. **O*NET Code:** 49-2022.01. **Average Salary:** $48,740. **Projected Growth:** –0.6%. **Annual Openings:** 23,000. **Education:** Postsecondary vocational training. **Job Zone:** 4. **Education/Training Program(s)**—Communications Systems Installation and Repair Technology. **Related Knowledge/Courses:** Telecommunications; Computers and Electronics; Design; Engineering and Technology; Physics. **Personality Type:** Realistic. **Skills Required:** Installation; Repairing; Troubleshooting; Technology Design; Operation Monitoring; Science; Equipment Maintenance; Quality Control Analysis. **Abilities:** Finger Dexterity; Hearing Sensitivity; Flexibility of Closure; Visual Color Discrimination; Arm-Hand Steadiness. **Occupational Values:** Supervision, Technical; Security; Moral Values; Company Policies and Practices; Variety; Supervision, Human Relations. **Interacting with Others:** Communicating with Supervisors, Peers, or Subordinates; Communicating with Persons Outside Organization; Performing Administrative Activities. **Physical Work Conditions:** Sitting; Hazardous Equipment; Kneeling, Crouching, Stooping, or Crawling; Standing; Hazardous Conditions.

Communication Equipment Mechanics, Installers, and Repairers

Install, maintain, test, and repair communication cables and equipment. **O*NET Code:** 49-2022.03. **Average Salary:** $48,740. **Projected Growth:** –0.6%. **Annual Openings:** 23,000. **Education:** Postsecondary vocational training. **Job Zone:** 3. **Education/Training Program(s)**—Communications Systems Installation and Repair Technology. **Related Knowledge/Courses:** Telecommunications; Computers and Electronics; Design; Mechanical; Engineering and Technology. **Personality Type:** Realistic. **Skills Required:** Repairing; Installation; Troubleshooting; Equipment Maintenance; Technology Design; Quality Control Analysis; Operation Monitoring; Operation and Control. **Abilities:** Dynamic Strength; Gross Body Equilibrium; Stamina; Explosive Strength; Gross Body Coordination. **Occupational Values:** Variety; Supervision, Technical; Security; Supervision, Human Relations; Social Service. **Interacting with Others:** Communicating with Persons Outside Organization; Establishing and Maintaining Interpersonal Relationships; Communicating with Supervisors, Peers, or Subordinates. **Physical Work Conditions:** Hazardous Conditions; High Places; Outdoors; Climbing Ladders, Scaffolds, or Poles; Common Protective or Safety Equipment.

Electric Meter Installers and Repairers

Install electric meters on customers' premises or on pole. Test meters and perform necessary repairs. Turn current on/off by connecting/disconnecting service drop. **O*NET Code:** 49-9012.01. **Average Salary:** $43,280. **Projected Growth:** 12.0%. **Annual Openings:** 5,000. **Education:** Moderate-term on-the-job training. **Job Zone:** 3. **Education/Training Program(s)**—Electromechanical and Instrumentation and Maintenance Technologies/Technicians, Other. **Related Knowledge/Courses:** Mechanical; Computers and Electronics; Engineering and Technology; Design; Geography; Telecommunications. **Personality Type:** Realistic. **Skills Required:** Installation; Troubleshooting; Repairing; Technology Design; Equipment Maintenance; Science; Quality Control Analysis; Operation Monitoring. **Abilities:** Visual Color Discrimination; Gross Body Equilibrium; Finger Dexterity; Extent Flexibility; Gross Body Coordination. **Occupational Values:** Independence; Moral Values; Supervision, Technical; Security; Company Policies and Practices. **Interacting with Others:** Communicating with Supervisors, Peers, or Subordinates; Establishing and Maintaining Interpersonal Relationships; Performing Administrative Activities. **Physical Work Conditions:** Hazardous Conditions; Outdoors; Minor Burns, Cuts, Bites, or Stings; Standing; Climbing Ladders, Scaffolds, or Poles.

Electrical and Electronics Repairers, Powerhouse, Substation, and Relay

Inspect, test, repair, or maintain electrical equipment in generating stations, substations, and in-service relays. **O*NET Code:** 49-2095.00. **Average Salary:** $52,720. **Projected Growth:** –0.6%. **Annual Openings:** 2,000. **Education:** Postsecondary vocational training. **Job Zone:** 5. **Education/Training Program(s)**—No data available. **Related Knowledge/Courses:** Computers and Electronics; Mechanical; Physics; Engineering and Technology; Mathematics. **Personality Type:** Realistic. **Skills Required:** Equipment Maintenance; Repairing; Installation; Troubleshooting; Science; Operation Monitoring; Quality Control Analysis; Equipment Selection. **Abilities:** Visual Color Discrimination; Hearing Sensitivity; Reaction Time; Extent Flexibility; Gross Body Equilibrium. **Occupational Values:** Variety; Moral Values; Supervision, Technical; Responsibility; Advancement. **Interacting with Others:** Communicating with Supervisors, Peers, or Subordinates; Performing Administrative Activities; Establishing and Maintaining Interpersonal Relationships; Providing Consultation and Advice to Others. **Physical Work Conditions:** Hazardous Conditions; Using Hands on Objects, Tools, or Controls; Spend Time Bending or Twisting the Body; Common Protective or Safety Equipment; Hazardous Equipment.

Electrical Power-Line Installers and Repairers

Install or repair cables or wires used in electrical power or distribution systems. May erect poles and light- or heavy-duty transmission towers. **O*NET Code:** 49-9051.00. **Average Salary:** $49,140. **Projected Growth:** 1.6%. **Annual Openings:** 9,000. **Education:** Long-term on-the-job training. **Job Zone:** 4. **Education/Training Program(s)**—Electrical and Power Transmission Installation/Installer, General; Electrical and

© 2006, JIST Works

Power Transmission Installers, Other; Lineworker. **Related Knowledge/Courses:** Public Safety and Security; Mechanical; Design; Engineering and Technology; Building and Construction; Computers and Electronics. **Personality Type:** Realistic. **Skills Required:** Installation; Repairing; Troubleshooting; Equipment Maintenance; Science; Quality Control Analysis; Technology Design; Operation and Control. **Abilities:** Dynamic Strength; Extent Flexibility; Gross Body Equilibrium; Visual Color Discrimination; Visualization. **Occupational Values:** Supervision, Technical; Security; Moral Values; Advancement; Supervision, Human Relations. **Interacting with Others:** Communicating with Supervisors, Peers, or Subordinates; Coordinating the Work and Activities of Others; Communicating with Persons Outside Organization; Establishing and Maintaining Interpersonal Relationships; Resolving Conflicts and Negotiating with Others; Coaching and Developing Others. **Physical Work Conditions:** Hazardous Conditions; Outdoors; Common Protective or Safety Equipment; High Places; Climbing Ladders, Scaffolds, or Poles.

Elevator Installers and Repairers

Assemble, install, repair, or maintain electric or hydraulic freight or passenger elevators, escalators, or dumbwaiters. **O*NET Code:** 47-4021.00. **Average Salary:** $55,910. **Projected Growth:** 17.1%. **Annual Openings:** 3,000. **Education:** Long-term on-the-job training. **Job Zone:** 4. **Education/Training Program(s)**—Industrial Mechanics and Maintenance Technology. **Related Knowledge/Courses:** Building and Construction; Mechanical; Engineering and Technology; Physics; Public Safety and Security; Telecommunications. **Personality Type:** Realistic. **Skills Required:** Installation; Repairing; Equipment Maintenance; Troubleshooting; Quality Control Analysis; Operation Monitoring; Systems Analysis; Operation and Control. **Abilities:** Night Vision; Extent Flexibility; Dynamic Strength; Gross Body Equilibrium; Hearing Sensitivity. **Occupational Values:** Moral Values; Independence; Supervision, Technical; Compensation; Company Policies and Practices; Responsibility. **Interacting with Others:** Communicating with Supervisors, Peers, or Subordinates; Communicating with Persons Outside Organization; Establishing and Maintaining Interpersonal Relationships. **Physical Work Conditions:** Hazardous Equipment; Minor Burns, Cuts, Bites, or Stings; Climbing Ladders, Scaffolds, or Poles; Hazardous Conditions; High Places.

Frame Wirers, Central Office

Connect wires from telephone lines and cables to distributing frames in telephone company central office, using soldering iron and other hand tools. **O*NET Code:** 49-2022.02. **Average Salary:** $48,740. **Projected Growth:** –0.6%. **Annual Openings:** 23,000. **Education:** Postsecondary vocational training. **Job Zone:** 2. **Education/Training Program(s)**—Communications Systems Installation and Repair Technology. **Related Knowledge/Courses:** Telecommunications; Engineering and Technology; Mechanical; Physics; Computers and Electronics; Design. **Personality Type:** Realistic. **Skills Required:** Installation; Repairing; Troubleshooting; Quality Control Analysis; Operation Monitoring; Equipment Maintenance; Equipment Selection.

Abilities: Extent Flexibility; Visualization; Multilimb Coordination; Arm-Hand Steadiness; Finger Dexterity; Trunk Strength. **Occupational Values:** Supervision, Technical; Security; Moral Values; Supervision, Human Relations; Company Policies and Practices. **Interacting with Others:** Communicating with Supervisors, Peers, or Subordinates; Establishing and Maintaining Interpersonal Relationships; Performing Administrative Activities. **Physical Work Conditions:** Climbing Ladders, Scaffolds, or Poles; Hazardous Conditions; Common Protective or Safety Equipment; Kneeling, Crouching, Stooping, or Crawling; Standing; Using Hands on Objects, Tools, or Controls.

Heating and Air Conditioning Mechanics

Install, service, and repair heating and air conditioning systems in residences and commercial establishments. **O*NET Code:** 49-9021.01. **Average Salary:** $35,670. **Projected Growth:** 31.8%. **Annual Openings:** 35,000. **Education:** Long-term on-the-job training. **Job Zone:** 3. **Education/Training Program(s)**—Heating, Air Conditioning and Refrigeration Technology/Technician (ACH/ACR/ACHR/HRAC/HVAC/AC Technology); Heating, Air Conditioning, Ventilation and Refrigeration Maintenance Technology/Technician (HAC, HACR, HVAC, HVACR); Solar Energy Technology/Technician. **Related Knowledge/Courses:** Mechanical; Building and Construction; Design; Customer and Personal Service; Engineering and Technology; Physics. **Personality Type:** Realistic. **Skills Required:** Installation; Repairing; Equipment Maintenance; Troubleshooting; Coordination; Systems Evaluation; Negotiation; Persuasion. **Abilities:** Extent Flexibility; Hearing Sensitivity; Finger Dexterity; Manual Dexterity; Gross Body Equilibrium. **Occupational Values:** Independence; Variety; Moral Values; Supervision, Technical; Responsibility. **Interacting with Others:** Establishing and Maintaining Interpersonal Relationships; Performing for or Working Directly with the Public; Communicating with Persons Outside Organization. **Physical Work Conditions:** Hazardous Conditions; Very Hot or Cold; Contaminants; Sounds, Noise Levels Are Distracting or Uncomfortable; Extremely Bright or Inadequate Lighting.

Home Appliance Installers

Install household appliances, such as refrigerators, washing machines, and stoves in mobile homes or customers' homes. **O*NET Code:** 49-9031.01. **Average Salary:** $30,290. **Projected Growth:** 5.5%. **Annual Openings:** 5,000. **Education:** Long-term on-the-job training. **Job Zone:** 3. **Education/Training Program(s)**—Appliance Installation and Repair Technology/Technician; Home Furnishings and Equipment Installers. **Related Knowledge/Courses:** Mechanical; Building and Construction; Transportation; Engineering and Technology. **Personality Type:** Realistic. **Skills Required:** Installation; Troubleshooting; Repairing; Operation Monitoring; Technology Design; Equipment Maintenance. **Abilities:** Static Strength; Dynamic Strength; Explosive Strength; Visualization; Wrist-Finger Speed; Extent Flexibility. **Occupational Values:** Social Service; Moral Values; Supervision, Technical; Advancement. **Interacting with Others:** Communicating with Persons Outside Organization; Performing for or Working Directly with the Public; Interpreting the Meaning of Information for Others. **Physical**

Work Conditions: Standing; Using Hands on Objects, Tools, or Controls; Kneeling, Crouching, Stooping, or Crawling; Spend Time Bending or Twisting the Body; Cramped Work Space, Awkward Positions.

Maintenance and Repair Workers, General

Perform work involving the skills of two or more maintenance or craft occupations to keep machines, mechanical equipment, or the structure of an establishment in repair. Duties may involve pipe fitting; boiler making; insulating; welding; machining; carpentry; repairing electrical or mechanical equipment; installing, aligning, and balancing new equipment; and repairing buildings, floors, or stairs. **O*NET Code:** 49-9042.00. **Average Salary:** $30,140. **Projected Growth:** 16.3%. **Annual Openings:** 155,000. **Education:** Long-term on-the-job training. **Job Zone:** 3. **Education/Training Program(s)**—Building/Construction Site Management/Manager. **Related Knowledge/Courses:** Mechanical; Building and Construction; Design; Public Safety and Security; Engineering and Technology; Physics. **Personality Type:** Realistic. **Skills Required:** Equipment Maintenance; Installation; Repairing; Troubleshooting; Operation Monitoring; Equipment Selection; Operation and Control; Critical Thinking. **Abilities:** Multilimb Coordination; Visual Color Discrimination; Extent Flexibility; Hearing Sensitivity; Static Strength. **Occupational Values:** Variety; Moral Values; Independence; Supervision, Human Relations; Supervision, Technical. **Interacting with Others:** Establishing and Maintaining Interpersonal Relationships; Communicating with Supervisors, Peers, or Subordinates; Coordinating the Work and Activities of Others. **Physical Work Conditions:** Very Hot or Cold; Sounds, Noise Levels Are Distracting or Uncomfortable; Contaminants; Minor Burns, Cuts, Bites, or Stings; Extremely Bright or Inadequate Lighting.

Meter Mechanics

Test, adjust, and repair gas, water, and oil meters. **O*NET Code:** 49-9012.03. **Average Salary:** $43,280. **Projected Growth:** 12.0%. **Annual Openings:** 5,000. **Education:** Moderate-term on-the-job training. **Job Zone:** 2. **Education/Training Program(s)**—Electromechanical and Instrumentation and Maintenance Technologies/Technicians, Other. **Related Knowledge/Courses:** Mechanical; Engineering and Technology. **Personality Type:** Realistic. **Skills Required:** Repairing; Installation; Equipment Maintenance; Quality Control Analysis; Troubleshooting; Operation Monitoring; Operation and Control. **Abilities:** Finger Dexterity; Arm-Hand Steadiness; Visualization; Flexibility of Closure; Control Precision; Wrist-Finger Speed. **Occupational Values:** Independence; Moral Values; Supervision, Technical; Security; Company Policies and Practices. **Interacting with Others:** Performing Administrative Activities; Interpreting the Meaning of Information for Others; Communicating with Supervisors, Peers, or Subordinates. **Physical Work Conditions:** Outdoors; Kneeling, Crouching, Stooping, or Crawling; Minor Burns, Cuts, Bites, or Stings; Walking and Running; Extremely Bright or Inadequate Lighting.

Refrigeration Mechanics

Install and repair industrial and commercial refrigerating systems. **O*NET Code:** 49-9021.02. **Average Salary:** $35,670. **Projected Growth:** 31.8%. **Annual Openings:** 35,000. **Education:** Long-term on-the-job training. **Job Zone:** 3. **Education/Training Program(s)**—Heating, Air Conditioning and Refrigeration Technology/Technician (ACH/ACR/ACHR/HRAC/HVAC/AC Technology); Heating, Air Conditioning, Ventilation and Refrigeration Maintenance Technology/Technician (HAC, HACR, HVAC, HVACR); Solar Energy Technology/Technician. **Related Knowledge/Courses:** Building and Construction; Mechanical; Engineering and Technology; Customer and Personal Service; Physics; Design. **Personality Type:** Realistic. **Skills Required:** Installation; Repairing; Equipment Maintenance; Operation Monitoring; Troubleshooting; Systems Evaluation; Science; Systems Analysis. **Abilities:** Extent Flexibility; Explosive Strength; Static Strength; Control Precision; Dynamic Strength. **Occupational Values:** Moral Values; Independence; Variety; Supervision, Technical; Security. **Interacting with Others:** Establishing and Maintaining Interpersonal Relationships; Coordinating the Work and Activities of Others; Communicating with Supervisors, Peers, or Subordinates. **Physical Work Conditions:** Very Hot or Cold; Extremely Bright or Inadequate Lighting; In an Enclosed Vehicle or Equipment; Cramped Work Space, Awkward Positions; Contaminants.

Station Installers and Repairers, Telephone

Install and repair telephone station equipment, such as telephones, coin collectors, telephone booths, and switching-key equipment. **O*NET Code:** 49-2022.05. **Average Salary:** $48,740. **Projected Growth:** -0.6%. **Annual Openings:** 23,000. **Education:** Postsecondary vocational training. **Job Zone:** 4. **Education/Training Program(s)**—Communications Systems Installation and Repair Technology. **Related Knowledge/Courses:** Telecommunications; Computers and Electronics; Mechanical; Engineering and Technology; Design; Geography. **Personality Type:** Realistic. **Skills Required:** Troubleshooting; Installation; Repairing; Equipment Maintenance; Quality Control Analysis; Operations Analysis; Technology Design; Operation Monitoring; Operation and Control. **Abilities:** Dynamic Strength; Gross Body Equilibrium; Stamina; Gross Body Coordination; Visual Color Discrimination. **Occupational Values:** Supervision, Technical; Security; Moral Values; Advancement; Independence; Variety; Supervision, Human Relations. **Interacting with Others:** Communicating with Supervisors, Peers, or Subordinates; Establishing and Maintaining Interpersonal Relationships; Performing for or Working Directly with the Public; Monitoring and Controlling Resources. **Physical Work Conditions:** Climbing Ladders, Scaffolds, or Poles; Common Protective or Safety Equipment; High Places; Standing; Very Hot or Cold.

Telecommunications Facility Examiners

Examine telephone transmission facilities to determine equipment requirements for providing subscribers with new or additional telephone services. **O*NET Code:** 49-2022.04. **Average Salary:** $48,740. **Projected Growth:** -0.6%. **Annual Openings:** 23,000. **Education:** Long-term on-the-job training. **Job Zone:** 3. **Education/Training Program(s)**—Communications Systems Installation and Repair Technology. **Related Knowledge/Courses:** Telecommunications; Computers and

Electronics; Engineering and Technology; Geography. **Personality Type:** Realistic. **Skills Required:** Technology Design; Installation. **Abilities:** Dynamic Strength; Gross Body Coordination; Gross Body Equilibrium; Stamina; Extent Flexibility. **Occupational Values:** Supervision, Technical; Moral Values; Responsibility; Independence; Supervision, Human Relations. **Interacting with Others:** Communicating with Persons Outside Organization; Establishing and Maintaining Interpersonal Relationships; Providing Consultation and Advice to Others. **Physical Work Conditions:** Climbing Ladders, Scaffolds, or Poles; High Places; Hazardous Conditions; Outdoors; Common Protective or Safety Equipment.

Telecommunications Line Installers and Repairers

String and repair telephone and television cable, including fiber optics and other equipment for transmitting messages or television programming. **O*NET Code:** 49-9052.00. **Average Salary:** $41,020. **Projected Growth:** 18.8%. **Annual Openings:** 13,000. **Education:** Long-term on-the-job training. **Job Zone:** 3. **Education/Training Program(s)**—Communications Systems Installation and Repair Technology. **Related Knowledge/Courses:** Telecommunications; Computers and Electronics; Mechanical; Physics; Sales and Marketing; Engineering and Technology. **Personality Type:** Realistic. **Skills Required:** Installation; Repairing; Troubleshooting; Equipment Maintenance; Operation Monitoring; Systems Evaluation; Mathematics; Operation and Control. **Abilities:** Gross Body Coordination; Manual Dexterity; Control Precision; Gross Body Equilibrium; Visual Color Discrimination. **Occupational Values:** Supervision, Technical; Independence; Security; Variety; Advancement; Supervision, Human Relations. **Interacting with Others:** Communicating with Supervisors, Peers, or Subordinates; Communicating with Persons Outside Organization; Establishing and Maintaining Interpersonal Relationships. **Physical Work Conditions:** Outdoors; Very Hot or Cold; Kneeling, Crouching, Stooping, or Crawling; High Places; Climbing Ladders, Scaffolds, or Poles; Spend Time Bending or Twisting the Body.

02.06 Construction Support/Labor

Carpenter Assemblers and Repairers

Perform a variety of tasks requiring a limited knowledge of carpentry, such as applying siding and weatherboard to building exteriors or assembling and erecting prefabricated buildings. **O*NET Code:** 47-2031.03. **Average Salary:** $34,870. **Projected Growth:** 10.1%. **Annual Openings:** 193,000. **Education:** Moderate-term on-the-job training. **Job Zone:** 2. **Education/Training Program(s)**—Carpentry/Carpenter. **Related Knowledge/Courses:** Building and Construction; Design; Engineering and Technology. **Personality Type:** Realistic. **Skills Required:** Repairing; Installation;

Management of Material Resources; Equipment Maintenance; Operation and Control. **Abilities:** Gross Body Equilibrium; Explosive Strength; Dynamic Strength; Static Strength; Manual Dexterity. **Occupational Values:** Moral Values; Variety; Activity; Co-workers; Advancement; Authority. **Interacting with Others:** Communicating with Supervisors, Peers, or Subordinates; Coordinating the Work and Activities of Others; Assisting and Caring for Others. **Physical Work Conditions:** Hazardous Equipment; High Places; Kneeling, Crouching, Stooping, or Crawling; Climbing Ladders, Scaffolds, or Poles; Standing.

Construction Laborers

Perform tasks involving physical labor at building, highway, and heavy construction projects; tunnel and shaft excavations; and demolition sites. May operate hand and power tools of all types: air hammers, earth tampers, cement mixers, small mechanical hoists, surveying and measuring equipment, and a variety of other equipment and instruments. May clean and prepare sites; dig trenches; set braces to support the sides of excavations; erect scaffolding; clean up rubble and debris; and remove asbestos, lead, and other hazardous waste materials. May assist other craft workers. **O*NET Code:** 47-2061.00. **Average Salary:** $25,030. **Projected Growth:** 14.2%. **Annual Openings:** 166,000. **Education:** Moderate-term on-the-job training. **Job Zone:** 2. **Education/Training Program(s)**—Construction Trades, Other. **Related Knowledge/Courses:** Building and Construction; Mechanical; Production and Processing; Engineering and Technology; Physics; Design. **Personality Type:** Realistic. **Skills Required:** Equipment Maintenance. **Abilities:** Static Strength; Trunk Strength; Dynamic Strength; Speed of Limb Movement; Stamina. **Occupational Values:** Co-workers; Supervision, Technical. **Interacting with Others:** Communicating with Supervisors, Peers, or Subordinates; Establishing and Maintaining Interpersonal Relationships; Communicating with Persons Outside Organization; Assisting and Caring for Others. **Physical Work Conditions:** Outdoors; Hazardous Equipment; Minor Burns, Cuts, Bites, or Stings; Standing; Very Hot or Cold.

Grips and Set-Up Workers, Motion Picture Sets, Studios, and Stages

Arrange equipment; raise and lower scenery; move dollies, cranes, and booms; and perform other duties for motion picture, recording, or television industry. **O*NET Code:** 53-7062.02. **Average Salary:** $19,980. **Projected Growth:** 6.6%. **Annual Openings:** 525,000. **Education:** Short-term on-the-job training. **Job Zone:** 2. **Education/Training Program(s)**—No data available. **Related Knowledge/Courses:** Building and Construction; Fine Arts; Mechanical. **Personality Type:** Realistic. **Skills Required:** Installation; Repairing; Technology Design; Operation and Control; Management of Material Resources; Operation Monitoring; Coordination; Monitoring. **Abilities:** Static Strength; Extent Flexibility; Spatial Orientation; Visualization; Trunk Strength; Depth Perception. **Occupational Values:** Advancement; Supervision, Technical; Co-workers; Company Policies and Practices; Variety; Recognition; Moral Values. **Interacting with Others:** Monitoring and Controlling Resources; Communicating with

Supervisors, Peers, or Subordinates; Establishing and Maintaining Interpersonal Relationships. **Physical Work Conditions:** Using Hands on Objects, Tools, or Controls; Standing; Climbing Ladders, Scaffolds, or Poles; High Places; Spend Time Bending or Twisting the Body.

Helpers—Brickmasons, Blockmasons, Stonemasons, and Tile and Marble Setters

Help brickmasons, blockmasons, stonemasons, or tile and marble setters by performing duties of lesser skill. Duties include using, supplying, or holding materials or tools and cleaning work area and equipment. **O*NET Code:** 47-3011.00. **Average Salary:** $24,650. **Projected Growth:** 2.2%. **Annual Openings:** 9,000. **Education:** Short-term on-the-job training. **Job Zone:** 1. **Education/Training Program(s)**— Mason/Masonry. **Related Knowledge/Courses:** Building and Construction; Mechanical. **Personality Type:** Realistic. **Skills Required:** Installation; Equipment Maintenance. **Abilities:** Static Strength; Dynamic Strength; Stamina; Extent Flexibility; Speed of Limb Movement. **Occupational Values:** Advancement; Supervision, Technical; Moral Values; Co-workers. **Interacting with Others:** Communicating with Supervisors, Peers, or Subordinates; Establishing and Maintaining Interpersonal Relationships; Assisting and Caring for Others. **Physical Work Conditions:** Outdoors; Kneeling, Crouching, Stooping, or Crawling; High Places; Spend Time Bending or Twisting the Body; Climbing Ladders, Scaffolds, or Poles; Walking and Running.

Helpers—Carpenters

Help carpenters by performing duties of lesser skill. Duties include using, supplying, or holding materials or tools and cleaning work area and equipment. **O*NET Code:** 47-3012.00. **Average Salary:** $21,870. **Projected Growth:** 14.0%. **Annual Openings:** 16,000. **Education:** Short-term on-the-job training. **Job Zone:** 1. **Education/Training Program(s)**— Carpentry/Carpenter. **Related Knowledge/Courses:** Building and Construction; Mechanical; Design; Physics; Public Safety and Security. **Personality Type:** Realistic. **Skills Required:** Repairing; Installation. **Abilities:** Static Strength; Dynamic Strength; Explosive Strength; Stamina; Trunk Strength. **Occupational Values:** Advancement; Co-workers; Supervision, Technical; Moral Values. **Interacting with Others:** Establishing and Maintaining Interpersonal Relationships; Communicating with Supervisors, Peers, or Subordinates; Assisting and Caring for Others. **Physical Work Conditions:** Hazardous Equipment; Common Protective or Safety Equipment; Kneeling, Crouching, Stooping, or Crawling; Very Hot or Cold; Outdoors.

Helpers—Electricians

Help electricians by performing duties of lesser skill. Duties include using, supplying, or holding materials or tools and cleaning work area and equipment. **O*NET Code:** 47-3013.00. **Average Salary:** $23,440. **Projected Growth:** 17.9%. **Annual Openings:** 17,000. **Education:** Short-term on-the-job training. **Job Zone:** 2. **Education/Training Program(s)**— Electrician. **Related Knowledge/Courses:** Building and Construction; Mechanical; Design; Mathematics; Public Safety and Security; Engineering and Technology. **Personality Type:** Realistic. **Skills Required:** Installation;

Troubleshooting; Repairing; Complex Problem Solving; Mathematics; Instructing; Critical Thinking; Equipment Selection; Time Management. **Abilities:** Explosive Strength; Dynamic Strength; Static Strength; Gross Body Equilibrium; Stamina. **Occupational Values:** Supervision, Technical; Advancement; Moral Values; Co-workers. **Interacting with Others:** Establishing and Maintaining Interpersonal Relationships; Communicating with Supervisors, Peers, or Subordinates; Coordinating the Work and Activities of Others. **Physical Work Conditions:** Very Hot or Cold; Extremely Bright or Inadequate Lighting; Contaminants; Outdoors; Hazardous Conditions.

Helpers—Installation, Maintenance, and Repair Workers

Help installation, maintenance, and repair workers in maintenance, parts replacement, and repair of vehicles, industrial machinery, and electrical and electronic equipment. Perform duties such as furnishing tools, materials, and supplies to other workers; cleaning work area, machines, and tools; and holding materials or tools for other workers. **O*NET Code:** 49-9098.00. **Average Salary:** $21,280. **Projected Growth:** 20.3%. **Annual Openings:** 33,000. **Education:** Short-term on-the-job training. **Job Zone:** 2. **Education/Training Program(s)**—Industrial Mechanics and Maintenance Technology. **Related Knowledge/Courses:** Mechanical; Engineering and Technology; Design; Chemistry; Public Safety and Security; Building and Construction. **Personality Type:** Realistic. **Skills Required:** Installation; Operation Monitoring; Repairing; Equipment Maintenance; Troubleshooting; Operations Analysis; Persuasion; Coordination. **Abilities:** Extent Flexibility; Hearing Sensitivity; Visual Color Discrimination; Static Strength; Stamina. **Occupational Values:** Advancement; Supervision, Technical; Co-workers; Moral Values; Variety. **Interacting with Others:** Establishing and Maintaining Interpersonal Relationships; Communicating with Supervisors, Peers, or Subordinates; Communicating with Persons Outside Organization. **Physical Work Conditions:** Hazardous Conditions; Hazardous Equipment; Extremely Bright or Inadequate Lighting; Very Hot or Cold; Sounds, Noise Levels Are Distracting or Uncomfortable.

Helpers—Painters, Paperhangers, Plasterers, and Stucco Masons

Help painters, paperhangers, plasterers, or stucco masons by performing duties of lesser skill. Duties include using, supplying, or holding materials or tools and cleaning work area and equipment. **O*NET Code:** 47-3014.00. **Average Salary:** $20,250. **Projected Growth:** 15.9%. **Annual Openings:** 5,000. **Education:** Short-term on-the-job training. **Job Zone:** 1. **Education/Training Program(s)**—Painting/Painter and Wall Coverer. **Related Knowledge/Courses:** Building and Construction; Economics and Accounting. **Personality Type:** Realistic. **Skills Required:** Repairing. **Abilities:** Static Strength; Dynamic Strength; Visual Color Discrimination; Explosive Strength; Extent Flexibility. **Occupational Values:** Supervision, Technical; Advancement; Moral Values; Co-workers. **Interacting with Others:** Communicating with Supervisors, Peers, or Subordinates; Establishing and Maintaining Interpersonal Relationships; Assisting and

Caring for Others. **Physical Work Conditions:** Climbing Ladders, Scaffolds, or Poles; Contaminants; High Places; Common Protective or Safety Equipment; Spend Time Bending or Twisting the Body.

Helpers—Pipelayers, Plumbers, Pipefitters, and Steamfitters

Help plumbers, pipefitters, steamfitters, or pipelayers by performing duties of lesser skill. Duties include using, supplying, or holding materials or tools and cleaning work area and equipment. **O*NET Code:** 47-3015.00. **Average Salary:** $22,610. **Projected Growth:** 10.9%. **Annual Openings:** 13,000. **Education:** Short-term on-the-job training. **Job Zone:** 2. **Education/Training Program(s)**—Plumbing Technology/ Plumber. **Related Knowledge/Courses:** Building and Construction; Mechanical; Public Safety and Security; Design; Law and Government; Engineering and Technology. **Personality Type:** Realistic. **Skills Required:** Installation; Repairing; Troubleshooting; Equipment Maintenance; Negotiation; Learning Strategies; Coordination; Mathematics. **Abilities:** Manual Dexterity; Static Strength; Explosive Strength; Dynamic Strength; Extent Flexibility. **Occupational Values:** Advancement; Supervision, Technical; Moral Values; Co-workers. **Interacting with Others:** Communicating with Supervisors, Peers, or Subordinates; Establishing and Maintaining Interpersonal Relationships; Coordinating the Work and Activities of Others. **Physical Work Conditions:** Very Hot or Cold; Sounds, Noise Levels Are Distracting or Uncomfortable; Outdoors; Contaminants; Hazardous Equipment.

Highway Maintenance Workers

Maintain highways, municipal and rural roads, airport runways, and rights-of-way. Duties include patching broken or eroded pavement and repairing guardrails, highway markers, and snow fences. May also mow or clear brush from along road or plow snow from roadway. **O*NET Code:** 47-4051.00. **Average Salary:** $29,120. **Projected Growth:** 10.4%. **Annual Openings:** 25,000. **Education:** Moderate-term on-the-job training. **Job Zone:** 2. **Education/Training Program(s)**— Construction/Heavy Equipment/Earthmoving Equipment Operation. **Related Knowledge/Courses:** Transportation; Building and Construction; Customer and Personal Service; Public Safety and Security; Mechanical; Geography. **Personality Type:** Realistic. **Skills Required:** Equipment Maintenance; Repairing; Installation; Troubleshooting; Management of Material Resources; Coordination; Management of Personnel Resources; Instructing. **Abilities:** Reaction Time; Rate Control; Response Orientation; Multilimb Coordination; Static Strength; Trunk Strength. **Occupational Values:** Moral Values; Supervision, Human Relations; Co-workers. **Interacting with Others:** Establishing and Maintaining Interpersonal Relationships; Coordinating the Work and Activities of Others; Communicating with Supervisors, Peers, or Subordinates. **Physical Work Conditions:** Very Hot or Cold; Outdoors; In an Open Vehicle or Equipment; Contaminants; In an Enclosed Vehicle or Equipment.

Septic Tank Servicers and Sewer Pipe Cleaners

Clean and repair septic tanks, sewer lines, or drains. May patch walls and partitions of tank, replace damaged drain tile, or repair breaks in underground piping. **O*NET Code:** 47-4071.00. **Average Salary:** $28,730. **Projected Growth:** 21.2%. **Annual Openings:** 3,000. **Education:** Moderate-term on-the-job training. **Job Zone:** 2. **Education/Training Program(s)**— Plumbing Technology/Plumber. **Related Knowledge/ Courses:** Mechanical; Building and Construction; Engineering and Technology; Economics and Accounting; Geography; Transportation. **Personality Type:** Realistic. **Skills Required:** Installation; Repairing; Operation and Control; Management of Material Resources; Equipment Maintenance; Mathematics; Equipment Selection; Troubleshooting. **Abilities:** Static Strength; Trunk Strength; Explosive Strength; Extent Flexibility; Gross Body Coordination. **Occupational Values:** Supervision, Technical; Independence. **Interacting with Others:** Communicating with Supervisors, Peers, or Subordinates; Communicating with Persons Outside Organization; Establishing and Maintaining Interpersonal Relationships; Coordinating the Work and Activities of Others. **Physical Work Conditions:** Outdoors; Contaminants; Common Protective or Safety Equipment; Kneeling, Crouching, Stooping, or Crawling; Spend Time Bending or Twisting the Body.

03 Arts and Communication

03.01   Managerial Work in Arts and Communication

03.02   Writing and Editing

03.03   News, Broadcasting, and Public Relations

03.04   Studio Art

03.05   Design

03.06   Drama

03.07   Music

03.08   Dance

03.09   Media Technology

03.10   Communications Technology

03.11   Musical Instrument Repair

03.01 Managerial Work in Arts and Communication

Agents and Business Managers of Artists, Performers, and Athletes

Represent and promote artists, performers, and athletes to prospective employers. May handle contract negotiation and other business matters for clients. O*NET Code: 13-1011.00. **Average Salary:** $55,700. **Projected Growth:** 27.8%. **Annual Openings:** 2,000. **Education:** Work experience plus degree. **Job Zone:** 3. **Education/Training Program(s)**—Arts Management; Purchasing, Procurement/Acquisitions, and Contracts Management. **Related Knowledge/Courses:** Sales and Marketing; Economics and Accounting; Personnel and Human Resources; Administration and Management; Fine Arts; Law and Government. **Personality Type:** Enterprising. **Skills Required:** Negotiation; Management of Financial Resources; Management of Personnel Resources; Time Management; Service Orientation; Speaking; Coordination; Persuasion. **Abilities:** Speech Clarity; Oral Expression; Mathematical Reasoning; Speech Recognition; Fluency of Ideas. **Occupational Values:** Social Service; Autonomy; Authority; Working Conditions; Variety. **Interacting with Others:** Resolving Conflicts and Negotiating with Others; Monitoring and Controlling Resources; Communicating with Persons Outside Organization; Establishing and Maintaining Interpersonal Relationships. **Physical Work Conditions:** Sitting; Outdoors; Walking and Running.

Art Directors

Formulate design concepts and presentation approaches and direct workers engaged in art work, layout design, and copy writing for visual communications media, such as magazines, books, newspapers, and packaging. O*NET Code: 27-1011.00. **Average Salary:** $63,170. **Projected Growth:** 11.4%. **Annual Openings:** 8,000. **Education:** Work experience plus degree. **Job Zone:** 4. **Education/Training Program(s)**—Graphic Design; Intermedia/Multimedia. **Related Knowledge/ Courses:** Design; Fine Arts; Computers and Electronics; Communications and Media; Production and Processing; Customer and Personal Service; Education and Training. **Personality Type:** Artistic. **Skills Required:** Coordination; Negotiation; Persuasion; Service Orientation; Management of Financial Resources; Instructing; Time Management; Operations Analysis. **Abilities:** Originality; Visual Color Discrimination; Fluency of Ideas; Category Flexibility; Visualization. **Occupational Values:** Creativity; Ability Utilization; Authority; Autonomy; Achievement. **Interacting with Others:** Providing Consultation and Advice to Others; Communicating with Supervisors, Peers, or Subordinates; Establishing and Maintaining Interpersonal Relationships. **Physical Work Conditions:** Sitting; Sounds, Noise Levels Are Distracting or Uncomfortable; Physical Proximity; Indoors.

Producers

Plan and coordinate various aspects of radio, television, stage, or motion picture production, such as selecting script; coordinating writing, directing, and editing; and arranging financing. O*NET Code: 27-2012.01. **Average Salary:** $51,870. **Projected Growth:** 18.3%. **Annual Openings:** 10,000. **Education:** Work experience plus degree. **Job Zone:** 4. **Education/Training Program(s)**—Cinematography and Film/Video Production; Directing and Theatrical Production; Drama and Dramatics/Theatre Arts, General; Dramatic/Theatre Arts and Stagecraft, Other; Film/Cinema Studies; Radio and Television; Theatre/Theatre Arts Management. **Related Knowledge/Courses:** Communications and Media; Clerical; Administration and Management; English Language; Fine Arts; Sales and Marketing. **Personality Type:** Artistic. **Skills Required:** Coordination; Negotiation; Monitoring; Management of Personnel Resources; Writing; Time Management; Social Perceptiveness; Management of Financial Resources. **Abilities:** Originality; Written Expression; Fluency of Ideas; Oral Comprehension; Written Comprehension; Oral Expression. **Occupational Values:** Authority; Creativity; Recognition; Responsibility; Autonomy. **Interacting with Others:** Communicating with Persons Outside Organization; Establishing and Maintaining Interpersonal Relationships; Communicating with Supervisors, Peers, or Subordinates. **Physical Work Conditions:** Sitting; Extremely Bright or Inadequate Lighting; Physical Proximity; Sounds, Noise Levels Are Distracting or Uncomfortable; In an Enclosed Vehicle or Equipment.

Program Directors

Direct and coordinate activities of personnel engaged in preparation of radio or television station program schedules and programs such as sports or news. O*NET Code: 27-2012.03. **Average Salary:** $51,870. **Projected Growth:** 18.3%. **Annual Openings:** 10,000. **Education:** Work experience plus degree. **Job Zone:** 5. **Education/Training Program(s)**—Cinematography and Film/Video Production; Directing and Theatrical Production; Drama and Dramatics/Theatre Arts, General; Dramatic/Theatre Arts and Stagecraft, Other; Film/Cinema Studies; Radio and Television; Theatre/Theatre Arts Management. **Related Knowledge/Courses:** Communications and Media; Administration and Management; Personnel and Human Resources; Economics and Accounting; Telecommunications; English Language. **Personality Type:** Enterprising. **Skills Required:** Management of Personnel Resources; Coordination; Management of Financial Resources; Management of Material Resources; Writing; Time Management; Active Learning; Reading Comprehension. **Abilities:** Written Expression; Originality; Oral Expression; Fluency of Ideas; Oral Comprehension. **Occupational Values:** Authority; Creativity; Variety; Autonomy; Responsibility. **Interacting with Others:** Communicating with Supervisors, Peers, or Subordinates; Monitoring and Controlling Resources; Coordinating the Work and Activities of Others; Guiding, Directing, and Motivating Subordinates; Staffing Organizational Units. **Physical Work Conditions:** Sitting; Indoors; Standing.

Public Relations Managers

Plan and direct public relations programs designed to create and maintain a favorable public image for employer or client or, if engaged in fundraising, plan and direct activities to solicit and maintain funds for special projects and nonprofit organizations. **O*NET Code:** 11-2031.00. **Average Salary:** $67,810. **Projected Growth:** 23.4%. **Annual Openings:** 10,000. **Education:** Work experience plus degree. **Job Zone:** 4. **Education/Training Program(s)**—Public Relations/Image Management. **Related Knowledge/Courses:** Sales and Marketing; Economics and Accounting; Education and Training; Law and Government; Customer and Personal Service; English Language; Foreign Language. **Personality Type:** No data available. **Skills Required:** Management of Financial Resources; Social Perceptiveness; Service Orientation; Monitoring; Persuasion; Coordination; Negotiation; Time Management. **Abilities:** No data available. **Occupational Values:** No data available. **Interacting with Others:** Establishing and Maintaining Interpersonal Relationships; Communicating with Persons Outside Organization; Communicating with Supervisors, Peers, or Subordinates. **Physical Work Conditions:** Sitting; Physical Proximity; In an Enclosed Vehicle or Equipment; Indoors; Extremely Bright or Inadequate Lighting.

Technical Directors/Managers

Coordinate activities of technical departments, such as taping, editing, engineering, and maintenance, to produce radio or television programs. **O*NET Code:** 27-2012.05. **Average Salary:** $51,870. **Projected Growth:** 18.3%. **Annual Openings:** 10,000. **Education:** Long-term on-the-job training. **Job Zone:** 3. **Education/Training Program(s)**—Cinematography and Film/Video Production; Directing and Theatrical Production; Drama and Dramatics/Theatre Arts, General; Dramatic/Theatre Arts and Stagecraft, Other; Film/Cinema Studies; Radio and Television; Theatre/Theatre Arts Management. **Related Knowledge/Courses:** Communications and Media; Computers and Electronics; Telecommunications; Philosophy and Theology; Sales and Marketing; Customer and Personal Service. **Personality Type:** Realistic. **Skills Required:** Time Management; Monitoring; Operation Monitoring; Operation and Control; Coordination; Management of Personnel Resources; Instructing; Troubleshooting. **Abilities:** Far Vision; Reaction Time; Selective Attention; Time Sharing; Sound Localization. **Occupational Values:** Authority; Autonomy; Creativity; Variety; Responsibility. **Interacting with Others:** Communicating with Supervisors, Peers, or Subordinates; Communicating with Persons Outside Organization; Guiding, Directing, and Motivating Subordinates. **Physical Work Conditions:** Sitting; Sounds, Noise Levels Are Distracting or Uncomfortable; Physical Proximity; Indoors; Very Hot or Cold; Extremely Bright or Inadequate Lighting.

03.02 Writing and Editing

Copy Writers

Write advertising copy for use by publication or broadcast media to promote sale of goods and services. **O*NET Code:** 27-3043.04. **Average Salary:** $43,340. **Projected Growth:** 16.1%. **Annual Openings:** 23,000. **Education:** Bachelor's degree. **Job Zone:** 4. **Education/Training Program(s)**—Broadcast Journalism; Business/Corporate Communications; Communication Studies/Speech Communication and Rhetoric; Communication, Journalism, and Related Programs, Other; Creative Writing; English Composition; Family and Consumer Sciences/Human Sciences Communication; Journalism; Mass Communication/Media Studies; Playwriting and Screenwriting; Technical and Business Writing. **Related Knowledge/Courses:** Sales and Marketing; Communications and Media; Sociology and Anthropology; English Language; Computers and Electronics; Administration and Management. **Personality Type:** Artistic. **Skills Required:** Persuasion; Time Management; Instructing; Coordination; Negotiation; Technology Design; Critical Thinking; Active Listening. **Abilities:** Originality; Fluency of Ideas; Written Expression; Oral Comprehension; Speech Recognition. **Occupational Values:** Creativity; Advancement; Recognition; Ability Utilization; Responsibility. **Interacting with Others:** Communicating with Persons Outside Organization; Communicating with Supervisors, Peers, or Subordinates; Establishing and Maintaining Interpersonal Relationships. **Physical Work Conditions:** Sitting; Contaminants; Physical Proximity; Sounds, Noise Levels Are Distracting or Uncomfortable; Indoors.

Creative Writers

Create original written works, such as plays or prose, for publication or performance. **O*NET Code:** 27-3043.02. **Average Salary:** $43,340. **Projected Growth:** 16.1%. **Annual Openings:** 23,000. **Education:** Bachelor's degree. **Job Zone:** 4. **Education/Training Program(s)**—Broadcast Journalism; Business/Corporate Communications; Communication Studies/Speech Communication and Rhetoric; Communication, Journalism, and Related Programs, Other; Creative Writing; English Composition; Family and Consumer Sciences/Human Sciences Communication; Journalism; Mass Communication/Media Studies; Playwriting and Screenwriting; Technical and Business Writing. **Related Knowledge/Courses:** English Language; Communications and Media; Fine Arts; Sociology and Anthropology; Computers and Electronics. **Personality Type:** Artistic. **Skills Required:** Writing; Reading Comprehension; Coordination; Critical Thinking; Complex Problem Solving; Social Perceptiveness; Monitoring; Negotiation. **Abilities:** Written Expression; Originality; Fluency of Ideas; Oral Comprehension; Written Comprehension. **Occupational Values:** Creativity; Ability Utilization; Achievement; Recognition; Autonomy. **Interacting with Others:**

Communicating with Persons Outside Organization; Communicating with Supervisors, Peers, or Subordinates; Establishing and Maintaining Interpersonal Relationships. **Physical Work Conditions:** Sitting; Indoors.

Editors

Perform variety of editorial duties, such as laying out, indexing, and revising content of written materials, in preparation for final publication. **O*NET Code:** 27-3041.00. **Average Salary:** $42,450. **Projected Growth:** 11.8%. **Annual Openings:** 14,000. **Education:** Bachelor's degree. **Job Zone:** 4. **Education/Training Program(s)**—Broadcast Journalism; Business/Corporate Communications; Communication, Journalism, and Related Programs, Other; Creative Writing; Journalism; Mass Communication/Media Studies; Publishing; Technical and Business Writing. **Related Knowledge/ Courses:** Communications and Media; English Language; Geography; History and Archeology; Clerical; Computers and Electronics. **Personality Type:** Artistic. **Skills Required:** Writing; Reading Comprehension; Active Listening; Time Management; Persuasion; Critical Thinking; Active Learning; Social Perceptiveness. **Abilities:** Originality; Written Expression; Written Comprehension; Fluency of Ideas; Visualization. **Occupational Values:** Creativity; Recognition; Responsibility; Autonomy; Ability Utilization; Achievement. **Interacting with Others:** Communicating with Persons Outside Organization; Establishing and Maintaining Interpersonal Relationships; Communicating with Supervisors, Peers, or Subordinates. **Physical Work Conditions:** Sitting; Physical Proximity; Sounds, Noise Levels Are Distracting or Uncomfortable; Contaminants.

Poets and Lyricists

Write poetry or song lyrics for publication or performance. **O*NET Code:** 27-3043.01. **Average Salary:** $43,340. **Projected Growth:** 16.1%. **Annual Openings:** 23,000. **Education:** Bachelor's degree. **Job Zone:** 4. **Education/Training Program(s)**—Broadcast Journalism; Business/Corporate Communications; Communication Studies/Speech Communication and Rhetoric; Communication, Journalism, and Related Programs, Other; Creative Writing; English Composition; Family and Consumer Sciences/Human Sciences Communication; Journalism; Mass Communication/Media Studies; Playwriting and Screenwriting; Technical and Business Writing. **Related Knowledge/Courses:** Fine Arts; Communications and Media; English Language. **Personality Type:** Artistic. **Skills Required:** Writing; Reading Comprehension; Learning Strategies. **Abilities:** Originality; Fluency of Ideas; Written Expression; Hearing Sensitivity; Category Flexibility. **Occupational Values:** Creativity; Ability Utilization; Independence; Recognition; Autonomy. **Interacting with Others:** Communicating with Persons Outside Organization; Establishing and Maintaining Interpersonal Relationships; Communicating with Supervisors, Peers, or Subordinates. **Physical Work Conditions:** Sitting; Indoors.

Technical Writers

Write technical materials, such as equipment manuals, appendices, or operating and maintenance instructions. May assist in layout work. **O*NET Code:** 27-3042.00. **Average Salary:**

$52,160. **Projected Growth:** 27.1%. **Annual Openings:** 6,000. **Education:** Bachelor's degree. **Job Zone:** 4. **Education/Training Program(s)**—Business/Corporate Communications; Family and Consumer Sciences/Human Sciences Communication; Technical and Business Writing. **Related Knowledge/Courses:** English Language; Clerical; Communications and Media; Computers and Electronics; Education and Training; Sales and Marketing. **Personality Type:** Artistic. **Skills Required:** Writing; Coordination; Active Learning; Active Listening; Reading Comprehension; Service Orientation; Technology Design; Speaking; Learning Strategies. **Abilities:** Written Expression; Originality; Information Ordering; Written Comprehension; Speed of Closure. **Occupational Values:** Creativity; Ability Utilization; Achievement; Responsibility; Recognition. **Interacting with Others:** Communicating with Supervisors, Peers, or Subordinates; Establishing and Maintaining Interpersonal Relationships; Coordinating the Work and Activities of Others. **Physical Work Conditions:** Sitting; Sounds, Noise Levels Are Distracting or Uncomfortable; Extremely Bright or Inadequate Lighting; Physical Proximity; Indoors.

03.03 News, Broadcasting, and Public Relations

Broadcast News Analysts

Analyze, interpret, and broadcast news received from various sources. **O*NET Code:** 27-3021.00. **Average Salary:** $31,720. **Projected Growth:** 6.2%. **Annual Openings:** 6,000. **Education:** Bachelor's degree. **Job Zone:** 4. **Education/Training Program(s)**—Broadcast Journalism; Journalism; Political Communication; Radio and Television. **Related Knowledge/Courses:** Communications and Media; English Language; Telecommunications; Computers and Electronics; Geography; Sociology and Anthropology. **Personality Type:** Artistic. **Skills Required:** Writing; Speaking; Reading Comprehension; Active Listening; Critical Thinking; Active Learning; Social Perceptiveness; Monitoring. **Abilities:** Written Expression; Speech Clarity; Oral Expression; Oral Comprehension; Written Comprehension. **Occupational Values:** Creativity; Recognition; Achievement; Social Status; Ability Utilization; Variety; Working Conditions. **Interacting with Others:** Performing for or Working Directly with the Public; Communicating with Persons Outside Organization; Establishing and Maintaining Interpersonal Relationships. **Physical Work Conditions:** Sitting; Indoors.

Caption Writers

Write caption phrases of dialogue for hearing-impaired and foreign language-speaking viewers of movie or television productions. **O*NET Code:** 27-3043.03. **Average Salary:** $43,340. **Projected Growth:** 16.1%. **Annual Openings:** 23,000. **Education:** Moderate-term on-the-job training. **Job Zone:** 3. **Education/Training Program(s)**—Broadcast Journalism;

Business/Corporate Communications; Communication, Journalism, and Related Programs, Other; Communication Studies/Speech Communication and Rhetoric; Creative Writing; English Composition; Family and Consumer Sciences/Human Sciences Communication; Journalism; Mass Communication/Media Studies; Playwriting and Screenwriting; Technical and Business Writing. **Related Knowledge/Courses:** Foreign Language; Communications and Media; English Language; Computers and Electronics; Telecommunications. **Personality Type:** Artistic. **Skills Required:** Writing; Reading Comprehension; Operation and Control; Management of Financial Resources. **Abilities:** Written Expression; Oral Comprehension; Written Comprehension; Wrist-Finger Speed; Near Vision. **Occupational Values:** Ability Utilization; Working Conditions; Achievement; Variety; Recognition; Autonomy. **Interacting with Others:** Communicating with Supervisors, Peers, or Subordinates; Interpreting the Meaning of Information for Others; Establishing and Maintaining Interpersonal Relationships. **Physical Work Conditions:** Sitting; Indoors; Spend Time Making Repetitive Motions; Extremely Bright or Inadequate Lighting.

Interpreters and Translators

Translate or interpret written, oral, or sign language text into another language for others. O*NET Code: 27-3091.00. **Average Salary:** $34,190. **Projected Growth:** 22.1%. **Annual Openings:** 4,000. **Education:** Long-term on-the-job training. **Job Zone:** 3. **Education/Training Program(s)—**African Languages, Literatures, and Linguistics; Albanian Language and Literature; American Indian/Native American Languages, Literatures, and Linguistics; Ancient Near Eastern and Biblical Languages, Literatures, and Linguistics; Ancient/Classical Greek Language and Literature; Arabic Language and Literature; Australian/Oceanic/Pacific Languages, Literatures, and Linguistics; Bahasa Indonesian/Bahasa Malay Languages and Literatures; Baltic Languages, Literatures, and Linguistics; Bengali Language and Literature; Bulgarian Language and Literature; Burmese Language and Literature; Catalan Language and Literature; Celtic Languages, Literatures, and Linguistics; Chinese Language and Literature; Classics and Classical Languages, Literatures, and Linguistics, General; Classics and Classical Languages, Literatures, and Linguistics, Other; Czech Language and Literature; Danish Language and Literature; Dutch/Flemish Language and Literature; East Asian Languages, Literatures, and Linguistics, General; East Asian Languages, Literatures, and Linguistics, Other; Filipino/Tagalog Language and Literature; Finnish and Related Languages, Literatures, and Linguistics; Foreign Languages and Literatures, General; Foreign Languages, Literatures, and Linguistics, Other; French Language and Literature; German Language and Literature; Germanic Languages, Literatures, and Linguistics, General; Germanic Languages, Literatures, and Linguistics, Other; Hebrew Language and Literature; Hindi Language and Literature; Hungarian/Magyar Language and Literature; Iranian/Persian Languages, Literatures, and Linguistics; Italian Language and Literature; Japanese Language and Literature; Khmer/Cambodian Language and Literature; Korean Language and Literature; Language Interpretation and Translation; Lao/Laotian Language and Literature; Latin

Language and Literature; Latin Teacher Education; Linguistics; Middle/Near Eastern and Semitic Languages, Literatures, and Linguistics, Other; others. **Related Knowledge/Courses:** Foreign Language; English Language; Communications and Media; Sociology and Anthropology; Geography; History and Archeology. **Personality Type:** Artistic. **Skills Required:** Active Listening; Writing; Reading Comprehension; Speaking; Service Orientation. **Abilities:** Speech Recognition; Written Expression; Written Comprehension; Oral Expression; Speech Clarity. **Occupational Values:** Social Service; Ability Utilization; Achievement; Working Conditions; Autonomy. **Interacting with Others:** Interpreting the Meaning of Information for Others; Establishing and Maintaining Interpersonal Relationships; Communicating with Persons Outside Organization. **Physical Work Conditions:** Sitting; Indoors; Outdoors.

Public Relations Specialists

Engage in promoting or creating good will for individuals, groups, or organizations by writing or selecting favorable publicity material and releasing it through various communications media. May prepare and arrange displays and make speeches. O*NET Code: 27-3031.00. **Average Salary:** $43,050. **Projected Growth:** 32.9%. **Annual Openings:** 28,000. **Education:** Bachelor's degree. **Job Zone:** 4. **Education/Training Program(s)—**Communication Studies/Speech Communication and Rhetoric; Family and Consumer Sciences/Human Sciences Communication; Health Communication; Political Communication; Public Relations/Image Management. **Related Knowledge/Courses:** Sales and Marketing; Customer and Personal Service; Communications and Media; Administration and Management; Clerical; English Language. **Personality Type:** Enterprising. **Skills Required:** Persuasion; Service Orientation; Negotiation; Social Perceptiveness; Coordination; Management of Financial Resources; Monitoring; Writing; Time Management. **Abilities:** Speech Clarity; Fluency of Ideas; Speech Recognition; Originality; Problem Sensitivity. **Occupational Values:** Creativity; Recognition; Ability Utilization; Achievement; Variety. **Interacting with Others:** Communicating with Persons Outside Organization; Communicating with Supervisors, Peers, or Subordinates; Establishing and Maintaining Interpersonal Relationships. **Physical Work Conditions:** Sitting; Physical Proximity.

Reporters and Correspondents

Collect and analyze facts about newsworthy events by interview, investigation, or observation. Report and write stories for newspaper, news magazine, radio, or television. O*NET Code: 27-3022.00. **Average Salary:** $31,720. **Projected Growth:** 6.2%. **Annual Openings:** 6,000. **Education:** Bachelor's degree. **Job Zone:** 4. **Education/Training Program(s)—**Agricultural Communication/Journalism; Broadcast Journalism; Journalism; Journalism, Other; Mass Communication/Media Studies; Photojournalism; Political Communication. **Related Knowledge/Courses:** Communications and Media; English Language; Geography; Sociology and Anthropology; Clerical; Customer and Personal Service. **Personality Type:** Artistic. **Skills Required:** Writing; Active

Listening; Critical Thinking; Reading Comprehension; Active Learning; Time Management; Speaking; Persuasion. **Abilities:** Written Expression; Oral Expression; Fluency of Ideas; Speech Clarity; Written Comprehension; Speech Recognition. **Occupational Values:** Creativity; Ability Utilization; Advancement; Recognition; Variety. **Interacting with Others:** Communicating with Persons Outside Organization; Establishing and Maintaining Interpersonal Relationships; Interpreting the Meaning of Information for Others; Performing for or Working Directly with the Public. **Physical Work Conditions:** Sounds, Noise Levels Are Distracting or Uncomfortable; Physical Proximity; Sitting; In an Enclosed Vehicle or Equipment; Outdoors.

03.04 Studio Art

Cartoonists

Create original artwork, using any of a wide variety of mediums and techniques such as painting and sculpture. **O*NET Code:** 27-1013.03. **Average Salary:** $37,030. **Projected Growth:** 16.5%. **Annual Openings:** 4,000. **Education:** Long-term on-the-job training. **Job Zone:** 4. **Education/Training Program(s)**—Art/Art Studies, General; Drawing; Fine Arts and Art Studies, Other; Fine/Studio Arts, General; Intermedia/Multimedia; Medical Illustration/Medical Illustrator; Painting; Visual and Performing Arts, General. **Related Knowledge/Courses:** Fine Arts; Communications and Media; Sales and Marketing; Design; Telecommunications. **Personality Type:** Artistic. **Skills Required:** Operations Analysis. **Abilities:** Visual Color Discrimination; Originality; Fluency of Ideas; Visualization; Arm-Hand Steadiness. **Occupational Values:** Creativity; Recognition; Autonomy; Ability Utilization; Achievement. **Interacting with Others:** Communicating with Supervisors, Peers, or Subordinates; Communicating with Persons Outside Organization; Establishing and Maintaining Interpersonal Relationships. **Physical Work Conditions:** Sitting; Indoors; Spend Time Making Repetitive Motions.

Craft Artists

Create or reproduce hand-made objects for sale and exhibition, using a variety of techniques such as welding, weaving, pottery, and needlecraft. **O*NET Code:** 27-1012.00. **Average Salary:** No data available. **Projected Growth:** 11.5%. **Annual Openings:** 13,000. **Education:** Associate degree. **Job Zone:** No data available. **Education/Training Program(s)**—Art/Art Studies, General; Ceramic Arts and Ceramics; Crafts/Craft Design, Folk Art and Artisanry; Drawing; Fiber, Textile and Weaving Arts; Metal and Jewelry Arts; Painting; Printmaking; Sculpture; Visual and Performing Arts, General. **Related Knowledge/Courses:** No data available. **Personality Type:** No data available. **Skills Required:** No data available. **Abilities:** No data available. **Occupational Values:** No data available. **Interacting with Others:** No data available. **Physical Work Conditions:** No data available.

Painters and Illustrators

Paint or draw subject material to produce original artwork or illustrations, using watercolors, oils, acrylics, tempera, or other paint mediums. **O*NET Code:** 27-1013.01. **Average Salary:** $37,030. **Projected Growth:** 16.5%. **Annual Openings:** 4,000. **Education:** Long-term on-the-job training. **Job Zone:** 4. **Education/Training Program(s)**—Art/Art Studies, General; Drawing; Fine Arts and Art Studies, Other; Fine/Studio Arts, General; Medical Illustration/Medical Illustrator; Painting; Visual and Performing Arts, General. **Related Knowledge/Courses:** Fine Arts; Design; Chemistry; History and Archeology; Communications and Media; Engineering and Technology. **Personality Type:** Artistic. **Skills Required:** Operations Analysis; Management of Material Resources; Installation; Quality Control Analysis; Repairing; Active Listening; Equipment Selection. **Abilities:** Visual Color Discrimination; Originality; Visualization; Fluency of Ideas; Extent Flexibility. **Occupational Values:** Creativity; Ability Utilization; Autonomy; Achievement; Independence. **Interacting with Others:** Communicating with Persons Outside Organization; Providing Consultation and Advice to Others; Communicating with Supervisors, Peers, or Subordinates; Establishing and Maintaining Interpersonal Relationships. **Physical Work Conditions:** Sitting; Spend Time Making Repetitive Motions; Standing; Indoors; Using Hands on Objects, Tools, or Controls.

Potters

Mold clay into ware as clay revolves on potter's wheel. **O*NET Code:** 51-9195.05. **Average Salary:** $24,470. **Projected Growth:** 6.4%. **Annual Openings:** 6,000. **Education:** Long-term on-the-job training. **Job Zone:** 4. **Education/Training Program(s)**—No data available. **Related Knowledge/Courses:** Fine Arts; Production and Processing. **Personality Type:** Realistic. **Skills Required:** Operation and Control. **Abilities:** Arm-Hand Steadiness; Manual Dexterity; Visualization; Rate Control; Multilimb Coordination. **Occupational Values:** Moral Values; Creativity; Independence; Variety; Recognition; Autonomy. **Interacting with Others:** Monitoring and Controlling Resources; Communicating with Supervisors, Peers, or Subordinates; Establishing and Maintaining Interpersonal Relationships; Coaching and Developing Others. **Physical Work Conditions:** Spend Time Making Repetitive Motions; Sitting; Spend Time Bending or Twisting the Body; Using Hands on Objects, Tools, or Controls; Contaminants.

Sculptors

Design and construct three-dimensional art works, using materials such as stone, wood, plaster, and metal and employing various manual and tool techniques. **O*NET Code:** 27-1013.04. **Average Salary:** $37,030. **Projected Growth:** 16.5%. **Annual Openings:** 4,000. **Education:** Long-term on-the-job training. **Job Zone:** 5. **Education/Training Program(s)**—Art/Art Studies, General; Ceramic Arts and Ceramics; Fine Arts and Art Studies, Other; Fine/Studio Arts, General; Sculpture; Visual and Performing Arts, General. **Related Knowledge/Courses:** Fine Arts; Design; Engineering and Technology; Building and Construction. **Personality Type:** Artistic. **Skills Required:** None met the criteria. **Abilities:** Originality; Visualization; Manual Dexterity; Fluency of Ideas; Finger Dexterity. **Occupational Values:** Creativity; Ability Utilization; Independence; Autonomy; Responsibility. **Interacting with Others:** Selling or Influencing Others;

Monitoring and Controlling Resources; Communicating with Persons Outside Organization. **Physical Work Conditions:** Using Hands on Objects, Tools, or Controls; Standing; Spend Time Bending or Twisting the Body; Minor Burns, Cuts, Bites, or Stings; Sitting; Kneeling, Crouching, Stooping, or Crawling.

Sketch Artists

Sketch likenesses of subjects according to observation or descriptions either to assist law enforcement agencies in identifying suspects, to depict courtroom scenes, or for entertainment purposes of patrons, using mediums such as pencil, charcoal, and pastels. **O*NET Code:** 27-1013.02. **Average Salary:** $37,030. **Projected Growth:** 16.5%. **Annual Openings:** 4,000. **Education:** Long-term on-the-job training. **Job Zone:** 3. **Education/Training Program(s)**—Art/Art Studies, General; Drawing; Fine Arts and Art Studies, Other; Fine/Studio Arts, General; Medical Illustration/Medical Illustrator; Visual and Performing Arts, General. **Related Knowledge/Courses:** Fine Arts; Design. **Personality Type:** Artistic. **Skills Required:** Active Listening; Social Perceptiveness; Speaking. **Abilities:** Visualization; Finger Dexterity; Arm-Hand Steadiness; Originality; Flexibility of Closure. **Occupational Values:** Creativity; Ability Utilization; Achievement; Variety; Autonomy. **Interacting with Others:** Communicating with Persons Outside Organization; Communicating with Supervisors, Peers, or Subordinates; Establishing and Maintaining Interpersonal Relationships. **Physical Work Conditions:** Sitting; Spend Time Making Repetitive Motions; Indoors; Extremely Bright or Inadequate Lighting; Using Hands on Objects, Tools, or Controls.

03.05 Design

Commercial and Industrial Designers

Develop and design manufactured products, such as cars, home appliances, and children's toys. Combine artistic talent with research on product use, marketing, and materials to create the most functional and appealing product design. **O*NET Code:** 27-1021.00. **Average Salary:** $52,080. **Projected Growth:** 14.7%. **Annual Openings:** 7,000. **Education:** Bachelor's degree. **Job Zone:** 4. **Education/Training Program(s)**—Commercial and Advertising Art; Design and Applied Arts, Other; Design and Visual Communications, General; Industrial Design. **Related Knowledge/Courses:** Design; Fine Arts; Production and Processing; Sales and Marketing; English Language; Communications and Media. **Personality Type:** Artistic. **Skills Required:** Operations Analysis; Management of Financial Resources; Active Learning; Equipment Selection; Persuasion; Systems Analysis; Systems Evaluation; Negotiation. **Abilities:** Visualization; Fluency of Ideas; Originality; Mathematical Reasoning; Visual Color Discrimination. **Occupational Values:** Creativity; Ability Utilization; Achievement; Recognition; Autonomy. **Interacting with Others:** Communicating with Persons Outside Organization; Communicating with Supervisors, Peers, or Subordinates; Establishing and Maintaining Interpersonal Relationships. **Physical Work Conditions:** Indoors; Sitting; Hazardous Equipment; Standing; Using Hands on Objects, Tools, or Controls.

Exhibit Designers

Plan, design, and oversee construction and installation of permanent and temporary exhibits and displays. **O*NET Code:** 27-1027.02. **Average Salary:** $35,710. **Projected Growth:** 20.9%. **Annual Openings:** 2,000. **Education:** Bachelor's degree. **Job Zone:** 4. **Education/Training Program(s)**—Design and Applied Arts, Other; Design and Visual Communications, General; Illustration; Technical Theatre/Theatre Design and Technology. **Related Knowledge/Courses:** Design; Fine Arts; Building and Construction; Sales and Marketing; Computers and Electronics; Customer and Personal Service. **Personality Type:** Artistic. **Skills Required:** Management of Financial Resources; Management of Material Resources; Negotiation; Systems Evaluation; Operations Analysis; Social Perceptiveness; Systems Analysis; Management of Personnel Resources. **Abilities:** Visual Color Discrimination; Visualization; Originality; Fluency of Ideas; Far Vision. **Occupational Values:** Creativity; Autonomy; Ability Utilization; Achievement; Recognition. **Interacting with Others:** Establishing and Maintaining Interpersonal Relationships; Coordinating the Work and Activities of Others; Communicating with Supervisors, Peers, or Subordinates; Communicating with Persons Outside Organization; Monitoring and Controlling Resources. **Physical Work Conditions:** Walking and Running; High Places; Standing; Climbing Ladders, Scaffolds, or Poles; Kneeling, Crouching, Stooping, or Crawling.

Fashion Designers

Design clothing and accessories. Create original garments or design garments that follow well-established fashion trends. May develop the line of color and kinds of materials. **O*NET Code:** 27-1022.00. **Average Salary:** $54,530. **Projected Growth:** 10.6%. **Annual Openings:** 2,000. **Education:** Bachelor's degree. **Job Zone:** 3. **Education/Training Program(s)**—Apparel and Textile Manufacture; Fashion and Fabric Consultant; Fashion/Apparel Design; Textile Science. **Related Knowledge/Courses:** Design; Fine Arts; Production and Processing; Sales and Marketing; Education and Training; Customer and Personal Service. **Personality Type:** Artistic. **Skills Required:** Persuasion; Management of Financial Resources; Operations Analysis; Systems Analysis; Negotiation; Management of Material Resources; Systems Evaluation; Coordination. **Abilities:** Visual Color Discrimination; Originality; Fluency of Ideas; Visualization; Finger Dexterity. **Occupational Values:** Creativity; Ability Utilization; Achievement; Recognition; Responsibility; Autonomy. **Interacting with Others:** Communicating with Supervisors, Peers, or Subordinates; Establishing and Maintaining Interpersonal Relationships; Communicating with Persons Outside Organization. **Physical Work Conditions:** Sitting; Kneeling, Crouching, Stooping, or Crawling; Indoors; Using Hands on Objects, Tools, or Controls; Walking and Running; Spend Time Bending or Twisting the Body.

© 2006, JIST Works

Floral Designers

Design, cut, and arrange live, dried, or artificial flowers and foliage. **O*NET Code:** 27-1023.00. **Average Salary:** $20,090. **Projected Growth:** 12.4%. **Annual Openings:** 13,000. **Education:** Moderate-term on-the-job training. **Job Zone:** 2. **Education/Training Program(s)**—Floriculture/Floristry Operations and Management. **Related Knowledge/Courses:** Customer and Personal Service; Sales and Marketing; Fine Arts; Personnel and Human Resources; Design; Production and Processing. **Personality Type:** Artistic. **Skills Required:** Management of Financial Resources; Management of Material Resources; Service Orientation; Management of Personnel Resources; Social Perceptiveness; Time Management; Instructing; Learning Strategies. **Abilities:** Visual Color Discrimination; Originality; Visualization; Fluency of Ideas; Category Flexibility. **Occupational Values:** Creativity; Achievement; Ability Utilization; Recognition; Autonomy. **Interacting with Others:** Performing for or Working Directly with the Public; Selling or Influencing Others; Establishing and Maintaining Interpersonal Relationships. **Physical Work Conditions:** Physical Proximity; Standing; In an Enclosed Vehicle or Equipment; Minor Burns, Cuts, Bites, or Stings; Very Hot or Cold.

Graphic Designers

Design or create graphics to meet specific commercial or pro-motional needs, such as packaging, displays, or logos. May use a variety of mediums to achieve artistic or decorative effects. **O*NET Code:** 27-1024.00. **Average Salary:** $36,930. **Projected Growth:** 21.9%. **Annual Openings:** 29,000. **Education:** Bachelor's degree. **Job Zone:** 4. **Education/Training Program(s)**—Agricultural Communication/Journalism; Commercial and Advertising Art; Computer Graphics; Design and Visual Communications, General; Graphic Design; Industrial Design; Web Page, Digital/Multimedia, and Information Resources Design. **Related Knowledge/Courses:** Fine Arts; Design; Computers and Electronics; Communications and Media; Sales and Marketing; Clerical. **Personality Type:** Artistic. **Skills Required:** Persuasion; Time Management; Troubleshooting; Instructing; Coordination; Social Perceptiveness; Operations Analysis; Complex Problem Solving. **Abilities:** Originality; Visual Color Discrimination; Visualization; Fluency of Ideas; Category Flexibility. **Occupational Values:** Creativity; Ability Utilization; Achievement; Recognition; Variety; Autonomy. **Interacting with Others:** Establishing and Maintaining Interpersonal Relationships; Communicating with Persons Outside Organization; Communicating with Supervisors, Peers, or Subordinates. **Physical Work Conditions:** Sitting; Sounds, Noise Levels Are Distracting or Uncomfortable; Physical Proximity; Indoors.

Interior Designers

Plan, design, and furnish interiors of residential, commercial, or industrial buildings. Formulate design that is practical, aes-thetic, and conducive to intended purposes, such as raising productivity, selling merchandise, or improving lifestyle. May specialize in a particular field, style, or phase of interior design. **O*NET Code:** 27-1025.00. **Average Salary:** $40,420. **Projected Growth:** 21.7%. **Annual Openings:** 8,000. **Education:** Bachelor's degree. **Job Zone:** 3. **Education/**

Training Program(s)—Facilities Planning and Management; Interior Architecture; Interior Design; Textile Science. **Related Knowledge/Courses:** Design; Sales and Marketing; Customer and Personal Service; Administration and Management; Clerical; Building and Construction. **Personality Type:** Artistic. **Skills Required:** Installation; Persuasion; Management of Financial Resources; Active Learning; Negotiation; Speaking; Troubleshooting; Critical Thinking. **Abilities:** Originality; Visualization; Visual Color Discrimination; Fluency of Ideas; Deductive Reasoning; Speech Recognition. **Occupational Values:** Creativity; Recognition; Ability Utilization; Achievement; Autonomy. **Interacting with Others:** Selling or Influencing Others; Communicating with Supervisors, Peers, or Subordinates; Establishing and Maintaining Interpersonal Relationships; Coordinating the Work and Activities of Others. **Physical Work Conditions:** Sitting; Physical Proximity; In an Enclosed Vehicle or Equipment; Extremely Bright or Inadequate Lighting.

Merchandise Displayers and Window Trimmers

Plan and erect commercial displays, such as those in windows and interiors of retail stores and at trade exhibitions. **O*NET Code:** 27-1026.00. **Average Salary:** $22,650. **Projected Growth:** 11.3%. **Annual Openings:** 10,000. **Education:** Moderate-term on-the-job training. **Job Zone:** 3. **Education/Training Program(s)**—No data available. **Related Knowledge/Courses:** Sales and Marketing; Fine Arts; Design; Sociology and Anthropology; Communications and Media; Building and Construction. **Personality Type:** Artistic. **Skills Required:** Installation; Operations Analysis; Equipment Selection. **Abilities:** Extent Flexibility; Visualization; Visual Color Discrimination; Originality; Depth Perception. **Occupational Values:** Creativity; Ability Utilization; Achievement; Recognition; Working Conditions. **Interacting with Others:** Communicating with Supervisors, Peers, or Subordinates; Communicating with Persons Outside Organization; Selling or Influencing Others. **Physical Work Conditions:** Climbing Ladders, Scaffolds, or Poles; Minor Burns, Cuts, Bites, or Stings; Spend Time Bending or Twisting the Body; Extremely Bright or Inadequate Lighting; Standing.

Set Designers

Design sets for theatrical, motion picture, and television pro-ductions. **O*NET Code:** 27-1027.01. **Average Salary:** $35,710. **Projected Growth:** 20.9%. **Annual Openings:** 2,000. **Education:** Bachelor's degree. **Job Zone:** 5. **Education/Training Program(s)**—Design and Applied Arts, Other; Design and Visual Communications, General; Illustration; Technical Theatre/Theatre Design and Technology. **Related Knowledge/Courses:** Fine Arts; Design; Building and Construction; Engineering and Technology; Geography; Communications and Media. **Personality Type:** Artistic. **Skills Required:** Management of Financial Resources; Management of Material Resources; Management of Personnel Resources; Persuasion; Operations Analysis; Systems Evaluation; Negotiation; Technology Design. **Abilities:** Visualization; Visual Color Discrimination; Originality; Auditory Attention; Fluency of Ideas; Time Sharing. **Occupational Values:** Creativity; Ability Utilization; Achievement; Authority; Autonomy. **Interacting with Others:**

Communicating with Supervisors, Peers, or Subordinates; Coordinating the Work and Activities of Others; Establishing and Maintaining Interpersonal Relationships. **Physical Work Conditions:** Standing; Climbing Ladders, Scaffolds, or Poles; Walking and Running; Spend Time Bending or Twisting the Body; High Places.

03.06 Drama

Actors

Play parts in stage, television, radio, video, or motion picture productions for entertainment, information, or instruction. Interpret serious or comic role by speech, gesture, and body movement to entertain or inform audience. May dance and sing. O*NET Code: 27-2011.00. **Average Salary:** $25,330. **Projected Growth:** 17.7%. **Annual Openings:** 8,000. **Education:** Long-term on-the-job training. **Job Zone:** 3. **Education/Training Program(s)**—Acting; Directing and Theatrical Production; Drama and Dramatics/Theatre Arts, General; Dramatic/Theatre Arts and Stagecraft, Other. **Related Knowledge/Courses:** Fine Arts; Communications and Media; English Language. **Personality Type:** Artistic. **Skills Required:** Speaking; Monitoring; Social Perceptiveness; Repairing; Coordination; Active Learning; Reading Comprehension; Equipment Maintenance. **Abilities:** Memorization; Gross Body Coordination; Originality; Spatial Orientation; Speech Clarity. **Occupational Values:** Ability Utilization; Recognition; Creativity; Variety; Achievement. **Interacting with Others:** Performing for or Working Directly with the Public; Communicating with Persons Outside Organization; Communicating with Supervisors, Peers, or Subordinates. **Physical Work Conditions:** Outdoors; Standing; Extremely Bright or Inadequate Lighting; Sitting; Very Hot or Cold.

Costume Attendants

Select, fit, and take care of costumes for cast members; aid entertainers. O*NET Code: 39-3092.00. **Average Salary:** $25,320. **Projected Growth:** 27.8%. **Annual Openings:** 66,000. **Education:** Moderate-term on-the-job training. **Job Zone:** 4. **Education/Training Program(s)**—No data available. **Related Knowledge/Courses:** Fine Arts; Design; Sociology and Anthropology; Geography; History and Archeology. **Personality Type:** Artistic. **Skills Required:** Management of Financial Resources; Management of Material Resources; Repairing. **Abilities:** Visual Color Discrimination; Arm-Hand Steadiness; Wrist-Finger Speed; Originality; Dynamic Flexibility. **Occupational Values:** Creativity; Social Service; Autonomy; Variety; Responsibility. **Interacting with Others:** Monitoring and Controlling Resources; Establishing and Maintaining Interpersonal Relationships; Communicating with Supervisors, Peers, or Subordinates; Coordinating the Work and Activities of Others; Providing Consultation and Advice to Others. **Physical Work Conditions:** Standing; Indoors; Kneeling, Crouching, Stooping, or Crawling; Sitting; Using Hands on Objects, Tools, or Controls; Spend Time Bending or Twisting the Body.

Directors—Stage, Motion Pictures, Television, and Radio

Interpret script, conduct rehearsals, and direct activities of cast and technical crew for stage, motion pictures, television, or radio programs. O*NET Code: 27-2012.02. **Average Salary:** $51,870. **Projected Growth:** 18.3%. **Annual Openings:** 10,000. **Education:** Work experience plus degree. **Job Zone:** 4. **Education/Training Program(s)**—Cinematography and Film/Video Production; Directing and Theatrical Production; Drama and Dramatics/Theatre Arts, General; Dramatic/Theatre Arts and Stagecraft, Other; Film/Cinema Studies; Radio and Television; Theatre/Theatre Arts Management. **Related Knowledge/Courses:** Communications and Media; Telecommunications; Computers and Electronics; Geography; Education and Training; Fine Arts. **Personality Type:** Artistic. **Skills Required:** Management of Personnel Resources; Time Management; Judgment and Decision Making; Critical Thinking; Active Listening; Operations Analysis; Speaking; Active Learning. **Abilities:** Originality; Visualization; Far Vision; Oral Expression; Fluency of Ideas. **Occupational Values:** Authority; Creativity; Recognition; Responsibility; Achievement. **Interacting with Others:** Communicating with Supervisors, Peers, or Subordinates; Establishing and Maintaining Interpersonal Relationships; Communicating with Persons Outside Organization. **Physical Work Conditions:** Sitting; Sounds, Noise Levels Are Distracting or Uncomfortable; Physical Proximity; Very Hot or Cold; In an Enclosed Vehicle or Equipment.

Makeup Artists, Theatrical and Performance

Apply makeup to performers to reflect period, setting, and situation of their role. O*NET Code: 39-5091.00. **Average Salary:** $23,860. **Projected Growth:** 18.2%. **Annual Openings:** Fewer than 500. **Education:** Postsecondary vocational training. **Job Zone:** 2. **Education/Training Program(s)**—Cosmetology/Cosmetologist, General; Makeup Artist/Specialist; Permanent Cosmetics/Makeup and Tattooing. **Related Knowledge/Courses:** Fine Arts; Sociology and Anthropology; Design; Communications and Media; History and Archeology; Geography. **Personality Type:** Artistic. **Skills Required:** Technology Design; Coordination; Management of Material Resources; Equipment Selection. **Abilities:** Visual Color Discrimination; Originality; Arm-Hand Steadiness; Finger Dexterity; Visualization. **Occupational Values:** Social Service; Creativity; Recognition; Ability Utilization; Achievement; Autonomy. **Interacting with Others:** Assisting and Caring for Others; Communicating with Supervisors, Peers, or Subordinates; Establishing and Maintaining Interpersonal Relationships. **Physical Work Conditions:** Using Hands on Objects, Tools, or Controls; Indoors; Contaminants; Extremely Bright or Inadequate Lighting; Sitting.

Public Address System and Other Announcers

Make announcements over loudspeaker at sporting or other public events. May act as master of ceremonies or disc jockey at weddings, parties, clubs, or other gathering places. O*NET Code: 27-3012.00. **Average Salary:** $21,490. **Projected Growth:** –10.1%. **Annual Openings:** 8,000. **Education:** Associate degree. **Job Zone:** 3. **Education/Training Program(s)**—Communication Studies/Speech Communication and Rhetoric. **Related Knowledge/Courses:** Communications and Media; Geography; English Language; Sales and Marketing. **Personality Type:** Social. **Skills Required:** Social Perceptiveness; Speaking; Service Orientation; Reading Comprehension; Monitoring. **Abilities:** Speech Clarity; Far Vision; Time Sharing; Peripheral Vision; Selective Attention. **Occupational Values:** Recognition; Creativity; Variety; Working Conditions; Social Status; Responsibility. **Interacting with Others:** Performing for or Working Directly with the Public; Communicating with Persons Outside Organization; Communicating with Supervisors, Peers, or Subordinates; Establishing and Maintaining Interpersonal Relationships. **Physical Work Conditions:** Sitting; Outdoors; Extremely Bright or Inadequate Lighting; Very Hot or Cold; Sounds, Noise Levels Are Distracting or Uncomfortable.

Radio and Television Announcers

Talk on radio or television. May interview guests, act as master of ceremonies, read news flashes, identify station by giving call letters, or announce song title and artist. **O*NET Code:** 27-3011.00. **Average Salary:** $21,490. **Projected Growth:** –10.1%. **Annual Openings:** 8,000. **Education:** Moderate-term on-the-job training. **Job Zone:** 3. **Education/Training Program(s)**—Broadcast Journalism; Radio and Television. **Related Knowledge/Courses:** Communications and Media; Telecommunications; English Language; Computers and Electronics; Geography; Fine Arts. **Personality Type:** Artistic. **Skills Required:** Speaking; Time Management; Social Perceptiveness; Writing; Coordination; Monitoring; Persuasion; Active Listening. **Abilities:** Speech Clarity; Memorization; Oral Expression; Oral Comprehension; Fluency of Ideas. **Occupational Values:** Recognition; Creativity; Working Conditions; Variety; Social Status. **Interacting with Others:** Performing for or Working Directly with the Public; Communicating with Persons Outside Organization; Establishing and Maintaining Interpersonal Relationships. **Physical Work Conditions:** Sitting; Physical Proximity; Sounds, Noise Levels Are Distracting or Uncomfortable; Extremely Bright or Inadequate Lighting; Indoors.

03.07 Music

Composers

Compose music for orchestra, choral group, or band. **O*NET Code:** 27-2041.03. **Average Salary:** $33,430. **Projected Growth:** 13.5%. **Annual Openings:** 8,000. **Education:** Master's degree. **Job Zone:** 5. **Education/Training Program(s)**—Conducting; Music Management and Merchandising; Music, Other; Music Performance, General; Music Theory and Composition; Musicology and Ethnomusicology; Religious/Sacred Music; Voice and Opera. **Related Knowledge/Courses:** Fine Arts; History and Archeology. **Personality Type:** Artistic. **Skills Required:** Equipment Selection. **Abilities:** Hearing Sensitivity; Originality; Fluency of Ideas; Auditory Attention; Sound Localization. **Occupational Values:** Creativity; Autonomy;

Ability Utilization; Responsibility; Independence. **Interacting with Others:** Interpreting the Meaning of Information for Others; Communicating with Persons Outside Organization; Performing for or Working Directly with the Public. **Physical Work Conditions:** Sitting; Indoors.

Music Arrangers and Orchestrators

Write and transcribe musical scores. **O*NET Code:** 27-2041.02. **Average Salary:** $33,430. **Projected Growth:** 13.5%. **Annual Openings:** 8,000. **Education:** Bachelor's degree. **Job Zone:** 4. **Education/Training Program(s)**—Conducting; Music Management and Merchandising; Music, Other; Music Performance, General; Music Theory and Composition; Musicology and Ethnomusicology; Religious/Sacred Music; Voice and Opera. **Related Knowledge/Courses:** Fine Arts; Foreign Language. **Personality Type:** Artistic. **Skills Required:** Coordination; Writing; Operations Analysis; Complex Problem Solving. **Abilities:** Hearing Sensitivity; Originality; Sound Localization; Fluency of Ideas; Auditory Attention. **Occupational Values:** Ability Utilization; Creativity; Autonomy; Achievement; Responsibility. **Interacting with Others:** Interpreting the Meaning of Information for Others; Establishing and Maintaining Interpersonal Relationships; Communicating with Supervisors, Peers, or Subordinates; Communicating with Persons Outside Organization. **Physical Work Conditions:** Sitting; Indoors.

Music Directors

Direct and conduct instrumental or vocal performances by musical groups, such as orchestras or choirs. **O*NET Code:** 27-2041.01. **Average Salary:** $33,430. **Projected Growth:** 13.5%. **Annual Openings:** 8,000. **Education:** Master's degree. **Job Zone:** 5. **Education/Training Program(s)**—Conducting; Music Management and Merchandising; Music, Other; Music Performance, General; Music Theory and Composition; Musicology and Ethnomusicology; Religious/Sacred Music; Voice and Opera. **Related Knowledge/Courses:** Fine Arts; Personnel and Human Resources; Administration and Management; Foreign Language; Transportation; English Language. **Personality Type:** Artistic. **Skills Required:** Management of Personnel Resources; Coordination; Instructing; Time Management; Monitoring; Learning Strategies; Social Perceptiveness; Operations Analysis. **Abilities:** Hearing Sensitivity; Sound Localization; Originality; Auditory Attention; Oral Expression. **Occupational Values:** Creativity; Authority; Responsibility; Autonomy; Ability Utilization. **Interacting with Others:** Coordinating the Work and Activities of Others; Establishing and Maintaining Interpersonal Relationships; Guiding, Directing, and Motivating Subordinates. **Physical Work Conditions:** Standing; Sitting; Spend Time Making Repetitive Motions; Indoors.

Musicians, Instrumental

Play one or more musical instruments in recital; in accompaniment; or as members of an orchestra, band, or other musical group. **O*NET Code:** 27-2042.02. **Average Salary:** $38,150. **Projected Growth:** 17.1%. **Annual Openings:** 25,000. **Education:** Long-term on-the-job training. **Job Zone:** 5. **Education/Training Program(s)**—Jazz/Jazz Studies; Music,

General; Music, Other; Music Pedagogy; Music Performance, General; Piano and Organ; Violin, Viola, Guitar, and Other Stringed Instruments. **Related Knowledge/Courses:** Fine Arts; Education and Training; Psychology; History and Archeology; Communications and Media; Sociology and Anthropology. **Personality Type:** Artistic. **Skills Required:** Instructing; Coordination; Active Learning; Learning Strategies; Management of Personnel Resources; Monitoring; Systems Analysis; Management of Material Resources. **Abilities:** Hearing Sensitivity; Sound Localization; Auditory Attention; Memorization; Originality. **Occupational Values:** Ability Utilization; Achievement; Creativity; Recognition; Moral Values; Autonomy. **Interacting with Others:** Performing for or Working Directly with the Public; Coordinating the Work and Activities of Others; Coaching and Developing Others. **Physical Work Conditions:** Sitting; Spend Time Making Repetitive Motions; Using Hands on Objects, Tools, or Controls; Indoors; Extremely Bright or Inadequate Lighting.

Singers

Sing songs on stage or radio or in television or motion pictures. **O*NET Code:** 27-2042.01. **Average Salary:** $38,150. **Projected Growth:** 17.1%. **Annual Openings:** 25,000. **Education:** Long-term on-the-job training. **Job Zone:** 2. **Education/Training Program(s)**—Jazz/Jazz Studies; Music, General; Music, Other; Music Pedagogy; Music Performance, General; Piano and Organ; Voice and Opera. **Related Knowledge/Courses:** Fine Arts; Communications and Media; Foreign Language. **Personality Type:** Artistic. **Skills Required:** None met the criteria. **Abilities:** Hearing Sensitivity; Auditory Attention; Originality; Sound Localization; Speech Clarity. **Occupational Values:** Ability Utilization; Achievement; Creativity; Recognition; Autonomy. **Interacting with Others:** Performing for or Working Directly with the Public; Communicating with Persons Outside Organization; Establishing and Maintaining Interpersonal Relationships. **Physical Work Conditions:** Standing; Sitting; Indoors.

Talent Directors

Audition and interview performers to select most appropriate talent for parts in stage, television, radio, or motion picture productions. **O*NET Code:** 27-2012.04. **Average Salary:** $51,870. **Projected Growth:** 18.3%. **Annual Openings:** 10,000. **Education:** Long-term on-the-job training. **Job Zone:** 3. **Education/Training Program(s)**—Cinematography and Film/Video Production; Directing and Theatrical Production; Drama and Dramatics/Theatre Arts, General; Dramatic/Theatre Arts and Stagecraft, Other; Film/Cinema Studies; Radio and Television; Theatre/Theatre Arts Management. **Related Knowledge/Courses:** Fine Arts; Sales and Marketing; Personnel and Human Resources; Administration and Management; Communications and Media; Economics and Accounting. **Personality Type:** Artistic. **Skills Required:** Negotiation; Management of Personnel Resources; Speaking; Social Perceptiveness; Persuasion; Active Listening; Writing; Reading Comprehension; Critical Thinking. **Abilities:** Hearing Sensitivity; Memorization; Oral Expression; Speech Clarity; Auditory Attention. **Occupational Values:** Authority; Responsibility; Autonomy; Variety; Creativity. **Interacting with Others:** Resolving Conflicts and Negotiating with Others; Communicating with Persons Outside Organization; Establishing and Maintaining Interpersonal Relationships; Selling or Influencing Others. **Physical Work Conditions:** Sitting; Indoors; Standing; Extremely Bright or Inadequate Lighting.

03.08 Dance

Choreographers

Create and teach dance. May direct and stage presentations. **O*NET Code:** 27-2032.00. **Average Salary:** $32,060. **Projected Growth:** 15.8%. **Annual Openings:** 3,000. **Education:** Work experience in a related occupation. **Job Zone:** 5. **Education/Training Program(s)**—Dance, General; Dance, Other. **Related Knowledge/Courses:** Fine Arts; Communications and Media; Personnel and Human Resources; Education and Training; Sociology and Anthropology. **Personality Type:** Artistic. **Skills Required:** Instructing; Coordination; Monitoring; Learning Strategies. **Abilities:** Gross Body Coordination; Dynamic Flexibility; Dynamic Strength; Stamina; Speed of Limb Movement. **Occupational Values:** Creativity; Authority; Responsibility; Ability Utilization; Recognition; Autonomy. **Interacting with Others:** Coaching and Developing Others; Coordinating the Work and Activities of Others; Training and Teaching Others. **Physical Work Conditions:** Spend Time Bending or Twisting the Body; Walking and Running; Standing; Keeping or Regaining Balance; Kneeling, Crouching, Stooping, or Crawling; Spend Time Making Repetitive Motions.

Dancers

Perform dances. May also sing or act. **O*NET Code:** 27-2031.00. **Average Salary:** $19,740. **Projected Growth:** 11.1%. **Annual Openings:** 3,000. **Education:** Long-term on-the-job training. **Job Zone:** 4. **Education/Training Program(s)**—Ballet; Dance, General; Dance, Other. **Related Knowledge/Courses:** Fine Arts; Administration and Management. **Personality Type:** Artistic. **Skills Required:** No data available. **Abilities:** Gross Body Coordination; Speed of Limb Movement; Dynamic Strength; Stamina; Dynamic Flexibility. **Occupational Values:** Ability Utilization; Recognition; Achievement; Creativity; Moral Values. **Interacting with Others:** Performing for or Working Directly with the Public; Coordinating the Work and Activities of Others; Communicating with Supervisors, Peers, or Subordinates. **Physical Work Conditions:** Walking and Running; Spend Time Bending or Twisting the Body; Keeping or Regaining Balance; Spend Time Making Repetitive Motions; Standing.

03.09 Media Technology

Audio and Video Equipment Technicians

Set up or set up and operate audio and video equipment, including microphones, sound speakers, video screens, projectors, video monitors, recording equipment, connecting wires and cables, sound and mixing boards, and related electronic equipment for concerts, sports events, meetings and conventions, presentations, and news conferences. May also set up and operate associated spotlights and other custom lighting systems. O*NET Code: 27-4011.00. **Average Salary:** $31,170. **Projected Growth:** 26.7%. **Annual Openings:** 5,000. **Education:** Long-term on-the-job training. **Job Zone:** 3. **Education/Training Program(s)**—Agricultural Communication/Journalism; Photographic and Film/Video Technology/Technician and Assistant; Recording Arts Technology/Technician. **Related Knowledge/Courses:** Computers and Electronics; Telecommunications; Engineering and Technology; Communications and Media; Mechanical; Customer and Personal Service. **Personality Type:** Conventional. **Skills Required:** Troubleshooting; Installation; Equipment Maintenance; Operation and Control; Service Orientation; Operation Monitoring; Repairing; Technology Design; Time Management. **Abilities:** Originality; Fluency of Ideas; Visualization; Speech Clarity; Written Expression. **Occupational Values:** Working Conditions; Authority; Co-workers; Social Service; Ability Utilization. **Interacting with Others:** Communicating with Supervisors, Peers, or Subordinates; Establishing and Maintaining Interpersonal Relationships; Communicating with Persons Outside Organization. **Physical Work Conditions:** Extremely Bright or Inadequate Lighting; Physical Proximity; Sounds, Noise Levels Are Distracting or Uncomfortable; Cramped Work Space, Awkward Positions; Sitting.

Broadcast Technicians

Set up, operate, and maintain the electronic equipment used to transmit radio and television programs. Control audio equipment to regulate volume level and quality of sound during radio and television broadcasts. Operate radio transmitter to broadcast radio and television programs. O*NET Code: 27-4012.00. **Average Salary:** $28,170. **Projected Growth:** 11.3%. **Annual Openings:** 4,000. **Education:** Postsecondary vocational training. **Job Zone:** 3. **Education/Training Program(s)**—Audiovisual Communications Technologies/Technicians, Other; Communications Technology/Technician; Radio and Television Broadcasting Technology/Technician. **Related Knowledge/Courses:** Telecommunications; Communications and Media; Computers and Electronics; Engineering and Technology; Mechanical; Education and Training. **Personality Type:** Realistic. **Skills Required:** Operation Monitoring; Troubleshooting; Instructing; Equipment Maintenance; Installation; Operation and Control; Coordination; Active Learning. **Abilities:** Response Orientation; Hearing Sensitivity; Reaction Time; Time Sharing; Control Precision. **Occupational Values:** Variety; Advancement; Ability Utilization; Achievement; Working Conditions; Recognition; Supervision, Human Relations. **Interacting with Others:** Establishing and Maintaining Interpersonal Relationships; Communicating with Supervisors, Peers, or Subordinates; Training and Teaching Others. **Physical Work Conditions:** Sitting; Sounds, Noise Levels Are Distracting or Uncomfortable; Physical Proximity; Extremely Bright or Inadequate Lighting; Indoors.

Camera Operators, Television, Video, and Motion Picture

Operate television, video, or motion picture camera to photograph images or scenes for various purposes, such as TV broadcasts, advertising, video production, or motion pictures. O*NET Code: 27-4031.00. **Average Salary:** $37,350. **Projected Growth:** 13.4%. **Annual Openings:** 4,000. **Education:** Moderate-term on-the-job training. **Job Zone:** 3. **Education/Training Program(s)**—Audiovisual Communications Technologies/Technicians, Other; Cinematography and Film/Video Production; Radio and Television Broadcasting Technology/Technician. **Related Knowledge/Courses:** Communications and Media; Computers and Electronics; Telecommunications; Customer and Personal Service; Sales and Marketing; Fine Arts. **Personality Type:** Artistic. **Skills Required:** Equipment Maintenance; Troubleshooting; Operation Monitoring; Coordination; Operation and Control; Active Listening; Time Management; Persuasion. **Abilities:** Spatial Orientation; Rate Control; Far Vision; Visual Color Discrimination; Visualization. **Occupational Values:** Ability Utilization; Variety; Recognition; Achievement; Authority; Creativity. **Interacting with Others:** Establishing and Maintaining Interpersonal Relationships; Performing for or Working Directly with the Public; Communicating with Supervisors, Peers, or Subordinates; Communicating with Persons Outside Organization. **Physical Work Conditions:** Extremely Bright or Inadequate Lighting; Physical Proximity; Outdoors; Very Hot or Cold; Sounds, Noise Levels Are Distracting or Uncomfortable.

Film and Video Editors

Edit motion picture soundtracks, film, and video. O*NET Code: 27-4032.00. **Average Salary:** $41,820. **Projected Growth:** 26.4%. **Annual Openings:** 3,000. **Education:** Bachelor's degree. **Job Zone:** 3. **Education/Training Program(s)**—Audiovisual Communications Technologies/Technicians, Other; Cinematography and Film/Video Production; Communications Technology/Technician; Photojournalism; Radio and Television; Radio and Television Broadcasting Technology/Technician. **Related Knowledge/Courses:** Communications and Media; Fine Arts; Computers and Electronics; Design; Education and Training; English Language. **Personality Type:** Artistic. **Skills Required:** Equipment Selection; Coordination; Time Management; Active Learning; Operations Analysis; Equipment Maintenance; Troubleshooting; Critical Thinking. **Abilities:** Night Vision; Visualization; Hearing Sensitivity; Information Ordering; Speed of Closure. **Occupational Values:** Authority; Creativity; Recognition; Social Status; Autonomy. **Interacting with Others:** Establishing and Maintaining Interpersonal Relationships; Providing Consultation and Advice to Others; Performing for or Working Directly with the Public. **Physical Work Conditions:** Sitting; Physical Proximity; Indoors; Sounds, Noise Levels Are Distracting or Uncomfortable.

Multi-Media Artists and Animators

Create special effects, animation, or other visual images, using film, video, computers, or other electronic tools and media for use in products or creations, such as computer games, movies, music videos, and commercials. **O*NET Code:** 27-1014.00. **Average Salary:** $46,770. **Projected Growth:** 15.8%. **Annual Openings:** 12,000. **Education:** Bachelor's degree. **Job Zone:** No data available. **Education/Training Program(s)**—Animation, Interactive Technology, Video Graphics, and Special Effects; Drawing; Graphic Design; Intermedia/Multimedia; Painting; Printmaking; Web Page, Digital/Multimedia, and Information Resources Design. **Related Knowledge/Courses:** No data available. **Personality Type:** No data available. **Skills Required:** No data available. **Abilities:** No data available. **Occupational Values:** No data available. **Interacting with Others:** No data available. **Physical Work Conditions:** No data available.

Photographic Hand Developers

Develop exposed photographic film or sensitized paper in series of chemical and water baths to produce negative or positive prints. **O*NET Code:** 51-9131.03. **Average Salary:** $20,470. **Projected Growth:** 5.4%. **Annual Openings:** 4,000. **Education:** Moderate-term on-the-job training. **Job Zone:** 2. **Education/Training Program(s)**—Photographic and Film/Video Technology/Technician and Assistant. **Related Knowledge/Courses:** Chemistry; Fine Arts. **Personality Type:** Realistic. **Skills Required:** None met the criteria. **Abilities:** Night Vision; Visual Color Discrimination; Wrist-Finger Speed; Reaction Time; Perceptual Speed. **Occupational Values:** Independence; Moral Values; Supervision, Technical. **Interacting with Others:** Communicating with Supervisors, Peers, or Subordinates; Performing Administrative Activities; Monitoring and Controlling Resources. **Physical Work Conditions:** Extremely Bright or Inadequate Lighting; Hazardous Conditions; Standing; Contaminants; Using Hands on Objects, Tools, or Controls.

Photographic Reproduction Technicians

Duplicate materials to produce prints on sensitized paper, cloth, or film, using photographic equipment. **O*NET Code:** 51-9131.02. **Average Salary:** $20,470. **Projected Growth:** 5.4%. **Annual Openings:** 4,000. **Education:** Moderate-term on-the-job training. **Job Zone:** 3. **Education/Training Program(s)**—Photographic and Film/Video Technology/Technician and Assistant. **Related Knowledge/Courses:** Chemistry; Fine Arts; Production and Processing; Engineering and Technology. **Personality Type:** Realistic. **Skills Required:** Technology Design; Installation; Mathematics; Equipment Selection; Operation and Control; Operations Analysis; Management of Material Resources. **Abilities:** Visual Color Discrimination; Night Vision; Near Vision; Information Ordering; Arm-Hand Steadiness. **Occupational Values:** Independence; Moral Values; Working Conditions; Supervision, Technical; Autonomy. **Interacting with Others:** Communicating with Supervisors, Peers, or Subordinates; Performing Administrative Activities; Interpreting the Meaning of Information for Others; Establishing and Maintaining Interpersonal Relationships; Assisting and Caring for Others; Coordinating the Work and Activities of Others. **Physical Work Conditions:** Hazardous Conditions; Extremely Bright or Inadequate Lighting; Indoors; Standing; Using Hands on Objects, Tools, or Controls.

Photographic Retouchers and Restorers

Retouch or restore photographic negatives and prints to accentuate desirable features of subject, using pencils, watercolors, or airbrushes. **O*NET Code:** 51-9131.01. **Average Salary:** $20,470. **Projected Growth:** 5.4%. **Annual Openings:** 4,000. **Education:** Moderate-term on-the-job training. **Job Zone:** 3. **Education/Training Program(s)**—Photographic and Film/Video Technology/Technician and Assistant. **Related Knowledge/Courses:** Fine Arts; Chemistry. **Personality Type:** Artistic. **Skills Required:** None met the criteria. **Abilities:** Visual Color Discrimination; Arm-Hand Steadiness; Finger Dexterity; Visualization; Wrist-Finger Speed. **Occupational Values:** Independence; Working Conditions; Creativity; Achievement; Variety. **Interacting with Others:** Establishing and Maintaining Interpersonal Relationships; Communicating with Supervisors, Peers, or Subordinates; Assisting and Caring for Others; Performing Administrative Activities. **Physical Work Conditions:** Using Hands on Objects, Tools, or Controls; Sitting; Extremely Bright or Inadequate Lighting; Spend Time Making Repetitive Motions; Contaminants.

Professional Photographers

Photograph subjects or newsworthy events, using still cameras, color or black-and-white film, and variety of photographic accessories. **O*NET Code:** 27-4021.01. **Average Salary:** $25,950. **Projected Growth:** 13.6%. **Annual Openings:** 18,000. **Education:** Long-term on-the-job training. **Job Zone:** 3. **Education/Training Program(s)**—Art/Art Studies, General; Commercial Photography; Film/Video and Photographic Arts, Other; Photography; Photojournalism; Visual and Performing Arts, General. **Related Knowledge/Courses:** Fine Arts; Communications and Media; Geography; Chemistry; Physics; Transportation. **Personality Type:** Artistic. **Skills Required:** Equipment Selection; Management of Material Resources; Technology Design; Operation and Control; Management of Personnel Resources; Social Perceptiveness; Science; Monitoring; Equipment Maintenance; Systems Analysis. **Abilities:** Rate Control; Depth Perception; Glare Sensitivity; Far Vision; Response Orientation. **Occupational Values:** Creativity; Ability Utilization; Achievement; Autonomy; Variety; Recognition; Responsibility. **Interacting with Others:** Establishing and Maintaining Interpersonal Relationships; Communicating with Persons Outside Organization; Coordinating the Work and Activities of Others. **Physical Work Conditions:** Standing; Extremely Bright or Inadequate Lighting; Very Hot or Cold; Outdoors; Kneeling, Crouching, Stooping, or Crawling.

Radio Operators

Receive and transmit communications, using radiotelegraph or radiotelephone equipment in accordance with government regulations. May repair equipment. **O*NET Code:** 27-4013.00. **Average Salary:** $31,040. **Projected Growth:** -6.2%. **Annual Openings:** Fewer than 500. **Education:** Long-term on-the-job training. **Job Zone:** 3. **Education/Training Program(s)**—Communications Systems Installation and Repair Technology. **Related Knowledge/Courses:** Telecommunications; Computers and Electronics; Geography; Communications and Media; Engineering and Technology;

Physics. **Personality Type:** Realistic. **Skills Required:** Operation Monitoring; Active Listening; Speaking; Operation and Control; Troubleshooting; Repairing; Coordination; Reading Comprehension; Equipment Maintenance. **Abilities:** Response Orientation; Reaction Time; Auditory Attention; Sound Localization; Control Precision. **Occupational Values:** Achievement; Supervision, Human Relations; Variety; Company Policies and Practices; Ability Utilization; Independence; Working Conditions; Recognition. **Interacting with Others:** Communicating with Supervisors, Peers, or Subordinates; Interpreting the Meaning of Information for Others; Establishing and Maintaining Interpersonal Relationships; Performing Administrative Activities. **Physical Work Conditions:** Sitting; Using Hands on Objects, Tools, or Controls; Indoors.

Sound Engineering Technicians

Operate machines and equipment to record, synchronize, mix, or reproduce music, voices, or sound effects in sporting arenas, theater productions, recording studios, or movie and video productions. **O*NET Code:** 27-4014.00. **Average Salary:** $37,220. **Projected Growth:** 25.5%. **Annual Openings:** 2,000. **Education:** Postsecondary vocational training. **Job Zone:** 3. **Education/Training Program(s)**—Communications Technology/Technician; Recording Arts Technology/Technician. **Related Knowledge/Courses:** Computers and Electronics; Engineering and Technology; Telecommunications; Communications and Media; Administration and Management; Fine Arts. **Personality Type:** Realistic. **Skills Required:** Operation and Control; Operation Monitoring; Equipment Maintenance; Management of Personnel Resources; Equipment Selection; Troubleshooting; Management of Material Resources; Quality Control Analysis. **Abilities:** Hearing Sensitivity; Auditory Attention; Sound Localization; Flexibility of Closure; Selective Attention; Response Orientation. **Occupational Values:** Authority; Working Conditions; Creativity; Moral Values; Company Policies and Practices. **Interacting with Others:** Communicating with Supervisors, Peers, or Subordinates; Establishing and Maintaining Interpersonal Relationships; Guiding, Directing, and Motivating Subordinates. **Physical Work Conditions:** Sitting; Using Hands on Objects, Tools, or Controls; Indoors; Spend Time Making Repetitive Motions; Standing.

03.10 Communications Technology

Air Traffic Controllers

Control air traffic on and within vicinity of airport and movement of air traffic between altitude sectors and control centers according to established procedures and policies. Authorize, regulate, and control commercial airline flights according to government or company regulations to expedite and ensure flight safety. **O*NET Code:** 53-2021.00. **Average Salary:** $97,020. **Projected Growth:** 12.6%. **Annual Openings:** 2,000. **Education:** Long-term on-the-job training.

Job Zone: 4. **Education/Training Program(s)**—Air Traffic Controller. **Related Knowledge/Courses:** Transportation; Physics; Telecommunications; Geography; Computers and Electronics; Clerical. **Personality Type:** Conventional. **Skills Required:** Operation and Control; Operation Monitoring; Active Listening; Coordination; Critical Thinking; Active Learning; Troubleshooting; Judgment and Decision Making; Systems Analysis. **Abilities:** Auditory Attention; Perceptual Speed; Spatial Orientation; Reaction Time; Time Sharing. **Occupational Values:** Authority; Supervision, Technical; Responsibility; Ability Utilization; Achievement. **Interacting with Others:** Communicating with Supervisors, Peers, or Subordinates; Assisting and Caring for Others; Coordinating the Work and Activities of Others. **Physical Work Conditions:** Sitting; Indoors; Using Hands on Objects, Tools, or Controls; Sounds, Noise Levels Are Distracting or Uncomfortable; Extremely Bright or Inadequate Lighting.

Airfield Operations Specialists

Ensure the safe takeoff and landing of commercial and military aircraft. Duties include coordination between air-traffic control and maintenance personnel; dispatching; using airfield landing and navigational aids; implementing airfield safety procedures; monitoring and maintaining flight records; and applying knowledge of weather information. **O*NET Code:** 53-2022.00. **Average Salary:** $36,710. **Projected Growth:** 17.2%. **Annual Openings:** 1,000. **Education:** Short-term on-the-job training. **Job Zone:** No data available. **Education/Training Program(s)**—Air Traffic Controller. **Related Knowledge/Courses:** No data available. **Personality Type:** No data available. **Skills Required:** No data available. **Abilities:** No data available. **Occupational Values:** No data available. **Interacting with Others:** No data available. **Physical Work Conditions:** No data available.

Central Office Operators

Operate telephone switchboard to establish or assist customers in establishing local or long-distance telephone connections. **O*NET Code:** 43-2021.02. **Average Salary:** $29,090. **Projected Growth:** –56.3%. **Annual Openings:** 6,000. **Education:** Short-term on-the-job training. **Job Zone:** 1. **Education/Training Program(s)**—Customer Service Support/Call Center/Teleservice Operation; Receptionist. **Related Knowledge/Courses:** Telecommunications; Administration and Management. **Personality Type:** Conventional. **Skills Required:** Service Orientation; Operation and Control. **Abilities:** Speech Recognition; Wrist-Finger Speed; Speech Clarity; Oral Expression. **Occupational Values:** Supervision, Technical; Social Service; Independence; Supervision, Human Relations; Activity. **Interacting with Others:** Communicating with Persons Outside Organization; Performing for or Working Directly with the Public; Assisting and Caring for Others. **Physical Work Conditions:** Sitting; Indoors; Using Hands on Objects, Tools, or Controls.

Directory Assistance Operators

Provide telephone information from central office switchboard. Refer to alphabetical or geographical reels or directories to answer questions or suggest answer sources. **O*NET Code:** 43-2021.01. **Average Salary:** $29,090. **Projected Growth:** –56.3%. **Annual Openings:** 6,000. **Education:**

Short-term on-the-job training. **Job Zone:** 1. **Education/Training Program(s)**—Customer Service Support/Call Center/Teleservice Operation; Receptionist. **Related Knowledge/Courses:** Telecommunications; Geography; Clerical; Computers and Electronics; Communications and Media; Foreign Language. **Personality Type:** Conventional. **Skills Required:** Service Orientation. **Abilities:** Reaction Time; Speech Recognition; Perceptual Speed; Wrist-Finger Speed; Speech Clarity. **Occupational Values:** Supervision, Technical; Independence; Activity; Social Service; Supervision, Human Relations. **Interacting with Others:** Communicating with Persons Outside Organization; Assisting and Caring for Others; Establishing and Maintaining Interpersonal Relationships. **Physical Work Conditions:** Sitting; Indoors; Spend Time Making Repetitive Motions; Using Hands on Objects, Tools, or Controls.

Dispatchers, Except Police, Fire, and Ambulance

Schedule and dispatch workers, work crews, equipment, or service vehicles for conveyance of materials, freight, or passengers or for normal installation, service, or emergency repairs rendered outside the place of business. Duties may include using radio, telephone, or computer to transmit assignments and compiling statistics and reports on work progress. **O*NET Code:** 43-5032.00. **Average Salary:** $30,610. **Projected Growth:** 14.4%. **Annual Openings:** 28,000. **Education:** Moderate-term on-the-job training. **Job Zone:** 2. **Education/Training Program(s)**—No data available. **Related Knowledge/Courses:** Transportation; Clerical; Public Safety and Security; Customer and Personal Service; Computers and Electronics; Geography; Communications and Media. **Personality Type:** Conventional. **Skills Required:** Service Orientation; Operations Analysis; Management of Personnel Resources; Critical Thinking; Learning Strategies; Instructing; Social Perceptiveness; Troubleshooting; Time Management. **Abilities:** Speech Recognition; Speech Clarity; Time Sharing; Auditory Attention; Oral Expression. **Occupational Values:** Authority; Supervision, Technical; Social Service; Supervision, Human Relations. **Interacting with Others:** Communicating with Supervisors, Peers, or Subordinates; Establishing and Maintaining Interpersonal Relationships; Performing Administrative Activities. **Physical Work Conditions:** Sitting; Sounds, Noise Levels Are Distracting or Uncomfortable; Physical Proximity; Contaminants; Indoors.

Police, Fire, and Ambulance Dispatchers

Receive complaints from public concerning crimes and police emergencies. Broadcast orders to police patrol units in vicinity of complaint to investigate. Operate radio, telephone, or computer equipment to receive reports of fires and medical emergencies and relay information or orders to proper officials. **O*NET Code:** 43-5031.00. **Average Salary:** $28,510. **Projected Growth:** 12.7%. **Annual Openings:** 15,000. **Education:** Moderate-term on-the-job training. **Job Zone:** 2. **Education/Training Program(s)**—No data available. **Related Knowledge/Courses:** Customer and Personal Service; Telecommunications; Clerical; Public Safety and Security; Law and Government; Computers and Electronics. **Personality Type:** Social. **Skills Required:** Active Listening; Speaking; Social Perceptiveness; Critical Thinking; Service Orientation; Judgment and Decision Making; Active Learning; Coordination. **Abilities:** Speech Recognition; Perceptual Speed; Speed of Closure; Category Flexibility; Flexibility of Closure; Selective Attention. **Occupational Values:** Authority; Social Service; Supervision, Technical; Supervision, Human Relations; Security. **Interacting with Others:** Performing for or Working Directly with the Public; Resolving Conflicts and Negotiating with Others; Communicating with Persons Outside Organization. **Physical Work Conditions:** Sitting; Sounds, Noise Levels Are Distracting or Uncomfortable; Physical Proximity; Indoors; Contaminants.

03.11 Musical Instrument Repair

Keyboard Instrument Repairers and Tuners

Repair, adjust, refinish, and tune musical keyboard instruments. **O*NET Code:** 49-9063.01. **Average Salary:** $28,440. **Projected Growth:** 6.3%. **Annual Openings:** 1,000. **Education:** Long-term on-the-job training. **Job Zone:** 3. **Education/Training Program(s)**—Musical Instrument Fabrication and Repair. **Related Knowledge/Courses:** Mechanical; Fine Arts; Engineering and Technology. **Personality Type:** Realistic. **Skills Required:** Repairing; Installation; Troubleshooting; Quality Control Analysis; Equipment Maintenance; Operation Monitoring; Equipment Selection. **Abilities:** Hearing Sensitivity; Sound Localization; Extent Flexibility; Dynamic Flexibility; Wrist-Finger Speed. **Occupational Values:** Independence; Moral Values; Working Conditions; Autonomy; Supervision, Technical. **Interacting with Others:** Communicating with Persons Outside Organization; Monitoring and Controlling Resources; Communicating with Supervisors, Peers, or Subordinates; Assisting and Caring for Others. **Physical Work Conditions:** Using Hands on Objects, Tools, or Controls; Indoors; Spend Time Making Repetitive Motions; Kneeling, Crouching, Stooping, or Crawling; Spend Time Bending or Twisting the Body.

Percussion Instrument Repairers and Tuners

Repair and tune musical percussion instruments. **O*NET Code:** 49-9063.04. **Average Salary:** $28,440. **Projected Growth:** 6.3%. **Annual Openings:** 1,000. **Education:** Long-term on-the-job training. **Job Zone:** 3. **Education/Training Program(s)**—Musical Instrument Fabrication and Repair. **Related Knowledge/Courses:** Fine Arts; Mechanical. **Personality Type:** Realistic. **Skills Required:** Repairing; Equipment Maintenance; Quality Control Analysis; Equipment Selection; Installation. **Abilities:** Hearing Sensitivity; Speed of Limb Movement; Auditory Attention; Finger Dexterity; Explosive Strength; Trunk Strength. **Occupational Values:** Independence; Moral Values; Working Conditions; Autonomy; Supervision, Technical; Responsibility. **Interacting with Others:** Monitoring and Controlling Resources; Communicating with Supervisors, Peers, or Subordinates; Providing Consultation and Advice to Others. **Physical Work Conditions:** Using Hands on Objects,

Tools, or Controls; Hazardous Equipment; Minor Burns, Cuts, Bites, or Stings; Indoors; Sitting.

Reed or Wind Instrument Repairers and Tuners

Repair, adjust, refinish, and tune musical reed and wind instruments. **O*NET Code:** 49-9063.03. **Average Salary:** $28,440. **Projected Growth:** 6.3%. **Annual Openings:** 1,000. **Education:** Long-term on-the-job training. **Job Zone:** 4. **Education/Training Program(s)**—Musical Instrument Fabrication and Repair. **Related Knowledge/Courses:** Mechanical; Administration and Management. **Personality Type:** Realistic. **Skills Required:** Repairing; Troubleshooting; Equipment Maintenance; Installation; Quality Control Analysis. **Abilities:** Hearing Sensitivity; Auditory Attention; Sound Localization; Speed of Limb Movement; Finger Dexterity; Depth Perception. **Occupational Values:** Independence; Moral Values; Working Conditions; Autonomy; Supervision, Technical; Responsibility. **Interacting with Others:** Communicating with Persons Outside Organization; Monitoring and Controlling Resources; Providing Consultation and Advice to Others. **Physical Work Conditions:** Using Hands on Objects, Tools, or Controls; Indoors; Sitting; Common Protective or Safety Equipment; Spend Time Making Repetitive Motions.

Stringed Instrument Repairers and Tuners

Repair, adjust, refinish, and tune musical stringed instruments. **O*NET Code:** 49-9063.02. **Average Salary:** $28,440. **Projected Growth:** 6.3%. **Annual Openings:** 1,000. **Education:** Long-term on-the-job training. **Job Zone:** 3. **Education/Training Program(s)**—Musical Instrument Fabrication and Repair. **Related Knowledge/Courses:** Fine Arts; Building and Construction. **Personality Type:** Realistic. **Skills Required:** Repairing; Technology Design; Equipment Maintenance; Troubleshooting; Quality Control Analysis. **Abilities:** Hearing Sensitivity; Auditory Attention; Sound Localization; Speed of Limb Movement; Visualization. **Occupational Values:** Independence; Moral Values; Working Conditions; Autonomy; Ability Utilization. **Interacting with Others:** Communicating with Supervisors, Peers, or Subordinates; Monitoring and Controlling Resources; Communicating with Persons Outside Organization; Establishing and Maintaining Interpersonal Relationships. **Physical Work Conditions:** Using Hands on Objects, Tools, or Controls; Indoors; Sitting; Spend Time Bending or Twisting the Body; Spend Time Making Repetitive Motions.

04 Business and Administration

04.01 **Managerial Work in General Business**

04.02 **Managerial Work in Business Detail**

04.03 **Human Resources Support**

04.04 **Secretarial Support**

04.05 **Accounting, Auditing, and Analytical Support**

04.06 **Mathematical Clerical Support**

04.07 **Records and Materials Processing**

04.08 **Clerical Machine Operation**

04.01 Managerial Work in General Business

Chief Executives

Determine and formulate policies and provide the overall direction of companies or private- and public-sector organizations within the guidelines set up by a board of directors or similar governing body. Plan, direct, or coordinate operational activities at the highest level of management with the help of subordinate executives and staff managers. **O*NET Code:** 11-1011.00. **Average Salary:** $136,400. **Projected Growth:** 16.7%. **Annual Openings:** 63,000. **Education:** Work experience plus degree. **Job Zone:** No data available. **Education/Training Program(s)**—Business Administration and Management, General; Business/Commerce, General; Entrepreneurship/Entrepreneurial Studies; International Business/Trade/Commerce; Public Administration; Public Administration and Social Service Professions, Other; Public Policy Analysis. **Related Knowledge/Courses:** No data available. **Personality Type:** No data available. **Skills Required:** No data available. **Abilities:** No data available. **Occupational Values:** No data available. **Interacting with Others:** No data available. **Physical Work Conditions:** No data available.

Compensation and Benefits Managers

Plan, direct, or coordinate compensation and benefits activities and staff of an organization. **O*NET Code:** 11-3041.00. **Average Salary:** $72,180. **Projected Growth:** 19.4%. **Annual Openings:** 21,000. **Education:** Work experience plus degree. **Job Zone:** 3. **Education/Training Program(s)**—Human Resources Management/Personnel Administration, General; Labor and Industrial Relations. **Related Knowledge/Courses:** Personnel and Human Resources; Clerical; Administration and Management; Economics and Accounting; Law and Government; Education and Training. **Personality Type:** Enterprising. **Skills Required:** Management of Personnel Resources; Management of Financial Resources; Time Management; Social Perceptiveness; Monitoring; Instructing; Management of Material Resources; Negotiation. **Abilities:** Originality; Written Expression; Mathematical Reasoning; Inductive Reasoning; Deductive Reasoning. **Occupational Values:** Authority; Working Conditions; Social Service; Ability Utilization; Autonomy. **Interacting with Others:** Communicating with Supervisors, Peers, or Subordinates; Establishing and Maintaining Interpersonal Relationships; Communicating with Persons Outside Organization. **Physical Work Conditions:** Sitting; Physical Proximity; Indoors; Sounds, Noise Levels Are Distracting or Uncomfortable; Contaminants.

General and Operations Managers

Plan, direct, or coordinate the operations of companies or public- and private-sector organizations. Duties and responsibilities include formulating policies, managing daily operations, and planning the use of materials and human resources, but are too diverse and general in nature to be classified in any one functional area of management or administration such as personnel, purchasing, or administrative services. Includes owners and managers who head small business establishments whose duties are primarily managerial. **O*NET Code:** 11-1021.00. **Average Salary:** $74,600. **Projected Growth:** 18.4%. **Annual Openings:** 260,000. **Education:** Work experience plus degree. **Job Zone:** 4. **Education/Training Program(s)**—Business Administration and Management, General; Business/Commerce, General; Entrepreneurship/Entrepreneurial Studies; International Business/Trade/Commerce; Public Administration. **Related Knowledge/Courses:** Sales and Marketing; Customer and Personal Service; Administration and Management; Personnel and Human Resources; Economics and Accounting; Law and Government. **Personality Type:** No data available. **Skills Required:** Management of Financial Resources; Management of Personnel Resources; Management of Material Resources; Negotiation; Monitoring; Persuasion; Coordination; Social Perceptiveness. **Abilities:** Speech Recognition; Mathematical Reasoning; Originality; Speech Clarity; Fluency of Ideas; Inductive Reasoning. **Occupational Values:** No data available. **Interacting with Others:** Establishing and Maintaining Interpersonal Relationships; Communicating with Supervisors, Peers, or Subordinates; Resolving Conflicts and Negotiating with Others. **Physical Work Conditions:** Sounds, Noise Levels Are Distracting or Uncomfortable; Sitting; Physical Proximity; Indoors, Not Environmentally Controlled; Very Hot or Cold; Walking and Running.

Human Resources Managers

Plan, direct, and coordinate human resource management activities of an organization to maximize the strategic use of human resources and maintain functions such as employee compensation, recruitment, personnel policies, and regulatory compliance. **O*NET Code:** 11-3040.00. **Average Salary:** $70,350. **Projected Growth:** 19.4%. **Annual Openings:** 21,000. **Education:** Work experience plus degree. **Job Zone:** 4. **Education/Training Program(s)**—Human Resources Development; Human Resources Management/Personnel Administration, General; Labor and Industrial Relations; Labor Studies. **Related Knowledge/Courses:** Personnel and Human Resources; Clerical; Education and Training; Law and Government; Customer and Personal Service; Economics and Accounting. **Personality Type:** Enterprising. **Skills Required:** Management of Personnel Resources; Negotiation; Persuasion; Time Management; Social Perceptiveness; Learning Strategies; Active Listening; Management of Financial Resources. **Abilities:** Speech Clarity; Speech Recognition; Category Flexibility; Mathematical Reasoning; Written Expression. **Occupational Values:** Authority; Working Conditions; Social Service; Ability Utilization; Autonomy. **Interacting with Others:** Establishing and Maintaining Interpersonal Relationships; Resolving Conflicts and Negotiating with Others; Staffing Organizational Units. **Physical Work Conditions:** Sitting; Indoors; Sounds, Noise Levels Are Distracting or Uncomfortable; Physical Proximity; Very Hot or Cold.

Private Sector Executives

Determine and formulate policies and business strategies and provide overall direction of private-sector organizations. Plan, direct, and coordinate operational activities at the highest level of management with the help of subordinate managers.

O*NET Code: 11-1011.02. **Average Salary:** $136,400. **Projected Growth:** 16.7%. **Annual Openings:** 63,000. **Education:** Work experience plus degree. **Job Zone:** 5. **Education/Training Program(s)**—Business Administration and Management, General; Business/Commerce, General; Entrepreneurship/Entrepreneurial Studies; International Business/Trade/Commerce; Public Administration; Public Administration and Social Service Professions, Other; Public Policy Analysis. **Related Knowledge/Courses:** Economics and Accounting; Production and Processing; Administration and Management; Sales and Marketing; Personnel and Human Resources; Psychology. **Personality Type:** Enterprising. **Skills Required:** Management of Financial Resources; Systems Evaluation; Systems Analysis; Management of Personnel Resources; Coordination; Judgment and Decision Making; Management of Material Resources; Negotiation. **Abilities:** Speech Clarity; Originality; Written Expression; Fluency of Ideas; Written Comprehension; Oral Expression. **Occupational Values:** Authority; Social Status; Autonomy; Compensation; Responsibility. **Interacting with Others:** Communicating with Supervisors, Peers, or Subordinates; Monitoring and Controlling Resources; Providing Consultation and Advice to Others. **Physical Work Conditions:** Sitting; Indoors; Walking and Running.

Training and Development Managers

Plan, direct, or coordinate the training and development activities and staff of an organization. O*NET Code: 11-3042.00. **Average Salary:** $72,180. **Projected Growth:** 19.4%. **Annual Openings:** 21,000. **Education:** Work experience plus degree. **Job Zone:** 4. **Education/Training Program(s)**—Human Resources Development; Human Resources Management/Personnel Administration, General. **Related Knowledge/Courses:** Clerical; Personnel and Human Resources; Administration and Management; Education and Training; Psychology; Computers and Electronics. **Personality Type:** Enterprising. **Skills Required:** Management of Personnel Resources; Management of Financial Resources; Learning Strategies; Negotiation; Instructing; Service Orientation; Social Perceptiveness; Persuasion. **Abilities:** Speech Clarity; Speech Recognition; Fluency of Ideas; Inductive Reasoning; Originality. **Occupational Values:** Authority; Social Service; Working Conditions; Co-workers; Creativity. **Interacting with Others:** Establishing and Maintaining Interpersonal Relationships; Communicating with Supervisors, Peers, or Subordinates; Training and Teaching Others. **Physical Work Conditions:** Physical Proximity; Sitting; Sounds, Noise Levels Are Distracting or Uncomfortable; Very Hot or Cold; Extremely Bright or Inadequate Lighting.

04.02 Managerial Work in Business Detail

Administrative Services Managers

Plan, direct, or coordinate supportive services of an organization, such as recordkeeping, mail distribution, telephone operator/receptionist, and other office support services. May oversee facilities planning and maintenance and custodial operations. O*NET Code: 11-3011.00. **Average Salary:** $58,130. **Projected Growth:** 19.8%. **Annual Openings:** 40,000. **Education:** Work experience plus degree. **Job Zone:** 4. **Education/Training Program(s)**—Business Administration and Management, General; Business/Commerce, General; Medical/Health Management and Clinical Assistant/Specialist; Public Administration; Purchasing, Procurement/Acquisitions, and Contracts Management. **Related Knowledge/Courses:** Personnel and Human Resources; Clerical; Customer and Personal Service; Economics and Accounting; Administration and Management; Public Safety and Security; Law and Government. **Personality Type:** Enterprising. **Skills Required:** Management of Personnel Resources; Service Orientation; Coordination; Management of Financial Resources; Monitoring; Social Perceptiveness; Speaking; Time Management. **Abilities:** Speech Recognition; Written Expression; Originality; Near Vision; Oral Expression; Far Vision. **Occupational Values:** Authority; Working Conditions; Responsibility; Autonomy; Advancement. **Interacting with Others:** Establishing and Maintaining Interpersonal Relationships; Communicating with Supervisors, Peers, or Subordinates; Resolving Conflicts and Negotiating with Others. **Physical Work Conditions:** Sitting; Sounds, Noise Levels Are Distracting or Uncomfortable; Contaminants; Indoors; Very Hot or Cold.

First-Line Supervisors, Administrative Support

Supervise and coordinate activities of workers involved in providing administrative support. O*NET Code: 43-1011.02. **Average Salary:** $39,920. **Projected Growth:** 6.6%. **Annual Openings:** 140,000. **Education:** Work experience in a related occupation. **Job Zone:** 3. **Education/Training Program(s)**—Agricultural Business Technology; Customer Service Management; Medical/Health Management and Clinical Assistant/Specialist; Office Management and Supervision. **Related Knowledge/Courses:** Clerical; Personnel and Human Resources; Transportation; Economics and Accounting; Administration and Management; Law and Government. **Personality Type:** Enterprising. **Skills Required:** Management of Personnel Resources; Management of Financial Resources; Management of Material Resources; Social Perceptiveness; Time Management; Monitoring; Instructing; Systems Evaluation. **Abilities:** Number Facility; Mathematical Reasoning; Wrist-Finger Speed; Written Expression; Memorization. **Occupational Values:** Authority; Autonomy; Creativity; Responsibility; Variety; Working Conditions; Advancement; Social Service. **Interacting with Others:** Communicating with Supervisors, Peers, or Subordinates; Establishing and Maintaining Interpersonal Relationships; Resolving Conflicts and Negotiating with Others; Guiding, Directing, and Motivating Subordinates. **Physical Work Conditions:** Sitting; Indoors; Walking and Running; Standing.

First-Line Supervisors, Customer Service

Supervise and coordinate activities of workers involved in providing customer service. O*NET Code: 43-1011.01. **Average Salary:** $39,920. **Projected Growth:** 6.6%. **Annual**

© 2006, JIST Works

Openings: 140,000. **Education:** Work experience in a related occupation. **Job Zone:** 3. **Education/Training Program(s)**— Agricultural Business Technology; Customer Service Management; Medical/Health Management and Clinical Assistant/Specialist; Office Management and Supervision. **Related Knowledge/Courses:** Customer and Personal Service; Personnel and Human Resources; Administration and Management; Clerical; Economics and Accounting; Education and Training. **Personality Type:** Enterprising. **Skills Required:** Management of Personnel Resources; Management of Financial Resources; Service Orientation; Social Perceptiveness; Coordination; Time Management; Systems Evaluation; Learning Strategies. **Abilities:** Speech Recognition; Memorization; Written Expression; Mathematical Reasoning; Originality; Speech Clarity. **Occupational Values:** Authority; Autonomy; Social Service; Creativity; Variety; Working Conditions; Advancement. **Interacting with Others:** Guiding, Directing, and Motivating Subordinates; Communicating with Supervisors, Peers, or Subordinates; Resolving Conflicts and Negotiating with Others; Coordinating the Work and Activities of Others. **Physical Work Conditions:** Sitting; Walking and Running; Indoors; Standing.

Housekeeping Supervisors

Supervise work activities of cleaning personnel to ensure clean, orderly, and attractive rooms in hotels, hospitals, educational institutions, and similar establishments. Assign duties, inspect work, and investigate complaints regarding housekeeping service and equipment and take corrective action. May purchase housekeeping supplies and equipment, take periodic inventories, screen applicants, train new employees, and recommend dismissals. **O*NET Code:** 37-1011.01. **Average Salary:** $29,170. **Projected Growth:** 16.2%. **Annual Openings:** 28,000. **Education:** Work experience in a related occupation. **Job Zone:** 4. **Education/Training Program(s)**—No data available. **Related Knowledge/Courses:** Personnel and Human Resources; Customer and Personal Service; Administration and Management; Clerical; Education and Training; Foreign Language. **Personality Type:** Enterprising. **Skills Required:** Management of Personnel Resources; Time Management; Management of Financial Resources; Management of Material Resources; Coordination; Speaking; Systems Evaluation; Systems Analysis. **Abilities:** Oral Expression; Written Expression; Oral Comprehension; Written Comprehension; Spatial Orientation. **Occupational Values:** Authority; Co-workers; Variety; Creativity; Responsibility; Autonomy. **Interacting with Others:** Communicating with Supervisors, Peers, or Subordinates; Guiding, Directing, and Motivating Subordinates; Establishing and Maintaining Interpersonal Relationships; Coordinating the Work and Activities of Others. **Physical Work Conditions:** Sitting; Indoors; Walking and Running; Standing; Climbing Ladders, Scaffolds, or Poles.

Janitorial Supervisors

Supervise work activities of janitorial personnel in commercial and industrial establishments. Assign duties, inspect work, and investigate complaints regarding janitorial services and take corrective action. May purchase janitorial supplies and equipment, take periodic inventories, screen applicants, train new employees, and recommend dismissals. **O*NET**

Code: 37-1011.02. **Average Salary:** $29,170. **Projected Growth:** 16.2%. **Annual Openings:** 28,000. **Education:** Work experience in a related occupation. **Job Zone:** 3. **Education/Training Program(s)**—No data available. **Related Knowledge/Courses:** Personnel and Human Resources; Administration and Management; Customer and Personal Service; Education and Training. **Personality Type:** Enterprising. **Skills Required:** Management of Personnel Resources; Coordination; Time Management; Social Perceptiveness; Persuasion; Negotiation; Instructing; Speaking; Management of Material Resources. **Abilities:** Oral Expression; Trunk Strength; Dynamic Strength; Manual Dexterity; Problem Sensitivity; Perceptual Speed. **Occupational Values:** Authority; Autonomy; Responsibility; Activity; Co-workers; Creativity. **Interacting with Others:** Establishing and Maintaining Interpersonal Relationships; Communicating with Supervisors, Peers, or Subordinates; Resolving Conflicts and Negotiating with Others; Coordinating the Work and Activities of Others; Staffing Organizational Units. **Physical Work Conditions:** Standing; Walking and Running; Contaminants; Spend Time Bending or Twisting the Body; Kneeling, Crouching, Stooping, or Crawling.

Meeting and Convention Planners

Coordinate activities of staff and convention personnel to make arrangements for group meetings and conventions. **O*NET Code:** 13-1121.00. **Average Salary:** $39,070. **Projected Growth:** 21.3%. **Annual Openings:** 7,000. **Education:** Bachelor's degree. **Job Zone:** 4. **Education/Training Program(s)**—Selling Skills and Sales Operations. **Related Knowledge/Courses:** Sales and Marketing; Customer and Personal Service; Personnel and Human Resources; Administration and Management; Education and Training; Clerical. **Personality Type:** Enterprising. **Skills Required:** Service Orientation; Coordination; Negotiation; Time Management; Persuasion; Social Perceptiveness; Operations Analysis; Management of Financial Resources. **Abilities:** Speech Recognition; Far Vision; Visualization; Fluency of Ideas; Memorization. **Occupational Values:** Authority; Creativity; Working Conditions; Variety; Recognition; Social Service. **Interacting with Others:** Establishing and Maintaining Interpersonal Relationships; Communicating with Supervisors, Peers, or Subordinates; Communicating with Persons Outside Organization. **Physical Work Conditions:** Sitting; Sounds, Noise Levels Are Distracting or Uncomfortable; Extremely Bright or Inadequate Lighting; Physical Proximity.

04.03 Human Resources Support

Compensation, Benefits, and Job Analysis Specialists

Conduct programs of compensation and benefits and job analysis for employer. May specialize in specific areas, such as position classification and pension programs. **O*NET Code:**

13-1072.00. **Average Salary:** $46,890. **Projected Growth:** 28.0%. **Annual Openings:** 15,000. **Education:** Bachelor's degree. **Job Zone:** 4. **Education/Training Program(s)—** Human Resources Management/Personnel Administration, General; Labor and Industrial Relations. **Related Knowledge/Courses:** Personnel and Human Resources; Clerical; Customer and Personal Service; English Language; Administration and Management; Education and Training. **Personality Type:** Investigative. **Skills Required:** Service Orientation; Persuasion; Coordination; Negotiation; Active Listening; Critical Thinking; Time Management; Social Perceptiveness. **Abilities:** Written Expression; Speech Clarity; Oral Expression; Deductive Reasoning; Originality. **Occupational Values:** Working Conditions; Authority; Co-workers; Responsibility; Ability Utilization; Autonomy. **Interacting with Others:** Establishing and Maintaining Interpersonal Relationships; Communicating with Supervisors, Peers, or Subordinates; Performing Administrative Activities. **Physical Work Conditions:** Sitting; Sounds, Noise Levels Are Distracting or Uncomfortable; Indoors; Contaminants; Physical Proximity.

Employment Interviewers, Private or Public Employment Service

Interview job applicants in employment office and refer them to prospective employers for consideration. Search application files, notify selected applicants of job openings, and refer qualified applicants to prospective employers. Contact employers to verify referral results. Record and evaluate various pertinent data. **O*NET Code:** 13-1071.01. **Average Salary:** $40,970. **Projected Growth:** 27.3%. **Annual Openings:** 29,000. **Education:** Bachelor's degree. **Job Zone:** 3. **Education/Training Program(s)—**Human Resources Management/Personnel Administration, General; Labor and Industrial Relations. **Related Knowledge/Courses:** Customer and Personal Service; Clerical; Foreign Language; Personnel and Human Resources; English Language; Sales and Marketing. **Personality Type:** Social. **Skills Required:** Service Orientation; Social Perceptiveness; Persuasion; Management of Personnel Resources; Negotiation; Instructing; Speaking; Time Management. **Abilities:** Speech Recognition; Category Flexibility; Speech Clarity; Oral Comprehension; Oral Expression. **Occupational Values:** Social Service; Working Conditions; Advancement; Co-workers; Supervision, Human Relations; Supervision, Technical. **Interacting with Others:** Establishing and Maintaining Interpersonal Relationships; Resolving Conflicts and Negotiating with Others; Performing for or Working Directly with the Public. **Physical Work Conditions:** Sitting; Physical Proximity; Sounds, Noise Levels Are Distracting or Uncomfortable; Extremely Bright or Inadequate Lighting; In an Enclosed Vehicle or Equipment.

Personnel Recruiters

Seek out, interview, and screen applicants to fill existing and future job openings and promote career opportunities within an organization. **O*NET Code:** 13-1071.02. **Average Salary:** $40,970. **Projected Growth:** 27.3%. **Annual Openings:** 29,000. **Education:** Bachelor's degree. **Job Zone:** 4. **Education/Training Program(s)—**Human Resources Management/Personnel Administration, General; Labor and Industrial Relations. **Related Knowledge/Courses:** Personnel

and Human Resources; Clerical; Education and Training; Sales and Marketing; Administration and Management; Computers and Electronics. **Personality Type:** Enterprising. **Skills Required:** Management of Personnel Resources; Negotiation; Persuasion; Service Orientation; Time Management; Management of Financial Resources; Monitoring; Social Perceptiveness. **Abilities:** Speech Recognition; Category Flexibility; Inductive Reasoning; Flexibility of Closure; Speed of Closure. **Occupational Values:** Working Conditions; Social Service; Supervision, Human Relations; Achievement; Advancement; Responsibility. **Interacting with Others:** Establishing and Maintaining Interpersonal Relationships; Communicating with Supervisors, Peers, or Subordinates; Communicating with Persons Outside Organization; Resolving Conflicts and Negotiating with Others. **Physical Work Conditions:** Sitting; Sounds, Noise Levels Are Distracting or Uncomfortable; Contaminants; Physical Proximity; Indoors.

Training and Development Specialists

Conduct training and development programs for employees. **O*NET Code:** 13-1073.00. **Average Salary:** $44,270. **Projected Growth:** 27.9%. **Annual Openings:** 35,000. **Education:** Bachelor's degree. **Job Zone:** 4. **Education/Training Program(s)—**Human Resources Management/Personnel Administration, General; Organizational Behavior Studies. **Related Knowledge/Courses:** Customer and Personal Service; Psychology; Sociology and Anthropology; Personnel and Human Resources; Education and Training; Clerical; Public Safety and Security. **Personality Type:** Social. **Skills Required:** Service Orientation; Instructing; Social Perceptiveness; Writing; Persuasion; Active Learning; Speaking; Time Management. **Abilities:** Speech Clarity; Originality; Oral Expression; Written Expression; Fluency of Ideas. **Occupational Values:** Authority; Social Service; Co-workers; Creativity; Working Conditions. **Interacting with Others:** Communicating with Supervisors, Peers, or Subordinates; Training and Teaching Others; Establishing and Maintaining Interpersonal Relationships. **Physical Work Conditions:** Physical Proximity; Sounds, Noise Levels Are Distracting or Uncomfortable; In an Enclosed Vehicle or Equipment; Sitting; Cramped Work Space, Awkward Positions.

04.04 Secretarial Support

Executive Secretaries and Administrative Assistants

Provide high-level administrative support by conducting research, preparing statistical reports, handling information requests, and performing clerical functions such as preparing correspondence, receiving visitors, arranging conference calls, and scheduling meetings. May also train and supervise lower-level clerical staff. **O*NET Code:** 43-6011.00. **Average Salary:** $34,350. **Projected Growth:** 8.7%. **Annual Openings:** 210,000. **Education:** Moderate-term on-the-job training. **Job Zone:** 3. **Education/Training Program(s)—**Administrative Assistant and Secretarial Science, General; Executive

© 2006, JIST Works

Assistant/Executive Secretary; Medical Administrative/Executive Assistant and Medical Secretary. **Related Knowledge/Courses:** Clerical; Customer and Personal Service; English Language; Computers and Electronics; Communications and Media; Administration and Management; Personnel and Human Resources. **Personality Type:** Conventional. **Skills Required:** Time Management; Active Listening; Writing; Speaking; Instructing; Service Orientation; Management of Financial Resources; Critical Thinking; Management of Material Resources. **Abilities:** Speech Recognition; Written Expression; Category Flexibility; Oral Comprehension; Time Sharing. **Occupational Values:** Working Conditions; Social Service; Advancement; Company Policies and Practices; Supervision, Human Relations. **Interacting with Others:** Establishing and Maintaining Interpersonal Relationships; Communicating with Supervisors, Peers, or Subordinates; Performing Administrative Activities. **Physical Work Conditions:** Sitting; Sounds, Noise Levels Are Distracting or Uncomfortable; Physical Proximity.

Legal Secretaries

Perform secretarial duties, utilizing legal terminology, procedures, and documents. Prepare legal papers and correspondence, such as summonses, complaints, motions, and subpoenas. May also assist with legal research. O*NET Code: 43-6012.00. **Average Salary:** $35,710. **Projected Growth:** 18.8%. **Annual Openings:** 39,000. **Education:** Postsecondary vocational training. **Job Zone:** 3. **Education/Training Program(s)**—Legal Administrative Assistant/Secretary. **Related Knowledge/Courses:** Clerical; Law and Government; Customer and Personal Service; Economics and Accounting; Computers and Electronics; English Language. **Personality Type:** Conventional. **Skills Required:** Time Management; Writing; Social Perceptiveness; Reading Comprehension; Negotiation; Learning Strategies; Persuasion; Active Learning; Instructing. **Abilities:** Speech Recognition; Near Vision; Written Expression; Oral Comprehension; Written Comprehension. **Occupational Values:** Working Conditions; Activity; Company Policies and Practices; Supervision, Technical; Security; Social Service. **Interacting with Others:** Performing Administrative Activities; Establishing and Maintaining Interpersonal Relationships; Communicating with Persons Outside Organization. **Physical Work Conditions:** Sitting.

Medical Secretaries

Perform secretarial duties, utilizing specific knowledge of medical terminology and hospital, clinic, or laboratory procedures. Duties include scheduling appointments, billing patients, and compiling and recording medical charts, reports, and correspondence. O*NET Code: 43-6013.00. **Average Salary:** $26,050. **Projected Growth:** 17.2%. **Annual Openings:** 50,000. **Education:** Postsecondary vocational training. **Job Zone:** 2. **Education/Training Program(s)**—Medical Administrative/Executive Assistant and Medical Secretary; Medical Insurance Specialist/Medical Biller; Medical Office Assistant/Specialist. **Related Knowledge/Courses:** Customer and Personal Service; Clerical; Telecommunications; English Language; Computers and Electronics; Communications and Media. **Personality Type:**

Conventional. **Skills Required:** Social Perceptiveness; Instructing; Active Listening; Time Management; Writing; Management of Personnel Resources; Reading Comprehension; Speaking; Management of Material Resources. **Abilities:** Speech Recognition; Category Flexibility; Near Vision; Information Ordering; Speech Clarity. **Occupational Values:** Working Conditions; Activity; Company Policies and Practices; Supervision, Technical; Security. **Interacting with Others:** Establishing and Maintaining Interpersonal Relationships; Assisting and Caring for Others; Communicating with Supervisors, Peers, or Subordinates; Performing Administrative Activities. **Physical Work Conditions:** Sounds, Noise Levels Are Distracting or Uncomfortable; Physical Proximity; Sitting; Disease or Infections; Cramped Work Space, Awkward Positions; Exposed to Radiation.

Secretaries, Except Legal, Medical, and Executive

Perform routine clerical and administrative functions such as drafting correspondence, scheduling appointments, organizing and maintaining paper and electronic files, or providing information to callers. O*NET Code: 43-6014.00. **Average Salary:** $25,570. **Projected Growth:** –2.9%. **Annual Openings:** 254,000. **Education:** Moderate-term on-the-job training. **Job Zone:** 2. **Education/Training Program(s)**—Administrative Assistant and Secretarial Science, General; Executive Assistant/Executive Secretary. **Related Knowledge/Courses:** Clerical; Customer and Personal Service; Computers and Electronics; English Language; Economics and Accounting; Personnel and Human Resources. **Personality Type:** Conventional. **Skills Required:** Writing; Social Perceptiveness; Instructing; Active Listening; Time Management; Speaking; Learning Strategies; Persuasion; Management of Financial Resources. **Abilities:** Speech Recognition; Written Expression; Category Flexibility; Time Sharing; Information Ordering; Speech Clarity. **Occupational Values:** Working Conditions; Activity; Company Policies and Practices; Supervision, Technical; Co-workers; Social Service; Moral Values. **Interacting with Others:** Establishing and Maintaining Interpersonal Relationships; Communicating with Supervisors, Peers, or Subordinates; Communicating with Persons Outside Organization. **Physical Work Conditions:** Sitting; Sounds, Noise Levels Are Distracting or Uncomfortable; Physical Proximity; Contaminants; Indoors.

04.05 Accounting, Auditing, and Analytical Support

Accountants

Analyze financial information and prepare financial reports to determine or maintain record of assets, liabilities, profit and loss, tax liability, or other financial activities within an organization. O*NET Code: 13-2011.01. **Average Salary:** $49,770. **Projected Growth:** 19.5%. **Annual Openings:**

119,000. **Education:** Bachelor's degree. **Job Zone:** 4. **Education/Training Program(s)**—Accounting; Accounting and Business/Management; Accounting and Computer Science; Accounting and Finance; Auditing; Taxation. **Related Knowledge/Courses:** Economics and Accounting; Clerical; Mathematics; Law and Government; Customer and Personal Service; Computers and Electronics. **Personality Type:** Conventional. **Skills Required:** Management of Financial Resources; Systems Evaluation; Systems Analysis; Operations Analysis; Judgment and Decision Making; Time Management; Monitoring; Negotiation. **Abilities:** Mathematical Reasoning; Number Facility; Deductive Reasoning; Flexibility of Closure; Inductive Reasoning; Category Flexibility. **Occupational Values:** Working Conditions; Compensation; Social Status; Security; Activity; Authority; Responsibility; Autonomy. **Interacting with Others:** Communicating with Supervisors, Peers, or Subordinates; Establishing and Maintaining Interpersonal Relationships; Providing Consultation and Advice to Others. **Physical Work Conditions:** Sitting; Indoors; Physical Proximity.

Auditors

Examine and analyze accounting records to determine financial status of establishment and prepare financial reports concerning operating procedures. **O*NET Code:** 13-2011.02. **Average Salary:** $49,770. **Projected Growth:** 19.5%. **Annual Openings:** 119,000. **Education:** Bachelor's degree. **Job Zone:** 4. **Education/Training Program(s)**—Accounting; Accounting and Business/Management; Accounting and Computer Science; Accounting and Finance; Auditing; Taxation. **Related Knowledge/Courses:** Economics and Accounting; Customer and Personal Service; Mathematics; Sales and Marketing; Law and Government; Computers and Electronics. **Personality Type:** Conventional. **Skills Required:** Management of Financial Resources; Time Management; Instructing; Negotiation; Service Orientation; Writing; Critical Thinking; Persuasion. **Abilities:** Number Facility; Mathematical Reasoning; Inductive Reasoning; Flexibility of Closure; Problem Sensitivity; Deductive Reasoning. **Occupational Values:** Advancement; Authority; Compensation; Working Conditions; Co-workers. **Interacting with Others:** Establishing and Maintaining Interpersonal Relationships; Communicating with Supervisors, Peers, or Subordinates; Providing Consultation and Advice to Others. **Physical Work Conditions:** Sitting; Sounds, Noise Levels Are Distracting or Uncomfortable; In an Enclosed Vehicle or Equipment; Indoors; Physical Proximity.

Budget Analysts

Examine budget estimates for completeness, accuracy, and conformance with procedures and regulations. Analyze budgeting and accounting reports for the purpose of maintaining expenditure controls. **O*NET Code:** 13-2031.00. **Average Salary:** $55,090. **Projected Growth:** 14.0%. **Annual Openings:** 8,000. **Education:** Bachelor's degree. **Job Zone:** 4. **Education/Training Program(s)**—Accounting; Finance, General. **Related Knowledge/Courses:** Economics and Accounting; Administration and Management; Clerical; Computers and Electronics; Mathematics; English Language. **Personality Type:** Conventional. **Skills Required:**

Management of Financial Resources; Operations Analysis; Mathematics; Service Orientation; Negotiation; Time Management; Active Learning; Monitoring. **Abilities:** Mathematical Reasoning; Number Facility; Written Comprehension; Written Expression; Oral Expression. **Occupational Values:** Advancement; Authority; Working Conditions; Supervision, Human Relations; Ability Utilization; Compensation; Autonomy. **Interacting with Others:** Monitoring and Controlling Resources; Establishing and Maintaining Interpersonal Relationships; Communicating with Supervisors, Peers, or Subordinates; Coordinating the Work and Activities of Others. **Physical Work Conditions:** Sitting; Indoors; Physical Proximity.

Industrial Engineering Technicians

Apply engineering theory and principles to problems of industrial layout or manufacturing production, usually under the direction of engineering staff. May study and record time, motion, method, and speed involved in performance of production, maintenance, clerical, and other worker operations for such purposes as establishing standard production rates or improving efficiency. **O*NET Code:** 17-3026.00. **Average Salary:** $42,870. **Projected Growth:** 8.7%. **Annual Openings:** 7,000. **Education:** Associate degree. **Job Zone:** 3. **Education/Training Program(s)**—Engineering/Industrial Management; Industrial Production Technologies/ Technicians, Other; Industrial Technology/Technician; Manufacturing Technology/Technician. **Related Knowledge/ Courses:** Production and Processing; Clerical; Engineering and Technology; Design; Mathematics; Education and Training. **Personality Type:** Investigative. **Skills Required:** Coordination; Persuasion; Troubleshooting; Instructing; Technology Design; Active Learning; Negotiation; Operations Analysis. **Abilities:** Mathematical Reasoning; Number Facility; Originality; Speed of Closure; Written Expression. **Occupational Values:** Advancement; Supervision, Human Relations; Ability Utilization; Achievement; Variety; Supervision, Technical. **Interacting with Others:** Communicating with Supervisors, Peers, or Subordinates; Establishing and Maintaining Interpersonal Relationships; Coordinating the Work and Activities of Others. **Physical Work Conditions:** Contaminants; Sounds, Noise Levels Are Distracting or Uncomfortable; Physical Proximity; Hazardous Equipment; Indoors, Not Environmentally Controlled.

Logisticians

Analyze and coordinate the logistical functions of a firm or organization. Responsible for the entire life cycle of a product, including acquisition, distribution, internal allocation, delivery, and final disposal of resources. **O*NET Code:** 13-1081.00. **Average Salary:** $49,740. **Projected Growth:** 27.5%. **Annual Openings:** 162,000. **Education:** Bachelor's degree. **Job Zone:** No data available. **Education/Training Program(s)**—Logistics and Materials Management; Operations Management and Supervision. **Related Knowledge/Courses:** No data available. **Personality Type:** No data available. **Skills Required:** No data available. **Abilities:** No data available. **Occupational Values:** No data available. **Interacting with Others:** No data available. **Physical Work Conditions:** No data available.

© 2006, JIST Works

Management Analysts

Conduct organizational studies and evaluations, design systems and procedures, conduct work simplifications and measurement studies, and prepare operations and procedures manuals to assist management in operating more efficiently and effectively. Includes program analysts and management consultants. **O*NET Code:** 13-1111.00. **Average Salary:** $63,090. **Projected Growth:** 30.4%. **Annual Openings:** 78,000. **Education:** Work experience plus degree. **Job Zone:** 4. **Education/Training Program(s)**—Business Administration and Management, General; Business/Commerce, General. **Related Knowledge/Courses:** Administration and Management; Personnel and Human Resources; Education and Training; Economics and Accounting; Clerical; English Language. **Personality Type:** Enterprising. **Skills Required:** Systems Evaluation; Management of Personnel Resources; Systems Analysis; Management of Material Resources; Operations Analysis; Judgment and Decision Making; Monitoring; Complex Problem Solving. **Abilities:** Originality; Written Expression; Fluency of Ideas; Visualization; Problem Sensitivity. **Occupational Values:** Creativity; Authority; Achievement; Working Conditions; Compensation; Social Status; Autonomy. **Interacting with Others:** Communicating with Supervisors, Peers, or Subordinates; Providing Consultation and Advice to Others; Establishing and Maintaining Interpersonal Relationships. **Physical Work Conditions:** Indoors; Sitting.

Operations Research Analysts

Formulate and apply mathematical modeling and other optimizing methods, using a computer to develop and interpret information that assists management with decision making, policy formulation, or other managerial functions. May develop related software, service, or products. Frequently concentrates on collecting and analyzing data and developing decision support software. May develop and supply optimal time, cost, or logistics networks for program evaluation, review, or implementation. **O*NET Code:** 15-2031.00. **Average Salary:** $59,090. **Projected Growth:** 6.2%. **Annual Openings:** 6,000. **Education:** Master's degree. **Job Zone:** 4. **Education/Training Program(s)**—Management Science, General; Management Sciences and Quantitative Methods, Other; Operations Research. **Related Knowledge/Courses:** Mathematics; Economics and Accounting; Administration and Management; Production and Processing; Computers and Electronics; Personnel and Human Resources. **Personality Type:** Investigative. **Skills Required:** Systems Evaluation; Systems Analysis; Mathematics; Judgment and Decision Making; Science; Monitoring; Critical Thinking; Complex Problem Solving. **Abilities:** Mathematical Reasoning; Number Facility; Written Expression; Fluency of Ideas; Deductive Reasoning. **Occupational Values:** Creativity; Autonomy; Responsibility; Ability Utilization; Recognition. **Interacting with Others:** Providing Consultation and Advice to Others; Communicating with Supervisors, Peers, or Subordinates; Communicating with Persons Outside Organization. **Physical Work Conditions:** Sitting; Indoors.

04.06 Mathematical Clerical Support

Billing, Cost, and Rate Clerks

Compile data, compute fees and charges, and prepare invoices for billing purposes. Duties include computing costs and calculating rates for goods, services, and shipment of goods; posting data; and keeping other relevant records. May involve use of computer or typewriter, calculator, and adding and bookkeeping machines. **O*NET Code:** 43-3021.02. **Average Salary:** $26,540. **Projected Growth:** 7.9%. **Annual Openings:** 78,000. **Education:** Short-term on-the-job training. **Job Zone:** 3. **Education/Training Program(s)**—Accounting Technology/Technician and Bookkeeping. **Related Knowledge/Courses:** Clerical; Computers and Electronics; Customer and Personal Service; Economics and Accounting; English Language; Mathematics. **Personality Type:** Conventional. **Skills Required:** Instructing; Service Orientation; Active Listening; Social Perceptiveness; Writing; Reading Comprehension; Negotiation; Learning Strategies. **Abilities:** Number Facility; Wrist-Finger Speed; Mathematical Reasoning; Written Expression; Near Vision. **Occupational Values:** Working Conditions; Independence; Advancement; Activity; Supervision, Human Relations; Supervision, Technical. **Interacting with Others:** Establishing and Maintaining Interpersonal Relationships; Communicating with Supervisors, Peers, or Subordinates; Performing Administrative Activities. **Physical Work Conditions:** Sitting; Physical Proximity; Contaminants; Indoors; Sounds, Noise Levels Are Distracting or Uncomfortable.

Bookkeeping, Accounting, and Auditing Clerks

Compute, classify, and record numerical data to keep financial records complete. Perform any combination of routine calculating, posting, and verifying duties to obtain primary financial data for use in maintaining accounting records. May also check the accuracy of figures, calculations, and postings pertaining to business transactions recorded by other workers. **O*NET Code:** 43-3031.00. **Average Salary:** $27,980. **Projected Growth:** 3.0%. **Annual Openings:** 274,000. **Education:** Moderate-term on-the-job training. **Job Zone:** 3. **Education/Training Program(s)**—Accounting and Related Services, Other; Accounting Technology/Technician and Bookkeeping. **Related Knowledge/Courses:** Clerical; Economics and Accounting; Computers and Electronics; Mathematics; Customer and Personal Service; English Language. **Personality Type:** Conventional. **Skills Required:** Management of Financial Resources; Time Management; Instructing; Critical Thinking; Negotiation; Active Learning; Persuasion; Mathematics; Learning Strategies. **Abilities:** Mathematical Reasoning; Category Flexibility; Number Facility; Speech Recognition; Near Vision. **Occupational Values:** Independence; Working Conditions; Advancement; Autonomy; Activity; Company Policies and Practices. **Interacting with Others:** Establishing and Maintaining Interpersonal Relationships; Communicating with

Supervisors, Peers, or Subordinates; Performing Administrative Activities. **Physical Work Conditions:** Sitting; Sounds, Noise Levels Are Distracting or Uncomfortable; Physical Proximity; Contaminants.

Brokerage Clerks

Perform clerical duties involving the purchase or sale of securities. Duties include writing orders for stock purchases and sales, computing transfer taxes, verifying stock transactions, accepting and delivering securities, tracking stock price fluctuations, computing equity, distributing dividends, and keeping records of daily transactions and holdings. **O*NET Code:** 43-4011.00. **Average Salary:** $34,480. **Projected Growth:** –14.7%. **Annual Openings:** 10,000. **Education:** Moderate-term on-the-job training. **Job Zone:** 2. **Education/Training Program(s)**—Accounting Technology/Technician and Bookkeeping. **Related Knowledge/Courses:** Clerical; Economics and Accounting; Mathematics; Sales and Marketing; Computers and Electronics; Communications and Media. **Personality Type:** Conventional. **Skills Required:** Service Orientation; Mathematics; Active Listening; Writing; Speaking; Management of Financial Resources; Reading Comprehension. **Abilities:** Mathematical Reasoning; Number Facility; Written Comprehension; Wrist-Finger Speed; Written Expression. **Occupational Values:** Working Conditions; Co-workers; Activity; Advancement; Supervision, Human Relations. **Interacting with Others:** Communicating with Persons Outside Organization; Communicating with Supervisors, Peers, or Subordinates; Establishing and Maintaining Interpersonal Relationships. **Physical Work Conditions:** Sitting; Indoors; Walking and Running.

Payroll and Timekeeping Clerks

Compile and post employee time and payroll data. May compute employees' time worked, production, and commission. May compute and post wages and deductions. May prepare paychecks. **O*NET Code:** 43-3051.00. **Average Salary:** $29,720. **Projected Growth:** 6.5%. **Annual Openings:** 19,000. **Education:** Short-term on-the-job training. **Job Zone:** 3. **Education/Training Program(s)**—Accounting Technology/Technician and Bookkeeping. **Related Knowledge/Courses:** Clerical; Customer and Personal Service; Administration and Management; Economics and Accounting; Personnel and Human Resources; Computers and Electronics; Mathematics. **Personality Type:** Conventional. **Skills Required:** Time Management; Learning Strategies; Social Perceptiveness; Instructing; Active Listening; Mathematics; Active Learning; Speaking; Critical Thinking. **Abilities:** Mathematical Reasoning; Oral Expression; Near Vision; Speech Recognition; Deductive Reasoning; Inductive Reasoning. **Occupational Values:** Working Conditions; Independence; Advancement; Supervision, Technical; Supervision, Human Relations. **Interacting with Others:** Establishing and Maintaining Interpersonal Relationships; Performing Administrative Activities; Communicating with Supervisors, Peers, or Subordinates. **Physical Work Conditions:** Sitting; Sounds, Noise Levels Are Distracting or Uncomfortable; Physical Proximity; Indoors.

Statement Clerks

Prepare and distribute bank statements to customers, answer inquiries, and reconcile discrepancies in records and accounts.

O*NET Code: 43-3021.01. **Average Salary:** $26,540. **Projected Growth:** 7.9%. **Annual Openings:** 78,000. **Education:** Short-term on-the-job training. **Job Zone:** 2. **Education/Training Program(s)**—Accounting Technology/Technician and Bookkeeping. **Related Knowledge/Courses:** Clerical; Computers and Electronics; Economics and Accounting; Telecommunications. **Personality Type:** Conventional. **Skills Required:** Active Listening; Reading Comprehension; Mathematics. **Abilities:** Perceptual Speed; Hearing Sensitivity; Written Comprehension; Number Facility; Wrist-Finger Speed. **Occupational Values:** Working Conditions; Supervision, Human Relations; Advancement; Supervision, Technical; Activity. **Interacting with Others:** Communicating with Persons Outside Organization; Establishing and Maintaining Interpersonal Relationships; Performing for or Working Directly with the Public. **Physical Work Conditions:** Sitting; Indoors; Spend Time Making Repetitive Motions; Using Hands on Objects, Tools, or Controls.

Tax Preparers

Prepare tax returns for individuals or small businesses but do not have the background or responsibilities of an accredited or certified public accountant. **O*NET Code:** 13-2082.00. **Average Salary:** $27,570. **Projected Growth:** 23.2%. **Annual Openings:** 11,000. **Education:** Moderate-term on-the-job training. **Job Zone:** 2. **Education/Training Program(s)**—Accounting Technology/Technician and Bookkeeping; Taxation. **Related Knowledge/Courses:** Economics and Accounting; Law and Government; Clerical; Mathematics; Computers and Electronics. **Personality Type:** Conventional. **Skills Required:** Mathematics; Reading Comprehension; Active Listening; Speaking; Active Learning; Judgment and Decision Making; Monitoring; Service Orientation. **Abilities:** Number Facility; Mathematical Reasoning; Deductive Reasoning; Written Comprehension; Oral Expression. **Occupational Values:** Working Conditions; Social Service; Independence; Co-workers; Supervision, Human Relations. **Interacting with Others:** Communicating with Persons Outside Organization; Performing Administrative Activities; Communicating with Supervisors, Peers, or Subordinates; Performing for or Working Directly with the Public. **Physical Work Conditions:** Sitting; Spend Time Making Repetitive Motions; Indoors.

04.07 Records and Materials Processing

Correspondence Clerks

Compose letters in reply to requests for merchandise, damage claims, credit and other information, delinquent accounts, incorrect billings, or unsatisfactory services. Duties may include gathering data to formulate reply and typing correspondence. **O*NET Code:** 43-4021.00. **Average Salary:** $27,330. **Projected Growth:** –1.4%. **Annual Openings:** 7,000. **Education:** Short-term on-the-job training. **Job Zone:** 2. **Education/Training Program(s)**—General Office Occupations and Clerical Services. **Related Knowledge/Courses:** Clerical; Communications and Media; English Language; Computers and Electronics; Economics and Accounting. **Personality Type:** Conventional. **Skills Required:** Writing; Reading Comprehension; Negotiation. **Abilities:** Wrist-Finger Speed; Written Expression; Written Comprehension; Near Vision; Fluency of Ideas. **Occupational Values:** Working Conditions; Social Service; Supervision, Human Relations; Activity; Company Policies and Practices. **Interacting with Others:** Communicating with Supervisors, Peers, or Subordinates; Communicating with Persons Outside Organization; Establishing and Maintaining Interpersonal Relationships; Performing Administrative Activities. **Physical Work Conditions:** Sitting; Indoors.

File Clerks

File correspondence, cards, invoices, receipts, and other records in alphabetical or numerical order or according to the filing system used. Locate and remove material from file when requested. **O*NET Code:** 43-4071.00. **Average Salary:** $20,610. **Projected Growth:** -0.3%. **Annual Openings:** 62,000. **Education:** Short-term on-the-job training. **Job Zone:** 3. **Education/Training Program(s)**—General Office Occupations and Clerical Services. **Related Knowledge/Courses:** Clerical; Computers and Electronics; English Language; Customer and Personal Service; Communications and Media; Administration and Management. **Personality Type:** Conventional. **Skills Required:** Instructing; Service Orientation; Learning Strategies; Time Management; Social Perceptiveness; Persuasion; Reading Comprehension; Active Listening. **Abilities:** Category Flexibility; Flexibility of Closure; Speech Recognition; Perceptual Speed; Finger Dexterity. **Occupational Values:** Working Conditions; Moral Values; Supervision, Human Relations; Activity; Company Policies and Practices. **Interacting with Others:** Establishing and Maintaining Interpersonal Relationships; Communicating with Supervisors, Peers, or Subordinates; Performing Administrative Activities. **Physical Work Conditions:** Sitting; Physical Proximity; Indoors; Sounds, Noise Levels Are Distracting or Uncomfortable; Walking and Running.

Human Resources Assistants, Except Payroll and Timekeeping

Compile and keep personnel records. Record data for each employee, such as address, weekly earnings, absences, amount of sales or production, supervisory reports on ability, and date of and reason for termination. Compile and type reports from employment records. File employment records. Search employee files and furnish information to authorized persons. **O*NET Code:** 43-4161.00. **Average Salary:** $31,320. **Projected Growth:** 19.3%. **Annual Openings:** 36,000. **Education:** Short-term on-the-job training. **Job Zone:** 3. **Education/Training Program(s)**—General Office Occupations and Clerical Services. **Related Knowledge/Courses:** Clerical; Personnel and Human Resources; Customer and Personal Service; Computers and Electronics; Education and Training; English Language. **Personality Type:** Conventional. **Skills Required:** Active Listening; Social Perceptiveness; Time Management; Management of Personnel Resources; Service Orientation; Instructing; Writing; Critical

Thinking. **Abilities:** Speech Recognition; Category Flexibility; Flexibility of Closure; Far Vision; Speed of Closure. **Occupational Values:** Working Conditions; Supervision, Human Relations; Social Service; Supervision, Technical; Activity; Company Policies and Practices. **Interacting with Others:** Establishing and Maintaining Interpersonal Relationships; Communicating with Supervisors, Peers, or Subordinates; Performing Administrative Activities. **Physical Work Conditions:** Sitting; Sounds, Noise Levels Are Distracting or Uncomfortable; Physical Proximity; Contaminants; Indoors.

Mail Clerks, Except Mail Machine Operators and Postal Service

Prepare incoming and outgoing mail for distribution. Duties include time-stamping, opening, reading, sorting, and routing incoming mail; sealing, stamping, and affixing postage to outgoing mail or packages; and keeping necessary records and completed forms. **O*NET Code:** 43-9051.02. **Average Salary:** $21,920. **Projected Growth:** -2.9%. **Annual Openings:** 29,000. **Education:** Short-term on-the-job training. **Job Zone:** 1. **Education/Training Program(s)**—General Office Occupations and Clerical Services. **Related Knowledge/Courses:** Geography; Clerical. **Personality Type:** Conventional. **Skills Required:** Service Orientation. **Abilities:** Wrist-Finger Speed; Perceptual Speed; Speed of Closure; Response Orientation; Dynamic Flexibility. **Occupational Values:** Supervision, Technical; Security; Supervision, Human Relations; Activity; Moral Values. **Interacting with Others:** Communicating with Persons Outside Organization; Communicating with Supervisors, Peers, or Subordinates; Performing for or Working Directly with the Public. **Physical Work Conditions:** Spend Time Making Repetitive Motions; Standing; Indoors; Walking and Running; Sitting.

Marking Clerks

Print and attach price tickets to articles of merchandise, using one or several methods, such as marking price on tickets by hand or using ticket-printing machine. **O*NET Code:** 43-5081.02. **Average Salary:** $19,860. **Projected Growth:** -4.2%. **Annual Openings:** 418,000. **Education:** Short-term on-the-job training. **Job Zone:** 1. **Education/Training Program(s)**—Retailing and Retail Operations. **Related Knowledge/Courses:** Clerical; Food Production. **Personality Type:** Conventional. **Skills Required:** None met the criteria. **Abilities:** None met the criteria. **Occupational Values:** Independence; Moral Values; Supervision, Technical. **Interacting with Others:** Communicating with Supervisors, Peers, or Subordinates; Performing Administrative Activities; Communicating with Persons Outside Organization. **Physical Work Conditions:** Indoors; Standing; Spend Time Making Repetitive Motions; Using Hands on Objects, Tools, or Controls; Walking and Running.

Meter Readers, Utilities

Read meter and record consumption of electricity, gas, water, or steam. **O*NET Code:** 43-5041.00. **Average Salary:** $29,660. **Projected Growth:** -14.1%. **Annual Openings:** 10,000. **Education:** Short-term on-the-job training. **Job Zone:** 1. **Education/Training Program(s)**—No data available. **Related Knowledge/Courses:** Transportation; Geography. **Personality**

Type: Conventional. **Skills Required:** Operation Monitoring. **Abilities:** Spatial Orientation; Rate Control. **Occupational Values:** Independence; Supervision, Technical; Supervision, Human Relations; Security; Company Policies and Practices. **Interacting with Others:** Communicating with Persons Outside Organization; Communicating with Supervisors, Peers, or Subordinates; Interpreting the Meaning of Information for Others; Performing Administrative Activities. **Physical Work Conditions:** Outdoors; Very Hot or Cold; Walking and Running; Standing; Extremely Bright or Inadequate Lighting.

Office Clerks, General

Perform duties too varied and diverse to be classified in any specific office clerical occupation that require limited knowledge of office management systems and procedures. Clerical duties may be assigned in accordance with the office procedures of individual establishments and may include a combination of answering telephones, bookkeeping, typing or word processing, stenography, office machine operation, and filing. **O*NET Code:** 43-9061.00. **Average Salary:** $22,440. **Projected Growth:** 10.4%. **Annual Openings:** 550,000. **Education:** Short-term on-the-job training. **Job Zone:** 2. **Education/Training Program(s)**—General Office Occupations and Clerical Services. **Related Knowledge/Courses:** Clerical; Customer and Personal Service; Economics and Accounting; Personnel and Human Resources; Computers and Electronics; English Language. **Personality Type:** Conventional. **Skills Required:** Active Listening; Reading Comprehension; Social Perceptiveness; Service Orientation; Writing; Speaking; Time Management; Learning Strategies. **Abilities:** Speech Recognition; Oral Expression; Category Flexibility; Near Vision; Far Vision. **Occupational Values:** Advancement; Co-workers; Working Conditions; Supervision, Human Relations; Supervision, Technical. **Interacting with Others:** Establishing and Maintaining Interpersonal Relationships; Communicating with Supervisors, Peers, or Subordinates; Performing for or Working Directly with the Public. **Physical Work Conditions:** Sitting; Physical Proximity; Sounds, Noise Levels Are Distracting or Uncomfortable; Indoors.

Order Fillers, Wholesale and Retail Sales

Fill customers' mail and telephone orders from stored merchandise in accordance with specifications on sales slips or order forms. Duties include computing prices of items, completing order receipts, keeping records of outgoing orders, and requisitioning additional materials, supplies, and equipment. **O*NET Code:** 43-5081.04. **Average Salary:** $19,860. **Projected Growth:** –4.2%. **Annual Openings:** 418,000. **Education:** Moderate-term on-the-job training. **Job Zone:** 2. **Education/Training Program(s)**—Retailing and Retail Operations. **Related Knowledge/Courses:** Sales and Marketing; Transportation; Education and Training; Production and Processing; Public Safety and Security; Communications and Media. **Personality Type:** Conventional. **Skills Required:** Troubleshooting; Social Perceptiveness; Quality Control Analysis; Repairing; Management of Personnel Resources; Learning Strategies; Time Management. **Abilities:** Static Strength. **Occupational Values:** Moral Values; Supervision, Human Relations.

Interacting with Others: Communicating with Persons Outside Organization; Establishing and Maintaining Interpersonal Relationships; Selling or Influencing Others. **Physical Work Conditions:** Sounds, Noise Levels Are Distracting or Uncomfortable; Contaminants; Physical Proximity; Sitting; Very Hot or Cold; Extremely Bright or Inadequate Lighting.

Postal Service Clerks

Perform any combination of tasks in a post office, such as receiving letters and parcels; selling postage and revenue stamps, postal cards, and stamped envelopes; filling out and selling money orders; placing mail in pigeon holes of mail rack or in bags according to state, address, or other scheme; and examining mail for correct postage. **O*NET Code:** 43-5051.00. **Average Salary:** $40,760. **Projected Growth:** –0.5%. **Annual Openings:** 5,000. **Education:** Short-term on-the-job training. **Job Zone:** 2. **Education/Training Program(s)**—General Office Occupations and Clerical Services. **Related Knowledge/Courses:** Clerical; Geography; Customer and Personal Service; Law and Government; Sales and Marketing. **Personality Type:** Conventional. **Skills Required:** Service Orientation. **Abilities:** Perceptual Speed; Time Sharing; Oral Expression; Extent Flexibility; Speech Clarity. **Occupational Values:** Security; Supervision, Technical; Supervision, Human Relations; Social Service; Company Policies and Practices. **Interacting with Others:** Performing for or Working Directly with the Public; Assisting and Caring for Others; Communicating with Persons Outside Organization; Establishing and Maintaining Interpersonal Relationships. **Physical Work Conditions:** Spend Time Making Repetitive Motions; Standing; Spend Time Bending or Twisting the Body; Indoors; Walking and Running.

Postal Service Mail Sorters, Processors, and Processing Machine Operators

Prepare incoming and outgoing mail for distribution. Examine, sort, and route mail by state, type of mail, or other scheme. Load, operate, and occasionally adjust and repair mail-processing, sorting, and canceling machinery. Keep records of shipments, pouches, and sacks and other duties related to mail handling within the postal service. Must complete a competitive exam. **O*NET Code:** 43-5053.00. **Average Salary:** $39,360. **Projected Growth:** –10.5%. **Annual Openings:** 18,000. **Education:** Short-term on-the-job training. **Job Zone:** No data available. **Education/Training Program(s)**—General Office Occupations and Clerical Services. **Related Knowledge/Courses:** No data available. **Personality Type:** No data available. **Skills Required:** No data available. **Abilities:** No data available. **Occupational Values:** No data available. **Interacting with Others:** No data available. **Physical Work Conditions:** No data available.

Procurement Clerks

Compile information and records to draw up purchase orders for procurement of materials and services. **O*NET Code:** 43-3061.00. **Average Salary:** $30,290. **Projected Growth:** –6.7%. **Annual Openings:** 13,000. **Education:** Short-term on-the-job training. **Job Zone:** 3. **Education/Training Program(s)**—General Office Occupations and Clerical Services. **Related Knowledge/Courses:** Clerical; Customer and Personal

Service; Administration and Management; Mathematics; English Language; Communications and Media. **Personality Type:** Conventional. **Skills Required:** Management of Financial Resources; Management of Material Resources; Time Management; Service Orientation; Persuasion; Monitoring; Negotiation; Operations Analysis. **Abilities:** Oral Comprehension; Speech Recognition; Near Vision; Deductive Reasoning; Inductive Reasoning; Mathematical Reasoning. **Occupational Values:** Working Conditions; Advancement; Supervision, Technical; Independence; Co-workers. **Interacting with Others:** Establishing and Maintaining Interpersonal Relationships; Communicating with Supervisors, Peers, or Subordinates; Communicating with Persons Outside Organization. **Physical Work Conditions:** Sitting; Sounds, Noise Levels Are Distracting or Uncomfortable; Contaminants; Indoors; Physical Proximity.

Production, Planning, and Expediting Clerks

Coordinate and expedite the flow of work and materials within or between departments of an establishment according to production schedule. Duties include reviewing and distributing production, work, and shipment schedules; conferring with department supervisors to determine progress of work and completion dates; and compiling reports on progress of work, inventory levels, costs, and production problems. **O*NET Code:** 43-5061.00. **Average Salary:** $35,260. **Projected Growth:** 14.1%. **Annual Openings:** 51,000. **Education:** Short-term on-the-job training. **Job Zone:** 2. **Education/Training Program(s)**—Parts, Warehousing, and Inventory Management Operations. **Related Knowledge/Courses:** Clerical; Production and Processing; Economics and Accounting; Mathematics; Computers and Electronics; Administration and Management. **Personality Type:** Conventional. **Skills Required:** Management of Material Resources; Management of Personnel Resources; Management of Financial Resources; Systems Analysis; Time Management; Systems Evaluation; Service Orientation; Negotiation. **Abilities:** Number Facility; Mathematical Reasoning; Near Vision; Wrist-Finger Speed; Speech Recognition. **Occupational Values:** Supervision, Technical; Advancement; Supervision, Human Relations; Activity; Authority; Co-workers; Company Policies and Practices. **Interacting with Others:** Communicating with Supervisors, Peers, or Subordinates; Establishing and Maintaining Interpersonal Relationships; Coordinating the Work and Activities of Others. **Physical Work Conditions:** Sitting; Indoors; Walking and Running; Disease or Infections; Standing.

Shipping, Receiving, and Traffic Clerks

Verify and keep records on incoming and outgoing shipments. Prepare items for shipment. Duties include assembling, addressing, stamping, and shipping merchandise or material; receiving, unpacking, verifying, and recording incoming merchandise or material; and arranging for the transportation of products. **O*NET Code:** 43-5071.00. **Average Salary:** $23,980. **Projected Growth:** 3.0%. **Annual Openings:** 154,000. **Education:** Short-term on-the-job training. **Job Zone:** 2. **Education/Training Program(s)**— General Office Occupations and Clerical Services; Traffic, Customs, and Transportation Clerk/Technician. **Related Knowledge/Courses:** Clerical; Transportation; Production

and Processing; Customer and Personal Service; Computers and Electronics; Education and Training. **Personality Type:** Conventional. **Skills Required:** Learning Strategies; Negotiation; Social Perceptiveness; Time Management; Mathematics; Instructing; Management of Financial Resources; Service Orientation. **Abilities:** Static Strength; Spatial Orientation; Stamina; Speech Recognition; Perceptual Speed. **Occupational Values:** Moral Values; Supervision, Human Relations; Supervision, Technical; Co-workers; Advancement. **Interacting with Others:** Establishing and Maintaining Interpersonal Relationships; Communicating with Supervisors, Peers, or Subordinates; Performing Administrative Activities. **Physical Work Conditions:** Sounds, Noise Levels Are Distracting or Uncomfortable; Contaminants; Physical Proximity; Sitting; Very Hot or Cold.

Stock Clerks, Sales Floor

Receive, store, and issue sales floor merchandise. Stock shelves, racks, cases, bins, and tables with merchandise and arrange merchandise displays to attract customers. May periodically take physical count of stock or check and mark merchandise. **O*NET Code:** 43-5081.01. **Average Salary:** $19,860. **Projected Growth:** –4.2%. **Annual Openings:** 418,000. **Education:** Short-term on-the-job training. **Job Zone:** 1. **Education/Training Program(s)**—Retailing and Retail Operations. **Related Knowledge/Courses:** Administration and Management; Customer and Personal Service; Sales and Marketing; Mathematics; Public Safety and Security; English Language. **Personality Type:** Realistic. **Skills Required:** Service Orientation; Learning Strategies; Negotiation; Active Learning; Instructing; Coordination; Management of Personnel Resources; Speaking. **Abilities:** Extent Flexibility; Trunk Strength; Speech Recognition; Oral Expression; Originality; Category Flexibility. **Occupational Values:** Independence; Advancement; Supervision, Technical; Activity; Moral Values. **Interacting with Others:** Establishing and Maintaining Interpersonal Relationships; Performing for or Working Directly with the Public; Communicating with Supervisors, Peers, or Subordinates. **Physical Work Conditions:** Walking and Running; Extremely Bright or Inadequate Lighting; Kneeling, Crouching, Stooping, or Crawling; Sounds, Noise Levels Are Distracting or Uncomfortable; Physical Proximity.

Stock Clerks—Stockroom, Warehouse, or Storage Yard

Receive, store, and issue materials, equipment, and other items from stockroom, warehouse, or storage yard. Keep records and compile stock reports. **O*NET Code:** 43-5081.03. **Average Salary:** $19,860. **Projected Growth:** –4.2%. **Annual Openings:** 418,000. **Education:** Moderate-term on-the-job training. **Job Zone:** 1. **Education/Training Program(s)**— Retailing and Retail Operations. **Related Knowledge/Courses:** Administration and Management; Production and Processing. **Personality Type:** Conventional. **Skills Required:** Service Orientation; Social Perceptiveness; Learning Strategies; Instructing; Negotiation; Critical Thinking; Reading Comprehension; Management of Financial Resources; Management of Personnel Resources. **Abilities:** Extent Flexibility; Multilimb Coordination; Static Strength; Stamina;

Depth Perception. **Occupational Values:** Moral Values; Supervision, Technical; Independence; Supervision, Human Relations; Advancement; Co-workers. **Interacting with Others:** Establishing and Maintaining Interpersonal Relationships; Performing for or Working Directly with the Public; Communicating with Supervisors, Peers, or Subordinates. **Physical Work Conditions:** Contaminants; Physical Proximity; Very Hot or Cold; Walking and Running; Sounds, Noise Levels Are Distracting or Uncomfortable.

Weighers, Measurers, Checkers, and Samplers, Recordkeeping

Weigh, measure, and check materials, supplies, and equipment for the purpose of keeping relevant records. Duties are primarily clerical by nature. **O*NET Code:** 43-5111.00. **Average Salary:** $24,640. **Projected Growth:** 14.6%. **Annual Openings:** 16,000. **Education:** Short-term on-the-job training. **Job Zone:** 1. **Education/Training Program(s)—**General Office Occupations and Clerical Services. **Related Knowledge/Courses:** Clerical; Design; Transportation; Production and Processing. **Personality Type:** Conventional. **Skills Required:** Operation and Control; Operation Monitoring; Equipment Selection. **Abilities:** Hearing Sensitivity; Multilimb Coordination; Manual Dexterity; Depth Perception; Control Precision; Extent Flexibility. **Occupational Values:** Supervision, Technical; Supervision, Human Relations; Moral Values; Co-workers; Independence. **Interacting with Others:** Communicating with Persons Outside Organization; Communicating with Supervisors, Peers, or Subordinates; Establishing and Maintaining Interpersonal Relationships; Performing Administrative Activities. **Physical Work Conditions:** Using Hands on Objects, Tools, or Controls; Standing; Spend Time Making Repetitive Motions; Indoors; Spend Time Bending or Twisting the Body.

04.08 Clerical Machine Operation

Billing, Posting, and Calculating Machine Operators

Operate machines that automatically perform mathematical processes, such as addition, subtraction, multiplication, and division, to calculate and record billing, accounting, statistical, and other numerical data. Duties include operating special billing machines to prepare statements, bills, and invoices and operating bookkeeping machines to copy and post data, make computations, and compile records of transactions. **O*NET Code:** 43-3021.03. **Average Salary:** $26,540. **Projected Growth:** 7.9%. **Annual Openings:** 78,000. **Education:** Short-term on-the-job training. **Job Zone:** 1. **Education/Training Program(s)—**Accounting Technology/ Technician and Bookkeeping. **Related Knowledge/Courses:** Clerical; Economics and Accounting; Computers and Electronics; Mathematics. **Personality Type:** Conventional. **Skills Required:** Mathematics; Management of Financial

Resources; Operation and Control; Operation Monitoring. **Abilities:** Wrist-Finger Speed; Mathematical Reasoning; Number Facility; Selective Attention; Time Sharing. **Occupational Values:** Independence; Supervision, Human Relations; Supervision, Technical; Advancement; Activity. **Interacting with Others:** Communicating with Supervisors, Peers, or Subordinates; Communicating with Persons Outside Organization; Establishing and Maintaining Interpersonal Relationships; Performing Administrative Activities. **Physical Work Conditions:** Spend Time Making Repetitive Motions; Sitting; Indoors.

Data Entry Keyers

Operate data-entry device, such as keyboard or photo-composing perforator. Duties may include verifying data and preparing materials for printing. **O*NET Code:** 43-9021.00. **Average Salary:** $22,730. **Projected Growth:** –5.4%. **Annual Openings:** 72,000. **Education:** Moderate-term on-the-job training. **Job Zone:** 2. **Education/Training Program(s)—**Business/Office Automation/Technology/Data Entry; Data Entry/Microcomputer Applications, General; Graphic and Printing Equipment Operator, General Production. **Related Knowledge/Courses:** Clerical; Computers and Electronics. **Personality Type:** Conventional. **Skills Required:** Reading Comprehension. **Abilities:** Wrist-Finger Speed; Written Comprehension. **Occupational Values:** Independence; Moral Values; Activity; Supervision, Human Relations; Working Conditions; Co-workers. **Interacting with Others:** Interpreting the Meaning of Information for Others; Performing Administrative Activities; Communicating with Supervisors, Peers, or Subordinates; Establishing and Maintaining Interpersonal Relationships. **Physical Work Conditions:** Sitting; Spend Time Making Repetitive Motions; Indoors; Using Hands on Objects, Tools, or Controls.

Duplicating Machine Operators

Operate one of a variety of office machines, such as photocopying, photographic, mimeograph, and duplicating machines, to make copies. **O*NET Code:** 43-9071.01. **Average Salary:** $22,940. **Projected Growth:** –4.6%. **Annual Openings:** 17,000. **Education:** Short-term on-the-job training. **Job Zone:** 1. **Education/Training Program(s)—**Agricultural Business Technology; General Office Occupations and Clerical Services. **Related Knowledge/Courses:** Personnel and Human Resources; Food Production. **Personality Type:** Conventional. **Skills Required:** Repairing; Equipment Maintenance; Operation Monitoring. **Abilities:** Visual Color Discrimination; Control Precision; Spatial Orientation; Finger Dexterity. **Occupational Values:** Independence; Supervision, Technical; Moral Values; Supervision, Human Relations. **Interacting with Others:** Performing Administrative Activities; Communicating with Supervisors, Peers, or Subordinates; Communicating with Persons Outside Organization; Establishing and Maintaining Interpersonal Relationships; Assisting and Caring for Others; Performing for or Working Directly with the Public. **Physical Work Conditions:** Spend Time Making Repetitive Motions; Standing; Using Hands on Objects, Tools, or Controls; Indoors; Spend Time Bending or Twisting the Body.

© 2006, JIST Works

Mail Machine Operators, Preparation and Handling

Operate machines that emboss names, addresses, and other matter onto metal plates for use in addressing machines; print names, addresses, and similar information onto items such as envelopes, accounting forms, and advertising literature; address, fold, stuff, seal, and stamp mail; and open envelopes. **O*NET Code:** 43-9051.01. **Average Salary:** $21,920. **Projected Growth:** –2.9%. **Annual Openings:** 29,000. **Education:** Short-term on-the-job training. **Job Zone:** 1. **Education/Training Program(s)**—General Office Occupations and Clerical Services. **Related Knowledge/Courses:** Production and Processing; Engineering and Technology. **Personality Type:** Realistic. **Skills Required:** Operation Monitoring; Operation and Control; Technology Design. **Abilities:** Manual Dexterity; Rate Control; Perceptual Speed; Dynamic Flexibility; Response Orientation. **Occupational Values:** Supervision, Technical; Independence; Moral Values; Supervision, Human Relations. **Interacting with Others:** Communicating with Supervisors, Peers, or Subordinates; Establishing and Maintaining Interpersonal Relationships; Interpreting the Meaning of Information for Others; Resolving Conflicts and Negotiating with Others. **Physical Work Conditions:** Spend Time Making Repetitive Motions; Using Hands on Objects, Tools, or Controls; Indoors; Standing; Spend Time Bending or Twisting the Body.

Switchboard Operators, Including Answering Service

Operate telephone business systems equipment or switch-boards to relay incoming, outgoing, and interoffice calls. May supply information to callers and record messages. **O*NET Code:** 43-2011.00. **Average Salary:** $21,500. **Projected Growth:** 0.3%. **Annual Openings:** 48,000. **Education:** Short-term on-the-job training. **Job Zone:** 2. **Education/Training Program(s)**—Receptionist. **Related Knowledge/Courses:** Customer and Personal Service; Clerical; English Language; Computers and Electronics; Telecommunications; Psychology; Communications and Media. **Personality Type:** Conventional. **Skills Required:** Service Orientation; Active Listening; Social Perceptiveness; Instructing; Critical Thinking; Learning Strategies; Speaking; Reading Comprehension. **Abilities:** Speech Recognition; Auditory Attention; Wrist-Finger Speed; Response Orientation; Hearing Sensitivity. **Occupational Values:** Independence; Activity; Supervision, Human Relations; Supervision, Technical; Working Conditions. **Interacting with Others:** Establishing and Maintaining Interpersonal Relationships; Performing for or Working Directly with the Public; Communicating with Persons Outside Organization. **Physical Work Conditions:** Sitting; Sounds, Noise Levels Are Distracting or Uncomfortable; Physical Proximity; Extremely Bright or Inadequate Lighting; Indoors.

Word Processors and Typists

Use word processor/computer or typewriter to type letters, reports, forms, or other material from rough draft, corrected copy, or voice recording. May perform other clerical duties as assigned. **O*NET Code:** 43-9022.00. **Average Salary:** $27,470. **Projected Growth:** –38.6%. **Annual Openings:** 45,000. **Education:** Moderate-term on-the-job training. **Job Zone:** 2. **Education/Training Program(s)**—General Office Occupations and Clerical Services; Word Processing. **Related Knowledge/Courses:** Clerical; Customer and Personal Service; Computers and Electronics; English Language; Sales and Marketing; Economics and Accounting. **Personality Type:** Conventional. **Skills Required:** Persuasion; Social Perceptiveness; Instructing; Learning Strategies; Coordination; Service Orientation; Time Management; Negotiation. **Abilities:** Wrist-Finger Speed; Speech Recognition; Near Vision; Perceptual Speed; Category Flexibility. **Occupational Values:** Working Conditions; Company Policies and Practices; Independence; Supervision, Human Relations; Activity. **Interacting with Others:** Establishing and Maintaining Interpersonal Relationships; Performing Administrative Activities; Communicating with Supervisors, Peers, or Subordinates. **Physical Work Conditions:** Sitting; Sounds, Noise Levels Are Distracting or Uncomfortable; Physical Proximity.

05 Education and Training

05.01 **Managerial Work in Education**

05.02 **Preschool, Elementary, and Secondary Teaching and Instructing**

05.03 **Postsecondary and Adult Teaching and Instructing**

05.04 **Library Services**

05.05 **Archival and Museum Services**

05.06 **Counseling, Health, and Fitness Education**

05.01 Managerial Work in Education

Education Administrators, Elementary and Secondary School

Plan, direct, or coordinate the academic, clerical, or auxiliary activities of public or private elementary or secondary-level schools. **O*NET Code:** 11-9032.00. **Average Salary:** $73,960. **Projected Growth:** 20.7%. **Annual Openings:** 31,000. **Education:** Work experience plus degree. **Job Zone:** 4. **Education/Training Program(s)**—Educational Administration and Supervision, Other; Educational Leadership and Administration, General; Educational, Instructional, and Curriculum Supervision; Elementary and Middle School Administration/Principalship; Secondary School Administration/Principalship. **Related Knowledge/Courses:** Education and Training; Sales and Marketing; Personnel and Human Resources; Administration and Management; Economics and Accounting; English Language. **Personality Type:** Social. **Skills Required:** Management of Financial Resources; Management of Personnel Resources; Management of Material Resources; Systems Analysis; Systems Evaluation; Coordination; Learning Strategies; Writing. **Abilities:** Written Expression; Originality; Speech Clarity; Fluency of Ideas; Oral Expression. **Occupational Values:** Authority; Ability Utilization; Creativity; Recognition; Social Status. **Interacting with Others:** Communicating with Supervisors, Peers, or Subordinates; Communicating with Persons Outside Organization; Establishing and Maintaining Interpersonal Relationships; Training and Teaching Others; Providing Consultation and Advice to Others; Monitoring and Controlling Resources. **Physical Work Conditions:** Sitting; Indoors; Walking and Running; Standing.

Education Administrators, Postsecondary

Plan, direct, or coordinate research, instructional, student administration and services, and other educational activities at postsecondary institutions, including universities, colleges, and junior and community colleges. **O*NET Code:** 11-9033.00. **Average Salary:** $67,760. **Projected Growth:** 25.9%. **Annual Openings:** 19,000. **Education:** Work experience plus degree. **Job Zone:** 5. **Education/Training Program(s)**—Community College Education; Educational Administration and Supervision, Other; Educational Leadership and Administration, General; Educational, Instructional, and Curriculum Supervision; Higher Education/Higher Education Administration. **Related Knowledge/Courses:** Education and Training; Administration and Management; Economics and Accounting; Personnel and Human Resources; Law and Government; English Language. **Personality Type:** Enterprising. **Skills Required:** Management of Financial Resources; Systems Evaluation; Management of Personnel Resources; Management of Material Resources; Coordination; Negotiation; Systems Analysis; Judgment and Decision Making. **Abilities:** Speech Clarity; Written Expression; Oral Expression; Oral Comprehension; Mathematical Reasoning. **Occupational Values:** Authority; Social Status; Working Conditions; Recognition; Ability Utilization; Creativity. **Interacting with Others:** Performing Administrative Activities; Communicating with Persons Outside Organization; Resolving Conflicts and Negotiating with Others; Providing Consultation and Advice to Others; Monitoring and Controlling Resources. **Physical Work Conditions:** Sitting; Walking and Running; Outdoors; Standing.

Education Administrators, Preschool and Child Care Center/Program

Plan, direct, or coordinate the academic and nonacademic activities of preschool and child care centers or programs. **O*NET Code:** 11-9031.00. **Average Salary:** $35,240. **Projected Growth:** 32.0%. **Annual Openings:** 9,000. **Education:** Work experience plus degree. **Job Zone:** 4. **Education/Training Program(s)**—Educational Administration and Supervision, Other; Educational Leadership and Administration, General; Educational, Instructional, and Curriculum Supervision. **Related Knowledge/Courses:** Education and Training; Sales and Marketing; Personnel and Human Resources; Administration and Management; Economics and Accounting; English Language. **Personality Type:** Social. **Skills Required:** Management of Financial Resources; Management of Personnel Resources; Management of Material Resources; Systems Analysis; Systems Evaluation; Coordination; Learning Strategies; Writing. **Abilities:** Written Expression; Originality; Speech Clarity; Fluency of Ideas; Oral Expression. **Occupational Values:** Authority; Ability Utilization; Creativity; Recognition; Social Status. **Interacting with Others:** Communicating with Supervisors, Peers, or Subordinates; Communicating with Persons Outside Organization; Establishing and Maintaining Interpersonal Relationships; Training and Teaching Others; Providing Consultation and Advice to Others; Monitoring and Controlling Resources. **Physical Work Conditions:** Sitting; Indoors; Walking and Running; Standing.

Instructional Coordinators

Develop instructional material, coordinate educational content, and incorporate current technology in specialized fields that provide guidelines to educators and instructors for developing curricula and conducting courses. **O*NET Code:** 25-9031.00. **Average Salary:** $47,550. **Projected Growth:** 25.4%. **Annual Openings:** 18,000. **Education:** Master's degree. **Job Zone:** 5. **Education/Training Program(s)**—Curriculum and Instruction; Educational/Instructional Media Design. **Related Knowledge/Courses:** Education and Training; Personnel and Human Resources; Psychology; Administration and Management; English Language; Economics and Accounting. **Personality Type:** Social. **Skills Required:** Learning Strategies; Instructing; Management of Personnel Resources; Speaking; Systems Analysis; Writing; Management of Financial Resources; Systems Evaluation. **Abilities:** Written Comprehension; Originality; Written Expression; Oral Expression; Fluency of Ideas. **Occupational Values:** Authority; Creativity; Autonomy; Achievement; Social Service. **Interacting with Others:** Communicating with Supervisors, Peers, or Subordinates; Communicating with

Persons Outside Organization; Providing Consultation and Advice to Others. **Physical Work Conditions:** Sitting; Indoors.

05.02 Preschool, Elementary, and Secondary Teaching and Instructing

Elementary School Teachers, Except Special Education

Teach pupils in public or private schools at the elementary level basic academic, social, and other formative skills. O*NET Code: 25-2021.00. **Average Salary:** $42,590. **Projected Growth:** 15.2%. **Annual Openings:** 183,000. **Education:** Bachelor's degree. **Job Zone:** 4. **Education/Training Program**(s)—Elementary Education and Teaching; Teacher Education, Multiple Levels. **Related Knowledge/Courses:** Geography; History and Archeology; Education and Training; Sociology and Anthropology; Therapy and Counseling; Psychology. **Personality Type:** Social. **Skills Required:** Learning Strategies; Social Perceptiveness; Instructing; Service Orientation; Science; Speaking; Coordination; Time Management. **Abilities:** Time Sharing; Speech Clarity; Far Vision; Originality; Number Facility. **Occupational Values:** Authority; Social Service; Creativity; Responsibility; Achievement. **Interacting with Others:** Establishing and Maintaining Interpersonal Relationships; Coaching and Developing Others; Communicating with Supervisors, Peers, or Subordinates; Communicating with Persons Outside Organization; Assisting and Caring for Others; Training and Teaching Others. **Physical Work Conditions:** Outdoors; Sitting; Walking and Running; Standing; Very Hot or Cold.

Kindergarten Teachers, Except Special Education

Teach elemental natural and social science, personal hygiene, music, art, and literature to children from 4 to 6 years old. Promote physical, mental, and social development. May be required to hold state certification. O*NET Code: 25-2012.00. **Average Salary:** $40,980. **Projected Growth:** 27.2%. **Annual Openings:** 34,000. **Education:** Bachelor's degree. **Job Zone:** 4. **Education/Training Program**(s)—Early Childhood Education and Teaching; Kindergarten/Preschool Education and Teaching. **Related Knowledge/Courses:** Education and Training; Sociology and Anthropology; Psychology; Customer and Personal Service; Therapy and Counseling; History and Archeology. **Personality Type:** Social. **Skills Required:** Learning Strategies; Service Orientation; Social Perceptiveness; Monitoring; Instructing; Speaking; Management of Personnel Resources; Active Listening. **Abilities:** Far Vision; Originality; Time Sharing; Peripheral Vision; Fluency of Ideas; Memorization. **Occupational Values:** Authority; Social Service; Creativity; Achievement;

Responsibility. **Interacting with Others:** Establishing and Maintaining Interpersonal Relationships; Communicating with Persons Outside Organization; Assisting and Caring for Others. **Physical Work Conditions:** Standing; Outdoors; Walking and Running; Disease or Infections; Sitting.

Middle School Teachers, Except Special and Vocational Education

Teach students in public or private schools in one or more subjects at the middle, intermediate, or junior high level, which falls between elementary and senior high school, as defined by applicable state laws and regulations. O*NET Code: 25-2022.00. **Average Salary:** $42,960. **Projected Growth:** 9.0%. **Annual Openings:** 69,000. **Education:** Bachelor's degree. **Job Zone:** 4. **Education/Training Program**(s)—Art Teacher Education; Computer Teacher Education; English/Language Arts Teacher Education; Family and Consumer Sciences/Home Economics Teacher Education; Foreign Language Teacher Education; Health Occupations Teacher Education; Health Teacher Education; History Teacher Education; Junior High/Intermediate/Middle School Education and Teaching; Mathematics Teacher Education; Music Teacher Education; Physical Education Teaching and Coaching; Reading Teacher Education; Science Teacher Education/General Science Teacher Education; Social Science Teacher Education; Social Studies Teacher Education; Teacher Education and Professional Development, Specific Subject Areas, Other; Technology Teacher Education/Industrial Arts Teacher Education. **Related Knowledge/Courses:** Education and Training; Therapy and Counseling; English Language; History and Archeology; Sociology and Anthropology; Geography. **Personality Type:** Social. **Skills Required:** Learning Strategies; Instructing; Speaking; Social Perceptiveness; Mathematics; Reading Comprehension; Monitoring; Active Learning. **Abilities:** Oral Comprehension; Written Comprehension; Oral Expression; Written Expression; Speech Clarity. **Occupational Values:** Authority; Social Service; Creativity; Responsibility; Achievement. **Interacting with Others:** Establishing and Maintaining Interpersonal Relationships; Communicating with Persons Outside Organization; Training and Teaching Others. **Physical Work Conditions:** Standing; Sitting; Disease or Infections; Outdoors.

Preschool Teachers, Except Special Education

Instruct children (normally up to 5 years of age) in activities designed to promote social, physical, and intellectual growth needed for primary school in preschool, day care center, or other child development facility. May be required to hold state certification. O*NET Code: 25-2011.00. **Average Salary:** $20,450. **Projected Growth:** 36.2%. **Annual Openings:** 88,000. **Education:** Bachelor's degree. **Job Zone:** 4. **Education/Training Program**(s)—Child Care and Support Services Management; Early Childhood Education and Teaching; Kindergarten/Preschool Education and Teaching. **Related Knowledge/Courses:** Customer and Personal Service; Education and Training; Psychology; Therapy and Counseling; Sociology and Anthropology; Fine Arts. **Personality Type:** Social. **Skills Required:** Social Perceptiveness; Learning Strategies; Monitoring; Instructing; Management of Personnel Resources; Speaking;

Coordination; Active Listening; Service Orientation; Management of Material Resources. **Abilities:** Time Sharing; Originality; Far Vision; Fluency of Ideas; Memorization. **Occupational Values:** Authority; Social Service; Creativity; Achievement; Responsibility. **Interacting with Others:** Assisting and Caring for Others; Establishing and Maintaining Interpersonal Relationships; Communicating with Persons Outside Organization; Resolving Conflicts and Negotiating with Others; Training and Teaching Others. **Physical Work Conditions:** Walking and Running; Standing; Kneeling, Crouching, Stooping, or Crawling; Outdoors; Sitting.

Secondary School Teachers, Except Special and Vocational Education

Instruct students in secondary public or private schools in one or more subjects at the secondary level, such as English, mathematics, or social studies. May be designated according to subject matter specialty, such as typing instructors, commercial teachers, or English teachers. **O*NET Code:** 25-2031.00. **Average Salary:** $45,180. **Projected Growth:** 18.2%. **Annual Openings:** 118,000. **Education:** Bachelor's degree. **Job Zone:** 4. **Education/Training Program(s)**—Agricultural Teacher Education; Art Teacher Education; Biology Teacher Education; Business Teacher Education; Chemistry Teacher Education; Computer Teacher Education; Drama and Dance Teacher Education; Driver and Safety Teacher Education; English/Language Arts Teacher Education; Family and Consumer Sciences/Home Economics Teacher Education; Foreign Language Teacher Education; French Language Teacher Education; Geography Teacher Education; German Language Teacher Education; Health Occupations Teacher Education; Health Teacher Education; History Teacher Education; Junior High/Intermediate/Middle School Education and Teaching; Latin Teacher Education; Mathematics Teacher Education; Music Teacher Education; Physical Education Teaching and Coaching; Physics Teacher Education; Reading Teacher Education; Sales and Marketing Operations/Marketing and Distribution Teacher Education; Science Teacher Education/General Science Teacher Education; Secondary Education and Teaching; Social Science Teacher Education; Social Studies Teacher Education; Spanish Language Teacher Education; Speech Teacher Education; Teacher Education and Professional Development, Specific Subject Areas, Other; Teacher Education, Multiple Levels; Technology Teacher Education/Industrial Arts Teacher Education. **Related Knowledge/Courses:** Education and Training; Therapy and Counseling; English Language; History and Archeology; Sociology and Anthropology; Geography. **Personality Type:** Social. **Skills Required:** Learning Strategies; Instructing; Speaking; Social Perceptiveness; Mathematics; Reading Comprehension; Monitoring; Active Learning. **Abilities:** Oral Comprehension; Written Comprehension; Oral Expression; Written Expression; Speech Clarity. **Occupational Values:** Authority; Social Service; Creativity; Responsibility; Achievement. **Interacting with Others:** Establishing and Maintaining Interpersonal Relationships; Communicating with Persons Outside Organization; Training and Teaching Others. **Physical Work Conditions:** Standing; Sitting; Disease or Infections; Outdoors.

Special Education Teachers, Middle School

Teach middle school subjects to educationally and physically handicapped students. Includes teachers who specialize and work with audibly and visually handicapped students and those who teach basic academic and life processes skills to the mentally impaired. **O*NET Code:** 25-2042.00. **Average Salary:** $43,260. **Projected Growth:** 30.0%. **Annual Openings:** 59,000. **Education:** Bachelor's degree. **Job Zone:** 4. **Education/Training Program(s)**—Special Education and Teaching, General. **Related Knowledge/Courses:** Therapy and Counseling; Education and Training; Psychology; Medicine and Dentistry; English Language; Customer and Personal Service. **Personality Type:** Social. **Skills Required:** Learning Strategies; Social Perceptiveness; Instructing; Monitoring; Speaking; Active Listening; Writing; Service Orientation; Complex Problem Solving. **Abilities:** Written Expression; Written Comprehension; Oral Expression; Oral Comprehension; Speech Clarity. **Occupational Values:** Social Service; Authority; Achievement; Creativity; Responsibility. **Interacting with Others:** Assisting and Caring for Others; Establishing and Maintaining Interpersonal Relationships; Performing for or Working Directly with the Public; Training and Teaching Others. **Physical Work Conditions:** Sitting; Standing; Disease or Infections; Indoors.

Special Education Teachers, Preschool, Kindergarten, and Elementary School

Teach elementary and preschool school subjects to educationally and physically handicapped students. Includes teachers who specialize and work with audibly and visually handicapped students and those who teach basic academic and life processes skills to the mentally impaired. **O*NET Code:** 25-2041.00. **Average Salary:** $42,630. **Projected Growth:** 30.0%. **Annual Openings:** 59,000. **Education:** Bachelor's degree. **Job Zone:** 4. **Education/Training Program(s)**—Education/Teaching of Individuals with Autism; Education/Teaching of Individuals with Emotional Disturbances; Education/Teaching of Individuals with Hearing Impairments, Including Deafness; Education/Teaching of Individuals with Mental Retardation; Education/Teaching of Individuals with Multiple Disabilities; Education/Teaching of Individuals with Orthopedic and Other Physical Health Impairments; Education/Teaching of Individuals with Specific Learning Disabilities; Education/Teaching of Individuals with Speech or Language Impairments; Education/Teaching of Individuals with Traumatic Brain Injuries; Education/Teaching of Individuals with Vision Impairments, Including Blindness; Special Education and Teaching, General; Special Education and Teaching, Other. **Related Knowledge/Courses:** Therapy and Counseling; Education and Training; Psychology; Medicine and Dentistry; English Language; Customer and Personal Service. **Personality Type:** Social. **Skills Required:** Learning Strategies; Social Perceptiveness; Instructing; Monitoring; Speaking; Active Listening; Writing; Service Orientation; Complex Problem Solving. **Abilities:** Written Expression; Written Comprehension; Oral Expression; Oral Comprehension; Speech Clarity. **Occupational Values:** Social Service; Authority; Achievement; Creativity; Responsibility. **Interacting with Others:** Assisting and Caring for Others; Establishing and Maintaining Interpersonal Relationships;

Performing for or Working Directly with the Public; Training and Teaching Others. **Physical Work Conditions:** Sitting; Standing; Disease or Infections; Indoors.

Special Education Teachers, Secondary School

Teach secondary school subjects to educationally and physically handicapped students. Includes teachers who specialize and work with audibly and visually handicapped students and those who teach basic academic and life processes skills to the mentally impaired. **O*NET Code:** 25-2043.00. **Average Salary:** $44,920. **Projected Growth:** 30.0%. **Annual Openings:** 59,000. **Education:** Bachelor's degree. **Job Zone:** 4. **Education/Training Program(s)**—Special Education and Teaching, General. **Related Knowledge/Courses:** Therapy and Counseling; Education and Training; Psychology; Medicine and Dentistry; English Language; Customer and Personal Service. **Personality Type:** Social. **Skills Required:** Learning Strategies; Social Perceptiveness; Instructing; Monitoring; Speaking; Active Listening; Writing; Service Orientation; Complex Problem Solving. **Abilities:** Written Expression; Written Comprehension; Oral Expression; Oral Comprehension; Speech Clarity. **Occupational Values:** Social Service; Authority; Achievement; Creativity; Responsibility. **Interacting with Others:** Assisting and Caring for Others; Establishing and Maintaining Interpersonal Relationships; Performing for or Working Directly with the Public; Training and Teaching Others. **Physical Work Conditions:** Sitting; Standing; Disease or Infections; Indoors.

Teacher Assistants

Perform duties that are instructional in nature or deliver direct services to students or parents. Serve in a position for which a teacher or another professional has ultimate responsibility for the design and implementation of educational programs and services. **O*NET Code:** 25-9041.00. **Average Salary:** $19,080. **Projected Growth:** 23.0%. **Annual Openings:** 259,000. **Education:** Short-term on-the-job training. **Job Zone:** 3. **Education/Training Program(s)**—Teacher Assistant/Aide; Teaching Assistants/Aides, Other. **Related Knowledge/Courses:** Education and Training; English Language; History and Archeology; Psychology; Sociology and Anthropology; Philosophy and Theology. **Personality Type:** Social. **Skills Required:** Instructing; Learning Strategies; Service Orientation; Speaking; Active Listening; Social Perceptiveness; Reading Comprehension; Writing. **Abilities:** Written Expression; Oral Expression; Speech Clarity; Fluency of Ideas; Auditory Attention. **Occupational Values:** Social Service; Authority; Co-workers; Achievement; Working Conditions. **Interacting with Others:** Communicating with Supervisors, Peers, or Subordinates; Communicating with Persons Outside Organization; Establishing and Maintaining Interpersonal Relationships. **Physical Work Conditions:** Sitting; Standing; Indoors; Walking and Running; Disease or Infections.

Vocational Education Teachers, Middle School

Teach or instruct vocational or occupational subjects at the middle school level. **O*NET Code:** 25-2023.00. **Average Salary:** $43,630. **Projected Growth:** 9.0%. **Annual Openings:** 2,000. **Education:** Bachelor's degree. **Job Zone:** 4. **Education/Training Program(s)**—Technology Teacher

Education/Industrial Arts Teacher Education. **Related Knowledge/Courses:** Education and Training; Therapy and Counseling; English Language; History and Archeology; Sociology and Anthropology; Geography. **Personality Type:** Social. **Skills Required:** Learning Strategies; Instructing; Speaking; Social Perceptiveness; Mathematics; Reading Comprehension; Monitoring; Active Learning. **Abilities:** Oral Comprehension; Written Comprehension; Oral Expression; Written Expression; Speech Clarity. **Occupational Values:** Authority; Social Service; Creativity; Responsibility; Achievement. **Interacting with Others:** Establishing and Maintaining Interpersonal Relationships; Communicating with Persons Outside Organization; Training and Teaching Others. **Physical Work Conditions:** Standing; Sitting; Disease or Infections; Outdoors.

Vocational Education Teachers, Secondary School

Teach or instruct vocational or occupational subjects at the secondary school level. **O*NET Code:** 25-2032.00. **Average Salary:** $45,140. **Projected Growth:** 9.0%. **Annual Openings:** 12,000. **Education:** Bachelor's degree. **Job Zone:** 4. **Education/Training Program(s)**—Technology Teacher Education/Industrial Arts Teacher Education. **Related Knowledge/Courses:** Education and Training; Therapy and Counseling; English Language; History and Archeology; Sociology and Anthropology; Geography. **Personality Type:** Social. **Skills Required:** Learning Strategies; Instructing; Speaking; Social Perceptiveness; Mathematics; Reading Comprehension; Monitoring; Active Learning. **Abilities:** Oral Comprehension; Written Comprehension; Oral Expression; Written Expression; Speech Clarity. **Occupational Values:** Authority; Social Service; Creativity; Responsibility; Achievement. **Interacting with Others:** Establishing and Maintaining Interpersonal Relationships; Communicating with Persons Outside Organization; Training and Teaching Others. **Physical Work Conditions:** Standing; Sitting; Disease or Infections; Outdoors.

05.03 Postsecondary and Adult Teaching and Instructing

Adult Literacy, Remedial Education, and GED Teachers and Instructors

Teach or instruct out-of-school youths and adults in remedial education classes, preparatory classes for the General Educational Development test, literacy, or English as a Second Language. Teaching may or may not take place in a traditional educational institution. **O*NET Code:** 25-3011.00. **Average Salary:** $37,910. **Projected Growth:** 20.4%. **Annual Openings:** 14,000. **Education:** Bachelor's degree. **Job Zone:** 4. **Education/Training Program(s)**—Adult and Continuing Education and Teaching; Adult Literacy Tutor/Instructor; Bilingual and Multilingual Education; Multicultural

© *2006, JIST Works*

Education; Teaching English as a Second or Foreign Language/ESL Language Instructor. **Related Knowledge/Courses:** Education and Training; English Language; Philosophy and Theology; Sociology and Anthropology; History and Archeology; Economics and Accounting. **Personality Type:** Social. **Skills Required:** Instructing; Writing; Speaking; Learning Strategies; Service Orientation; Systems Evaluation; Reading Comprehension; Active Listening; Judgment and Decision Making; Management of Material Resources. **Abilities:** Written Expression; Speech Clarity; Oral Expression; Oral Comprehension; Fluency of Ideas. **Occupational Values:** Authority; Social Service; Creativity; Achievement; Responsibility. **Interacting with Others:** Training and Teaching Others; Communicating with Persons Outside Organization; Coaching and Developing Others. **Physical Work Conditions:** Sitting; Standing; Indoors; Walking and Running.

Agricultural Sciences Teachers, Postsecondary

Teach courses in the agricultural sciences. Includes teachers of agronomy, dairy sciences, fisheries management, horticultural sciences, poultry sciences, range management, and agricultural soil conservation. **O*NET Code:** 25-1041.00. **Average Salary:** $64,970. **Projected Growth:** 38.1%. **Annual Openings:** 216,000. **Education:** Master's degree. **Job Zone:** 5. **Education/Training Program(s)—**Agribusiness/Agricultural Business Operations; Agricultural and Domestic Animal Services, Other; Agricultural and Food Products Processing; Agricultural and Horticultural Plant Breeding; Agricultural Animal Breeding; Agricultural Business and Management, General; Agricultural Business and Management, Other; Agricultural Economics; Agricultural Mechanization, General; Agricultural Mechanization, Other; Agricultural Power Machinery Operation; Agricultural Production Operations, General; Agricultural Production Operations, Other; Agricultural Teacher Education; Agricultural/Farm Supplies Retailing and Wholesaling; Agriculture, Agriculture Operations, and Related Sciences, Other; Agriculture, General; Agronomy and Crop Science; Animal Health; Animal Nutrition; Animal Sciences, General; Animal Sciences, Other; Animal Training; Animal/Livestock Husbandry and Production; Applied Horticulture/Horticultural Business Services, Other; Applied Horticulture/Horticultural Operations, General; Aquaculture; Crop Production; Dairy Science; Equestrian/Equine Studies; Farm/Farm and Ranch Management; Food Science; Greenhouse Operations and Management; Horticultural Science; International Agriculture; Landscaping and Groundskeeping; Livestock Management; Ornamental Horticulture; Plant Nursery Operations and Management; Plant Protection and Integrated Pest Management; Plant Sciences, General; Plant Sciences, Other; Poultry Science; Range Science and Management; Soil Science and Agronomy, General; Turf and Turfgrass Management. **Related Knowledge/Courses:** Biology; Education and Training; Medicine and Dentistry; Chemistry; Therapy and Counseling; Psychology. **Personality Type:** Investigative. **Skills Required:** Science; Instructing; Learning Strategies; Reading Comprehension; Active Learning; Writing; Critical Thinking; Mathematics. **Abilities:** Speech Clarity; Written Expression; Oral Expression; Oral Comprehension; Written Comprehension. **Occupational Values:** Authority; Social Service; Creativity; Achievement; Social Status. **Interacting with Others:** Training and Teaching Others; Coaching and Developing Others; Interpreting the Meaning of Information for Others; Communicating with Supervisors, Peers, or Subordinates; Providing Consultation and Advice to Others. **Physical Work Conditions:** Sitting; Indoors; Standing.

Anthropology and Archeology Teachers, Postsecondary

Teach courses in anthropology or archeology. **O*NET Code:** 25-1061.00. **Average Salary:** $60,290. **Projected Growth:** 38.1%. **Annual Openings:** 216,000. **Education:** Master's degree. **Job Zone:** 5. **Education/Training Program(s)—**Anthropology; Archeology; Physical Anthropology; Social Science Teacher Education. **Related Knowledge/Courses:** Sociology and Anthropology; History and Archeology; Education and Training; Psychology; Economics and Accounting; English Language. **Personality Type:** Social. **Skills Required:** Instructing; Learning Strategies; Reading Comprehension; Active Learning; Speaking; Writing; Science; Active Listening; Critical Thinking. **Abilities:** Written Expression; Speech Clarity; Oral Expression; Oral Comprehension; Written Comprehension. **Occupational Values:** Authority; Social Service; Creativity; Achievement; Social Status. **Interacting with Others:** Training and Teaching Others; Coaching and Developing Others; Communicating with Supervisors, Peers, or Subordinates; Providing Consultation and Advice to Others. **Physical Work Conditions:** Indoors; Sitting; Standing.

Architecture Teachers, Postsecondary

Teach courses in architecture and architectural design, such as architectural environmental design, interior architecture/design, and landscape architecture. **O*NET Code:** 25-1031.00. **Average Salary:** $59,120. **Projected Growth:** 38.1%. **Annual Openings:** 216,000. **Education:** Master's degree. **Job Zone:** No data available. **Education/Training Program(s)—**Architectural Engineering; Architecture (BArch, BA/BS, MArch, MA/MS, PhD); City/Urban, Community, and Regional Planning; Environmental Design/Architecture; Interior Architecture; Landscape Architecture (BS, BSLA, BLA, MSLA, MLA, PhD); Teacher Education and Professional Development, Specific Subject Areas, Other. **Related Knowledge/Courses:** No data available. **Personality Type:** No data available. **Skills Required:** No data available. **Abilities:** No data available. **Occupational Values:** No data available. **Interacting with Others:** No data available. **Physical Work Conditions:** No data available.

Area, Ethnic, and Cultural Studies Teachers, Postsecondary

Teach courses pertaining to the culture and development of an area (e.g., Latin America), an ethnic group, or any other group (e.g., women's studies, urban affairs). **O*NET Code:** 25-1062.00. **Average Salary:** $55,760. **Projected Growth:** 38.1%. **Annual Openings:** 216,000. **Education:** Master's degree. **Job Zone:** 5. **Education/Training Program(s)—**African Studies; African-American/Black Studies; American Indian/Native American Studies; American/United States

Studies/Civilization; Area Studies, Other; Area, Ethnic, Cultural, and Gender Studies, Other; Asian Studies/Civilization; Asian-American Studies; Balkans Studies; Baltic Studies; Canadian Studies; Caribbean Studies; Central/Middle and Eastern European Studies; Chinese Studies; Commonwealth Studies; East Asian Studies; Ethnic, Cultural Minority, and Gender Studies, Other; European Studies/Civilization; French Studies; Gay/Lesbian Studies; German Studies; Hispanic-American, Puerto Rican, and Mexican-American/Chicano Studies; Intercultural/ Multicultural and Diversity Studies; Islamic Studies; Italian Studies; Japanese Studies; Jewish/Judaic Studies; Korean Studies; Latin American Studies; Near and Middle Eastern Studies; Pacific Area/Pacific Rim Studies; Polish Studies; Regional Studies (U.S., Canadian, Foreign); Religion/Religious Studies, Other; Russian Studies; Scandinavian Studies; Slavic Studies; Social Studies Teacher Education; South Asian Studies; Southeast Asian Studies; Spanish and Iberian Studies; Tibetan Studies; Ukraine Studies; Ural-Altaic and Central Asian Studies; Western European Studies; Women's Studies. **Related Knowledge/Courses:** Sociology and Anthropology; History and Archeology; Education and Training; Psychology; Economics and Accounting; English Language. **Personality Type:** Social. **Skills Required:** Instructing; Learning Strategies; Reading Comprehension; Active Learning; Speaking; Writing; Science; Active Listening; Critical Thinking. **Abilities:** Written Expression; Speech Clarity; Oral Expression; Oral Comprehension; Written Comprehension. **Occupational Values:** Authority; Social Service; Creativity; Achievement; Social Status. **Interacting with Others:** Training and Teaching Others; Coaching and Developing Others; Communicating with Supervisors, Peers, or Subordinates; Providing Consultation and Advice to Others. **Physical Work Conditions:** Indoors; Sitting; Standing.

Art, Drama, and Music Teachers, Postsecondary

Teach courses in drama, music, and the arts, including fine and applied art, such as painting and sculpture, or design and crafts. **O*NET Code:** 25-1121.00. **Average Salary:** $48,150. **Projected Growth:** 38.1%. **Annual Openings:** 216,000. **Education:** Master's degree. **Job Zone:** 5. **Education/Training Program(s)**—Art History, Criticism and Conservation; Art/Art Studies, General; Arts Management; Ceramic Arts and Ceramics; Cinematography and Film/Video Production; Commercial Photography; Conducting; Crafts/Craft Design, Folk Art, and Artisanry; Dance, General; Design and Applied Arts, Other; Design and Visual Communications, General; Directing and Theatrical Production; Drama and Dramatics/Theatre Arts, General; Dramatic/Theatre Arts and Stagecraft, Other; Fashion/Apparel Design; Fiber, Textile, and Weaving Arts; Film/Cinema Studies; Film/Video and Photographic Arts, Other; Fine Arts and Art Studies, Other; Fine/Studio Arts, General; Graphic Design; Industrial Design; Interior Design; Intermedia/Multimedia; Jazz/Jazz Studies; Metal and Jewelry Arts; Music History, Literature, and Theory; Music Management and Merchandising; Music Pedagogy; Music Performance, General; Music Theory and Composition; Music, Other; Musicology and Ethnomusicology; Painting; Photography; Piano and Organ; Playwriting and Screenwriting; Printmaking; Sculpture;

Technical Theatre/Theatre Design and Technology; Theatre Literature, History, and Criticism; Theatre/Theatre Arts Management; Violin, Viola, Guitar, and Other Stringed Instruments; Visual and Performing Arts, General; Visual and Performing Arts, Other; Voice and Opera. **Related Knowledge/Courses:** Fine Arts; Education and Training; English Language; Communications and Media; Administration and Management; Clerical. **Personality Type:** Artistic. **Skills Required:** Instructing; Learning Strategies; Writing; Speaking; Reading Comprehension; Complex Problem Solving; Time Management; Active Learning. **Abilities:** Visual Color Discrimination; Written Expression; Oral Expression; Written Comprehension; Originality. **Occupational Values:** Authority; Social Service; Creativity; Ability Utilization; Achievement. **Interacting with Others:** Training and Teaching Others; Coaching and Developing Others; Communicating with Supervisors, Peers, or Subordinates; Providing Consultation and Advice to Others. **Physical Work Conditions:** Indoors; Sitting; Standing; Using Hands on Objects, Tools, or Controls.

Atmospheric, Earth, Marine, and Space Sciences Teachers, Postsecondary

Teach courses in the physical sciences, except chemistry and physics. **O*NET Code:** 25-1051.00. **Average Salary:** $64,080. **Projected Growth:** 38.1%. **Annual Openings:** 216,000. **Education:** Master's degree. **Job Zone:** No data available. **Education/Training Program(s)**—Acoustics; Astronomy; Astrophysics; Atmospheric Chemistry and Climatology; Atmospheric Physics and Dynamics; Atmospheric Sciences and Meteorology, General; Atmospheric Sciences and Meteorology, Other; Atomic/Molecular Physics; Elementary Particle Physics; Geochemistry; Geochemistry and Petrology; Geological and Earth Sciences/Geosciences, Other; Geology/Earth Science, General; Geophysics and Seismology; Hydrology and Water Resources Science; Meteorology; Nuclear Physics; Oceanography, Chemical and Physical; Optics/Optical Sciences; Paleontology; Physics Teacher Education; Physics, Other; Planetary Astronomy and Science; Plasma and High-Temperature Physics; Science Teacher Education/General Science Teacher Education; Solid State and Low-Temperature Physics; Theoretical and Mathematical Physics. **Related Knowledge/Courses:** No data available. **Personality Type:** No data available. **Skills Required:** No data available. **Abilities:** No data available. **Occupational Values:** No data available. **Interacting with Others:** No data available. **Physical Work Conditions:** No data available.

Biological Science Teachers, Postsecondary

Teach courses in biological sciences. **O*NET Code:** 25-1042.00. **Average Salary:** $60,850. **Projected Growth:** 38.1%. **Annual Openings:** 216,000. **Education:** Master's degree. **Job Zone:** 5. **Education/Training Program(s)**—Anatomy; Animal Physiology; Biochemistry; Biological and Biomedical Sciences, Other; Biology/Biological Sciences, General; Biometry/Biometrics; Biophysics; Biotechnology; Botany/Plant Biology; Cell/Cellular Biology and Histology; Ecology; Ecology, Evolution, Systematics, and Population Biology, Other; Entomology; Evolutionary Biology; Immunology; Marine Biology and Biological Oceanography; Microbiology, General; Molecular Biology; Neuroscience;

Nutrition Sciences; Parasitology; Pathology/Experimental Pathology; Pharmacology; Plant Genetics; Plant Pathology/Phytopathology; Plant Physiology; Radiation Biology/Radiobiology; Toxicology; Virology; Zoology/Animal Biology. **Related Knowledge/Courses:** Biology; Education and Training; Medicine and Dentistry; Chemistry; Therapy and Counseling; Psychology. **Personality Type:** Investigative. **Skills Required:** Science; Instructing; Learning Strategies; Reading Comprehension; Active Learning; Writing; Critical Thinking; Mathematics. **Abilities:** Speech Clarity; Written Expression; Oral Expression; Oral Comprehension; Written Comprehension. **Occupational Values:** Authority; Social Service; Creativity; Achievement; Social Status. **Interacting with Others:** Training and Teaching Others; Coaching and Developing Others; Interpreting the Meaning of Information for Others; Communicating with Supervisors, Peers, or Subordinates; Providing Consultation and Advice to Others. **Physical Work Conditions:** Sitting; Indoors; Standing.

Business Teachers, Postsecondary

Teach courses in business administration and management, such as accounting, finance, human resources, labor relations, marketing, and operations research. **O*NET Code:** 25-1011.00. **Average Salary:** $56,560. **Projected Growth:** 38.1%. **Annual Openings:** 216,000. **Education:** Master's degree. **Job Zone:** No data available. **Education/Training Program(s)—**Accounting; Actuarial Science; Business Administration and Management, General; Business Statistics; Business Teacher Education; Business/Commerce, General; Business/Corporate Communications; Entrepreneurship/Entrepreneurial Studies; Finance, General; Financial Planning and Services; Franchising and Franchise Operations; Human Resources Management/Personnel Administration, General; Insurance; International Business/Trade/Commerce; International Finance; International Marketing; Investments and Securities; Labor and Industrial Relations; Logistics and Materials Management; Management Science, General; Marketing Research; Marketing/Marketing Management, General; Operations Management and Supervision; Organizational Behavior Studies; Public Finance; Purchasing, Procurement/Acquisitions, and Contracts Management. **Related Knowledge/Courses:** No data available. **Personality Type:** No data available. **Skills Required:** No data available. **Abilities:** No data available. **Occupational Values:** No data available. **Interacting with Others:** No data available. **Physical Work Conditions:** No data available.

Chemistry Teachers, Postsecondary

Teach courses pertaining to the chemical and physical properties and compositional changes of substances. Work may include instruction in the methods of qualitative and quantitative chemical analysis. Includes both teachers primarily engaged in teaching and those who do a combination of both teaching and research. **O*NET Code:** 25-1052.00. **Average Salary:** $56,190. **Projected Growth:** 38.1%. **Annual Openings:** 216,000. **Education:** Master's degree. **Job Zone:** 5. **Education/Training Program(s)—**Analytical Chemistry; Chemical Physics; Chemistry, General; Chemistry, Other; Geochemistry; Inorganic Chemistry; Organic Chemistry; Physical and Theoretical Chemistry; Polymer Chemistry.

Related Knowledge/Courses: Chemistry; Mathematics; Education and Training; English Language; Physics; Administration and Management. **Personality Type:** Investigative. **Skills Required:** Science; Instructing; Writing; Learning Strategies; Reading Comprehension; Active Learning; Speaking; Management of Personnel Resources. **Abilities:** Written Expression; Originality; Oral Expression; Fluency of Ideas; Inductive Reasoning. **Occupational Values:** Authority; Social Service; Creativity; Achievement; Social Status. **Interacting with Others:** Training and Teaching Others; Communicating with Persons Outside Organization; Interpreting the Meaning of Information for Others. **Physical Work Conditions:** Hazardous Conditions; Sitting; Contaminants; Indoors; Standing; Common Protective or Safety Equipment.

Communications Teachers, Postsecondary

Teach courses in communications, such as organizational communications, public relations, radio/television broadcasting, and journalism. **O*NET Code:** 25-1122.00. **Average Salary:** $49,420. **Projected Growth:** 38.1%. **Annual Openings:** 216,000. **Education:** Master's degree. **Job Zone:** No data available. **Education/Training Program(s)—**Advertising; Broadcast Journalism; Communication Studies/Speech Communication and Rhetoric; Communication, Journalism, and Related Programs, Other; Digital Communication and Media/Multimedia; Health Communication; Journalism; Journalism, Other; Mass Communication/Media Studies; Political Communication; Public Relations/Image Management; Radio and Television. **Related Knowledge/Courses:** No data available. **Personality Type:** No data available. **Skills Required:** No data available. **Abilities:** No data available. **Occupational Values:** No data available. **Interacting with Others:** No data available. **Physical Work Conditions:** No data available.

Computer Science Teachers, Postsecondary

Teach courses in computer science. May specialize in a field of computer science such as the design and function of computers or operations and research analysis. **O*NET Code:** 25-1021.00. **Average Salary:** $52,040. **Projected Growth:** 38.1%. **Annual Openings:** 216,000. **Education:** Master's degree. **Job Zone:** 5. **Education/Training Program(s)—**Computer and Information Sciences, General; Computer Programming/Programmer, General; Computer Science; Computer Systems Analysis/Analyst; Information Science/Studies. **Related Knowledge/Courses:** Computers and Electronics; Education and Training; Mathematics; Physics; English Language; Administration and Management; Telecommunications. **Personality Type:** Investigative. **Skills Required:** Programming; Instructing; Writing; Learning Strategies; Active Learning; Reading Comprehension; Mathematics; Science. **Abilities:** Written Expression; Speech Clarity; Oral Expression; Originality; Written Comprehension. **Occupational Values:** Authority; Social Service; Creativity; Ability Utilization; Achievement. **Interacting with Others:** Training and Teaching Others; Communicating with Persons Outside Organization; Providing Consultation and Advice to Others. **Physical Work Conditions:** Sitting; Indoors; Using Hands on Objects, Tools, or Controls; Extremely Bright or Inadequate Lighting; Walking and Running.

© 2006, JIST Works

299

Criminal Justice and Law Enforcement Teachers, Postsecondary

Teach courses in criminal justice, corrections, and law enforcement administration. **O*NET Code:** 25-1111.00. **Average Salary:** $46,030. **Projected Growth:** 38.1%. **Annual Openings:** 216,000. **Education:** Master's degree. **Job Zone:** No data available. **Education/Training Program(s)—** Corrections; Corrections Administration; Corrections and Criminal Justice, Other; Criminal Justice/Law Enforcement Administration; Criminal Justice/Police Science; Criminal Justice/Safety Studies; Criminalistics and Criminal Science; Forensic Science and Technology; Juvenile Corrections; Security and Loss Prevention Services; Teacher Education and Professional Development, Specific Subject Areas, Other. **Related Knowledge/Courses:** No data available. **Personality Type:** No data available. **Skills Required:** No data available. **Abilities:** No data available. **Occupational Values:** No data available. **Interacting with Others:** No data available. **Physical Work Conditions:** No data available.

Economics Teachers, Postsecondary

Teach courses in economics. **O*NET Code:** 25-1063.00. **Average Salary:** $66,300. **Projected Growth:** 38.1%. **Annual Openings:** 216,000. **Education:** Master's degree. **Job Zone:** 5. **Education/Training Program(s)—**Applied Economics; Business/Managerial Economics; Development Economics and International Development; Econometrics and Quantitative Economics; Economics, General; Economics, Other; International Economics; Social Science Teacher Education. **Related Knowledge/Courses:** Sociology and Anthropology; History and Archeology; Education and Training; Psychology; Economics and Accounting; English Language. **Personality Type:** Social. **Skills Required:** Instructing; Learning Strategies; Reading Comprehension; Active Learning; Speaking; Writing; Science; Active Listening; Critical Thinking. **Abilities:** Written Expression; Speech Clarity; Oral Expression; Oral Comprehension; Written Comprehension. **Occupational Values:** Authority; Social Service; Creativity; Achievement; Social Status. **Interacting with Others:** Training and Teaching Others; Coaching and Developing Others; Communicating with Supervisors, Peers, or Subordinates; Providing Consultation and Advice to Others. **Physical Work Conditions:** Indoors; Sitting; Standing.

Education Teachers, Postsecondary

Teach courses pertaining to education, such as counseling, curriculum, guidance, instruction, teacher education, and teaching English as a second language. **O*NET Code:** 25-1081.00. **Average Salary:** $48,180. **Projected Growth:** 38.1%. **Annual Openings:** 216,000. **Education:** Master's degree. **Job Zone:** No data available. **Education/Training Program(s)—** Agricultural Teacher Education; Art Teacher Education; Biology Teacher Education; Business Teacher Education; Chemistry Teacher Education; Computer Teacher Education; Drama and Dance Teacher Education; Driver and Safety Teacher Education; Education, General; English/Language Arts Teacher Education; Family and Consumer Sciences/Home Economics Teacher Education; Foreign Language Teacher Education; French Language Teacher Education; Geography Teacher Education; German Language Teacher Education; Health Occupations Teacher Education; Health Teacher Education; History Teacher Education; Mathematics Teacher Education; Music Teacher Education; Physical Education Teaching and Coaching; Physics Teacher Education; Reading Teacher Education; Sales and Marketing Operations/Marketing and Distribution Teacher Education; Science Teacher Education/General Science Teacher Education; Social Science Teacher Education; Social Studies Teacher Education; Spanish Language Teacher Education; Speech Teacher Education; Teacher Education and Professional Development, Specific Subject Areas, Other; Technical Teacher Education; Technology Teacher Education/Industrial Arts Teacher Education; Trade and Industrial Teacher Education. **Related Knowledge/Courses:** No data available. **Personality Type:** No data available. **Skills Required:** No data available. **Abilities:** No data available. **Occupational Values:** No data available. **Interacting with Others:** No data available. **Physical Work Conditions:** No data available.

Engineering Teachers, Postsecondary

Teach courses pertaining to the application of physical laws and principles of engineering for the development of machines, materials, instruments, processes, and services. Includes teachers of subjects such as chemical, civil, electrical, industrial, mechanical, mineral, and petroleum engineering. Includes both teachers primarily engaged in teaching and those who do a combination of both teaching and research. **O*NET Code:** 25-1032.00. **Average Salary:** $71,070. **Projected Growth:** 38.1%. **Annual Openings:** 216,000. **Education:** Master's degree. **Job Zone:** 5. **Education/Training Program(s)—**Aerospace, Aeronautical, and Astronautical Engineering; Agricultural/Biological Engineering and Bioengineering; Architectural Engineering; Biomedical/Medical Engineering; Ceramic Sciences and Engineering; Chemical Engineering; Civil Engineering, General; Civil Engineering, Other; Computer Engineering, General; Computer Engineering, Other; Computer Hardware Engineering; Computer Software Engineering; Construction Engineering; Electrical, Electronics, and Communications Engineering; Engineering Mechanics; Engineering Physics; Engineering Science; Engineering, General; Engineering, Other; Environmental/Environmental Health Engineering; Forest Engineering; Geological/Geophysical Engineering; Geotechnical Engineering; Industrial Engineering; Manufacturing Engineering; Materials Engineering; Materials Science; Mechanical Engineering; Metallurgical Engineering; Mining and Mineral Engineering; Naval Architecture and Marine Engineering; Nuclear Engineering; Ocean Engineering; Petroleum Engineering; Polymer/Plastics Engineering; Structural Engineering; Surveying Engineering; Systems Engineering; Teacher Education and Professional Development, Specific Subject Areas, Other; Textile Sciences and Engineering; Transportation and Highway Engineering; Water Resources Engineering. **Related Knowledge/Courses:** Engineering and Technology; Education and Training; Physics; Chemistry; Design; Mathematics. **Personality Type:** Investigative. **Skills Required:** Science; Mathematics; Instructing; Technology Design; Active Learning; Critical Thinking; Learning Strategies; Reading Comprehension; Operations Analysis. **Abilities:** Speech Clarity; Written

Expression; Oral Expression; Mathematical Reasoning; Written Comprehension. **Occupational Values:** Authority; Social Service; Creativity; Ability Utilization; Achievement. **Interacting with Others:** Training and Teaching Others; Communicating with Supervisors, Peers, or Subordinates; Coaching and Developing Others. **Physical Work Conditions:** Sitting; Indoors; Standing.

English Language and Literature Teachers, Postsecondary

Teach courses in English language and literature, including linguistics and comparative literature. **O*NET Code:** 25-1123.00. **Average Salary:** $47,560. **Projected Growth:** 38.1%. **Annual Openings:** 216,000. **Education:** Master's degree. **Job Zone:** 5. **Education/Training Program(s)**—American Literature (Canadian); American Literature (United States); Comparative Literature; Creative Writing; English Composition; English Language and Literature, General; English Language and Literature/Letters, Other; English Literature (British and Commonwealth); Technical and Business Writing. **Related Knowledge/Courses:** Foreign Language; Education and Training; English Language; Communications and Media; Therapy and Counseling; Clerical. **Personality Type:** Artistic. **Skills Required:** Instructing; Learning Strategies; Speaking; Reading Comprehension; Writing; Critical Thinking; Active Learning; Active Listening. **Abilities:** Speech Clarity; Written Expression; Speech Recognition; Oral Expression; Written Comprehension. **Occupational Values:** Authority; Social Service; Achievement; Creativity; Social Status; Autonomy. **Interacting with Others:** Training and Teaching Others; Communicating with Supervisors, Peers, or Subordinates; Communicating with Persons Outside Organization. **Physical Work Conditions:** Indoors; Sitting; Standing.

Environmental Science Teachers, Postsecondary

Teach courses in environmental science. **O*NET Code:** 25-1053.00. **Average Salary:** $60,660. **Projected Growth:** 38.1%. **Annual Openings:** 216,000. **Education:** Master's degree. **Job Zone:** No data available. **Education/Training Program(s)**—Environmental Science; Environmental Studies; Science Teacher Education/General Science Teacher Education. **Related Knowledge/Courses:** No data available. **Personality Type:** No data available. **Skills Required:** No data available. **Abilities:** No data available. **Occupational Values:** No data available. **Interacting with Others:** No data available. **Physical Work Conditions:** No data available.

Farm and Home Management Advisors

Advise, instruct, and assist individuals and families engaged in agriculture, agricultural-related processes, or home economics activities. Demonstrate procedures and apply research findings to solve problems; instruct and train in product development, sales, and the utilization of machinery and equipment to promote general welfare. Includes county agricultural agents, feed and farm management advisers, home economists, and extension service advisors. **O*NET Code:** 25-9021.00. **Average Salary:** $39,930. **Projected Growth:** 6.9%. **Annual Openings:** 3,000. **Education:** Bachelor's degree. **Job Zone:** 4. **Education/Training Program(s)**—Adult Development and Aging; Agricultural and Extension Education Services; Animal Nutrition; Animal/Livestock Husbandry and Production; Apparel and Textiles, General; Business Family and Consumer Sciences/Human Sciences; Child Development; Consumer Economics; Consumer Merchandising/Retailing Management; Consumer Services and Advocacy; Crop Production; Family and Community Services; Family and Consumer Economics and Related Services, Other; Family and Consumer Sciences/Human Sciences, General; Family and Consumer Sciences/Human Sciences, Other; Family Resource Management Studies, General; Family Systems; Farm/Farm and Ranch Management; Home Furnishings and Equipment Installers; Housing and Human Environments, General; Housing and Human Environments, Other; Human Development, Family Studies, and Related Services, Other. **Related Knowledge/Courses:** Food Production; Education and Training; Economics and Accounting; Mathematics; Administration and Management; Communications and Media. **Personality Type:** Social. **Skills Required:** Persuasion; Service Orientation; Instructing; Systems Analysis; Learning Strategies; Writing; Operations Analysis; Active Learning; Systems Evaluation. **Abilities:** Speech Clarity; Mathematical Reasoning; Oral Expression; Written Expression; Originality. **Occupational Values:** Social Service; Authority; Creativity; Autonomy; Achievement. **Interacting with Others:** Communicating with Persons Outside Organization; Providing Consultation and Advice to Others; Establishing and Maintaining Interpersonal Relationships. **Physical Work Conditions:** Very Hot or Cold; Extremely Bright or Inadequate Lighting; Standing; Outdoors; Contaminants.

Foreign Language and Literature Teachers, Postsecondary

Teach courses in foreign (i.e., other than English) languages and literature. **O*NET Code:** 25-1124.00. **Average Salary:** $47,060. **Projected Growth:** 38.1%. **Annual Openings:** 216,000. **Education:** Master's degree. **Job Zone:** 5. **Education/Training Program(s)**—African Languages, Literatures, and Linguistics; Albanian Language and Literature; American Indian/Native American Languages, Literatures, and Linguistics; Ancient Near Eastern and Biblical Languages, Literatures, and Linguistics; Ancient/Classical Greek Language and Literature; Arabic Language and Literature; Australian/Oceanic/Pacific Languages, Literatures, and Linguistics; Bahasa Indonesian/Bahasa Malay Languages and Literatures; Baltic Languages, Literatures, and Linguistics; Bengali Language and Literature; Bulgarian Language and Literature; Burmese Language and Literature; Catalan Language and Literature; Celtic Languages, Literatures, and Linguistics; Chinese Language and Literature; Classics and Classical Languages, Literatures, and Linguistics, General; Classics and Classical Languages, Literatures, and Linguistics, Other; Czech Language and Literature; Danish Language and Literature; Dutch/Flemish Language and Literature; East Asian Languages, Literatures, and Linguistics, General; East Asian Languages, Literatures, and Linguistics, Other; Filipino/Tagalog Language and Literature; Finnish and Related Languages, Literatures, and Linguistics; Foreign Languages and Literatures, General; Foreign Languages, Literatures, and Linguistics, Other; French Language and Literature; German Language and Literature; Germanic

Languages, Literatures, and Linguistics, General; Germanic Languages, Literatures, and Linguistics, Other; Hebrew Language and Literature; Hindi Language and Literature; Hungarian/Magyar Language and Literature; Iranian/Persian Languages, Literatures, and Linguistics; Italian Language and Literature; Japanese Language and Literature; Khmer/Cambodian Language and Literature; Korean Language and Literature; Language Interpretation and Translation; Lao/Laotian Language and Literature; Latin Language and Literature; Latin Teacher Education; Linguistics; Middle/Near Eastern and Semitic Languages, Literatures, and Linguistics, Other; others. **Related Knowledge/Courses:** Foreign Language; Education and Training; English Language; Communications and Media; Therapy and Counseling; Clerical. **Personality Type:** Artistic. **Skills Required:** Instructing; Learning Strategies; Speaking; Reading Comprehension; Writing; Critical Thinking; Active Learning; Active Listening. **Abilities:** Speech Clarity; Written Expression; Speech Recognition; Oral Expression; Written Comprehension. **Occupational Values:** Authority; Social Service; Achievement; Creativity; Social Status; Autonomy. **Interacting with Others:** Training and Teaching Others; Communicating with Supervisors, Peers, or Subordinates; Communicating with Persons Outside Organization. **Physical Work Conditions:** Indoors; Sitting; Standing.

Forestry and Conservation Science Teachers, Postsecondary

Teach courses in environmental and conservation science. **O*NET Code:** 25-1043.00. **Average Salary:** $64,350. **Projected Growth:** 38.1%. **Annual Openings:** 216,000. **Education:** Master's degree. **Job Zone:** 5. **Education/Training Program(s)**—Science Teacher Education/General Science Teacher Education. **Related Knowledge/Courses:** Biology; Education and Training; Medicine and Dentistry; Chemistry; Therapy and Counseling; Psychology. **Personality Type:** Investigative. **Skills Required:** Science; Instructing; Learning Strategies; Reading Comprehension; Active Learning; Writing; Critical Thinking; Mathematics. **Abilities:** Speech Clarity; Written Expression; Oral Expression; Oral Comprehension; Written Comprehension. **Occupational Values:** Authority; Social Service; Creativity; Achievement; Social Status. **Interacting with Others:** Training and Teaching Others; Coaching and Developing Others; Interpreting the Meaning of Information for Others; Communicating with Supervisors, Peers, or Subordinates; Providing Consultation and Advice to Others. **Physical Work Conditions:** Sitting; Indoors; Standing.

Geography Teachers, Postsecondary

Teach courses in geography. **O*NET Code:** 25-1064.00. **Average Salary:** $56,810. **Projected Growth:** 38.1%. **Annual Openings:** 216,000. **Education:** Master's degree. **Job Zone:** No data available. **Education/Training Program(s)**— Geography; Geography Teacher Education. **Related Knowledge/Courses:** No data available. **Personality Type:** No data available. **Skills Required:** No data available. **Abilities:** No data available. **Occupational Values:** No data available. **Interacting with Others:** No data available. **Physical Work Conditions:** No data available.

Graduate Teaching Assistants

Assist department chairperson, faculty members, or other professional staff members in college or university by performing teaching or teaching-related duties, such as teaching lower-level courses, developing teaching materials, preparing and giving examinations, and grading examinations or papers. Graduate assistants must be enrolled in a graduate school program. Graduate assistants who primarily perform non-teaching duties, such as laboratory research, should be reported in the occupational category related to the work performed. **O*NET Code:** 25-1191.00. **Average Salary:** $25,550. **Projected Growth:** 38.1%. **Annual Openings:** 216,000. **Education:** Master's degree. **Job Zone:** 5. **Education/Training Program(s)**—No data available. **Related Knowledge/Courses:** Education and Training; English Language; Clerical; Mathematics; Administration and Management; Computers and Electronics. **Personality Type:** Social. **Skills Required:** Instructing; Learning Strategies; Speaking; Reading Comprehension; Science; Writing; Critical Thinking; Mathematics; Active Learning. **Abilities:** Speech Clarity; Oral Expression; Oral Comprehension; Written Comprehension; Written Expression. **Occupational Values:** Social Service; Authority; Co-workers; Working Conditions; Achievement; Creativity. **Interacting with Others:** Training and Teaching Others; Communicating with Supervisors, Peers, or Subordinates; Communicating with Persons Outside Organization. **Physical Work Conditions:** Indoors; Standing; Sitting.

Health Specialties Teachers, Postsecondary

Teach courses in health specialties, such as veterinary medicine, dentistry, pharmacy, therapy, laboratory technology, and public health. **O*NET Code:** 25-1071.00. **Average Salary:** $63,250. **Projected Growth:** 38.1%. **Annual Openings:** 216,000. **Education:** Master's degree. **Job Zone:** 5. **Education/Training Program(s)**—Allied Health and Medical Assisting Services, Other; Allied Health Diagnostic, Intervention, and Treatment Professions, Other; Art Therapy/Therapist; Asian Bodywork Therapy; Audiology/Audiologist and Hearing Sciences; Audiology/Audiologist and Speech-Language Pathology/Pathologist; Biostatistics; Blood Bank Technology Specialist; Cardiovascular Technology/Technologist; Chiropractic (DC); Clinical Laboratory Science/Medical Technology/Technologist; Clinical/Medical Laboratory Assistant; Clinical/Medical Laboratory Technician; Communication Disorders, General; Cytotechnology/Cytotechnologist; Dance Therapy/Therapist; Dental Assisting/Assistant; Dental Clinical Sciences, General (MS, PhD); Dental Hygiene/Hygienist; Dental Laboratory Technology/Technician; Dental Services and Allied Professions, Other; Dentistry (DDS, DMD); Diagnostic Medical Sonography/Sonographer and Ultrasound Technician; Electrocardiograph Technology/Technician; Electroneurodiagnostic/Electroencephalographic Technology/Technologist; Emergency Medical Technology/Technician (EMT Paramedic); Environmental Health; Epidemiology; Health Occupations Teacher Education; Health/Medical Physics; Health/Medical Preparatory Programs, Other; Hematology Technology/Technician; Hypnotherapy/Hypnotherapist; Massage

Therapy/Therapeutic Massage; Medical Radiologic Technology/Science—Radiation Therapist; Music Therapy/Therapist; Nuclear Medical Technology/Technologist; Occupational Health and Industrial Hygiene; Occupational Therapist Assistant; Occupational Therapy/Therapist; Orthotist/Prosthetist; Perfusion Technology/Perfusionist; Pharmacy (PharmD [USA]; PharmD, BS/BPharm [Canada]); Pharmacy Administration and Pharmacy Policy and Regulatory Affairs (MS, PhD); Pharmacy Technician/Assistant; Pharmacy, Pharmaceutical Sciences, and Administration, Other; Physical Therapist Assistant; Physical Therapy/Therapist; Physician Assistant; Pre-Dentistry Studies; Pre-Medicine/Pre-Medical Studies; Pre-Nursing Studies; others. **Related Knowledge/Courses:** Biology; Education and Training; Medicine and Dentistry; Therapy and Counseling; English Language; Chemistry. **Personality Type:** Investigative. **Skills Required:** Science; Instructing; Writing; Reading Comprehension; Active Learning; Critical Thinking; Learning Strategies; Speaking. **Abilities:** Written Expression; Speech Clarity; Oral Expression; Written Comprehension; Mathematical Reasoning. **Occupational Values:** Authority; Social Service; Creativity; Achievement; Social Status. **Interacting with Others:** Training and Teaching Others; Coaching and Developing Others; Communicating with Supervisors, Peers, or Subordinates. **Physical Work Conditions:** Standing; Indoors; Disease or Infections; Sitting; Exposed to Radiation.

History Teachers, Postsecondary

Teach courses in human history and historiography. **O*NET Code:** 25-1125.00. **Average Salary:** $53,130. **Projected Growth:** 38.1%. **Annual Openings:** 216,000. **Education:** Master's degree. **Job Zone:** 5. **Education/Training Program(s)**—American History (United States); Asian History; Canadian History; European History; History and Philosophy of Science and Technology; History, General; History, Other; Public/Applied History and Archival Administration. **Related Knowledge/Courses:** Sociology and Anthropology; History and Archeology; Education and Training; Psychology; Economics and Accounting; English Language. **Personality Type:** Social. **Skills Required:** Instructing; Learning Strategies; Reading Comprehension; Active Learning; Speaking; Writing; Science; Active Listening; Critical Thinking. **Abilities:** Written Expression; Speech Clarity; Oral Expression; Oral Comprehension; Written Comprehension. **Occupational Values:** Authority; Social Service; Creativity; Achievement; Social Status. **Interacting with Others:** Training and Teaching Others; Coaching and Developing Others; Communicating with Supervisors, Peers, or Subordinates; Providing Consultation and Advice to Others. **Physical Work Conditions:** Indoors; Sitting; Standing.

Home Economics Teachers, Postsecondary

Teach courses in child care, family relations, finance, nutrition, and related subjects as pertaining to home management. **O*NET Code:** 25-1192.00. **Average Salary:** $46,780. **Projected Growth:** 38.1%. **Annual Openings:** 216,000. **Education:** Master's degree. **Job Zone:** No data available. **Education/Training Program(s)**—Business Family and Consumer Sciences/Human Sciences; Child Care and Support Services Management; Family and Consumer Sciences/Human Sciences, General; Foodservice Systems Administration/Management; Human Development and Family Studies, General. **Related Knowledge/Courses:** No data available. **Personality Type:** No data available. **Skills Required:** No data available. **Abilities:** No data available. **Occupational Values:** No data available. **Interacting with Others:** No data available. **Physical Work Conditions:** No data available.

Law Teachers, Postsecondary

Teach courses in law. **O*NET Code:** 25-1112.00. **Average Salary:** $86,360. **Projected Growth:** 38.1%. **Annual Openings:** 216,000. **Education:** First professional degree. **Job Zone:** No data available. **Education/Training Program(s)**—Law (LL.B., J.D.); Legal Studies, General. **Related Knowledge/Courses:** No data available. **Personality Type:** No data available. **Skills Required:** No data available. **Abilities:** No data available. **Occupational Values:** No data available. **Interacting with Others:** No data available. **Physical Work Conditions:** No data available.

Library Science Teachers, Postsecondary

Teach courses in library science. **O*NET Code:** 25-1082.00. **Average Salary:** $51,340. **Projected Growth:** 38.1%. **Annual Openings:** 216,000. **Education:** Master's degree. **Job Zone:** No data available. **Education/Training Program(s)**—Library Science/Librarianship; Teacher Education and Professional Development, Specific Subject Areas, Other. **Related Knowledge/Courses:** No data available. **Personality Type:** No data available. **Skills Required:** No data available. **Abilities:** No data available. **Occupational Values:** No data available. **Interacting with Others:** No data available. **Physical Work Conditions:** No data available.

Mathematical Science Teachers, Postsecondary

Teach courses pertaining to mathematical concepts, statistics, and actuarial science and to the application of original and standardized mathematical techniques in solving specific problems and situations. **O*NET Code:** 25-1022.00. **Average Salary:** $51,820. **Projected Growth:** 38.1%. **Annual Openings:** 216,000. **Education:** Master's degree. **Job Zone:** 5. **Education/Training Program(s)**—Algebra and Number Theory; Analysis and Functional Analysis; Applied Mathematics; Business Statistics; Geometry/Geometric Analysis; Logic; Mathematical Statistics and Probability; Mathematics and Statistics, Other; Mathematics, General; Mathematics, Other; Statistics, General; Topology and Foundations. **Related Knowledge/Courses:** Mathematics; Education and Training; English Language; Clerical; Communications and Media; Administration and Management. **Personality Type:** Investigative. **Skills Required:** Mathematics; Instructing; Learning Strategies; Active Learning; Reading Comprehension; Writing; Critical Thinking; Speaking. **Abilities:** Mathematical Reasoning; Number Facility; Written Expression; Oral Expression; Written Comprehension. **Occupational Values:** Authority; Social Service; Ability Utilization; Achievement; Creativity. **Interacting with Others:** Training and Teaching Others; Communicating with Supervisors, Peers, or Subordinates; Coaching and Developing Others; Providing Consultation and Advice to Others. **Physical Work Conditions:** Sitting; Standing.

Nursing Instructors and Teachers, Postsecondary

Demonstrate and teach patient care in classroom and clinical units to nursing students. Includes both teachers primarily engaged in teaching and those who do a combination of both teaching and research. O*NET Code: 25-1072.00. **Average Salary:** $51,310. **Projected Growth:** 38.1%. **Annual Openings:** 216,000. **Education:** Master's degree. **Job Zone:** 5. **Education/Training Program(s)**—Adult Health Nurse/Nursing; Clinical Nurse Specialist; Family Practice Nurse/Nurse Practitioner; Maternal/Child Health and Neonatal Nurse/Nursing; Nurse Anesthetist; Nurse Midwife/Nursing Midwifery; Nursing, Other; Nursing—Registered Nurse Training (RN, ASN, BSN, MSN); Nursing Science (MS, PhD); Pediatric Nurse/Nursing; Perioperative/Operating Room and Surgical Nurse/Nursing; Pre-Nursing Studies; Psychiatric/Mental Health Nurse/Nursing; Public Health/Community Nurse/Nursing. **Related Knowledge/Courses:** Education and Training; Medicine and Dentistry; Biology; Psychology; Chemistry; Therapy and Counseling. **Personality Type:** Social. **Skills Required:** Learning Strategies; Instructing; Management of Personnel Resources; Science; Reading Comprehension; Service Orientation; Social Perceptiveness; Speaking; Time Management. **Abilities:** Speech Clarity; Oral Expression; Written Expression; Deductive Reasoning; Static Strength. **Occupational Values:** Authority; Social Service; Achievement; Social Status; Autonomy. **Interacting with Others:** Training and Teaching Others; Communicating with Supervisors, Peers, or Subordinates; Coaching and Developing Others. **Physical Work Conditions:** Disease or Infections; Indoors; Common Protective or Safety Equipment; Walking and Running; Standing.

Philosophy and Religion Teachers, Postsecondary

Teach courses in philosophy, religion, and theology. O*NET Code: 25-1126.00. **Average Salary:** $50,110. **Projected Growth:** 38.1%. **Annual Openings:** 216,000. **Education:** Master's degree. **Job Zone:** No data available. **Education/Training Program(s)**—Bible/Biblical Studies; Buddhist Studies; Christian Studies; Divinity/Ministry (BD, MDiv.); Ethics; Hindu Studies; Missions/Missionary Studies and Missiology; Pastoral Counseling and Specialized Ministries, Other; Pastoral Studies/Counseling; Philosophy; Philosophy and Religious Studies, Other; Philosophy, Other; Pre-Theology/Pre-Ministerial Studies; Rabbinical Studies; Religion/Religious Studies; Religious Education; Religious/Sacred Music; Talmudic Studies; Theological and Ministerial Studies, Other; Theology and Religious Vocations, Other; Theology/Theological Studies. **Related Knowledge/Courses:** No data available. **Personality Type:** No data available. **Skills Required:** No data available. **Abilities:** No data available. **Occupational Values:** No data available. **Interacting with Others:** No data available. **Physical Work Conditions:** No data available.

Physics Teachers, Postsecondary

Teach courses pertaining to the laws of matter and energy. Includes both teachers primarily engaged in teaching and those who do a combination of both teaching and research. O*NET Code: 25-1054.00. **Average Salary:** $63,790. **Projected Growth:** 38.1%. **Annual Openings:** 216,000. **Education:** Master's degree. **Job Zone:** 5. **Education/Training Program(s)**—Acoustics; Atomic/Molecular Physics; Elementary Particle Physics; Nuclear Physics; Optics/Optical Sciences; Physics, General; Physics, Other; Plasma and High-Temperature Physics; Solid State and Low-Temperature Physics; Theoretical and Mathematical Physics. **Related Knowledge/Courses:** Physics; Education and Training; Mathematics; English Language; Administration and Management; Chemistry. **Personality Type:** Investigative. **Skills Required:** Science; Instructing; Writing; Learning Strategies; Reading Comprehension; Active Learning; Critical Thinking; Complex Problem Solving; Judgment and Decision Making. **Abilities:** Mathematical Reasoning; Number Facility; Written Expression; Speech Clarity; Oral Expression. **Occupational Values:** Authority; Social Service; Achievement; Creativity; Social Status. **Interacting with Others:** Training and Teaching Others; Communicating with Persons Outside Organization; Interpreting the Meaning of Information for Others. **Physical Work Conditions:** Sitting; Indoors; Standing; Common Protective or Safety Equipment; Very Hot or Cold.

Political Science Teachers, Postsecondary

Teach courses in political science, international affairs, and international relations. O*NET Code: 25-1065.00. **Average Salary:** $58,530. **Projected Growth:** 38.1%. **Annual Openings:** 216,000. **Education:** Master's degree. **Job Zone:** 5. **Education/Training Program(s)**—American Government and Politics (United States); Political Science and Government, General; Political Science and Government, Other; Social Science Teacher Education. **Related Knowledge/Courses:** Sociology and Anthropology; History and Archeology; Education and Training; Psychology; Economics and Accounting; English Language. **Personality Type:** Social. **Skills Required:** Instructing; Learning Strategies; Reading Comprehension; Active Learning; Speaking; Writing; Science; Active Listening; Critical Thinking. **Abilities:** Written Expression; Speech Clarity; Oral Expression; Oral Comprehension; Written Comprehension. **Occupational Values:** Authority; Social Service; Creativity; Achievement; Social Status. **Interacting with Others:** Training and Teaching Others; Coaching and Developing Others; Communicating with Supervisors, Peers, or Subordinates; Providing Consultation and Advice to Others. **Physical Work Conditions:** Indoors; Sitting; Standing.

Psychology Teachers, Postsecondary

Teach courses in psychology, such as child, clinical, and developmental psychology and psychological counseling. O*NET Code: 25-1066.00. **Average Salary:** $54,530. **Projected Growth:** 38.1%. **Annual Openings:** 216,000. **Education:** Master's degree. **Job Zone:** 5. **Education/Training Program(s)**—Clinical Psychology; Cognitive Psychology and Psycholinguistics; Community Psychology; Comparative Psychology; Counseling Psychology; Developmental and Child Psychology; Educational Psychology; Experimental Psychology; Industrial and Organizational Psychology; Marriage and Family Therapy/Counseling; Personality Psychology; Physiological Psychology/Psychobiology; Psychology Teacher Education; Psychology, General; Psychology, Other; Psychometrics and Quantitative Psychology; School Psychology; Social Psychology; Social

Science Teacher Education. **Related Knowledge/Courses:** Sociology and Anthropology; History and Archeology; Education and Training; Psychology; Economics and Accounting; English Language. **Personality Type:** Social. **Skills Required:** Instructing; Learning Strategies; Reading Comprehension; Active Learning; Speaking; Writing; Science; Active Listening; Critical Thinking. **Abilities:** Written Expression; Speech Clarity; Oral Expression; Oral Comprehension; Written Comprehension. **Occupational Values:** Authority; Social Service; Creativity; Achievement; Social Status. **Interacting with Others:** Training and Teaching Others; Coaching and Developing Others; Communicating with Supervisors, Peers, or Subordinates; Providing Consultation and Advice to Others. **Physical Work Conditions:** Indoors; Sitting; Standing.

Recreation and Fitness Studies Teachers, Postsecondary

Teach courses pertaining to recreation, leisure, and fitness studies, including exercise physiology and facilities management. O*NET Code: 25-1193.00. **Average Salary:** $44,180. **Projected Growth:** 38.1%. **Annual Openings:** 216,000. **Education:** Master's degree. **Job Zone:** No data available. **Education/Training Program(s)—**Health and Physical Education, General; Parks, Recreation and Leisure Studies; Sport and Fitness Administration/Management. **Related Knowledge/Courses:** No data available. **Personality Type:** No data available. **Skills Required:** No data available. **Abilities:** No data available. **Occupational Values:** No data available. **Interacting with Others:** No data available. **Physical Work Conditions:** No data available.

Self-Enrichment Education Teachers

Teach or instruct courses other than those that normally lead to an occupational objective or degree. Courses may include self-improvement, nonvocational, and nonacademic subjects. Teaching may or may not take place in a traditional educational institution. O*NET Code: 25-3021.00. **Average Salary:** $30,560. **Projected Growth:** 40.1%. **Annual Openings:** 39,000. **Education:** Work experience in a related occupation. **Job Zone:** 4. **Education/Training Program(s)—**Adult and Continuing Education and Teaching. **Related Knowledge/Courses:** Education and Training; English Language; Philosophy and Theology; Sociology and Anthropology; History and Archeology; Economics and Accounting. **Personality Type:** Social. **Skills Required:** Instructing; Writing; Speaking; Learning Strategies; Service Orientation; Systems Evaluation; Reading Comprehension; Active Listening; Judgment and Decision Making; Management of Material Resources. **Abilities:** Written Expression; Speech Clarity; Oral Expression; Oral Comprehension; Fluency of Ideas. **Occupational Values:** Authority; Social Service; Creativity; Achievement; Responsibility. **Interacting with Others:** Training and Teaching Others; Communicating with Persons Outside Organization; Coaching and Developing Others. **Physical Work Conditions:** Sitting; Standing; Indoors; Walking and Running.

Social Work Teachers, Postsecondary

Teach courses in social work. O*NET Code: 25-1113.00. **Average Salary:** $51,190. **Projected Growth:** 38.1%. **Annual**
Openings: 216,000. **Education:** Master's degree. **Job Zone:** No data available. **Education/Training Program(s)—**Clinical/Medical Social Work; Social Work; Teacher Education and Professional Development, Specific Subject Areas, Other. **Related Knowledge/Courses:** No data available. **Personality Type:** No data available. **Skills Required:** No data available. **Abilities:** No data available. **Occupational Values:** No data available. **Interacting with Others:** No data available. **Physical Work Conditions:** No data available.

Sociology Teachers, Postsecondary

Teach courses in sociology. O*NET Code: 25-1067.00. **Average Salary:** $53,870. **Projected Growth:** 38.1%. **Annual Openings:** 216,000. **Education:** Master's degree. **Job Zone:** 5. **Education/Training Program(s)—**Social Science Teacher Education; Sociology. **Related Knowledge/Courses:** Sociology and Anthropology; History and Archeology; Education and Training; Psychology; Economics and Accounting; English Language. **Personality Type:** Social. **Skills Required:** Instructing; Learning Strategies; Reading Comprehension; Active Learning; Speaking; Writing; Science; Active Listening; Critical Thinking. **Abilities:** Written Expression; Speech Clarity; Oral Expression; Oral Comprehension; Written Comprehension. **Occupational Values:** Authority; Social Service; Creativity; Achievement; Social Status. **Interacting with Others:** Training and Teaching Others; Coaching and Developing Others; Communicating with Supervisors, Peers, or Subordinates; Providing Consultation and Advice to Others. **Physical Work Conditions:** Indoors; Sitting; Standing.

Vocational Education Teachers, Postsecondary

Teach or instruct vocational or occupational subjects at the postsecondary level (but at less than the baccalaureate) to students who have graduated or left high school. Includes correspondence school instructors; industrial, commercial and government training instructors; and adult education teachers and instructors who prepare persons to operate industrial machinery and equipment and transportation and communications equipment. Teaching may take place in public or private schools whose primary business is education or in a school associated with an organization whose primary business is other than education. O*NET Code: 25-1194.00. **Average Salary:** $40,040. **Projected Growth:** 38.1%. **Annual Openings:** 216,000. **Education:** Work experience in a related occupation. **Job Zone:** 4. **Education/Training Program(s)—**Agricultural Teacher Education; Business Teacher Education; Health Occupations Teacher Education; Sales and Marketing Operations/Marketing and Distribution Teacher Education; Teacher Education and Professional Development, Specific Subject Areas, Other; Technical Teacher Education; Technology Teacher Education/Industrial Arts Teacher Education; Trade and Industrial Teacher Education. **Related Knowledge/Courses:** Education and Training; English Language; Philosophy and Theology; Sociology and Anthropology; Communications and Media; Administration and Management. **Personality Type:** Social. **Skills Required:** Instructing; Service Orientation; Writing; Speaking; Learning Strategies; Judgment and Decision Making; Active Listening; Reading Comprehension; Complex Problem Solving; Technology Design. **Abilities:** Speech Clarity; Oral

Expression; Originality; Fluency of Ideas; Written Expression. **Occupational Values:** Authority; Social Service; Creativity; Achievement; Responsibility. **Interacting with Others:** Training and Teaching Others; Communicating with Persons Outside Organization; Communicating with Supervisors, Peers, or Subordinates; Assisting and Caring for Others. **Physical Work Conditions:** Standing; Walking and Running; Indoors; Sitting; Spend Time Making Repetitive Motions.

05.04 Library Services

Librarians

Administer libraries and perform related library services. Work in a variety of settings, including public libraries, schools, colleges and universities, museums, corporations, government agencies, law firms, non-profit organizations, and health care providers. Tasks may include selecting, acquiring, cataloguing, classifying, circulating, and maintaining library materials and furnishing reference, bibliographical, and readers' advisory services. May perform in-depth strategic research and synthesize, analyze, edit, and filter information. May set up or work with databases and information systems to catalogue and access information. **O*NET Code:** 25-4021.00. **Average Salary:** $44,730. **Projected Growth:** 10.1%. **Annual Openings:** 15,000. **Education:** Master's degree. **Job Zone:** 5. **Education/Training Program(s)**—Library Science/ Librarianship; Library Science, Other; School Librarian/ School Library Media Specialist. **Related Knowledge/Courses:** Customer and Personal Service; Clerical; English Language; Personnel and Human Resources; Communications and Media; Geography. **Personality Type:** Artistic. **Skills Required:** Management of Financial Resources; Learning Strategies; Service Orientation; Instructing; Persuasion; Management of Material Resources; Monitoring; Social Perceptiveness. **Abilities:** Flexibility of Closure; Speech Recognition; Far Vision; Category Flexibility; Near Vision. **Occupational Values:** Working Conditions; Authority; Social Service; Co-workers; Responsibility; Autonomy. **Interacting with Others:** Establishing and Maintaining Interpersonal Relationships; Communicating with Supervisors, Peers, or Subordinates; Performing for or Working Directly with the Public; Training and Teaching Others. **Physical Work Conditions:** Physical Proximity; Sitting; Sounds, Noise Levels Are Distracting or Uncomfortable; Indoors; Contaminants.

Library Assistants, Clerical

Compile records, sort and shelve books, and issue and receive library materials such as pictures, cards, slides, and microfilm. Locate library materials for loan and replace material in shelving area, stacks, or files according to identification number and title. Register patrons to permit them to borrow books, periodicals, and other library materials. **O*NET Code:** 43-4121.00. **Average Salary:** $19,980. **Projected Growth:** 21.5%. **Annual Openings:** 27,000. **Education:** Short-term on-the-job training. **Job Zone:** 3. **Education/Training Program(s)**— Library Assistant/Technician. **Related Knowledge/Courses:** Clerical; Computers and Electronics; Customer and Personal Service; English Language; History and Archeology;

Geography; Communications and Media. **Personality Type:** Conventional. **Skills Required:** Service Orientation; Instructing; Reading Comprehension; Time Management; Learning Strategies; Social Perceptiveness; Active Listening; Writing. **Abilities:** Speech Recognition; Far Vision; Category Flexibility; Extent Flexibility; Flexibility of Closure; Near Vision. **Occupational Values:** Supervision, Technical; Social Service; Working Conditions; Supervision, Human Relations; Security; Co-workers. **Interacting with Others:** Establishing and Maintaining Interpersonal Relationships; Communicating with Supervisors, Peers, or Subordinates; Performing for or Working Directly with the Public. **Physical Work Conditions:** Physical Proximity; Sitting; Contaminants; Sounds, Noise Levels Are Distracting or Uncomfortable.

Library Technicians

Assist librarians by helping readers in the use of library catalogs, databases, and indexes to locate books and other materials and by answering questions that require only brief consultation of standard reference. Compile records; sort and shelve books; remove or repair damaged books; register patrons; check materials in and out of the circulation process. Replace materials in shelving area (stacks) or files. Includes bookmobile drivers who operate bookmobiles or light trucks that pull trailers to specific locations on a predetermined schedule and assist with providing services in mobile libraries. **O*NET Code:** 25-4031.00. **Average Salary:** $24,850. **Projected Growth:** 16.8%. **Annual Openings:** 22,000. **Education:** Short-term on-the-job training. **Job Zone:** 3. **Education/Training Program(s)**—Library Assistant/Technician. **Related Knowledge/Courses:** Clerical; Customer and Personal Service; Computers and Electronics; Geography; Education and Training; English Language. **Personality Type:** Conventional. **Skills Required:** Service Orientation; Instructing; Social Perceptiveness; Reading Comprehension; Learning Strategies; Active Listening; Critical Thinking; Time Management. **Abilities:** Category Flexibility; Fluency of Ideas; Flexibility of Closure; Speech Recognition; Written Expression; Near Vision. **Occupational Values:** Working Conditions; Social Service; Authority; Co-workers; Advancement. **Interacting with Others:** Establishing and Maintaining Interpersonal Relationships; Performing for or Working Directly with the Public; Communicating with Supervisors, Peers, or Subordinates. **Physical Work Conditions:** Sitting; Contaminants; Physical Proximity; Indoors; Sounds, Noise Levels Are Distracting or Uncomfortable.

05.05 Archival and Museum Services

Archivists

Appraise, edit, and direct safekeeping of permanent records and historically valuable documents. Participate in research activities based on archival materials. **O*NET Code:** 25-4011.00. **Average Salary:** $36,160. **Projected Growth:** 17.0%.

Annual Openings: 2,000. **Education:** Master's degree. **Job Zone:** 5. **Education/Training Program(s)**—Art History, Criticism, and Conservation; Cultural Resource Management and Policy Analysis; Historic Preservation and Conservation; Historic Preservation and Conservation, Other; Museology/Museum Studies; Public/Applied History and Archival Administration. **Related Knowledge/Courses:** History and Archeology; Sociology and Anthropology; Communications and Media; Administration and Management; English Language; Clerical. **Personality Type:** Investigative. **Skills Required:** Management of Personnel Resources; Writing; Management of Material Resources; Judgment and Decision Making; Reading Comprehension; Systems Evaluation; Operations Analysis; Speaking; Coordination. **Abilities:** Written Comprehension; Memorization; Written Expression; Visualization; Oral Expression; Category Flexibility. **Occupational Values:** Working Conditions; Authority; Creativity; Autonomy; Co-workers. **Interacting with Others:** Communicating with Supervisors, Peers, or Subordinates; Communicating with Persons Outside Organization; Monitoring and Controlling Resources. **Physical Work Conditions:** Sitting; Indoors; Walking and Running; Standing.

Audio-Visual Collections Specialists

Prepare, plan, and operate audio-visual teaching aids for use in education. May record, catalogue, and file audio-visual materials. **O*NET Code:** 25-9011.00. **Average Salary:** $34,040. **Projected Growth:** 16.3%. **Annual Openings:** 2,000. **Education:** Moderate-term on-the-job training. **Job Zone:** 5. **Education/Training Program(s)**—No data available. **Related Knowledge/Courses:** Education and Training; Customer and Personal Service; Communications and Media; Computers and Electronics; Telecommunications; Clerical. **Personality Type:** Conventional. **Skills Required:** Troubleshooting; Instructing; Technology Design; Installation; Equipment Selection; Operations Analysis; Writing; Active Learning. **Abilities:** Originality; Fluency of Ideas; Visualization; Speech Clarity; Written Expression. **Occupational Values:** Working Conditions; Authority; Co-workers; Social Service; Ability Utilization. **Interacting with Others:** Communicating with Supervisors, Peers, or Subordinates; Performing for or Working Directly with the Public; Establishing and Maintaining Interpersonal Relationships. **Physical Work Conditions:** Sitting; Physical Proximity; Very Hot or Cold; Sounds, Noise Levels Are Distracting or Uncomfortable; Extremely Bright or Inadequate Lighting.

Curators

Administer affairs of museum and conduct research programs. Direct instructional, research, and public service activities of institution. **O*NET Code:** 25-4012.00. **Average Salary:** $36,160. **Projected Growth:** 17.0%. **Annual Openings:** 2,000. **Education:** Master's degree. **Job Zone:** 4. **Education/Training Program(s)**—Art History, Criticism, and Conservation; Museology/Museum Studies; Public/Applied History and Archival Administration. **Related Knowledge/Courses:** Clerical; History and Archeology; Fine Arts; Sociology and Anthropology; Philosophy and Theology; Education and Training. **Personality Type:** Artistic. **Skills Required:** Management of Financial Resources; Management of

Personnel Resources; Time Management; Persuasion; Writing; Negotiation; Service Orientation; Monitoring. **Abilities:** Visual Color Discrimination; Speech Recognition; Far Vision; Written Expression; Visualization; Speech Clarity. **Occupational Values:** Authority; Creativity; Working Conditions; Co-workers; Responsibility. **Interacting with Others:** Communicating with Supervisors, Peers, or Subordinates; Communicating with Persons Outside Organization; Establishing and Maintaining Interpersonal Relationships. **Physical Work Conditions:** Sitting; Physical Proximity; Sounds, Noise Levels Are Distracting or Uncomfortable; Contaminants; Extremely Bright or Inadequate Lighting.

Museum Technicians and Conservators

Prepare specimens, such as fossils, skeletal parts, lace, and textiles, for museum collection and exhibits. May restore documents or install, arrange, and exhibit materials. **O*NET Code:** 25-4013.00. **Average Salary:** $36,160. **Projected Growth:** 17.0%. **Annual Openings:** 2,000. **Education:** Master's degree. **Job Zone:** 3. **Education/Training Program(s)**—Art History, Criticism, and Conservation; Museology/Museum Studies; Public/Applied History and Archival Administration. **Related Knowledge/Courses:** History and Archeology; Sociology and Anthropology; Design; Fine Arts; Education and Training; Geography. **Personality Type:** Artistic. **Skills Required:** Management of Material Resources; Time Management; Repairing; Critical Thinking; Instructing; Installation; Technology Design; Equipment Maintenance. **Abilities:** Visual Color Discrimination; Visualization; Wrist-Finger Speed; Written Expression; Manual Dexterity. **Occupational Values:** Working Conditions; Co-workers; Authority; Ability Utilization; Achievement. **Interacting with Others:** Establishing and Maintaining Interpersonal Relationships; Communicating with Supervisors, Peers, or Subordinates; Communicating with Persons Outside Organization. **Physical Work Conditions:** Contaminants; Sounds, Noise Levels Are Distracting or Uncomfortable; Physical Proximity; Sitting; Cramped Work Space, Awkward Positions.

05.06 Counseling, Health, and Fitness Education

Educational, Vocational, and School Counselors

Counsel individuals and provide group educational and vocational guidance services. **O*NET Code:** 21-1012.00. **Average Salary:** $44,990. **Projected Growth:** 15.0%. **Annual Openings:** 32,000. **Education:** Master's degree. **Job Zone:** 4. **Education/Training Program(s)**—College Student Counseling and Personnel Services; Counselor Education/School Counseling and Guidance Services. **Related Knowledge/Courses:** Therapy and Counseling; Psychology; Education and Training; Sociology and Anthropology; English Language; Personnel and Human Resources. **Personality Type:** Social. **Skills Required:** Service Orientation; Social Perceptiveness; Active Listening; Speaking; Systems Evaluation; Instructing; Reading

Comprehension; Active Learning. **Abilities:** Oral Expression; Oral Comprehension; Written Expression; Fluency of Ideas; Written Comprehension. **Occupational Values:** Social Service; Authority; Achievement; Creativity; Working Conditions. **Interacting with Others:** Establishing and Maintaining Interpersonal Relationships; Communicating with Persons Outside Organization; Assisting and Caring for Others. **Physical Work Conditions:** Sitting; Indoors.

Fitness Trainers and Aerobics Instructors

Instruct or coach groups or individuals in exercise activities and the fundamentals of sports. Demonstrate techniques and methods of participation. Observe participants and inform them of corrective measures necessary to improve their skills. Those required to hold teaching degrees should be reported in the appropriate teaching category. **O*NET Code:** 39-9031.00. **Average Salary:** $24,610. **Projected Growth:** 44.5%. **Annual Openings:** 38,000. **Education:** Postsecondary vocational training. **Job Zone:** 3. **Education/Training Program(s)**—Health and Physical Education, General; Physical Education Teaching and Coaching; Sport and Fitness Administration/Management. **Related Knowledge/Courses:** Customer and Personal Service; Education and Training; Psychology; Medicine and Dentistry; Sociology and Anthropology; Fine Arts. **Personality Type:** Social. **Skills Required:** Instructing; Service Orientation; Coordination; Monitoring; Equipment Selection; Time Management; Social Perceptiveness; Learning Strategies. **Abilities:** Stamina; Explosive Strength; Dynamic Strength; Time Sharing; Speed of Limb Movement; Peripheral Vision. **Occupational Values:** Authority; Social Service; Creativity; Responsibility; Achievement. **Interacting with Others:** Coaching and Developing Others; Performing for or Working Directly with the Public; Establishing and Maintaining Interpersonal Relationships; Assisting and Caring for Others. **Physical Work Conditions:** Physical Proximity; Walking and Running; Standing; Keeping or Regaining Balance; Indoors.

Health Educators

Promote, maintain, and improve individual and community health by assisting individuals and communities in adopting healthy behaviors. Collect and analyze data to identify community needs prior to planning, implementing, monitoring, and evaluating programs designed to encourage healthy lifestyles, policies, and environments. May also serve as a resource to assist individuals, other professionals, or the community and may administer fiscal resources for health education programs. **O*NET Code:** 21-1091.00. **Average Salary:** $38,100. **Projected Growth:** 21.9%. **Annual Openings:** 8,000. **Education:** Master's degree. **Job Zone:** 5. **Education/Training Program(s)**—Community Health Services/Liaison/Counseling; Health Communication; International Public Health/International Health; Maternal and Child Health; Public Health Education and Promotion. **Related Knowledge/Courses:** Education and Training; Communications and Media; Sales and Marketing; Therapy and Counseling; Medicine and Dentistry; English Language. **Personality Type:** Social. **Skills Required:** Speaking; Coordination; Writing; Persuasion; Systems Analysis; Active Learning; Systems Evaluation; Service Orientation; Complex Problem Solving. **Abilities:** Speech Clarity; Oral Expression; Written Expression; Originality; Inductive Reasoning. **Occupational Values:** Social Service; Authority; Creativity; Achievement; Social Status. **Interacting with Others:** Communicating with Persons Outside Organization; Communicating with Supervisors, Peers, or Subordinates; Establishing and Maintaining Interpersonal Relationships; Training and Teaching Others. **Physical Work Conditions:** Sitting; Indoors.

© 2006, JIST Works

06 Finance and Insurance

06.01   **Managerial Work in Finance and Insurance**

06.02   **Finance/Insurance Investigation and Analysis**

06.03   **Finance/Insurance Records Processing**

06.04   **Finance/Insurance Customer Service**

06.05   **Finance/Insurance Sales and Support**

06.01 Managerial Work in Finance and Insurance

Financial Managers, Branch or Department

Direct and coordinate financial activities of workers in a branch, office, or department of an establishment, such as branch bank, brokerage firm, risk and insurance department, or credit department. **O*NET Code: 11-3031.02. Average Salary: $79,090. Projected Growth: 18.3%. Annual Openings: 71,000. Education:** Work experience plus degree. **Job Zone: 4. Education/Training Program(s)**—Accounting and Business/Management; Accounting and Finance; Credit Management; Finance and Financial Management Services, Other; Finance, General; International Finance; Public Finance. **Related Knowledge/Courses:** Economics and Accounting; Administration and Management; Law and Government; Mathematics; Personnel and Human Resources; Psychology. **Personality Type:** Enterprising. **Skills Required:** Management of Financial Resources; Management of Personnel Resources; Systems Analysis; Systems Evaluation; Judgment and Decision Making; Monitoring; Writing; Negotiation. **Abilities:** Written Expression; Mathematical Reasoning; Number Facility; Speed of Closure; Written Comprehension. **Occupational Values:** Authority; Working Conditions; Ability Utilization; Recognition; Responsibility; Autonomy. **Interacting with Others:** Communicating with Supervisors, Peers, or Subordinates; Monitoring and Controlling Resources; Performing Administrative Activities. **Physical Work Conditions:** Sitting; Indoors; Walking and Running.

Treasurers, Controllers, and Chief Financial Officers

Plan, direct, and coordinate the financial activities of an organization at the highest level of management. Includes financial reserve officers. **O*NET Code: 11-3031.01. Average Salary: $79,090. Projected Growth: 18.3%. Annual Openings: 71,000. Education:** Work experience plus degree. **Job Zone: 5. Education/Training Program(s)**—Accounting and Business/Management; Accounting and Finance; Credit Management; Finance and Financial Management Services, Other; Finance, General; International Finance; Public Finance. **Related Knowledge/Courses:** Economics and Accounting; Administration and Management; Law and Government; Mathematics; English Language; Personnel and Human Resources. **Personality Type:** Enterprising. **Skills Required:** Management of Financial Resources; Systems Analysis; Systems Evaluation; Judgment and Decision Making; Complex Problem Solving; Mathematics; Management of Personnel Resources; Critical Thinking. **Abilities:** Mathematical Reasoning; Deductive Reasoning; Number Facility; Fluency of Ideas; Originality. **Occupational Values:** Authority; Working Conditions; Advancement; Ability Utilization; Activity. **Interacting with Others:** Providing Consultation and Advice to Others; Monitoring and Controlling Resources; Communicating with Supervisors, Peers, or Subordinates. **Physical Work Conditions:** Sitting; Indoors; Walking and Running; Standing.

06.02 Finance/Insurance Investigation and Analysis

Appraisers, Real Estate

Appraise real property to determine its value for purchase, sales, investment, mortgage, or loan purposes. **O*NET Code: 13-2021.02. Average Salary: $42,900. Projected Growth: 17.6%. Annual Openings: 11,000. Education:** Postsecondary vocational training. **Job Zone: 4. Education/Training Program(s)**—Real Estate. **Related Knowledge/Courses:** Personnel and Human Resources; Building and Construction; Economics and Accounting; Law and Government; Geography; Administration and Management; Communications and Media. **Personality Type:** Enterprising. **Skills Required:** Writing; Mathematics; Management of Personnel Resources; Speaking; Time Management; Management of Financial Resources; Reading Comprehension; Systems Analysis. **Abilities:** Number Facility; Deductive Reasoning; Written Expression; Mathematical Reasoning; Written Comprehension; Far Vision. **Occupational Values:** Responsibility; Autonomy; Independence; Ability Utilization; Working Conditions; Social Status. **Interacting with Others:** Communicating with Supervisors, Peers, or Subordinates; Communicating with Persons Outside Organization; Guiding, Directing, and Motivating Subordinates. **Physical Work Conditions:** Sitting; Outdoors; Walking and Running; Standing; Extremely Bright or Inadequate Lighting.

Assessors

Appraise real and personal property to determine its fair value. May assess taxes in accordance with prescribed schedules. **O*NET Code: 13-2021.01. Average Salary: $42,900. Projected Growth: 17.6%. Annual Openings: 11,000. Education:** Postsecondary vocational training. **Job Zone: 3. Education/Training Program(s)**—Real Estate. **Related Knowledge/Courses:** Customer and Personal Service; Clerical; Building and Construction; Law and Government; Mathematics; Computers and Electronics. **Personality Type:** Conventional. **Skills Required:** Negotiation; Social Perceptiveness; Persuasion; Mathematics; Active Listening; Speaking; Service Orientation; Instructing. **Abilities:** Mathematical Reasoning; Written Expression; Number Facility; Inductive Reasoning; Written Comprehension; Category Flexibility. **Occupational Values:** Responsibility; Independence; Autonomy; Compensation; Security. **Interacting with Others:** Resolving Conflicts and Negotiating with Others; Performing for or Working Directly with the Public; Communicating with Persons Outside Organization. **Physical Work Conditions:** In an Enclosed Vehicle or Equipment; Very Hot or Cold; Physical Proximity; Sitting; Outdoors.

Claims Examiners, Property and Casualty Insurance

Review settled insurance claims to determine that payments and settlements have been made in accordance with company practices and procedures. Report overpayments, underpayments, and other irregularities. Confer with legal counsel on claims requiring litigation. **O*NET Code:** 13-1031.01. **Average Salary:** $44,020. **Projected Growth:** 14.2%. **Annual Openings:** 31,000. **Education:** Long-term on-the-job training. **Job Zone:** 4. **Education/Training Program(s)—** Health/Medical Claims Examiner; Insurance. **Related Knowledge/Courses:** Law and Government; Mathematics; Economics and Accounting; Communications and Media. **Personality Type:** Conventional. **Skills Required:** Mathematics; Reading Comprehension; Writing; Judgment and Decision Making; Monitoring; Critical Thinking; Systems Evaluation; Speaking. **Abilities:** Number Facility; Mathematical Reasoning; Oral Comprehension; Written Comprehension; Oral Expression. **Occupational Values:** Advancement; Supervision, Human Relations; Company Policies and Practices; Working Conditions; Responsibility. **Interacting with Others:** Communicating with Supervisors, Peers, or Subordinates; Communicating with Persons Outside Organization; Interpreting the Meaning of Information for Others. **Physical Work Conditions:** Sitting; Indoors.

Cost Estimators

Prepare cost estimates for product manufacturing, construction projects, or services to aid management in bidding on or determining price of product or service. May specialize according to particular service performed or type of product manufactured. **O*NET Code:** 13-1051.00. **Average Salary:** $49,220. **Projected Growth:** 18.6%. **Annual Openings:** 25,000. **Education:** Bachelor's degree. **Job Zone:** 4. **Education/Training Program(s)—**Business Administration and Management, General; Business/Commerce, General; Construction Engineering; Construction Engineering Technology/Technician; Manufacturing Engineering; Materials Engineering; Mechanical Engineering. **Related Knowledge/Courses:** Administration and Management; Sales and Marketing; Production and Processing; Clerical; Economics and Accounting; Personnel and Human Resources; Mathematics. **Personality Type:** Conventional. **Skills Required:** Management of Financial Resources; Negotiation; Coordination; Management of Personnel Resources; Persuasion; Time Management; Mathematics; Active Listening. **Abilities:** Mathematical Reasoning; Number Facility; Inductive Reasoning; Oral Comprehension; Oral Expression; Originality. **Occupational Values:** Working Conditions; Independence; Advancement; Responsibility; Autonomy. **Interacting with Others:** Communicating with Supervisors, Peers, or Subordinates; Resolving Conflicts and Negotiating with Others; Coordinating the Work and Activities of Others. **Physical Work Conditions:** Contaminants; Sitting; Very Hot or Cold; In an Enclosed Vehicle or Equipment; Physical Proximity.

Credit Analysts

Analyze current credit data and financial statements of individuals or firms to determine the degree of risk involved in extending credit or lending money. Prepare reports with this credit information for use in decision making. **O*NET Code:** 13-2041.00. **Average Salary:** $46,640. **Projected Growth:** 18.7%. **Annual Openings:** 9,000. **Education:** Bachelor's degree. **Job Zone:** 4. **Education/Training Program(s)—** Accounting; Credit Management; Finance, General. **Related Knowledge/Courses:** Economics and Accounting; Clerical; Mathematics; Customer and Personal Service; Administration and Management; English Language; Law and Government. **Personality Type:** Conventional. **Skills Required:** Speaking; Negotiation; Writing; Instructing; Social Perceptiveness; Active Listening; Monitoring; Service Orientation; Operations Analysis; Judgment and Decision Making. **Abilities:** Mathematical Reasoning; Number Facility; Speech Recognition; Flexibility of Closure; Deductive Reasoning. **Occupational Values:** Advancement; Working Conditions; Supervision, Human Relations; Activity; Company Policies and Practices. **Interacting with Others:** Establishing and Maintaining Interpersonal Relationships; Communicating with Supervisors, Peers, or Subordinates; Training and Teaching Others. **Physical Work Conditions:** Sitting; Indoors; Physical Proximity; Sounds, Noise Levels Are Distracting or Uncomfortable.

Financial Analysts

Conduct quantitative analyses of information affecting investment programs of public or private institutions. **O*NET Code:** 13-2051.00. **Average Salary:** $61,130. **Projected Growth:** 18.7%. **Annual Openings:** 22,000. **Education:** Bachelor's degree. **Job Zone:** 5. **Education/Training Program(s)—**Accounting and Business/Management; Accounting and Finance; Finance, General. **Related Knowledge/Courses:** Economics and Accounting; Mathematics; Law and Government; Computers and Electronics; Sales and Marketing; English Language. **Personality Type:** Investigative. **Skills Required:** Judgment and Decision Making; Systems Analysis; Critical Thinking; Active Learning; Systems Evaluation; Reading Comprehension; Mathematics; Management of Financial Resources. **Abilities:** Number Facility; Mathematical Reasoning; Deductive Reasoning; Written Expression; Speed of Closure. **Occupational Values:** Autonomy; Compensation; Creativity; Recognition; Advancement; Social Status. **Interacting with Others:** Communicating with Supervisors, Peers, or Subordinates; Providing Consultation and Advice to Others; Communicating with Persons Outside Organization. **Physical Work Conditions:** Sitting; Indoors; Walking and Running.

Insurance Adjusters, Examiners, and Investigators

Investigate, analyze, and determine the extent of insurance company's liability concerning personal, casualty, or property loss or damages and attempt to effect settlement with claimants. Correspond with or interview medical specialists, agents, witnesses, or claimants to compile information. Calculate benefit payments and approve payment of claims within a certain monetary limit. **O*NET Code:** 13-1031.02. **Average Salary:** $44,020. **Projected Growth:** 14.2%. **Annual Openings:** 31,000. **Education:** Long-term on-the-job training. **Job Zone:** 3. **Education/Training Program(s)—** Health/Medical Claims Examiner; Insurance. **Related**

Knowledge/Courses: Customer and Personal Service; Clerical; Computers and Electronics; Law and Government; English Language; Mathematics. **Personality Type:** Enterprising. **Skills Required:** Negotiation; Persuasion; Time Management; Judgment and Decision Making; Social Perceptiveness; Service Orientation; Management of Financial Resources; Critical Thinking. **Abilities:** Far Vision; Speech Recognition; Inductive Reasoning; Near Vision; Written Expression; Flexibility of Closure. **Occupational Values:** Advancement; Company Policies and Practices; Ability Utilization; Supervision, Human Relations; Responsibility. **Interacting with Others:** Establishing and Maintaining Interpersonal Relationships; Communicating with Persons Outside Organization; Communicating with Supervisors, Peers, or Subordinates. **Physical Work Conditions:** Sitting; Sounds, Noise Levels Are Distracting or Uncomfortable; Physical Proximity; Extremely Bright or Inadequate Lighting; Indoors.

Insurance Appraisers, Auto Damage

Appraise automobile or other vehicle damage to determine cost of repair for insurance claim settlement and seek agreement with automotive repair shop on cost of repair. Prepare insurance forms to indicate repair cost or cost estimates and recommendations. **O*NET Code:** 13-1032.00. **Average Salary:** $44,650. **Projected Growth:** 11.7%. **Annual Openings:** 2,000. **Education:** Long-term on-the-job training. **Job Zone:** 4. **Education/Training Program(s)**—Insurance. **Related Knowledge/Courses:** Economics and Accounting; Mechanical; Clerical; Mathematics; Administration and Management; Telecommunications. **Personality Type:** Conventional. **Skills Required:** Negotiation; Mathematics; Management of Financial Resources; Judgment and Decision Making; Writing; Speaking; Systems Evaluation; Reading Comprehension. **Abilities:** Mathematical Reasoning; Number Facility; Written Expression; Written Comprehension; Gross Body Coordination. **Occupational Values:** Advancement; Company Policies and Practices; Supervision, Human Relations; Responsibility; Variety; Social Service; Supervision, Technical. **Interacting with Others:** Communicating with Supervisors, Peers, or Subordinates; Establishing and Maintaining Interpersonal Relationships; Communicating with Persons Outside Organization; Performing Administrative Activities. **Physical Work Conditions:** Sitting; Outdoors; Spend Time Bending or Twisting the Body; Kneeling, Crouching, Stooping, or Crawling; Standing.

Insurance Underwriters

Review individual applications for insurance to evaluate degree of risk involved and determine acceptance of applications. **O*NET Code:** 13-2053.00. **Average Salary:** $48,370. **Projected Growth:** 10.0%. **Annual Openings:** 12,000. **Education:** Bachelor's degree. **Job Zone:** 3. **Education/Training Program(s)**—Insurance. **Related Knowledge/Courses:** Customer and Personal Service; Clerical; Sales and Marketing; Economics and Accounting; Computers and Electronics; Law and Government. **Personality Type:** Conventional. **Skills Required:** Service Orientation; Writing; Active Learning; Learning Strategies; Persuasion; Active Listening; Monitoring; Negotiation. **Abilities:** Flexibility of Closure; Speech Recognition;

Deductive Reasoning; Inductive Reasoning; Category Flexibility. **Occupational Values:** Advancement; Responsibility; Supervision, Human Relations; Working Conditions; Company Policies and Practices. **Interacting with Others:** Establishing and Maintaining Interpersonal Relationships; Communicating with Supervisors, Peers, or Subordinates; Communicating with Persons Outside Organization. **Physical Work Conditions:** Sitting; Physical Proximity; Sounds, Noise Levels Are Distracting or Uncomfortable.

Loan Counselors

Provide guidance to prospective loan applicants who have problems qualifying for traditional loans. Guidance may include determining the best type of loan and explaining loan requirements or restrictions. **O*NET Code:** 13-2071.00. **Average Salary:** $33,660. **Projected Growth:** 17.8%. **Annual Openings:** 4,000. **Education:** Bachelor's degree. **Job Zone:** 4. **Education/Training Program(s)**—Banking and Financial Support Services; Finance and Financial Management Services, Other. **Related Knowledge/Courses:** Economics and Accounting; Mathematics; Law and Government; Sales and Marketing; Clerical; Personnel and Human Resources. **Personality Type:** Enterprising. **Skills Required:** Management of Personnel Resources; Speaking; Judgment and Decision Making; Reading Comprehension; Mathematics; Active Listening; Writing; Critical Thinking; Active Learning; Systems Evaluation. **Abilities:** Number Facility; Written Expression; Oral Expression; Mathematical Reasoning; Speech Recognition; Speech Clarity. **Occupational Values:** Advancement; Working Conditions; Co-workers; Social Service; Responsibility. **Interacting with Others:** Communicating with Persons Outside Organization; Communicating with Supervisors, Peers, or Subordinates; Establishing and Maintaining Interpersonal Relationships. **Physical Work Conditions:** Sitting; Indoors; Walking and Running.

Loan Officers

Evaluate, authorize, or recommend approval of commercial, real estate, or credit loans. Advise borrowers on financial status and methods of payments. Includes mortgage loan officers and agents, collection analysts, loan servicing officers, and loan underwriters. **O*NET Code:** 13-2072.00. **Average Salary:** $47,530. **Projected Growth:** 18.8%. **Annual Openings:** 30,000. **Education:** Bachelor's degree. **Job Zone:** 3. **Education/Training Program(s)**—Credit Management; Finance, General. **Related Knowledge/Courses:** Economics and Accounting; Sales and Marketing; Customer and Personal Service; Law and Government; English Language; Mathematics. **Personality Type:** Enterprising. **Skills Required:** Persuasion; Social Perceptiveness; Service Orientation; Instructing; Negotiation; Learning Strategies; Complex Problem Solving; Coordination. **Abilities:** Number Facility; Written Expression; Oral Expression; Mathematical Reasoning; Speech Recognition; Speech Clarity. **Occupational Values:** Advancement; Working Conditions; Co-workers; Social Service; Responsibility. **Interacting with Others:** Performing for or Working Directly with the Public; Communicating with Persons Outside Organization; Establishing and Maintaining Interpersonal Relationships.

Physical Work Conditions: Sitting; Sounds, Noise Levels Are Distracting or Uncomfortable; Physical Proximity; Very Hot or Cold; In an Enclosed Vehicle or Equipment.

Market Research Analysts

Research market conditions in local, regional, or national areas to determine potential sales of a product or service. May gather information on competitors, prices, sales, and methods of marketing and distribution. May use survey results to create a marketing campaign based on regional preferences and buying habits. **O*NET Code:** 19-3021.00. **Average Salary:** $54,830. **Projected Growth:** 23.4%. **Annual Openings:** 18,000. **Education:** Bachelor's degree. **Job Zone:** 4. **Education/Training Program(s)**—Applied Economics; Business/Managerial Economics; Econometrics and Quantitative Economics; Economics, General; International Economics; Marketing Research. **Related Knowledge/Courses:** Sales and Marketing; Psychology; Mathematics; Economics and Accounting; Computers and Electronics; Food Production. **Personality Type:** Investigative. **Skills Required:** Programming; Writing; Systems Analysis; Mathematics; Operations Analysis; Systems Evaluation; Monitoring; Active Learning; Complex Problem Solving. **Abilities:** Number Facility; Mathematical Reasoning; Inductive Reasoning; Speed of Closure; Deductive Reasoning. **Occupational Values:** Autonomy; Working Conditions; Advancement; Recognition; Variety. **Interacting with Others:** Communicating with Supervisors, Peers, or Subordinates; Interpreting the Meaning of Information for Others; Communicating with Persons Outside Organization. **Physical Work Conditions:** Sitting; Indoors; Disease or Infections; Walking and Running.

Survey Researchers

Design or conduct surveys. May supervise interviewers who conduct the survey in person or over the telephone. May present survey results to client. **O*NET Code:** 19-3022.00. **Average Salary:** $26,990. **Projected Growth:** 33.6%. **Annual Openings:** 3,000. **Education:** Bachelor's degree. **Job Zone:** No data available. **Education/Training Program(s)**—Applied Economics; Business/Managerial Economics; Economics, General; Marketing Research. **Related Knowledge/Courses:** No data available. **Personality Type:** No data available. **Skills Required:** No data available. **Abilities:** No data available. **Occupational Values:** No data available. **Interacting with Others:** No data available. **Physical Work Conditions:** No data available.

06.03 Finance/Insurance Records Processing

Credit Authorizers

Authorize credit charges against customers' accounts. **O*NET Code:** 43-4041.01. **Average Salary:** $27,640. **Projected Growth:** -6.7%. **Annual Openings:** 15,000. **Education:** Short-term on-the-job training. **Job Zone:** 1. **Education/Training Program(s)**—Banking and Financial Support Services. **Related Knowledge/Courses:** Clerical; Economics and Accounting; Computers and Electronics; Telecommunications. **Personality Type:** Conventional. **Skills Required:** Active Listening. **Abilities:** Wrist-Finger Speed; Number Facility; Perceptual Speed; Glare Sensitivity. **Occupational Values:** Working Conditions; Supervision, Human Relations; Security; Advancement; Supervision, Technical. **Interacting with Others:** Establishing and Maintaining Interpersonal Relationships; Communicating with Persons Outside Organization; Communicating with Supervisors, Peers, or Subordinates. **Physical Work Conditions:** Sitting; Indoors.

Credit Checkers

Investigate history and credit standing of individuals or business establishments applying for credit. Telephone or write to credit departments of business and service establishments to obtain information about applicant's credit standing. **O*NET Code:** 43-4041.02. **Average Salary:** $27,640. **Projected Growth:** -6.7%. **Annual Openings:** 15,000. **Education:** Short-term on-the-job training. **Job Zone:** 1. **Education/Training Program(s)**—Banking and Financial Support Services. **Related Knowledge/Courses:** Clerical; Economics and Accounting; Law and Government; Computers and Electronics; Mathematics; Telecommunications. **Personality Type:** Conventional. **Skills Required:** Speaking; Active Listening; Writing; Judgment and Decision Making. **Abilities:** Speech Clarity; Written Expression; Number Facility; Oral Comprehension; Oral Expression. **Occupational Values:** Working Conditions; Advancement; Supervision, Human Relations; Activity; Co-workers; Supervision, Technical. **Interacting with Others:** Communicating with Persons Outside Organization; Establishing and Maintaining Interpersonal Relationships; Communicating with Supervisors, Peers, or Subordinates. **Physical Work Conditions:** Sitting; Indoors.

Insurance Claims Clerks

Obtain information from insured or designated persons for purpose of settling claim with insurance carrier. **O*NET Code:** 43-9041.01. **Average Salary:** $28,840. **Projected Growth:** 3.6%. **Annual Openings:** 41,000. **Education:** Moderate-term on-the-job training. **Job Zone:** 2. **Education/Training Program(s)**—General Office Occupations and Clerical Services. **Related Knowledge/Courses:** Clerical; Law and Government; Economics and Accounting; Telecommunications; Geography; Mathematics. **Personality Type:** Conventional. **Skills Required:** Speaking; Active Listening; Reading Comprehension; Mathematics. **Abilities:** Speech Recognition; Number Facility; Near Vision; Mathematical Reasoning; Written Comprehension. **Occupational Values:** Supervision, Human Relations; Working Conditions; Advancement; Moral Values; Activity; Company Policies and Practices. **Interacting with Others:** Communicating with Persons Outside Organization; Establishing and Maintaining Interpersonal Relationships; Performing Administrative Activities. **Physical Work Conditions:** Sitting; Indoors.

Insurance Policy Processing Clerks

Process applications for, changes to, reinstatement of, and cancellation of insurance policies. Duties include reviewing insurance applications to ensure that all questions have been answered, compiling data on insurance policy changes, changing policy records to conform to insured party's specifications, compiling data on lapsed insurance policies to determine automatic reinstatement according to company policies, canceling insurance policies as requested by agents, and verifying the accuracy of insurance company records. **O*NET Code:** 43-9041.02. **Average Salary:** $28,840. **Projected Growth:** 3.6%. **Annual Openings:** 41,000. **Education:** Moderate-term on-the-job training. **Job Zone:** 2. **Education/Training Program(s)**—General Office Occupations and Clerical Services. **Related Knowledge/Courses:** Clerical; Customer and Personal Service; Computers and Electronics; Sales and Marketing; Economics and Accounting; Production and Processing. **Personality Type:** Conventional. **Skills Required:** Critical Thinking; Social Perceptiveness; Learning Strategies; Service Orientation; Instructing; Active Learning; Coordination; Reading Comprehension. **Abilities:** Speech Recognition; Near Vision; Mathematical Reasoning; Deductive Reasoning; Oral Expression; Written Expression. **Occupational Values:** Working Conditions; Supervision, Human Relations; Advancement; Co-workers; Supervision, Technical. **Interacting with Others:** Communicating with Supervisors, Peers, or Subordinates; Establishing and Maintaining Interpersonal Relationships; Communicating with Persons Outside Organization. **Physical Work Conditions:** Sitting; Physical Proximity; Sounds, Noise Levels Are Distracting or Uncomfortable.

Proofreaders and Copy Markers

Read transcript or proof type setup to detect and mark for correction any grammatical, typographical, or compositional errors. **O*NET Code:** 43-9081.00. **Average Salary:** $24,550. **Projected Growth:** –4.8%. **Annual Openings:** 5,000. **Education:** Short-term on-the-job training. **Job Zone:** 2. **Education/Training Program(s)**—Graphic and Printing Equipment Operator, General Production. **Related Knowledge/Courses:** English Language; Food Production. **Personality Type:** Conventional. **Skills Required:** Reading Comprehension. **Abilities:** Written Comprehension; Memorization; Perceptual Speed; Near Vision; Written Expression. **Occupational Values:** Working Conditions; Independence; Moral Values; Supervision, Human Relations; Activity; Company Policies and Practices. **Interacting with Others:** Communicating with Supervisors, Peers, or Subordinates; Providing Consultation and Advice to Others; Establishing and Maintaining Interpersonal Relationships. **Physical Work Conditions:** Sitting; Indoors; Spend Time Making Repetitive Motions.

06.04 Finance/Insurance Customer Service

Bill and Account Collectors

Locate and notify customers of delinquent accounts by mail, telephone, or personal visit to solicit payment. Duties include receiving payment and posting amount to customer's account; preparing statements to credit department if customer fails to respond; initiating repossession proceedings or service disconnection; keeping records of collection and status of accounts. **O*NET Code:** 43-3011.00. **Average Salary:** $27,210. **Projected Growth:** 24.5%. **Annual Openings:** 76,000. **Education:** Short-term on-the-job training. **Job Zone:** 3. **Education/Training Program(s)**—Banking and Financial Support Services. **Related Knowledge/Courses:** Clerical; Customer and Personal Service; Computers and Electronics; Law and Government; Economics and Accounting; Personnel and Human Resources. **Personality Type:** Conventional. **Skills Required:** Social Perceptiveness; Time Management; Management of Financial Resources; Service Orientation; Persuasion; Management of Personnel Resources; Speaking; Instructing; Judgment and Decision Making. **Abilities:** Speech Recognition; Written Expression; Oral Expression; Time Sharing; Oral Comprehension. **Occupational Values:** Supervision, Human Relations; Authority; Variety; Supervision, Technical; Activity. **Interacting with Others:** Establishing and Maintaining Interpersonal Relationships; Resolving Conflicts and Negotiating with Others; Communicating with Persons Outside Organization; Performing for or Working Directly with the Public. **Physical Work Conditions:** Sitting; Physical Proximity; Sounds, Noise Levels Are Distracting or Uncomfortable; Contaminants; Indoors.

Loan Interviewers and Clerks

Interview loan applicants to elicit information; investigate applicants' backgrounds and verify references; prepare loan request papers; and forward findings, reports, and documents to appraisal department. Review loan papers to ensure completeness and complete transactions between loan establishment, borrowers, and sellers upon approval of loan. **O*NET Code:** 43-4131.00. **Average Salary:** $28,490. **Projected Growth:** –14.3%. **Annual Openings:** 31,000. **Education:** Short-term on-the-job training. **Job Zone:** 2. **Education/Training Program(s)**—Banking and Financial Support Services. **Related Knowledge/Courses:** Clerical; Economics and Accounting; Law and Government; Customer and Personal Service; Computers and Electronics; Mathematics. **Personality Type:** Conventional. **Skills Required:** Active Listening; Speaking; Mathematics; Service Orientation; Reading Comprehension; Management of Financial Resources. **Abilities:** Number Facility; Mathematical Reasoning; Near Vision; Speech Recognition; Perceptual Speed; Wrist-Finger Speed. **Occupational Values:** Working Conditions; Advancement; Co-workers; Social Service; Supervision, Human Relations. **Interacting with Others:** Communicating with Persons Outside Organization; Establishing and Maintaining Interpersonal Relationships; Performing Administrative Activities. **Physical Work Conditions:** Sitting; Indoors.

New Accounts Clerks

Interview persons desiring to open bank accounts. Explain banking services available to prospective customers and assist them in preparing application form. **O*NET Code:** 43-4141.00. **Average Salary:** $26,200. **Projected Growth:** 11.2%. **Annual Openings:** 24,000. **Education:** Work experience in a related occupation. **Job Zone:** 2. **Education/Training Program(s)**—Banking and Financial Support Services. **Related Knowledge/Courses:** Customer and Personal Service; Sales and Marketing; Economics and Accounting; Mathematics; Clerical; Personnel and Human Resources. **Personality Type:** Conventional. **Skills Required:** Service Orientation; Social Perceptiveness; Active Listening; Critical Thinking; Writing; Speaking; Judgment and Decision Making; Reading Comprehension. **Abilities:** Number Facility; Oral Expression; Memorization; Mathematical Reasoning; Oral Comprehension. **Occupational Values:** Working Conditions; Social Service; Co-workers; Supervision, Technical; Supervision, Human Relations. **Interacting with Others:** Establishing and Maintaining Interpersonal Relationships; Performing for or Working Directly with the Public; Communicating with Supervisors, Peers, or Subordinates. **Physical Work Conditions:** Sitting; Sounds, Noise Levels Are Distracting or Uncomfortable; Physical Proximity; Indoors.

Tellers

Receive and pay out money. Keep records of money and negotiable instruments involved in a financial institution's various transactions. **O*NET Code:** 43-3071.00. **Average Salary:** $20,810. **Projected Growth:** 9.4%. **Annual Openings:** 127,000. **Education:** Short-term on-the-job training. **Job Zone:** 2. **Education/Training Program(s)**—Banking and Financial Support Services. **Related Knowledge/Courses:** Customer and Personal Service; English Language; Sales and Marketing; Clerical; Public Safety and Security; Economics and Accounting; Law and Government. **Personality Type:** Conventional. **Skills Required:** Service Orientation; Active Learning; Social Perceptiveness; Instructing; Active Listening; Time Management; Mathematics; Learning Strategies. **Abilities:** Perceptual Speed; Near Vision; Speech Recognition; Selective Attention; Oral Comprehension; Oral Expression. **Occupational Values:** Working Conditions; Co-workers; Social Service; Supervision, Technical; Supervision, Human Relations. **Interacting with Others:** Performing for or Working Directly with the Public; Establishing and Maintaining Interpersonal Relationships; Communicating with Supervisors, Peers, or Subordinates. **Physical Work Conditions:** Physical Proximity; Sitting; Keeping or Regaining Balance; Contaminants; Minor Burns, Cuts, Bites, or Stings.

06.05 Finance/Insurance Sales and Support

Advertising Sales Agents

Sell or solicit advertising, including graphic art, advertising space in publications, custom-made signs, or TV and radio advertising time. May obtain leases for outdoor advertising sites or persuade retailer to use sales promotion display items. **O*NET Code:** 41-3011.00. **Average Salary:** $39,210. **Projected Growth:** 13.4%. **Annual Openings:** 24,000. **Education:** Moderate-term on-the-job training. **Job Zone:** 3. **Education/Training Program(s)**—Advertising. **Related**

Knowledge/Courses: Sales and Marketing; Customer and Personal Service; Economics and Accounting; English Language; Communications and Media; Administration and Management. **Personality Type:** Enterprising. **Skills Required:** Negotiation; Persuasion; Social Perceptiveness; Service Orientation; Management of Financial Resources; Speaking; Instructing; Monitoring. **Abilities:** Oral Expression; Originality; Written Expression; Visualization; Speech Recognition. **Occupational Values:** Creativity; Variety; Social Status; Autonomy; Ability Utilization; Achievement; Working Conditions. **Interacting with Others:** Selling or Influencing Others; Communicating with Persons Outside Organization; Establishing and Maintaining Interpersonal Relationships. **Physical Work Conditions:** In an Enclosed Vehicle or Equipment; Outdoors; Physical Proximity; Very Hot or Cold; Sounds, Noise Levels Are Distracting or Uncomfortable.

Insurance Sales Agents

Sell life, property, casualty, health, automotive, or other types of insurance. May refer clients to independent brokers, work as independent broker, or be employed by an insurance company. **O*NET Code:** 41-3021.00. **Average Salary:** $40,370. **Projected Growth:** 8.4%. **Annual Openings:** 52,000. **Education:** Bachelor's degree. **Job Zone:** 3. **Education/Training Program(s)**—Insurance. **Related Knowledge/Courses:** Sales and Marketing; Customer and Personal Service; Economics and Accounting; Computers and Electronics; Clerical; Mathematics; Law and Government. **Personality Type:** Enterprising. **Skills Required:** Persuasion; Time Management; Negotiation; Service Orientation; Social Perceptiveness; Judgment and Decision Making; Active Listening; Speaking. **Abilities:** Speech Recognition; Deductive Reasoning; Mathematical Reasoning; Originality; Inductive Reasoning; Number Facility. **Occupational Values:** Working Conditions; Advancement; Responsibility; Social Service; Autonomy. **Interacting with Others:** Establishing and Maintaining Interpersonal Relationships; Communicating with Persons Outside Organization; Communicating with Supervisors, Peers, or Subordinates; Selling or Influencing Others; Resolving Conflicts and Negotiating with Others. **Physical Work Conditions:** Sitting; Physical Proximity; In an Enclosed Vehicle or Equipment; Extremely Bright or Inadequate Lighting; Sounds, Noise Levels Are Distracting or Uncomfortable.

Personal Financial Advisors

Advise clients on financial plans, utilizing knowledge of tax and investment strategies, securities, insurance, pension plans, and real estate. Duties include assessing clients' assets, liabilities, cash flow, insurance coverage, tax status, and financial objectives to establish investment strategies. **O*NET Code:** 13-2052.00. **Average Salary:** $60,230. **Projected Growth:** 34.6%. **Annual Openings:** 18,000. **Education:** Bachelor's degree. **Job Zone:** 3. **Education/Training Program(s)**—Finance, General; Financial Planning and Services. **Related Knowledge/Courses:** Economics and Accounting; Mathematics; Administration and Management; Law and Government; Customer and Personal Service; Therapy and Counseling. **Personality Type:** Social. **Skills Required:** Service Orientation; Speaking; Management of Financial Resources; Active Listening; Judgment and Decision

Making; Mathematics; Critical Thinking; Reading Comprehension; Writing. **Abilities:** Mathematical Reasoning; Number Facility; Speech Clarity; Problem Sensitivity; Written Expression. **Occupational Values:** Social Service; Working Conditions; Authority; Social Status; Co-workers. **Interacting with Others:** Communicating with Persons Outside Organization; Communicating with Supervisors, Peers, or Subordinates; Establishing and Maintaining Interpersonal Relationships; Assisting and Caring for Others; Providing Consultation and Advice to Others. **Physical Work Conditions:** Sitting; Indoors.

Sales Agents, Financial Services

Sell financial services such as loan, tax, and securities counseling to customers of financial institutions and business establishments. **O*NET Code:** 41-3031.02. **Average Salary:** $62,680. **Projected Growth:** 13.0%. **Annual Openings:** 39,000. **Education:** Bachelor's degree. **Job Zone:** 3. **Education/Training Program(s)**—Business and Personal/Financial Services Marketing Operations; Financial Planning and Services; Investments and Securities. **Related Knowledge/Courses:** Economics and Accounting; Sales and Marketing; Computers and Electronics; Mathematics; Law and Government; Communications and Media. **Personality Type:** Enterprising. **Skills Required:** Persuasion; Systems Analysis; Management of Financial Resources; Service Orientation; Negotiation; Systems Evaluation; Active Learning; Monitoring. **Abilities:** Number Facility; Mathematical Reasoning; Speech Recognition; Speech Clarity; Written Expression. **Occupational Values:** Recognition; Compensation; Responsibility; Autonomy; Working Conditions. **Interacting with Others:** Communicating with Persons Outside Organization; Establishing and Maintaining Interpersonal Relationships; Selling or Influencing Others. **Physical Work Conditions:** Sitting; Indoors; Disease or Infections.

Sales Agents, Securities and Commodities

Buy and sell securities in investment and trading firms and develop and implement financial plans for individuals, businesses, and organizations. **O*NET Code:** 41-3031.01. **Average Salary:** $62,680. **Projected Growth:** 13.0%. **Annual Openings:** 39,000. **Education:** Bachelor's degree. **Job Zone:** 4. **Education/Training Program(s)**—Business and Personal/Financial Services Marketing Operations; Financial Planning and Services; Investments and Securities. **Related Knowledge/Courses:** Economics and Accounting; Sales and Marketing; Mathematics; Computers and Electronics; Customer and Personal Service; Personnel and Human Resources. **Personality Type:** Enterprising. **Skills Required:** Management of Financial Resources; Systems Analysis; Systems Evaluation; Persuasion; Service Orientation; Negotiation; Active Learning; Judgment and Decision Making. **Abilities:** Number Facility; Deductive Reasoning; Written Expression; Mathematical Reasoning; Speech Recognition. **Occupational Values:** Recognition; Compensation; Responsibility; Working Conditions; Autonomy. **Interacting with Others:** Communicating with Persons Outside Organization; Monitoring and Controlling Resources; Providing Consultation and Advice to Others. **Physical Work Conditions:** Sitting; Indoors.

© 2006, JIST Works

07 Government and Public Administration

07.01 **Managerial Work in Government and Public Administration**

07.02 **Public Planning**

07.03 **Regulations Enforcement**

07.04 **Public Administration Clerical Support**

07.01 Managerial Work in Government and Public Administration

Government Service Executives

Determine and formulate policies and provide overall direction of federal, state, local, or international government activities. Plan, direct, and coordinate operational activities at the highest level of management with the help of subordinate managers. **O*NET Code:** 11-1011.01. **Average Salary:** $136,400. **Projected Growth:** 16.7%. **Annual Openings:** 63,000. **Education:** Work experience plus degree. **Job Zone:** 4. **Education/Training Program(s)**—Business Administration and Management, General; Business/Commerce, General; Entrepreneurship/Entrepreneurial Studies; International Business/Trade/Commerce; Public Administration; Public Administration and Social Service Professions, Other; Public Policy Analysis. **Related Knowledge/Courses:** Administration and Management; Law and Government; Personnel and Human Resources; Economics and Accounting; Education and Training; Psychology. **Personality Type:** Enterprising. **Skills Required:** Management of Financial Resources; Systems Evaluation; Coordination; Systems Analysis; Management of Personnel Resources; Judgment and Decision Making; Negotiation; Persuasion. **Abilities:** Speech Clarity; Written Expression; Mathematical Reasoning; Speech Recognition; Originality; Deductive Reasoning. **Occupational Values:** Authority; Variety; Social Status; Working Conditions; Creativity. **Interacting with Others:** Performing Administrative Activities; Communicating with Persons Outside Organization; Communicating with Supervisors, Peers, or Subordinates; Coordinating the Work and Activities of Others. **Physical Work Conditions:** Sitting; Walking and Running; Indoors; Standing.

Social and Community Service Managers

Plan, organize, or coordinate the activities of a social service program or community outreach organization. Oversee the program or organization's budget and policies regarding participant involvement, program requirements, and benefits. Work may involve directing social workers, counselors, or probation officers. **O*NET Code:** 11-9151.00. **Average Salary:** $46,200. **Projected Growth:** 27.7%. **Annual Openings:** 19,000. **Education:** Bachelor's degree. **Job Zone:** 4. **Education/Training Program(s)**—Business Administration and Management, General; Business, Management, Marketing, and Related Support Services, Other; Business/Commerce, General; Community Organization and Advocacy; Entrepreneurship/Entrepreneurial Studies; Human Services, General; Non-Profit/Public/Organizational Management; Public Administration. **Related Knowledge/Courses:** Customer and Personal Service; Sociology and Anthropology; Psychology; Education and Training; Clerical; Therapy and Counseling. **Personality Type:** Social. **Skills Required:** Social Perceptiveness; Service Orientation; Negotiation; Management of Personnel Resources; Persuasion; Instructing; Monitoring; Learning Strategies; Time Management. **Abilities:** Speech Clarity; Speech Recognition; Originality; Category Flexibility; Mathematical Reasoning. **Occupational Values:** Social Service; Authority; Autonomy; Security; Creativity. **Interacting with Others:** Establishing and Maintaining Interpersonal Relationships; Communicating with Persons Outside Organization; Coordinating the Work and Activities of Others. **Physical Work Conditions:** Sitting; Sounds, Noise Levels Are Distracting or Uncomfortable; In an Enclosed Vehicle or Equipment; Physical Proximity; Indoors.

07.02 Public Planning

City Planning Aides

Compile data from various sources, such as maps, reports, and field and file investigations, for use by city planner in making planning studies. **O*NET Code:** 19-4061.01. **Average Salary:** $48,660. **Projected Growth:** 17.5%. **Annual Openings:** 18,000. **Education:** Associate degree. **Job Zone:** 3. **Education/Training Program(s)**—Social Sciences, General. **Related Knowledge/Courses:** Geography; Mathematics; Clerical; Sociology and Anthropology; Law and Government; Communications and Media. **Personality Type:** Conventional. **Skills Required:** Writing; Mathematics; Speaking; Active Listening; Reading Comprehension; Critical Thinking. **Abilities:** Written Expression; Oral Comprehension; Speech Clarity; Mathematical Reasoning; Written Comprehension; Oral Expression. **Occupational Values:** Advancement; Working Conditions; Supervision, Human Relations; Variety; Company Policies and Practices. **Interacting with Others:** Communicating with Supervisors, Peers, or Subordinates; Communicating with Persons Outside Organization; Establishing and Maintaining Interpersonal Relationships. **Physical Work Conditions:** Sitting; Outdoors; Indoors; Standing.

Urban and Regional Planners

Develop comprehensive plans and programs for use of land and physical facilities of local jurisdictions, such as towns, cities, counties, and metropolitan areas. **O*NET Code:** 19-3051.00. **Average Salary:** $52,680. **Projected Growth:** 10.7%. **Annual Openings:** 5,000. **Education:** Master's degree. **Job Zone:** 4. **Education/Training Program(s)**—City/Urban, Community and Regional Planning. **Related Knowledge/Courses:** Design; Geography; Customer and Personal Service; Building and Construction; Law and Government; Clerical. **Personality Type:** Investigative. **Skills Required:** Persuasion; Coordination; Complex Problem Solving; Service Orientation; Time Management; Social Perceptiveness; Writing; Speaking; Negotiation. **Abilities:** Originality; Written Expression; Visualization; Category Flexibility; Inductive Reasoning. **Occupational Values:** Creativity; Autonomy; Ability Utilization; Achievement; Authority; Social Status. **Interacting with Others:** Communicating with Persons Outside Organization; Establishing and Maintaining Interpersonal Relationships;

© 2006, JIST Works

Performing for or Working Directly with the Public. **Physical Work Conditions:** Sitting; Extremely Bright or Inadequate Lighting; Sounds, Noise Levels Are Distracting or Uncomfortable; Contaminants; In an Enclosed Vehicle or Equipment.

07.03 Regulations Enforcement

Agricultural Inspectors

Inspect agricultural commodities, processing equipment and facilities, and fish and logging operations to ensure compliance with regulations and laws governing health, quality, and safety. **O*NET Code:** 45-2011.00. **Average Salary:** $29,150. **Projected Growth:** 6.7%. **Annual Openings:** 3,000. **Education:** Work experience in a related occupation. **Job Zone:** 4. **Education/Training Program(s)**—Agricultural and Food Products Processing. **Related Knowledge/Courses:** Food Production; Production and Processing; Biology; Law and Government; Chemistry; English Language. **Personality Type:** Realistic. **Skills Required:** Quality Control Analysis; Science; Reading Comprehension; Writing; Speaking; Critical Thinking; Operation Monitoring; Systems Evaluation. **Abilities:** Written Expression; Inductive Reasoning; Problem Sensitivity; Flexibility of Closure; Originality. **Occupational Values:** Responsibility; Autonomy; Security; Independence; Variety. **Interacting with Others:** Providing Consultation and Advice to Others; Communicating with Persons Outside Organization; Interpreting the Meaning of Information for Others. **Physical Work Conditions:** Outdoors; Walking and Running; Standing; Very Hot or Cold; Disease or Infections.

Aviation Inspectors

Inspect aircraft, maintenance procedures, air navigational aids, air traffic controls, and communications equipment to ensure conformance with federal safety regulations. **O*NET Code:** 53-6051.01. **Average Salary:** $49,480. **Projected Growth:** 7.7%. **Annual Openings:** 5,000. **Education:** Work experience in a related occupation. **Job Zone:** 4. **Education/Training Program(s)**—No data available. **Related Knowledge/Courses:** Engineering and Technology; Public Safety and Security; Mechanical; Law and Government; Physics; Education and Training. **Personality Type:** Realistic. **Skills Required:** Operation Monitoring; Quality Control Analysis; Science; Systems Analysis; Systems Evaluation; Writing; Critical Thinking; Reading Comprehension. **Abilities:** Problem Sensitivity; Written Expression; Inductive Reasoning; Flexibility of Closure; Response Orientation. **Occupational Values:** Supervision, Technical; Responsibility; Supervision, Human Relations; Authority; Compensation; Autonomy. **Interacting with Others:** Communicating with Supervisors, Peers, or Subordinates; Providing Consultation and Advice to Others; Coordinating the Work and Activities of Others. **Physical Work Conditions:** Outdoors; Sounds, Noise Levels Are Distracting or Uncomfortable; Hazardous Equipment; Standing; Extremely Bright or Inadequate Lighting.

Child Support, Missing Persons, and Unemployment Insurance Fraud Investigators

Conduct investigations to locate, arrest, and return fugitives and persons wanted for non-payment of support payments and unemployment insurance fraud and to locate missing persons. **O*NET Code:** 33-3021.04. **Average Salary:** $53,350. **Projected Growth:** 22.4%. **Annual Openings:** 11,000. **Education:** Work experience in a related occupation. **Job Zone:** 4. **Education/Training Program(s)**—Criminal Justice/Police Science; Criminalistics and Criminal Science. **Related Knowledge/Courses:** Law and Government; Public Safety and Security; Geography; English Language; Economics and Accounting; Sociology and Anthropology. **Personality Type:** Enterprising. **Skills Required:** Negotiation; Active Listening; Speaking; Critical Thinking; Reading Comprehension; Judgment and Decision Making; Writing; Persuasion. **Abilities:** Oral Expression; Speech Clarity; Oral Comprehension; Written Comprehension; Problem Sensitivity. **Occupational Values:** Achievement; Social Service; Social Status; Ability Utilization; Authority; Supervision, Human Relations; Responsibility. **Interacting with Others:** Communicating with Persons Outside Organization; Establishing and Maintaining Interpersonal Relationships; Communicating with Supervisors, Peers, or Subordinates. **Physical Work Conditions:** Sitting; Walking and Running; Indoors; Outdoors; Extremely Bright or Inadequate Lighting.

Environmental Compliance Inspectors

Inspect and investigate sources of pollution to protect the public and environment and ensure conformance with federal, state, and local regulations and ordinances. **O*NET Code:** 13-1041.01. **Average Salary:** $46,420. **Projected Growth:** 9.8%. **Annual Openings:** 20,000. **Education:** Long-term on-the-job training. **Job Zone:** 3. **Education/Training Program(s)**—No data available. **Related Knowledge/Courses:** Chemistry; Public Safety and Security; Law and Government; Physics; Production and Processing; Biology. **Personality Type:** Investigative. **Skills Required:** Science; Systems Evaluation; Reading Comprehension; Negotiation; Speaking; Critical Thinking; Systems Analysis; Writing; Persuasion; Judgment and Decision Making. **Abilities:** Problem Sensitivity; Written Expression; Written Comprehension; Inductive Reasoning; Information Ordering. **Occupational Values:** Supervision, Human Relations; Authority; Achievement; Advancement; Co-workers; Autonomy. **Interacting with Others:** Communicating with Persons Outside Organization; Communicating with Supervisors, Peers, or Subordinates; Providing Consultation and Advice to Others. **Physical Work Conditions:** Contaminants; Disease or Infections; Climbing Ladders, Scaffolds, or Poles; Walking and Running; Hazardous Conditions.

Equal Opportunity Representatives and Officers

Monitor and evaluate compliance with equal opportunity laws, guidelines, and policies to ensure that employment practices and contracting arrangements give equal opportunity without regard to race, religion, color, national origin, sex, age, or disability. **O*NET Code:** 13-1041.03. **Average Salary:** $46,420. **Projected Growth:** 9.8%. **Annual**

Openings: 20,000. **Education:** Long-term on-the-job training. **Job Zone:** 4. **Education/Training Program(s)**—No data available. **Related Knowledge/Courses:** Personnel and Human Resources; Law and Government; Sociology and Anthropology; English Language; Mathematics; Communications and Media. **Personality Type:** Social. **Skills Required:** Negotiation; Writing; Speaking; Persuasion; Reading Comprehension; Active Listening; Systems Analysis; Systems Evaluation. **Abilities:** Written Comprehension; Written Expression; Oral Expression; Deductive Reasoning; Inductive Reasoning. **Occupational Values:** Working Conditions; Social Service; Social Status; Responsibility; Achievement; Supervision, Human Relations; Autonomy. **Interacting with Others:** Communicating with Supervisors, Peers, or Subordinates; Communicating with Persons Outside Organization; Resolving Conflicts and Negotiating with Others. **Physical Work Conditions:** Sitting; Indoors; Walking and Running; Standing; Extremely Bright or Inadequate Lighting.

Financial Examiners

Enforce or ensure compliance with laws and regulations governing financial and securities institutions and financial and real estate transactions. May examine, verify correctness of, or establish authenticity of records. **O*NET Code:** 13-2061.00. **Average Salary:** $59,050. **Projected Growth:** 8.9%. **Annual Openings:** 3,000. **Education:** Bachelor's degree. **Job Zone:** 4. **Education/Training Program(s)**—Accounting; Taxation. **Related Knowledge/Courses:** Economics and Accounting; Education and Training; Mathematics; Law and Government; Administration and Management; English Language. **Personality Type:** Enterprising. **Skills Required:** Reading Comprehension; Negotiation; Judgment and Decision Making; Writing; Management of Financial Resources; Mathematics; Speaking; Active Listening; Persuasion; Systems Analysis. **Abilities:** Mathematical Reasoning; Number Facility; Written Expression; Written Comprehension; Inductive Reasoning. **Occupational Values:** Authority; Working Conditions; Advancement; Social Status; Compensation; Responsibility; Autonomy. **Interacting with Others:** Communicating with Persons Outside Organization; Providing Consultation and Advice to Others; Communicating with Supervisors, Peers, or Subordinates. **Physical Work Conditions:** Sitting; Indoors; Walking and Running; Extremely Bright or Inadequate Lighting.

Fire Inspectors

Inspect buildings and equipment to detect fire hazards and enforce state and local regulations. **O*NET Code:** 33-2021.01. **Average Salary:** $45,810. **Projected Growth:** 11.6%. **Annual Openings:** 1,000. **Education:** Moderate-term on-the-job training. **Job Zone:** 3. **Education/Training Program(s)**—Fire Protection and Safety Technology/Technician; Fire Science/Firefighting. **Related Knowledge/Courses:** Customer and Personal Service; Building and Construction; Public Safety and Security; Law and Government; Education and Training; Physics. **Personality Type:** Conventional. **Skills Required:** Persuasion; Service Orientation; Negotiation; Instructing; Coordination; Social Perceptiveness; Learning Strategies; Science. **Abilities:** Stamina; Flexibility of Closure; Visual Color Discrimination; Gross Body Equilibrium; Far

Vision. **Occupational Values:** Achievement; Social Status; Authority; Ability Utilization; Security; Responsibility. **Interacting with Others:** Communicating with Persons Outside Organization; Establishing and Maintaining Interpersonal Relationships; Performing for or Working Directly with the Public. **Physical Work Conditions:** In an Enclosed Vehicle or Equipment; Sounds, Noise Levels Are Distracting or Uncomfortable; Outdoors; Extremely Bright or Inadequate Lighting; Very Hot or Cold.

Fish and Game Wardens

Patrol assigned area to prevent fish and game law violations. Investigate reports of damage to crops or property by wildlife. Compile biological data. **O*NET Code:** 33-3031.00. **Average Salary:** $42,430. **Projected Growth:** 7.1%. **Annual Openings:** 1,000. **Education:** Long-term on-the-job training. **Job Zone:** 3. **Education/Training Program(s)**—Fishing and Fisheries Sciences and Management; Natural Resource Economics; Wildlife and Wildlands Science and Management. **Related Knowledge/Courses:** Biology; Law and Government; Geography; Public Safety and Security; Food Production; Transportation. **Personality Type:** Realistic. **Skills Required:** Persuasion; Negotiation; Systems Analysis; Systems Evaluation; Speaking; Social Perceptiveness; Active Listening; Critical Thinking; Judgment and Decision Making. **Abilities:** Night Vision; Peripheral Vision; Speech Clarity; Rate Control; Sound Localization. **Occupational Values:** Authority; Responsibility; Variety; Security; Social Status. **Interacting with Others:** Performing for or Working Directly with the Public; Communicating with Persons Outside Organization; Resolving Conflicts and Negotiating with Others. **Physical Work Conditions:** Outdoors; Minor Burns, Cuts, Bites, or Stings; Extremely Bright or Inadequate Lighting; Walking and Running; Very Hot or Cold.

Forest Fire Inspectors and Prevention Specialists

Enforce fire regulations and inspect for forest fire hazards. Report forest fires and weather conditions. **O*NET Code:** 33-2022.00. **Average Salary:** $38,530. **Projected Growth:** 11.6%. **Annual Openings:** 1,000. **Education:** Moderate-term on-the-job training. **Job Zone:** 2. **Education/Training Program(s)**—Fire Science/Firefighting. **Related Knowledge/Courses:** Geography; Public Safety and Security; Physics; Telecommunications; Medicine and Dentistry; Biology. **Personality Type:** Realistic. **Skills Required:** Management of Personnel Resources; Management of Material Resources; Service Orientation; Coordination; Monitoring; Instructing; Critical Thinking; Systems Analysis. **Abilities:** Night Vision; Glare Sensitivity; Far Vision; Sound Localization; Peripheral Vision. **Occupational Values:** Achievement; Authority; Ability Utilization; Social Status; Variety; Responsibility. **Interacting with Others:** Communicating with Persons Outside Organization; Assisting and Caring for Others; Establishing and Maintaining Interpersonal Relationships. **Physical Work Conditions:** Outdoors; Very Hot or Cold; Minor Burns, Cuts, Bites, or Stings; Specialized Protective or Safety Equipment; Extremely Bright or Inadequate Lighting.

Government Property Inspectors and Investigators

Investigate or inspect government property to ensure compliance with contract agreements and government regulations. **O*NET Code:** 13-1041.04. **Average Salary:** $46,420. **Projected Growth:** 9.8%. **Annual Openings:** 20,000. **Education:** Long-term on-the-job training. **Job Zone:** 3. **Education/Training Program(s)**—No data available. **Related Knowledge/Courses:** Law and Government; Personnel and Human Resources; Public Safety and Security; English Language; Communications and Media; Mathematics. **Personality Type:** Enterprising. **Skills Required:** Negotiation; Speaking; Systems Analysis; Judgment and Decision Making; Writing; Critical Thinking; Reading Comprehension; Systems Evaluation. **Abilities:** Oral Expression; Written Expression; Written Comprehension; Problem Sensitivity; Memorization. **Occupational Values:** Advancement; Variety; Supervision, Human Relations; Social Status; Security; Company Policies and Practices. **Interacting with Others:** Communicating with Supervisors, Peers, or Subordinates; Communicating with Persons Outside Organization; Interpreting the Meaning of Information for Others. **Physical Work Conditions:** Walking and Running; Standing; Extremely Bright or Inadequate Lighting; Sitting; Very Hot or Cold.

Immigration and Customs Inspectors

Investigate and inspect persons, common carriers, goods, and merchandise arriving in or departing from the United States or moving between states to detect violations of immigration and customs laws and regulations. **O*NET Code:** 33-3021.05. **Average Salary:** $53,350. **Projected Growth:** 22.4%. **Annual Openings:** 11,000. **Education:** Work experience in a related occupation. **Job Zone:** 3. **Education/Training Program(s)**—Criminal Justice/Police Science; Criminalistics and Criminal Science. **Related Knowledge/Courses:** Law and Government; Geography; Public Safety and Security; Foreign Language; Transportation; Communications and Media. **Personality Type:** Conventional. **Skills Required:** Writing; Speaking; Negotiation; Judgment and Decision Making; Systems Analysis. **Abilities:** Memorization; Written Comprehension; Written Expression; Problem Sensitivity; Number Facility. **Occupational Values:** Supervision, Human Relations; Supervision, Technical; Advancement; Authority; Security. **Interacting with Others:** Communicating with Supervisors, Peers, or Subordinates; Interpreting the Meaning of Information for Others; Communicating with Persons Outside Organization. **Physical Work Conditions:** Standing; Walking and Running; Kneeling, Crouching, Stooping, or Crawling; Indoors; Climbing Ladders, Scaffolds, or Poles; Spend Time Bending or Twisting the Body.

Licensing Examiners and Inspectors

Examine, evaluate, and investigate eligibility for, conformity with, or liability under licenses or permits. **O*NET Code:** 13-1041.02. **Average Salary:** $46,420. **Projected Growth:** 9.8%. **Annual Openings:** 20,000. **Education:** Long-term on-the-job training. **Job Zone:** 3. **Education/Training Program(s)**—No data available. **Related Knowledge/Courses:** Law and Government; Transportation; Clerical; English Language; Communications and Media. **Personality Type:** Conventional. **Skills Required:** Speaking; Monitoring; Reading Comprehension; Active Listening; Writing; Judgment and Decision Making; Critical Thinking; Mathematics. **Abilities:** Written Expression; Oral Expression; Written Comprehension; Problem Sensitivity; Perceptual Speed. **Occupational Values:** Authority; Social Service; Supervision, Human Relations; Security; Company Policies and Practices; Supervision, Technical; Responsibility; Autonomy. **Interacting with Others:** Communicating with Persons Outside Organization; Interpreting the Meaning of Information for Others; Communicating with Supervisors, Peers, or Subordinates; Performing for or Working Directly with the Public. **Physical Work Conditions:** Sitting; Outdoors; Walking and Running; Standing; Very Hot or Cold.

Marine Cargo Inspectors

Inspect cargoes of seagoing vessels to certify compliance with health and safety regulations in cargo handling and stowage. **O*NET Code:** 53-6051.03. **Average Salary:** $49,480. **Projected Growth:** 7.7%. **Annual Openings:** 5,000. **Education:** Work experience in a related occupation. **Job Zone:** 5. **Education/Training Program(s)**—No data available. **Related Knowledge/Courses:** Public Safety and Security; Mathematics; Transportation; Design; Physics; Law and Government. **Personality Type:** Conventional. **Skills Required:** Mathematics; Writing; Systems Evaluation; Reading Comprehension; Speaking; Critical Thinking; Persuasion; Judgment and Decision Making. **Abilities:** Number Facility; Mathematical Reasoning; Spatial Orientation; Perceptual Speed; Speed of Closure. **Occupational Values:** Responsibility; Autonomy; Independence; Supervision, Technical; Security. **Interacting with Others:** Communicating with Supervisors, Peers, or Subordinates; Interpreting the Meaning of Information for Others; Communicating with Persons Outside Organization; Performing Administrative Activities. **Physical Work Conditions:** Outdoors; Walking and Running; Extremely Bright or Inadequate Lighting; Very Hot or Cold; Standing; Climbing Ladders, Scaffolds, or Poles.

Mechanical Inspectors

Inspect and test mechanical assemblies and systems, such as motors, vehicles, and transportation equipment, for defects and wear to ensure compliance with specifications. **O*NET Code:** 51-9061.02. **Average Salary:** $28,200. **Projected Growth:** 4.7%. **Annual Openings:** 87,000. **Education:** Long-term on-the-job training. **Job Zone:** 4. **Education/Training Program(s)**—Quality Control Technology/Technician. **Related Knowledge/Courses:** Mechanical; Design; Engineering and Technology; Production and Processing; Public Safety and Security; Physics. **Personality Type:** Realistic. **Skills Required:** Quality Control Analysis; Science; Installation; Operation Monitoring; Troubleshooting; Operation and Control; Equipment Maintenance; Repairing. **Abilities:** Hearing Sensitivity; Perceptual Speed; Sound Localization; Visualization; Auditory Attention. **Occupational Values:** Responsibility; Independence; Supervision, Technical; Autonomy; Activity. **Interacting with Others:** Communicating with Persons Outside Organization; Communicating with Supervisors, Peers, or Subordinates; Providing Consultation and Advice to Others. **Physical Work**

Conditions: Standing; Sounds, Noise Levels Are Distracting or Uncomfortable; Hazardous Equipment; Walking and Running; Common Protective or Safety Equipment.

Motor Vehicle Inspectors

Inspect automotive vehicles to ensure compliance with governmental regulations and safety standards. **O*NET Code:** 53-6051.05. **Average Salary:** $49,480. **Projected Growth:** 7.7%. **Annual Openings:** 5,000. **Education:** Work experience in a related occupation. **Job Zone:** 2. **Education/Training Program(s)**—No data available. **Related Knowledge/Courses:** Public Safety and Security; Mechanical; Computers and Electronics; Engineering and Technology; Law and Government; Transportation. **Personality Type:** Realistic. **Skills Required:** Science; Troubleshooting; Quality Control Analysis; Operation Monitoring; Technology Design; Equipment Maintenance; Systems Evaluation. **Abilities:** Hearing Sensitivity; Sound Localization; Extent Flexibility; Visual Color Discrimination; Flexibility of Closure. **Occupational Values:** Responsibility; Supervision, Technical; Security; Autonomy; Independence. **Interacting with Others:** Communicating with Persons Outside Organization; Communicating with Supervisors, Peers, or Subordinates; Performing for or Working Directly with the Public; Performing Administrative Activities. **Physical Work Conditions:** Outdoors; Standing; Spend Time Bending or Twisting the Body; Hazardous Equipment; Minor Burns, Cuts, Bites, or Stings; Kneeling, Crouching, Stooping, or Crawling.

Nuclear Monitoring Technicians

Collect and test samples to monitor results of nuclear experiments and contamination of humans, facilities, and environment. **O*NET Code:** 19-4051.02. **Average Salary:** $60,250. **Projected Growth:** 1.5%. **Annual Openings:** 1,000. **Education:** Associate degree. **Job Zone:** 3. **Education/Training Program(s)**—Industrial Radiologic Technology/Technician; Nuclear and Industrial Radiologic Technologies/Technicians, Other; Nuclear Engineering Technology/Technician; Nuclear/Nuclear Power Technology/Technician; Radiation Protection/Health Physics Technician. **Related Knowledge/Courses:** Physics; Chemistry; Public Safety and Security; Mathematics; Biology; Education and Training. **Personality Type:** Realistic. **Skills Required:** Science; Operation Monitoring; Mathematics; Operation and Control; Installation; Speaking; Writing; Critical Thinking. **Abilities:** Problem Sensitivity; Number Facility; Inductive Reasoning; Mathematical Reasoning; Written Comprehension; Category Flexibility. **Occupational Values:** Compensation; Supervision, Technical; Social Status; Company Policies and Practices; Advancement; Supervision, Human Relations. **Interacting with Others:** Communicating with Supervisors, Peers, or Subordinates; Interpreting the Meaning of Information for Others; Providing Consultation and Advice to Others. **Physical Work Conditions:** Specialized Protective or Safety Equipment; Hazardous Conditions; Exposed to Radiation; Contaminants; Hazardous Equipment.

Occupational Health and Safety Specialists

Review, evaluate, and analyze work environments and design programs and procedures to control, eliminate, and prevent disease or injury caused by chemical, physical, and biological agents or ergonomic factors. May conduct inspections and enforce adherence to laws and regulations governing the health and safety of individuals. May be employed in the public or private sector. **O*NET Code:** 29-9011.00. **Average Salary:** $48,330. **Projected Growth:** 13.2%. **Annual Openings:** 6,000. **Education:** Master's degree. **Job Zone:** 5. **Education/Training Program(s)**—Environmental Health; Industrial Safety Technology/Technician; Occupational Health and Industrial Hygiene; Occupational Safety and Health Technology/Technician; Quality Control and Safety Technologies/Technicians, Other. **Related Knowledge/Courses:** Public Safety and Security; Medicine and Dentistry; Chemistry; Physics; Law and Government; Economics and Accounting; Biology. **Personality Type:** Social. **Skills Required:** Science; Writing; Speaking; Mathematics; Management of Financial Resources; Reading Comprehension; Operation Monitoring; Systems Analysis. **Abilities:** Written Expression; Number Facility; Written Comprehension; Mathematical Reasoning; Oral Expression. **Occupational Values:** Autonomy; Creativity; Authority; Variety; Recognition. **Interacting with Others:** Communicating with Supervisors, Peers, or Subordinates; Communicating with Persons Outside Organization; Providing Consultation and Advice to Others. **Physical Work Conditions:** Disease or Infections; Contaminants; Common Protective or Safety Equipment; Walking and Running; Hazardous Conditions.

Pressure Vessel Inspectors

Inspect pressure vessel equipment for conformance with safety laws and standards regulating their design, fabrication, installation, repair, and operation. **O*NET Code:** 13-1041.05. **Average Salary:** $46,420. **Projected Growth:** 9.8%. **Annual Openings:** 20,000. **Education:** Long-term on-the-job training. **Job Zone:** 4. **Education/Training Program(s)**—No data available. **Related Knowledge/Courses:** Physics; Public Safety and Security; Mechanical; Engineering and Technology; Law and Government; Design; Mathematics. **Personality Type:** Realistic. **Skills Required:** Quality Control Analysis; Operation Monitoring; Mathematics; Science; Operations Analysis; Systems Evaluation; Writing; Troubleshooting; Systems Analysis. **Abilities:** Mathematical Reasoning; Oral Expression; Deductive Reasoning; Written Expression; Number Facility. **Occupational Values:** Autonomy; Independence; Responsibility; Supervision, Human Relations; Authority. **Interacting with Others:** Communicating with Supervisors, Peers, or Subordinates; Communicating with Persons Outside Organization; Establishing and Maintaining Interpersonal Relationships. **Physical Work Conditions:** Standing; Very Hot or Cold; Extremely Bright or Inadequate Lighting; Common Protective or Safety Equipment; Indoors.

Railroad Inspectors

Inspect railroad equipment, roadbed, and track to ensure safe transport of people or cargo. **O*NET Code:** 53-6051.04. **Average Salary:** $49,480. **Projected Growth:** 7.7%. **Annual Openings:** 5,000. **Education:** Work experience in a related occupation. **Job Zone:** 2. **Education/Training Program(s)**—No data available. **Related Knowledge/Courses:** Transportation; Public Safety and Security; Mechanical; Engineering and Technology; Building and Construction;

Geography. **Personality Type:** Realistic. **Skills Required:** Repairing; Troubleshooting; Operation Monitoring; Equipment Maintenance; Management of Personnel Resources; Quality Control Analysis; Systems Analysis; Time Management. **Abilities:** Response Orientation; Control Precision; Extent Flexibility; Hearing Sensitivity; Reaction Time. **Occupational Values:** Authority; Responsibility; Co-workers; Supervision, Technical; Autonomy. **Interacting with Others:** Communicating with Supervisors, Peers, or Subordinates; Coordinating the Work and Activities of Others; Establishing and Maintaining Interpersonal Relationships. **Physical Work Conditions:** Outdoors; Hazardous Equipment; Standing; Walking and Running; Spend Time Bending or Twisting the Body.

Tax Examiners, Collectors, and Revenue Agents

Determine tax liability or collect taxes from individuals or business firms according to prescribed laws and regulations. **O*NET Code:** 13-2081.00. **Average Salary:** $43,230. **Projected Growth:** 5.0%. **Annual Openings:** 9,000. **Education:** Bachelor's degree. **Job Zone:** 4. **Education/Training Program(s)**—Accounting; Taxation. **Related Knowledge/Courses:** Economics and Accounting; Law and Government; Mathematics; Communications and Media; English Language; Administration and Management. **Personality Type:** Conventional. **Skills Required:** Mathematics; Judgment and Decision Making; Reading Comprehension; Critical Thinking; Management of Financial Resources; Complex Problem Solving; Active Listening; Writing; Speaking. **Abilities:** Mathematical Reasoning; Number Facility; Written Comprehension; Oral Expression; Deductive Reasoning. **Occupational Values:** Working Conditions; Supervision, Human Relations; Authority; Security; Company Policies and Practices. **Interacting with Others:** Communicating with Persons Outside Organization; Providing Consultation and Advice to Others; Interpreting the Meaning of Information for Others; Communicating with Supervisors, Peers, or Subordinates; Resolving Conflicts and Negotiating with Others. **Physical Work Conditions:** Sitting; Indoors.

07.04 Public Administration Clerical Support

Court Clerks

Perform clerical duties in court of law; prepare docket of cases to be called; secure information for judges; and contact witnesses, attorneys, and litigants to obtain information for court. **O*NET Code:** 43-4031.01. **Average Salary:** $27,890. **Projected Growth:** 12.3%. **Annual Openings:** 14,000. **Education:** Short-term on-the-job training. **Job Zone:** 2. **Education/Training Program(s)**—General Office Occupations and Clerical Services. **Related Knowledge/Courses:** Clerical; Customer and Personal Service; Law and

Government; Computers and Electronics; English Language; Public Safety and Security. **Personality Type:** Conventional. **Skills Required:** Instructing; Service Orientation; Active Listening; Coordination; Critical Thinking; Learning Strategies; Time Management; Writing. **Abilities:** Wrist-Finger Speed; Oral Comprehension; Near Vision; Written Expression; Written Comprehension; Oral Expression. **Occupational Values:** Working Conditions; Authority; Supervision, Human Relations; Activity; Security. **Interacting with Others:** Establishing and Maintaining Interpersonal Relationships; Communicating with Persons Outside Organization; Performing for or Working Directly with the Public. **Physical Work Conditions:** Sitting; Physical Proximity; Sounds, Noise Levels Are Distracting or Uncomfortable; Contaminants; Extremely Bright or Inadequate Lighting.

Court Reporters

Use verbatim methods and equipment to capture, store, retrieve, and transcribe pretrial and trial proceedings or other information. Includes stenocaptioners who operate comput-erized stenographic captioning equipment to provide cap-tions of live or prerecorded broadcasts for hearing-impaired viewers. **O*NET Code:** 23-2091.00. **Average Salary:** $42,200. **Projected Growth:** 12.7%. **Annual Openings:** 2,000. **Education:** Postsecondary vocational training. **Job Zone:** No data available. **Education/Training Program(s)**—Court Reporting/Court Reporter. **Related Knowledge/Courses:** No data available. **Personality Type:** No data available. **Skills Required:** No data available. **Abilities:** No data available. **Occupational Values:** No data available. **Interacting with Others:** No data available. **Physical Work Conditions:** No data available.

License Clerks

Issue licenses or permits to qualified applicants. Obtain nec-essary information; record data; advise applicants on require-ments; collect fees; and issue licenses. May conduct oral, writ-ten, visual, or performance testing. **O*NET Code:** 43-4031.03. **Average Salary:** $27,890. **Projected Growth:** 12.3%. **Annual Openings:** 14,000. **Education:** Short-term on-the-job train-ing. **Job Zone:** 2. **Education/Training Program(s)**—General Office Occupations and Clerical Services. **Related Knowledge/Courses:** Clerical; Law and Government; Economics and Accounting; Transportation; Sociology and Anthropology; English Language; Telecommunications. **Personality Type:** Conventional. **Skills Required:** Speaking; Active Listening. **Abilities:** Far Vision; Glare Sensitivity; Perceptual Speed; Written Expression; Auditory Attention. **Occupational Values:** Social Service; Supervision, Human Relations; Working Conditions; Supervision, Technical; Activity. **Interacting with Others:** Performing for or Working Directly with the Public; Communicating with Persons Outside Organization; Establishing and Maintaining Interpersonal Relationships. **Physical Work Conditions:** Sitting; Indoors; Standing; Disease or Infections; Spend Time Bending or Twisting the Body.

Municipal Clerks

Draft agendas and bylaws for town or city council, record minutes of council meetings, answer official correspondence, keep fiscal records and accounts, and prepare reports on civic needs. **O*NET Code:** 43-4031.02. **Average Salary:** $27,890. **Projected Growth:** 12.3%. **Annual Openings:** 14,000. **Education:** Short-term on-the-job training. **Job Zone:** 3. **Education/Training Program(s)**—General Office Occupations and Clerical Services. **Related Knowledge/Courses:** Clerical; Law and Government; English Language; Customer and Personal Service; Personnel and Human Resources; Administration and Management. **Personality Type:** Conventional. **Skills Required:** Service Orientation; Social Perceptiveness; Management of Financial Resources; Persuasion; Active Listening; Writing; Time Management; Instructing. **Abilities:** Selective Attention; Written Expression; Wrist-Finger Speed; Night Vision; Memorization. **Occupational Values:** Working Conditions; Supervision, Human Relations; Security; Company Policies and Practices; Social Service. **Interacting with Others:** Performing for or Working Directly with the Public; Communicating with Persons Outside Organization; Communicating with Supervisors, Peers, or Subordinates. **Physical Work Conditions:** Sitting; Physical Proximity; Sounds, Noise Levels Are Distracting or Uncomfortable; Indoors.

© 2006, JIST Works

08 Health Science

08.01   **Managerial Work in Medical and Health Services**

08.02   **Medicine and Surgery**

08.03   **Dentistry**

08.04   **Health Specialties**

08.05   **Animal Care**

08.06   **Medical Technology**

08.07   **Medical Therapy**

08.08   **Patient Care and Assistance**

08.09   **Health Protection and Promotion**

08.01 Managerial Work in Medical and Health Services

Coroners

Direct activities such as autopsies, pathological and toxicological analyses, and inquests relating to the investigation of deaths occurring within a legal jurisdiction to determine cause of death or to fix responsibility for accidental, violent, or unexplained deaths. **O*NET Code:** 13-1041.06. **Average Salary:** $46,420. **Projected Growth:** 9.8%. **Annual Openings:** 20,000. **Education:** Work experience in a related occupation. **Job Zone:** 4. **Education/Training Program(s)—** No data available. **Related Knowledge/Courses:** Medicine and Dentistry; Biology; Chemistry; Administration and Management; Law and Government; English Language. **Personality Type:** Investigative. **Skills Required:** Science; Reading Comprehension; Speaking; Writing; Critical Thinking; Mathematics; Management of Personnel Resources; Active Listening; Coordination; Complex Problem Solving. **Abilities:** Inductive Reasoning; Written Expression; Speed of Closure; Flexibility of Closure; Oral Expression. **Occupational Values:** Authority; Autonomy; Responsibility; Security; Ability Utilization. **Interacting with Others:** Communicating with Supervisors, Peers, or Subordinates; Coordinating the Work and Activities of Others; Interpreting the Meaning of Information for Others; Communicating with Persons Outside Organization; Providing Consultation and Advice to Others. **Physical Work Conditions:** Disease or Infections; Common Protective or Safety Equipment; Contaminants; Hazardous Equipment; Standing.

First-Line Supervisors and Manager/Supervisors—Animal Care Workers, Except Livestock

Directly supervise and coordinate activities of animal care workers. Manager/Supervisors are generally found in smaller establishments, where they perform both supervisory and management functions, such as accounting, marketing, and personnel work, and may also engage in the same animal care work as the workers they supervise. **O*NET Code:** 45-1011.03. **Average Salary:** $35,540. **Projected Growth:** 11.4%. **Annual Openings:** 6,000. **Education:** Associate degree. **Job Zone:** 3. **Education/Training Program(s)—**Agricultural Business and Management, Other; Agricultural Production Operations, General; Agricultural Production Operations, Other; Agriculture, Agriculture Operations, and Related Sciences, Other; Animal Nutrition; Animal Sciences, General; Aquaculture; Farm/Farm and Ranch Management; Fishing and Fisheries Sciences and Management; Range Science and Management. **Related Knowledge/Courses:** Administration and Management; Biology; Medicine and Dentistry; Economics and Accounting; Personnel and Human Resources; Education and Training. **Personality Type:** Realistic. **Skills Required:** Management of Financial Resources; Management of Personnel Resources; Instructing; Management of Material

Resources; Systems Evaluation; Time Management; Writing; Speaking; Coordination. **Abilities:** Problem Sensitivity; Gross Body Coordination; Peripheral Vision; Manual Dexterity; Speed of Closure. **Occupational Values:** Authority; Responsibility; Autonomy; Creativity; Activity. **Interacting with Others:** Communicating with Supervisors, Peers, or Subordinates; Coordinating the Work and Activities of Others; Communicating with Persons Outside Organization. **Physical Work Conditions:** Minor Burns, Cuts, Bites, or Stings; Disease or Infections; Outdoors; Standing; Hazardous Conditions; Kneeling, Crouching, Stooping, or Crawling.

Medical and Health Services Managers

Plan, direct, or coordinate medicine and health services in hospitals, clinics, managed care organizations, public health agencies, or similar organizations. **O*NET Code:** 11-9111.00. **Average Salary:** $66,360. **Projected Growth:** 29.3%. **Annual Openings:** 33,000. **Education:** Work experience plus degree. **Job Zone:** 5. **Education/Training Program(s)—**Community Health and Preventive Medicine; Health and Medical Administrative Services, Other; Health Information/Medical Records Administration/Administrator; Health Services Administration; Health Unit Manager/Ward Supervisor; Health/Health Care Administration/Management; Hospital and Health Care Facilities Administration/Management; Medical Staff Services Technology/Technician; Nursing Administration (MSN, MS, PhD); Public Health, General (MPH, DPH). **Related Knowledge/Courses:** Therapy and Counseling; Customer and Personal Service; Personnel and Human Resources; Medicine and Dentistry; Psychology; Sociology and Anthropology; Education and Training; Philosophy and Theology. **Personality Type:** Enterprising. **Skills Required:** Persuasion; Management of Personnel Resources; Service Orientation; Management of Material Resources; Monitoring; Social Perceptiveness; Management of Financial Resources; Critical Thinking; Learning Strategies. **Abilities:** Mathematical Reasoning; Originality; Oral Comprehension; Speech Recognition; Deductive Reasoning. **Occupational Values:** Authority; Social Service; Creativity; Working Conditions; Social Status. **Interacting with Others:** Establishing and Maintaining Interpersonal Relationships; Resolving Conflicts and Negotiating with Others; Guiding, Directing, and Motivating Subordinates. **Physical Work Conditions:** Sounds, Noise Levels Are Distracting or Uncomfortable; Physical Proximity; Sitting; Disease or Infections; Exposed to Radiation.

08.02 Medicine and Surgery

Anesthesiologists

Administer anesthetics during surgery or other medical procedures. **O*NET Code:** 29-1061.00. **Average Salary:** More than $145,000. **Projected Growth:** 19.5%. **Annual Openings:** 38,000. **Education:** First professional degree. **Job Zone:** 5. **Education/Training Program(s)—**Anesthesiology; Critical Care Anesthesiology. **Related Knowledge/Courses:** Medicine and Dentistry; Biology; Chemistry; English Language; Mathematics; Physics. **Personality Type:** Investigative. **Skills Required:** Operation Monitoring; Judgment and Decision Making; Reading Comprehension; Instructing; Critical Thinking; Coordination; Systems Evaluation; Active Learning; Monitoring. **Abilities:** Problem Sensitivity; Control Precision; Speech Clarity; Oral Expression; Time Sharing. **Occupational Values:** Social Service; Social Status; Ability Utilization; Compensation; Achievement. **Interacting with Others:** Assisting and Caring for Others; Communicating with Supervisors, Peers, or Subordinates; Interpreting the Meaning of Information for Others. **Physical Work Conditions:** Common Protective or Safety Equipment; Disease or Infections; Indoors; Standing; Hazardous Conditions.

Family and General Practitioners

Diagnose, treat, and help prevent diseases and injuries that commonly occur in the general population. O*NET Code: 29-1062.00. **Average Salary:** $137,670. **Projected Growth:** 19.5%. **Annual Openings:** 38,000. **Education:** First professional degree. **Job Zone:** 5. **Education/Training Program(s)—** Family Medicine; Medicine (MD); Osteopathic Medicine/Osteopathy (DO). **Related Knowledge/Courses:** Medicine and Dentistry; Biology; Therapy and Counseling; Chemistry; Administration and Management; Personnel and Human Resources; Physics. **Personality Type:** Investigative. **Skills Required:** Science; Reading Comprehension; Systems Evaluation; Active Learning; Judgment and Decision Making; Management of Personnel Resources; Social Perceptiveness; Systems Analysis. **Abilities:** Manual Dexterity; Inductive Reasoning; Arm-Hand Steadiness; Finger Dexterity; Oral Expression. **Occupational Values:** Social Service; Social Status; Ability Utilization; Achievement; Recognition. **Interacting with Others:** Assisting and Caring for Others; Communicating with Persons Outside Organization; Communicating with Supervisors, Peers, or Subordinates; Performing for or Working Directly with the Public. **Physical Work Conditions:** Disease or Infections; Common Protective or Safety Equipment; Indoors; Walking and Running; Spend Time Bending or Twisting the Body.

Internists, General

Diagnose and provide non-surgical treatment of diseases and injuries of internal organ systems. Provide care mainly for adults who have a wide range of problems associated with the internal organs. O*NET Code: 29-1063.00. **Average Salary:** More than $145,000. **Projected Growth:** 19.5%. **Annual Openings:** 38,000. **Education:** First professional degree. **Job Zone:** 5. **Education/Training Program(s)—**Cardiology; Critical Care Medicine; Endocrinology and Metabolism; Gastroenterology; Geriatric Medicine; Hematology; Infectious Disease; Internal Medicine; Nephrology; Neurology; Nuclear Medicine; Oncology; Pulmonary Disease; Rheumatology. **Related Knowledge/Courses:** Medicine and Dentistry; Biology; Therapy and Counseling; Chemistry; Administration and Management; Personnel and Human Resources; Physics. **Personality Type:** Investigative. **Skills Required:** Science; Reading Comprehension; Systems Evaluation; Active Learning; Judgment and Decision Making; Management of Personnel Resources; Social Perceptiveness; Systems Analysis. **Abilities:** Manual Dexterity; Inductive

Reasoning; Arm-Hand Steadiness; Finger Dexterity; Oral Expression. **Occupational Values:** Social Service; Social Status; Ability Utilization; Achievement; Recognition. **Interacting with Others:** Assisting and Caring for Others; Communicating with Persons Outside Organization; Communicating with Supervisors, Peers, or Subordinates; Performing for or Working Directly with the Public. **Physical Work Conditions:** Disease or Infections; Common Protective or Safety Equipment; Indoors; Walking and Running; Spend Time Bending or Twisting the Body.

Medical Assistants

Perform administrative and certain clinical duties under the direction of physician. Administrative duties may include scheduling appointments, maintaining medical records, billing, and coding for insurance purposes. Clinical duties may include taking and recording vital signs and medical histories, preparing patients for examination, drawing blood, and administering medications as directed by physician. O*NET Code: 31-9092.00. **Average Salary:** $24,310. **Projected Growth:** 58.9%. **Annual Openings:** 78,000. **Education:** Moderate-term on-the-job training. **Job Zone:** 3. **Education/Training Program(s)—**Allied Health and Medical Assisting Services, Other; Anesthesiologist Assistant; Chiropractic Assistant/Technician; Medical Administrative/Executive Assistant and Medical Secretary; Medical Insurance Coding Specialist/Coder; Medical Office Assistant/Specialist; Medical Office Management/Administration; Medical Reception/Receptionist; Medical/Clinical Assistant; Opthalmic Technician/Technologist; Optomeric Technician/Assistant; Orthoptics/Orthoptist. **Related Knowledge/Courses:** Medicine and Dentistry; Customer and Personal Service; Clerical; Psychology; Therapy and Counseling; English Language. **Personality Type:** Social. **Skills Required:** Social Perceptiveness; Service Orientation; Instructing; Active Listening; Learning Strategies; Negotiation; Active Learning; Persuasion; Troubleshooting; Time Management. **Abilities:** Arm-Hand Steadiness; Oral Comprehension; Speech Recognition; Oral Expression; Written Comprehension. **Occupational Values:** Social Service; Co-workers; Variety; Supervision, Human Relations; Security; Social Status. **Interacting with Others:** Assisting and Caring for Others; Establishing and Maintaining Interpersonal Relationships; Communicating with Supervisors, Peers, or Subordinates. **Physical Work Conditions:** Physical Proximity; Disease or Infections; Indoors; Sounds, Noise Levels Are Distracting or Uncomfortable; Walking and Running.

Medical Transcriptionists

Use transcribing machines with headset and foot pedal to listen to recordings by physicians and other health care professionals dictating a variety of medical reports, such as emergency room visits, diagnostic imaging studies, operations, chart reviews, and final summaries. Transcribe dictated reports and translate medical jargon and abbreviations into their expanded forms. Edit as necessary and return reports in either printed or electronic form to the dictator for review and signature or correction. O*NET Code: 31-9094.00. **Average Salary:** $27,790. **Projected Growth:** 22.6%. **Annual Openings:** 18,000. **Education:** Associate degree. **Job Zone:** No data available. **Education/Training Program(s)—**Medical

Transcription/Transcriptionist. **Related Knowledge/Courses:** No data available. **Personality Type:** No data available. **Skills Required:** No data available. **Abilities:** No data available. **Occupational Values:** No data available. **Interacting with Others:** No data available. **Physical Work Conditions:** No data available.

Obstetricians and Gynecologists

Diagnose, treat, and help prevent diseases of women, especially those affecting the reproductive system and the process of childbirth. **O*NET Code:** 29-1064.00. **Average Salary:** More than $145,000. **Projected Growth:** 19.5%. **Annual Openings:** 38,000. **Education:** First professional degree. **Job Zone:** 5. **Education/Training Program(s)**—Neonatal-Perinatal Medicine; Obstetrics and Gynecology. **Related Knowledge/Courses:** Medicine and Dentistry; Biology; Therapy and Counseling; Chemistry; Administration and Management; Personnel and Human Resources; Physics. **Personality Type:** Investigative. **Skills Required:** Science; Reading Comprehension; Systems Evaluation; Active Learning; Judgment and Decision Making; Management of Personnel Resources; Social Perceptiveness; Systems Analysis. **Abilities:** Manual Dexterity; Inductive Reasoning; Arm-Hand Steadiness; Finger Dexterity; Oral Expression. **Occupational Values:** Social Service; Social Status; Ability Utilization; Achievement; Recognition. **Interacting with Others:** Assisting and Caring for Others; Communicating with Persons Outside Organization; Communicating with Supervisors, Peers, or Subordinates; Performing for or Working Directly with the Public. **Physical Work Conditions:** Disease or Infections; Common Protective or Safety Equipment; Indoors; Walking and Running; Spend Time Bending or Twisting the Body.

Pediatricians, General

Diagnose, treat, and help prevent children's diseases and injuries. **O*NET Code:** 29-1065.00. **Average Salary:** $136,490. **Projected Growth:** 19.5%. **Annual Openings:** 38,000. **Education:** First professional degree. **Job Zone:** 5. **Education/Training Program(s)**—Child/Pediatric Neurology; Family Medicine; Neonatal-Perinatal Medicine; Pediatric Cardiology; Pediatric Endocrinology; Pediatric Hemato-Oncology; Pediatric Nephrology; Pediatric Orthopedics; Pediatric Surgery; Pediatrics. **Related Knowledge/Courses:** Medicine and Dentistry; Biology; Therapy and Counseling; Chemistry; Administration and Management; Personnel and Human Resources; Physics. **Personality Type:** Investigative. **Skills Required:** Science; Reading Comprehension; Systems Evaluation; Active Learning; Judgment and Decision Making; Management of Personnel Resources; Social Perceptiveness; Systems Analysis. **Abilities:** Manual Dexterity; Inductive Reasoning; Arm-Hand Steadiness; Finger Dexterity; Oral Expression. **Occupational Values:** Social Service; Social Status; Ability Utilization; Achievement; Recognition. **Interacting with Others:** Assisting and Caring for Others; Communicating with Persons Outside Organization; Communicating with Supervisors, Peers, or Subordinates; Performing for or Working Directly with the Public. **Physical Work Conditions:** Disease or Infections; Common Protective or Safety Equipment; Indoors; Walking and Running; Spend Time Bending or Twisting the Body.

Pharmacists

Compound and dispense medications, following prescriptions issued by physicians, dentists, or other authorized medical practitioners. **O*NET Code:** 29-1051.00. **Average Salary:** $82,520. **Projected Growth:** 30.1%. **Annual Openings:** 23,000. **Education:** First professional degree. **Job Zone:** 5. **Education/Training Program(s)**—Clinical and Industrial Drug Development (MS, PhD); Clinical, Hospital, and Managed Care Pharmacy (MS, PhD); Industrial and Physical Pharmacy and Cosmetic Sciences (MS, PhD); Medicinal and Pharmaceutical Chemistry (MS, PhD); Natural Products Chemistry and Pharmacognosy (MS, PhD); Pharmaceutics and Drug Design (MS, PhD); Pharmacoeconomics/Pharmaceutical Economics (MS, PhD); Pharmacy (PharmD [USA]; PharmD, BS/BPharm [Canada]); Pharmacy Administration and Pharmacy Policy and Regulatory Affairs (MS, PhD); Pharmacy, Pharmaceutical Sciences, and Administration, Other. **Related Knowledge/Courses:** Medicine and Dentistry; Chemistry; Customer and Personal Service; Psychology; Therapy and Counseling; Mathematics. **Personality Type:** Investigative. **Skills Required:** Instructing; Social Perceptiveness; Reading Comprehension; Active Listening; Critical Thinking; Science; Speaking; Active Learning. **Abilities:** Problem Sensitivity; Oral Comprehension; Written Expression; Category Flexibility; Oral Expression; Inductive Reasoning. **Occupational Values:** Authority; Social Service; Social Status; Ability Utilization; Achievement; Working Conditions. **Interacting with Others:** Establishing and Maintaining Interpersonal Relationships; Assisting and Caring for Others; Performing for or Working Directly with the Public. **Physical Work Conditions:** Physical Proximity; Disease or Infections; Sounds, Noise Levels Are Distracting or Uncomfortable; Standing; Indoors.

Pharmacy Aides

Record drugs delivered to the pharmacy, store incoming merchandise, and inform the supervisor of stock needs. May operate cash register and accept prescriptions for filling. **O*NET Code:** 31-9095.00. **Average Salary:** $18,500. **Projected Growth:** 17.6%. **Annual Openings:** 10,000. **Education:** Moderate-term on-the-job training. **Job Zone:** 2. **Education/Training Program(s)**—Pharmacy Technician/Assistant. **Related Knowledge/Courses:** Customer and Personal Service; Medicine and Dentistry; Clerical; Computers and Electronics; Mathematics; Chemistry; English Language. **Personality Type:** No data available. **Skills Required:** Instructing; Service Orientation; Active Learning; Learning Strategies; Social Perceptiveness; Judgment and Decision Making; Critical Thinking; Monitoring. **Abilities:** Speech Recognition; Oral Comprehension; Problem Sensitivity; Trunk Strength; Speech Clarity. **Occupational Values:** No data available. **Interacting with Others:** Establishing and Maintaining Interpersonal Relationships; Performing for or Working Directly with the Public; Resolving Conflicts and Negotiating with Others. **Physical Work Conditions:** Physical Proximity; Disease or Infections; Standing; Walking and Running; Sounds, Noise Levels Are Distracting or Uncomfortable.

Pharmacy Technicians

Prepare medications under the direction of a pharmacist. May measure, mix, count out, label, and record amounts and dosages of medications. **O*NET Code:** 29-2052.00. **Average Salary:** $23,430. **Projected Growth:** 28.8%. **Annual Openings:** 39,000. **Education:** Moderate-term on-the-job training. **Job Zone:** 2. **Education/Training Program(s)—** Pharmacy Technician/Assistant. **Related Knowledge/Courses:** Customer and Personal Service; Chemistry; Medicine and Dentistry; Mathematics; Clerical; Therapy and Counseling. **Personality Type:** Conventional. **Skills Required:** Instructing; Service Orientation; Active Listening; Active Learning; Critical Thinking; Speaking; Mathematics; Troubleshooting. **Abilities:** Speech Recognition; Category Flexibility; Speech Clarity; Oral Comprehension; Oral Expression; Near Vision. **Occupational Values:** Working Conditions; Co-workers; Social Service; Activity; Security. **Interacting with Others:** Establishing and Maintaining Interpersonal Relationships; Performing for or Working Directly with the Public; Communicating with Supervisors, Peers, or Subordinates. **Physical Work Conditions:** Physical Proximity; Standing; Sounds, Noise Levels Are Distracting or Uncomfortable; Extremely Bright or Inadequate Lighting; Very Hot or Cold.

Physician Assistants

Provide health care services typically performed by a physician under the supervision of a physician. Conduct complete physicals, provide treatment, and counsel patients. May, in some cases, prescribe medication. Must graduate from an accredited educational program for physician assistants. **O*NET Code:** 29-1071.00. **Average Salary:** $68,200. **Projected Growth:** 48.9%. **Annual Openings:** 7,000. **Education:** Bachelor's degree. **Job Zone:** 4. **Education/Training Program(s)—**Physician Assistant. **Related Knowledge/ Courses:** Medicine and Dentistry; Biology; Psychology; Therapy and Counseling; Customer and Personal Service; Chemistry. **Personality Type:** Investigative. **Skills Required:** Social Perceptiveness; Science; Instructing; Critical Thinking; Reading Comprehension; Time Management; Active Listening; Active Learning. **Abilities:** Inductive Reasoning; Problem Sensitivity; Speed of Closure; Oral Comprehension; Oral Expression; Arm-Hand Steadiness. **Occupational Values:** Social Service; Achievement; Co-workers; Ability Utilization; Activity; Social Status. **Interacting with Others:** Assisting and Caring for Others; Communicating with Supervisors, Peers, or Subordinates; Establishing and Maintaining Interpersonal Relationships. **Physical Work Conditions:** Physical Proximity; Disease or Infections; Indoors; Contaminants; Sitting.

Psychiatrists

Diagnose, treat, and help prevent disorders of the mind. **O*NET Code:** 29-1066.00. **Average Salary:** $135,440. **Projected Growth:** 19.5%. **Annual Openings:** 38,000. **Education:** First professional degree. **Job Zone:** 5. **Education/Training Program(s)—**Child Psychiatry; Physical, Medical, and Rehabilitation/Psychiatry; Psychiatry. **Related Knowledge/Courses:** Therapy and Counseling; Medicine and Dentistry; Psychology; Biology; Philosophy and Theology; Sociology and Anthropology. **Personality Type:** Investigative.

Skills Required: Social Perceptiveness; Persuasion; Active Learning; Science; Active Listening; Negotiation; Critical Thinking; Learning Strategies; Complex Problem Solving. **Abilities:** Inductive Reasoning; Problem Sensitivity; Written Expression; Speech Recognition; Deductive Reasoning. **Occupational Values:** Social Service; Responsibility; Social Status; Autonomy; Ability Utilization; Achievement. **Interacting with Others:** Establishing and Maintaining Interpersonal Relationships; Assisting and Caring for Others; Training and Teaching Others. **Physical Work Conditions:** Sitting; Physical Proximity; Disease or Infections; Sounds, Noise Levels Are Distracting or Uncomfortable; Indoors.

Registered Nurses

Assess patient health problems and needs, develop and implement nursing care plans, and maintain medical records. Administer nursing care to ill, injured, convalescent, or disabled patients. May advise patients on health maintenance and disease prevention or provide case management. Licensing or registration required. Includes advance practice nurses, such as nurse practitioners, clinical nurse specialists, certified nurse midwives, and certified registered nurse anesthetists. Advanced practice nursing is practiced by RNs who have specialized formal, post-basic education and who function in highly autonomous and specialized roles. **O*NET Code:** 29-1111.00. **Average Salary:** $51,020. **Projected Growth:** 27.3%. **Annual Openings:** 215,000. **Education:** Associate degree. **Job Zone:** 3. **Education/Training Program(s)—**Adult Health Nurse/Nursing; Clinical Nurse Specialist; Critical Care Nursing; Family Practice Nurse/Nurse Practitioner; Maternal/Child Health and Neonatal Nurse/Nursing; Nurse Anesthetist; Nurse Midwife/Nursing Midwifery; Nursing—Registered Nurse Training (RN, ASN, BSN, MSN); Nursing Science (MS, PhD); Nursing, Other; Occupational and Environmental Health Nursing; Pediatric Nurse/Nursing; Perioperative/Operating Room and Surgical Nurse/Nursing; Psychiatric/Mental Health Nurse/Nursing; Public Health/Community Nurse/Nursing. **Related Knowledge/Courses:** Psychology; Medicine and Dentistry; Customer and Personal Service; Therapy and Counseling; Sociology and Anthropology; Philosophy and Theology. **Personality Type:** Social. **Skills Required:** Social Perceptiveness; Service Orientation; Instructing; Time Management; Critical Thinking; Learning Strategies; Coordination; Active Learning; Monitoring. **Abilities:** Problem Sensitivity; Inductive Reasoning; Flexibility of Closure; Speech Recognition; Deductive Reasoning. **Occupational Values:** Social Service; Co-workers; Ability Utilization; Achievement; Activity. **Interacting with Others:** Assisting and Caring for Others; Establishing and Maintaining Interpersonal Relationships; Performing for or Working Directly with the Public. **Physical Work Conditions:** Physical Proximity; Disease or Infections; Contaminants; Sounds, Noise Levels Are Distracting or Uncomfortable; Cramped Work Space, Awkward Positions.

Surgeons

Treat diseases, injuries, and deformities by invasive methods, such as manual manipulation or by using instruments and appliances. **O*NET Code:** 29-1067.00. **Average Salary:** More than $145,000. **Projected Growth:** 19.5%. **Annual Openings:**

38,000. **Education:** First professional degree. **Job Zone:** 5. **Education/Training Program(s)**—Adult Reconstructive Orthopedics (Orthopedic Surgery); Colon and Rectal Surgery; Critical Care Surgery; General Surgery; Hand Surgery; Neurological Surgery/Neurosurgery; Orthopedic Surgery of the Spine; Orthopedics/Orthopedic Surgery; Otolaryngology; Pediatric Orthopedics; Pediatric Surgery; Plastic Surgery; Sports Medicine; Thoracic Surgery; Urology; Vascular Surgery. **Related Knowledge/Courses:** Medicine and Dentistry; Biology; Chemistry; Administration and Management; Therapy and Counseling; Physics; Psychology. **Personality Type:** Investigative. **Skills Required:** Science; Management of Personnel Resources; Systems Evaluation; Judgment and Decision Making; Systems Analysis; Reading Comprehension; Operation and Control; Coordination. **Abilities:** Manual Dexterity; Arm-Hand Steadiness; Finger Dexterity; Speed of Closure; Flexibility of Closure. **Occupational Values:** Social Service; Recognition; Social Status; Ability Utilization; Achievement. **Interacting with Others:** Assisting and Caring for Others; Communicating with Supervisors, Peers, or Subordinates; Communicating with Persons Outside Organization; Coordinating the Work and Activities of Others. **Physical Work Conditions:** Disease or Infections; Common Protective or Safety Equipment; Standing; Specialized Protective or Safety Equipment; Using Hands on Objects, Tools, or Controls.

Surgical Technologists

Assist in operations under the supervision of surgeons, registered nurses, or other surgical personnel. May help set up operating room, prepare and transport patients for surgery, adjust lights and equipment, pass instruments and other supplies to surgeons and surgeon's assistants, hold retractors, cut sutures, and help count sponges, needles, supplies, and instruments. **O*NET Code:** 29-2055.00. **Average Salary:** $33,150. **Projected Growth:** 27.9%. **Annual Openings:** 13,000. **Education:** Postsecondary vocational training. **Job Zone:** 3. **Education/Training Program(s)**—Pathology/Pathologist Assistant; Surgical Technology/Technologist. **Related Knowledge/Courses:** Medicine and Dentistry; Customer and Personal Service; Psychology; Chemistry; Philosophy and Theology; Education and Training. **Personality Type:** Realistic. **Skills Required:** Instructing; Troubleshooting; Learning Strategies; Equipment Selection; Active Learning; Social Perceptiveness; Reading Comprehension; Coordination. **Abilities:** Arm-Hand Steadiness; Selective Attention; Speech Recognition; Problem Sensitivity; Time Sharing; Finger Dexterity. **Occupational Values:** Social Service; Security; Co-workers; Supervision, Human Relations; Company Policies and Practices. **Interacting with Others:** Assisting and Caring for Others; Establishing and Maintaining Interpersonal Relationships; Communicating with Supervisors, Peers, or Subordinates. **Physical Work Conditions:** Physical Proximity; Contaminants; Hazardous Conditions; Disease or Infections; Exposed to Radiation.

08.03 Dentistry

Dental Assistants

Assist dentist, set up patient and equipment, and keep records. **O*NET Code:** 31-9091.00. **Average Salary:** $27,900. **Projected Growth:** 42.5%. **Annual Openings:** 35,000. **Education:** Moderate-term on-the-job training. **Job Zone:** 2. **Education/Training Program(s)**—Dental Assisting/Assistant. **Related Knowledge/Courses:** Medicine and Dentistry; Customer and Personal Service; Clerical; Chemistry; Psychology; Computers and Electronics. **Personality Type:** Social. **Skills Required:** Social Perceptiveness; Equipment Maintenance; Instructing; Management of Material Resources; Persuasion; Service Orientation; Time Management; Operation and Control. **Abilities:** Finger Dexterity; Speech Recognition; Arm-Hand Steadiness; Manual Dexterity; Flexibility of Closure. **Occupational Values:** Social Service; Working Conditions; Security; Co-workers; Variety; Recognition. **Interacting with Others:** Assisting and Caring for Others; Communicating with Supervisors, Peers, or Subordinates; Coordinating the Work and Activities of Others. **Physical Work Conditions:** Physical Proximity; Contaminants; Disease or Infections; Exposed to Radiation; Extremely Bright or Inadequate Lighting.

Dental Hygienists

Clean teeth and examine oral areas, head, and neck for signs of oral disease. May educate patients about oral hygiene, take and develop X rays, or apply fluoride or sealants. **O*NET Code:** 29-2021.00. **Average Salary:** $56,680. **Projected Growth:** 43.1%. **Annual Openings:** 9,000. **Education:** Associate degree. **Job Zone:** 3. **Education/Training Program(s)**—Dental Hygiene/Hygienist. **Related Knowledge/Courses:** Biology; Medicine and Dentistry; Customer and Personal Service; Psychology; Chemistry; Sales and Marketing. **Personality Type:** Social. **Skills Required:** Time Management; Active Learning; Social Perceptiveness; Instructing; Persuasion; Learning Strategies; Reading Comprehension; Service Orientation. **Abilities:** Finger Dexterity; Control Precision; Manual Dexterity; Arm-Hand Steadiness; Problem Sensitivity. **Occupational Values:** Social Service; Co-workers; Security; Authority; Social Status. **Interacting with Others:** Establishing and Maintaining Interpersonal Relationships; Assisting and Caring for Others; Performing for or Working Directly with the Public. **Physical Work Conditions:** Sitting; Physical Proximity; Exposed to Radiation; Disease or Infections; Contaminants.

Dentists, General

Diagnose and treat diseases, injuries, and malformations of teeth and gums and related oral structures. May treat diseases of nerve, pulp, and other dental tissues affecting vitality of teeth. **O*NET Code:** 29-1021.00. **Average Salary:** $120,420. **Projected Growth:** 4.1%. **Annual Openings:** 7,000. **Education:** First professional degree. **Job Zone:** 5. **Education/Training Program(s)**—Advanced General Dentistry (Cert, MS, PhD); Dental Public Health and Education (Cert, MS/MPH, PhD/DPH); Dental Public Health

Specialty; Dentistry (DDS, DMD); Pediatric Dentistry/Pedodontics (Cert, MS, PhD); Pedodontics Specialty. **Related Knowledge/Courses:** Medicine and Dentistry; Biology; Chemistry; English Language; Administration and Management; Psychology. **Personality Type:** Investigative. **Skills Required:** Science; Reading Comprehension; Active Learning; Service Orientation; Critical Thinking; Judgment and Decision Making; Learning Strategies; Writing; Monitoring; Management of Financial Resources. **Abilities:** Arm-Hand Steadiness; Control Precision; Finger Dexterity; Oral Expression; Manual Dexterity. **Occupational Values:** Social Service; Social Status; Recognition; Responsibility; Ability Utilization; Achievement. **Interacting with Others:** Assisting and Caring for Others; Establishing and Maintaining Interpersonal Relationships; Communicating with Persons Outside Organization. **Physical Work Conditions:** Common Protective or Safety Equipment; Indoors; Exposed to Radiation; Disease or Infections; Sitting.

Oral and Maxillofacial Surgeons

Perform surgery on mouth, jaws, and related head and neck structure to execute difficult and multiple extractions of teeth, to remove tumors and other abnormal growths, to correct abnormal jaw relations by mandibular or maxillary revision, to prepare mouth for insertion of dental prosthesis, or to treat fractured jaws. **O*NET Code:** 29-1022.00. **Average Salary:** $120,420. **Projected Growth:** 4.1%. **Annual Openings:** 7,000. **Education:** First professional degree. **Job Zone:** 5. **Education/Training Program(s)**—Dental/Oral Surgery Specialty; Oral/Maxillofacial Surgery (Cert, MS, PhD). **Related Knowledge/Courses:** Medicine and Dentistry; Chemistry; Biology; Psychology; Therapy and Counseling; English Language. **Personality Type:** Investigative. **Skills Required:** Science; Reading Comprehension; Judgment and Decision Making; Critical Thinking; Active Learning; Learning Strategies; Service Orientation; Monitoring. **Abilities:** Arm-Hand Steadiness; Finger Dexterity; Visualization; Manual Dexterity; Control Precision. **Occupational Values:** Social Service; Social Status; Recognition; Responsibility; Achievement. **Interacting with Others:** Assisting and Caring for Others; Providing Consultation and Advice to Others; Establishing and Maintaining Interpersonal Relationships. **Physical Work Conditions:** Common Protective or Safety Equipment; Disease or Infections; Indoors; Standing; Using Hands on Objects, Tools, or Controls.

Orthodontists

Examine, diagnose, and treat dental malocclusions and oral cavity anomalies. Design and fabricate appliances to realign teeth and jaws to produce and maintain normal function and to improve appearance. **O*NET Code:** 29-1023.00. **Average Salary:** $120,420. **Projected Growth:** 4.1%. **Annual Openings:** 7,000. **Education:** First professional degree. **Job Zone:** 5. **Education/Training Program(s)**—Orthodontics Specialty; Orthodontics/Orthodontology (Cert, MS, PhD). **Related Knowledge/Courses:** Medicine and Dentistry; Biology; Therapy and Counseling; Chemistry; Administration and Management; Design. **Personality Type:** Investigative. **Skills Required:** Science; Technology Design; Reading Comprehension; Active Learning; Service Orientation;

Operations Analysis; Critical Thinking; Complex Problem Solving; Equipment Selection; Judgment and Decision Making. **Abilities:** Arm-Hand Steadiness; Control Precision; Manual Dexterity; Finger Dexterity; Problem Sensitivity. **Occupational Values:** Social Service; Social Status; Recognition; Responsibility; Ability Utilization; Achievement. **Interacting with Others:** Assisting and Caring for Others; Establishing and Maintaining Interpersonal Relationships; Communicating with Supervisors, Peers, or Subordinates. **Physical Work Conditions:** Common Protective or Safety Equipment; Indoors; Disease or Infections; Standing; Sitting.

Prosthodontists

Construct oral prostheses to replace missing teeth and other oral structures to correct natural and acquired deformation of mouth and jaws; to restore and maintain oral function, such as chewing and speaking; and to improve appearance. **O*NET Code:** 29-1024.00. **Average Salary:** $120,420. **Projected Growth:** 4.1%. **Annual Openings:** 7,000. **Education:** First professional degree. **Job Zone:** 5. **Education/Training Program(s)**—Prosthodontics Specialty; Prosthodontics/Prosthodontology (Cert, MS, PhD). **Related Knowledge/Courses:** Medicine and Dentistry; Chemistry; Biology; English Language; Design. **Personality Type:** Investigative. **Skills Required:** Science; Technology Design; Reading Comprehension; Critical Thinking; Judgment and Decision Making; Service Orientation; Equipment Selection; Mathematics; Active Learning; Operations Analysis. **Abilities:** Finger Dexterity; Visualization; Arm-Hand Steadiness; Control Precision; Wrist-Finger Speed; Near Vision. **Occupational Values:** Social Service; Responsibility; Ability Utilization; Achievement; Autonomy. **Interacting with Others:** Assisting and Caring for Others; Communicating with Persons Outside Organization; Establishing and Maintaining Interpersonal Relationships. **Physical Work Conditions:** Common Protective or Safety Equipment; Indoors; Sitting; Standing; Spend Time Bending or Twisting the Body.

08.04 Health Specialties

Chiropractors

Adjust spinal column and other articulations of the body to correct abnormalities of the human body believed to be caused by interference with the nervous system. Examine patient to determine nature and extent of disorder. Manipulate spine or other involved area. May utilize supplementary measures, such as exercise, rest, water, light, heat, and nutritional therapy. **O*NET Code:** 29-1011.00. **Average Salary:** $66,610. **Projected Growth:** 23.3%. **Annual Openings:** 3,000. **Education:** First professional degree. **Job Zone:** 5. **Education/Training Program(s)**—Chiropractic (DC). **Related Knowledge/Courses:** Medicine and Dentistry; Biology; Therapy and Counseling; English Language; Customer and Personal Service; Chemistry. **Personality Type:** Investigative. **Skills Required:** Science; Reading Comprehension; Judgment and Decision Making; Active Learning; Complex Problem Solving; Social Perceptiveness;

Persuasion; Systems Analysis. **Abilities:** Problem Sensitivity; Inductive Reasoning; Manual Dexterity; Finger Dexterity; Wrist-Finger Speed. **Occupational Values:** Social Service; Responsibility; Autonomy; Recognition; Compensation; Social Status. **Interacting with Others:** Assisting and Caring for Others; Establishing and Maintaining Interpersonal Relationships; Communicating with Persons Outside Organization. **Physical Work Conditions:** Disease or Infections; Spend Time Bending or Twisting the Body; Exposed to Radiation; Indoors; Common Protective or Safety Equipment.

Optometrists

Diagnose, manage, and treat conditions and diseases of the human eye and visual system. Examine eyes and visual system, diagnose problems or impairments, prescribe corrective lenses, and provide treatment. May prescribe therapeutic drugs to treat specific eye conditions. **O*NET Code:** 29-1041.00. **Average Salary:** $87,340. **Projected Growth:** 17.1%. **Annual Openings:** 2,000. **Education:** First professional degree. **Job Zone:** 5. **Education/Training Program(s)—** Optometry (OD). **Related Knowledge/Courses:** Medicine and Dentistry; Biology; Psychology; Customer and Personal Service; Personnel and Human Resources; Sales and Marketing. **Personality Type:** Investigative. **Skills Required:** Science; Persuasion; Judgment and Decision Making; Management of Personnel Resources; Service Orientation; Active Listening; Reading Comprehension; Active Learning; Instructing. **Abilities:** Inductive Reasoning; Problem Sensitivity; Speed of Closure; Finger Dexterity; Flexibility of Closure; Arm-Hand Steadiness. **Occupational Values:** Social Service; Social Status; Responsibility; Ability Utilization; Recognition; Autonomy. **Interacting with Others:** Performing for or Working Directly with the Public; Establishing and Maintaining Interpersonal Relationships; Training and Teaching Others. **Physical Work Conditions:** Physical Proximity; Disease or Infections; Sitting; Indoors.

Podiatrists

Diagnose and treat diseases and deformities of the human foot. **O*NET Code:** 29-1081.00. **Average Salary:** $95,550. **Projected Growth:** 15.0%. **Annual Openings:** 1,000. **Education:** First professional degree. **Job Zone:** 4. **Education/Training Program(s)—**Podiatric Medicine/ Podiatry (DPM). **Related Knowledge/Courses:** Medicine and Dentistry; Biology; Chemistry; Therapy and Counseling; English Language; Physics. **Personality Type:** Social. **Skills Required:** Active Learning; Reading Comprehension; Technology Design; Judgment and Decision Making; Service Orientation; Equipment Selection; Active Listening; Critical Thinking; Complex Problem Solving; Systems Evaluation. **Abilities:** Manual Dexterity; Speed of Closure; Finger Dexterity; Inductive Reasoning; Control Precision. **Occupational Values:** Social Service; Recognition; Responsibility; Social Status; Autonomy. **Interacting with Others:** Assisting and Caring for Others; Communicating with Persons Outside Organization; Performing for or Working Directly with the Public. **Physical Work Conditions:** Disease or Infections; Common Protective or Safety Equipment; Exposed to Radiation; Minor Burns, Cuts, Bites, or Stings; Indoors.

08.05 Animal Care

Animal Breeders

Breed animals, including cattle, goats, horses, sheep, swine, poultry, dogs, cats, or pet birds. Select and breed animals according to their genealogy, characteristics, and offspring. May require a knowledge of artificial insemination techniques and equipment use. May involve keeping records on heats, birth intervals, or pedigree. **O*NET Code:** 45-2021.00. **Average Salary:** $25,560. **Projected Growth:** 6.1%. **Annual Openings:** 1,000. **Education:** Associate degree. **Job Zone:** 3. **Education/Training Program(s)—**Animal/Livestock Husbandry and Production; Horse Husbandry/Equine Science and Management. **Related Knowledge/Courses:** Food Production; Sales and Marketing; Biology; Medicine and Dentistry; Clerical; Building and Construction. **Personality Type:** Realistic. **Skills Required:** Science; Management of Material Resources; Equipment Selection; Systems Analysis; Negotiation. **Abilities:** Static Strength; Extent Flexibility; Trunk Strength; Explosive Strength; Dynamic Strength. **Occupational Values:** Responsibility; Independence; Autonomy; Creativity; Activity. **Interacting with Others:** Monitoring and Controlling Resources; Selling or Influencing Others; Communicating with Persons Outside Organization. **Physical Work Conditions:** Minor Burns, Cuts, Bites, or Stings; Outdoors; Kneeling, Crouching, Stooping, or Crawling; Spend Time Bending or Twisting the Body; Sounds, Noise Levels Are Distracting or Uncomfortable; Walking and Running.

Animal Trainers

Train animals for riding, harness, security, performance, or obedience or for assisting persons with disabilities. Accustom animals to human voice and contact; condition animals to respond to commands. Train animals according to prescribed standards for show or competition. May train animals to carry pack loads or work as part of pack team. **O*NET Code:** 39-2011.00. **Average Salary:** $22,870. **Projected Growth:** 14.3%. **Annual Openings:** 4,000. **Education:** Moderate-term on-the-job training. **Job Zone:** 3. **Education/Training Program(s)—**Animal Training; Equestrian/Equine Studies. **Related Knowledge/Courses:** Biology; Education and Training; Sales and Marketing; Medicine and Dentistry; Customer and Personal Service; Public Safety and Security. **Personality Type:** Social. **Skills Required:** Instructing; Learning Strategies; Monitoring; Persuasion; Social Perceptiveness; Systems Evaluation; Systems Analysis; Active Learning; Coordination. **Abilities:** Memorization; Speed of Limb Movement; Peripheral Vision; Flexibility of Closure; Far Vision. **Occupational Values:** Responsibility; Creativity; Autonomy; Independence; Compensation. **Interacting with Others:** Providing Consultation and Advice to Others; Communicating with Persons Outside Organization; Establishing and Maintaining Interpersonal Relationships. **Physical Work Conditions:** Minor Burns, Cuts, Bites, or Stings; Kneeling, Crouching, Stooping, or Crawling; Disease or Infections; Outdoors; Walking and Running.

Nonfarm Animal Caretakers

Feed, water, groom, bathe, exercise, or otherwise care for pets and other nonfarm animals, such as dogs, cats, ornamental fish or birds, zoo animals, and mice. Work in settings such as kennels, animal shelters, zoos, circuses, and aquariums. May keep records of feedings, treatments, and animals received or discharged. May clean, disinfect, and repair cages, pens, or fish tanks. **O*NET Code:** 39-2021.00. **Average Salary:** $17,470. **Projected Growth:** 22.2%. **Annual Openings:** 32,000. **Education:** Short-term on-the-job training. **Job Zone:** 1. **Education/Training Program(s)**—Agricultural/Farm Supplies Retailing and Wholesaling; Dog/Pet/Animal Grooming. **Related Knowledge/Courses:** Medicine and Dentistry; Building and Construction; Biology; Chemistry. **Personality Type:** Realistic. **Skills Required:** Installation; Repairing; Service Orientation; Equipment Maintenance; Troubleshooting; Technology Design. **Abilities:** Dynamic Strength; Static Strength; Explosive Strength; Spatial Orientation; Rate Control; Speed of Limb Movement. **Occupational Values:** Independence; Supervision, Technical; Activity. **Interacting with Others:** Communicating with Persons Outside Organization; Establishing and Maintaining Interpersonal Relationships; Communicating with Supervisors, Peers, or Subordinates; Assisting and Caring for Others. **Physical Work Conditions:** Outdoors; Disease or Infections; Minor Burns, Cuts, Bites, or Stings; Contaminants; Standing.

Veterinarians

Diagnose and treat diseases and dysfunctions of animals. May engage in a particular function, such as research and development, consultation, administration, technical writing, sale or production of commercial products, or rendering of technical services to commercial firms or other organizations. Includes veterinarians who inspect livestock. **O*NET Code:** 29-1131.00. **Average Salary:** $65,290. **Projected Growth:** 25.1%. **Annual Openings:** 4,000. **Education:** First professional degree. **Job Zone:** 5. **Education/Training Program(s)**—Comparative and Laboratory Animal Medicine (Cert, MS, PhD); Laboratory Animal Medicine; Large Animal/Food Animal and Equine Surgery and Medicine (Cert, MS, PhD); Small/Companion Animal Surgery and Medicine (Cert, MS, PhD); Theriogenology; Veterinary Anatomy (Cert, MS, PhD); Veterinary Anesthesiology; Veterinary Biomedical and Clinical Sciences, Other (Cert, MS, PhD); Veterinary Dentistry; Veterinary Dermatology; Veterinary Emergency and Critical Care Medicine; Veterinary Infectious Diseases (Cert, MS, PhD); Veterinary Internal Medicine; Veterinary Medicine (DVM); Veterinary Microbiology; Veterinary Microbiology and Immunobiology (Cert, MS, PhD); Veterinary Nutrition; Veterinary Ophthalmology; Veterinary Pathology; Veterinary Pathology and Pathobiology (Cert, MS, PhD); Veterinary Physiology (Cert, MS, PhD); Veterinary Practice; Veterinary Preventive Medicine; Veterinary Preventive Medicine Epidemiology and Public Health (Cert, MS, PhD); Veterinary Radiology; Veterinary Residency Programs, Other; Veterinary Sciences/Veterinary Clinical Sciences, General (Cert, MS, PhD); Veterinary Surgery; Veterinary Toxicology; Veterinary Toxicology and Pharmacology (Cert, MS, PhD); Zoological Medicine. **Related Knowledge/Courses:** Medicine and Dentistry; Biology; Customer and Personal Service; Chemistry; Sales and Marketing; Education and Training. **Personality Type:** Investigative. **Skills Required:** Science; Instructing; Management of Financial Resources; Reading Comprehension; Active Learning; Service Orientation; Complex Problem Solving; Judgment and Decision Making; Time Management; Management of Personnel Resources. **Abilities:** Speed of Closure; Inductive Reasoning; Originality; Manual Dexterity; Fluency of Ideas. **Occupational Values:** Recognition; Social Status; Responsibility; Autonomy; Ability Utilization; Achievement. **Interacting with Others:** Assisting and Caring for Others; Performing for or Working Directly with the Public; Establishing and Maintaining Interpersonal Relationships. **Physical Work Conditions:** Contaminants; Physical Proximity; Sounds, Noise Levels Are Distracting or Uncomfortable; Exposed to Radiation; Disease or Infections.

Veterinary Assistants and Laboratory Animal Caretakers

Feed, water, and examine pets and other nonfarm animals for signs of illness, disease, or injury in laboratories and animal hospitals and clinics. Clean and disinfect cages and work areas; sterilize laboratory and surgical equipment. May provide routine post-operative care, administer medication orally or topically, or prepare samples for laboratory examination under the supervision of veterinary or laboratory animal technologists or technicians, veterinarians, or scientists. **O*NET Code:** 31-9096.00. **Average Salary:** $18,370. **Projected Growth:** 26.2%. **Annual Openings:** 11,000. **Education:** Short-term on-the-job training. **Job Zone:** 2. **Education/Training Program(s)**—Veterinary/Animal Health Technology/Technician and Veterinary Assistant. **Related Knowledge/Courses:** Medicine and Dentistry; Biology; Chemistry; Customer and Personal Service; Clerical; Sales and Marketing. **Personality Type:** Realistic. **Skills Required:** Instructing; Science; Service Orientation; Social Perceptiveness; Active Listening; Reading Comprehension; Active Learning; Troubleshooting. **Abilities:** Visual Color Discrimination; Oral Comprehension; Response Orientation; Speed of Closure; Finger Dexterity; Static Strength. **Occupational Values:** Variety; Supervision, Technical. **Interacting with Others:** Assisting and Caring for Others; Establishing and Maintaining Interpersonal Relationships; Communicating with Supervisors, Peers, or Subordinates. **Physical Work Conditions:** Contaminants; Minor Burns, Cuts, Bites, or Stings; Exposed to Radiation; Walking and Running; Disease or Infections.

Veterinary Technologists and Technicians

Perform medical tests in a laboratory environment for use in the treatment and diagnosis of diseases in animals. Prepare vaccines and serums for prevention of diseases. Prepare tissue samples, take blood samples, and execute laboratory tests, such as urinalysis and blood counts. Clean and sterilize instruments and materials and maintain equipment and machines. **O*NET Code:** 29-2056.00. **Average Salary:** $24,190. **Projected Growth:** 44.1%. **Annual Openings:** 11,000. **Education:** Associate degree. **Job Zone:** 3. **Education/Training Program(s)**—Veterinary/Animal Health Technology/Technician and Veterinary Assistant. **Related Knowledge/Courses:** Biology; Customer and Personal

Service; Medicine and Dentistry; Chemistry; Sales and Marketing; Mathematics. **Personality Type:** No data available. **Skills Required:** Instructing; Social Perceptiveness; Science; Active Learning; Operation Monitoring; Time Management; Reading Comprehension; Service Orientation; Equipment Maintenance. **Abilities:** No data available. **Occupational Values:** No data available. **Interacting with Others:** Establishing and Maintaining Interpersonal Relationships; Assisting and Caring for Others; Performing for or Working Directly with the Public. **Physical Work Conditions:** Contaminants; Physical Proximity; Minor Burns, Cuts, Bites, or Stings; Exposed to Radiation; Sounds, Noise Levels Are Distracting or Uncomfortable.

08.06 Medical Technology

Biological Technicians

Assist biological and medical scientists in laboratories. Set up, operate, and maintain laboratory instruments and equipment; monitor experiments; make observations; and calculate and record results. May analyze organic substances, such as blood, food, and drugs. **O*NET Code:** 19-4021.00. **Average Salary:** $33,360. **Projected Growth:** 19.4%. **Annual Openings:** 7,000. **Education:** Associate degree. **Job Zone:** 4. **Education/Training Program(s)**—Biology Technician/Biotechnology Laboratory Technician. **Related Knowledge/Courses:** Chemistry; Biology; Mathematics; English Language; Production and Processing; Geography. **Personality Type:** Realistic. **Skills Required:** Science; Active Learning; Instructing; Learning Strategies; Equipment Maintenance; Troubleshooting; Technology Design; Service Orientation; Quality Control Analysis. **Abilities:** Static Strength; Mathematical Reasoning; Dynamic Strength; Reaction Time; Dynamic Flexibility; Sound Localization. **Occupational Values:** Supervision, Technical; Variety; Advancement. **Interacting with Others:** Communicating with Supervisors, Peers, or Subordinates; Establishing and Maintaining Interpersonal Relationships; Coaching and Developing Others. **Physical Work Conditions:** Contaminants; Physical Proximity; Hazardous Conditions; Indoors; Sitting.

Cardiovascular Technologists and Technicians

Conduct tests on pulmonary or cardiovascular systems of patients for diagnostic purposes. May conduct or assist in electrocardiograms, cardiac catheterizations, pulmonary-functions, lung capacity, and similar tests. **O*NET Code:** 29-2031.00. **Average Salary:** $37,800. **Projected Growth:** 33.5%. **Annual Openings:** 6,000. **Education:** Associate degree. **Job Zone:** 3. **Education/Training Program(s)**—Cardiopulmonary Technology/Technologist; Cardiovascular Technology/Technologist; Electrocardiograph Technology/Technician; Perfusion Technology/Perfusionist. **Related Knowledge/Courses:** Customer and Personal Service; Medicine and Dentistry; Psychology; Education and Training; Physics; Computers and Electronics; English Language.

Personality Type: Investigative. **Skills Required:** Instructing; Service Orientation; Active Learning; Operation Monitoring; Equipment Maintenance; Time Management; Social Perceptiveness; Learning Strategies. **Abilities:** Oral Comprehension; Written Comprehension; Hearing Sensitivity; Oral Expression; Problem Sensitivity. **Occupational Values:** Social Service; Social Status; Recognition; Compensation; Ability Utilization; Achievement; Co-workers. **Interacting with Others:** Assisting and Caring for Others; Establishing and Maintaining Interpersonal Relationships; Performing for or Working Directly with the Public. **Physical Work Conditions:** Physical Proximity; Disease or Infections; Exposed to Radiation; Contaminants; Hazardous Conditions.

Diagnostic Medical Sonographers

Produce ultrasonic recordings of internal organs for use by physicians. **O*NET Code:** 29-2032.00. **Average Salary:** $50,980. **Projected Growth:** 24.0%. **Annual Openings:** 4,000. **Education:** Associate degree. **Job Zone:** 3. **Education/Training Program(s)**—Allied Health Diagnostic, Intervention, and Treatment Professions, Other; Diagnostic Medical Sonography/Sonographer and Ultrasound Technician. **Related Knowledge/Courses:** Medicine and Dentistry; Biology; Physics; Customer and Personal Service; Education and Training; Clerical; Psychology. **Personality Type:** No data available. **Skills Required:** Social Perceptiveness; Reading Comprehension; Instructing; Learning Strategies; Active Learning; Service Orientation; Operation and Control; Active Listening. **Abilities:** Flexibility of Closure; Control Precision; Inductive Reasoning; Problem Sensitivity; Perceptual Speed; Response Orientation. **Occupational Values:** No data available. **Interacting with Others:** Assisting and Caring for Others; Establishing and Maintaining Interpersonal Relationships; Communicating with Supervisors, Peers, or Subordinates. **Physical Work Conditions:** Physical Proximity; Disease or Infections; Cramped Work Space, Awkward Positions; Sounds, Noise Levels Are Distracting or Uncomfortable; Contaminants.

Medical and Clinical Laboratory Technicians

Perform routine medical laboratory tests for the diagnosis, treatment, and prevention of disease. May work under the supervision of a medical technologist. **O*NET Code:** 29-2012.00. **Average Salary:** $30,140. **Projected Growth:** 19.4%. **Annual Openings:** 21,000. **Education:** Associate degree. **Job Zone:** 2. **Education/Training Program(s)**—Blood Bank Technology Specialist; Clinical/Medical Laboratory Assistant; Clinical/Medical Laboratory Technician; Hematology Technology/Technician; Histologic Technician. **Related Knowledge/Courses:** Medicine and Dentistry; Clerical; Therapy and Counseling; Biology; Chemistry; Customer and Personal Service. **Personality Type:** Realistic. **Skills Required:** Equipment Maintenance; Science; Troubleshooting; Instructing; Monitoring; Time Management; Service Orientation; Active Learning. **Abilities:** Inductive Reasoning; Visual Color Discrimination; Finger Dexterity; Flexibility of Closure; Near Vision. **Occupational Values:** Ability Utilization; Co-workers; Achievement; Activity; Security. **Interacting with Others:** Communicating with Supervisors, Peers, or Subordinates; Establishing and Maintaining

© 2006, JIST Works

Interpersonal Relationships; Assisting and Caring for Others. **Physical Work Conditions:** Disease or Infections; Physical Proximity; Hazardous Conditions; Contaminants; Indoors.

Medical and Clinical Laboratory Technologists

Perform complex medical laboratory tests for diagnosis, treatment, and prevention of disease. May train or supervise staff. **O*NET Code:** 29-2011.00. **Average Salary:** $44,460. **Projected Growth:** 19.3%. **Annual Openings:** 21,000. **Education:** Bachelor's degree. **Job Zone:** 4. **Education/ Training Program(s)**—Clinical Laboratory Science/Medical Technology/Technologist; Clinical/Medical Laboratory Science and Allied Professions, Other; Cytogenetics/Genetics/ Clinical Genetics Technology/Technologist; Cytotechnology/ Cytotechnologist; Histologic Technology/Histotechnologist; Renal/Dialysis Technologist/Technician. **Related Knowledge/ Courses:** Biology; Chemistry; Computers and Electronics; Public Safety and Security; Customer and Personal Service; Mathematics. **Personality Type:** Investigative. **Skills Required:** Equipment Maintenance; Operation Monitoring; Quality Control Analysis; Science; Troubleshooting; Instructing; Repairing; Operation and Control. **Abilities:** Inductive Reasoning; Flexibility of Closure; Near Vision; Finger Dexterity; Category Flexibility. **Occupational Values:** Ability Utilization; Achievement; Co-workers; Social Service; Variety. **Interacting with Others:** Establishing and Maintaining Interpersonal Relationships; Communicating with Supervisors, Peers, or Subordinates; Coordinating the Work and Activities of Others; Guiding, Directing, and Motivating Subordinates. **Physical Work Conditions:** Contaminants; Disease or Infections; Hazardous Conditions; Sounds, Noise Levels Are Distracting or Uncomfortable; Physical Proximity.

Medical Equipment Preparers

Prepare, sterilize, install, or clean laboratory or health care equipment. May perform routine laboratory tasks and operate or inspect equipment. **O*NET Code:** 31-9093.00. **Average Salary:** $23,940. **Projected Growth:** 18.1%. **Annual Openings:** 6,000. **Education:** Short-term on-the-job training. **Job Zone:** 2. **Education/Training Program(s)**—Allied Health and Medical Assisting Services, Other; Medical/Clinical Assistant. **Related Knowledge/Courses:** Chemistry; Customer and Personal Service; Education and Training; Production and Processing; Biology; Medicine and Dentistry. **Personality Type:** Realistic. **Skills Required:** Operation Monitoring; Service Orientation; Management of Material Resources; Instructing; Learning Strategies; Equipment Maintenance; Active Learning; Monitoring. **Abilities:** Static Strength; Response Orientation; Rate Control; Reaction Time; Extent Flexibility; Hearing Sensitivity. **Occupational Values:** Independence; Supervision, Technical; Security; Moral Values; Supervision, Human Relations. **Interacting with Others:** Communicating with Supervisors, Peers, or Subordinates; Assisting and Caring for Others; Establishing and Maintaining Interpersonal Relationships. **Physical Work Conditions:** Contaminants; Disease or Infections; Physical Proximity; Minor Burns, Cuts, Bites, or Stings; Hazardous Conditions.

Medical Records and Health Information Technicians

Compile, process, and maintain medical records of hospital and clinic patients in a manner consistent with medical, administrative, ethical, legal, and regulatory requirements of the health care system. Process, maintain, compile, and report patient information for health requirements and standards. **O*NET Code:** 29-2071.00. **Average Salary:** $24,920. **Projected Growth:** 46.8%. **Annual Openings:** 24,000. **Education:** Associate degree. **Job Zone:** 3. **Education/Training Program(s)**—Health Information/Medical Records Technology/Technician; Medical Insurance Coding Specialist/Coder. **Related Knowledge/Courses:** Clerical; Customer and Personal Service; Personnel and Human Resources; Medicine and Dentistry; Administration and Management; Computers and Electronics. **Personality Type:** Conventional. **Skills Required:** Instructing; Systems Evaluation; Time Management; Active Listening; Critical Thinking; Learning Strategies; Service Orientation; Reading Comprehension; Active Learning; Social Perceptiveness. **Abilities:** Category Flexibility; Speech Recognition; Perceptual Speed; Near Vision; Written Expression. **Occupational Values:** Working Conditions; Activity; Security; Moral Values; Supervision, Human Relations. **Interacting with Others:** Communicating with Supervisors, Peers, or Subordinates; Establishing and Maintaining Interpersonal Relationships; Communicating with Persons Outside Organization. **Physical Work Conditions:** Physical Proximity; Sitting; Sounds, Noise Levels Are Distracting or Uncomfortable; Contaminants; Indoors.

Nuclear Medicine Technologists

Prepare, administer, and measure radioactive isotopes in therapeutic, diagnostic, and tracer studies, utilizing a variety of radioisotope equipment. Prepare stock solutions of radioactive materials and calculate doses to be administered by radiologists. Subject patients to radiation. Execute blood volume, red cell survival, and fat absorption studies, following standard laboratory techniques. **O*NET Code:** 29-2033.00. **Average Salary:** $53,680. **Projected Growth:** 23.6%. **Annual Openings:** 2,000. **Education:** Associate degree. **Job Zone:** 3. **Education/Training Program(s)**—Nuclear Medical Technology/Technologist; Radiation Protection/Health Physics Technician. **Related Knowledge/Courses:** Medicine and Dentistry; Customer and Personal Service; Biology; Physics; Chemistry; Computers and Electronics. **Personality Type:** Investigative. **Skills Required:** Science; Social Perceptiveness; Operation Monitoring; Service Orientation; Instructing; Active Learning; Coordination; Operation and Control. **Abilities:** Oral Comprehension; Written Comprehension; Written Expression; Oral Expression; Problem Sensitivity. **Occupational Values:** Social Service; Ability Utilization; Achievement; Authority; Co-workers. **Interacting with Others:** Assisting and Caring for Others; Performing for or Working Directly with the Public; Establishing and Maintaining Interpersonal Relationships. **Physical Work Conditions:** Exposed to Radiation; Physical Proximity; Disease or Infections; Contaminants; Indoors.

Opticians, Dispensing

Design, measure, fit, and adapt lenses and frames for client according to written optical prescription or specification. Assist client with selecting frames. Measure customer for size of eyeglasses and coordinate frames with facial and eye measurements and optical prescription. Prepare work order for optical laboratory containing instructions for grinding and mounting lenses in frames. Verify exactness of finished lens spectacles. Adjust frame and lens position to fit client. May shape or reshape frames. **O*NET Code:** 29-2081.00. **Average Salary:** $27,360. **Projected Growth:** 18.2%. **Annual Openings:** 10,000. **Education:** Long-term on-the-job training. **Job Zone:** 3. **Education/Training Program(s)**—Opticianry/Ophthalmic Dispensing Optician. **Related Knowledge/Courses:** Sales and Marketing; Customer and Personal Service; Clerical; Production and Processing; Administration and Management; Psychology. **Personality Type:** Enterprising. **Skills Required:** Persuasion; Service Orientation; Technology Design; Speaking; Social Perceptiveness; Active Learning; Instructing; Management of Financial Resources. **Abilities:** Oral Expression; Control Precision; Oral Comprehension; Arm-Hand Steadiness; Finger Dexterity. **Occupational Values:** Social Service; Social Status; Achievement; Responsibility; Authority. **Interacting with Others:** Performing for or Working Directly with the Public; Communicating with Supervisors, Peers, or Subordinates; Establishing and Maintaining Interpersonal Relationships; Assisting and Caring for Others. **Physical Work Conditions:** Physical Proximity; Sitting; Minor Burns, Cuts, Bites, or Stings; Contaminants.

Orthotists and Prosthetists

Assist patients with disabling conditions of limbs and spine or with partial or total absence of limb by fitting and preparing orthopedic braces or prostheses. **O*NET Code:** 29-2091.00. **Average Salary:** $49,860. **Projected Growth:** 18.9%. **Annual Openings:** 1,000. **Education:** Bachelor's degree. **Job Zone:** 3. **Education/Training Program(s)**—Assistive/Augmentative Technology and Rehabilitation Engineering; Orthotist/Prosthetist. **Related Knowledge/Courses:** Medicine and Dentistry; Design; Building and Construction; Therapy and Counseling; Engineering and Technology; Customer and Personal Service; Physics; Education and Training. **Personality Type:** Social. **Skills Required:** Technology Design; Social Perceptiveness; Speaking; Instructing; Science; Management of Personnel Resources; Active Listening; Service Orientation. **Abilities:** Speech Clarity; Oral Expression; Originality; Visualization; Control Precision. **Occupational Values:** Social Service; Achievement; Ability Utilization; Recognition; Authority. **Interacting with Others:** Assisting and Caring for Others; Communicating with Supervisors, Peers, or Subordinates; Communicating with Persons Outside Organization. **Physical Work Conditions:** Disease or Infections; Indoors; Spend Time Bending or Twisting the Body; Kneeling, Crouching, Stooping, or Crawling; Standing; Using Hands on Objects, Tools, or Controls.

Radiologic Technicians

Maintain and use equipment and supplies necessary to demonstrate portions of the human body on X-ray film or fluoroscopic screen for diagnostic purposes. **O*NET Code:** 29-2034.02. **Average Salary:** $41,850. **Projected Growth:** 22.9%. **Annual Openings:** 21,000. **Education:** Associate degree. **Job Zone:** 3. **Education/Training Program(s)**—Allied Health Diagnostic, Intervention, and Treatment Professions, Other; Medical Radiologic Technology/Science—Radiation Therapist; Radiologic Technology/Science—Radiographer. **Related Knowledge/Courses:** Clerical; Psychology; Medicine and Dentistry; Customer and Personal Service; Physics; English Language. **Personality Type:** Realistic. **Skills Required:** Service Orientation; Science; Instructing; Negotiation; Social Perceptiveness; Active Listening; Equipment Selection; Speaking; Learning Strategies; Coordination. **Abilities:** Control Precision; Oral Comprehension; Flexibility of Closure; Extent Flexibility; Time Sharing. **Occupational Values:** Social Service; Co-workers; Moral Values; Security; Advancement; Authority; Supervision, Human Relations. **Interacting with Others:** Assisting and Caring for Others; Establishing and Maintaining Interpersonal Relationships; Performing for or Working Directly with the Public. **Physical Work Conditions:** Exposed to Radiation; Physical Proximity; Disease or Infections; Contaminants; Walking and Running.

Radiologic Technologists

Take X rays and CAT scans or administer nonradioactive materials into patient's bloodstream for diagnostic purposes. Includes technologists who specialize in other modalities, such as computed tomography, ultrasound, and magnetic resonance. **O*NET Code:** 29-2034.01. **Average Salary:** $41,850. **Projected Growth:** 22.9%. **Annual Openings:** 21,000. **Education:** Associate degree. **Job Zone:** 3. **Education/Training Program(s)**—Allied Health Diagnostic, Intervention, and Treatment Professions, Other; Medical Radiologic Technology/Science—Radiation Therapist; Radiologic Technology/Science—Radiographer. **Related Knowledge/Courses:** Medicine and Dentistry; Customer and Personal Service; Psychology; Physics; Biology; Chemistry. **Personality Type:** Realistic. **Skills Required:** Instructing; Social Perceptiveness; Service Orientation; Reading Comprehension; Active Listening; Operation Monitoring; Speaking; Critical Thinking; Coordination. **Abilities:** Flexibility of Closure; Rate Control; Speed of Closure; Far Vision; Depth Perception. **Occupational Values:** Social Service; Ability Utilization; Authority; Co-workers; Security. **Interacting with Others:** Assisting and Caring for Others; Performing for or Working Directly with the Public; Establishing and Maintaining Interpersonal Relationships. **Physical Work Conditions:** Disease or Infections; Physical Proximity; Contaminants; Sounds, Noise Levels Are Distracting or Uncomfortable; Exposed to Radiation.

08.07 Medical Therapy

Audiologists

Assess and treat persons with hearing and related disorders. May fit hearing aids and provide auditory training. May perform research related to hearing problems. **O*NET Code:** 29-1121.00. **Average Salary:** $50,000. **Projected Growth:** 29.0%. **Annual Openings:** 1,000. **Education:** Master's degree. **Job**

© 2006, JIST Works

Zone: 4. **Education/Training Program(s)**—Audiology/Audiologist and Hearing Sciences; Audiology/Audiologist and Speech-Language Pathology/Pathologist; Communication Disorders Sciences and Services, Other; Communication Disorders, General. **Related Knowledge/Courses:** Therapy and Counseling; Medicine and Dentistry; Education and Training; Personnel and Human Resources; Economics and Accounting; Biology. **Personality Type:** Social. **Skills Required:** Instructing; Management of Personnel Resources; Management of Financial Resources; Writing; Service Orientation; Learning Strategies; Speaking; Reading Comprehension; Active Learning; Social Perceptiveness. **Abilities:** Speech Clarity; Oral Expression; Oral Comprehension; Speech Recognition; Written Expression. **Occupational Values:** Social Service; Authority; Achievement; Creativity; Ability Utilization; Co-workers. **Interacting with Others:** Interpreting the Meaning of Information for Others; Assisting and Caring for Others; Communicating with Persons Outside Organization; Coordinating the Work and Activities of Others. **Physical Work Conditions:** Sitting; Indoors.

Massage Therapists

Massage customers for hygienic or remedial purposes. **O*NET Code:** 31-9011.00. **Average Salary:** $29,950. **Projected Growth:** 27.1%. **Annual Openings:** 24,000. **Education:** Postsecondary vocational training. **Job Zone:** No data available. **Education/Training Program(s)**—Asian Bodywork Therapy; Massage Therapy/Therapeutic Massage; Somatic Bodywork; Somatic Bodywork and Related Therapeutic Services, Other. **Related Knowledge/Courses:** No data available. **Personality Type:** No data available. **Skills Required:** No data available. **Abilities:** No data available. **Occupational Values:** No data available. **Interacting with Others:** No data available. **Physical Work Conditions:** No data available.

Occupational Therapist Aides

Under close supervision of an occupational therapist or occupational therapy assistant, perform only delegated, selected, or routine tasks in specific situations. These duties include preparing patient and treatment room. **O*NET Code:** 31-2012.00. **Average Salary:** $23,070. **Projected Growth:** 42.6%. **Annual Openings:** 1,000. **Education:** Short-term on-the-job training. **Job Zone:** 2. **Education/Training Program(s)**—Occupational Therapist Assistant. **Related Knowledge/Courses:** Therapy and Counseling; Medicine and Dentistry; Psychology; Education and Training; Clerical; Biology. **Personality Type:** Social. **Skills Required:** Social Perceptiveness; Service Orientation; Technology Design; Instructing; Reading Comprehension; Speaking; Writing; Active Listening. **Abilities:** Static Strength; Gross Body Coordination; Extent Flexibility; Speech Recognition; Oral Expression. **Occupational Values:** Social Service; Achievement; Co-workers; Security; Supervision, Human Relations. **Interacting with Others:** Assisting and Caring for Others; Establishing and Maintaining Interpersonal Relationships; Communicating with Supervisors, Peers, or Subordinates. **Physical Work Conditions:** Disease or Infections; Kneeling, Crouching, Stooping, or Crawling; Spend Time Bending or Twisting the Body; Standing; Sitting.

Occupational Therapist Assistants

Assist occupational therapists in providing occupational therapy treatments and procedures. May, in accordance with state laws, assist in development of treatment plans, carry out routine functions, direct activity programs, and document the progress of treatments. Generally requires formal training. **O*NET Code:** 31-2011.00. **Average Salary:** $38,120. **Projected Growth:** 39.2%. **Annual Openings:** 3,000. **Education:** Associate degree. **Job Zone:** 3. **Education/Training Program(s)**—Occupational Therapist Assistant. **Related Knowledge/Courses:** Psychology; Therapy and Counseling; Sociology and Anthropology; Philosophy and Theology; Customer and Personal Service; Medicine and Dentistry. **Personality Type:** Social. **Skills Required:** Social Perceptiveness; Instructing; Service Orientation; Persuasion; Time Management; Learning Strategies; Monitoring; Active Listening; Writing; Critical Thinking. **Abilities:** Static Strength; Gross Body Coordination; Extent Flexibility; Speech Recognition; Oral Expression. **Occupational Values:** Social Service; Achievement; Co-workers; Security; Supervision, Human Relations. **Interacting with Others:** Assisting and Caring for Others; Establishing and Maintaining Interpersonal Relationships; Communicating with Supervisors, Peers, or Subordinates. **Physical Work Conditions:** Physical Proximity; Disease or Infections; Walking and Running; Contaminants; Very Hot or Cold; Cramped Work Space, Awkward Positions.

Occupational Therapists

Assess, plan, organize, and participate in rehabilitative programs that help restore vocational, homemaking, and daily living skills, as well as general independence, to disabled persons. **O*NET Code:** 29-1122.00. **Average Salary:** $53,320. **Projected Growth:** 35.2%. **Annual Openings:** 10,000. **Education:** Bachelor's degree. **Job Zone:** 4. **Education/Training Program(s)**—Occupational Therapy/Therapist. **Related Knowledge/Courses:** Therapy and Counseling; Psychology; Customer and Personal Service; Medicine and Dentistry; Education and Training; Sociology and Anthropology. **Personality Type:** Social. **Skills Required:** Social Perceptiveness; Service Orientation; Instructing; Science; Coordination; Technology Design; Persuasion; Reading Comprehension; Active Learning. **Abilities:** Inductive Reasoning; Problem Sensitivity; Speech Recognition; Originality; Deductive Reasoning; Speed of Closure. **Occupational Values:** Social Service; Achievement; Co-workers; Ability Utilization; Authority. **Interacting with Others:** Establishing and Maintaining Interpersonal Relationships; Assisting and Caring for Others; Communicating with Supervisors, Peers, or Subordinates; Training and Teaching Others. **Physical Work Conditions:** Physical Proximity; Disease or Infections; Sitting; Sounds, Noise Levels Are Distracting or Uncomfortable; Contaminants.

Physical Therapist Aides

Under close supervision of a physical therapist or physical therapy assistant, perform only delegated, selected, or routine tasks in specific situations. These duties include preparing the patient and the treatment area. **O*NET Code:** 31-2022.00. **Average Salary:** $21,070. **Projected Growth:** 46.4%. **Annual**

Openings: 8,000. **Education:** Associate degree. **Job Zone:** 2. **Education/Training Program(s)**—Physical Therapist Assistant. **Related Knowledge/Courses:** Psychology; Customer and Personal Service; Medicine and Dentistry; Therapy and Counseling; Philosophy and Theology; Clerical. **Personality Type:** Social. **Skills Required:** Social Perceptiveness; Service Orientation; Time Management; Learning Strategies; Negotiation; Persuasion; Operation Monitoring; Equipment Maintenance. **Abilities:** Oral Expression; Wrist-Finger Speed; Oral Comprehension; Static Strength. **Occupational Values:** Social Service; Achievement; Co-workers; Security; Supervision, Human Relations. **Interacting with Others:** Assisting and Caring for Others; Establishing and Maintaining Interpersonal Relationships; Performing for or Working Directly with the Public. **Physical Work Conditions:** Physical Proximity; Disease or Infections; Contaminants; Cramped Work Space, Awkward Positions; Sounds, Noise Levels Are Distracting or Uncomfortable.

Physical Therapist Assistants

Assist physical therapists in providing physical therapy treatments and procedures. May, in accordance with state laws, assist in the development of treatment plans, carry out routine functions, document the progress of treatment, and modify specific treatments in accordance with patient status and within the scope of treatment plans established by a physical therapist. Generally requires formal training. **O*NET Code:** 31-2021.00. **Average Salary:** $37,280. **Projected Growth:** 44.6%. **Annual Openings:** 10,000. **Education:** Associate degree. **Job Zone:** 3. **Education/Training Program(s)**— Physical Therapist Assistant. **Related Knowledge/Courses:** Psychology; Therapy and Counseling; Medicine and Dentistry; Education and Training; Customer and Personal Service; Sociology and Anthropology. **Personality Type:** Social. **Skills Required:** Social Perceptiveness; Service Orientation; Instructing; Time Management; Active Learning; Critical Thinking; Learning Strategies; Writing; Speaking. **Abilities:** Static Strength; Gross Body Coordination; Dynamic Strength; Trunk Strength; Extent Flexibility; Gross Body Equilibrium. **Occupational Values:** Social Service; Achievement; Co-workers; Security; Supervision, Human Relations. **Interacting with Others:** Assisting and Caring for Others; Performing for or Working Directly with the Public; Establishing and Maintaining Interpersonal Relationships. **Physical Work Conditions:** Physical Proximity; Disease or Infections; Keeping or Regaining Balance; Walking and Running; Cramped Work Space, Awkward Positions.

Physical Therapists

Assess, plan, organize, and participate in rehabilitative programs that improve mobility, relieve pain, increase strength, and decrease or prevent deformity of patients suffering from disease or injury. **O*NET Code:** 29-1123.00. **Average Salary:** $58,700. **Projected Growth:** 35.3%. **Annual Openings:** 16,000. **Education:** Master's degree. **Job Zone:** 5. **Education/Training Program(s)**—Kinesiotherapy/ Kinesiotherapist; Physical Therapy/Therapist. **Related Knowledge/Courses:** Psychology; Therapy and Counseling; Customer and Personal Service; Medicine and Dentistry; Biology; Sociology and Anthropology. **Personality Type:** Social. **Skills Required:** Instructing; Social Perceptiveness;

Reading Comprehension; Learning Strategies; Science; Service Orientation; Time Management; Critical Thinking; Coordination. **Abilities:** Problem Sensitivity; Inductive Reasoning; Deductive Reasoning; Stamina; Speed of Closure; Speech Recognition. **Occupational Values:** Social Service; Achievement; Co-workers; Ability Utilization; Authority. **Interacting with Others:** Assisting and Caring for Others; Establishing and Maintaining Interpersonal Relationships; Communicating with Supervisors, Peers, or Subordinates. **Physical Work Conditions:** Physical Proximity; Disease or Infections; Contaminants; Keeping or Regaining Balance; Cramped Work Space, Awkward Positions.

Radiation Therapists

Provide radiation therapy to patients as prescribed by a radiologist according to established practices and standards. Duties may include reviewing prescription and diagnosis; acting as liaison with physician and supportive care personnel; preparing equipment, such as immobilization, treatment, and protection devices; and maintaining records, reports, and files. May assist in dosimetry procedures and tumor localization. **O*NET Code:** 29-1124.00. **Average Salary:** $55,550. **Projected Growth:** 31.6%. **Annual Openings:** 1,000. **Education:** Associate degree. **Job Zone:** 3. **Education/Training Program(s)**—Medical Radiologic Technology/Science—Radiation Therapist. **Related Knowledge/Courses:** Medicine and Dentistry; Customer and Personal Service; Psychology; Biology; Physics; Mathematics. **Personality Type:** Social. **Skills Required:** Operation Monitoring; Technology Design; Operation and Control; Time Management; Instructing; Service Orientation; Management of Personnel Resources; Social Perceptiveness. **Abilities:** Speed of Closure; Oral Comprehension; Visualization; Response Orientation; Speech Clarity. **Occupational Values:** Social Service; Co-workers; Ability Utilization; Security; Achievement. **Interacting with Others:** Assisting and Caring for Others; Establishing and Maintaining Interpersonal Relationships; Performing for or Working Directly with the Public. **Physical Work Conditions:** Physical Proximity; Disease or Infections; Exposed to Radiation; Walking and Running; Sounds, Noise Levels Are Distracting or Uncomfortable.

Recreational Therapists

Plan, direct, or coordinate medically-approved recreation programs for patients in hospitals, nursing homes, or other institutions. Activities include sports, trips, dramatics, social activities, and arts and crafts. May assess a patient condition and recommend appropriate recreational activity. **O*NET Code:** 29-1125.00. **Average Salary:** $32,540. **Projected Growth:** 9.1%. **Annual Openings:** 3,000. **Education:** Bachelor's degree. **Job Zone:** 4. **Education/Training Program(s)**—Therapeutic Recreation/Recreational Therapy. **Related Knowledge/Courses:** Psychology; Therapy and Counseling; Sociology and Anthropology; Customer and Personal Service; Philosophy and Theology; Fine Arts. **Personality Type:** Social. **Skills Required:** Social Perceptiveness; Instructing; Persuasion; Writing; Learning Strategies; Coordination; Service Orientation; Active Listening. **Abilities:** Originality; Speech Recognition; Gross Body Coordination; Problem Sensitivity; Written Expression.

© 2006, JIST Works

Occupational Values: Social Service; Achievement; Co-workers; Creativity; Authority. **Interacting with Others:** Assisting and Caring for Others; Establishing and Maintaining Interpersonal Relationships; Communicating with Supervisors, Peers, or Subordinates. **Physical Work Conditions:** Physical Proximity; Disease or Infections; Contaminants; Sounds, Noise Levels Are Distracting or Uncomfortable; Extremely Bright or Inadequate Lighting.

Respiratory Therapists

Assess, treat, and care for patients with breathing disorders. Assume primary responsibility for all respiratory care modalities, including the supervision of respiratory therapy technicians. Initiate and conduct therapeutic procedures; maintain patient records; and select, assemble, check, and operate equipment. **O*NET Code:** 29-1126.00. **Average Salary:** $42,050. **Projected Growth:** 34.8%. **Annual Openings:** 10,000. **Education:** Associate degree. **Job Zone:** 3. **Education/Training Program(s)**—Respiratory Care Therapy/Therapist. **Related Knowledge/Courses:** Customer and Personal Service; Medicine and Dentistry; Psychology; Biology; Education and Training; Chemistry. **Personality Type:** Investigative. **Skills Required:** Instructing; Science; Active Learning; Service Orientation; Time Management; Reading Comprehension; Troubleshooting; Mathematics. **Abilities:** Inductive Reasoning; Problem Sensitivity; Speed of Closure; Category Flexibility; Flexibility of Closure. **Occupational Values:** Social Service; Co-workers; Achievement; Social Status; Authority. **Interacting with Others:** Assisting and Caring for Others; Establishing and Maintaining Interpersonal Relationships; Communicating with Supervisors, Peers, or Subordinates. **Physical Work Conditions:** Physical Proximity; Disease or Infections; Indoors; Standing; Exposed to Radiation; Hazardous Conditions.

Respiratory Therapy Technicians

Provide specific, well-defined respiratory care procedures under the direction of respiratory therapists and physicians. **O*NET Code:** 29-2054.00. **Average Salary:** $35,960. **Projected Growth:** 34.2%. **Annual Openings:** 5,000. **Education:** Postsecondary vocational training. **Job Zone:** 3. **Education/Training Program(s)**—Respiratory Care Therapy/Therapist; Respiratory Therapy Technician/Assistant. **Related Knowledge/Courses:** Medicine and Dentistry; Psychology; Customer and Personal Service; Chemistry; Physics; Biology. **Personality Type:** No data available. **Skills Required:** Troubleshooting; Time Management; Operation Monitoring; Social Perceptiveness; Instructing; Learning Strategies; Operation and Control; Service Orientation; Equipment Maintenance. **Abilities:** Perceptual Speed; Auditory Attention; Inductive Reasoning; Problem Sensitivity; Flexibility of Closure. **Occupational Values:** No data available. **Interacting with Others:** Assisting and Caring for Others; Establishing and Maintaining Interpersonal Relationships; Communicating with Supervisors, Peers, or Subordinates. **Physical Work Conditions:** Contaminants; Physical Proximity; Disease or Infections; Sounds, Noise Levels Are Distracting or Uncomfortable; Cramped Work Space, Awkward Positions.

Speech-Language Pathologists

Assess and treat persons with speech, language, voice, and fluency disorders. May select alternative communication systems and teach their use. May perform research related to speech and language problems. **O*NET Code:** 29-1127.00. **Average Salary:** $50,890. **Projected Growth:** 27.2%. **Annual Openings:** 10,000. **Education:** Master's degree. **Job Zone:** 5. **Education/Training Program(s)**—Audiology/Audiologist and Speech-Language Pathology/Pathologist; Communication Disorders Sciences and Services, Other; Communication Disorders, General; Speech-Language Pathology/Pathologist. **Related Knowledge/Courses:** Therapy and Counseling; Psychology; Education and Training; English Language; Sociology and Anthropology; Medicine and Dentistry. **Personality Type:** Social. **Skills Required:** Instructing; Social Perceptiveness; Learning Strategies; Service Orientation; Time Management; Active Learning; Coordination; Speaking. **Abilities:** Speech Recognition; Hearing Sensitivity; Inductive Reasoning; Flexibility of Closure; Originality. **Occupational Values:** Social Service; Authority; Achievement; Creativity; Ability Utilization; Co-workers. **Interacting with Others:** Establishing and Maintaining Interpersonal Relationships; Communicating with Supervisors, Peers, or Subordinates; Performing for or Working Directly with the Public; Coaching and Developing Others. **Physical Work Conditions:** Physical Proximity; Sitting; Sounds, Noise Levels Are Distracting or Uncomfortable; Contaminants; Disease or Infections.

08.08 Patient Care and Assistance

Home Health Aides

Provide routine, personal health care, such as bathing, dressing, or grooming, to elderly, convalescent, or disabled persons in the home of patients or in a residential care facility. **O*NET Code:** 31-1011.00. **Average Salary:** $18,200. **Projected Growth:** 48.1%. **Annual Openings:** 141,000. **Education:** Short-term on-the-job training. **Job Zone:** 2. **Education/Training Program(s)**—Home Health Aide/Home Attendant. **Related Knowledge/Courses:** Medicine and Dentistry; Psychology; Therapy and Counseling; Philosophy and Theology; Customer and Personal Service; Public Safety and Security. **Personality Type:** Social. **Skills Required:** Social Perceptiveness; Service Orientation; Instructing; Reading Comprehension; Writing; Persuasion; Active Listening; Learning Strategies; Monitoring. **Abilities:** Static Strength; Dynamic Strength; Sound Localization; Stamina; Time Sharing. **Occupational Values:** Social Service; Variety. **Interacting with Others:** Assisting and Caring for Others; Establishing and Maintaining Interpersonal Relationships; Communicating with Supervisors, Peers, or Subordinates. **Physical Work Conditions:** Physical Proximity; Contaminants; Disease or Infections; In an Enclosed Vehicle or Equipment; Walking and Running.

Licensed Practical and Licensed Vocational Nurses

Care for ill, injured, convalescent, or disabled persons in hospitals, nursing homes, clinics, private homes, group homes, and similar institutions. May work under the supervision of a registered nurse. Licensing required. **O*NET Code:** 29-2061.00. **Average Salary:** $33,110. **Projected Growth:** 20.2%. **Annual Openings:** 105,000. **Education:** Postsecondary vocational training. **Job Zone:** 3. **Education/Training Program(s)**—Licensed Practical /Vocational Nurse Training (LPN, LVN, Cert, Dipl, AAS). **Related Knowledge/Courses:** Psychology; Customer and Personal Service; Therapy and Counseling; Medicine and Dentistry; Philosophy and Theology; Sociology and Anthropology; Education and Training. **Personality Type:** Social. **Skills Required:** Service Orientation; Science; Active Listening; Time Management; Judgment and Decision Making; Instructing; Management of Personnel Resources; Writing; Operation Monitoring. **Abilities:** Problem Sensitivity; Speed of Closure; Speech Recognition; Inductive Reasoning; Perceptual Speed. **Occupational Values:** Social Service; Co-workers; Achievement; Ability Utilization; Activity; Social Status. **Interacting with Others:** Assisting and Caring for Others; Training and Teaching Others; Establishing and Maintaining Interpersonal Relationships. **Physical Work Conditions:** Physical Proximity; Disease or Infections; Walking and Running; Sounds, Noise Levels Are Distracting or Uncomfortable; Sitting.

Nursing Aides, Orderlies, and Attendants

Provide basic patient care under direction of nursing staff. Perform duties such as feeding, bathing, dressing, grooming, or moving patients or changing linens. **O*NET Code:** 31-1012.00. **Average Salary:** $20,760. **Projected Growth:** 24.9%. **Annual Openings:** 302,000. **Education:** Short-term on-the-job training. **Job Zone:** 2. **Education/Training Program(s)**—Health Aide; Nurse/Nursing Assistant/Aide and Patient Care Assistant. **Related Knowledge/Courses:** Psychology; Customer and Personal Service; Medicine and Dentistry; Education and Training; English Language; Foreign Language. **Personality Type:** Social. **Skills Required:** Social Perceptiveness; Time Management; Instructing; Service Orientation; Monitoring; Coordination; Operation Monitoring; Persuasion. **Abilities:** Speech Recognition; Static Strength; Extent Flexibility; Arm-Hand Steadiness; Perceptual Speed. **Occupational Values:** Social Service; Co-workers; Supervision, Technical; Security; Variety. **Interacting with Others:** Establishing and Maintaining Interpersonal Relationships; Assisting and Caring for Others; Training and Teaching Others. **Physical Work Conditions:** Physical Proximity; Disease or Infections; Walking and Running; Sounds, Noise Levels Are Distracting or Uncomfortable; Contaminants.

Psychiatric Aides

Assist mentally impaired or emotionally disturbed patients, working under direction of nursing and medical staff. **O*NET Code:** 31-1013.00. **Average Salary:** $23,110. **Projected Growth:** 14.5%. **Annual Openings:** 12,000. **Education:** Short-term on-the-job training. **Job Zone:** 2. **Education/Training Program(s)**—Health Aide; Psychiatric/ Mental Health Services Technician. **Related Knowledge/ Courses:** Psychology; Therapy and Counseling; Philosophy and Theology; Customer and Personal Service; Sociology and Anthropology; Medicine and Dentistry; Education and Training; Public Safety and Security. **Personality Type:** Social. **Skills Required:** Social Perceptiveness; Persuasion; Negotiation; Service Orientation; Instructing; Learning Strategies; Active Listening; Coordination. **Abilities:** Speech Recognition; Static Strength; Problem Sensitivity; Oral Expression; Inductive Reasoning. **Occupational Values:** Social Service; Co-workers; Supervision, Human Relations; Security; Variety; Supervision, Technical. **Interacting with Others:** Assisting and Caring for Others; Establishing and Maintaining Interpersonal Relationships; Resolving Conflicts and Negotiating with Others. **Physical Work Conditions:** Physical Proximity; Sounds, Noise Levels Are Distracting or Uncomfortable; Contaminants; Disease or Infections; Sitting; Walking and Running.

Psychiatric Technicians

Care for mentally impaired or emotionally disturbed individuals, following physician instructions and hospital procedures. Monitor patients' physical and emotional well-being and report to medical staff. May participate in rehabilitation and treatment programs, help with personal hygiene, and administer oral medications and hypodermic injections. **O*NET Code:** 29-2053.00. **Average Salary:** $25,670. **Projected Growth:** 5.9%. **Annual Openings:** 10,000. **Education:** Postsecondary vocational training. **Job Zone:** 3. **Education/Training Program(s)**—Psychiatric/Mental Health Services Technician. **Related Knowledge/Courses:** Therapy and Counseling; Psychology; Customer and Personal Service; Medicine and Dentistry; Biology; Clerical. **Personality Type:** Social. **Skills Required:** Social Perceptiveness; Service Orientation; Reading Comprehension; Science; Active Listening; Speaking; Critical Thinking; Learning Strategies. **Abilities:** Explosive Strength; Problem Sensitivity; Time Sharing; Oral Expression; Oral Comprehension. **Occupational Values:** Social Service; Co-workers; Supervision, Human Relations; Security; Advancement. **Interacting with Others:** Assisting and Caring for Others; Communicating with Supervisors, Peers, or Subordinates; Establishing and Maintaining Interpersonal Relationships. **Physical Work Conditions:** Indoors; Disease or Infections; Standing; Minor Burns, Cuts, Bites, or Stings; Common Protective or Safety Equipment.

08.09 Health Protection and Promotion

Athletic Trainers

Evaluate, advise, and treat athletes to assist in recovery from injury, avoid injury, or maintain peak physical fitness. **O*NET Code:** 29-9091.00. **Average Salary:** $32,990. **Projected Growth:** 29.9%. **Annual Openings:** 2,000. **Education:** Bachelor's degree. **Job Zone:** 5. **Education/Training Program(s)**—Athletic Training/Trainer.

© 2006, JIST Works

Related Knowledge/Courses: Therapy and Counseling; Medicine and Dentistry; Psychology; Customer and Personal Service; Biology; Education and Training. **Personality Type:** Social. **Skills Required:** Social Perceptiveness; Time Management; Service Orientation; Instructing; Management of Material Resources; Coordination; Management of Personnel Resources; Management of Financial Resources. **Abilities:** Stamina; Extent Flexibility; Static Strength; Dynamic Flexibility; Problem Sensitivity; Speed of Closure. **Occupational Values:** Social Service; Authority; Variety; Creativity; Autonomy. **Interacting with Others:** Assisting and Caring for Others; Establishing and Maintaining Interpersonal Relationships; Coaching and Developing Others. **Physical Work Conditions:** Physical Proximity; Outdoors; Very Hot or Cold; Contaminants; Disease or Infections.

Dietetic Technicians

Assist dietitians in the provision of food service and nutritional programs. Under the supervision of dietitians, may plan and produce meals based on established guidelines, teach principles of food and nutrition, or counsel individuals. **O*NET Code:** 29-2051.00. **Average Salary:** $22,870. **Projected Growth:** 20.2%. **Annual Openings:** 5,000. **Education:** Moderate-term on-the-job training. **Job Zone:** 3. **Education/Training Program(s)**—Dietetic Technician (DTR); Dietetics/Dietitian (RD); Dietitian Assistant; Foods, Nutrition, and Wellness Studies, General; Nutrition Sciences. **Related Knowledge/Courses:** Food Production; Medicine and Dentistry; Public Safety and Security. **Personality Type:** Social. **Skills Required:** Social Perceptiveness; Active Learning; Service Orientation; Reading Comprehension; Negotiation; Learning Strategies; Instructing; Management of Personnel Resources. **Abilities:** Originality; Fluency of Ideas; Oral Expression; Speech Clarity; Written Expression. **Occupational Values:** Social Service; Co-workers; Working Conditions; Authority; Variety. **Interacting with Others:** Establishing and Maintaining Interpersonal Relationships; Communicating with Supervisors, Peers, or Subordinates; Assisting and Caring for Others. **Physical Work Conditions:** Physical Proximity; Minor Burns, Cuts, Bites, or Stings; Sounds, Noise Levels Are Distracting or Uncomfortable; Disease or Infections; Walking and Running.

Dietitians and Nutritionists

Plan and conduct food service or nutritional programs to assist in the promotion of health and control of disease. May supervise activities of a department providing quantity food services, counsel individuals, or conduct nutritional research.

O*NET Code: 29-1031.00. **Average Salary:** $42,630. **Projected Growth:** 17.8%. **Annual Openings:** 8,000. **Education:** Bachelor's degree. **Job Zone:** 5. **Education/Training Program(s)**—Clinical Nutrition/Nutritionist; Dietetics and Clinical Nutrition Services, Other; Dietetics/Dietitian (RD); Foods, Nutrition, and Related Services, Other; Foods, Nutrition, and Wellness Studies, General; Foodservice Systems Administration/Management; Human Nutrition; Nutrition Sciences. **Related Knowledge/Courses:** Sociology and Anthropology; Food Production; Therapy and Counseling; Psychology; Education and Training; Customer and Personal Service. **Personality Type:** Investigative. **Skills Required:** Instructing; Social Perceptiveness; Persuasion; Learning Strategies; Science; Writing; Service Orientation; Speaking; Time Management. **Abilities:** Category Flexibility; Written Expression; Inductive Reasoning; Speech Recognition; Deductive Reasoning; Speech Clarity. **Occupational Values:** Social Service; Authority; Ability Utilization; Creativity; Achievement. **Interacting with Others:** Communicating with Supervisors, Peers, or Subordinates; Establishing and Maintaining Interpersonal Relationships; Training and Teaching Others. **Physical Work Conditions:** Sitting; Physical Proximity; Very Hot or Cold; Sounds, Noise Levels Are Distracting or Uncomfortable.

Embalmers

Prepare bodies for interment in conformity with legal requirements. **O*NET Code:** 39-4011.00. **Average Salary:** $34,500. **Projected Growth:** 8.3%. **Annual Openings:** 1,000. **Education:** Postsecondary vocational training. **Job Zone:** 3. **Education/Training Program(s)**—Funeral Service and Mortuary Science, General; Mortuary Science and Embalming/Embalmer. **Related Knowledge/Courses:** Customer and Personal Service; Chemistry; Biology; Philosophy and Theology; Clerical; Psychology. **Personality Type:** Realistic. **Skills Required:** Service Orientation; Social Perceptiveness; Management of Financial Resources; Instructing; Science; Management of Material Resources; Management of Personnel Resources; Time Management. **Abilities:** Static Strength; Visual Color Discrimination; Finger Dexterity; Arm-Hand Steadiness; Manual Dexterity. **Occupational Values:** Independence; Social Service; Autonomy; Security; Supervision, Technical. **Interacting with Others:** Assisting and Caring for Others; Establishing and Maintaining Interpersonal Relationships; Performing for or Working Directly with the Public. **Physical Work Conditions:** Hazardous Conditions; Contaminants; In an Enclosed Vehicle or Equipment; Physical Proximity; Disease or Infections.

09 Hospitality, Tourism, and Recreation

09.01 **Managerial Work in Hospitality and Tourism**

09.02 **Recreational Services**

09.03 **Hospitality and Travel Services**

09.04 **Food and Beverage Preparation**

09.05 **Food and Beverage Service**

09.06 **Sports**

09.07 **Barber and Beauty Services**

09.01 Managerial Work in Hospitality and Tourism

First-Line Supervisors/Managers of Food Preparation and Serving Workers

Supervise workers engaged in preparing and serving food. O*NET Code: 35-1012.00. **Average Salary:** $24,990. **Projected Growth:** 15.5%. **Annual Openings:** 154,000. **Education:** Work experience in a related occupation. **Job Zone:** 2. **Education/Training Program(s)**—Cooking and Related Culinary Arts, General; Foodservice Systems Administration/Management; Restaurant, Culinary, and Catering Management/Manager. **Related Knowledge/Courses:** Customer and Personal Service; Food Production; Administration and Management; Sales and Marketing; Personnel and Human Resources; Education and Training. **Personality Type:** Enterprising. **Skills Required:** Management of Personnel Resources; Management of Financial Resources; Instructing; Equipment Maintenance; Learning Strategies; Monitoring; Service Orientation; Negotiation. **Abilities:** Speech Recognition; Time Sharing; Deductive Reasoning; Oral Expression; Category Flexibility. **Occupational Values:** Authority; Co-workers; Responsibility; Creativity; Autonomy. **Interacting with Others:** Communicating with Supervisors, Peers, or Subordinates; Establishing and Maintaining Interpersonal Relationships; Performing for or Working Directly with the Public. **Physical Work Conditions:** Physical Proximity; Very Hot or Cold; Sounds, Noise Levels Are Distracting or Uncomfortable; Minor Burns, Cuts, Bites, or Stings; Walking and Running.

First-Line Supervisors/Managers of Personal Service Workers

Supervise and coordinate activities of personal service workers such as flight attendants, hairdressers, or caddies. O*NET Code: 39-1021.00. **Average Salary:** $29,860. **Projected Growth:** 9.4%. **Annual Openings:** 26,000. **Education:** Work experience in a related occupation. **Job Zone:** 3. **Education/Training Program(s)**—No data available. **Related Knowledge/Courses:** Administration and Management; Customer and Personal Service; Personnel and Human Resources; Psychology; Education and Training; Economics and Accounting. **Personality Type:** Enterprising. **Skills Required:** Service Orientation; Management of Personnel Resources; Coordination; Time Management; Management of Financial Resources; Management of Material Resources; Negotiation; Learning Strategies. **Abilities:** Time Sharing; Fluency of Ideas; Written Expression; Originality; Far Vision. **Occupational Values:** Authority; Co-workers; Autonomy; Working Conditions; Responsibility. **Interacting with Others:** Communicating with Supervisors, Peers, or Subordinates; Coordinating the Work and Activities of Others; Establishing and Maintaining Interpersonal Relationships; Guiding, Directing, and Motivating Subordinates. **Physical Work Conditions:** Indoors; Standing; Sitting.

Food Service Managers

Plan, direct, or coordinate activities of an organization or department that serves food and beverages. O*NET Code: 11-9051.00. **Average Salary:** $37,950. **Projected Growth:** 11.5%. **Annual Openings:** 58,000. **Education:** Work experience in a related occupation. **Job Zone:** 3. **Education/Training Program(s)**—Hospitality Administration/Management, General; Hotel/Motel Administration/Management; Restaurant, Culinary, and Catering Management/Manager; Restaurant/Food Services Management. **Related Knowledge/Courses:** Customer and Personal Service; Sales and Marketing; Food Production; Production and Processing; Administration and Management; Personnel and Human Resources. **Personality Type:** Enterprising. **Skills Required:** Management of Personnel Resources; Management of Financial Resources; Time Management; Monitoring; Instructing; Service Orientation; Learning Strategies; Management of Material Resources. **Abilities:** Speech Recognition; Mathematical Reasoning; Perceptual Speed; Visual Color Discrimination; Originality. **Occupational Values:** Authority; Creativity; Autonomy; Responsibility; Security. **Interacting with Others:** Establishing and Maintaining Interpersonal Relationships; Resolving Conflicts and Negotiating with Others; Communicating with Supervisors, Peers, or Subordinates. **Physical Work Conditions:** Very Hot or Cold; Physical Proximity; Walking and Running; Minor Burns, Cuts, Bites, or Stings; Sounds, Noise Levels Are Distracting or Uncomfortable.

Gaming Managers

Plan, organize, direct, control, or coordinate gaming operations in a casino. Formulate gaming policies for their area of responsibility. O*NET Code: 11-9071.00. **Average Salary:** $57,930. **Projected Growth:** 12.4%. **Annual Openings:** 1,000. **Education:** Work experience plus degree. **Job Zone:** 3. **Education/Training Program(s)**—Personal and Culinary Services, Other. **Related Knowledge/Courses:** Economics and Accounting; Administration and Management; Personnel and Human Resources; Customer and Personal Service; Mathematics; Education and Training. **Personality Type:** Enterprising. **Skills Required:** Management of Financial Resources; Management of Personnel Resources; Negotiation; Management of Material Resources; Time Management; Speaking; Critical Thinking; Social Perceptiveness. **Abilities:** Mathematical Reasoning; Number Facility; Time Sharing; Oral Comprehension; Oral Expression; Far Vision. **Occupational Values:** Authority; Social Service; Responsibility; Creativity; Autonomy. **Interacting with Others:** Monitoring and Controlling Resources; Communicating with Supervisors, Peers, or Subordinates; Establishing and Maintaining Interpersonal Relationships. **Physical Work Conditions:** Indoors; Sitting; Standing; Walking and Running; Extremely Bright or Inadequate Lighting.

Gaming Supervisors

Supervise gaming operations and personnel in an assigned area. Circulate among tables and observe operations. Ensure that stations and games are covered for each shift. May explain and interpret operating rules of house to patrons. May plan and organize activities and create friendly atmosphere for guests in hotels/casinos. May adjust service complaints. **O*NET Code:** 39-1011.00. **Average Salary:** $40,650. **Projected Growth:** 15.7%. **Annual Openings:** 6,000. **Education:** Postsecondary vocational training. **Job Zone:** 2. **Education/Training Program(s)**—No data available. **Related Knowledge/Courses:** Customer and Personal Service; Psychology; Education and Training; Mathematics; Personnel and Human Resources; Law and Government. **Personality Type:** Enterprising. **Skills Required:** Instructing; Management of Personnel Resources; Service Orientation; Social Perceptiveness; Monitoring; Critical Thinking; Persuasion; Learning Strategies; Time Management. **Abilities:** Mathematical Reasoning; Number Facility; Time Sharing; Oral Comprehension; Oral Expression; Far Vision. **Occupational Values:** Authority; Social Service; Responsibility; Creativity; Autonomy. **Interacting with Others:** Guiding, Directing, and Motivating Subordinates; Performing for or Working Directly with the Public; Communicating with Supervisors, Peers, or Subordinates; Establishing and Maintaining Interpersonal Relationships. **Physical Work Conditions:** Sounds, Noise Levels Are Distracting or Uncomfortable; Physical Proximity; Contaminants; Extremely Bright or Inadequate Lighting; Standing.

Lodging Managers

Plan, direct, or coordinate activities of an organization or department that provides lodging and other accommodations. **O*NET Code:** 11-9081.00. **Average Salary:** $36,350. **Projected Growth:** 6.6%. **Annual Openings:** 10,000. **Education:** Work experience in a related occupation. **Job Zone:** 3. **Education/Training Program(s)**—Hospitality Administration/Management, General; Hospitality and Recreation Marketing Operations; Hotel/Motel Administration/Management; Resort Management; Selling Skills and Sales Operations. **Related Knowledge/Courses:** Clerical; Sales and Marketing; Customer and Personal Service; Personnel and Human Resources; Psychology; Administration and Management; Economics and Accounting. **Personality Type:** Enterprising. **Skills Required:** Management of Financial Resources; Negotiation; Social Perceptiveness; Management of Material Resources; Monitoring; Persuasion; Time Management; Management of Personnel Resources. **Abilities:** Speech Recognition; Written Expression; Oral Comprehension; Problem Sensitivity; Deductive Reasoning; Memorization. **Occupational Values:** Authority; Autonomy; Social Service; Responsibility; Working Conditions; Creativity. **Interacting with Others:** Establishing and Maintaining Interpersonal Relationships; Resolving Conflicts and Negotiating with Others; Performing for or Working Directly with the Public. **Physical Work Conditions:** Physical Proximity; Sitting; Very Hot or Cold; Sounds, Noise Levels Are Distracting or Uncomfortable; Indoors.

09.02 Recreational Services

Amusement and Recreation Attendants

Perform variety of attending duties at amusement or recreation facility. May schedule use of recreation facilities, maintain and provide equipment to participants of sporting events or recreational pursuits, or operate amusement concessions and rides. **O*NET Code:** 39-3091.00. **Average Salary:** $15,300. **Projected Growth:** 27.8%. **Annual Openings:** 66,000. **Education:** Short-term on-the-job training. **Job Zone:** 1. **Education/Training Program(s)**—No data available. **Related Knowledge/Courses:** Customer and Personal Service; Sales and Marketing; Mechanical; Public Safety and Security; Communications and Media; Economics and Accounting; Psychology. **Personality Type:** Realistic. **Skills Required:** Repairing; Service Orientation; Operation and Control; Operation Monitoring; Equipment Maintenance; Management of Material Resources. **Abilities:** Rate Control; Reaction Time; Peripheral Vision; Spatial Orientation; Night Vision. **Occupational Values:** Social Service; Co-workers; Supervision, Technical; Moral Values; Authority. **Interacting with Others:** Performing for or Working Directly with the Public; Establishing and Maintaining Interpersonal Relationships; Communicating with Persons Outside Organization. **Physical Work Conditions:** Outdoors; Very Hot or Cold; Walking and Running; Standing; Extremely Bright or Inadequate Lighting.

Gaming and Sports Book Writers and Runners

Assist in the operation of games such as keno and bingo. Scan winning tickets presented by patrons, calculate amount of winnings, and pay patrons. May operate keno and bingo equipment. May start gaming equipment that randomly selects numbers. May announce number selected until total numbers specified for each game are selected. May pick up tickets from players; collect bets; and receive, verify, and record patrons' cash wagers. **O*NET Code:** 39-3012.00. **Average Salary:** $18,980. **Projected Growth:** 24.4%. **Annual Openings:** 5,000. **Education:** Postsecondary vocational training. **Job Zone:** 2. **Education/Training Program(s)**—No data available. **Related Knowledge/Courses:** Sales and Marketing; Law and Government; Psychology; Foreign Language; Customer and Personal Service; Mathematics; Sociology and Anthropology. **Personality Type:** Enterprising. **Skills Required:** Service Orientation. **Abilities:** Perceptual Speed; Memorization; Auditory Attention; Wrist-Finger Speed; Peripheral Vision. **Occupational Values:** Supervision, Technical; Co-workers; Compensation; Working Conditions. **Interacting with Others:** Performing for or Working Directly with the Public; Establishing and Maintaining Interpersonal Relationships; Communicating with Persons Outside Organization. **Physical Work Conditions:** Spend Time Making Repetitive Motions; Standing; Indoors; Sitting; Walking and Running.

© 2006, JIST Works

Gaming Dealers

Operate table games. Stand or sit behind table and operate games of chance by dispensing the appropriate number of cards or blocks to players or operating other gaming equipment. Compare the house's hand against players' hands and pay off or collect players' money or chips. O*NET Code: 39-3011.00. **Average Salary:** $14,230. **Projected Growth:** 24.7%. **Annual Openings:** 26,000. **Education:** Postsecondary vocational training. **Job Zone:** 2. **Education/Training Program(s)**—No data available. **Related Knowledge/Courses:** Customer and Personal Service; Psychology; Mathematics; Sales and Marketing; Sociology and Anthropology; Education and Training; Law and Government. **Personality Type:** Enterprising. **Skills Required:** Service Orientation; Speaking; Social Perceptiveness; Coordination; Mathematics; Critical Thinking; Active Listening; Instructing. **Abilities:** Perceptual Speed; Memorization; Auditory Attention; Wrist-Finger Speed; Peripheral Vision. **Occupational Values:** Supervision, Technical; Co-workers; Compensation; Working Conditions. **Interacting with Others:** Performing for or Working Directly with the Public; Communicating with Supervisors, Peers, or Subordinates; Establishing and Maintaining Interpersonal Relationships. **Physical Work Conditions:** Sounds, Noise Levels Are Distracting or Uncomfortable; Physical Proximity; Standing; Extremely Bright or Inadequate Lighting; Contaminants.

Locker Room, Coatroom, and Dressing Room Attendants

Provide personal items to patrons or customers in locker rooms, dressing rooms, or coatrooms. O*NET Code: 39-3093.00. **Average Salary:** $17,480. **Projected Growth:** 27.8%. **Annual Openings:** 66,000. **Education:** Short-term on-the-job training. **Job Zone:** 1. **Education/Training Program(s)**—No data available. **Related Knowledge/Courses:** Customer and Personal Service; Sales and Marketing; Personnel and Human Resources. **Personality Type:** Social. **Skills Required:** Service Orientation; Negotiation; Instructing; Social Perceptiveness; Critical Thinking; Persuasion; Reading Comprehension; Speaking; Time Management. **Abilities:** Auditory Attention; Speech Recognition; Night Vision; Response Orientation; Speech Clarity. **Occupational Values:** Social Service; Variety; Working Conditions; Co-workers. **Interacting with Others:** Establishing and Maintaining Interpersonal Relationships; Performing for or Working Directly with the Public; Communicating with Supervisors, Peers, or Subordinates; Training and Teaching Others. **Physical Work Conditions:** Walking and Running; Keeping or Regaining Balance; Physical Proximity; Standing; Kneeling, Crouching, Stooping, or Crawling.

Motion Picture Projectionists

Set up and operate motion picture projection and related sound reproduction equipment. O*NET Code: 39-3021.00. **Average Salary:** $17,070. **Projected Growth:** 0.4%. **Annual Openings:** 1,000. **Education:** Short-term on-the-job training. **Job Zone:** 2. **Education/Training Program(s)**—No data available. **Related Knowledge/Courses:** Communications and Media; Fine Arts; Telecommunications. **Personality Type:** Realistic. **Skills Required:** Installation; Repairing; Operation Monitoring; Equipment Maintenance; Operation and Control;

Technology Design. **Abilities:** Hearing Sensitivity; Rate Control; Sound Localization; Night Vision; Arm-Hand Steadiness; Response Orientation. **Occupational Values:** Independence; Working Conditions; Moral Values; Supervision, Technical; Supervision, Human Relations. **Interacting with Others:** Communicating with Supervisors, Peers, or Subordinates; Establishing and Maintaining Interpersonal Relationships; Interpreting the Meaning of Information for Others; Selling or Influencing Others; Resolving Conflicts and Negotiating with Others; Performing for or Working Directly with the Public. **Physical Work Conditions:** Sitting; Sounds, Noise Levels Are Distracting or Uncomfortable; Extremely Bright or Inadequate Lighting; Indoors; Using Hands on Objects, Tools, or Controls; Spend Time Bending or Twisting the Body.

Recreation Workers

Conduct recreation activities with groups in public, private, or volunteer agencies or recreation facilities. Organize and promote activities such as arts and crafts, sports, games, music, dramatics, social recreation, camping, and hobbies, taking into account the needs and interests of individual members. O*NET Code: 39-9032.00. **Average Salary:** $18,950. **Projected Growth:** 20.5%. **Annual Openings:** 56,000. **Education:** Bachelor's degree. **Job Zone:** 4. **Education/Training Program(s)**—Health and Physical Education/Fitness, Other; Parks, Recreation and Leisure Facilities Management; Parks, Recreation and Leisure Studies; Parks, Recreation, Leisure and Fitness Studies, Other; Sport and Fitness Administration/Management. **Related Knowledge/Courses:** Customer and Personal Service; Psychology; Education and Training; Clerical; Sales and Marketing; Sociology and Anthropology. **Personality Type:** Social. **Skills Required:** Management of Personnel Resources; Service Orientation; Management of Financial Resources; Social Perceptiveness; Time Management; Management of Material Resources; Instructing; Coordination. **Abilities:** Memorization; Originality; Speech Recognition; Speech Clarity; Fluency of Ideas. **Occupational Values:** Social Service; Creativity; Authority; Co-workers; Variety; Autonomy. **Interacting with Others:** Establishing and Maintaining Interpersonal Relationships; Communicating with Persons Outside Organization; Communicating with Supervisors, Peers, or Subordinates; Resolving Conflicts and Negotiating with Others. **Physical Work Conditions:** Sounds, Noise Levels Are Distracting or Uncomfortable; Physical Proximity; Sitting; Contaminants; Very Hot or Cold.

Slot Key Persons

Coordinate/supervise functions of slot department workers to provide service to patrons. Handle and settle complaints of players. Verify and pay off jackpots. Reset slot machines after payoffs. Make minor repairs or adjustments to slot machines. Recommend removal of slot machines for repair. Report hazards and enforce safety rules. O*NET Code: 39-1012.00. **Average Salary:** $22,770. **Projected Growth:** 14.8%. **Annual Openings:** 3,000. **Education:** Short-term on-the-job training. **Job Zone:** 2. **Education/Training Program(s)**—No data available. **Related Knowledge/Courses:** Customer and Personal Service; Administration and Management; Public Safety and Security; Sales and Marketing; Education and Training;

Personnel and Human Resources. **Personality Type:** No data available. **Skills Required:** Social Perceptiveness; Service Orientation; Negotiation; Learning Strategies; Time Management; Management of Personnel Resources; Instructing; Critical Thinking. **Abilities:** No data available. **Occupational Values:** No data available. **Interacting with Others:** Communicating with Supervisors, Peers, or Subordinates; Establishing and Maintaining Interpersonal Relationships; Performing for or Working Directly with the Public. **Physical Work Conditions:** Sounds, Noise Levels Are Distracting or Uncomfortable; Physical Proximity; Walking and Running; Contaminants; Cramped Work Space, Awkward Positions.

Ushers, Lobby Attendants, and Ticket Takers

Assist patrons at entertainment events by performing duties such as collecting admission tickets and passes from patrons, assisting in finding seats, searching for lost articles, and locating such facilities as rest rooms and telephones. **O*NET Code:** 39-3031.00. **Average Salary:** $14,910. **Projected Growth:** 15.5%. **Annual Openings:** 27,000. **Education:** Short-term on-the-job training. **Job Zone:** 1. **Education/Training Program(s)**—No data available. **Related Knowledge/Courses:** Sales and Marketing; Customer and Personal Service; Foreign Language; Telecommunications. **Personality Type:** Social. **Skills Required:** Service Orientation. **Abilities:** Spatial Orientation; Night Vision. **Occupational Values:** Social Service; Co-workers; Supervision, Technical; Working Conditions. **Interacting with Others:** Performing for or Working Directly with the Public; Establishing and Maintaining Interpersonal Relationships; Assisting and Caring for Others. **Physical Work Conditions:** Standing; Walking and Running; Spend Time Bending or Twisting the Body; Indoors; Extremely Bright or Inadequate Lighting.

09.03 Hospitality and Travel Services

Baggage Porters and Bellhops

Handle baggage for travelers at transportation terminals or for guests at hotels or similar establishments. **O*NET Code:** 39-6011.00. **Average Salary:** $18,030. **Projected Growth:** 14.4%. **Annual Openings:** 15,000. **Education:** Short-term on-the-job training. **Job Zone:** 1. **Education/Training Program(s)**—No data available. **Related Knowledge/Courses:** Transportation; Public Safety and Security; Geography. **Personality Type:** Enterprising. **Skills Required:** Social Perceptiveness; Critical Thinking; Service Orientation; Coordination; Management of Personnel Resources; Instructing; Reading Comprehension; Negotiation. **Abilities:** Static Strength; Speech Recognition; Stamina; Gross Body Coordination; Extent Flexibility. **Occupational Values:** Social Service; Supervision, Technical; Co-workers; Independence; Working Conditions. **Interacting with Others:** Performing for or Working Directly with the Public; Establishing and Maintaining Interpersonal Relationships; Assisting and Caring for Others. **Physical Work Conditions:** Very Hot or Cold; Extremely Bright or Inadequate Lighting; Outdoors, Under Cover; Outdoors; Contaminants.

Concierges

Assist patrons at hotel, apartment, or office building with personal services. May take messages; arrange or give advice on transportation, business services, or entertainment; or monitor guest requests for housekeeping and maintenance. **O*NET Code:** 39-6012.00. **Average Salary:** $22,940. **Projected Growth:** 15.3%. **Annual Openings:** 4,000. **Education:** Short-term on-the-job training. **Job Zone:** 2. **Education/Training Program(s)**—No data available. **Related Knowledge/Courses:** Customer and Personal Service; Philosophy and Theology; Clerical; Psychology; Public Safety and Security; Communications and Media. **Personality Type:** No data available. **Skills Required:** Service Orientation; Social Perceptiveness; Management of Personnel Resources; Instructing; Persuasion; Critical Thinking; Learning Strategies; Time Management. **Abilities:** No data available. **Occupational Values:** No data available. **Interacting with Others:** Performing for or Working Directly with the Public; Establishing and Maintaining Interpersonal Relationships; Communicating with Supervisors, Peers, or Subordinates; Communicating with Persons Outside Organization. **Physical Work Conditions:** Physical Proximity; Sounds, Noise Levels Are Distracting or Uncomfortable; Sitting; Very Hot or Cold; Cramped Work Space, Awkward Positions; Standing.

Flight Attendants

Provide personal services to ensure the safety and comfort of airline passengers during flight. Greet passengers, verify tickets, explain use of safety equipment, and serve food or beverages. **O*NET Code:** 39-6031.00. **Average Salary:** $42,000. **Projected Growth:** 15.9%. **Annual Openings:** 23,000. **Education:** Long-term on-the-job training. **Job Zone:** 2. **Education/Training Program(s)**—Airline Flight Attendant. **Related Knowledge/Courses:** Customer and Personal Service; Medicine and Dentistry; Transportation; Geography; Public Safety and Security; Psychology. **Personality Type:** Enterprising. **Skills Required:** Service Orientation; Social Perceptiveness; Coordination; Negotiation. **Abilities:** Reaction Time; Gross Body Equilibrium; Speech Recognition; Speech Clarity; Gross Body Coordination. **Occupational Values:** Social Service; Supervision, Technical; Co-workers; Supervision, Human Relations; Company Policies and Practices. **Interacting with Others:** Performing for or Working Directly with the Public; Assisting and Caring for Others; Establishing and Maintaining Interpersonal Relationships. **Physical Work Conditions:** Standing; Walking and Running; Spend Time Bending or Twisting the Body; High Places; Indoors.

Hotel, Motel, and Resort Desk Clerks

Accommodate hotel, motel, and resort patrons by registering and assigning rooms to guests, issuing room keys, transmitting and receiving messages, keeping records of occupied rooms and guests' accounts, making and confirming reservations, and presenting statements to and collecting payments from departing guests. **O*NET Code:** 43-4081.00. **Average Salary:** $17,530. **Projected Growth:** 23.9%. **Annual Openings:** 46,000. **Education:** Short-term on-the-job training. **Job Zone:** 2. **Education/Training Program(s)**—Selling Skills and Sales Operations. **Related Knowledge/Courses:** Customer and Personal Service; Clerical; Sales and Marketing; Computers and Electronics; Administration and Management; Geography. **Personality Type:** Conventional. **Skills Required:** Service Orientation; Instructing; Critical Thinking; Learning Strategies; Social Perceptiveness; Persuasion; Negotiation; Active Listening. **Abilities:** Speech Recognition; Time Sharing; Speed of Closure; Speech Clarity; Oral Comprehension; Oral Expression. **Occupational Values:** Social Service; Working Conditions; Supervision, Human Relations; Supervision, Technical; Co-workers. **Interacting with Others:** Performing for or Working Directly with the Public; Establishing and Maintaining Interpersonal Relationships; Assisting and Caring for Others. **Physical Work Conditions:** Physical Proximity; Standing; Sounds, Noise Levels Are Distracting or Uncomfortable; Very Hot or Cold; Extremely Bright or Inadequate Lighting; Sitting.

Janitors and Cleaners, Except Maids and Housekeeping Cleaners

Keep buildings in clean and orderly condition. Perform heavy cleaning duties, such as cleaning floors, shampooing rugs, washing walls and glass, and removing rubbish. Duties may include tending furnace and boiler, performing routine maintenance activities, notifying management of need for repairs, and cleaning snow or debris from sidewalk. **O*NET Code:** 37-2011.00. **Average Salary:** $18,680. **Projected Growth:** 18.3%. **Annual Openings:** 454,000. **Education:** Short-term on-the-job training. **Job Zone:** 1. **Education/Training Program(s)**—No data available. **Related Knowledge/Courses:** Mechanical; Chemistry; Building and Construction; Transportation; Public Safety and Security; Physics. **Personality Type:** Realistic. **Skills Required:** Repairing; Equipment Maintenance; Installation; Troubleshooting. **Abilities:** Static Strength; Extent Flexibility; Stamina; Multilimb Coordination; Trunk Strength. **Occupational Values:** Independence; Moral Values; Co-workers. **Interacting with Others:** Communicating with Supervisors, Peers, or Subordinates; Establishing and Maintaining Interpersonal Relationships; Monitoring and Controlling Resources. **Physical Work Conditions:** Contaminants; Standing; Very Hot or Cold; Hazardous Conditions; Extremely Bright or Inadequate Lighting.

Maids and Housekeeping Cleaners

Perform any combination of light cleaning duties to maintain private households or commercial establishments, such as hotels, restaurants, and hospitals, in a clean and orderly manner. Duties include making beds, replenishing linens, cleaning rooms and halls, and vacuuming. **O*NET Code:** 37-2012.00. **Average Salary:** $16,770. **Projected Growth:** 9.2%. **Annual Openings:** 352,000. **Education:** Short-term on-the-job training. **Job Zone:** 1. **Education/Training Program(s)**—No data available. **Related Knowledge/Courses:** Customer and Personal Service; Chemistry. **Personality Type:** Realistic. **Skills Required:** None met the criteria. **Abilities:** Spatial Orientation; Trunk Strength; Stamina; Wrist-Finger Speed; Static Strength. **Occupational Values:** Independence; Moral Values; Social Service; Activity; Co-workers. **Interacting with Others:** Communicating with Supervisors, Peers, or Subordinates; Assisting and Caring for Others;

Communicating with Persons Outside Organization; Performing for or Working Directly with the Public. **Physical Work Conditions:** Standing; Walking and Running; Kneeling, Crouching, Stooping, or Crawling; Spend Time Making Repetitive Motions; Spend Time Bending or Twisting the Body.

Reservation and Transportation Ticket Agents

Make and confirm reservations for passengers and sell tickets for transportation agencies such as airlines, bus companies, railroads, and steamship lines. May check baggage and direct passengers to designated concourse, pier, or track. **O*NET Code:** 43-4181.02. **Average Salary:** $26,440. **Projected Growth:** 12.2%. **Annual Openings:** 35,000. **Education:** Short-term on-the-job training. **Job Zone:** 2. **Education/Training Program(s)**—Selling Skills and Sales Operations; Tourism and Travel Services Marketing Operations; Tourism Promotion Operations. **Related Knowledge/Courses:** Geography; Transportation; Sales and Marketing; Clerical; Computers and Electronics; Foreign Language; Telecommunications; Communications and Media. **Personality Type:** Conventional. **Skills Required:** Service Orientation; Active Listening; Speaking. **Abilities:** Speech Recognition; Memorization; Speech Clarity; Auditory Attention; Oral Expression. **Occupational Values:** Social Service; Supervision, Human Relations; Working Conditions; Supervision, Technical; Company Policies and Practices. **Interacting with Others:** Assisting and Caring for Others; Performing for or Working Directly with the Public; Communicating with Persons Outside Organization; Establishing and Maintaining Interpersonal Relationships. **Physical Work Conditions:** Standing; Indoors; Walking and Running; Sitting; Spend Time Making Repetitive Motions.

Tour Guides and Escorts

Escort individuals or groups on sightseeing tours or through places of interest, such as industrial establishments, public buildings, and art galleries. **O*NET Code:** 39-6021.00. **Average Salary:** $19,080. **Projected Growth:** 11.0%. **Annual Openings:** 9,000. **Education:** Short-term on-the-job training. **Job Zone:** 3. **Education/Training Program(s)**—Tourism and Travel Services Management. **Related Knowledge/Courses:** History and Archeology; Customer and Personal Service; Geography; Philosophy and Theology; Sociology and Anthropology; Fine Arts. **Personality Type:** Social. **Skills Required:** Speaking; Social Perceptiveness; Instructing; Reading Comprehension; Active Listening; Active Learning; Learning Strategies; Service Orientation. **Abilities:** Speech Clarity; Speech Recognition; Memorization; Spatial Orientation; Night Vision. **Occupational Values:** Social Service; Authority; Variety; Recognition; Supervision, Technical. **Interacting with Others:** Performing for or Working Directly with the Public; Establishing and Maintaining Interpersonal Relationships; Communicating with Persons Outside Organization. **Physical Work Conditions:** Physical Proximity; Indoors, Not Environmentally Controlled; Very Hot or Cold; Extremely Bright or Inadequate Lighting; Outdoors, Under Cover; Sounds, Noise Levels Are Distracting or Uncomfortable.

Transportation Attendants, Except Flight Attendants and Baggage Porters

Provide services to ensure the safety and comfort of passengers aboard ships, buses, or trains or within the station or terminal. Perform duties such as greeting passengers, explaining the use of safety equipment, serving meals or beverages, or answering questions related to travel. **O*NET Code:** 39-6032.00. **Average Salary:** $18,900. **Projected Growth:** 18.9%. **Annual Openings:** 6,000. **Education:** Short-term on-the-job training. **Job Zone:** 1. **Education/Training Program(s)—** Selling Skills and Sales Operations. **Related Knowledge/Courses:** Customer and Personal Service; Transportation; Foreign Language; Public Safety and Security; Communications and Media; Geography. **Personality Type:** Enterprising. **Skills Required:** Service Orientation. **Abilities:** Gross Body Equilibrium; Reaction Time; Night Vision; Glare Sensitivity; Speech Clarity. **Occupational Values:** Social Service; Co-workers; Supervision, Technical; Security; Supervision, Human Relations. **Interacting with Others:** Performing for or Working Directly with the Public; Assisting and Caring for Others; Establishing and Maintaining Interpersonal Relationships. **Physical Work Conditions:** Walking and Running; Spend Time Bending or Twisting the Body; Standing; Kneeling, Crouching, Stooping, or Crawling; Indoors.

Travel Agents

Plan and sell transportation and accommodations for travel agency customers. Determine destination, modes of transportation, travel dates, costs, and accommodations required. **O*NET Code:** 41-3041.00. **Average Salary:** $27,270. **Projected Growth:** –13.8%. **Annual Openings:** 14,000. **Education:** Postsecondary vocational training. **Job Zone:** 3. **Education/Training Program(s)—**Selling Skills and Sales Operations; Tourism and Travel Services Marketing Operations. **Related Knowledge/Courses:** Geography; Sales and Marketing; Clerical; Transportation; Customer and Personal Service; Computers and Electronics. **Personality Type:** Enterprising. **Skills Required:** Service Orientation; Persuasion; Negotiation; Active Listening; Time Management; Social Perceptiveness; Speaking; Critical Thinking. **Abilities:** Speech Recognition; Fluency of Ideas; Originality; Time Sharing; Oral Expression; Category Flexibility. **Occupational Values:** Social Service; Working Conditions; Autonomy; Recognition; Variety. **Interacting with Others:** Performing for or Working Directly with the Public; Establishing and Maintaining Interpersonal Relationships; Communicating with Persons Outside Organization. **Physical Work Conditions:** Sitting; Sounds, Noise Levels Are Distracting or Uncomfortable; Physical Proximity.

Travel Clerks

Provide tourists with travel information, such as points of interest, restaurants, rates, and emergency service. Duties include answering inquiries, offering suggestions, and providing literature pertaining to trips, excursions, sporting events, concerts, and plays. May make reservations, deliver tickets, arrange for visas, or contact individuals and groups to inform them of package tours. **O*NET Code:** 43-4181.01. **Average Salary:** $26,440. **Projected Growth:** 12.2%. **Annual Openings:** 35,000. **Education:** Short-term on-the-job training. **Job Zone:** 2. **Education/Training Program(s)—** Selling Skills and Sales Operations; Tourism and Travel Services Marketing Operations; Tourism Promotion Operations. **Related Knowledge/Courses:** Geography; Transportation; Customer and Personal Service; Clerical; Telecommunications. **Personality Type:** Conventional. **Skills Required:** Service Orientation; Speaking; Active Listening; Social Perceptiveness; Coordination; Mathematics. **Abilities:** Wrist-Finger Speed; Fluency of Ideas; Oral Expression; Oral Comprehension; Near Vision. **Occupational Values:** Social Service; Working Conditions; Supervision, Human Relations; Activity; Variety; Supervision, Technical. **Interacting with Others:** Assisting and Caring for Others; Establishing and Maintaining Interpersonal Relationships; Communicating with Persons Outside Organization; Performing for or Working Directly with the Public. **Physical Work Conditions:** Sitting; Indoors.

Travel Guides

Plan, organize, and conduct long distance cruises, tours, and expeditions for individuals and groups. **O*NET Code:** 39-6022.00. **Average Salary:** $28,020. **Projected Growth:** –0.3%. **Annual Openings:** 2,000. **Education:** Moderate-term on-the-job training. **Job Zone:** 2. **Education/Training Program(s)—** Selling Skills and Sales Operations. **Related Knowledge/Courses:** Geography; Transportation; Customer and Personal Service; Sales and Marketing; Medicine and Dentistry; Foreign Language; Communications and Media. **Personality Type:** Enterprising. **Skills Required:** Service Orientation; Management of Material Resources; Instructing; Operation and Control; Time Management; Coordination; Persuasion; Judgment and Decision Making. **Abilities:** Glare Sensitivity; Reaction Time; Stamina; Auditory Attention; Rate Control; Night Vision. **Occupational Values:** Social Service; Variety; Authority; Creativity; Autonomy. **Interacting with Others:** Performing for or Working Directly with the Public; Assisting and Caring for Others; Communicating with Persons Outside Organization. **Physical Work Conditions:** Outdoors; Walking and Running; Standing; Minor Burns, Cuts, Bites, or Stings; Specialized Protective or Safety Equipment.

09.04 Food and Beverage Preparation

Bakers, Bread and Pastry

Mix and bake ingredients according to recipes to produce small quantities of breads, pastries, and other baked goods for consumption on premises or for sale as specialty baked goods. **O*NET Code:** 51-3011.01. **Average Salary:** $21,070. **Projected Growth:** 11.2%. **Annual Openings:** 29,000. **Education:** Long-term on-the-job training. **Job Zone:** 3. **Education/Training Program(s)—**Baking and Pastry Arts/Baker/Pastry Chef. **Related Knowledge/Courses:** Food Production; Production and Processing. **Personality Type:** Realistic. **Skills Required:** None met the criteria. **Abilities:** Wrist-Finger Speed; Finger Dexterity. **Occupational Values:** Moral Values; Supervision,

© 2006, JIST Works

Technical; Independence; Supervision, Human Relations. **Interacting with Others:** Communicating with Persons Outside Organization; Communicating with Supervisors, Peers, or Subordinates; Performing for or Working Directly with the Public. **Physical Work Conditions:** Standing; Minor Burns, Cuts, Bites, or Stings; Indoors; Very Hot or Cold; Spend Time Making Repetitive Motions.

Butchers and Meat Cutters

Cut, trim, or prepare consumer-sized portions of meat for use or sale in retail establishments. **O*NET Code:** 51-3021.00. **Average Salary:** $26,020. **Projected Growth:** –2.5%. **Annual Openings:** 21,000. **Education:** Long-term on-the-job training. **Job Zone:** 3. **Education/Training Program(s)**—Meat Cutting/Meat Cutter. **Related Knowledge/Courses:** Food Production; Biology; Sales and Marketing. **Personality Type:** Realistic. **Skills Required:** Management of Personnel Resources; Management of Financial Resources. **Abilities:** Dynamic Strength; Manual Dexterity; Finger Dexterity. **Occupational Values:** Independence; Social Service; Moral Values; Responsibility. **Interacting with Others:** Performing for or Working Directly with the Public; Monitoring and Controlling Resources; Communicating with Persons Outside Organization. **Physical Work Conditions:** Minor Burns, Cuts, Bites, or Stings; Standing; Hazardous Equipment; Indoors; Spend Time Making Repetitive Motions.

Chefs and Head Cooks

Direct the preparation, seasoning, and cooking of salads, soups, fish, meats, vegetables, desserts, or other foods. May plan and price menu items, order supplies, and keep records and accounts. May participate in cooking. **O*NET Code:** 35-1011.00. **Average Salary:** $29,520. **Projected Growth:** 15.8%. **Annual Openings:** 33,000. **Education:** Postsecondary vocational training. **Job Zone:** 4. **Education/Training Program(s)**—Cooking and Related Culinary Arts, General; Culinary Arts/Chef Training. **Related Knowledge/Courses:** Administration and Management; Personnel and Human Resources; Economics and Accounting; Education and Training; Biology; Food Production. **Personality Type:** Enterprising. **Skills Required:** Management of Financial Resources; Management of Material Resources; Management of Personnel Resources; Coordination; Instructing; Time Management; Systems Evaluation; Negotiation. **Abilities:** Manual Dexterity; Perceptual Speed; Originality; Time Sharing; Finger Dexterity. **Occupational Values:** Authority; Responsibility; Creativity; Co-workers; Autonomy. **Interacting with Others:** Establishing and Maintaining Interpersonal Relationships; Communicating with Supervisors, Peers, or Subordinates; Monitoring and Controlling Resources. **Physical Work Conditions:** Minor Burns, Cuts, Bites, or Stings; Standing; Hazardous Equipment; Using Hands on Objects, Tools, or Controls; Very Hot or Cold.

Cooks, Fast Food

Prepare and cook food in a fast food restaurant with a limited menu. Duties of the cooks are limited to preparation of a few basic items and normally involve operating large-volume single-purpose cooking equipment. **O*NET Code:** 35-2011.00. **Average Salary:** $14,580. **Projected Growth:** 4.9%. **Annual Openings:** 165,000. **Education:** Short-term on-the-job training. **Job Zone:** 2. **Education/Training Program(s)**—

Food Preparation/Professional Cooking/Kitchen Assistant; Institutional Food Workers. **Related Knowledge/Courses:** Customer and Personal Service; Economics and Accounting. **Personality Type:** Realistic. **Skills Required:** None met the criteria. **Abilities:** Wrist-Finger Speed. **Occupational Values:** Moral Values; Co-workers; Supervision, Technical; Activity; Social Service. **Interacting with Others:** Performing for or Working Directly with the Public; Communicating with Persons Outside Organization; Establishing and Maintaining Interpersonal Relationships. **Physical Work Conditions:** Standing; Minor Burns, Cuts, Bites, or Stings; Indoors; Very Hot or Cold; Spend Time Making Repetitive Motions.

Cooks, Institution and Cafeteria

Prepare and cook large quantities of food for institutions such as schools, hospitals, or cafeterias. **O*NET Code:** 35-2012.00. **Average Salary:** $18,570. **Projected Growth:** 2.1%. **Annual Openings:** 121,000. **Education:** Short-term on-the-job training. **Job Zone:** 2. **Education/Training Program(s)**—Cooking and Related Culinary Arts, General; Culinary Arts and Related Services, Other; Food Preparation/Professional Cooking/Kitchen Assistant; Foodservice Systems Administration/Management; Institutional Food Workers. **Related Knowledge/Courses:** Customer and Personal Service; Food Production; Administration and Management; Economics and Accounting; Personnel and Human Resources; Production and Processing. **Personality Type:** Realistic. **Skills Required:** Management of Financial Resources; Management of Personnel Resources; Management of Material Resources; Active Learning. **Abilities:** Wrist-Finger Speed; Originality; Oral Expression; Fluency of Ideas; Time Sharing. **Occupational Values:** Authority; Co-workers; Supervision, Technical; Social Service; Responsibility. **Interacting with Others:** Monitoring and Controlling Resources; Coordinating the Work and Activities of Others; Communicating with Supervisors, Peers, or Subordinates; Establishing and Maintaining Interpersonal Relationships. **Physical Work Conditions:** Standing; Minor Burns, Cuts, Bites, or Stings; Using Hands on Objects, Tools, or Controls; Indoors; Very Hot or Cold.

Cooks, Restaurant

Prepare, season, and cook soups, meats, vegetables, desserts, or other foodstuffs in restaurants. May order supplies, keep records and accounts, price items on menu, or plan menu. **O*NET Code:** 35-2014.00. **Average Salary:** $19,400. **Projected Growth:** 15.9%. **Annual Openings:** 211,000. **Education:** Long-term on-the-job training. **Job Zone:** 2. **Education/Training Program(s)**—Cooking and Related Culinary Arts, General; Culinary Arts/Chef Training. **Related Knowledge/Courses:** Food Production; Production and Processing; Customer and Personal Service; Foreign Language; Chemistry; Education and Training. **Personality Type:** Realistic. **Skills Required:** Equipment Maintenance; Instructing; Active Learning; Time Management; Learning Strategies; Management of Personnel Resources; Social Perceptiveness; Troubleshooting. **Abilities:** Time Sharing; Manual Dexterity; Originality; Perceptual Speed; Multilimb Coordination. **Occupational Values:** Creativity; Authority; Co-workers; Responsibility; Social Service. **Interacting with Others:** Establishing and Maintaining Interpersonal

Relationships; Coordinating the Work and Activities of Others; Training and Teaching Others. **Physical Work Conditions:** Very Hot or Cold; Minor Burns, Cuts, Bites, or Stings; Physical Proximity; Standing; Sounds, Noise Levels Are Distracting or Uncomfortable.

Cooks, Short Order

Prepare and cook to order a variety of foods that require only a short preparation time. May take orders from customers and serve patrons at counters or tables. **O*NET Code:** 35-2015.00. **Average Salary:** $16,650. **Projected Growth:** 9.0%. **Annual Openings:** 64,000. **Education:** Short-term on-the-job training. **Job Zone:** 1. **Education/Training Program(s)**—Food Preparation/Professional Cooking/Kitchen Assistant; Institutional Food Workers. **Related Knowledge/Courses:** Food Production; Production and Processing; Customer and Personal Service; Foreign Language. **Personality Type:** Realistic. **Skills Required:** Time Management; Troubleshooting; Instructing; Management of Personnel Resources; Service Orientation; Learning Strategies; Judgment and Decision Making; Active Learning. **Abilities:** Speech Recognition; Time Sharing; Reaction Time; Wrist-Finger Speed; Visual Color Discrimination. **Occupational Values:** Moral Values; Social Service; Co-workers; Activity. **Interacting with Others:** Establishing and Maintaining Interpersonal Relationships; Performing for or Working Directly with the Public; Communicating with Supervisors, Peers, or Subordinates; Assisting and Caring for Others. **Physical Work Conditions:** Very Hot or Cold; Physical Proximity; Minor Burns, Cuts, Bites, or Stings; Standing; Indoors.

Dishwashers

Clean dishes, kitchen, food preparation equipment, or utensils. **O*NET Code:** 35-9021.00. **Average Salary:** $15,120. **Projected Growth:** 9.0%. **Annual Openings:** 166,000. **Education:** Short-term on-the-job training. **Job Zone:** 1. **Education/Training Program(s)**—Food Preparation/ Professional Cooking/Kitchen Assistant. **Related Knowledge/Courses:** Food Production. **Personality Type:** Realistic. **Skills Required:** None met the criteria. **Abilities:** Trunk Strength; Extent Flexibility; Peripheral Vision; Dynamic Strength; Static Strength. **Occupational Values:** Moral Values; Co-workers. **Interacting with Others:** Establishing and Maintaining Interpersonal Relationships; Communicating with Supervisors, Peers, or Subordinates; Assisting and Caring for Others. **Physical Work Conditions:** Standing; Minor Burns, Cuts, Bites, or Stings; Walking and Running; Indoors; Spend Time Making Repetitive Motions.

Food Preparation Workers

Perform a variety of food preparation duties other than cooking, such as preparing cold foods and shellfish, slicing meat, and brewing coffee or tea. **O*NET Code:** 35-2021.00. **Average Salary:** $16,590. **Projected Growth:** 20.2%. **Annual Openings:** 267,000. **Education:** Short-term on-the-job training. **Job Zone:** 1. **Education/Training Program(s)**—Cooking and Related Culinary Arts, General; Food Preparation/Professional Cooking/Kitchen Assistant; Institutional Food Workers. **Related Knowledge/Courses:** Food Production; Customer and Personal Service; Sales and Marketing; Production and Processing; Administration and

Management; Personnel and Human Resources. **Personality Type:** Realistic. **Skills Required:** Management of Personnel Resources; Instructing; Service Orientation; Social Perceptiveness; Negotiation; Learning Strategies; Persuasion; Management of Financial Resources. **Abilities:** Extent Flexibility; Auditory Attention; Speed of Limb Movement; Perceptual Speed; Static Strength; Trunk Strength. **Occupational Values:** Co-workers; Social Service; Supervision, Technical. **Interacting with Others:** Establishing and Maintaining Interpersonal Relationships; Performing for or Working Directly with the Public; Communicating with Supervisors, Peers, or Subordinates. **Physical Work Conditions:** Physical Proximity; Walking and Running; Very Hot or Cold; Minor Burns, Cuts, Bites, or Stings; Standing.

09.05 Food and Beverage Service

Bartenders

Mix and serve drinks to patrons directly or through waitstaff. **O*NET Code:** 35-3011.00. **Average Salary:** $15,170. **Projected Growth:** 8.6%. **Annual Openings:** 100,000. **Education:** Short-term on-the-job training. **Job Zone:** 2. **Education/Training Program(s)**—Bartending/Bartender. **Related Knowledge/Courses:** Customer and Personal Service; Psychology; Food Production; Sales and Marketing; Sociology and Anthropology; Philosophy and Theology. **Personality Type:** Enterprising. **Skills Required:** Social Perceptiveness; Persuasion; Service Orientation; Negotiation; Critical Thinking; Learning Strategies; Speaking; Active Learning; Instructing. **Abilities:** Speech Recognition; Problem Sensitivity; Static Strength; Gross Body Coordination; Category Flexibility. **Occupational Values:** Social Service; Supervision, Technical; Co-workers; Working Conditions. **Interacting with Others:** Performing for or Working Directly with the Public; Establishing and Maintaining Interpersonal Relationships; Communicating with Persons Outside Organization; Selling or Influencing Others. **Physical Work Conditions:** Physical Proximity; Walking and Running; Standing; Sounds, Noise Levels Are Distracting or Uncomfortable; Contaminants.

Combined Food Preparation and Serving Workers, Including Fast Food

Perform duties which combine both food preparation and food service. **O*NET Code:** 35-3021.00. **Average Salary:** $14,660. **Projected Growth:** 22.8%. **Annual Openings:** 734,000. **Education:** Short-term on-the-job training. **Job Zone:** 1. **Education/Training Program(s)**—Food Preparation/Professional Cooking/Kitchen Assistant; Institutional Food Workers. **Related Knowledge/Courses:** Food Production; Sales and Marketing; Customer and Personal Service; Personnel and Human Resources; Production and Processing; Economics and Accounting. **Personality Type:** Realistic. **Skills Required:** Instructing; Service Orientation; Social Perceptiveness; Time Management; Management of Personnel Resources. **Abilities:**

Speech Recognition; Speech Clarity; Trunk Strength; Multilimb Coordination; Auditory Attention. **Occupational Values:** Moral Values; Co-workers; Advancement. **Interacting with Others:** Performing for or Working Directly with the Public; Establishing and Maintaining Interpersonal Relationships; Coordinating the Work and Activities of Others. **Physical Work Conditions:** Physical Proximity; Walking and Running; Minor Burns, Cuts, Bites, or Stings; Standing; Very Hot or Cold.

Counter Attendants, Cafeteria, Food Concession, and Coffee Shop

Serve food to diners at counter or from a steam table. **O*NET Code:** 35-3022.00. **Average Salary:** $15,530. **Projected Growth:** 16.7%. **Annual Openings:** 190,000. **Education:** Short-term on-the-job training. **Job Zone:** 1. **Education/Training Program(s)**—Food Service, Waiter/ Waitress, and Dining Room Management/Manager. **Related Knowledge/Courses:** Sales and Marketing; Customer and Personal Service; Food Production; Psychology; Public Safety and Security; Administration and Management. **Personality Type:** Social. **Skills Required:** Social Perceptiveness; Negotiation; Management of Personnel Resources; Equipment Maintenance; Service Orientation; Troubleshooting; Persuasion; Instructing. **Abilities:** Extent Flexibility; Speech Recognition; Stamina; Time Sharing; Trunk Strength; Gross Body Coordination. **Occupational Values:** Social Service; Co-workers; Supervision, Technical; Moral Values. **Interacting with Others:** Performing for or Working Directly with the Public; Establishing and Maintaining Interpersonal Relationships; Communicating with Supervisors, Peers, or Subordinates; Selling or Influencing Others. **Physical Work Conditions:** Physical Proximity; Standing; Walking and Running; Sounds, Noise Levels Are Distracting or Uncomfortable; Minor Burns, Cuts, Bites, or Stings.

Dining Room and Cafeteria Attendants and Bartender Helpers

Facilitate food service. Clean tables; carry dirty dishes; replace soiled table linens; set tables; replenish supply of clean linens, silverware, glassware, and dishes; supply service bar with food; and serve water, butter, and coffee to patrons. **O*NET Code:** 35-9011.00. **Average Salary:** $14,680. **Projected Growth:** 14.9%. **Annual Openings:** 143,000. **Education:** Short-term on-the-job training. **Job Zone:** 1. **Education/ Training Program(s)**—Food Service, Waiter/Waitress, and Dining Room Management/Manager. **Related Knowledge/ Courses:** Administration and Management; Clerical. **Personality Type:** Realistic. **Skills Required:** Service Orientation. **Abilities:** Static Strength; Stamina; Wrist-Finger Speed; Speed of Limb Movement; Gross Body Coordination. **Occupational Values:** Supervision, Technical; Co-workers; Social Service; Moral Values. **Interacting with Others:** Communicating with Persons Outside Organization; Performing for or Working Directly with the Public; Establishing and Maintaining Interpersonal Relationships. **Physical Work Conditions:** Standing; Walking and Running; Indoors; Spend Time Bending or Twisting the Body; Minor Burns, Cuts, Bites, or Stings.

Food Servers, Nonrestaurant

Serve food to patrons outside of a restaurant environment, such as in hotels, hospital rooms, or cars. **O*NET Code:** 35-3041.00. **Average Salary:** $16,260. **Projected Growth:** 10.4%. **Annual Openings:** 47,000. **Education:** Short-term on-the-job training. **Job Zone:** 1. **Education/Training Program(s)**—Food Service, Waiter/Waitress, and Dining Room Management/Manager. **Related Knowledge/Courses:** Sales and Marketing; Food Production; Customer and Personal Service. **Personality Type:** Social. **Skills Required:** Service Orientation. **Abilities:** Wrist-Finger Speed; Speed of Limb Movement; Stamina; Static Strength; Sound Localization. **Occupational Values:** Social Service; Supervision, Technical; Co-workers; Moral Values. **Interacting with Others:** Performing for or Working Directly with the Public; Communicating with Persons Outside Organization; Assisting and Caring for Others. **Physical Work Conditions:** Standing; Walking and Running; Outdoors; Very Hot or Cold; Extremely Bright or Inadequate Lighting.

Hosts and Hostesses, Restaurant, Lounge, and Coffee Shop

Welcome patrons, seat them at tables or in lounge, and help ensure quality of facilities and service. **O*NET Code:** 35-9031.00. **Average Salary:** $15,500. **Projected Growth:** 16.4%. **Annual Openings:** 95,000. **Education:** Short-term on-the-job training. **Job Zone:** 1. **Education/Training Program(s)**—Food Service, Waiter/Waitress, and Dining Room Management/Manager. **Related Knowledge/Courses:** Customer and Personal Service; Food Production; Sales and Marketing; Administration and Management; Public Safety and Security. **Personality Type:** Enterprising. **Skills Required:** Service Orientation; Persuasion; Instructing; Social Perceptiveness; Negotiation; Learning Strategies. **Abilities:** Speech Recognition; Time Sharing; Trunk Strength; Far Vision; Stamina. **Occupational Values:** Supervision, Technical; Social Service; Co-workers; Authority; Working Conditions; Responsibility. **Interacting with Others:** Establishing and Maintaining Interpersonal Relationships; Performing for or Working Directly with the Public; Assisting and Caring for Others. **Physical Work Conditions:** Physical Proximity; Walking and Running; Standing; Sounds, Noise Levels Are Distracting or Uncomfortable; Indoors.

Waiters and Waitresses

Take orders and serve food and beverages to patrons at tables in dining establishment. **O*NET Code:** 35-3031.00. **Average Salary:** $14,130. **Projected Growth:** 17.5%. **Annual Openings:** 721,000. **Education:** Short-term on-the-job training. **Job Zone:** 1. **Education/Training Program(s)**—Food Service, Waiter/Waitress, and Dining Room Management/Manager. **Related Knowledge/Courses:** Customer and Personal Service; Food Production; Sales and Marketing; Psychology; Education and Training; Personnel and Human Resources. **Personality Type:** Social. **Skills Required:** Service Orientation; Persuasion; Instructing; Social Perceptiveness; Negotiation; Learning Strategies; Coordination; Speaking; Critical Thinking. **Abilities:** Gross Body Coordination; Speech Recognition; Stamina; Trunk Strength; Extent Flexibility. **Occupational Values:** Social Service; Supervision, Technical; Co-workers. **Interacting with**

Others: Performing for or Working Directly with the Public; Establishing and Maintaining Interpersonal Relationships; Communicating with Supervisors, Peers, or Subordinates. **Physical Work Conditions:** Physical Proximity; Walking and Running; Standing; Minor Burns, Cuts, Bites, or Stings; Very Hot or Cold; Keeping or Regaining Balance.

09.06 Sports

Athletes and Sports Competitors

Compete in athletic events. **O*NET Code:** 27-2021.00. **Average Salary:** $46,320. **Projected Growth:** 19.2%. **Annual Openings:** 3,000. **Education:** Long-term on-the-job training. **Job Zone:** 3. **Education/Training Program(s)**—Health and Physical Education, General. **Related Knowledge/Courses:** Biology; Communications and Media; Medicine and Dentistry. **Personality Type:** Enterprising. **Skills Required:** Monitoring; Coordination; Social Perceptiveness; Active Learning; Negotiation; Learning Strategies. **Abilities:** Stamina; Dynamic Strength; Dynamic Flexibility; Gross Body Coordination; Explosive Strength. **Occupational Values:** Recognition; Social Status; Ability Utilization; Compensation; Achievement; Co-workers. **Interacting with Others:** Communicating with Persons Outside Organization; Performing for or Working Directly with the Public; Establishing and Maintaining Interpersonal Relationships. **Physical Work Conditions:** Minor Burns, Cuts, Bites, or Stings; Walking and Running; Outdoors; Standing; Spend Time Bending or Twisting the Body.

Coaches and Scouts

Instruct or coach groups or individuals in the fundamentals of sports. Demonstrate techniques and methods of participation. May evaluate athletes' strengths and weaknesses as possible recruits or to improve the athletes' technique to prepare them for competition. Those required to hold teaching degrees should be reported in the appropriate teaching category. **O*NET Code:** 27-2022.00. **Average Salary:** $26,740. **Projected Growth:** 18.3%. **Annual Openings:** 26,000. **Education:** Long-term on-the-job training. **Job Zone:** 5. **Education/Training Program(s)**—Health and Physical Education, General; Physical Education Teaching and Coaching; Sport and Fitness Administration/Management. **Related Knowledge/Courses:** Education and Training; Psychology; Sales and Marketing; Personnel and Human Resources; Therapy and Counseling; Customer and Personal Service. **Personality Type:** Enterprising. **Skills Required:** Social Perceptiveness; Instructing; Persuasion; Negotiation; Management of Personnel Resources; Time Management; Learning Strategies; Management of Financial Resources. **Abilities:** Visualization; Gross Body Coordination; Fluency of Ideas; Speech Clarity; Speech Recognition. **Occupational Values:** Authority; Responsibility; Recognition; Autonomy; Creativity. **Interacting with Others:** Coaching and Developing Others; Communicating with Persons Outside Organization; Establishing and Maintaining Interpersonal Relationships; Coordinating the Work and Activities of Others; Developing and Building Teams. **Physical Work**

Conditions: Physical Proximity; Very Hot or Cold; Sounds, Noise Levels Are Distracting or Uncomfortable; Outdoors; Extremely Bright or Inadequate Lighting.

Umpires, Referees, and Other Sports Officials

Officiate at competitive athletic or sporting events. Detect infractions of rules and decide penalties according to established regulations. **O*NET Code:** 27-2023.00. **Average Salary:** $21,550. **Projected Growth:** 16.9%. **Annual Openings:** 3,000. **Education:** Long-term on-the-job training. **Job Zone:** 2. **Education/Training Program(s)**—No data available. **Related Knowledge/Courses:** Psychology; Sociology and Anthropology; Customer and Personal Service; Administration and Management; Personnel and Human Resources; English Language. **Personality Type:** Enterprising. **Skills Required:** Negotiation; Persuasion; Social Perceptiveness; Judgment and Decision Making; Coordination; Monitoring; Active Listening; Active Learning. **Abilities:** Far Vision; Glare Sensitivity; Peripheral Vision; Memorization; Perceptual Speed. **Occupational Values:** Authority; Responsibility; Ability Utilization; Achievement; Autonomy. **Interacting with Others:** Resolving Conflicts and Negotiating with Others; Establishing and Maintaining Interpersonal Relationships; Developing and Building Teams; Coaching and Developing Others. **Physical Work Conditions:** Sounds, Noise Levels Are Distracting or Uncomfortable; Physical Proximity; Walking and Running; Very Hot or Cold; Keeping or Regaining Balance.

09.07 Barber and Beauty Services

Barbers

Provide barbering services, such as cutting, trimming, shampooing, and styling hair; trimming beards; or giving shaves. **O*NET Code:** 39-5011.00. **Average Salary:** $20,280. **Projected Growth:** 6.5%. **Annual Openings:** 7,000. **Education:** Postsecondary vocational training. **Job Zone:** 3. **Education/Training Program(s)**—Barbering/Barber; Cosmetology, Barber/Styling, and Nail Instructor; Hair Styling/Stylist and Hair Design; Salon/Beauty Salon Management/Manager. **Related Knowledge/Courses:** Customer and Personal Service; Sales and Marketing; Economics and Accounting. **Personality Type:** Realistic. **Skills Required:** Service Orientation; Management of Financial Resources; Management of Material Resources. **Abilities:** Finger Dexterity; Arm-Hand Steadiness; Extent Flexibility; Visualization; Manual Dexterity. **Occupational Values:** Social Service; Autonomy; Recognition; Creativity; Moral Values. **Interacting with Others:** Establishing and Maintaining Interpersonal Relationships; Performing for or Working Directly with the Public; Assisting and Caring for Others; Monitoring and Controlling Resources. **Physical Work Conditions:** Standing; Minor Burns, Cuts, Bites, or Stings; Spend Time Making Repetitive Motions; Indoors; Using Hands on Objects, Tools, or Controls; Spend Time Bending or Twisting the Body.

© 2006, JIST Works

Hairdressers, Hairstylists, and Cosmetologists

Provide beauty services, such as shampooing, cutting, coloring, and styling hair and massaging and treating scalp. May also apply makeup, dress wigs, perform hair removal, and provide nail and skin care services. **O*NET Code:** 39-5012.00. **Average Salary:** $19,300. **Projected Growth:** 14.7%. **Annual Openings:** 68,000. **Education:** Postsecondary vocational training. **Job Zone:** 3. **Education/Training Program(s)—**Cosmetology and Related Personal Grooming Arts, Other; Cosmetology, Barber/Styling, and Nail Instructor; Cosmetology/Cosmetologist, General; Electrolysis/Electrology and Electrolysis Technician; Hair Styling/Stylist and Hair Design; Make-Up Artist/Specialist; Permanent Cosmetics/Makeup and Tattooing; Salon/Beauty Salon Management/Manager. **Related Knowledge/Courses:** Chemistry; Customer and Personal Service; Sales and Marketing; Education and Training; Administration and Management; English Language. **Personality Type:** Enterprising. **Skills Required:** Learning Strategies; Social Perceptiveness; Time Management; Management of Financial Resources; Service Orientation; Science; Persuasion; Active Learning; Operations Analysis. **Abilities:** Arm-Hand Steadiness; Visual Color Discrimination; Finger Dexterity; Manual Dexterity; Visualization; Speech Recognition. **Occupational Values:** Social Service; Autonomy; Achievement; Creativity; Recognition. **Interacting with Others:** Performing for or Working Directly with the Public; Providing Consultation and Advice to Others; Establishing and Maintaining Interpersonal Relationships. **Physical Work Conditions:** Contaminants; Hazardous Conditions; Minor Burns, Cuts, Bites, or Stings; Physical Proximity; Standing.

Manicurists and Pedicurists

Clean and shape customers' fingernails and toenails. May polish or decorate nails. **O*NET Code:** 39-5092.00. **Average Salary:** $17,490. **Projected Growth:** 22.7%. **Annual Openings:** 7,000. **Education:** Postsecondary vocational training. **Job Zone:** 1. **Education/Training Program(s)—**Cosmetology/Cosmetologist, General; Nail Technician/Specialist and Manicurist. **Related Knowledge/Courses:** Customer and Personal Service; Chemistry; Sociology and Anthropology. **Personality Type:** Enterprising. **Skills Required:** Service Orientation. **Abilities:** Visual Color Discrimination; Arm-Hand Steadiness; Finger Dexterity; Glare Sensitivity; Hearing Sensitivity. **Occupational Values:** Social Service; Autonomy; Moral Values; Independence; Working Conditions. **Interacting with Others:** Performing for or Working Directly with the Public; Establishing and Maintaining Interpersonal Relationships; Assisting and Caring for Others. **Physical Work Conditions:** Sitting; Using Hands on Objects, Tools, or Controls; Indoors; Hazardous Conditions; Minor Burns, Cuts, Bites, or Stings.

Shampooers

Shampoo and rinse customers' hair. **O*NET Code:** 39-5093.00. **Average Salary:** $14,560. **Projected Growth:** 16.6%. **Annual Openings:** 3,000. **Education:** Short-term on-the-job training. **Job Zone:** No data available. **Education/Training Program(s)—**Hair Styling/Stylist and Hair Design. **Related Knowledge/Courses:** No data available. **Personality Type:** No data available. **Skills Required:** No data available. **Abilities:** No data available. **Occupational Values:** No data available. **Interacting with Others:** No data available. **Physical Work Conditions:** No data available.

Skin Care Specialists

Provide skin care treatments to face and body to enhance an individual's appearance. **O*NET Code:** 39-5094.00. **Average Salary:** $23,670. **Projected Growth:** 19.4%. **Annual Openings:** 3,000. **Education:** Short-term on-the-job training. **Job Zone:** No data available. **Education/Training Program(s)—**Cosmetology/Cosmetologist, General; Facial Treatment Specialist/Facialist. **Related Knowledge/Courses:** No data available. **Personality Type:** No data available. **Skills Required:** No data available. **Abilities:** No data available. **Occupational Values:** No data available. **Interacting with Others:** No data available. **Physical Work Conditions:** No data available.

10 Human Service

10.01 **Counseling and Social Work**

10.02 **Religious Work**

10.03 **Child/Personal Care and Services**

10.04 **Client Interviewing**

10.01 Counseling and Social Work

Child, Family, and School Social Workers

Provide social services and assistance to improve the social and psychological functioning of children and their families and to maximize the family well-being and the academic functioning of children. May assist single parents, arrange adoptions, and find foster homes for abandoned or abused children. In schools, they address such problems as teenage pregnancy, misbehavior, and truancy. May also advise teachers on how to deal with problem children. **O*NET Code:** 21-1021.00. **Average Salary:** $34,300. **Projected Growth:** 23.2%. **Annual Openings:** 45,000. **Education:** Bachelor's degree. **Job Zone:** 5. **Education/Training Program(s)**—Juvenile Corrections; Social Work; Youth Services/Administration. **Related Knowledge/Courses:** Therapy and Counseling; Psychology; Sociology and Anthropology; Customer and Personal Service; Law and Government; Philosophy and Theology. **Personality Type:** Social. **Skills Required:** Social Perceptiveness; Service Orientation; Learning Strategies; Negotiation; Monitoring; Speaking; Active Listening; Persuasion. **Abilities:** Speech Recognition; Problem Sensitivity; Originality; Inductive Reasoning; Written Expression. **Occupational Values:** Social Service; Autonomy; Activity; Achievement; Variety; Authority. **Interacting with Others:** Establishing and Maintaining Interpersonal Relationships; Communicating with Supervisors, Peers, or Subordinates; Resolving Conflicts and Negotiating with Others. **Physical Work Conditions:** Sitting; Sounds, Noise Levels Are Distracting or Uncomfortable; In an Enclosed Vehicle or Equipment; Physical Proximity; Outdoors.

Clinical Psychologists

Diagnose or evaluate mental and emotional disorders of individuals through observation, interview, and psychological tests and formulate and administer programs of treatment. **O*NET Code:** 19-3031.02. **Average Salary:** $53,230. **Projected Growth:** 24.4%. **Annual Openings:** 17,000. **Education:** Master's degree. **Job Zone:** 4. **Education/Training Program(s)**—Clinical Child Psychology; Clinical Psychology; Counseling Psychology; Developmental and Child Psychology; Psychoanalysis and Psychotherapy; Psychology, General; School Psychology. **Related Knowledge/Courses:** Therapy and Counseling; Psychology; Administration and Management; Sociology and Anthropology; Customer and Personal Service; English Language. **Personality Type:** Investigative. **Skills Required:** Social Perceptiveness; Active Listening; Systems Evaluation; Persuasion; Speaking; Reading Comprehension; Systems Analysis; Science. **Abilities:** Written Expression; Inductive Reasoning; Oral Comprehension; Written Comprehension; Originality; Problem Sensitivity. **Occupational Values:** Social Service; Creativity; Autonomy; Responsibility; Ability Utilization. **Interacting with Others:** Communicating with Persons Outside Organization; Communicating with Supervisors, Peers, or Subordinates; Assisting and Caring for Others. **Physical Work Conditions:** Sitting; Indoors; Disease or Infections.

Counseling Psychologists

Assess and evaluate individuals' problems through the use of case history, interview, and observation and provide individual or group counseling services to assist individuals in achieving more effective personal, social, educational, and vocational development and adjustment. **O*NET Code:** 19-3031.03. **Average Salary:** $53,230. **Projected Growth:** 24.4%. **Annual Openings:** 17,000. **Education:** Master's degree. **Job Zone:** 5. **Education/Training Program(s)**—Clinical Child Psychology; Clinical Psychology; Counseling Psychology; Developmental and Child Psychology; Psychoanalysis and Psychotherapy; Psychology, General; School Psychology. **Related Knowledge/Courses:** Therapy and Counseling; Psychology; Sociology and Anthropology; Philosophy and Theology; Mathematics; Education and Training. **Personality Type:** Social. **Skills Required:** Social Perceptiveness; Active Listening; Learning Strategies; Critical Thinking; Persuasion; Reading Comprehension; Active Learning; Science; Monitoring. **Abilities:** Problem Sensitivity; Inductive Reasoning; Oral Expression; Oral Comprehension; Written Comprehension. **Occupational Values:** Social Service; Creativity; Autonomy; Achievement; Ability Utilization; Working Conditions. **Interacting with Others:** Communicating with Persons Outside Organization; Establishing and Maintaining Interpersonal Relationships; Assisting and Caring for Others; Providing Consultation and Advice to Others. **Physical Work Conditions:** Sitting; Indoors; Disease or Infections.

Marriage and Family Therapists

Diagnose and treat mental and emotional disorders, whether cognitive, affective, or behavioral, within the context of marriage and family systems. Apply psychotherapeutic and family systems theories and techniques in the delivery of professional services to individuals, couples, and families for the purpose of treating such diagnosed nervous and mental disorders. **O*NET Code:** 21-1013.00. **Average Salary:** $38,210. **Projected Growth:** 22.4%. **Annual Openings:** 3,000. **Education:** Master's degree. **Job Zone:** No data available. **Education/Training Program(s)**—Clinical Pastoral Counseling/Patient Counseling; Marriage and Family Therapy/Counseling; Social Work. **Related Knowledge/Courses:** No data available. **Personality Type:** No data available. **Skills Required:** No data available. **Abilities:** No data available. **Occupational Values:** No data available. **Interacting with Others:** No data available. **Physical Work Conditions:** No data available.

Medical and Public Health Social Workers

Provide persons, families, or vulnerable populations with the psychosocial support needed to cope with chronic, acute, or terminal illnesses, such as Alzheimer's, cancer, or AIDS. Services include advising family caregivers, providing patient education and counseling, and making necessary referrals for other social services. **O*NET Code:** 21-1022.00. **Average Salary:** $39,160. **Projected Growth:** 28.6%. **Annual Openings:** 18,000. **Education:** Bachelor's degree. **Job Zone:** 5. **Education/Training Program(s)**—Clinical/Medical Social

Work. **Related Knowledge/Courses:** Psychology; Therapy and Counseling; Customer and Personal Service; Sociology and Anthropology; Philosophy and Theology; Medicine and Dentistry. **Personality Type:** Social. **Skills Required:** Social Perceptiveness; Service Orientation; Negotiation; Coordination; Active Listening; Critical Thinking; Learning Strategies; Instructing. **Abilities:** Speech Recognition; Problem Sensitivity; Speed of Closure; Inductive Reasoning; Originality; Category Flexibility. **Occupational Values:** Social Service; Creativity; Autonomy; Achievement; Authority. **Interacting with Others:** Establishing and Maintaining Interpersonal Relationships; Resolving Conflicts and Negotiating with Others; Communicating with Supervisors, Peers, or Subordinates; Communicating with Persons Outside Organization. **Physical Work Conditions:** Physical Proximity; Disease or Infections; Sounds, Noise Levels Are Distracting or Uncomfortable; Sitting; Contaminants.

Mental Health and Substance Abuse Social Workers

Assess and treat individuals with mental, emotional, or substance abuse problems, including abuse of alcohol, tobacco, and/or other drugs. Activities may include individual and group therapy, crisis intervention, case management, client advocacy, prevention, and education. **O*NET Code:** 21-1023.00. **Average Salary:** $33,650. **Projected Growth:** 34.5%. **Annual Openings:** 17,000. **Education:** Master's degree. **Job Zone:** 5. **Education/Training Program(s)**—Clinical/Medical Social Work. **Related Knowledge/Courses:** Psychology; Therapy and Counseling; Customer and Personal Service; Sociology and Anthropology; Medicine and Dentistry; Philosophy and Theology. **Personality Type:** Social. **Skills Required:** Social Perceptiveness; Service Orientation; Negotiation; Persuasion; Active Listening; Critical Thinking; Coordination; Judgment and Decision Making. **Abilities:** Speech Recognition; Problem Sensitivity; Originality; Speech Clarity; Inductive Reasoning. **Occupational Values:** Social Service; Creativity; Autonomy; Achievement; Authority. **Interacting with Others:** Establishing and Maintaining Interpersonal Relationships; Assisting and Caring for Others; Resolving Conflicts and Negotiating with Others. **Physical Work Conditions:** Sounds, Noise Levels Are Distracting or Uncomfortable; Sitting; Physical Proximity; In an Enclosed Vehicle or Equipment; Extremely Bright or Inadequate Lighting.

Mental Health Counselors

Counsel with emphasis on prevention. Work with individuals and groups to promote optimum mental health. May help individuals deal with addictions and substance abuse; family, parenting, and marital problems; suicide; stress management; problems with self-esteem; and issues associated with aging and mental and emotional health. **O*NET Code:** 21-1014.00. **Average Salary:** $32,040. **Projected Growth:** 26.7%. **Annual Openings:** 13,000. **Education:** Master's degree. **Job Zone:** 5. **Education/Training Program(s)**—Clinical/Medical Social Work; Mental and Social Health Services and Allied Professions, Other; Mental Health Counseling/Counselor; Substance Abuse/Addiction Counseling. **Related Knowledge/Courses:** Therapy and Counseling; Psychology; Sociology and Anthropology; Customer and Personal Service;

Philosophy and Theology; Education and Training. **Personality Type:** Social. **Skills Required:** Social Perceptiveness; Service Orientation; Negotiation; Learning Strategies; Persuasion; Active Listening; Critical Thinking; Active Learning; Instructing. **Abilities:** Inductive Reasoning; Speech Recognition; Problem Sensitivity; Oral Expression; Originality; Deductive Reasoning. **Occupational Values:** Social Service; Creativity; Autonomy; Achievement; Authority. **Interacting with Others:** Establishing and Maintaining Interpersonal Relationships; Resolving Conflicts and Negotiating with Others; Communicating with Supervisors, Peers, or Subordinates. **Physical Work Conditions:** Sitting; Physical Proximity; Sounds, Noise Levels Are Distracting or Uncomfortable; Very Hot or Cold; Contaminants.

Probation Officers and Correctional Treatment Specialists

Provide social services to assist in rehabilitation of law offenders in custody or on probation or parole. Make recommendations for actions involving formulation of rehabilitation plan and treatment of offender, including conditional release and education and employment stipulations. **O*NET Code:** 21-1092.00. **Average Salary:** $39,200. **Projected Growth:** 14.7%. **Annual Openings:** 15,000. **Education:** Bachelor's degree. **Job Zone:** 4. **Education/Training Program(s)**—Social Work. **Related Knowledge/Courses:** Therapy and Counseling; Psychology; Sociology and Anthropology; Public Safety and Security; Philosophy and Theology; Law and Government. **Personality Type:** Social. **Skills Required:** Social Perceptiveness; Persuasion; Time Management; Negotiation; Learning Strategies; Coordination; Management of Personnel Resources; Instructing. **Abilities:** Speech Recognition; Inductive Reasoning; Deductive Reasoning; Originality; Problem Sensitivity. **Occupational Values:** Social Service; Authority; Supervision, Human Relations; Autonomy; Activity; Security. **Interacting with Others:** Establishing and Maintaining Interpersonal Relationships; Resolving Conflicts and Negotiating with Others; Communicating with Supervisors, Peers, or Subordinates. **Physical Work Conditions:** Disease or Infections; Very Hot or Cold; Physical Proximity; Contaminants; Indoors, Not Environmentally Controlled; Outdoors.

Rehabilitation Counselors

Counsel individuals to maximize the independence and employability of persons coping with personal, social, and vocational difficulties that result from birth defects, illness, disease, accidents, or the stress of daily life. Coordinate activities for residents of care and treatment facilities. Assess client needs and design and implement rehabilitation programs that may include personal and vocational counseling, training, and job placement. **O*NET Code:** 21-1015.00. **Average Salary:** $27,410. **Projected Growth:** 33.8%. **Annual Openings:** 19,000. **Education:** Bachelor's degree. **Job Zone:** No data available. **Education/Training Program(s)**—Assistive/Augmentative Technology and Rehabilitation Engineering; Vocational Rehabilitation Counseling/Counselor. **Related Knowledge/Courses:** No data available. **Personality Type:** No data available. **Skills Required:** No data available. **Abilities:**

© 2006, JIST Works

No data available. **Occupational Values:** No data available. **Interacting with Others:** No data available. **Physical Work Conditions:** No data available.

Residential Advisors

Coordinate activities for residents of boarding schools, college fraternities or sororities, college dormitories, or similar establishments. Order supplies and determine need for maintenance, repairs, and furnishings. May maintain household records and assign rooms. May refer residents to counseling resources if needed. O*NET Code: 39-9041.00. **Average Salary:** $21,370. **Projected Growth:** 33.6%. **Annual Openings:** 12,000. **Education:** Moderate-term on-the-job training. **Job Zone:** 3. **Education/Training Program(s)—** Hotel/Motel Administration/Management. **Related Knowledge/Courses:** Psychology; Customer and Personal Service; Sociology and Anthropology; Therapy and Counseling; Personnel and Human Resources; Administration and Management. **Personality Type:** Social. **Skills Required:** Social Perceptiveness; Negotiation; Management of Personnel Resources; Coordination; Management of Material Resources; Management of Financial Resources; Speaking; Persuasion; Service Orientation; Time Management. **Abilities:** Originality; Fluency of Ideas; Night Vision; Far Vision; Memorization; Speed of Closure. **Occupational Values:** Social Service; Authority; Supervision, Human Relations; Working Conditions; Autonomy. **Interacting with Others:** Establishing and Maintaining Interpersonal Relationships; Assisting and Caring for Others; Providing Consultation and Advice to Others. **Physical Work Conditions:** Disease or Infections; Outdoors; Sitting; Walking and Running; Standing.

Social and Human Service Assistants

Assist professionals from a wide variety of fields, such as psychology, rehabilitation, or social work, to provide client services as well as support for families. May assist clients in identifying available benefits and social and community services and help clients obtain them. May assist social workers with developing, organizing, and conducting programs to prevent and resolve problems relevant to substance abuse, human relationships, rehabilitation, or adult daycare. O*NET Code: 21-1093.00. **Average Salary:** $23,990. **Projected Growth:** 48.7%. **Annual Openings:** 63,000. **Education:** Moderate-term on-the-job training. **Job Zone:** 3. **Education/Training Program(s)—**Mental and Social Health Services and Allied Professions, Other. **Related Knowledge/Courses:** Therapy and Counseling; Psychology; Customer and Personal Service; Clerical; Sociology and Anthropology; Philosophy and Theology. **Personality Type:** Social. **Skills Required:** Social Perceptiveness; Service Orientation; Management of Financial Resources; Time Management; Instructing; Learning Strategies; Active Listening; Speaking; Critical Thinking. **Abilities:** Oral Expression; Oral Comprehension; Time Sharing; Speech Recognition; Written Comprehension. **Occupational Values:** Social Service; Authority; Variety; Supervision, Human Relations; Supervision, Technical. **Interacting with Others:** Establishing and Maintaining Interpersonal Relationships; Resolving Conflicts and Negotiating with Others; Assisting and Caring for Others. **Physical Work Conditions:** Sitting; Sounds, Noise Levels Are Distracting or Uncomfortable; In an Enclosed Vehicle or Equipment; Physical Proximity; Extremely Bright or Inadequate Lighting.

Substance Abuse and Behavioral Disorder Counselors

Counsel and advise individuals with alcohol, tobacco, drug, or other problems, such as gambling and eating disorders. May counsel individuals, families, or groups or engage in prevention programs. O*NET Code: 21-1011.00. **Average Salary:** $31,510. **Projected Growth:** 23.3%. **Annual Openings:** 10,000. **Education:** Master's degree. **Job Zone:** 4. **Education/Training Program(s)—**Clinical/Medical Social Work; Mental and Social Health Services and Allied Professions, Other; Substance Abuse/Addiction Counseling. **Related Knowledge/Courses:** Therapy and Counseling; Psychology; Customer and Personal Service; Medicine and Dentistry; Education and Training; Communications and Media. **Personality Type:** Social. **Skills Required:** Social Perceptiveness; Management of Financial Resources; Service Orientation; Management of Personnel Resources; Instructing; Systems Analysis; Systems Evaluation; Negotiation. **Abilities:** Oral Expression; Speech Recognition; Speech Clarity; Fluency of Ideas; Problem Sensitivity. **Occupational Values:** Social Service; Creativity; Autonomy; Achievement; Authority. **Interacting with Others:** Establishing and Maintaining Interpersonal Relationships; Communicating with Persons Outside Organization; Assisting and Caring for Others. **Physical Work Conditions:** Sitting; Disease or Infections; Walking and Running.

10.02 Religious Work

Clergy

Conduct religious worship and perform other spiritual functions associated with beliefs and practices of religious faith or denomination. Provide spiritual and moral guidance and assistance to members. O*NET Code: 21-2011.00. **Average Salary:** $34,930. **Projected Growth:** 15.5%. **Annual Openings:** 34,000. **Education:** First professional degree. **Job Zone:** 5. **Education/Training Program(s)—**Clinical Pastoral Counseling/Patient Counseling; Divinity/Ministry (BD, MDiv.); Pastoral Counseling and Specialized Ministries, Other; Pastoral Studies/Counseling; Pre-Theology/Pre-Ministerial Studies; Rabbinical Studies; Theological and Ministerial Studies, Other; Theology and Religious Vocations, Other; Theology/Theological Studies; Youth Ministry. **Related Knowledge/Courses:** Philosophy and Theology; Education and Training; Therapy and Counseling; Psychology; English Language; Communications and Media. **Personality Type:** Social. **Skills Required:** Service Orientation; Social Perceptiveness; Speaking; Writing; Active Listening; Reading Comprehension; Persuasion; Learning Strategies. **Abilities:** Speech Clarity; Oral Expression; Written Expression; Fluency of Ideas; Written Comprehension. **Occupational Values:** Social Status; Social Service; Autonomy; Achievement; Recognition. **Interacting with Others:** Assisting and Caring for Others; Establishing and Maintaining Interpersonal

Relationships; Performing for or Working Directly with the Public. **Physical Work Conditions:** Standing; Indoors; Sitting.

Directors, Religious Activities and Education

Direct and coordinate activities of a denominational group to meet religious needs of students. Plan, direct, or coordinate church school programs designed to promote religious education among church membership. May provide counseling and guidance relative to marital, health, financial, and religious problems. **O*NET Code:** 21-2021.00. **Average Salary:** $29,240. **Projected Growth:** 24.1%. **Annual Openings:** 16,000. **Education:** Bachelor's degree. **Job Zone:** 5. **Education/Training Program(s)**—Bible/Biblical Studies; Missions/Missionary Studies and Missiology; Religious Education; Youth Ministry. **Related Knowledge/Courses:** Therapy and Counseling; Philosophy and Theology; Administration and Management; Sociology and Anthropology; Psychology; Education and Training. **Personality Type:** Social. **Skills Required:** Management of Financial Resources; Social Perceptiveness; Management of Personnel Resources; Service Orientation; Management of Material Resources; Instructing; Systems Analysis; Coordination; Judgment and Decision Making. **Abilities:** Speech Clarity; Oral Expression; Fluency of Ideas; Oral Comprehension; Mathematical Reasoning. **Occupational Values:** Social Service; Social Status; Creativity; Autonomy; Achievement. **Interacting with Others:** Communicating with Supervisors, Peers, or Subordinates; Communicating with Persons Outside Organization; Establishing and Maintaining Interpersonal Relationships; Assisting and Caring for Others; Providing Consultation and Advice to Others. **Physical Work Conditions:** Sitting; Indoors; Walking and Running; Standing.

10.03 Child/Personal Care and Services

Child Care Workers

Attend to children at schools, businesses, private households, and child care institutions. Perform a variety of tasks, such as dressing, feeding, bathing, and overseeing play. **O*NET Code:** 39-9011.00. **Average Salary:** $16,570. **Projected Growth:** 11.7%. **Annual Openings:** 406,000. **Education:** Short-term on-the-job training. **Job Zone:** 2. **Education/Training Program(s)**—Child Care Provider/Assistant. **Related Knowledge/Courses:** Customer and Personal Service; Psychology; Sociology and Anthropology; Philosophy and Theology; Public Safety and Security; Geography; Education and Training. **Personality Type:** Social. **Skills Required:** Social Perceptiveness; Negotiation; Learning Strategies; Service Orientation; Persuasion; Time Management; Critical Thinking; Monitoring. **Abilities:** Speech Recognition; Originality; Fluency of Ideas; Inductive Reasoning; Flexibility of Closure; Time Sharing. **Occupational Values:** Social Service; Activity; Variety; Authority; Co-workers. **Interacting with Others:** Assisting and Caring for Others; Establishing

and Maintaining Interpersonal Relationships; Communicating with Supervisors, Peers, or Subordinates. **Physical Work Conditions:** Physical Proximity; Sounds, Noise Levels Are Distracting or Uncomfortable; Minor Burns, Cuts, Bites, or Stings; Kneeling, Crouching, Stooping, or Crawling; Disease or Infections.

Funeral Attendants

Perform variety of tasks during funeral, such as placing casket in parlor or chapel prior to service, arranging floral offerings or lights around casket, directing or escorting mourners, closing casket, and issuing and storing funeral equipment. **O*NET Code:** 39-4021.00. **Average Salary:** $19,030. **Projected Growth:** 18.9%. **Annual Openings:** 3,000. **Education:** Short-term on-the-job training. **Job Zone:** 2. **Education/Training Program(s)**—Funeral Service and Mortuary Science, General. **Related Knowledge/Courses:** Customer and Personal Service; Philosophy and Theology; Transportation; Psychology; Clerical; Law and Government. **Personality Type:** Social. **Skills Required:** Social Perceptiveness; Service Orientation; Coordination; Reading Comprehension; Active Listening; Speaking; Instructing; Learning Strategies. **Abilities:** Static Strength; Gross Body Coordination; Dynamic Strength; Extent Flexibility; Trunk Strength. **Occupational Values:** Social Service; Security. **Interacting with Others:** Assisting and Caring for Others; Performing for or Working Directly with the Public; Establishing and Maintaining Interpersonal Relationships. **Physical Work Conditions:** Physical Proximity; In an Enclosed Vehicle or Equipment; Outdoors; Very Hot or Cold; Contaminants.

Nannies

Care for children in private households and provide support and expertise to parents in satisfying children's physical, emotional, intellectual, and social needs. Duties may include meal planning and preparation, laundry and clothing care, organization of play activities and outings, discipline, intellectual stimulation, language activities, and transportation. **O*NET Code:** 39-9011.01. **Average Salary:** No data available. **Projected Growth:** 11.7%. **Annual Openings:** 406,000. **Education:** Short-term on-the-job training. **Job Zone:** 3. **Education/Training Program(s)**—Child Care Provider/ Assistant. **Related Knowledge/Courses:** Philosophy and Theology; Psychology; Geography; Medicine and Dentistry; Sociology and Anthropology; Therapy and Counseling. **Personality Type:** No data available. **Skills Required:** Negotiation; Social Perceptiveness; Time Management; Persuasion; Instructing; Management of Financial Resources; Speaking; Service Orientation. **Abilities:** Response Orientation; Speech Recognition; Flexibility of Closure; Originality; Extent Flexibility. **Occupational Values:** No data available. **Interacting with Others:** Assisting and Caring for Others; Establishing and Maintaining Interpersonal Relationships; Coaching and Developing Others. **Physical Work Conditions:** In an Enclosed Vehicle or Equipment; Physical Proximity; Outdoors; Very Hot or Cold; Sounds, Noise Levels Are Distracting or Uncomfortable.

Personal and Home Care Aides

Assist elderly or disabled adults with daily living activities at the person's home or in a daytime non-residential facility.

Duties performed at a place of residence may include keeping house (making beds, doing laundry, washing dishes) and preparing meals. May provide meals and supervised activities at non-residential care facilities. May advise families, the elderly, and disabled on such things as nutrition, cleanliness, and household utilities. **O*NET Code:** 39-9021.00. **Average Salary:** $16,750. **Projected Growth:** 40.5%. **Annual Openings:** 154,000. **Education:** Short-term on-the-job training. **Job Zone:** 2. **Education/Training Program(s)**—No data available. **Related Knowledge/Courses:** Customer and Personal Service; Medicine and Dentistry; Therapy and Counseling; Psychology. **Personality Type:** Social. **Skills Required:** Social Perceptiveness; Persuasion; Service Orientation; Learning Strategies; Coordination; Instructing; Critical Thinking; Monitoring. **Abilities:** Speech Recognition; Static Strength; Trunk Strength; Dynamic Strength; Hearing Sensitivity; Speech Clarity. **Occupational Values:** Social Service; Variety; Authority; Autonomy; Independence. **Interacting with Others:** Assisting and Caring for Others; Establishing and Maintaining Interpersonal Relationships; Communicating with Supervisors, Peers, or Subordinates. **Physical Work Conditions:** Physical Proximity; In an Enclosed Vehicle or Equipment; Disease or Infections; Minor Burns, Cuts, Bites, or Stings; Sitting.

10.04 Client Interviewing

Claims Takers, Unemployment Benefits

Interview unemployed workers and compile data to determine eligibility for unemployment benefits. **O*NET Code:** 43-4061.01. **Average Salary:** $32,630. **Projected Growth:** –11.6%. **Annual Openings:** 12,000. **Education:** Moderate-term on-the-job training. **Job Zone:** 2. **Education/Training Program(s)**—Community Organization and Advocacy. **Related Knowledge/Courses:** Personnel and Human Resources; Clerical; Therapy and Counseling; Foreign Language; Law and Government; Customer and Personal Service. **Personality Type:** Conventional. **Skills Required:** Speaking; Service Orientation; Social Perceptiveness; Active Listening; Reading Comprehension. **Abilities:** Speech Clarity; Written Expression; Oral Comprehension; Written Comprehension; Oral Expression. **Occupational Values:** Social Service; Supervision, Technical; Authority; Security; Supervision, Human Relations. **Interacting with Others:** Communicating with Persons Outside Organization; Performing for or Working Directly with the Public; Interpreting the Meaning of Information for Others; Communicating with Supervisors, Peers, or Subordinates. **Physical Work Conditions:** Sitting; Indoors.

Interviewers, Except Eligibility and Loan

Interview persons by telephone, by mail, in person, or by other means for the purpose of completing forms, applications, or questionnaires. Ask specific questions, record answers, and assist persons with completing form. May sort, classify, and file forms. **O*NET Code:** 43-4111.00. **Average Salary:** $22,910. **Projected Growth:** 28.0%. **Annual Openings:** 46,000. **Education:** Short-term on-the-job training. **Job Zone:** 3. **Education/Training Program(s)**—Receptionist. **Related Knowledge/Courses:** Customer and Personal Service; Therapy and Counseling; Sales and Marketing; Education and Training; Psychology; Philosophy and Theology. **Personality Type:** Conventional. **Skills Required:** Service Orientation; Social Perceptiveness; Speaking; Persuasion; Active Listening; Negotiation; Learning Strategies; Writing; Critical Thinking. **Abilities:** Speech Recognition; Oral Comprehension; Oral Expression; Written Expression; Category Flexibility. **Occupational Values:** Independence; Working Conditions; Supervision, Technical. **Interacting with Others:** Establishing and Maintaining Interpersonal Relationships; Communicating with Supervisors, Peers, or Subordinates; Assisting and Caring for Others. **Physical Work Conditions:** Sitting; Physical Proximity; Sounds, Noise Levels Are Distracting or Uncomfortable.

Welfare Eligibility Workers and Interviewers

Interview and investigate applicants and recipients to determine eligibility for use of social programs and agency resources. Duties include recording and evaluating personal and financial data obtained from individuals; initiating procedures to grant, modify, deny, or terminate eligibility for various aid programs; authorizing grant amounts; and preparing reports. These workers generally receive specialized training and assist social service caseworkers. **O*NET Code:** 43-4061.02. **Average Salary:** $32,630. **Projected Growth:** –11.6%. **Annual Openings:** 12,000. **Education:** Moderate-term on-the-job training. **Job Zone:** 2. **Education/Training Program(s)**—Community Organization and Advocacy. **Related Knowledge/Courses:** Therapy and Counseling; Sociology and Anthropology; Law and Government; Administration and Management; Clerical; Psychology. **Personality Type:** Social. **Skills Required:** Service Orientation; Judgment and Decision Making; Systems Evaluation; Active Listening; Writing; Speaking; Social Perceptiveness; Management of Financial Resources. **Abilities:** Written Expression; Written Comprehension; Oral Expression; Oral Comprehension; Speech Clarity. **Occupational Values:** Social Service; Achievement; Security; Authority; Supervision, Technical. **Interacting with Others:** Communicating with Persons Outside Organization; Assisting and Caring for Others; Establishing and Maintaining Interpersonal Relationships. **Physical Work Conditions:** Sitting; Indoors; Walking and Running.

11 Information Technology

11.01   **Managerial Work in Information Technology**

11.02   **Information Technology Specialties**

11.03   **Digital Equipment Repair**

11.01 Managerial Work in Information Technology

Computer and Information Systems Managers

Plan, direct, or coordinate activities in such fields as electronic data processing, information systems, systems analysis, and computer programming. **O*NET Code:** 11-3021.00. **Average Salary:** $90,490. **Projected Growth:** 36.1%. **Annual Openings:** 39,000. **Education:** Work experience plus degree. **Job Zone:** 5. **Education/Training Program(s)**—Computer and Information Sciences, General; Computer Science; Information Resources Management/CIO Training; Information Science/Studies; Knowledge Management; Management Information Systems, General; Operations Management and Supervision; System Administration/Administrator. **Related Knowledge/Courses:** Clerical; Computers and Electronics; Economics and Accounting; Engineering and Technology; Administration and Management; Design. **Personality Type:** Enterprising. **Skills Required:** Management of Financial Resources; Negotiation; Operations Analysis; Persuasion; Programming; Management of Material Resources; Systems Analysis; Technology Design; Systems Evaluation. **Abilities:** Originality; Deductive Reasoning; Oral Comprehension; Inductive Reasoning; Problem Sensitivity. **Occupational Values:** Authority; Creativity; Responsibility; Working Conditions; Ability Utilization; Advancement. **Interacting with Others:** Communicating with Supervisors, Peers, or Subordinates; Resolving Conflicts and Negotiating with Others; Establishing and Maintaining Interpersonal Relationships; Training and Teaching Others. **Physical Work Conditions:** Sitting; Sounds, Noise Levels Are Distracting or Uncomfortable; Cramped Work Space, Awkward Positions; Indoors; Physical Proximity.

Network and Computer Systems Administrators

Install, configure, and support an organization's local area network (LAN), wide area network (WAN), and Internet system or a segment of a network system. Maintain network hardware and software. Monitor network to ensure network availability to all system users and perform necessary maintenance to support network availability. May supervise other network support and client server specialists and plan, coordinate, and implement network security measures. **O*NET Code:** 15-1071.00. **Average Salary:** $57,060. **Projected Growth:** 37.4%. **Annual Openings:** 35,000. **Education:** Bachelor's degree. **Job Zone:** 4. **Education/Training Program(s)**—Computer and Information Sciences and Support Services, Other; Computer and Information Sciences, General; Computer and Information Systems Security; Computer Systems Analysis/Analyst; Computer Systems Networking and Telecommunications; Information Science/Studies; System Administration/Administrator; System, Networking, and LAN/WAN Management/Manager.

Related Knowledge/Courses: Computers and Electronics; Telecommunications; Customer and Personal Service; Education and Training; Engineering and Technology; Administration and Management. **Personality Type:** No data available. **Skills Required:** Troubleshooting; Installation; Repairing; Service Orientation; Technology Design; Systems Evaluation; Programming; Systems Analysis. **Abilities:** Inductive Reasoning; Finger Dexterity; Flexibility of Closure; Deductive Reasoning; Speed of Closure. **Occupational Values:** No data available. **Interacting with Others:** Communicating with Supervisors, Peers, or Subordinates; Establishing and Maintaining Interpersonal Relationships; Providing Consultation and Advice to Others. **Physical Work Conditions:** Sitting; Physical Proximity; Sounds, Noise Levels Are Distracting or Uncomfortable; Indoors; Contaminants.

11.02 Information Technology Specialties

Computer Operators

Monitor and control electronic computer and peripheral electronic data processing equipment to process business, scientific, engineering, and other data according to operating instructions. May enter commands at a computer terminal and set controls on computer and peripheral devices. Monitor and respond to operating and error messages. **O*NET Code:** 43-9011.00. **Average Salary:** $30,340. **Projected Growth:** –16.7%. **Annual Openings:** 27,000. **Education:** Moderate-term on-the-job training. **Job Zone:** 3. **Education/Training Program(s)**—Data Processing and Data Processing Technology/Technician. **Related Knowledge/Courses:** Computers and Electronics; Sales and Marketing; Clerical; Administration and Management; Telecommunications; Customer and Personal Service. **Personality Type:** Conventional. **Skills Required:** Instructing; Service Orientation; Critical Thinking; Troubleshooting; Time Management; Social Perceptiveness; Active Learning; Negotiation. **Abilities:** Speed of Closure; Wrist-Finger Speed; Speech Recognition; Near Vision; Memorization. **Occupational Values:** Working Conditions; Supervision; Human Relations; Independence; Advancement; Recognition. **Interacting with Others:** Communicating with Supervisors, Peers, or Subordinates; Establishing and Maintaining Interpersonal Relationships; Providing Consultation and Advice to Others. **Physical Work Conditions:** Sitting; Sounds, Noise Levels Are Distracting or Uncomfortable; Indoors; In an Enclosed Vehicle or Equipment; Physical Proximity.

Computer Programmers

Convert project specifications and statements of problems and procedures to detailed logical flow charts for coding into computer language. Develop and write computer programs to store, locate, and retrieve specific documents, data, and information. May program web sites. **O*NET Code:** 15-1021.00. **Average Salary:** $61,730. **Projected Growth:** 14.6%. **Annual Openings:** 45,000. **Education:** Bachelor's degree. **Job Zone:** 4.

Education/Training Program(s)—Artificial Intelligence and Robotics; Bioinformatics; Computer Graphics; Computer Programming, Specific Applications; Computer Programming, Vendor/Product Certification; Computer Programming/Programmer, General; E-Commerce/Electronic Commerce; Management Information Systems, General; Medical Informatics; Medical Office Computer Specialist/Assistant; Web Page, Digital/Multimedia and Information Resources Design; Web/Multimedia Management and Webmaster. Related Knowledge/Courses: Computers and Electronics; Design; Mathematics; Telecommunications; English Language; Customer and Personal Service. Personality Type: Investigative. Skills Required: Programming; Operations Analysis; Technology Design; Troubleshooting; Critical Thinking; Active Learning; Complex Problem Solving; Systems Analysis. Abilities: Written Expression; Information Ordering; Originality; Oral Comprehension; Written Comprehension. Occupational Values: Creativity; Ability Utilization; Advancement; Autonomy; Compensation. Interacting with Others: Communicating with Supervisors, Peers, or Subordinates; Establishing and Maintaining Interpersonal Relationships; Providing Consultation and Advice to Others. Physical Work Conditions: Sitting; Physical Proximity; Sounds, Noise Levels Are Distracting or Uncomfortable; Indoors; In an Enclosed Vehicle or Equipment.

Computer Security Specialists

Plan, coordinate, and implement security measures for information systems to regulate access to computer data files and prevent unauthorized modification, destruction, or disclosure of information. O*NET Code: 15-1071.01. Average Salary: $57,060. Projected Growth: 37.4%. Annual Openings: 35,000. Education: Bachelor's degree. Job Zone: 4. Education/Training Program(s)—Computer and Information Sciences and Support Services, Other; Computer and Information Sciences, General; Computer and Information Systems Security; Computer Systems Analysis/Analyst; Computer Systems Networking and Telecommunications; Information Science/Studies; System Administration/Administrator; System, Networking, and LAN/WAN Management/Manager. Related Knowledge/ Courses: Computers and Electronics; Public Safety and Security; Administration and Management; Telecommunications. Personality Type: Investigative. Skills Required: Programming; Technology Design; Installation; Operations Analysis; Management of Material Resources; Science; Writing; Mathematics; Quality Control Analysis. Abilities: Deductive Reasoning; Fluency of Ideas; Information Ordering; Written Comprehension; Written Expression. Occupational Values: Working Conditions; Compensation; Creativity; Responsibility; Autonomy. Interacting with Others: Communicating with Supervisors, Peers, or Subordinates; Providing Consultation and Advice to Others; Coordinating the Work and Activities of Others. Physical Work Conditions: Indoors; Sitting; Standing.

Computer Software Engineers, Applications

Develop, create, and modify general computer applications software or specialized utility programs. Analyze user needs and develop software solutions. Design software or customize software for client use with the aim of optimizing operational efficiency. May analyze and design databases within an application area, working individually or coordinating database development as part of a team. O*NET Code: 15-1031.00. Average Salary: $73,410. Projected Growth: 45.5%. Annual Openings: 55,000. Education: Bachelor's degree. Job Zone: 4. Education/Training Program(s)—Artificial Intelligence and Robotics; Bioinformatics; Computer Engineering Technologies/Technicians, Other; Computer Engineering, General; Computer Science; Computer Software Engineering; Information Technology; Medical Illustration and Informatics, Other; Medical Informatics. Related Knowledge/Courses: Computers and Electronics; Telecommunications; Engineering and Technology; Mathematics; Design; English Language. Personality Type: Investigative. Skills Required: Programming; Troubleshooting; Technology Design; Systems Analysis; Quality Control Analysis; Operations Analysis; Complex Problem Solving; Critical Thinking. Abilities: Mathematical Reasoning; Inductive Reasoning; Deductive Reasoning; Oral Expression; Written Expression. Occupational Values: Creativity; Ability Utilization; Working Conditions; Authority; Social Status; Responsibility. Interacting with Others: Communicating with Supervisors, Peers, or Subordinates; Interpreting the Meaning of Information for Others; Establishing and Maintaining Interpersonal Relationships. Physical Work Conditions: Sitting; Sounds, Noise Levels Are Distracting or Uncomfortable; Physical Proximity; Indoors.

Computer Software Engineers, Systems Software

Research, design, develop, and test operating systems-level software, compilers, and network distribution software for medical, industrial, military, communications, aerospace, business, scientific, and general computing applications. Set operational specifications and formulate and analyze software requirements. Apply principles and techniques of computer science, engineering, and mathematical analysis. O*NET Code: 15-1032.00. Average Salary: $77,250. Projected Growth: 45.5%. Annual Openings: 39,000. Education: Bachelor's degree. Job Zone: 4. Education/Training Program(s)—Artificial Intelligence and Robotics; Computer Engineering Technologies/Technicians, Other; Computer Engineering, General; Computer Science; Information Science/Studies; Information Technology. Related Knowledge/Courses: Computers and Electronics; Design; Engineering and Technology; Telecommunications; Mathematics; Education and Training. Personality Type: Investigative. Skills Required: Programming; Technology Design; Troubleshooting; Systems Analysis; Complex Problem Solving; Operations Analysis; Active Learning; Critical Thinking. Abilities: Mathematical Reasoning; Inductive Reasoning; Deductive Reasoning; Oral Expression; Written Expression. Occupational Values: Creativity; Ability Utilization; Working Conditions; Authority; Social Status; Responsibility. Interacting with Others: Establishing and Maintaining Interpersonal Relationships; Providing Consultation and Advice to Others; Communicating with Supervisors, Peers, or Subordinates. Physical Work Conditions: Sitting; Extremely Bright or Inadequate Lighting; Physical Proximity; Indoors; Sounds, Noise Levels Are Distracting or Uncomfortable.

© 2006, JIST Works

Computer Support Specialists

Provide technical assistance to computer system users. Answer questions or resolve computer problems for clients in person, via telephone, or from remote location. May provide assistance concerning the use of computer hardware and software, including printing, installation, word processing, electronic mail, and operating systems. **O*NET Code:** 15-1041.00. **Average Salary:** $39,900. **Projected Growth:** 30.3%. **Annual Openings:** 71,000. **Education:** Associate degree. **Job Zone:** 3. **Education/Training Program(s)**—Accounting and Computer Science; Agricultural Business Technology; Computer Hardware Technology/Technician; Computer Software Technology/Technician; Data Processing and Data Processing Technology/Technician; Medical Office Computer Specialist/Assistant. **Related Knowledge/Courses:** Computers and Electronics; Customer and Personal Service; Telecommunications; Production and Processing; Engineering and Technology; Design. **Personality Type:** Investigative. **Skills Required:** Troubleshooting; Repairing; Persuasion; Social Perceptiveness; Installation; Instructing; Equipment Maintenance; Writing; Service Orientation. **Abilities:** Inductive Reasoning; Written Comprehension; Deductive Reasoning; Oral Comprehension; Originality; Visualization. **Occupational Values:** Advancement; Creativity; Variety; Autonomy; Working Conditions; Social Service. **Interacting with Others:** Establishing and Maintaining Interpersonal Relationships; Communicating with Supervisors, Peers, or Subordinates; Developing and Building Teams. **Physical Work Conditions:** Sounds, Noise Levels Are Distracting or Uncomfortable; Physical Proximity; Sitting; Indoors; Contaminants; Keeping or Regaining Balance.

Computer Systems Analysts

Analyze science, engineering, business, and all other data processing problems for application to electronic data processing systems. Analyze user requirements, procedures, and problems to automate or improve existing systems and review computer system capabilities, workflow, and scheduling limitations. May analyze or recommend commercially available software. May supervise computer programmers. **O*NET Code:** 15-1051.00. **Average Salary:** $65,050. **Projected Growth:** 39.4%. **Annual Openings:** 68,000. **Education:** Bachelor's degree. **Job Zone:** 4. **Education/Training Program(s)**—Computer and Information Sciences, General; Computer Systems Analysis/Analyst; Information Technology; Web/Multimedia Management and Webmaster. **Related Knowledge/Courses:** Computers and Electronics; Customer and Personal Service; Telecommunications; Design; Education and Training; English Language. **Personality Type:** Investigative. **Skills Required:** Quality Control Analysis; Installation; Troubleshooting; Technology Design; Time Management; Service Orientation; Systems Analysis; Operations Analysis. **Abilities:** Written Expression; Mathematical Reasoning; Deductive Reasoning; Originality; Speed of Closure. **Occupational Values:** Creativity; Ability Utilization; Compensation; Responsibility; Autonomy. **Interacting with Others:** Interpreting the Meaning of Information for Others; Establishing and Maintaining Interpersonal Relationships; Communicating with Supervisors, Peers, or Subordinates. **Physical Work**

Conditions: Sitting; Physical Proximity; Very Hot or Cold; Extremely Bright or Inadequate Lighting; Sounds, Noise Levels Are Distracting or Uncomfortable.

Database Administrators

Coordinate changes to computer databases. Test and implement the database, applying knowledge of database management systems. May plan, coordinate, and implement security measures to safeguard computer databases. **O*NET Code:** 15-1061.00. **Average Salary:** $59,150. **Projected Growth:** 44.2%. **Annual Openings:** 16,000. **Education:** Bachelor's degree. **Job Zone:** 4. **Education/Training Program(s)**—Computer and Information Sciences, General; Computer and Information Systems Security; Computer Systems Analysis/Analyst; Data Modeling/Warehousing and Database Administration; Management Information Systems, General. **Related Knowledge/Courses:** Computers and Electronics; Clerical; Customer and Personal Service; Economics and Accounting; Administration and Management; Mathematics. **Personality Type:** Investigative. **Skills Required:** Troubleshooting; Persuasion; Operations Analysis; Instructing; Systems Evaluation; Management of Personnel Resources; Time Management; Technology Design. **Abilities:** Originality; Category Flexibility; Flexibility of Closure; Fluency of Ideas; Visualization. **Occupational Values:** Creativity; Compensation; Security; Authority; Company Policies and Practices; Responsibility. **Interacting with Others:** Establishing and Maintaining Interpersonal Relationships; Communicating with Supervisors, Peers, or Subordinates; Training and Teaching Others. **Physical Work Conditions:** Sitting; Sounds, Noise Levels Are Distracting or Uncomfortable; Physical Proximity.

Network Systems and Data Communications Analysts

Analyze, design, test, and evaluate network systems, such as local area networks (LAN), wide area networks (WAN), Internet, intranet, and other data communications systems. Perform network modeling, analysis, and planning. Research and recommend network and data communications hardware and software. Includes telecommunications specialists who deal with the interfacing of computer and communications equipment. May supervise computer programmers. **O*NET Code:** 15-1081.00. **Average Salary:** $59,300. **Projected Growth:** 57.0%. **Annual Openings:** 29,000. **Education:** Bachelor's degree. **Job Zone:** 3. **Education/Training Program(s)**—Computer and Information Sciences, General; Computer and Information Systems Security; Computer Systems Analysis/Analyst; Computer Systems Networking and Telecommunications; Information Technology. **Related Knowledge/Courses:** Customer and Personal Service; Computers and Electronics; Telecommunications; Education and Training; Engineering and Technology; Design. **Personality Type:** Investigative. **Skills Required:** Installation; Troubleshooting; Technology Design; Management of Material Resources; Systems Analysis; Systems Evaluation; Operations Analysis; Equipment Maintenance. **Abilities:** Written Expression; Originality; Speech Clarity; Oral Comprehension; Written Comprehension; Oral Expression. **Occupational Values:** Compensation; Advancement; Creativity; Ability Utilization; Autonomy. **Interacting with**

Others: Establishing and Maintaining Interpersonal Relationships; Communicating with Supervisors, Peers, or Subordinates; Communicating with Persons Outside Organization. **Physical Work Conditions:** Sitting; Physical Proximity; Cramped Work Space, Awkward Positions; Indoors; Sounds, Noise Levels Are Distracting or Uncomfortable.

11.03 Digital Equipment Repair

Automatic Teller Machine Servicers

Collect deposits and replenish automatic teller machines with cash and supplies. **O*NET Code:** 49-2011.01. **Average Salary:** $33,950. **Projected Growth:** 15.1%. **Annual Openings:** 19,000. **Education:** Long-term on-the-job training. **Job Zone:** 3. **Education/Training Program(s)—** Business Machine Repair; Computer Installation and Repair Technology/Technician. **Related Knowledge/Courses:** Computers and Electronics; Telecommunications; Philosophy and Theology; Geography. **Personality Type:** Realistic. **Skills Required:** Management of Financial Resources; Repairing; Programming. **Abilities:** Number Facility; Perceptual Speed; Wrist-Finger Speed; Visual Color Discrimination; Manual Dexterity. **Occupational Values:** Independence; Supervision, Technical; Supervision, Human Relations. **Interacting with Others:** Communicating with Supervisors, Peers, or Subordinates; Performing Administrative Activities; Establishing and Maintaining Interpersonal Relationships. **Physical Work Conditions:** Standing; Outdoors; Very Hot or Cold; Extremely Bright or Inadequate Lighting; Kneeling, Crouching, Stooping, or Crawling; Spend Time Making Repetitive Motions.

Coin, Vending, and Amusement Machine Servicers and Repairers

Install, service, adjust, or repair coin, vending, or amusement machines, including video games, jukeboxes, pinball machines, or slot machines. **O*NET Code:** 49-9091.00. **Average Salary:** $27,710. **Projected Growth:** 15.2%. **Annual Openings:** 7,000. **Education:** Moderate-term on-the-job training. **Job Zone:** 2. **Education/Training Program(s)—** Electrical/Electronics Maintenance and Repair Technology, Other. **Related Knowledge/Courses:** Mechanical; Engineering and Technology. **Personality Type:** Realistic. **Skills Required:** Repairing; Installation; Equipment Maintenance; Troubleshooting; Quality Control Analysis. **Abilities:** Static Strength; Wrist-Finger Speed; Finger Dexterity; Trunk Strength; Control Precision. **Occupational Values:** Independence; Supervision, Technical; Moral Values; Security; Responsibility. **Interacting with Others:** Communicating with Persons Outside Organization; Establishing and Maintaining Interpersonal Relationships;

Communicating with Supervisors, Peers, or Subordinates; Selling or Influencing Others; Performing Administrative Activities. **Physical Work Conditions:** Spend Time Bending or Twisting the Body; Kneeling, Crouching, Stooping, or Crawling; Standing; Walking and Running; Spend Time Making Repetitive Motions.

Data Processing Equipment Repairers

Repair, maintain, and install computer hardware such as peripheral equipment and word-processing systems. **O*NET Code:** 49-2011.02. **Average Salary:** $33,950. **Projected Growth:** 15.1%. **Annual Openings:** 19,000. **Education:** Postsecondary vocational training. **Job Zone:** 4. **Education/Training Program(s)—** Business Machine Repair; Computer Installation and Repair Technology/Technician. **Related Knowledge/Courses:** Computers and Electronics; Telecommunications; Design; Mechanical; Physics; Engineering and Technology. **Personality Type:** Realistic. **Skills Required:** Installation; Repairing; Troubleshooting; Science; Equipment Maintenance; Operation Monitoring; Quality Control Analysis; Operation and Control. **Abilities:** Hearing Sensitivity; Visual Color Discrimination; Visualization; Finger Dexterity; Inductive Reasoning; Mathematical Reasoning. **Occupational Values:** Variety; Advancement; Supervision, Technical; Security; Moral Values. **Interacting with Others:** Communicating with Supervisors, Peers, or Subordinates; Establishing and Maintaining Interpersonal Relationships; Interpreting the Meaning of Information for Others. **Physical Work Conditions:** Indoors; Hazardous Conditions; Kneeling, Crouching, Stooping, or Crawling; Using Hands on Objects, Tools, or Controls; Sitting.

Office Machine and Cash Register Servicers

Repair and service office machines, such as adding, accounting, calculating, duplicating, and typewriting machines. Includes the repair of manual, electrical, and electronic office machines. **O*NET Code:** 49-2011.03. **Average Salary:** $33,950. **Projected Growth:** 15.1%. **Annual Openings:** 19,000. **Education:** Long-term on-the-job training. **Job Zone:** 3. **Education/Training Program(s)—** Business Machine Repair; Computer Installation and Repair Technology/Technician. **Related Knowledge/Courses:** Computers and Electronics; Mechanical; Engineering and Technology; Design; Telecommunications; Education and Training. **Personality Type:** Realistic. **Skills Required:** Installation; Repairing; Instructing; Equipment Maintenance; Technology Design; Troubleshooting; Quality Control Analysis; Science. **Abilities:** Finger Dexterity; Visual Color Discrimination; Visualization; Arm-Hand Steadiness; Manual Dexterity; Control Precision. **Occupational Values:** Supervision, Technical; Independence; Moral Values; Authority; Responsibility. **Interacting with Others:** Training and Teaching Others; Communicating with Supervisors, Peers, or Subordinates; Communicating with Persons Outside Organization. **Physical Work Conditions:** Hazardous Equipment; Using Hands on Objects, Tools, or Controls; Indoors; Spend Time Bending or Twisting the Body; Minor Burns, Cuts, Bites, or Stings; Sitting.

© 2006, JIST Works

12 Law and Public Safety

12.01   **Managerial Work in Law and Public Safety**

12.02   **Legal Practice and Justice Administration**

12.03   **Legal Support**

12.04   **Law Enforcement and Public Safety**

12.05   **Safety and Security**

12.06   **Emergency Responding**

12.07   **Military**

12.01 Managerial Work in Law and Public Safety

Emergency Management Specialists

Coordinate disaster response or crisis management activities, provide disaster preparedness training, and prepare emergency plans and procedures for natural (e.g., hurricanes, floods, earthquakes), wartime, or technological (e.g., nuclear power plant emergencies, hazardous materials spills) disasters or hostage situations. **O*NET Code:** 13-1061.00. **Average Salary:** $45,120. **Projected Growth:** 28.2%. **Annual Openings:** 2,000. **Education:** Work experience in a related occupation. **Job Zone:** No data available. **Education/Training Program(s)**—Community Organization and Advocacy; Public Administration. **Related Knowledge/Courses:** No data available. **Personality Type:** No data available. **Skills Required:** No data available. **Abilities:** No data available. **Occupational Values:** No data available. **Interacting with Others:** No data available. **Physical Work Conditions:** No data available.

First-Line Supervisors/Managers of Correctional Officers

Supervise and coordinate activities of correctional officers and jailers. **O*NET Code:** 33-1011.00. **Average Salary:** $44,280. **Projected Growth:** 19.0%. **Annual Openings:** 4,000. **Education:** Work experience in a related occupation. **Job Zone:** No data available. **Education/Training Program(s)**—Corrections; Corrections Administration. **Related Knowledge/Courses:** No data available. **Personality Type:** No data available. **Skills Required:** No data available. **Abilities:** No data available. **Occupational Values:** No data available. **Interacting with Others:** No data available. **Physical Work Conditions:** No data available.

First-Line Supervisors/Managers of Police and Detectives

Supervise and coordinate activities of members of police force. **O*NET Code:** 33-1012.00. **Average Salary:** $63,190. **Projected Growth:** 15.3%. **Annual Openings:** 14,000. **Education:** Work experience in a related occupation. **Job Zone:** 4. **Education/Training Program(s)**—Corrections; Criminal Justice/Law Enforcement Administration; Criminal Justice/Safety Studies. **Related Knowledge/Courses:** Public Safety and Security; Psychology; Law and Government; Customer and Personal Service; Personnel and Human Resources; Education and Training. **Personality Type:** Enterprising. **Skills Required:** Management of Personnel Resources; Persuasion; Negotiation; Social Perceptiveness; Service Orientation; Monitoring; Instructing; Coordination. **Abilities:** Reaction Time; Response Orientation; Rate Control; Glare Sensitivity; Explosive Strength; Stamina. **Occupational Values:** Authority; Social Status; Social Service; Responsibility; Autonomy. **Interacting with Others:** Guiding, Directing, and Motivating Subordinates; Performing for or Working Directly with the Public; Communicating with Supervisors, Peers, or Subordinates; Resolving Conflicts and Negotiating with Others. **Physical Work Conditions:** Very Hot or Cold; In an Enclosed Vehicle or Equipment; Outdoors; Extremely Bright or Inadequate Lighting; Physical Proximity.

Forest Fire Fighting and Prevention Supervisors

Supervise fire fighters who control and suppress fires in forests or vacant public land. **O*NET Code:** 33-1021.02. **Average Salary:** $57,320. **Projected Growth:** 18.7%. **Annual Openings:** 8,000. **Education:** Work experience in a related occupation. **Job Zone:** 5. **Education/Training Program(s)**—Fire Protection and Safety Technology/Technician; Fire Services Administration. **Related Knowledge/Courses:** Public Safety and Security; Transportation; Education and Training; Geography; Administration and Management; Chemistry. **Personality Type:** Realistic. **Skills Required:** Management of Personnel Resources; Management of Material Resources; Service Orientation; Systems Evaluation; Coordination; Systems Analysis; Instructing; Judgment and Decision Making; Time Management. **Abilities:** Spatial Orientation; Far Vision; Night Vision; Auditory Attention; Stamina. **Occupational Values:** Authority; Social Status; Responsibility; Autonomy; Achievement; Co-workers. **Interacting with Others:** Coordinating the Work and Activities of Others; Communicating with Supervisors, Peers, or Subordinates; Training and Teaching Others. **Physical Work Conditions:** Specialized Protective or Safety Equipment; Common Protective or Safety Equipment; Outdoors; Very Hot or Cold; Minor Burns, Cuts, Bites, or Stings.

Municipal Fire Fighting and Prevention Supervisors

Supervise fire fighters who control and extinguish municipal fires, protect life and property, and conduct rescue efforts. **O*NET Code:** 33-1021.01. **Average Salary:** $57,320. **Projected Growth:** 18.7%. **Annual Openings:** 8,000. **Education:** Work experience in a related occupation. **Job Zone:** 3. **Education/Training Program(s)**—Fire Protection and Safety Technology/Technician; Fire Services Administration. **Related Knowledge/Courses:** Public Safety and Security; Customer and Personal Service; Education and Training; Building and Construction; Medicine and Dentistry; Psychology. **Personality Type:** Realistic. **Skills Required:** Service Orientation; Management of Personnel Resources; Equipment Maintenance; Coordination; Instructing; Judgment and Decision Making; Management of Material Resources; Social Perceptiveness. **Abilities:** Auditory Attention; Stamina; Sound Localization; Time Sharing; Explosive Strength; Night Vision. **Occupational Values:** Authority; Social Status; Achievement; Co-workers; Social Service; Responsibility. **Interacting with Others:** Assisting and Caring for Others; Resolving Conflicts and Negotiating with Others; Establishing and Maintaining Interpersonal Relationships. **Physical Work Conditions:** Sounds, Noise Levels Are Distracting or Uncomfortable; Physical Proximity; Very Hot or Cold; Contaminants; Outdoors; In an Enclosed Vehicle or Equipment.

© 2006, JIST Works

12.02 Legal Practice and Justice Administration

Administrative Law Judges, Adjudicators, and Hearing Officers

Conduct hearings to decide or recommend decisions on claims concerning government programs or other government-related matters and prepare decisions. Determine penalties or the existence and the amount of liability or recommend the acceptance or rejection of claims or compromise settlements. **O*NET Code:** 23-1021.00. **Average Salary:** $67,340. **Projected Growth:** 5.8%. **Annual Openings:** 1,000. **Education:** Work experience plus degree. **Job Zone:** 5. **Education/Training Program(s)**—Law (LL.B., J.D.); Legal Professions and Studies, Other. **Related Knowledge/Courses:** Law and Government; Therapy and Counseling; Psychology; English Language; Administration and Management; Sociology and Anthropology. **Personality Type:** Enterprising. **Skills Required:** Judgment and Decision Making; Critical Thinking; Active Listening; Writing; Reading Comprehension; Active Learning; Speaking; Negotiation. **Abilities:** Written Comprehension; Oral Comprehension; Memorization; Deductive Reasoning; Written Expression; Inductive Reasoning. **Occupational Values:** Autonomy; Working Conditions; Responsibility; Security; Authority. **Interacting with Others:** Communicating with Supervisors, Peers, or Subordinates; Communicating with Persons Outside Organization; Resolving Conflicts and Negotiating with Others; Providing Consultation and Advice to Others. **Physical Work Conditions:** Sitting; Indoors.

Arbitrators, Mediators, and Conciliators

Facilitate negotiation and conflict resolution through dialogue. Resolve conflicts outside of the court system by mutual consent of parties involved. **O*NET Code:** 23-1022.00. **Average Salary:** $53,670. **Projected Growth:** 13.7%. **Annual Openings:** Fewer than 500. **Education:** Work experience plus degree. **Job Zone:** 5. **Education/Training Program(s)**—Law (LL.B., J.D.); Legal Professions and Studies, Other. **Related Knowledge/Courses:** Law and Government; Therapy and Counseling; Psychology; English Language; Administration and Management; Sociology and Anthropology. **Personality Type:** Enterprising. **Skills Required:** Judgment and Decision Making; Critical Thinking; Active Listening; Writing; Reading Comprehension; Active Learning; Speaking; Negotiation. **Abilities:** Written Comprehension; Oral Comprehension; Memorization; Deductive Reasoning; Written Expression; Inductive Reasoning. **Occupational Values:** Autonomy; Working Conditions; Responsibility; Security; Authority. **Interacting with Others:** Communicating with Supervisors, Peers, or Subordinates; Communicating with Persons Outside Organization; Resolving Conflicts and Negotiating with Others; Providing Consultation and Advice to Others. **Physical Work Conditions:** Sitting; Indoors.

Judges, Magistrate Judges, and Magistrates

Arbitrate, advise, adjudicate, or administer justice in a court of law. May sentence defendant in criminal cases according to government statutes. May determine liability of defendant in civil cases. May issue marriage licenses and perform wedding ceremonies. **O*NET Code:** 23-1023.00. **Average Salary:** $91,230. **Projected Growth:** 8.7%. **Annual Openings:** 2,000. **Education:** Work experience plus degree. **Job Zone:** 5. **Education/Training Program(s)**—Law (LL.B., J.D.); Legal Professions and Studies, Other. **Related Knowledge/Courses:** Law and Government; Sociology and Anthropology; Philosophy and Theology; Public Safety and Security; English Language; History and Archeology. **Personality Type:** Enterprising. **Skills Required:** Judgment and Decision Making; Active Listening; Critical Thinking; Reading Comprehension; Active Learning; Systems Analysis; Writing; Speaking; Negotiation. **Abilities:** Speed of Closure; Memorization; Written Comprehension; Problem Sensitivity; Deductive Reasoning. **Occupational Values:** Responsibility; Social Status; Autonomy; Recognition; Authority. **Interacting with Others:** Resolving Conflicts and Negotiating with Others; Interpreting the Meaning of Information for Others; Communicating with Supervisors, Peers, or Subordinates; Performing for or Working Directly with the Public. **Physical Work Conditions:** Sitting; Indoors; Disease or Infections.

Lawyers

Represent clients in criminal and civil litigation and other legal proceedings, draw up legal documents, and manage or advise clients on legal transactions. May specialize in a single area or may practice broadly in many areas of law. **O*NET Code:** 23-1011.00. **Average Salary:** $92,730. **Projected Growth:** 17.0%. **Annual Openings:** 53,000. **Education:** First professional degree. **Job Zone:** 5. **Education/Training Program(s)**—Advanced Legal Research/Studies, General (LL.M., M.C.L., M.L.I., M.S.L., J.S.D./S.J.D.); American/U.S. Law/Legal Studies/Jurisprudence (LL.M., M.C.J., J.S.D./S.J.D.); Banking, Corporate, Finance, and Securities Law (LL.M., J.S.D./S.J.D.); Canadian Law/Legal Studies/Jurisprudence (LL.M., M.C.J., J.S.D./S.J.D.); Comparative Law (LL.M., M.C.L., J.S.D./S.J.D.); Energy, Environment, and Natural Resources Law (LL.M., M.S., J.S.D./S.J.D.); Health Law (LL.M., M.J., J.S.D./S.J.D.); International Business, Trade, and Tax Law (LL.M., J.S.D./S.J.D.); International Law and Legal Studies (LL.M., J.S.D./S.J.D.); Law (LL.B., J.D.); Legal Professions and Studies, Other; Legal Research and Advanced Professional Studies, Other; Programs for Foreign Lawyers (LL.M., M.C.L.); Tax Law/Taxation (LL.M, J.S.D./S.J.D.). **Related Knowledge/Courses:** Law and Government; English Language; Customer and Personal Service; Personnel and Human Resources; Administration and Management; Psychology. **Personality Type:** Enterprising. **Skills Required:** Persuasion; Negotiation; Critical Thinking; Active Learning; Social Perceptiveness; Writing; Judgment and Decision Making; Time Management. **Abilities:** Oral Expression; Speech Clarity; Written Expression; Written Comprehension; Oral Comprehension. **Occupational Values:** Autonomy; Compensation; Ability Utilization; Social Service; Creativity. **Interacting with Others:** Resolving Conflicts and Negotiating with Others; Communicating with Persons Outside Organization; Providing Consultation and Advice to Others.

Physical Work Conditions: Sitting; Indoors; In an Enclosed Vehicle or Equipment; Physical Proximity; Extremely Bright or Inadequate Lighting.

12.03 Legal Support

Law Clerks

Assist lawyers or judges by researching or preparing legal documents. May meet with clients or assist lawyers and judges in court. **O*NET Code:** 23-2092.00. **Average Salary:** $32,750. **Projected Growth:** 3.7%. **Annual Openings:** 6,000. **Education:** Bachelor's degree. **Job Zone:** 4. **Education/Training Program(s)**—Law (LL.B., J.D.). **Related Knowledge/Courses:** Law and Government; Clerical; English Language; Customer and Personal Service; Computers and Electronics; Psychology. **Personality Type:** Enterprising. **Skills Required:** Critical Thinking; Active Learning; Writing; Time Management; Judgment and Decision Making; Persuasion; Reading Comprehension; Active Listening. **Abilities:** Written Comprehension; Number Facility; Written Expression; Speech Recognition; Oral Comprehension; Oral Expression. **Occupational Values:** Working Conditions; Social Service; Advancement; Variety; Activity; Social Status. **Interacting with Others:** Establishing and Maintaining Interpersonal Relationships; Communicating with Supervisors, Peers, or Subordinates; Resolving Conflicts and Negotiating with Others. **Physical Work Conditions:** Sitting; Indoors; Physical Proximity; Sounds, Noise Levels Are Distracting or Uncomfortable.

Paralegals and Legal Assistants

Assist lawyers by researching legal precedent, investigating facts, or preparing legal documents. Conduct research to support a legal proceeding, to formulate a defense, or to initiate legal action. **O*NET Code:** 23-2011.00. **Average Salary:** $38,440. **Projected Growth:** 28.7%. **Annual Openings:** 29,000. **Education:** Associate degree. **Job Zone:** 3. **Education/Training Program(s)**—Legal Assistant/Paralegal. **Related Knowledge/Courses:** Clerical; Law and Government; Customer and Personal Service; Computers and Electronics; English Language; Personnel and Human Resources. **Personality Type:** Enterprising. **Skills Required:** Time Management; Instructing; Active Listening; Writing; Speaking; Monitoring; Social Perceptiveness; Service Orientation. **Abilities:** Flexibility of Closure; Speech Recognition; Inductive Reasoning; Written Expression; Category Flexibility; Near Vision. **Occupational Values:** Working Conditions; Social Service; Advancement; Autonomy; Variety. **Interacting with Others:** Communicating with Supervisors, Peers, or Subordinates; Establishing and Maintaining Interpersonal Relationships; Communicating with Persons Outside Organization. **Physical Work Conditions:** Sitting; Sounds, Noise Levels Are Distracting or Uncomfortable; Indoors; Physical Proximity.

Title Examiners and Abstractors

Title Examiners: Search public records and examine titles to determine legal condition of property title. Copy or summarize (abstract) recorded documents which affect condition of title to property (e.g., mortgages, trust deeds, and contracts). May prepare and issue policy that guarantees legality of title. Abstractors: Summarize pertinent legal or insurance details or sections of statutes or case law from reference books for purpose of examination, proof, or ready reference. Search out titles to determine if title deed is correct. **O*NET Code:** 23-2093.02. **Average Salary:** $33,910. **Projected Growth:** –2.7%. **Annual Openings:** 6,000. **Education:** Long-term on-the-job training. **Job Zone:** 3. **Education/Training Program(s)**—Legal Assistant/Paralegal. **Related Knowledge/Courses:** Law and Government; Clerical; English Language; Geography; Economics and Accounting; Administration and Management. **Personality Type:** Conventional. **Skills Required:** Management of Personnel Resources; Reading Comprehension; Writing; Critical Thinking; Speaking; Mathematics; Active Listening; Active Learning. **Abilities:** Written Comprehension; Written Expression; Near Vision; Speed of Closure; Number Facility. **Occupational Values:** Independence; Company Policies and Practices; Autonomy; Working Conditions; Advancement; Social Service; Supervision, Human Relations; Supervision, Technical. **Interacting with Others:** Communicating with Persons Outside Organization; Communicating with Supervisors, Peers, or Subordinates; Resolving Conflicts and Negotiating with Others. **Physical Work Conditions:** Sitting; Indoors; Disease or Infections; Minor Burns, Cuts, Bites, or Stings.

Title Searchers

Compile list of mortgages, deeds, contracts, judgments, and other instruments (chain) pertaining to title by searching public and private records of real estate or title insurance company. **O*NET Code:** 23-2093.01. **Average Salary:** $33,910. **Projected Growth:** –2.7%. **Annual Openings:** 6,000. **Education:** Moderate-term on-the-job training. **Job Zone:** 2. **Education/Training Program(s)**—Legal Assistant/Paralegal. **Related Knowledge/Courses:** Law and Government; Clerical; Geography; English Language; Economics and Accounting; Computers and Electronics; Sociology and Anthropology. **Personality Type:** Conventional. **Skills Required:** Writing; Speaking; Reading Comprehension; Critical Thinking; Active Listening; Judgment and Decision Making; Complex Problem Solving. **Abilities:** Written Expression; Written Comprehension; Wrist-Finger Speed; Near Vision; Speed of Closure. **Occupational Values:** Independence; Working Conditions; Advancement; Supervision, Technical; Company Policies and Practices. **Interacting with Others:** Communicating with Persons Outside Organization; Communicating with Supervisors, Peers, or Subordinates; Establishing and Maintaining Interpersonal Relationships. **Physical Work Conditions:** Sitting; Indoors; Disease or Infections.

12.04 Law Enforcement and Public Safety

Bailiffs

Maintain order in courts of law. **O*NET Code:** 33-3011.00. **Average Salary:** $34,280. **Projected Growth:** 9.5%. **Annual Openings:** 2,000. **Education:** Moderate-term on-the-job training. **Job Zone:** 2. **Education/Training Program(s)**—Criminal Justice/Police Science. **Related Knowledge/Courses:** Public Safety and Security; Customer and Personal Service; Law and Government; Psychology; Philosophy and Theology; Sociology and Anthropology. **Personality Type:** Social. **Skills Required:** Persuasion; Social Perceptiveness; Negotiation; Active Listening; Service Orientation; Learning Strategies; Active Learning; Monitoring; Time Management. **Abilities:** Static Strength; Reaction Time; Gross Body Coordination; Response Orientation; Selective Attention. **Occupational Values:** Security; Authority; Supervision, Human Relations; Co-workers; Company Policies and Practices. **Interacting with Others:** Resolving Conflicts and Negotiating with Others; Performing for or Working Directly with the Public; Communicating with Persons Outside Organization. **Physical Work Conditions:** Contaminants; Physical Proximity; Sitting; Sounds, Noise Levels Are Distracting or Uncomfortable; Outdoors.

Correctional Officers and Jailers

Guard inmates in penal or rehabilitative institution in accordance with established regulations and procedures. May guard prisoners in transit between jail, courtroom, prison, or other point. Includes deputy sheriffs and police who spend the majority of their time guarding prisoners in correctional institutions. **O*NET Code:** 33-3012.00. **Average Salary:** $33,240. **Projected Growth:** 24.2%. **Annual Openings:** 49,000. **Education:** Moderate-term on-the-job training. **Job Zone:** 3. **Education/Training Program(s)**—Corrections; Corrections and Criminal Justice, Other; Juvenile Corrections. **Related Knowledge/Courses:** Psychology; Public Safety and Security; Law and Government; Philosophy and Theology; Sociology and Anthropology; Transportation; Education and Training. **Personality Type:** Realistic. **Skills Required:** Social Perceptiveness; Persuasion; Negotiation; Instructing; Monitoring; Speaking; Writing; Critical Thinking; Coordination. **Abilities:** Reaction Time; Response Orientation; Static Strength; Flexibility of Closure; Stamina; Far Vision. **Occupational Values:** Security; Authority; Supervision, Human Relations; Co-workers; Company Policies and Practices. **Interacting with Others:** Establishing and Maintaining Interpersonal Relationships; Communicating with Supervisors, Peers, or Subordinates; Resolving Conflicts and Negotiating with Others. **Physical Work Conditions:** Sounds, Noise Levels Are Distracting or Uncomfortable; Physical Proximity; Contaminants; Disease or Infections; Very Hot or Cold.

Criminal Investigators and Special Agents

Investigate alleged or suspected criminal violations of federal, state, or local laws to determine if evidence is sufficient to recommend prosecution. **O*NET Code:** 33-3021.03. **Average Salary:** $53,350. **Projected Growth:** 22.4%. **Annual Openings:** 11,000. **Education:** Work experience in a related occupation. **Job Zone:** 4. **Education/Training Program(s)**—Criminal Justice/Police Science; Criminalistics and Criminal Science. **Related Knowledge/Courses:** Public Safety and Security; Law and Government; Psychology; Sociology and Anthropology; Telecommunications; Geography. **Personality Type:** Enterprising. **Skills Required:** Social Perceptiveness; Speaking; Persuasion; Active Listening; Writing; Critical Thinking; Coordination; Judgment and Decision Making. **Abilities:** Night Vision; Speech Recognition; Inductive Reasoning; Flexibility of Closure; Sound Localization. **Occupational Values:** Achievement; Social Status; Ability Utilization; Security; Authority. **Interacting with Others:** Communicating with Supervisors, Peers, or Subordinates; Interpreting the Meaning of Information for Others; Establishing and Maintaining Interpersonal Relationships. **Physical Work Conditions:** Outdoors; Walking and Running; Kneeling, Crouching, Stooping, or Crawling; Standing; Spend Time Bending or Twisting the Body; Specialized Protective or Safety Equipment.

Fire Investigators

Conduct investigations to determine causes of fires and explosions. **O*NET Code:** 33-2021.02. **Average Salary:** $45,810. **Projected Growth:** 11.6%. **Annual Openings:** 1,000. **Education:** Bachelor's degree. **Job Zone:** 4. **Education/Training Program(s)**—Fire Protection and Safety Technology/Technician; Fire Science/Firefighting. **Related Knowledge/Courses:** Public Safety and Security; Law and Government; Chemistry; Building and Construction; Education and Training; Telecommunications. **Personality Type:** Investigative. **Skills Required:** Science; Active Listening; Critical Thinking; Persuasion; Systems Evaluation; Writing; Speaking; Judgment and Decision Making. **Abilities:** Speed of Closure; Inductive Reasoning; Flexibility of Closure; Spatial Orientation; Written Expression. **Occupational Values:** Achievement; Responsibility; Ability Utilization; Social Status; Variety. **Interacting with Others:** Communicating with Persons Outside Organization; Communicating with Supervisors, Peers, or Subordinates; Establishing and Maintaining Interpersonal Relationships; Performing Administrative Activities. **Physical Work Conditions:** Very Hot or Cold; Kneeling, Crouching, Stooping, or Crawling; Common Protective or Safety Equipment; Extremely Bright or Inadequate Lighting; Outdoors; Contaminants.

Forensic Science Technicians

Collect, identify, classify, and analyze physical evidence related to criminal investigations. Perform tests on weapons or substances such as fiber, hair, and tissue to determine significance to investigation. May testify as expert witnesses on evidence or crime laboratory techniques. May serve as specialists in area of expertise, such as ballistics, fingerprinting, handwriting, or biochemistry. **O*NET Code:** 19-4092.00. **Average**

Salary: $43,200. **Projected Growth:** 18.9%. **Annual Openings:** 1,000. **Education:** Associate degree. **Job Zone:** 4. **Education/Training Program(s)**—Forensic Science and Technology. **Related Knowledge/Courses:** Chemistry; Law and Government; Customer and Personal Service; English Language; Public Safety and Security; Biology. **Personality Type:** Investigative. **Skills Required:** Science; Quality Control Analysis; Troubleshooting; Active Learning; Instructing; Speaking; Critical Thinking; Monitoring. **Abilities:** Inductive Reasoning; Category Flexibility; Flexibility of Closure; Near Vision; Oral Expression. **Occupational Values:** Autonomy; Achievement; Variety; Recognition; Creativity. **Interacting with Others:** Communicating with Persons Outside Organization; Interpreting the Meaning of Information for Others; Communicating with Supervisors, Peers, or Subordinates. **Physical Work Conditions:** Contaminants; Hazardous Conditions; Sitting; In an Enclosed Vehicle or Equipment; Cramped Work Space, Awkward Positions.

Highway Patrol Pilots

Pilot aircraft to patrol highway and enforce traffic laws. O*NET Code: 33-3051.02. **Average Salary:** $44,530. **Projected Growth:** 24.7%. **Annual Openings:** 67,000. **Education:** Long-term on-the-job training. **Job Zone:** 3. **Education/Training Program(s)**—Criminal Justice/Police Science; Criminalistics and Criminal Science. **Related Knowledge/Courses:** Public Safety and Security; Transportation; Law and Government; Customer and Personal Service; Medicine and Dentistry; Psychology; Geography. **Personality Type:** Realistic. **Skills Required:** Operation and Control; Social Perceptiveness; Service Orientation; Operation Monitoring; Judgment and Decision Making; Active Listening; Critical Thinking; Reading Comprehension. **Abilities:** Far Vision; Rate Control; Glare Sensitivity; Response Orientation; Night Vision. **Occupational Values:** Social Service; Achievement; Security; Authority; Variety. **Interacting with Others:** Performing for or Working Directly with the Public; Communicating with Persons Outside Organization; Assisting and Caring for Others. **Physical Work Conditions:** Outdoors; Common Protective or Safety Equipment; Sounds, Noise Levels Are Distracting or Uncomfortable; High Places; Sitting.

Parking Enforcement Workers

Patrol assigned area, such as public parking lot or section of city, to issue tickets to overtime parking violators and illegally parked vehicles. O*NET Code: 33-3041.00. **Average Salary:** $28,370. **Projected Growth:** 11.5%. **Annual Openings:** 1,000. **Education:** Short-term on-the-job training. **Job Zone:** 1. **Education/Training Program(s)**—Security and Protective Services, Other. **Related Knowledge/Courses:** Law and Government; Geography; Clerical. **Personality Type:** Conventional. **Skills Required:** None met the criteria. **Abilities:** Gross Body Coordination; Glare Sensitivity; Spatial Orientation; Finger Dexterity; Stamina. **Occupational Values:** Independence; Security; Supervision, Technical; Supervision, Human Relations; Co-workers. **Interacting with Others:** Communicating with Supervisors, Peers, or Subordinates; Communicating with Persons Outside Organization; Performing for or Working Directly with the Public; Performing Administrative Activities. **Physical Work**

Conditions: Outdoors; Very Hot or Cold; Standing; Walking and Running; Extremely Bright or Inadequate Lighting.

Police Detectives

Conduct investigations to prevent crimes or solve criminal cases. O*NET Code: 33-3021.01. **Average Salary:** $53,350. **Projected Growth:** 22.4%. **Annual Openings:** 11,000. **Education:** Work experience in a related occupation. **Job Zone:** 4. **Education/Training Program(s)**—Criminal Justice/Police Science; Criminalistics and Criminal Science. **Related Knowledge/Courses:** Public Safety and Security; Law and Government; Psychology; Customer and Personal Service; Education and Training; Philosophy and Theology. **Personality Type:** Enterprising. **Skills Required:** Persuasion; Negotiation; Social Perceptiveness; Coordination; Service Orientation; Active Listening; Speaking; Critical Thinking; Time Management. **Abilities:** Response Orientation; Flexibility of Closure; Speech Recognition; Speed of Closure; Explosive Strength. **Occupational Values:** Variety; Responsibility; Ability Utilization; Achievement; Social Status. **Interacting with Others:** Communicating with Persons Outside Organization; Performing for or Working Directly with the Public; Communicating with Supervisors, Peers, or Subordinates; Establishing and Maintaining Interpersonal Relationships. **Physical Work Conditions:** In an Enclosed Vehicle or Equipment; Very Hot or Cold; Outdoors; Extremely Bright or Inadequate Lighting; Indoors, Not Environmentally Controlled; Physical Proximity.

Police Identification and Records Officers

Collect evidence at crime scene, classify and identify fingerprints, and photograph evidence for use in criminal and civil cases. O*NET Code: 33-3021.02. **Average Salary:** $53,350. **Projected Growth:** 22.4%. **Annual Openings:** 11,000. **Education:** Work experience in a related occupation. **Job Zone:** 3. **Education/Training Program(s)**—Criminal Justice/Police Science; Criminalistics and Criminal Science. **Related Knowledge/Courses:** Law and Government; Customer and Personal Service; Public Safety and Security; Telecommunications; Computers and Electronics; Psychology; English Language. **Personality Type:** Conventional. **Skills Required:** Persuasion; Negotiation; Service Orientation; Judgment and Decision Making; Social Perceptiveness; Critical Thinking; Time Management; Learning Strategies; Coordination. **Abilities:** Flexibility of Closure; Near Vision; Visual Color Discrimination; Speech Recognition; Glare Sensitivity. **Occupational Values:** Advancement; Co-workers; Supervision, Human Relations; Supervision, Technical; Security; Company Policies and Practices. **Interacting with Others:** Performing for or Working Directly with the Public; Resolving Conflicts and Negotiating with Others; Communicating with Supervisors, Peers, or Subordinates; Establishing and Maintaining Interpersonal Relationships. **Physical Work Conditions:** Very Hot or Cold; Extremely Bright or Inadequate Lighting; In an Enclosed Vehicle or Equipment; Sounds, Noise Levels Are Distracting or Uncomfortable; Outdoors; Contaminants.

Police Patrol Officers

Patrol assigned area to enforce laws and ordinances, regulate traffic, control crowds, prevent crime, and arrest violators.

O*NET Code: 33-3051.01. **Average Salary:** $44,530. **Projected Growth:** 24.7%. **Annual Openings:** 67,000. **Education:** Long-term on-the-job training. **Job Zone:** 3. **Education/Training Program(s)**—Criminal Justice/Police Science; Criminalistics and Criminal Science. **Related Knowledge/Courses:** Public Safety and Security; Law and Government; Customer and Personal Service; Psychology; Sociology and Anthropology; Telecommunications. **Personality Type:** Social. **Skills Required:** Persuasion; Negotiation; Social Perceptiveness; Judgment and Decision Making; Service Orientation; Active Listening; Critical Thinking; Coordination. **Abilities:** Reaction Time; Rate Control; Response Orientation; Night Vision; Stamina; Far Vision. **Occupational Values:** Social Service; Variety; Security; Social Status; Achievement; Authority; Supervision, Human Relations. **Interacting with Others:** Resolving Conflicts and Negotiating with Others; Performing for or Working Directly with the Public; Communicating with Persons Outside Organization. **Physical Work Conditions:** In an Enclosed Vehicle or Equipment; Contaminants; Outdoors; Very Hot or Cold; Sounds, Noise Levels Are Distracting or Uncomfortable; Extremely Bright or Inadequate Lighting.

Sheriffs and Deputy Sheriffs

Enforce law and order in rural or unincorporated districts or serve legal processes of courts. May patrol courthouse, guard court or grand jury, or escort defendants. O*NET Code: 33-3051.03. **Average Salary:** $44,530. **Projected Growth:** 24.7%. **Annual Openings:** 67,000. **Education:** Long-term on-the-job training. **Job Zone:** 2. **Education/Training Program(s)**—Criminal Justice/Police Science; Criminalistics and Criminal Science. **Related Knowledge/Courses:** Public Safety and Security; Law and Government; Psychology; Geography; Sociology and Anthropology; Clerical. **Personality Type:** Social. **Skills Required:** Social Perceptiveness; Service Orientation; Active Listening; Speaking; Coordination; Judgment and Decision Making; Writing; Critical Thinking. **Abilities:** Inductive Reasoning; Night Vision; Multilimb Coordination; Rate Control; Glare Sensitivity. **Occupational Values:** Authority; Security; Variety; Social Status; Social Service. **Interacting with Others:** Performing for or Working Directly with the Public; Assisting and Caring for Others; Communicating with Supervisors, Peers, or Subordinates. **Physical Work Conditions:** Specialized Protective or Safety Equipment; Outdoors; Minor Burns, Cuts, Bites, or Stings; Walking and Running; Kneeling, Crouching, Stooping, or Crawling.

Transit and Railroad Police

Protect and police railroad and transit property, employees, or passengers. O*NET Code: 33-3052.00. **Average Salary:** $44,260. **Projected Growth:** 15.9%. **Annual Openings:** 1,000. **Education:** Long-term on-the-job training. **Job Zone:** 2. **Education/Training Program(s)**—Security and Loss Prevention Services; Security and Protective Services, Other. **Related Knowledge/Courses:** Public Safety and Security; Law and Government; Transportation; Administration and Management; Personnel and Human Resources; Sociology and Anthropology. **Personality Type:** Enterprising. **Skills Required:** Management of Personnel Resources; Active Listening; Speaking; Social Perceptiveness; Coordination;

Writing; Critical Thinking; Instructing. **Abilities:** Night Vision; Speed of Limb Movement; Explosive Strength; Sound Localization; Stamina. **Occupational Values:** Authority; Responsibility; Creativity; Variety; Security; Social Status; Co-workers. **Interacting with Others:** Communicating with Supervisors, Peers, or Subordinates; Establishing and Maintaining Interpersonal Relationships; Coordinating the Work and Activities of Others. **Physical Work Conditions:** Outdoors; Walking and Running; Standing; Spend Time Bending or Twisting the Body; Extremely Bright or Inadequate Lighting.

12.05 Safety and Security

Animal Control Workers

Handle animals for the purpose of investigations of mistreatment or control of abandoned, dangerous, or unattended animals. O*NET Code: 33-9011.00. **Average Salary:** $25,870. **Projected Growth:** 12.6%. **Annual Openings:** 2,000. **Education:** Moderate-term on-the-job training. **Job Zone:** 2. **Education/Training Program(s)**—Security and Protective Services, Other. **Related Knowledge/Courses:** Education and Training; Biology; Sales and Marketing; Communications and Media; Public Safety and Security; Chemistry; Law and Government. **Personality Type:** Social. **Skills Required:** Instructing; Learning Strategies; Social Perceptiveness; Service Orientation; Critical Thinking; Active Listening; Speaking; Persuasion; Systems Analysis. **Abilities:** Reaction Time; Rate Control; Far Vision; Explosive Strength; Stamina. **Occupational Values:** Authority; Social Service; Supervision, Technical; Variety; Security. **Interacting with Others:** Assisting and Caring for Others; Communicating with Persons Outside Organization; Training and Teaching Others. **Physical Work Conditions:** Minor Burns, Cuts, Bites, or Stings; Outdoors; Common Protective or Safety Equipment; Standing; Walking and Running.

Crossing Guards

Guide or control vehicular or pedestrian traffic at such places as streets, schools, railroad crossings, or construction sites. O*NET Code: 33-9091.00. **Average Salary:** $19,090. **Projected Growth:** 16.5%. **Annual Openings:** 19,000. **Education:** Short-term on-the-job training. **Job Zone:** 1. **Education/Training Program(s)**—Security and Protective Services, Other. **Related Knowledge/Courses:** Public Safety and Security; Law and Government; Geography. **Personality Type:** Social. **Skills Required:** Service Orientation. **Abilities:** Peripheral Vision; Reaction Time; Night Vision; Far Vision; Glare Sensitivity. **Occupational Values:** Authority; Social Service; Independence; Supervision, Technical; Moral Values. **Interacting with Others:** Communicating with Supervisors, Peers, or Subordinates; Communicating with Persons Outside Organization; Assisting and Caring for Others; Performing for or Working Directly with the Public. **Physical Work Conditions:** Outdoors; Standing; Walking and Running; Common Protective or Safety Equipment; Sounds, Noise Levels Are Distracting or Uncomfortable; Contaminants.

Gaming Surveillance Officers and Gaming Investigators

Act as oversight and security agent for management and customers. Observe casino or casino hotel operation for irregular activities such as cheating or theft by either employees or patrons. May utilize one-way mirrors above the casino floor and cashier's cage and from desk. Use of audio/video equipment is also common to observe operation of the business. Usually required to provide verbal and written reports of all violations and suspicious behavior to supervisor. **O*NET Code:** 33-9031.00. **Average Salary:** $25,770. **Projected Growth:** 24.6%. **Annual Openings:** 2,000. **Education:** Long-term on-the-job training. **Job Zone:** 2. **Education/Training Program(s)**—No data available. **Related Knowledge/Courses:** Public Safety and Security; Computers and Electronics; Law and Government; Clerical; Education and Training; Telecommunications. **Personality Type:** No data available. **Skills Required:** Management of Personnel Resources; Active Listening; Social Perceptiveness; Instructing; Negotiation; Learning Strategies; Writing; Critical Thinking. **Abilities:** No data available. **Occupational Values:** No data available. **Interacting with Others:** Communicating with Supervisors, Peers, or Subordinates; Coaching and Developing Others; Coordinating the Work and Activities of Others; Guiding, Directing, and Motivating Subordinates; Monitoring and Controlling Resources. **Physical Work Conditions:** Physical Proximity; Sitting; Contaminants; Sounds, Noise Levels Are Distracting or Uncomfortable; Extremely Bright or Inadequate Lighting.

Lifeguards, Ski Patrol, and Other Recreational Protective Service Workers

Monitor recreational areas, such as pools, beaches, or ski slopes, to provide assistance and protection to participants. **O*NET Code:** 33-9092.00. **Average Salary:** $29,900. **Projected Growth:** 14.3%. **Annual Openings:** 60,000. **Education:** Short-term on-the-job training. **Job Zone:** 2. **Education/Training Program(s)**—Security and Protective Services, Other. **Related Knowledge/Courses:** Medicine and Dentistry; Public Safety and Security; Psychology; Telecommunications; Customer and Personal Service; Engineering and Technology; Communications and Media. **Personality Type:** Realistic. **Skills Required:** Service Orientation; Instructing; Learning Strategies; Social Perceptiveness; Persuasion; Science; Critical Thinking; Systems Analysis. **Abilities:** Glare Sensitivity; Sound Localization; Night Vision; Stamina; Far Vision. **Occupational Values:** Social Service; Authority; Variety; Supervision, Technical; Achievement. **Interacting with Others:** Assisting and Caring for Others; Performing for or Working Directly with the Public; Communicating with Persons Outside Organization. **Physical Work Conditions:** Outdoors; Very Hot or Cold; Walking and Running; Extremely Bright or Inadequate Lighting; Climbing Ladders, Scaffolds, or Poles.

Private Detectives and Investigators

Detect occurrences of unlawful acts or infractions of rules in private establishment or seek, examine, and compile information for client. **O*NET Code:** 33-9021.00. **Average Salary:** $30,460. **Projected Growth:** 25.3%. **Annual Openings:**

9,000. **Education:** Work experience in a related occupation. **Job Zone:** 2. **Education/Training Program(s)**—Criminal Justice/Police Science. **Related Knowledge/Courses:** Public Safety and Security; Psychology; Law and Government; Telecommunications; Medicine and Dentistry; Therapy and Counseling; Communications and Media. **Personality Type:** Enterprising. **Skills Required:** Persuasion; Systems Evaluation; Critical Thinking; Social Perceptiveness; Active Listening; Writing; Speaking; Judgment and Decision Making; Systems Analysis. **Abilities:** Night Vision; Far Vision; Speed of Limb Movement; Sound Localization; Peripheral Vision. **Occupational Values:** Ability Utilization; Responsibility; Achievement; Authority; Creativity. **Interacting with Others:** Communicating with Supervisors, Peers, or Subordinates; Assisting and Caring for Others; Communicating with Persons Outside Organization. **Physical Work Conditions:** Standing; Outdoors; Walking and Running; Climbing Ladders, Scaffolds, or Poles; Spend Time Bending or Twisting the Body.

Security Guards

Guard, patrol, or monitor premises to prevent theft, violence, or infractions of rules. **O*NET Code:** 33-9032.00. **Average Salary:** $19,970. **Projected Growth:** 31.9%. **Annual Openings:** 228,000. **Education:** Short-term on-the-job training. **Job Zone:** 2. **Education/Training Program(s)**—Securities Services Administration/Management; Security and Loss Prevention Services. **Related Knowledge/Courses:** Public Safety and Security; Customer and Personal Service; Law and Government; Clerical; Telecommunications; English Language. **Personality Type:** Social. **Skills Required:** Social Perceptiveness; Negotiation; Learning Strategies; Speaking; Time Management; Monitoring; Active Listening; Critical Thinking. **Abilities:** Flexibility of Closure; Selective Attention; Far Vision; Stamina; Speech Recognition. **Occupational Values:** Authority; Social Service; Supervision, Human Relations; Supervision, Technical. **Interacting with Others:** Communicating with Supervisors, Peers, or Subordinates; Resolving Conflicts and Negotiating with Others; Performing for or Working Directly with the Public. **Physical Work Conditions:** Very Hot or Cold; Sounds, Noise Levels Are Distracting or Uncomfortable; Physical Proximity; Extremely Bright or Inadequate Lighting; Outdoors.

12.06 Emergency Responding

Emergency Medical Technicians and Paramedics

Assess injuries, administer emergency medical care, and extricate trapped individuals. Transport injured or sick persons to medical facilities. **O*NET Code:** 29-2041.00. **Average Salary:** $24,760. **Projected Growth:** 33.1%. **Annual Openings:** 32,000. **Education:** Postsecondary vocational training. **Job Zone:** 2. **Education/Training Program(s)**—Emergency Care Attendant (EMT Ambulance); Emergency Medical Technology/Technician (EMT Paramedic). **Related Knowledge/Courses:** Customer and Personal Service;

Medicine and Dentistry; Psychology; Public Safety and Security; Chemistry; Therapy and Counseling. **Personality Type:** Social. **Skills Required:** Equipment Maintenance; Social Perceptiveness; Service Orientation; Coordination; Instructing; Negotiation; Critical Thinking; Speaking; Persuasion. **Abilities:** Reaction Time; Response Orientation; Rate Control; Manual Dexterity; Stamina. **Occupational Values:** Social Service; Achievement; Co-workers; Variety; Ability Utilization. **Interacting with Others:** Assisting and Caring for Others; Performing for or Working Directly with the Public; Establishing and Maintaining Interpersonal Relationships. **Physical Work Conditions:** Extremely Bright or Inadequate Lighting; Physical Proximity; Sounds, Noise Levels Are Distracting or Uncomfortable; Very Hot or Cold; Contaminants.

Forest Fire Fighters

Control and suppress fires in forests or on vacant public land. **O*NET Code:** 33-2011.02. **Average Salary:** $37,410. **Projected Growth:** 20.7%. **Annual Openings:** 29,000. **Education:** Long-term on-the-job training. **Job Zone:** 2. **Education/Training Program(s)**—Fire Protection, Other; Fire Science/Firefighting. **Related Knowledge/Courses:** Customer and Personal Service; Geography; Education and Training; Public Safety and Security; Mechanical; Personnel and Human Resources. **Personality Type:** Realistic. **Skills Required:** Management of Personnel Resources; Service Orientation; Equipment Maintenance; Coordination; Repairing; Instructing; Equipment Selection; Operation Monitoring. **Abilities:** Spatial Orientation; Stamina; Explosive Strength; Gross Body Coordination; Static Strength. **Occupational Values:** Achievement; Co-workers; Social Status; Supervision, Technical; Supervision, Human Relations. **Interacting with Others:** Establishing and Maintaining Interpersonal Relationships; Assisting and Caring for Others; Coordinating the Work and Activities of Others. **Physical Work Conditions:** Very Hot or Cold; Contaminants; Outdoors; Hazardous Conditions; Extremely Bright or Inadequate Lighting.

Municipal Fire Fighters

Control and extinguish municipal fires, protect life and property, and conduct rescue efforts. **O*NET Code:** 33-2011.01. **Average Salary:** $37,410. **Projected Growth:** 20.7%. **Annual Openings:** 29,000. **Education:** Long-term on-the-job training. **Job Zone:** 3. **Education/Training Program(s)**—Fire Protection, Other; Fire Science/Firefighting. **Related Knowledge/Courses:** Customer and Personal Service; Medicine and Dentistry; Physics; Public Safety and Security; Psychology; Building and Construction. **Personality Type:** Realistic. **Skills Required:** Service Orientation; Equipment Maintenance; Social Perceptiveness; Equipment Selection; Coordination; Learning Strategies; Critical Thinking; Complex Problem Solving; Operation Monitoring. **Abilities:** Static Strength; Dynamic Strength; Stamina; Trunk Strength; Flexibility of Closure. **Occupational Values:** Social Status; Achievement; Co-workers; Social Service; Supervision, Technical. **Interacting with Others:** Communicating with Supervisors, Peers, or Subordinates; Establishing and Maintaining Interpersonal Relationships; Assisting and Caring for Others. **Physical Work Conditions:** Physical Proximity; Very Hot or Cold; Contaminants; Outdoors; Hazardous Conditions.

12.07 Military

Air Crew Members

Perform in-flight duties to ensure the successful completion of combat, reconnaissance, transport, and search and rescue missions. Duties include operating aircraft communications and detection equipment, including establishing satellite linkages and jamming enemy communications capabilities; conducting pre-flight, in-flight, and post-flight inspections of onboard equipment; operating and maintaining aircraft weapons and defensive systems; operating and maintaining aircraft in-flight refueling systems; executing aircraft safety and emergency procedures; computing and verifying passenger, cargo, fuel, and emergency and special equipment weight and balance data; and conducting cargo and personnel drops. **O*NET Code:** 55-3011.00. **Average Salary:** No data available. **Projected Growth:** No data available. **Annual Openings:** No data available. **Education:** Moderate-term on-the-job training. **Job Zone:** No data available. **Education/Training Program(s)**—No data available. **Related Knowledge/Courses:** No data available. **Personality Type:** No data available. **Skills Required:** No data available. **Abilities:** No data available. **Occupational Values:** No data available. **Interacting with Others:** No data available. **Physical Work Conditions:** No data available.

Air Crew Officers

Perform and direct in-flight duties to ensure the successful completion of combat, reconnaissance, transport, and search and rescue missions. Duties include operating aircraft communications and radar equipment, such as establishing satellite linkages and jamming enemy communications capabilities; operating aircraft weapons and defensive systems; conducting pre-flight, in-flight, and post-flight inspections of onboard equipment; and directing cargo and personnel drops. **O*NET Code:** 55-1011.00. **Average Salary:** No data available. **Projected Growth:** No data available. **Annual Openings:** No data available. **Education:** Long-term on-the-job training. **Job Zone:** No data available. **Education/Training Program(s)**—No data available. **Related Knowledge/Courses:** No data available. **Personality Type:** No data available. **Skills Required:** No data available. **Abilities:** No data available. **Occupational Values:** No data available. **Interacting with Others:** No data available. **Physical Work Conditions:** No data available.

Aircraft Launch and Recovery Officers

Plan and direct the operation and maintenance of catapults; arresting gear; and associated mechanical, hydraulic, and control systems involved primarily in aircraft carrier takeoff and landing operations. Duties include supervision of readiness and safety of arresting gear, launching equipment, barricades, and visual landing aid systems; planning and coordinating the design, development, and testing of launch and recovery systems; preparing specifications for catapult and arresting gear installations; evaluating design proposals; determining handling equipment needed for new aircraft; preparing technical data and instructions for operation of landing aids; and training personnel in carrier takeoff and landing procedures. **O*NET Code:** 55-1012.00. **Average Salary:** No data available. **Projected Growth:** No data available. **Annual Openings:** No data available. **Education:** Long-term on-the-job training. **Job Zone:** No data available. **Education/Training Program(s)—** No data available. **Related Knowledge/Courses:** No data available. **Personality Type:** No data available. **Skills Required:** No data available. **Abilities:** No data available. **Occupational Values:** No data available. **Interacting with Others:** No data available. **Physical Work Conditions:** No data available.

Aircraft Launch and Recovery Specialists

Operate and maintain catapults; arresting gear; and associated mechanical, hydraulic, and control systems involved primarily in aircraft carrier takeoff and landing operations. Duties include installing and maintaining visual landing aids; testing and maintaining launch and recovery equipment, using electric and mechanical test equipment and hand tools; activating airfield arresting systems, such as crash barriers and cables, during emergency landing situations; directing aircraft launch and recovery operations, using hand or light signals; and maintaining logs of airplane launches, recoveries, and equipment maintenance. **O*NET Code:** 55-3012.00. **Average Salary:** No data available. **Projected Growth:** No data available. **Annual Openings:** No data available. **Education:** Moderate-term on-the-job training. **Job Zone:** No data available. **Education/Training Program(s)—**No data available. **Related Knowledge/Courses:** No data available. **Personality Type:** No data available. **Skills Required:** No data available. **Abilities:** No data available. **Occupational Values:** No data available. **Interacting with Others:** No data available. **Physical Work Conditions:** No data available.

Armored Assault Vehicle Crew Members

Operate tanks, light armor, and amphibious assault vehicles during combat situations on land or in aquatic environments. Duties include driving armored vehicles that require specialized training; operating and maintaining targeting and firing systems; operating and maintaining advanced onboard communications and navigation equipment; transporting personnel and equipment in a combat environment; and operating and maintaining auxiliary weapons, including machine guns and grenade launchers. **O*NET Code:** 55-3013.00. **Average Salary:** No data available. **Projected Growth:** No data available. **Annual Openings:** No data available. **Education:** Moderate-term on-the-job training. **Job Zone:** No data available. **Education/Training Program(s)—**No data available. **Related Knowledge/Courses:** No data available. **Personality Type:** No data available. **Skills Required:** No data available. **Abilities:** No data available. **Occupational Values:** No data available. **Interacting with Others:** No data available. **Physical Work Conditions:** No data available.

Armored Assault Vehicle Officers

Direct the operation of tanks, light armor, and amphibious assault vehicle units during combat situations on land or in aquatic environments. Duties include directing crew members in the operation of targeting and firing systems; coordinating the operation of advanced onboard communications

and navigation equipment; directing the transport of personnel and equipment during combat; formulating and implementing battle plans, including the tactical employment of armored vehicle units; and coordinating with infantry, artillery, and air support units. **O*NET Code:** 55-1013.00. **Average Salary:** No data available. **Projected Growth:** No data available. **Annual Openings:** No data available. **Education:** Long-term on-the-job training. **Job Zone:** No data available. **Education/Training Program(s)—**No data available. **Related Knowledge/Courses:** No data available. **Personality Type:** No data available. **Skills Required:** No data available. **Abilities:** No data available. **Occupational Values:** No data available. **Interacting with Others:** No data available. **Physical Work Conditions:** No data available.

Artillery and Missile Crew Members

Target, fire, and maintain weapons used to destroy enemy positions, aircraft, and vessels. Field artillery crew members predominantly use guns, cannons, and howitzers in ground combat operations, while air defense artillery crew members predominantly use missiles and rockets. Naval artillery crew members predominantly use torpedoes and missiles launched from a ship or submarine. Duties include testing, inspecting, and storing ammunition, missiles, and torpedoes; conducting preventive and routine maintenance on weapons and related equipment; establishing and maintaining radio and wire communications; and operating weapons-targeting, -firing, and -launch computer systems. **O*NET Code:** 55-3014.00. **Average Salary:** No data available. **Projected Growth:** No data available. **Annual Openings:** No data available. **Education:** Moderate-term on-the-job training. **Job Zone:** No data available. **Education/Training Program(s)—**No data available. **Related Knowledge/Courses:** No data available. **Personality Type:** No data available. **Skills Required:** No data available. **Abilities:** No data available. **Occupational Values:** No data available. **Interacting with Others:** No data available. **Physical Work Conditions:** No data available.

Artillery and Missile Officers

Manage personnel and weapons operations to destroy enemy positions, aircraft, and vessels. Duties include planning, targeting, and coordinating the tactical deployment of field artillery and air defense artillery missile systems units; directing the establishment and operation of fire control communications systems; targeting and launching intercontinental ballistic missiles; directing the storage and handling of nuclear munitions and components; overseeing security of weapons storage and launch facilities; and managing maintenance of weapons systems. **O*NET Code:** 55-1014.00. **Average Salary:** No data available. **Projected Growth:** No data available. **Annual Openings:** No data available. **Education:** Long-term on-the-job training. **Job Zone:** No data available. **Education/Training Program(s)—**No data available. **Related Knowledge/Courses:** No data available. **Personality Type:** No data available. **Skills Required:** No data available. **Abilities:** No data available. **Occupational Values:** No data available. **Interacting with Others:** No data available. **Physical Work Conditions:** No data available.

Command and Control Center Officers

Manage the operation of communications, detection, and weapons systems essential for controlling air, ground, and naval operations. Duties include managing critical communication links between air, naval, and ground forces; formulating and implementing emergency plans for natural and wartime disasters; coordinating emergency response teams and agencies; evaluating command center information and need for high-level military and government reporting; managing the operation of surveillance and detection systems; providing technical information and advice on capabilities and operational readiness; and directing operation of weapons-targeting, -firing, and -launch computer systems. **O*NET Code:** 55-1015.00. **Average Salary:** No data available. **Projected Growth:** No data available. **Annual Openings:** No data available. **Education:** Long-term on-the-job training. **Job Zone:** No data available. **Education/Training Program(s)—** No data available. **Related Knowledge/Courses:** No data available. **Personality Type:** No data available. **Skills Required:** No data available. **Abilities:** No data available. **Occupational Values:** No data available. **Interacting with Others:** No data available. **Physical Work Conditions:** No data available.

Command and Control Center Specialists

Operate and monitor communications, detection, and weapons systems essential for controlling air, ground, and naval operations. Duties include maintaining and relaying critical communications between air, naval, and ground forces; implementing emergency plans for natural and wartime disasters; relaying command center information to high-level military and government decision makers; monitoring surveillance and detection systems, such as air defense; interpreting and evaluating tactical situations and making recommendations to superiors; and operating weapons-targeting, -firing, and -launch computer systems. **O*NET Code:** 55-3015.00. **Average Salary:** No data available. **Projected Growth:** No data available. **Annual Openings:** No data available. **Education:** Moderate-term on-the-job training. **Job Zone:** No data available. **Education/Training Program(s)—** No data available. **Related Knowledge/Courses:** No data available. **Personality Type:** No data available. **Skills Required:** No data available. **Abilities:** No data available. **Occupational Values:** No data available. **Interacting with Others:** No data available. **Physical Work Conditions:** No data available.

First-Line Supervisors/Managers of Air Crew Members

Supervise and coordinate the activities of air crew members. Supervisors may also perform the same activities as the workers they supervise. **O*NET Code:** 55-2011.00. **Average Salary:** No data available. **Projected Growth:** No data available. **Annual Openings:** No data available. **Education:** Work experience in a related occupation. **Job Zone:** No data available. **Education/Training Program(s)—**No data available. **Related Knowledge/Courses:** No data available. **Personality Type:** No data available. **Skills Required:** No data available. **Abilities:** No data available. **Occupational Values:** No data available. **Interacting with Others:** No data available. **Physical Work Conditions:** No data available.

First-Line Supervisors/Managers of Weapons Specialists/Crew Members

Supervise and coordinate the activities of weapons specialists/crew members. Supervisors may also perform the same activities as the workers they supervise. **O*NET Code:** 55-2012.00. **Average Salary:** No data available. **Projected Growth:** No data available. **Annual Openings:** No data available. **Education:** Work experience in a related occupation. **Job Zone:** No data available. **Education/Training Program(s)—** No data available. **Related Knowledge/Courses:** No data available. **Personality Type:** No data available. **Skills Required:** No data available. **Abilities:** No data available. **Occupational Values:** No data available. **Interacting with Others:** No data available. **Physical Work Conditions:** No data available.

Infantry

Operate weapons and equipment in ground combat operations. Duties include operating and maintaining weapons, such as rifles, machine guns, mortars, and hand grenades; locating, constructing, and camouflaging infantry positions and equipment; evaluating terrain and recording topographical information; operating and maintaining field communications equipment; assessing need for and directing supporting fire; placing explosives and performing minesweeping activities on land; and participating in basic reconnaissance operations. **O*NET Code:** 55-3016.00. **Average Salary:** No data available. **Projected Growth:** No data available. **Annual Openings:** No data available. **Education:** Moderate-term on-the-job training. **Job Zone:** No data available. **Education/Training Program(s)—**No data available. **Related Knowledge/Courses:** No data available. **Personality Type:** No data available. **Skills Required:** No data available. **Abilities:** No data available. **Occupational Values:** No data available. **Interacting with Others:** No data available. **Physical Work Conditions:** No data available.

Infantry Officers

Direct, train, and lead infantry units in ground combat operations. Duties include directing deployment of infantry weapons, vehicles, and equipment; directing location, construction, and camouflage of infantry positions and equipment; managing field communications operations; coordinating with armor, artillery, and air support units; performing strategic and tactical planning, including battle plan development; and leading basic reconnaissance operations. **O*NET Code:** 55-1016.00. **Average Salary:** No data available. **Projected Growth:** No data available. **Annual Openings:** No data available. **Education:** Long-term on-the-job training. **Job Zone:** No data available. **Education/Training Program(s)—** No data available. **Related Knowledge/Courses:** No data available. **Personality Type:** No data available. **Skills Required:** No data available. **Abilities:** No data available. **Occupational Values:** No data available. **Interacting with Others:** No data available. **Physical Work Conditions:** No data available.

Radar and Sonar Technicians

Operate equipment, using radio or sound wave technology to identify, track, and analyze objects or natural phenomena of military interest. Includes airborne, shipboard, and terrestrial positions. May perform minor maintenance. **O*NET Code:** 55-3017.00. **Average Salary:** No data available. **Projected Growth:** No data available. **Annual Openings:** No data available. **Education:** Moderate-term on-the-job training. **Job Zone:** No data available. **Education/Training Program(s)—** No data available. **Related Knowledge/Courses:** No data available. **Personality Type:** No data available. **Skills Required:** No data available. **Abilities:** No data available. **Occupational Values:** No data available. **Interacting with Others:** No data available. **Physical Work Conditions:** No data available.

Special Forces

Implement unconventional operations by air, land, or sea during combat or peacetime as members of elite teams. These activities include offensive raids, demolitions, reconnaissance, search and rescue, and counterterrorism. In addition to their combat training, Special Forces members often have specialized training in swimming, diving, parachuting, survival, emergency medicine, and foreign languages. Duties include conducting advanced reconnaissance operations and collecting intelligence information; recruiting, training, and equipping friendly forces; conducting raids and invasions on enemy territories; laying and detonating explosives for demolition targets; locating, identifying, defusing, and disposing of ordnance; and operating and maintaining sophisticated communications equipment. **O*NET Code:** 55-3018.00. **Average Salary:** No data available. **Projected Growth:** No data available. **Annual Openings:** No data available. **Education:** Long-term on-the-job training. **Job Zone:** No data available. **Education/Training Program(s)—**No data available. **Related Knowledge/Courses:** No data available. **Personality Type:** No data available. **Skills Required:** No data available. **Abilities:** No data available. **Occupational Values:** No data available. **Interacting with Others:** No data available. **Physical Work Conditions:** No data available.

Special Forces Officers

Lead elite teams that implement unconventional operations by air, land, or sea during combat or peacetime. These activities include offensive raids, demolitions, reconnaissance, search and rescue, and counterterrorism. In addition to their combat training, special forces officers often have specialized training in swimming, diving, parachuting, survival, emergency medicine, and foreign languages. Duties include directing advanced reconnaissance operations and evaluating intelligence information; recruiting, training, and equipping friendly forces; leading raids and invasions on enemy territories; training personnel to implement individual missions and contingency plans; performing strategic and tactical planning for politically sensitive missions; and operating sophisticated communications equipment. **O*NET Code:** 55-1017.00. **Average Salary:** No data available. **Projected Growth:** No data available. **Annual Openings:** No data available. **Education:** Long-term on-the-job training. **Job Zone:** No data available. **Education/Training Program(s)—**No data available. **Related Knowledge/Courses:** No data available. **Personality Type:** No data available. **Skills Required:** No data available. **Abilities:** No data available. **Occupational Values:** No data available. **Interacting with Others:** No data available. **Physical Work Conditions:** No data available.

© 2006, JIST Works

13 Manufacturing

13.01   **Managerial Work in Manufacturing**

13.02   **Machine Setup and Operation**

13.03   **Production Work, Assorted Materials Processing**

13.04   **Welding, Brazing, and Soldering**

13.05   **Production Machining Technology**

13.06   **Production Precision Work**

13.07   **Production Quality Control**

13.08   **Graphic Arts Production**

13.09   **Hands-On Work, Assorted Materials**

13.10   **Woodworking Technology**

13.11   **Apparel, Shoes, Leather, and Fabric Care**

13.12   **Electrical and Electronic Repair**

13.13   **Machinery Repair**

13.14   **Vehicle and Facility Mechanical Work**

13.15   **Medical and Technical Equipment Repair**

13.16   **Utility Operation and Energy Distribution**

13.17   **Loading, Moving, Hoisting, and Conveying**

13.01 Managerial Work in Manufacturing

First-Line Supervisors/Managers of Helpers, Laborers, and Material Movers, Hand

Supervise and coordinate the activities of helpers, laborers, or material movers. **O*NET Code:** 53-1021.00. **Average Salary:** $38,210. **Projected Growth:** 14.0%. **Annual Openings:** 16,000. **Education:** Work experience in a related occupation. **Job Zone:** 3. **Education/Training Program(s)**—No data available. **Related Knowledge/Courses:** Production and Processing; Economics and Accounting; Personnel and Human Resources; Administration and Management; Education and Training; Mathematics. **Personality Type:** Enterprising. **Skills Required:** Management of Personnel Resources; Social Perceptiveness; Instructing; Systems Analysis; Systems Evaluation; Learning Strategies; Time Management; Coordination; Management of Financial Resources. **Abilities:** Oral Expression; Mathematical Reasoning; Oral Comprehension; Fluency of Ideas; Static Strength. **Occupational Values:** Authority; Responsibility; Co-workers; Variety; Autonomy. **Interacting with Others:** Communicating with Supervisors, Peers, or Subordinates; Establishing and Maintaining Interpersonal Relationships; Guiding, Directing, and Motivating Subordinates. **Physical Work Conditions:** Sitting; Indoors; Standing.

First-Line Supervisors/Managers of Mechanics, Installers, and Repairers

Supervise and coordinate the activities of mechanics, installers, and repairers. **O*NET Code:** 49-1011.00. **Average Salary:** $49,290. **Projected Growth:** 15.4%. **Annual Openings:** 42,000. **Education:** Work experience in a related occupation. **Job Zone:** 4. **Education/Training Program(s)**— Operations Management and Supervision. **Related Knowledge/Courses:** Mechanical; Building and Construction; Personnel and Human Resources; Design; Administration and Management; Customer and Personal Service. **Personality Type:** Enterprising. **Skills Required:** Management of Personnel Resources; Installation; Management of Financial Resources; Management of Material Resources; Repairing; Equipment Maintenance; Negotiation; Troubleshooting. **Abilities:** Hearing Sensitivity; Speech Recognition; Visualization; Originality; Auditory Attention. **Occupational Values:** Authority; Responsibility; Autonomy; Variety; Co-workers. **Interacting with Others:** Coordinating the Work and Activities of Others; Communicating with Supervisors, Peers, or Subordinates; Establishing and Maintaining Interpersonal Relationships. **Physical Work Conditions:** Contaminants; Outdoors; Very Hot or Cold; Indoors, Not Environmentally Controlled; In an Enclosed Vehicle or Equipment.

First-Line Supervisors/Managers of Production and Operating Workers

Supervise and coordinate the activities of production and operating workers, such as inspectors, precision workers, machine setters and operators, assemblers, fabricators, and plant and system operators. **O*NET Code:** 51-1011.00. **Average Salary:** $44,160. **Projected Growth:** 9.5%. **Annual Openings:** 66,000. **Education:** Work experience in a related occupation. **Job Zone:** 3. **Education/Training Program(s)**— Operations Management and Supervision. **Related Knowledge/Courses:** Production and Processing; Personnel and Human Resources; Administration and Management; Economics and Accounting; Psychology; Mathematics. **Personality Type:** Enterprising. **Skills Required:** Management of Personnel Resources; Management of Material Resources; Systems Analysis; Negotiation; Coordination; Management of Financial Resources; Social Perceptiveness; Instructing; Operation Monitoring. **Abilities:** Auditory Attention; Oral Comprehension; Oral Expression; Mathematical Reasoning; Number Facility; Speech Clarity. **Occupational Values:** Authority; Responsibility; Variety; Co-workers; Autonomy. **Interacting with Others:** Communicating with Supervisors, Peers, or Subordinates; Coordinating the Work and Activities of Others; Monitoring and Controlling Resources. **Physical Work Conditions:** Walking and Running; Sitting; Indoors; Hazardous Equipment; Common Protective or Safety Equipment.

Industrial Production Managers

Plan, direct, or coordinate the work activities and resources necessary for manufacturing products in accordance with cost, quality, and quantity specifications. **O*NET Code:** 11-3051.00. **Average Salary:** $71,650. **Projected Growth:** 7.9%. **Annual Openings:** 18,000. **Education:** Bachelor's degree. **Job Zone:** 4. **Education/Training Program(s)**—Business Administration and Management, General; Business/Commerce, General; Operations Management and Supervision. **Related Knowledge/Courses:** Production and Processing; Personnel and Human Resources; Education and Training; Administration and Management; Mechanical; Engineering and Technology. **Personality Type:** Enterprising. **Skills Required:** Management of Material Resources; Persuasion; Management of Personnel Resources; Coordination; Monitoring; Systems Evaluation; Time Management; Negotiation. **Abilities:** Mathematical Reasoning; Originality; Deductive Reasoning; Visualization; Inductive Reasoning. **Occupational Values:** Authority; Autonomy; Creativity; Responsibility; Variety. **Interacting with Others:** Guiding, Directing, and Motivating Subordinates; Coordinating the Work and Activities of Others; Developing and Building Teams. **Physical Work Conditions:** Sitting; Sounds, Noise Levels Are Distracting or Uncomfortable; Contaminants; Physical Proximity; Indoors, Not Environmentally Controlled.

13.02 Machine Setup and Operation

Bindery Machine Setters and Set-Up Operators

Set up or set up and operate machines that perform some or all of the following functions in order to produce books, magazines, pamphlets, catalogs, and other printed materials: gathering, folding, cutting, stitching, rounding and backing, supering, casing-in, lining, pressing, and trimming. **O*NET Code:** 51-5011.01. **Average Salary:** $22,950. **Projected Growth:** -5.2%. **Annual Openings:** 6,000. **Education:** Moderate-term on-the-job training. **Job Zone:** 2. **Education/Training Program(s)**—Graphic Communications, Other. **Related Knowledge/Courses:** Production and Processing; Mechanical. **Personality Type:** Realistic. **Skills Required:** Installation; Operation Monitoring; Repairing; Operation and Control; Equipment Maintenance; Operations Analysis; Quality Control Analysis; Instructing. **Abilities:** Control Precision; Static Strength; Arm-Hand Steadiness; Perceptual Speed; Response Orientation. **Occupational Values:** Moral Values; Independence; Supervision, Technical; Activity; Company Policies and Practices. **Interacting with Others:** Communicating with Supervisors, Peers, or Subordinates; Training and Teaching Others; Interpreting the Meaning of Information for Others; Coaching and Developing Others; Performing Administrative Activities. **Physical Work Conditions:** Using Hands on Objects, Tools, or Controls; Standing; Indoors; Hazardous Equipment; Spend Time Making Repetitive Motions.

Buffing and Polishing Set-Up Operators

Set up and operate buffing or polishing machine. **O*NET Code:** 51-4033.02. **Average Salary:** $27,010. **Projected Growth:** 2.4%. **Annual Openings:** 9,000. **Education:** Moderate-term on-the-job training. **Job Zone:** 2. **Education/Training Program(s)**—Machine Shop Technology/Assistant; Machine Tool Technology/Machinist. **Related Knowledge/Courses:** Mechanical; Production and Processing. **Personality Type:** Realistic. **Skills Required:** Repairing; Operation and Control; Equipment Maintenance; Installation; Operation Monitoring. **Abilities:** Dynamic Flexibility; Control Precision; Rate Control; Speed of Limb Movement; Manual Dexterity; Extent Flexibility. **Occupational Values:** Independence; Moral Values; Supervision, Technical; Activity; Supervision, Human Relations. **Interacting with Others:** Communicating with Supervisors, Peers, or Subordinates; Coordinating the Work and Activities of Others; Establishing and Maintaining Interpersonal Relationships; Assisting and Caring for Others; Performing Administrative Activities; Monitoring and Controlling Resources. **Physical Work Conditions:** Hazardous Equipment; Standing; Using Hands on Objects, Tools, or Controls; Sounds, Noise Levels Are Distracting or Uncomfortable; Common Protective or Safety Equipment.

Casting Machine Set-Up Operators

Set up and operate machines to cast and assemble printing type. **O*NET Code:** 51-4072.05. **Average Salary:** $24,070. **Projected Growth:** 8.9%. **Annual Openings:** 18,000. **Education:** Postsecondary vocational training. **Job Zone:** 3. **Education/Training Program(s)**—No data available. **Related Knowledge/Courses:** Production and Processing; Mechanical. **Personality Type:** Realistic. **Skills Required:** Operation Monitoring; Operation and Control; Installation; Equipment Maintenance; Repairing. **Abilities:** Manual Dexterity; Reaction Time; Arm-Hand Steadiness; Control Precision; Wrist-Finger Speed. **Occupational Values:** Independence;

Moral Values; Supervision, Human Relations; Supervision, Technical; Activity; Company Policies and Practices. **Interacting with Others:** Communicating with Supervisors, Peers, or Subordinates; Establishing and Maintaining Interpersonal Relationships; Coordinating the Work and Activities of Others; Performing Administrative Activities. **Physical Work Conditions:** Hazardous Equipment; Sounds, Noise Levels Are Distracting or Uncomfortable; Standing; Using Hands on Objects, Tools, or Controls; Indoors.

Coating, Painting, and Spraying Machine Setters and Set-Up Operators

Set up or set up and operate machines to coat or paint any of a wide variety of products, such as food products; glassware; and cloth, ceramic, metal, plastic, paper, and wood products, with lacquer, silver and copper solution, rubber, paint, varnish, glaze, enamel, oil, or rust-proofing materials. **O*NET Code:** 51-9121.01. **Average Salary:** $25,920. **Projected Growth:** 9.4%. **Annual Openings:** 17,000. **Education:** Moderate-term on-the-job training. **Job Zone:** 2. **Education/Training Program(s)**—No data available. **Related Knowledge/Courses:** Production and Processing; Chemistry; Mechanical; Physics. **Personality Type:** Realistic. **Skills Required:** Operation Monitoring; Operation and Control; Installation; Equipment Maintenance; Equipment Selection; Quality Control Analysis. **Abilities:** Visual Color Discrimination; Manual Dexterity; Rate Control; Trunk Strength; Explosive Strength. **Occupational Values:** Moral Values; Independence; Activity; Supervision, Technical; Supervision, Human Relations. **Interacting with Others:** Communicating with Supervisors, Peers, or Subordinates; Performing Administrative Activities; Coordinating the Work and Activities of Others. **Physical Work Conditions:** Contaminants; Hazardous Conditions; Hazardous Equipment; Common Protective or Safety Equipment; Standing.

Combination Machine Tool Setters and Set-Up Operators, Metal and Plastic

Set up or set up and operate more than one type of cutting or forming machine tool, such as gear hobbers, lathes, press brakes, and shearing and boring machines. **O*NET Code:** 51-4081.01. **Average Salary:** $28,790. **Projected Growth:** 8.3%. **Annual Openings:** 8,000. **Education:** Moderate-term on-the-job training. **Job Zone:** 3. **Education/Training Program(s)**—Machine Shop Technology/Assistant; Machine Tool Technology/Machinist. **Related Knowledge/Courses:** Mechanical; Design; Production and Processing; Building and Construction; Education and Training; Foreign Language. **Personality Type:** Realistic. **Skills Required:** Operation Monitoring; Quality Control Analysis; Operation and Control; Equipment Maintenance; Installation; Repairing; Mathematics; Instructing; Troubleshooting. **Abilities:** Reaction Time; Static Strength; Visual Color Discrimination; Control Precision; Visualization; Extent Flexibility. **Occupational Values:** Moral Values; Supervision, Technical; Activity; Company Policies and Practices; Supervision, Human Relations. **Interacting with Others:** Training and Teaching Others; Communicating with Supervisors, Peers, or Subordinates; Establishing and Maintaining Interpersonal Relationships. **Physical Work Conditions:** Hazardous Equipment; Minor Burns, Cuts, Bites, or Stings; Common

Protective or Safety Equipment; Sounds, Noise Levels Are Distracting or Uncomfortable; Standing.

Crushing, Grinding, and Polishing Machine Setters, Operators, and Tenders

Set up, operate, or tend machines to crush, grind, or polish materials such as coal, glass, grain, stone, food, or rubber. **O*NET Code:** 51-9021.00. **Average Salary:** $26,370. **Projected Growth:** –2.8%. **Annual Openings:** 6,000. **Education:** Moderate-term on-the-job training. **Job Zone:** 1. **Education/Training Program(s)**—No data available. **Related Knowledge/Courses:** Production and Processing; Mechanical; Chemistry; Physics. **Personality Type:** Realistic. **Skills Required:** Operation Monitoring; Operation and Control; Equipment Maintenance; Quality Control Analysis. **Abilities:** Control Precision; Reaction Time; Static Strength; Rate Control; Explosive Strength. **Occupational Values:** Moral Values; Independence; Supervision, Technical; Supervision, Human Relations; Company Policies and Practices. **Interacting with Others:** Communicating with Supervisors, Peers, or Subordinates; Establishing and Maintaining Interpersonal Relationships; Interpreting the Meaning of Information for Others. **Physical Work Conditions:** Common Protective or Safety Equipment; Hazardous Equipment; Sounds, Noise Levels Are Distracting or Uncomfortable; Extremely Bright or Inadequate Lighting; Standing; Spend Time Bending or Twisting the Body.

Drilling and Boring Machine Tool Setters, Operators, and Tenders, Metal and Plastic

Set up, operate, or tend drilling machines to drill, bore, ream, mill, or countersink metal or plastic workpieces. **O*NET Code:** 51-4032.00. **Average Salary:** $27,990. **Projected Growth:** 2.1%. **Annual Openings:** 5,000. **Education:** Moderate-term on-the-job training. **Job Zone:** 2. **Education/Training Program(s)**—Machine Tool Technology/Machinist. **Related Knowledge/Courses:** Mechanical; Building and Construction; Design; Foreign Language; Mathematics; Public Safety and Security. **Personality Type:** Realistic. **Skills Required:** Operation Monitoring; Quality Control Analysis; Science; Installation; Operation and Control; Mathematics; Technology Design; Equipment Selection. **Abilities:** Static Strength; Visualization; Dynamic Strength; Arm-Hand Steadiness; Control Precision. **Occupational Values:** Independence; Supervision, Technical; Moral Values; Supervision, Human Relations; Activity; Advancement. **Interacting with Others:** Communicating with Supervisors, Peers, or Subordinates; Establishing and Maintaining Interpersonal Relationships; Coordinating the Work and Activities of Others. **Physical Work Conditions:** Hazardous Equipment; Minor Burns, Cuts, Bites, or Stings; Common Protective or Safety Equipment; Standing; Sounds, Noise Levels Are Distracting or Uncomfortable.

Electrolytic Plating and Coating Machine Setters and Set-Up Operators, Metal and Plastic

Set up or set up and operate electrolytic plating or coating machines, such as continuous multistrand electrogalvanizing machines, to coat metal or plastic products electrolytically with chromium, copper, cadmium, or other metal to provide protective or decorative surfaces or to build up worn surfaces.

O*NET Code: 51-4193.01. **Average Salary:** $26,250. **Projected Growth:** –2.6%. **Annual Openings:** 6,000. **Education:** Postsecondary vocational training. **Job Zone:** 3. **Education/Training Program(s)**—No data available. **Related Knowledge/Courses:** Chemistry; Mechanical; Production and Processing; Physics. **Personality Type:** Realistic. **Skills Required:** Operation Monitoring; Operation and Control; Quality Control Analysis; Science. **Abilities:** Control Precision; Static Strength; Gross Body Coordination; Extent Flexibility; Multilimb Coordination. **Occupational Values:** Moral Values; Independence; Supervision, Human Relations; Supervision, Technical; Activity. **Interacting with Others:** Communicating with Supervisors, Peers, or Subordinates; Establishing and Maintaining Interpersonal Relationships; Coordinating the Work and Activities of Others; Coaching and Developing Others. **Physical Work Conditions:** Common Protective or Safety Equipment; Minor Burns, Cuts, Bites, or Stings; Standing; Indoors; Spend Time Bending or Twisting the Body.

Extruding and Drawing Machine Setters, Operators, and Tenders, Metal and Plastic

Set up, operate, or tend machines to extrude or draw thermoplastic or metal materials into tubes, rods, hoses, wire, bars, or structural shapes. **O*NET Code:** 51-4021.00. **Average Salary:** $26,670. **Projected Growth:** 7.1%. **Annual Openings:** 14,000. **Education:** Moderate-term on-the-job training. **Job Zone:** 2. **Education/Training Program(s)**—Machine Tool Technology/Machinist. **Related Knowledge/Courses:** Production and Processing; Mechanical; Physics; Engineering and Technology. **Personality Type:** Realistic. **Skills Required:** Quality Control Analysis; Operation Monitoring; Installation; Operation and Control; Equipment Maintenance; Repairing; Science; Equipment Selection. **Abilities:** Control Precision; Rate Control; Static Strength; Stamina; Visualization; Wrist-Finger Speed. **Occupational Values:** Moral Values; Independence; Supervision, Technical; Activity; Supervision, Human Relations. **Interacting with Others:** Communicating with Supervisors, Peers, or Subordinates; Monitoring and Controlling Resources; Establishing and Maintaining Interpersonal Relationships. **Physical Work Conditions:** Hazardous Equipment; Common Protective or Safety Equipment; Sounds, Noise Levels Are Distracting or Uncomfortable; Standing; Indoors.

Extruding and Forming Machine Setters, Operators, and Tenders, Synthetic and Glass Fibers

Set up, operate, or tend machines that extrude and form continuous filaments from synthetic materials, such as liquid polymer, rayon, and fiberglass. **O*NET Code:** 51-6091.00. **Average Salary:** $28,380. **Projected Growth:** –13.1%. **Annual Openings:** 4,000. **Education:** Moderate-term on-the-job training. **Job Zone:** No data available. **Education/Training Program(s)**—No data available. **Related Knowledge/Courses:** No data available. **Personality Type:** No data available. **Skills Required:** No data available. **Abilities:** No data available. **Occupational Values:** No data available. **Interacting with Others:** No data available. **Physical Work Conditions:** No data available.

© 2006, JIST Works

Extruding, Forming, Pressing, and Compacting Machine Setters and Set-Up Operators

Set up or set up and operate machines, such as glass forming machines, plodder machines, and tuber machines, to manufacture any of a wide variety of products, such as soap bars, formed rubber, glassware, food, brick, and tile, by means of extruding, compressing, or compacting. **O*NET Code:** 51-9041.01. **Average Salary:** $27,180. **Projected Growth:** -0.1%. **Annual Openings:** 10,000. **Education:** Moderate-term on-the-job training. **Job Zone:** 2. **Education/Training Program(s)**—No data available. **Related Knowledge/Courses:** Production and Processing; Mechanical; Physics; Chemistry; Engineering and Technology. **Personality Type:** Realistic. **Skills Required:** Installation; Operation Monitoring; Equipment Maintenance; Repairing; Operation and Control; Quality Control Analysis; Troubleshooting; Technology Design. **Abilities:** Rate Control; Static Strength; Reaction Time; Hearing Sensitivity; Control Precision. **Occupational Values:** Moral Values; Independence; Supervision, Technical; Supervision, Human Relations; Company Policies and Practices. **Interacting with Others:** Communicating with Supervisors, Peers, or Subordinates; Establishing and Maintaining Interpersonal Relationships; Assisting and Caring for Others; Coaching and Developing Others. **Physical Work Conditions:** Hazardous Equipment; Sounds, Noise Levels Are Distracting or Uncomfortable; Indoors; Standing; Using Hands on Objects, Tools, or Controls.

Fiber Product Cutting Machine Setters and Set-Up Operators

Set up and operate machine to cut or slice fiber material, such as paper, wallboard, and insulation material. **O*NET Code:** 51-9032.01. **Average Salary:** $26,500. **Projected Growth:** 6.6%. **Annual Openings:** 12,000. **Education:** Moderate-term on-the-job training. **Job Zone:** 2. **Education/Training Program(s)**—No data available. **Related Knowledge/Courses:** Production and Processing; Mechanical; Design; Clerical; Building and Construction. **Personality Type:** Realistic. **Skills Required:** Operation Monitoring; Operation and Control; Equipment Maintenance; Repairing; Installation. **Abilities:** Rate Control; Explosive Strength; Control Precision; Static Strength; Reaction Time. **Occupational Values:** Moral Values; Independence; Supervision, Technical; Activity; Company Policies and Practices. **Interacting with Others:** Communicating with Supervisors, Peers, or Subordinates; Performing Administrative Activities; Establishing and Maintaining Interpersonal Relationships. **Physical Work Conditions:** Hazardous Equipment; Minor Burns, Cuts, Bites, or Stings; Standing; Sounds, Noise Levels Are Distracting or Uncomfortable; Using Hands on Objects, Tools, or Controls.

Forging Machine Setters, Operators, and Tenders, Metal and Plastic

Set up, operate, or tend forging machines to taper, shape, or form metal or plastic parts. **O*NET Code:** 51-4022.00. **Average Salary:** $26,850. **Projected Growth:** 5.9%. **Annual Openings:** 3,000. **Education:** Moderate-term on-the-job training. **Job Zone:** 2. **Education/Training Program(s)**—Machine Tool Technology/Machinist. **Related Knowledge/Courses:** Design; Mechanical; Physics; Engineering and Technology.

Personality Type: Realistic. **Skills Required:** Installation; Operation Monitoring; Operation and Control; Equipment Maintenance; Repairing; Quality Control Analysis; Troubleshooting; Equipment Selection. **Abilities:** Control Precision; Visualization; Static Strength; Extent Flexibility; Gross Body Equilibrium. **Occupational Values:** Moral Values; Independence; Supervision, Human Relations; Supervision, Technical; Activity; Company Policies and Practices. **Interacting with Others:** Communicating with Supervisors, Peers, or Subordinates; Establishing and Maintaining Interpersonal Relationships; Coordinating the Work and Activities of Others; Providing Consultation and Advice to Others. **Physical Work Conditions:** Using Hands on Objects, Tools, or Controls; Common Protective or Safety Equipment; Hazardous Equipment; Standing; Very Hot or Cold.

Glass Cutting Machine Setters and Set-Up Operators

Set up and operate machines to cut glass. **O*NET Code:** 51-9032.03. **Average Salary:** $26,500. **Projected Growth:** 6.6%. **Annual Openings:** 12,000. **Education:** Short-term on-the-job training. **Job Zone:** 1. **Education/Training Program(s)**—No data available. **Related Knowledge/Courses:** Production and Processing; Mechanical. **Personality Type:** Realistic. **Skills Required:** Operation Monitoring; Operation and Control; Equipment Maintenance; Installation; Repairing; Quality Control Analysis. **Abilities:** Arm-Hand Steadiness; Rate Control; Manual Dexterity; Control Precision; Depth Perception. **Occupational Values:** Authority; Supervision, Technical; Moral Values; Activity; Co-workers. **Interacting with Others:** Guiding, Directing, and Motivating Subordinates; Communicating with Supervisors, Peers, or Subordinates; Coordinating the Work and Activities of Others. **Physical Work Conditions:** Hazardous Equipment; Minor Burns, Cuts, Bites, or Stings; Using Hands on Objects, Tools, or Controls; Common Protective or Safety Equipment; Indoors; Sounds, Noise Levels Are Distracting or Uncomfortable.

Grinding, Honing, Lapping, and Deburring Machine Set-Up Operators

Set up and operate grinding, honing, lapping, or deburring machines to remove excess materials or burrs from internal and external surfaces. **O*NET Code:** 51-4033.01. **Average Salary:** $27,010. **Projected Growth:** 2.4%. **Annual Openings:** 9,000. **Education:** Moderate-term on-the-job training. **Job Zone:** 3. **Education/Training Program(s)**—Machine Shop Technology/Assistant; Machine Tool Technology/Machinist. **Related Knowledge/Courses:** Mechanical; Production and Processing; Engineering and Technology; Physics. **Personality Type:** Realistic. **Skills Required:** Equipment Maintenance; Installation; Operation and Control; Repairing; Operation Monitoring; Troubleshooting; Quality Control Analysis; Equipment Selection. **Abilities:** Control Precision; Static Strength; Visualization; Manual Dexterity; Number Facility. **Occupational Values:** Independence; Moral Values; Supervision, Technical; Activity; Supervision, Human Relations. **Interacting with Others:** Monitoring and Controlling Resources; Communicating with Supervisors, Peers, or Subordinates; Coordinating the Work and Activities of Others. **Physical Work Conditions:** Hazardous Equipment;

Using Hands on Objects, Tools, or Controls; Indoors; Sounds, Noise Levels Are Distracting or Uncomfortable; Standing.

Heating Equipment Setters and Set-Up Operators, Metal and Plastic

Set up or set up and operate heating equipment, such as heat-treating furnaces, flame-hardening machines, and induction machines, that anneal or heat-treat metal objects. **O*NET Code:** 51-4191.01. **Average Salary:** $29,140. **Projected Growth:** -0.6%. **Annual Openings:** 4,000. **Education:** Postsecondary vocational training. **Job Zone:** 3. **Education/Training Program(s)**—Machine Shop Technology/Assistant; Machine Tool Technology/Machinist. **Related Knowledge/Courses:** Mechanical; Physics; Production and Processing; Education and Training; Engineering and Technology; Building and Construction. **Personality Type:** Realistic. **Skills Required:** Operation Monitoring; Operation and Control; Equipment Maintenance; Quality Control Analysis; Installation; Science. **Abilities:** Manual Dexterity; Control Precision; Explosive Strength; Arm-Hand Steadiness; Reaction Time. **Occupational Values:** Moral Values; Supervision, Human Relations; Supervision, Technical; Activity; Company Policies and Practices. **Interacting with Others:** Communicating with Supervisors, Peers, or Subordinates; Training and Teaching Others; Interpreting the Meaning of Information for Others; Assisting and Caring for Others; Coordinating the Work and Activities of Others. **Physical Work Conditions:** Hazardous Equipment; Minor Burns, Cuts, Bites, or Stings; Common Protective or Safety Equipment; Very Hot or Cold; Using Hands on Objects, Tools, or Controls.

Lathe and Turning Machine Tool Setters, Operators, and Tenders, Metal and Plastic

Set up, operate, or tend lathe and turning machines to turn, bore, thread, form, or face metal or plastic materials such as wire, rod, or bar stock. **O*NET Code:** 51-4034.00. **Average Salary:** $30,120. **Projected Growth:** 0.8%. **Annual Openings:** 7,000. **Education:** Moderate-term on-the-job training. **Job Zone:** 3. **Education/Training Program(s)**—Machine Tool Technology/Machinist. **Related Knowledge/Courses:** Production and Processing; Mechanical; Engineering and Technology; Physics; Design; Mathematics. **Personality Type:** Realistic. **Skills Required:** Installation; Equipment Maintenance; Technology Design; Operation Monitoring; Operation and Control; Operations Analysis; Quality Control Analysis; Repairing. **Abilities:** Visualization; Control Precision; Static Strength; Multilimb Coordination; Stamina. **Occupational Values:** Moral Values; Supervision, Technical; Independence; Supervision, Human Relations; Advancement; Company Policies and Practices. **Interacting with Others:** Communicating with Supervisors, Peers, or Subordinates; Establishing and Maintaining Interpersonal Relationships; Assisting and Caring for Others. **Physical Work Conditions:** Hazardous Equipment; Common Protective or Safety Equipment; Sounds, Noise Levels Are Distracting or Uncomfortable; Using Hands on Objects, Tools, or Controls; Indoors; Standing.

Metal Molding, Coremaking, and Casting Machine Operators and Tenders

Operate or tend metal molding, casting, or coremaking machines to mold or cast metal products, such as pipes, brake drums, and rods, and metal parts, such as automobile trim, carburetor housings, and motor parts. Machines include centrifugal casting machines, vacuum casting machines, turnover draw-type coremaking machines, conveyor-screw coremaking machines, and die casting machines. **O*NET Code:** 51-4072.04. **Average Salary:** $24,070. **Projected Growth:** 8.9%. **Annual Openings:** 18,000. **Education:** Short-term on-the-job training. **Job Zone:** 1. **Education/Training Program(s)**—No data available. **Related Knowledge/Courses:** Mechanical; Production and Processing; Building and Construction; Public Safety and Security; Foreign Language; Physics. **Personality Type:** Realistic. **Skills Required:** Operation Monitoring; Equipment Maintenance; Repairing; Operation and Control; Quality Control Analysis; Installation; Technology Design; Science; Troubleshooting. **Abilities:** Static Strength; Reaction Time; Auditory Attention; Response Orientation; Gross Body Equilibrium. **Occupational Values:** Moral Values; Supervision, Human Relations; Company Policies and Practices; Activity; Supervision, Technical. **Interacting with Others:** Communicating with Supervisors, Peers, or Subordinates; Monitoring and Controlling Resources; Coordinating the Work and Activities of Others; Performing Administrative Activities. **Physical Work Conditions:** Hazardous Equipment; Common Protective or Safety Equipment; Very Hot or Cold; Minor Burns, Cuts, Bites, or Stings; Standing.

Metal Molding, Coremaking, and Casting Machine Setters and Set-Up Operators

Set up or set up and operate metal casting, molding, and coremaking machines to mold or cast metal parts and products, such as tubes, rods, automobile trim, carburetor housings, and motor parts. Machines include die casting and continuous casting machines and roll-over, squeeze, and shell molding machines. **O*NET Code:** 51-4072.03. **Average Salary:** $24,070. **Projected Growth:** 8.9%. **Annual Openings:** 18,000. **Education:** Moderate-term on-the-job training. **Job Zone:** 2. **Education/Training Program(s)**—No data available. **Related Knowledge/Courses:** Production and Processing; Mechanical; Physics. **Personality Type:** Realistic. **Skills Required:** Operation Monitoring; Installation; Operation and Control; Equipment Maintenance; Equipment Selection; Repairing; Quality Control Analysis. **Abilities:** Explosive Strength; Control Precision; Static Strength; Gross Body Coordination; Extent Flexibility. **Occupational Values:** Independence; Moral Values; Supervision, Human Relations; Company Policies and Practices; Supervision, Technical. **Interacting with Others:** Communicating with Supervisors, Peers, or Subordinates; Assisting and Caring for Others; Coordinating the Work and Activities of Others. **Physical Work Conditions:** Hazardous Equipment; Minor Burns, Cuts, Bites, or Stings; Common Protective or Safety Equipment; Very Hot or Cold; Using Hands on Objects, Tools, or Controls.

© 2006, JIST Works

Milling and Planing Machine Setters, Operators, and Tenders, Metal and Plastic

Set up, operate, or tend milling or planing machines to mill, plane, shape, groove, or profile metal or plastic workpieces. **O*NET Code:** 51-4035.00. **Average Salary:** $30,130. **Projected Growth:** 0.8%. **Annual Openings:** 2,000. **Education:** Moderate-term on-the-job training. **Job Zone:** 3. **Education/Training Program(s)**—Machine Tool Technology/Machinist. **Related Knowledge/Courses:** Production and Processing; Mechanical; Physics; Design; Engineering and Technology; Mathematics. **Personality Type:** Realistic. **Skills Required:** Equipment Maintenance; Technology Design; Operation and Control; Repairing; Operation Monitoring; Installation; Mathematics; Equipment Selection. **Abilities:** Control Precision; Static Strength; Reaction Time; Wrist-Finger Speed; Rate Control. **Occupational Values:** Independence; Moral Values; Supervision, Technical; Advancement; Supervision, Human Relations. **Interacting with Others:** Communicating with Supervisors, Peers, or Subordinates; Establishing and Maintaining Interpersonal Relationships; Coaching and Developing Others. **Physical Work Conditions:** Hazardous Equipment; Common Protective or Safety Equipment; Standing; Sounds, Noise Levels Are Distracting or Uncomfortable; Using Hands on Objects, Tools, or Controls.

Multiple Machine Tool Setters, Operators, and Tenders, Metal and Plastic

Set up, operate, or tend more than one type of cutting or forming machine tool or robot. **O*NET Code:** 51-4081.00. **Average Salary:** $28,790. **Projected Growth:** 8.3%. **Annual Openings:** 8,000. **Education:** Postsecondary vocational training. **Job Zone:** No data available. **Education/Training Program(s)**—Machine Shop Technology/Assistant; Machine Tool Technology/Machinist. **Related Knowledge/Courses:** No data available. **Personality Type:** No data available. **Skills Required:** No data available. **Abilities:** No data available. **Occupational Values:** No data available. **Interacting with Others:** No data available. **Physical Work Conditions:** No data available.

Nonelectrolytic Plating and Coating Machine Setters and Set-Up Operators, Metal and Plastic

Set up or set up and operate nonelectrolytic plating or coating machines, such as hot-dip lines and metal-spraying machines, to coat metal or plastic products or parts with metal. **O*NET Code:** 51-4193.03. **Average Salary:** $26,250. **Projected Growth:** –2.6%. **Annual Openings:** 6,000. **Education:** Postsecondary vocational training. **Job Zone:** 3. **Education/Training Program(s)**—No data available. **Related Knowledge/Courses:** Production and Processing; Mechanical; Chemistry. **Personality Type:** Realistic. **Skills Required:** Installation; Operation Monitoring; Operation and Control; Technology Design; Equipment Maintenance; Quality Control Analysis; Equipment Selection. **Abilities:** Control Precision; Rate Control; Visual Color Discrimination; Manual Dexterity; Reaction Time. **Occupational Values:** Moral Values; Independence; Supervision, Human Relations; Supervision, Technical; Activity; Company Policies and Practices. **Interacting with Others:** Communicating with

Supervisors, Peers, or Subordinates; Establishing and Maintaining Interpersonal Relationships; Interpreting the Meaning of Information for Others; Selling or Influencing Others; Coordinating the Work and Activities of Others; Coaching and Developing Others. **Physical Work Conditions:** Hazardous Equipment; Common Protective or Safety Equipment; Minor Burns, Cuts, Bites, or Stings; Standing; Using Hands on Objects, Tools, or Controls.

Paper Goods Machine Setters, Operators, and Tenders

Set up, operate, or tend paper goods machines that perform a variety of functions, such as converting, sawing, corrugating, banding, wrapping, boxing, stitching, forming, or sealing paper or paperboard sheets into products. **O*NET Code:** 51-9196.00. **Average Salary:** $29,350. **Projected Growth:** –2.8%. **Annual Openings:** 16,000. **Education:** Moderate-term on-the-job training. **Job Zone:** 2. **Education/Training Program(s)**—No data available. **Related Knowledge/Courses:** Production and Processing; Mechanical. **Personality Type:** Realistic. **Skills Required:** Operation Monitoring; Equipment Maintenance; Installation; Operation and Control; Repairing; Troubleshooting; Quality Control Analysis; Technology Design. **Abilities:** Rate Control; Control Precision; Manual Dexterity; Finger Dexterity; Static Strength. **Occupational Values:** Moral Values; Independence; Supervision, Human Relations; Supervision, Technical; Company Policies and Practices. **Interacting with Others:** Communicating with Supervisors, Peers, or Subordinates; Performing Administrative Activities; Monitoring and Controlling Resources. **Physical Work Conditions:** Hazardous Equipment; Sounds, Noise Levels Are Distracting or Uncomfortable; Standing; Common Protective or Safety Equipment; Indoors.

Plastic Molding and Casting Machine Setters and Set-Up Operators

Set up or set up and operate plastic molding machines, such as compression or injection molding machines, to mold, form, or cast thermoplastic materials to specified shape. **O*NET Code:** 51-4072.01. **Average Salary:** $24,070. **Projected Growth:** 8.9%. **Annual Openings:** 18,000. **Education:** Moderate-term on-the-job training. **Job Zone:** 2. **Education/Training Program(s)**—No data available. **Related Knowledge/Courses:** Mechanical; Production and Processing; Chemistry. **Personality Type:** Realistic. **Skills Required:** Equipment Maintenance; Operation Monitoring; Repairing; Operation and Control; Troubleshooting; Installation; Quality Control Analysis. **Abilities:** Control Precision; Static Strength; Explosive Strength; Wrist-Finger Speed; Visual Color Discrimination. **Occupational Values:** Moral Values; Independence; Supervision, Human Relations; Company Policies and Practices; Activity. **Interacting with Others:** Communicating with Supervisors, Peers, or Subordinates; Establishing and Maintaining Interpersonal Relationships; Assisting and Caring for Others. **Physical Work Conditions:** Hazardous Equipment; Contaminants; Common Protective or Safety Equipment; Sounds, Noise Levels Are Distracting or Uncomfortable; Hazardous Conditions; Minor Burns, Cuts, Bites, or Stings.

Press and Press Brake Machine Setters and Set-Up Operators, Metal and Plastic

Set up or set up and operate power-press machines or power-brake machines to bend, form, stretch, notch, punch, or straighten metal or plastic plate and structural shapes as specified by work order, blueprints, drawing, templates, or layout. O*NET Code: 51-4031.03. **Average Salary:** $25,440. **Projected Growth:** 6.8%. **Annual Openings:** 37,000. **Education:** Moderate-term on-the-job training. **Job Zone:** 2. **Education/Training Program(s)**—Machine Tool Technology/Machinist; Sheet Metal Technology/Sheetworking. **Related Knowledge/Courses:** Mechanical; Building and Construction; Production and Processing; Public Safety and Security; Design; Physics. **Personality Type:** Realistic. **Skills Required:** Science; Installation; Operation Monitoring; Technology Design; Operation and Control; Equipment Maintenance; Quality Control Analysis; Repairing. **Abilities:** Visualization; Multilimb Coordination; Depth Perception; Manual Dexterity; Dynamic Strength; Extent Flexibility. **Occupational Values:** Independence; Moral Values; Activity; Supervision, Technical; Supervision, Human Relations. **Interacting with Others:** Communicating with Supervisors, Peers, or Subordinates; Providing Consultation and Advice to Others; Establishing and Maintaining Interpersonal Relationships; Coordinating the Work and Activities of Others; Monitoring and Controlling Resources. **Physical Work Conditions:** Hazardous Equipment; Common Protective or Safety Equipment; Minor Burns, Cuts, Bites, or Stings; Sounds, Noise Levels Are Distracting or Uncomfortable; Standing.

Punching Machine Setters and Set-Up Operators, Metal and Plastic

Set up or set up and operate machines to punch, crimp, cut blanks, or notch metal or plastic workpieces between preset dies according to specifications. O*NET Code: 51-4031.02. **Average Salary:** $25,440. **Projected Growth:** 6.8%. **Annual Openings:** 37,000. **Education:** Moderate-term on-the-job training. **Job Zone:** 2. **Education/Training Program(s)**—Machine Tool Technology/Machinist; Sheet Metal Technology/Sheetworking. **Related Knowledge/Courses:** Mechanical; Production and Processing; Physics; Engineering and Technology. **Personality Type:** Realistic. **Skills Required:** Equipment Maintenance; Installation; Operation and Control; Repairing; Operation Monitoring; Troubleshooting. **Abilities:** Control Precision; Manual Dexterity; Finger Dexterity; Visualization; Response Orientation. **Occupational Values:** Independence; Moral Values; Supervision, Technical; Activity; Supervision, Human Relations. **Interacting with Others:** Monitoring and Controlling Resources; Communicating with Supervisors, Peers, or Subordinates; Communicating with Persons Outside Organization; Establishing and Maintaining Interpersonal Relationships; Assisting and Caring for Others; Selling or Influencing Others. **Physical Work Conditions:** Hazardous Equipment; Standing; Using Hands on Objects, Tools, or Controls; Common Protective or Safety Equipment; Indoors.

Rolling Machine Setters, Operators, and Tenders, Metal and Plastic

Set up, operate, or tend machines to roll steel or plastic, forming bends, beads, knurls, rolls, or plate, or to flatten, temper, or reduce gauge of material. O*NET Code: 51-4023.00. **Average Salary:** $29,150. **Projected Growth:** 2.0%. **Annual Openings:** 3,000. **Education:** Moderate-term on-the-job training. **Job Zone:** 2. **Education/Training Program(s)**—Machine Tool Technology/Machinist; Sheet Metal Technology/Sheetworking. **Related Knowledge/Courses:** Production and Processing; Mechanical; Physics; Education and Training; Design; Mathematics. **Personality Type:** Realistic. **Skills Required:** Operation Monitoring; Operation and Control; Equipment Maintenance; Installation; Quality Control Analysis; Management of Personnel Resources; Repairing; Mathematics. **Abilities:** Rate Control; Manual Dexterity; Control Precision; Static Strength; Extent Flexibility. **Occupational Values:** Supervision, Technical; Supervision, Human Relations; Activity; Independence; Moral Values. **Interacting with Others:** Guiding, Directing, and Motivating Subordinates; Communicating with Supervisors, Peers, or Subordinates; Coordinating the Work and Activities of Others. **Physical Work Conditions:** Hazardous Equipment; Sounds, Noise Levels Are Distracting or Uncomfortable; Standing; Using Hands on Objects, Tools, or Controls; Common Protective or Safety Equipment.

Sawing Machine Setters and Set-Up Operators

Set up or set up and operate wood-sawing machines. Examine blueprints, drawings, work orders, and patterns to determine size and shape of items to be sawed, sawing machines to set up, and sequence of sawing operations. O*NET Code: 51-7041.01. **Average Salary:** $22,490. **Projected Growth:** -0.2%. **Annual Openings:** 10,000. **Education:** Moderate-term on-the-job training. **Job Zone:** 2. **Education/Training Program(s)**—Cabinetmaking and Millwork/Millwright. **Related Knowledge/Courses:** Building and Construction; Mechanical; Engineering and Technology; Design; Production and Processing; Mathematics. **Personality Type:** Realistic. **Skills Required:** Operation and Control; Equipment Selection. **Abilities:** Hearing Sensitivity; Manual Dexterity; Control Precision; Speed of Limb Movement; Static Strength; Depth Perception. **Occupational Values:** Moral Values; Independence; Company Policies and Practices; Supervision, Technical; Supervision, Human Relations. **Interacting with Others:** Communicating with Supervisors, Peers, or Subordinates; Establishing and Maintaining Interpersonal Relationships; Coaching and Developing Others. **Physical Work Conditions:** Hazardous Equipment; Minor Burns, Cuts, Bites, or Stings; Common Protective or Safety Equipment; Sounds, Noise Levels Are Distracting or Uncomfortable; Standing.

Sawing Machine Tool Setters and Set-Up Operators, Metal and Plastic

Set up or set up and operate metal or plastic sawing machines to cut straight, curved, irregular, or internal patterns in metal or plastic stock or to trim edges of metal or plastic objects. Involves the use of such machines as band saws, circular saws, friction saws, hacksawing machines, and jigsaws. **O*NET**

Code: 51-4031.01. **Average Salary:** $25,440. **Projected Growth:** 6.8%. **Annual Openings:** 37,000. **Education:** Moderate-term on-the-job training. **Job Zone:** 2. **Education/Training Program(s)**—Machine Tool Technology/Machinist; Sheet Metal Technology/Sheetworking. **Related Knowledge/Courses:** Production and Processing; Mechanical; Engineering and Technology; Design; Building and Construction. **Personality Type:** Realistic. **Skills Required:** Operation Monitoring; Equipment Maintenance; Installation; Operation and Control; Repairing; Equipment Selection; Quality Control Analysis. **Abilities:** Rate Control; Arm-Hand Steadiness; Manual Dexterity; Control Precision; Explosive Strength. **Occupational Values:** Moral Values; Supervision, Technical; Independence; Supervision, Human Relations; Activity; Company Policies and Practices. **Interacting with Others:** Communicating with Supervisors, Peers, or Subordinates; Coordinating the Work and Activities of Others; Performing Administrative Activities. **Physical Work Conditions:** Hazardous Equipment; Minor Burns, Cuts, Bites, or Stings; Sounds, Noise Levels Are Distracting or Uncomfortable; Common Protective or Safety Equipment; Standing.

Screen Printing Machine Setters and Set-Up Operators

Set up or set up and operate screen printing machines to print designs onto articles and materials such as glass or plasticware, cloth, and paper. **O*NET Code:** 51-5023.06. **Average Salary:** $29,750. **Projected Growth:** 4.6%. **Annual Openings:** 30,000. **Education:** Moderate-term on-the-job training. **Job Zone:** 3. **Education/Training Program(s)**—Graphic and Printing Equipment Operator, General Production; Graphic Communications, Other; Printing Management; Printing Press Operator. **Related Knowledge/Courses:** Production and Processing; Mechanical; Fine Arts; Education and Training; Communications and Media; Design. **Personality Type:** Realistic. **Skills Required:** Repairing; Equipment Maintenance; Operation Monitoring; Troubleshooting; Operation and Control; Instructing; Quality Control Analysis; Systems Analysis. **Abilities:** Visual Color Discrimination; Speech Clarity; Perceptual Speed; Finger Dexterity; Multilimb Coordination. **Occupational Values:** Company Policies and Practices; Authority; Supervision, Technical; Activity; Moral Values. **Interacting with Others:** Establishing and Maintaining Interpersonal Relationships; Training and Teaching Others; Communicating with Supervisors, Peers, or Subordinates. **Physical Work Conditions:** Hazardous Equipment; Hazardous Conditions; Sounds, Noise Levels Are Distracting or Uncomfortable; Contaminants; Standing; Common Protective or Safety Equipment.

Shear and Slitter Machine Setters and Set-Up Operators, Metal and Plastic

Set up or set up and operate power-shear or slitting machines to cut metal or plastic material, such as plates, sheets, slabs, billets or bars, to specified dimensions and angles. **O*NET Code:** 51-4031.04. **Average Salary:** $25,440. **Projected Growth:** 6.8%. **Annual Openings:** 37,000. **Education:** Moderate-term on-the-job training. **Job Zone:** 2. **Education/Training Program(s)**—Machine Tool Technology/Machinist; Sheet Metal Technology/Sheetworking. **Related**

Knowledge/Courses: Mechanical; Production and Processing; Building and Construction; Public Safety and Security; Engineering and Technology; Foreign Language. **Personality Type:** Realistic. **Skills Required:** Operation Monitoring; Installation; Operation and Control; Quality Control Analysis; Equipment Maintenance; Technology Design; Troubleshooting; Repairing. **Abilities:** Reaction Time; Control Precision; Extent Flexibility; Static Strength; Visualization. **Occupational Values:** Moral Values; Activity; Independence; Supervision, Human Relations; Supervision, Technical. **Interacting with Others:** Communicating with Supervisors, Peers, or Subordinates; Establishing and Maintaining Interpersonal Relationships; Communicating with Persons Outside Organization; Coordinating the Work and Activities of Others. **Physical Work Conditions:** Hazardous Equipment; Minor Burns, Cuts, Bites, or Stings; Common Protective or Safety Equipment; Sounds, Noise Levels Are Distracting or Uncomfortable; Standing.

Soldering and Brazing Machine Setters and Set-Up Operators

Set up or set up and operate soldering or brazing machines to braze, solder, heat treat, or spot weld fabricated metal products or components as specified by work orders, blueprints, and layout specifications. **O*NET Code:** 51-4122.03. **Average Salary:** $29,180. **Projected Growth:** 0.9%. **Annual Openings:** 10,000. **Education:** Moderate-term on-the-job training. **Job Zone:** 2. **Education/Training Program(s)**—Welding Technology/Welder. **Related Knowledge/Courses:** Mechanical; Building and Construction; Engineering and Technology; Design; Physics; Production and Processing. **Personality Type:** Realistic. **Skills Required:** Installation; Operation Monitoring; Quality Control Analysis; Operation and Control; Repairing; Instructing; Troubleshooting; Equipment Maintenance. **Abilities:** Reaction Time; Wrist-Finger Speed; Manual Dexterity; Rate Control; Speed of Limb Movement; Explosive Strength. **Occupational Values:** Moral Values; Independence; Company Policies and Practices; Supervision, Human Relations; Supervision, Technical. **Interacting with Others:** Coaching and Developing Others; Communicating with Supervisors, Peers, or Subordinates; Training and Teaching Others. **Physical Work Conditions:** Common Protective or Safety Equipment; Hazardous Conditions; Hazardous Equipment; Extremely Bright or Inadequate Lighting; Very Hot or Cold.

Textile Cutting Machine Setters, Operators, and Tenders

Set up, operate, or tend machines that cut textiles. **O*NET Code:** 51-6062.00. **Average Salary:** $20,600. **Projected Growth:** -22.6%. **Annual Openings:** 4,000. **Education:** Moderate-term on-the-job training. **Job Zone:** 3. **Education/Training Program(s)**—Industrial Mechanics and Maintenance Technology. **Related Knowledge/Courses:** Mechanical; Design; Public Safety and Security; Engineering and Technology; Foreign Language. **Personality Type:** Realistic. **Skills Required:** Installation; Operation Monitoring; Equipment Maintenance; Operation and Control; Repairing; Quality Control Analysis; Troubleshooting; Technology Design. **Abilities:** Control Precision; Arm-Hand Steadiness; Auditory Attention; Finger Dexterity; Extent

Flexibility; Hearing Sensitivity. **Occupational Values:** Moral Values; Supervision, Technical; Supervision, Human Relations; Independence; Activity; Company Policies and Practices. **Interacting with Others:** Communicating with Supervisors, Peers, or Subordinates; Establishing and Maintaining Interpersonal Relationships; Providing Consultation and Advice to Others. **Physical Work Conditions:** Hazardous Equipment; Minor Burns, Cuts, Bites, or Stings; Standing; Common Protective or Safety Equipment; Using Hands on Objects, Tools, or Controls.

Textile Knitting and Weaving Machine Setters, Operators, and Tenders

Set up, operate, or tend machines that knit, loop, weave, or draw in textiles. **O*NET Code:** 51-6063.00. **Average Salary:** $23,550. **Projected Growth:** –38.6%. **Annual Openings:** 6,000. **Education:** Long-term on-the-job training. **Job Zone:** 3. **Education/Training Program(s)**—Industrial Mechanics and Maintenance Technology. **Related Knowledge/Courses:** Mechanical; Design; Public Safety and Security; Engineering and Technology; Foreign Language. **Personality Type:** Realistic. **Skills Required:** Installation; Operation Monitoring; Equipment Maintenance; Operation and Control; Repairing; Quality Control Analysis; Troubleshooting; Technology Design. **Abilities:** Control Precision; Arm-Hand Steadiness; Auditory Attention; Finger Dexterity; Extent Flexibility; Hearing Sensitivity. **Occupational Values:** Moral Values; Supervision, Technical; Supervision, Human Relations; Independence; Activity; Company Policies and Practices. **Interacting with Others:** Communicating with Supervisors, Peers, or Subordinates; Establishing and Maintaining Interpersonal Relationships; Providing Consultation and Advice to Others. **Physical Work Conditions:** Hazardous Equipment; Minor Burns, Cuts, Bites, or Stings; Standing; Common Protective or Safety Equipment; Using Hands on Objects, Tools, or Controls.

Textile Winding, Twisting, and Drawing Out Machine Setters, Operators, and Tenders

Set up, operate, or tend machines that wind or twist textiles or draw out and combine sliver, such as wool, hemp, or synthetic fibers. **O*NET Code:** 51-6064.00. **Average Salary:** $22,310. **Projected Growth:** –30.3%. **Annual Openings:** 10,000. **Education:** Moderate-term on-the-job training. **Job Zone:** 3. **Education/Training Program(s)**—Industrial Mechanics and Maintenance Technology. **Related Knowledge/Courses:** Mechanical; Design; Public Safety and Security; Engineering and Technology; Foreign Language. **Personality Type:** Realistic. **Skills Required:** Installation; Operation Monitoring; Equipment Maintenance; Operation and Control; Repairing; Quality Control Analysis; Troubleshooting; Technology Design. **Abilities:** Control Precision; Arm-Hand Steadiness; Auditory Attention; Finger Dexterity; Extent Flexibility; Hearing Sensitivity. **Occupational Values:** Moral Values; Supervision, Technical; Supervision, Human Relations; Independence; Activity; Company Policies and Practices. **Interacting with Others:** Communicating with Supervisors, Peers, or Subordinates; Establishing and Maintaining Interpersonal Relationships; Providing Consultation and Advice to Others. **Physical Work Conditions:** Hazardous Equipment; Minor Burns, Cuts, Bites,

or Stings; Standing; Common Protective or Safety Equipment; Using Hands on Objects, Tools, or Controls.

Woodworking Machine Setters and Set-Up Operators, Except Sawing

Set up or set up and operate woodworking machines, such as lathes, drill presses, sanders, shapers, and planing machines, to perform woodworking operations. **O*NET Code:** 51-7042.01. **Average Salary:** $22,430. **Projected Growth:** 3.0%. **Annual Openings:** 14,000. **Education:** Moderate-term on-the-job training. **Job Zone:** 2. **Education/Training Program(s)**—Cabinetmaking and Millwork/Millwright; Woodworking, General. **Related Knowledge/Courses:** Mechanical; Engineering and Technology; Design; Production and Processing. **Personality Type:** Realistic. **Skills Required:** Operation Monitoring; Operation and Control; Installation; Troubleshooting; Repairing; Equipment Selection; Equipment Maintenance. **Abilities:** Wrist-Finger Speed; Manual Dexterity; Control Precision; Finger Dexterity; Rate Control. **Occupational Values:** Independence; Moral Values; Supervision, Technical; Activity; Company Policies and Practices. **Interacting with Others:** Communicating with Supervisors, Peers, or Subordinates; Establishing and Maintaining Interpersonal Relationships; Monitoring and Controlling Resources. **Physical Work Conditions:** Hazardous Equipment; Minor Burns, Cuts, Bites, or Stings; Common Protective or Safety Equipment; Using Hands on Objects, Tools, or Controls; Spend Time Bending or Twisting the Body.

13.03 Production Work, Assorted Materials Processing

Bakers, Manufacturing

Mix and bake ingredients according to recipes to produce breads, pastries, and other baked goods. Goods are produced in large quantities for sale through establishments such as grocery stores. Generally, high-volume production equipment is used. **O*NET Code:** 51-3011.02. **Average Salary:** $21,070. **Projected Growth:** 11.2%. **Annual Openings:** 29,000. **Education:** Long-term on-the-job training. **Job Zone:** 3. **Education/Training Program(s)**—Baking and Pastry Arts/Baker/Pastry Chef. **Related Knowledge/Courses:** Production and Processing; Food Production. **Personality Type:** Realistic. **Skills Required:** Operation Monitoring. **Abilities:** Visual Color Discrimination; Information Ordering; Gross Body Coordination; Manual Dexterity; Originality. **Occupational Values:** Supervision, Technical; Moral Values; Company Policies and Practices; Independence; Co-workers; Supervision, Human Relations. **Interacting with Others:** Monitoring and Controlling Resources; Communicating with Supervisors, Peers, or Subordinates; Establishing and Maintaining Interpersonal Relationships. **Physical Work Conditions:** Minor Burns, Cuts, Bites, or Stings; Standing;

Very Hot or Cold; Indoors; Spend Time Making Repetitive Motions.

Cementing and Gluing Machine Operators and Tenders

Operate or tend cementing and gluing machines to join items for further processing or to form a completed product. Processes include joining veneer sheets into plywood; gluing paper; and joining rubber and rubberized fabric parts, plastic, simulated leather, or other materials. **O*NET Code:** 51-9191.00. **Average Salary:** $23,480. **Projected Growth:** 1.1%. **Annual Openings:** 4,000. **Education:** Moderate-term on-the-job training. **Job Zone:** 1. **Education/Training Program(s)—** No data available. **Related Knowledge/Courses:** Production and Processing; Mechanical; Chemistry. **Personality Type:** Realistic. **Skills Required:** Operation Monitoring; Equipment Maintenance; Operation and Control; Troubleshooting; Quality Control Analysis; Technology Design; Repairing; Equipment Selection. **Abilities:** Arm-Hand Steadiness; Dynamic Flexibility; Control Precision; Static Strength; Manual Dexterity. **Occupational Values:** Moral Values; Supervision, Human Relations; Supervision, Technical; Company Policies and Practices; Independence. **Interacting with Others:** Communicating with Supervisors, Peers, or Subordinates; Establishing and Maintaining Interpersonal Relationships; Performing Administrative Activities. **Physical Work Conditions:** Hazardous Equipment; Minor Burns, Cuts, Bites, or Stings; Common Protective or Safety Equipment; Sounds, Noise Levels Are Distracting or Uncomfortable; Contaminants; Spend Time Bending or Twisting the Body.

Chemical Equipment Controllers and Operators

Control or operate equipment to control chemical changes or reactions in the processing of industrial or consumer products. Typical equipment used are reaction kettles, catalytic converters, continuous or batch-treating equipment, saturator tanks, electrolytic cells, reactor vessels, recovery units, and fermentation chambers. **O*NET Code:** 51-9011.01. **Average Salary:** $38,760. **Projected Growth:** –3.8%. **Annual Openings:** 8,000. **Education:** Moderate-term on-the-job training. **Job Zone:** 2. **Education/Training Program(s)—**Chemical Technology/Technician. **Related Knowledge/Courses:** Chemistry; Mechanical; Public Safety and Security; Telecommunications; Engineering and Technology; Production and Processing. **Personality Type:** Realistic. **Skills Required:** Operation Monitoring; Science; Operation and Control; Quality Control Analysis; Management of Personnel Resources; Equipment Maintenance; Repairing; Mathematics. **Abilities:** Reaction Time; Information Ordering; Control Precision; Selective Attention; Response Orientation. **Occupational Values:** Supervision, Technical; Moral Values; Company Policies and Practices; Advancement; Supervision, Human Relations. **Interacting with Others:** Coordinating the Work and Activities of Others; Communicating with Supervisors, Peers, or Subordinates; Establishing and Maintaining Interpersonal Relationships. **Physical Work Conditions:** Hazardous Conditions; Minor Burns, Cuts, Bites, or Stings; Common Protective or Safety Equipment; Hazardous Equipment; Using Hands on Objects, Tools, or Controls.

Chemical Equipment Tenders

Tend equipment in which a chemical change or reaction takes place in the processing of industrial or consumer products. Typical equipment used are devulcanizers, batch stills, fermenting tanks, steam-jacketed kettles, and reactor vessels. **O*NET Code:** 51-9011.02. **Average Salary:** $38,760. **Projected Growth:** –3.8%. **Annual Openings:** 8,000. **Education:** Moderate-term on-the-job training. **Job Zone:** 2. **Education/Training Program(s)—**Chemical Technology/Technician. **Related Knowledge/Courses:** Chemistry; Public Safety and Security; Mechanical; Production and Processing. **Personality Type:** Realistic. **Skills Required:** Operation Monitoring; Operation and Control; Science; Quality Control Analysis; Repairing; Equipment Maintenance; Troubleshooting. **Abilities:** Reaction Time; Speed of Limb Movement; Control Precision; Response Orientation; Rate Control. **Occupational Values:** Moral Values; Advancement; Supervision, Technical; Company Policies and Practices; Activity. **Interacting with Others:** Communicating with Supervisors, Peers, or Subordinates; Assisting and Caring for Others; Establishing and Maintaining Interpersonal Relationships. **Physical Work Conditions:** Hazardous Conditions; Common Protective or Safety Equipment; Contaminants; Hazardous Equipment; Walking and Running.

Cleaning, Washing, and Metal Pickling Equipment Operators and Tenders

Operate or tend machines to wash or clean products, such as barrels or kegs, glass items, tin plate, food, pulp, coal, plastic, or rubber, to remove impurities. **O*NET Code:** 51-9192.00. **Average Salary:** $23,840. **Projected Growth:** 6.9%. **Annual Openings:** 3,000. **Education:** Moderate-term on-the-job training. **Job Zone:** 1. **Education/Training Program(s)—**No data available. **Related Knowledge/Courses:** Production and Processing; Chemistry; Mechanical. **Personality Type:** Realistic. **Skills Required:** Operation Monitoring; Operation and Control; Equipment Maintenance; Quality Control Analysis; Troubleshooting; Repairing. **Abilities:** Rate Control; Control Precision; Multilimb Coordination; Information Ordering; Arm-Hand Steadiness. **Occupational Values:** Moral Values; Independence; Supervision, Human Relations; Supervision, Technical; Company Policies and Practices. **Interacting with Others:** Performing Administrative Activities; Communicating with Supervisors, Peers, or Subordinates; Establishing and Maintaining Interpersonal Relationships. **Physical Work Conditions:** Hazardous Equipment; Standing; Sounds, Noise Levels Are Distracting or Uncomfortable; Common Protective or Safety Equipment; Minor Burns, Cuts, Bites, or Stings.

Coating, Painting, and Spraying Machine Operators and Tenders

Coating Machine Operators and Tenders: Operate or tend machines to coat any of a wide variety of items: Coat food products with sugar, chocolate, or butter; coat paper and paper products with chemical solutions, wax, or glazes; or coat fabric with rubber or plastic. Painting and Spraying Machine Operators and Tenders: Operate or tend machines to spray or paint decorative, protective, or other coating or finish, such as adhesive, lacquer, paint, stain, latex, preservative, oil, or other solutions. May apply coating or finish to any of a wide variety of items or materials, such as wood and wood products, ceramics, and glass. Includes workers who apply coating or finish to materials preparatory to further processing or to consumer use. **O*NET Code:** 51-9121.02. **Average Salary:** $25,920. **Projected Growth:** 9.4%. **Annual Openings:** 17,000. **Education:** Moderate-term on-the-job training. **Job Zone:** 1. **Education/Training Program(s)**—No data available. **Related Knowledge/Courses:** Chemistry; Production and Processing; Physics; Food Production; Engineering and Technology; Mechanical. **Personality Type:** Realistic. **Skills Required:** Operation Monitoring; Operation and Control; Technology Design; Equipment Maintenance. **Abilities:** Rate Control; Reaction Time; Dynamic Strength; Multilimb Coordination; Arm-Hand Steadiness; Control Precision. **Occupational Values:** Moral Values; Independence; Supervision, Technical; Supervision, Human Relations; Activity; Company Policies and Practices. **Interacting with Others:** Communicating with Supervisors, Peers, or Subordinates; Establishing and Maintaining Interpersonal Relationships; Assisting and Caring for Others; Coordinating the Work and Activities of Others; Monitoring and Controlling Resources. **Physical Work Conditions:** Contaminants; Hazardous Conditions; Hazardous Equipment; Common Protective or Safety Equipment; Standing.

Combination Machine Tool Operators and Tenders, Metal and Plastic

Operate or tend more than one type of cutting or forming machine tool, which has been previously set up. Includes such machine tools as band saws, press brakes, slitting machines, drills, lathes, and boring machines. **O*NET Code:** 51-4081.02. **Average Salary:** $28,790. **Projected Growth:** 8.3%. **Annual Openings:** 8,000. **Education:** Moderate-term on-the-job training. **Job Zone:** 2. **Education/Training Program(s)**—Machine Shop Technology/Assistant; Machine Tool Technology/Machinist. **Related Knowledge/Courses:** Production and Processing; Mechanical; Building and Construction. **Personality Type:** Realistic. **Skills Required:** Operation Monitoring; Installation; Operation and Control; Equipment Maintenance; Quality Control Analysis; Repairing. **Abilities:** Rate Control; Manual Dexterity; Control Precision; Multilimb Coordination; Reaction Time; Speed of Limb Movement. **Occupational Values:** Moral Values; Independence; Company Policies and Practices; Supervision, Human Relations; Activity. **Interacting with Others:** Communicating with Supervisors, Peers, or Subordinates; Coordinating the Work and Activities of Others; Performing Administrative Activities. **Physical Work Conditions:** Hazardous Equipment; Minor Burns, Cuts, Bites, or Stings; Standing; Sounds, Noise Levels Are Distracting or Uncomfortable; Common Protective or Safety Equipment.

Cooling and Freezing Equipment Operators and Tenders

Operate or tend equipment, such as cooling and freezing units, refrigerators, batch freezers, and freezing tunnels, to cool or freeze products, food, blood plasma, and chemicals. **O*NET Code:** 51-9193.00. **Average Salary:** $22,140. **Projected Growth:** 7.1%. **Annual Openings:** 1,000. **Education:** Moderate-term on-the-job training. **Job Zone:** 1.

Education/Training Program(s)—No data available. **Related Knowledge/Courses:** Chemistry; Mechanical; Food Production; Public Safety and Security; Engineering and Technology; Physics. **Personality Type:** Realistic. **Skills Required:** Operation Monitoring; Repairing; Operation and Control; Equipment Maintenance; Quality Control Analysis; Troubleshooting; Science; Installation. **Abilities:** Extent Flexibility; Reaction Time; Stamina; Manual Dexterity; Finger Dexterity; Static Strength. **Occupational Values:** Moral Values; Independence; Supervision, Technical; Company Policies and Practices; Supervision, Human Relations. **Interacting with Others:** Communicating with Supervisors, Peers, or Subordinates; Performing Administrative Activities; Communicating with Persons Outside Organization; Establishing and Maintaining Interpersonal Relationships; Coordinating the Work and Activities of Others. **Physical Work Conditions:** Very Hot or Cold; Hazardous Equipment; Standing; Indoors; Using Hands on Objects, Tools, or Controls.

Cutting and Slicing Machine Operators and Tenders

Operate or tend machines to cut or slice any of a wide variety of products or materials, such as tobacco, food, paper, roofing slate, glass, stone, rubber, cork, and insulating material. **O*NET Code:** 51-9032.04. **Average Salary:** $26,500. **Projected Growth:** 6.6%. **Annual Openings:** 12,000. **Education:** Short-term on-the-job training. **Job Zone:** 1. **Education/Training Program(s)**—No data available. **Related Knowledge/Courses:** Production and Processing; Food Production; Design; Physics; Mechanical. **Personality Type:** Realistic. **Skills Required:** Operation Monitoring; Operation and Control; Installation; Equipment Maintenance; Troubleshooting. **Abilities:** Reaction Time; Extent Flexibility; Perceptual Speed; Static Strength; Explosive Strength. **Occupational Values:** Moral Values; Independence; Supervision, Technical; Activity; Company Policies and Practices. **Interacting with Others:** Establishing and Maintaining Interpersonal Relationships; Communicating with Supervisors, Peers, or Subordinates; Coordinating the Work and Activities of Others. **Physical Work Conditions:** Hazardous Equipment; Minor Burns, Cuts, Bites, or Stings; Common Protective or Safety Equipment; Using Hands on Objects, Tools, or Controls; Standing.

Electrolytic Plating and Coating Machine Operators and Tenders, Metal and Plastic

Operate or tend electrolytic plating or coating machines, such as zinc-plating machines and anodizing machines, to coat metal or plastic products electrolytically with chromium, zinc, copper, cadmium, or other metal to provide protective or decorative surfaces or to build up worn surfaces. **O*NET Code:** 51-4193.02. **Average Salary:** $26,250. **Projected Growth:** –2.6%. **Annual Openings:** 6,000. **Education:** Moderate-term on-the-job training. **Job Zone:** 2. **Education/Training Program(s)**—No data available. **Related Knowledge/Courses:** Chemistry; Production and Processing; Physics; Mechanical. **Personality Type:** Realistic. **Skills Required:** Operation and Control; Quality Control Analysis; Equipment Maintenance; Operation Monitoring; Repairing. **Abilities:** Mathematical Reasoning; Control Precision;

© 2006, JIST Works

Reaction Time; Dynamic Flexibility; Dynamic Strength. **Occupational Values:** Moral Values; Independence; Supervision, Human Relations; Activity; Supervision, Technical. **Interacting with Others:** Communicating with Supervisors, Peers, or Subordinates; Establishing and Maintaining Interpersonal Relationships; Resolving Conflicts and Negotiating with Others; Coordinating the Work and Activities of Others. **Physical Work Conditions:** Hazardous Conditions; Common Protective or Safety Equipment; Using Hands on Objects, Tools, or Controls; Indoors; Walking and Running.

Extruding and Forming Machine Operators and Tenders, Synthetic or Glass Fibers

Operate or tend machines that extrude and form continuous filaments from synthetic materials, such as liquid polymer, rayon, and fiberglass, preparatory to further processing. **O*NET Code:** 51-6091.01. **Average Salary:** $28,380. **Projected Growth:** –13.1%. **Annual Openings:** 4,000. **Education:** Moderate-term on-the-job training. **Job Zone:** 1. **Education/Training Program(s)**—No data available. **Related Knowledge/Courses:** Production and Processing; Mechanical; Engineering and Technology. **Personality Type:** Realistic. **Skills Required:** Equipment Maintenance; Operation Monitoring; Operation and Control; Repairing; Installation. **Abilities:** Control Precision; Perceptual Speed; Wrist-Finger Speed; Static Strength; Extent Flexibility. **Occupational Values:** Moral Values; Supervision, Technical; Independence; Supervision, Human Relations; Company Policies and Practices. **Interacting with Others:** Communicating with Supervisors, Peers, or Subordinates; Establishing and Maintaining Interpersonal Relationships; Coordinating the Work and Activities of Others. **Physical Work Conditions:** Using Hands on Objects, Tools, or Controls; Common Protective or Safety Equipment; Indoors; Standing; Hazardous Equipment; Spend Time Making Repetitive Motions.

Extruding, Forming, Pressing, and Compacting Machine Operators and Tenders

Operate or tend machines to shape and form any of a wide variety of manufactured products, such as glass bulbs, molded food and candy, rubber goods, clay products, wax products, tobacco plugs, cosmetics, or paper products, by means of extruding, compressing or compacting. **O*NET Code:** 51-9041.02. **Average Salary:** $27,180. **Projected Growth:** –0.1%. **Annual Openings:** 10,000. **Education:** Short-term on-the-job training. **Job Zone:** 1. **Education/Training Program(s)**—No data available. **Related Knowledge/Courses:** Production and Processing; Mechanical. **Personality Type:** Realistic. **Skills Required:** Operation Monitoring; Operation and Control; Equipment Maintenance; Repairing; Installation; Troubleshooting; Quality Control Analysis. **Abilities:** Dynamic Strength; Rate Control; Control Precision; Perceptual Speed; Reaction Time; Speed of Limb Movement. **Occupational Values:** Moral Values; Independence; Supervision, Technical; Supervision, Human Relations; Activity; Company Policies and Practices. **Interacting with Others:** Performing Administrative Activities; Communicating with Supervisors, Peers, or Subordinates; Interpreting the Meaning of Information for Others; Coordinating the Work and Activities of Others. **Physical**

Work Conditions: Hazardous Equipment; Standing; Using Hands on Objects, Tools, or Controls; Sounds, Noise Levels Are Distracting or Uncomfortable; Spend Time Making Repetitive Motions.

Food and Tobacco Roasting, Baking, and Drying Machine Operators and Tenders

Operate or tend food or tobacco roasting, baking, or drying equipment, including hearth ovens, kiln driers, roasters, char kilns, and vacuum-drying equipment. **O*NET Code:** 51-3091.00. **Average Salary:** $24,260. **Projected Growth:** 4.2%. **Annual Openings:** 3,000. **Education:** Short-term on-the-job training. **Job Zone:** 1. **Education/Training Program(s)**—Agricultural and Food Products Processing. **Related Knowledge/Courses:** Food Production; Production and Processing; Mechanical; Chemistry. **Personality Type:** Realistic. **Skills Required:** Operation Monitoring; Installation; Operation and Control; Quality Control Analysis; Troubleshooting; Equipment Maintenance; Science; Systems Analysis. **Abilities:** Static Strength; Hearing Sensitivity; Sound Localization; Visual Color Discrimination; Reaction Time. **Occupational Values:** Moral Values; Supervision, Technical; Company Policies and Practices; Independence; Supervision, Human Relations. **Interacting with Others:** Communicating with Supervisors, Peers, or Subordinates; Establishing and Maintaining Interpersonal Relationships; Performing Administrative Activities. **Physical Work Conditions:** Minor Burns, Cuts, Bites, or Stings; Hazardous Equipment; Common Protective or Safety Equipment; Standing; Using Hands on Objects, Tools, or Controls.

Food Batchmakers

Set up and operate equipment that mixes or blends ingredients used in the manufacturing of food products. Includes candy makers and cheese makers. **O*NET Code:** 51-3092.00. **Average Salary:** $22,190. **Projected Growth:** 7.2%. **Annual Openings:** 10,000. **Education:** Short-term on-the-job training. **Job Zone:** 2. **Education/Training Program(s)**—Agricultural and Food Products Processing; Foodservice Systems Administration/Management. **Related Knowledge/Courses:** Public Safety and Security; Production and Processing; Food Production; Mathematics; Foreign Language; Chemistry. **Personality Type:** Realistic. **Skills Required:** Operation Monitoring; Equipment Maintenance; Troubleshooting; Operation and Control; Quality Control Analysis; Time Management; Repairing; Instructing. **Abilities:** Information Ordering; Visual Color Discrimination; Memorization; Manual Dexterity; Wrist-Finger Speed. **Occupational Values:** Supervision, Technical; Authority; Variety; Co-workers; Moral Values; Company Policies and Practices. **Interacting with Others:** Establishing and Maintaining Interpersonal Relationships; Communicating with Supervisors, Peers, or Subordinates; Training and Teaching Others. **Physical Work Conditions:** Sounds, Noise Levels Are Distracting or Uncomfortable; Contaminants; Very Hot or Cold; Standing; Indoors, Not Environmentally Controlled.

Food Cooking Machine Operators and Tenders

Operate or tend cooking equipment, such as steam cooking

vats, deep fry cookers, pressure cookers, kettles, and boilers, to prepare food products. **O*NET Code:** 51-3093.00. **Average Salary:** $20,910. **Projected Growth:** 8.8%. **Annual Openings:** 6,000. **Education:** Short-term on-the-job training. **Job Zone:** 2. **Education/Training Program(s)**—Agricultural and Food Products Processing. **Related Knowledge/Courses:** Food Production; Production and Processing; Chemistry; Administration and Management; Computers and Electronics. **Personality Type:** Realistic. **Skills Required:** Operation Monitoring; Instructing; Quality Control Analysis; Learning Strategies; Coordination; Negotiation; Management of Personnel Resources; Operations Analysis. **Abilities:** Reaction Time; Response Orientation; Auditory Attention; Sound Localization; Rate Control. **Occupational Values:** Moral Values; Supervision, Technical; Company Policies and Practices; Supervision, Human Relations; Independence. **Interacting with Others:** Communicating with Supervisors, Peers, or Subordinates; Establishing and Maintaining Interpersonal Relationships; Coaching and Developing Others. **Physical Work Conditions:** Very Hot or Cold; Sounds, Noise Levels Are Distracting or Uncomfortable; Physical Proximity; Minor Burns, Cuts, Bites, or Stings; Walking and Running.

Furnace, Kiln, Oven, Drier, and Kettle Operators and Tenders

Operate or tend heating equipment other than basic metal, plastic, or food processing equipment. Includes activities such as annealing glass, drying lumber, curing rubber, removing moisture from materials, or boiling soap. **O*NET Code:** 51-9051.00. **Average Salary:** $29,620. **Projected Growth:** –4.9%. **Annual Openings:** 4,000. **Education:** Moderate-term on-the-job training. **Job Zone:** 2. **Education/Training Program(s)**—No data available. **Related Knowledge/Courses:** Production and Processing; Mechanical; Public Safety and Security; Engineering and Technology; Education and Training; Administration and Management; Physics. **Personality Type:** Realistic. **Skills Required:** Operation Monitoring; Operation and Control; Instructing; Equipment Maintenance; Troubleshooting; Repairing; Learning Strategies; Coordination. **Abilities:** Static Strength; Trunk Strength; Stamina; Control Precision. **Occupational Values:** Moral Values; Supervision, Technical; Company Policies and Practices; Supervision, Human Relations; Independence; Advancement. **Interacting with Others:** Communicating with Supervisors, Peers, or Subordinates; Establishing and Maintaining Interpersonal Relationships; Training and Teaching Others; Coaching and Developing Others. **Physical Work Conditions:** Hazardous Conditions; Sounds, Noise Levels Are Distracting or Uncomfortable; Contaminants; In an Open Vehicle or Equipment; Hazardous Equipment.

Heat Treating, Annealing, and Tempering Machine Operators and Tenders, Metal and Plastic

Operate or tend machines, such as furnaces, baths, flame-hardening machines, and electronic induction machines, to harden, anneal, and heat-treat metal products or metal parts. **O*NET Code:** 51-4191.02. **Average Salary:** $29,140. **Projected Growth:** –0.6%. **Annual Openings:** 4,000. **Education:** Moderate-term on-the-job training. **Job Zone:** 2.

Education/Training Program(s)—Machine Shop Technology/Assistant; Machine Tool Technology/Machinist. **Related Knowledge/Courses:** Production and Processing; Mechanical; Physics; Chemistry; Building and Construction. **Personality Type:** Realistic. **Skills Required:** Operation Monitoring; Quality Control Analysis; Installation; Operation and Control; Science; Equipment Maintenance; Repairing; Equipment Selection. **Abilities:** Rate Control; Static Strength; Dynamic Strength; Visual Color Discrimination; Dynamic Flexibility. **Occupational Values:** Moral Values; Independence; Supervision, Human Relations; Supervision, Technical; Company Policies and Practices. **Interacting with Others:** Communicating with Supervisors, Peers, or Subordinates; Coordinating the Work and Activities of Others; Establishing and Maintaining Interpersonal Relationships. **Physical Work Conditions:** Hazardous Equipment; Hazardous Conditions; Minor Burns, Cuts, Bites, or Stings; Very Hot or Cold; Standing.

Heaters, Metal and Plastic

Operate or tend heating equipment, such as soaking pits, reheating furnaces, and heating and vacuum equipment, to heat metal sheets, blooms, billets, bars, plate, and rods to a specified temperature for rolling or processing or to heat and cure preformed plastic parts. **O*NET Code:** 51-4191.03. **Average Salary:** $29,140. **Projected Growth:** –0.6%. **Annual Openings:** 4,000. **Education:** Moderate-term on-the-job training. **Job Zone:** 2. **Education/Training Program(s)**—Machine Shop Technology/Assistant; Machine Tool Technology/Machinist. **Related Knowledge/Courses:** Production and Processing; Mechanical; Physics; Engineering and Technology. **Personality Type:** Realistic. **Skills Required:** Equipment Maintenance; Repairing; Operation and Control; Operation Monitoring. **Abilities:** Control Precision; Extent Flexibility; Multilimb Coordination; Static Strength; Gross Body Coordination. **Occupational Values:** Moral Values; Supervision, Technical; Supervision, Human Relations; Company Policies and Practices; Activity. **Interacting with Others:** Communicating with Supervisors, Peers, or Subordinates; Assisting and Caring for Others; Establishing and Maintaining Interpersonal Relationships. **Physical Work Conditions:** Hazardous Equipment; Minor Burns, Cuts, Bites, or Stings; Hazardous Conditions; Standing; Very Hot or Cold.

Meat, Poultry, and Fish Cutters and Trimmers

Use hand tools to perform routine cutting and trimming of meat, poultry, and fish. **O*NET Code:** 51-3022.00. **Average Salary:** $18,500. **Projected Growth:** 16.4%. **Annual Openings:** 27,000. **Education:** Short-term on-the-job training. **Job Zone:** 1. **Education/Training Program(s)**—Meat Cutting/Meat Cutter. **Related Knowledge/Courses:** Food Production; Biology; Production and Processing; Law and Government; Public Safety and Security. **Personality Type:** Realistic. **Skills Required:** None met the criteria. **Abilities:** Static Strength; Wrist-Finger Speed; Dynamic Strength; Manual Dexterity; Speed of Limb Movement. **Occupational Values:** Supervision, Technical; Independence. **Interacting with Others:** Communicating with Supervisors, Peers, or Subordinates; Monitoring and Controlling Resources; Performing Administrative Activities. **Physical Work Conditions:** Minor Burns, Cuts, Bites, or Stings; Standing;

© 2006, JIST Works

Common Protective or Safety Equipment; Spend Time Making Repetitive Motions; Contaminants.

Metal-Refining Furnace Operators and Tenders

Operate or tend furnaces, such as gas, oil, coal, electric-arc or electric induction, open-hearth, or oxygen furnaces, to melt and refine metal before casting or to produce specified types of steel. **O*NET Code:** 51-4051.00. **Average Salary:** $32,340. **Projected Growth:** -0.8%. **Annual Openings:** 2,000. **Education:** Moderate-term on-the-job training. **Job Zone:** 2. **Education/Training Program(s)**—No data available. **Related Knowledge/Courses:** Production and Processing; Physics; Mechanical; Chemistry; Engineering and Technology. **Personality Type:** Realistic. **Skills Required:** Operation Monitoring; Operation and Control; Equipment Maintenance; Science; Troubleshooting; Quality Control Analysis. **Abilities:** Static Strength; Dynamic Flexibility; Dynamic Strength; Stamina; Explosive Strength; Gross Body Coordination. **Occupational Values:** Independence; Moral Values; Supervision, Human Relations; Activity; Company Policies and Practices. **Interacting with Others:** Communicating with Supervisors, Peers, or Subordinates; Performing Administrative Activities; Coordinating the Work and Activities of Others. **Physical Work Conditions:** Hazardous Equipment; Very Hot or Cold; Minor Burns, Cuts, Bites, or Stings; Hazardous Conditions; Contaminants.

Mixing and Blending Machine Setters, Operators, and Tenders

Set up, operate, or tend machines to mix or blend materials such as chemicals, tobacco, liquids, color pigments, or explosive ingredients. **O*NET Code:** 51-9023.00. **Average Salary:** $27,890. **Projected Growth:** -6.5%. **Annual Openings:** 14,000. **Education:** Moderate-term on-the-job training. **Job Zone:** 1. **Education/Training Program(s)**—Agricultural and Food Products Processing. **Related Knowledge/Courses:** Production and Processing; Mechanical; Chemistry; Physics. **Personality Type:** Realistic. **Skills Required:** Operation Monitoring; Operation and Control; Equipment Maintenance; Quality Control Analysis. **Abilities:** Control Precision; Reaction Time; Static Strength; Rate Control; Explosive Strength. **Occupational Values:** Moral Values; Independence; Supervision, Technical; Supervision, Human Relations; Company Policies and Practices. **Interacting with Others:** Communicating with Supervisors, Peers, or Subordinates; Establishing and Maintaining Interpersonal Relationships; Interpreting the Meaning of Information for Others. **Physical Work Conditions:** Common Protective or Safety Equipment; Hazardous Equipment; Sounds, Noise Levels Are Distracting or Uncomfortable; Extremely Bright or Inadequate Lighting; Standing; Spend Time Bending or Twisting the Body.

Nonelectrolytic Plating and Coating Machine Operators and Tenders, Metal and Plastic

Operate or tend nonelectrolytic plating or coating machines, such as metal-spraying machines and vacuum metalizing machines, to coat metal or plastic products or parts with metal. **O*NET Code:** 51-4193.04. **Average Salary:** $26,250. **Projected Growth:** -2.6%. **Annual Openings:** 6,000. **Education:** Short-term on-the-job training. **Job Zone:** 1. **Education/Training Program(s)**—No data available. **Related**

Knowledge/Courses: Production and Processing; Chemistry; Physics; Mechanical; Engineering and Technology. **Personality Type:** Realistic. **Skills Required:** Operation Monitoring; Equipment Maintenance; Operation and Control; Repairing. **Abilities:** Extent Flexibility; Trunk Strength; Speed of Limb Movement; Explosive Strength; Multilimb Coordination. **Occupational Values:** Moral Values; Independence; Supervision, Human Relations; Supervision, Technical; Activity; Company Policies and Practices. **Interacting with Others:** Communicating with Supervisors, Peers, or Subordinates; Establishing and Maintaining Interpersonal Relationships; Assisting and Caring for Others; Coaching and Developing Others; Performing Administrative Activities. **Physical Work Conditions:** Standing; Minor Burns, Cuts, Bites, or Stings; Common Protective or Safety Equipment; Indoors; Using Hands on Objects, Tools, or Controls.

Packaging and Filling Machine Operators and Tenders

Operate or tend machines to prepare industrial or consumer products for storage or shipment. Includes cannery workers who pack food products. **O*NET Code:** 51-9111.00. **Average Salary:** $21,970. **Projected Growth:** 21.1%. **Annual Openings:** 69,000. **Education:** Short-term on-the-job training. **Job Zone:** 2. **Education/Training Program(s)**—No data available. **Related Knowledge/Courses:** Production and Processing; Mechanical; Psychology; Sociology and Anthropology; Education and Training; Public Safety and Security. **Personality Type:** Realistic. **Skills Required:** Equipment Maintenance; Instructing; Troubleshooting; Quality Control Analysis; Coordination; Operation Monitoring; Operation and Control; Learning Strategies. **Abilities:** Perceptual Speed; Reaction Time; Auditory Attention; Static Strength; Response Orientation. **Occupational Values:** Moral Values; Independence; Supervision, Technical; Supervision, Human Relations; Activity. **Interacting with Others:** Communicating with Supervisors, Peers, or Subordinates; Establishing and Maintaining Interpersonal Relationships; Training and Teaching Others. **Physical Work Conditions:** Contaminants; Sounds, Noise Levels Are Distracting or Uncomfortable; Hazardous Conditions; Hazardous Equipment; Standing.

Plastic Molding and Casting Machine Operators and Tenders

Operate or tend plastic molding machines, such as compression or injection molding machines, to mold, form, or cast thermoplastic materials to specified shape. **O*NET Code:** 51-4072.02. **Average Salary:** $24,070. **Projected Growth:** 8.9%. **Annual Openings:** 18,000. **Education:** Short-term on-the-job training. **Job Zone:** 1. **Education/Training Program(s)**—No data available. **Related Knowledge/Courses:** Production and Processing; Mechanical; Physics. **Personality Type:** Realistic. **Skills Required:** Operation Monitoring; Operation and Control; Quality Control Analysis; Equipment Maintenance; Science. **Abilities:** Rate Control; Static Strength; Control Precision; Reaction Time; Perceptual Speed. **Occupational Values:** Moral Values; Independence; Company Policies and Practices; Supervision, Human Relations; Supervision, Technical. **Interacting with Others:** Communicating with

Supervisors, Peers, or Subordinates; Establishing and Maintaining Interpersonal Relationships; Coordinating the Work and Activities of Others. **Physical Work Conditions:** Hazardous Equipment; Standing; Sounds, Noise Levels Are Distracting or Uncomfortable; Using Hands on Objects, Tools, or Controls; Indoors; Spend Time Bending or Twisting the Body.

Pourers and Casters, Metal

Operate hand-controlled mechanisms to pour and regulate the flow of molten metal into molds to produce castings or ingots. **O*NET Code:** 51-4052.00. **Average Salary:** $28,480. **Projected Growth:** -2.0%. **Annual Openings:** 2,000. **Education:** Moderate-term on-the-job training. **Job Zone:** 1. **Education/Training Program(s)**—No data available. **Related Knowledge/Courses:** Production and Processing; Mechanical; Physics. **Personality Type:** Realistic. **Skills Required:** Operation Monitoring; Repairing; Operation and Control; Equipment Maintenance; Installation; Troubleshooting; Science; Quality Control Analysis. **Abilities:** Depth Perception; Visual Color Discrimination; Speed of Limb Movement; Hearing Sensitivity; Dynamic Flexibility; Sound Localization. **Occupational Values:** Moral Values; Supervision, Technical; Independence; Supervision, Human Relations. **Interacting with Others:** Communicating with Supervisors, Peers, or Subordinates; Establishing and Maintaining Interpersonal Relationships; Assisting and Caring for Others. **Physical Work Conditions:** Common Protective or Safety Equipment; Minor Burns, Cuts, Bites, or Stings; Very Hot or Cold; Using Hands on Objects, Tools, or Controls; Hazardous Equipment.

Pressing Machine Operators and Tenders—Textile, Garment, and Related Materials

Operate or tend pressing machines, such as hot-head pressing, steam pressing, automatic pressing, ironing, plunger pressing, and hydraulic pressing machines, to press and shape articles such as leather, fur, and cloth garments, drapes, slipcovers, handkerchiefs, and millinery. **O*NET Code:** 51-6021.02. **Average Salary:** $17,050. **Projected Growth:** -0.2%. **Annual Openings:** 19,000. **Education:** Short-term on-the-job training. **Job Zone:** 1. **Education/Training Program(s)**—No data available. **Related Knowledge/Courses:** Engineering and Technology; Food Production. **Personality Type:** Realistic. **Skills Required:** Operation Monitoring; Operation and Control; Installation; Quality Control Analysis; Repairing. **Abilities:** Arm-Hand Steadiness; Control Precision; Manual Dexterity; Visual Color Discrimination; Reaction Time. **Occupational Values:** Moral Values; Independence; Company Policies and Practices; Supervision, Human Relations; Supervision, Technical. **Interacting with Others:** Communicating with Supervisors, Peers, or Subordinates; Establishing and Maintaining Interpersonal Relationships; Communicating with Persons Outside Organization; Coaching and Developing Others; Monitoring and Controlling Resources. **Physical Work Conditions:** Minor Burns, Cuts, Bites, or Stings; Very Hot or Cold; Hazardous Equipment; Using Hands on Objects, Tools, or Controls; Indoors.

Production Helpers

Perform variety of tasks requiring limited knowledge of production processes in support of skilled production workers. **O*NET Code:** 51-9198.02. **Average Salary:** $19,940. **Projected Growth:** 7.7%. **Annual Openings:** 134,000. **Education:** Short-term on-the-job training. **Job Zone:** 1. **Education/Training Program(s)**—No data available. **Related Knowledge/Courses:** Mechanical; Production and Processing; Engineering and Technology. **Personality Type:** Realistic. **Skills Required:** Equipment Maintenance; Repairing; Operation Monitoring; Installation; Operation and Control. **Abilities:** Auditory Attention; Static Strength; Reaction Time; Stamina; Speed of Limb Movement. **Occupational Values:** Supervision, Technical; Moral Values; Activity; Supervision, Human Relations; Advancement; Co-workers. **Interacting with Others:** Communicating with Supervisors, Peers, or Subordinates; Establishing and Maintaining Interpersonal Relationships; Assisting and Caring for Others; Coordinating the Work and Activities of Others; Performing Administrative Activities. **Physical Work Conditions:** Hazardous Equipment; Minor Burns, Cuts, Bites, or Stings; Standing; Using Hands on Objects, Tools, or Controls; Walking and Running; Spend Time Bending or Twisting the Body.

Production Laborers

Perform variety of routine tasks to assist in production activities. **O*NET Code:** 51-9198.01. **Average Salary:** $19,940. **Projected Growth:** 11.3%. **Annual Openings:** 67,000. **Education:** Short-term on-the-job training. **Job Zone:** 1. **Education/Training Program(s)**—No data available. **Related Knowledge/Courses:** Production and Processing; Administration and Management. **Personality Type:** Realistic. **Skills Required:** Installation; Equipment Maintenance; Repairing. **Abilities:** Dynamic Strength; Static Strength; Dynamic Flexibility; Explosive Strength; Stamina. **Occupational Values:** Moral Values; Activity; Co-workers; Supervision, Technical. **Interacting with Others:** Performing Administrative Activities; Assisting and Caring for Others; Communicating with Supervisors, Peers, or Subordinates. **Physical Work Conditions:** Hazardous Equipment; Spend Time Bending or Twisting the Body; Standing; Spend Time Making Repetitive Motions; Very Hot or Cold.

Sawing Machine Operators and Tenders

Operate or tend wood-sawing machines, such as circular saws, band saws, multiple-blade sawing machines, scroll saws, ripsaws, equalizer saws, power saws, and crozer machines. Duties include sawing logs to specifications; cutting lumber to specified dimensions; sawing curved or irregular designs; trimming edges and removing defects from lumber; or cutting grooves, bevel, and miter according to specifications or work orders. **O*NET Code:** 51-7041.02. **Average Salary:** $22,490. **Projected Growth:** -0.2%. **Annual Openings:** 10,000. **Education:** Moderate-term on-the-job training. **Job Zone:** 2. **Education/Training Program(s)**—Cabinetmaking and Millwork/Millwright. **Related Knowledge/Courses:** Production and Processing; Mechanical; Building and Construction; Design. **Personality Type:** Realistic. **Skills Required:** Equipment Maintenance; Repairing; Operation and Control; Installation; Operation Monitoring; Equipment Selection; Quality Control Analysis. **Abilities:** Rate Control;

Static Strength; Stamina; Control Precision; Manual Dexterity. **Occupational Values:** Moral Values; Independence; Supervision, Technical; Activity; Company Policies and Practices. **Interacting with Others:** Communicating with Supervisors, Peers, or Subordinates; Performing Administrative Activities; Interpreting the Meaning of Information for Others. **Physical Work Conditions:** Hazardous Equipment; Minor Burns, Cuts, Bites, or Stings; Sounds, Noise Levels Are Distracting or Uncomfortable; Contaminants; Common Protective or Safety Equipment.

Separating, Filtering, Clarifying, Precipitating, and Still Machine Setters, Operators, and Tenders

Set up, operate, or tend continuous flow or vat-type equipment; filter presses; shaker screens; centrifuges; condenser tubes; precipitating, fermenting, or evaporating tanks; scrubbing towers; or batch stills. These machines extract, sort, or separate liquids, gases, or solids from other materials to recover a refined product. Includes dairy processing equipment operators. **O*NET Code:** 51-9012.00. **Average Salary:** $32,310. **Projected Growth:** 0.8%. **Annual Openings:** 5,000. **Education:** Moderate-term on-the-job training. **Job Zone:** 1. **Education/Training Program(s)**—No data available. **Related Knowledge/Courses:** Chemistry; Mechanical; Production and Processing. **Personality Type:** Realistic. **Skills Required:** Operation Monitoring; Repairing; Equipment Maintenance; Operation and Control; Quality Control Analysis; Installation; Troubleshooting; Science. **Abilities:** Control Precision; Trunk Strength; Response Orientation; Wrist-Finger Speed; Perceptual Speed. **Occupational Values:** Moral Values; Supervision, Human Relations; Supervision, Technical; Advancement; Company Policies and Practices. **Interacting with Others:** Communicating with Supervisors, Peers, or Subordinates; Performing Administrative Activities; Interpreting the Meaning of Information for Others; Establishing and Maintaining Interpersonal Relationships; Assisting and Caring for Others; Coordinating the Work and Activities of Others. **Physical Work Conditions:** Common Protective or Safety Equipment; Standing; Contaminants; Using Hands on Objects, Tools, or Controls; Hazardous Conditions; Hazardous Equipment.

Sewing Machine Operators, Garment

Operate or tend sewing machines to perform garment sewing operations, such as joining, reinforcing, or decorating garments or garment parts. **O*NET Code:** 51-6031.01. **Average Salary:** $17,740. **Projected Growth:** –31.5%. **Annual Openings:** 39,000. **Education:** Moderate-term on-the-job training. **Job Zone:** 1. **Education/Training Program(s)**—Apparel and Textile Manufacture. **Related Knowledge/ Courses:** Production and Processing; Administration and Management. **Personality Type:** Realistic. **Skills Required:** Repairing; Operation and Control; Equipment Maintenance; Equipment Selection; Operation Monitoring. **Abilities:** Visual Color Discrimination; Hearing Sensitivity; Sound Localization; Arm-Hand Steadiness; Reaction Time. **Occupational Values:** Moral Values; Activity; Independence; Supervision, Human Relations; Company Policies and Practices. **Interacting with Others:** Establishing and

Maintaining Interpersonal Relationships; Communicating with Supervisors, Peers, or Subordinates; Monitoring and Controlling Resources. **Physical Work Conditions:** Sitting; Spend Time Making Repetitive Motions; Hazardous Equipment; Using Hands on Objects, Tools, or Controls; Sounds, Noise Levels Are Distracting or Uncomfortable.

Sewing Machine Operators, Non-Garment

Operate or tend sewing machines to join together, reinforce, decorate, or perform related sewing operations in the manufacture of nongarment products, such as upholstery, draperies, linens, carpets, and mattresses. **O*NET Code:** 51-6031.02. **Average Salary:** $17,740. **Projected Growth:** –31.5%. **Annual Openings:** 39,000. **Education:** Moderate-term on-the-job training. **Job Zone:** 1. **Education/Training Program(s)**—Apparel and Textile Manufacture. **Related Knowledge/Courses:** Production and Processing; Mechanical. **Personality Type:** Realistic. **Skills Required:** Operation and Control; Equipment Maintenance; Operation Monitoring. **Abilities:** Rate Control; Manual Dexterity; Visual Color Discrimination; Arm-Hand Steadiness; Finger Dexterity. **Occupational Values:** Moral Values; Independence; Supervision, Human Relations; Activity; Company Policies and Practices. **Interacting with Others:** Performing Administrative Activities; Communicating with Supervisors, Peers, or Subordinates; Coordinating the Work and Activities of Others. **Physical Work Conditions:** Hazardous Equipment; Sitting; Using Hands on Objects, Tools, or Controls; Spend Time Making Repetitive Motions; Indoors.

Shoe Machine Operators and Tenders

Operate or tend a variety of machines to join, decorate, reinforce, or finish shoes and shoe parts. **O*NET Code:** 51-6042.00. **Average Salary:** $20,400. **Projected Growth:** –26.1%. **Annual Openings:** 1,000. **Education:** Moderate-term on-the-job training. **Job Zone:** 1. **Education/Training Program(s)**—Shoe, Boot and Leather Repair. **Related Knowledge/Courses:** Production and Processing; Economics and Accounting. **Personality Type:** Realistic. **Skills Required:** Operation and Control; Operation Monitoring. **Abilities:** Finger Dexterity; Arm-Hand Steadiness; Manual Dexterity; Wrist-Finger Speed; Visual Color Discrimination. **Occupational Values:** Moral Values; Independence; Activity; Supervision, Human Relations; Company Policies and Practices. **Interacting with Others:** Communicating with Supervisors, Peers, or Subordinates; Establishing and Maintaining Interpersonal Relationships; Assisting and Caring for Others; Performing Administrative Activities; Monitoring and Controlling Resources. **Physical Work Conditions:** Sitting; Minor Burns, Cuts, Bites, or Stings; Spend Time Making Repetitive Motions; Hazardous Equipment; Indoors.

Slaughterers and Meat Packers

Work in slaughtering, meat packing, or wholesale establishments performing precision functions involving the preparation of meat. Work may include specialized slaughtering tasks, cutting standard or premium cuts of meat for marketing, making sausage, or wrapping meats. **O*NET Code:** 51-3023.00. **Average Salary:** $20,700. **Projected Growth:** 18.1%. **Annual Openings:** 23,000. **Education:** Moderate-term on-

© 2006, JIST Works

the-job training. **Job Zone:** 2. **Education/Training Program(s)**—Meat Cutting/Meat Cutter. **Related Knowledge/Courses:** Food Production; Biology; Philosophy and Theology; Public Safety and Security; Production and Processing; Law and Government. **Personality Type:** Realistic. **Skills Required:** None met the criteria. **Abilities:** Static Strength; Dynamic Strength; Trunk Strength; Extent Flexibility; Wrist-Finger Speed. **Occupational Values:** Independence; Security. **Interacting with Others:** Communicating with Supervisors, Peers, or Subordinates; Establishing and Maintaining Interpersonal Relationships; Assisting and Caring for Others; Coordinating the Work and Activities of Others. **Physical Work Conditions:** Common Protective or Safety Equipment; Minor Burns, Cuts, Bites, or Stings; Spend Time Making Repetitive Motions; Standing; Sounds, Noise Levels Are Distracting or Uncomfortable; Contaminants.

Stone Sawyers

Set up and operate gang saws, reciprocating saws, circular saws, or wire saws to cut blocks of stone into specified dimensions. **O*NET Code:** 51-9032.02. **Average Salary:** $26,500. **Projected Growth:** 6.6%. **Annual Openings:** 12,000. **Education:** Moderate-term on-the-job training. **Job Zone:** 2. **Education/Training Program(s)**—No data available. **Related Knowledge/Courses:** Mechanical; Building and Construction; Production and Processing; Physics. **Personality Type:** Realistic. **Skills Required:** Operation Monitoring; Equipment Maintenance; Operation and Control; Repairing; Equipment Selection. **Abilities:** Depth Perception; Control Precision; Reaction Time; Stamina; Explosive Strength. **Occupational Values:** Moral Values; Supervision, Technical; Activity; Company Policies and Practices; Independence; Supervision, Human Relations. **Interacting with Others:** Communicating with Supervisors, Peers, or Subordinates; Coordinating the Work and Activities of Others; Assisting and Caring for Others. **Physical Work Conditions:** Hazardous Equipment; Sounds, Noise Levels Are Distracting or Uncomfortable; Common Protective or Safety Equipment; Standing; Minor Burns, Cuts, Bites, or Stings.

Team Assemblers

Work as part of a team having responsibility for assembling an entire product or component of a product. Team assemblers can perform all tasks conducted by the team in the assembly process and rotate through all or most of them rather than being assigned to a specific task on a permanent basis. May participate in making management decisions affecting the work. Team leaders who work as part of the team should be included. **O*NET Code:** 51-2092.00. **Average Salary:** $23,420. **Projected Growth:** -1.6%. **Annual Openings:** 143,000. **Education:** Moderate-term on-the-job training. **Job Zone:** No data available. **Education/Training Program(s)**—No data available. **Related Knowledge/Courses:** No data available. **Personality Type:** No data available. **Skills Required:** No data available. **Abilities:** No data available. **Occupational Values:** No data available. **Interacting with Others:** No data available. **Physical Work Conditions:** No data available.

Textile Bleaching and Dyeing Machine Operators and Tenders

Operate or tend machines to bleach, shrink, wash, dye, or finish textiles or synthetic or glass fibers. **O*NET Code:** 51-6061.00. **Average Salary:** $21,710. **Projected Growth:** -28.7%. **Annual Openings:** 4,000. **Education:** Moderate-term on-the-job training. **Job Zone:** 1. **Education/Training Program(s)**—No data available. **Related Knowledge/Courses:** Production and Processing; Chemistry. **Personality Type:** Realistic. **Skills Required:** Operation Monitoring; Operation and Control; Equipment Maintenance; Quality Control Analysis; Installation. **Abilities:** Visual Color Discrimination; Rate Control; Arm-Hand Steadiness; Control Precision; Dynamic Flexibility. **Occupational Values:** Moral Values; Supervision, Technical; Supervision, Human Relations; Company Policies and Practices; Advancement. **Interacting with Others:** Communicating with Supervisors, Peers, or Subordinates; Establishing and Maintaining Interpersonal Relationships; Coordinating the Work and Activities of Others; Performing Administrative Activities. **Physical Work Conditions:** Hazardous Equipment; Hazardous Conditions; Minor Burns, Cuts, Bites, or Stings; Contaminants; Using Hands on Objects, Tools, or Controls.

Tire Builders

Operate machines to build tires from rubber components. **O*NET Code:** 51-9197.00. **Average Salary:** $38,760. **Projected Growth:** 6.6%. **Annual Openings:** 2,000. **Education:** Moderate-term on-the-job training. **Job Zone:** 1. **Education/Training Program(s)**—No data available. **Related Knowledge/Courses:** Production and Processing; Mechanical. **Personality Type:** Realistic. **Skills Required:** Operation and Control; Operation Monitoring. **Abilities:** Static Strength; Speed of Limb Movement; Explosive Strength; Wrist-Finger Speed; Dynamic Strength; Hearing Sensitivity. **Occupational Values:** Moral Values; Independence; Supervision, Human Relations; Supervision, Technical; Activity; Company Policies and Practices. **Interacting with Others:** Communicating with Supervisors, Peers, or Subordinates; Establishing and Maintaining Interpersonal Relationships; Monitoring and Controlling Resources. **Physical Work Conditions:** Hazardous Equipment; Minor Burns, Cuts, Bites, or Stings; Contaminants; Standing; Common Protective or Safety Equipment.

Woodworking Machine Operators and Tenders, Except Sawing

Operate or tend woodworking machines, such as drill presses, lathes, shapers, routers, sanders, planers, and wood-nailing machines, to perform woodworking operations. **O*NET Code:** 51-7042.02. **Average Salary:** $22,430. **Projected Growth:** 3.0%. **Annual Openings:** 14,000. **Education:** Moderate-term on-the-job training. **Job Zone:** 1. **Education/Training Program(s)**—Cabinetmaking and Millwork/Millwright; Woodworking, General. **Related Knowledge/Courses:** Mechanical; Production and Processing; Building and Construction; Design; Engineering and Technology; Foreign Language. **Personality Type:** Realistic. **Skills Required:** Operation Monitoring; Operation and Control; Equipment Maintenance; Quality Control Analysis;

Installation; Repairing; Technology Design; Science. **Abilities:** Visualization; Arm-Hand Steadiness; Static Strength; Speed of Limb Movement; Extent Flexibility. **Occupational Values:** Independence; Moral Values; Supervision, Technical; Activity; Company Policies and Practices. **Interacting with Others:** Communicating with Supervisors, Peers, or Subordinates; Establishing and Maintaining Interpersonal Relationships; Monitoring and Controlling Resources. **Physical Work Conditions:** Hazardous Equipment; Common Protective or Safety Equipment; Minor Burns, Cuts, Bites, or Stings; Sounds, Noise Levels Are Distracting or Uncomfortable; Contaminants; Using Hands on Objects, Tools, or Controls.

13.04 Welding, Brazing, and Soldering

Brazers

Braze together components to assemble fabricated metal parts, using torch or welding machine and flux. **O*NET Code:** 51-4121.05. **Average Salary:** $29,940. **Projected Growth:** 17.0%. **Annual Openings:** 71,000. **Education:** Short-term on-the-job training. **Job Zone:** 2. **Education/Training Program(s)**—Welding Technology/Welder. **Related Knowledge/Courses:** Engineering and Technology; Building and Construction; Mechanical; Chemistry. **Personality Type:** Realistic. **Skills Required:** Operation and Control; Operation Monitoring; Installation; Equipment Selection; Science; Quality Control Analysis. **Abilities:** Arm-Hand Steadiness; Speed of Limb Movement; Glare Sensitivity; Visualization; Visual Color Discrimination. **Occupational Values:** Moral Values; Activity; Company Policies and Practices; Independence; Supervision, Technical. **Interacting with Others:** Communicating with Supervisors, Peers, or Subordinates; Establishing and Maintaining Interpersonal Relationships; Coordinating the Work and Activities of Others. **Physical Work Conditions:** Common Protective or Safety Equipment; Hazardous Conditions; Hazardous Equipment; Using Hands on Objects, Tools, or Controls; Standing.

Fitters, Structural Metal—Precision

Lay out, position, align, and fit together fabricated parts of structural metal products preparatory to welding or riveting. **O*NET Code:** 51-2041.02. **Average Salary:** $29,190. **Projected Growth:** 6.2%. **Annual Openings:** 14,000. **Education:** Moderate-term on-the-job training. **Job Zone:** 4. **Education/Training Program(s)**—Machine Shop Technology/Assistant. **Related Knowledge/Courses:** Building and Construction; Mechanical; Physics; Design; Mathematics; Production and Processing; Engineering and Technology. **Personality Type:** Realistic. **Skills Required:** Mathematics; Equipment Selection. **Abilities:** Depth Perception; Static Strength; Multilimb Coordination; Glare Sensitivity; Control Precision. **Occupational Values:** Moral Values; Supervision, Technical; Independence; Advancement; Supervision, Human

Relations. **Interacting with Others:** Communicating with Supervisors, Peers, or Subordinates; Coordinating the Work and Activities of Others; Guiding, Directing, and Motivating Subordinates. **Physical Work Conditions:** Hazardous Equipment; Minor Burns, Cuts, Bites, or Stings; Common Protective or Safety Equipment; Sounds, Noise Levels Are Distracting or Uncomfortable; Spend Time Bending or Twisting the Body.

Metal Fabricators, Structural Metal Products

Fabricate and assemble structural metal products, such as frameworks or shells for machinery, ovens, tanks, and stacks and metal parts for buildings and bridges, according to job order or blueprints. **O*NET Code:** 51-2041.01. **Average Salary:** $29,190. **Projected Growth:** 6.2%. **Annual Openings:** 14,000. **Education:** Moderate-term on-the-job training. **Job Zone:** 4. **Education/Training Program(s)**—Machine Shop Technology/Assistant. **Related Knowledge/Courses:** Design; Building and Construction; Production and Processing; Mechanical; Engineering and Technology; Mathematics; Physics. **Personality Type:** Realistic. **Skills Required:** Operation and Control; Mathematics; Quality Control Analysis; Operations Analysis; Equipment Selection; Operation Monitoring; Technology Design; Science. **Abilities:** Extent Flexibility; Static Strength; Control Precision; Explosive Strength; Visualization; Dynamic Strength. **Occupational Values:** Independence; Supervision, Human Relations; Moral Values; Activity; Company Policies and Practices. **Interacting with Others:** Communicating with Supervisors, Peers, or Subordinates; Establishing and Maintaining Interpersonal Relationships; Coordinating the Work and Activities of Others; Monitoring and Controlling Resources. **Physical Work Conditions:** Hazardous Equipment; Standing; Common Protective or Safety Equipment; Minor Burns, Cuts, Bites, or Stings; Using Hands on Objects, Tools, or Controls.

Solderers

Solder together components to assemble fabricated metal products, using soldering iron. **O*NET Code:** 51-4121.04. **Average Salary:** $29,940. **Projected Growth:** 17.0%. **Annual Openings:** 71,000. **Education:** Short-term on-the-job training. **Job Zone:** 1. **Education/Training Program(s)**—Welding Technology/Welder. **Related Knowledge/Courses:** Building and Construction; Mechanical; Production and Processing. **Personality Type:** Realistic. **Skills Required:** Operation and Control; Equipment Maintenance; Equipment Selection; Installation; Operation Monitoring; Science; Repairing. **Abilities:** Manual Dexterity; Finger Dexterity; Wrist-Finger Speed; Arm-Hand Steadiness; Visual Color Discrimination. **Occupational Values:** Moral Values; Activity; Company Policies and Practices; Independence; Supervision, Human Relations. **Interacting with Others:** Communicating with Supervisors, Peers, or Subordinates; Establishing and Maintaining Interpersonal Relationships; Monitoring and Controlling Resources. **Physical Work Conditions:** Common Protective or Safety Equipment; Using Hands on Objects, Tools, or Controls; Hazardous Equipment; Minor Burns, Cuts, Bites, or Stings; Contaminants.

Soldering and Brazing Machine Operators and Tenders

Operate or tend soldering and brazing machines that braze, solder, or spot-weld fabricated metal products or components as specified by work orders, blueprints, and layout specifications. **O*NET Code:** 51-4122.04. **Average Salary:** $29,180. **Projected Growth:** 0.9%. **Annual Openings:** 10,000. **Education:** Short-term on-the-job training. **Job Zone:** 1. **Education/Training Program(s)—**Welding Technology/ Welder. **Related Knowledge/Courses:** Mechanical; Production and Processing; Chemistry. **Personality Type:** Realistic. **Skills Required:** Operation Monitoring; Equipment Maintenance; Operation and Control; Repairing; Quality Control Analysis; Equipment Selection; Science; Troubleshooting. **Abilities:** Control Precision; Perceptual Speed; Wrist-Finger Speed; Extent Flexibility; Static Strength; Trunk Strength. **Occupational Values:** Moral Values; Independence; Company Policies and Practices; Supervision, Human Relations; Activity. **Interacting with Others:** Performing Administrative Activities; Communicating with Supervisors, Peers, or Subordinates; Establishing and Maintaining Interpersonal Relationships; Monitoring and Controlling Resources. **Physical Work Conditions:** Common Protective or Safety Equipment; Hazardous Equipment; Using Hands on Objects, Tools, or Controls; Indoors; Very Hot or Cold.

Welder-Fitters

Lay out, fit, and fabricate metal components to assemble structural forms, such as machinery frames, bridge parts, and pressure vessels, using knowledge of welding techniques, metallurgy, and engineering requirements. Includes experimental welders who analyze engineering drawings and specifications to plan welding operations where procedural information is unavailable. **O*NET Code:** 51-4121.03. **Average Salary:** $29,940. **Projected Growth:** 17.0%. **Annual Openings:** 71,000. **Education:** Long-term on-the-job training. **Job Zone:** 4. **Education/Training Program(s)—**Welding Technology/Welder. **Related Knowledge/Courses:** Design; Building and Construction; Mechanical; Production and Processing; Engineering and Technology; Physics. **Personality Type:** Realistic. **Skills Required:** Repairing; Installation; Equipment Maintenance; Equipment Selection; Quality Control Analysis; Mathematics; Operation Monitoring; Science. **Abilities:** Extent Flexibility; Gross Body Equilibrium; Arm-Hand Steadiness; Dynamic Strength; Originality. **Occupational Values:** Activity; Company Policies and Practices; Advancement; Moral Values; Supervision, Technical. **Interacting with Others:** Communicating with Supervisors, Peers, or Subordinates; Coordinating the Work and Activities of Others; Training and Teaching Others. **Physical Work Conditions:** Hazardous Equipment; Minor Burns, Cuts, Bites, or Stings; Common Protective or Safety Equipment; Very Hot or Cold; Hazardous Conditions.

Welders and Cutters

Use hand welding and flame-cutting equipment to weld together metal components and parts or to cut, trim, or scarf metal objects to dimensions as specified by layouts, work orders, or blueprints. **O*NET Code:** 51-4121.02. **Average Salary:** $29,940. **Projected Growth:** 17.0%. **Annual Openings:** 71,000. **Education:** Long-term on-the-job training. **Job Zone:** 2. **Education/Training Program(s)—**Welding Technology/Welder. **Related Knowledge/Courses:** Building and Construction; Mechanical; Design; Production and Processing; Physics; Chemistry. **Personality Type:** Realistic. **Skills Required:** Operation Monitoring; Repairing; Equipment Maintenance; Operation and Control; Installation; Quality Control Analysis; Mathematics; Equipment Selection. **Abilities:** Arm-Hand Steadiness; Rate Control; Manual Dexterity; Control Precision; Extent Flexibility. **Occupational Values:** Activity; Moral Values; Company Policies and Practices; Advancement; Independence; Supervision, Human Relations. **Interacting with Others:** Communicating with Supervisors, Peers, or Subordinates; Coordinating the Work and Activities of Others; Performing Administrative Activities. **Physical Work Conditions:** Hazardous Equipment; Minor Burns, Cuts, Bites, or Stings; Common Protective or Safety Equipment; Using Hands on Objects, Tools, or Controls; Hazardous Conditions.

Welders, Production

Assemble and weld metal parts on production line, using welding equipment requiring only a limited knowledge of welding techniques. **O*NET Code:** 51-4121.01. **Average Salary:** $29,940. **Projected Growth:** 17.0%. **Annual Openings:** 71,000. **Education:** Short-term on-the-job training. **Job Zone:** 1. **Education/Training Program(s)—**Welding Technology/Welder. **Related Knowledge/Courses:** Mechanical; Production and Processing; Building and Construction; Physics. **Personality Type:** Realistic. **Skills Required:** Operation Monitoring; Equipment Maintenance; Operation and Control; Troubleshooting; Repairing; Installation; Quality Control Analysis; Equipment Selection. **Abilities:** Dynamic Strength; Arm-Hand Steadiness; Manual Dexterity; Explosive Strength; Rate Control. **Occupational Values:** Moral Values; Activity; Company Policies and Practices; Supervision, Technical; Independence; Advancement; Supervision, Human Relations. **Interacting with Others:** Communicating with Supervisors, Peers, or Subordinates; Coordinating the Work and Activities of Others; Assisting and Caring for Others. **Physical Work Conditions:** Common Protective or Safety Equipment; Hazardous Equipment; Standing; Very Hot or Cold; Sounds, Noise Levels Are Distracting or Uncomfortable.

Welding Machine Operators and Tenders

Operate or tend welding machines that join or bond together components to fabricate metal products and assemblies according to specifications and blueprints. **O*NET Code:** 51-4122.02. **Average Salary:** $29,180. **Projected Growth:** 0.9%. **Annual Openings:** 10,000. **Education:** Moderate-term on-the-job training. **Job Zone:** 2. **Education/Training Program(s)—**Welding Technology/Welder. **Related Knowledge/Courses:** Production and Processing; Chemistry; Engineering and Technology; Design; Building and Construction. **Personality Type:** Realistic. **Skills Required:** Operation Monitoring; Operation and Control; Equipment Maintenance; Quality Control Analysis; Repairing; Equipment Selection. **Abilities:** Control Precision; Manual Dexterity; Reaction Time; Speed of Limb Movement; Arm-Hand Steadiness; Hearing Sensitivity. **Occupational Values:**

© 2006, JIST Works

Moral Values; Independence; Company Policies and Practices; Supervision, Human Relations; Activity. **Interacting with Others:** Communicating with Supervisors, Peers, or Subordinates; Coordinating the Work and Activities of Others; Performing Administrative Activities. **Physical Work Conditions:** Hazardous Equipment; Common Protective or Safety Equipment; Standing; Sounds, Noise Levels Are Distracting or Uncomfortable; Using Hands on Objects, Tools, or Controls.

Welding Machine Setters and Set-Up Operators

Set up or set up and operate welding machines that join or bond together components to fabricate metal products or assemblies according to specifications and blueprints. **O*NET Code:** 51-4122.01. **Average Salary:** $29,180. **Projected Growth:** 0.9%. **Annual Openings:** 10,000. **Education:** Postsecondary vocational training. **Job Zone:** 3. **Education/Training Program(s)**—Welding Technology/Welder. **Related Knowledge/Courses:** Mechanical; Production and Processing; Chemistry; Design; Building and Construction; Physics. **Personality Type:** Realistic. **Skills Required:** Operation Monitoring; Equipment Selection; Quality Control Analysis; Equipment Maintenance; Operation and Control; Installation; Mathematics; Repairing. **Abilities:** Manual Dexterity; Hearing Sensitivity; Rate Control; Sound Localization; Static Strength; Dynamic Flexibility. **Occupational Values:** Moral Values; Independence; Company Policies and Practices; Supervision, Human Relations; Supervision, Technical. **Interacting with Others:** Communicating with Supervisors, Peers, or Subordinates; Performing Administrative Activities; Establishing and Maintaining Interpersonal Relationships. **Physical Work Conditions:** Hazardous Equipment; Sounds, Noise Levels Are Distracting or Uncomfortable; Common Protective or Safety Equipment; Standing; Using Hands on Objects, Tools, or Controls.

13.05 Production Machining Technology

Foundry Mold and Coremakers

Make or form wax or sand cores or molds used in the production of metal castings in foundries. **O*NET Code:** 51-4071.00. **Average Salary:** $27,100. **Projected Growth:** 3.6%. **Annual Openings:** 3,000. **Education:** Moderate-term on-the-job training. **Job Zone:** 2. **Education/Training Program(s)**—Ironworking/Ironworker. **Related Knowledge/Courses:** Mechanical; Building and Construction; Design; Production and Processing. **Personality Type:** Realistic. **Skills Required:** Operation and Control; Science; Technology Design; Operation Monitoring; Operations Analysis. **Abilities:** Static Strength; Arm-Hand Steadiness; Multilimb Coordination; Speed of Limb Movement; Stamina. **Occupational Values:** Moral Values; Supervision, Human Relations; Supervision, Technical; Advancement; Co-workers; Company Policies and Practices. **Interacting with Others:** Communicating with Supervisors, Peers, or Subordinates; Establishing and

Maintaining Interpersonal Relationships; Coordinating the Work and Activities of Others. **Physical Work Conditions:** Common Protective or Safety Equipment; Hazardous Equipment; Very Hot or Cold; Minor Burns, Cuts, Bites, or Stings; Extremely Bright or Inadequate Lighting.

Lay-Out Workers, Metal and Plastic

Lay out reference points and dimensions on metal or plastic stock or workpieces, such as sheets, plates, tubes, structural shapes, castings, or machine parts, for further processing. Includes shipfitters. **O*NET Code:** 51-4192.00. **Average Salary:** $32,000. **Projected Growth:** 15.6%. **Annual Openings:** 1,000. **Education:** Postsecondary vocational training. **Job Zone:** 3. **Education/Training Program(s)**—Machine Shop Technology/Assistant; Machine Tool Technology/Machinist. **Related Knowledge/Courses:** Design; Production and Processing; Mathematics; Physics; Engineering and Technology; Chemistry. **Personality Type:** Realistic. **Skills Required:** Mathematics; Technology Design; Operations Analysis; Science; Equipment Selection; Quality Control Analysis. **Abilities:** Mathematical Reasoning; Visualization; Multilimb Coordination; Arm-Hand Steadiness; Manual Dexterity. **Occupational Values:** Independence; Moral Values; Supervision, Technical; Company Policies and Practices; Advancement. **Interacting with Others:** Communicating with Supervisors, Peers, or Subordinates; Establishing and Maintaining Interpersonal Relationships; Coordinating the Work and Activities of Others; Providing Consultation and Advice to Others; Performing Administrative Activities. **Physical Work Conditions:** Standing; Using Hands on Objects, Tools, or Controls; Hazardous Equipment; Kneeling, Crouching, Stooping, or Crawling; Very Hot or Cold.

Machinists

Set up and operate a variety of machine tools to produce precision parts and instruments. Includes precision instrument makers who fabricate, modify, or repair mechanical instruments. May also fabricate and modify parts to make or repair machine tools or maintain industrial machines, applying knowledge of mechanics, shop mathematics, metal properties, layout, and machining procedures. **O*NET Code:** 51-4041.00. **Average Salary:** $33,590. **Projected Growth:** 8.2%. **Annual Openings:** 30,000. **Education:** Long-term on-the-job training. **Job Zone:** 3. **Education/Training Program(s)**—Machine Shop Technology/Assistant; Machine Tool Technology/Machinist. **Related Knowledge/Courses:** Mechanical; Mathematics; Engineering and Technology; Design; Production and Processing; Computers and Electronics. **Personality Type:** Realistic. **Skills Required:** Operation Monitoring; Operation and Control; Equipment Maintenance; Quality Control Analysis; Installation; Troubleshooting; Equipment Selection; Technology Design. **Abilities:** Hearing Sensitivity; Auditory Attention; Visualization; Multilimb Coordination; Control Precision. **Occupational Values:** Moral Values; Supervision, Technical; Company Policies and Practices; Supervision, Human Relations; Creativity. **Interacting with Others:** Communicating with Supervisors, Peers, or Subordinates; Establishing and Maintaining Interpersonal Relationships; Training and Teaching Others. **Physical Work Conditions:**

Sounds, Noise Levels Are Distracting or Uncomfortable; Hazardous Equipment; Contaminants; Indoors, Not Environmentally Controlled; Physical Proximity.

Model Makers, Metal and Plastic

Set up and operate machines, such as lathes, milling and engraving machines, and jig borers, to make working models of metal or plastic objects. **O*NET Code:** 51-4061.00. **Average Salary:** $44,560. **Projected Growth:** 14.6%. **Annual Openings:** 1,000. **Education:** Moderate-term on-the-job training. **Job Zone:** 4. **Education/Training Program(s)**—Sheet Metal Technology/Sheetworking. **Related Knowledge/Courses:** Mechanical; Design; Building and Construction; Engineering and Technology; Computers and Electronics; Telecommunications. **Personality Type:** Realistic. **Skills Required:** Technology Design; Quality Control Analysis; Operations Analysis; Equipment Selection; Troubleshooting; Operation Monitoring; Operation and Control; Systems Analysis. **Abilities:** Control Precision; Mathematical Reasoning; Visualization; Visual Color Discrimination; Oral Expression; Number Facility. **Occupational Values:** Ability Utilization; Creativity; Moral Values; Achievement; Variety; Supervision, Human Relations. **Interacting with Others:** Communicating with Supervisors, Peers, or Subordinates; Providing Consultation and Advice to Others; Establishing and Maintaining Interpersonal Relationships; Performing Administrative Activities. **Physical Work Conditions:** Hazardous Equipment; Minor Burns, Cuts, Bites, or Stings; Common Protective or Safety Equipment; Using Hands on Objects, Tools, or Controls; Indoors; Standing.

Numerical Control Machine Tool Operators and Tenders, Metal and Plastic

Set up and operate numerical control (magnetic- or punched-tape-controlled) machine tools that automatically mill, drill, broach, and ream metal and plastic parts. May adjust machine feed and speed, change cutting tools, or adjust machine controls when automatic programming is faulty or if machine malfunctions. **O*NET Code:** 51-4011.01. **Average Salary:** $30,020. **Projected Growth:** 9.3%. **Annual Openings:** 11,000. **Education:** Long-term on-the-job training. **Job Zone:** 2. **Education/Training Program(s)**—Machine Shop Technology/Assistant. **Related Knowledge/Courses:** Production and Processing; Mechanical; Design; Engineering and Technology; Computers and Electronics; Physics. **Personality Type:** Realistic. **Skills Required:** Operation Monitoring; Equipment Maintenance; Operation and Control; Quality Control Analysis; Installation; Mathematics; Equipment Selection; Troubleshooting. **Abilities:** Rate Control; Reaction Time; Dynamic Strength; Wrist-Finger Speed; Response Orientation. **Occupational Values:** Moral Values; Supervision, Technical; Activity; Independence; Supervision, Human Relations. **Interacting with Others:** Communicating with Supervisors, Peers, or Subordinates; Establishing and Maintaining Interpersonal Relationships; Coordinating the Work and Activities of Others. **Physical Work Conditions:** Hazardous Equipment; Standing; Common Protective or Safety Equipment; Minor Burns, Cuts, Bites, or Stings; Indoors; Sounds, Noise Levels Are Distracting or Uncomfortable.

Numerical Tool and Process Control Programmers

Develop programs to control machining or processing of parts by automatic machine tools, equipment, or systems. **O*NET Code:** 51-4012.00. **Average Salary:** $39,070. **Projected Growth:** 13.0%. **Annual Openings:** 2,000. **Education:** Long-term on-the-job training. **Job Zone:** 3. **Education/Training Program(s)**—Computer Programming/Programmer, General; Data Processing and Data Processing Technology/Technician. **Related Knowledge/Courses:** Computers and Electronics; Design; Mathematics; Production and Processing; Engineering and Technology; Foreign Language. **Personality Type:** Realistic. **Skills Required:** Programming; Troubleshooting; Operations Analysis; Technology Design; Mathematics; Quality Control Analysis; Operation Monitoring; Operation and Control. **Abilities:** Number Facility; Mathematical Reasoning; Information Ordering; Speed of Closure; Deductive Reasoning. **Occupational Values:** Creativity; Compensation; Autonomy; Independence; Advancement. **Interacting with Others:** Communicating with Supervisors, Peers, or Subordinates; Providing Consultation and Advice to Others; Performing Administrative Activities. **Physical Work Conditions:** Sitting; Indoors; Using Hands on Objects, Tools, or Controls; Walking and Running; Spend Time Bending or Twisting the Body.

Patternmakers, Metal and Plastic

Lay out, machine, fit, and assemble castings and parts to metal or plastic foundry patterns, core boxes, or match plates. **O*NET Code:** 51-4062.00. **Average Salary:** $37,660. **Projected Growth:** 3.6%. **Annual Openings:** Fewer than 500. **Education:** Moderate-term on-the-job training. **Job Zone:** 4. **Education/Training Program(s)**—Sheet Metal Technology/Sheetworking. **Related Knowledge/Courses:** Design; Production and Processing; Mechanical; Engineering and Technology; Foreign Language; Telecommunications. **Personality Type:** Realistic. **Skills Required:** Technology Design; Operation Monitoring; Repairing; Operation and Control; Quality Control Analysis; Operations Analysis; Equipment Maintenance; Installation. **Abilities:** Visualization; Arm-Hand Steadiness; Wrist-Finger Speed; Control Precision; Auditory Attention. **Occupational Values:** Moral Values; Independence; Supervision, Technical; Company Policies and Practices; Ability Utilization; Advancement; Supervision, Human Relations; Creativity. **Interacting with Others:** Communicating with Supervisors, Peers, or Subordinates; Establishing and Maintaining Interpersonal Relationships; Communicating with Persons Outside Organization; Coordinating the Work and Activities of Others; Training and Teaching Others. **Physical Work Conditions:** Hazardous Equipment; Minor Burns, Cuts, Bites, or Stings; Common Protective or Safety Equipment; Using Hands on Objects, Tools, or Controls; Indoors; Sounds, Noise Levels Are Distracting or Uncomfortable.

Tool and Die Makers

Analyze specifications, lay out metal stock, set up and operate machine tools, and fit and assemble parts to make and repair dies, cutting tools, jigs, fixtures, gauges, and machinists' hand tools. **O*NET Code:** 51-4111.00. **Average Salary:** $42,830.

Projected Growth: 0.4%. **Annual Openings:** 3,000. **Education:** Long-term on-the-job training. **Job Zone:** 4. **Education/Training Program(s)**—Tool and Die Technology/Technician. **Related Knowledge/Courses:** Mechanical; Production and Processing; Building and Construction; Design; Engineering and Technology; Mathematics. **Personality Type:** Realistic. **Skills Required:** Installation; Operation and Control; Repairing; Technology Design; Equipment Selection; Equipment Maintenance; Operations Analysis; Quality Control Analysis. **Abilities:** Mathematical Reasoning; Manual Dexterity; Wrist-Finger Speed; Number Facility; Control Precision. **Occupational Values:** Moral Values; Supervision, Technical; Company Policies and Practices; Advancement; Independence; Compensation; Supervision, Human Relations. **Interacting with Others:** Communicating with Supervisors, Peers, or Subordinates; Coordinating the Work and Activities of Others; Performing Administrative Activities. **Physical Work Conditions:** Hazardous Equipment; Using Hands on Objects, Tools, or Controls; Common Protective or Safety Equipment; Indoors; Standing.

Tool Grinders, Filers, and Sharpeners

Perform precision smoothing, sharpening, polishing, or grinding of metal objects. **O*NET Code:** 51-4194.00. **Average Salary:** $29,980. **Projected Growth:** –7.7%. **Annual Openings:** 2,000. **Education:** Moderate-term on-the-job training. **Job Zone:** 3. **Education/Training Program(s)**—Machine Shop Technology/Assistant. **Related Knowledge/Courses:** Mechanical; Design; Building and Construction; Public Safety and Security; Engineering and Technology; Foreign Language. **Personality Type:** Realistic. **Skills Required:** Operation Monitoring; Quality Control Analysis; Equipment Maintenance; Technology Design; Operation and Control; Repairing; Equipment Selection; Science. **Abilities:** Hearing Sensitivity; Auditory Attention; Sound Localization; Wrist-Finger Speed; Static Strength. **Occupational Values:** Moral Values; Supervision, Technical; Company Policies and Practices; Supervision, Human Relations; Independence. **Interacting with Others:** Establishing and Maintaining Interpersonal Relationships; Communicating with Supervisors, Peers, or Subordinates; Interpreting the Meaning of Information for Others; Communicating with Persons Outside Organization; Assisting and Caring for Others; Resolving Conflicts and Negotiating with Others. **Physical Work Conditions:** Hazardous Equipment; Minor Burns, Cuts, Bites, or Stings; Common Protective or Safety Equipment; Indoors; Sounds, Noise Levels Are Distracting or Uncomfortable; Standing.

13.06 Production Precision Work

Bench Workers, Jewelry

Cut, file, form, and solder parts for jewelry. **O*NET Code:** 51-9071.04. **Average Salary:** $27,500. **Projected Growth:** 4.5%. **Annual Openings:** 3,000. **Education:** Long-term on-the-job

training. **Job Zone:** 3. **Education/Training Program(s)**—Watchmaking and Jewelrymaking. **Related Knowledge/Courses:** Fine Arts; Production and Processing; Design; Chemistry. **Personality Type:** Realistic. **Skills Required:** Quality Control Analysis; Technology Design; Operations Analysis; Operation and Control; Repairing. **Abilities:** Finger Dexterity; Arm-Hand Steadiness; Visual Color Discrimination; Manual Dexterity; Near Vision. **Occupational Values:** Independence; Working Conditions; Creativity; Ability Utilization; Variety. **Interacting with Others:** Communicating with Persons Outside Organization; Communicating with Supervisors, Peers, or Subordinates; Establishing and Maintaining Interpersonal Relationships. **Physical Work Conditions:** Sitting; Using Hands on Objects, Tools, or Controls; Indoors; Hazardous Equipment; Spend Time Making Repetitive Motions.

Bookbinders

Perform highly skilled hand-finishing operations, such as grooving and lettering, to bind books. **O*NET Code:** 51-5012.00. **Average Salary:** $29,250. **Projected Growth:** 1.3%. **Annual Openings:** Fewer than 500. **Education:** Moderate-term on-the-job training. **Job Zone:** 4. **Education/Training Program(s)**—Precision Production, Other. **Related Knowledge/Courses:** Production and Processing; Communications and Media; Mechanical; Engineering and Technology. **Personality Type:** Realistic. **Skills Required:** Operation and Control. **Abilities:** Visual Color Discrimination; Static Strength; Wrist-Finger Speed; Manual Dexterity; Explosive Strength; Dynamic Flexibility. **Occupational Values:** Supervision, Technical; Moral Values; Independence; Working Conditions; Supervision, Human Relations. **Interacting with Others:** Communicating with Supervisors, Peers, or Subordinates; Establishing and Maintaining Interpersonal Relationships; Training and Teaching Others; Coaching and Developing Others. **Physical Work Conditions:** Minor Burns, Cuts, Bites, or Stings; Contaminants; Hazardous Conditions; Indoors; Hazardous Equipment; Using Hands on Objects, Tools, or Controls.

Dental Laboratory Technicians

Construct and repair full or partial dentures or dental appliances. **O*NET Code:** 51-9081.00. **Average Salary:** $30,400. **Projected Growth:** 3.6%. **Annual Openings:** 3,000. **Education:** Long-term on-the-job training. **Job Zone:** 3. **Education/Training Program(s)**—Dental Laboratory Technology/Technician. **Related Knowledge/Courses:** Medicine and Dentistry; Design; Biology; Telecommunications; Mechanical; Engineering and Technology; Chemistry. **Personality Type:** Realistic. **Skills Required:** Technology Design; Science; Quality Control Analysis; Operations Analysis; Reading Comprehension; Mathematics; Writing; Active Learning; Monitoring. **Abilities:** Finger Dexterity; Arm-Hand Steadiness; Visualization; Control Precision; Wrist-Finger Speed; Near Vision. **Occupational Values:** Independence; Working Conditions; Supervision, Technical; Recognition; Moral Values. **Interacting with Others:** Communicating with Supervisors, Peers, or Subordinates; Communicating with Persons Outside Organization; Establishing and Maintaining Interpersonal Relationships. **Physical Work Conditions:** Sitting; Using

Hands on Objects, Tools, or Controls; Indoors; Common Protective or Safety Equipment; Spend Time Bending or Twisting the Body.

Electrical and Electronic Equipment Assemblers

Assemble or modify electrical or electronic equipment, such as computers, test equipment telemetering systems, electric motors, and batteries. **O*NET Code:** 51-2022.00. **Average Salary:** $23,990. **Projected Growth:** –18.3%. **Annual Openings:** 19,000. **Education:** Short-term on-the-job training. **Job Zone:** 3. **Education/Training Program(s)—** Communications Systems Installation and Repair Technology; Industrial Electronics Technology/Technician. **Related Knowledge/Courses:** Computers and Electronics; Engineering and Technology; Production and Processing; Design; Mechanical; Building and Construction. **Personality Type:** Realistic. **Skills Required:** Installation; Science; Equipment Maintenance; Quality Control Analysis; Instructing; Operation Monitoring; Repairing; Equipment Selection. **Abilities:** Visual Color Discrimination; Finger Dexterity; Control Precision; Visualization; Manual Dexterity; Hearing Sensitivity. **Occupational Values:** Advancement; Moral Values; Company Policies and Practices; Authority; Supervision, Technical. **Interacting with Others:** Communicating with Supervisors, Peers, or Subordinates; Communicating with Persons Outside Organization; Providing Consultation and Advice to Others. **Physical Work Conditions:** Using Hands on Objects, Tools, or Controls; Hazardous Equipment; Indoors; Common Protective or Safety Equipment; Sitting.

Electromechanical Equipment Assemblers

Assemble or modify electromechanical equipment or devices, such as servomechanisms, gyros, dynamometers, magnetic drums, tape drives, brakes, control linkage, actuators, and appliances. **O*NET Code:** 51-2023.00. **Average Salary:** $26,200. **Projected Growth:** –8.3%. **Annual Openings:** 4,000. **Education:** Short-term on-the-job training. **Job Zone:** 3. **Education/Training Program(s)—**Electromechanical and Instrumentation and Maintenance Technologies/Technicians, Other; Electromechanical Technology/Electromechanical Engineering Technology; Robotics Technology/Technician. **Related Knowledge/Courses:** Computers and Electronics; Mechanical; Production and Processing; Design; Physics; Engineering and Technology. **Personality Type:** Realistic. **Skills Required:** Installation; Quality Control Analysis; Technology Design; Operation Monitoring; Equipment Maintenance; Repairing; Operation and Control; Troubleshooting. **Abilities:** Manual Dexterity; Visual Color Discrimination; Arm-Hand Steadiness; Visualization; Multilimb Coordination. **Occupational Values:** Independence; Advancement; Supervision, Technical; Moral Values; Company Policies and Practices. **Interacting with Others:** Communicating with Supervisors, Peers, or Subordinates; Coordinating the Work and Activities of Others; Performing Administrative Activities. **Physical Work Conditions:** Hazardous Equipment; Sounds, Noise Levels Are Distracting or Uncomfortable; Using Hands on Objects, Tools, or Controls; Hazardous Conditions; Minor Burns, Cuts, Bites, or Stings.

Engine and Other Machine Assemblers

Construct, assemble, or rebuild machines such as engines, turbines, and similar equipment used in such industries as construction, extraction, textiles, and paper manufacturing. **O*NET Code:** 51-2031.00. **Average Salary:** $33,900. **Projected Growth:** –1.9%. **Annual Openings:** 3,000. **Education:** Short-term on-the-job training. **Job Zone:** 3. **Education/Training Program(s)—**Engine Machinist; Heavy Equipment Maintenance Technology/Technician; Industrial Mechanics and Maintenance Technology. **Related Knowledge/Courses:** Mechanical; Design; Building and Construction; Engineering and Technology; Public Safety and Security; Computers and Electronics. **Personality Type:** Realistic. **Skills Required:** Installation; Equipment Maintenance; Repairing; Quality Control Analysis; Technology Design; Operation Monitoring; Operation and Control; Troubleshooting. **Abilities:** Extent Flexibility; Visualization; Visual Color Discrimination; Static Strength; Multilimb Coordination. **Occupational Values:** Moral Values; Independence; Advancement; Supervision, Human Relations; Supervision, Technical. **Interacting with Others:** Communicating with Supervisors, Peers, or Subordinates; Establishing and Maintaining Interpersonal Relationships; Communicating with Persons Outside Organization. **Physical Work Conditions:** Hazardous Equipment; Minor Burns, Cuts, Bites, or Stings; Kneeling, Crouching, Stooping, or Crawling; Common Protective or Safety Equipment; Extremely Bright or Inadequate Lighting.

Gem and Diamond Workers

Split, saw, cut, shape, polish, or drill gems and diamonds used in jewelry or industrial tools. **O*NET Code:** 51-9071.06. **Average Salary:** $27,500. **Projected Growth:** 4.5%. **Annual Openings:** 3,000. **Education:** Moderate-term on-the-job training. **Job Zone:** 2. **Education/Training Program(s)—**Watchmaking and Jewelrymaking. **Related Knowledge/ Courses:** Mechanical; Production and Processing; Engineering and Technology; Physics; Fine Arts. **Personality Type:** Realistic. **Skills Required:** Equipment Maintenance; Repairing; Operation and Control; Equipment Selection. **Abilities:** Arm-Hand Steadiness; Control Precision; Near Vision; Finger Dexterity; Manual Dexterity. **Occupational Values:** Independence; Ability Utilization; Compensation; Supervision, Technical; Working Conditions; Recognition; Creativity. **Interacting with Others:** Communicating with Supervisors, Peers, or Subordinates; Monitoring and Controlling Resources; Interpreting the Meaning of Information for Others; Communicating with Persons Outside Organization; Establishing and Maintaining Interpersonal Relationships; Assisting and Caring for Others. **Physical Work Conditions:** Hazardous Equipment; Sitting; Minor Burns, Cuts, Bites, or Stings; Using Hands on Objects, Tools, or Controls; Indoors.

Jewelers

Fabricate and repair jewelry articles. **O*NET Code:** 51-9071.01. **Average Salary:** $27,500. **Projected Growth:** 4.5%. **Annual Openings:** 3,000. **Education:** Postsecondary vocational training. **Job Zone:** 4. **Education/Training Program(s)—**Watchmaking and Jewelrymaking. **Related**

Knowledge/Courses: Fine Arts; Production and Processing; Design; Physics; Chemistry; Economics and Accounting. **Personality Type:** Realistic. **Skills Required:** Repairing; Quality Control Analysis; Science; Installation; Operation Monitoring; Equipment Maintenance; Operation and Control; Troubleshooting. **Abilities:** Finger Dexterity; Arm-Hand Steadiness; Visual Color Discrimination; Manual Dexterity; Near Vision. **Occupational Values:** Working Conditions; Autonomy; Ability Utilization; Independence; Variety; Creativity. **Interacting with Others:** Interpreting the Meaning of Information for Others; Communicating with Persons Outside Organization; Communicating with Supervisors, Peers, or Subordinates; Monitoring and Controlling Resources. **Physical Work Conditions:** Using Hands on Objects, Tools, or Controls; Sitting; Hazardous Conditions; Indoors; Hazardous Equipment; Minor Burns, Cuts, Bites, or Stings.

Medical Appliance Technicians

Construct, fit, maintain, or repair medical supportive devices, such as braces, artificial limbs, joints, arch supports, and other surgical and medical appliances. **O*NET Code:** 51-9082.00. **Average Salary:** $28,450. **Projected Growth:** 16.1%. **Annual Openings:** 1,000. **Education:** Long-term on-the-job training. **Job Zone:** 2. **Education/Training Program(s)—** Assistive/Augmentative Technology and Rehabilitation Engineering; Orthotist/Prosthetist. **Related Knowledge/Courses:** Design; Mechanical; Medicine and Dentistry; Engineering and Technology; Physics; Therapy and Counseling. **Personality Type:** Realistic. **Skills Required:** Technology Design; Operations Analysis; Repairing; Equipment Maintenance; Quality Control Analysis; Equipment Selection; Instructing; Science. **Abilities:** Visualization; Manual Dexterity; Visual Color Discrimination; Finger Dexterity; Arm-Hand Steadiness; Control Precision. **Occupational Values:** Independence; Social Service; Achievement; Recognition; Working Conditions; Social Status; Supervision, Technical. **Interacting with Others:** Assisting and Caring for Others; Communicating with Persons Outside Organization; Training and Teaching Others. **Physical Work Conditions:** Hazardous Equipment; Minor Burns, Cuts, Bites, or Stings; Spend Time Bending or Twisting the Body; Spend Time Making Repetitive Motions; Common Protective or Safety Equipment.

Model and Mold Makers, Jewelry

Make models or molds to create jewelry items. **O*NET Code:** 51-9071.03. **Average Salary:** $27,500. **Projected Growth:** 4.5%. **Annual Openings:** 3,000. **Education:** Long-term on-the-job training. **Job Zone:** 3. **Education/Training Program(s)—**Watchmaking and Jewelrymaking. **Related Knowledge/Courses:** Design; Fine Arts; Production and Processing; Building and Construction; Economics and Accounting; Engineering and Technology. **Personality Type:** Realistic. **Skills Required:** Technology Design; Repairing; Management of Material Resources; Operations Analysis; Operation and Control; Installation; Equipment Maintenance; Equipment Selection. **Abilities:** Arm-Hand Steadiness; Finger Dexterity; Near Vision; Manual Dexterity; Wrist-Finger Speed. **Occupational Values:** Independence; Working Conditions; Variety; Creativity; Moral Values.

Interacting with Others: Communicating with Supervisors, Peers, or Subordinates; Performing Administrative Activities; Interpreting the Meaning of Information for Others; Monitoring and Controlling Resources. **Physical Work Conditions:** Minor Burns, Cuts, Bites, or Stings; Hazardous Equipment; Using Hands on Objects, Tools, or Controls; Common Protective or Safety Equipment; Sitting.

Optical Instrument Assemblers

Assemble optical instruments, such as telescopes, level-transits, and gunsights. **O*NET Code:** 51-9083.02. **Average Salary:** $22,950. **Projected Growth:** 9.2%. **Annual Openings:** 2,000. **Education:** Moderate-term on-the-job training. **Job Zone:** 4. **Education/Training Program(s)—**Ophthalmic Laboratory Technology/Technician. **Related Knowledge/Courses:** Physics; Mathematics; Mechanical; Design; Production and Processing; Building and Construction. **Personality Type:** Realistic. **Skills Required:** Mathematics; Science; Equipment Selection; Operation Monitoring; Operation and Control; Technology Design; Installation; Quality Control Analysis. **Abilities:** Finger Dexterity; Arm-Hand Steadiness; Manual Dexterity; Number Facility; Mathematical Reasoning. **Occupational Values:** Independence; Working Conditions; Moral Values; Supervision, Technical; Advancement; Supervision, Human Relations. **Interacting with Others:** Performing Administrative Activities; Communicating with Supervisors, Peers, or Subordinates; Interpreting the Meaning of Information for Others. **Physical Work Conditions:** Using Hands on Objects, Tools, or Controls; Hazardous Equipment; Indoors; Common Protective or Safety Equipment; Sitting.

Pewter Casters and Finishers

Cast and finish pewter alloy to form parts for goblets, candlesticks, and other pewterware. **O*NET Code:** 51-9071.05. **Average Salary:** $27,500. **Projected Growth:** 4.5%. **Annual Openings:** 3,000. **Education:** Postsecondary vocational training. **Job Zone:** 4. **Education/Training Program(s)—** Watchmaking and Jewelrymaking. **Related Knowledge/Courses:** Fine Arts; Design; Production and Processing; Building and Construction; Chemistry. **Personality Type:** Realistic. **Skills Required:** Technology Design; Operation and Control; Science; Installation; Reading Comprehension; Operations Analysis. **Abilities:** Auditory Attention; Originality; Visualization; Arm-Hand Steadiness; Control Precision. **Occupational Values:** Independence; Creativity; Ability Utilization; Variety; Moral Values. **Interacting with Others:** Communicating with Persons Outside Organization; Communicating with Supervisors, Peers, or Subordinates; Establishing and Maintaining Interpersonal Relationships; Performing Administrative Activities. **Physical Work Conditions:** Very Hot or Cold; Minor Burns, Cuts, Bites, or Stings; Hazardous Equipment; Common Protective or Safety Equipment; Extremely Bright or Inadequate Lighting.

Precision Lens Grinders and Polishers

Set up and operate variety of machines and equipment to grind and polish lens and other optical elements. **O*NET Code:** 51-9083.01. **Average Salary:** $22,950. **Projected Growth:** 9.2%. **Annual Openings:** 2,000. **Education:** Moderate-term on-the-job training. **Job Zone:** 3.

Education/Training Program(s)—Ophthalmic Laboratory Technology/Technician. **Related Knowledge/Courses:** Physics; Mechanical; Production and Processing; Chemistry. **Personality Type:** Realistic. **Skills Required:** Operation Monitoring; Operation and Control; Equipment Selection; Quality Control Analysis; Technology Design; Equipment Maintenance. **Abilities:** Finger Dexterity; Arm-Hand Steadiness; Manual Dexterity; Near Vision; Control Precision. **Occupational Values:** Independence; Compensation; Working Conditions; Moral Values; Supervision, Technical. **Interacting with Others:** Communicating with Supervisors, Peers, or Subordinates; Coordinating the Work and Activities of Others; Performing Administrative Activities. **Physical Work Conditions:** Using Hands on Objects, Tools, or Controls; Sitting; Indoors; Hazardous Equipment; Minor Burns, Cuts, Bites, or Stings; Common Protective or Safety Equipment.

Precision Mold and Pattern Casters, Except Nonferrous Metals

Cast molds and patterns from a variety of materials, except nonferrous metals, according to blueprints and specifications. **O*NET Code:** 51-9195.01. **Average Salary:** $24,470. **Projected Growth:** 6.4%. **Annual Openings:** 6,000. **Education:** Moderate-term on-the-job training. **Job Zone:** 3. **Education/Training Program(s)**—No data available. **Related Knowledge/Courses:** Production and Processing; Design; Building and Construction; Engineering and Technology; Mechanical; Physics. **Personality Type:** Realistic. **Skills Required:** Installation. **Abilities:** Wrist-Finger Speed; Visualization; Arm-Hand Steadiness; Speed of Limb Movement; Manual Dexterity. **Occupational Values:** Moral Values; Supervision, Technical; Independence; Supervision, Human Relations; Advancement. **Interacting with Others:** Communicating with Supervisors, Peers, or Subordinates; Establishing and Maintaining Interpersonal Relationships; Assisting and Caring for Others; Coaching and Developing Others. **Physical Work Conditions:** Standing; Hazardous Equipment; Indoors; Sounds, Noise Levels Are Distracting or Uncomfortable; Common Protective or Safety Equipment.

Precision Pattern and Die Casters, Nonferrous Metals

Cast metal patterns and dies according to specifications from a variety of nonferrous metals, such as aluminum or bronze. **O*NET Code:** 51-9195.02. **Average Salary:** $24,470. **Projected Growth:** 6.4%. **Annual Openings:** 6,000. **Education:** Long-term on-the-job training. **Job Zone:** 4. **Education/Training Program(s)**—No data available. **Related Knowledge/Courses:** Production and Processing; Building and Construction; Design; Engineering and Technology; Physics. **Personality Type:** Realistic. **Skills Required:** Operation and Control. **Abilities:** Explosive Strength; Dynamic Strength; Manual Dexterity; Depth Perception; Reaction Time. **Occupational Values:** Moral Values; Independence; Supervision, Human Relations; Supervision, Technical. **Interacting with Others:** Communicating with Supervisors, Peers, or Subordinates; Establishing and Maintaining Interpersonal Relationships; Assisting and Caring for Others; Coaching and Developing Others. **Physical Work Conditions:** Very Hot or Cold; Common Protective or Safety Equipment; Hazardous Equipment; Contaminants; Hazardous Conditions.

Semiconductor Processors

Perform any or all of the following functions in the manufacture of electronic semiconductors: load semiconductor material into furnace; saw formed ingots into segments; load individual segment into crystal-growing chamber and monitor controls; locate crystal axis in ingot, using X-ray equipment, and saw ingots into wafers; clean, polish, and load wafers into series of special-purpose furnaces, chemical baths, and equipment used to form circuitry and change conductive properties. **O*NET Code:** 51-9141.00. **Average Salary:** $27,480. **Projected Growth:** –10.6%. **Annual Openings:** 4,000. **Education:** Associate degree. **Job Zone:** 1. **Education/Training Program(s)**—Industrial Electronics Technology/Technician. **Related Knowledge/Courses:** Production and Processing; Physics; Computers and Electronics; Mechanical; Engineering and Technology. **Personality Type:** Realistic. **Skills Required:** Operation Monitoring; Operation and Control; Science; Quality Control Analysis; Equipment Maintenance; Equipment Selection; Mathematics; Repairing. **Abilities:** Control Precision; Wrist-Finger Speed; Number Facility; Written Comprehension; Near Vision. **Occupational Values:** Moral Values; Independence; Company Policies and Practices; Advancement; Supervision, Human Relations. **Interacting with Others:** Communicating with Supervisors, Peers, or Subordinates; Establishing and Maintaining Interpersonal Relationships; Performing Administrative Activities; Monitoring and Controlling Resources. **Physical Work Conditions:** Using Hands on Objects, Tools, or Controls; Hazardous Equipment; Indoors; Common Protective or Safety Equipment; Standing.

Silversmiths

Anneal, solder, hammer, shape, and glue silver articles. **O*NET Code:** 51-9071.02. **Average Salary:** $27,500. **Projected Growth:** 4.5%. **Annual Openings:** 3,000. **Education:** Long-term on-the-job training. **Job Zone:** 3. **Education/Training Program(s)**—Watchmaking and Jewelrymaking. **Related Knowledge/Courses:** Mechanical; Fine Arts; Production and Processing; Physics; Design; Building and Construction. **Personality Type:** Realistic. **Skills Required:** Equipment Maintenance; Technology Design; Management of Material Resources; Science; Repairing; Equipment Selection. **Abilities:** Arm-Hand Steadiness; Manual Dexterity; Explosive Strength; Finger Dexterity; Visualization. **Occupational Values:** Independence; Variety; Autonomy; Creativity; Recognition. **Interacting with Others:** Communicating with Supervisors, Peers, or Subordinates; Communicating with Persons Outside Organization; Performing Administrative Activities. **Physical Work Conditions:** Hazardous Equipment; Very Hot or Cold; Using Hands on Objects, Tools, or Controls; Indoors; Standing.

Timing Device Assemblers, Adjusters, and Calibrators

Perform precision assembling or adjusting, within narrow tolerances, of timing devices, such as watches, clocks, or chronometers. **O*NET Code:** 51-2093.00. **Average Salary:** $26,740. **Projected Growth:** –3.0%. **Annual Openings:** 1,000.

Education: Moderate-term on-the-job training. **Job Zone:** 2. **Education/Training Program(s)**—Watchmaking and Jewelrymaking. **Related Knowledge/Courses:** Mechanical; Design; Engineering and Technology. **Personality Type:** Realistic. **Skills Required:** Repairing; Installation; Technology Design; Science; Equipment Maintenance; Operation Monitoring; Troubleshooting; Equipment Selection; Quality Control Analysis. **Abilities:** Finger Dexterity; Manual Dexterity; Arm-Hand Steadiness; Visualization; Near Vision. **Occupational Values:** Independence; Moral Values; Ability Utilization; Working Conditions; Achievement. **Interacting with Others:** Communicating with Persons Outside Organization; Establishing and Maintaining Interpersonal Relationships; Communicating with Supervisors, Peers, or Subordinates. **Physical Work Conditions:** Sitting; Using Hands on Objects, Tools, or Controls; Indoors; Spend Time Making Repetitive Motions; Extremely Bright or Inadequate Lighting; Common Protective or Safety Equipment.

13.07 Production Quality Control

Electrical and Electronic Inspectors and Testers

Inspect and test electrical and electronic systems, such as radar navigational equipment, computer memory units, and television and radio transmitters, using precision measuring instruments. **O*NET Code:** 51-9061.04. **Average Salary:** $28,200. **Projected Growth:** 4.7%. **Annual Openings:** 87,000. **Education:** Moderate-term on-the-job training. **Job Zone:** 3. **Education/Training Program(s)**—Quality Control Technology/Technician. **Related Knowledge/Courses:** Computers and Electronics; Telecommunications; Design; Mechanical; Engineering and Technology; Production and Processing. **Personality Type:** Realistic. **Skills Required:** Programming; Quality Control Analysis; Installation; Troubleshooting; Repairing; Operation Monitoring; Science; Equipment Maintenance. **Abilities:** Perceptual Speed; Reaction Time; Finger Dexterity; Control Precision; Mathematical Reasoning. **Occupational Values:** Responsibility; Supervision, Technical; Advancement; Co-workers; Activity. **Interacting with Others:** Establishing and Maintaining Interpersonal Relationships; Communicating with Supervisors, Peers, or Subordinates; Communicating with Persons Outside Organization. **Physical Work Conditions:** Common Protective or Safety Equipment; Hazardous Conditions; Hazardous Equipment; Standing; Walking and Running.

Graders and Sorters, Agricultural Products

Grade, sort, or classify unprocessed food and other agricultural products by size, weight, color, or condition. **O*NET Code:** 45-2041.00. **Average Salary:** $16,530. **Projected Growth:** 6.7%. **Annual Openings:** 11,000. **Education:** Work experience in a related occupation. **Job Zone:** 1. **Education/Training Program(s)**—Agricultural/Farm Supplies Retailing and Wholesaling. **Related Knowledge/Courses:** Production and Processing; Food Production. **Personality

Type: Realistic. **Skills Required:** None met the criteria. **Abilities:** Perceptual Speed; Category Flexibility; Speed of Limb Movement; Flexibility of Closure; Speed of Closure. **Occupational Values:** Independence; Supervision, Technical; Moral Values; Supervision, Human Relations; Activity; Responsibility. **Interacting with Others:** Establishing and Maintaining Interpersonal Relationships; Communicating with Supervisors, Peers, or Subordinates; Performing Administrative Activities; Monitoring and Controlling Resources. **Physical Work Conditions:** Using Hands on Objects, Tools, or Controls; Spend Time Making Repetitive Motions; Standing; Indoors; Contaminants.

Materials Inspectors

Examine and inspect materials and finished parts and products for defects and wear and to ensure conformance with work orders, diagrams, blueprints, and template specifications. Usually specialize in a single phase of inspection. **O*NET Code:** 51-9061.01. **Average Salary:** $28,200. **Projected Growth:** 4.7%. **Annual Openings:** 87,000. **Education:** Moderate-term on-the-job training. **Job Zone:** 3. **Education/Training Program(s)**—Quality Control Technology/Technician. **Related Knowledge/Courses:** Design; Mechanical; Production and Processing; Engineering and Technology; Physics; Public Safety and Security. **Personality Type:** Realistic. **Skills Required:** Quality Control Analysis; Operation Monitoring; Troubleshooting; Technology Design; Installation; Operation and Control; Science; Mathematics. **Abilities:** Perceptual Speed; Visual Color Discrimination; Inductive Reasoning; Reaction Time; Auditory Attention. **Occupational Values:** Responsibility; Independence; Supervision, Technical; Autonomy; Activity. **Interacting with Others:** Providing Consultation and Advice to Others; Establishing and Maintaining Interpersonal Relationships; Communicating with Supervisors, Peers, or Subordinates; Communicating with Persons Outside Organization; Coordinating the Work and Activities of Others. **Physical Work Conditions:** Hazardous Equipment; Standing; Common Protective or Safety Equipment; Walking and Running; Very Hot or Cold.

Precision Devices Inspectors and Testers

Verify accuracy of and adjust precision devices, such as meters and gauges, testing instruments, and clock and watch mechanisms, to ensure operation of device is in accordance with design specifications. **O*NET Code:** 51-9061.03. **Average Salary:** $28,200. **Projected Growth:** 4.7%. **Annual Openings:** 87,000. **Education:** Moderate-term on-the-job training. **Job Zone:** 3. **Education/Training Program(s)**—Quality Control Technology/Technician. **Related Knowledge/Courses:** Design; Mechanical; Production and Processing; Mathematics; Engineering and Technology; Physics. **Personality Type:** Realistic. **Skills Required:** Quality Control Analysis; Operation Monitoring; Technology Design; Installation; Science; Troubleshooting; Equipment Maintenance; Operation and Control. **Abilities:** Perceptual Speed; Finger Dexterity; Control Precision; Visual Color Discrimination; Arm-Hand Steadiness. **Occupational Values:** Responsibility; Independence; Supervision, Technical; Autonomy; Activity. **Interacting with Others:** Communicating with Supervisors, Peers, or Subordinates;

Communicating with Persons Outside Organization; Establishing and Maintaining Interpersonal Relationships. **Physical Work Conditions:** Sitting; Common Protective or Safety Equipment; Spend Time Making Repetitive Motions; Walking and Running; Indoors; Kneeling, Crouching, Stooping, or Crawling.

Production Inspectors, Testers, Graders, Sorters, Samplers, Weighers

Inspect, test, grade, sort, sample, or weigh nonagricultural raw materials or processed, machined, fabricated, or assembled parts or products. Work may be performed before, during, or after processing. **O*NET Code:** 51-9061.05. **Average Salary:** $28,200. **Projected Growth:** 4.7%. **Annual Openings:** 87,000. **Education:** Short-term on-the-job training. **Job Zone:** 1. **Education/Training Program(s)**—Quality Control Technology/Technician. **Related Knowledge/Courses:** Production and Processing; Engineering and Technology; Mechanical. **Personality Type:** Realistic. **Skills Required:** Quality Control Analysis; Operation Monitoring; Operation and Control; Troubleshooting; Management of Material Resources; Equipment Maintenance; Repairing; Science. **Abilities:** Visual Color Discrimination; Perceptual Speed; Category Flexibility; Control Precision; Auditory Attention. **Occupational Values:** Supervision, Technical; Responsibility; Activity; Compensation; Security; Co-workers; Company Policies and Practices. **Interacting with Others:** Communicating with Supervisors, Peers, or Subordinates; Interpreting the Meaning of Information for Others; Performing Administrative Activities. **Physical Work Conditions:** Using Hands on Objects, Tools, or Controls; Indoors; Walking and Running; Spend Time Bending or Twisting the Body; Hazardous Equipment.

13.08 Graphic Arts Production

Bindery Machine Operators and Tenders

Operate or tend binding machines that round, back, case, line stitch, press, fold, trim, or perform other binding operations on books and related articles. **O*NET Code:** 51-5011.02. **Average Salary:** $22,950. **Projected Growth:** -5.2%. **Annual Openings:** 6,000. **Education:** Short-term on-the-job training. **Job Zone:** 1. **Education/Training Program(s)**—Graphic Communications, Other. **Related Knowledge/Courses:** Production and Processing; Mechanical; Clerical. **Personality Type:** Realistic. **Skills Required:** Operation Monitoring; Equipment Maintenance; Operation and Control; Quality Control Analysis; Installation. **Abilities:** Manual Dexterity; Control Precision; Explosive Strength; Rate Control; Dynamic Strength. **Occupational Values:** Moral Values; Independence; Supervision, Technical; Supervision, Human Relations; Activity. **Interacting with Others:** Communicating with Supervisors, Peers, or Subordinates; Performing Administrative Activities; Coordinating the Work and Activities of Others. **Physical Work Conditions:** Hazardous Equipment; Standing; Sounds, Noise Levels Are Distracting or Uncomfortable; Using Hands on Objects, Tools, or Controls; Minor Burns, Cuts, Bites, or Stings.

Camera Operators

Operate process camera and related darkroom equipment to photograph and develop negatives of material to be printed. **O*NET Code:** 51-5022.04. **Average Salary:** $31,560. **Projected Growth:** -11.2%. **Annual Openings:** 6,000. **Education:** Long-term on-the-job training. **Job Zone:** 4. **Education/Training Program(s)**—Graphic and Printing Equipment Operator, General Production; Graphic Communications, General; Graphic Communications, Other; Graphic Design; Platemaker/Imager; Prepress/Desktop Publishing and Digital Imaging Design; Printing Management. **Related Knowledge/Courses:** Fine Arts; Chemistry. **Personality Type:** Realistic. **Skills Required:** Technology Design; Equipment Selection; Operations Analysis; Operation and Control; Quality Control Analysis. **Abilities:** Visual Color Discrimination; Visualization; Arm-Hand Steadiness; Night Vision; Glare Sensitivity. **Occupational Values:** Independence; Creativity; Autonomy; Social Status; Moral Values. **Interacting with Others:** Communicating with Supervisors, Peers, or Subordinates; Communicating with Persons Outside Organization; Establishing and Maintaining Interpersonal Relationships. **Physical Work Conditions:** Indoors; Extremely Bright or Inadequate Lighting; Standing; Spend Time Bending or Twisting the Body; Using Hands on Objects, Tools, or Controls.

Design Printing Machine Setters and Set-Up Operators

Set up or set up and operate machines to print designs on materials. **O*NET Code:** 51-5023.04. **Average Salary:** $29,750. **Projected Growth:** 4.6%. **Annual Openings:** 30,000. **Education:** Postsecondary vocational training. **Job Zone:** 3. **Education/Training Program(s)**—Graphic and Printing Equipment Operator, General Production; Graphic Communications, Other; Printing Management; Printing Press Operator. **Related Knowledge/Courses:** Mechanical; Engineering and Technology; Production and Processing. **Personality Type:** Realistic. **Skills Required:** Repairing; Operation Monitoring; Equipment Maintenance; Operation and Control; Technology Design; Installation; Troubleshooting; Equipment Selection. **Abilities:** Visual Color Discrimination; Rate Control; Multilimb Coordination; Control Precision; Dynamic Strength. **Occupational Values:** Independence; Moral Values; Supervision, Technical; Company Policies and Practices; Activity. **Interacting with Others:** Communicating with Supervisors, Peers, or Subordinates; Performing Administrative Activities; Communicating with Persons Outside Organization; Establishing and Maintaining Interpersonal Relationships. **Physical Work Conditions:** Hazardous Equipment; Indoors; Spend Time Bending or Twisting the Body; Spend Time Making Repetitive Motions; Common Protective or Safety Equipment.

Desktop Publishers

Format typescript and graphic elements, using computer software, to produce publication-ready material. **O*NET Code:**

43-9031.00. **Average Salary:** $31,410. **Projected Growth:** 29.2%. **Annual Openings:** 4,000. **Education:** Postsecondary vocational training. **Job Zone:** 3. **Education/Training Program(s)**—Prepress/Desktop Publishing and Digital Imaging Design. **Related Knowledge/Courses:** Computers and Electronics; Production and Processing; English Language; Customer and Personal Service; Clerical; Administration and Management; Telecommunications. **Personality Type:** Realistic. **Skills Required:** Time Management; Service Orientation; Instructing; Operation and Control; Active Listening; Operations Analysis; Reading Comprehension; Technology Design. **Abilities:** Visualization; Fluency of Ideas; Originality; Flexibility of Closure; Visual Color Discrimination. **Occupational Values:** Working Conditions; Independence; Variety; Supervision, Human Relations; Recognition; Supervision, Technical; Autonomy. **Interacting with Others:** Establishing and Maintaining Interpersonal Relationships; Communicating with Supervisors, Peers, or Subordinates; Communicating with Persons Outside Organization. **Physical Work Conditions:** Sitting; Indoors; Physical Proximity; Sounds, Noise Levels Are Distracting or Uncomfortable; Contaminants.

Dot Etchers

Increase or reduce size of photographic dots by chemical or photomechanical methods to make color corrections on halftone negatives or positives to be used in preparation of lithographic printing plates. **O*NET Code:** 51-5022.08. **Average Salary:** $31,560. **Projected Growth:** –11.2%. **Annual Openings:** 6,000. **Education:** Long-term on-the-job training. **Job Zone:** 5. **Education/Training Program(s)**—Graphic and Printing Equipment Operator, General Production; Graphic Communications, General; Graphic Communications, Other; Graphic Design; Platemaker/Imager; Prepress/Desktop Publishing and Digital Imaging Design; Printing Management. **Related Knowledge/Courses:** Fine Arts; Chemistry; Production and Processing. **Personality Type:** Realistic. **Skills Required:** Equipment Selection; Operations Analysis. **Abilities:** Visual Color Discrimination; Night Vision; Flexibility of Closure; Visualization; Near Vision. **Occupational Values:** Moral Values; Independence; Autonomy; Responsibility; Working Conditions; Creativity. **Interacting with Others:** Communicating with Supervisors, Peers, or Subordinates; Establishing and Maintaining Interpersonal Relationships; Training and Teaching Others; Coaching and Developing Others; Performing Administrative Activities; Monitoring and Controlling Resources. **Physical Work Conditions:** Extremely Bright or Inadequate Lighting; Sitting; Using Hands on Objects, Tools, or Controls; Exposed to Radiation; Indoors.

Electronic Masking System Operators

Operate computerized masking system to produce stripping masks used in production of offset lithographic printing plates. **O*NET Code:** 51-5022.09. **Average Salary:** $31,560. **Projected Growth:** –11.2%. **Annual Openings:** 6,000. **Education:** Long-term on-the-job training. **Job Zone:** 4. **Education/Training Program(s)**—Graphic and Printing Equipment Operator, General Production; Graphic Communications, General; Graphic Communications, Other; Graphic Design; Platemaker/Imager; Prepress/Desktop Publishing and Digital Imaging Design; Printing Management. **Related Knowledge/Courses:** Design; Computers and Electronics; Production and Processing; Fine Arts. **Personality Type:** Realistic. **Skills Required:** Operation and Control; Technology Design. **Abilities:** Visualization; Arm-Hand Steadiness; Fluency of Ideas. **Occupational Values:** Moral Values; Independence; Working Conditions; Supervision, Technical; Social Status. **Interacting with Others:** Communicating with Supervisors, Peers, or Subordinates; Establishing and Maintaining Interpersonal Relationships; Assisting and Caring for Others. **Physical Work Conditions:** Sitting; Using Hands on Objects, Tools, or Controls; Indoors.

Electrotypers and Stereotypers

Fabricate and finish electrotype and stereotype printing plates. **O*NET Code:** 51-5022.10. **Average Salary:** $31,560. **Projected Growth:** –11.2%. **Annual Openings:** 6,000. **Education:** Long-term on-the-job training. **Job Zone:** 5. **Education/Training Program(s)**—Graphic and Printing Equipment Operator, General Production; Graphic Communications, General; Graphic Communications, Other; Graphic Design; Platemaker/Imager; Prepress/Desktop Publishing and Digital Imaging Design; Printing Management. **Related Knowledge/Courses:** Mechanical; Engineering and Technology; Production and Processing. **Personality Type:** Realistic. **Skills Required:** Operation and Control; Operation Monitoring; Troubleshooting; Quality Control Analysis. **Abilities:** Arm-Hand Steadiness; Visual Color Discrimination; Manual Dexterity; Visualization; Explosive Strength. **Occupational Values:** Independence; Supervision, Technical; Moral Values; Supervision, Human Relations; Working Conditions; Advancement. **Interacting with Others:** Establishing and Maintaining Interpersonal Relationships; Communicating with Supervisors, Peers, or Subordinates; Coordinating the Work and Activities of Others. **Physical Work Conditions:** Hazardous Equipment; Common Protective or Safety Equipment; Using Hands on Objects, Tools, or Controls; Spend Time Making Repetitive Motions; Sounds, Noise Levels Are Distracting or Uncomfortable; Spend Time Bending or Twisting the Body.

Embossing Machine Set-Up Operators

Set up and operate embossing machines. **O*NET Code:** 51-5023.07. **Average Salary:** $29,750. **Projected Growth:** 4.6%. **Annual Openings:** 30,000. **Education:** Postsecondary vocational training. **Job Zone:** 3. **Education/Training Program(s)**—Graphic and Printing Equipment Operator, General Production; Graphic Communications, Other; Printing Management; Printing Press Operator. **Related Knowledge/Courses:** Production and Processing; Administration and Management. **Personality Type:** Realistic. **Skills Required:** Installation; Operation and Control; Equipment Maintenance; Operation Monitoring; Repairing. **Abilities:** Manual Dexterity; Control Precision; Trunk Strength; Speed of Limb Movement; Wrist-Finger Speed. **Occupational Values:** Independence; Moral Values; Supervision, Technical; Supervision, Human Relations; Activity. **Interacting with Others:** Communicating with Supervisors, Peers, or Subordinates; Coordinating the Work and Activities of Others; Interpreting the Meaning of

Information for Others; Establishing and Maintaining Interpersonal Relationships; Assisting and Caring for Others; Monitoring and Controlling Resources. **Physical Work Conditions:** Hazardous Equipment; Using Hands on Objects, Tools, or Controls; Common Protective or Safety Equipment; Indoors; Standing.

Engraver Set-Up Operators

Set up and operate machines to transfer printing designs. O*NET Code: 51-5023.08. **Average Salary:** $29,750. **Projected Growth:** 4.6%. **Annual Openings:** 30,000. **Education:** Long-term on-the-job training. **Job Zone:** 4. **Education/Training Program(s)**—Graphic and Printing Equipment Operator, General Production; Graphic Communications, Other; Printing Management; Printing Press Operator. **Related Knowledge/Courses:** Production and Processing; Mechanical. **Personality Type:** Realistic. **Skills Required:** Operation and Control; Installation; Operation Monitoring. **Abilities:** Visual Color Discrimination; Control Precision; Arm-Hand Steadiness; Manual Dexterity; Wrist-Finger Speed. **Occupational Values:** Independence; Moral Values; Supervision, Human Relations; Supervision, Technical; Activity; Company Policies and Practices. **Interacting with Others:** Performing Administrative Activities; Communicating with Supervisors, Peers, or Subordinates; Establishing and Maintaining Interpersonal Relationships; Coordinating the Work and Activities of Others. **Physical Work Conditions:** Hazardous Equipment; Minor Burns, Cuts, Bites, or Stings; Using Hands on Objects, Tools, or Controls; Indoors; Standing.

Engravers, Hand

Engrave designs and identifying information onto rollers or plates used in printing. O*NET Code: 51-9194.06. **Average Salary:** $22,590. **Projected Growth:** 6.1%. **Annual Openings:** 1,000. **Education:** Long-term on-the-job training. **Job Zone:** 3. **Education/Training Program(s)**—Graphic Communications, Other. **Related Knowledge/Courses:** Fine Arts; Design; Production and Processing. **Personality Type:** Realistic. **Skills Required:** Equipment Maintenance. **Abilities:** Depth Perception; Visual Color Discrimination; Arm-Hand Steadiness; Manual Dexterity; Finger Dexterity. **Occupational Values:** Moral Values; Independence; Supervision, Technical. **Interacting with Others:** Communicating with Supervisors, Peers, or Subordinates; Coordinating the Work and Activities of Others; Performing for or Working Directly with the Public; Performing Administrative Activities. **Physical Work Conditions:** Using Hands on Objects, Tools, or Controls; Hazardous Equipment; Sitting; Indoors; Minor Burns, Cuts, Bites, or Stings; Spend Time Making Repetitive Motions.

Engravers/Carvers

Engrave or carve designs or lettering onto objects, using hand-held power tools. O*NET Code: 51-9194.02. **Average Salary:** $22,590. **Projected Growth:** 6.1%. **Annual Openings:** 1,000. **Education:** Long-term on-the-job training. **Job Zone:** 3. **Education/Training Program(s)**—Graphic Communications, Other. **Related Knowledge/Courses:** Fine Arts; Production and Processing; Design. **Personality Type:** Realistic. **Skills Required:** Equipment Maintenance; Operation and Control; Equipment Selection; Installation. **Abilities:** Arm-Hand Steadiness; Originality; Finger Dexterity;

Manual Dexterity; Control Precision; Wrist-Finger Speed. **Occupational Values:** Independence; Moral Values; Creativity; Variety; Ability Utilization; Achievement; Working Conditions. **Interacting with Others:** Communicating with Persons Outside Organization; Communicating with Supervisors, Peers, or Subordinates; Providing Consultation and Advice to Others. **Physical Work Conditions:** Hazardous Equipment; Using Hands on Objects, Tools, or Controls; Minor Burns, Cuts, Bites, or Stings; Indoors; Common Protective or Safety Equipment.

Etchers

Etch or cut artistic designs in glass articles, using acid solutions, sandblasting equipment, and design patterns. O*NET Code: 51-9194.03. **Average Salary:** $22,590. **Projected Growth:** 6.1%. **Annual Openings:** 1,000. **Education:** Long-term on-the-job training. **Job Zone:** 3. **Education/Training Program(s)**—Graphic Communications, Other. **Related Knowledge/Courses:** Fine Arts; Chemistry; Production and Processing; Design. **Personality Type:** Realistic. **Skills Required:** Operation Monitoring; Equipment Maintenance; Operation and Control; Equipment Selection. **Abilities:** Arm-Hand Steadiness; Manual Dexterity; Wrist-Finger Speed; Control Precision; Depth Perception. **Occupational Values:** Independence; Creativity; Moral Values; Variety; Achievement; Autonomy. **Interacting with Others:** Communicating with Supervisors, Peers, or Subordinates; Performing for or Working Directly with the Public; Communicating with Persons Outside Organization; Coordinating the Work and Activities of Others; Performing Administrative Activities. **Physical Work Conditions:** Hazardous Equipment; Using Hands on Objects, Tools, or Controls; Common Protective or Safety Equipment; Contaminants; Spend Time Making Repetitive Motions.

Etchers, Hand

Etch patterns, designs, lettering, or figures onto a variety of materials and products. O*NET Code: 51-9194.05. **Average Salary:** $22,590. **Projected Growth:** 6.1%. **Annual Openings:** 1,000. **Education:** Moderate-term on-the-job training. **Job Zone:** 1. **Education/Training Program(s)**—Graphic Communications, Other. **Related Knowledge/Courses:** Fine Arts; Design; Production and Processing; Chemistry. **Personality Type:** Realistic. **Skills Required:** Equipment Selection; Equipment Maintenance; Technology Design; Systems Analysis. **Abilities:** Arm-Hand Steadiness; Manual Dexterity; Visualization; Control Precision; Visual Color Discrimination. **Occupational Values:** Moral Values; Independence; Supervision, Technical. **Interacting with Others:** Communicating with Supervisors, Peers, or Subordinates; Performing Administrative Activities; Communicating with Persons Outside Organization; Performing for or Working Directly with the Public; Coordinating the Work and Activities of Others. **Physical Work Conditions:** Hazardous Conditions; Using Hands on Objects, Tools, or Controls; Minor Burns, Cuts, Bites, or Stings; Contaminants; Indoors.

Film Laboratory Technicians

Evaluate motion picture film to determine characteristics such as sensitivity to light, density, and exposure time required for printing. O*NET Code: 51-9131.04. **Average**

Salary: $20,470. **Projected Growth:** 5.4%. **Annual Openings:** 4,000. **Education:** Moderate-term on-the-job training. **Job Zone:** 4. **Education/Training Program(s)**—Photographic and Film/Video Technology/Technician and Assistant. **Related Knowledge/Courses:** Physics; Fine Arts; Production and Processing; Engineering and Technology. **Personality Type:** Realistic. **Skills Required:** Science; Management of Material Resources; Quality Control Analysis. **Abilities:** Visual Color Discrimination; Night Vision; Arm-Hand Steadiness; Far Vision; Near Vision. **Occupational Values:** Independence; Supervision, Technical; Moral Values; Working Conditions; Autonomy. **Interacting with Others:** Interpreting the Meaning of Information for Others; Communicating with Supervisors, Peers, or Subordinates; Performing Administrative Activities. **Physical Work Conditions:** Extremely Bright or Inadequate Lighting; Sitting; Indoors; Using Hands on Objects, Tools, or Controls; Minor Burns, Cuts, Bites, or Stings.

Hand Compositors and Typesetters

Set up and arrange type by hand. Assemble and lock setup of type, cuts, and headings. Pull proofs. **O*NET Code:** 51-5022.01. **Average Salary:** $31,560. **Projected Growth:** –11.2%. **Annual Openings:** 6,000. **Education:** Long-term on-the-job training. **Job Zone:** 4. **Education/Training Program(s)**—Graphic and Printing Equipment Operator, General Production; Graphic Communications, General; Graphic Communications, Other; Graphic Design; Platemaker/Imager; Prepress/Desktop Publishing and Digital Imaging Design; Printing Management. **Related Knowledge/Courses:** Production and Processing; Communications and Media; English Language; Clerical. **Personality Type:** Realistic. **Skills Required:** None met the criteria. **Abilities:** Finger Dexterity; Perceptual Speed; Wrist-Finger Speed; Visualization; Peripheral Vision. **Occupational Values:** Moral Values; Independence; Supervision, Technical; Working Conditions; Supervision, Human Relations. **Interacting with Others:** Establishing and Maintaining Interpersonal Relationships; Communicating with Supervisors, Peers, or Subordinates; Assisting and Caring for Others; Training and Teaching Others; Monitoring and Controlling Resources. **Physical Work Conditions:** Hazardous Equipment; Using Hands on Objects, Tools, or Controls; Indoors; Sounds, Noise Levels Are Distracting or Uncomfortable; Sitting.

Job Printers

Set type according to copy, operate press to print job order, read proof for errors and clarity of impression, and correct imperfections. Job printers are often found in small establishments where work combines several job skills. **O*NET Code:** 51-5021.00. **Average Salary:** $31,310. **Projected Growth:** 9.2%. **Annual Openings:** 7,000. **Education:** Long-term on-the-job training. **Job Zone:** 5. **Education/Training Program(s)**—Graphic and Printing Equipment Operator, General Production; Printing Management. **Related Knowledge/Courses:** Production and Processing; Communications and Media; English Language; Mechanical; Clerical. **Personality Type:** Realistic. **Skills Required:** Operation and Control; Operation Monitoring; Quality Control Analysis. **Abilities:** Finger Dexterity; Perceptual Speed; Manual Dexterity; Wrist-Finger Speed; Control

Precision; Near Vision. **Occupational Values:** Independence; Moral Values; Variety; Supervision, Technical; Activity. **Interacting with Others:** Establishing and Maintaining Interpersonal Relationships; Communicating with Supervisors, Peers, or Subordinates; Monitoring and Controlling Resources. **Physical Work Conditions:** Hazardous Equipment; Hazardous Conditions; Contaminants; Indoors; Sounds, Noise Levels Are Distracting or Uncomfortable; Spend Time Bending or Twisting the Body.

Letterpress Setters and Set-Up Operators

Set up or set up and operate direct relief letterpresses, either sheet- or roll (web)-fed, to produce single-color or multicolor printed material, such as newspapers, books, and periodicals. **O*NET Code:** 51-5023.03. **Average Salary:** $29,750. **Projected Growth:** 4.6%. **Annual Openings:** 30,000. **Education:** Moderate-term on-the-job training. **Job Zone:** 3. **Education/Training Program(s)**—Graphic and Printing Equipment Operator, General Production; Graphic Communications, Other; Printing Management; Printing Press Operator. **Related Knowledge/Courses:** Production and Processing; Economics and Accounting. **Personality Type:** Realistic. **Skills Required:** Installation; Operation Monitoring; Equipment Maintenance; Operation and Control; Troubleshooting; Quality Control Analysis; Management of Personnel Resources; Equipment Selection. **Abilities:** Visual Color Discrimination; Perceptual Speed; Static Strength; Trunk Strength; Control Precision. **Occupational Values:** Independence; Supervision, Technical; Activity; Moral Values; Authority; Company Policies and Practices. **Interacting with Others:** Communicating with Supervisors, Peers, or Subordinates; Establishing and Maintaining Interpersonal Relationships; Coordinating the Work and Activities of Others; Guiding, Directing, and Motivating Subordinates; Coaching and Developing Others. **Physical Work Conditions:** Hazardous Equipment; Standing; Using Hands on Objects, Tools, or Controls; Indoors; Common Protective or Safety Equipment.

Marking and Identification Printing Machine Setters and Set-Up Operators

Set up or set up and operate machines to print trademarks, labels, or multicolored identification symbols on materials. **O*NET Code:** 51-5023.05. **Average Salary:** $29,750. **Projected Growth:** 4.6%. **Annual Openings:** 30,000. **Education:** Short-term on-the-job training. **Job Zone:** 1. **Education/Training Program(s)**—Graphic and Printing Equipment Operator, General Production; Graphic Communications, Other; Printing Management; Printing Press Operator. **Related Knowledge/Courses:** Sales and Marketing; Personnel and Human Resources. **Personality Type:** Realistic. **Skills Required:** Operation Monitoring; Operation and Control; Equipment Maintenance; Quality Control Analysis. **Abilities:** Visual Color Discrimination; Rate Control; Speed of Limb Movement; Response Orientation; Arm-Hand Steadiness. **Occupational Values:** Independence; Moral Values; Supervision, Technical; Company Policies and Practices; Activity. **Interacting with Others:** Communicating with Supervisors, Peers, or Subordinates; Establishing and Maintaining Interpersonal Relationships; Communicating with Persons Outside Organization. **Physical Work**

Conditions: Standing; Using Hands on Objects, Tools, or Controls; Hazardous Equipment; Spend Time Making Repetitive Motions; Kneeling, Crouching, Stooping, or Crawling.

Offset Lithographic Press Setters and Set-Up Operators

Set up or set up and operate offset printing press, either sheet- or web-fed, to print single-color and multicolor copy from lithographic plates. Examine job order to determine press operating time, quantity to be printed, and stock specifications. **O*NET Code:** 51-5023.02. **Average Salary:** $29,750. **Projected Growth:** 4.6%. **Annual Openings:** 30,000. **Education:** Long-term on-the-job training. **Job Zone:** 5. **Education/Training Program(s)**—Graphic and Printing Equipment Operator, General Production; Graphic Communications, Other; Printing Management; Printing Press Operator. **Related Knowledge/Courses:** Production and Processing; Mechanical. **Personality Type:** Realistic. **Skills Required:** Operation Monitoring; Operation and Control; Installation; Equipment Maintenance; Management of Personnel Resources; Equipment Selection; Quality Control Analysis. **Abilities:** Visual Color Discrimination; Control Precision; Finger Dexterity. **Occupational Values:** Independence; Moral Values; Activity; Supervision, Technical; Company Policies and Practices. **Interacting with Others:** Guiding, Directing, and Motivating Subordinates; Coordinating the Work and Activities of Others; Communicating with Supervisors, Peers, or Subordinates. **Physical Work Conditions:** Standing; Indoors; Hazardous Equipment; Sounds, Noise Levels Are Distracting or Uncomfortable; Spend Time Making Repetitive Motions.

Pantograph Engravers

Affix identifying information onto a variety of materials and products, using engraving machines or equipment. **O*NET Code:** 51-9194.04. **Average Salary:** $22,590. **Projected Growth:** 6.1%. **Annual Openings:** 1,000. **Education:** Moderate-term on-the-job training. **Job Zone:** 1. **Education/Training Program(s)**—Graphic Communications, Other. **Related Knowledge/Courses:** Mechanical; Production and Processing; Design. **Personality Type:** Realistic. **Skills Required:** Equipment Maintenance; Operation Monitoring; Operation and Control; Quality Control Analysis. **Abilities:** Rate Control; Arm-Hand Steadiness; Control Precision; Manual Dexterity; Visualization; Wrist-Finger Speed. **Occupational Values:** Moral Values; Independence; Supervision, Technical. **Interacting with Others:** Communicating with Supervisors, Peers, or Subordinates; Performing Administrative Activities; Establishing and Maintaining Interpersonal Relationships; Assisting and Caring for Others; Performing for or Working Directly with the Public; Coordinating the Work and Activities of Others. **Physical Work Conditions:** Hazardous Equipment; Minor Burns, Cuts, Bites, or Stings; Using Hands on Objects, Tools, or Controls; Indoors; Hazardous Conditions.

Paste-Up Workers

Arrange and mount typeset material and illustrations into pasteup for printing reproduction, based on artist's or editor's layout. **O*NET Code:** 51-5022.02. **Average Salary:** $31,560. **Projected Growth:** –11.2%. **Annual Openings:** 6,000. **Education:** Long-term on-the-job training. **Job Zone:** 4. **Education/Training Program(s)**—Graphic and Printing Equipment Operator, General Production; Graphic Communications, General; Graphic Communications, Other; Graphic Design; Platemaker/Imager; Prepress/Desktop Publishing and Digital Imaging Design; Printing Management. **Related Knowledge/Courses:** Communications and Media; Design; Clerical; Fine Arts; Production and Processing; Computers and Electronics. **Personality Type:** Realistic. **Skills Required:** Operation Monitoring; Operation and Control. **Abilities:** Visual Color Discrimination; Arm-Hand Steadiness; Wrist-Finger Speed; Visualization; Manual Dexterity. **Occupational Values:** Independence; Working Conditions; Variety; Moral Values; Activity. **Interacting with Others:** Communicating with Supervisors, Peers, or Subordinates; Establishing and Maintaining Interpersonal Relationships; Interpreting the Meaning of Information for Others. **Physical Work Conditions:** Minor Burns, Cuts, Bites, or Stings; Indoors; Contaminants; Sitting; Using Hands on Objects, Tools, or Controls.

Photoengravers

Photograph copy, develop negatives, and prepare photosensitized metal plates for use in letterpress and gravure printing. **O*NET Code:** 51-5022.03. **Average Salary:** $31,560. **Projected Growth:** –11.2%. **Annual Openings:** 6,000. **Education:** Long-term on-the-job training. **Job Zone:** 4. **Education/Training Program(s)**—Graphic and Printing Equipment Operator, General Production; Graphic Communications, General; Graphic Communications, Other; Graphic Design; Platemaker/Imager; Prepress/Desktop Publishing and Digital Imaging Design; Printing Management. **Related Knowledge/Courses:** Chemistry; Fine Arts; Computers and Electronics; Design; Physics. **Personality Type:** Realistic. **Skills Required:** Equipment Maintenance; Operation and Control; Repairing. **Abilities:** Night Vision; Visual Color Discrimination; Finger Dexterity; Near Vision; Flexibility of Closure; Arm-Hand Steadiness. **Occupational Values:** Independence; Supervision, Technical; Variety; Moral Values; Autonomy. **Interacting with Others:** Establishing and Maintaining Interpersonal Relationships; Communicating with Supervisors, Peers, or Subordinates; Communicating with Persons Outside Organization; Assisting and Caring for Others; Coordinating the Work and Activities of Others; Coaching and Developing Others. **Physical Work Conditions:** Contaminants; Hazardous Conditions; Minor Burns, Cuts, Bites, or Stings; Common Protective or Safety Equipment; Extremely Bright or Inadequate Lighting.

Photoengraving and Lithographing Machine Operators and Tenders

Operate or tend photoengraving and lithographing equipment, such as plate graining, pantograph, roll varnishing, and routing machines. **O*NET Code:** 51-5022.13. **Average Salary:** $31,560. **Projected Growth:** –11.2%. **Annual Openings:** 6,000. **Education:** Moderate-term on-the-job training. **Job Zone:** 2. **Education/Training Program(s)**—Graphic and Printing Equipment Operator, General Production; Graphic Communications, General; Graphic Communications, Other; Graphic Design; Platemaker/Imager; Prepress/Desktop

© 2006, JIST Works

Publishing and Digital Imaging Design; Printing Management. **Related Knowledge/Courses:** Production and Processing; Chemistry; Physics; Mechanical; Fine Arts; Engineering and Technology. **Personality Type:** Realistic. **Skills Required:** Equipment Maintenance; Operation and Control; Repairing. **Abilities:** Visual Color Discrimination; Control Precision; Near Vision; Visualization; Finger Dexterity. **Occupational Values:** Moral Values; Independence; Supervision, Technical; Supervision, Human Relations; Activity. **Interacting with Others:** Communicating with Supervisors, Peers, or Subordinates; Establishing and Maintaining Interpersonal Relationships; Assisting and Caring for Others; Coaching and Developing Others; Monitoring and Controlling Resources. **Physical Work Conditions:** Hazardous Equipment; Indoors; Sitting; Standing; Using Hands on Objects, Tools, or Controls.

Photographic Processing Machine Operators

Operate photographic processing machines, such as photographic printing machines, film developing machines, and mounting presses. **O*NET Code:** 51-9132.00. **Average Salary:** $19,030. **Projected Growth:** 9.2%. **Annual Openings:** 9,000. **Education:** Short-term on-the-job training. **Job Zone:** 2. **Education/Training Program(s)**—Photographic and Film/Video Technology/Technician and Assistant. **Related Knowledge/Courses:** Production and Processing; Chemistry; Mechanical; Computers and Electronics; Fine Arts. **Personality Type:** Realistic. **Skills Required:** Operation Monitoring; Operation and Control; Equipment Maintenance; Science; Quality Control Analysis. **Abilities:** Night Vision; Visual Color Discrimination; Manual Dexterity; Rate Control; Arm-Hand Steadiness; Control Precision. **Occupational Values:** Moral Values; Independence; Working Conditions; Supervision, Technical; Company Policies and Practices. **Interacting with Others:** Performing Administrative Activities; Communicating with Supervisors, Peers, or Subordinates; Coordinating the Work and Activities of Others. **Physical Work Conditions:** Hazardous Conditions; Standing; Contaminants; Using Hands on Objects, Tools, or Controls; Extremely Bright or Inadequate Lighting.

Plate Finishers

Set up and operate equipment to trim and mount electrotype or stereotype plates. **O*NET Code:** 51-5022.11. **Average Salary:** $31,560. **Projected Growth:** –11.2%. **Annual Openings:** 6,000. **Education:** Long-term on-the-job training. **Job Zone:** 5. **Education/Training Program(s)**—Graphic and Printing Equipment Operator, General Production; Graphic Communications, General; Graphic Communications, Other; Graphic Design; Platemaker/Imager; Prepress/Desktop Publishing and Digital Imaging Design; Printing Management. **Related Knowledge/Courses:** Production and Processing; Mechanical. **Personality Type:** Realistic. **Skills Required:** Operation and Control; Equipment Maintenance; Installation; Quality Control Analysis; Repairing. **Abilities:** Rate Control; Reaction Time; Explosive Strength; Manual Dexterity; Control Precision; Dynamic Strength. **Occupational Values:** Independence; Moral Values; Supervision, Human Relations; Supervision, Technical; Activity; Company Policies and Practices. **Interacting with Others:** Communicating with Supervisors, Peers, or

Subordinates; Assisting and Caring for Others; Coordinating the Work and Activities of Others. **Physical Work Conditions:** Hazardous Equipment; Using Hands on Objects, Tools, or Controls; Standing; Spend Time Making Repetitive Motions; Sounds, Noise Levels Are Distracting or Uncomfortable.

Platemakers

Produce printing plates by exposing sensitized metal sheets to special light through a photographic negative. May operate machines that process plates automatically. **O*NET Code:** 51-5022.07. **Average Salary:** $31,560. **Projected Growth:** –11.2%. **Annual Openings:** 6,000. **Education:** Long-term on-the-job training. **Job Zone:** 3. **Education/Training Program(s)**—Graphic and Printing Equipment Operator, General Production; Graphic Communications, General; Graphic Communications, Other; Graphic Design; Platemaker/Imager; Prepress/Desktop Publishing and Digital Imaging Design; Printing Management. **Related Knowledge/Courses:** Chemistry; Production and Processing; Fine Arts; Physics; Engineering and Technology. **Personality Type:** Realistic. **Skills Required:** Quality Control Analysis; Installation; Operation Monitoring; Operation and Control; Repairing. **Abilities:** Arm-Hand Steadiness; Extent Flexibility; Visualization; Wrist-Finger Speed. **Occupational Values:** Independence; Creativity; Moral Values; Supervision, Technical; Responsibility; Autonomy. **Interacting with Others:** Communicating with Supervisors, Peers, or Subordinates; Establishing and Maintaining Interpersonal Relationships; Coordinating the Work and Activities of Others. **Physical Work Conditions:** Using Hands on Objects, Tools, or Controls; Minor Burns, Cuts, Bites, or Stings; Sitting; Standing; Indoors; Spend Time Bending or Twisting the Body.

Precision Etchers and Engravers, Hand or Machine

Engrave or etch flat or curved metal, wood, rubber, or other materials by hand or machine for printing, identification, or decorative purposes. Includes etchers and engravers of both hard and soft metals or materials and jewelry and seal engravers. **O*NET Code:** 51-9194.01. **Average Salary:** $22,590. **Projected Growth:** 6.1%. **Annual Openings:** 1,000. **Education:** Long-term on-the-job training. **Job Zone:** 3. **Education/Training Program(s)**—Graphic Communications, Other. **Related Knowledge/Courses:** Design; Fine Arts; Mechanical; Production and Processing. **Personality Type:** Realistic. **Skills Required:** Operation and Control; Equipment Selection. **Abilities:** Arm-Hand Steadiness; Control Precision; Finger Dexterity; Depth Perception; Manual Dexterity. **Occupational Values:** Independence; Moral Values; Creativity; Ability Utilization; Achievement; Working Conditions; Autonomy. **Interacting with Others:** Communicating with Supervisors, Peers, or Subordinates; Communicating with Persons Outside Organization; Establishing and Maintaining Interpersonal Relationships. **Physical Work Conditions:** Standing; Minor Burns, Cuts, Bites, or Stings; Spend Time Making Repetitive Motions; Using Hands on Objects, Tools, or Controls; Sitting.

Precision Printing Workers

Perform variety of precision printing activities, such as duplication of microfilm and reproduction of graphic arts materials. **O*NET Code:** 51-5023.01. **Average Salary:** $29,750. **Projected Growth:** 4.6%. **Annual Openings:** 30,000. **Education:** Moderate-term on-the-job training. **Job Zone:** 2. **Education/Training Program(s)**—Graphic and Printing Equipment Operator, General Production; Graphic Communications, Other; Printing Management; Printing Press Operator. **Related Knowledge/Courses:** Computers and Electronics; Chemistry; Production and Processing; Communications and Media; Fine Arts. **Personality Type:** Realistic. **Skills Required:** Technology Design; Quality Control Analysis; Equipment Maintenance; Operation and Control; Equipment Selection; Operation Monitoring; Troubleshooting; Operations Analysis; Repairing. **Abilities:** Visual Color Discrimination; Visualization; Control Precision; Depth Perception; Reaction Time. **Occupational Values:** Supervision, Technical; Independence; Variety; Moral Values; Social Status. **Interacting with Others:** Communicating with Supervisors, Peers, or Subordinates; Communicating with Persons Outside Organization; Establishing and Maintaining Interpersonal Relationships. **Physical Work Conditions:** Standing; Spend Time Making Repetitive Motions; Using Hands on Objects, Tools, or Controls; Kneeling, Crouching, Stooping, or Crawling; Walking and Running; Spend Time Bending or Twisting the Body.

Printing Press Machine Operators and Tenders

Operate or tend various types of printing machines, such as offset lithographic presses, letter or letterset presses, and flexographic or gravure presses, to produce print on paper or other materials such as plastic, cloth, or rubber. **O*NET Code:** 51-5023.09. **Average Salary:** $29,750. **Projected Growth:** 4.6%. **Annual Openings:** 30,000. **Education:** Short-term on-the-job training. **Job Zone:** 1. **Education/Training Program(s)**—Graphic and Printing Equipment Operator, General Production; Graphic Communications, Other; Printing Management; Printing Press Operator. **Related Knowledge/Courses:** Production and Processing; Mechanical; Chemistry. **Personality Type:** Realistic. **Skills Required:** Operation Monitoring; Management of Personnel Resources; Equipment Maintenance; Operation and Control; Installation; Quality Control Analysis; Repairing; Troubleshooting. **Abilities:** Visual Color Discrimination; Visualization; Manual Dexterity; Control Precision; Perceptual Speed; Finger Dexterity. **Occupational Values:** Advancement; Authority; Supervision, Human Relations; Supervision, Technical; Activity; Company Policies and Practices. **Interacting with Others:** Establishing and Maintaining Interpersonal Relationships; Communicating with Supervisors, Peers, or Subordinates; Coordinating the Work and Activities of Others. **Physical Work Conditions:** Hazardous Equipment; Common Protective or Safety Equipment; Indoors; Spend Time Bending or Twisting the Body; Standing.

Scanner Operators

Operate electronic or computerized scanning equipment to produce and screen film separations of photographs or art for use in producing lithographic printing plates. Evaluate and correct for deficiencies in the film. **O*NET Code:** 51-5022.05. **Average Salary:** $31,560. **Projected Growth:** –11.2%. **Annual Openings:** 6,000. **Education:** Long-term on-the-job training. **Job Zone:** 4. **Education/Training Program(s)**—Graphic and Printing Equipment Operator, General Production; Graphic Communications, General; Graphic Communications, Other; Graphic Design; Platemaker/Imager; Prepress/Desktop Publishing and Digital Imaging Design; Printing Management. **Related Knowledge/Courses:** Fine Arts; Production and Processing; Computers and Electronics; Communications and Media; Physics; Chemistry. **Personality Type:** Realistic. **Skills Required:** Quality Control Analysis; Operation and Control; Monitoring; Operation Monitoring. **Abilities:** Visual Color Discrimination; Night Vision; Perceptual Speed; Near Vision; Response Orientation. **Occupational Values:** Moral Values; Independence; Autonomy; Working Conditions; Social Status. **Interacting with Others:** Communicating with Supervisors, Peers, or Subordinates; Communicating with Persons Outside Organization; Establishing and Maintaining Interpersonal Relationships. **Physical Work Conditions:** Sitting; Using Hands on Objects, Tools, or Controls; Extremely Bright or Inadequate Lighting.

Strippers

Cut and arrange film into flats (layout sheets resembling a film negative of text in its final form), which are used to make plates. Prepare separate flat for each color. **O*NET Code:** 51-5022.06. **Average Salary:** $31,560. **Projected Growth:** –11.2%. **Annual Openings:** 6,000. **Education:** Long-term on-the-job training. **Job Zone:** 4. **Education/Training Program(s)**—Graphic and Printing Equipment Operator, General Production; Graphic Communications, General; Graphic Communications, Other; Graphic Design; Platemaker/Imager; Prepress/Desktop Publishing and Digital Imaging Design; Printing Management. **Related Knowledge/Courses:** Fine Arts; Chemistry; Production and Processing; Design. **Personality Type:** Realistic. **Skills Required:** Equipment Selection; Operation and Control; Operations Analysis; Science; Critical Thinking. **Abilities:** Visual Color Discrimination; Visualization; Arm-Hand Steadiness; Finger Dexterity; Fluency of Ideas. **Occupational Values:** Independence; Creativity; Moral Values; Supervision, Technical; Social Status. **Interacting with Others:** Communicating with Supervisors, Peers, or Subordinates; Communicating with Persons Outside Organization; Performing Administrative Activities. **Physical Work Conditions:** Sitting; Indoors; Extremely Bright or Inadequate Lighting; Using Hands on Objects, Tools, or Controls; Spend Time Making Repetitive Motions.

Typesetting and Composing Machine Operators and Tenders

Operate or tend typesetting and composing equipment, such as phototypesetters, linotype or monotype keyboard machines, photocomposers, linocasters, and photoletterers. **O*NET Code:** 51-5022.12. **Average Salary:** $31,560. **Projected Growth:** –11.2%. **Annual Openings:** 6,000. **Education:** Moderate-term on-the-job training. **Job Zone:** 2. **Education/Training Program(s)**—Graphic and Printing Equipment Operator, General Production; Graphic

Communications, General; Graphic Communications, Other; Graphic Design; Platemaker/Imager; Prepress/Desktop Publishing and Digital Imaging Design; Printing Management. **Related Knowledge/Courses:** Computers and Electronics; Economics and Accounting. **Personality Type:** Realistic. **Skills Required:** Operation Monitoring; Operation and Control; Equipment Maintenance. **Abilities:** Visual Color Discrimination; Information Ordering; Arm-Hand Steadiness; Wrist-Finger Speed; Reaction Time. **Occupational Values:** Independence; Moral Values; Supervision, Human Relations; Supervision, Technical; Activity; Company Policies and Practices. **Interacting with Others:** Communicating with Supervisors, Peers, or Subordinates; Establishing and Maintaining Interpersonal Relationships; Training and Teaching Others. **Physical Work Conditions:** Hazardous Equipment; Using Hands on Objects, Tools, or Controls; Indoors; Minor Burns, Cuts, Bites, or Stings; Hazardous Conditions.

13.09 Hands-On Work, Assorted Materials

Coil Winders, Tapers, and Finishers

Wind wire coils used in electrical components, such as resistors and transformers, and in electrical equipment and instruments, such as field cores, bobbins, armature cores, electrical motors, generators, and control equipment. **O*NET Code:** 51-2021.00. **Average Salary:** $24,450. **Projected Growth:** –13.9%. **Annual Openings:** 2,000. **Education:** Short-term on-the-job training. **Job Zone:** 2. **Education/Training Program(s)—** Industrial Electronics Technology/Technician. **Related Knowledge/Courses:** Production and Processing; Mechanical; Physics. **Personality Type:** Realistic. **Skills Required:** Equipment Maintenance; Repairing; Operation Monitoring; Installation; Operation and Control; Equipment Selection; Quality Control Analysis. **Abilities:** Control Precision; Manual Dexterity; Speed of Limb Movement; Rate Control; Arm-Hand Steadiness. **Occupational Values:** Supervision, Technical; Moral Values; Activity; Company Policies and Practices; Independence. **Interacting with Others:** Communicating with Supervisors, Peers, or Subordinates; Performing Administrative Activities; Interpreting the Meaning of Information for Others; Coordinating the Work and Activities of Others. **Physical Work Conditions:** Hazardous Equipment; Standing; Using Hands on Objects, Tools, or Controls; Indoors; Sounds, Noise Levels Are Distracting or Uncomfortable.

Cutters and Trimmers, Hand

Use hand tools or hand-held power tools to cut and trim a variety of manufactured items, such as carpet, fabric, stone, glass, or rubber. **O*NET Code:** 51-9031.00. **Average Salary:** $22,260. **Projected Growth:** 7.6%. **Annual Openings:** 5,000. **Education:** Short-term on-the-job training. **Job Zone:** 1. **Education/Training Program(s)—**No data available. **Related Knowledge/Courses:** Production and Processing; Building and Construction. **Personality Type:** Realistic. **Skills**

Required: Equipment Maintenance; Repairing. **Abilities:** Visualization; Wrist-Finger Speed; Manual Dexterity; Trunk Strength; Speed of Limb Movement. **Occupational Values:** Independence; Moral Values; Supervision, Technical. **Interacting with Others:** Communicating with Supervisors, Peers, or Subordinates; Performing Administrative Activities; Monitoring and Controlling Resources. **Physical Work Conditions:** Hazardous Equipment; Minor Burns, Cuts, Bites, or Stings; Using Hands on Objects, Tools, or Controls; Common Protective or Safety Equipment; Spend Time Making Repetitive Motions.

Fabric and Apparel Patternmakers

Draw and construct sets of precision master fabric patterns or layouts. May also mark and cut fabrics and apparel. **O*NET Code:** 51-6092.00. **Average Salary:** $29,510. **Projected Growth:** –24.6%. **Annual Openings:** 1,000. **Education:** Long-term on-the-job training. **Job Zone:** 2. **Education/Training Program(s)—**Apparel and Textile Manufacture. **Related Knowledge/Courses:** Design; Production and Processing; Mathematics. **Personality Type:** Realistic. **Skills Required:** Operations Analysis; Technology Design; Mathematics; Management of Material Resources. **Abilities:** Arm-Hand Steadiness; Visualization; Wrist-Finger Speed; Mathematical Reasoning; Visual Color Discrimination. **Occupational Values:** Moral Values; Independence; Working Conditions; Achievement; Advancement. **Interacting with Others:** Communicating with Supervisors, Peers, or Subordinates; Providing Consultation and Advice to Others; Establishing and Maintaining Interpersonal Relationships. **Physical Work Conditions:** Sitting; Using Hands on Objects, Tools, or Controls; Indoors; Minor Burns, Cuts, Bites, or Stings; Spend Time Bending or Twisting the Body.

Glass Blowers, Molders, Benders, and Finishers

Shape molten glass according to patterns. **O*NET Code:** 51-9195.04. **Average Salary:** $24,470. **Projected Growth:** 6.4%. **Annual Openings:** 6,000. **Education:** Long-term on-the-job training. **Job Zone:** 4. **Education/Training Program(s)—**No data available. **Related Knowledge/Courses:** Production and Processing; Physics; Design; Engineering and Technology; Fine Arts. **Personality Type:** Realistic. **Skills Required:** None met the criteria. **Abilities:** Arm-Hand Steadiness; Visualization; Wrist-Finger Speed; Manual Dexterity; Control Precision. **Occupational Values:** Independence; Ability Utilization; Achievement; Moral Values; Recognition; Supervision, Technical. **Interacting with Others:** Establishing and Maintaining Interpersonal Relationships; Communicating with Supervisors, Peers, or Subordinates; Assisting and Caring for Others; Coaching and Developing Others. **Physical Work Conditions:** Standing; Very Hot or Cold; Minor Burns, Cuts, Bites, or Stings; Using Hands on Objects, Tools, or Controls; Indoors.

Grinding and Polishing Workers, Hand

Grind, sand, or polish, using hand tools or hand-held power tools, a variety of metal, wood, stone, clay, plastic, or glass objects. **O*NET Code:** 51-9022.00. **Average Salary:** $23,220. **Projected Growth:** 9.0%. **Annual Openings:** 6,000. **Education:** Moderate-term on-the-job training. **Job Zone:** 1. **Education/Training Program(s)—**No data available. **Related**

Knowledge/Courses: Production and Processing; Chemistry; Mechanical; Physics. **Personality Type:** Realistic. **Skills Required:** Operation Monitoring; Repairing; Operation and Control; Equipment Maintenance. **Abilities:** Wrist-Finger Speed; Trunk Strength; Extent Flexibility; Control Precision; Multilimb Coordination; Stamina. **Occupational Values:** Moral Values; Independence; Supervision, Technical. **Interacting with Others:** Communicating with Supervisors, Peers, or Subordinates; Establishing and Maintaining Interpersonal Relationships; Performing Administrative Activities. **Physical Work Conditions:** Common Protective or Safety Equipment; Hazardous Equipment; Sounds, Noise Levels Are Distracting or Uncomfortable; Spend Time Making Repetitive Motions; Using Hands on Objects, Tools, or Controls.

Mold Makers, Hand

Construct or form molds from existing forms for use in casting objects. **O*NET Code:** 51-9195.06. **Average Salary:** $24,470. **Projected Growth:** 6.4%. **Annual Openings:** 6,000. **Education:** Moderate-term on-the-job training. **Job Zone:** 2. **Education/Training Program(s)**—No data available. **Related Knowledge/Courses:** Building and Construction; Production and Processing. **Personality Type:** Realistic. **Skills Required:** Repairing; Science; Equipment Selection. **Abilities:** Visualization; Hearing Sensitivity; Explosive Strength; Extent Flexibility; Speed of Limb Movement; Dynamic Flexibility. **Occupational Values:** Moral Values; Supervision, Technical; Independence; Supervision, Human Relations. **Interacting with Others:** Communicating with Supervisors, Peers, or Subordinates; Establishing and Maintaining Interpersonal Relationships; Communicating with Persons Outside Organization; Providing Consultation and Advice to Others; Performing Administrative Activities; Monitoring and Controlling Resources. **Physical Work Conditions:** Common Protective or Safety Equipment; Using Hands on Objects, Tools, or Controls; Hazardous Equipment; Contaminants; Indoors.

Molding and Casting Workers

Perform a variety of duties, such as mixing materials, assembling mold parts, filling molds, and stacking molds, to mold and cast a wide range of products. **O*NET Code:** 51-9195.07. **Average Salary:** $24,470. **Projected Growth:** 6.4%. **Annual Openings:** 6,000. **Education:** Moderate-term on-the-job training. **Job Zone:** 2. **Education/Training Program(s)**—No data available. **Related Knowledge/Courses:** Building and Construction; Production and Processing. **Personality Type:** Realistic. **Skills Required:** Operation Monitoring; Operation and Control; Quality Control Analysis; Installation; Repairing; Equipment Maintenance; Equipment Selection. **Abilities:** Visualization; Manual Dexterity; Memorization; Static Strength; Trunk Strength. **Occupational Values:** Moral Values; Independence; Supervision, Technical; Supervision, Human Relations. **Interacting with Others:** Establishing and Maintaining Interpersonal Relationships; Communicating with Supervisors, Peers, or Subordinates; Coordinating the Work and Activities of Others; Monitoring and Controlling Resources. **Physical Work Conditions:** Using Hands on Objects, Tools, or Controls; Spend Time Making Repetitive Motions; Indoors; Standing; Spend Time Bending or Twisting the Body.

Painters, Transportation Equipment

Operate or tend painting machines to paint surfaces of transportation equipment, such as automobiles, buses, trucks, trains, boats, and airplanes. **O*NET Code:** 51-9122.00. **Average Salary:** $34,360. **Projected Growth:** 17.5%. **Annual Openings:** 9,000. **Education:** Moderate-term on-the-job training. **Job Zone:** 2. **Education/Training Program(s)**—Autobody/Collision and Repair Technology/Technician. **Related Knowledge/Courses:** Design; Mechanical; Fine Arts; Chemistry. **Personality Type:** Realistic. **Skills Required:** Operation and Control; Equipment Maintenance. **Abilities:** Visual Color Discrimination; Dynamic Flexibility; Gross Body Equilibrium; Arm-Hand Steadiness; Static Strength. **Occupational Values:** Moral Values; Independence; Supervision, Human Relations; Supervision, Technical; Company Policies and Practices. **Interacting with Others:** Communicating with Supervisors, Peers, or Subordinates; Establishing and Maintaining Interpersonal Relationships; Assisting and Caring for Others; Selling or Influencing Others; Resolving Conflicts and Negotiating with Others; Monitoring and Controlling Resources. **Physical Work Conditions:** Spend Time Making Repetitive Motions; Spend Time Bending or Twisting the Body; Climbing Ladders, Scaffolds, or Poles; Contaminants; High Places.

Painting, Coating, and Decorating Workers

Paint, coat, or decorate articles such as furniture, glass, plateware, pottery, jewelry, cakes, toys, books, or leather. **O*NET Code:** 51-9123.00. **Average Salary:** $22,310. **Projected Growth:** 17.6%. **Annual Openings:** 6,000. **Education:** Short-term on-the-job training. **Job Zone:** 1. **Education/Training Program(s)**—Graphic Design. **Related Knowledge/Courses:** Production and Processing; Fine Arts; Building and Construction. **Personality Type:** Realistic. **Skills Required:** None met the criteria. **Abilities:** Visual Color Discrimination; Manual Dexterity; Wrist-Finger Speed; Arm-Hand Steadiness; Finger Dexterity. **Occupational Values:** Moral Values; Independence; Supervision, Technical. **Interacting with Others:** Communicating with Supervisors, Peers, or Subordinates; Coordinating the Work and Activities of Others; Establishing and Maintaining Interpersonal Relationships; Assisting and Caring for Others; Performing Administrative Activities. **Physical Work Conditions:** Using Hands on Objects, Tools, or Controls; Common Protective or Safety Equipment; Contaminants; Indoors; Standing.

Sewers, Hand

Sew, join, reinforce, or finish, usually with needle and thread, a variety of manufactured items. Includes weavers and stitchers. **O*NET Code:** 51-6051.00. **Average Salary:** $18,210. **Projected Growth:** –21.2%. **Annual Openings:** 6,000. **Education:** Short-term on-the-job training. **Job Zone:** 1. **Education/Training Program(s)**—No data available. **Related Knowledge/Courses:** Production and Processing; Fine Arts; Design. **Personality Type:** Realistic. **Skills Required:** None met the criteria. **Abilities:** Visual Color Discrimination; Arm-Hand Steadiness; Wrist-Finger Speed; Finger Dexterity; Near Vision. **Occupational Values:** Independence; Moral Values; Activity. **Interacting with Others:** Communicating with Supervisors, Peers, or Subordinates; Monitoring and Controlling Resources; Coordinating the Work and Activities

© 2006, JIST Works

of Others; Performing Administrative Activities. **Physical Work Conditions:** Spend Time Making Repetitive Motions; Using Hands on Objects, Tools, or Controls; Sitting; Indoors; Common Protective or Safety Equipment.

13.10 Woodworking Technology

Cabinetmakers and Bench Carpenters

Cut, shape, and assemble wooden articles or set up and operate a variety of woodworking machines, such as power saws, jointers, and mortisers, to surface, cut, or shape lumber or to fabricate parts for wood products. **O*NET Code:** 51-7011.00. **Average Salary:** $24,920. **Projected Growth:** 9.4%. **Annual Openings:** 15,000. **Education:** Long-term on-the-job training. **Job Zone:** 3. **Education/Training Program(s)—** Cabinetmaking and Millwork/Millwright. **Related Knowledge/Courses:** Building and Construction; Design; Engineering and Technology; Production and Processing; Mechanical; Fine Arts. **Personality Type:** Realistic. **Skills Required:** Installation; Operation and Control; Equipment Selection; Equipment Maintenance. **Abilities:** Explosive Strength; Visualization; Arm-Hand Steadiness; Control Precision; Extent Flexibility. **Occupational Values:** Independence; Recognition; Social Status; Moral Values; Ability Utilization; Achievement; Compensation; Autonomy. **Interacting with Others:** Communicating with Supervisors, Peers, or Subordinates; Communicating with Persons Outside Organization; Establishing and Maintaining Interpersonal Relationships; Coordinating the Work and Activities of Others; Training and Teaching Others; Performing Administrative Activities. **Physical Work Conditions:** Hazardous Equipment; Kneeling, Crouching, Stooping, or Crawling; Using Hands on Objects, Tools, or Controls; Standing; Spend Time Bending or Twisting the Body.

Furniture Finishers

Shape, finish, and refinish damaged, worn, or used furniture or new high-grade furniture to specified color or finish. **O*NET Code:** 51-7021.00. **Average Salary:** $23,230. **Projected Growth:** 3.3%. **Annual Openings:** 3,000. **Education:** Long-term on-the-job training. **Job Zone:** 2. **Education/Training Program(s)—**Furniture Design and Manufacturing. **Related Knowledge/Courses:** Building and Construction; Fine Arts; Chemistry; Production and Processing; Engineering and Technology. **Personality Type:** Realistic. **Skills Required:** Repairing; Equipment Selection. **Abilities:** Visual Color Discrimination; Dynamic Flexibility; Speed of Limb Movement; Wrist-Finger Speed; Extent Flexibility. **Occupational Values:** Independence; Recognition; Moral Values; Autonomy; Creativity. **Interacting with Others:** Communicating with Persons Outside Organization; Monitoring and Controlling Resources; Communicating with Supervisors, Peers, or Subordinates; Establishing and Maintaining Interpersonal Relationships. **Physical Work Conditions:** Hazardous Conditions; Kneeling, Crouching,

Stooping, or Crawling; Contaminants; Minor Burns, Cuts, Bites, or Stings; Using Hands on Objects, Tools, or Controls.

Model Makers, Wood

Construct full-size and scale wooden precision models of products. Includes wood jig builders and loft workers. **O*NET Code:** 51-7031.00. **Average Salary:** $25,170. **Projected Growth:** 10.3%. **Annual Openings:** Fewer than 500. **Education:** Long-term on-the-job training. **Job Zone:** 4. **Education/Training Program(s)—**Cabinetmaking and Millwork/Millwright. **Related Knowledge/Courses:** Design; Building and Construction; Engineering and Technology; Mechanical; Production and Processing. **Personality Type:** Realistic. **Skills Required:** Mathematics; Operation and Control; Equipment Selection; Installation; Quality Control Analysis. **Abilities:** Visualization; Multilimb Coordination; Extent Flexibility; Control Precision; Explosive Strength; Trunk Strength. **Occupational Values:** Moral Values; Independence; Ability Utilization; Supervision, Technical. **Interacting with Others:** Communicating with Supervisors, Peers, or Subordinates; Establishing and Maintaining Interpersonal Relationships; Interpreting the Meaning of Information for Others; Providing Consultation and Advice to Others. **Physical Work Conditions:** Minor Burns, Cuts, Bites, or Stings; Hazardous Equipment; Indoors; Standing; Using Hands on Objects, Tools, or Controls.

Patternmakers, Wood

Plan, lay out, and construct wooden unit or sectional patterns used in forming sand molds for castings. **O*NET Code:** 51-7032.00. **Average Salary:** $30,890. **Projected Growth:** 11.8%. **Annual Openings:** Fewer than 500. **Education:** Long-term on-the-job training. **Job Zone:** 4. **Education/Training Program(s)—**Cabinetmaking and Millwork/Millwright. **Related Knowledge/Courses:** Design; Building and Construction; Engineering and Technology; Mechanical; Production and Processing. **Personality Type:** Realistic. **Skills Required:** Mathematics; Operation and Control; Equipment Selection; Installation; Quality Control Analysis. **Abilities:** Visualization; Multilimb Coordination; Extent Flexibility; Control Precision; Explosive Strength; Trunk Strength. **Occupational Values:** Moral Values; Independence; Ability Utilization; Supervision, Technical. **Interacting with Others:** Communicating with Supervisors, Peers, or Subordinates; Establishing and Maintaining Interpersonal Relationships; Interpreting the Meaning of Information for Others; Providing Consultation and Advice to Others. **Physical Work Conditions:** Minor Burns, Cuts, Bites, or Stings; Hazardous Equipment; Indoors; Standing; Using Hands on Objects, Tools, or Controls.

13.11 Apparel, Shoes, Leather, and Fabric Care

Custom Tailors

Design/make tailored garments, applying knowledge of garment design, construction, styling, and fabrics. **O*NET Code:**

51-6052.02. **Average Salary:** $21,690. **Projected Growth:** –9.1%. **Annual Openings:** 9,000. **Education:** Work experience in a related occupation. **Job Zone:** 4. **Education/Training Program(s)**—No data available. **Related Knowledge/Courses:** Design; Customer and Personal Service; Production and Processing; Fine Arts; Sales and Marketing. **Personality Type:** Realistic. **Skills Required:** Service Orientation; Operations Analysis; Operation and Control; Management of Financial Resources. **Abilities:** Originality; Arm-Hand Steadiness; Fluency of Ideas; Finger Dexterity; Visualization; Wrist-Finger Speed. **Occupational Values:** Autonomy; Creativity; Working Conditions; Social Service; Responsibility. **Interacting with Others:** Communicating with Persons Outside Organization; Establishing and Maintaining Interpersonal Relationships; Performing for or Working Directly with the Public. **Physical Work Conditions:** Sitting; Indoors; Using Hands on Objects, Tools, or Controls; Kneeling, Crouching, Stooping, or Crawling; Spend Time Making Repetitive Motions.

Fabric Menders, Except Garment

Repair tears, holes, and other defects in fabrics, such as draperies, linens, parachutes, and tents. **O*NET Code:** 49-9093.00. **Average Salary:** $29,260. **Projected Growth:** –2.2%. **Annual Openings:** Fewer than 500. **Education:** Short-term on-the-job training. **Job Zone:** 1. **Education/Training Program(s)**—No data available. **Related Knowledge/Courses:** Administration and Management; Fine Arts. **Personality Type:** Realistic. **Skills Required:** None met the criteria. **Abilities:** Finger Dexterity; Arm-Hand Steadiness; Wrist-Finger Speed; Visual Color Discrimination; Manual Dexterity. **Occupational Values:** Moral Values; Independence; Supervision, Technical; Activity. **Interacting with Others:** Communicating with Supervisors, Peers, or Subordinates; Communicating with Persons Outside Organization; Establishing and Maintaining Interpersonal Relationships. **Physical Work Conditions:** Sitting; Spend Time Making Repetitive Motions; Using Hands on Objects, Tools, or Controls; Indoors; Spend Time Bending or Twisting the Body.

Laundry and Drycleaning Machine Operators and Tenders, Except Pressing

Operate or tend washing or drycleaning machines to wash or dryclean commercial, industrial, or household articles, such as cloth garments, suede, leather, furs, blankets, draperies, fine linens, rugs, and carpets. **O*NET Code:** 51-6011.03. **Average Salary:** $16,970. **Projected Growth:** 12.3%. **Annual Openings:** 47,000. **Education:** Moderate-term on-the-job training. **Job Zone:** 1. **Education/Training Program(s)**—No data available. **Related Knowledge/Courses:** Chemistry; Production and Processing. **Personality Type:** Realistic. **Skills Required:** Operation Monitoring; Equipment Maintenance; Operation and Control; Installation. **Abilities:** Gross Body Coordination; Dynamic Strength; Trunk Strength; Speed of Limb Movement; Stamina; Visual Color Discrimination. **Occupational Values:** Supervision, Technical; Moral Values; Company Policies and Practices; Supervision, Human Relations; Independence; Social Service. **Interacting with Others:** Communicating with Supervisors, Peers, or Subordinates; Guiding, Directing, and Motivating Subordinates; Coordinating the Work and Activities of Others.

Physical Work Conditions: Hazardous Equipment; Very Hot or Cold; Contaminants; Hazardous Conditions; Using Hands on Objects, Tools, or Controls.

Precision Dyers

Change or restore the color of articles, such as garments, drapes, and slipcovers, by means of dyes. Work requires knowledge of the composition of the textiles being dyed or restored and the chemical properties of bleaches and dyes and their effects upon such textiles. **O*NET Code:** 51-6011.02. **Average Salary:** $16,970. **Projected Growth:** 12.3%. **Annual Openings:** 47,000. **Education:** Postsecondary vocational training. **Job Zone:** 3. **Education/Training Program(s)**—No data available. **Related Knowledge/Courses:** Chemistry; Production and Processing. **Personality Type:** Realistic. **Skills Required:** Science. **Abilities:** Visual Color Discrimination; Extent Flexibility; Trunk Strength; Gross Body Coordination; Category Flexibility. **Occupational Values:** Supervision, Technical; Independence; Moral Values. **Interacting with Others:** Communicating with Supervisors, Peers, or Subordinates; Coordinating the Work and Activities of Others; Performing Administrative Activities. **Physical Work Conditions:** Standing; Spend Time Bending or Twisting the Body; Indoors; Hazardous Conditions; Walking and Running.

Pressers, Delicate Fabrics

Press drycleaned and wet-cleaned silk and synthetic fiber garments by hand or machine, applying knowledge of fabrics and heat, to produce high-quality finish. Finish pleated or fancy garments, normally by hand. **O*NET Code:** 51-6021.01. **Average Salary:** $17,050. **Projected Growth:** -0.2%. **Annual Openings:** 19,000. **Education:** Moderate-term on-the-job training. **Job Zone:** 2. **Education/Training Program(s)**—No data available. **Related Knowledge/Courses:** Economics and Accounting; Sales and Marketing. **Personality Type:** Realistic. **Skills Required:** None met the criteria. **Abilities:** Dynamic Flexibility; Manual Dexterity; Reaction Time; Speed of Limb Movement; Wrist-Finger Speed. **Occupational Values:** Moral Values; Independence; Supervision, Technical. **Interacting with Others:** Communicating with Supervisors, Peers, or Subordinates; Monitoring and Controlling Resources; Establishing and Maintaining Interpersonal Relationships; Assisting and Caring for Others. **Physical Work Conditions:** Minor Burns, Cuts, Bites, or Stings; Very Hot or Cold; Standing; Indoors; Using Hands on Objects, Tools, or Controls.

Pressers, Hand

Press articles to remove wrinkles, flatten seams, and give shape by using hand iron. Articles pressed include drapes; knit goods; millinery parts; parachutes; garments; slipcovers; and textiles such as lace, rayon, and silk. May block (shape) knitted garments after cleaning. May press leather goods. **O*NET Code:** 51-6021.03. **Average Salary:** $17,050. **Projected Growth:** -0.2%. **Annual Openings:** 19,000. **Education:** Short-term on-the-job training. **Job Zone:** 1. **Education/Training Program(s)**—No data available. **Related Knowledge/Courses:** Administration and Management; Economics and Accounting. **Personality Type:** Realistic. **Skills Required:** None met the criteria. **Abilities:** Manual Dexterity; Speed of Limb Movement; Multilimb

Coordination; Depth Perception; Wrist-Finger Speed. **Occupational Values:** Moral Values; Independence. **Interacting with Others:** Communicating with Supervisors, Peers, or Subordinates; Establishing and Maintaining Interpersonal Relationships; Monitoring and Controlling Resources. **Physical Work Conditions:** Minor Burns, Cuts, Bites, or Stings; Standing; Using Hands on Objects, Tools, or Controls; Indoors; Very Hot or Cold.

Shoe and Leather Workers and Repairers

Construct, decorate, or repair leather and leather-like products, such as luggage, shoes, and saddles. **O*NET Code:** 51-6041.00. **Average Salary:** $19,540. **Projected Growth:** –16.1%. **Annual Openings:** 2,000. **Education:** Long-term on-the-job training. **Job Zone:** 2. **Education/Training Program(s)—** Leatherworking and Upholstery, Other; Shoe, Boot and Leather Repair. **Related Knowledge/Courses:** Production and Processing; Design; Fine Arts; Engineering and Technology. **Personality Type:** Realistic. **Skills Required:** Repairing; Operations Analysis. **Abilities:** Arm-Hand Steadiness; Visual Color Discrimination; Wrist-Finger Speed; Finger Dexterity; Visualization; Manual Dexterity. **Occupational Values:** Independence; Moral Values; Autonomy; Ability Utilization; Creativity. **Interacting with Others:** Performing for or Working Directly with the Public; Communicating with Supervisors, Peers, or Subordinates; Communicating with Persons Outside Organization. **Physical Work Conditions:** Sitting; Using Hands on Objects, Tools, or Controls; Spend Time Making Repetitive Motions; Indoors; Hazardous Equipment; Minor Burns, Cuts, Bites, or Stings.

Shop and Alteration Tailors

Make tailored garments from existing patterns. Alter, repair, or fit made-to-measure or ready-to-wear garments. **O*NET Code:** 51-6052.01. **Average Salary:** $21,690. **Projected Growth:** –9.1%. **Annual Openings:** 9,000. **Education:** Work experience in a related occupation. **Job Zone:** 3. **Education/Training Program(s)—**No data available. **Related Knowledge/Courses:** Customer and Personal Service; Production and Processing. **Personality Type:** Realistic. **Skills Required:** Operations Analysis. **Abilities:** Arm-Hand Steadiness; Finger Dexterity; Wrist-Finger Speed; Control Precision; Manual Dexterity. **Occupational Values:** Social Service; Independence; Working Conditions; Autonomy; Variety. **Interacting with Others:** Performing for or Working Directly with the Public; Communicating with Persons Outside Organization; Communicating with Supervisors, Peers, or Subordinates; Establishing and Maintaining Interpersonal Relationships. **Physical Work Conditions:** Sitting; Indoors; Spend Time Making Repetitive Motions; Kneeling, Crouching, Stooping, or Crawling; Hazardous Equipment; Minor Burns, Cuts, Bites, or Stings.

Spotters, Dry Cleaning

Identify stains in wool, synthetic, and silk garments and household fabrics and apply chemical solutions to remove stains. Determine spotting procedures on basis of type of fabric and nature of stain. **O*NET Code:** 51-6011.01. **Average Salary:** $16,970. **Projected Growth:** 12.3%. **Annual Openings:** 47,000. **Education:** Short-term on-the-job training. **Job Zone:** 1. **Education/Training Program(s)—**No data

available. **Related Knowledge/Courses:** Chemistry; Food Production. **Personality Type:** Realistic. **Skills Required:** Operation Monitoring. **Abilities:** Visual Color Discrimination; Wrist-Finger Speed; Glare Sensitivity; Hearing Sensitivity; Dynamic Flexibility. **Occupational Values:** Independence; Moral Values; Supervision, Technical. **Interacting with Others:** Establishing and Maintaining Interpersonal Relationships; Communicating with Supervisors, Peers, or Subordinates; Assisting and Caring for Others; Monitoring and Controlling Resources. **Physical Work Conditions:** Hazardous Conditions; Contaminants; Minor Burns, Cuts, Bites, or Stings; Using Hands on Objects, Tools, or Controls; Indoors.

Upholsterers

Make, repair, or replace upholstery for household furniture or transportation vehicles. **O*NET Code:** 51-6093.00. **Average Salary:** $25,170. **Projected Growth:** –8.7%. **Annual Openings:** 9,000. **Education:** Long-term on-the-job training. **Job Zone:** 3. **Education/Training Program(s)—** Upholstery/Upholsterer. **Related Knowledge/Courses:** Building and Construction; Production and Processing. **Personality Type:** Realistic. **Skills Required:** Repairing; Technology Design. **Abilities:** Static Strength; Extent Flexibility; Finger Dexterity; Manual Dexterity; Wrist-Finger Speed. **Occupational Values:** Autonomy; Creativity; Moral Values; Independence; Working Conditions. **Interacting with Others:** Communicating with Supervisors, Peers, or Subordinates; Establishing and Maintaining Interpersonal Relationships; Performing Administrative Activities. **Physical Work Conditions:** Spend Time Bending or Twisting the Body; Using Hands on Objects, Tools, or Controls; Kneeling, Crouching, Stooping, or Crawling; Standing; Indoors.

13.12 Electrical and Electronic Repair

Avionics Technicians

Install, inspect, test, adjust, or repair avionics equipment, such as radar, radio, navigation, and missile control systems in aircraft or space vehicles. **O*NET Code:** 49-2091.00. **Average Salary:** $43,580. **Projected Growth:** 3.4%. **Annual Openings:** 3,000. **Education:** Postsecondary vocational training. **Job Zone:** 4. **Education/Training Program(s)—**Airframe Mechanics and Aircraft Maintenance Technology/Technician; Avionics Maintenance Technology/Technician. **Related Knowledge/Courses:** Computers and Electronics; Physics; Design; Engineering and Technology; Telecommunications; Mechanical. **Personality Type:** Realistic. **Skills Required:** Repairing; Installation; Troubleshooting; Equipment Maintenance; Operation Monitoring; Science; Quality Control Analysis; Operation and Control. **Abilities:** Finger Dexterity; Extent Flexibility; Arm-Hand Steadiness; Spatial Orientation; Visual Color Discrimination. **Occupational Values:** Compensation; Supervision, Human Relations; Variety; Supervision, Technical; Independence; Advancement;

Moral Values. **Interacting with Others:** Interpreting the Meaning of Information for Others; Communicating with Supervisors, Peers, or Subordinates; Coordinating the Work and Activities of Others. **Physical Work Conditions:** Hazardous Conditions; Using Hands on Objects, Tools, or Controls; Hazardous Equipment; Minor Burns, Cuts, Bites, or Stings; Kneeling, Crouching, Stooping, or Crawling; Common Protective or Safety Equipment.

Battery Repairers

Inspect, repair, recharge, and replace batteries. **O*NET Code:** 49-2092.03. **Average Salary:** $32,820. **Projected Growth:** 5.3%. **Annual Openings:** 3,000. **Education:** Moderate-term on-the-job training. **Job Zone:** 2. **Education/Training Program(s)**—Electrical/Electronics Equipment Installation and Repair, General. **Related Knowledge/Courses:** Computers and Electronics; Mechanical; Chemistry; Engineering and Technology. **Personality Type:** Realistic. **Skills Required:** Repairing; Installation; Quality Control Analysis; Troubleshooting; Equipment Maintenance; Science; Operation and Control; Equipment Selection. **Abilities:** Explosive Strength; Manual Dexterity; Dynamic Strength; Visual Color Discrimination; Static Strength. **Occupational Values:** Supervision, Technical; Moral Values; Security; Independence; Supervision, Human Relations. **Interacting with Others:** Communicating with Supervisors, Peers, or Subordinates; Establishing and Maintaining Interpersonal Relationships; Performing Administrative Activities. **Physical Work Conditions:** Minor Burns, Cuts, Bites, or Stings; Kneeling, Crouching, Stooping, or Crawling; Spend Time Bending or Twisting the Body; Contaminants; Hazardous Conditions; Common Protective or Safety Equipment.

Electric Home Appliance and Power Tool Repairers

Repair, adjust, and install all types of electric household appliances. **O*NET Code:** 49-2092.01. **Average Salary:** $32,820. **Projected Growth:** 5.3%. **Annual Openings:** 3,000. **Education:** Long-term on-the-job training. **Job Zone:** 3. **Education/Training Program(s)**—Electrical/Electronics Equipment Installation and Repair, General. **Related Knowledge/Courses:** Mechanical; Building and Construction; Design; Engineering and Technology; Computers and Electronics; Physics. **Personality Type:** Realistic. **Skills Required:** Installation; Troubleshooting; Repairing; Equipment Maintenance; Technology Design; Operation Monitoring; Quality Control Analysis; Science. **Abilities:** Visual Color Discrimination; Static Strength; Arm-Hand Steadiness; Finger Dexterity; Visualization; Extent Flexibility. **Occupational Values:** Variety; Social Service; Independence; Supervision, Technical; Moral Values. **Interacting with Others:** Communicating with Persons Outside Organization; Performing for or Working Directly with the Public; Interpreting the Meaning of Information for Others; Establishing and Maintaining Interpersonal Relationships; Performing Administrative Activities. **Physical Work Conditions:** Using Hands on Objects, Tools, or Controls; Sitting; Indoors; Hazardous Equipment; Kneeling, Crouching, Stooping, or Crawling.

Electric Motor and Switch Assemblers and Repairers

Test, repair, rebuild, and assemble electric motors, generators, and equipment. **O*NET Code:** 49-2092.02. **Average Salary:** $32,820. **Projected Growth:** 5.3%. **Annual Openings:** 3,000. **Education:** Long-term on-the-job training. **Job Zone:** 3. **Education/Training Program(s)**—Electrical/Electronics Equipment Installation and Repair, General. **Related Knowledge/Courses:** Mechanical; Computers and Electronics; Design; Engineering and Technology; Public Safety and Security; Foreign Language. **Personality Type:** Realistic. **Skills Required:** Installation; Repairing; Science; Troubleshooting; Technology Design; Operation Monitoring; Quality Control Analysis; Equipment Maintenance. **Abilities:** Hearing Sensitivity; Visual Color Discrimination; Extent Flexibility; Finger Dexterity; Arm-Hand Steadiness. **Occupational Values:** Supervision, Technical; Independence; Variety; Moral Values; Advancement. **Interacting with Others:** Communicating with Supervisors, Peers, or Subordinates; Establishing and Maintaining Interpersonal Relationships; Performing Administrative Activities. **Physical Work Conditions:** Hazardous Equipment; Hazardous Conditions; Using Hands on Objects, Tools, or Controls; Minor Burns, Cuts, Bites, or Stings; Common Protective or Safety Equipment.

Electrical and Electronics Installers and Repairers, Transportation Equipment

Install, adjust, or maintain mobile electronics communication equipment, including sound, sonar, security, navigation, and surveillance systems on trains, watercraft, or other mobile equipment. **O*NET Code:** 49-2093.00. **Average Salary:** $39,870. **Projected Growth:** 7.1%. **Annual Openings:** 2,000. **Education:** Postsecondary vocational training. **Job Zone:** 3. **Education/Training Program(s)**—Automobile/Automotive Mechanics Technology/Technician. **Related Knowledge/Courses:** Mechanical; Computers and Electronics; Building and Construction; Engineering and Technology; Physics; Public Safety and Security; Telecommunications. **Personality Type:** Realistic. **Skills Required:** Repairing; Installation; Equipment Maintenance; Equipment Selection; Troubleshooting; Science; Quality Control Analysis. **Abilities:** Extent Flexibility; Manual Dexterity; Visual Color Discrimination; Finger Dexterity; Explosive Strength. **Occupational Values:** Variety; Advancement; Supervision, Human Relations; Supervision, Technical; Security; Moral Values. **Interacting with Others:** Communicating with Persons Outside Organization; Interpreting the Meaning of Information for Others; Communicating with Supervisors, Peers, or Subordinates. **Physical Work Conditions:** Hazardous Equipment; Hazardous Conditions; Kneeling, Crouching, Stooping, or Crawling; Using Hands on Objects, Tools, or Controls; Minor Burns, Cuts, Bites, or Stings.

Electrical and Electronics Repairers, Commercial and Industrial Equipment

Repair, test, adjust, or install electronic equipment, such as industrial controls, transmitters, and antennas. **O*NET Code:** 49-2094.00. **Average Salary:** $41,690. **Projected Growth:**

© 2006, JIST Works

10.3%. **Annual Openings:** 10,000. **Education:** Postsecondary vocational training. **Job Zone:** 3. **Education/Training Program(s)**—Computer Installation and Repair Technology/Technician; Industrial Electronics Technology/Technician. **Related Knowledge/Courses:** Computers and Electronics; Mechanical; Telecommunications; Design; Transportation; Engineering and Technology. **Personality Type:** Realistic. **Skills Required:** Installation; Troubleshooting; Repairing; Operation Monitoring; Equipment Maintenance; Operation and Control; Coordination; Systems Analysis. **Abilities:** Extent Flexibility; Visualization; Visual Color Discrimination; Auditory Attention; Perceptual Speed; Finger Dexterity. **Occupational Values:** Authority; Variety; Creativity; Compensation; Co-workers. **Interacting with Others:** Communicating with Supervisors, Peers, or Subordinates; Establishing and Maintaining Interpersonal Relationships; Communicating with Persons Outside Organization. **Physical Work Conditions:** Cramped Work Space, Awkward Positions; Sounds, Noise Levels Are Distracting or Uncomfortable; Hazardous Conditions; Physical Proximity; Contaminants.

Electrical Parts Reconditioners

Recondition and rebuild salvaged electrical parts of equipment and wind new coils on armatures of used generators and motors. **O*NET Code:** 49-2092.05. **Average Salary:** $32,820. **Projected Growth:** 5.3%. **Annual Openings:** 3,000. **Education:** Moderate-term on-the-job training. **Job Zone:** 2. **Education/Training Program(s)**—Electrical/Electronics Equipment Installation and Repair, General. **Related Knowledge/Courses:** Mechanical; Engineering and Technology. **Personality Type:** Realistic. **Skills Required:** Repairing; Installation; Equipment Maintenance; Quality Control Analysis; Technology Design; Troubleshooting; Equipment Selection. **Abilities:** Speed of Limb Movement; Finger Dexterity; Wrist-Finger Speed; Manual Dexterity; Explosive Strength; Dynamic Flexibility. **Occupational Values:** Moral Values; Independence; Supervision, Technical; Supervision, Human Relations; Responsibility. **Interacting with Others:** Communicating with Supervisors, Peers, or Subordinates; Interpreting the Meaning of Information for Others; Establishing and Maintaining Interpersonal Relationships. **Physical Work Conditions:** Common Protective or Safety Equipment; Minor Burns, Cuts, Bites, or Stings; Hazardous Equipment; Spend Time Making Repetitive Motions; Sitting.

Electronic Equipment Installers and Repairers, Motor Vehicles

Install, diagnose, or repair communications, sound, security, or navigation equipment in motor vehicles. **O*NET Code:** 49-2096.00. **Average Salary:** $26,040. **Projected Growth:** 14.8%. **Annual Openings:** 1,000. **Education:** Postsecondary vocational training. **Job Zone:** 3. **Education/Training Program(s)**—Automobile/Automotive Mechanics Technology/Technician. **Related Knowledge/Courses:** Mechanical; Computers and Electronics; Building and Construction; Engineering and Technology; Physics; Public Safety and Security; Telecommunications. **Personality Type:** Realistic. **Skills Required:** Repairing; Installation; Equipment Maintenance; Equipment Selection; Troubleshooting; Science; Quality Control Analysis. **Abilities:** Extent Flexibility;

Manual Dexterity; Visual Color Discrimination; Finger Dexterity; Explosive Strength. **Occupational Values:** Variety; Advancement; Supervision, Human Relations; Supervision, Technical; Security; Moral Values. **Interacting with Others:** Communicating with Persons Outside Organization; Interpreting the Meaning of Information for Others; Communicating with Supervisors, Peers, or Subordinates. **Physical Work Conditions:** Hazardous Equipment; Hazardous Conditions; Kneeling, Crouching, Stooping, or Crawling; Using Hands on Objects, Tools, or Controls; Minor Burns, Cuts, Bites, or Stings.

Electronic Home Entertainment Equipment Installers and Repairers

Repair, adjust, or install audio or television receivers, stereo systems, camcorders, video systems, or other electronic home entertainment equipment. **O*NET Code:** 49-2097.00. **Average Salary:** $27,800. **Projected Growth:** 8.6%. **Annual Openings:** 5,000. **Education:** Postsecondary vocational training. **Job Zone:** 3. **Education/Training Program(s)**—Communications Systems Installation and Repair Technology. **Related Knowledge/Courses:** Computers and Electronics; Telecommunications; Design; Mechanical; Engineering and Technology; Geography. **Personality Type:** Realistic. **Skills Required:** Installation; Science; Troubleshooting; Repairing; Equipment Maintenance; Technology Design; Quality Control Analysis; Management of Financial Resources. **Abilities:** Visual Color Discrimination; Finger Dexterity; Static Strength; Sound Localization; Visualization. **Occupational Values:** Variety; Independence; Supervision, Technical; Social Service; Security. **Interacting with Others:** Communicating with Persons Outside Organization; Establishing and Maintaining Interpersonal Relationships; Performing for or Working Directly with the Public. **Physical Work Conditions:** Spend Time Bending or Twisting the Body; Climbing Ladders, Scaffolds, or Poles; Keeping or Regaining Balance; Minor Burns, Cuts, Bites, or Stings; Kneeling, Crouching, Stooping, or Crawling.

Radio Mechanics

Test or repair mobile or stationary radio transmitting and receiving equipment and two-way radio communications systems used in ship-to-shore communications and found in service and emergency vehicles. **O*NET Code:** 49-2021.00. **Average Salary:** $36,490. **Projected Growth:** –29.3%. **Annual Openings:** 1,000. **Education:** Postsecondary vocational training. **Job Zone:** 3. **Education/Training Program(s)**—Communications Systems Installation and Repair Technology. **Related Knowledge/Courses:** Telecommunications; Computers and Electronics; Engineering and Technology; Physics; Mechanical; Design. **Personality Type:** Realistic. **Skills Required:** Installation; Repairing; Troubleshooting; Quality Control Analysis; Equipment Maintenance; Operation Monitoring; Technology Design; Systems Analysis; Systems Evaluation. **Abilities:** Finger Dexterity; Visual Color Discrimination; Speed of Closure; Hearing Sensitivity; Flexibility of Closure. **Occupational Values:** Independence; Variety; Moral Values; Supervision, Technical; Security. **Interacting with Others:** Communicating with Supervisors, Peers, or Subordinates;

Providing Consultation and Advice to Others; Communicating with Persons Outside Organization; Coaching and Developing Others. **Physical Work Conditions:** Minor Burns, Cuts, Bites, or Stings; Using Hands on Objects, Tools, or Controls; Sitting; Kneeling, Crouching, Stooping, or Crawling; Extremely Bright or Inadequate Lighting.

Transformer Repairers

Clean and repair electrical transformers. **O*NET Code:** 49-2092.04. **Average Salary:** $32,820. **Projected Growth:** 5.3%. **Annual Openings:** 3,000. **Education:** Long-term on-the-job training. **Job Zone:** 4. **Education/Training Program(s)—** Electrical/Electronics Equipment Installation and Repair, General. **Related Knowledge/Courses:** Mechanical; Engineering and Technology; Telecommunications; Computers and Electronics. **Personality Type:** Realistic. **Skills Required:** Repairing; Installation; Troubleshooting; Equipment Maintenance. **Abilities:** Manual Dexterity; Dynamic Strength; Dynamic Flexibility; Gross Body Equilibrium; Reaction Time. **Occupational Values:** Supervision, Technical; Moral Values; Security; Supervision, Human Relations; Activity; Company Policies and Practices. **Interacting with Others:** Communicating with Supervisors, Peers, or Subordinates; Establishing and Maintaining Interpersonal Relationships; Coordinating the Work and Activities of Others. **Physical Work Conditions:** Outdoors; Hazardous Conditions; Climbing Ladders, Scaffolds, or Poles; Common Protective or Safety Equipment; Hazardous Equipment.

13.13 Machinery Repair

Bicycle Repairers

Repair and service bicycles. **O*NET Code:** 49-3091.00. **Average Salary:** $19,800. **Projected Growth:** 18.8%. **Annual Openings:** 2,000. **Education:** Moderate-term on-the-job training. **Job Zone:** 2. **Education/Training Program(s)—**Bicycle Mechanics and Repair Technology/Technician. **Related Knowledge/Courses:** Mechanical; Sales and Marketing; Engineering and Technology; Physics; Transportation; Building and Construction. **Personality Type:** Realistic. **Skills Required:** Repairing; Installation; Technology Design; Troubleshooting; Equipment Maintenance. **Abilities:** Extent Flexibility; Finger Dexterity; Manual Dexterity; Static Strength; Visualization; Wrist-Finger Speed. **Occupational Values:** Social Service; Independence; Responsibility; Moral Values; Autonomy. **Interacting with Others:** Selling or Influencing Others; Performing for or Working Directly with the Public; Communicating with Persons Outside Organization; Establishing and Maintaining Interpersonal Relationships. **Physical Work Conditions:** Kneeling, Crouching, Stooping, or Crawling; Hazardous Equipment; Using Hands on Objects, Tools, or Controls; Standing; Minor Burns, Cuts, Bites, or Stings.

Gas Appliance Repairers

Repair and install gas appliances and equipment, such as ovens, dryers, and hot water heaters. **O*NET Code:** 49-

9031.02. **Average Salary:** $30,290. **Projected Growth:** 5.5%. **Annual Openings:** 5,000. **Education:** Long-term on-the-job training. **Job Zone:** 4. **Education/Training Program(s)—** Appliance Installation and Repair Technology/Technician; Home Furnishings and Equipment Installers. **Related Knowledge/Courses:** Mechanical; Physics; Building and Construction; Engineering and Technology; Chemistry; Economics and Accounting. **Personality Type:** Realistic. **Skills Required:** Repairing; Installation; Troubleshooting; Operation Monitoring; Equipment Maintenance; Operation and Control; Quality Control Analysis; Systems Evaluation. **Abilities:** Sound Localization; Extent Flexibility; Static Strength; Depth Perception; Visualization; Hearing Sensitivity. **Occupational Values:** Moral Values; Independence; Supervision, Technical; Responsibility; Compensation; Supervision, Human Relations. **Interacting with Others:** Communicating with Persons Outside Organization; Establishing and Maintaining Interpersonal Relationships; Performing for or Working Directly with the Public. **Physical Work Conditions:** Kneeling, Crouching, Stooping, or Crawling; Hazardous Conditions; Minor Burns, Cuts, Bites, or Stings; Using Hands on Objects, Tools, or Controls; Hazardous Equipment.

Hand and Portable Power Tool Repairers

Repair and adjust hand and power tools. **O*NET Code:** 49-2092.06. **Average Salary:** $32,820. **Projected Growth:** 5.3%. **Annual Openings:** 3,000. **Education:** Moderate-term on-the-job training. **Job Zone:** 2. **Education/Training Program(s)—** Electrical/Electronics Equipment Installation and Repair, General. **Related Knowledge/Courses:** Mechanical; Engineering and Technology; Design. **Personality Type:** Realistic. **Skills Required:** Repairing; Technology Design; Management of Material Resources; Equipment Maintenance; Operation and Control; Troubleshooting; Quality Control Analysis. **Abilities:** Manual Dexterity; Finger Dexterity; Visualization; Wrist-Finger Speed; Speed of Limb Movement. **Occupational Values:** Independence; Moral Values; Activity; Supervision, Technical; Responsibility. **Interacting with Others:** Monitoring and Controlling Resources; Performing Administrative Activities; Communicating with Supervisors, Peers, or Subordinates. **Physical Work Conditions:** Hazardous Equipment; Common Protective or Safety Equipment; Using Hands on Objects, Tools, or Controls; Minor Burns, Cuts, Bites, or Stings; Spend Time Making Repetitive Motions.

Industrial Machinery Mechanics

Repair, install, adjust, or maintain industrial production and processing machinery or refinery and pipeline distribution systems. **O*NET Code:** 49-9041.00. **Average Salary:** $38,740. **Projected Growth:** 5.5%. **Annual Openings:** 19,000. **Education:** Long-term on-the-job training. **Job Zone:** 3. **Education/Training Program(s)—**Heavy/Industrial Equipment Maintenance Technologies, Other; Industrial Mechanics and Maintenance Technology. **Related Knowledge/Courses:** Mechanical; Engineering and Technology; Computers and Electronics; Physics; Public Safety and Security; Design. **Personality Type:** Realistic. **Skills Required:** Equipment Maintenance; Repairing; Troubleshooting; Operation Monitoring; Quality Control Analysis; Installation; Technology Design; Operation and Control. **Abilities:**

© 2006, JIST Works

Hearing Sensitivity; Extent Flexibility; Auditory Attention; Visual Color Discrimination; Static Strength. **Occupational Values:** Independence; Variety; Moral Values; Activity; Advancement. **Interacting with Others:** Communicating with Supervisors, Peers, or Subordinates; Monitoring and Controlling Resources; Interpreting the Meaning of Information for Others. **Physical Work Conditions:** Hazardous Equipment; Common Protective or Safety Equipment; Sounds, Noise Levels Are Distracting or Uncomfortable; Minor Burns, Cuts, Bites, or Stings; Using Hands on Objects, Tools, or Controls; Spend Time Bending or Twisting the Body.

Locksmiths and Safe Repairers

Repair and open locks, make keys, change locks and safe combinations, and install and repair safes. **O*NET Code:** 49-9094.00. **Average Salary:** $29,350. **Projected Growth:** 21.0%. **Annual Openings:** 3,000. **Education:** Moderate-term on-the-job training. **Job Zone:** 3. **Education/Training Program(s)—** Locksmithing and Safe Repair. **Related Knowledge/Courses:** Mechanical; Engineering and Technology; Clerical; Building and Construction. **Personality Type:** Realistic. **Skills Required:** Installation; Repairing; Technology Design; Troubleshooting. **Abilities:** Finger Dexterity; Arm-Hand Steadiness; Manual Dexterity; Control Precision; Wrist-Finger Speed. **Occupational Values:** Independence; Responsibility; Supervision, Technical; Security; Moral Values. **Interacting with Others:** Communicating with Persons Outside Organization; Establishing and Maintaining Interpersonal Relationships; Performing Administrative Activities. **Physical Work Conditions:** Using Hands on Objects, Tools, or Controls; Minor Burns, Cuts, Bites, or Stings; Kneeling, Crouching, Stooping, or Crawling; Standing; Very Hot or Cold.

Maintenance Workers, Machinery

Lubricate machinery, change parts, or perform other routine machinery maintenance. **O*NET Code:** 49-9043.00. **Average Salary:** $32,720. **Projected Growth:** 5.9%. **Annual Openings:** 5,000. **Education:** Long-term on-the-job training. **Job Zone:** 1. **Education/Training Program(s)—** Heavy/Industrial Equipment Maintenance Technologies, Other; Industrial Mechanics and Maintenance Technology. **Related Knowledge/Courses:** Mechanical; Chemistry; Production and Processing; Engineering and Technology; Physics; Transportation. **Personality Type:** Realistic. **Skills Required:** Equipment Maintenance; Repairing; Installation; Operation Monitoring; Troubleshooting; Technology Design; Operation and Control; Quality Control Analysis. **Abilities:** Extent Flexibility; Static Strength; Reaction Time; Rate Control; Dynamic Strength. **Occupational Values:** Variety; Moral Values; Supervision, Human Relations; Co-workers; Supervision, Technical. **Interacting with Others:** Communicating with Supervisors, Peers, or Subordinates; Establishing and Maintaining Interpersonal Relationships; Assisting and Caring for Others. **Physical Work Conditions:** Hazardous Equipment; Common Protective or Safety Equipment; Spend Time Bending or Twisting the Body; Sounds, Noise Levels Are Distracting or Uncomfortable; Minor Burns, Cuts, Bites, or Stings; Kneeling, Crouching, Stooping, or Crawling.

Mechanical Door Repairers

Install, service, or repair opening and closing mechanisms of automatic doors and hydraulic door-closers. Includes garage door mechanics. **O*NET Code:** 49-9011.00. **Average Salary:** $29,340. **Projected Growth:** 21.8%. **Annual Openings:** 1,000. **Education:** Moderate-term on-the-job training. **Job Zone:** 3. **Education/Training Program(s)—**No data available. **Related Knowledge/Courses:** Mechanical; Engineering and Technology; Building and Construction; Physics; Design. **Personality Type:** Realistic. **Skills Required:** Installation; Repairing; Equipment Maintenance; Technology Design; Troubleshooting. **Abilities:** Visual Color Discrimination; Extent Flexibility; Speed of Limb Movement; Visualization; Arm-Hand Steadiness. **Occupational Values:** Independence; Moral Values; Supervision, Technical; Supervision, Human Relations; Responsibility. **Interacting with Others:** Communicating with Supervisors, Peers, or Subordinates; Communicating with Persons Outside Organization; Coordinating the Work and Activities of Others; Performing Administrative Activities. **Physical Work Conditions:** Hazardous Equipment; Standing; Kneeling, Crouching, Stooping, or Crawling; Spend Time Bending or Twisting the Body; Using Hands on Objects, Tools, or Controls.

Millwrights

Install, dismantle, or move machinery and heavy equipment according to layout plans, blueprints, or other drawings. **O*NET Code:** 49-9044.00. **Average Salary:** $43,180. **Projected Growth:** 5.3%. **Annual Openings:** 7,000. **Education:** Long-term on-the-job training. **Job Zone:** 3. **Education/Training Program(s)—**Heavy/Industrial Equipment Maintenance Technologies, Other; Industrial Mechanics and Maintenance Technology. **Related Knowledge/Courses:** Mechanical; Building and Construction; Engineering and Technology; Design; Physics; Public Safety and Security. **Personality Type:** Realistic. **Skills Required:** Installation; Repairing; Troubleshooting; Equipment Maintenance; Mathematics; Equipment Selection; Coordination; Technology Design. **Abilities:** Auditory Attention; Extent Flexibility; Static Strength; Rate Control; Multilimb Coordination. **Occupational Values:** Variety; Moral Values; Supervision, Human Relations; Compensation; Supervision, Technical. **Interacting with Others:** Establishing and Maintaining Interpersonal Relationships; Communicating with Supervisors, Peers, or Subordinates; Coordinating the Work and Activities of Others. **Physical Work Conditions:** Very Hot or Cold; Sounds, Noise Levels Are Distracting or Uncomfortable; Extremely Bright or Inadequate Lighting; Contaminants; Hazardous Conditions.

Signal and Track Switch Repairers

Install, inspect, test, maintain, or repair electric gate crossings, signals, signal equipment, track switches, section lines, or intercommunications systems within a railroad system. **O*NET Code:** 49-9097.00. **Average Salary:** $43,930. **Projected Growth:** –3.1%. **Annual Openings:** 1,000. **Education:** Postsecondary vocational training. **Job Zone:** 4. **Education/Training Program(s)—**Electrician. **Related Knowledge/Courses:** Transportation; Mechanical; Telecommunications; Engineering and Technology; Physics; Public Safety and Security. **Personality Type:** Realistic. **Skills**

Required: Installation; Equipment Maintenance; Repairing; Troubleshooting; Quality Control Analysis; Operation Monitoring; Science; Systems Evaluation. **Abilities:** Peripheral Vision; Sound Localization; Visual Color Discrimination; Finger Dexterity; Depth Perception. **Occupational Values:** Supervision, Technical; Moral Values; Supervision, Human Relations; Security; Variety. **Interacting with Others:** Communicating with Supervisors, Peers, or Subordinates; Establishing and Maintaining Interpersonal Relationships; Monitoring and Controlling Resources. **Physical Work Conditions:** Outdoors; Hazardous Conditions; Hazardous Equipment; Minor Burns, Cuts, Bites, or Stings; Standing; Common Protective or Safety Equipment.

Valve and Regulator Repairers

Test, repair, and adjust mechanical regulators and valves. **O*NET Code:** 49-9012.02. **Average Salary:** $43,280. **Projected Growth:** 12.0%. **Annual Openings:** 5,000. **Education:** Moderate-term on-the-job training. **Job Zone:** 3. **Education/Training Program(s)**—Electromechanical and Instrumentation and Maintenance Technologies/Technicians, Other. **Related Knowledge/Courses:** Mechanical; Physics; Mathematics; Engineering and Technology; Chemistry; Building and Construction. **Personality Type:** Realistic. **Skills Required:** Repairing; Equipment Maintenance; Installation; Quality Control Analysis; Troubleshooting; Mathematics; Writing; Science. **Abilities:** Manual Dexterity; Wrist-Finger Speed; Finger Dexterity; Extent Flexibility; Arm-Hand Steadiness. **Occupational Values:** Supervision, Technical; Independence; Moral Values; Security; Authority; Responsibility. **Interacting with Others:** Communicating with Persons Outside Organization; Providing Consultation and Advice to Others; Establishing and Maintaining Interpersonal Relationships. **Physical Work Conditions:** Hazardous Equipment; Hazardous Conditions; Standing; Spend Time Bending or Twisting the Body; Climbing Ladders, Scaffolds, or Poles; Using Hands on Objects, Tools, or Controls.

13.14 Vehicle and Facility Mechanical Work

Aircraft Body and Bonded Structure Repairers

Repair body or structure of aircraft according to specifications. **O*NET Code:** 49-3011.03. **Average Salary:** $43,980. **Projected Growth:** 11.0%. **Annual Openings:** 12,000. **Education:** Postsecondary vocational training. **Job Zone:** 3. **Education/Training Program(s)**—Agricultural Mechanics and Equipment/Machine Technology; Airframe Mechanics and Aircraft Maintenance Technology/Technician. **Related Knowledge/Courses:** Mechanical; Building and Construction; Design; Engineering and Technology; Production and Processing; Physics; Public Safety and Security. **Personality Type:** Realistic. **Skills Required:** Installation; Repairing; Equipment Maintenance; Equipment Selection; Mathematics; Operation Monitoring; Operation and Control; Troubleshooting. **Abilities:** Extent Flexibility; Wrist-Finger

Speed; Gross Body Equilibrium; Finger Dexterity; Manual Dexterity. **Occupational Values:** Compensation; Moral Values; Security; Variety; Supervision, Technical. **Interacting with Others:** Communicating with Supervisors, Peers, or Subordinates; Establishing and Maintaining Interpersonal Relationships; Coordinating the Work and Activities of Others. **Physical Work Conditions:** Hazardous Equipment; Climbing Ladders, Scaffolds, or Poles; Using Hands on Objects, Tools, or Controls; Minor Burns, Cuts, Bites, or Stings; Kneeling, Crouching, Stooping, or Crawling.

Aircraft Engine Specialists

Repair and maintain the operating condition of aircraft engines. Includes helicopter engine mechanics. **O*NET Code:** 49-3011.02. **Average Salary:** $43,980. **Projected Growth:** 11.0%. **Annual Openings:** 12,000. **Education:** Postsecondary vocational training. **Job Zone:** 4. **Education/Training Program(s)**—Agricultural Mechanics and Equipment/Machine Technology; Aircraft Powerplant Technology/Technician. **Related Knowledge/Courses:** Mechanical; Engineering and Technology; Physics; Building and Construction; Mathematics; Transportation; Computers and Electronics; Design. **Personality Type:** Realistic. **Skills Required:** Equipment Maintenance; Repairing; Installation; Troubleshooting; Operation Monitoring; Quality Control Analysis; Judgment and Decision Making; Equipment Selection; Systems Analysis; Systems Evaluation. **Abilities:** Hearing Sensitivity; Sound Localization; Extent Flexibility; Auditory Attention; Static Strength. **Occupational Values:** Compensation; Ability Utilization; Moral Values; Security; Company Policies and Practices. **Interacting with Others:** Communicating with Supervisors, Peers, or Subordinates; Interpreting the Meaning of Information for Others; Training and Teaching Others; Coaching and Developing Others; Providing Consultation and Advice to Others. **Physical Work Conditions:** Hazardous Equipment; Minor Burns, Cuts, Bites, or Stings; Hazardous Conditions; Using Hands on Objects, Tools, or Controls; Extremely Bright or Inadequate Lighting.

Aircraft Rigging Assemblers

Fabricate and assemble aircraft tubing or cable components or assemblies. **O*NET Code:** 51-2011.03. **Average Salary:** $35,260. **Projected Growth:** -9.4%. **Annual Openings:** 2,000. **Education:** Long-term on-the-job training. **Job Zone:** 3. **Education/Training Program(s)**—Aircraft Powerplant Technology/Technician; Airframe Mechanics and Aircraft Maintenance Technology/Technician; Avionics Maintenance Technology/Technician. **Related Knowledge/Courses:** Physics; Production and Processing; Engineering and Technology; Design; Mechanical; Building and Construction. **Personality Type:** Realistic. **Skills Required:** Installation; Repairing; Operation Monitoring; Operation and Control; Troubleshooting; Equipment Selection; Quality Control Analysis; Equipment Maintenance. **Abilities:** Manual Dexterity; Explosive Strength; Arm-Hand Steadiness; Static Strength; Dynamic Flexibility. **Occupational Values:** Moral Values; Independence; Advancement; Supervision, Technical; Supervision, Human Relations. **Interacting with Others:** Communicating with Supervisors, Peers, or Subordinates; Coordinating the Work and Activities of Others; Assisting and Caring for Others. **Physical Work Conditions:** Hazardous

 © 2006, JIST Works

Equipment; Using Hands on Objects, Tools, or Controls; Minor Burns, Cuts, Bites, or Stings; Outdoors; Standing.

Aircraft Structure Assemblers, Precision

Assemble tail, wing, fuselage, or other structural section of aircraft, space vehicles, and missiles from parts, subassemblies, and components and install functional units, parts, or equipment, such as landing gear, control surfaces, doors, and floorboards. **O*NET Code:** 51-2011.01. **Average Salary:** $35,260. **Projected Growth:** –9.4%. **Annual Openings:** 2,000. **Education:** Long-term on-the-job training. **Job Zone:** 3. **Education/Training Program(s)**—Aircraft Powerplant Technology/Technician; Airframe Mechanics and Aircraft Maintenance Technology/Technician; Avionics Maintenance Technology/Technician. **Related Knowledge/Courses:** Mechanical; Production and Processing; Engineering and Technology; Building and Construction; Design; Physics. **Personality Type:** Realistic. **Skills Required:** Installation; Troubleshooting; Quality Control Analysis; Repairing; Equipment Maintenance; Equipment Selection; Mathematics; Science. **Abilities:** Extent Flexibility; Visualization; Arm-Hand Steadiness; Manual Dexterity; Gross Body Equilibrium. **Occupational Values:** Moral Values; Independence; Advancement; Supervision, Human Relations; Supervision, Technical. **Interacting with Others:** Communicating with Supervisors, Peers, or Subordinates; Coordinating the Work and Activities of Others; Performing Administrative Activities. **Physical Work Conditions:** Hazardous Equipment; Standing; Spend Time Bending or Twisting the Body; Outdoors; Using Hands on Objects, Tools, or Controls.

Aircraft Systems Assemblers, Precision

Lay out, assemble, install, and test aircraft systems, such as armament, environmental control, plumbing and hydraulic. **O*NET Code:** 51-2011.02. **Average Salary:** $35,260. **Projected Growth:** –9.4%. **Annual Openings:** 2,000. **Education:** Long-term on-the-job training. **Job Zone:** 3. **Education/Training Program(s)**—Aircraft Powerplant Technology/Technician; Airframe Mechanics and Aircraft Maintenance Technology/Technician; Avionics Maintenance Technology/Technician. **Related Knowledge/Courses:** Mechanical; Design; Production and Processing; Building and Construction; Engineering and Technology; Physics. **Personality Type:** Realistic. **Skills Required:** Installation; Equipment Maintenance; Repairing; Troubleshooting; Quality Control Analysis; Technology Design; Operation Monitoring; Operation and Control. **Abilities:** Explosive Strength; Manual Dexterity; Dynamic Strength; Static Strength; Visualization; Extent Flexibility. **Occupational Values:** Moral Values; Independence; Advancement; Compensation; Supervision, Human Relations; Supervision, Technical. **Interacting with Others:** Communicating with Supervisors, Peers, or Subordinates; Coordinating the Work and Activities of Others; Performing Administrative Activities. **Physical Work Conditions:** Hazardous Equipment; Kneeling, Crouching, Stooping, or Crawling; Sounds, Noise Levels Are Distracting or Uncomfortable; Using Hands on Objects, Tools, or Controls; Standing; Spend Time Bending or Twisting the Body.

Airframe-and-Power-Plant Mechanics

Inspect, test, repair, maintain, and service aircraft. **O*NET Code:** 49-3011.01. **Average Salary:** $43,980. **Projected Growth:** 11.0%. **Annual Openings:** 12,000. **Education:** Postsecondary vocational training. **Job Zone:** 4. **Education/Training Program(s)**—Agricultural Mechanics and Equipment/Machine Technology; Aircraft Powerplant Technology/Technician; Airframe Mechanics and Aircraft Maintenance Technology/Technician. **Related Knowledge/Courses:** Mechanical; Engineering and Technology; Building and Construction; Design; Physics; Public Safety and Security. **Personality Type:** Realistic. **Skills Required:** Equipment Maintenance; Installation; Repairing; Troubleshooting; Operation Monitoring; Quality Control Analysis; Science; Equipment Selection. **Abilities:** Manual Dexterity; Hearing Sensitivity; Visual Color Discrimination; Control Precision; Explosive Strength. **Occupational Values:** Compensation; Moral Values; Security; Variety; Advancement. **Interacting with Others:** Communicating with Supervisors, Peers, or Subordinates; Coordinating the Work and Activities of Others; Performing Administrative Activities. **Physical Work Conditions:** Hazardous Equipment; Kneeling, Crouching, Stooping, or Crawling; Common Protective or Safety Equipment; Very Hot or Cold; Spend Time Bending or Twisting the Body.

Automotive Body and Related Repairers

Repair and refinish automotive vehicle bodies and straighten vehicle frames. **O*NET Code:** 49-3021.00. **Average Salary:** $33,360. **Projected Growth:** 13.2%. **Annual Openings:** 23,000. **Education:** Long-term on-the-job training. **Job Zone:** 2. **Education/Training Program(s)**—Autobody/Collision and Repair Technology/Technician. **Related Knowledge/Courses:** Mechanical; Building and Construction; Customer and Personal Service; Administration and Management; Chemistry; Transportation. **Personality Type:** Realistic. **Skills Required:** Repairing; Installation; Equipment Maintenance; Troubleshooting; Equipment Selection; Learning Strategies; Negotiation; Management of Financial Resources. **Abilities:** Extent Flexibility; Hearing Sensitivity; Depth Perception; Static Strength; Reaction Time. **Occupational Values:** Variety; Compensation; Moral Values; Independence; Ability Utilization; Achievement. **Interacting with Others:** Establishing and Maintaining Interpersonal Relationships; Communicating with Persons Outside Organization; Communicating with Supervisors, Peers, or Subordinates. **Physical Work Conditions:** Contaminants; Sounds, Noise Levels Are Distracting or Uncomfortable; Hazardous Conditions; Minor Burns, Cuts, Bites, or Stings; Hazardous Equipment.

Automotive Glass Installers and Repairers

Replace or repair broken windshields and window glass in motor vehicles. **O*NET Code:** 49-3022.00. **Average Salary:** $27,210. **Projected Growth:** 10.7%. **Annual Openings:** 3,000. **Education:** Long-term on-the-job training. **Job Zone:** 2. **Education/Training Program(s)**—Autobody/Collision and Repair Technology/Technician. **Related Knowledge/Courses:** Mechanical; Engineering and Technology. **Personality Type:** Realistic. **Skills Required:** Installation; Repairing; Technology Design. **Abilities:** Static Strength; Extent Flexibility; Stamina;

Arm-Hand Steadiness; Gross Body Coordination. **Occupational Values:** Independence; Moral Values; Security; Compensation; Responsibility. **Interacting with Others:** Communicating with Supervisors, Peers, or Subordinates; Communicating with Persons Outside Organization; Establishing and Maintaining Interpersonal Relationships; Performing for or Working Directly with the Public. **Physical Work Conditions:** Common Protective or Safety Equipment; Minor Burns, Cuts, Bites, or Stings; Standing; Using Hands on Objects, Tools, or Controls; Outdoors.

Automotive Master Mechanics

Repair automobiles, trucks, buses, and other vehicles. Master mechanics repair virtually any part on the vehicle or specialize in the transmission system. **O*NET Code:** 49-3023.01. **Average Salary:** $31,570. **Projected Growth:** 12.4%. **Annual Openings:** 100,000. **Education:** Postsecondary vocational training. **Job Zone:** 3. **Education/Training Program(s)—** Alternative Fuel Vehicle Technology/Technician; Automobile/Automotive Mechanics Technology/Technician; Automotive Engineering Technology/Technician; Medium/Heavy Vehicle and Truck Technology/Technician; Vehicle Emissions Inspection and Maintenance Technology/Technician. **Related Knowledge/Courses:** Mechanical; Computers and Electronics; Physics; Engineering and Technology; Education and Training; Customer and Personal Service. **Personality Type:** Realistic. **Skills Required:** Troubleshooting; Repairing; Installation; Equipment Maintenance; Active Learning; Complex Problem Solving; Instructing; Equipment Selection. **Abilities:** Extent Flexibility; Hearing Sensitivity; Reaction Time; Finger Dexterity; Visual Color Discrimination; Auditory Attention. **Occupational Values:** Compensation; Ability Utilization; Independence; Variety; Responsibility. **Interacting with Others:** Communicating with Supervisors, Peers, or Subordinates; Interpreting the Meaning of Information for Others; Establishing and Maintaining Interpersonal Relationships. **Physical Work Conditions:** Contaminants; In an Enclosed Vehicle or Equipment; Sounds, Noise Levels Are Distracting or Uncomfortable; Cramped Work Space, Awkward Positions; Minor Burns, Cuts, Bites, or Stings.

Automotive Specialty Technicians

Repair only one system or component on a vehicle, such as brakes, suspension, or radiator. **O*NET Code:** 49-3023.02. **Average Salary:** $31,570. **Projected Growth:** 12.4%. **Annual Openings:** 100,000. **Education:** Postsecondary vocational training. **Job Zone:** 2. **Education/Training Program(s)—** Alternative Fuel Vehicle Technology/Technician; Automobile/Automotive Mechanics Technology/Technician; Automotive Engineering Technology/Technician; Medium/Heavy Vehicle and Truck Technology/Technician; Vehicle Emissions Inspection and Maintenance Technology/Technician. **Related Knowledge/Courses:** Mechanical; Computers and Electronics; Design; Physics; Engineering and Technology; Chemistry. **Personality Type:** Realistic. **Skills Required:** Installation; Repairing; Troubleshooting; Equipment Maintenance; Quality Control Analysis; Technology Design; Operation Monitoring; Management of Material Resources. **Abilities:** Extent Flexibility; Hearing Sensitivity; Explosive Strength; Static Strength; Trunk Strength. **Occupational**

Values: Responsibility; Independence; Ability Utilization; Achievement; Compensation; Autonomy. **Interacting with Others:** Communicating with Persons Outside Organization; Establishing and Maintaining Interpersonal Relationships; Communicating with Supervisors, Peers, or Subordinates; Monitoring and Controlling Resources. **Physical Work Conditions:** Common Protective or Safety Equipment; Contaminants; Standing; Kneeling, Crouching, Stooping, or Crawling; Hazardous Equipment; Minor Burns, Cuts, Bites, or Stings.

Bus and Truck Mechanics and Diesel Engine Specialists

Diagnose, adjust, repair, or overhaul trucks, buses, and all types of diesel engines. Includes mechanics working primarily with automobile diesel engines. **O*NET Code:** 49-3031.00. **Average Salary:** $35,160. **Projected Growth:** 14.2%. **Annual Openings:** 28,000. **Education:** Postsecondary vocational training. **Job Zone:** 3. **Education/Training Program(s)—** Diesel Mechanics Technology/Technician; Medium/Heavy Vehicle and Truck Technology/Technician. **Related Knowledge/Courses:** Mechanical; Transportation; Public Safety and Security; Engineering and Technology; Law and Government; Physics; Chemistry. **Personality Type:** Realistic. **Skills Required:** Equipment Maintenance; Repairing; Troubleshooting; Installation; Learning Strategies; Coordination; Instructing; Technology Design. **Abilities:** Hearing Sensitivity; Extent Flexibility; Visualization; Static Strength; Auditory Attention. **Occupational Values:** Variety; Compensation; Responsibility; Independence; Achievement. **Interacting with Others:** Establishing and Maintaining Interpersonal Relationships; Communicating with Supervisors, Peers, or Subordinates; Interpreting the Meaning of Information for Others. **Physical Work Conditions:** Extremely Bright or Inadequate Lighting; Contaminants; Sounds, Noise Levels Are Distracting or Uncomfortable; Very Hot or Cold; In an Open Vehicle or Equipment.

Farm Equipment Mechanics

Diagnose, adjust, repair, or overhaul farm machinery and vehicles, such as tractors, harvesters, dairy equipment, and irrigation systems. **O*NET Code:** 49-3041.00. **Average Salary:** $27,660. **Projected Growth:** 7.7%. **Annual Openings:** 3,000. **Education:** Postsecondary vocational training. **Job Zone:** 3. **Education/Training Program(s)—** Agricultural Mechanics and Equipment/Machine Technology; Agricultural Mechanization, General; Agricultural Mechanization, Other; Agricultural Power Machinery Operation. **Related Knowledge/Courses:** Mechanical; Engineering and Technology; Physics; Transportation; Computers and Electronics; Chemistry. **Personality Type:** Realistic. **Skills Required:** Installation; Repairing; Technology Design; Equipment Maintenance; Troubleshooting; Operation Monitoring; Quality Control Analysis; Operation and Control. **Abilities:** Extent Flexibility; Hearing Sensitivity; Visual Color Discrimination; Control Precision; Sound Localization. **Occupational Values:** Moral Values; Variety; Responsibility; Independence; Ability Utilization; Achievement. **Interacting with Others:** Communicating with Supervisors, Peers, or Subordinates; Assisting and Caring for Others; Performing for or Working Directly with the Public;

© 2006, JIST Works

Providing Consultation and Advice to Others. **Physical Work Conditions:** Hazardous Equipment; Outdoors; Minor Burns, Cuts, Bites, or Stings; Spend Time Bending or Twisting the Body; Using Hands on Objects, Tools, or Controls.

Fiberglass Laminators and Fabricators

Laminate layers of fiberglass on molds to form boat decks and hulls, bodies for golf carts, automobiles, or other products. **O*NET Code:** 51-2091.00. **Average Salary:** $24,840. **Projected Growth:** 5.6%. **Annual Openings:** 5,000. **Education:** Moderate-term on-the-job training. **Job Zone:** No data available. **Education/Training Program(s)**—Marine Maintenance/Fitter and Ship Repair Technology/Technician. **Related Knowledge/Courses:** No data available. **Personality Type:** No data available. **Skills Required:** No data available. **Abilities:** No data available. **Occupational Values:** No data available. **Interacting with Others:** No data available. **Physical Work Conditions:** No data available.

Mobile Heavy Equipment Mechanics, Except Engines

Diagnose, adjust, repair, or overhaul mobile mechanical, hydraulic, and pneumatic equipment, such as cranes, bulldozers, graders, and conveyors, used in construction, logging, and surface mining. **O*NET Code:** 49-3042.00. **Average Salary:** $37,170. **Projected Growth:** 9.6%. **Annual Openings:** 12,000. **Education:** Postsecondary vocational training. **Job Zone:** 4. **Education/Training Program(s)**—Agricultural Mechanics and Equipment/Machine Technology; Heavy Equipment Maintenance Technology/Technician. **Related Knowledge/Courses:** Mechanical; Engineering and Technology; Physics; Customer and Personal Service; Transportation; Chemistry. **Personality Type:** Realistic. **Skills Required:** Installation; Equipment Maintenance; Repairing; Troubleshooting; Operation Monitoring; Equipment Selection; Operation and Control; Persuasion. **Abilities:** Auditory Attention; Multilimb Coordination; Hearing Sensitivity; Extent Flexibility; Depth Perception. **Occupational Values:** Compensation; Moral Values; Authority; Variety; Co-workers; Responsibility. **Interacting with Others:** Communicating with Supervisors, Peers, or Subordinates; Guiding, Directing, and Motivating Subordinates; Resolving Conflicts and Negotiating with Others. **Physical Work Conditions:** Sounds, Noise Levels Are Distracting or Uncomfortable; Contaminants; Very Hot or Cold; In an Open Vehicle or Equipment; Hazardous Equipment.

Motorboat Mechanics

Repairs and adjusts electrical and mechanical equipment of gasoline- or diesel-powered inboard or inboard-outboard boat engines. **O*NET Code:** 49-3051.00. **Average Salary:** $29,740. **Projected Growth:** 18.3%. **Annual Openings:** 2,000. **Education:** Long-term on-the-job training. **Job Zone:** 3. **Education/Training Program(s)**—Marine Maintenance/Fitter and Ship Repair Technology/Technician; Small Engine Mechanics and Repair Technology/Technician. **Related Knowledge/Courses:** Mechanical; Engineering and Technology; Physics. **Personality Type:** Realistic. **Skills Required:** Repairing; Troubleshooting; Quality Control Analysis; Equipment Maintenance; Installation; Operation

Monitoring; Operation and Control; Equipment Selection. **Abilities:** Hearing Sensitivity; Static Strength; Control Precision; Sound Localization; Extent Flexibility. **Occupational Values:** Variety; Moral Values; Security; Compensation; Company Policies and Practices. **Interacting with Others:** Communicating with Supervisors, Peers, or Subordinates; Performing Administrative Activities; Communicating with Persons Outside Organization. **Physical Work Conditions:** Outdoors; Kneeling, Crouching, Stooping, or Crawling; Using Hands on Objects, Tools, or Controls; Very Hot or Cold; Spend Time Bending or Twisting the Body.

Motorcycle Mechanics

Diagnose, adjust, repair, or overhaul motorcycles, scooters, mopeds, dirt bikes, or similar motorized vehicles. **O*NET Code:** 49-3052.00. **Average Salary:** $27,850. **Projected Growth:** 18.7%. **Annual Openings:** 1,000. **Education:** Long-term on-the-job training. **Job Zone:** 2. **Education/Training Program(s)**—Motorcycle Maintenance and Repair Technology/Technician. **Related Knowledge/Courses:** Mechanical; Engineering and Technology; Physics. **Personality Type:** Realistic. **Skills Required:** Repairing; Troubleshooting; Equipment Maintenance; Technology Design; Installation; Operation Monitoring; Quality Control Analysis; Operation and Control. **Abilities:** Static Strength; Hearing Sensitivity; Control Precision; Finger Dexterity; Manual Dexterity. **Occupational Values:** Variety; Compensation; Responsibility; Independence; Achievement. **Interacting with Others:** Communicating with Persons Outside Organization; Providing Consultation and Advice to Others; Interpreting the Meaning of Information for Others; Communicating with Supervisors, Peers, or Subordinates. **Physical Work Conditions:** Kneeling, Crouching, Stooping, or Crawling; Contaminants; Minor Burns, Cuts, Bites, or Stings; Using Hands on Objects, Tools, or Controls; Cramped Work Space, Awkward Positions.

Outdoor Power Equipment and Other Small Engine Mechanics

Diagnose, adjust, repair, or overhaul small engines used to power lawn mowers, chain saws, and related equipment. **O*NET Code:** 49-3053.00. **Average Salary:** $24,730. **Projected Growth:** 18.9%. **Annual Openings:** 3,000. **Education:** Moderate-term on-the-job training. **Job Zone:** 3. **Education/Training Program(s)**—Small Engine Mechanics and Repair Technology/Technician. **Related Knowledge/Courses:** Mechanical; Engineering and Technology. **Personality Type:** Realistic. **Skills Required:** Repairing; Equipment Maintenance; Troubleshooting; Installation; Quality Control Analysis; Operation Monitoring; Operation and Control; Systems Evaluation. **Abilities:** Extent Flexibility; Static Strength; Explosive Strength; Sound Localization; Finger Dexterity. **Occupational Values:** Moral Values; Company Policies and Practices; Variety; Compensation; Security. **Interacting with Others:** Communicating with Persons Outside Organization; Interpreting the Meaning of Information for Others; Communicating with Supervisors, Peers, or Subordinates; Providing Consultation and Advice to Others. **Physical Work Conditions:** Hazardous Equipment; Kneeling, Crouching, Stooping, or Crawling; Contaminants; Minor Burns, Cuts, Bites, or Stings; Very Hot or Cold.

Rail Car Repairers

Diagnose, adjust, repair, or overhaul railroad rolling stock, mine cars, or mass-transit rail cars. **O*NET Code:** 49-3043.00. **Average Salary:** $40,400. **Projected Growth:** 4.5%. **Annual Openings:** 1,000. **Education:** Long-term on-the-job training. **Job Zone:** 3. **Education/Training Program(s)**—Heavy Equipment Maintenance Technology/Technician. **Related Knowledge/Courses:** Mechanical; Building and Construction; Engineering and Technology; Design; Transportation; Physics. **Personality Type:** Realistic. **Skills Required:** Repairing; Installation; Equipment Maintenance; Troubleshooting; Quality Control Analysis; Equipment Selection; Operation Monitoring. **Abilities:** Extent Flexibility; Depth Perception; Static Strength; Explosive Strength; Multilimb Coordination. **Occupational Values:** Variety; Moral Values; Independence; Compensation; Responsibility. **Interacting with Others:** Communicating with Supervisors, Peers, or Subordinates; Establishing and Maintaining Interpersonal Relationships; Assisting and Caring for Others. **Physical Work Conditions:** Hazardous Equipment; Minor Burns, Cuts, Bites, or Stings; Outdoors; Kneeling, Crouching, Stooping, or Crawling; Sounds, Noise Levels Are Distracting or Uncomfortable.

Recreational Vehicle Service Technicians

Diagnose, inspect, adjust, repair, or overhaul recreational vehicles, including travel trailers. May specialize in maintaining gas, electrical, hydraulic, plumbing, or chassis/towing systems as well as repairing generators, appliances, and interior components. **O*NET Code:** 49-3092.00. **Average Salary:** $28,350. **Projected Growth:** 21.8%. **Annual Openings:** 4,000. **Education:** Long-term on-the-job training. **Job Zone:** 2. **Education/Training Program(s)**—Vehicle Maintenance and Repair Technologies, Other.. **Related Knowledge/Courses:** Building and Construction; Mechanical; Design; Engineering and Technology; Physics. **Personality Type:** Realistic. **Skills Required:** Installation; Repairing; Troubleshooting; Equipment Maintenance; Quality Control Analysis; Equipment Selection; Systems Evaluation; Technology Design; Management of Material Resources. **Abilities:** Extent Flexibility; Control Precision; Static Strength; Trunk Strength; Visualization. **Occupational Values:** Variety; Supervision, Technical; Moral Values; Supervision, Human Relations. **Interacting with Others:** Establishing and Maintaining Interpersonal Relationships; Communicating with Supervisors, Peers, or Subordinates; Communicating with Persons Outside Organization. **Physical Work Conditions:** Standing; Hazardous Conditions; Outdoors; Kneeling, Crouching, Stooping, or Crawling; Climbing Ladders, Scaffolds, or Poles.

Tire Repairers and Changers

Repair and replace tires. **O*NET Code:** 49-3093.00. **Average Salary:** $20,810. **Projected Growth:** 8.0%. **Annual Openings:** 22,000. **Education:** Short-term on-the-job training. **Job Zone:** 1. **Education/Training Program(s)**—No data available. **Related Knowledge/Courses:** Mechanical; Administration and Management. **Personality Type:** Realistic. **Skills Required:** Repairing; Installation; Equipment Maintenance; Operation and Control. **Abilities:** Static Strength; Control Precision; Response Orientation; Wrist-Finger Speed;

Explosive Strength. **Occupational Values:** Moral Values; Independence; Supervision, Technical; Security; Social Service. **Interacting with Others:** Performing for or Working Directly with the Public; Communicating with Persons Outside Organization; Assisting and Caring for Others. **Physical Work Conditions:** Standing; Kneeling, Crouching, Stooping, or Crawling; Using Hands on Objects, Tools, or Controls; Outdoors; Hazardous Equipment.

13.15 Medical and Technical Equipment Repair

Camera and Photographic Equipment Repairers

Repair and adjust cameras and photographic equipment, including commercial video and motion picture camera equipment. **O*NET Code:** 49-9061.00. **Average Salary:** $30,810. **Projected Growth:** –7.1%. **Annual Openings:** 1,000. **Education:** Moderate-term on-the-job training. **Job Zone:** 4. **Education/Training Program(s)**—Communications Systems Installation and Repair Technology. **Related Knowledge/Courses:** Mechanical; Engineering and Technology; Design; Fine Arts; Physics; Computers and Electronics. **Personality Type:** Realistic. **Skills Required:** Repairing; Troubleshooting; Installation; Technology Design; Quality Control Analysis; Operation Monitoring; Speaking; Reading Comprehension; Active Learning; Equipment Maintenance. **Abilities:** Finger Dexterity; Visual Color Discrimination; Control Precision; Night Vision; Depth Perception. **Occupational Values:** Working Conditions; Autonomy; Ability Utilization; Independence; Variety. **Interacting with Others:** Communicating with Persons Outside Organization; Establishing and Maintaining Interpersonal Relationships; Providing Consultation and Advice to Others. **Physical Work Conditions:** Minor Burns, Cuts, Bites, or Stings; Using Hands on Objects, Tools, or Controls; Extremely Bright or Inadequate Lighting; Sitting; Hazardous Conditions; Hazardous Equipment.

Medical Equipment Repairers

Test, adjust, or repair biomedical or electromedical equipment. **O*NET Code:** 49-9062.00. **Average Salary:** $38,250. **Projected Growth:** 14.8%. **Annual Openings:** 4,000. **Education:** Moderate-term on-the-job training. **Job Zone:** 3. **Education/Training Program(s)**—Biomedical Technology/Technician. **Related Knowledge/Courses:** Computers and Electronics; Mechanical; Customer and Personal Service; Engineering and Technology; Physics; Clerical; Public Safety and Security. **Personality Type:** Realistic. **Skills Required:** Repairing; Installation; Equipment Maintenance; Troubleshooting; Instructing; Service Orientation; Operation Monitoring; Quality Control Analysis; Systems Analysis. **Abilities:** Hearing Sensitivity; Finger Dexterity; Visual Color Discrimination; Visualization; Control Precision. **Occupational Values:** Compensation; Moral Values; Variety; Supervision, Technical; Security; Authority; Co-workers.

Interacting with Others: Establishing and Maintaining Interpersonal Relationships; Communicating with Supervisors, Peers, or Subordinates; Communicating with Persons Outside Organization. **Physical Work Conditions:** Contaminants; Physical Proximity; Extremely Bright or Inadequate Lighting; Cramped Work Space, Awkward Positions; Hazardous Conditions.

Watch Repairers

Repair, clean, and adjust mechanisms of timing instruments, such as watches and clocks. **O*NET Code:** 49-9064.00. **Average Salary:** $28,210. **Projected Growth:** 3.5%. **Annual Openings:** 1,000. **Education:** Long-term on-the-job training. **Job Zone:** 3. **Education/Training Program(s)**—Watchmaking and Jewelrymaking. **Related Knowledge/Courses:** Mechanical; Personnel and Human Resources. **Personality Type:** Realistic. **Skills Required:** Repairing; Troubleshooting; Equipment Maintenance; Quality Control Analysis; Installation; Equipment Selection. **Abilities:** Finger Dexterity; Arm-Hand Steadiness; Near Vision; Manual Dexterity; Control Precision. **Occupational Values:** Independence; Working Conditions; Moral Values; Ability Utilization; Compensation; Autonomy. **Interacting with Others:** Communicating with Persons Outside Organization; Performing for or Working Directly with the Public; Establishing and Maintaining Interpersonal Relationships; Performing Administrative Activities. **Physical Work Conditions:** Sitting; Using Hands on Objects, Tools, or Controls; Indoors; Spend Time Making Repetitive Motions; Minor Burns, Cuts, Bites, or Stings.

13.16 Utility Operation and Energy Distribution

Auxiliary Equipment Operators, Power

Control and maintain auxiliary equipment, such as pumps, fans, compressors, condensers, feedwater heaters, filters, and chlorinators, that supply water, fuel, lubricants, air, and auxiliary power for turbines, generators, boilers, and other power-generating plant facilities. **O*NET Code:** 51-8013.02. **Average Salary:** $51,540. **Projected Growth:** 0.3%. **Annual Openings:** 3,000. **Education:** Long-term on-the-job training. **Job Zone:** 2. **Education/Training Program(s)**—No data available. **Related Knowledge/Courses:** Mechanical; Physics; Engineering and Technology; Chemistry. **Personality Type:** Realistic. **Skills Required:** Operation Monitoring; Operation and Control; Equipment Maintenance; Troubleshooting; Repairing. **Abilities:** Control Precision; Sound Localization; Extent Flexibility; Reaction Time; Gross Body Coordination. **Occupational Values:** Supervision, Technical; Supervision, Human Relations; Moral Values; Security; Advancement. **Interacting with Others:** Communicating with Supervisors, Peers, or Subordinates; Performing Administrative Activities; Communicating with Persons Outside Organization; Establishing and Maintaining Interpersonal Relationships. **Physical Work Conditions:** Hazardous Equipment;

Hazardous Conditions; Kneeling, Crouching, Stooping, or Crawling; Minor Burns, Cuts, Bites, or Stings; Standing.

Boiler Operators and Tenders, Low Pressure

Operate or tend low-pressure stationary steam boilers and auxiliary steam equipment, such as pumps, compressors and air-conditioning equipment, to supply steam heat for office buildings, apartment houses, or industrial establishments; to maintain steam at specified pressure aboard marine vessels; or to generate and supply compressed air for operation of pneumatic tools, hoists, and air lances. **O*NET Code:** 51-8021.01. **Average Salary:** $43,880. **Projected Growth:** 0.3%. **Annual Openings:** 4,000. **Education:** Moderate-term on-the-job training. **Job Zone:** 2. **Education/Training Program(s)**—No data available. **Related Knowledge/Courses:** Mechanical; Physics; Production and Processing; Engineering and Technology. **Personality Type:** Realistic. **Skills Required:** Installation; Equipment Maintenance; Operation Monitoring; Operation and Control; Repairing; Troubleshooting; Quality Control Analysis; Equipment Selection. **Abilities:** Explosive Strength; Dynamic Strength; Trunk Strength; Control Precision; Extent Flexibility. **Occupational Values:** Moral Values; Independence; Supervision, Technical; Company Policies and Practices. **Interacting with Others:** Communicating with Supervisors, Peers, or Subordinates; Performing Administrative Activities; Coordinating the Work and Activities of Others. **Physical Work Conditions:** Very Hot or Cold; Hazardous Equipment; Minor Burns, Cuts, Bites, or Stings; Standing; Spend Time Bending or Twisting the Body.

Chemical Plant and System Operators

Control or operate an entire chemical process or system of machines. **O*NET Code:** 51-8091.00. **Average Salary:** $44,280. **Projected Growth:** –12.3%. **Annual Openings:** 4,000. **Education:** Long-term on-the-job training. **Job Zone:** 2. **Education/Training Program(s)**—Chemical Technology/Technician. **Related Knowledge/Courses:** Production and Processing; Chemistry; Mechanical; Public Safety and Security; Engineering and Technology; Mathematics. **Personality Type:** Realistic. **Skills Required:** Operation Monitoring; Operation and Control; Science; Troubleshooting; Quality Control Analysis; Mathematics; Systems Analysis; Equipment Maintenance. **Abilities:** Reaction Time; Control Precision; Information Ordering; Response Orientation; Oral Comprehension; Written Comprehension. **Occupational Values:** Compensation; Supervision, Technical; Security; Advancement; Supervision, Human Relations. **Interacting with Others:** Communicating with Supervisors, Peers, or Subordinates; Establishing and Maintaining Interpersonal Relationships; Performing Administrative Activities. **Physical Work Conditions:** Hazardous Conditions; Standing; Common Protective or Safety Equipment; Sitting; Walking and Running.

Gas Compressor Operators

Operate steam or internal combustion engines to transmit, compress, or recover gases, such as butane, nitrogen, hydrogen, and natural gas, in various production processes. **O*NET Code:** 53-7071.02. **Average Salary:** $43,830. **Projected Growth:** 1.0%. **Annual Openings:** 1,000. **Education:** Moderate-term on-the-job training. **Job Zone:** 4.

Education/Training Program(s)—No data available. **Related Knowledge/Courses:** Chemistry; Mechanical; Physics; Production and Processing; Engineering and Technology; Clerical. **Personality Type:** Realistic. **Skills Required:** Repairing; Operation Monitoring; Operation and Control; Troubleshooting; Quality Control Analysis. **Abilities:** Control Precision; Extent Flexibility. **Occupational Values:** Independence; Supervision, Human Relations; Supervision, Technical; Moral Values; Security. **Interacting with Others:** Communicating with Supervisors, Peers, or Subordinates; Establishing and Maintaining Interpersonal Relationships; Performing Administrative Activities. **Physical Work Conditions:** Contaminants; Hazardous Conditions; Common Protective or Safety Equipment; Climbing Ladders, Scaffolds, or Poles; Kneeling, Crouching, Stooping, or Crawling.

Gas Distribution Plant Operators

Control equipment to regulate flow and pressure of gas for utility companies and industrial use. May control distribution of gas for a municipal or industrial plant or a single process in an industrial plant. **O*NET Code:** 51-8092.02. **Average Salary:** $49,630. **Projected Growth:** 6.7%. **Annual Openings:** 1,000. **Education:** Long-term on-the-job training. **Job Zone:** 3. **Education/Training Program(s)**—No data available. **Related Knowledge/Courses:** Mechanical; Physics; Engineering and Technology; Production and Processing; Clerical. **Personality Type:** Realistic. **Skills Required:** Operation and Control; Operation Monitoring; Equipment Maintenance; Troubleshooting; Operations Analysis; Repairing; Installation; Systems Evaluation. **Abilities:** Control Precision; Extent Flexibility; Inductive Reasoning. **Occupational Values:** Security; Advancement; Supervision, Human Relations; Supervision, Technical; Company Policies and Practices. **Interacting with Others:** Communicating with Supervisors, Peers, or Subordinates; Performing Administrative Activities; Interpreting the Meaning of Information for Others; Establishing and Maintaining Interpersonal Relationships. **Physical Work Conditions:** Hazardous Conditions; Contaminants; Common Protective or Safety Equipment; Walking and Running; Standing.

Gas Processing Plant Operators

Control equipment, such as compressors, evaporators, heat exchangers, and refrigeration equipment, to process gas for utility companies and for industrial use. **O*NET Code:** 51-8092.01. **Average Salary:** $49,630. **Projected Growth:** 6.7%. **Annual Openings:** 1,000. **Education:** Long-term on-the-job training. **Job Zone:** 2. **Education/Training Program(s)**—No data available. **Related Knowledge/Courses:** Mechanical; Chemistry; Engineering and Technology; Production and Processing; Physics; Mathematics. **Personality Type:** Realistic. **Skills Required:** Operation Monitoring; Repairing; Operation and Control; Equipment Maintenance; Mathematics; Science; Troubleshooting; Quality Control Analysis. **Abilities:** Control Precision; Gross Body Coordination; Mathematical Reasoning. **Occupational Values:** Security; Supervision, Human Relations; Advancement; Supervision, Technical; Company Policies and Practices. **Interacting with Others:** Communicating with Supervisors, Peers, or Subordinates; Establishing and Maintaining Interpersonal Relationships; Coordinating the Work and Activities of Others; Performing

Administrative Activities. **Physical Work Conditions:** Specialized Protective or Safety Equipment; Hazardous Conditions; Common Protective or Safety Equipment; Contaminants; Standing.

Gas Pumping Station Operators

Control the operation of steam, gas, or electric-motor-driven compressor to maintain specified pressures on high- and low-pressure mains dispensing gas from gasholders. **O*NET Code:** 53-7071.01. **Average Salary:** $43,830. **Projected Growth:** 1.0%. **Annual Openings:** 1,000. **Education:** Moderate-term on-the-job training. **Job Zone:** 2. **Education/Training Program(s)**—No data available. **Related Knowledge/Courses:** Mechanical; Engineering and Technology; Physics. **Personality Type:** Realistic. **Skills Required:** Operation Monitoring; Operation and Control; Equipment Maintenance. **Abilities:** Control Precision; Static Strength; Reaction Time. **Occupational Values:** Independence; Supervision, Human Relations; Supervision, Technical. **Interacting with Others:** Performing Administrative Activities; Communicating with Supervisors, Peers, or Subordinates; Monitoring and Controlling Resources. **Physical Work Conditions:** Standing; Contaminants; Very Hot or Cold; Outdoors; Hazardous Conditions.

Gaugers

Gauge and test oil in storage tanks. Regulate flow of oil into pipelines at wells, tank farms, refineries, and marine and rail terminals, following prescribed standards and regulations. **O*NET Code:** 51-8093.03. **Average Salary:** $50,050. **Projected Growth:** –11.0%. **Annual Openings:** 3,000. **Education:** Long-term on-the-job training. **Job Zone:** 3. **Education/Training Program(s)**—No data available. **Related Knowledge/Courses:** Mechanical; Physics; Engineering and Technology; Public Safety and Security; Production and Processing; Mathematics. **Personality Type:** Realistic. **Skills Required:** Operation Monitoring; Equipment Maintenance; Science; Operation and Control; Mathematics; Troubleshooting; Quality Control Analysis; Repairing. **Abilities:** Response Orientation; Control Precision; Perceptual Speed; Static Strength; Extent Flexibility. **Occupational Values:** Independence; Supervision, Technical; Moral Values; Supervision, Human Relations. **Interacting with Others:** Communicating with Supervisors, Peers, or Subordinates; Establishing and Maintaining Interpersonal Relationships; Monitoring and Controlling Resources. **Physical Work Conditions:** Hazardous Conditions; Contaminants; Outdoors; Common Protective or Safety Equipment; Standing.

Nuclear Power Reactor Operators

Control nuclear reactors. **O*NET Code:** 51-8011.00. **Average Salary:** $63,270. **Projected Growth:** –3.2%. **Annual Openings:** Fewer than 500. **Education:** Long-term on-the-job training. **Job Zone:** 4. **Education/Training Program(s)**—Nuclear/Nuclear Power Technology/Technician. **Related Knowledge/Courses:** Telecommunications; Engineering and Technology; Physics; Chemistry; Computers and Electronics; Public Safety and Security. **Personality Type:** Realistic. **Skills Required:** Operation Monitoring; Operation and Control;

Coordination; Instructing; Systems Analysis; Management of Personnel Resources; Speaking; Troubleshooting; Judgment and Decision Making. **Abilities:** Control Precision; Multilimb Coordination; Reaction Time; Written Comprehension; Oral Comprehension. **Occupational Values:** Supervision, Technical; Authority; Supervision, Human Relations; Advancement; Co-workers. **Interacting with Others:** Communicating with Supervisors, Peers, or Subordinates; Establishing and Maintaining Interpersonal Relationships; Interpreting the Meaning of Information for Others; Coordinating the Work and Activities of Others. **Physical Work Conditions:** Hazardous Conditions; Specialized Protective or Safety Equipment; Exposed to Radiation; Standing; Using Hands on Objects, Tools, or Controls.

Petroleum Pump System Operators

Control or operate manifold and pumping systems to circulate liquids through a petroleum refinery. **O*NET Code:** 51-8093.01. **Average Salary:** $50,050. **Projected Growth:** –11.0%. **Annual Openings:** 3,000. **Education:** Long-term on-the-job training. **Job Zone:** 3. **Education/Training Program(s)**—No data available. **Related Knowledge/Courses:** Mechanical; Chemistry; Production and Processing; Clerical; Telecommunications; Engineering and Technology. **Personality Type:** Realistic. **Skills Required:** Operation and Control; Operation Monitoring; Repairing; Troubleshooting; Coordination; Equipment Maintenance; Systems Analysis. **Abilities:** Rate Control; Control Precision; Information Ordering; Gross Body Coordination; Wrist-Finger Speed; Extent Flexibility. **Occupational Values:** Supervision, Technical; Supervision, Human Relations; Compensation; Security; Company Policies and Practices. **Interacting with Others:** Communicating with Supervisors, Peers, or Subordinates; Establishing and Maintaining Interpersonal Relationships; Performing Administrative Activities. **Physical Work Conditions:** Contaminants; Standing; Hazardous Conditions; Kneeling, Crouching, Stooping, or Crawling; Using Hands on Objects, Tools, or Controls; Spend Time Bending or Twisting the Body.

Petroleum Refinery and Control Panel Operators

Analyze specifications and control continuous operation of petroleum refining and processing units. Operate control panel to regulate temperature, pressure, rate of flow, and tank level in petroleum refining unit according to process schedules. **O*NET Code:** 51-8093.02. **Average Salary:** $50,050. **Projected Growth:** –11.0%. **Annual Openings:** 3,000. **Education:** Long-term on-the-job training. **Job Zone:** 4. **Education/Training Program(s)**—No data available. **Related Knowledge/Courses:** Chemistry; Mechanical; Physics; Production and Processing; Engineering and Technology; Public Safety and Security. **Personality Type:** Realistic. **Skills Required:** Operation Monitoring; Operation and Control; Equipment Maintenance; Repairing; Troubleshooting; Science; Quality Control Analysis; Mathematics. **Abilities:** Sound Localization; Reaction Time; Rate Control; Auditory Attention; Hearing Sensitivity. **Occupational Values:** Supervision, Technical; Advancement; Supervision, Human Relations; Security; Company Policies and Practices. **Interacting with Others:** Communicating with Supervisors, Peers, or Subordinates; Interpreting the Meaning of Information for Others; Establishing and Maintaining Interpersonal Relationships. **Physical Work Conditions:** Hazardous Conditions; Walking and Running; Common Protective or Safety Equipment; Standing; Sounds, Noise Levels Are Distracting or Uncomfortable; Contaminants.

Power Distributors and Dispatchers

Coordinate, regulate, or distribute electricity or steam. **O*NET Code:** 51-8012.00. **Average Salary:** $56,910. **Projected Growth:** –3.0%. **Annual Openings:** 1,000. **Education:** Long-term on-the-job training. **Job Zone:** 4. **Education/Training Program(s)**—No data available. **Related Knowledge/Courses:** Mechanical; Physics; Engineering and Technology; Telecommunications; Computers and Electronics. **Personality Type:** Realistic. **Skills Required:** Operation Monitoring; Equipment Maintenance; Repairing; Management of Personnel Resources; Operation and Control; Troubleshooting; Instructing; Installation. **Abilities:** Reaction Time; Sound Localization; Perceptual Speed; Hearing Sensitivity; Response Orientation. **Occupational Values:** Authority; Supervision, Technical; Compensation; Security; Supervision, Human Relations. **Interacting with Others:** Communicating with Supervisors, Peers, or Subordinates; Coordinating the Work and Activities of Others; Guiding, Directing, and Motivating Subordinates. **Physical Work Conditions:** Hazardous Conditions; Sitting; Using Hands on Objects, Tools, or Controls; Spend Time Bending or Twisting the Body; Extremely Bright or Inadequate Lighting.

Power Generating Plant Operators, Except Auxiliary Equipment Operators

Control or operate machinery, such as steam-driven turbo-generators, to generate electric power, often through the use of panelboards, control boards, or semi-automatic equipment. **O*NET Code:** 51-8013.01. **Average Salary:** $51,540. **Projected Growth:** 0.3%. **Annual Openings:** 3,000. **Education:** Long-term on-the-job training. **Job Zone:** 4. **Education/Training Program(s)**—No data available. **Related Knowledge/Courses:** Mechanical; Engineering and Technology; Physics; Computers and Electronics. **Personality Type:** Realistic. **Skills Required:** Operation Monitoring; Operation and Control; Troubleshooting; Equipment Maintenance; Repairing; Science; Quality Control Analysis; Installation. **Abilities:** Sound Localization; Selective Attention; Reaction Time; Hearing Sensitivity; Perceptual Speed. **Occupational Values:** Supervision, Technical; Supervision, Human Relations; Moral Values; Independence; Security. **Interacting with Others:** Establishing and Maintaining Interpersonal Relationships; Communicating with Supervisors, Peers, or Subordinates; Performing Administrative Activities. **Physical Work Conditions:** Common Protective or Safety Equipment; Hazardous Equipment; Hazardous Conditions; Standing; Using Hands on Objects, Tools, or Controls; Specialized Protective or Safety Equipment.

Ship Engineers

Supervise and coordinate activities of crew engaged in operating and maintaining engines; boilers; deck machinery; and electrical, sanitary, and refrigeration equipment aboard ship. **O*NET Code:** 53-5031.00. **Average Salary:** $54,560.

Projected Growth: 4.5%. **Annual Openings:** 1,000. **Education:** Postsecondary vocational training. **Job Zone:** 5. **Education/Training Program(s)**—No data available. **Related Knowledge/Courses:** Mechanical; Transportation; Engineering and Technology; Telecommunications; Public Safety and Security; Physics. **Personality Type:** Realistic. **Skills Required:** Operation and Control; Operation Monitoring; Repairing; Management of Personnel Resources; Equipment Maintenance; Coordination; Troubleshooting; Systems Evaluation. **Abilities:** Control Precision; Glare Sensitivity; Explosive Strength; Oral Expression; Gross Body Coordination; Auditory Attention. **Occupational Values:** Authority; Responsibility; Compensation; Social Status; Autonomy. **Interacting with Others:** Coordinating the Work and Activities of Others; Communicating with Supervisors, Peers, or Subordinates; Establishing and Maintaining Interpersonal Relationships; Guiding, Directing, and Motivating Subordinates. **Physical Work Conditions:** Standing; Very Hot or Cold; Extremely Bright or Inadequate Lighting; Kneeling, Crouching, Stooping, or Crawling; Cramped Work Space, Awkward Positions; Climbing Ladders, Scaffolds, or Poles.

Stationary Engineers

Operate and maintain stationary engines and mechanical equipment to provide utilities for buildings or industrial processes. Operate equipment such as steam engines, generators, motors, turbines, and steam boilers. **O*NET Code:** 51-8021.02. **Average Salary:** $43,880. **Projected Growth:** 0.3%. **Annual Openings:** 4,000. **Education:** Long-term on-the-job training. **Job Zone:** 3. **Education/Training Program(s)**—No data available. **Related Knowledge/Courses:** Mechanical; Physics; Engineering and Technology; Computers and Electronics; Chemistry; Production and Processing. **Personality Type:** Realistic. **Skills Required:** Equipment Maintenance; Operation Monitoring; Repairing; Operation and Control; Troubleshooting; Quality Control Analysis; Technology Design; Systems Evaluation. **Abilities:** Control Precision; Finger Dexterity; Manual Dexterity; Static Strength; Sound Localization. **Occupational Values:** Supervision, Technical; Supervision, Human Relations; Moral Values; Autonomy; Independence; Advancement. **Interacting with Others:** Communicating with Supervisors, Peers, or Subordinates; Interpreting the Meaning of Information for Others; Establishing and Maintaining Interpersonal Relationships. **Physical Work Conditions:** Sounds, Noise Levels Are Distracting or Uncomfortable; Hazardous Conditions; Minor Burns, Cuts, Bites, or Stings; Specialized Protective or Safety Equipment; Contaminants.

Water and Liquid Waste Treatment Plant and System Operators

Operate or control an entire process or system of machines, often through the use of control boards, to transfer or treat water or liquid waste. **O*NET Code:** 51-8031.00. **Average Salary:** $34,180. **Projected Growth:** 16.0%. **Annual Openings:** 9,000. **Education:** Long-term on-the-job training. **Job Zone:** 3. **Education/Training Program(s)**—Water Quality and Wastewater Treatment Management and Recycling Technology/Technician. **Related Knowledge/Courses:** Biology; Chemistry; Physics; Public Safety and Security;

Mathematics; Law and Government. **Personality Type:** Realistic. **Skills Required:** Operation Monitoring; Installation; Operation and Control; Troubleshooting; Management of Material Resources; Management of Personnel Resources; Operations Analysis; Equipment Maintenance. **Abilities:** Flexibility of Closure; Multilimb Coordination; Extent Flexibility; Depth Perception; Control Precision. **Occupational Values:** Security; Authority; Supervision, Technical; Co-workers; Company Policies and Practices. **Interacting with Others:** Communicating with Supervisors, Peers, or Subordinates; Establishing and Maintaining Interpersonal Relationships; Monitoring and Controlling Resources. **Physical Work Conditions:** Outdoors; Contaminants; In an Enclosed Vehicle or Equipment; Sounds, Noise Levels Are Distracting or Uncomfortable; Very Hot or Cold.

13.17 Loading, Moving, Hoisting, and Conveying

Conveyor Operators and Tenders

Control or tend conveyors or conveyor systems that move materials or products to and from stockpiles, processing stations, departments, or vehicles. May control speed and routing of materials or products. **O*NET Code:** 53-7011.00. **Average Salary:** $25,310. **Projected Growth:** 12.4%. **Annual Openings:** 9,000. **Education:** Short-term on-the-job training. **Job Zone:** 1. **Education/Training Program(s)**—Ground Transportation, Other. **Related Knowledge/Courses:** Production and Processing; Mechanical. **Personality Type:** Realistic. **Skills Required:** Operation Monitoring; Equipment Maintenance; Operation and Control; Repairing; Troubleshooting. **Abilities:** Perceptual Speed; Static Strength; Multilimb Coordination; Rate Control; Trunk Strength. **Occupational Values:** Supervision, Technical; Supervision, Human Relations; Activity; Moral Values; Co-workers; Company Policies and Practices. **Interacting with Others:** Communicating with Supervisors, Peers, or Subordinates; Establishing and Maintaining Interpersonal Relationships; Coordinating the Work and Activities of Others; Performing Administrative Activities. **Physical Work Conditions:** Hazardous Equipment; Using Hands on Objects, Tools, or Controls; Contaminants; Spend Time Bending or Twisting the Body; Spend Time Making Repetitive Motions.

Freight, Stock, and Material Movers, Hand

Load, unload and move materials at plant, yard, or other work site. **O*NET Code:** 53-7062.03. **Average Salary:** $19,980. **Projected Growth:** 6.6%. **Annual Openings:** 525,000. **Education:** Short-term on-the-job training. **Job Zone:** 1. **Education/Training Program(s)**—No data available. **Related Knowledge/Courses:** Production and Processing; Transportation; Mechanical; Physics. **Personality Type:** Realistic. **Skills Required:** Installation. **Abilities:** Static Strength; Trunk Strength; Extent Flexibility; Gross Body Equilibrium; Multilimb Coordination. **Occupational Values:** Supervision, Technical; Moral Values; Co-workers;

Advancement; Supervision, Human Relations. **Interacting with Others:** Communicating with Supervisors, Peers, or Subordinates; Performing Administrative Activities; Establishing and Maintaining Interpersonal Relationships; Assisting and Caring for Others. **Physical Work Conditions:** Climbing Ladders, Scaffolds, or Poles; Standing; Common Protective or Safety Equipment; Walking and Running; Minor Burns, Cuts, Bites, or Stings; Kneeling, Crouching, Stooping, or Crawling.

Hoist and Winch Operators

Operate or tend hoists or winches to lift and pull loads, using power-operated cable equipment. **O*NET Code:** 53-7041.00. **Average Salary:** $31,570. **Projected Growth:** 13.0%. **Annual Openings:** 1,000. **Education:** Moderate-term on-the-job training. **Job Zone:** 2. **Education/Training Program(s)—**Construction/Heavy Equipment/Earthmoving Equipment Operation. **Related Knowledge/Courses:** Mechanical; Public Safety and Security; Transportation; Customer and Personal Service; Design; Administration and Management; Physics. **Personality Type:** Realistic. **Skills Required:** Equipment Maintenance; Operation and Control; Coordination; Equipment Selection; Repairing; Troubleshooting; Monitoring; Operation Monitoring; Time Management. **Abilities:** Depth Perception; Multilimb Coordination; Reaction Time; Control Precision; Static Strength. **Occupational Values:** Independence; Moral Values; Supervision, Technical; Advancement. **Interacting with Others:** Communicating with Supervisors, Peers, or Subordinates; Training and Teaching Others; Guiding, Directing, and Motivating Subordinates; Monitoring and Controlling Resources. **Physical Work Conditions:** Sounds, Noise Levels Are Distracting or Uncomfortable; Contaminants; Hazardous Conditions; Hazardous Equipment; Very Hot or Cold; Cramped Work Space, Awkward Positions.

Industrial Truck and Tractor Operators

Operate industrial trucks or tractors equipped to move materials around a warehouse, storage yard, factory, construction site, or similar location. **O*NET Code:** 53-7051.00. **Average Salary:** $26,450. **Projected Growth:** 11.1%. **Annual Openings:** 94,000. **Education:** Short-term on-the-job training. **Job Zone:** 2. **Education/Training Program(s)—**Ground Transportation, Other. **Related Knowledge/Courses:** Transportation; Mechanical; Geography; Chemistry; Mathematics; Production and Processing. **Personality Type:** Realistic. **Skills Required:** Operation Monitoring; Equipment Maintenance; Instructing; Repairing; Troubleshooting; Operation and Control; Systems Analysis; Learning Strategies; Equipment Selection; Installation. **Abilities:** Static Strength; Response Orientation; Reaction Time; Stamina; Depth Perception. **Occupational Values:** Supervision, Technical; Supervision, Human Relations; Moral Values; Advancement. **Interacting with Others:** Establishing and Maintaining Interpersonal Relationships; Communicating with Supervisors, Peers, or Subordinates; Resolving Conflicts and Negotiating with Others. **Physical Work Conditions:** In an Open Vehicle or Equipment; Sounds, Noise Levels Are Distracting or Uncomfortable; Contaminants; Very Hot or Cold; Indoors, Not Environmentally Controlled.

Irradiated-Fuel Handlers

Package, store, and convey irradiated fuels and wastes, using hoists, mechanical arms, shovels, and industrial truck. **O*NET Code:** 47-4041.01. **Average Salary:** $33,080. **Projected Growth:** 43.1%. **Annual Openings:** 8,000. **Education:** Moderate-term on-the-job training. **Job Zone:** 2. **Education/Training Program(s)—**Hazardous Materials Management and Waste Technology/Technician. **Related Knowledge/Courses:** Transportation; Production and Processing; Chemistry; Public Safety and Security; Law and Government; Building and Construction. **Personality Type:** Realistic. **Skills Required:** Operation and Control. **Abilities:** Static Strength; Control Precision; Spatial Orientation; Multilimb Coordination; Reaction Time. **Occupational Values:** Supervision, Technical; Independence; Supervision, Human Relations; Compensation; Advancement. **Interacting with Others:** Establishing and Maintaining Interpersonal Relationships; Communicating with Supervisors, Peers, or Subordinates; Assisting and Caring for Others. **Physical Work Conditions:** Exposed to Radiation; Contaminants; Outdoors; Specialized Protective or Safety Equipment; Common Protective or Safety Equipment.

Machine Feeders and Offbearers

Feed materials into or remove materials from machines or equipment that is automatic or tended by other workers. **O*NET Code:** 53-7063.00. **Average Salary:** $22,030. **Projected Growth:** –1.4%. **Annual Openings:** 31,000. **Education:** Short-term on-the-job training. **Job Zone:** 1. **Education/Training Program(s)—**No data available. **Related Knowledge/Courses:** Production and Processing; Mechanical; Chemistry. **Personality Type:** Realistic. **Skills Required:** Equipment Maintenance; Operation Monitoring; Operation and Control; Repairing. **Abilities:** Static Strength; Dynamic Strength; Extent Flexibility; Stamina; Manual Dexterity. **Occupational Values:** Activity; Moral Values; Supervision, Technical; Co-workers; Advancement; Supervision, Human Relations. **Interacting with Others:** Performing Administrative Activities; Communicating with Supervisors, Peers, or Subordinates; Establishing and Maintaining Interpersonal Relationships; Assisting and Caring for Others; Coordinating the Work and Activities of Others. **Physical Work Conditions:** Hazardous Equipment; Standing; Using Hands on Objects, Tools, or Controls; Spend Time Making Repetitive Motions; Spend Time Bending or Twisting the Body.

Packers and Packagers, Hand

Pack or package by hand a wide variety of products and materials. **O*NET Code:** 53-7064.00. **Average Salary:** $16,980. **Projected Growth:** 14.4%. **Annual Openings:** 198,000. **Education:** Short-term on-the-job training. **Job Zone:** 1. **Education/Training Program(s)—**No data available. **Related Knowledge/Courses:** Production and Processing; Public Safety and Security; Sales and Marketing; Food Production; Administration and Management; Clerical; Transportation. **Personality Type:** Realistic. **Skills Required:** Persuasion; Management of Personnel Resources; Active Listening; Social Perceptiveness; Instructing; Coordination; Learning Strategies; Service Orientation. **Abilities:** Extent Flexibility; Manual Dexterity; Static Strength; Stamina; Trunk Strength.

Occupational Values: Supervision, Technical; Activity; Moral Values; Co-workers; Advancement; Supervision, Human Relations. **Interacting with Others:** Establishing and Maintaining Interpersonal Relationships; Communicating with Supervisors, Peers, or Subordinates; Assisting and Caring for Others. **Physical Work Conditions:** Physical Proximity; Sounds, Noise Levels Are Distracting or Uncomfortable; Standing; Contaminants; Very Hot or Cold.

Pump Operators, Except Wellhead Pumpers

Tend, control, or operate power-driven, stationary, or portable pumps and manifold systems to transfer gases, oil, other liquids, slurries, or powdered materials to and from various vessels and processes. **O*NET Code:** 53-7072.00. **Average Salary:** $35,440. **Projected Growth:** –5.0%. **Annual Openings:** 2,000. **Education:** Moderate-term on-the-job training. **Job Zone:** 2. **Education/Training Program(s)**—No data available. **Related Knowledge/Courses:** Mechanical; Physics; Chemistry; Production and Processing. **Personality Type:** Realistic. **Skills Required:** Operation Monitoring; Operation and Control; Equipment Maintenance; Repairing; Science; Troubleshooting; Quality Control Analysis. **Abilities:** Control Precision; Rate Control; Gross Body Coordination; Stamina; Speed of Limb Movement. **Occupational Values:** Supervision, Technical; Supervision, Human Relations; Moral Values; Advancement; Independence; Authority. **Interacting with Others:** Communicating with Supervisors, Peers, or Subordinates; Establishing and Maintaining Interpersonal Relationships; Coordinating the Work and Activities of Others. **Physical Work Conditions:** Hazardous Equipment; Hazardous Conditions; Standing; Using Hands on Objects, Tools, or Controls; Sounds, Noise Levels Are Distracting or Uncomfortable.

Refuse and Recyclable Material Collectors

Collect and dump refuse or recyclable materials from containers into truck. May drive truck. **O*NET Code:** 53-7081.00. **Average Salary:** $25,080. **Projected Growth:** 17.6%. **Annual Openings:** 42,000. **Education:** Short-term on-the-job training. **Job Zone:** 1. **Education/Training Program(s)**—No data

available. **Related Knowledge/Courses:** Transportation; Administration and Management. **Personality Type:** Realistic. **Skills Required:** Operation and Control. **Abilities:** Static Strength; Rate Control; Stamina; Trunk Strength; Gross Body Coordination. **Occupational Values:** Supervision, Human Relations; Supervision, Technical; Company Policies and Practices; Security. **Interacting with Others:** Communicating with Supervisors, Peers, or Subordinates; Establishing and Maintaining Interpersonal Relationships; Communicating with Persons Outside Organization; Assisting and Caring for Others; Performing for or Working Directly with the Public; Performing Administrative Activities. **Physical Work Conditions:** Outdoors; Very Hot or Cold; Standing; Contaminants; Minor Burns, Cuts, Bites, or Stings.

Tank Car, Truck, and Ship Loaders

Load and unload chemicals and bulk solids such as coal, sand, and grain into or from tank cars, trucks, or ships, using material-moving equipment. May perform a variety of other tasks relating to shipment of products. May gauge or sample shipping tanks and test them for leaks. **O*NET Code:** 53-7121.00. **Average Salary:** $32,430. **Projected Growth:** –2.1%. **Annual Openings:** 3,000. **Education:** Moderate-term on-the-job training. **Job Zone:** 3. **Education/Training Program(s)**—No data available. **Related Knowledge/Courses:** Chemistry; Transportation; Production and Processing; Physics; Mechanical; Public Safety and Security. **Personality Type:** Realistic. **Skills Required:** Operation Monitoring; Operation and Control; Quality Control Analysis; Repairing; Troubleshooting. **Abilities:** Static Strength; Reaction Time; Rate Control; Response Orientation; Control Precision. **Occupational Values:** Independence; Supervision, Technical; Moral Values; Supervision, Human Relations. **Interacting with Others:** Communicating with Supervisors, Peers, or Subordinates; Coordinating the Work and Activities of Others; Establishing and Maintaining Interpersonal Relationships. **Physical Work Conditions:** Hazardous Conditions; Outdoors; Contaminants; Common Protective or Safety Equipment; Standing.

© 2006, JIST Works

14 Retail and Wholesale Sales and Service

14.01   **Managerial Work in Retail/Wholesale Sales and Service**

14.02   **Technical Sales**

14.03   **General Sales**

14.04   **Personal Soliciting**

14.05   **Purchasing**

14.06   **Customer Service**

14.01 Managerial Work in Retail/Wholesale Sales and Service

Advertising and Promotions Managers

Plan and direct advertising policies and programs or produce collateral materials, such as posters, contests, coupons, or giveaways, to create extra interest in the purchase of a product or service for a department or an entire organization or on an account basis. **O*NET Code:** 11-2011.00. **Average Salary:** $61,400. **Projected Growth:** 25.0%. **Annual Openings:** 13,000. **Education:** Work experience plus degree. **Job Zone:** 4. **Education/Training Program(s)**—Advertising; Marketing/Marketing Management, General; Public Relations/Image Management. **Related Knowledge/Courses:** Sales and Marketing; Customer and Personal Service; Communications and Media; Production and Processing; Design; Clerical. **Personality Type:** Artistic. **Skills Required:** Service Orientation; Management of Financial Resources; Persuasion; Negotiation; Time Management; Coordination; Management of Personnel Resources; Monitoring. **Abilities:** Originality; Fluency of Ideas; Speech Clarity; Written Expression; Oral Expression. **Occupational Values:** Authority; Creativity; Working Conditions; Ability Utilization; Achievement. **Interacting with Others:** Communicating with Supervisors, Peers, or Subordinates; Establishing and Maintaining Interpersonal Relationships; Resolving Conflicts and Negotiating with Others. **Physical Work Conditions:** Sitting; Contaminants; Keeping or Regaining Balance; In an Enclosed Vehicle or Equipment; Very Hot or Cold.

First-Line Supervisors/Managers of Non-Retail Sales Workers

Directly supervise and coordinate activities of sales workers other than retail sales workers. May perform duties such as budgeting, accounting, and personnel work in addition to supervisory duties. **O*NET Code:** 41-1012.00. **Average Salary:** $56,700. **Projected Growth:** 6.8%. **Annual Openings:** 72,000. **Education:** Work experience in a related occupation. **Job Zone:** 3. **Education/Training Program(s)**—Business, Management, Marketing, and Related Support Services, Other; General Merchandising, Sales, and Related Marketing Operations, Other; Special Products Marketing Operations; Specialized Merchandising, Sales, and Related Marketing Operations, Other. **Related Knowledge/Courses:** Sales and Marketing; Economics and Accounting; Personnel and Human Resources; Administration and Management; Mathematics; Customer and Personal Service. **Personality Type:** Enterprising. **Skills Required:** Management of Personnel Resources; Management of Financial Resources; Management of Material Resources; Systems Evaluation; Systems Analysis; Negotiation; Coordination; Social Perceptiveness. **Abilities:** Oral Expression; Number Facility; Fluency of Ideas; Originality; Written Expression.

Occupational Values: Authority; Responsibility; Creativity; Autonomy; Variety; Advancement. **Interacting with Others:** Communicating with Supervisors, Peers, or Subordinates; Monitoring and Controlling Resources; Staffing Organizational Units. **Physical Work Conditions:** Walking and Running; Standing; Sitting.

First-Line Supervisors/Managers of Retail Sales Workers

Directly supervise sales workers in a retail establishment or department. Duties may include management functions, such as purchasing, budgeting, accounting, and personnel work, in addition to supervisory duties. **O*NET Code:** 41-1011.00. **Average Salary:** $31,570. **Projected Growth:** 9.1%. **Annual Openings:** 251,000. **Education:** Work experience in a related occupation. **Job Zone:** 2. **Education/Training Program(s)**—Business, Management, Marketing, and Related Support Services, Other; Consumer Merchandising/Retailing Management; E-Commerce/Electronic Commerce; Floriculture/Floristry Operations and Management; Retailing and Retail Operations; Selling Skills and Sales Operations; Special Products Marketing Operations; Specialized Merchandising, Sales, and Related Marketing Operations, Other. **Related Knowledge/Courses:** Sales and Marketing; Customer and Personal Service; Administration and Management; Personnel and Human Resources; Public Safety and Security; English Language; Communications and Media. **Personality Type:** Enterprising. **Skills Required:** Management of Personnel Resources; Persuasion; Instructing; Management of Financial Resources; Time Management; Social Perceptiveness; Service Orientation; Monitoring. **Abilities:** Speech Recognition; Originality; Mathematical Reasoning; Extent Flexibility; Time Sharing; Trunk Strength. **Occupational Values:** Authority; Responsibility; Creativity; Autonomy; Variety; Advancement. **Interacting with Others:** Establishing and Maintaining Interpersonal Relationships; Communicating with Supervisors, Peers, or Subordinates; Resolving Conflicts and Negotiating with Others; Performing for or Working Directly with the Public. **Physical Work Conditions:** Physical Proximity; Walking and Running; Standing; Indoors; Hazardous Equipment.

Funeral Directors

Perform various tasks to arrange and direct funeral services, such as coordinating transportation of body to mortuary for embalming, interviewing family or other authorized person to arrange details, selecting pallbearers, procuring official for religious rites, and providing transportation for mourners. **O*NET Code:** 11-9061.00. **Average Salary:** $46,120. **Projected Growth:** 6.6%. **Annual Openings:** 3,000. **Education:** Associate degree. **Job Zone:** 3. **Education/Training Program(s)**—Funeral Direction/Service; Funeral Service and Mortuary Science, General. **Related Knowledge/Courses:** Customer and Personal Service; Philosophy and Theology; Clerical; Sales and Marketing; Psychology; Therapy and Counseling. **Personality Type:** Enterprising. **Skills Required:** Service Orientation; Social Perceptiveness; Management of Financial Resources; Coordination; Management of Personnel Resources; Negotiation; Time Management; Management of Material Resources. **Abilities:** Oral Comprehension; Oral Expression; Memorization; Written Comprehension; Written

Expression. **Occupational Values:** Social Service; Autonomy; Authority; Security; Compensation. **Interacting with Others:** Performing for or Working Directly with the Public; Assisting and Caring for Others; Establishing and Maintaining Interpersonal Relationships. **Physical Work Conditions:** In an Enclosed Vehicle or Equipment; Contaminants; Outdoors; Physical Proximity; Very Hot or Cold.

Marketing Managers

Determine the demand for products and services offered by a firm and its competitors and identify potential customers. Develop pricing strategies with the goal of maximizing the firm's profits or share of the market while ensuring the firm's customers are satisfied. Oversee product development or monitor trends that indicate the need for new products and services. **O*NET Code:** 11-2021.00. **Average Salary:** $85,220. **Projected Growth:** 21.3%. **Annual Openings:** 30,000. **Education:** Work experience plus degree. **Job Zone:** 4. **Education/Training Program(s)**—Apparel and Textile Marketing Management; Consumer Merchandising/Retailing Management; International Marketing; Marketing Research; Marketing, Other; Marketing/Marketing Management, General. **Related Knowledge/Courses:** Sales and Marketing; Customer and Personal Service; Administration and Management; Personnel and Human Resources; Education and Training; English Language. **Personality Type:** Enterprising. **Skills Required:** Management of Financial Resources; Management of Personnel Resources; Negotiation; Operations Analysis; Persuasion; Coordination; Instructing; Time Management. **Abilities:** Fluency of Ideas; Originality; Deductive Reasoning; Inductive Reasoning; Mathematical Reasoning. **Occupational Values:** Creativity; Authority; Working Conditions; Recognition; Autonomy. **Interacting with Others:** Communicating with Persons Outside Organization; Establishing and Maintaining Interpersonal Relationships; Resolving Conflicts and Negotiating with Others. **Physical Work Conditions:** Sitting; Indoors; In an Enclosed Vehicle or Equipment.

Property, Real Estate, and Community Association Managers

Plan, direct, or coordinate selling, buying, leasing, or governance activities of commercial, industrial, or residential real estate properties. **O*NET Code:** 11-9141.00. **Average Salary:** $38,750. **Projected Growth:** 12.8%. **Annual Openings:** 35,000. **Education:** Bachelor's degree. **Job Zone:** 4. **Education/Training Program(s)**—Real Estate. **Related Knowledge/Courses:** Administration and Management; Law and Government; Sales and Marketing; Personnel and Human Resources; Economics and Accounting; Building and Construction. **Personality Type:** Enterprising. **Skills Required:** Management of Financial Resources; Management of Personnel Resources; Negotiation; Management of Material Resources; Coordination; Systems Evaluation; Judgment and Decision Making; Time Management. **Abilities:** Mathematical Reasoning; Number Facility; Written Expression; Speech Recognition; Oral Expression. **Occupational Values:** Authority; Autonomy; Responsibility; Variety; Activity. **Interacting with Others:** Communicating with Supervisors, Peers, or Subordinates; Monitoring and Controlling Resources; Communicating with Persons Outside Organization; Resolving Conflicts and Negotiating with Others. **Physical Work Conditions:** Sitting; Walking and Running; Outdoors; Indoors; Spend Time Bending or Twisting the Body.

Purchasing Managers

Plan, direct, or coordinate the activities of buyers, purchasing officers, and related workers involved in purchasing materials, products, and services. **O*NET Code:** 11-3061.00. **Average Salary:** $67,830. **Projected Growth:** 4.8%. **Annual Openings:** 9,000. **Education:** Work experience plus degree. **Job Zone:** 4. **Education/Training Program(s)**—Purchasing, Procurement/ Acquisitions and Contracts Management. **Related Knowledge/Courses:** Personnel and Human Resources; Economics and Accounting; Administration and Management; Production and Processing; Education and Training; Computers and Electronics. **Personality Type:** Enterprising. **Skills Required:** Negotiation; Management of Financial Resources; Management of Material Resources; Operations Analysis; Persuasion; Time Management; Active Learning; Coordination. **Abilities:** Speech Recognition; Mathematical Reasoning; Number Facility; Category Flexibility; Flexibility of Closure. **Occupational Values:** Authority; Working Conditions; Activity; Advancement; Coworkers. **Interacting with Others:** Communicating with Supervisors, Peers, or Subordinates; Providing Consultation and Advice to Others; Establishing and Maintaining Interpersonal Relationships. **Physical Work Conditions:** Sitting; Sounds, Noise Levels Are Distracting or Uncomfortable; Very Hot or Cold; Contaminants; Physical Proximity.

Sales Managers

Direct the actual distribution or movement of a product or service to the customer. Coordinate sales distribution by establishing sales territories, quotas, and goals and establish training programs for sales representatives. Analyze sales statistics gathered by staff to determine sales potential and inventory requirements and monitor the preferences of customers. **O*NET Code:** 11-2022.00. **Average Salary:** $81,970. **Projected Growth:** 30.5%. **Annual Openings:** 54,000. **Education:** Work experience plus degree. **Job Zone:** 4. **Education/Training Program(s)**—Business Administration and Management, General; Business/Commerce, General; Consumer Merchandising/Retailing Management; Marketing, Other; Marketing/Marketing Management, General. **Related Knowledge/Courses:** Sales and Marketing; Computers and Electronics; Mathematics; Customer and Personal Service; Administration and Management; Law and Government. **Personality Type:** Enterprising. **Skills Required:** Negotiation; Service Orientation; Persuasion; Management of Personnel Resources; Time Management; Monitoring; Instructing; Social Perceptiveness. **Abilities:** Mathematical Reasoning; Speech Recognition; Originality; Fluency of Ideas; Speech Clarity. **Occupational Values:** Authority; Creativity; Compensation; Advancement; Recognition; Autonomy. **Interacting with Others:** Communicating with Persons Outside Organization; Establishing and Maintaining Interpersonal Relationships; Communicating with Supervisors, Peers, or Subordinates; Selling or Influencing Others. **Physical Work Conditions:** In an Enclosed Vehicle or Equipment; Sitting; Sounds, Noise

Levels Are Distracting or Uncomfortable; Physical Proximity; Very Hot or Cold; Extremely Bright or Inadequate Lighting.

14.02 Technical Sales

Sales Engineers

Sell business goods or services, the selling of which requires a technical background equivalent to a baccalaureate degree in engineering. **O*NET Code:** 41-9031.00. **Average Salary:** $68,510. **Projected Growth:** 19.9%. **Annual Openings:** 7,000. **Education:** Bachelor's degree. **Job Zone:** 5. **Education/Training Program(s)**—Selling Skills and Sales Operations. **Related Knowledge/Courses:** Sales and Marketing; Design; Engineering and Technology; Production and Processing; Physics; Customer and Personal Service. **Personality Type:** Enterprising. **Skills Required:** Technology Design; Troubleshooting; Operations Analysis; Persuasion; Negotiation; Management of Material Resources; Service Orientation; Speaking. **Abilities:** Mathematical Reasoning; Visualization; Number Facility; Speech Clarity; Written Comprehension; Written Expression. **Occupational Values:** Ability Utilization; Creativity; Variety; Recognition; Social Service; Responsibility. **Interacting with Others:** Communicating with Persons Outside Organization; Providing Consultation and Advice to Others; Selling or Influencing Others. **Physical Work Conditions:** Sitting; Walking and Running; Indoors; Standing; Extremely Bright or Inadequate Lighting; Spend Time Bending or Twisting the Body.

Sales Representatives, Agricultural

Sell agricultural products and services, such as animal feeds; farm and garden equipment; and dairy, poultry, and veterinarian supplies. **O*NET Code:** 41-4011.01. **Average Salary:** $57,820. **Projected Growth:** 19.3%. **Annual Openings:** 44,000. **Education:** Moderate-term on-the-job training. **Job Zone:** 2. **Education/Training Program(s)**—Business, Management, Marketing, and Related Support Services, Other; Selling Skills and Sales Operations. **Related Knowledge/Courses:** Sales and Marketing; Economics and Accounting; Mathematics; Food Production; Telecommunications; Communications and Media. **Personality Type:** Enterprising. **Skills Required:** Persuasion; Negotiation; Speaking; Writing; Active Listening; Mathematics; Instructing; Service Orientation. **Abilities:** Oral Expression; Speech Recognition; Written Comprehension; Fluency of Ideas; Written Expression. **Occupational Values:** Achievement; Advancement; Creativity; Responsibility; Variety; Recognition; Autonomy. **Interacting with Others:** Selling or Influencing Others; Communicating with Persons Outside Organization; Establishing and Maintaining Interpersonal Relationships. **Physical Work Conditions:** Standing; Outdoors; Hazardous Equipment; Sitting; Walking and Running.

Sales Representatives, Chemical and Pharmaceutical

Sell chemical or pharmaceutical products or services, such as acids, industrial chemicals, agricultural chemicals, medicines,

drugs, and water treatment supplies. **O*NET Code:** 41-4011.02. **Average Salary:** $57,820. **Projected Growth:** 19.3%. **Annual Openings:** 44,000. **Education:** Moderate-term on-the-job training. **Job Zone:** 3. **Education/Training Program(s)**—Business, Management, Marketing, and Related Support Services, Other; Selling Skills and Sales Operations. **Related Knowledge/Courses:** Sales and Marketing; Chemistry; Biology; Mathematics; Medicine and Dentistry; Economics and Accounting. **Personality Type:** Enterprising. **Skills Required:** Persuasion; Science; Speaking; Social Perceptiveness; Negotiation; Active Listening; Critical Thinking; Instructing. **Abilities:** Oral Expression; Written Comprehension; Number Facility; Speech Clarity; Oral Comprehension. **Occupational Values:** Recognition; Compensation; Creativity; Ability Utilization; Achievement; Advancement; Responsibility; Autonomy. **Interacting with Others:** Communicating with Persons Outside Organization; Selling or Influencing Others; Establishing and Maintaining Interpersonal Relationships. **Physical Work Conditions:** Sitting; Standing; Walking and Running.

Sales Representatives, Electrical/Electronic

Sell electrical, electronic, or related products or services, such as communication equipment, radiographic-inspection equipment and services, ultrasonic equipment, electronics parts, computers, and EDP systems. **O*NET Code:** 41-4011.03. **Average Salary:** $57,820. **Projected Growth:** 19.3%. **Annual Openings:** 44,000. **Education:** Moderate-term on-the-job training. **Job Zone:** 2. **Education/Training Program(s)**—Business, Management, Marketing, and Related Support Services, Other; Selling Skills and Sales Operations. **Related Knowledge/Courses:** Sales and Marketing; Computers and Electronics; Education and Training; Economics and Accounting; Telecommunications; Mathematics. **Personality Type:** Enterprising. **Skills Required:** Persuasion; Negotiation; Instructing; Operations Analysis; Active Listening; Equipment Selection; Speaking; Technology Design. **Abilities:** Oral Expression; Speech Clarity; Speech Recognition; Oral Comprehension; Memorization. **Occupational Values:** Variety; Recognition; Advancement; Achievement; Compensation; Working Conditions; Autonomy. **Interacting with Others:** Communicating with Persons Outside Organization; Selling or Influencing Others; Performing for or Working Directly with the Public. **Physical Work Conditions:** Standing; Indoors; Sitting; Walking and Running.

Sales Representatives, Instruments

Sell precision instruments, such as dynamometers and spring scales and laboratory, navigation, and surveying instruments. **O*NET Code:** 41-4011.06. **Average Salary:** $57,820. **Projected Growth:** 19.3%. **Annual Openings:** 44,000. **Education:** Moderate-term on-the-job training. **Job Zone:** 3. **Education/Training Program(s)**—Business, Management, Marketing, and Related Support Services, Other; Selling Skills and Sales Operations. **Related Knowledge/Courses:** Sales and Marketing; Engineering and Technology; Customer and Personal Service. **Personality Type:** Enterprising. **Skills Required:** Persuasion; Service Orientation; Active Listening; Speaking; Negotiation; Instructing. **Abilities:** Oral Expression; Mathematical Reasoning; Oral Comprehension.

© 2006, JIST Works

Occupational Values: Autonomy; Recognition; Creativity; Achievement; Compensation; Working Conditions; Responsibility. **Interacting with Others:** Selling or Influencing Others; Communicating with Persons Outside Organization; Establishing and Maintaining Interpersonal Relationships. **Physical Work Conditions:** Standing; Sitting; Indoors.

Sales Representatives, Mechanical Equipment and Supplies

Sell mechanical equipment, machinery, materials, and supplies, such as aircraft and railroad equipment and parts, construction machinery, material-handling equipment, industrial machinery, and welding equipment. **O*NET Code:** 41-4011.04. **Average Salary:** $57,820. **Projected Growth:** 19.3%. **Annual Openings:** 44,000. **Education:** Moderate-term on-the-job training. **Job Zone:** 2. **Education/Training Program(s)**—Business, Management, Marketing, and Related Support Services, Other; Selling Skills and Sales Operations. **Related Knowledge/Courses:** Sales and Marketing; Mathematics; Economics and Accounting; Design; Telecommunications; Engineering and Technology. **Personality Type:** Enterprising. **Skills Required:** Operations Analysis; Persuasion; Negotiation; Equipment Selection; Instructing; Active Listening; Speaking; Reading Comprehension. **Abilities:** Speech Clarity; Oral Expression; Written Expression; Mathematical Reasoning; Memorization. **Occupational Values:** Autonomy; Variety; Recognition; Compensation; Achievement. **Interacting with Others:** Selling or Influencing Others; Communicating with Persons Outside Organization; Establishing and Maintaining Interpersonal Relationships. **Physical Work Conditions:** Walking and Running; Standing; Sitting; Indoors; Outdoors.

Sales Representatives, Medical

Sell medical equipment, products, and services. Does not include pharmaceutical sales representatives. **O*NET Code:** 41-4011.05. **Average Salary:** $57,820. **Projected Growth:** 19.3%. **Annual Openings:** 44,000. **Education:** Moderate-term on-the-job training. **Job Zone:** 3. **Education/Training Program(s)**—Business, Management, Marketing, and Related Support Services, Other; Selling Skills and Sales Operations. **Related Knowledge/Courses:** Sales and Marketing; Design; Mathematics; Economics and Accounting; Engineering and Technology; Medicine and Dentistry. **Personality Type:** Enterprising. **Skills Required:** Technology Design; Persuasion; Negotiation; Operations Analysis; Active Listening; Writing; Speaking; Service Orientation. **Abilities:** Oral Comprehension; Oral Expression; Mathematical Reasoning; Speech Recognition; Number Facility. **Occupational Values:** Autonomy; Recognition; Variety; Compensation; Achievement; Creativity. **Interacting with Others:** Selling or Influencing Others; Communicating with Persons Outside Organization; Establishing and Maintaining Interpersonal Relationships. **Physical Work Conditions:** Standing; Indoors; Walking and Running; Sitting.

14.03 General Sales

Parts Salespersons

Sell spare and replacement parts and equipment in repair shop or parts store. **O*NET Code:** 41-2022.00. **Average Salary:** $24,820. **Projected Growth:** –2.0%. **Annual Openings:** 37,000. **Education:** Moderate-term on-the-job training. **Job Zone:** 2. **Education/Training Program(s)**—Selling Skills and Sales Operations; Vehicle and Vehicle Parts and Accessories Marketing Operations. **Related Knowledge/Courses:** Customer and Personal Service; Sales and Marketing; Computers and Electronics; Mechanical; Production and Processing; Personnel and Human Resources; Mathematics. **Personality Type:** Enterprising. **Skills Required:** Service Orientation; Negotiation; Management of Personnel Resources; Social Perceptiveness; Persuasion; Instructing; Management of Financial Resources; Critical Thinking; Time Management. **Abilities:** Speech Recognition; Category Flexibility; Near Vision; Flexibility of Closure; Hearing Sensitivity. **Occupational Values:** Co-workers; Social Service; Working Conditions; Advancement; Supervision, Technical. **Interacting with Others:** Establishing and Maintaining Interpersonal Relationships; Performing for or Working Directly with the Public; Communicating with Persons Outside Organization. **Physical Work Conditions:** Contaminants; Sounds, Noise Levels Are Distracting or Uncomfortable; Physical Proximity; Indoors, Not Environmentally Controlled; Very Hot or Cold.

Real Estate Brokers

Operate real estate office or work for commercial real estate firm, overseeing real estate transactions. Other duties usually include selling real estate or renting properties and arranging loans. **O*NET Code:** 41-9021.00. **Average Salary:** $54,370. **Projected Growth:** 2.4%. **Annual Openings:** 11,000. **Education:** Work experience in a related occupation. **Job Zone:** 3. **Education/Training Program(s)**—Real Estate. **Related Knowledge/Courses:** Sales and Marketing; Customer and Personal Service; Law and Government; Personnel and Human Resources; Administration and Management; Building and Construction. **Personality Type:** No data available. **Skills Required:** Management of Financial Resources; Negotiation; Persuasion; Service Orientation; Active Listening; Judgment and Decision Making; Time Management; Mathematics. **Abilities:** No data available. **Occupational Values:** No data available. **Interacting with Others:** Communicating with Persons Outside Organization; Resolving Conflicts and Negotiating with Others; Performing for or Working Directly with the Public. **Physical Work Conditions:** In an Enclosed Vehicle or Equipment; Outdoors; Physical Proximity; Sitting; Very Hot or Cold.

Real Estate Sales Agents

Rent, buy, or sell property for clients. Perform duties such as study property listings, interview prospective clients, accompany clients to property site, discuss conditions of sale, and draw up real estate contracts. Includes agents who represent buyer. **O*NET Code:** 41-9022.00. **Average Salary:** $33,830.

Projected Growth: 5.7%. **Annual Openings:** 34,000. **Education:** Postsecondary vocational training. **Job Zone:** 2. **Education/Training Program(s)**—Real Estate. **Related Knowledge/Courses:** Sales and Marketing; Customer and Personal Service; Clerical; Law and Government; Economics and Accounting; Administration and Management. **Personality Type:** Enterprising. **Skills Required:** Negotiation; Coordination; Time Management; Service Orientation; Social Perceptiveness; Speaking; Management of Financial Resources; Active Listening. **Abilities:** Speech Recognition; Near Vision; Far Vision; Flexibility of Closure; Speech Clarity. **Occupational Values:** Responsibility; Compensation; Recognition; Variety; Social Status; Social Service. **Interacting with Others:** Performing for or Working Directly with the Public; Resolving Conflicts and Negotiating with Others; Communicating with Persons Outside Organization. **Physical Work Conditions:** In an Enclosed Vehicle or Equipment; Very Hot or Cold; Sitting; Outdoors; Physical Proximity.

Retail Salespersons

Sell merchandise such as furniture, motor vehicles, appliances, or apparel in a retail establishment. **O*NET Code:** 41-2031.00. **Average Salary:** $18,340. **Projected Growth:** 14.6%. **Annual Openings:** 1014000. **Education:** Short-term on-the-job training. **Job Zone:** 2. **Education/Training Program(s)**—Floriculture/Floristry Operations and Management; Retailing and Retail Operations; Sales, Distribution, and Marketing Operations, General; Selling Skills and Sales Operations. **Related Knowledge/Courses:** Sales and Marketing; Customer and Personal Service; Administration and Management; Education and Training; Personnel and Human Resources; Clerical. **Personality Type:** Enterprising. **Skills Required:** Social Perceptiveness; Writing; Speaking; Critical Thinking; Negotiation; Instructing; Management of Personnel Resources; Service Orientation. **Abilities:** Speech Recognition; Trunk Strength; Category Flexibility; Extent Flexibility; Far Vision. **Occupational Values:** Supervision, Technical; Advancement; Co-workers; Social Service; Working Conditions; Supervision, Human Relations. **Interacting with Others:** Performing for or Working Directly with the Public; Establishing and Maintaining Interpersonal Relationships; Selling or Influencing Others. **Physical Work Conditions:** Physical Proximity; Standing; Walking and Running; Very Hot or Cold; Keeping or Regaining Balance.

Sales Representatives, Wholesale and Manufacturing, Except Technical and Scientific Products

Sell goods for wholesalers or manufacturers to businesses or groups of individuals. Work requires substantial knowledge of items sold. **O*NET Code:** 41-4012.00. **Average Salary:** $44,530. **Projected Growth:** 19.1%. **Annual Openings:** 160,000. **Education:** Moderate-term on-the-job training. **Job Zone:** 2. **Education/Training Program(s)**—Apparel and Accessories Marketing Operations; Business, Management, Marketing, and Related Support Services, Other; Fashion Merchandising; General Merchandising, Sales, and Related Marketing Operations, Other; Sales, Distribution, and Marketing Operations, General; Special Products Marketing Operations; Specialized Merchandising, Sales, and Related

Marketing Operations, Other. **Related Knowledge/Courses:** Sales and Marketing; Customer and Personal Service; Communications and Media; Transportation; Economics and Accounting; Psychology. **Personality Type:** Enterprising. **Skills Required:** Negotiation; Management of Material Resources; Persuasion; Service Orientation; Speaking; Social Perceptiveness; Instructing; Writing. **Abilities:** Speech Recognition; Memorization; Speech Clarity; Fluency of Ideas; Mathematical Reasoning. **Occupational Values:** Autonomy; Variety; Recognition; Achievement; Compensation; Authority; Creativity. **Interacting with Others:** Selling or Influencing Others; Communicating with Persons Outside Organization; Communicating with Supervisors, Peers, or Subordinates; Establishing and Maintaining Interpersonal Relationships; Performing for or Working Directly with the Public. **Physical Work Conditions:** Sitting; Walking and Running; Standing; Outdoors; Indoors.

Service Station Attendants

Service automobiles, buses, trucks, boats, and other automotive or marine vehicles with fuel, lubricants, and accessories. Collect payment for services and supplies. May lubricate vehicle; change motor oil; install antifreeze; or replace lights or other accessories, such as windshield wiper blades or fan belts. May repair or replace tires. **O*NET Code:** 53-6031.00. **Average Salary:** $17,090. **Projected Growth:** 3.3%. **Annual Openings:** 23,000. **Education:** Short-term on-the-job training. **Job Zone:** 1. **Education/Training Program(s)**—No data available. **Related Knowledge/Courses:** Sales and Marketing; Physics; Mechanical; Transportation; Chemistry; Mathematics. **Personality Type:** Realistic. **Skills Required:** Repairing; Installation; Equipment Maintenance; Troubleshooting; Service Orientation; Quality Control Analysis. **Abilities:** Extent Flexibility; Hearing Sensitivity; Static Strength; Reaction Time; Rate Control. **Occupational Values:** Social Service; Co-workers. **Interacting with Others:** Communicating with Persons Outside Organization; Performing for or Working Directly with the Public; Establishing and Maintaining Interpersonal Relationships. **Physical Work Conditions:** Contaminants; Hazardous Conditions; Outdoors; Kneeling, Crouching, Stooping, or Crawling; Minor Burns, Cuts, Bites, or Stings.

14.04 Personal Soliciting

Demonstrators and Product Promoters

Demonstrate merchandise and answer questions for the purpose of creating public interest in buying the product. May sell demonstrated merchandise. **O*NET Code:** 41-9011.00. **Average Salary:** $20,270. **Projected Growth:** 17.0%. **Annual Openings:** 38,000. **Education:** Moderate-term on-the-job training. **Job Zone:** 1. **Education/Training Program(s)**—Retailing and Retail Operations. **Related Knowledge/Courses:** Sales and Marketing; Communications and Media; Education and Training; English Language; Sociology and Anthropology; Clerical. **Personality Type:** Enterprising. **Skills Required:** Persuasion; Speaking; Social Perceptiveness; Instructing; Learning Strategies; Active Learning; Writing;

Technology Design. **Abilities:** Fluency of Ideas; Speech Clarity; Originality; Written Expression; Oral Expression. **Occupational Values:** Variety; Social Service; Independence; Supervision, Technical. **Interacting with Others:** Communicating with Persons Outside Organization; Establishing and Maintaining Interpersonal Relationships; Performing for or Working Directly with the Public. **Physical Work Conditions:** Outdoors; Walking and Running; Standing; Extremely Bright or Inadequate Lighting; Very Hot or Cold.

Door-To-Door Sales Workers, News and Street Vendors, and Related Workers

Sell goods or services door-to-door or on the street. **O*NET Code:** 41-9091.00. **Average Salary:** $23,000. **Projected Growth:** –11.8%. **Annual Openings:** 39,000. **Education:** Short-term on-the-job training. **Job Zone:** 1. **Education/Training Program(s)**—Selling Skills and Sales Operations. **Related Knowledge/Courses:** Sales and Marketing; Communications and Media; Economics and Accounting; Customer and Personal Service; Telecommunications; Geography. **Personality Type:** Enterprising. **Skills Required:** Persuasion; Service Orientation; Social Perceptiveness; Technology Design; Negotiation; Speaking; Management of Financial Resources. **Abilities:** Speech Clarity; Originality; Memorization; Number Facility; Speech Recognition. **Occupational Values:** Independence; Social Service. **Interacting with Others:** Selling or Influencing Others; Communicating with Persons Outside Organization; Performing for or Working Directly with the Public. **Physical Work Conditions:** Outdoors; Walking and Running; Standing; Extremely Bright or Inadequate Lighting; Very Hot or Cold.

Models

Model garments and other apparel to display clothing before prospective buyers at fashion shows, private showings, or retail establishments or for photographer. May pose for photos to be used for advertising purposes. May pose as subject for paintings, sculptures, and other types of artistic expression. **O*NET Code:** 41-9012.00. **Average Salary:** $22,630. **Projected Growth:** 14.5%. **Annual Openings:** 1,000. **Education:** Moderate-term on-the-job training. **Job Zone:** 1. **Education/Training Program(s)**—Fashion Modeling. **Related Knowledge/Courses:** Fine Arts; Sales and Marketing; Communications and Media; Sociology and Anthropology. **Personality Type:** Artistic. **Skills Required:** Social Perceptiveness. **Abilities:** Glare Sensitivity; Gross Body Coordination; Dynamic Flexibility; Visual Color Discrimination; Peripheral Vision. **Occupational Values:** Recognition; Social Status; Compensation. **Interacting with Others:** Performing for or Working Directly with the Public; Establishing and Maintaining Interpersonal Relationships; Communicating with Persons Outside Organization. **Physical Work Conditions:** Walking and Running; Standing; Extremely Bright or Inadequate Lighting; Outdoors; Very Hot or Cold.

Telemarketers

Solicit orders for goods or services over the telephone. **O*NET Code:** 41-9041.00. **Average Salary:** $20,280. **Projected Growth:** –4.9%. **Annual Openings:** 90,000. **Education:** Short-term on-the-job training. **Job Zone:** 2. **Education/Training Program(s)**—Sales, Distribution, and Marketing Operations, General; Selling Skills and Sales Operations. **Related Knowledge/Courses:** Sales and Marketing; Communications and Media; English Language; Customer and Personal Service; Computers and Electronics; Telecommunications. **Personality Type:** Enterprising. **Skills Required:** Persuasion; Negotiation; Service Orientation; Speaking; Active Listening; Social Perceptiveness; Learning Strategies; Monitoring. **Abilities:** Speech Clarity; Originality; Memorization; Number Facility; Speech Recognition. **Occupational Values:** Independence; Social Service. **Interacting with Others:** Selling or Influencing Others; Establishing and Maintaining Interpersonal Relationships; Communicating with Persons Outside Organization. **Physical Work Conditions:** Sitting; Physical Proximity; Sounds, Noise Levels Are Distracting or Uncomfortable.

14.05 Purchasing

Purchasing Agents, Except Wholesale, Retail, and Farm Products

Purchase machinery, equipment, tools, parts, supplies, or services necessary for the operation of an establishment. Purchase raw or semi-finished materials for manufacturing. **O*NET Code:** 13-1023.00. **Average Salary:** $47,250. **Projected Growth:** 11.2%. **Annual Openings:** 29,000. **Education:** Bachelor's degree. **Job Zone:** 3. **Education/Training Program(s)**—Sales, Distribution, and Marketing Operations, General. **Related Knowledge/Courses:** Clerical; Economics and Accounting; Production and Processing; Administration and Management; Computers and Electronics; Mathematics. **Personality Type:** Enterprising. **Skills Required:** Time Management; Negotiation; Management of Personnel Resources; Persuasion; Coordination; Monitoring; Management of Financial Resources; Speaking. **Abilities:** Deductive Reasoning; Category Flexibility; Written Expression; Inductive Reasoning; Speech Recognition. **Occupational Values:** Authority; Advancement; Variety; Compensation; Autonomy. **Interacting with Others:** Establishing and Maintaining Interpersonal Relationships; Communicating with Supervisors, Peers, or Subordinates; Communicating with Persons Outside Organization. **Physical Work Conditions:** Sitting; Physical Proximity; Sounds, Noise Levels Are Distracting or Uncomfortable; Very Hot or Cold; Cramped Work Space, Awkward Positions.

Wholesale and Retail Buyers, Except Farm Products

Buy merchandise or commodities, other than farm products, for resale to consumers at the wholesale or retail level, including both durable and nondurable goods. Analyze past buying trends, sales records, price, and quality of merchandise to determine value and yield. Select, order, and authorize payment for merchandise according to contractual agreements. May conduct meetings with sales personnel and introduce new products. **O*NET Code:** 13-1022.00. **Average Salary:** $42,200. **Projected Growth:** 4.3%. **Annual Openings:**

24,000. **Education:** Bachelor's degree. **Job Zone:** 3. **Education/Training Program(s)**—Apparel and Accessories Marketing Operations; Apparel and Textile Marketing Management; Fashion Merchandising; Merchandising and Buying Operations; Sales, Distribution, and Marketing Operations, General. **Related Knowledge/Courses:** Sales and Marketing; Customer and Personal Service; Clerical; Economics and Accounting; Administration and Management; Mathematics. **Personality Type:** Enterprising. **Skills Required:** Management of Financial Resources; Negotiation; Management of Material Resources; Service Orientation; Instructing; Management of Personnel Resources; Learning Strategies; Operations Analysis. **Abilities:** Mathematical Reasoning; Speech Recognition; Inductive Reasoning; Deductive Reasoning; Category Flexibility. **Occupational Values:** Advancement; Working Conditions; Authority; Co-workers; Creativity; Responsibility. **Interacting with Others:** Establishing and Maintaining Interpersonal Relationships; Performing for or Working Directly with the Public; Selling or Influencing Others. **Physical Work Conditions:** Sitting; Physical Proximity; Sounds, Noise Levels Are Distracting or Uncomfortable; Indoors.

14.06 Customer Service

Adjustment Clerks

Investigate and resolve customers' inquiries concerning merchandise, service, billing, or credit rating. Examine pertinent information to determine accuracy of customers' complaints and responsibility for errors. Notify customers and appropriate personnel of findings, adjustments, and recommendations, such as exchange of merchandise, refund of money, credit to customers' accounts, or adjustment to customers' bills. **O*NET Code:** 43-4051.01. **Average Salary:** $26,600. **Projected Growth:** 24.3%. **Annual Openings:** 419,000. **Education:** Moderate-term on-the-job training. **Job Zone:** 2. **Education/Training Program(s)**—Customer Service Support/Call Center/Teleservice Operation; Receptionist. **Related Knowledge/Courses:** Economics and Accounting; Clerical; Education and Training; Customer and Personal Service. **Personality Type:** Conventional. **Skills Required:** Instructing; Speaking; Writing; Service Orientation; Active Listening; Persuasion; Negotiation; Critical Thinking. **Abilities:** Number Facility; Oral Comprehension; Written Expression; Speech Recognition; Written Comprehension; Oral Expression. **Occupational Values:** Working Conditions; Authority; Co-workers; Social Service; Supervision, Human Relations. **Interacting with Others:** Performing for or Working Directly with the Public; Communicating with Persons Outside Organization; Resolving Conflicts and Negotiating with Others. **Physical Work Conditions:** Sitting; Indoors.

Cashiers

Receive and disburse money in establishments other than financial institutions. Usually involves use of electronic scanners, cash registers, or related equipment. Often involved in processing credit or debit card transactions and validating checks. **O*NET Code:** 41-2011.00. **Average Salary:** $15,970. **Projected Growth:** 13.2%. **Annual Openings:** 1221000. **Education:** Short-term on-the-job training. **Job Zone:** 1. **Education/Training Program(s)**—Retailing and Retail Operations. **Related Knowledge/Courses:** Customer and Personal Service; Education and Training; Foreign Language; English Language; Administration and Management; Mathematics. **Personality Type:** Conventional. **Skills Required:** Social Perceptiveness; Service Orientation; Learning Strategies; Management of Personnel Resources; Instructing; Negotiation; Persuasion; Systems Analysis. **Abilities:** Speech Recognition; Extent Flexibility; Wrist-Finger Speed; Speed of Closure; Trunk Strength; Speech Clarity. **Occupational Values:** Co-workers; Supervision, Technical; Social Service; Advancement; Supervision, Human Relations. **Interacting with Others:** Establishing and Maintaining Interpersonal Relationships; Performing for or Working Directly with the Public; Assisting and Caring for Others. **Physical Work Conditions:** Physical Proximity; Standing; Contaminants; Sounds, Noise Levels Are Distracting or Uncomfortable; Very Hot or Cold.

Counter and Rental Clerks

Receive orders for repairs, rentals, and services. May describe available options, compute cost, and accept payment. **O*NET Code:** 41-2021.00. **Average Salary:** $17,780. **Projected Growth:** 26.3%. **Annual Openings:** 144,000. **Education:** Short-term on-the-job training. **Job Zone:** 1. **Education/Training Program(s)**—Selling Skills and Sales Operations. **Related Knowledge/Courses:** Administration and Management; Food Production; Sales and Marketing; Personnel and Human Resources; English Language; Clerical; Mathematics. **Personality Type:** Conventional. **Skills Required:** Instructing; Service Orientation. **Abilities:** Extent Flexibility; Trunk Strength; Speech Recognition; Oral Expression; Category Flexibility. **Occupational Values:** Social Service; Working Conditions; Co-workers; Supervision, Technical; Advancement. **Interacting with Others:** Performing for or Working Directly with the Public; Establishing and Maintaining Interpersonal Relationships; Coaching and Developing Others. **Physical Work Conditions:** Physical Proximity; Sounds, Noise Levels Are Distracting or Uncomfortable; Walking and Running; Contaminants; Standing.

Customer Service Representatives, Utilities

Interview applicants for water, gas, electric, or telephone service. Talk with customer by phone or in person and receive orders for installation, turn-on, discontinuance, or change in services. **O*NET Code:** 43-4051.02. **Average Salary:** $26,600. **Projected Growth:** 24.3%. **Annual Openings:** 419,000. **Education:** Moderate-term on-the-job training. **Job Zone:** 2. **Education/Training Program(s)**—Customer Service Support/Call Center/Teleservice Operation; Receptionist. **Related Knowledge/Courses:** Sales and Marketing; Customer and Personal Service; Economics and Accounting; Clerical; Telecommunications. **Personality Type:** Conventional. **Skills Required:** Service Orientation; Active Listening; Speaking; Negotiation. **Abilities:** Wrist-Finger Speed; Auditory Attention; Number Facility; Speech Clarity; Oral Expression; Mathematical Reasoning. **Occupational Values:** Supervision,

Technical; Supervision, Human Relations; Security; Working Conditions; Social Service. **Interacting with Others:** Performing for or Working Directly with the Public; Communicating with Persons Outside Organization; Resolving Conflicts and Negotiating with Others. **Physical Work Conditions:** Sitting; Indoors; Spend Time Making Repetitive Motions; Disease or Infections; Using Hands on Objects, Tools, or Controls.

Gaming Change Persons and Booth Cashiers

Exchange coins and tokens for patrons' money. May issue pay-offs and obtain customer's signature on receipt when winnings exceed the amount held in the slot machine. May operate a booth in the slot machine area and furnish change persons with money bank at the start of the shift or count and audit money in drawers. **O*NET Code:** 41-2012.00. **Average Salary:** $20,370. **Projected Growth:** 24.1%. **Annual Openings:** 12,000. **Education:** Short-term on-the-job training. **Job Zone:** No data available. **Education/Training Program(s)**—Retailing and Retail Operations. **Related Knowledge/Courses:** No data available. **Personality Type:** No data available. **Skills Required:** No data available. **Abilities:** No data available. **Occupational Values:** No data available. **Interacting with Others:** No data available. **Physical Work Conditions:** No data available.

Order Clerks

Receive and process incoming orders for materials; merchandise; classified ads; or services such as repairs, installations, or rental of facilities. Duties include informing customers of receipt, prices, shipping dates, and delays; preparing contracts; and handling complaints. **O*NET Code:** 43-4151.00. **Average Salary:** $25,150. **Projected Growth:** –5.7%. **Annual Openings:** 61,000. **Education:** Short-term on-the-job training. **Job Zone:** 2. **Education/Training Program(s)**—General Office Occupations and Clerical Services. **Related Knowledge/Courses:** Customer and Personal Service; Clerical; Sales and Marketing; Computers and Electronics; Production and Processing; Administration and Management. **Personality Type:** Conventional. **Skills Required:** Service Orientation; Time Management; Active Listening; Negotia-tion; Coordination; Persuasion; Reading Comprehension; Speaking. **Abilities:** Speech Recognition; Flexibility of Closure; Near Vision; Auditory Attention; Category Flexibility. **Occupational Values:** Supervision, Technical; Advancement; Supervision, Human Relations; Co-workers; Social Service. **Interacting with Others:** Establishing and Maintaining Interpersonal Relationships; Communicating with Supervisors, Peers, or Subordinates; Communicating with Persons Outside Organization; Performing Administrative Activities. **Physical Work Conditions:** Very Hot or Cold; Contaminants; Sitting; Physical Proximity; Sounds, Noise Levels Are Distracting or Uncomfortable.

Receptionists and Information Clerks

Answer inquiries and obtain information for general public, customers, visitors, and other interested parties. Provide information regarding activities conducted at establishment and location of departments, offices, and employees within organization. **O*NET Code:** 43-4171.00. **Average Salary:** $21,440. **Projected Growth:** 29.5%. **Annual Openings:** 296,000. **Education:** Short-term on-the-job training. **Job Zone:** 2. **Education/Training Program(s)**—General Office Occupations and Clerical Services; Health Unit Coordinator/Ward Clerk; Medical Reception/Receptionist; Receptionist. **Related Knowledge/Courses:** Customer and Personal Service; Clerical; Computers and Electronics; Transportation; Administration and Management; English Language. **Personality Type:** Conventional. **Skills Required:** Service Orientation; Social Perceptiveness; Active Listening; Writing; Critical Thinking; Reading Comprehension; Speaking; Persuasion. **Abilities:** Speech Recognition; Speech Clarity; Oral Expression; Category Flexibility; Far Vision. **Occupational Values:** Social Service; Working Conditions; Supervision, Technical; Company Policies and Practices; Activity. **Interacting with Others:** Establishing and Maintaining Interpersonal Relationships; Communicating with Supervisors, Peers, or Subordinates; Communicating with Persons Outside Organization. **Physical Work Conditions:** Sitting; Physical Proximity; Contaminants; Sounds, Noise Levels Are Distracting or Uncomfortable; Extremely Bright or Inadequate Lighting.

15 Scientific Research, Engineering, and Mathematics

15.01   **Managerial Work in Scientific Research, Engineering, and Mathematics**

15.02   **Physical Sciences**

15.03   **Life Sciences**

15.04   **Social Sciences**

15.05   **Physical Science Laboratory Technology**

15.06   **Mathematics and Data Analysis**

15.07   **Research and Design Engineering**

15.08   **Industrial and Safety Engineering**

15.09   **Engineering Technology**

15.01 Managerial Work in Scientific Research, Engineering, and Mathematics

Engineering Managers

Plan, direct, or coordinate activities in such fields as architecture and engineering or research and development in these fields. **O*NET Code:** 11-9041.00. **Average Salary:** $95,630. **Projected Growth:** 9.2%. **Annual Openings:** 16,000. **Education:** Work experience plus degree. **Job Zone:** 5. **Education/Training Program(s)**—Aerospace, Aeronautical and Astronautical Engineering; Agricultural/Biological Engineering and Bioengineering; Architectural Engineering; Architecture (BArch, BA/BS, MArch, MA/MS, PhD); Biomedical/Medical Engineering; Ceramic Sciences and Engineering; Chemical Engineering; City/Urban, Community and Regional Planning; Civil Engineering, General; Civil Engineering, Other; Computer Engineering, General; Computer Engineering, Other; Computer Hardware Engineering; Computer Software Engineering; Construction Engineering; Electrical, Electronics and Communications Engineering; Engineering Mechanics; Engineering Physics; Engineering Science; Engineering, General; Engineering, Other; Environmental Design/Architecture; Environmental/Environmental Health Engineering; Forest Engineering; Geological/Geophysical Engineering; Geotechnical Engineering; Industrial Engineering; Interior Architecture; Landscape Architecture (BS, BSLA, BLA, MSLA, MLA, PhD); Manufacturing Engineering; Materials Engineering; Materials Science; Mechanical Engineering; Metallurgical Engineering; Mining and Mineral Engineering; Naval Architecture and Marine Engineering; Nuclear Engineering; Ocean Engineering; Petroleum Engineering; Polymer/Plastics Engineering; Structural Engineering; Surveying Engineering; Systems Engineering; Textile Sciences and Engineering; Transportation and Highway Engineering; Water Resources Engineering. **Related Knowledge/Courses:** Engineering and Technology; Design; Physics; Mathematics; Personnel and Human Resources; Administration and Management; Building and Construction. **Personality Type:** Enterprising. **Skills Required:** Technology Design; Operations Analysis; Science; Management of Financial Resources; Installation; Negotiation; Persuasion; Time Management. **Abilities:** Fluency of Ideas; Mathematical Reasoning; Originality; Oral Comprehension; Written Comprehension. **Occupational Values:** Authority; Compensation; Autonomy; Creativity; Ability Utilization; Working Conditions. **Interacting with Others:** Communicating with Supervisors, Peers, or Subordinates; Establishing and Maintaining Interpersonal Relationships; Resolving Conflicts and Negotiating with Others. **Physical Work Conditions:** Indoors, Not Environmentally Controlled; Sounds, Noise Levels Are Distracting or Uncomfortable; Sitting; Extremely Bright or Inadequate Lighting; Contaminants.

Natural Sciences Managers

Plan, direct, or coordinate activities in such fields as life sciences, physical sciences, mathematics, and statistics and research and development in these fields. **O*NET Code:** 11-9121.00. **Average Salary:** $86,910. **Projected Growth:** 11.3%. **Annual Openings:** 5,000. **Education:** Work experience plus degree. **Job Zone:** 5. **Education/Training Program(s)**—Acoustics; Algebra and Number Theory; Analysis and Functional Analysis; Analytical Chemistry; Anatomy; Animal Genetics; Animal Physiology; Applied Mathematics; Applied Mathematics, Other; Astronomy; Astrophysics; Atmospheric Chemistry and Climatology; Atmospheric Physics and Dynamics; Atmospheric Sciences and Meteorology, General; Atmospheric Sciences and Meteorology, Other; Atomic/Molecular Physics; Biochemistry; Biological and Biomedical Sciences, Other; Biological and Physical Sciences; Biology/Biological Sciences, General; Biometry/Biometrics; Biophysics; Biopsychology; Biostatistics; Biotechnology; Botany/Plant Biology; Botany/Plant Biology, Other; Cell/Cellular Biology and Anatomical Sciences, Other; Cell/Cellular Biology and Histology; Chemical Physics; Chemistry, General; Chemistry, Other; Computational Mathematics; Ecology; Ecology, Evolution, Systematics and Population Biology, Other; Elementary Particle Physics; Entomology; Evolutionary Biology; Geochemistry; Geochemistry and Petrology; Geological and Earth Sciences/Geosciences, Other; Geology/Earth Science, General; Geometry/Geometric Analysis; Geophysics and Seismology; Hydrology and Water Resources Science; Immunology; Inorganic Chemistry; Logic; Marine Biology and Biological Oceanography; Mathematics and Computer Science; Mathematics and Statistics, Other; Mathematics, General; Medical Microbiology and Bacteriology; Meteorology; Microbiology, General; Molecular Biology; Natural Sciences; Neuroscience; Nuclear Physics; Nutrition Sciences; Oceanography, Chemical and Physical; Operations Research; Optics/Optical Sciences; Organic Chemistry; Paleontology; Parasitology; Pathology/Experimental Pathology; Pharmacology; Physical and Theoretical Chemistry; Physical Sciences; Physical Sciences, Other; Physics, General; Physics, Other; Planetary Astronomy and Science; Plant Genetics; Plant Pathology/Phytopathology; Plant Physiology; Plasma and High-Temperature Physics; Polymer Chemistry; others. **Related Knowledge/Courses:** Chemistry; Administration and Management; Economics and Accounting; Physics; Law and Government; Mathematics. **Personality Type:** Investigative. **Skills Required:** Management of Material Resources; Management of Financial Resources; Science; Management of Personnel Resources; Coordination; Systems Analysis; Systems Evaluation; Time Management. **Abilities:** Mathematical Reasoning; Written Comprehension; Written Expression; Fluency of Ideas; Originality. **Occupational Values:** Authority; Creativity; Responsibility; Autonomy; Working Conditions. **Interacting with Others:** Communicating with Supervisors, Peers, or Subordinates; Providing Consultation and Advice to Others; Developing and Building Teams. **Physical Work Conditions:** Sitting; Indoors; Extremely Bright or Inadequate Lighting; Walking and

Running; Common Protective or Safety Equipment; Specialized Protective or Safety Equipment.

15.02 Physical Sciences

Astronomers

Observe, research, and interpret celestial and astronomical phenomena to increase basic knowledge and apply such information to practical problems. **O*NET Code:** 19-2011.00. **Average Salary:** $85,910. **Projected Growth:** 4.9%. **Annual Openings:** Fewer than 500. **Education:** Doctoral degree. **Job Zone:** 5. **Education/Training Program(s)**—Astronomy; Astronomy and Astrophysics, Other; Astrophysics; Planetary Astronomy and Science. **Related Knowledge/Courses:** Physics; Mathematics; History and Archeology; Design; Engineering and Technology; Geography. **Personality Type:** Investigative. **Skills Required:** Science; Technology Design; Mathematics; Active Learning; Programming; Critical Thinking; Operations Analysis; Reading Comprehension. **Abilities:** Mathematical Reasoning; Night Vision; Depth Perception; Number Facility; Written Expression; Inductive Reasoning. **Occupational Values:** Autonomy; Independence; Creativity; Ability Utilization; Responsibility. **Interacting with Others:** Interpreting the Meaning of Information for Others; Providing Consultation and Advice to Others; Communicating with Supervisors, Peers, or Subordinates. **Physical Work Conditions:** Outdoors; Sitting; Extremely Bright or Inadequate Lighting; Standing; Very Hot or Cold.

Atmospheric and Space Scientists

Investigate atmospheric phenomena and interpret meteorological data gathered by surface and air stations, satellites, and radar to prepare reports and forecasts for public and other uses. **O*NET Code:** 19-2021.00. **Average Salary:** $65,400. **Projected Growth:** 16.2%. **Annual Openings:** 1,000. **Education:** Bachelor's degree. **Job Zone:** 4. **Education/Training Program(s)**—Atmospheric Chemistry and Climatology; Atmospheric Physics and Dynamics; Atmospheric Sciences and Meteorology, General; Atmospheric Sciences and Meteorology, Other; Meteorology. **Related Knowledge/Courses:** Physics; Geography; Communications and Media; Telecommunications; Administration and Management; Mathematics. **Personality Type:** Investigative. **Skills Required:** Science; Active Learning; Management of Personnel Resources; Critical Thinking; Speaking; Judgment and Decision Making; Systems Analysis; Complex Problem Solving. **Abilities:** Speed of Closure; Speech Clarity; Inductive Reasoning; Written Expression; Originality. **Occupational Values:** Recognition; Social Status; Responsibility; Autonomy; Ability Utilization. **Interacting with Others:** Communicating with Supervisors, Peers, or Subordinates; Interpreting the Meaning of Information for Others; Communicating with Persons Outside Organization; Performing for or Working Directly with the Public. **Physical Work Conditions:** Sitting; Extremely Bright or Inadequate Lighting; Very Hot or Cold; Outdoors; Indoors.

Chemists

Conduct qualitative and quantitative chemical analyses or chemical experiments in laboratories for quality or process control or to develop new products or knowledge. **O*NET Code:** 19-2031.00. **Average Salary:** $54,960. **Projected Growth:** 12.7%. **Annual Openings:** 7,000. **Education:** Bachelor's degree. **Job Zone:** 4. **Education/Training Program(s)**—Analytical Chemistry; Chemical Physics; Chemistry, General; Chemistry, Other; Inorganic Chemistry; Organic Chemistry; Physical and Theoretical Chemistry; Polymer Chemistry. **Related Knowledge/Courses:** Chemistry; Mathematics; Engineering and Technology; Computers and Electronics; Education and Training; English Language. **Personality Type:** Investigative. **Skills Required:** Science; Quality Control Analysis; Technology Design; Time Management; Instructing; Management of Financial Resources; Management of Material Resources; Equipment Selection; Operation Monitoring; Troubleshooting. **Abilities:** Oral Comprehension; Written Expression; Inductive Reasoning; Deductive Reasoning; Category Flexibility. **Occupational Values:** Creativity; Ability Utilization; Responsibility; Autonomy; Achievement. **Interacting with Others:** Establishing and Maintaining Interpersonal Relationships; Communicating with Supervisors, Peers, or Subordinates; Providing Consultation and Advice to Others. **Physical Work Conditions:** Hazardous Conditions; Contaminants; Physical Proximity; Sounds, Noise Levels Are Distracting or Uncomfortable; Sitting.

Geographers

Study nature and use of areas of earth's surface, relating and interpreting interactions of physical and cultural phenomena. Conduct research on physical aspects of a region, including land forms, climates, soils, plants, and animals, and conduct research on the spatial implications of human activities within a given area, including social characteristics, economic activities, and political organization, as well as researching interdependence between regions at scales ranging from local to global. **O*NET Code:** 19-3092.00. **Average Salary:** $56,290. **Projected Growth:** 19.5%. **Annual Openings:** Fewer than 500. **Education:** Bachelor's degree. **Job Zone:** 4. **Education/Training Program(s)**—Geography. **Related Knowledge/Courses:** Geography; Sociology and Anthropology; Biology; Physics; History and Archeology; Design. **Personality Type:** Investigative. **Skills Required:** Writing; Reading Comprehension; Mathematics; Science; Critical Thinking; Active Learning; Speaking; Systems Evaluation. **Abilities:** Night Vision; Written Expression; Spatial Orientation; Far Vision; Flexibility of Closure. **Occupational Values:** Autonomy; Ability Utilization; Creativity; Responsibility; Social Status. **Interacting with Others:** Communicating with Supervisors, Peers, or Subordinates; Communicating with Persons Outside Organization; Interpreting the Meaning of Information for Others. **Physical Work Conditions:** Outdoors; Spend Time Bending or Twisting the Body; Sitting; Kneeling, Crouching, Stooping, or Crawling; Very Hot or Cold.

© 2006, JIST Works

Geologists

Study composition, structure, and history of the earth's crust; examine rocks, minerals, and fossil remains to identify and determine the sequence of processes affecting the development of the earth; apply knowledge of chemistry, physics, biology, and mathematics to explain these phenomena and to help locate mineral and petroleum deposits and underground water resources; prepare geologic reports and maps; and interpret research data to recommend further action for study. **O*NET Code:** 19-2042.01. **Average Salary:** $68,570. **Projected Growth:** 11.5%. **Annual Openings:** 2,000. **Education:** Bachelor's degree. **Job Zone:** 5. **Education/Training Program(s)**—Geochemistry; Geochemistry and Petrology; Geological and Earth Sciences/Geosciences, Other; Geology/Earth Science, General; Geophysics and Seismology; Oceanography, Chemical and Physical; Paleontology. **Related Knowledge/Courses:** Geography; Physics; Chemistry; Engineering and Technology; Mathematics; Biology. **Personality Type:** Investigative. **Skills Required:** Science; Management of Financial Resources; Time Management; Active Learning; Coordination; Critical Thinking; Persuasion; Negotiation. **Abilities:** Written Expression; Mathematical Reasoning; Category Flexibility; Number Facility; Written Comprehension. **Occupational Values:** Responsibility; Autonomy; Ability Utilization; Creativity; Achievement. **Interacting with Others:** Interpreting the Meaning of Information for Others; Communicating with Supervisors, Peers, or Subordinates; Establishing and Maintaining Interpersonal Relationships. **Physical Work Conditions:** Sitting; Very Hot or Cold; Extremely Bright or Inadequate Lighting; Contaminants; Sounds, Noise Levels Are Distracting or Uncomfortable.

Hydrologists

Research the distribution, circulation, and physical properties of underground and surface waters; study the form and intensity of precipitation, its rate of infiltration into the soil, its movement through the earth, and its return to the ocean and atmosphere. **O*NET Code:** 19-2043.00. **Average Salary:** $59,010. **Projected Growth:** 21.0%. **Annual Openings:** 1,000. **Education:** Bachelor's degree. **Job Zone:** 5. **Education/Training Program(s)**—Geology/Earth Science, General; Hydrology and Water Resources Science; Oceanography, Chemical and Physical. **Related Knowledge/Courses:** Physics; Geography; Mathematics; Chemistry; History and Archeology; Communications and Media. **Personality Type:** Investigative. **Skills Required:** Science; Mathematics; Active Learning; Writing; Critical Thinking; Systems Analysis; Complex Problem Solving; Judgment and Decision Making. **Abilities:** Written Comprehension; Mathematical Reasoning; Deductive Reasoning; Oral Comprehension; Flexibility of Closure. **Occupational Values:** Autonomy; Ability Utilization; Creativity; Responsibility; Independence. **Interacting with Others:** Interpreting the Meaning of Information for Others; Providing Consultation and Advice to Others; Communicating with Supervisors, Peers, or Subordinates. **Physical Work Conditions:** Outdoors; Very Hot or Cold; Sitting; Extremely Bright or Inadequate Lighting; Standing.

Materials Scientists

Research and study the structures and chemical properties of various natural and manmade materials, including metals, alloys, rubber, ceramics, semiconductors, polymers, and glass. Determine ways to strengthen or combine materials or develop new materials with new or specific properties for use in a variety of products and applications. **O*NET Code:** 19-2032.00. **Average Salary:** $71,090. **Projected Growth:** 8.5%. **Annual Openings:** 1,000. **Education:** Bachelor's degree. **Job Zone:** 4. **Education/Training Program(s)**—Materials Science. **Related Knowledge/Courses:** Chemistry; Physics; Engineering and Technology; Mathematics; Administration and Management; English Language. **Personality Type:** Investigative. **Skills Required:** Science; Active Learning; Writing; Mathematics; Reading Comprehension; Operations Analysis; Quality Control Analysis; Speaking; Critical Thinking; Systems Evaluation. **Abilities:** Originality; Mathematical Reasoning; Written Expression; Number Facility; Fluency of Ideas. **Occupational Values:** Creativity; Autonomy; Ability Utilization; Social Status; Responsibility. **Interacting with Others:** Communicating with Supervisors, Peers, or Subordinates; Interpreting the Meaning of Information for Others; Guiding, Directing, and Motivating Subordinates. **Physical Work Conditions:** Sitting; Indoors; Common Protective or Safety Equipment; Using Hands on Objects, Tools, or Controls.

Physicists

Conduct research into the phases of physical phenomena, develop theories and laws on the basis of observation and experiments, and devise methods to apply laws and theories to industry and other fields. **O*NET Code:** 19-2012.00. **Average Salary:** $83,570. **Projected Growth:** 6.9%. **Annual Openings:** 1,000. **Education:** Doctoral degree. **Job Zone:** 5. **Education/Training Program(s)**—Acoustics; Astrophysics; Atomic/Molecular Physics; Elementary Particle Physics; Health/Medical Physics; Nuclear Physics; Optics/Optical Sciences; Physics, General; Physics, Other; Plasma and High-Temperature Physics; Solid State and Low-Temperature Physics; Theoretical and Mathematical Physics. **Related Knowledge/Courses:** Physics; Mathematics; Education and Training; Engineering and Technology; Design; English Language. **Personality Type:** Investigative. **Skills Required:** Science; Mathematics; Writing; Active Learning; Technology Design; Reading Comprehension; Critical Thinking; Operations Analysis. **Abilities:** Mathematical Reasoning; Deductive Reasoning; Written Comprehension; Written Expression; Inductive Reasoning. **Occupational Values:** Creativity; Autonomy; Ability Utilization; Recognition; Social Status. **Interacting with Others:** Interpreting the Meaning of Information for Others; Communicating with Persons Outside Organization; Providing Consultation and Advice to Others. **Physical Work Conditions:** Sitting; Specialized Protective or Safety Equipment; Indoors; Exposed to Radiation; Hazardous Conditions.

15.03 Life Sciences

Biochemists

Research or study chemical composition and processes of living organisms that affect vital processes such as growth and aging to determine chemical actions and effects on organisms such as the action of foods, drugs, or other substances on body functions and tissues. **O*NET Code:** 19-1021.01. **Average Salary:** $64,390. **Projected Growth:** 22.9%. **Annual Openings:** 2,000. **Education:** Doctoral degree. **Job Zone:** 5. **Education/Training Program(s)**—Biochemistry; Biochemistry/Biophysics and Molecular Biology; Biophysics; Cell/Cellular Biology and Anatomical Sciences, Other; Molecular Biochemistry; Molecular Biophysics; Soil Chemistry and Physics; Soil Microbiology. **Related Knowledge/Courses:** Biology; Chemistry; Mathematics; Building and Construction; Engineering and Technology; English Language. **Personality Type:** Investigative. **Skills Required:** Science; Writing; Reading Comprehension; Active Learning; Programming; Critical Thinking; Mathematics; Equipment Selection. **Abilities:** Inductive Reasoning; Written Expression; Written Comprehension; Deductive Reasoning; Category Flexibility. **Occupational Values:** Creativity; Autonomy; Ability Utilization; Responsibility; Independence. **Interacting with Others:** Interpreting the Meaning of Information for Others; Providing Consultation and Advice to Others; Communicating with Supervisors, Peers, or Subordinates. **Physical Work Conditions:** Disease or Infections; Common Protective or Safety Equipment; Indoors; Contaminants; Sitting.

Biologists

Research or study basic principles of plant and animal life, such as origin, relationship, development, anatomy, and functions. **O*NET Code:** 19-1020.01. **Average Salary:** $64,390. **Projected Growth:** 22.3%. **Annual Openings:** 3,000. **Education:** Doctoral degree. **Job Zone:** 5. **Education/Training Program(s)**—Biochemistry; Biochemistry/Biophysics and Molecular Biology; Biology/Biological Sciences, General; Biophysics; Cell/Cellular Biology and Anatomical Sciences, Other; Molecular Biochemistry; Soil Microbiology. **Related Knowledge/Courses:** Biology; Law and Government; Chemistry; Geography; Computers and Electronics; Physics; Public Safety and Security. **Personality Type:** Investigative. **Skills Required:** Negotiation; Persuasion; Management of Financial Resources; Science; Judgment and Decision Making; Active Learning; Management of Material Resources; Critical Thinking. **Abilities:** Inductive Reasoning; Category Flexibility; Oral Expression; Written Expression; Flexibility of Closure. **Occupational Values:** Autonomy; Creativity; Ability Utilization; Recognition; Responsibility. **Interacting with Others:** Establishing and Maintaining Interpersonal Relationships; Communicating with Supervisors, Peers, or Subordinates; Communicating with Persons Outside Organization. **Physical Work Conditions:** Sitting; Sounds, Noise Levels Are Distracting or Uncomfortable; Indoors; In an Enclosed Vehicle or Equipment; Outdoors; Physical Proximity.

Biophysicists

Research or study physical principles of living cells and organisms, their electrical and mechanical energy, and related phenomena. **O*NET Code:** 19-1021.02. **Average Salary:** $64,390. **Projected Growth:** 22.9%. **Annual Openings:** 2,000. **Education:** Doctoral degree. **Job Zone:** 5. **Education/Training Program(s)**—Biochemistry; Biochemistry/Biophysics and Molecular Biology; Biophysics; Cell/Cellular Biology and Anatomical Sciences, Other; Molecular Biochemistry; Molecular Biophysics; Soil Chemistry and Physics; Soil Microbiology. **Related Knowledge/Courses:** Biology; Physics; Mathematics; Chemistry. **Personality Type:** Investigative. **Skills Required:** Science; Reading Comprehension; Writing; Mathematics; Active Learning; Critical Thinking; Complex Problem Solving; Programming. **Abilities:** Inductive Reasoning; Written Expression; Category Flexibility; Written Comprehension; Oral Comprehension. **Occupational Values:** Autonomy; Ability Utilization; Responsibility; Independence; Creativity. **Interacting with Others:** Interpreting the Meaning of Information for Others; Communicating with Supervisors, Peers, or Subordinates; Providing Consultation and Advice to Others. **Physical Work Conditions:** Common Protective or Safety Equipment; Indoors; Exposed to Radiation; Disease or Infections; Contaminants; Using Hands on Objects, Tools, or Controls.

Environmental Scientists and Specialists, Including Health

Conduct research or perform investigation for the purpose of identifying, abating, or eliminating sources of pollutants or hazards that affect either the environment or the health of the population. Utilizing knowledge of various scientific disciplines, may collect, synthesize, study, report, and take action based on data derived from measurements or observations of air, food, soil, water, and other sources. **O*NET Code:** 19-2041.00. **Average Salary:** $50,070. **Projected Growth:** 23.7%. **Annual Openings:** 6,000. **Education:** Bachelor's degree. **Job Zone:** 5. **Education/Training Program(s)**—Environmental Science; Environmental Studies. **Related Knowledge/Courses:** Biology; Geography; Law and Government; Chemistry; Customer and Personal Service; Education and Training. **Personality Type:** Investigative. **Skills Required:** Service Orientation; Science; Coordination; Negotiation; Persuasion; Reading Comprehension; Active Learning; Time Management. **Abilities:** Inductive Reasoning; Problem Sensitivity; Speech Clarity; Mathematical Reasoning; Oral Comprehension; Oral Expression. **Occupational Values:** Autonomy; Creativity; Ability Utilization; Achievement; Recognition. **Interacting with Others:** Establishing and Maintaining Interpersonal Relationships; Communicating with Supervisors, Peers, or Subordinates; Communicating with Persons Outside Organization. **Physical Work Conditions:** Very Hot or Cold; In an Enclosed Vehicle or Equipment; Sitting; Sounds, Noise Levels Are Distracting or Uncomfortable; Contaminants.

Epidemiologists

Investigate and describe the determinants and distribution of disease, disability, and other health outcomes and develop the means for prevention and control. **O*NET Code:** 19-1041.00. **Average Salary:** $53,660. **Projected Growth:** 32.5%. **Annual Openings:** Fewer than 500. **Education:** Doctoral degree. **Job**

Zone: 4. Education/Training Program(s)—Cell/Cellular Biology and Histology; Epidemiology; Medical Scientist (MS, PhD). Related Knowledge/Courses: Biology; Medicine and Dentistry; Chemistry; Mathematics; Education and Training; Communications and Media. Personality Type: Investigative. Skills Required: Instructing; Science; Active Learning; Systems Evaluation; Writing; Systems Analysis; Reading Comprehension; Service Orientation. Abilities: Written Expression; Inductive Reasoning; Speech Clarity; Fluency of Ideas; Originality. Occupational Values: Social Status; Achievement; Creativity; Ability Utilization; Recognition. Interacting with Others: Training and Teaching Others; Interpreting the Meaning of Information for Others; Communicating with Supervisors, Peers, or Subordinates. Physical Work Conditions: Disease or Infections; Common Protective or Safety Equipment; Sitting; Specialized Protective or Safety Equipment; Indoors.

Medical Scientists, Except Epidemiologists

Conduct research dealing with the understanding of human diseases and the improvement of human health. Engage in clinical investigation or other research, production, technical writing, or related activities. O*NET Code: 19-1042.00. Average Salary: $60,200. Projected Growth: 26.9%. Annual Openings: 6,000. Education: Doctoral degree. Job Zone: 4. Education/Training Program(s)—Anatomy; Biochemistry; Biomedical Sciences, General; Biophysics; Biostatistics; Cardiovascular Science; Cell Physiology; Cell/Cellular Biology and Histology; Endocrinology; Environmental Toxicology; Epidemiology; Exercise Physiology; Human/Medical Genetics; Immunology; Medical Microbiology and Bacteriology; Medical Scientist (MS, PhD); Molecular Biology; Molecular Pharmacology; Molecular Physiology; Molecular Toxicology; Neurobiology and Neurophysiology; Neuropharmacology; Oncology and Cancer Biology; Pathology/Experimental Pathology; Pharmacology; Pharmacology and Toxicology; Pharmacology and Toxicology, Other; Physiology, General; Physiology, Pathology, and Related Sciences, Other; Reproductive Biology; Toxicology; Vision Science/Physiological Optics. Related Knowledge/Courses: Biology; Medicine and Dentistry; Chemistry; Mathematics; Education and Training; Communications and Media. Personality Type: Investigative. Skills Required: Instructing; Science; Active Learning; Systems Evaluation; Writing; Systems Analysis; Reading Comprehension; Service Orientation. Abilities: Written Expression; Inductive Reasoning; Speech Clarity; Fluency of Ideas; Originality. Occupational Values: Social Status; Achievement; Creativity; Ability Utilization; Recognition. Interacting with Others: Training and Teaching Others; Interpreting the Meaning of Information for Others; Communicating with Supervisors, Peers, or Subordinates. Physical Work Conditions: Disease or Infections; Common Protective or Safety Equipment; Sitting; Specialized Protective or Safety Equipment; Indoors.

Microbiologists

Investigate the growth, structure, development, and other characteristics of microscopic organisms, such as bacteria, algae, or fungi. Includes medical microbiologists who study the relationship between organisms and disease or the effects of antibiotics on microorganisms. O*NET Code: 19-1022.00. Average Salary: $52,100. Projected Growth: 20.0%. Annual Openings: 1,000. Education: Doctoral degree. Job Zone: 4. Education/Training Program(s)—Biochemistry/Biophysics and Molecular Biology; Cell/Cellular Biology and Anatomical Sciences, Other; Microbiology, General; Neuroanatomy; Soil Microbiology; Structural Biology. Related Knowledge/Courses: Biology; Chemistry; Clerical; English Language; Computers and Electronics; Administration and Management. Personality Type: Investigative. Skills Required: Science; Operation Monitoring; Instructing; Equipment Maintenance; Active Listening; Troubleshooting; Time Management; Technology Design. Abilities: Inductive Reasoning; Category Flexibility; Speed of Closure; Written Expression; Oral Comprehension; Oral Expression. Occupational Values: Autonomy; Creativity; Ability Utilization; Social Status; Independence. Interacting with Others: Interpreting the Meaning of Information for Others; Communicating with Supervisors, Peers, or Subordinates; Establishing and Maintaining Interpersonal Relationships; Training and Teaching Others. Physical Work Conditions: Contaminants; Hazardous Conditions; Disease or Infections; Sitting; Indoors.

15.04 Social Sciences

Anthropologists

Research or study the origins and physical, social, and cultural development and behavior of humans and the cultures and organizations they have created. O*NET Code: 19-3091.01. Average Salary: $41,260. Projected Growth: 12.8%. Annual Openings: 1,000. Education: Bachelor's degree. Job Zone: 4. Education/Training Program(s)—Anthropology; Archeology; Physical Anthropology. Related Knowledge/Courses: Sociology and Anthropology; History and Archeology; Geography; Biology; Philosophy and Theology; Foreign Language. Personality Type: Investigative. Skills Required: Science; Writing; Active Learning; Social Perceptiveness; Critical Thinking; Complex Problem Solving; Reading Comprehension; Instructing. Abilities: Written Expression; Oral Comprehension; Written Comprehension; Inductive Reasoning; Fluency of Ideas. Occupational Values: Autonomy; Creativity; Ability Utilization; Responsibility; Achievement; Variety. Interacting with Others: Interpreting the Meaning of Information for Others; Providing Consultation and Advice to Others; Communicating with Supervisors, Peers, or Subordinates. Physical Work Conditions: Sitting; Outdoors; Walking and Running; Kneeling, Crouching, Stooping, or Crawling.

Archeologists

Conduct research to reconstruct record of past human life and culture from human remains, artifacts, architectural features, and structures recovered through excavation, underwater recovery, or other means of discovery. O*NET Code: 19-3091.02. Average Salary: $41,260. Projected Growth: 12.8%. Annual Openings: 1,000. Education: Bachelor's degree. Job Zone: 4. Education/Training Program(s)—Anthropology; Archeology; Physical Anthropology. Related Knowledge/

Courses: History and Archeology; Sociology and Anthropology; Geography; Foreign Language; Philosophy and Theology; English Language. **Personality Type:** Investigative. **Skills Required:** Science; Active Learning; Writing; Critical Thinking; Reading Comprehension; Complex Problem Solving; Judgment and Decision Making; Management of Material Resources. **Abilities:** Inductive Reasoning; Deductive Reasoning; Category Flexibility; Written Comprehension; Written Expression. **Occupational Values:** Autonomy; Creativity; Achievement; Responsibility; Recognition. **Interacting with Others:** Interpreting the Meaning of Information for Others; Communicating with Supervisors, Peers, or Subordinates; Communicating with Persons Outside Organization. **Physical Work Conditions:** Outdoors; Kneeling, Crouching, Stooping, or Crawling; Very Hot or Cold; Spend Time Bending or Twisting the Body; Extremely Bright or Inadequate Lighting.

Economists

Conduct research, prepare reports, or formulate plans to aid in solution of economic problems arising from production and distribution of goods and services. May collect and process economic and statistical data using econometric and sampling techniques. **O*NET Code:** 19-3011.00. **Average Salary:** $70,520. **Projected Growth:** 13.4%. **Annual Openings:** 2,000. **Education:** Bachelor's degree. **Job Zone:** 5. **Education/Training Program(s)**—Agricultural Economics; Applied Economics; Business/Managerial Economics; Development Economics and International Development; Econometrics and Quantitative Economics; Economics, General; Economics, Other; International Economics. **Related Knowledge/Courses:** Economics and Accounting; Mathematics; Education and Training; Personnel and Human Resources; Production and Processing; Computers and Electronics. **Personality Type:** Investigative. **Skills Required:** Systems Evaluation; Systems Analysis; Persuasion; Judgment and Decision Making; Complex Problem Solving; Instructing; Writing; Learning Strategies. **Abilities:** Speech Clarity; Written Expression; Mathematical Reasoning; Number Facility; Oral Expression. **Occupational Values:** Autonomy; Authority; Ability Utilization; Creativity; Working Conditions. **Interacting with Others:** Providing Consultation and Advice to Others; Training and Teaching Others; Communicating with Supervisors, Peers, or Subordinates; Communicating with Persons Outside Organization. **Physical Work Conditions:** Sitting; Indoors; Standing.

Educational Psychologists

Investigate processes of learning and teaching and develop psychological principles and techniques applicable to educational problems. **O*NET Code:** 19-3031.01. **Average Salary:** $53,230. **Projected Growth:** 24.4%. **Annual Openings:** 17,000. **Education:** Master's degree. **Job Zone:** 4. **Education/Training Program(s)**—Clinical Child Psychology; Clinical Psychology; Counseling Psychology; Developmental and Child Psychology; Psychoanalysis and Psychotherapy; Psychology, General; School Psychology. **Related Knowledge/Courses:** Psychology; Education and Training; Therapy and Counseling; Sociology and Anthropology; Mathematics; English Language. **Personality Type:**

Investigative. **Skills Required:** Social Perceptiveness; Systems Evaluation; Science; Learning Strategies; Systems Analysis; Writing; Complex Problem Solving; Mathematics; Service Orientation. **Abilities:** Written Expression; Category Flexibility; Speed of Closure; Inductive Reasoning; Written Comprehension; Oral Expression. **Occupational Values:** Social Service; Creativity; Autonomy; Ability Utilization; Achievement. **Interacting with Others:** Communicating with Supervisors, Peers, or Subordinates; Interpreting the Meaning of Information for Others; Communicating with Persons Outside Organization; Providing Consultation and Advice to Others. **Physical Work Conditions:** Sitting; Walking and Running; Indoors; Extremely Bright or Inadequate Lighting.

Historians

Research, analyze, record, and interpret the past as recorded in sources such as government and institutional records, newspapers and other periodicals, photographs, interviews, films, and unpublished manuscripts, such as personal diaries and letters. **O*NET Code:** 19-3093.00. **Average Salary:** $42,370. **Projected Growth:** 6.6%. **Annual Openings:** Fewer than 500. **Education:** Bachelor's degree. **Job Zone:** 5. **Education/Training Program(s)**—American History (United States); Ancient Studies/Civilization; Architectural History and Criticism, General; Asian History; Canadian History; Classical, Ancient Mediterranean and Near Eastern Studies and Archaeology; Cultural Resource Management and Policy Analysis; European History; Historic Preservation and Conservation; Historic Preservation and Conservation, Other; History and Philosophy of Science and Technology; History, General; History, Other; Holocaust and Related Studies; Medieval and Renaissance Studies. **Related Knowledge/Courses:** History and Archeology; Computers and Electronics; English Language; Clerical; Communications and Media; Geography. **Personality Type:** Investigative. **Skills Required:** Reading Comprehension; Social Perceptiveness; Instructing; Management of Financial Resources; Time Management; Management of Personnel Resources; Persuasion; Active Learning. **Abilities:** Written Expression; Written Comprehension; Memorization; Oral Comprehension; Oral Expression. **Occupational Values:** Autonomy; Working Conditions; Creativity; Responsibility; Achievement. **Interacting with Others:** Communicating with Persons Outside Organization; Providing Consultation and Advice to Others; Establishing and Maintaining Interpersonal Relationships. **Physical Work Conditions:** Contaminants; Sounds, Noise Levels Are Distracting or Uncomfortable; Extremely Bright or Inadequate Lighting; Physical Proximity; Cramped Work Space, Awkward Positions.

Industrial-Organizational Psychologists

Apply principles of psychology to personnel, administration, management, sales, and marketing problems. Activities may include policy planning; employee screening, training, and development; and organizational development and analysis. May work with management to reorganize the work setting to improve worker productivity. **O*NET Code:** 19-3032.00. **Average Salary:** $67,740. **Projected Growth:** 16.0%. **Annual Openings:** Fewer than 500. **Education:** Master's degree. **Job Zone:** 5. **Education/Training Program(s)**—Industrial and Organizational Psychology; Psychology, General. **Related**

Knowledge/Courses: Personnel and Human Resources; Psychology; Education and Training; Administration and Management; Mathematics; Sales and Marketing; Therapy and Counseling. **Personality Type:** Investigative. **Skills Required:** Systems Evaluation; Management of Personnel Resources; Science; Systems Analysis; Complex Problem Solving; Mathematics; Active Learning; Social Perceptiveness. **Abilities:** Originality; Written Expression; Mathematical Reasoning; Oral Expression; Oral Comprehension. **Occupational Values:** Creativity; Autonomy; Working Conditions; Compensation; Authority. **Interacting with Others:** Communicating with Supervisors, Peers, or Subordinates; Providing Consultation and Advice to Others; Communicating with Persons Outside Organization; Training and Teaching Others. **Physical Work Conditions:** Indoors; Sitting.

Political Scientists

Study the origin, development, and operation of political systems. Research a wide range of subjects, such as relations between the United States and foreign countries, the beliefs and institutions of foreign nations, or the politics of small towns or a major metropolis. May study topics such as public opinion, political decision making, and ideology. May analyze the structure and operation of governments as well as various political entities. May conduct public opinion surveys, analyze election results, or analyze public documents. **O*NET Code:** 19-3094.00. **Average Salary:** $81,670. **Projected Growth:** 5.9%. **Annual Openings:** 1,000. **Education:** Master's degree. **Job Zone:** 5. **Education/Training Program(s)**—American Government and Politics (United States); Canadian Government and Politics; International/Global Studies; Political Science and Government, General; Political Science and Government, Other. **Related Knowledge/Courses:** Law and Government; Philosophy and Theology; History and Archeology; Sociology and Anthropology; Communications and Media; Geography; English Language. **Personality Type:** Investigative. **Skills Required:** Systems Analysis; Writing; Mathematics; Active Learning; Social Perceptiveness; Systems Evaluation; Reading Comprehension; Speaking. **Abilities:** Written Expression; Written Comprehension; Inductive Reasoning; Oral Comprehension; Oral Expression. **Occupational Values:** Autonomy; Creativity; Working Conditions; Responsibility; Ability Utilization. **Interacting with Others:** Providing Consultation and Advice to Others; Communicating with Persons Outside Organization; Communicating with Supervisors, Peers, or Subordinates. **Physical Work Conditions:** Sitting; Indoors.

Sociologists

Study human society and social behavior by examining the groups and social institutions that people form as well as various social, religious, political, and business organizations. May study the behavior and interaction of groups, trace their origin and growth, and analyze the influence of group activities on individual members. **O*NET Code:** 19-3041.00. **Average Salary:** $55,630. **Projected Growth:** 13.4%. **Annual Openings:** Fewer than 500. **Education:** Master's degree. **Job Zone:** 3. **Education/Training Program(s)**—Criminology; Demography and Population Studies; Sociology; Urban

Studies/Affairs. **Related Knowledge/Courses:** Sociology and Anthropology; Education and Training; Philosophy and Theology; English Language; Psychology; History and Archeology. **Personality Type:** Investigative. **Skills Required:** Writing; Social Perceptiveness; Mathematics; Systems Analysis; Active Learning; Critical Thinking; Complex Problem Solving; Systems Evaluation. **Abilities:** Written Expression; Mathematical Reasoning; Oral Comprehension; Written Comprehension; Originality. **Occupational Values:** Creativity; Autonomy; Responsibility; Working Conditions; Ability Utilization. **Interacting with Others:** Communicating with Supervisors, Peers, or Subordinates; Providing Consultation and Advice to Others; Interpreting the Meaning of Information for Others; Communicating with Persons Outside Organization. **Physical Work Conditions:** Sitting; Indoors.

15.05 Physical Science Laboratory Technology

Chemical Technicians

Conduct chemical and physical laboratory tests to assist scientists in making qualitative and quantitative analyses of solids, liquids, and gaseous materials for purposes such as research and development of new products or processes; quality control; maintenance of environmental standards; and other work involving experimental, theoretical, or practical application of chemistry and related sciences. **O*NET Code:** 19-4031.00. **Average Salary:** $37,620. **Projected Growth:** 4.7%. **Annual Openings:** 9,000. **Education:** Associate degree. **Job Zone:** 3. **Education/Training Program(s)**—Chemical Technology/Technician; Food Science. **Related Knowledge/Courses:** Chemistry; Computers and Electronics; Mechanical; Mathematics; Customer and Personal Service; English Language. **Personality Type:** Realistic. **Skills Required:** Operation Monitoring; Science; Quality Control Analysis; Equipment Maintenance; Troubleshooting; Repairing; Time Management; Mathematics; Active Learning; Operation and Control. **Abilities:** Category Flexibility; Inductive Reasoning; Flexibility of Closure; Oral Comprehension; Near Vision. **Occupational Values:** Advancement; Variety; Supervision, Human Relations; Supervision, Technical; Co-workers. **Interacting with Others:** Communicating with Supervisors, Peers, or Subordinates; Establishing and Maintaining Interpersonal Relationships; Training and Teaching Others. **Physical Work Conditions:** Hazardous Conditions; Contaminants; Sounds, Noise Levels Are Distracting or Uncomfortable; Indoors; Very Hot or Cold.

Nuclear Equipment Operation Technicians

Operate equipment used for the release, control, and utilization of nuclear energy to assist scientists in laboratory and production activities. **O*NET Code:** 19-4051.01. **Average Salary:** $60,250. **Projected Growth:** 1.5%. **Annual Openings:** 1,000. **Education:** Associate degree. **Job Zone:** 3. **Education/Training Program(s)**—Industrial Radiologic Technology/Technician; Nuclear and Industrial

Radiologic Technologies/Technicians, Other; Nuclear Engineering Technology/Technician; Nuclear/Nuclear Power Technology/Technician; Radiation Protection/Health Physics Technician. **Related Knowledge/Courses:** Physics; Engineering and Technology; Chemistry; Public Safety and Security; Production and Processing; Design. **Personality Type:** Realistic. **Skills Required:** Science; Installation; Mathematics; Operation Monitoring; Operation and Control; Equipment Maintenance; Quality Control Analysis; Troubleshooting. **Abilities:** Reaction Time; Control Precision; Perceptual Speed; Number Facility; Information Ordering; Arm-Hand Steadiness. **Occupational Values:** Compensation; Supervision, Technical; Ability Utilization; Advancement; Supervision, Human Relations. **Interacting with Others:** Communicating with Supervisors, Peers, or Subordinates; Interpreting the Meaning of Information for Others; Coordinating the Work and Activities of Others. **Physical Work Conditions:** Exposed to Radiation; Specialized Protective or Safety Equipment; Hazardous Conditions; Hazardous Equipment; Common Protective or Safety Equipment.

Photographers, Scientific

Photograph variety of subject material to illustrate or record scientific/medical data or phenomena, utilizing knowledge of scientific procedures and photographic technology and techniques. **O*NET Code:** 27-4021.02. **Average Salary:** $25,950. **Projected Growth:** 13.6%. **Annual Openings:** 18,000. **Education:** Long-term on-the-job training. **Job Zone:** 3. **Education/Training Program(s)**—Art/Art Studies, General; Commercial Photography; Film/Video and Photographic Arts, Other; Photography; Photojournalism; Visual and Performing Arts, General. **Related Knowledge/Courses:** Fine Arts; Chemistry; Physics; Engineering and Technology; Medicine and Dentistry; Communications and Media. **Personality Type:** Artistic. **Skills Required:** Science; Reading Comprehension; Equipment Selection; Technology Design; Active Learning; Operation and Control; Management of Material Resources; Writing. **Abilities:** Visual Color Discrimination; Night Vision; Far Vision; Fluency of Ideas; Rate Control. **Occupational Values:** Creativity; Ability Utilization; Achievement; Autonomy; Independence; Recognition. **Interacting with Others:** Communicating with Persons Outside Organization; Communicating with Supervisors, Peers, or Subordinates; Establishing and Maintaining Interpersonal Relationships. **Physical Work Conditions:** Standing; Extremely Bright or Inadequate Lighting; Hazardous Conditions; Using Hands on Objects, Tools, or Controls; Outdoors; Walking and Running.

15.06 Mathematics and Data Analysis

Actuaries

Analyze statistical data such as mortality, accident, sickness, disability, and retirement rates and construct probability tables to forecast risk and liability for payment of future ben-

efits. May ascertain premium rates required and cash reserves necessary to ensure payment of future benefits. **O*NET Code:** 15-2011.00. **Average Salary:** $75,280. **Projected Growth:** 14.9%. **Annual Openings:** 2,000. **Education:** Work experience plus degree. **Job Zone:** 5. **Education/Training Program(s)**—Actuarial Science. **Related Knowledge/Courses:** Mathematics; Economics and Accounting; Computers and Electronics; Sales and Marketing; English Language; Personnel and Human Resources. **Personality Type:** Conventional. **Skills Required:** Mathematics; Programming; Active Learning; Complex Problem Solving; Critical Thinking; Operations Analysis; Monitoring; Instructing. **Abilities:** Number Facility; Mathematical Reasoning; Deductive Reasoning; Written Expression; Speed of Closure. **Occupational Values:** Autonomy; Working Conditions; Advancement; Ability Utilization; Independence; Supervision, Human Relations. **Interacting with Others:** Communicating with Supervisors, Peers, or Subordinates; Establishing and Maintaining Interpersonal Relationships; Providing Consultation and Advice to Others. **Physical Work Conditions:** Sitting; Indoors; Sounds, Noise Levels Are Distracting or Uncomfortable; Physical Proximity.

Mathematical Technicians

Apply standardized mathematical formulas, principles, and methodology to technological problems in engineering and physical sciences in relation to specific industrial and research objectives, processes, equipment, and products. **O*NET Code:** 15-2091.00. **Average Salary:** $37,370. **Projected Growth:** 11.8%. **Annual Openings:** 1,000. **Education:** Bachelor's degree. **Job Zone:** 4. **Education/Training Program(s)**—Applied Mathematics. **Related Knowledge/Courses:** Mathematics; Computers and Electronics; Engineering and Technology; English Language; Physics; Clerical. **Personality Type:** Investigative. **Skills Required:** Mathematics; Programming; Science; Critical Thinking; Active Learning; Complex Problem Solving; Operations Analysis; Judgment and Decision Making. **Abilities:** Mathematical Reasoning; Number Facility; Deductive Reasoning; Oral Comprehension; Oral Expression. **Occupational Values:** Advancement; Ability Utilization; Working Conditions; Supervision, Human Relations; Creativity. **Interacting with Others:** Communicating with Supervisors, Peers, or Subordinates; Interpreting the Meaning of Information for Others; Establishing and Maintaining Interpersonal Relationships. **Physical Work Conditions:** Sitting; Indoors.

Mathematicians

Conduct research in fundamental mathematics or in application of mathematical techniques to science, management, and other fields. Solve or direct solutions to problems in various fields by mathematical methods. **O*NET Code:** 15-2021.00. **Average Salary:** $77,670. **Projected Growth:** –1.0%. **Annual Openings:** Fewer than 500. **Education:** Master's degree. **Job Zone:** 5. **Education/Training Program(s)**—Algebra and Number Theory; Analysis and Functional Analysis; Applied Mathematics; Applied Mathematics, Other; Computational Mathematics; Geometry/Geometric Analysis; Logic; Mathematical Statistics and Probability; Mathematics and Statistics, Other; Mathematics, General; Mathematics, Other;

Topology and Foundations. **Related Knowledge/Courses:** Mathematics; Engineering and Technology; Economics and Accounting; Computers and Electronics; Physics; Administration and Management. **Personality Type:** Investigative. **Skills Required:** Mathematics; Active Learning; Learning Strategies; Critical Thinking; Complex Problem Solving; Reading Comprehension; Writing; Operations Analysis. **Abilities:** Mathematical Reasoning; Number Facility; Originality; Written Expression; Fluency of Ideas; Inductive Reasoning. **Occupational Values:** Autonomy; Ability Utilization; Creativity; Independence; Working Conditions. **Interacting with Others:** Interpreting the Meaning of Information for Others; Communicating with Supervisors, Peers, or Subordinates; Providing Consultation and Advice to Others. **Physical Work Conditions:** Sitting; Indoors.

Social Science Research Assistants

Assist social scientists in laboratory, survey, and other social research. May perform publication activities, laboratory analysis, quality control, or data management. Normally these individuals work under the direct supervision of a social scientist and assist in those activities which are more routine. **O*NET Code:** 19-4061.00. **Average Salary:** $48,660. **Projected Growth:** 17.5%. **Annual Openings:** 18,000. **Education:** Associate degree. **Job Zone:** No data available. **Education/Training Program(s)**—Social Sciences, General. **Related Knowledge/Courses:** No data available. **Personality Type:** No data available. **Skills Required:** No data available. **Abilities:** No data available. **Occupational Values:** No data available. **Interacting with Others:** No data available. **Physical Work Conditions:** No data available.

Statistical Assistants

Compile and compute data according to statistical formulas for use in statistical studies. May perform actuarial computations and compile charts and graphs for use by actuaries. Includes actuarial clerks. **O*NET Code:** 43-9111.00. **Average Salary:** $29,990. **Projected Growth:** –7.2%. **Annual Openings:** 2,000. **Education:** Moderate-term on-the-job training. **Job Zone:** 2. **Education/Training Program(s)**—Accounting Technology/Technician and Bookkeeping. **Related Knowledge/Courses:** Mathematics; Computers and Electronics; Clerical; Communications and Media. **Personality Type:** Conventional. **Skills Required:** Mathematics; Writing; Programming. **Abilities:** Mathematical Reasoning; Number Facility; Wrist-Finger Speed; Category Flexibility; Written Expression. **Occupational Values:** Independence; Working Conditions; Advancement; Supervision, Human Relations; Autonomy. **Interacting with Others:** Interpreting the Meaning of Information for Others; Communicating with Supervisors, Peers, or Subordinates; Providing Consultation and Advice to Others. **Physical Work Conditions:** Sitting; Indoors; Spend Time Making Repetitive Motions; Spend Time Bending or Twisting the Body.

Statisticians

Engage in the development of mathematical theory or apply statistical theory and methods to collect, organize, interpret, and summarize numerical data to provide usable information. May specialize in fields such as bio-statistics, agricultural statistics, business statistics, economic statistics, or other fields. **O*NET Code:** 15-2041.00. **Average Salary:** $64,320. **Projected Growth:** 4.8%. **Annual Openings:** 2,000. **Education:** Master's degree. **Job Zone:** 4. **Education/Training Program(s)**—Applied Mathematics; Biostatistics; Business Statistics; Mathematical Statistics and Probability; Mathematics, General; Statistics, General; Statistics, Other. **Related Knowledge/Courses:** Mathematics; Computers and Electronics; English Language; Economics and Accounting; Administration and Management; Clerical. **Personality Type:** Investigative. **Skills Required:** Mathematics; Science; Systems Evaluation; Active Learning; Critical Thinking; Complex Problem Solving; Judgment and Decision Making; Systems Analysis. **Abilities:** Number Facility; Mathematical Reasoning; Speed of Closure; Written Expression; Inductive Reasoning. **Occupational Values:** Autonomy; Ability Utilization; Creativity; Independence; Responsibility. **Interacting with Others:** Interpreting the Meaning of Information for Others; Communicating with Supervisors, Peers, or Subordinates; Communicating with Persons Outside Organization. **Physical Work Conditions:** Sitting; Indoors.

15.07 Research and Design Engineering

Aerospace Engineers

Perform a variety of engineering work in designing, constructing, and testing aircraft, missiles, and spacecraft. May conduct basic and applied research to evaluate adaptability of materials and equipment to aircraft design and manufacture. May recommend improvements in testing equipment and techniques. **O*NET Code:** 17-2011.00. **Average Salary:** $77,340. **Projected Growth:** –5.2%. **Annual Openings:** 5,000. **Education:** Bachelor's degree. **Job Zone:** 5. **Education/Training Program(s)**—Aerospace, Aeronautical and Astronautical Engineering. **Related Knowledge/Courses:** Engineering and Technology; Design; Physics; Mechanical; Computers and Electronics; Mathematics. **Personality Type:** Investigative. **Skills Required:** Systems Evaluation; Systems Analysis; Science; Persuasion; Judgment and Decision Making; Time Management; Management of Personnel Resources; Technology Design. **Abilities:** Mathematical Reasoning; Deductive Reasoning; Inductive Reasoning; Written Expression; Information Ordering. **Occupational Values:** Creativity; Social Status; Ability Utilization; Authority; Responsibility; Autonomy. **Interacting with Others:** Establishing and Maintaining Interpersonal Relationships; Communicating with Supervisors, Peers, or Subordinates; Coordinating the Work and Activities of Others. **Physical Work Conditions:** Sitting; Sounds, Noise Levels Are Distracting or Uncomfortable; Indoors; Physical Proximity; Very Hot or Cold.

Biomedical Engineers

Apply knowledge of engineering, biology, and biomechanical principles to the design, development, and evaluation of biological and health systems and products, such as artificial organs, prostheses, instrumentation, medical information systems, and health management and care delivery systems. **O*NET Code:** 17-2031.00. **Average Salary:** $64,780. **Projected Growth:** 26.1%. **Annual Openings:** Fewer than 500. **Education:** Bachelor's degree. **Job Zone:** No data available. **Education/Training Program(s)**—Biomedical/Medical Engineering. **Related Knowledge/Courses:** No data available. **Personality Type:** No data available. **Skills Required:** No data available. **Abilities:** No data available. **Occupational Values:** No data available. **Interacting with Others:** No data available. **Physical Work Conditions:** No data available.

Chemical Engineers

Design chemical plant equipment and devise processes for manufacturing chemicals and products, such as gasoline, synthetic rubber, plastics, detergents, cement, paper, and pulp, by applying principles and technology of chemistry, physics, and engineering. **O*NET Code:** 17-2041.00. **Average Salary:** $75,310. **Projected Growth:** 0.4%. **Annual Openings:** 2,000. **Education:** Bachelor's degree. **Job Zone:** 4. **Education/Training Program(s)**—Chemical Engineering. **Related Knowledge/Courses:** Engineering and Technology; Chemistry; Physics; Design; Production and Processing; Mathematics. **Personality Type:** Investigative. **Skills Required:** Science; Technology Design; Troubleshooting; Mathematics; Operations Analysis; Systems Analysis; Active Learning; Installation; Systems Evaluation. **Abilities:** Mathematical Reasoning; Originality; Category Flexibility; Deductive Reasoning; Written Comprehension. **Occupational Values:** Creativity; Ability Utilization; Authority; Social Status; Responsibility; Autonomy. **Interacting with Others:** Communicating with Supervisors, Peers, or Subordinates; Providing Consultation and Advice to Others; Establishing and Maintaining Interpersonal Relationships. **Physical Work Conditions:** Sitting; Sounds, Noise Levels Are Distracting or Uncomfortable; Hazardous Conditions; Contaminants; Very Hot or Cold.

Civil Engineers

Perform engineering duties in planning, designing, and overseeing construction and maintenance of building structures and facilities, such as roads, railroads, airports, bridges, harbors, channels, dams, irrigation projects, pipelines, power plants, water and sewage systems, and waste disposal units. Includes architectural, structural, traffic, ocean, and geo-technical engineers. **O*NET Code:** 17-2051.00. **Average Salary:** $62,840. **Projected Growth:** 8.0%. **Annual Openings:** 17,000. **Education:** Bachelor's degree. **Job Zone:** 4. **Education/Training Program(s)**—Civil Engineering, General; Civil Engineering, Other; Transportation and Highway Engineering; Water Resources Engineering. **Related Knowledge/Courses:** Engineering and Technology; Design; Building and Construction; Mathematics; Customer and Personal Service; Transportation; Physics. **Personality Type:** Realistic. **Skills Required:** Coordination; Science; Persuasion; Negotiation; Mathematics; Instructing; Operations Analysis; Monitoring; Service Orientation; Technology Design. **Abilities:** Originality; Deductive Reasoning; Visualization; Mathematical Reasoning; Speed of Closure. **Occupational Values:** Ability Utilization; Creativity; Authority; Social Status; Autonomy. **Interacting with Others:** Resolving Conflicts and Negotiating with Others; Communicating with Supervisors, Peers, or Subordinates; Communicating with Persons Outside Organization; Coordinating the Work and Activities of Others. **Physical Work Conditions:** In an Enclosed Vehicle or Equipment; Sitting; Very Hot or Cold; Outdoors; Contaminants.

Computer Hardware Engineers

Research, design, develop, and test computer or computer-related equipment for commercial, industrial, military, or scientific use. May supervise the manufacturing and installation of computer or computer-related equipment and components. **O*NET Code:** 17-2061.00. **Average Salary:** $79,090. **Projected Growth:** 6.1%. **Annual Openings:** 6,000. **Education:** Bachelor's degree. **Job Zone:** 4. **Education/Training Program(s)**—Computer Engineering, General; Computer Hardware Engineering. **Related Knowledge/Courses:** Computers and Electronics; Mathematics; Engineering and Technology; Design; Telecommunications; Education and Training. **Personality Type:** Investigative. **Skills Required:** Programming; Troubleshooting; Installation; Science; Operations Analysis; Technology Design; Management of Material Resources; Active Learning. **Abilities:** Mathematical Reasoning; Inductive Reasoning; Deductive Reasoning; Oral Expression; Written Expression. **Occupational Values:** Creativity; Ability Utilization; Working Conditions; Authority; Social Status; Responsibility. **Interacting with Others:** Providing Consultation and Advice to Others; Communicating with Supervisors, Peers, or Subordinates; Communicating with Persons Outside Organization. **Physical Work Conditions:** Sitting; Indoors; Walking and Running; Spend Time Making Repetitive Motions.

Electrical Engineers

Design, develop, test, or supervise the manufacturing and installation of electrical equipment, components, or systems for commercial, industrial, military, or scientific use. **O*NET Code:** 17-2071.00. **Average Salary:** $70,830. **Projected Growth:** 2.5%. **Annual Openings:** 11,000. **Education:** Bachelor's degree. **Job Zone:** 4. **Education/Training Program(s)**—Electrical, Electronics and Communications Engineering. **Related Knowledge/Courses:** Engineering and Technology; Design; Computers and Electronics; Physics; Mathematics; Telecommunications. **Personality Type:** Investigative. **Skills Required:** Troubleshooting; Technology Design; Systems Analysis; Science; Systems Evaluation; Management of Material Resources; Complex Problem Solving; Equipment Selection. **Abilities:** Mathematical Reasoning; Visualization; Oral Comprehension; Originality; Deductive Reasoning. **Occupational Values:** Creativity; Ability Utilization; Social Status; Responsibility; Autonomy. **Interacting with Others:** Communicating with Supervisors, Peers, or Subordinates; Establishing and Maintaining Interpersonal Relationships; Interpreting the Meaning of Information for Others. **Physical Work Conditions:** Sitting; Sounds, Noise Levels Are Distracting or Uncomfortable; Indoors; Physical Proximity; Hazardous Conditions.

Electronics Engineers, Except Computer

Research, design, develop, and test electronic components and systems for commercial, industrial, military, or scientific use, utilizing knowledge of electronic theory and materials properties. Design electronic circuits and components for use in fields such as telecommunications, aerospace guidance and propulsion control, acoustics, or instruments and controls. **O*NET Code:** 17-2072.00. **Average Salary:** $73,470. **Projected Growth:** 9.4%. **Annual Openings:** 11,000. **Education:** Bachelor's degree. **Job Zone:** 5. **Education/Training Program(s)**—Electrical, Electronics and Communications Engineering. **Related Knowledge/Courses:** Engineering and Technology; Design; Computers and Electronics; Telecommunications; Production and Processing; Mathematics. **Personality Type:** Investigative. **Skills Required:** Science; Mathematics; Writing; Judgment and Decision Making; Management of Financial Resources; Reading Comprehension; Technology Design; Systems Analysis. **Abilities:** Mathematical Reasoning; Originality; Number Facility; Written Expression; Visualization. **Occupational Values:** Creativity; Ability Utilization; Social Status; Responsibility; Autonomy. **Interacting with Others:** Communicating with Supervisors, Peers, or Subordinates; Communicating with Persons Outside Organization; Coordinating the Work and Activities of Others. **Physical Work Conditions:** Hazardous Conditions; Sitting; Standing; Using Hands on Objects, Tools, or Controls; Walking and Running.

Marine Architects

Design and oversee construction and repair of marine craft and floating structures, such as ships, barges, tugs, dredges, submarines, torpedoes, floats, and buoys. May confer with marine engineers. **O*NET Code:** 17-2121.02. **Average Salary:** $71,290. **Projected Growth:** –5.0%. **Annual Openings:** Fewer than 500. **Education:** Bachelor's degree. **Job Zone:** 5. **Education/Training Program(s)**—Naval Architecture and Marine Engineering. **Related Knowledge/Courses:** Design; Physics; Engineering and Technology; Building and Construction; Mathematics; Transportation. **Personality Type:** Realistic. **Skills Required:** Technology Design; Quality Control Analysis; Mathematics; Science; Active Learning; Systems Analysis; Monitoring; Judgment and Decision Making. **Abilities:** Originality; Visualization; Fluency of Ideas; Written Comprehension; Mathematical Reasoning. **Occupational Values:** Creativity; Ability Utilization; Social Status; Achievement; Recognition. **Interacting with Others:** Communicating with Supervisors, Peers, or Subordinates; Coordinating the Work and Activities of Others; Communicating with Persons Outside Organization. **Physical Work Conditions:** Sitting; Hazardous Equipment; Extremely Bright or Inadequate Lighting; Very Hot or Cold; Minor Burns, Cuts, Bites, or Stings.

Marine Engineers

Design, develop, and take responsibility for the installation of ship machinery and related equipment, including propulsion machines and power supply systems. **O*NET Code:** 17-2121.01. **Average Salary:** $71,290. **Projected Growth:** –5.0%. **Annual Openings:** Fewer than 500. **Education:** Bachelor's degree. **Job Zone:** 5. **Education/Training Program(s)**—Naval Architecture and Marine Engineering. **Related Knowledge/ Courses:** Engineering and Technology; Mechanical; Physics; Design; Mathematics; Transportation. **Personality Type:**

Realistic. **Skills Required:** Science; Troubleshooting; Quality Control Analysis; Mathematics; Operations Analysis; Installation; Systems Analysis; Systems Evaluation. **Abilities:** Written Expression; Originality; Speed of Closure; Visualization; Inductive Reasoning. **Occupational Values:** Creativity; Ability Utilization; Authority; Social Status; Autonomy. **Interacting with Others:** Communicating with Supervisors, Peers, or Subordinates; Coordinating the Work and Activities of Others; Communicating with Persons Outside Organization. **Physical Work Conditions:** Hazardous Equipment; Sitting; Hazardous Conditions; Minor Burns, Cuts, Bites, or Stings; Extremely Bright or Inadequate Lighting.

Materials Engineers

Evaluate materials and develop machinery and processes to manufacture materials for use in products that must meet specialized design and performance specifications. Develop new uses for known materials. Includes those working with composite materials or specializing in one type of material, such as graphite, metal and metal alloys, ceramics and glass, plastics and polymers, and naturally occurring materials. **O*NET Code:** 17-2131.00. **Average Salary:** $65,010. **Projected Growth:** 4.1%. **Annual Openings:** 2,000. **Education:** Bachelor's degree. **Job Zone:** 5. **Education/Training Program(s)**—Ceramic Sciences and Engineering; Materials Engineering; Metallurgical Engineering. **Related Knowledge/Courses:** Engineering and Technology; Design; Mathematics; Production and Processing; Physics; Economics and Accounting. **Personality Type:** Investigative. **Skills Required:** Science; Operations Analysis; Technology Design; Mathematics; Judgment and Decision Making; Systems Evaluation; Active Learning; Complex Problem Solving. **Abilities:** Mathematical Reasoning; Written Expression; Number Facility; Visualization; Written Comprehension. **Occupational Values:** Creativity; Responsibility; Autonomy; Ability Utilization; Social Status. **Interacting with Others:** Communicating with Supervisors, Peers, or Subordinates; Providing Consultation and Advice to Others; Communicating with Persons Outside Organization. **Physical Work Conditions:** Sitting; Indoors; Common Protective or Safety Equipment.

Mechanical Engineers

Perform engineering duties in planning and designing tools, engines, machines, and other mechanically functioning equipment. Oversee installation, operation, maintenance, and repair of such equipment as centralized heat, gas, water, and steam systems. **O*NET Code:** 17-2141.00. **Average Salary:** $65,210. **Projected Growth:** 4.8%. **Annual Openings:** 14,000. **Education:** Bachelor's degree. **Job Zone:** 4. **Education/Training Program(s)**—Mechanical Engineering. **Related Knowledge/Courses:** Design; Engineering and Technology; Mechanical; Production and Processing; Administration and Management; Physics. **Personality Type:** Realistic. **Skills Required:** Science; Operations Analysis; Complex Problem Solving; Installation; Coordination; Mathematics; Negotiation; Judgment and Decision Making. **Abilities:** Mathematical Reasoning; Originality; Number Facility; Oral Comprehension; Category Flexibility. **Occupational Values:** Creativity; Autonomy; Authority;

Social Status; Responsibility. **Interacting with Others:** Communicating with Supervisors, Peers, or Subordinates; Establishing and Maintaining Interpersonal Relationships; Communicating with Persons Outside Organization. **Physical Work Conditions:** Sitting; Sounds, Noise Levels Are Distracting or Uncomfortable; Contaminants; Indoors; Physical Proximity.

Nuclear Engineers

Conduct research on nuclear engineering problems or apply principles and theory of nuclear science to problems concerned with release, control, and utilization of nuclear energy and nuclear waste disposal. **O*NET Code:** 17-2161.00. **Average Salary:** $83,260. **Projected Growth:** -0.1%. **Annual Openings:** 1,000. **Education:** Bachelor's degree. **Job Zone:** 5. **Education/Training Program(s)**—Nuclear Engineering. **Related Knowledge/Courses:** Engineering and Technology; Physics; Design; Mathematics; Chemistry; Administration and Management. **Personality Type:** Investigative. **Skills Required:** Science; Technology Design; Operations Analysis; Quality Control Analysis; Systems Evaluation; Operation Monitoring; Systems Analysis; Mathematics. **Abilities:** Mathematical Reasoning; Deductive Reasoning; Written Expression; Number Facility; Originality. **Occupational Values:** Ability Utilization; Creativity; Social Status; Authority; Responsibility. **Interacting with Others:** Communicating with Supervisors, Peers, or Subordinates; Interpreting the Meaning of Information for Others; Providing Consultation and Advice to Others. **Physical Work Conditions:** Hazardous Conditions; Exposed to Radiation; Specialized Protective or Safety Equipment; Sitting; Common Protective or Safety Equipment.

15.08 Industrial and Safety Engineering

Fire-Prevention and Protection Engineers

Research causes of fires, determine fire protection methods, and design or recommend materials or equipment such as structural components or fire-detection equipment to assist organizations in safeguarding life and property against fire, explosion, and related hazards. **O*NET Code:** 17-2111.02. **Average Salary:** $61,430. **Projected Growth:** 7.9%. **Annual Openings:** 4,000. **Education:** Bachelor's degree. **Job Zone:** 4. **Education/Training Program(s)**—Environmental/Environmental Health Engineering. **Related Knowledge/Courses:** Public Safety and Security; Engineering and Technology; Education and Training; Design; Chemistry; Law and Government. **Personality Type:** Investigative. **Skills Required:** Technology Design; Instructing; Operations Analysis; Science; Systems Evaluation; Active Learning; Speaking; Quality Control Analysis. **Abilities:** Inductive Reasoning; Deductive Reasoning; Category Flexibility; Written Expression; Oral Expression. **Occupational Values:** Authority; Social Status; Creativity; Responsibility; Autonomy. **Interacting with Others:** Providing Consultation and Advice to Others; Communicating with Persons Outside Organization; Training and Teaching Others. **Physical Work Conditions:** Specialized Protective or Safety Equipment; Sitting; Climbing Ladders, Scaffolds, or Poles; Kneeling, Crouching, Stooping, or Crawling; Very Hot or Cold.

Industrial Engineers

Design, develop, test, and evaluate integrated systems for managing industrial production processes, including human work factors, quality control, inventory control, logistics and material flow, cost analysis, and production coordination. **O*NET Code:** 17-2112.00. **Average Salary:** $64,050. **Projected Growth:** 10.6%. **Annual Openings:** 16,000. **Education:** Bachelor's degree. **Job Zone:** 4. **Education/Training Program(s)**—Industrial Engineering. **Related Knowledge/Courses:** Engineering and Technology; Design; Production and Processing; Mathematics; Education and Training; Mechanical. **Personality Type:** Enterprising. **Skills Required:** Equipment Selection; Negotiation; Technology Design; Troubleshooting; Active Learning; Persuasion; Judgment and Decision Making; Complex Problem Solving. **Abilities:** Mathematical Reasoning; Visualization; Deductive Reasoning; Inductive Reasoning; Fluency of Ideas. **Occupational Values:** Authority; Creativity; Ability Utilization; Social Status; Autonomy. **Interacting with Others:** Communicating with Supervisors, Peers, or Subordinates; Establishing and Maintaining Interpersonal Relationships; Resolving Conflicts and Negotiating with Others; Coordinating the Work and Activities of Others. **Physical Work Conditions:** Sounds, Noise Levels Are Distracting or Uncomfortable; Contaminants; Sitting; Extremely Bright or Inadequate Lighting; Very Hot or Cold.

Industrial Safety and Health Engineers

Plan, implement, and coordinate safety programs requiring application of engineering principles and technology to prevent or correct unsafe environmental working conditions. **O*NET Code:** 17-2111.01. **Average Salary:** $61,430. **Projected Growth:** 7.9%. **Annual Openings:** 4,000. **Education:** Bachelor's degree. **Job Zone:** 4. **Education/Training Program(s)**—Environmental/Environmental Health Engineering. **Related Knowledge/Courses:** Engineering and Technology; Design; Public Safety and Security; Physics; Administration and Management; Chemistry. **Personality Type:** Investigative. **Skills Required:** Operations Analysis; Technology Design; Mathematics; Science; Instructing; Systems Evaluation; Systems Analysis; Quality Control Analysis. **Abilities:** Mathematical Reasoning; Written Expression; Inductive Reasoning; Number Facility; Oral Comprehension. **Occupational Values:** Creativity; Authority; Social Status; Responsibility; Autonomy. **Interacting with Others:** Providing Consultation and Advice to Others; Interpreting the Meaning of Information for Others; Communicating with Supervisors, Peers, or Subordinates; Communicating with Persons Outside Organization. **Physical Work Conditions:** Specialized Protective or Safety Equipment; Sitting; Indoors; Common Protective or Safety Equipment; Standing.

Product Safety Engineers

Develop and conduct tests to evaluate product safety levels and recommend measures to reduce or eliminate hazards.

© 2006, JIST Works

O*NET Code: 17-2111.03. **Average Salary:** $61,430. **Projected Growth:** 7.9%. **Annual Openings:** 4,000. **Education:** Bachelor's degree. **Job Zone:** 5. **Education/Training Program(s)**—Environmental/Environmental Health Engineering. **Related Knowledge/Courses:** Chemistry; Engineering and Technology; Physics; Public Safety and Security; Production and Processing; Biology. **Personality Type:** Investigative. **Skills Required:** Quality Control Analysis; Operations Analysis; Science; Mathematics; Technology Design; Active Learning; Writing; Troubleshooting. **Abilities:** Written Expression; Deductive Reasoning; Fluency of Ideas; Problem Sensitivity; Inductive Reasoning. **Occupational Values:** Creativity; Ability Utilization; Achievement; Autonomy; Responsibility. **Interacting with Others:** Interpreting the Meaning of Information for Others; Providing Consultation and Advice to Others; Communicating with Supervisors, Peers, or Subordinates. **Physical Work Conditions:** Specialized Protective or Safety Equipment; Sitting; Indoors; Standing; Walking and Running.

15.09 Engineering Technology

Aerospace Engineering and Operations Technicians

Operate, install, calibrate, and maintain integrated computer/communications systems consoles; simulators; and other data acquisition, test, and measurement instruments and equipment to launch, track, position, and evaluate air and space vehicles. May record and interpret test data. **O*NET Code:** 17-3021.00. **Average Salary:** $51,690. **Projected Growth:** 1.5%. **Annual Openings:** 2,000. **Education:** Associate degree. **Job Zone:** 4. **Education/Training Program(s)**—Aeronautical/Aerospace Engineering Technology/Technician. **Related Knowledge/Courses:** Computers and Electronics; Engineering and Technology; Physics; Mechanical; Mathematics. **Personality Type:** Investigative. **Skills Required:** Science; Programming; Equipment Maintenance; Installation; Mathematics; Operation Monitoring; Technology Design; Quality Control Analysis. **Abilities:** Number Facility; Mathematical Reasoning; Written Expression; Written Comprehension; Inductive Reasoning. **Occupational Values:** Activity; Achievement; Compensation; Working Conditions; Advancement. **Interacting with Others:** Communicating with Supervisors, Peers, or Subordinates; Interpreting the Meaning of Information for Others; Providing Consultation and Advice to Others. **Physical Work Conditions:** Hazardous Equipment; Sitting; Standing; Using Hands on Objects, Tools, or Controls; Indoors.

Calibration and Instrumentation Technicians

Develop, test, calibrate, operate, and repair electrical, mechanical, electromechanical, electrohydraulic, or electronic measuring and recording instruments, apparatus, and equipment. **O*NET Code:** 17-3023.02. **Average Salary:**

$45,390. **Projected Growth:** 10.0%. **Annual Openings:** 24,000. **Education:** Associate degree. **Job Zone:** 4. **Education/Training Program(s)**—Computer Engineering Technology/Technician; Computer Technology/Computer Systems Technology; Electrical and Electronic Engineering Technologies/Technicians, Other; Electrical, Electronic and Communications Engineering Technology/Technician; Telecommunications Technology/Technician. **Related Knowledge/Courses:** Design; Mathematics; Computers and Electronics; Engineering and Technology; Mechanical; Physics. **Personality Type:** Realistic. **Skills Required:** Technology Design; Equipment Maintenance; Quality Control Analysis; Science; Equipment Selection; Troubleshooting; Installation; Operations Analysis. **Abilities:** Mathematical Reasoning; Information Ordering; Deductive Reasoning; Written Comprehension; Control Precision. **Occupational Values:** Supervision, Human Relations; Working Conditions; Social Status; Achievement; Advancement; Supervision, Technical. **Interacting with Others:** Communicating with Supervisors, Peers, or Subordinates; Establishing and Maintaining Interpersonal Relationships; Interpreting the Meaning of Information for Others. **Physical Work Conditions:** Indoors; Sitting; Standing; Hazardous Equipment.

Cartographers and Photogrammetrists

Collect, analyze, and interpret geographic information provided by geodetic surveys, aerial photographs, and satellite data. Research, study, and prepare maps and other spatial data in digital or graphic form for legal, social, political, educational, and design purposes. May work with Geographic Information Systems (GIS). May design and evaluate algorithms, data structures, and user interfaces for GIS and mapping systems. **O*NET Code:** 17-1021.00. **Average Salary:** $45,550. **Projected Growth:** 15.1%. **Annual Openings:** 1,000. **Education:** Bachelor's degree. **Job Zone:** 3. **Education/Training Program(s)**—Cartography; Surveying Technology/Surveying. **Related Knowledge/Courses:** Geography; Design; Computers and Electronics; Engineering and Technology; Mathematics; Production and Processing. **Personality Type:** Conventional. **Skills Required:** Active Learning; Technology Design; Science; Mathematics; Troubleshooting; Critical Thinking; Reading Comprehension; Complex Problem Solving. **Abilities:** Far Vision; Spatial Orientation; Flexibility of Closure; Mathematical Reasoning; Visual Color Discrimination. **Occupational Values:** Autonomy; Responsibility; Ability Utilization; Achievement; Working Conditions; Creativity. **Interacting with Others:** Establishing and Maintaining Interpersonal Relationships; Communicating with Supervisors, Peers, or Subordinates; Interpreting the Meaning of Information for Others. **Physical Work Conditions:** Sitting; Indoors; Sounds, Noise Levels Are Distracting or Uncomfortable; Physical Proximity.

Civil Engineering Technicians

Apply theory and principles of civil engineering in planning, designing, and overseeing construction and maintenance of structures and facilities under the direction of engineering staff or physical scientists. **O*NET Code:** 17-3022.00. **Average Salary:** $38,220. **Projected Growth:** 7.6%. **Annual Openings:** 10,000. **Education:** Associate degree. **Job Zone:** 3.

Education/Training Program(s)—Civil Engineering Technology/Technician; Construction Engineering Technology/Technician. **Related Knowledge/Courses:** Design; Building and Construction; Engineering and Technology; Mathematics; Computers and Electronics; Transportation. **Personality Type:** Realistic. **Skills Required:** Mathematics; Instructing; Active Learning; Critical Thinking; Operations Analysis; Writing; Complex Problem Solving; Science; Time Management. **Abilities:** Mathematical Reasoning; Visualization; Deductive Reasoning; Written Expression; Oral Comprehension; Category Flexibility. **Occupational Values:** Advancement; Working Conditions; Ability Utilization; Supervision, Human Relations; Achievement; Activity. **Interacting with Others:** Communicating with Supervisors, Peers, or Subordinates; Establishing and Maintaining Interpersonal Relationships; Interpreting the Meaning of Information for Others. **Physical Work Conditions:** Sitting; Very Hot or Cold; Physical Proximity; Sounds, Noise Levels Are Distracting or Uncomfortable; Outdoors; In an Enclosed Vehicle or Equipment.

Electrical Engineering Technicians

Apply electrical theory and related knowledge to test and modify developmental or operational electrical machinery and electrical control equipment and circuitry in industrial or commercial plants and laboratories. Usually work under direction of engineering staff. **O*NET Code:** 17-3023.03. **Average Salary:** $45,390. **Projected Growth:** 10.0%. **Annual Openings:** 24,000. **Education:** Associate degree. **Job Zone:** 3. **Education/Training Program(s)**—Computer Engineering Technology/Technician; Computer Technology/Computer Systems Technology; Electrical and Electronic Engineering Technologies/Technicians, Other; Electrical, Electronic and Communications Engineering Technology/Technician; Telecommunications Technology/Technician. **Related Knowledge/Courses:** Engineering and Technology; Design; Computers and Electronics; Physics; Mechanical; Telecommunications. **Personality Type:** Realistic. **Skills Required:** Troubleshooting; Repairing; Installation; Technology Design; Operations Analysis; Equipment Maintenance; Mathematics; Science. **Abilities:** Mathematical Reasoning; Visualization; Deductive Reasoning; Information Ordering; Fluency of Ideas. **Occupational Values:** Advancement; Working Conditions; Ability Utilization; Achievement; Activity. **Interacting with Others:** Communicating with Supervisors, Peers, or Subordinates; Establishing and Maintaining Interpersonal Relationships; Providing Consultation and Advice to Others. **Physical Work Conditions:** Sitting; Sounds, Noise Levels Are Distracting or Uncomfortable; Indoors; Hazardous Conditions; Contaminants.

Electro-Mechanical Technicians

Operate, test, and maintain unmanned, automated, servo-mechanical, or electromechanical equipment. May operate unmanned submarines, aircraft, or other equipment at worksites, such as oil rigs, deep ocean exploration, or hazardous waste removal. May assist engineers in testing and designing robotics equipment. **O*NET Code:** 17-3024.00. **Average Salary:** $40,720. **Projected Growth:** 11.5%. **Annual**

Openings: 4,000. **Education:** Associate degree. **Job Zone:** 4. **Education/Training Program(s)**—Engineering Technologies/Technicians, Other. **Related Knowledge/Courses:** Mechanical; Production and Processing; Engineering and Technology; Computers and Electronics; Design; Physics. **Personality Type:** Realistic. **Skills Required:** Repairing; Troubleshooting; Equipment Maintenance; Installation; Quality Control Analysis; Operation Monitoring; Science; Operation and Control. **Abilities:** Finger Dexterity; Arm-Hand Steadiness; Manual Dexterity; Visualization; Visual Color Discrimination. **Occupational Values:** Independence; Moral Values; Advancement; Supervision, Human Relations; Supervision, Technical. **Interacting with Others:** Communicating with Supervisors, Peers, or Subordinates; Interpreting the Meaning of Information for Others; Performing Administrative Activities. **Physical Work Conditions:** Hazardous Equipment; Using Hands on Objects, Tools, or Controls; Minor Burns, Cuts, Bites, or Stings; Sitting; Standing.

Electronic Drafters

Draw wiring diagrams, circuit board assembly diagrams, schematics, and layout drawings used for manufacture, installation, and repair of electronic equipment. **O*NET Code:** 17-3012.01. **Average Salary:** $42,620. **Projected Growth:** 0.7%. **Annual Openings:** 5,000. **Education:** Postsecondary vocational training. **Job Zone:** 3. **Education/Training Program(s)**—Electrical/Electronics Drafting and Electrical/Electronics CAD/CADD. **Related Knowledge/Courses:** Design; Computers and Electronics; Engineering and Technology; Mathematics; Administration and Management; Physics; Telecommunications. **Personality Type:** Realistic. **Skills Required:** Programming; Technology Design; Operations Analysis; Mathematics; Management of Material Resources; Science; Troubleshooting; Quality Control Analysis. **Abilities:** Visualization; Number Facility; Information Ordering; Category Flexibility; Mathematical Reasoning; Arm-Hand Steadiness. **Occupational Values:** Working Conditions; Ability Utilization; Social Status; Compensation; Authority. **Interacting with Others:** Communicating with Supervisors, Peers, or Subordinates; Coordinating the Work and Activities of Others; Providing Consultation and Advice to Others. **Physical Work Conditions:** Sitting; Using Hands on Objects, Tools, or Controls; Indoors; Walking and Running; Hazardous Equipment; Spend Time Making Repetitive Motions.

Electronics Engineering Technicians

Lay out, build, test, troubleshoot, repair, and modify developmental and production electronic components, parts, equipment, and systems, such as computer equipment, missile control instrumentation, electron tubes, test equipment, and machine tool numerical controls, applying principles and theories of electronics, electrical circuitry, engineering mathematics, electronic and electrical testing, and physics. Usually work under direction of engineering staff. **O*NET Code:** 17-3023.01. **Average Salary:** $45,390. **Projected Growth:** 10.0%. **Annual Openings:** 24,000. **Education:** Associate degree. **Job Zone:** 3. **Education/Training Program(s)**—Computer Engineering Technology/Technician; Computer Technology/Computer Systems Technology; Electrical and Electronic

© 2006, JIST Works

Engineering Technologies/Technicians, Other; Electrical, Electronic, and Communications Engineering Technology/Technician; Telecommunications Technology/Technician. **Related Knowledge/Courses:** Engineering and Technology; Computers and Electronics; Mechanical; Mathematics; Design; Telecommunications. **Personality Type:** Realistic. **Skills Required:** Repairing; Troubleshooting; Equipment Maintenance; Installation; Technology Design; Operation Monitoring; Service Orientation; Systems Evaluation. **Abilities:** Mathematical Reasoning; Visualization; Written Comprehension; Arm-Hand Steadiness; Speech Clarity. **Occupational Values:** Advancement; Working Conditions; Ability Utilization; Achievement; Activity. **Interacting with Others:** Communicating with Supervisors, Peers, or Subordinates; Establishing and Maintaining Interpersonal Relationships; Providing Consultation and Advice to Others. **Physical Work Conditions:** Contaminants; Hazardous Equipment; Hazardous Conditions; Physical Proximity; Sitting.

Environmental Engineering Technicians

Apply theory and principles of environmental engineering to modify, test, and operate equipment and devices used in the prevention, control, and remediation of environmental pollution, including waste treatment and site remediation. May assist in the development of environmental pollution remediation devices under direction of engineer. **O*NET Code:** 17-3025.00. **Average Salary:** $38,180. **Projected Growth:** 28.4%. **Annual Openings:** 3,000. **Education:** Associate degree. **Job Zone:** 3. **Education/Training Program(s)—** Environmental Engineering Technology/Environmental Technology; Hazardous Materials Information Systems Technology/Technician. **Related Knowledge/Courses:** Engineering and Technology; Design; Building and Construction; Physics; Customer and Personal Service; Law and Government. **Personality Type:** No data available. **Skills Required:** Troubleshooting; Science; Coordination; Repairing; Equipment Maintenance; Time Management; Management of Financial Resources; Service Orientation. **Abilities:** No data available. **Occupational Values:** No data available. **Interacting with Others:** Communicating with Supervisors, Peers, or Subordinates; Establishing and Maintaining Interpersonal Relationships; Communicating with Persons Outside Organization. **Physical Work Conditions:** Indoors, Not Environmentally Controlled; Hazardous Conditions; Contaminants; Outdoors, Under Cover; Outdoors; Hazardous Equipment.

Mapping Technicians

Calculate mapmaking information from field notes and draw and verify accuracy of topographical maps. **O*NET Code:** 17-3031.02. **Average Salary:** $29,970. **Projected Growth:** 23.1%. **Annual Openings:** 10,000. **Education:** Moderate-term on-the-job training. **Job Zone:** 3. **Education/Training Program(s)—**Cartography; Surveying Technology/Surveying. **Related Knowledge/Courses:** Geography; Design; Mathematics; Computers and Electronics; Administration and Management; Engineering and Technology. **Personality Type:** Conventional. **Skills Required:** Mathematics; Technology Design; Management of Personnel Resources; Operations Analysis; Active Learning; Monitoring. **Abilities:** Spatial Orientation; Mathematical Reasoning; Number Facility; Near Vision; Flexibility of Closure. **Occupational Values:** Authority; Moral Values; Autonomy; Achievement; Activity. **Interacting with Others:** Communicating with Supervisors, Peers, or Subordinates; Coordinating the Work and Activities of Others; Guiding, Directing, and Motivating Subordinates. **Physical Work Conditions:** Sitting; Indoors; Using Hands on Objects, Tools, or Controls; Spend Time Making Repetitive Motions.

Mechanical Drafters

Prepare detailed working diagrams of machinery and mechanical devices, including dimensions, fastening methods, and other engineering information. **O*NET Code:** 17-3013.00. **Average Salary:** $42,380. **Projected Growth:** 1.9%. **Annual Openings:** 9,000. **Education:** Postsecondary vocational training. **Job Zone:** 3. **Education/Training Program(s)—**Mechanical Drafting and Mechanical Drafting CAD/CADD. **Related Knowledge/Courses:** Design; Engineering and Technology; Building and Construction; Mathematics; Physics; English Language. **Personality Type:** Realistic. **Skills Required:** Technology Design; Installation; Equipment Selection; Quality Control Analysis; Operations Analysis; Mathematics; Persuasion; Instructing; Troubleshooting. **Abilities:** Mathematical Reasoning; Visualization; Originality; Visual Color Discrimination; Written Expression; Category Flexibility. **Occupational Values:** Authority; Ability Utilization; Working Conditions; Creativity; Achievement; Moral Values; Autonomy. **Interacting with Others:** Establishing and Maintaining Interpersonal Relationships; Communicating with Supervisors, Peers, or Subordinates; Communicating with Persons Outside Organization. **Physical Work Conditions:** Sitting; Sounds, Noise Levels Are Distracting or Uncomfortable; Physical Proximity; Contaminants; Indoors; Indoors, Not Environmentally Controlled.

Mechanical Engineering Technicians

Apply theory and principles of mechanical engineering to modify, develop, and test machinery and equipment under direction of engineering staff or physical scientists. **O*NET Code:** 17-3027.00. **Average Salary:** $42,650. **Projected Growth:** 11.0%. **Annual Openings:** 6,000. **Education:** Associate degree. **Job Zone:** 3. **Education/Training Program(s)—**Mechanical Engineering–Related Technologies/Technicians, Other; Mechanical Engineering/Mechanical Technology/Technician. **Related Knowledge/Courses:** Engineering and Technology; Design; Mechanical; Computers and Electronics; Physics; Mathematics. **Personality Type:** Realistic. **Skills Required:** Troubleshooting; Coordination; Installation; Technology Design; Service Orientation; Time Management; Equipment Selection; Active Learning; Instructing; Operations Analysis. **Abilities:** Mathematical Reasoning; Deductive Reasoning; Visualization; Inductive Reasoning; Flexibility of Closure. **Occupational Values:** Advancement; Achievement; Supervision, Human Relations; Variety; Ability Utilization; Activity; Social Status; Supervision, Technical. **Interacting with Others:** Communicating with Supervisors, Peers, or Subordinates; Establishing and Maintaining Interpersonal Relationships; Interpreting the Meaning of Information for Others. **Physical**

Work Conditions: Contaminants; Sounds, Noise Levels Are Distracting or Uncomfortable; Very Hot or Cold; Hazardous Equipment; Sitting.

Surveying Technicians

Adjust and operate surveying instruments, such as the theodolite and electronic distance-measuring equipment, and compile notes, make sketches, and enter data into computers. **O*NET Code:** 17-3031.01. **Average Salary:** $29,970. **Projected Growth:** 23.1%. **Annual Openings:** 10,000. **Education:** Long-term on-the-job training. **Job Zone:** 4. **Education/Training Program(s)—**Cartography; Surveying Technology/Surveying. **Related Knowledge/Courses:** Design; Engineering and Technology; Geography; Mathematics; Computers and Electronics. **Personality Type:** Realistic. **Skills Required:** Mathematics. **Abilities:** Spatial Orientation; Written Expression; Far Vision; Mathematical Reasoning. **Occupational Values:** Authority; Advancement; Moral Values; Supervision, Technical; Social Status; Company Policies and Practices. **Interacting with Others:** Communicating with Supervisors, Peers, or Subordinates; Guiding, Directing, and Motivating Subordinates; Coordinating the Work and Activities of Others. **Physical Work Conditions:** Outdoors; Very Hot or Cold; Standing; Extremely Bright or Inadequate Lighting; Walking and Running.

© 2006, JIST Works

16 Transportation, Distribution, and Logistics

16.01   **Managerial Work in Transportation**

16.02   **Air Vehicle Operation**

16.03   **Truck Driving**

16.04   **Rail Vehicle Operation**

16.05   **Water Vehicle Operation**

16.06   **Other Services Requiring Driving**

16.07   **Transportation Support Work**

16.01 Managerial Work in Transportation

Aircraft Cargo Handling Supervisors

Direct ground crew in the loading, unloading, securing, and staging of aircraft cargo or baggage. Determine the quantity and orientation of cargo and compute aircraft center of gravity. May accompany aircraft as member of flight crew, monitor and handle cargo in flight, and assist and brief passengers on safety and emergency procedures. **O*NET Code:** 53-1011.00. **Average Salary:** $34,620. **Projected Growth:** 15.6%. **Annual Openings:** 1,000. **Education:** Work experience in a related occupation. **Job Zone:** No data available. **Education/Training Program(s)**—No data available. **Related Knowledge/Courses:** No data available. **Personality Type:** No data available. **Skills Required:** No data available. **Abilities:** No data available. **Occupational Values:** No data available. **Interacting with Others:** No data available. **Physical Work Conditions:** No data available.

First-Line Supervisors/Managers of Transportation and Material-Moving Machine and Vehicle Operators

Directly supervise and coordinate activities of transportation and material-moving machine and vehicle operators and helpers. **O*NET Code:** 53-1031.00. **Average Salary:** $44,340. **Projected Growth:** 12.1%. **Annual Openings:** 23,000. **Education:** Work experience in a related occupation. **Job Zone:** 3. **Education/Training Program(s)**—No data available. **Related Knowledge/Courses:** Economics and Accounting; Transportation; Personnel and Human Resources; Administration and Management; Production and Processing; Sales and Marketing. **Personality Type:** Enterprising. **Skills Required:** Management of Financial Resources; Management of Personnel Resources; Management of Material Resources; Systems Analysis; Operations Analysis; Equipment Maintenance; Negotiation; Coordination. **Abilities:** Mathematical Reasoning; Number Facility; Written Expression; Oral Expression; Speech Recognition. **Occupational Values:** Authority; Responsibility; Variety; Autonomy; Co-workers. **Interacting with Others:** Communicating with Supervisors, Peers, or Subordinates; Coordinating the Work and Activities of Others; Guiding, Directing, and Motivating Subordinates. **Physical Work Conditions:** Very Hot or Cold; Sitting; Outdoors; Walking and Running; Extremely Bright or Inadequate Lighting.

Postmasters and Mail Superintendents

Direct and coordinate operational, administrative, management, and supportive services of a U.S. post office or coordinate activities of workers engaged in postal and related work in assigned post office. **O*NET Code:** 11-9131.00. **Average Salary:** $50,720. **Projected Growth:** -0.5%. **Annual Openings:** 3,000. **Education:** Work experience in a related occupation. **Job Zone:** 4. **Education/Training Program(s)**— Public Administration. **Related Knowledge/Courses:**

Personnel and Human Resources; Administration and Management; Transportation; Economics and Accounting; Education and Training; Geography. **Personality Type:** Enterprising. **Skills Required:** Management of Financial Resources; Negotiation; Management of Personnel Resources; Systems Evaluation; Management of Material Resources; Systems Analysis; Coordination; Monitoring. **Abilities:** Written Expression; Oral Comprehension; Oral Expression; Written Comprehension; Time Sharing. **Occupational Values:** Authority; Security; Company Policies and Practices; Compensation; Working Conditions. **Interacting with Others:** Resolving Conflicts and Negotiating with Others; Communicating with Supervisors, Peers, or Subordinates; Guiding, Directing, and Motivating Subordinates. **Physical Work Conditions:** Indoors; Sitting.

Railroad Conductors and Yardmasters

Conductors coordinate activities of train crew on passenger or freight train. Coordinate activities of switch-engine crew within yard of railroad, industrial plant, or similar location. Yardmasters coordinate activities of workers engaged in railroad traffic operations, such as the makeup or breakup of trains and yard switching, and review train schedules and switching orders. **O*NET Code:** 53-4031.00. **Average Salary:** $46,290. **Projected Growth:** -4.2%. **Annual Openings:** 5,000. **Education:** Work experience in a related occupation. **Job Zone:** 4. **Education/Training Program(s)**—Truck and Bus Driver/Commercial Vehicle Operation. **Related Knowledge/Courses:** Transportation; Administration and Management; Geography; Public Safety and Security; Telecommunications; Mechanical. **Personality Type:** Realistic. **Skills Required:** Coordination; Management of Personnel Resources; Operation Monitoring; Operation and Control; Equipment Maintenance; Troubleshooting; Systems Evaluation; Instructing. **Abilities:** Rate Control; Speech Clarity; Far Vision; Reaction Time; Written Expression. **Occupational Values:** Authority; Supervision, Technical; Security; Company Policies and Practices; Autonomy. **Interacting with Others:** Communicating with Supervisors, Peers, or Subordinates; Coordinating the Work and Activities of Others; Communicating with Persons Outside Organization; Establishing and Maintaining Interpersonal Relationships. **Physical Work Conditions:** Outdoors; Walking and Running; Keeping or Regaining Balance; Hazardous Conditions; Kneeling, Crouching, Stooping, or Crawling.

Storage and Distribution Managers

Plan, direct, and coordinate the storage and distribution operations within an organization or the activities of organizations that are engaged in storing and distributing materials and products. **O*NET Code:** 11-3071.02. **Average Salary:** $64,870. **Projected Growth:** 19.7%. **Annual Openings:** 13,000. **Education:** Work experience in a related occupation. **Job Zone:** 3. **Education/Training Program(s)**—Aeronautics/ Aviation/Aerospace Science and Technology, General; Aviation/Airway Management and Operations; Business Administration and Management, General; Business/ Commerce, General; Logistics and Materials Management; Public Administration. **Related Knowledge/Courses:** Customer and Personal Service; Administration and

Management; Sales and Marketing; Personnel and Human Resources; Education and Training; Production and Processing. **Personality Type:** Enterprising. **Skills Required:** Management of Personnel Resources; Operations Analysis; Monitoring; Persuasion; Service Orientation; Management of Material Resources; Social Perceptiveness; Negotiation. **Abilities:** Mathematical Reasoning; Visualization; Written Comprehension; Written Expression; Oral Expression; Number Facility. **Occupational Values:** Authority; Creativity; Autonomy; Responsibility; Security; Company Policies and Practices. **Interacting with Others:** Communicating with Supervisors, Peers, or Subordinates; Monitoring and Controlling Resources; Establishing and Maintaining Interpersonal Relationships; Resolving Conflicts and Negotiating with Others; Guiding, Directing, and Motivating Subordinates. **Physical Work Conditions:** Very Hot or Cold; Contaminants; Sounds, Noise Levels Are Distracting or Uncomfortable; Indoors, Not Environmentally Controlled; Sitting.

Transportation Managers

Plan, direct, and coordinate the transportation operations within an organization or the activities of organizations that provide transportation services. **O*NET Code:** 11-3071.01. **Average Salary:** $64,870. **Projected Growth:** 19.7%. **Annual Openings:** 13,000. **Education:** Work experience in a related occupation. **Job Zone:** 3. **Education/Training Program(s)—** Aeronautics/Aviation/Aerospace Science and Technology, General; Aviation/Airway Management and Operations; Business Administration and Management, General; Business/Commerce, General; Logistics and Materials Management; Public Administration. **Related Knowledge/ Courses:** Transportation; Customer and Personal Service; Clerical; Sales and Marketing; Administration and Management; Psychology. **Personality Type:** Enterprising. **Skills Required:** Negotiation; Time Management; Coordination; Instructing; Monitoring; Critical Thinking; Management of Financial Resources; Active Learning. **Abilities:** Speech Recognition; Mathematical Reasoning; Originality; Selective Attention; Auditory Attention. **Occupational Values:** Authority; Autonomy; Ability Utilization; Variety; Activity; Security; Responsibility. **Interacting with Others:** Communicating with Persons Outside Organization; Providing Consultation and Advice to Others; Resolving Conflicts and Negotiating with Others. **Physical Work Conditions:** Sitting; Sounds, Noise Levels Are Distracting or Uncomfortable; Physical Proximity; Very Hot or Cold; Indoors.

16.02 Air Vehicle Operation

Airline Pilots, Copilots, and Flight Engineers

Pilot and navigate the flight of multi-engine aircraft in regularly scheduled service for the transport of passengers and cargo. Requires Federal Air Transport rating and certification in specific aircraft type used. **O*NET Code:** 53-2011.00.

Average Salary: $128,140. **Projected Growth:** 18.5%. **Annual Openings:** 6,000. **Education:** Bachelor's degree. **Job Zone:** 4. **Education/Training Program(s)—**Airline/Commercial/Professional Pilot and Flight Crew; Flight Instructor. **Related Knowledge/Courses:** Transportation; Geography; Public Safety and Security; Education and Training; Mechanical; Physics. **Personality Type:** Realistic. **Skills Required:** Operation and Control; Operation Monitoring; Instructing; Science; Coordination; Systems Evaluation; Judgment and Decision Making; Systems Analysis. **Abilities:** Night Vision; Far Vision; Peripheral Vision; Spatial Orientation; Rate Control. **Occupational Values:** Authority; Recognition; Compensation; Ability Utilization; Social Status. **Interacting with Others:** Training and Teaching Others; Communicating with Supervisors, Peers, or Subordinates; Coordinating the Work and Activities of Others. **Physical Work Conditions:** High Places; Sitting; Exposed to Whole Body Vibration; Hazardous Equipment; Using Hands on Objects, Tools, or Controls.

Commercial Pilots

Pilot and navigate the flight of small fixed or rotary-winged aircraft, primarily for the transport of cargo and passengers. Requires Commercial Rating. **O*NET Code:** 53-2012.00. **Average Salary:** $51,000. **Projected Growth:** 14.9%. **Annual Openings:** 2,000. **Education:** Postsecondary vocational training. **Job Zone:** 4. **Education/Training Program(s)—** Airline/Commercial/Professional Pilot and Flight Crew; Flight Instructor. **Related Knowledge/Courses:** Transportation; Geography; Public Safety and Security; Education and Training; Mechanical; Physics. **Personality Type:** Realistic. **Skills Required:** Operation and Control; Operation Monitoring; Instructing; Science; Coordination; Systems Evaluation; Judgment and Decision Making; Systems Analysis. **Abilities:** Night Vision; Far Vision; Peripheral Vision; Spatial Orientation; Rate Control. **Occupational Values:** Authority; Recognition; Compensation; Ability Utilization; Social Status. **Interacting with Others:** Training and Teaching Others; Communicating with Supervisors, Peers, or Subordinates; Coordinating the Work and Activities of Others. **Physical Work Conditions:** High Places; Sitting; Exposed to Whole Body Vibration; Hazardous Equipment; Using Hands on Objects, Tools, or Controls.

16.03 Truck Driving

Tractor-Trailer Truck Drivers

Drive tractor-trailer truck to transport products, livestock, or materials to specified destinations. **O*NET Code:** 53-3032.02. **Average Salary:** $33,240. **Projected Growth:** 19.0%. **Annual Openings:** 299,000. **Education:** Moderate-term on-the-job training. **Job Zone:** 2. **Education/Training Program(s)—** Truck and Bus Driver/Commercial Vehicle Operation. **Related Knowledge/Courses:** Transportation; Geography; Mechanical; Law and Government; Public Safety and Security; Telecommunications. **Personality Type:** Realistic. **Skills Required:** Operation and Control; Equipment Maintenance; Repairing; Troubleshooting; Management of Material

Resources; Operation Monitoring. **Abilities:** Static Strength; Reaction Time; Response Orientation; Spatial Orientation; Rate Control. **Occupational Values:** Compensation; Company Policies and Practices; Autonomy; Independence; Supervision, Human Relations. **Interacting with Others:** Establishing and Maintaining Interpersonal Relationships; Communicating with Supervisors, Peers, or Subordinates; Performing Administrative Activities. **Physical Work Conditions:** Sitting; Extremely Bright or Inadequate Lighting; Outdoors; Very Hot or Cold; Sounds, Noise Levels Are Distracting or Uncomfortable; Spend Time Bending or Twisting the Body.

Truck Drivers, Heavy

Drive truck with capacity of more than three tons to transport materials to specified destinations. **O*NET Code:** 53-3032.01. **Average Salary:** $33,240. **Projected Growth:** 19.0%. **Annual Openings:** 299,000. **Education:** Short-term on-the-job training. **Job Zone:** 1. **Education/Training Program(s)—**Truck and Bus Driver/Commercial Vehicle Operation. **Related Knowledge/Courses:** Transportation; Geography; Telecommunications; Mechanical; Public Safety and Security; Law and Government. **Personality Type:** Realistic. **Skills Required:** Equipment Maintenance; Repairing; Operation Monitoring; Operation and Control; Management of Financial Resources. **Abilities:** Response Orientation; Static Strength; Reaction Time; Rate Control; Spatial Orientation; Night Vision. **Occupational Values:** Compensation; Independence; Company Policies and Practices; Autonomy; Supervision, Human Relations. **Interacting with Others:** Communicating with Persons Outside Organization; Communicating with Supervisors, Peers, or Subordinates; Establishing and Maintaining Interpersonal Relationships; Monitoring and Controlling Resources. **Physical Work Conditions:** Sitting; Outdoors; Extremely Bright or Inadequate Lighting; Very Hot or Cold; Hazardous Equipment.

Truck Drivers, Light or Delivery Services

Drive a truck or van with a capacity of under 26,000 GVW, primarily to deliver or pick up merchandise or to deliver packages within a specified area. May require use of automatic routing or location software. May load and unload truck. **O*NET Code:** 53-3033.00. **Average Salary:** $24,230. **Projected Growth:** 23.2%. **Annual Openings:** 219,000. **Education:** Short-term on-the-job training. **Job Zone:** 1. **Education/Training Program(s)—**Truck and Bus Driver/ Commercial Vehicle Operation. **Related Knowledge/Courses:** Transportation; Geography; Telecommunications; Mechanical; Law and Government; Public Safety and Security. **Personality Type:** Realistic. **Skills Required:** Equipment Maintenance; Repairing; Operation Monitoring; Operation and Control; Troubleshooting. **Abilities:** Response Orientation; Reaction Time; Static Strength; Rate Control; Explosive Strength. **Occupational Values:** Independence; Compensation; Supervision, Technical; Company Policies and Practices; Supervision, Human Relations. **Interacting with Others:** Communicating with Persons Outside Organization; Performing for or Working Directly with the Public; Communicating with Supervisors, Peers, or Subordinates; Establishing and Maintaining Interpersonal Relationships.

Physical Work Conditions: Outdoors; Sitting; Very Hot or Cold; Extremely Bright or Inadequate Lighting; Spend Time Bending or Twisting the Body.

16.04 Rail Vehicle Operation

Locomotive Engineers

Drive electric, diesel-electric, steam, or gas-turbine-electric locomotives to transport passengers or freight. Interpret train orders, electronic or manual signals, and railroad rules and regulations. **O*NET Code:** 53-4011.00. **Average Salary:** $50,850. **Projected Growth:** –7.2%. **Annual Openings:** 4,000. **Education:** Work experience in a related occupation. **Job Zone:** 4. **Education/Training Program(s)—**Transportation and Materials Moving, Other. **Related Knowledge/Courses:** Transportation; Geography; Public Safety and Security; Engineering and Technology; Telecommunications; Mechanical. **Personality Type:** Realistic. **Skills Required:** Operation and Control; Operation Monitoring; Equipment Maintenance; Systems Analysis; Troubleshooting; Reading Comprehension; Writing; Time Management. **Abilities:** Night Vision; Sound Localization; Response Orientation; Reaction Time; Auditory Attention. **Occupational Values:** Supervision, Technical; Supervision, Human Relations; Compensation; Security; Company Policies and Practices. **Interacting with Others:** Communicating with Supervisors, Peers, or Subordinates; Establishing and Maintaining Interpersonal Relationships; Interpreting the Meaning of Information for Others; Performing Administrative Activities. **Physical Work Conditions:** Hazardous Equipment; Hazardous Conditions; Sounds, Noise Levels Are Distracting or Uncomfortable; Contaminants; Extremely Bright or Inadequate Lighting.

Locomotive Firers

Monitor locomotive instruments and watch for dragging equipment, obstacles on rights-of-way, and train signals during run. Watch for and relay traffic signals from yard workers to yard engineer in railroad yard. **O*NET Code:** 53-4012.00. **Average Salary:** $46,220. **Projected Growth:** –7.2%. **Annual Openings:** 4,000. **Education:** Postsecondary vocational training. **Job Zone:** 3. **Education/Training Program(s)—**Transportation and Materials Moving, Other. **Related Knowledge/Courses:** Transportation; Geography; Mechanical; Physics; Public Safety and Security; Engineering and Technology. **Personality Type:** Realistic. **Skills Required:** Operation Monitoring; Operation and Control; Coordination; Systems Analysis; Management of Material Resources. **Abilities:** Far Vision; Night Vision; Peripheral Vision; Reaction Time; Response Orientation. **Occupational Values:** Supervision, Technical; Supervision, Human Relations; Company Policies and Practices; Security; Moral Values. **Interacting with Others:** Establishing and Maintaining Interpersonal Relationships; Communicating with Supervisors, Peers, or Subordinates; Interpreting the Meaning of Information for Others. **Physical Work Conditions:**

Hazardous Equipment; Outdoors; Sounds, Noise Levels Are Distracting or Uncomfortable; Very Hot or Cold; Exposed to Whole Body Vibration.

Rail Yard Engineers, Dinkey Operators, and Hostlers

Drive switching or other locomotive or dinkey engines within railroad yard, industrial plant, quarry, construction project, or similar location. **O*NET Code:** 53-4013.00. **Average Salary:** $36,600. **Projected Growth:** -7.2%. **Annual Openings:** 4,000. **Education:** Work experience in a related occupation. **Job Zone:** 2. **Education/Training Program(s)—** Truck and Bus Driver/Commercial Vehicle Operation. **Related Knowledge/Courses:** Transportation; Mechanical; Telecommunications; Engineering and Technology; Public Safety and Security. **Personality Type:** Realistic. **Skills Required:** Operation and Control; Operation Monitoring; Equipment Maintenance; Installation; Repairing; Troubleshooting; Technology Design. **Abilities:** Control Precision; Reaction Time; Rate Control; Response Orientation; Depth Perception. **Occupational Values:** Supervision, Technical; Supervision, Human Relations; Security; Company Policies and Practices; Advancement. **Interacting with Others:** Communicating with Supervisors, Peers, or Subordinates; Establishing and Maintaining Interpersonal Relationships; Interpreting the Meaning of Information for Others. **Physical Work Conditions:** Outdoors; Sounds, Noise Levels Are Distracting or Uncomfortable; Spend Time Making Repetitive Motions; Spend Time Bending or Twisting the Body; Contaminants; Walking and Running.

Subway and Streetcar Operators

Operate subway, elevated suburban train with no separate locomotive, or electric-powered streetcar to transport passengers. May handle fares. **O*NET Code:** 53-4041.00. **Average Salary:** $48,870. **Projected Growth:** 13.2%. **Annual Openings:** 2,000. **Education:** Moderate-term on-the-job training. **Job Zone:** 2. **Education/Training Program(s)—**Truck and Bus Driver/Commercial Vehicle Operation. **Related Knowledge/Courses:** Transportation; Geography; Clerical; Customer and Personal Service; Foreign Language; Telecommunications. **Personality Type:** Realistic. **Skills Required:** Operation and Control; Operation Monitoring. **Abilities:** Reaction Time; Control Precision; Spatial Orientation; Response Orientation; Night Vision; Glare Sensitivity. **Occupational Values:** Supervision, Technical; Supervision, Human Relations; Independence; Security; Social Service; Company Policies and Practices. **Interacting with Others:** Performing for or Working Directly with the Public; Communicating with Persons Outside Organization; Communicating with Supervisors, Peers, or Subordinates. **Physical Work Conditions:** Sitting; Using Hands on Objects, Tools, or Controls; Outdoors; Spend Time Making Repetitive Motions; Very Hot or Cold.

16.05 Water Vehicle Operation

Able Seamen

Stand watch at bow or on wing of bridge to look for obstructions in path of vessel. Measure water depth. Turn wheel on bridge or use emergency equipment as directed by mate. Break out, rig, overhaul, and store cargo-handling gear, stationary rigging, and running gear. Chip rust from and paint deck or ship's structure. Must hold government-issued certification. Must hold certification when working aboard liquid-carrying vessels. **O*NET Code:** 53-5011.01. **Average Salary:** $29,810. **Projected Growth:** 4.0%. **Annual Openings:** 3,000. **Education:** Short-term on-the-job training. **Job Zone:** 2. **Education/Training Program(s)—**Marine Transportation, Other. **Related Knowledge/Courses:** Transportation; Geography; Mechanical; Telecommunications; Physics; Public Safety and Security. **Personality Type:** Realistic. **Skills Required:** Operation and Control; Operation Monitoring; Equipment Maintenance; Coordination; Management of Personnel Resources; Repairing; Systems Analysis. **Abilities:** Night Vision; Glare Sensitivity; Far Vision; Peripheral Vision; Depth Perception. **Occupational Values:** Advancement; Co-workers; Supervision, Technical; Authority; Supervision, Human Relations. **Interacting with Others:** Communicating with Supervisors, Peers, or Subordinates; Establishing and Maintaining Interpersonal Relationships; Communicating with Persons Outside Organization; Coordinating the Work and Activities of Others. **Physical Work Conditions:** Outdoors; Extremely Bright or Inadequate Lighting; Standing; Keeping or Regaining Balance; Very Hot or Cold.

Dredge Operators

Operate dredge to remove sand, gravel, or other materials from lakes, rivers, or streams and to excavate and maintain navigable channels in waterways. **O*NET Code:** 53-7031.00. **Average Salary:** $27,850. **Projected Growth:** 8.9%. **Annual Openings:** 14,000. **Education:** Moderate-term on-the-job training. **Job Zone:** 2. **Education/Training Program(s)—** Construction/Heavy Equipment/Earthmoving Equipment Operation. **Related Knowledge/Courses:** Engineering and Technology; Mechanical; Physics; Transportation; Geography; Telecommunications. **Personality Type:** Realistic. **Skills Required:** Operation Monitoring; Operation and Control; Management of Personnel Resources. **Abilities:** Depth Perception; Glare Sensitivity; Static Strength; Peripheral Vision; Sound Localization. **Occupational Values:** Authority; Supervision, Technical; Moral Values. **Interacting with Others:** Communicating with Supervisors, Peers, or Subordinates; Coordinating the Work and Activities of Others; Establishing and Maintaining Interpersonal Relationships; Guiding, Directing, and Motivating Subordinates. **Physical Work Conditions:** Outdoors; Hazardous Equipment; Minor Burns, Cuts, Bites, or Stings; Using Hands on Objects, Tools, or Controls; Extremely Bright or Inadequate Lighting.

Mates—Ship, Boat, and Barge

Supervise and coordinate activities of crew aboard ships, boats, barges, or dredges. **O*NET Code:** 53-5021.02. **Average Salary:** $50,900. **Projected Growth:** 2.4%. **Annual Openings:** 3,000. **Education:** Work experience in a related occupation. **Job Zone:** 3. **Education/Training Program(s)—** Commercial Fishing; Marine Science/Merchant Marine Officer; Marine Transportation, Other. **Related Knowledge/ Courses:** Transportation; Geography; Mechanical; Public Safety and Security; Administration and Management; Physics. **Personality Type:** Realistic. **Skills Required:** Management of Personnel Resources; Operation and Control; Repairing; Coordination; Operation Monitoring; Systems Analysis; Systems Evaluation; Time Management. **Abilities:** Spatial Orientation; Far Vision; Glare Sensitivity; Night Vision; Control Precision. **Occupational Values:** Authority; Advancement; Co-workers; Supervision, Technical; Autonomy. **Interacting with Others:** Guiding, Directing, and Motivating Subordinates; Establishing and Maintaining Interpersonal Relationships; Coordinating the Work and Activities of Others. **Physical Work Conditions:** Outdoors; Very Hot or Cold; Climbing Ladders, Scaffolds, or Poles; Standing; Extremely Bright or Inadequate Lighting.

Motorboat Operators

Operate small motor-driven boats to carry passengers and freight between ships or from ship to shore. May patrol harbors and beach areas. May assist in navigational activities. **O*NET Code:** 53-5022.00. **Average Salary:** $33,360. **Projected Growth:** 2.7%. **Annual Openings:** 1,000. **Education:** Moderate-term on-the-job training. **Job Zone:** 2. **Education/Training Program(s)—** Marine Transportation, Other. **Related Knowledge/Courses:** Transportation; Mechanical; Geography; Public Safety and Security; Telecommunications; Physics. **Personality Type:** Realistic. **Skills Required:** Equipment Maintenance; Repairing; Operation and Control; Operation Monitoring; Troubleshooting. **Abilities:** Night Vision; Sound Localization; Peripheral Vision; Far Vision; Glare Sensitivity. **Occupational Values:** Autonomy; Independence; Recognition; Authority; Responsibility. **Interacting with Others:** Performing for or Working Directly with the Public; Communicating with Persons Outside Organization; Establishing and Maintaining Interpersonal Relationships. **Physical Work Conditions:** Outdoors; Common Protective or Safety Equipment; Hazardous Equipment; Minor Burns, Cuts, Bites, or Stings; Keeping or Regaining Balance.

Ordinary Seamen and Marine Oilers

Stand deck department watches and perform a variety of tasks to preserve the painted surface of the ship and to maintain lines and ship equipment, such as running and cargo-handling gear. May oil and grease moving parts of engines and auxiliary equipment. Must hold government-issued certification. Must hold certification when working aboard liquid-carrying vessels. **O*NET Code:** 53-5011.02. **Average Salary:** $29,810. **Projected Growth:** 4.0%. **Annual Openings:** 3,000. **Education:** Short-term on-the-job training. **Job Zone:** 2. **Education/Training Program(s)—** Marine Transportation, Other. **Related Knowledge/Courses:** Transportation; Geography; Mechanical; Building and Construction; Public

Safety and Security; Engineering and Technology. **Personality Type:** Realistic. **Skills Required:** Repairing; Equipment Maintenance; Operation and Control; Operation Monitoring; Troubleshooting; Installation; Systems Analysis. **Abilities:** Night Vision; Peripheral Vision; Depth Perception; Sound Localization; Far Vision. **Occupational Values:** Advancement; Supervision, Technical; Co-workers. **Interacting with Others:** Establishing and Maintaining Interpersonal Relationships; Communicating with Supervisors, Peers, or Subordinates; Assisting and Caring for Others. **Physical Work Conditions:** Outdoors; Hazardous Equipment; Minor Burns, Cuts, Bites, or Stings; Spend Time Bending or Twisting the Body; Common Protective or Safety Equipment.

Pilots, Ship

Command ships to steer them into and out of harbors, estuaries, straits, and sounds and on rivers, lakes, and bays. Must be licensed by U.S. Coast Guard with limitations indicating class and tonnage of vessels for which license is valid and route and waters that may be piloted. **O*NET Code:** 53-5021.03. **Average Salary:** $50,900. **Projected Growth:** 2.4%. **Annual Openings:** 3,000. **Education:** Work experience plus degree. **Job Zone:** 5. **Education/Training Program(s)—** Commercial Fishing; Marine Science/Merchant Marine Officer; Marine Transportation, Other. **Related Knowledge/Courses:** Transportation; Geography; Physics; Law and Government; Public Safety and Security; Telecommunications. **Personality Type:** Realistic. **Skills Required:** Operation and Control; Operation Monitoring; Judgment and Decision Making; Systems Analysis; Management of Personnel Resources; Systems Evaluation; Monitoring; Mathematics; Science. **Abilities:** Far Vision; Night Vision; Spatial Orientation; Rate Control; Depth Perception; Glare Sensitivity. **Occupational Values:** Authority; Responsibility; Autonomy; Social Status; Recognition. **Interacting with Others:** Communicating with Supervisors, Peers, or Subordinates; Communicating with Persons Outside Organization; Establishing and Maintaining Interpersonal Relationships. **Physical Work Conditions:** Keeping or Regaining Balance; Very Hot or Cold; Extremely Bright or Inadequate Lighting; Outdoors; Standing.

Ship and Boat Captains

Command vessels in oceans, bays, lakes, rivers, and coastal waters. **O*NET Code:** 53-5021.01. **Average Salary:** $50,900. **Projected Growth:** 2.4%. **Annual Openings:** 3,000. **Education:** Long-term on-the-job training. **Job Zone:** 4. **Education/Training Program(s)—** Commercial Fishing; Marine Science/Merchant Marine Officer; Marine Transportation, Other. **Related Knowledge/Courses:** Transportation; Geography; Physics; Administration and Management; Personnel and Human Resources; Mathematics. **Personality Type:** Enterprising. **Skills Required:** Management of Personnel Resources; Operation Monitoring; Operation and Control; Coordination; Troubleshooting; Management of Material Resources; Judgment and Decision Making; Management of Financial Resources. **Abilities:** Night Vision; Far Vision; Spatial Orientation; Glare Sensitivity; Response Orientation. **Occupational Values:** Authority; Responsibility; Autonomy; Recognition; Social Status. **Interacting with**

Others: Communicating with Supervisors, Peers, or Subordinates; Coordinating the Work and Activities of Others; Staffing Organizational Units. **Physical Work Conditions:** Outdoors; Extremely Bright or Inadequate Lighting; Very Hot or Cold; Standing; Keeping or Regaining Balance.

16.06 Other Services Requiring Driving

Ambulance Drivers and Attendants, Except Emergency Medical Technicians

Drive ambulance or assist ambulance driver in transporting sick, injured, or convalescent persons. Assist in lifting patients. **O*NET Code:** 53-3011.00. **Average Salary:** $18,920. **Projected Growth:** 26.7%. **Annual Openings:** 4,000. **Education:** Moderate-term on-the-job training. **Job Zone:** 1. **Education/Training Program(s)**—Emergency Medical Technology/Technician (EMT Paramedic). **Related Knowledge/Courses:** Medicine and Dentistry; Geography; Transportation; Biology; Telecommunications; Physics. **Personality Type:** Social. **Skills Required:** Service Orientation; Operation and Control; Coordination; Speaking; Persuasion. **Abilities:** Reaction Time; Sound Localization; Response Orientation; Peripheral Vision; Spatial Orientation; Static Strength. **Occupational Values:** Social Service; Variety; Security; Achievement; Co-workers; Supervision, Technical. **Interacting with Others:** Assisting and Caring for Others; Establishing and Maintaining Interpersonal Relationships; Performing for or Working Directly with the Public. **Physical Work Conditions:** Disease or Infections; Outdoors; Contaminants; Sitting; Spend Time Bending or Twisting the Body.

Bus Drivers, School

Transport students or special clients, such as the elderly or persons with disabilities. Ensure adherence to safety rules. May assist passengers in boarding or exiting. **O*NET Code:** 53-3022.00. **Average Salary:** $22,720. **Projected Growth:** 16.7%. **Annual Openings:** 76,000. **Education:** Short-term on-the-job training. **Job Zone:** 2. **Education/Training Program(s)**—Truck and Bus Driver/Commercial Vehicle Operation. **Related Knowledge/Courses:** Transportation; Customer and Personal Service; Public Safety and Security; Geography; Law and Government; Mechanical. **Personality Type:** Realistic. **Skills Required:** Repairing; Operation and Control; Operation Monitoring; Equipment Maintenance. **Abilities:** Response Orientation; Reaction Time; Sound Localization; Rate Control; Peripheral Vision. **Occupational Values:** Supervision, Technical; Supervision, Human Relations; Independence; Company Policies and Practices; Social Service. **Interacting with Others:** Resolving Conflicts and Negotiating with Others; Performing for or Working Directly with the Public; Assisting and Caring for Others. **Physical Work Conditions:** Sitting; Sounds, Noise Levels Are Distracting or Uncomfortable; Outdoors; Extremely Bright or Inadequate Lighting; Spend Time Making Repetitive Motions.

Bus Drivers, Transit and Intercity

Drive bus or motor coach, including regular route operations, charters, and private carriage. May assist passengers with baggage. May collect fares or tickets. **O*NET Code:** 53-3021.00. **Average Salary:** $29,030. **Projected Growth:** 15.2%. **Annual Openings:** 33,000. **Education:** Moderate-term on-the-job training. **Job Zone:** 2. **Education/Training Program(s)**—Truck and Bus Driver/Commercial Vehicle Operation. **Related Knowledge/Courses:** Transportation; Customer and Personal Service; Geography; Public Safety and Security; Psychology; Law and Government. **Personality Type:** Realistic. **Skills Required:** Social Perceptiveness; Equipment Maintenance; Troubleshooting; Operation and Control; Negotiation; Instructing; Service Orientation; Operation Monitoring. **Abilities:** Peripheral Vision; Response Orientation; Rate Control; Reaction Time; Spatial Orientation; Hearing Sensitivity. **Occupational Values:** Supervision, Technical; Supervision, Human Relations; Company Policies and Practices; Independence; Social Service. **Interacting with Others:** Establishing and Maintaining Interpersonal Relationships; Performing for or Working Directly with the Public; Communicating with Persons Outside Organization. **Physical Work Conditions:** Sounds, Noise Levels Are Distracting or Uncomfortable; In an Enclosed Vehicle or Equipment; Sitting; Contaminants; Physical Proximity.

Couriers and Messengers

Pick up and carry messages, documents, packages, and other items between offices or departments within an establishment or to other business concerns, traveling by foot, bicycle, motorcycle, automobile, or public conveyance. **O*NET Code:** 43-5021.00. **Average Salary:** $19,880. **Projected Growth:** 4.0%. **Annual Openings:** 25,000. **Education:** Short-term on-the-job training. **Job Zone:** 1. **Education/Training Program(s)**—No data available. **Related Knowledge/Courses:** Transportation; Geography. **Personality Type:** Realistic. **Skills Required:** Service Orientation; Equipment Maintenance. **Abilities:** Response Orientation; Stamina; Spatial Orientation; Reaction Time; Night Vision. **Occupational Values:** Independence; Social Service. **Interacting with Others:** Communicating with Persons Outside Organization; Establishing and Maintaining Interpersonal Relationships; Communicating with Supervisors, Peers, or Subordinates. **Physical Work Conditions:** Hazardous Equipment; Outdoors; Walking and Running; Standing; Very Hot or Cold.

Driver/Sales Workers

Drive truck or other vehicle over established routes or within an established territory and sell goods such as food products, including restaurant take-out items, or pick up and deliver items such as laundry. May also take orders and collect payments. Includes newspaper delivery drivers. **O*NET Code:** 53-3031.00. **Average Salary:** $20,360. **Projected Growth:** 4.3%. **Annual Openings:** 67,000. **Education:** Short-term on-the-job training. **Job Zone:** 1. **Education/Training Program(s)**—Retailing and Retail Operations. **Related Knowledge/Courses:** Transportation; Sales and Marketing; Customer and Personal Service; Public Safety and Security; English Language; Geography. **Personality Type:** Enterprising. **Skills Required:** Social Perceptiveness;

Negotiation; Persuasion; Speaking; Coordination; Active Listening; Critical Thinking; Active Learning; Service Orientation. **Abilities:** Response Orientation; Speech Recognition; Reaction Time; Peripheral Vision; Hearing Sensitivity. **Occupational Values:** Independence; Supervision, Technical; Social Service. **Interacting with Others:** Communicating with Persons Outside Organization; Establishing and Maintaining Interpersonal Relationships; Communicating with Supervisors, Peers, or Subordinates; Selling or Influencing Others. **Physical Work Conditions:** In an Enclosed Vehicle or Equipment; Very Hot or Cold; Outdoors; Physical Proximity; Sitting.

Parking Lot Attendants

Park automobiles or issue tickets for customers in a parking lot or garage. May collect fee. **O*NET Code:** 53-6021.00. **Average Salary:** $16,800. **Projected Growth:** 19.2%. **Annual Openings:** 19,000. **Education:** Short-term on-the-job training. **Job Zone:** 1. **Education/Training Program(s)**—No data available. **Related Knowledge/Courses:** Customer and Personal Service; Public Safety and Security; Transportation; Geography; Psychology; English Language. **Personality Type:** Realistic. **Skills Required:** Service Orientation; Critical Thinking; Systems Evaluation; Management of Personnel Resources; Coordination; Instructing; Time Management; Learning Strategies; Social Perceptiveness. **Abilities:** Depth Perception; Stamina; Far Vision; Speech Recognition; Response Orientation; Peripheral Vision. **Occupational Values:** Social Service; Independence. **Interacting with Others:** Establishing and Maintaining Interpersonal Relationships; Performing for or Working Directly with the Public; Assisting and Caring for Others. **Physical Work Conditions:** Very Hot or Cold; Contaminants; Physical Proximity; Outdoors; In an Enclosed Vehicle or Equipment.

Postal Service Mail Carriers

Sort mail for delivery. Deliver mail on established route by vehicle or on foot. **O*NET Code:** 43-5052.00. **Average Salary:** $44,540. **Projected Growth:** -0.5%. **Annual Openings:** 20,000. **Education:** Short-term on-the-job training. **Job Zone:** 1. **Education/Training Program(s)**—General Office Occupations and Clerical Services. **Related Knowledge/Courses:** Transportation; Geography; Clerical. **Personality Type:** Conventional. **Skills Required:** None met the criteria. **Abilities:** Spatial Orientation; Static Strength; Stamina; Perceptual Speed; Response Orientation. **Occupational Values:** Independence; Security; Supervision, Human Relations; Social Service; Compensation; Company Policies and Practices; Supervision, Technical. **Interacting with Others:** Communicating with Persons Outside Organization; Performing for or Working Directly with the Public; Establishing and Maintaining Interpersonal Relationships; Performing Administrative Activities. **Physical Work Conditions:** Outdoors; Walking and Running; Very Hot or Cold; Minor Burns, Cuts, Bites, or Stings; Standing.

Taxi Drivers and Chauffeurs

Drive automobiles, vans, or limousines to transport passengers. May occasionally carry cargo. **O*NET Code:** 53-3041.00. **Average Salary:** $19,230. **Projected Growth:** 21.7%. **Annual Openings:** 28,000. **Education:** Short-term on-the-job training. **Job Zone:** 1. **Education/Training Program(s)**—Truck and Bus Driver/Commercial Vehicle Operation. **Related Knowledge/Courses:** Transportation; Economics and Accounting; English Language; Clerical; Sales and Marketing; Public Safety and Security. **Personality Type:** Realistic. **Skills Required:** Service Orientation; Installation; Equipment Maintenance; Operation and Control; Social Perceptiveness; Negotiation; Coordination; Instructing. **Abilities:** Reaction Time; Sound Localization; Response Orientation; Rate Control; Spatial Orientation; Peripheral Vision. **Occupational Values:** Social Service; Independence. **Interacting with Others:** Performing for or Working Directly with the Public; Assisting and Caring for Others; Establishing and Maintaining Interpersonal Relationships. **Physical Work Conditions:** In an Enclosed Vehicle or Equipment; Sitting; Contaminants; Physical Proximity; Extremely Bright or Inadequate Lighting.

16.07 Transportation Support Work

Bridge and Lock Tenders

Operate and tend bridges, canal locks, and lighthouses to permit marine passage on inland waterways, near shores, and at danger points in waterway passages. May supervise such operations. Includes drawbridge operators, lock tenders and operators, and slip bridge operators. **O*NET Code:** 53-6011.00. **Average Salary:** $36,640. **Projected Growth:** -17.4%. **Annual Openings:** Fewer than 500. **Education:** Short-term on-the-job training. **Job Zone:** 2. **Education/Training Program(s)**—No data available. **Related Knowledge/Courses:** Mechanical; Transportation; Engineering and Technology; Physics; Public Safety and Security; Telecommunications. **Personality Type:** Realistic. **Skills Required:** Repairing; Installation; Equipment Maintenance; Operation and Control; Troubleshooting; Operation Monitoring; Systems Analysis; Writing; Management of Personnel Resources. **Abilities:** Far Vision; Night Vision; Depth Perception; Glare Sensitivity; Reaction Time. **Occupational Values:** Independence; Security; Moral Values; Supervision, Human Relations; Autonomy. **Interacting with Others:** Communicating with Persons Outside Organization; Communicating with Supervisors, Peers, or Subordinates; Assisting and Caring for Others. **Physical Work Conditions:** Hazardous Equipment; Extremely Bright or Inadequate Lighting; Outdoors; Very Hot or Cold; Minor Burns, Cuts, Bites, or Stings; Using Hands on Objects, Tools, or Controls.

Cargo and Freight Agents

Expedite and route movement of incoming and outgoing cargo and freight shipments in airline, train, and trucking terminals and shipping docks. Take orders from customers and arrange pickup of freight and cargo for delivery to loading platform. Prepare and examine bills of lading to determine shipping charges and tariffs. **O*NET Code:** 43-5011.00. **Average Salary:** $33,850. **Projected Growth:** 15.5%. **Annual Openings:** 8,000. **Education:** Moderate-term on-the-job training. **Job Zone:** 2. **Education/Training Program(s)**—General Office Occupations and Clerical Services. **Related**

© 2006, JIST Works

Knowledge/Courses: Transportation; Geography; Clerical; Telecommunications; Customer and Personal Service. **Personality Type:** Conventional. **Skills Required:** Service Orientation; Operation and Control; Coordination. **Abilities:** Static Strength; Trunk Strength; Manual Dexterity; Dynamic Strength; Stamina. **Occupational Values:** Supervision, Technical; Supervision, Human Relations; Company Policies and Practices; Moral Values; Co-workers. **Interacting with Others:** Communicating with Supervisors, Peers, or Subordinates; Communicating with Persons Outside Organization; Assisting and Caring for Others. **Physical Work Conditions:** Sounds, Noise Levels Are Distracting or Uncomfortable; Standing; Walking and Running; Very Hot or Cold; Outdoors.

Cleaners of Vehicles and Equipment

Wash or otherwise clean vehicles, machinery, and other equipment. Use such materials as water, cleaning agents, brushes, cloths, and hoses. **O*NET Code:** 53-7061.00. **Average Salary:** $17,340. **Projected Growth:** 8.7%. **Annual Openings:** 74,000. **Education:** Short-term on-the-job training. **Job Zone:** 1. **Education/Training Program(s)**—No data available. **Related Knowledge/Courses:** Public Safety and Security; Chemistry; Transportation; Administration and Management; Mechanical; Customer and Personal Service. **Personality Type:** Realistic. **Skills Required:** Equipment Maintenance; Repairing; Troubleshooting; Instructing; Quality Control Analysis. **Abilities:** Extent Flexibility; Stamina; Speed of Limb Movement; Static Strength; Trunk Strength. **Occupational Values:** Independence; Moral Values; Supervision, Technical. **Interacting with Others:** Establishing and Maintaining Interpersonal Relationships; Communicating with Supervisors, Peers, or Subordinates; Performing for or Working Directly with the Public. **Physical Work Conditions:** Contaminants; In an Enclosed Vehicle or Equipment; Sounds, Noise Levels Are Distracting or Uncomfortable; Very Hot or Cold; Extremely Bright or Inadequate Lighting.

Freight Inspectors

Inspect freight for proper storage according to specifications. **O*NET Code:** 53-6051.06. **Average Salary:** $49,480. **Projected Growth:** 7.7%. **Annual Openings:** 5,000. **Education:** Work experience in a related occupation. **Job Zone:** 2. **Education/Training Program(s)**—No data available. **Related Knowledge/Courses:** Transportation; Public Safety and Security; Production and Processing; Geography. **Personality Type:** Conventional. **Skills Required:** Writing; Mathematics; Systems Analysis. **Abilities:** Category Flexibility; Spatial Orientation; Sound Localization; Stamina; Far Vision. **Occupational Values:** Supervision, Technical; Security; Co-workers; Company Policies and Practices; Responsibility. **Interacting with Others:** Performing Administrative Activities; Communicating with Supervisors, Peers, or Subordinates; Coordinating the Work and Activities of Others. **Physical Work Conditions:** Outdoors; Standing; Climbing Ladders, Scaffolds, or Poles; Very Hot or Cold; Walking and Running; Spend Time Bending or Twisting the Body.

Public Transportation Inspectors

Monitor operation of public transportation systems to ensure good service and compliance with regulations. Investigate accidents, equipment failures, and complaints. **O*NET Code:** 53-6051.02. **Average Salary:** $49,480. **Projected Growth:** 7.7%. **Annual Openings:** 5,000. **Education:** Work experience in a related occupation. **Job Zone:** 4. **Education/Training Program(s)**—No data available. **Related Knowledge/Courses:** Transportation; Personnel and Human Resources; Public Safety and Security; Law and Government; Geography; Administration and Management. **Personality Type:** Enterprising. **Skills Required:** Operations Analysis; Writing; Management of Personnel Resources; Systems Evaluation; Monitoring; Speaking; Negotiation; Reading Comprehension; Systems Analysis. **Abilities:** Written Expression; Oral Expression; Response Orientation; Fluency of Ideas; Inductive Reasoning; Time Sharing. **Occupational Values:** Authority; Supervision, Human Relations; Supervision, Technical; Responsibility; Security; Company Policies and Practices. **Interacting with Others:** Communicating with Supervisors, Peers, or Subordinates; Establishing and Maintaining Interpersonal Relationships; Interpreting the Meaning of Information for Others; Communicating with Persons Outside Organization; Performing Administrative Activities. **Physical Work Conditions:** Outdoors; Sitting; Walking and Running; Very Hot or Cold; Extremely Bright or Inadequate Lighting.

Railroad Yard Workers

Perform a variety of activities such as coupling railcars and operating railroad track switches in railroad yard to facilitate the movement of railcars within the yard. **O*NET Code:** 53-4021.02. **Average Salary:** $45,700. **Projected Growth:** –22.8%. **Annual Openings:** 2,000. **Education:** Work experience in a related occupation. **Job Zone:** 1. **Education/Training Program(s)**—Truck and Bus Driver/Commercial Vehicle Operation. **Related Knowledge/Courses:** Transportation; Mechanical; Engineering and Technology. **Personality Type:** Realistic. **Skills Required:** Operation and Control; Repairing. **Abilities:** Response Orientation; Rate Control; Reaction Time; Gross Body Equilibrium; Far Vision. **Occupational Values:** Supervision, Technical; Supervision, Human Relations; Company Policies and Practices; Advancement; Moral Values. **Interacting with Others:** Communicating with Supervisors, Peers, or Subordinates; Coordinating the Work and Activities of Others; Establishing and Maintaining Interpersonal Relationships. **Physical Work Conditions:** Outdoors; Hazardous Equipment; Climbing Ladders, Scaffolds, or Poles; High Places; Standing.

Stevedores, Except Equipment Operators

Manually load and unload ship cargo. Stack cargo in transit shed or in hold of ship, using pallet or cargo board. Attach and move slings to lift cargo. Guide load lift. **O*NET Code:** 53-7062.01. **Average Salary:** $19,980. **Projected Growth:** 6.6%. **Annual Openings:** 525,000. **Education:** Short-term on-the-job training. **Job Zone:** 1. **Education/Training Program(s)**—No data available. **Related Knowledge/Courses:** Transportation; Production and Processing; Physics. **Personality Type:** Realistic. **Skills Required:** None met the criteria. **Abilities:** Static Strength; Stamina; Dynamic

Strength; Explosive Strength; Trunk Strength. **Occupational Values:** Supervision, Technical; Moral Values; Co-workers. **Interacting with Others:** Communicating with Supervisors, Peers, or Subordinates; Establishing and Maintaining Interpersonal Relationships; Assisting and Caring for Others. **Physical Work Conditions:** Outdoors; Spend Time Bending or Twisting the Body; Standing; Hazardous Equipment; Extremely Bright or Inadequate Lighting.

Traffic Technicians

Conduct field studies to determine traffic volume, speed, effectiveness of signals, adequacy of lighting, and other factors influencing traffic conditions under direction of traffic engineer. **O*NET Code:** 53-6041.00. **Average Salary:** $33,700. **Projected Growth:** 9.3%. **Annual Openings:** 1,000. **Education:** Short-term on-the-job training. **Job Zone:** 4. **Education/Training Program(s)**—Traffic, Customs, and Transportation Clerk/Technician. **Related Knowledge/Courses:** Transportation; Design; Mathematics; Engineering and Technology; Public Safety and Security; Geography. **Personality Type:** Realistic. **Skills Required:** Mathematics; Critical Thinking; Writing; Complex Problem Solving; Operations Analysis; Systems Analysis; Systems Evaluation; Speaking. **Abilities:** Number Facility; Reaction Time; Fluency of Ideas; Mathematical Reasoning; Inductive Reasoning; Glare Sensitivity. **Occupational Values:** Independence; Variety; Supervision, Human Relations; Supervision, Technical; Company Policies and Practices. **Interacting with Others:** Communicating with Supervisors, Peers, or Subordinates; Communicating with Persons Outside Organization; Providing Consultation and Advice to Others. **Physical Work Conditions:** Standing; Very Hot or Cold; Extremely Bright or Inadequate Lighting; Outdoors; Sounds, Noise Levels Are Distracting or Uncomfortable; Contaminants.

Train Crew Members

Inspect couplings, airhoses, journal boxes, and handbrakes on trains to ensure that they function properly. **O*NET Code:** 53-4021.01. **Average Salary:** $45,700. **Projected Growth:** –22.8%. **Annual Openings:** 2,000. **Education:** Work experience in a related occupation. **Job Zone:** 2. **Education/Training Program(s)**—Truck and Bus Driver/Commercial Vehicle Operation. **Related Knowledge/Courses:** Transportation; Mechanical; Customer and Personal Service; Public Safety and Security; Geography; Building and Construction. **Personality Type:** Realistic. **Skills Required:** Equipment Maintenance; Repairing; Service Orientation; Operation and Control; Troubleshooting; Operation Monitoring; Installation; Quality Control Analysis. **Abilities:** Auditory Attention; Spatial Orientation; Gross Body Equilibrium; Gross Body Coordination; Dynamic Strength; Far Vision. **Occupational Values:** Supervision, Technical; Social Service; Supervision, Human Relations; Advancement; Company Policies and Practices. **Interacting with Others:** Performing for or Working Directly with the Public; Communicating with Supervisors, Peers, or Subordinates; Communicating with Persons Outside Organization; Establishing and Maintaining Interpersonal Relationships. **Physical Work Conditions:** Walking and Running; Standing; Outdoors; Hazardous Equipment; Sounds, Noise Levels Are Distracting or Uncomfortable; Climbing Ladders, Scaffolds, or Poles.

© 2006, JIST Works

PART 3

Crosswalks to Careers

by Work Values, Leisure Activities, School Subjects, Work Settings, Skills, Abilities, Knowledges, and Military Occupations

We mentioned the importance of these crosswalks in the quick summary of the table of contents as well as in the introduction. You can use these crosswalks to help you identify GOE Work Groups that you should consider. In some cases, using the crosswalks will help you identify options you had overlooked. There are eight crosswalks:

Work Values with Corresponding Work Groups

Leisure Activities with Corresponding Work Groups

School Subjects with Corresponding Work Groups

Work Settings with Corresponding Work Groups

Skills with Corresponding Work Groups

Abilities with Corresponding Work Groups

Knowledges with Corresponding Work Groups

Military Occupations with Corresponding Work Groups

Using the Crosswalks

Look at the first crosswalk, "Work Values with Corresponding Work Groups," to see how the crosswalks work. You will see a work value in bold followed by a list of Work Groups. Only the Work Groups whose occupations offer a lot of that particular work value are included. Look at each bold work value and identify three or four that you most want to include in your long-term career plan. List these work values on a sheet of paper. (This book will probably be used by other people, so don't mark in it.) Next, look at the Work Group numbers and names listed for each work value. Write down the Work Group information for the work values you chose. You can then refer to Part 1 to learn more about the Work Groups you have listed.

© 2006 JIST Works

Crosswalk A: Work Values with Corresponding Work Groups

Ability Utilization: Making use of your individual abilities

01.02 Resource Science/Engineering for Plants, Animals, and the Environment

02.02 Architectural Design

03.02 Writing and Editing

03.03 News, Broadcasting, and Public Relations

03.04 Studio Art

03.05 Design

03.07 Music

03.08 Dance

05.01 Managerial Work in Education

05.03 Postsecondary and Adult Teaching and Instructing

08.02 Medicine and Surgery

08.03 Dentistry

09.06 Sports

11.02 Information Technology Specialties

15.02 Physical Sciences

15.03 Life Sciences

15.04 Social Sciences

15.07 Research and Design Engineering

15.08 Industrial and Safety Engineering

16.02 Air Vehicle Operation

Achievement: Getting a feeling of accomplishment

02.02 Architectural Design

03.01 Managerial Work in Arts and Communication

03.02 Writing and Editing

03.04 Studio Art

03.05 Design

03.07 Music

03.08 Dance

05.02 Preschool, Elementary, and Secondary Teaching and Instructing

05.03 Postsecondary and Adult Teaching and Instructing

05.06 Counseling, Health, and Fitness Education

08.02 Medicine and Surgery

08.03 Dentistry

08.04 Health Specialties

08.07 Medical Therapy

09.06 Sports

10.02 Religious Work

12.01 Managerial Work in Law and Public Safety

12.06 Emergency Responding

15.04 Social Sciences

Activity: Being busy all the time

04.01 Managerial Work in General Business

04.02 Managerial Work in Business Detail

04.04 Secretarial Support

05.01 Managerial Work in Education

05.02 Preschool, Elementary, and Secondary Teaching and Instructing

06.01 Managerial Work in Finance and Insurance

07.01 Managerial Work in Government and Public Administration

07.04 Public Administration Clerical Support

08.05 Animal Care

13.01 Managerial Work in Manufacturing

13.04 Welding, Brazing, and Soldering

13.07 Production Quality Control

15.08 Industrial and Safety Engineering

15.09 Engineering Technology

Advancement: Having opportunities for advancement

01.03 Resource Technologies for Plants, Animals, and the Environment

02.03 Architecture/Construction Engineering Technologies

02.06 Construction Support/Labor

03.03 News, Broadcasting, and Public Relations

04.05 Accounting, Auditing, and Analytical Support

04.06 Mathematical Clerical Support

06.01 Managerial Work in Finance and Insurance

06.02 Finance/Insurance Investigation and Analysis

06.05 Finance/Insurance Sales and Support

07.02 Public Planning

11.01 Managerial Work in Information Technology

11.02 Information Technology Specialties

12.03 Legal Support

13.01 Managerial Work in Manufacturing

14.01 Managerial Work in Retail/Wholesale Sales and Service

14.02 Technical Sales

14.03 General Sales

14.05 Purchasing

15.05 Physical Science Laboratory Technology

15.06 Mathematics and Data Analysis

15.09 Engineering Technology

16.02 Air Vehicle Operation

16.05 Water Vehicle Operation

Authority: Giving directions and instructions to others

01.01 Managerial Work in Agriculture and Natural Resources

02.01 Managerial Work in Architecture/Construction

03.01 Managerial Work in Arts and Communication

04.01 Managerial Work in General Business

04.02 Managerial Work in Business Detail

05.01 Managerial Work in Education

05.02 Preschool, Elementary, and Secondary Teaching and Instructing

05.03 Postsecondary and Adult Teaching and Instructing

05.05 Archival and Museum Services

05.06 Counseling, Health, and Fitness Education

06.01 Managerial Work in Finance and Insurance

07.01 Managerial Work in Government and Public Administration

08.01 Managerial Work in Medical and Health Services

09.01 Managerial Work in Hospitality and Tourism

11.01 Managerial Work in Information Technology

12.01 Managerial Work in Law and Public Safety

12.05 Safety and Security

13.01 Managerial Work in Manufacturing

14.01 Managerial Work in Retail/Wholesale Sales and Service

15.01 Managerial Work in Scientific Research, Engineering, and Mathematics

15.08 Industrial and Safety Engineering

16.01 Managerial Work in Transportation

16.02 Air Vehicle Operation

16.05 Water Vehicle Operation

Autonomy: Planning your work with little supervision

01.01 Managerial Work in Agriculture and Natural Resources

01.02 Resource Science/Engineering for Plants, Animals, and the Environment

02.01 Managerial Work in Architecture/Construction

03.01 Managerial Work in Arts and Communication

03.02 Writing and Editing

03.04 Studio Art

03.05 Design

03.07 Music

04.01 Managerial Work in General Business

07.01 Managerial Work in Government and Public Administration

08.01 Managerial Work in Medical and Health Services

08.04 Health Specialties

10.01 Counseling and Social Work

10.02 Religious Work

12.01 Managerial Work in Law and Public Safety

12.02 Legal Practice and Justice Administration

13.01 Managerial Work in Manufacturing

14.01 Managerial Work in Retail/Wholesale Sales and Service

15.01 Managerial Work in Scientific Research, Engineering, and Mathematics

15.02 Physical Sciences

15.03 Life Sciences

15.04 Social Sciences

15.06 Mathematics and Data Analysis

15.07 Research and Design Engineering

15.08 Industrial and Safety Engineering

16.01 Managerial Work in Transportation

Company Policies and Practices: Being treated fairly by the company

06.01 Managerial Work in Finance and Insurance

06.02 Finance/Insurance Investigation and Analysis

07.01 Managerial Work in Government and Public Administration

11.02 Information Technology Specialties

13.05 Production Machining Technology

15.01 Managerial Work in Scientific Research, Engineering, and Mathematics

16.01 Managerial Work in Transportation

16.02 Air Vehicle Operation

Compensation: Being paid well in comparison with other workers

02.02 Architectural Design

02.03 Architecture/Construction Engineering Technologies

04.05 Accounting, Auditing, and Analytical Support

06.01 Managerial Work in Finance and Insurance

06.05 Finance/Insurance Sales and Support

08.02 Medicine and Surgery

08.03 Dentistry

08.04 Health Specialties

09.06 Sports

11.01 Managerial Work in Information Technology

11.02 Information Technology Specialties

12.02 Legal Practice and Justice Administration

13.14 Vehicle and Facility Mechanical Work

14.01 Managerial Work in Retail/Wholesale Sales and Service

14.02 Technical Sales

15.01 Managerial Work in Scientific Research, Engineering, and Mathematics

15.05 Physical Science Laboratory Technology

15.07 Research and Design Engineering

16.01 Managerial Work in Transportation

16.02 Air Vehicle Operation

16.03 Truck Driving

© 2006, JIST Works

Co-workers: Having co-workers who are easy to get along with

04.02 Managerial Work in Business Detail
04.03 Human Resources Support
05.01 Managerial Work in Education
05.03 Postsecondary and Adult Teaching and Instructing
05.04 Library Services
05.05 Archival and Museum Services
08.02 Medicine and Surgery
08.07 Medical Therapy
08.08 Patient Care and Assistance
09.02 Recreational Services
09.04 Food and Beverage Preparation
09.05 Food and Beverage Service
09.06 Sports
11.01 Managerial Work in Information Technology
12.01 Managerial Work in Law and Public Safety
12.06 Emergency Responding
13.01 Managerial Work in Manufacturing
14.03 General Sales
15.01 Managerial Work in Scientific Research, Engineering, and Mathematics

Creativity: Trying out your own ideas

01.02 Resource Science/Engineering for Plants, Animals, and the Environment
02.02 Architectural Design
03.01 Managerial Work in Arts and Communication
03.02 Writing and Editing
03.04 Studio Art
03.05 Design
03.06 Drama
03.07 Music
03.08 Dance
05.01 Managerial Work in Education
05.02 Preschool, Elementary, and Secondary Teaching and Instructing
05.03 Postsecondary and Adult Teaching and Instructing
05.06 Counseling, Health, and Fitness Education
10.01 Counseling and Social Work
10.02 Religious Work
11.02 Information Technology Specialties
15.01 Managerial Work in Scientific Research, Engineering, and Mathematics
15.02 Physical Sciences
15.03 Life Sciences
15.04 Social Sciences
15.07 Research and Design Engineering
15.08 Industrial and Safety Engineering

Independence: Doing your work alone

01.05 Nursery, Groundskeeping, and Pest Control
01.07 Hunting and Fishing
03.04 Studio Art
03.11 Musical Instrument Repair
04.08 Clerical Machine Operation
11.03 Digital Equipment Repair
13.02 Machine Setup and Operation
13.06 Production Precision Work
13.08 Graphic Arts Production
13.09 Hands-On Work, Assorted Materials
13.10 Woodworking Technology
13.11 Apparel, Shoes, Leather, and Fabric Care
13.13 Machinery Repair
13.15 Medical and Technical Equipment Repair
14.04 Personal Soliciting
15.02 Physical Sciences
15.06 Mathematics and Data Analysis
16.03 Truck Driving
16.06 Other Services Requiring Driving

Moral Values: Never being pressured to do things that go against your sense of right and wrong

01.04 General Farming
01.05 Nursery, Groundskeeping, and Pest Control
01.06 Forestry and Logging
01.08 Mining and Drilling
02.04 Construction Crafts
02.05 Systems and Equipment Installation, Maintenance, and Repair
03.08 Dance
03.11 Musical Instrument Repair
09.04 Food and Beverage Preparation
09.07 Barber and Beauty Services
13.02 Machine Setup and Operation
13.03 Production Work, Assorted Materials Processing
13.04 Welding, Brazing, and Soldering
13.05 Production Machining Technology
13.06 Production Precision Work
13.08 Graphic Arts Production
13.09 Hands-On Work, Assorted Materials
13.10 Woodworking Technology
13.11 Apparel, Shoes, Leather, and Fabric Care
13.12 Electrical and Electronic Repair
13.13 Machinery Repair
13.14 Vehicle and Facility Mechanical Work
13.15 Medical and Technical Equipment Repair

Responsibility: Making decisions on your own

01.01 Managerial Work in Agriculture and Natural Resources

01.02 Resource Science/Engineering for Plants, Animals, and the Environment

02.01 Managerial Work in Architecture/Construction

03.01 Managerial Work in Arts and Communication

03.02 Writing and Editing

03.07 Music

05.02 Preschool, Elementary, and Secondary Teaching and Instructing

05.06 Counseling, Health, and Fitness Education

08.01 Managerial Work in Medical and Health Services

08.04 Health Specialties

09.01 Managerial Work in Hospitality and Tourism

11.01 Managerial Work in Information Technology

12.01 Managerial Work in Law and Public Safety

12.02 Legal Practice and Justice Administration

13.01 Managerial Work in Manufacturing

15.02 Physical Sciences

15.03 Life Sciences

15.04 Social Sciences

15.07 Research and Design Engineering

15.08 Industrial and Safety Engineering

Security: Having steady employment

01.03 Resource Technologies for Plants, Animals, and the Environment

07.01 Managerial Work in Government and Public Administration

07.03 Regulations Enforcement

08.01 Managerial Work in Medical and Health Services

08.02 Medicine and Surgery

08.03 Dentistry

08.06 Medical Technology

10.02 Religious Work

10.03 Child/Personal Care and Services

11.01 Managerial Work in Information Technology

11.02 Information Technology Specialties

12.01 Managerial Work in Law and Public Safety

12.02 Legal Practice and Justice Administration

12.04 Law Enforcement and Public Safety

15.03 Life Sciences

16.01 Managerial Work in Transportation

Social Service: Having work where you do things for other people

05.02 Preschool, Elementary, and Secondary Teaching and Instructing

05.03 Postsecondary and Adult Teaching and Instructing

05.04 Library Services

05.06 Counseling, Health, and Fitness Education

08.02 Medicine and Surgery

08.03 Dentistry

08.04 Health Specialties

08.06 Medical Technology

08.07 Medical Therapy

08.08 Patient Care and Assistance

08.09 Health Protection and Promotion

09.03 Hospitality and Travel Services

09.07 Barber and Beauty Services

10.01 Counseling and Social Work

10.02 Religious Work

10.03 Child/Personal Care and Services

10.04 Client Interviewing

12.05 Safety and Security

12.06 Emergency Responding

16.06 Other Services Requiring Driving

Social Status: Being looked up to by others in your company and your community

02.02 Architectural Design

05.01 Managerial Work in Education

05.03 Postsecondary and Adult Teaching and Instructing

06.05 Finance/Insurance Sales and Support

07.01 Managerial Work in Government and Public Administration

08.02 Medicine and Surgery

08.03 Dentistry

08.04 Health Specialties

09.06 Sports

10.02 Religious Work

12.01 Managerial Work in Law and Public Safety

12.02 Legal Practice and Justice Administration

12.06 Emergency Responding

15.02 Physical Sciences

15.03 Life Sciences

15.07 Research and Design Engineering

15.08 Industrial and Safety Engineering

16.02 Air Vehicle Operation

Variety: Having something different to do every day

01.04 General Farming

01.07 Hunting and Fishing

02.01 Managerial Work in Architecture/Construction

03.01 Managerial Work in Arts and Communication

03.03 News, Broadcasting, and Public Relations

03.04 Studio Art

03.05 Design

03.06 Drama

03.09 Media Technology

04.01 Managerial Work in General Business

05.06 Counseling, Health, and Fitness Education

06.01 Managerial Work in Finance and Insurance

07.01 Managerial Work in Government and Public Administration

08.05 Animal Care

08.09 Health Protection and Promotion

10.01 Counseling and Social Work

13.01 Managerial Work in Manufacturing

14.01 Managerial Work in Retail/Wholesale Sales and Service

14.02 Technical Sales

14.05 Purchasing

Working Conditions: Having good working conditions

03.02 Writing and Editing

03.05 Design

03.09 Media Technology

04.01 Managerial Work in General Business

04.03 Human Resources Support

04.04 Secretarial Support

04.05 Accounting, Auditing, and Analytical Support

04.06 Mathematical Clerical Support

05.02 Preschool, Elementary, and Secondary Teaching and Instructing

05.04 Library Services

05.05 Archival and Museum Services

06.01 Managerial Work in Finance and Insurance

06.03 Finance/Insurance Records Processing

06.04 Finance/Insurance Customer Service

06.05 Finance/Insurance Sales and Support

07.02 Public Planning

11.01 Managerial Work in Information Technology

11.02 Information Technology Specialties

12.02 Legal Practice and Justice Administration

12.03 Legal Support

14.01 Managerial Work in Retail/Wholesale Sales and Service

15.01 Managerial Work in Scientific Research, Engineering, and Mathematics

15.04 Social Sciences

15.06 Mathematics and Data Analysis

Crosswalk B: Leisure Activities with Corresponding Work Groups

Acting in a play or amateur variety show

03.06 Drama

Addressing letters for an organization

04.02 Managerial Work in Business Detail

04.08 Clerical Machine Operation

Announcing or emceeing a program

03.03 News, Broadcasting, and Public Relations

03.06 Drama

Applying first aid in emergencies as a volunteer

12.01 Managerial Work in Law and Public Safety

12.06 Emergency Responding

Applying makeup for amateur theater

03.06 Drama

08.09 Health Protection and Promotion

09.07 Barber and Beauty Services

Assembling radios, computers, and other devices from kits

11.03 Digital Equipment Repair

13.12 Electrical and Electronic Repair

13.15 Medical and Technical Equipment Repair

Assembling toys, shelving, furniture, and other items around the house

13.06 Production Precision Work

13.10 Woodworking Technology

13.13 Machinery Repair

Babysitting or caring for children

10.03 Child/Personal Care and Services

Baking and decorating cakes

09.04 Food and Beverage Preparation

Balancing checkbooks for family members

04.01 Managerial Work in General Business

04.02 Managerial Work in Business Detail

04.03 Human Resources Support

04.05 Accounting, Auditing, and Analytical Support

04.06 Mathematical Clerical Support

04.07 Records and Materials Processing

Being a member of the school safety patrol

12.01 Managerial Work in Law and Public Safety

Being on the debate team

12.02 Legal Practice and Justice Administration

Belonging to a 4-H club, a garden club, or Future Farmers of America

01.01 Managerial Work in Agriculture and Natural Resources

01.02 Resource Science/Engineering for Plants, Animals, and the Environment

01.03 Resource Technologies for Plants, Animals, and the Environment

01.04 General Farming

01.05 Nursery, Groundskeeping, and Pest Control

Belonging to a computer club

11.01 Managerial Work in Information Technology

11.02 Information Technology Specialties

15.02 Physical Sciences

15.07 Research and Design Engineering

15.08 Industrial and Safety Engineering

Belonging to a literary or book club

03.02 Writing and Editing

Belonging to a political science club

07.01 Managerial Work in Government and Public Administration

15.04 Social Sciences

Breeding animals

01.01 Managerial Work in Agriculture and Natural Resources

01.04 General Farming

08.05 Animal Care

Budgeting the family income

04.01 Managerial Work in General Business

04.02 Managerial Work in Business Detail

04.05 Accounting, Auditing, and Analytical Support

15.01 Managerial Work in Scientific Research, Engineering, and Mathematics

Building cabinets or furniture

02.01 Managerial Work in Architecture/Construction

13.01 Managerial Work in Manufacturing

13.10 Woodworking Technology

Building model airplanes, automobiles, or boats

13.02 Machine Setup and Operation

13.04 Welding, Brazing, and Soldering

13.05 Production Machining Technology

13.06 Production Precision Work

13.14 Vehicle and Facility Mechanical Work

13.17 Loading, Moving, Hoisting, and Conveying

16.02 Air Vehicle Operation

16.05 Water Vehicle Operation

16.07 Transportation Support Work

Building or repairing radios or television sets

02.05 Systems and Equipment Installation, Maintenance, and Repair

13.12 Electrical and Electronic Repair

15.09 Engineering Technology

Building robots or electronic devices

13.06 Production Precision Work

13.12 Electrical and Electronic Repair

13.15 Medical and Technical Equipment Repair

Buying large quantities of food or other products for an organization

13.07 Production Quality Control

14.05 Purchasing

Calculating sports statistics

09.06 Sports

15.06 Mathematics and Data Analysis

Campaigning for political candidates or issues

07.01 Managerial Work in Government and Public Administration

14.04 Personal Soliciting

15.04 Social Sciences

Camping, hiking, or engaging in other outdoor activities

16.05 Water Vehicle Operation

Canning and preserving food

09.04 Food and Beverage Preparation

13.03 Production Work, Assorted Materials Processing

Carving small wooden objects

03.04 Studio Art

03.11 Musical Instrument Repair

05.05 Archival and Museum Services

08.06 Medical Technology

13.03 Production Work, Assorted Materials Processing

13.06 Production Precision Work

13.08 Graphic Arts Production

13.10 Woodworking Technology

Chauffeuring special groups, such as children, older people, or people with disabilities

16.01 Managerial Work in Transportation

16.06 Other Services Requiring Driving

Coaching children or youth in sports activities

05.06 Counseling, Health, and Fitness Education

09.06 Sports

10.03 Child/Personal Care and Services

Collecting and arranging stamps, coins, or other items

04.07 Records and Materials Processing

Collecting rocks or minerals

01.01 Managerial Work in Agriculture and Natural Resources

01.02 Resource Science/Engineering for Plants, Animals, and the Environment

01.08 Mining and Drilling

15.02 Physical Sciences

Conducting experiments involving plants

14.02 Technical Sales

15.01 Managerial Work in Scientific Research, Engineering, and Mathematics

15.03 Life Sciences

Conducting house-to-house or telephone surveys for a PTA or other organization

04.02 Managerial Work in Business Detail

06.02 Finance/Insurance Investigation and Analysis

14.01 Managerial Work in Retail/Wholesale Sales and Service

14.04 Personal Soliciting

14.06 Customer Service

15.04 Social Sciences

15.06 Mathematics and Data Analysis

Constructing stage sets for school or other amateur theater

02.01 Managerial Work in Architecture/Construction

02.02 Architectural Design

02.04 Construction Crafts

02.06 Construction Support/Labor

Cooking and baking

09.04 Food and Beverage Preparation

Cooking large quantities of food for community events

09.01 Managerial Work in Hospitality and Tourism

09.04 Food and Beverage Preparation

13.03 Production Work, Assorted Materials Processing

Creating dance steps for school or other amateur musicals

03.08 Dance

Creating or styling hairdos for friends

09.07 Barber and Beauty Services

Creating unusual lighting effects for school or other amateur plays

03.09 Media Technology

Creating Web pages

03.05 Design

11.02 Information Technology Specialties

Cutting and trimming hair for family and friends

09.07 Barber and Beauty Services

Designing and building an addition or remodeling the interior of a home

02.01 Managerial Work in Architecture/Construction

02.02 Architectural Design

02.03 Architecture/Construction Engineering Technologies

15.07 Research and Design Engineering

Designing and landscaping a flower garden

01.01 Managerial Work in Agriculture and Natural Resources

Designing and making costumes for school plays, festivals, and other events

03.05 Design

Designing stage sets for school or community plays

03.01 Managerial Work in Arts and Communication

03.05 Design

Designing your own greeting cards and writing original verses

03.01 Managerial Work in Arts and Communication

03.02 Writing and Editing

Developing film

03.09 Media Technology

15.05 Physical Science Laboratory Technology

Developing publicity fliers for a school or community event

03.01 Managerial Work in Arts and Communication

03.03 News, Broadcasting, and Public Relations

03.05 Design

14.01 Managerial Work in Retail/Wholesale Sales and Service

Directing school or other amateur plays or musicals

03.01 Managerial Work in Arts and Communication

03.06 Drama

Directing traffic at community events

12.04 Law Enforcement and Public Safety

12.05 Safety and Security

16.06 Other Services Requiring Driving

Doing crafts

03.04 Studio Art

13.06 Production Precision Work

Doing crossword puzzles

03.02 Writing and Editing

Doing desktop publishing for a school or community publication

03.02 Writing and Editing

03.03 News, Broadcasting, and Public Relations

13.08 Graphic Arts Production

Doing electrical wiring and repairs in the home

02.01 Managerial Work in Architecture/Construction

02.04 Construction Crafts

02.05 Systems and Equipment Installation, Maintenance, and Repair

13.16 Utility Operation and Energy Distribution

15.09 Engineering Technology

Doing fundraising for school groups, teams, or community organizations

06.04 Finance/Insurance Customer Service

06.05 Finance/Insurance Sales and Support

Doing impersonations

03.06 Drama

Doing makeup, hair, and nails for family and friends

09.07 Barber and Beauty Services

Doing public speaking or debating

05.02 Preschool, Elementary, and Secondary Teaching and Instructing

05.03 Postsecondary and Adult Teaching and Instructing

07.02 Public Planning

12.02 Legal Practice and Justice Administration

14.02 Technical Sales

14.04 Personal Soliciting

Doing strenuous activities, such as dancing, climbing, backpacking, running, swimming, and skiing

01.06 Forestry and Logging

01.07 Hunting and Fishing

02.06 Construction Support/Labor

05.06 Counseling, Health, and Fitness Education

12.07 Military

Doing volunteer work for the Red Cross

12.06 Emergency Responding

Drawing posters for an organization or political campaign

02.02 Architectural Design

02.03 Architecture/Construction Engineering Technologies

03.01 Managerial Work in Arts and Communication

03.04 Studio Art

Driving a bus as a volunteer for an organization

16.01 Managerial Work in Transportation

16.04 Rail Vehicle Operation

16.05 Water Vehicle Operation

16.06 Other Services Requiring Driving

Driving a truck and tractor to harvest crops on a family farm

16.03 Truck Driving

Driving an ambulance as a volunteer

16.01 Managerial Work in Transportation

16.03 Truck Driving

16.04 Rail Vehicle Operation

16.06 Other Services Requiring Driving

Driving go-karts

16.03 Truck Driving

16.04 Rail Vehicle Operation

16.06 Other Services Requiring Driving

Editing or proofreading a school or organizational newspaper, yearbook, or magazine

03.01 Managerial Work in Arts and Communication

03.02 Writing and Editing

06.03 Finance/Insurance Records Processing

Entertaining at parties or other events

03.06 Drama

03.07 Music

Experimenting with a chemistry set

08.02 Medicine and Surgery

08.06 Medical Technology

12.04 Law Enforcement and Public Safety

15.01 Managerial Work in Scientific Research, Engineering, and Mathematics

15.02 Physical Sciences

15.03 Life Sciences

15.05 Physical Science Laboratory Technology

15.07 Research and Design Engineering

Fishing

01.07 Hunting and Fishing

© 2006, JIST Works

Gardening

01.05 Nursery, Groundskeeping, and Pest Control

Handling equipment for a local athletic team

09.06 Sports

13.17 Loading, Moving, Hoisting, and Conveying

Helping conduct physical exercises for people with disabilities

08.07 Medical Therapy

Helping friends and others with math

05.03 Postsecondary and Adult Teaching and Instructing

15.06 Mathematics and Data Analysis

Helping friends and relatives with their tax reports

04.06 Mathematical Clerical Support

10.04 Client Interviewing

Helping members of the family with their English lessons

05.01 Managerial Work in Education

05.02 Preschool, Elementary, and Secondary Teaching and Instructing

05.03 Postsecondary and Adult Teaching and Instructing

Helping people with disabilities take walks

10.01 Counseling and Social Work

Helping persuade people to sign petitions or support a cause

06.05 Finance/Insurance Sales and Support

14.01 Managerial Work in Retail/Wholesale Sales and Service

14.02 Technical Sales

14.03 General Sales

14.04 Personal Soliciting

Helping run a school or community fair or carnival

04.01 Managerial Work in General Business

04.02 Managerial Work in Business Detail

06.01 Managerial Work in Finance and Insurance

07.01 Managerial Work in Government and Public Administration

08.01 Managerial Work in Medical and Health Services

09.01 Managerial Work in Hospitality and Tourism

09.02 Recreational Services

14.03 General Sales

15.01 Managerial Work in Scientific Research, Engineering, and Mathematics

15.08 Industrial and Safety Engineering

Helping sick relatives, friends, and neighbors

08.01 Managerial Work in Medical and Health Services

08.02 Medicine and Surgery

08.03 Dentistry

08.04 Health Specialties

08.06 Medical Technology

08.07 Medical Therapy

08.08 Patient Care and Assistance

Helping to organize things at home, such as shopping lists and budgets

07.02 Public Planning

09.01 Managerial Work in Hospitality and Tourism

10.03 Child/Personal Care and Services

13.01 Managerial Work in Manufacturing

Hunting or target shooting

01.07 Hunting and Fishing

12.07 Military

Illustrating the school yearbook

03.04 Studio Art

Installing and repairing home stereo equipment

01.03 Resource Technologies for Plants, Animals, and the Environment

02.05 Systems and Equipment Installation, Maintenance, and Repair

03.09 Media Technology

15.07 Research and Design Engineering

15.09 Engineering Technology

Instructing family members in observing traffic regulations

05.01 Managerial Work in Education

05.02 Preschool, Elementary, and Secondary Teaching and Instructing

07.03 Regulations Enforcement

12.04 Law Enforcement and Public Safety

12.05 Safety and Security

16.03 Truck Driving

16.06 Other Services Requiring Driving

Keeping a journal or diary

03.02 Writing and Editing

03.03 News, Broadcasting, and Public Relations

Keeping score for athletic events

09.06 Sports

Keyboarding papers and letters for others

04.04 Secretarial Support

04.07 Records and Materials Processing

Keying in text for a school or community publication

04.04 Secretarial Support

04.06 Mathematical Clerical Support

04.07 Records and Materials Processing

04.08 Clerical Machine Operation

Learning first aid and CPR

12.06 Emergency Responding

Learning to use new features of word-processing and other programs

12.03 Legal Support

13.08 Graphic Arts Production

Listening to friends and helping them with their personal problems

05.06 Counseling, Health, and Fitness Education

08.08 Patient Care and Assistance

10.01 Counseling and Social Work

Making belts or other leather articles

13.11 Apparel, Shoes, Leather, and Fabric Care

Making ceramic objects

03.04 Studio Art

13.06 Production Precision Work

13.09 Hands-On Work, Assorted Materials

Making jewelry or stringing beads

13.06 Production Precision Work

Making sketches of machines or other mechanical equipment

13.01 Managerial Work in Manufacturing

13.02 Machine Setup and Operation

13.04 Welding, Brazing, and Soldering

13.05 Production Machining Technology

13.07 Production Quality Control

13.08 Graphic Arts Production

13.16 Utility Operation and Energy Distribution

15.09 Engineering Technology

Making tie-dyed clothes

03.05 Design

13.11 Apparel, Shoes, Leather, and Fabric Care

Making videos of family activities

03.01 Managerial Work in Arts and Communication

03.09 Media Technology

Mixing drinks for family or friends

09.05 Food and Beverage Service

Modeling clothes for a fashion show

14.04 Personal Soliciting

Mounting and framing pictures

03.05 Design

Mowing the lawn

01.05 Nursery, Groundskeeping, and Pest Control

Nursing sick pets

08.01 Managerial Work in Medical and Health Services

08.05 Animal Care

15.03 Life Sciences

Operating a calculator or adding machine for an organization

04.06 Mathematical Clerical Support

04.08 Clerical Machine Operation

06.03 Finance/Insurance Records Processing

Operating a CB or ham radio

03.10 Communications Technology

15.09 Engineering Technology

16.02 Air Vehicle Operation

16.05 Water Vehicle Operation

16.07 Transportation Support Work

Operating a model train layout

13.17 Loading, Moving, Hoisting, and Conveying

16.01 Managerial Work in Transportation

16.04 Rail Vehicle Operation

16.07 Transportation Support Work

Operating a motorboat or other pleasure boat

12.07 Military

16.01 Managerial Work in Transportation

16.05 Water Vehicle Operation

Operating flight or driving simulators on the computer

16.02 Air Vehicle Operation

16.03 Truck Driving

16.04 Rail Vehicle Operation

Operating power tools for household projects

01.06 Forestry and Logging

01.08 Mining and Drilling

02.04 Construction Crafts

13.02 Machine Setup and Operation

13.03 Production Work, Assorted Materials Processing

13.05 Production Machining Technology

13.10 Woodworking Technology

Organizing your room, CDs, DVDs, tools, books, and other items

05.04 Library Services

05.05 Archival and Museum Services

09.03 Hospitality and Travel Services

15.08 Industrial and Safety Engineering

Painting landscapes, seascapes, or portraits

03.04 Studio Art

© 2006, JIST Works

Painting the interior or exterior of a home

02.04 Construction Crafts

02.06 Construction Support/Labor

Painting, refinishing, or reupholstering furniture

13.09 Hands-On Work, Assorted Materials

13.11 Apparel, Shoes, Leather, and Fabric Care

Participating in gymnastics

05.06 Counseling, Health, and Fitness Education

Performing experiments for a science fair

01.02 Resource Science/Engineering for Plants, Animals, and the Environment

01.03 Resource Technologies for Plants, Animals, and the Environment

08.03 Dentistry

14.02 Technical Sales

15.02 Physical Sciences

15.03 Life Sciences

15.05 Physical Science Laboratory Technology

15.07 Research and Design Engineering

15.09 Engineering Technology

Performing magic tricks for friends

03.06 Drama

Planning advertisements for a school or community newspaper

03.02 Writing and Editing

03.03 News, Broadcasting, and Public Relations

14.01 Managerial Work in Retail/Wholesale Sales and Service

Planning and arranging programs for school or community organizations

03.01 Managerial Work in Arts and Communication

04.01 Managerial Work in General Business

05.01 Managerial Work in Education

Planning and cooking meals

10.03 Child/Personal Care and Services

Planning family recreational activities

08.07 Medical Therapy

09.02 Recreational Services

Planning parties and outings

09.03 Hospitality and Travel Services

Planting trees

01.01 Managerial Work in Agriculture and Natural Resources

01.03 Resource Technologies for Plants, Animals, and the Environment

01.05 Nursery, Groundskeeping, and Pest Control

01.06 Forestry and Logging

Playing a musical instrument

03.07 Music

03.11 Musical Instrument Repair

Playing baseball, basketball, football, or other sports

09.06 Sports

Playing chess or solving complex puzzles

11.02 Information Technology Specialties

12.02 Legal Practice and Justice Administration

Posing for an artist or photographer

14.04 Personal Soliciting

Preparing family income tax returns

04.05 Accounting, Auditing, and Analytical Support

Racing midget or stock cars

16.02 Air Vehicle Operation

16.03 Truck Driving

16.06 Other Services Requiring Driving

Raising or caring for animals

01.01 Managerial Work in Agriculture and Natural Resources

01.02 Resource Science/Engineering for Plants, Animals, and the Environment

01.03 Resource Technologies for Plants, Animals, and the Environment

01.04 General Farming

08.05 Animal Care

Raising vegetables in a home garden

01.01 Managerial Work in Agriculture and Natural Resources

01.02 Resource Science/Engineering for Plants, Animals, and the Environment

01.03 Resource Technologies for Plants, Animals, and the Environment

01.04 General Farming

Reading about religious issues

10.02 Religious Work

Reading about technological developments, such as computer science or aerospace

01.02 Resource Science/Engineering for Plants, Animals, and the Environment

01.03 Resource Technologies for Plants, Animals, and the Environment

02.03 Architecture/Construction Engineering Technologies

11.01 Managerial Work in Information Technology

13.16 Utility Operation and Energy Distribution

15.01 Managerial Work in Scientific Research, Engineering, and Mathematics

15.02 Physical Sciences

15.05 Physical Science Laboratory Technology
15.06 Mathematics and Data Analysis
15.07 Research and Design Engineering
15.08 Industrial and Safety Engineering
15.09 Engineering Technology

Reading airplane or boat magazines

16.01 Managerial Work in Transportation
16.02 Air Vehicle Operation
16.05 Water Vehicle Operation
16.07 Transportation Support Work

Reading business magazines and newspapers

04.01 Managerial Work in General Business
04.03 Human Resources Support
04.05 Accounting, Auditing, and Analytical Support
06.01 Managerial Work in Finance and Insurance
06.02 Finance/Insurance Investigation and Analysis
06.05 Finance/Insurance Sales and Support
14.01 Managerial Work in Retail/Wholesale Sales and Service
14.02 Technical Sales
14.05 Purchasing
15.04 Social Sciences
15.08 Industrial and Safety Engineering

Reading detective stories; watching television detective shows

07.03 Regulations Enforcement
12.01 Managerial Work in Law and Public Safety
12.04 Law Enforcement and Public Safety
12.05 Safety and Security

Reading farm magazines

01.01 Managerial Work in Agriculture and Natural Resources

Reading mechanical or automotive magazines

13.01 Managerial Work in Manufacturing
13.14 Vehicle and Facility Mechanical Work
13.17 Loading, Moving, Hoisting, and Conveying
16.04 Rail Vehicle Operation

Reading medical or scientific magazines

08.02 Medicine and Surgery
08.03 Dentistry
08.04 Health Specialties
08.05 Animal Care
08.06 Medical Technology
08.07 Medical Therapy
08.09 Health Protection and Promotion
15.02 Physical Sciences
15.03 Life Sciences
15.05 Physical Science Laboratory Technology

15.07 Research and Design Engineering
15.09 Engineering Technology

Reading military stories; watching television shows and movies about the military

12.07 Military

Recruiting members for a club or other organization

14.03 General Sales
14.04 Personal Soliciting

Repairing electrical household appliances

02.05 Systems and Equipment Installation, Maintenance, and Repair
11.03 Digital Equipment Repair
13.13 Machinery Repair
13.16 Utility Operation and Energy Distribution

Repairing or assembling bicycles or tricycles

13.01 Managerial Work in Manufacturing
13.13 Machinery Repair
16.07 Transportation Support Work

Repairing plumbing in the home

02.01 Managerial Work in Architecture/Construction
02.04 Construction Crafts
02.06 Construction Support/Labor
13.13 Machinery Repair
13.16 Utility Operation and Energy Distribution

Repairing the family car

13.14 Vehicle and Facility Mechanical Work
16.03 Truck Driving

Researching things that sound interesting to you

05.04 Library Services
12.03 Legal Support
12.04 Law Enforcement and Public Safety
14.05 Purchasing
15.04 Social Sciences

Selling advertising space for a school newspaper or yearbook

06.05 Finance/Insurance Sales and Support
14.01 Managerial Work in Retail/Wholesale Sales and Service
14.02 Technical Sales

Serving as a host or hostess for houseguests

09.01 Managerial Work in Hospitality and Tourism
09.03 Hospitality and Travel Services

Serving as a leader of a scouting or other group

02.01 Managerial Work in Architecture/Construction
04.01 Managerial Work in General Business
04.02 Managerial Work in Business Detail

© 2006, JIST Works

05.01 Managerial Work in Education

06.01 Managerial Work in Finance and Insurance

07.01 Managerial Work in Government and Public Administration

08.01 Managerial Work in Medical and Health Services

10.01 Counseling and Social Work

10.02 Religious Work

11.01 Managerial Work in Information Technology

13.01 Managerial Work in Manufacturing

14.01 Managerial Work in Retail/Wholesale Sales and Service

16.01 Managerial Work in Transportation

Serving as a salesperson or clerk in a store run by a charity organization

14.03 General Sales

14.06 Customer Service

Serving as a volunteer counselor at a youth camp or center

05.06 Counseling, Health, and Fitness Education

10.01 Counseling and Social Work

Serving as a volunteer in a fire department or emergency rescue squad

12.01 Managerial Work in Law and Public Safety

12.06 Emergency Responding

Serving as a volunteer in a hospital, nursing home, or retirement home

08.01 Managerial Work in Medical and Health Services

08.02 Medicine and Surgery

08.03 Dentistry

08.04 Health Specialties

08.06 Medical Technology

08.08 Patient Care and Assistance

10.01 Counseling and Social Work

Serving as a volunteer interviewer in a social service organization

04.03 Human Resources Support

06.04 Finance/Insurance Customer Service

07.02 Public Planning

10.01 Counseling and Social Work

10.04 Client Interviewing

14.06 Customer Service

Serving as president of a club or other organization

01.01 Managerial Work in Agriculture and Natural Resources

04.01 Managerial Work in General Business

07.01 Managerial Work in Government and Public Administration

09.01 Managerial Work in Hospitality and Tourism

11.01 Managerial Work in Information Technology

12.01 Managerial Work in Law and Public Safety

15.01 Managerial Work in Scientific Research, Engineering, and Mathematics

Serving as secretary of a club or other organization

04.04 Secretarial Support

07.04 Public Administration Clerical Support

Serving as treasurer of a club or other organization

04.01 Managerial Work in General Business

04.05 Accounting, Auditing, and Analytical Support

06.01 Managerial Work in Finance and Insurance

14.05 Purchasing

Setting tables for club or organizational functions

09.05 Food and Beverage Service

Setting the table and serving family meals

09.01 Managerial Work in Hospitality and Tourism

09.05 Food and Beverage Service

Sewing, knitting, or doing needlework

13.09 Hands-On Work, Assorted Materials

13.11 Apparel, Shoes, Leather, and Fabric Care

Singing in a choir or other group

03.07 Music

Soliciting clothes, food, and other supplies for needy people

14.03 General Sales

14.04 Personal Soliciting

Soliciting funds for community organizations

14.01 Managerial Work in Retail/Wholesale Sales and Service

14.04 Personal Soliciting

Speaking on radio or television

03.03 News, Broadcasting, and Public Relations

03.06 Drama

Staying fit, eating right, and taking care of your health

08.09 Health Protection and Promotion

Studying plants in gardens, parks, or forests

01.02 Resource Science/Engineering for Plants, Animals, and the Environment

15.03 Life Sciences

Studying the habits of wildlife

15.03 Life Sciences

Taking apart or fixing mechanical and electronic devices

11.03 Digital Equipment Repair

13.02 Machine Setup and Operation

13.04 Welding, Brazing, and Soldering

13.05 Production Machining Technology

13.06 Production Precision Work

13.07 Production Quality Control

13.12 Electrical and Electronic Repair

13.13 Machinery Repair

13.15 Medical and Technical Equipment Repair

Taking ballet or other dancing lessons

03.08 Dance

Taking lessons in singing or in playing a musical instrument

03.07 Music

Taking photographs

03.09 Media Technology

15.05 Physical Science Laboratory Technology

Taking trips

09.03 Hospitality and Travel Services

Talking on the phone

03.10 Communications Technology

Teaching dancing as a volunteer in an after-school center

03.08 Dance

Teaching games to children as a volunteer aide in a nursery school

05.01 Managerial Work in Education

05.02 Preschool, Elementary, and Secondary Teaching and Instructing

10.03 Child/Personal Care and Services

Teaching immigrants or other individuals to speak, write, or read English

03.03 News, Broadcasting, and Public Relations

05.01 Managerial Work in Education

05.03 Postsecondary and Adult Teaching and Instructing

Teaching in a religious school

10.02 Religious Work

Training dogs or other animals to perform on command

08.05 Animal Care

Trimming shrubs and hedges

01.05 Nursery, Groundskeeping, and Pest Control

Tutoring pupils in school subjects

05.02 Preschool, Elementary, and Secondary Teaching and Instructing

Umpiring or refereeing amateur sporting events

09.06 Sports

Upgrading hardware in personal computers

11.03 Digital Equipment Repair

15.07 Research and Design Engineering

Ushering for school or community events

09.02 Recreational Services

Using a pocket calculator or spreadsheet to figure out income and expenses for an organization

04.02 Managerial Work in Business Detail

04.05 Accounting, Auditing, and Analytical Support

04.06 Mathematical Clerical Support

06.02 Finance/Insurance Investigation and Analysis

06.03 Finance/Insurance Records Processing

06.04 Finance/Insurance Customer Service

14.03 General Sales

15.01 Managerial Work in Scientific Research, Engineering, and Mathematics

15.06 Mathematics and Data Analysis

15.08 Industrial and Safety Engineering

Visiting museums or historic sites

05.05 Archival and Museum Services

15.04 Social Sciences

Volunteering at a house of worship

10.02 Religious Work

Volunteering at the library

05.04 Library Services

14.06 Customer Service

Waiting on tables at club or organizational functions

09.05 Food and Beverage Service

Washing and waxing the family car

16.07 Transportation Support Work

Weaving rugs or making quilts

13.11 Apparel, Shoes, Leather, and Fabric Care

Working on bicycles, minibikes, lawn mowers, or cars

13.14 Vehicle and Facility Mechanical Work

Writing articles, stories, or plays

03.01 Managerial Work in Arts and Communication

03.02 Writing and Editing

03.03 News, Broadcasting, and Public Relations

12.02 Legal Practice and Justice Administration

© 2006, JIST Works

Writing computer programs

11.01 Managerial Work in Information Technology

11.02 Information Technology Specialties

15.06 Mathematics and Data Analysis

Writing letters and e-mails to friends and family

07.04 Public Administration Clerical Support

Writing songs for club socials or amateur performances

03.07 Music

Crosswalk C: School Subjects with Corresponding Work Groups

Abnormal Psychology

08.02 Medicine and Surgery

10.01 Counseling and Social Work

Abstract Writing

03.02 Writing and Editing

03.03 News, Broadcasting, and Public Relations

Accounting

01.01 Managerial Work in Agriculture and Natural Resources

03.01 Managerial Work in Arts and Communication

04.01 Managerial Work in General Business

04.02 Managerial Work in Business Detail

04.03 Human Resources Support

04.04 Secretarial Support

04.05 Accounting, Auditing, and Analytical Support

04.06 Mathematical Clerical Support

06.01 Managerial Work in Finance and Insurance

06.02 Finance/Insurance Investigation and Analysis

07.01 Managerial Work in Government and Public Administration

08.01 Managerial Work in Medical and Health Services

09.01 Managerial Work in Hospitality and Tourism

11.01 Managerial Work in Information Technology

12.01 Managerial Work in Law and Public Safety

13.01 Managerial Work in Manufacturing

14.01 Managerial Work in Retail/Wholesale Sales and Service

15.01 Managerial Work in Scientific Research, Engineering, and Mathematics

16.01 Managerial Work in Transportation

Acoustics

03.09 Media Technology

Acting Techniques

03.06 Drama

Advertising

03.02 Writing and Editing

14.01 Managerial Work in Retail/Wholesale Sales and Service

Advertising Art/Production

03.05 Design

03.09 Media Technology

Aeronautical Charts

16.02 Air Vehicle Operation

Agribusiness

01.01 Managerial Work in Agriculture and Natural Resources

01.04 General Farming

01.05 Nursery, Groundskeeping, and Pest Control

14.02 Technical Sales

14.05 Purchasing

Agricultural Systems

01.02 Resource Science/Engineering for Plants, Animals, and the Environment

Agriculture, Mechanized

01.01 Managerial Work in Agriculture and Natural Resources

01.04 General Farming

Agronomy

01.01 Managerial Work in Agriculture and Natural Resources

01.05 Nursery, Groundskeeping, and Pest Control

Aircraft Mechanics

13.14 Vehicle and Facility Mechanical Work

Airport Safety

16.01 Managerial Work in Transportation

Anatomy

08.02 Medicine and Surgery

08.07 Medical Therapy

08.08 Patient Care and Assistance

08.09 Health Protection and Promotion

Anatomy, Specialized/Advanced

08.04 Health Specialties

08.05 Animal Care

08.07 Medical Therapy

Anesthesia

08.02 Medicine and Surgery

Animal Breeding

08.05 Animal Care

Animal Grooming

08.05 Animal Care

Animal Obedience Training

08.05 Animal Care

Animal Science

01.01 Managerial Work in Agriculture and Natural Resources

01.02 Resource Science/Engineering for Plants, Animals, and the Environment

01.03 Resource Technologies for Plants, Animals, and the Environment

01.04 General Farming

Arbitration/Negotiation

12.02 Legal Practice and Justice Administration

Archeology

05.05 Archival and Museum Services

15.04 Social Sciences

Architectural Drafting

02.02 Architectural Design

02.03 Architecture/Construction Engineering Technologies

Architectural History

02.01 Managerial Work in Architecture/Construction

02.02 Architectural Design

07.02 Public Planning

Art

02.02 Architectural Design

03.09 Media Technology

Arts and Crafts

03.04 Studio Art

05.05 Archival and Museum Services

Astronomy

15.02 Physical Sciences

Auditing Procedures

04.06 Mathematical Clerical Support

Auditory Development

08.07 Medical Therapy

Auto Mechanics

13.14 Vehicle and Facility Mechanical Work

Baking

09.04 Food and Beverage Preparation

Band

03.07 Music

03.11 Musical Instrument Repair

Biochemistry

08.02 Medicine and Surgery

08.03 Dentistry

08.04 Health Specialties

08.05 Animal Care

08.06 Medical Technology

08.07 Medical Therapy

15.03 Life Sciences

15.07 Research and Design Engineering

Biology

01.02 Resource Science/Engineering for Plants, Animals, and the Environment

01.03 Resource Technologies for Plants, Animals, and the Environment

01.05 Nursery, Groundskeeping, and Pest Control

01.06 Forestry and Logging

01.07 Hunting and Fishing

05.02 Preschool, Elementary, and Secondary Teaching and Instructing

05.03 Postsecondary and Adult Teaching and Instructing

05.05 Archival and Museum Services

07.03 Regulations Enforcement

08.01 Managerial Work in Medical and Health Services

08.02 Medicine and Surgery

08.03 Dentistry

08.04 Health Specialties

08.05 Animal Care

08.06 Medical Technology

08.07 Medical Therapy

08.08 Patient Care and Assistance

08.09 Health Protection and Promotion

15.01 Managerial Work in Scientific Research, Engineering, and Mathematics

15.03 Life Sciences

Biostatistics and Epidemiology

15.03 Life Sciences

Blueprint/Schematic Reading

02.01 Managerial Work in Architecture/Construction

02.03 Architecture/Construction Engineering Technologies

© 2006, JIST Works

02.04 Construction Crafts

02.05 Systems and Equipment Installation, Maintenance, and Repair

13.02 Machine Setup and Operation

13.03 Production Work, Assorted Materials Processing

13.04 Welding, Brazing, and Soldering

13.05 Production Machining Technology

13.10 Woodworking Technology

13.12 Electrical and Electronic Repair

13.13 Machinery Repair

13.15 Medical and Technical Equipment Repair

13.16 Utility Operation and Energy Distribution

Bookbinding

13.06 Production Precision Work

Bookkeeping

04.06 Mathematical Clerical Support

04.07 Records and Materials Processing

04.08 Clerical Machine Operation

07.03 Regulations Enforcement

Botany

15.03 Life Sciences

Bricklaying

02.04 Construction Crafts

02.06 Construction Support/Labor

Broadcast Journalism

03.03 News, Broadcasting, and Public Relations

Business Analysis

04.01 Managerial Work in General Business

04.05 Accounting, Auditing, and Analytical Support

06.01 Managerial Work in Finance and Insurance

09.01 Managerial Work in Hospitality and Tourism

14.05 Purchasing

Business Computer Applications

02.01 Managerial Work in Architecture/Construction

04.01 Managerial Work in General Business

04.02 Managerial Work in Business Detail

04.06 Mathematical Clerical Support

04.07 Records and Materials Processing

04.08 Clerical Machine Operation

05.01 Managerial Work in Education

05.04 Library Services

06.01 Managerial Work in Finance and Insurance

06.03 Finance/Insurance Records Processing

07.01 Managerial Work in Government and Public Administration

07.04 Public Administration Clerical Support

12.03 Legal Support

Business Law

03.01 Managerial Work in Arts and Communication

04.01 Managerial Work in General Business

04.02 Managerial Work in Business Detail

04.03 Human Resources Support

04.04 Secretarial Support

04.05 Accounting, Auditing, and Analytical Support

05.01 Managerial Work in Education

06.01 Managerial Work in Finance and Insurance

06.02 Finance/Insurance Investigation and Analysis

07.01 Managerial Work in Government and Public Administration

08.01 Managerial Work in Medical and Health Services

09.01 Managerial Work in Hospitality and Tourism

12.02 Legal Practice and Justice Administration

12.03 Legal Support

14.01 Managerial Work in Retail/Wholesale Sales and Service

Business Machine Operating

04.04 Secretarial Support

06.04 Finance/Insurance Customer Service

12.03 Legal Support

14.06 Customer Service

Business Machine Repair

11.03 Digital Equipment Repair

Business Math

04.07 Records and Materials Processing

06.04 Finance/Insurance Customer Service

Business Organization

04.01 Managerial Work in General Business

04.03 Human Resources Support

04.05 Accounting, Auditing, and Analytical Support

09.01 Managerial Work in Hospitality and Tourism

Business Writing

02.01 Managerial Work in Architecture/Construction

03.01 Managerial Work in Arts and Communication

04.01 Managerial Work in General Business

04.02 Managerial Work in Business Detail

04.04 Secretarial Support

06.01 Managerial Work in Finance and Insurance

07.01 Managerial Work in Government and Public Administration

08.01 Managerial Work in Medical and Health Services

09.01 Managerial Work in Hospitality and Tourism

12.03 Legal Support

Cabinetmaking

13.10 Woodworking Technology

Cake Decorating

09.04 Food and Beverage Preparation

Calculus

01.02 Resource Science/Engineering for Plants, Animals, and the Environment

02.02 Architectural Design

02.03 Architecture/Construction Engineering Technologies

11.02 Information Technology Specialties

15.01 Managerial Work in Scientific Research, Engineering, and Mathematics

15.02 Physical Sciences

15.03 Life Sciences

15.07 Research and Design Engineering

15.08 Industrial and Safety Engineering

15.09 Engineering Technology

Carpentry

02.04 Construction Crafts

02.06 Construction Support/Labor

13.10 Woodworking Technology

Cashiering

14.03 General Sales

14.04 Personal Soliciting

14.06 Customer Service

Ceramics

03.04 Studio Art

Chemical Safety

01.05 Nursery, Groundskeeping, and Pest Control

13.02 Machine Setup and Operation

13.03 Production Work, Assorted Materials Processing

15.05 Physical Science Laboratory Technology

Chemistry

05.03 Postsecondary and Adult Teaching and Instructing

08.01 Managerial Work in Medical and Health Services

08.02 Medicine and Surgery

08.03 Dentistry

08.04 Health Specialties

08.05 Animal Care

08.06 Medical Technology

08.07 Medical Therapy

08.08 Patient Care and Assistance

08.09 Health Protection and Promotion

14.02 Technical Sales

15.03 Life Sciences

15.05 Physical Science Laboratory Technology

15.07 Research and Design Engineering

Child Development/Care

05.02 Preschool, Elementary, and Secondary Teaching and Instructing

05.06 Counseling, Health, and Fitness Education

10.01 Counseling and Social Work

10.02 Religious Work

10.03 Child/Personal Care and Services

Choir/Chorus

03.07 Music

Cinematography

03.01 Managerial Work in Arts and Communication

03.09 Media Technology

Clerical Practices/Office Practices

04.04 Secretarial Support

04.06 Mathematical Clerical Support

04.07 Records and Materials Processing

04.08 Clerical Machine Operation

05.04 Library Services

06.03 Finance/Insurance Records Processing

06.04 Finance/Insurance Customer Service

07.04 Public Administration Clerical Support

Clothing

13.09 Hands-On Work, Assorted Materials

13.11 Apparel, Shoes, Leather, and Fabric Care

Coaching

09.06 Sports

Computer Concepts/Methods

03.09 Media Technology

11.03 Digital Equipment Repair

15.07 Research and Design Engineering

Computer Graphics

03.09 Media Technology

Computer Network Management

11.01 Managerial Work in Information Technology

Computer Programming

11.02 Information Technology Specialties

Computer Science

01.02 Resource Science/Engineering for Plants, Animals, and the Environment

11.01 Managerial Work in Information Technology

11.02 Information Technology Specialties

Computerized Drafting and Design

02.02 Architectural Design

02.03 Architecture/Construction Engineering Technologies

© 2006, JIST Works

Construction Shop

02.04 Construction Crafts

02.05 Systems and Equipment Installation, Maintenance, and Repair

02.06 Construction Support/Labor

Construction Technology

02.01 Managerial Work in Architecture/Construction

02.02 Architectural Design

02.04 Construction Crafts

02.05 Systems and Equipment Installation, Maintenance, and Repair

15.07 Research and Design Engineering

15.09 Engineering Technology

Consumer Behavior

06.02 Finance/Insurance Investigation and Analysis

09.07 Barber and Beauty Services

14.01 Managerial Work in Retail/Wholesale Sales and Service

14.03 General Sales

14.04 Personal Soliciting

14.05 Purchasing

14.06 Customer Service

Contract Law

03.01 Managerial Work in Arts and Communication

04.01 Managerial Work in General Business

04.02 Managerial Work in Business Detail

04.03 Human Resources Support

05.01 Managerial Work in Education

12.02 Legal Practice and Justice Administration

12.03 Legal Support

Cookery, Quantity

09.04 Food and Beverage Preparation

Cooking

09.05 Food and Beverage Service

Copy Writing

03.02 Writing and Editing

Cosmetology

09.07 Barber and Beauty Services

Costuming

03.06 Drama

Counseling Techniques

05.06 Counseling, Health, and Fitness Education

10.01 Counseling and Social Work

10.02 Religious Work

Crafts Shop

13.09 Hands-On Work, Assorted Materials

13.11 Apparel, Shoes, Leather, and Fabric Care

Creative Writing

03.01 Managerial Work in Arts and Communication

03.02 Writing and Editing

Criminal Investigating

06.02 Finance/Insurance Investigation and Analysis

07.03 Regulations Enforcement

12.04 Law Enforcement and Public Safety

12.05 Safety and Security

Criminology

10.01 Counseling and Social Work

12.01 Managerial Work in Law and Public Safety

12.04 Law Enforcement and Public Safety

Crystallography

15.02 Physical Sciences

Culinary Arts

09.04 Food and Beverage Preparation

Customs Law

07.03 Regulations Enforcement

Dairy Science/Technology

01.01 Managerial Work in Agriculture and Natural Resources

Dance

03.08 Dance

Data Entry

04.06 Mathematical Clerical Support

04.07 Records and Materials Processing

04.08 Clerical Machine Operation

Data Retrieval Techniques

05.04 Library Services

12.03 Legal Support

12.04 Law Enforcement and Public Safety

12.05 Safety and Security

14.05 Purchasing

Database Theory/Design

11.02 Information Technology Specialties

Dental Anatomy

08.03 Dentistry

Design Graphics

03.05 Design

Design Media

03.05 Design

Diesel Mechanics/Diesels

13.14 Vehicle and Facility Mechanical Work

Diet and Therapy

08.08 Patient Care and Assistance

08.09 Health Protection and Promotion

Directing

03.06 Drama

Drafting

01.03 Resource Technologies for Plants, Animals, and the Environment

02.03 Architecture/Construction Engineering Technologies

03.05 Design

15.09 Engineering Technology

Drama

03.06 Drama

Driver Education

16.03 Truck Driving

16.06 Other Services Requiring Driving

Earth Science

01.03 Resource Technologies for Plants, Animals, and the Environment

01.08 Mining and Drilling

15.02 Physical Sciences

Ecology/Environmental Science

01.07 Hunting and Fishing

Economics

03.03 News, Broadcasting, and Public Relations

15.04 Social Sciences

Editing

03.01 Managerial Work in Arts and Communication

03.02 Writing and Editing

03.03 News, Broadcasting, and Public Relations

Education

04.03 Human Resources Support

05.01 Managerial Work in Education

05.02 Preschool, Elementary, and Secondary Teaching and Instructing

05.03 Postsecondary and Adult Teaching and Instructing

05.04 Library Services

10.02 Religious Work

Educational Psychology

05.01 Managerial Work in Education

05.02 Preschool, Elementary, and Secondary Teaching and Instructing

05.03 Postsecondary and Adult Teaching and Instructing

15.04 Social Sciences

Electric/Electronic Shop

13.12 Electrical and Electronic Repair

13.13 Machinery Repair

Electric/Electronic Theory

15.07 Research and Design Engineering

Electrical Circuits

02.04 Construction Crafts

02.05 Systems and Equipment Installation, Maintenance, and Repair

11.03 Digital Equipment Repair

13.12 Electrical and Electronic Repair

13.13 Machinery Repair

Electricity/Electronics

03.09 Media Technology

13.14 Vehicle and Facility Mechanical Work

14.02 Technical Sales

15.09 Engineering Technology

Electronic Devices

11.03 Digital Equipment Repair

13.12 Electrical and Electronic Repair

13.15 Medical and Technical Equipment Repair

Emergency Care/Rescue

03.10 Communications Technology

12.01 Managerial Work in Law and Public Safety

12.05 Safety and Security

12.06 Emergency Responding

Engine Mechanics

13.14 Vehicle and Facility Mechanical Work

Farm and Ranch Management

01.01 Managerial Work in Agriculture and Natural Resources

Fashion Illustration

03.04 Studio Art

03.05 Design

Fiction Writing

03.02 Writing and Editing

Finance

06.01 Managerial Work in Finance and Insurance

06.02 Finance/Insurance Investigation and Analysis

06.05 Finance/Insurance Sales and Support

07.01 Managerial Work in Government and Public Administration

07.02 Public Planning

08.01 Managerial Work in Medical and Health Services

09.01 Managerial Work in Hospitality and Tourism

Financial Information Systems

04.06 Mathematical Clerical Support

Fine Arts

03.04 Studio Art

03.05 Design

Fire Fighting

12.01 Managerial Work in Law and Public Safety

12.06 Emergency Responding

Fire Safety

15.08 Industrial and Safety Engineering

First Aid

12.05 Safety and Security

12.06 Emergency Responding

Flight Safety

16.02 Air Vehicle Operation

Flight Training/Pilot Training

16.02 Air Vehicle Operation

Floral Arranging

03.05 Design

Food and Fiber Crops

01.04 General Farming

Food Preparation/Service

09.04 Food and Beverage Preparation

09.05 Food and Beverage Service

Food Science

01.03 Resource Technologies for Plants, Animals, and the Environment

Foreign Languages

01.01 Managerial Work in Agriculture and Natural Resources

05.02 Preschool, Elementary, and Secondary Teaching and Instructing

05.03 Postsecondary and Adult Teaching and Instructing

09.03 Hospitality and Travel Services

Forestry

01.06 Forestry and Logging

Genetics

08.05 Animal Care

08.06 Medical Technology

15.03 Life Sciences

Geographic Information Systems

07.02 Public Planning

15.02 Physical Sciences

15.09 Engineering Technology

Geography

15.02 Physical Sciences

Geology

01.02 Resource Science/Engineering for Plants, Animals, and the Environment

01.03 Resource Technologies for Plants, Animals, and the Environment

Government

07.01 Managerial Work in Government and Public Administration

07.02 Public Planning

07.03 Regulations Enforcement

07.04 Public Administration Clerical Support

Grammar

03.02 Writing and Editing

03.03 News, Broadcasting, and Public Relations

06.03 Finance/Insurance Records Processing

Graphic Arts

13.08 Graphic Arts Production

Guidance

05.06 Counseling, Health, and Fitness Education

Health

05.06 Counseling, Health, and Fitness Education

08.01 Managerial Work in Medical and Health Services

08.02 Medicine and Surgery

08.03 Dentistry

08.04 Health Specialties

08.06 Medical Technology

08.07 Medical Therapy

08.08 Patient Care and Assistance

08.09 Health Protection and Promotion

12.06 Emergency Responding

Health Law

08.02 Medicine and Surgery

Heavy Equipment Operating

01.08 Mining and Drilling

02.04 Construction Crafts

Hematology

08.06 Medical Technology

History

05.05 Archival and Museum Services

15.04 Social Sciences

Home Management

10.03 Child/Personal Care and Services

Home/Consumer Economics

05.02 Preschool, Elementary, and Secondary Teaching and Instructing

Horticulture

01.04 General Farming

01.05 Nursery, Groundskeeping, and Pest Control

Hotel Administration

09.01 Managerial Work in Hospitality and Tourism

Human Growth and Development

05.02 Preschool, Elementary, and Secondary Teaching and Instructing

15.04 Social Sciences

Hydraulics/Hydraulic Shop

13.14 Vehicle and Facility Mechanical Work

Industrial Arts

02.04 Construction Crafts

02.05 Systems and Equipment Installation, Maintenance, and Repair

02.06 Construction Support/Labor

Industrial Distribution

16.01 Managerial Work in Transportation

Industrial Hygiene

15.03 Life Sciences

Industrial Materials

13.02 Machine Setup and Operation

13.03 Production Work, Assorted Materials Processing

13.04 Welding, Brazing, and Soldering

13.05 Production Machining Technology

13.06 Production Precision Work

13.07 Production Quality Control

13.09 Hands-On Work, Assorted Materials

13.11 Apparel, Shoes, Leather, and Fabric Care

Industrial Organization

13.01 Managerial Work in Manufacturing

15.08 Industrial and Safety Engineering

Industrial Safety

13.01 Managerial Work in Manufacturing

13.02 Machine Setup and Operation

13.03 Production Work, Assorted Materials Processing

13.04 Welding, Brazing, and Soldering

13.05 Production Machining Technology

13.06 Production Precision Work

13.07 Production Quality Control

13.08 Graphic Arts Production

13.09 Hands-On Work, Assorted Materials

13.10 Woodworking Technology

13.12 Electrical and Electronic Repair

13.13 Machinery Repair

13.14 Vehicle and Facility Mechanical Work

13.17 Loading, Moving, Hoisting, and Conveying

15.08 Industrial and Safety Engineering

Instrument Repair

13.15 Medical and Technical Equipment Repair

Insurance

06.02 Finance/Insurance Investigation and Analysis

06.03 Finance/Insurance Records Processing

06.05 Finance/Insurance Sales and Support

15.06 Mathematics and Data Analysis

Jewelry

13.06 Production Precision Work

Journalism

03.03 News, Broadcasting, and Public Relations

Kinesiology

08.08 Patient Care and Assistance

08.09 Health Protection and Promotion

Labor and Industry

13.01 Managerial Work in Manufacturing

Laboratory Science

08.01 Managerial Work in Medical and Health Services

08.02 Medicine and Surgery

08.03 Dentistry

08.04 Health Specialties

08.05 Animal Care

08.06 Medical Technology

12.04 Law Enforcement and Public Safety

15.05 Physical Science Laboratory Technology

Landscaping

01.05 Nursery, Groundskeeping, and Pest Control

02.02 Architectural Design

Laser Electronics/Optics

13.06 Production Precision Work

Law, Comprehensive

12.02 Legal Practice and Justice Administration

Law Enforcement

07.03 Regulations Enforcement

12.01 Managerial Work in Law and Public Safety

12.04 Law Enforcement and Public Safety

12.05 Safety and Security

© 2006, JIST Works

Leathercraft

13.11 Apparel, Shoes, Leather, and Fabric Care

Legal Terminology

07.04 Public Administration Clerical Support

12.03 Legal Support

Literature

03.02 Writing and Editing

03.06 Drama

05.03 Postsecondary and Adult Teaching and Instructing

Lithography

13.08 Graphic Arts Production

Locksmithing/Lock Repair

13.13 Machinery Repair

Locomotive Equipment/Operating

16.04 Rail Vehicle Operation

Machine Operating

13.02 Machine Setup and Operation

13.03 Production Work, Assorted Materials Processing

13.04 Welding, Brazing, and Soldering

13.05 Production Machining Technology

13.06 Production Precision Work

13.09 Hands-On Work, Assorted Materials

13.11 Apparel, Shoes, Leather, and Fabric Care

Management

01.01 Managerial Work in Agriculture and Natural Resources

02.01 Managerial Work in Architecture/Construction

03.01 Managerial Work in Arts and Communication

04.01 Managerial Work in General Business

04.02 Managerial Work in Business Detail

05.01 Managerial Work in Education

06.01 Managerial Work in Finance and Insurance

07.01 Managerial Work in Government and Public Administration

08.01 Managerial Work in Medical and Health Services

09.01 Managerial Work in Hospitality and Tourism

11.01 Managerial Work in Information Technology

12.01 Managerial Work in Law and Public Safety

13.01 Managerial Work in Manufacturing

14.01 Managerial Work in Retail/Wholesale Sales and Service

15.01 Managerial Work in Scientific Research, Engineering, and Mathematics

16.01 Managerial Work in Transportation

Manufacturing Processes

13.01 Managerial Work in Manufacturing

13.02 Machine Setup and Operation

13.03 Production Work, Assorted Materials Processing

13.04 Welding, Brazing, and Soldering

13.05 Production Machining Technology

13.06 Production Precision Work

13.07 Production Quality Control

13.09 Hands-On Work, Assorted Materials

13.10 Woodworking Technology

13.17 Loading, Moving, Hoisting, and Conveying

Marketing/Merchandising

03.05 Design

04.01 Managerial Work in General Business

04.02 Managerial Work in Business Detail

06.02 Finance/Insurance Investigation and Analysis

06.05 Finance/Insurance Sales and Support

09.02 Recreational Services

14.01 Managerial Work in Retail/Wholesale Sales and Service

14.02 Technical Sales

14.03 General Sales

14.05 Purchasing

Masonry

02.04 Construction Crafts

Math Computing, Advanced/Special

01.03 Resource Technologies for Plants, Animals, and the Environment

05.03 Postsecondary and Adult Teaching and Instructing

15.06 Mathematics and Data Analysis

Math Computing, Standard Formula

04.05 Accounting, Auditing, and Analytical Support

04.06 Mathematical Clerical Support

06.01 Managerial Work in Finance and Insurance

06.02 Finance/Insurance Investigation and Analysis

06.03 Finance/Insurance Records Processing

Mechanical Drawing

01.03 Resource Technologies for Plants, Animals, and the Environment

Mechanics/Mechanics of Materials

01.02 Resource Science/Engineering for Plants, Animals, and the Environment

02.02 Architectural Design

15.07 Research and Design Engineering

15.09 Engineering Technology

Medical Record Science

08.06 Medical Technology

Medical Terminology

04.04 Secretarial Support

08.06 Medical Technology

08.07 Medical Therapy

08.08 Patient Care and Assistance

08.09 Health Protection and Promotion

Menu Planning

09.01 Managerial Work in Hospitality and Tourism

09.04 Food and Beverage Preparation

Metal Forming and Fabrication/Technology

03.11 Musical Instrument Repair

13.02 Machine Setup and Operation

13.03 Production Work, Assorted Materials Processing

13.04 Welding, Brazing, and Soldering

13.05 Production Machining Technology

Metal Shop

03.11 Musical Instrument Repair

Metallurgy/Metal Properties

15.02 Physical Sciences

Metalsmithing

13.04 Welding, Brazing, and Soldering

13.06 Production Precision Work

Meteorology

15.02 Physical Sciences

Microbiology

15.03 Life Sciences

Mining Practices

01.08 Mining and Drilling

Model Making

13.05 Production Machining Technology

13.10 Woodworking Technology

Modeling, Personal

14.04 Personal Soliciting

Moldmaking

13.02 Machine Setup and Operation

13.03 Production Work, Assorted Materials Processing

13.05 Production Machining Technology

13.06 Production Precision Work

Money and Banking

06.01 Managerial Work in Finance and Insurance

06.02 Finance/Insurance Investigation and Analysis

06.03 Finance/Insurance Records Processing

Music Composition/Arranging

03.07 Music

Music: Theory and History

03.07 Music

03.08 Dance

Naval Architecture

15.07 Research and Design Engineering

Navigation

16.02 Air Vehicle Operation

16.05 Water Vehicle Operation

News Writing

03.03 News, Broadcasting, and Public Relations

Newscasting

03.03 News, Broadcasting, and Public Relations

Nuclear Safety

13.16 Utility Operation and Energy Distribution

13.17 Loading, Moving, Hoisting, and Conveying

15.05 Physical Science Laboratory Technology

Nursing Care

08.02 Medicine and Surgery

08.08 Patient Care and Assistance

Nutrition

08.09 Health Protection and Promotion

Officiating

09.06 Sports

Offset Printing

13.08 Graphic Arts Production

Oilfield Practices

01.08 Mining and Drilling

Opera

03.07 Music

Operations Research

04.05 Accounting, Auditing, and Analytical Support

Optics

08.04 Health Specialties

13.15 Medical and Technical Equipment Repair

Oral Anatomy

08.03 Dentistry

Oral Development

08.03 Dentistry

Oral Hygiene

08.03 Dentistry

Orchestra

03.07 Music

Painting, Fine Arts and Applied

03.04 Studio Art

Pathology

05.03 Postsecondary and Adult Teaching and Instructing

08.06 Medical Technology

Penology

12.01 Managerial Work in Law and Public Safety

Personal Grooming

14.04 Personal Soliciting

Personnel Management

01.01 Managerial Work in Agriculture and Natural Resources

02.01 Managerial Work in Architecture/Construction

03.01 Managerial Work in Arts and Communication

04.01 Managerial Work in General Business

04.02 Managerial Work in Business Detail

04.03 Human Resources Support

05.01 Managerial Work in Education

06.01 Managerial Work in Finance and Insurance

07.01 Managerial Work in Government and Public Administration

08.01 Managerial Work in Medical and Health Services

09.01 Managerial Work in Hospitality and Tourism

11.01 Managerial Work in Information Technology

12.01 Managerial Work in Law and Public Safety

13.01 Managerial Work in Manufacturing

14.01 Managerial Work in Retail/Wholesale Sales and Service

15.01 Managerial Work in Scientific Research, Engineering, and Mathematics

16.01 Managerial Work in Transportation

Pharmacology

08.02 Medicine and Surgery

08.03 Dentistry

08.04 Health Specialties

08.05 Animal Care

Philosophy

10.02 Religious Work

12.02 Legal Practice and Justice Administration

Photography

03.09 Media Technology

05.05 Archival and Museum Services

13.08 Graphic Arts Production

15.05 Physical Science Laboratory Technology

Physical Education

03.08 Dance

05.02 Preschool, Elementary, and Secondary Teaching and Instructing

05.03 Postsecondary and Adult Teaching and Instructing

05.06 Counseling, Health, and Fitness Education

08.09 Health Protection and Promotion

09.06 Sports

Physical Science

01.02 Resource Science/Engineering for Plants, Animals, and the Environment

01.03 Resource Technologies for Plants, Animals, and the Environment

07.03 Regulations Enforcement

Physical Therapy

08.07 Medical Therapy

Physics

01.02 Resource Science/Engineering for Plants, Animals, and the Environment

01.03 Resource Technologies for Plants, Animals, and the Environment

02.02 Architectural Design

05.03 Postsecondary and Adult Teaching and Instructing

08.06 Medical Technology

15.02 Physical Sciences

15.07 Research and Design Engineering

15.08 Industrial and Safety Engineering

15.09 Engineering Technology

Plant Pest Management/Pathology

01.01 Managerial Work in Agriculture and Natural Resources

01.04 General Farming

01.05 Nursery, Groundskeeping, and Pest Control

Plumbing

02.04 Construction Crafts

02.06 Construction Support/Labor

Police Science

12.01 Managerial Work in Law and Public Safety

12.04 Law Enforcement and Public Safety

Political Science

15.04 Social Sciences

Power Systems/Technology

13.16 Utility Operation and Energy Distribution

Print Shop/Printing

13.08 Graphic Arts Production

Printmaking

13.08 Graphic Arts Production

Production/Inventory Control

04.06 Mathematical Clerical Support

04.07 Records and Materials Processing

Property Management

04.02 Managerial Work in Business Detail

Psychology

03.02 Writing and Editing
05.01 Managerial Work in Education
05.06 Counseling, Health, and Fitness Education
08.02 Medicine and Surgery
08.04 Health Specialties
08.07 Medical Therapy
08.08 Patient Care and Assistance
08.09 Health Protection and Promotion
10.01 Counseling and Social Work
15.04 Social Sciences

Public Health

07.03 Regulations Enforcement
08.01 Managerial Work in Medical and Health Services
10.01 Counseling and Social Work
15.03 Life Sciences

Public Speaking

03.03 News, Broadcasting, and Public Relations
03.06 Drama
03.10 Communications Technology
05.02 Preschool, Elementary, and Secondary Teaching and Instructing
05.03 Postsecondary and Adult Teaching and Instructing
06.04 Finance/Insurance Customer Service
06.05 Finance/Insurance Sales and Support
07.01 Managerial Work in Government and Public Administration
07.02 Public Planning
10.02 Religious Work
10.04 Client Interviewing
14.04 Personal Soliciting

Pump Operation

01.08 Mining and Drilling
13.16 Utility Operation and Energy Distribution
13.17 Loading, Moving, Hoisting, and Conveying

Quality Control

13.07 Production Quality Control
15.08 Industrial and Safety Engineering

Radio/TV Operations

03.09 Media Technology

Railroad Safety

16.04 Rail Vehicle Operation

Real Estate Laws/Regulations

06.02 Finance/Insurance Investigation and Analysis
14.03 General Sales

Record Keeping

04.04 Secretarial Support
04.06 Mathematical Clerical Support
04.07 Records and Materials Processing
04.08 Clerical Machine Operation
05.04 Library Services
06.04 Finance/Insurance Customer Service
06.05 Finance/Insurance Sales and Support
09.03 Hospitality and Travel Services
10.04 Client Interviewing
12.04 Law Enforcement and Public Safety
14.02 Technical Sales
14.03 General Sales

Recreation

08.07 Medical Therapy
09.02 Recreational Services

Religion

10.02 Religious Work

Research Methods

07.02 Public Planning
15.04 Social Sciences
15.06 Mathematics and Data Analysis

Retailing

14.01 Managerial Work in Retail/Wholesale Sales and Service
14.03 General Sales

Safety Regulations

07.03 Regulations Enforcement
12.05 Safety and Security

Scheduling

13.01 Managerial Work in Manufacturing
16.01 Managerial Work in Transportation

Sculpture/Sculpting

03.04 Studio Art

Selling

06.05 Finance/Insurance Sales and Support
09.02 Recreational Services
09.03 Hospitality and Travel Services
09.05 Food and Beverage Service
14.01 Managerial Work in Retail/Wholesale Sales and Service
14.02 Technical Sales
14.03 General Sales
14.04 Personal Soliciting
14.06 Customer Service

© 2006, JIST Works

Sewing

13.03 Production Work, Assorted Materials Processing

13.09 Hands-On Work, Assorted Materials

Ship Systems

13.16 Utility Operation and Energy Distribution

16.05 Water Vehicle Operation

Shipping Regulations

04.07 Records and Materials Processing

04.08 Clerical Machine Operation

16.07 Transportation Support Work

Shop Math

02.04 Construction Crafts

02.05 Systems and Equipment Installation, Maintenance, and Repair

03.11 Musical Instrument Repair

13.01 Managerial Work in Manufacturing

13.02 Machine Setup and Operation

13.03 Production Work, Assorted Materials Processing

13.04 Welding, Brazing, and Soldering

13.05 Production Machining Technology

13.06 Production Precision Work

13.07 Production Quality Control

13.08 Graphic Arts Production

13.10 Woodworking Technology

13.12 Electrical and Electronic Repair

13.13 Machinery Repair

13.14 Vehicle and Facility Mechanical Work

Social Anthropology

15.04 Social Sciences

Social Problems

10.02 Religious Work

Social Work

10.01 Counseling and Social Work

Sociology

07.02 Public Planning

Soil Science

01.02 Resource Science/Engineering for Plants, Animals, and the Environment

01.03 Resource Technologies for Plants, Animals, and the Environment

01.05 Nursery, Groundskeeping, and Pest Control

01.06 Forestry and Logging

Spelling

04.04 Secretarial Support

06.03 Finance/Insurance Records Processing

Statistics

04.05 Accounting, Auditing, and Analytical Support

04.06 Mathematical Clerical Support

06.02 Finance/Insurance Investigation and Analysis

07.02 Public Planning

15.04 Social Sciences

15.06 Mathematics and Data Analysis

Surveying

02.03 Architecture/Construction Engineering Technologies

15.09 Engineering Technology

Systems Analysis

11.02 Information Technology Specialties

Technical Writing

03.02 Writing and Editing

11.01 Managerial Work in Information Technology

12.01 Managerial Work in Law and Public Safety

Theater Arts

03.01 Managerial Work in Arts and Communication

03.05 Design

03.06 Drama

03.09 Media Technology

Tool Design

13.05 Production Machining Technology

Traffic Control/Management

16.01 Managerial Work in Transportation

16.07 Transportation Support Work

Truck Operating

16.03 Truck Driving

16.06 Other Services Requiring Driving

Turf Management

01.05 Nursery, Groundskeeping, and Pest Control

Typing

04.04 Secretarial Support

Veterinary Sciences

08.05 Animal Care

Vocational Agriculture

01.04 General Farming

01.05 Nursery, Groundskeeping, and Pest Control

Voice

03.07 Music

Wastewater/Water Treatment Processing

13.16 Utility Operation and Energy Distribution

Watchmaking/Watch Repair Shop

13.15 Medical and Technical Equipment Repair

Water Safety

01.07 Hunting and Fishing

Welding

13.04 Welding, Brazing, and Soldering

Wood Machining

03.11 Musical Instrument Repair

Wood Shop/Woodworking

02.04 Construction Crafts

X-ray Technology

08.06 Medical Technology

Zoology

01.02 Resource Science/Engineering for Plants, Animals, and the Environment

Crosswalk D: Work Settings with Corresponding Work Groups

Airplanes

09.03 Hospitality and Travel Services

12.07 Military

13.12 Electrical and Electronic Repair

13.14 Vehicle and Facility Mechanical Work

15.07 Research and Design Engineering

16.02 Air Vehicle Operation

Airports

03.10 Communications Technology

16.01 Managerial Work in Transportation

16.02 Air Vehicle Operation

16.07 Transportation Support Work

Amusement parks, circuses, and carnivals

08.05 Animal Care

09.02 Recreational Services

Animal hospitals, boarding kennels, and grooming parlors

08.01 Managerial Work in Medical and Health Services

08.05 Animal Care

Artists' studios and craft workshops

03.01 Managerial Work in Arts and Communication

03.04 Studio Art

03.11 Musical Instrument Repair

08.06 Medical Technology

13.08 Graphic Arts Production

13.09 Hands-On Work, Assorted Materials

13.10 Woodworking Technology

Auto service stations and repair shops

13.12 Electrical and Electronic Repair

13.14 Vehicle and Facility Mechanical Work

Barber shops and beauty salons

09.01 Managerial Work in Hospitality and Tourism

09.07 Barber and Beauty Services

Bowling alleys

09.02 Recreational Services

Bus and train stations

03.06 Drama

09.03 Hospitality and Travel Services

12.04 Law Enforcement and Public Safety

13.17 Loading, Moving, Hoisting, and Conveying

16.01 Managerial Work in Transportation

16.06 Other Services Requiring Driving

16.07 Transportation Support Work

Buses and trolleys

13.14 Vehicle and Facility Mechanical Work

16.06 Other Services Requiring Driving

Business offices

02.01 Managerial Work in Architecture/Construction

02.02 Architectural Design

02.03 Architecture/Construction Engineering Technologies

03.01 Managerial Work in Arts and Communication

03.02 Writing and Editing

03.03 News, Broadcasting, and Public Relations

03.04 Studio Art

03.05 Design

04.01 Managerial Work in General Business

04.02 Managerial Work in Business Detail

04.03 Human Resources Support

04.04 Secretarial Support

04.05 Accounting, Auditing, and Analytical Support

© 2006, JIST Works

04.06 Mathematical Clerical Support

04.07 Records and Materials Processing

04.08 Clerical Machine Operation

05.04 Library Services

05.05 Archival and Museum Services

06.01 Managerial Work in Finance and Insurance

06.02 Finance/Insurance Investigation and Analysis

06.03 Finance/Insurance Records Processing

06.04 Finance/Insurance Customer Service

06.05 Finance/Insurance Sales and Support

07.01 Managerial Work in Government and Public Administration

07.02 Public Planning

07.03 Regulations Enforcement

08.01 Managerial Work in Medical and Health Services

09.06 Sports

10.01 Counseling and Social Work

10.04 Client Interviewing

11.01 Managerial Work in Information Technology

11.02 Information Technology Specialties

11.03 Digital Equipment Repair

12.02 Legal Practice and Justice Administration

12.03 Legal Support

12.05 Safety and Security

13.01 Managerial Work in Manufacturing

13.08 Graphic Arts Production

14.01 Managerial Work in Retail/Wholesale Sales and Service

14.02 Technical Sales

14.03 General Sales

14.04 Personal Soliciting

14.05 Purchasing

14.06 Customer Service

15.01 Managerial Work in Scientific Research, Engineering, and Mathematics

15.02 Physical Sciences

15.04 Social Sciences

15.06 Mathematics and Data Analysis

15.07 Research and Design Engineering

15.08 Industrial and Safety Engineering

15.09 Engineering Technology

16.01 Managerial Work in Transportation

Colleges and universities

01.02 Resource Science/Engineering for Plants, Animals, and the Environment

03.07 Music

03.08 Dance

05.01 Managerial Work in Education

05.03 Postsecondary and Adult Teaching and Instructing

05.06 Counseling, Health, and Fitness Education

09.06 Sports

10.01 Counseling and Social Work

15.01 Managerial Work in Scientific Research, Engineering, and Mathematics

15.02 Physical Sciences

15.03 Life Sciences

15.04 Social Sciences

15.06 Mathematics and Data Analysis

15.07 Research and Design Engineering

Construction sites

01.08 Mining and Drilling

02.01 Managerial Work in Architecture/Construction

02.02 Architectural Design

02.03 Architecture/Construction Engineering Technologies

02.04 Construction Crafts

02.05 Systems and Equipment Installation, Maintenance, and Repair

02.06 Construction Support/Labor

13.04 Welding, Brazing, and Soldering

15.01 Managerial Work in Scientific Research, Engineering, and Mathematics

15.07 Research and Design Engineering

15.09 Engineering Technology

Convention and trade show centers

04.02 Managerial Work in Business Detail

14.01 Managerial Work in Retail/Wholesale Sales and Service

14.02 Technical Sales

14.03 General Sales

14.04 Personal Soliciting

14.05 Purchasing

Country clubs and resorts

09.02 Recreational Services

09.05 Food and Beverage Service

09.06 Sports

12.05 Safety and Security

Courthouses

03.03 News, Broadcasting, and Public Relations

07.04 Public Administration Clerical Support

12.02 Legal Practice and Justice Administration

12.03 Legal Support

Design studios

02.02 Architectural Design

02.03 Architecture/Construction Engineering Technologies

03.05 Design

15.09 Engineering Technology

Doctors' and dentists' offices and clinics

04.04 Secretarial Support
08.02 Medicine and Surgery
08.03 Dentistry
08.04 Health Specialties
08.06 Medical Technology
08.07 Medical Therapy
08.08 Patient Care and Assistance
14.02 Technical Sales
15.09 Engineering Technology

Drug stores

08.02 Medicine and Surgery

Elementary schools

05.01 Managerial Work in Education
05.02 Preschool, Elementary, and Secondary Teaching and Instructing
10.02 Religious Work

Factories and plants

01.03 Resource Technologies for Plants, Animals, and the Environment
03.05 Design
04.02 Managerial Work in Business Detail
04.03 Human Resources Support
04.05 Accounting, Auditing, and Analytical Support
04.06 Mathematical Clerical Support
04.07 Records and Materials Processing
07.03 Regulations Enforcement
11.01 Managerial Work in Information Technology
11.02 Information Technology Specialties
12.05 Safety and Security
13.01 Managerial Work in Manufacturing
13.02 Machine Setup and Operation
13.03 Production Work, Assorted Materials Processing
13.04 Welding, Brazing, and Soldering
13.05 Production Machining Technology
13.06 Production Precision Work
13.07 Production Quality Control
13.09 Hands-On Work, Assorted Materials
13.10 Woodworking Technology
13.11 Apparel, Shoes, Leather, and Fabric Care
13.12 Electrical and Electronic Repair
13.13 Machinery Repair
13.14 Vehicle and Facility Mechanical Work
13.15 Medical and Technical Equipment Repair
13.17 Loading, Moving, Hoisting, and Conveying
14.02 Technical Sales

14.05 Purchasing
15.01 Managerial Work in Scientific Research, Engineering, and Mathematics
15.02 Physical Sciences
15.03 Life Sciences
15.04 Social Sciences
15.05 Physical Science Laboratory Technology
15.07 Research and Design Engineering
15.08 Industrial and Safety Engineering
15.09 Engineering Technology

Farms

01.01 Managerial Work in Agriculture and Natural Resources
01.02 Resource Science/Engineering for Plants, Animals, and the Environment
01.03 Resource Technologies for Plants, Animals, and the Environment
01.04 General Farming
01.05 Nursery, Groundskeeping, and Pest Control
07.03 Regulations Enforcement
08.05 Animal Care
13.07 Production Quality Control
13.14 Vehicle and Facility Mechanical Work
14.05 Purchasing

Fire stations

03.10 Communications Technology
12.01 Managerial Work in Law and Public Safety
12.06 Emergency Responding

Fish hatcheries

01.01 Managerial Work in Agriculture and Natural Resources
01.03 Resource Technologies for Plants, Animals, and the Environment
08.05 Animal Care
08.06 Medical Technology

Forests

01.01 Managerial Work in Agriculture and Natural Resources
01.02 Resource Science/Engineering for Plants, Animals, and the Environment
01.03 Resource Technologies for Plants, Animals, and the Environment
01.06 Forestry and Logging
01.07 Hunting and Fishing
07.03 Regulations Enforcement
12.06 Emergency Responding

Freight terminals

16.01 Managerial Work in Transportation
16.03 Truck Driving
16.07 Transportation Support Work

Funeral homes

08.09 Health Protection and Promotion

10.03 Child/Personal Care and Services

14.01 Managerial Work in Retail/Wholesale Sales and Service

Gambling casinos and card clubs

09.01 Managerial Work in Hospitality and Tourism

09.02 Recreational Services

12.05 Safety and Security

14.06 Customer Service

Golf courses and tennis courts

01.01 Managerial Work in Agriculture and Natural Resources

02.02 Architectural Design

Government offices

01.02 Resource Science/Engineering for Plants, Animals, and the Environment

04.01 Managerial Work in General Business

04.02 Managerial Work in Business Detail

04.03 Human Resources Support

04.04 Secretarial Support

04.05 Accounting, Auditing, and Analytical Support

04.06 Mathematical Clerical Support

04.07 Records and Materials Processing

04.08 Clerical Machine Operation

06.01 Managerial Work in Finance and Insurance

07.01 Managerial Work in Government and Public Administration

07.02 Public Planning

07.03 Regulations Enforcement

07.04 Public Administration Clerical Support

10.01 Counseling and Social Work

10.04 Client Interviewing

11.01 Managerial Work in Information Technology

11.02 Information Technology Specialties

11.03 Digital Equipment Repair

12.01 Managerial Work in Law and Public Safety

12.02 Legal Practice and Justice Administration

12.03 Legal Support

14.06 Customer Service

15.01 Managerial Work in Scientific Research, Engineering, and Mathematics

15.03 Life Sciences

15.04 Social Sciences

15.06 Mathematics and Data Analysis

15.07 Research and Design Engineering

15.08 Industrial and Safety Engineering

Gymnasiums and health clubs

05.06 Counseling, Health, and Fitness Education

08.09 Health Protection and Promotion

High schools

05.01 Managerial Work in Education

05.02 Preschool, Elementary, and Secondary Teaching and Instructing

05.06 Counseling, Health, and Fitness Education

10.01 Counseling and Social Work

10.02 Religious Work

Hospitals and nursing homes

04.04 Secretarial Support

07.03 Regulations Enforcement

08.01 Managerial Work in Medical and Health Services

08.02 Medicine and Surgery

08.04 Health Specialties

08.06 Medical Technology

08.07 Medical Therapy

08.08 Patient Care and Assistance

08.09 Health Protection and Promotion

10.01 Counseling and Social Work

11.01 Managerial Work in Information Technology

11.02 Information Technology Specialties

14.02 Technical Sales

14.06 Customer Service

15.03 Life Sciences

15.07 Research and Design Engineering

15.09 Engineering Technology

Hotels and motels

04.02 Managerial Work in Business Detail

09.01 Managerial Work in Hospitality and Tourism

09.03 Hospitality and Travel Services

Houses of worship

10.02 Religious Work

Jails and reformatories

10.01 Counseling and Social Work

12.01 Managerial Work in Law and Public Safety

Kindergartens and day care centers

05.01 Managerial Work in Education

05.02 Preschool, Elementary, and Secondary Teaching and Instructing

10.03 Child/Personal Care and Services

Laboratories

01.02 Resource Science/Engineering for Plants, Animals, and the Environment

01.03 Resource Technologies for Plants, Animals, and the Environment

08.05 Animal Care

08.06 Medical Technology

13.08 Graphic Arts Production

15.01 Managerial Work in Scientific Research, Engineering, and Mathematics

15.02 Physical Sciences

15.03 Life Sciences

15.05 Physical Science Laboratory Technology

15.07 Research and Design Engineering

15.08 Industrial and Safety Engineering

Laundries and dry cleaners

13.11 Apparel, Shoes, Leather, and Fabric Care

Libraries

05.04 Library Services

05.05 Archival and Museum Services

15.04 Social Sciences

Media workstation labs

03.09 Media Technology

Military installations

12.07 Military

Mines and quarries

01.01 Managerial Work in Agriculture and Natural Resources

01.02 Resource Science/Engineering for Plants, Animals, and the Environment

01.03 Resource Technologies for Plants, Animals, and the Environment

01.08 Mining and Drilling

15.02 Physical Sciences

15.07 Research and Design Engineering

15.09 Engineering Technology

Movie studios

02.06 Construction Support/Labor

03.01 Managerial Work in Arts and Communication

03.02 Writing and Editing

03.04 Studio Art

03.06 Drama

03.09 Media Technology

Museums

05.05 Archival and Museum Services

15.04 Social Sciences

Music studios

03.01 Managerial Work in Arts and Communication

03.07 Music

03.08 Dance

Nightclubs

03.07 Music

03.08 Dance

Office buildings

02.05 Systems and Equipment Installation, Maintenance, and Repair

03.10 Communications Technology

07.03 Regulations Enforcement

09.03 Hospitality and Travel Services

12.05 Safety and Security

13.13 Machinery Repair

13.16 Utility Operation and Energy Distribution

Oil fields

01.01 Managerial Work in Agriculture and Natural Resources

01.02 Resource Science/Engineering for Plants, Animals, and the Environment

01.03 Resource Technologies for Plants, Animals, and the Environment

01.08 Mining and Drilling

13.16 Utility Operation and Energy Distribution

15.01 Managerial Work in Scientific Research, Engineering, and Mathematics

15.02 Physical Sciences

15.07 Research and Design Engineering

15.09 Engineering Technology

Parks and campgrounds

01.01 Managerial Work in Agriculture and Natural Resources

01.02 Resource Science/Engineering for Plants, Animals, and the Environment

01.05 Nursery, Groundskeeping, and Pest Control

09.02 Recreational Services

12.05 Safety and Security

Photographers' studios

03.09 Media Technology

14.04 Personal Soliciting

Plant nurseries

01.01 Managerial Work in Agriculture and Natural Resources

01.02 Resource Science/Engineering for Plants, Animals, and the Environment

01.03 Resource Technologies for Plants, Animals, and the Environment

01.04 General Farming

01.05 Nursery, Groundskeeping, and Pest Control

Police headquarters

03.10 Communications Technology

12.01 Managerial Work in Law and Public Safety

12.04 Law Enforcement and Public Safety

© 2006, JIST Works

Ports and harbors

07.03 Regulations Enforcement

13.17 Loading, Moving, Hoisting, and Conveying

16.01 Managerial Work in Transportation

16.05 Water Vehicle Operation

16.07 Transportation Support Work

Post offices

04.07 Records and Materials Processing

16.01 Managerial Work in Transportation

16.06 Other Services Requiring Driving

Print shops

13.08 Graphic Arts Production

Private homes

01.05 Nursery, Groundskeeping, and Pest Control

02.02 Architectural Design

02.04 Construction Crafts

02.05 Systems and Equipment Installation, Maintenance, and Repair

02.06 Construction Support/Labor

03.05 Design

06.05 Finance/Insurance Sales and Support

08.08 Patient Care and Assistance

09.03 Hospitality and Travel Services

10.03 Child/Personal Care and Services

13.13 Machinery Repair

14.03 General Sales

14.04 Personal Soliciting

Race tracks

09.01 Managerial Work in Hospitality and Tourism

14.06 Customer Service

Radio studios

03.03 News, Broadcasting, and Public Relations

03.06 Drama

03.07 Music

03.09 Media Technology

13.12 Electrical and Electronic Repair

Railroad tracks and yards

07.03 Regulations Enforcement

13.13 Machinery Repair

13.17 Loading, Moving, Hoisting, and Conveying

16.01 Managerial Work in Transportation

16.04 Rail Vehicle Operation

16.07 Transportation Support Work

Recreation centers and playgrounds

09.02 Recreational Services

10.03 Child/Personal Care and Services

Rehearsal halls

03.01 Managerial Work in Arts and Communication

03.06 Drama

03.07 Music

03.08 Dance

Restaurants, cafeterias, and other eating places

09.01 Managerial Work in Hospitality and Tourism

09.04 Food and Beverage Preparation

09.05 Food and Beverage Service

Scenes of crimes or emergencies

12.01 Managerial Work in Law and Public Safety

12.04 Law Enforcement and Public Safety

12.06 Emergency Responding

Schools and homes for people with disabilities

05.01 Managerial Work in Education

05.02 Preschool, Elementary, and Secondary Teaching and Instructing

08.07 Medical Therapy

Ships and boats

01.01 Managerial Work in Agriculture and Natural Resources

01.07 Hunting and Fishing

07.03 Regulations Enforcement

12.07 Military

13.14 Vehicle and Facility Mechanical Work

13.16 Utility Operation and Energy Distribution

15.07 Research and Design Engineering

16.05 Water Vehicle Operation

Sports stadiums

03.03 News, Broadcasting, and Public Relations

08.09 Health Protection and Promotion

09.06 Sports

Stores and shopping malls

03.05 Design

04.02 Managerial Work in Business Detail

04.07 Records and Materials Processing

06.02 Finance/Insurance Investigation and Analysis

11.03 Digital Equipment Repair

12.05 Safety and Security

13.11 Apparel, Shoes, Leather, and Fabric Care

13.15 Medical and Technical Equipment Repair

14.01 Managerial Work in Retail/Wholesale Sales and Service

14.03 General Sales

14.04 Personal Soliciting

14.05 Purchasing

14.06 Customer Service

15.04 Social Sciences

Streets and highways

06.02 Finance/Insurance Investigation and Analysis

07.02 Public Planning

09.03 Hospitality and Travel Services

12.04 Law Enforcement and Public Safety

12.05 Safety and Security

16.03 Truck Driving

16.06 Other Services Requiring Driving

Television and video studios

03.01 Managerial Work in Arts and Communication

03.02 Writing and Editing

03.03 News, Broadcasting, and Public Relations

03.05 Design

03.06 Drama

03.07 Music

03.08 Dance

03.09 Media Technology

14.04 Personal Soliciting

Theaters

02.06 Construction Support/Labor

03.01 Managerial Work in Arts and Communication

03.02 Writing and Editing

03.05 Design

03.06 Drama

03.07 Music

03.08 Dance

03.11 Musical Instrument Repair

09.02 Recreational Services

Trains

13.14 Vehicle and Facility Mechanical Work

16.04 Rail Vehicle Operation

16.07 Transportation Support Work

Travel agencies

09.03 Hospitality and Travel Services

Warehouses

04.07 Records and Materials Processing

13.17 Loading, Moving, Hoisting, and Conveying

14.05 Purchasing

16.01 Managerial Work in Transportation

16.03 Truck Driving

Waterworks and light and power plants

07.03 Regulations Enforcement

13.13 Machinery Repair

13.16 Utility Operation and Energy Distribution

13.17 Loading, Moving, Hoisting, and Conveying

14.02 Technical Sales

14.06 Customer Service

15.05 Physical Science Laboratory Technology

15.07 Research and Design Engineering

Zoos and aquariums

08.01 Managerial Work in Medical and Health Services

08.05 Animal Care

Crosswalk E: Skills with Corresponding Work Groups

Active Learning: Understanding the implications of new information for both current and future problem solving and decision making

01.02 Resource Science/Engineering for Plants, Animals, and the Environment

02.03 Architecture/Construction Engineering Technologies

05.03 Postsecondary and Adult Teaching and Instructing

08.02 Medicine and Surgery

08.03 Dentistry

08.04 Health Specialties

12.02 Legal Practice and Justice Administration

15.02 Physical Sciences

15.03 Life Sciences

15.04 Social Sciences

15.06 Mathematics and Data Analysis

Active Listening: Giving full attention to what other people are saying, taking time to understand the points being made, asking questions as appropriate, and not interrupting at inappropriate times

02.03 Architecture/Construction Engineering Technologies

03.03 News, Broadcasting, and Public Relations

03.10 Communications Technology

04.03 Human Resources Support

04.04 Secretarial Support

04.06 Mathematical Clerical Support

05.04 Library Services

06.03 Finance/Insurance Records Processing

06.04 Finance/Insurance Customer Service

07.04 Public Administration Clerical Support

08.02 Medicine and Surgery

08.04 Health Specialties

08.08 Patient Care and Assistance

09.03 Hospitality and Travel Services

10.01 Counseling and Social Work

10.02 Religious Work

10.04 Client Interviewing

12.02 Legal Practice and Justice Administration

12.03 Legal Support

12.04 Law Enforcement and Public Safety

14.06 Customer Service

Complex Problem Solving: Identifying complex problems and reviewing related information to develop and evaluate options and implement solutions

01.02 Resource Science/Engineering for Plants, Animals, and the Environment

02.02 Architectural Design

04.05 Accounting, Auditing, and Analytical Support

06.01 Managerial Work in Finance and Insurance

06.05 Finance/Insurance Sales and Support

08.04 Health Specialties

11.02 Information Technology Specialties

15.03 Life Sciences

15.04 Social Sciences

15.06 Mathematics and Data Analysis

15.08 Industrial and Safety Engineering

Coordination: Adjusting actions in relation to others' actions

02.01 Managerial Work in Architecture/Construction

02.02 Architectural Design

02.03 Architecture/Construction Engineering Technologies

03.01 Managerial Work in Arts and Communication

03.02 Writing and Editing

03.07 Music

03.08 Dance

04.02 Managerial Work in Business Detail

05.01 Managerial Work in Education

05.06 Counseling, Health, and Fitness Education

09.06 Sports

12.01 Managerial Work in Law and Public Safety

12.06 Emergency Responding

13.01 Managerial Work in Manufacturing

14.01 Managerial Work in Retail/Wholesale Sales and Service

15.01 Managerial Work in Scientific Research, Engineering, and Mathematics

16.01 Managerial Work in Transportation

16.02 Air Vehicle Operation

Critical Thinking: Using logic and reasoning to identify the strengths and weaknesses of alternative solutions, conclusions, or approaches to problems

08.03 Dentistry

12.02 Legal Practice and Justice Administration

12.03 Legal Support

15.02 Physical Sciences

15.03 Life Sciences

Equipment Maintenance: Performing routine maintenance on equipment and determining when and what kind of maintenance is needed

01.04 General Farming

01.05 Nursery, Groundskeeping, and Pest Control

01.07 Hunting and Fishing

01.08 Mining and Drilling

02.05 Systems and Equipment Installation, Maintenance, and Repair

02.06 Construction Support/Labor

03.09 Media Technology

03.11 Musical Instrument Repair

08.06 Medical Technology

11.03 Digital Equipment Repair

12.06 Emergency Responding

13.02 Machine Setup and Operation

13.03 Production Work, Assorted Materials Processing

13.09 Hands-On Work, Assorted Materials

13.12 Electrical and Electronic Repair

13.13 Machinery Repair

13.14 Vehicle and Facility Mechanical Work

13.15 Medical and Technical Equipment Repair

13.16 Utility Operation and Energy Distribution

13.17 Loading, Moving, Hoisting, and Conveying

16.03 Truck Driving

16.04 Rail Vehicle Operation

16.05 Water Vehicle Operation

16.06 Other Services Requiring Driving

16.07 Transportation Support Work

Equipment Selection: Determining the kind of tools and equipment needed to do a job

01.05 Nursery, Groundskeeping, and Pest Control

01.06 Forestry and Logging

01.07 Hunting and Fishing

02.04 Construction Crafts

03.09 Media Technology

05.05 Archival and Museum Services

08.03 Dentistry

12.06 Emergency Responding

13.04 Welding, Brazing, and Soldering

13.10 Woodworking Technology

13.11 Apparel, Shoes, Leather, and Fabric Care

15.05 Physical Science Laboratory Technology

Installation: Installing equipment, machines, wiring, or programs to meet specifications

02.01 Managerial Work in Architecture/Construction

02.04 Construction Crafts

02.05 Systems and Equipment Installation, Maintenance, and Repair

02.06 Construction Support/Labor

11.01 Managerial Work in Information Technology

11.02 Information Technology Specialties

11.03 Digital Equipment Repair

13.10 Woodworking Technology

13.12 Electrical and Electronic Repair

13.13 Machinery Repair

13.14 Vehicle and Facility Mechanical Work

13.15 Medical and Technical Equipment Repair

15.05 Physical Science Laboratory Technology

15.09 Engineering Technology

Instructing: Teaching others how to do something

03.08 Dance

04.03 Human Resources Support

05.02 Preschool, Elementary, and Secondary Teaching and Instructing

05.03 Postsecondary and Adult Teaching and Instructing

05.04 Library Services

05.05 Archival and Museum Services

05.06 Counseling, Health, and Fitness Education

08.02 Medicine and Surgery

08.05 Animal Care

08.06 Medical Technology

08.07 Medical Therapy

08.08 Patient Care and Assistance

08.09 Health Protection and Promotion

12.01 Managerial Work in Law and Public Safety

12.06 Emergency Responding

16.02 Air Vehicle Operation

Judgment and Decision Making: Considering the relative costs and benefits of potential actions to choose the most appropriate one

01.02 Resource Science/Engineering for Plants, Animals, and the Environment

04.05 Accounting, Auditing, and Analytical Support

06.01 Managerial Work in Finance and Insurance

06.02 Finance/Insurance Investigation and Analysis

06.05 Finance/Insurance Sales and Support

08.04 Health Specialties

12.01 Managerial Work in Law and Public Safety

12.02 Legal Practice and Justice Administration

15.07 Research and Design Engineering

Learning Strategies: Selecting and using training/instructional methods and procedures appropriate for the situation when learning or teaching new things

05.01 Managerial Work in Education

05.02 Preschool, Elementary, and Secondary Teaching and Instructing

05.03 Postsecondary and Adult Teaching and Instructing

05.04 Library Services

08.06 Medical Technology

08.07 Medical Therapy

08.08 Patient Care and Assistance

08.09 Health Protection and Promotion

09.06 Sports

10.01 Counseling and Social Work

10.02 Religious Work

Management of Financial Resources: Determining how money will be spent to get the work done and accounting for these expenditures

01.01 Managerial Work in Agriculture and Natural Resources

02.01 Managerial Work in Architecture/Construction

02.02 Architectural Design

03.01 Managerial Work in Arts and Communication

03.05 Design

04.01 Managerial Work in General Business

04.02 Managerial Work in Business Detail

04.05 Accounting, Auditing, and Analytical Support

05.01 Managerial Work in Education

06.01 Managerial Work in Finance and Insurance

06.05 Finance/Insurance Sales and Support

07.01 Managerial Work in Government and Public Administration

08.01 Managerial Work in Medical and Health Services

09.01 Managerial Work in Hospitality and Tourism

09.04 Food and Beverage Preparation

09.07 Barber and Beauty Services

10.02 Religious Work

13.01 Managerial Work in Manufacturing

14.01 Managerial Work in Retail/Wholesale Sales and Service

© 2006, JIST Works

14.05 Purchasing

15.01 Managerial Work in Scientific Research, Engineering, and Mathematics

16.01 Managerial Work in Transportation

Management of Material Resources: Obtaining and seeing to the appropriate use of equipment, facilities, and materials needed to do certain work

01.01 Managerial Work in Agriculture and Natural Resources

02.01 Managerial Work in Architecture/Construction

03.04 Studio Art

03.05 Design

04.01 Managerial Work in General Business

04.02 Managerial Work in Business Detail

05.01 Managerial Work in Education

05.05 Archival and Museum Services

08.01 Managerial Work in Medical and Health Services

08.05 Animal Care

09.01 Managerial Work in Hospitality and Tourism

09.04 Food and Beverage Preparation

09.07 Barber and Beauty Services

12.01 Managerial Work in Law and Public Safety

13.01 Managerial Work in Manufacturing

14.05 Purchasing

15.01 Managerial Work in Scientific Research, Engineering, and Mathematics

16.01 Managerial Work in Transportation

Management of Personnel Resources: Motivating, developing, and directing people as they work, identifying the best people for the job

01.01 Managerial Work in Agriculture and Natural Resources

02.01 Managerial Work in Architecture/Construction

02.02 Architectural Design

03.01 Managerial Work in Arts and Communication

03.07 Music

04.01 Managerial Work in General Business

04.02 Managerial Work in Business Detail

05.01 Managerial Work in Education

05.05 Archival and Museum Services

06.01 Managerial Work in Finance and Insurance

07.01 Managerial Work in Government and Public Administration

08.01 Managerial Work in Medical and Health Services

09.01 Managerial Work in Hospitality and Tourism

09.04 Food and Beverage Preparation

12.01 Managerial Work in Law and Public Safety

13.01 Managerial Work in Manufacturing

14.01 Managerial Work in Retail/Wholesale Sales and Service

14.05 Purchasing

16.01 Managerial Work in Transportation

Mathematics: Using mathematics to solve problems

01.02 Resource Science/Engineering for Plants, Animals, and the Environment

01.03 Resource Technologies for Plants, Animals, and the Environment

02.03 Architecture/Construction Engineering Technologies

04.06 Mathematical Clerical Support

06.02 Finance/Insurance Investigation and Analysis

07.02 Public Planning

15.02 Physical Sciences

15.03 Life Sciences

15.06 Mathematics and Data Analysis

15.07 Research and Design Engineering

15.08 Industrial and Safety Engineering

15.09 Engineering Technology

Monitoring: Monitoring/assessing your performance or that of other individuals or organizations to make improvements or take corrective action

03.01 Managerial Work in Arts and Communication

03.06 Drama

03.07 Music

04.01 Managerial Work in General Business

04.05 Accounting, Auditing, and Analytical Support

05.02 Preschool, Elementary, and Secondary Teaching and Instructing

05.06 Counseling, Health, and Fitness Education

06.01 Managerial Work in Finance and Insurance

07.01 Managerial Work in Government and Public Administration

08.08 Patient Care and Assistance

09.01 Managerial Work in Hospitality and Tourism

09.06 Sports

Negotiation: Bringing others together and trying to reconcile differences

02.01 Managerial Work in Architecture/Construction

02.02 Architectural Design

03.01 Managerial Work in Arts and Communication

03.05 Design

04.01 Managerial Work in General Business

04.03 Human Resources Support

04.07 Records and Materials Processing

05.04 Library Services

06.02 Finance/Insurance Investigation and Analysis

06.05 Finance/Insurance Sales and Support

07.01 Managerial Work in Government and Public Administration

09.01 Managerial Work in Hospitality and Tourism

09.06 Sports

10.01 Counseling and Social Work

10.03 Child/Personal Care and Services

12.02 Legal Practice and Justice Administration

12.04 Law Enforcement and Public Safety

14.01 Managerial Work in Retail/Wholesale Sales and Service

14.02 Technical Sales

14.03 General Sales

14.05 Purchasing

16.01 Managerial Work in Transportation

Operation and Control: Controlling operations of equipment or systems

01.04 General Farming

01.05 Nursery, Groundskeeping, and Pest Control

01.06 Forestry and Logging

01.08 Mining and Drilling

03.09 Media Technology

03.10 Communications Technology

04.08 Clerical Machine Operation

13.02 Machine Setup and Operation

13.03 Production Work, Assorted Materials Processing

13.04 Welding, Brazing, and Soldering

13.05 Production Machining Technology

13.06 Production Precision Work

13.08 Graphic Arts Production

13.09 Hands-On Work, Assorted Materials

13.10 Woodworking Technology

13.11 Apparel, Shoes, Leather, and Fabric Care

13.16 Utility Operation and Energy Distribution

13.17 Loading, Moving, Hoisting, and Conveying

15.05 Physical Science Laboratory Technology

16.02 Air Vehicle Operation

16.03 Truck Driving

16.04 Rail Vehicle Operation

16.05 Water Vehicle Operation

16.07 Transportation Support Work

Operation Monitoring: Watching gauges, dials, or other indicators to make sure a machine is working properly

04.08 Clerical Machine Operation

12.06 Emergency Responding

13.02 Machine Setup and Operation

13.03 Production Work, Assorted Materials Processing

13.04 Welding, Brazing, and Soldering

13.05 Production Machining Technology

13.07 Production Quality Control

13.08 Graphic Arts Production

13.16 Utility Operation and Energy Distribution

13.17 Loading, Moving, Hoisting, and Conveying

15.05 Physical Science Laboratory Technology

16.02 Air Vehicle Operation

16.04 Rail Vehicle Operation

16.05 Water Vehicle Operation

Operations Analysis: Analyzing needs and product requirements to create a design

01.02 Resource Science/Engineering for Plants, Animals, and the Environment

02.02 Architectural Design

02.03 Architecture/Construction Engineering Technologies

03.04 Studio Art

03.05 Design

04.05 Accounting, Auditing, and Analytical Support

05.05 Archival and Museum Services

11.01 Managerial Work in Information Technology

11.02 Information Technology Specialties

14.02 Technical Sales

14.05 Purchasing

15.01 Managerial Work in Scientific Research, Engineering, and Mathematics

15.02 Physical Sciences

15.07 Research and Design Engineering

15.08 Industrial and Safety Engineering

Persuasion: Persuading others to change their minds or behavior

02.02 Architectural Design

03.01 Managerial Work in Arts and Communication

03.05 Design

04.01 Managerial Work in General Business

04.03 Human Resources Support

05.06 Counseling, Health, and Fitness Education

06.05 Finance/Insurance Sales and Support

07.01 Managerial Work in Government and Public Administration

08.07 Medical Therapy

08.08 Patient Care and Assistance

08.09 Health Protection and Promotion

09.06 Sports

10.01 Counseling and Social Work

10.03 Child/Personal Care and Services

12.01 Managerial Work in Law and Public Safety

12.04 Law Enforcement and Public Safety

© 2006, JIST Works

12.05 Safety and Security

14.01 Managerial Work in Retail/Wholesale Sales and Service

14.02 Technical Sales

14.04 Personal Soliciting

14.05 Purchasing

Programming: Writing computer programs for various purposes

01.03 Resource Technologies for Plants, Animals, and the Environment

01.06 Forestry and Logging

03.04 Studio Art

03.08 Dance

04.08 Clerical Machine Operation

05.03 Postsecondary and Adult Teaching and Instructing

09.02 Recreational Services

09.05 Food and Beverage Service

11.01 Managerial Work in Information Technology

11.02 Information Technology Specialties

13.11 Apparel, Shoes, Leather, and Fabric Care

14.06 Customer Service

15.06 Mathematics and Data Analysis

15.09 Engineering Technology

Quality Control Analysis: Conducting tests and inspections of products, services, or processes to evaluate quality or performance

03.11 Musical Instrument Repair

08.06 Medical Technology

13.05 Production Machining Technology

13.06 Production Precision Work

13.07 Production Quality Control

13.08 Graphic Arts Production

13.15 Medical and Technical Equipment Repair

15.05 Physical Science Laboratory Technology

15.08 Industrial and Safety Engineering

15.09 Engineering Technology

Reading Comprehension: Understanding written sentences and paragraphs in work-related documents

03.02 Writing and Editing

03.03 News, Broadcasting, and Public Relations

05.03 Postsecondary and Adult Teaching and Instructing

06.03 Finance/Insurance Records Processing

08.02 Medicine and Surgery

08.03 Dentistry

08.04 Health Specialties

08.09 Health Protection and Promotion

12.02 Legal Practice and Justice Administration

15.02 Physical Sciences

15.03 Life Sciences

15.04 Social Sciences

Repairing: Repairing machines or systems, using the needed tools

01.04 General Farming

01.07 Hunting and Fishing

01.08 Mining and Drilling

02.04 Construction Crafts

02.05 Systems and Equipment Installation, Maintenance, and Repair

02.06 Construction Support/Labor

03.11 Musical Instrument Repair

11.03 Digital Equipment Repair

13.09 Hands-On Work, Assorted Materials

13.12 Electrical and Electronic Repair

13.13 Machinery Repair

13.14 Vehicle and Facility Mechanical Work

13.15 Medical and Technical Equipment Repair

13.16 Utility Operation and Energy Distribution

15.09 Engineering Technology

16.03 Truck Driving

Science: Using scientific rules and methods to solve problems

01.02 Resource Science/Engineering for Plants, Animals, and the Environment

01.03 Resource Technologies for Plants, Animals, and the Environment

08.01 Managerial Work in Medical and Health Services

08.02 Medicine and Surgery

08.03 Dentistry

08.04 Health Specialties

08.05 Animal Care

08.06 Medical Technology

15.01 Managerial Work in Scientific Research, Engineering, and Mathematics

15.02 Physical Sciences

15.03 Life Sciences

15.05 Physical Science Laboratory Technology

15.07 Research and Design Engineering

15.08 Industrial and Safety Engineering

16.02 Air Vehicle Operation

Service Orientation: Actively looking for ways to help people

03.10 Communications Technology

04.02 Managerial Work in Business Detail

04.03 Human Resources Support

04.06 Mathematical Clerical Support

04.07 Records and Materials Processing

05.04 Library Services

05.06 Counseling, Health, and Fitness Education

06.04 Finance/Insurance Customer Service

06.05 Finance/Insurance Sales and Support

07.04 Public Administration Clerical Support

08.02 Medicine and Surgery

08.03 Dentistry

08.04 Health Specialties

08.06 Medical Technology

08.07 Medical Therapy

08.08 Patient Care and Assistance

08.09 Health Protection and Promotion

09.01 Managerial Work in Hospitality and Tourism

09.02 Recreational Services

09.03 Hospitality and Travel Services

09.05 Food and Beverage Service

09.07 Barber and Beauty Services

10.01 Counseling and Social Work

10.02 Religious Work

10.03 Child/Personal Care and Services

10.04 Client Interviewing

12.01 Managerial Work in Law and Public Safety

12.05 Safety and Security

12.06 Emergency Responding

14.01 Managerial Work in Retail/Wholesale Sales and Service

14.03 General Sales

14.06 Customer Service

16.06 Other Services Requiring Driving

Social Perceptiveness: Being aware of others' reactions and understanding why they react as they do

04.02 Managerial Work in Business Detail

04.03 Human Resources Support

04.04 Secretarial Support

05.02 Preschool, Elementary, and Secondary Teaching and Instructing

05.04 Library Services

05.06 Counseling, Health, and Fitness Education

07.01 Managerial Work in Government and Public Administration

07.04 Public Administration Clerical Support

08.02 Medicine and Surgery

08.06 Medical Technology

08.07 Medical Therapy

08.08 Patient Care and Assistance

08.09 Health Protection and Promotion

09.02 Recreational Services

09.03 Hospitality and Travel Services

09.05 Food and Beverage Service

09.06 Sports

10.01 Counseling and Social Work

10.02 Religious Work

10.03 Child/Personal Care and Services

12.04 Law Enforcement and Public Safety

12.05 Safety and Security

12.06 Emergency Responding

14.03 General Sales

14.04 Personal Soliciting

15.04 Social Sciences

16.06 Other Services Requiring Driving

Speaking: Talking to others to convey information effectively

03.03 News, Broadcasting, and Public Relations

03.06 Drama

05.02 Preschool, Elementary, and Secondary Teaching and Instructing

05.03 Postsecondary and Adult Teaching and Instructing

05.06 Counseling, Health, and Fitness Education

06.03 Finance/Insurance Records Processing

06.04 Finance/Insurance Customer Service

06.05 Finance/Insurance Sales and Support

07.02 Public Planning

08.01 Managerial Work in Medical and Health Services

10.01 Counseling and Social Work

10.02 Religious Work

10.04 Client Interviewing

14.04 Personal Soliciting

Systems Analysis: Determining how a system should work and how changes in conditions, operations, and the environment will affect outcomes

01.02 Resource Science/Engineering for Plants, Animals, and the Environment

04.05 Accounting, Auditing, and Analytical Support

05.01 Managerial Work in Education

06.01 Managerial Work in Finance and Insurance

07.03 Regulations Enforcement

11.01 Managerial Work in Information Technology

11.02 Information Technology Specialties

13.01 Managerial Work in Manufacturing

15.04 Social Sciences

15.07 Research and Design Engineering

© 2006, JIST Works

16.01 Managerial Work in Transportation

16.02 Air Vehicle Operation

Systems Evaluation: Identifying measures or indicators of system performance and the actions needed to improve or correct performance relative to the goals of the system

04.05 Accounting, Auditing, and Analytical Support

05.01 Managerial Work in Education

06.01 Managerial Work in Finance and Insurance

07.01 Managerial Work in Government and Public Administration

07.03 Regulations Enforcement

08.01 Managerial Work in Medical and Health Services

11.01 Managerial Work in Information Technology

13.01 Managerial Work in Manufacturing

15.04 Social Sciences

15.07 Research and Design Engineering

15.08 Industrial and Safety Engineering

16.01 Managerial Work in Transportation

16.02 Air Vehicle Operation

Technology Design: Generating or adapting equipment and technology to serve user needs

02.03 Architecture/Construction Engineering Technologies

08.03 Dentistry

08.07 Medical Therapy

11.01 Managerial Work in Information Technology

11.02 Information Technology Specialties

13.05 Production Machining Technology

13.06 Production Precision Work

13.15 Medical and Technical Equipment Repair

15.01 Managerial Work in Scientific Research, Engineering, and Mathematics

15.07 Research and Design Engineering

15.08 Industrial and Safety Engineering

15.09 Engineering Technology

Time Management: Managing one's own time and the time of others

02.03 Architecture/Construction Engineering Technologies

03.01 Managerial Work in Arts and Communication

03.06 Drama

04.01 Managerial Work in General Business

04.02 Managerial Work in Business Detail

04.03 Human Resources Support

04.04 Secretarial Support

04.07 Records and Materials Processing

05.04 Library Services

05.05 Archival and Museum Services

08.01 Managerial Work in Medical and Health Services

08.07 Medical Therapy

08.09 Health Protection and Promotion

09.01 Managerial Work in Hospitality and Tourism

10.03 Child/Personal Care and Services

13.01 Managerial Work in Manufacturing

14.01 Managerial Work in Retail/Wholesale Sales and Service

14.05 Purchasing

15.01 Managerial Work in Scientific Research, Engineering, and Mathematics

Troubleshooting: Determining causes of operating errors and deciding what to do about them

02.01 Managerial Work in Architecture/Construction

02.05 Systems and Equipment Installation, Maintenance, and Repair

11.01 Managerial Work in Information Technology

11.02 Information Technology Specialties

11.03 Digital Equipment Repair

13.07 Production Quality Control

13.12 Electrical and Electronic Repair

13.13 Machinery Repair

13.14 Vehicle and Facility Mechanical Work

13.15 Medical and Technical Equipment Repair

15.09 Engineering Technology

16.07 Transportation Support Work

Writing: Communicating effectively in writing as appropriate for the needs of the audience

03.02 Writing and Editing

03.03 News, Broadcasting, and Public Relations

04.04 Secretarial Support

05.03 Postsecondary and Adult Teaching and Instructing

05.05 Archival and Museum Services

07.02 Public Planning

07.03 Regulations Enforcement

10.02 Religious Work

12.02 Legal Practice and Justice Administration

12.03 Legal Support

15.02 Physical Sciences

15.03 Life Sciences

15.04 Social Sciences

Crosswalk F: Abilities with Corresponding Work Groups

Arm-Hand Steadiness: Keeping your hand and arm steady while moving your arm or while holding your arm and hand in one position

03.04 Studio Art

08.02 Medicine and Surgery

08.03 Dentistry

08.04 Health Specialties

08.06 Medical Technology

09.07 Barber and Beauty Services

13.04 Welding, Brazing, and Soldering

13.06 Production Precision Work

13.08 Graphic Arts Production

13.09 Hands-On Work, Assorted Materials

13.11 Apparel, Shoes, Leather, and Fabric Care

13.15 Medical and Technical Equipment Repair

15.05 Physical Science Laboratory Technology

Auditory Attention: Focusing on a single source of sound in the presence of other distracting sounds

03.07 Music

03.10 Communications Technology

03.11 Musical Instrument Repair

09.02 Recreational Services

13.01 Managerial Work in Manufacturing

Category Flexibility: Generating or using different sets of rules for combining or grouping things in different ways

01.02 Resource Science/Engineering for Plants, Animals, and the Environment

01.03 Resource Technologies for Plants, Animals, and the Environment

02.02 Architectural Design

04.01 Managerial Work in General Business

04.03 Human Resources Support

04.07 Records and Materials Processing

05.04 Library Services

05.05 Archival and Museum Services

08.06 Medical Technology

08.09 Health Protection and Promotion

11.01 Managerial Work in Information Technology

14.05 Purchasing

15.02 Physical Sciences

15.03 Life Sciences

15.05 Physical Science Laboratory Technology

15.08 Industrial and Safety Engineering

Control Precision: Quickly and repeatedly adjusting the controls of a machine or a vehicle to exact positions

08.03 Dentistry

08.04 Health Specialties

13.02 Machine Setup and Operation

13.03 Production Work, Assorted Materials Processing

13.05 Production Machining Technology

13.07 Production Quality Control

13.15 Medical and Technical Equipment Repair

13.16 Utility Operation and Energy Distribution

Deductive Reasoning: Applying general rules to specific problems to produce answers that make sense

01.02 Resource Science/Engineering for Plants, Animals, and the Environment

02.02 Architectural Design

04.05 Accounting, Auditing, and Analytical Support

06.01 Managerial Work in Finance and Insurance

06.02 Finance/Insurance Investigation and Analysis

07.01 Managerial Work in Government and Public Administration

08.01 Managerial Work in Medical and Health Services

11.01 Managerial Work in Information Technology

11.02 Information Technology Specialties

12.02 Legal Practice and Justice Administration

14.05 Purchasing

15.01 Managerial Work in Scientific Research, Engineering, and Mathematics

15.02 Physical Sciences

15.04 Social Sciences

15.06 Mathematics and Data Analysis

15.07 Research and Design Engineering

15.08 Industrial and Safety Engineering

Depth Perception: Judging which of several objects is closer or farther away from you or judging the distance between you and an object

01.08 Mining and Drilling

16.05 Water Vehicle Operation

© 2006, JIST Works

Dynamic Flexibility: Quickly and repeatedly bending, stretching, twisting, or reaching out with your body, arms, and/or legs

01.05 Nursery, Groundskeeping, and Pest Control

03.08 Dance

09.04 Food and Beverage Preparation

13.02 Machine Setup and Operation

13.03 Production Work, Assorted Materials Processing

13.04 Welding, Brazing, and Soldering

13.09 Hands-On Work, Assorted Materials

13.10 Woodworking Technology

Dynamic Strength: Exerting muscle force repeatedly or continuously over time

01.04 General Farming

01.05 Nursery, Groundskeeping, and Pest Control

01.06 Forestry and Logging

01.07 Hunting and Fishing

02.04 Construction Crafts

02.05 Systems and Equipment Installation, Maintenance, and Repair

02.06 Construction Support/Labor

03.08 Dance

09.06 Sports

12.06 Emergency Responding

Explosive Strength: Using short bursts of muscle force to propel yourself or to throw an object

01.04 General Farming

01.05 Nursery, Groundskeeping, and Pest Control

01.06 Forestry and Logging

01.07 Hunting and Fishing

01.08 Mining and Drilling

03.08 Dance

12.05 Safety and Security

13.02 Machine Setup and Operation

13.04 Welding, Brazing, and Soldering

13.10 Woodworking Technology

16.03 Truck Driving

Extent Flexibility: Bending, stretching, twisting, or reaching with your body, arms, and/or legs

02.04 Construction Crafts

02.05 Systems and Equipment Installation, Maintenance, and Repair

02.06 Construction Support/Labor

08.05 Animal Care

13.12 Electrical and Electronic Repair

13.13 Machinery Repair

13.14 Vehicle and Facility Mechanical Work

Far Vision: Seeing details of objects at a distance

02.02 Architectural Design

02.03 Architecture/Construction Engineering Technologies

05.04 Library Services

12.04 Law Enforcement and Public Safety

12.05 Safety and Security

16.02 Air Vehicle Operation

16.04 Rail Vehicle Operation

16.05 Water Vehicle Operation

Finger Dexterity: Making precisely coordinated movements of the fingers of one or both hands to grasp, manipulate, or assemble very small objects

08.02 Medicine and Surgery

08.03 Dentistry

08.04 Health Specialties

08.06 Medical Technology

09.07 Barber and Beauty Services

11.03 Digital Equipment Repair

13.06 Production Precision Work

13.07 Production Quality Control

13.12 Electrical and Electronic Repair

13.13 Machinery Repair

13.15 Medical and Technical Equipment Repair

Flexibility of Closure: Identifying or detecting a known pattern

02.03 Architecture/Construction Engineering Technologies

05.04 Library Services

07.03 Regulations Enforcement

08.01 Managerial Work in Medical and Health Services

08.06 Medical Technology

11.01 Managerial Work in Information Technology

12.04 Law Enforcement and Public Safety

Fluency of Ideas: Coming up with a number of ideas about a topic

01.02 Resource Science/Engineering for Plants, Animals, and the Environment

02.02 Architectural Design

03.01 Managerial Work in Arts and Communication

03.02 Writing and Editing

03.05 Design

04.01 Managerial Work in General Business

04.05 Accounting, Auditing, and Analytical Support

05.01 Managerial Work in Education

05.03 Postsecondary and Adult Teaching and Instructing

07.01 Managerial Work in Government and Public Administration

10.02 Religious Work

11.01 Managerial Work in Information Technology

14.01 Managerial Work in Retail/Wholesale Sales and Service

15.01 Managerial Work in Scientific Research, Engineering, and Mathematics

15.04 Social Sciences

15.08 Industrial and Safety Engineering

Glare Sensitivity: Seeing objects in the presence of glare or bright lighting

01.01 Managerial Work in Agriculture and Natural Resources

01.07 Hunting and Fishing

12.01 Managerial Work in Law and Public Safety

12.04 Law Enforcement and Public Safety

12.06 Emergency Responding

14.04 Personal Soliciting

16.02 Air Vehicle Operation

16.04 Rail Vehicle Operation

16.05 Water Vehicle Operation

16.07 Transportation Support Work

Gross Body Coordination: Coordinating the movement of your arms, legs, and torso together when the whole body is in motion

03.08 Dance

08.05 Animal Care

09.05 Food and Beverage Service

09.06 Sports

Gross Body Equilibrium: Keeping or regaining your body balance or staying upright when in an unstable position

02.04 Construction Crafts

02.05 Systems and Equipment Installation, Maintenance, and Repair

02.06 Construction Support/Labor

03.08 Dance

12.01 Managerial Work in Law and Public Safety

12.06 Emergency Responding

Hearing Sensitivity: Detecting or telling the differences between sounds that vary in pitch and loudness

03.07 Music

03.09 Media Technology

03.11 Musical Instrument Repair

13.07 Production Quality Control

13.14 Vehicle and Facility Mechanical Work

Inductive Reasoning: Combining pieces of information to form general rules or conclusions

01.02 Resource Science/Engineering for Plants, Animals, and the Environment

01.03 Resource Technologies for Plants, Animals, and the Environment

04.05 Accounting, Auditing, and Analytical Support

08.01 Managerial Work in Medical and Health Services

08.02 Medicine and Surgery

08.04 Health Specialties

08.07 Medical Therapy

10.01 Counseling and Social Work

11.01 Managerial Work in Information Technology

12.02 Legal Practice and Justice Administration

14.05 Purchasing

15.02 Physical Sciences

15.03 Life Sciences

15.04 Social Sciences

15.07 Research and Design Engineering

15.08 Industrial and Safety Engineering

Information Ordering: Arranging things or actions in a certain order or pattern according to a specific rule or set of rules

01.01 Managerial Work in Agriculture and Natural Resources

02.01 Managerial Work in Architecture/Construction

02.02 Architectural Design

02.03 Architecture/Construction Engineering Technologies

11.02 Information Technology Specialties

15.05 Physical Science Laboratory Technology

15.07 Research and Design Engineering

15.09 Engineering Technology

Manual Dexterity: Quickly moving your hand, your hand together with your arm, or your two hands to grasp, manipulate, or assemble objects

08.02 Medicine and Surgery

08.04 Health Specialties

09.04 Food and Beverage Preparation

13.06 Production Precision Work

Mathematical Reasoning: Choosing the right mathematical methods or formulas to solve a problem

01.03 Resource Technologies for Plants, Animals, and the Environment

02.03 Architecture/Construction Engineering Technologies

04.01 Managerial Work in General Business

04.05 Accounting, Auditing, and Analytical Support

04.06 Mathematical Clerical Support

05.03 Postsecondary and Adult Teaching and Instructing

06.01 Managerial Work in Finance and Insurance

06.02 Finance/Insurance Investigation and Analysis

06.05 Finance/Insurance Sales and Support

07.01 Managerial Work in Government and Public Administration

13.01 Managerial Work in Manufacturing

14.01 Managerial Work in Retail/Wholesale Sales and Service

© 2006, JIST Works

14.05 Purchasing

15.01 Managerial Work in Scientific Research, Engineering, and Mathematics

15.02 Physical Sciences

15.03 Life Sciences

15.06 Mathematics and Data Analysis

15.07 Research and Design Engineering

15.08 Industrial and Safety Engineering

15.09 Engineering Technology

Memorization: Remembering information such as words, numbers, pictures, and procedures

03.06 Drama

03.07 Music

04.01 Managerial Work in General Business

04.02 Managerial Work in Business Detail

05.01 Managerial Work in Education

05.02 Preschool, Elementary, and Secondary Teaching and Instructing

06.01 Managerial Work in Finance and Insurance

06.03 Finance/Insurance Records Processing

07.01 Managerial Work in Government and Public Administration

07.03 Regulations Enforcement

09.01 Managerial Work in Hospitality and Tourism

12.02 Legal Practice and Justice Administration

14.02 Technical Sales

14.03 General Sales

Multilimb Coordination: Coordinating two or more limbs while sitting, standing, or lying down

01.04 General Farming

01.08 Mining and Drilling

13.10 Woodworking Technology

13.14 Vehicle and Facility Mechanical Work

13.17 Loading, Moving, Hoisting, and Conveying

Near Vision: Seeing details of objects at close range

04.04 Secretarial Support

04.05 Accounting, Auditing, and Analytical Support

04.06 Mathematical Clerical Support

04.07 Records and Materials Processing

04.08 Clerical Machine Operation

05.04 Library Services

06.03 Finance/Insurance Records Processing

06.04 Finance/Insurance Customer Service

06.05 Finance/Insurance Sales and Support

07.04 Public Administration Clerical Support

08.06 Medical Technology

12.03 Legal Support

13.15 Medical and Technical Equipment Repair

14.03 General Sales

14.06 Customer Service

15.05 Physical Science Laboratory Technology

Night Vision: Seeing under low light conditions

12.01 Managerial Work in Law and Public Safety

12.04 Law Enforcement and Public Safety

12.05 Safety and Security

16.02 Air Vehicle Operation

16.04 Rail Vehicle Operation

16.05 Water Vehicle Operation

16.06 Other Services Requiring Driving

16.07 Transportation Support Work

Number Facility: Adding, subtracting, multiplying, or dividing quickly and correctly

01.01 Managerial Work in Agriculture and Natural Resources

01.03 Resource Technologies for Plants, Animals, and the Environment

02.03 Architecture/Construction Engineering Technologies

04.05 Accounting, Auditing, and Analytical Support

04.06 Mathematical Clerical Support

06.01 Managerial Work in Finance and Insurance

06.02 Finance/Insurance Investigation and Analysis

06.03 Finance/Insurance Records Processing

06.05 Finance/Insurance Sales and Support

14.01 Managerial Work in Retail/Wholesale Sales and Service

14.02 Technical Sales

15.06 Mathematics and Data Analysis

Oral Comprehension: Listening to and understanding information and ideas presented through spoken words and sentences

03.03 News, Broadcasting, and Public Relations

05.02 Preschool, Elementary, and Secondary Teaching and Instructing

05.03 Postsecondary and Adult Teaching and Instructing

05.06 Counseling, Health, and Fitness Education

07.02 Public Planning

10.04 Client Interviewing

12.02 Legal Practice and Justice Administration

15.01 Managerial Work in Scientific Research, Engineering, and Mathematics

15.02 Physical Sciences

15.03 Life Sciences

15.04 Social Sciences

Oral Expression: Communicating information and ideas in speaking so others will understand

05.01 Managerial Work in Education

05.03 Postsecondary and Adult Teaching and Instructing

05.06 Counseling, Health, and Fitness Education

08.02 Medicine and Surgery

10.02 Religious Work

14.02 Technical Sales

15.04 Social Sciences

Originality: Coming up with unusual or clever ideas about a given topic or situation or developing creative ways to solve a problem

01.02 Resource Science/Engineering for Plants, Animals, and the Environment

02.01 Managerial Work in Architecture/Construction

02.02 Architectural Design

03.01 Managerial Work in Arts and Communication

03.02 Writing and Editing

03.04 Studio Art

03.05 Design

03.06 Drama

03.07 Music

04.01 Managerial Work in General Business

05.01 Managerial Work in Education

07.01 Managerial Work in Government and Public Administration

10.01 Counseling and Social Work

11.01 Managerial Work in Information Technology

11.02 Information Technology Specialties

14.04 Personal Soliciting

15.01 Managerial Work in Scientific Research, Engineering, and Mathematics

15.07 Research and Design Engineering

Perceptual Speed: Quickly and accurately comparing similarities and differences among sets of letters, numbers, objects, pictures, or patterns

03.10 Communications Technology

04.07 Records and Materials Processing

06.04 Finance/Insurance Customer Service

08.01 Managerial Work in Medical and Health Services

08.06 Medical Technology

13.07 Production Quality Control

15.05 Physical Science Laboratory Technology

Peripheral Vision: Seeing objects or movement of objects to your side when your eyes are looking ahead

01.07 Hunting and Fishing

01.08 Mining and Drilling

09.02 Recreational Services

12.04 Law Enforcement and Public Safety

12.05 Safety and Security

16.02 Air Vehicle Operation

16.03 Truck Driving

16.04 Rail Vehicle Operation

16.05 Water Vehicle Operation

16.06 Other Services Requiring Driving

Problem Sensitivity: Telling when something is wrong or is likely to go wrong

01.02 Resource Science/Engineering for Plants, Animals, and the Environment

04.05 Accounting, Auditing, and Analytical Support

07.03 Regulations Enforcement

08.01 Managerial Work in Medical and Health Services

08.02 Medicine and Surgery

08.04 Health Specialties

08.05 Animal Care

08.06 Medical Technology

08.07 Medical Therapy

08.08 Patient Care and Assistance

10.01 Counseling and Social Work

11.01 Managerial Work in Information Technology

15.01 Managerial Work in Scientific Research, Engineering, and Mathematics

15.03 Life Sciences

Rate Control: Timing your movements or the movement of a piece of equipment in anticipation of changes in the speed and/or direction of a moving object or scene

01.04 General Farming

01.08 Mining and Drilling

12.06 Emergency Responding

13.03 Production Work, Assorted Materials Processing

13.17 Loading, Moving, Hoisting, and Conveying

16.02 Air Vehicle Operation

16.03 Truck Driving

16.04 Rail Vehicle Operation

16.06 Other Services Requiring Driving

Reaction Time: Quickly responding with your hand, finger, or foot to a signal when it appears

12.01 Managerial Work in Law and Public Safety

12.05 Safety and Security

13.16 Utility Operation and Energy Distribution

16.03 Truck Driving

16.04 Rail Vehicle Operation

16.06 Other Services Requiring Driving

Response Orientation: Choosing quickly between two or more movements in response to two or more different signals

01.08 Mining and Drilling

03.09 Media Technology

12.01 Managerial Work in Law and Public Safety

© 2006, JIST Works

12.04 Law Enforcement and Public Safety

16.02 Air Vehicle Operation

16.03 Truck Driving

16.04 Rail Vehicle Operation

16.06 Other Services Requiring Driving

Selective Attention: Concentrating on a task over a period of time without being distracted

04.08 Clerical Machine Operation

09.01 Managerial Work in Hospitality and Tourism

09.02 Recreational Services

13.07 Production Quality Control

Sound Localization: Telling the direction from which a sound originated

03.07 Music

03.11 Musical Instrument Repair

12.05 Safety and Security

13.07 Production Quality Control

13.13 Machinery Repair

13.16 Utility Operation and Energy Distribution

16.05 Water Vehicle Operation

16.06 Other Services Requiring Driving

Spatial Orientation: Knowing your location in relation to the environment or knowing where other objects are in relation to you

01.01 Managerial Work in Agriculture and Natural Resources

01.06 Forestry and Logging

01.07 Hunting and Fishing

12.01 Managerial Work in Law and Public Safety

12.04 Law Enforcement and Public Safety

16.02 Air Vehicle Operation

16.03 Truck Driving

16.05 Water Vehicle Operation

16.06 Other Services Requiring Driving

16.07 Transportation Support Work

Speech Clarity: Speaking clearly so others can understand you

03.03 News, Broadcasting, and Public Relations

03.06 Drama

04.01 Managerial Work in General Business

04.03 Human Resources Support

05.01 Managerial Work in Education

05.03 Postsecondary and Adult Teaching and Instructing

05.05 Archival and Museum Services

05.06 Counseling, Health, and Fitness Education

07.01 Managerial Work in Government and Public Administration

08.09 Health Protection and Promotion

10.02 Religious Work

12.02 Legal Practice and Justice Administration

14.04 Personal Soliciting

14.06 Customer Service

16.01 Managerial Work in Transportation

Speech Recognition: Identifying and understanding the speech of another person

03.01 Managerial Work in Arts and Communication

03.03 News, Broadcasting, and Public Relations

03.10 Communications Technology

04.01 Managerial Work in General Business

04.02 Managerial Work in Business Detail

04.03 Human Resources Support

04.04 Secretarial Support

05.04 Library Services

06.04 Finance/Insurance Customer Service

06.05 Finance/Insurance Sales and Support

07.01 Managerial Work in Government and Public Administration

07.04 Public Administration Clerical Support

08.07 Medical Therapy

08.08 Patient Care and Assistance

08.09 Health Protection and Promotion

09.03 Hospitality and Travel Services

10.01 Counseling and Social Work

10.03 Child/Personal Care and Services

10.04 Client Interviewing

14.01 Managerial Work in Retail/Wholesale Sales and Service

14.03 General Sales

14.05 Purchasing

14.06 Customer Service

16.01 Managerial Work in Transportation

Speed of Closure: Quickly making sense of, combining, and organizing information into meaningful patterns

02.03 Architecture/Construction Engineering Technologies

06.01 Managerial Work in Finance and Insurance

08.01 Managerial Work in Medical and Health Services

08.02 Medicine and Surgery

08.04 Health Specialties

Speed of Limb Movement: Quickly moving your arms and legs

01.07 Hunting and Fishing

03.08 Dance

03.11 Musical Instrument Repair

12.06 Emergency Responding

Stamina: Exerting yourself physically over long periods of time without getting winded or out of breath

01.04 General Farming

01.05 Nursery, Groundskeeping, and Pest Control

02.04 Construction Crafts

02.06 Construction Support/Labor

03.08 Dance

09.05 Food and Beverage Service

09.06 Sports

12.01 Managerial Work in Law and Public Safety

12.05 Safety and Security

12.06 Emergency Responding

Static Strength: Exerting maximum muscle force to lift, push, pull, or carry objects

01.04 General Farming

01.06 Forestry and Logging

01.07 Hunting and Fishing

01.08 Mining and Drilling

02.04 Construction Crafts

02.06 Construction Support/Labor

10.03 Child/Personal Care and Services

12.06 Emergency Responding

13.14 Vehicle and Facility Mechanical Work

13.17 Loading, Moving, Hoisting, and Conveying

16.03 Truck Driving

Time Sharing: Shifting back and forth between two or more activities or sources of information

04.02 Managerial Work in Business Detail

04.04 Secretarial Support

05.02 Preschool, Elementary, and Secondary Teaching and Instructing

08.08 Patient Care and Assistance

09.01 Managerial Work in Hospitality and Tourism

09.03 Hospitality and Travel Services

13.01 Managerial Work in Manufacturing

15.05 Physical Science Laboratory Technology

16.01 Managerial Work in Transportation

Trunk Strength: Using your abdominal and lower back muscles to support part of the body repeatedly or continuously over time without tiring

01.04 General Farming

02.06 Construction Support/Labor

09.03 Hospitality and Travel Services

09.05 Food and Beverage Service

10.03 Child/Personal Care and Services

Visual Color Discrimination: Matching or detecting differences between colors, including shades of color and brightness

03.05 Design

03.09 Media Technology

09.07 Barber and Beauty Services

11.03 Digital Equipment Repair

13.07 Production Quality Control

13.08 Graphic Arts Production

13.11 Apparel, Shoes, Leather, and Fabric Care

13.12 Electrical and Electronic Repair

15.05 Physical Science Laboratory Technology

Visualization: Imagining how something will look after it is moved around or when its parts are moved or rearranged

02.01 Managerial Work in Architecture/Construction

02.02 Architectural Design

02.03 Architecture/Construction Engineering Technologies

03.04 Studio Art

03.05 Design

05.05 Archival and Museum Services

13.05 Production Machining Technology

15.07 Research and Design Engineering

15.09 Engineering Technology

Wrist-Finger Speed: Making fast, simple, repeated movements of your fingers, hands, and wrists

04.08 Clerical Machine Operation

09.04 Food and Beverage Preparation

11.03 Digital Equipment Repair

13.05 Production Machining Technology

13.06 Production Precision Work

13.08 Graphic Arts Production

13.09 Hands-On Work, Assorted Materials

13.11 Apparel, Shoes, Leather, and Fabric Care

Written Comprehension: Reading and understanding information and ideas presented in writing

03.03 News, Broadcasting, and Public Relations

05.01 Managerial Work in Education

05.03 Postsecondary and Adult Teaching and Instructing

06.01 Managerial Work in Finance and Insurance

07.02 Public Planning

11.02 Information Technology Specialties

12.02 Legal Practice and Justice Administration

12.03 Legal Support

15.01 Managerial Work in Scientific Research, Engineering, and Mathematics

15.02 Physical Sciences

15.03 Life Sciences

15.04 Social Sciences

15.07 Research and Design Engineering

Written Expression: Communicating information and ideas in writing so others will understand

01.02 Resource Science/Engineering for Plants, Animals, and the Environment

03.01 Managerial Work in Arts and Communication

03.02 Writing and Editing

03.03 News, Broadcasting, and Public Relations

05.01 Managerial Work in Education

05.03 Postsecondary and Adult Teaching and Instructing

06.01 Managerial Work in Finance and Insurance

07.02 Public Planning

07.04 Public Administration Clerical Support

08.01 Managerial Work in Medical and Health Services

10.04 Client Interviewing

12.02 Legal Practice and Justice Administration

12.03 Legal Support

15.02 Physical Sciences

15.03 Life Sciences

15.04 Social Sciences

15.08 Industrial and Safety Engineering

Crosswalk G: Knowledges with Corresponding Work Groups

Administration and Management: Business and management principles involved in strategic planning, resource allocation, human resources modeling, leadership techniques, production methods, and coordination of people and resources

01.01 Managerial Work in Agriculture and Natural Resources

02.01 Managerial Work in Architecture/Construction

03.01 Managerial Work in Arts and Communication

04.01 Managerial Work in General Business

04.02 Managerial Work in Business Detail

04.03 Human Resources Support

04.05 Accounting, Auditing, and Analytical Support

05.01 Managerial Work in Education

06.01 Managerial Work in Finance and Insurance

07.01 Managerial Work in Government and Public Administration

08.01 Managerial Work in Medical and Health Services

09.01 Managerial Work in Hospitality and Tourism

11.01 Managerial Work in Information Technology

13.01 Managerial Work in Manufacturing

14.01 Managerial Work in Retail/Wholesale Sales and Service

14.05 Purchasing

15.01 Managerial Work in Scientific Research, Engineering, and Mathematics

15.07 Research and Design Engineering

16.01 Managerial Work in Transportation

Biology: Plant and animal organisms and their tissues, cells, functions, interdependencies, and interactions with each other and the environment

01.01 Managerial Work in Agriculture and Natural Resources

01.02 Resource Science/Engineering for Plants, Animals, and the Environment

01.03 Resource Technologies for Plants, Animals, and the Environment

01.04 General Farming

01.05 Nursery, Groundskeeping, and Pest Control

01.06 Forestry and Logging

01.07 Hunting and Fishing

08.01 Managerial Work in Medical and Health Services

08.02 Medicine and Surgery

08.03 Dentistry

08.04 Health Specialties

08.05 Animal Care

08.06 Medical Technology

08.07 Medical Therapy

08.09 Health Protection and Promotion

15.03 Life Sciences

Building and Construction: The materials, methods, and tools involved in the construction or repair of houses; buildings; or other structures, such as highways and roads

02.01 Managerial Work in Architecture/Construction

02.02 Architectural Design

02.03 Architecture/Construction Engineering Technologies

02.04 Construction Crafts

02.06 Construction Support/Labor

07.02 Public Planning

13.04 Welding, Brazing, and Soldering

13.10 Woodworking Technology

13.14 Vehicle and Facility Mechanical Work

Chemistry: The chemical composition, structure, and properties of substances and of the chemical processes and transformations that they undergo; this includes uses of chemicals and their danger signs, production techniques, and disposal methods

01.02 Resource Science/Engineering for Plants, Animals, and the Environment

01.03 Resource Technologies for Plants, Animals, and the Environment

01.04 General Farming

01.05 Nursery, Groundskeeping, and Pest Control

08.01 Managerial Work in Medical and Health Services

08.02 Medicine and Surgery

08.03 Dentistry

08.04 Health Specialties

08.06 Medical Technology

09.07 Barber and Beauty Services

12.06 Emergency Responding

15.01 Managerial Work in Scientific Research, Engineering, and Mathematics

15.02 Physical Sciences

15.03 Life Sciences

15.05 Physical Science Laboratory Technology

15.08 Industrial and Safety Engineering

Clerical Practices: Administrative and clerical procedures and systems such as word processing, managing files and records, stenography and transcription, designing forms, and other office procedures and terminology

04.02 Managerial Work in Business Detail

04.03 Human Resources Support

04.04 Secretarial Support

04.05 Accounting, Auditing, and Analytical Support

04.06 Mathematical Clerical Support

04.07 Records and Materials Processing

04.08 Clerical Machine Operation

05.04 Library Services

05.05 Archival and Museum Services

06.03 Finance/Insurance Records Processing

06.04 Finance/Insurance Customer Service

07.02 Public Planning

07.04 Public Administration Clerical Support

11.01 Managerial Work in Information Technology

12.03 Legal Support

14.05 Purchasing

Communications and Media: Media production, communication, and dissemination techniques and methods; this includes alternative ways to inform and entertain via written, oral, and visual media

03.01 Managerial Work in Arts and Communication

03.02 Writing and Editing

03.03 News, Broadcasting, and Public Relations

03.06 Drama

03.07 Music

03.08 Dance

03.09 Media Technology

05.03 Postsecondary and Adult Teaching and Instructing

05.05 Archival and Museum Services

10.02 Religious Work

14.01 Managerial Work in Retail/Wholesale Sales and Service

14.04 Personal Soliciting

15.02 Physical Sciences

Computers and Electronics: Circuit boards; processors; chips; electronic equipment; and computer hardware and software, including applications and programming

02.03 Architecture/Construction Engineering Technologies

04.04 Secretarial Support

04.05 Accounting, Auditing, and Analytical Support

04.08 Clerical Machine Operation

05.04 Library Services

11.01 Managerial Work in Information Technology

11.02 Information Technology Specialties

11.03 Digital Equipment Repair

13.12 Electrical and Electronic Repair

15.06 Mathematics and Data Analysis

15.07 Research and Design Engineering

15.09 Engineering Technology

Customer and Personal Service: Principles and processes for providing customer and personal services; this includes customer needs assessment, meeting quality standards for services, and evaluation of customer satisfaction

04.02 Managerial Work in Business Detail

04.03 Human Resources Support

04.04 Secretarial Support

05.04 Library Services

06.04 Finance/Insurance Customer Service

06.05 Finance/Insurance Sales and Support

08.02 Medicine and Surgery

08.06 Medical Technology

© 2006, JIST Works

08.07 Medical Therapy

08.08 Patient Care and Assistance

08.09 Health Protection and Promotion

09.01 Managerial Work in Hospitality and Tourism

09.02 Recreational Services

09.03 Hospitality and Travel Services

09.05 Food and Beverage Service

09.07 Barber and Beauty Services

10.01 Counseling and Social Work

10.03 Child/Personal Care and Services

11.02 Information Technology Specialties

12.06 Emergency Responding

14.01 Managerial Work in Retail/Wholesale Sales and Service

14.03 General Sales

14.06 Customer Service

Design: Design techniques, tools, and principles involved in production of precision technical plans, blueprints, drawings, and models

02.01 Managerial Work in Architecture/Construction

02.02 Architectural Design

02.03 Architecture/Construction Engineering Technologies

02.04 Construction Crafts

02.06 Construction Support/Labor

03.04 Studio Art

03.05 Design

07.02 Public Planning

11.01 Managerial Work in Information Technology

11.02 Information Technology Specialties

13.05 Production Machining Technology

13.07 Production Quality Control

13.10 Woodworking Technology

15.07 Research and Design Engineering

15.08 Industrial and Safety Engineering

15.09 Engineering Technology

Economics and Accounting: Economic and accounting principles and practices, the financial markets, banking, and the analysis and reporting of financial data

03.01 Managerial Work in Arts and Communication

04.01 Managerial Work in General Business

04.02 Managerial Work in Business Detail

04.05 Accounting, Auditing, and Analytical Support

04.06 Mathematical Clerical Support

05.01 Managerial Work in Education

06.01 Managerial Work in Finance and Insurance

06.02 Finance/Insurance Investigation and Analysis

06.03 Finance/Insurance Records Processing

06.04 Finance/Insurance Customer Service

06.05 Finance/Insurance Sales and Support

07.01 Managerial Work in Government and Public Administration

09.01 Managerial Work in Hospitality and Tourism

12.03 Legal Support

13.01 Managerial Work in Manufacturing

14.01 Managerial Work in Retail/Wholesale Sales and Service

14.02 Technical Sales

14.03 General Sales

14.05 Purchasing

15.01 Managerial Work in Scientific Research, Engineering, and Mathematics

15.06 Mathematics and Data Analysis

16.01 Managerial Work in Transportation

Education and Training: Principles and methods for curriculum and training design, teaching and instruction for individuals and groups, and the measurement of training effects

04.01 Managerial Work in General Business

04.03 Human Resources Support

05.01 Managerial Work in Education

05.02 Preschool, Elementary, and Secondary Teaching and Instructing

05.03 Postsecondary and Adult Teaching and Instructing

05.05 Archival and Museum Services

05.06 Counseling, Health, and Fitness Education

07.01 Managerial Work in Government and Public Administration

10.02 Religious Work

11.01 Managerial Work in Information Technology

12.01 Managerial Work in Law and Public Safety

13.01 Managerial Work in Manufacturing

15.04 Social Sciences

16.02 Air Vehicle Operation

Engineering and Technology: The practical application of engineering science and technology; this includes applying principles, techniques, procedures, and equipment to the design and production of various goods and services

01.02 Resource Science/Engineering for Plants, Animals, and the Environment

02.01 Managerial Work in Architecture/Construction

02.02 Architectural Design

02.03 Architecture/Construction Engineering Technologies

02.05 Systems and Equipment Installation, Maintenance, and Repair

11.01 Managerial Work in Information Technology

11.02 Information Technology Specialties

13.10 Woodworking Technology

13.13 Machinery Repair

13.14 Vehicle and Facility Mechanical Work

13.15 Medical and Technical Equipment Repair

13.16 Utility Operation and Energy Distribution

15.01 Managerial Work in Scientific Research, Engineering, and Mathematics

15.02 Physical Sciences

15.05 Physical Science Laboratory Technology

15.07 Research and Design Engineering

15.08 Industrial and Safety Engineering

15.09 Engineering Technology

English Language: The structure and content of the English language, including the meaning and spelling of words, rules of composition, and grammar

03.02 Writing and Editing

03.03 News, Broadcasting, and Public Relations

04.04 Secretarial Support

05.01 Managerial Work in Education

05.03 Postsecondary and Adult Teaching and Instructing

05.04 Library Services

06.01 Managerial Work in Finance and Insurance

08.02 Medicine and Surgery

08.04 Health Specialties

10.02 Religious Work

11.02 Information Technology Specialties

12.02 Legal Practice and Justice Administration

12.03 Legal Support

15.04 Social Sciences

Fine Arts: The theory and techniques required to compose, produce, and perform works of music, dance, visual arts, drama, and sculpture

02.02 Architectural Design

03.01 Managerial Work in Arts and Communication

03.02 Writing and Editing

03.04 Studio Art

03.05 Design

03.06 Drama

03.07 Music

03.08 Dance

03.09 Media Technology

03.11 Musical Instrument Repair

05.05 Archival and Museum Services

13.06 Production Precision Work

13.08 Graphic Arts Production

13.09 Hands-On Work, Assorted Materials

13.11 Apparel, Shoes, Leather, and Fabric Care

14.04 Personal Soliciting

Food Production: Techniques and equipment for planting, growing, and harvesting food products (both plant and animal) for consumption, including storage/handling techniques

01.01 Managerial Work in Agriculture and Natural Resources

01.02 Resource Science/Engineering for Plants, Animals, and the Environment

01.03 Resource Technologies for Plants, Animals, and the Environment

01.04 General Farming

01.05 Nursery, Groundskeeping, and Pest Control

01.06 Forestry and Logging

01.07 Hunting and Fishing

07.03 Regulations Enforcement

09.01 Managerial Work in Hospitality and Tourism

09.04 Food and Beverage Preparation

09.05 Food and Beverage Service

13.03 Production Work, Assorted Materials Processing

Foreign Language: The structure and content of a foreign (non-English) language, including the meaning and spelling of words, rules of composition and grammar, and pronunciation

01.06 Forestry and Logging

03.03 News, Broadcasting, and Public Relations

03.07 Music

03.11 Musical Instrument Repair

04.03 Human Resources Support

04.07 Records and Materials Processing

04.08 Clerical Machine Operation

05.02 Preschool, Elementary, and Secondary Teaching and Instructing

07.04 Public Administration Clerical Support

09.02 Recreational Services

09.04 Food and Beverage Preparation

10.04 Client Interviewing

13.02 Machine Setup and Operation

13.08 Graphic Arts Production

13.09 Hands-On Work, Assorted Materials

13.11 Apparel, Shoes, Leather, and Fabric Care

14.06 Customer Service

15.04 Social Sciences

Geography: Principles and methods for describing the features of land, sea, and air masses, including their physical characteristics; locations; interrelationships; and distribution of plant, animal, and human life

01.02 Resource Science/Engineering for Plants, Animals, and the Environment

02.02 Architectural Design

02.03 Architecture/Construction Engineering Technologies

03.10 Communications Technology

05.04 Library Services

07.02 Public Planning

09.03 Hospitality and Travel Services

15.02 Physical Sciences

15.04 Social Sciences

16.02 Air Vehicle Operation

16.03 Truck Driving

16.04 Rail Vehicle Operation

16.05 Water Vehicle Operation

16.06 Other Services Requiring Driving

16.07 Transportation Support Work

History and Archeology: Historical events and their causes, indicators, and effects on civilizations and cultures

03.04 Studio Art

05.02 Preschool, Elementary, and Secondary Teaching and Instructing

05.03 Postsecondary and Adult Teaching and Instructing

05.04 Library Services

05.05 Archival and Museum Services

06.01 Managerial Work in Finance and Insurance

07.02 Public Planning

12.02 Legal Practice and Justice Administration

15.02 Physical Sciences

15.04 Social Sciences

Law and Government: Laws, legal codes, court procedures, precedents, government regulations, executive orders, agency rules, and the democratic political process

02.02 Architectural Design

04.01 Managerial Work in General Business

06.01 Managerial Work in Finance and Insurance

06.02 Finance/Insurance Investigation and Analysis

06.04 Finance/Insurance Customer Service

07.01 Managerial Work in Government and Public Administration

07.02 Public Planning

07.03 Regulations Enforcement

07.04 Public Administration Clerical Support

12.01 Managerial Work in Law and Public Safety

12.02 Legal Practice and Justice Administration

12.03 Legal Support

12.04 Law Enforcement and Public Safety

12.05 Safety and Security

14.01 Managerial Work in Retail/Wholesale Sales and Service

Mathematics: Arithmetic, algebra, geometry, calculus, and statistics and their applications

01.02 Resource Science/Engineering for Plants, Animals, and the Environment

02.03 Architecture/Construction Engineering Technologies

04.05 Accounting, Auditing, and Analytical Support

04.06 Mathematical Clerical Support

06.01 Managerial Work in Finance and Insurance

06.02 Finance/Insurance Investigation and Analysis

07.02 Public Planning

11.02 Information Technology Specialties

14.05 Purchasing

15.01 Managerial Work in Scientific Research, Engineering, and Mathematics

15.02 Physical Sciences

15.03 Life Sciences

15.06 Mathematics and Data Analysis

15.07 Research and Design Engineering

15.09 Engineering Technology

Mechanical Devices: Machines and tools, including their designs, uses, repair, and maintenance

01.08 Mining and Drilling

02.01 Managerial Work in Architecture/Construction

02.04 Construction Crafts

02.05 Systems and Equipment Installation, Maintenance, and Repair

02.06 Construction Support/Labor

03.11 Musical Instrument Repair

11.03 Digital Equipment Repair

13.02 Machine Setup and Operation

13.03 Production Work, Assorted Materials Processing

13.04 Welding, Brazing, and Soldering

13.05 Production Machining Technology

13.06 Production Precision Work

13.12 Electrical and Electronic Repair

13.13 Machinery Repair

13.14 Vehicle and Facility Mechanical Work

13.15 Medical and Technical Equipment Repair

13.16 Utility Operation and Energy Distribution

13.17 Loading, Moving, Hoisting, and Conveying

16.02 Air Vehicle Operation

16.05 Water Vehicle Operation

Medicine and Dentistry: The information and techniques needed to diagnose and treat human injuries, diseases, and deformities; this includes symptoms, treatment alternatives, drug properties and interactions, and preventive health care measures

08.01 Managerial Work in Medical and Health Services

08.02 Medicine and Surgery

08.03 Dentistry

08.04 Health Specialties

08.05 Animal Care

08.06 Medical Technology

08.07 Medical Therapy

08.08 Patient Care and Assistance

08.09 Health Protection and Promotion

12.06 Emergency Responding

15.03 Life Sciences

Personnel and Human Resources: Principles and procedures for personnel recruitment, selection, training, compensation and benefits, labor relations and negotiation, and personnel information systems

01.01 Managerial Work in Agriculture and Natural Resources

02.01 Managerial Work in Architecture/Construction

03.01 Managerial Work in Arts and Communication

04.01 Managerial Work in General Business

04.02 Managerial Work in Business Detail

04.03 Human Resources Support

04.05 Accounting, Auditing, and Analytical Support

05.01 Managerial Work in Education

06.01 Managerial Work in Finance and Insurance

07.01 Managerial Work in Government and Public Administration

08.01 Managerial Work in Medical and Health Services

09.01 Managerial Work in Hospitality and Tourism

10.04 Client Interviewing

12.01 Managerial Work in Law and Public Safety

13.01 Managerial Work in Manufacturing

14.01 Managerial Work in Retail/Wholesale Sales and Service

15.01 Managerial Work in Scientific Research, Engineering, and Mathematics

16.01 Managerial Work in Transportation

Philosophy and Theology: Different philosophical systems and religions; this includes their basic principles, values, ethics, ways of thinking, customs, practices, and impact on human culture

03.08 Dance

05.02 Preschool, Elementary, and Secondary Teaching and Instructing

05.04 Library Services

05.05 Archival and Museum Services

08.01 Managerial Work in Medical and Health Services

08.07 Medical Therapy

08.08 Patient Care and Assistance

08.09 Health Protection and Promotion

10.01 Counseling and Social Work

10.02 Religious Work

10.03 Child/Personal Care and Services

12.02 Legal Practice and Justice Administration

12.04 Law Enforcement and Public Safety

15.04 Social Sciences

Physics: Physical principles and laws and their interrelationships and applications to understanding fluid, material, and atmospheric dynamics and mechanical, electrical, atomic, and subatomic structures and processes

01.02 Resource Science/Engineering for Plants, Animals, and the Environment

01.08 Mining and Drilling

08.04 Health Specialties

13.13 Machinery Repair

13.15 Medical and Technical Equipment Repair

13.16 Utility Operation and Energy Distribution

15.01 Managerial Work in Scientific Research, Engineering, and Mathematics

15.02 Physical Sciences

15.03 Life Sciences

15.05 Physical Science Laboratory Technology

15.07 Research and Design Engineering

15.08 Industrial and Safety Engineering

15.09 Engineering Technology

16.02 Air Vehicle Operation

Production and Processing: Raw materials, production processes, quality control, costs, and other techniques for maximizing the effective manufacture and distribution of goods

04.05 Accounting, Auditing, and Analytical Support

09.04 Food and Beverage Preparation

13.01 Managerial Work in Manufacturing

13.02 Machine Setup and Operation

13.03 Production Work, Assorted Materials Processing

13.04 Welding, Brazing, and Soldering

13.05 Production Machining Technology

13.06 Production Precision Work

13.07 Production Quality Control

13.08 Graphic Arts Production

13.09 Hands-On Work, Assorted Materials

13.11 Apparel, Shoes, Leather, and Fabric Care

13.17 Loading, Moving, Hoisting, and Conveying

14.05 Purchasing

15.07 Research and Design Engineering

Psychology: Human behavior and performance; individual differences in ability, personality, and interests; learning and motivation; psychological research methods; and the assessment and treatment of behavioral and affective disorders

04.01 Managerial Work in General Business

05.01 Managerial Work in Education

05.02 Preschool, Elementary, and Secondary Teaching and Instructing

05.03 Postsecondary and Adult Teaching and Instructing

05.06 Counseling, Health, and Fitness Education

07.01 Managerial Work in Government and Public Administration

08.02 Medicine and Surgery

08.04 Health Specialties

08.07 Medical Therapy

08.08 Patient Care and Assistance

08.09 Health Protection and Promotion

09.06 Sports

10.01 Counseling and Social Work

10.02 Religious Work

12.02 Legal Practice and Justice Administration

12.04 Law Enforcement and Public Safety

12.06 Emergency Responding

13.01 Managerial Work in Manufacturing

Public Safety and Security: Relevant equipment, policies, procedures, and strategies to promote effective local, state, or national security operations for the protection of people, data, property, and institutions

02.01 Managerial Work in Architecture/Construction

02.03 Architecture/Construction Engineering Technologies

07.03 Regulations Enforcement

12.01 Managerial Work in Law and Public Safety

12.04 Law Enforcement and Public Safety

12.05 Safety and Security

12.06 Emergency Responding

15.08 Industrial and Safety Engineering

16.02 Air Vehicle Operation

16.06 Other Services Requiring Driving

16.07 Transportation Support Work

Sales and Marketing: Principles and methods for showing, promoting, and selling products or services; this includes marketing strategy and tactics, product demonstrations, sales techniques, and sales control systems

02.02 Architectural Design

03.01 Managerial Work in Arts and Communication

03.05 Design

04.01 Managerial Work in General Business

05.01 Managerial Work in Education

06.02 Finance/Insurance Investigation and Analysis

06.05 Finance/Insurance Sales and Support

08.05 Animal Care

09.01 Managerial Work in Hospitality and Tourism

09.02 Recreational Services

09.05 Food and Beverage Service

09.07 Barber and Beauty Services

14.01 Managerial Work in Retail/Wholesale Sales and Service

14.02 Technical Sales

14.03 General Sales

14.04 Personal Soliciting

14.05 Purchasing

14.06 Customer Service

16.01 Managerial Work in Transportation

Sociology and Anthropology: Group behavior and dynamics, societal trends and influences, human migrations, ethnicity, and cultures and their history and origins

04.03 Human Resources Support

05.02 Preschool, Elementary, and Secondary Teaching and Instructing

05.03 Postsecondary and Adult Teaching and Instructing

05.05 Archival and Museum Services

05.06 Counseling, Health, and Fitness Education

07.01 Managerial Work in Government and Public Administration

08.07 Medical Therapy

08.08 Patient Care and Assistance

08.09 Health Protection and Promotion

09.06 Sports

10.01 Counseling and Social Work

10.02 Religious Work

12.02 Legal Practice and Justice Administration

12.04 Law Enforcement and Public Safety

15.04 Social Sciences

Telecommunications: Transmission, broadcasting, switching, control, and operation of telecommunications systems

02.05 Systems and Equipment Installation, Maintenance, and Repair

03.06 Drama

03.09 Media Technology

03.10 Communications Technology

06.03 Finance/Insurance Records Processing

11.01 Managerial Work in Information Technology

11.02 Information Technology Specialties

11.03 Digital Equipment Repair

12.01 Managerial Work in Law and Public Safety

12.04 Law Enforcement and Public Safety

12.05 Safety and Security

13.07 Production Quality Control

13.12 Electrical and Electronic Repair

14.02 Technical Sales

16.02 Air Vehicle Operation

16.03 Truck Driving

16.04 Rail Vehicle Operation

Therapy and Counseling: Principles, methods, and procedures for diagnosis, treatment, and rehabilitation of physical and mental dysfunctions and for career counseling and guidance

05.02 Preschool, Elementary, and Secondary Teaching and Instructing

05.03 Postsecondary and Adult Teaching and Instructing

05.06 Counseling, Health, and Fitness Education

08.01 Managerial Work in Medical and Health Services

08.02 Medicine and Surgery

08.04 Health Specialties

08.07 Medical Therapy

08.08 Patient Care and Assistance

08.09 Health Protection and Promotion

09.06 Sports

10.01 Counseling and Social Work

10.02 Religious Work

10.03 Child/Personal Care and Services

10.04 Client Interviewing

12.01 Managerial Work in Law and Public Safety

Transportation: Principles and methods for moving people or goods by air, rail, sea, or road, including the relative costs and benefits

01.07 Hunting and Fishing

01.08 Mining and Drilling

03.10 Communications Technology

04.07 Records and Materials Processing

09.03 Hospitality and Travel Services

12.01 Managerial Work in Law and Public Safety

12.04 Law Enforcement and Public Safety

12.06 Emergency Responding

13.01 Managerial Work in Manufacturing

13.17 Loading, Moving, Hoisting, and Conveying

14.05 Purchasing

16.01 Managerial Work in Transportation

16.02 Air Vehicle Operation

16.03 Truck Driving

16.04 Rail Vehicle Operation

16.05 Water Vehicle Operation

16.06 Other Services Requiring Driving

16.07 Transportation Support Work

Crosswalk H: Military Occupations with Corresponding Work Groups

This crosswalk identifies the GOE Work Groups that are related to military occupations. If you have military experience, you may find this crosswalk helpful as a guide to Work Groups where your experience is most likely to be relevant.

Administrators, General

03.01 Managerial Work in Arts and Communication

04.01 Managerial Work in General Business

04.02 Managerial Work in Business Detail

04.04 Secretarial Support

04.05 Accounting, Auditing, and Analytical Support

04.07 Records and Materials Processing

04.08 Clerical Machine Operation

11.01 Managerial Work in Information Technology

11.02 Information Technology Specialties

13.08 Graphic Arts Production

15.01 Managerial Work in Scientific Research, Engineering, and Mathematics

15.07 Research and Design Engineering

15.08 Industrial and Safety Engineering

16.01 Managerial Work in Transportation

16.06 Other Services Requiring Driving

ADP Computers, General

02.05 Systems and Equipment Installation, Maintenance, and Repair

04.07 Records and Materials Processing

11.01 Managerial Work in Information Technology

11.02 Information Technology Specialties

11.03 Digital Equipment Repair

13.01 Managerial Work in Manufacturing

13.12 Electrical and Electronic Repair

Aerospace and Underseas Medicine

02.04 Construction Crafts

07.03 Regulations Enforcement

08.02 Medicine and Surgery

12.06 Emergency Responding

Air Crew, General

13.14 Vehicle and Facility Mechanical Work

16.01 Managerial Work in Transportation

Air Traffic Control

03.10 Communications Technology

11.02 Information Technology Specialties

11.03 Digital Equipment Repair

13.12 Electrical and Electronic Repair

Air Traffic Control Radar

11.03 Digital Equipment Repair

13.01 Managerial Work in Manufacturing

13.12 Electrical and Electronic Repair

Airborne Fire Control

13.12 Electrical and Electronic Repair

Aircraft Accessories

02.05 Systems and Equipment Installation, Maintenance, and Repair

11.03 Digital Equipment Repair

12.06 Emergency Responding

13.01 Managerial Work in Manufacturing

13.12 Electrical and Electronic Repair

13.13 Machinery Repair

13.14 Vehicle and Facility Mechanical Work

14.03 General Sales

Aircraft Crews

15.07 Research and Design Engineering

16.01 Managerial Work in Transportation

16.02 Air Vehicle Operation

Aircraft Engines

13.01 Managerial Work in Manufacturing

13.14 Vehicle and Facility Mechanical Work

Aircraft, General

04.07 Records and Materials Processing

09.03 Hospitality and Travel Services

13.01 Managerial Work in Manufacturing

13.12 Electrical and Electronic Repair

13.14 Vehicle and Facility Mechanical Work

15.09 Engineering Technology

16.01 Managerial Work in Transportation

Aircraft Launch Equipment

12.06 Emergency Responding

13.17 Loading, Moving, Hoisting, and Conveying

Aircraft Structures

13.01 Managerial Work in Manufacturing

13.07 Production Quality Control

13.09 Hands-On Work, Assorted Materials

13.12 Electrical and Electronic Repair

13.14 Vehicle and Facility Mechanical Work

15.09 Engineering Technology

Ammunition Repair

01.08 Mining and Drilling

02.05 Systems and Equipment Installation, Maintenance, and Repair

13.01 Managerial Work in Manufacturing

Analysis

03.03 News, Broadcasting, and Public Relations

03.09 Media Technology

11.01 Managerial Work in Information Technology

11.02 Information Technology Specialties

15.06 Mathematics and Data Analysis

Anesthesiology

08.02 Medicine and Surgery

Armament Maintenance, General

13.01 Managerial Work in Manufacturing

Armor and Amphibious, General

02.01 Managerial Work in Architecture and Construction

02.04 Construction Crafts

13.14 Vehicle and Facility Mechanical Work

Audiology and Speech

08.07 Medical Therapy

Auditing and Accounting

04.02 Managerial Work in Business Detail

04.06 Mathematical Clerical Support

Automotive and Allied Officers

13.01 Managerial Work in Manufacturing

15.07 Research and Design Engineering

Automotive, General

01.01 Managerial Work in Agriculture and Natural Resources

02.01 Managerial Work in Architecture and Construction

02.05 Systems and Equipment Installation, Maintenance, and Repair

13.01 Managerial Work in Manufacturing

13.12 Electrical and Electronic Repair

13.13 Machinery Repair

13.14 Vehicle and Facility Mechanical Work

Auxiliaries

02.05 Systems and Equipment Installation, Maintenance, and Repair

13.01 Managerial Work in Manufacturing

13.12 Electrical and Electronic Repair

13.13 Machinery Repair

13.14 Vehicle and Facility Mechanical Work

13.16 Utility Operation and Energy Distribution

Auxiliary Labor, General

02.04 Construction Crafts

10.01 Counseling and Social Work

Aviation Maintenance and Allied Officers

04.01 Managerial Work in General Business

04.05 Accounting, Auditing, and Analytical Support

13.01 Managerial Work in Manufacturing

15.01 Managerial Work in Scientific Research, Engineering, and Mathematics

15.07 Research and Design Engineering

15.08 Industrial and Safety Engineering

16.01 Managerial Work in Transportation

Aviation Maintenance Records and Reports

04.07 Records and Materials Processing

11.01 Managerial Work in Information Technology

11.02 Information Technology Specialties

Aviation Ordnance

01.08 Mining and Drilling

02.05 Systems and Equipment Installation, Maintenance, and Repair

13.01 Managerial Work in Manufacturing

13.12 Electrical and Electronic Repair

13.14 Vehicle and Facility Mechanical Work

Behavioral Sciences

08.08 Patient Care and Assistance

Biomedical Laboratory Services

08.01 Managerial Work in Medical and Health Services

08.02 Medicine and Surgery

08.04 Health Specialties

08.06 Medical Technology

08.09 Health Protection and Promotion

13.06 Production Precision Work

13.15 Medical and Technical Equipment Repair

15.02 Physical Sciences

15.03 Life Sciences

Biomedical Science and Allied Health

13.01 Managerial Work in Manufacturing

13.15 Medical and Technical Equipment Repair

Boatswains

12.05 Safety and Security

16.05 Water Vehicle Operation

Cardiology

08.02 Medicine and Surgery

Central Office

02.05 Systems and Equipment Installation, Maintenance, and Repair

Chaplains

10.02 Religious Work

Chaplain's Assistants

04.07 Records and Materials Processing

10.02 Religious Work

12.05 Safety and Security

Colon and Rectal Surgery

08.02 Medicine and Surgery

Combat Engineering, General

01.01 Managerial Work in Agriculture and Natural Resources

01.08 Mining and Drilling

02.01 Managerial Work in Architecture and Construction

02.04 Construction Crafts

Combat Operations Control, General

13.12 Electrical and Electronic Repair

15.09 Engineering Technology

Combined Personnel and Administration, General

04.02 Managerial Work in Business Detail

04.07 Records and Materials Processing

11.02 Information Technology Specialties

Communications and Radar

04.05 Accounting, Auditing, and Analytical Support

11.01 Managerial Work in Information Technology

11.02 Information Technology Specialties

13.01 Managerial Work in Manufacturing

15.07 Research and Design Engineering

16.01 Managerial Work in Transportation

Communications Center Operations, General

02.05 Systems and Equipment Installation, Maintenance, and Repair

03.09 Media Technology

04.02 Managerial Work in Business Detail

11.02 Information Technology Specialties

11.03 Digital Equipment Repair

13.01 Managerial Work in Manufacturing

Communications Intelligence

03.03 News, Broadcasting, and Public Relations

04.01 Managerial Work in General Business

11.01 Managerial Work in Information Technology

15.06 Mathematics and Data Analysis

© 2006, JIST Works

Communications Radio

02.05 Systems and Equipment Installation, Maintenance, and Repair

03.09 Media Technology

11.02 Information Technology Specialties

11.03 Digital Equipment Repair

13.01 Managerial Work in Manufacturing

13.12 Electrical and Electronic Repair

Community Activities Officers

10.01 Counseling and Social Work

Comprehensive Dental Officers

08.03 Dentistry

Comptrollers and Fiscal Officers

04.05 Accounting, Auditing, and Analytical Support

06.01 Managerial Work in Finance and Insurance

Construction and Utilities

01.02 Resource Science/Engineering for Plants, Animals, and the Environment

02.01 Managerial Work in Architecture and Construction

02.02 Architectural Design

04.02 Managerial Work in Business Detail

13.01 Managerial Work in Manufacturing

15.01 Managerial Work in Scientific Research, Engineering, and Mathematics

15.07 Research and Design Engineering

15.08 Industrial and Safety Engineering

Construction Equipment

01.01 Managerial Work in Agriculture and Natural Resources

02.01 Managerial Work in Architecture and Construction

13.14 Vehicle and Facility Mechanical Work

Construction Equipment Operation

01.01 Managerial Work in Agriculture and Natural Resources

01.08 Mining and Drilling

02.01 Managerial Work in Architecture and Construction

02.04 Construction Crafts

13.05 Production Machining Technology

13.12 Electrical and Electronic Repair

13.13 Machinery Repair

Construction, General

01.01 Managerial Work in Agriculture and Natural Resources

01.08 Mining and Drilling

02.01 Managerial Work in Architecture and Construction

02.03 Architecture/Construction Engineering Technologies

02.04 Construction Crafts

02.06 Construction Support/Labor

12.01 Managerial Work in Law and Public Safety

13.14 Vehicle and Facility Mechanical Work

15.09 Engineering Technology

Corrections

10.01 Counseling and Social Work

12.01 Managerial Work in Law and Public Safety

12.04 Law Enforcement and Public Safety

Counterintelligence

11.01 Managerial Work in Information Technology

11.02 Information Technology Specialties

12.01 Managerial Work in Law and Public Safety

Critical Care Nurses

08.02 Medicine and Surgery

Data Processing

04.05 Accounting, Auditing, and Analytical Support

11.01 Managerial Work in Information Technology

11.02 Information Technology Specialties

15.07 Research and Design Engineering

Dental Care, General

08.02 Medicine and Surgery

08.03 Dentistry

Dental Laboratory

13.06 Production Precision Work

Diet Therapy

08.09 Health Protection and Promotion

09.01 Managerial Work in Hospitality and Tourism

09.04 Food and Beverage Preparation

Disbursing

04.02 Managerial Work in Business Detail

04.06 Mathematical Clerical Support

06.04 Finance/Insurance Customer Service

Divers

01.08 Mining and Drilling

02.04 Construction Crafts

08.05 Animal Care

Drafting

02.03 Architecture/Construction Engineering Technologies

15.09 Engineering Technology

Educators and Instructors

04.01 Managerial Work in General Business

04.03 Human Resources Support

05.03 Postsecondary and Adult Teaching and Instructing

15.02 Physical Sciences

15.07 Research and Design Engineering

16.02 Air Vehicle Operation

Electric Power

02.04 Construction Crafts

02.05 Systems and Equipment Installation, Maintenance, and Repair

13.12 Electrical and Electronic Repair

13.13 Machinery Repair

13.14 Vehicle and Facility Mechanical Work

13.16 Utility Operation and Energy Distribution

Electrical/Electronic

11.01 Managerial Work in Information Technology

11.02 Information Technology Specialties

13.01 Managerial Work in Manufacturing

15.01 Managerial Work in Scientific Research, Engineering, and Mathematics

15.07 Research and Design Engineering

16.01 Managerial Work in Transportation

Electricians

02.04 Construction Crafts

02.05 Systems and Equipment Installation, Maintenance, and Repair

13.01 Managerial Work in Manufacturing

13.12 Electrical and Electronic Repair

13.13 Machinery Repair

13.14 Vehicle and Facility Mechanical Work

Electronic Countermeasures

13.12 Electrical and Electronic Repair

15.09 Engineering Technology

Electronic Instruments, Not Elsewhere Classified

11.02 Information Technology Specialties

11.03 Digital Equipment Repair

13.01 Managerial Work in Manufacturing

13.07 Production Quality Control

13.12 Electrical and Electronic Repair

Emergency Medicine

08.01 Managerial Work in Medical and Health Services

Endocrinology

08.02 Medicine and Surgery

Endodontics

08.03 Dentistry

Environmental Health Services

01.02 Resource Science/Engineering for Plants, Animals, and the Environment

02.02 Architectural Design

07.03 Regulations Enforcement

08.06 Medical Technology

08.07 Medical Therapy

15.03 Life Sciences

15.07 Research and Design Engineering

15.08 Industrial and Safety Engineering

EOD/UDT

01.08 Mining and Drilling

12.01 Managerial Work in Law and Public Safety

Exchange and Commissary

14.01 Managerial Work in Retail/Wholesale Sales and Service

Executive Dentistry

08.01 Managerial Work in Medical and Health Services

Executive Medicine

08.01 Managerial Work in Medical and Health Services

08.02 Medicine and Surgery

Executives, Not Elsewhere Classified

04.01 Managerial Work in General Business

04.05 Accounting, Auditing, and Analytical Support

07.01 Managerial Work in Government and Public Administration

11.01 Managerial Work in Information Technology

12.02 Legal Practice and Justice Administration

15.01 Managerial Work in Scientific Research, Engineering, and Mathematics

15.07 Research and Design Engineering

16.01 Managerial Work in Transportation

16.02 Air Vehicle Operation

Fabric, Leather, and Rubber, General

13.03 Production Work, Assorted Materials Processing

13.07 Production Quality Control

13.11 Apparel, Shoes, Leather, and Fabric Care

13.13 Machinery Repair

Family Practice

08.02 Medicine and Surgery

Firefighting and Damage Control

12.01 Managerial Work in Law and Public Safety

12.06 Emergency Responding

First Sergeants, Sergeants Major, and Leading Chiefs

04.03 Human Resources Support

16.05 Water Vehicle Operation

Fixed-Wing Fighter and Bomber Pilots

04.01 Managerial Work in General Business

16.02 Air Vehicle Operation

Flight Nurses

08.02 Medicine and Surgery

Flight Operations

03.10 Communications Technology

16.01 Managerial Work in Transportation

Food Service, General

09.01 Managerial Work in Hospitality and Tourism

09.02 Recreational Services

09.03 Hospitality and Travel Services

09.04 Food and Beverage Preparation

09.05 Food and Beverage Service

14.01 Managerial Work in Retail/Wholesale Sales and Service

14.03 General Sales

Forward Area Equipment Support, General

02.05 Systems and Equipment Installation, Maintenance, and Repair

13.01 Managerial Work in Manufacturing

13.07 Production Quality Control

13.11 Apparel, Shoes, Leather, and Fabric Care

Functional Analysis

04.02 Managerial Work in Business Detail

04.05 Accounting, Auditing, and Analytical Support

04.07 Records and Materials Processing

11.02 Information Technology Specialties

Gastroenterology

08.02 Medicine and Surgery

General and Flag Officers

04.01 Managerial Work in General Business

07.01 Managerial Work in Government and Public Administration

General and Other Nurses

08.01 Managerial Work in Medical and Health Services

08.02 Medicine and Surgery

General Dentistry

08.03 Dentistry

General Internist

08.02 Medicine and Surgery

General Medicine

08.02 Medicine and Surgery

General Surgery

08.02 Medicine and Surgery

Ground and Naval Arms

02.01 Managerial Work in Architecture and Construction

04.01 Managerial Work in General Business

15.07 Research and Design Engineering

16.05 Water Vehicle Operation

Health Services Administration Officers

04.02 Managerial Work in Business Detail

04.05 Accounting, Auditing, and Analytical Support

06.01 Managerial Work in Finance and Insurance

08.01 Managerial Work in Medical and Health Services

08.02 Medicine and Surgery

11.01 Managerial Work in Information Technology

Helicopter Pilots

04.05 Accounting, Auditing, and Analytical Support

16.02 Air Vehicle Operation

Hematology and Oncology

08.02 Medicine and Surgery

Illustrating

03.05 Design

03.09 Media Technology

13.08 Graphic Arts Production

Image Interpretation

15.09 Engineering Technology

Industrial Gas and Fuel Production, General

13.13 Machinery Repair

13.16 Utility Operation and Energy Distribution

Infantry, General

02.04 Construction Crafts

Infectious Disease

08.02 Medicine and Surgery

Information

03.01 Managerial Work in Arts and Communication

03.02 Writing and Editing

03.03 News, Broadcasting, and Public Relations

04.01 Managerial Work in General Business

Information and Education, General

03.01 Managerial Work in Arts and Communication

03.02 Writing and Editing

03.03 News, Broadcasting, and Public Relations

03.06 Drama

03.09 Media Technology

04.03 Human Resources Support

04.07 Records and Materials Processing

12.01 Managerial Work in Law and Public Safety

15.04 Social Sciences

Inspection

04.01 Managerial Work in General Business

07.03 Regulations Enforcement

Intelligence, General

03.03 News, Broadcasting, and Public Relations

04.01 Managerial Work in General Business

11.01 Managerial Work in Information Technology

15.01 Managerial Work in Scientific Research, Engineering, and Mathematics

15.04 Social Sciences

15.09 Engineering Technology

Intercept Operators (Code and Non-Code)

03.03 News, Broadcasting, and Public Relations

03.09 Media Technology

04.05 Accounting, Auditing, and Analytical Support

11.02 Information Technology Specialties

Interior Communications

02.04 Construction Crafts

02.05 Systems and Equipment Installation, Maintenance, and Repair

13.01 Managerial Work in Manufacturing

13.12 Electrical and Electronic Repair

Investigations

12.01 Managerial Work in Law and Public Safety

12.04 Law Enforcement and Public Safety

Language Interrogation/Interpretation

03.03 News, Broadcasting, and Public Relations

04.07 Records and Materials Processing

Laundry and Personal Service, General

02.04 Construction Crafts

09.07 Barber and Beauty Services

13.03 Production Work, Assorted Materials Processing

13.11 Apparel, Shoes, Leather, and Fabric Care

Law Enforcement, General

12.01 Managerial Work in Law and Public Safety

12.04 Law Enforcement and Public Safety

12.05 Safety and Security

Legal

04.02 Managerial Work in Business Detail

04.04 Secretarial Support

07.04 Public Administration Clerical Support

12.02 Legal Practice and Justice Administration

12.03 Legal Support

Linemen

02.05 Systems and Equipment Installation, Maintenance, and Repair

13.01 Managerial Work in Manufacturing

13.12 Electrical and Electronic Repair

Lithography, General

13.02 Machine Setup and Operation

13.08 Graphic Arts Production

13.13 Machinery Repair

Logistics, General

04.05 Accounting, Auditing, and Analytical Support

16.01 Managerial Work in Transportation

Machinists

13.02 Machine Setup and Operation

13.03 Production Work, Assorted Materials Processing

13.05 Production Machining Technology

13.13 Machinery Repair

13.16 Utility Operation and Energy Distribution

Main Propulsion

02.04 Construction Crafts

02.05 Systems and Equipment Installation, Maintenance, and Repair

13.01 Managerial Work in Manufacturing

13.05 Production Machining Technology

13.12 Electrical and Electronic Repair

13.13 Machinery Repair

13.14 Vehicle and Facility Mechanical Work

13.16 Utility Operation and Energy Distribution

Manpower and Personnel

04.01 Managerial Work in General Business

04.03 Human Resources Support

04.05 Accounting, Auditing, and Analytical Support

11.01 Managerial Work in Information Technology

15.04 Social Sciences

Mapping

02.03 Architecture/Construction Engineering Technologies

15.09 Engineering Technology

Mathematicians and Statisticians

04.05 Accounting, Auditing, and Analytical Support

15.06 Mathematics and Data Analysis

Medical Administration

04.02 Managerial Work in Business Detail

08.06 Medical Technology

Medical Care and Treatment, General

07.03 Regulations Enforcement

08.01 Managerial Work in Medical and Health Services

08.02 Medicine and Surgery

08.06 Medical Technology

08.07 Medical Therapy

08.08 Patient Care and Assistance

12.06 Emergency Responding

Medical Logistics

04.02 Managerial Work in Business Detail

04.07 Records and Materials Processing

Memorial Activities and Embalming

08.09 Health Protection and Promotion

10.03 Child/Personal Care and Services

14.01 Managerial Work in Retail/Wholesale Sales and Service

© 2006, JIST Works

Mental Health Nursing

08.02 Medicine and Surgery

Metal Body Repair

13.01 Managerial Work in Manufacturing

13.04 Welding, Brazing, and Soldering

13.14 Vehicle and Facility Mechanical Work

Metalworking, General

13.01 Managerial Work in Manufacturing

13.02 Machine Setup and Operation

13.03 Production Work, Assorted Materials Processing

13.04 Welding, Brazing, and Soldering

13.05 Production Machining Technology

13.07 Production Quality Control

13.14 Vehicle and Facility Mechanical Work

15.05 Physical Science Laboratory Technology

Meteorologists

15.01 Managerial Work in Scientific Research, Engineering, and Mathematics

15.02 Physical Sciences

Military Training Instructors

04.03 Human Resources Support

Mines and Degaussing

01.08 Mining and Drilling

13.12 Electrical and Electronic Repair

Missile Artillery, Operating Crew

13.01 Managerial Work in Manufacturing

Missile Checkout Equipment, Test Equipment, and Calibration

11.03 Digital Equipment Repair

13.01 Managerial Work in Manufacturing

13.12 Electrical and Electronic Repair

Missile Fuel and Petroleum

13.01 Managerial Work in Manufacturing

13.16 Utility Operation and Energy Distribution

Missile Guidance and Control

11.03 Digital Equipment Repair

13.01 Managerial Work in Manufacturing

13.12 Electrical and Electronic Repair

Missile Launch and Support Facilities

04.02 Managerial Work in Business Detail

Missile Maintenance

13.01 Managerial Work in Manufacturing

Missile Mechanics

11.03 Digital Equipment Repair

13.12 Electrical and Electronic Repair

13.14 Vehicle and Facility Mechanical Work

Missiles

15.01 Managerial Work in Scientific Research, Engineering, and Mathematics

Morale and Welfare

03.07 Music

Motor Vehicle Operators

13.17 Loading, Moving, Hoisting, and Conveying

16.01 Managerial Work in Transportation

16.03 Truck Driving

16.06 Other Services Requiring Driving

Musicians, General

03.07 Music

03.09 Media Technology

03.11 Musical Instrument Repair

Navigation, Communication, and Countermeasure, Not Elsewhere Classified

02.05 Systems and Equipment Installation, Maintenance, and Repair

03.09 Media Technology

11.03 Digital Equipment Repair

13.01 Managerial Work in Manufacturing

13.12 Electrical and Electronic Repair

13.14 Vehicle and Facility Mechanical Work

13.15 Medical and Technical Equipment Repair

Navigators

16.05 Water Vehicle Operation

Nephrology

08.02 Medicine and Surgery

Neurological Surgery

08.02 Medicine and Surgery

Non-Code Radio

03.09 Media Technology

Non-Radio Communications (Visual)

03.09 Media Technology

11.01 Managerial Work in Information Technology

11.02 Information Technology Specialties

Nuclear, Biological, and Chemical Warfare Specialists

01.01 Managerial Work in Agriculture and Natural Resources

02.01 Managerial Work in Architecture and Construction

12.01 Managerial Work in Law and Public Safety

Nuclear Power

13.01 Managerial Work in Manufacturing

13.04 Welding, Brazing, and Soldering

13.13 Machinery Repair

13.16 Utility Operation and Energy Distribution

15.05 Physical Science Laboratory Technology

Nuclear Weapons Equipment Repair, General

01.08 Mining and Drilling

02.05 Systems and Equipment Installation, Maintenance, and Repair

13.01 Managerial Work in Manufacturing

Nurse Anesthetists

08.02 Medicine and Surgery

Nurse Midwives

08.02 Medicine and Surgery

Nurse Practitioners

08.02 Medicine and Surgery

Nursing Education

08.02 Medicine and Surgery

Nursing Service Administration

08.02 Medicine and Surgery

Obstetrics and Gynecology

08.02 Medicine and Surgery

Oncology Surgery

08.02 Medicine and Surgery

Operating Room Nurses

08.02 Medicine and Surgery

Operational Intelligence

03.09 Media Technology

12.01 Managerial Work in Law and Public Safety

15.09 Engineering Technology

Operations Staff

03.10 Communications Technology

04.01 Managerial Work in General Business

04.05 Accounting, Auditing, and Analytical Support

07.03 Regulations Enforcement

12.01 Managerial Work in Law and Public Safety

16.01 Managerial Work in Transportation

16.02 Air Vehicle Operation

16.05 Water Vehicle Operation

Operators/Analysts

04.02 Managerial Work in Business Detail

04.07 Records and Materials Processing

11.01 Managerial Work in Information Technology

11.02 Information Technology Specialties

11.03 Digital Equipment Repair

13.01 Managerial Work in Manufacturing

Ophthalmology/Optometry

08.02 Medicine and Surgery

08.06 Medical Technology

13.06 Production Precision Work

Optometry

08.04 Health Specialties

Oral Maxillofacial Surgery

08.03 Dentistry

Oral Pathology

08.03 Dentistry

Ordnance

04.05 Accounting, Auditing, and Analytical Support

12.01 Managerial Work in Law and Public Safety

13.01 Managerial Work in Manufacturing

14.01 Managerial Work in Retail/Wholesale Sales and Service

15.01 Managerial Work in Scientific Research, Engineering, and Mathematics

15.07 Research and Design Engineering

15.08 Industrial and Safety Engineering

16.01 Managerial Work in Transportation

Orthodontics

08.03 Dentistry

Orthopedic

08.06 Medical Technology

13.06 Production Precision Work

Orthopedic Surgery

08.02 Medicine and Surgery

Other Biomedical Science and Allied Health

03.09 Media Technology

13.08 Graphic Arts Production

15.05 Physical Science Laboratory Technology

Other Biomedical Science and Allied Health Officers

08.01 Managerial Work in Medical and Health Services

13.01 Managerial Work in Manufacturing

15.03 Life Sciences

Other Craftsworkers, Not Elsewhere Classified, General

02.04 Construction Crafts

12.01 Managerial Work in Law and Public Safety

12.06 Emergency Responding

13.04 Welding, Brazing, and Soldering

13.05 Production Machining Technology

Other Fixed-Wing Pilots

16.02 Air Vehicle Operation

Other Mechanical and Electrical Equipment, General

02.04 Construction Crafts

02.05 Systems and Equipment Installation, Maintenance, and Repair

© 2006, JIST Works

13.12 Electrical and Electronic Repair

13.13 Machinery Repair

13.14 Vehicle and Facility Mechanical Work

Pediatric Surgery

08.02 Medicine and Surgery

Pediatrics

08.02 Medicine and Surgery

15.03 Life Sciences

Pedodontics

08.03 Dentistry

Periodontics

08.03 Dentistry

Peripheral Vascular Surgery

08.02 Medicine and Surgery

Personnel, General

04.03 Human Resources Support

04.05 Accounting, Auditing, and Analytical Support

04.07 Records and Materials Processing

11.02 Information Technology Specialties

Pharmacy

08.02 Medicine and Surgery

Photography, General

03.01 Managerial Work in Arts and Communication

03.03 News, Broadcasting, and Public Relations

03.04 Studio Art

03.05 Design

03.06 Drama

03.09 Media Technology

13.08 Graphic Arts Production

13.12 Electrical and Electronic Repair

13.15 Medical and Technical Equipment Repair

Physical and Occupational Therapy

08.07 Medical Therapy

Physical Science Laboratory

07.03 Regulations Enforcement

13.07 Production Quality Control

13.16 Utility Operation and Energy Distribution

15.05 Physical Science Laboratory Technology

Physical Scientists

04.01 Managerial Work in General Business

13.01 Managerial Work in Manufacturing

14.01 Managerial Work in Retail/Wholesale Sales and Service

15.01 Managerial Work in Scientific Research, Engineering, and Mathematics

15.02 Physical Sciences

15.07 Research and Design Engineering

Physician Assistants

08.02 Medicine and Surgery

Physiology

07.03 Regulations Enforcement

08.02 Medicine and Surgery

15.03 Life Sciences

Pictorial

03.01 Managerial Work in Arts and Communication

03.04 Studio Art

03.09 Media Technology

04.01 Managerial Work in General Business

Pilots and Navigators

16.02 Air Vehicle Operation

Plastic Surgery

08.02 Medicine and Surgery

Podiatry

08.04 Health Specialties

Police

03.01 Managerial Work in Arts and Communication

12.01 Managerial Work in Law and Public Safety

12.04 Law Enforcement and Public Safety

Postal

04.02 Managerial Work in Business Detail

04.07 Records and Materials Processing

Precision Equipment, General

07.03 Regulations Enforcement

13.13 Machinery Repair

Preventive Medicine

07.03 Regulations Enforcement

08.01 Managerial Work in Medical and Health Services

08.02 Medicine and Surgery

Procurement and Production

04.05 Accounting, Auditing, and Analytical Support

13.01 Managerial Work in Manufacturing

14.01 Managerial Work in Retail/Wholesale Sales and Service

15.07 Research and Design Engineering

15.08 Industrial and Safety Engineering

Programmers

04.02 Managerial Work in Business Detail

11.01 Managerial Work in Information Technology

11.02 Information Technology Specialties

Prosthodontics

08.03 Dentistry

Psychiatry

08.02 Medicine and Surgery

Psychologists

15.01 Managerial Work in Scientific Research, Engineering, and Mathematics

Psychology and Social Work

10.01 Counseling and Social Work

Public Health

08.01 Managerial Work in Medical and Health Services

08.03 Dentistry

Pulmonary Disease

08.02 Medicine and Surgery

Radar

03.10 Communications Technology

11.02 Information Technology Specialties

Radio Code

03.09 Media Technology

04.02 Managerial Work in Business Detail

11.01 Managerial Work in Information Technology

11.02 Information Technology Specialties

13.12 Electrical and Electronic Repair

Radio/Radar, General

11.03 Digital Equipment Repair

13.01 Managerial Work in Manufacturing

13.12 Electrical and Electronic Repair

Radiology

08.06 Medical Technology

Railway Operators

16.01 Managerial Work in Transportation

16.07 Transportation Support Work

Recreation and Welfare

09.02 Recreational Services

Recruiting and Counseling

04.03 Human Resources Support

10.01 Counseling and Social Work

Research and Development Coordinators

02.01 Managerial Work in Architecture and Construction

04.01 Managerial Work in General Business

15.01 Managerial Work in Scientific Research, Engineering, and Mathematics

15.03 Life Sciences

15.07 Research and Design Engineering

15.08 Industrial and Safety Engineering

Rheumatology

08.02 Medicine and Surgery

Safety

02.04 Construction Crafts

07.03 Regulations Enforcement

12.01 Managerial Work in Law and Public Safety

15.08 Industrial and Safety Engineering

16.01 Managerial Work in Transportation

Sales Store

04.07 Records and Materials Processing

14.01 Managerial Work in Retail/Wholesale Sales and Service

14.03 General Sales

Scientists and Professionals, Not Elsewhere Classified

04.05 Accounting, Auditing, and Analytical Support

15.01 Managerial Work in Scientific Research, Engineering, and Mathematics

Seamanship, General

16.05 Water Vehicle Operation

Security Guards

12.04 Law Enforcement and Public Safety

12.05 Safety and Security

Ship Construction and Maintenance

04.01 Managerial Work in General Business

13.01 Managerial Work in Manufacturing

13.16 Utility Operation and Energy Distribution

15.01 Managerial Work in Scientific Research, Engineering, and Mathematics

15.07 Research and Design Engineering

15.08 Industrial and Safety Engineering

16.01 Managerial Work in Transportation

Ship Machinery

13.01 Managerial Work in Manufacturing

13.16 Utility Operation and Energy Distribution

15.07 Research and Design Engineering

16.01 Managerial Work in Transportation

Shipboard and Other Fire Control

11.02 Information Technology Specialties

11.03 Digital Equipment Repair

13.01 Managerial Work in Manufacturing

13.12 Electrical and Electronic Repair

Shipboard Inertial Navigation Systems

11.03 Digital Equipment Repair

13.12 Electrical and Electronic Repair

Signal Intelligence/Electronic Warfare, General

03.03 News, Broadcasting, and Public Relations

04.05 Accounting, Auditing, and Analytical Support

11.02 Information Technology Specialties

13.12 Electrical and Electronic Repair

Small Boat Operators

16.05 Water Vehicle Operation

Social Scientists

03.03 News, Broadcasting, and Public Relations

12.01 Managerial Work in Law and Public Safety

15.04 Social Sciences

Sonar, General

02.05 Systems and Equipment Installation, Maintenance, and Repair

11.01 Managerial Work in Information Technology

11.03 Digital Equipment Repair

13.12 Electrical and Electronic Repair

Sonar Operators, General

13.12 Electrical and Electronic Repair

Steelworking

02.04 Construction Crafts

Stenography

04.07 Records and Materials Processing

11.02 Information Technology Specialties

Stewards and Enlisted Aides

04.02 Managerial Work in Business Detail

04.04 Secretarial Support

Supply

04.05 Accounting, Auditing, and Analytical Support

14.01 Managerial Work in Retail/Wholesale Sales and Service

16.01 Managerial Work in Transportation

Supply Administration

01.08 Mining and Drilling

02.05 Systems and Equipment Installation, Maintenance, and Repair

04.02 Managerial Work in Business Detail

04.05 Accounting, Auditing, and Analytical Support

04.06 Mathematical Clerical Support

04.07 Records and Materials Processing

09.04 Food and Beverage Preparation

11.02 Information Technology Specialties

14.05 Purchasing

16.07 Transportation Support Work

Surgery

08.02 Medicine and Surgery

08.06 Medical Technology

Surveillance/Target Acquisition and Tracking Radar

11.03 Digital Equipment Repair

13.01 Managerial Work in Manufacturing

13.12 Electrical and Electronic Repair

Surveying

02.03 Architecture/Construction Engineering Technologies

15.09 Engineering Technology

Teletype and Cryptographic Equipment, General

02.05 Systems and Equipment Installation, Maintenance, and Repair

03.09 Media Technology

11.02 Information Technology Specialties

11.03 Digital Equipment Repair

13.01 Managerial Work in Manufacturing

13.12 Electrical and Electronic Repair

Therapy

08.06 Medical Technology

08.07 Medical Therapy

Thoracic and Cardiac Surgery

08.02 Medicine and Surgery

Tracked Vehicles

13.01 Managerial Work in Manufacturing

13.12 Electrical and Electronic Repair

13.14 Vehicle and Facility Mechanical Work

Training Administrators

03.02 Writing and Editing

04.01 Managerial Work in General Business

04.03 Human Resources Support

04.05 Accounting, Auditing, and Analytical Support

05.01 Managerial Work in Education

05.03 Postsecondary and Adult Teaching and Instructing

16.01 Managerial Work in Transportation

Training Devices

02.05 Systems and Equipment Installation, Maintenance, and Repair

11.03 Digital Equipment Repair

13.01 Managerial Work in Manufacturing

13.12 Electrical and Electronic Repair

Transportation

04.01 Managerial Work in General Business

04.02 Managerial Work in Business Detail

04.05 Accounting, Auditing, and Analytical Support

04.07 Records and Materials Processing

09.01 Managerial Work in Hospitality and Tourism

09.03 Hospitality and Travel Services

13.01 Managerial Work in Manufacturing

15.07 Research and Design Engineering

16.01 Managerial Work in Transportation

16.05 Water Vehicle Operation

16.07 Transportation Support Work

Undesignated Occupations, General

04.03 Human Resources Support

16.05 Water Vehicle Operation

Unit Supply

04.05 Accounting, Auditing, and Analytical Support

Urology

08.02 Medicine and Surgery

Utilities, General

01.01 Managerial Work in Agriculture and Natural Resources

01.05 Nursery, Groundskeeping, and Pest Control

02.01 Managerial Work in Architecture and Construction

02.04 Construction Crafts

02.05 Systems and Equipment Installation, Maintenance, and Repair

13.01 Managerial Work in Manufacturing

13.13 Machinery Repair

13.16 Utility Operation and Energy Distribution

Veterinarians

01.03 Resource Technologies for Plants, Animals, and the Environment

08.05 Animal Care

Veterinary Medicine

07.03 Regulations Enforcement

08.05 Animal Care

Warehousing and Equipment Handling

04.07 Records and Materials Processing

13.17 Loading, Moving, Hoisting, and Conveying

16.01 Managerial Work in Transportation

Weather, General

15.02 Physical Sciences

Welding

13.04 Welding, Brazing, and Soldering

Wire Communications, General

04.07 Records and Materials Processing

11.02 Information Technology Specialties

Woodworking

02.04 Construction Crafts

© 2006, JIST Works

Appendix

Information for Vocational Counselors and Other Professionals

The appendix is divided into two sections: The first provides information for individuals who want to use the revised GOE structure in other publications and databases; the second offers tips on how to use the *GOE* in counseling.

Guidelines for Use of the GOE Structure by Other Developers

With this fourth edition of the *GOE*, we introduce a GOE structure that is both old and new. It uses the popular occupational clustering scheme developed by the U.S. Department of Education, but it improves on that scheme by dividing each of the 16 clusters into Work Groups, as the *GOE* has done in all its previous versions.

As the U.S. Department of Labor does not plan to revise the GOE, we believe this new GOE structure can become the de facto standard. We believe that many developers of occupational instruments, publications, software, and Internet systems will want to abandon the old GOE numbering references and replace them with the new ones presented in this revised edition. To encourage this, we present the following answers to questions developers have asked us.

Who owns the new GOE structure and content?

The GOE was originally developed by the U.S. Department of Labor, and its content and structure were in the public domain. The 16-cluster scheme developed by the U.S. Department of Education is also in the public domain. However, JIST's revised *GOE* represents a combination of these two, together with many changes, and this allows us to copyright the revised structure and text, which we have done. What this means is that the new GOE Work Group structure and content are *not* in the public domain, and rights to this structure and content are protected under copyright laws.

Can others use the GOE structure in their own materials?

Yes. We encourage other developers and publishers to refer to and use the revised GOE structure in their materials and products. We want to do this because of the GOE's importance to other systems that have traditionally cross-referenced it. Also, we believe that allowing its use by others is in keeping with the GOE's original spirit and intent.

Is there a cost for using the new GOE structure in our products?

A small charge covers the costs of our negotiating and recording permissions. This is not a small matter, as we anticipate numerous inquiries regarding use of the new GOE structure. We also want to know who is using the new GOE structure and how it is being used—an essential requirement for protecting our copyrights. For those wanting to use the new GOE structure, there is a one-time fee of $250 for most printed products and an annual licensing fee of

$200 for most software. These fees cover the use of the revised GOE Interest Area names, numbers, and brief descriptions; Work Group names and numbers; and related O*NET job title names arranged within the Work Groups. This fee does not cover use of the longer descriptive text for the Interest Areas, Work Groups, or job descriptions. Also, these fees do not include the use of the GOE structure in consumable items such as printed interest inventories. These other uses will be negotiated separately.

Are there other restrictions?

For the preceding uses, we require that a statement be included with each use that identifies JIST as the material's source and the copyright owner. We will provide you with this statement and will advise you of certain easy-to-follow guidelines for using the material in your product.

I work for the government. Why can't I use the new GOE structure for free?

JIST has invested a great deal of time and money in producing the new GOE structure. This material was not produced by any government agency. Even so, we will consider your special circumstances, particularly for uses by the good people at the U.S. Department of Labor.

Can we use the revised *GOE* text?

Perhaps, depending on the situation. It took us several years to develop this revised text, so we do not want someone to use it to create a product that directly competes with our products. Let us know what you want to do, and we will consider it. Additional fees would likely apply to these situations.

Can we arrange for custom variations of the text and database information?

Anything is possible, so you can ask; however, custom work depends on our resource availability. Programming and writing costs would be charged to you at an hourly rate, and these tasks are expensive due to the high skill levels required.

Will we have access to future changes to the GOE structure?

Sure. We expect to make improvements in all GOE elements over time, and these changes will be available to you as they are made. Note that it will be your responsibility to be aware of the newest changes because we have no mechanism to keep you informed. Check with us if you are creating or revising a product, and we'll give you the latest version.

Can we suggest changes to the GOE?

Of course. We are interested in any suggestions for improving the GOE. We prefer that you submit your suggestions via e-mail to info@jist.com, but we will be happy to take them via letter.

Are fees and other details subject to change?

Yes. As we gain experience with the various uses of the GOE, we will revise our licensing fees and restrictions. This means that the terms and conditions noted here are subject to change without notice. Check with us for the latest changes.

How do we contact you for permissions?

Please contact us in writing, providing clear information on the following:

* What GOE content or rights you want to use or obtain.
* The product in which you will be using our materials. A clear, complete description of your product or a sample draft would be helpful, if available.
* The nature and size of the population you expect to use your product.
* Any other information you think we should know.

Send your inquiry to Rights Editor, JIST Publishing, 8902 Otis Ave., Indianapolis, Indiana 46216-1033. Or contact us by e-mail at info@jist.com.

Information for Vocational Counselors

Note: This content comes, with few changes, from the original edition of the *Guide for Occupational Exploration,* published by the U.S. Department of Labor in 1979.

An essential ingredient of vocational counseling is providing occupational and labor market information. Although career decision making involves far more than just these elements, any instrument that organizes the world of work and provides information about occupational duties and requirements is valuable. Because vocational counseling services are not available to a large number of potential counselees, the *Guide for Occupational Exploration* was intended to help such persons make more-informed vocational decisions.

The counselor who assists individuals in choosing a suitable occupational or vocational goal may function in any setting—the school, the college, the public employment service, the private employment service, the vocational rehabilitation agency, or the community or private vocational guidance center.

In virtually every setting in which such counselors operate, they wish to help the individual evaluate his or her occupational interests, skills, and potentials; relate them to occupational requirements and opportunities; arrive at a suitable occupational goal; and establish a plan for achieving it.

To assist the counselee in this analysis, the counselor uses various tools and sources of information. The counselor helps the applicant or client analyze his or her work experience (regular, casual, part-time, summer, military), education and training, volunteer and leisure-time activities, and other relevant experiences that may provide evidence of occupational preferences, skills, and potentialities. The counselor may administer or arrange the administration of interest inventories or checklists; aptitude tests, such as the U.S. Employment Service's General Aptitude Test Battery; or other tests and inventories.

Note: The GATB has been discontinued from widespread use as an assessment instrument.

Employment or vocational counseling, however, cannot be effective if it is limited to information about the counselee. The counselor and counselee must also have information about the world of work. Information about the counselee must be related to information about the world of work to help the individual determine a promising occupational choice.

For some time now, the counselor has had available sources of occupational information. Some sources published by the U.S. Department of Labor include the _Occupational Outlook Handbook,_ the _Occupational Outlook Quarterly,_ the _Dictionary of Occupational Titles,_ and most recently the computer-accessed O*NET database. Other sources are state occupational guides and labor market reports prepared by state employment agencies. These and similar publications provide useful information about labor market trends and opportunities as well as descriptions of occupations. However, a practical grouping of jobs in terms of occupational interest and work requirements did not exist until the development of the GOE in 1979. That publication and its revisions filled this long-expressed need of vocational counselors. The thousands of occupations in the world of work are now grouped by interests and traits required for successful job performance. Hence, the GOE provides a convenient connection between information about the counselee and potentially suitable fields of work.

Role of the GOE in Counseling and Guidance

Note: We have revised the text that follows to eliminate reference to the old GOE system that included Subgroups. We did this to avoid confusion, since this information can be helpful to career counselors and the historical reference to the old GOE system is not useful here.

The GOE groups occupations into fields of work within 16 major Interest Areas, containing broad fields (four-digit Work Groups). The counselor and counselee can explore and relate occupationally significant information about the counselee. Rather than attempting to explore the entire world of work, the counselor and counselee can identify those areas of work in which the counselee has the strongest interest. They can also identify within the Interest Areas those Work Groups that are most closely related to the interests, skills, aptitudes, education and training, and physical abilities of the counselee.

The GOE may be used particularly (1) to give the counselee an overview of the world of work and thus widen his or her understanding of occupations and (2) to help the counselee determine his or her occupational goal by offering a choice of fields of work and occupations that best reflect the interests, abilities, and potentials of the counselee.

Widening the Understanding of the World of Work

If the counselee's experience and understanding of the world of work are limited, it will be desirable for him or her, during the early stages of the counseling process, to obtain an overview of the various Interest Areas and Work Groups covered in the GOE.

The counselor may review these sections with the counselee and suggest that the counselee review them independently. This will help the counselee become familiar with the various Interest Areas and the Work Groups covered in each area, especially those areas in which the counselee has a particular interest.

This overview should be helpful not only in giving the counselee an overall feel for the world of work but also in providing a background against which to relate elements of the counselee's work experience, education and training, leisure-time activities, and other experiences that point to possibly suitable fields of work and occupations.

Determining Occupational Goal

During the counseling process, the counselor assists the counselee in choosing an occupational field that best represents the counselee's interests, skills, and potential abilities and that offers opportunity for employment. Analysis of occupation-related experiences, application of aptitude and interest tests, and relation of the resulting information to occupational groupings in the GOE are major steps in this process.

Analysis of Occupationally Related Experiences

The counselor assists the counselee in analyzing occupation-related experiences that may indicate the counselee's true occupational interests, aptitudes, acquired skills, personal traits, and any environmental and financial factors that may have vocational significance. Thus, the counselor explores with the counselee past work history, school courses, leisure-time activities, hobbies, volunteer activities, and other experiences for indications of the kinds of work the counselee particularly liked and seemed to do well in and the types he or she disliked or did poorly in. From this analysis will emerge indications of types of work for the counselee either to consider seriously or avoid altogether.

When the counselee receives an overview of the world of work early in the counseling process, he or she will have an occupational information base for analyzing past experiences in light of their occupational significance.

Aptitude and Interest Testing

In addition to obtaining information about the counselee's background during the counseling interview, the counselor will often administer or arrange for the administration of assessment tests for further indications of interests and potential ability. The occupational preferences that derive from the interview(s) and the use of the interest tools will serve as entries to the 16 Interest Areas in the *New Guide for Occupational Exploration*.

Uses of the GOE in Determining Occupational Goals

After occupationally significant information is obtained about the counselee through the counseling interview(s) and the use of the various tools, the counselor and the counselee can use the GOE to explore fields of work and help the counselee select a suitable occupational goal. The following steps are suggested:

STEP 1. Help the Counselee Identify Areas to Be Considered. Information obtained about the counselee will reveal broad areas that are of particular interest to him or her. Making a list of these Interest Areas will ensure exploration of all pertinent areas. The counselee should be encouraged to read the description of the selected areas to further verify the relevance of his or her interests. Reviewing the descriptions of other Interest Areas will also identify possible areas to explore.

STEP 2. Help the Counselee Select and Explore Work Groups. When the counselee chooses further Interest Areas to explore, he or she may review all Work Group descriptions (indicated by the four-digit code) within these Interest Areas to decide which Work Groups to explore. Sometimes, glancing at the Work Group title may be enough to identify a type of activity the counselee does not wish to investigate further. The counselee may then turn to the next Group selected for further exploration. Alternatively, when the counselee reads a Group title and description and expresses interest in the Work Group, he or she may explore it immediately before moving on to the next Work Group.

In the counselee's exploration of the Work Group, the counselor should help the counselee determine suitability of the Group from the standpoint of his or her true interests, aptitudes, skills and traits required, further preparation needed, and other relevant considerations.

To explore a selected Work Group, the counselee should review the information provided under the Work Group description. During the discussion of this information, the counselor should help the counselee try to relate occupationally significant information about himself or herself to the information in that Work Group.

* **ITEM 1. What kind of work would you do?** This item provides examples of some specific work tasks of occupations within the Group, such as "Design structures for crop storage, animal shelter and loading, and animal and crop processing," or "Care for athletic injuries, using physical therapy equipment, techniques, and medication." These examples, along with the description of the Work Group, will help the counselee get a feel for the kind of work involved and determine whether it is a type of activity in line with his or her interests, skills, and potentials. These activities may apply to just one occupation but usually are illustrative of the kind of work performed in various jobs in this Group.

✳ **ITEM 2. What things about you point to this kind of work?** This item mentions work experience, extracurricular activities, hobbies, and other activities and experiences, as well as work values, physical and mental abilities, and preferences for work settings relevant to occupations in this Work Group. This item provides clues concerning the counselee's possible ability to do or to learn to do this kind of work and his or her desire to do it.

Included in this item are questions such as "Is it important for you to plan your work with little supervision?" "Have you enjoyed raising or caring for animals as a leisure-time activity?" "Have you liked and done well in accounting as a school subject?" "Are you able to see details at close range?" and "Would you work in places such as railroad tracks and yards?" These questions help the counselee think through whether he or she has the interest and ability to do or to learn to do types of work included in this Group. These questions also help the counselee think about certain issues of personal likes and dislikes that may affect the desirability of the occupations in this Group. The counselor should help the counselee relate these kinds of personal experiences and interests to the Work Groups being explored.

✳ **ITEM 3. What skills and knowledges do you need for this kind of work?** This item names the worker characteristics required to perform successfully in occupations in this Group. For example, it points to actual or potential abilities such as "Information Gathering—knowing how to find information and identifying essential information" and "Time Management—managing your own time and the time of others." It also points to actual or potential knowledges such as "Communications and Media—media production, communication, and dissemination techniques and methods; this includes alternative ways to inform and entertain via written, oral, and visual media" and "Public Safety and Security—relevant equipment, policies, procedures, and strategies to promote effective local, state, or national security operations for the protection of people, data, property, and institutions." This information should help the counselee determine whether these are the kind of work requirements that he or she is capable of handling.

✳ **ITEM 4. What else should you consider about this kind of work?** This item provides a number of other considerations that the counselee will want to weigh in making up his or her mind about the satisfactions and suitability of this kind of work. For example, the counselee may be advised "Many of these jobs require work on evenings and weekends," "The work environment may be hot, cold, noisy, or dusty, and workers may need to exercise caution because of hazardous equipment or materials," or "Competition for most of these jobs is likely to be keen."

✳ **ITEM 5. How can you prepare for jobs of this kind?** This item describes the kind of training, work, and other experiences usually required by or acceptable to employers. It tells the counselee how to enter the field. Counselees who are interested in this Work Group should consider whether they have the kind of preparation usually needed or the willingness to take further training if needed.

The counselee should keep a simple record of all Work Groups he or she reviewed and those he or she identified for further exploration.

STEP 3. Help the Counselee Explore Specific Occupations. After exploring the Work Groups, the counselee will usually find that he or she either is not seriously interested in the type of work in the Group or will want to explore it still further. If the counselee is still interested in the Work Group, the counselor should help him or her examine specific occupations within the Work Group and choose one or more for further investigation.

The counselee should be encouraged to identify occupations that seem interesting and potentially suitable, based on all the information that the counselee now has about himself or herself. The counselee should be instructed how to look up information on occupations that seem particularly interesting in a print, software, or Internet source, such as this book, the O*NET Web site, America's Career InfoNet, or the *O*NET Dictionary of Occupational Titles*. The counselee should then consider the specific occupations from the standpoint of opportunities available for placement or training, the counselee's interests and qualifications, and the occupational requirements.

STEP 4. Help the Counselee Select His or Her Vocational Goal. The counselee, working with the counselor, should compile a list of specific occupations that appear to be particularly interesting to the counselee. With the counselor's help, the counselee should weigh the pros and cons of each desirable and suitable Work Group or occupation.

STEP 5. Help the Counselee Develop a Plan for Attaining the Goal. As usual, the counselor will assist the counselee in developing a realistic vocational plan for reaching the goal. The plan should reflect actions to be taken by the counselee, by the counselor, or by other resources to enable the counselee to enter a training program, obtain suitable employment, or take some other step toward attaining the goal. A thoughtful plan will include a contingency plan for what to do if the intended goal proves unattainable or loses its appeal.

STEP 6. Assign Appropriate Occupational Titles. If the counselee's thinking remains at the Group level and the counselee does not select a specific occupational goal, the counselor should assign one or more occupational titles to the counselee. The assigned titles should reflect the counselee's goals and facilitate his or her selection for suitable employment.

Two or more counseling interviews are usually required to help the counselee make a suitable occupational choice and plan to implement that choice. The counselor may wish to suggest that the counselee review the *New GOE* during one of the interviews or between interviews. The introduction provides helpful suggestions for reviewing the book.

The GOE thus serves as a useful reference tool in career exploration and can help the individual and the counselor develop a sound and realistic vocational goal for the counselee.

GOSHEN PUBLIC LIBRARY
601 SOUTH FIFTH STREET
GOSHEN, IN 46526

© 2006 JIST Works

Index of Interest Areas, Work Groups, and Jobs

A

Able Seamen, 220, 461

Accountants, 77, 283–284

Accounting, Auditing, and Analytical Support Work Group, 76–77, 283–285

Actors, 62, 270

Actuaries, 207, 448

Adjustment Clerks, 196, 438

Administrative Law Judges, Adjudicators, and Hearing Officers, 153, 367

Administrative Services Managers, 73, 280

Adult Literacy, Remedial Education, and GED Teachers and Instructors, 88, 296–297

Advertising and Promotions Managers, 189, 432

Advertising Sales Agents, 100, 315

Aerospace Engineering and Operations Technicians, 212, 453

Aerospace Engineers, 209, 449

Agents and Business Managers of Artists, Performers, and Athletes, 55, 263

Agricultural Crop Farm Managers, 31, 228

Agricultural Engineers, 33, 232

Agricultural Equipment Operators, 36, 236

Agricultural Inspectors, 106, 319

Agricultural Sciences Teachers, Postsecondary, 88, 297

Agricultural Technicians, 35, 234–235

Agriculture and Natural Resources Interest Area, 29–41, 227–243

Air Crew Members, 159, 373

Air Crew Officers, 159, 373

Air Traffic Controllers, 67, 275

Air Vehicle Operation Work Group, 215–216, 459

Aircraft Body and Bonded Structure Repairers, 182, 420

Aircraft Cargo Handling Supervisors, 215, 458

Aircraft Engine Specialists, 182, 420

Aircraft Launch and Recovery Officers, 159, 373–374

Aircraft Launch and Recovery Specialists, 159, 374

Aircraft Rigging Assemblers, 182, 420–421

Aircraft Structure Assemblers, Precision, 182, 421

Aircraft Systems Assemblers, Precision, 182, 421

Airfield Operations Specialists, 67, 275

Airframe-and-Power-Plant Mechanics, 182, 421

Airline Pilots, Copilots, and Flight Engineers, 216, 459

Ambulance Drivers and Attendants, Except Emergency Medical Technicians, 222, 463

Amusement and Recreation Attendants, 128, 344

Anesthesiologists, 113, 326–327

Animal Breeders, 118, 332

Animal Care Work Group, 116–118, 332–334

Animal Control Workers, 157, 371

Animal Scientists, 33, 232

Animal Trainers, 118, 332

Anthropologists, 204, 445

Anthropology and Archeology Teachers, Postsecondary, 88, 297

Apparel, Shoes, Leather, and Fabric Care Work Group, 176–177, 413–415

Appraisers, Real Estate, 96, 310

Arbitrators, Mediators, and Conciliators, 153, 367

Archeologists, 204, 445–446

Architects, Except Landscape and Naval, 45, 244

Architectural Design Work Group, 44–45, 244–245

Architectural Drafters, 47, 245

Architecture and Construction Interest Area, 42–52, 243–261

Architecture Teachers, Postsecondary, 88, 297

Architecture/Construction Engineering Technologies Work Group, 45–47, 245–246

Archival and Museum Services Work Group, 89–91, 306–307

Archivists, 91, 306–307

Area, Ethnic, and Cultural Studies Teachers, Postsecondary, 88, 297–298

Armored Assault Vehicle Crew Members, 159, 374

Armored Assault Vehicle Officers, 159, 374

Art Directors, 55, 263

Art, Drama, and Music Teachers, Postsecondary, 88, 298

Artillery and Missile Crew Members, 159, 374

Artillery and Missile Officers, 159, 374

Arts and Communication Interest Area, 53–68, 262–277

Assessors, 96, 310

Astronomers, 201, 442

Athletes and Sports Competitors, 134, 352

Athletic Trainers, 124, 340–341

Atmospheric and Space Scientists, 201, 442

Atmospheric, Earth, Marine, and Space Sciences Teachers, Postsecondary, 88, 298

Audio and Video Equipment Technicians, 66, 272–273

Audio-Visual Collections Specialists, 91, 307

Audiologists, 121, 336–337

Auditors, 77, 284

Automatic Teller Machine Servicers, 148, 364

Automotive Body and Related Repairers, 182, 421

Automotive Glass Installers and Repairers, 182, 421–422

Automotive Master Mechanics, 182, 422

Automotive Specialty Technicians, 182, 422

Auxiliary Equipment Operators, Power, 184, 425

Aviation Inspectors, 106, 319

Avionics Technicians, 179, 415–416

B

Baggage Porters and Bellhops, 130, 346

Bailiffs, 156, 369

Bakers, Bread and Pastry, 131, 348–349

Bakers, Manufacturing, 166, 386–387

Barber and Beauty Services Work Group, 134–135, 352–353

Barbers, 135, 352

Bartenders, 132, 350

Battery Repairers, 179, 416

Bench Workers, Jewelry, 171, 399

Bicycle Repairers, 180, 418

Bill and Account Collectors, 99, 314

Billing, Cost, and Rate Clerks, 78, 285

Billing, Posting, and Calculating Machine Operators, 81, 290

Bindery Machine Operators and Tenders, 173, 404

Bindery Machine Setters and Set-Up Operators, 164, 378–379

Biochemists, 202, 444

Biological Science Teachers, Postsecondary, 88, 298–299

Biological Technicians, 120, 334

Biologists, 202, 444

Biomedical Engineers, 209, 449–450

Biophysicists, 202, 444

Boat Builders and Shipwrights, 49, 246

Boiler Operators and Tenders, Low Pressure, 184, 425

Boilermakers, 49, 246

Bookbinders, 171, 399

Bookkeeping, Accounting, and Auditing Clerks, 78, 285–286

Brattice Builders, 48, 246–247

Brazers, 168, 395

Brickmasons and Blockmasons, 49, 247

Bridge and Lock Tenders, 223, 464

Broadcast News Analysts, 58, 265

Broadcast Technicians, 66, 273

Brokerage Clerks, 78, 286

Budget Analysts, 77, 284

Buffing and Polishing Set-Up Operators, 164, 379

Bus and Truck Mechanics and Diesel Engine Specialists, 182, 422

Bus Drivers, School, 221, 463

Bus Drivers, Transit and Intercity, 222, 463

Business and Administration Interest Area, 69–81, 278–291

Business Teachers, Postsecondary, 88, 299

Butchers and Meat Cutters, 131, 349

C

Cabinetmakers and Bench Carpenters, 176, 413

Calibration and Instrumentation Technicians, 212, 453

Camera and Photographic Equipment Repairers, 183, 424

Camera Operators, 173, 404

Camera Operators, Television, Video, and Motion Picture, 66, 273

Caption Writers, 58, 265–266

Cardiovascular Technologists and Technicians, 120, 334

Cargo and Freight Agents, 223, 464–465

Carpenter Assemblers and Repairers, 52, 259

Carpet Installers, 48, 247

Cartographers and Photogrammetrists, 212, 453

Cartoonists, 59, 267

Cashiers, 196, 438

Casting Machine Set-Up Operators, 165, 379

Ceiling Tile Installers, 48, 247

Cement Masons and Concrete Finishers, 49, 247

Cementing and Gluing Machine Operators and Tenders, 166, 387

Central Office and PBX Installers and Repairers, 50, 256

Central Office Operators, 67, 275

Chefs and Head Cooks, 131, 349

Chemical Engineers, 209, 450

Chemical Equipment Controllers and Operators, 166, 387

Chemical Equipment Tenders, 166, 387

Chemical Plant and System Operators, 184, 425

Chemical Technicians, 205, 447

Chemistry Teachers, Postsecondary, 88, 299

Chemists, 201, 442

Chief Executives, 71, 279

Child Care Workers, 141, 358

Child Support, Missing Persons, and Unemployment Insurance Fraud Investigators, 106, 319

Child, Family, and School Social Workers, 138, 355

Child/Personal Care and Services Work Group, 140–141, 358–359

Chiropractors, 116, 331–332

Choreographers, 64, 272

City Planning Aides, 104, 318

Civil Drafters, 47, 245

Civil Engineering Technicians, 212, 453–454

Civil Engineers, 209, 450

Claims Examiners, Property and Casualty Insurance, 96, 311

Claims Takers, Unemployment Benefits, 142, 359

Cleaners of Vehicles and Equipment, 223, 465

Cleaning, Washing, and Metal Pickling Equipment Operators and Tenders, 166, 387

Clergy, 140, 357–358

Clerical Machine Operation Work Group, 80–81, 290–291

Client Interviewing Work Group, 141–142, 359

Clinical Psychologists, 138, 355

Coaches and Scouts, 134, 352

Coating, Painting, and Spraying Machine Operators and Tenders, 166, 387–388

Coating, Painting, and Spraying Machine Setters and Set-Up Operators, 164, 379

Coil Winders, Tapers, and Finishers, 175, 411

Coin, Vending, and Amusement Machine Servicers and Repairers, 148, 362

Combination Machine Tool Operators and Tenders, Metal and Plastic, 166, 388

Combination Machine Tool Setters and Set-Up Operators, Metal and Plastic, 164, 379–380

Combined Food Preparation and Serving Workers, Including Fast Food, 132, 350–351

Command and Control Center Officers, 159, 374–375

Command and Control Center Specialists, 159, 375

Commercial and Industrial Designers, 60, 268

Commercial Divers, 48, 248

Commercial Pilots, 216, 459

Communication Equipment Mechanics, Installers, and Repairers, 50, 256

Communications Teachers, Postsecondary, 88, 299

Communications Technology Work Group, 66–67, 275–276

Compensation and Benefits Managers, 71, 279

Compensation, Benefits, and Job Analysis Specialists, 74, 281–282

Composers, 63, 271

Computer and Information Systems Managers, 145, 361

Computer Hardware Engineers, 209, 405

Computer Operators, 147, 361

Computer Programmers, 147, 361–362

Computer Science Teachers, Postsecondary, 88, 299

Computer Security Specialists, 147, 362

Computer Software Engineers, Applications, 147, 362

Computer Software Engineers, Systems Software, 147, 362

Computer Support Specialists, 147, 363

Computer Systems Analysts, 147, 363

Concierges, 130, 346

Construction and Building Inspectors, 47, 245

Construction Carpenters, 49, 248

Construction Crafts Work Group, 47–49, 246–255

Construction Drillers, 41, 239

Construction Laborers, 52, 259

Construction Managers, 44, 244

Construction Support/Labor Work Group, 50–52, 259–261

Continuous Mining Machine Operators, 41, 239–240

Conveyor Operators and Tenders, 186, 428

Cooks, Fast Food, 131, 349

Cooks, Institution and Cafeteria, 131, 349

Cooks, Restaurant, 131, 349–350

Cooks, Short Order, 131, 350

Cooling and Freezing Equipment Operators and Tenders, 166, 388

Copy Writers, 56, 265

Coroners, 110, 326

Correctional Officers and Jailers, 156, 369

Correspondence Clerks, 80, 286–287

Cost Estimators, 96, 311

© 2006 JIST Works

Costume Attendants, 62, 270

Counseling and Social Work Work Group, 137–138, 355–357

Counseling Psychologists, 138, 355

Counseling, Health, and Fitness Education Work Group, 91–92, 307–308

Counter and Rental Clerks, 196, 438

Counter Attendants, Cafeteria, Food Concession, and Coffee Shop, 132, 351

Couriers and Messengers, 221, 463

Court Clerks, 107, 323

Court Reporters, 107, 323

Craft Artists, 59, 267

Crane and Tower Operators, 48, 248

Creative Writers, 56, 264–265

Credit Analysts, 96, 311

Credit Authorizers, 98, 313

Credit Checkers, 98, 313

Criminal Investigators and Special Agents, 156, 369

Criminal Justice and Law Enforcement Teachers, Postsecondary, 88, 300

Crossing Guards, 157, 371

Crushing, Grinding, and Polishing Machine Setters, Operators, and Tenders, 164, 380

Curators, 91, 307

Custom Tailors, 177, 413–414

Customer Service Representatives, Utilities, 196, 438–439

Customer Service Work Group, 195–196, 438–439

Cutters and Trimmers, Hand, 175, 411

Cutting and Slicing Machine Operators and Tenders, 166, 388

D

Dance Work Group, 63–64, 272

Dancers, 64, 272

Data Entry Keyers, 81, 290

Data Processing Equipment Repairers, 148, 364

Database Administrators, 147, 363

Demonstrators and Product Promoters, 194, 436–437

Dental Assistants, 114, 330

Dental Hygienists, 114, 330

Dental Laboratory Technicians, 171, 399–400

Dentistry Work Group, 113–114, 330–331

Dentists, General, 114, 330–331

Derrick Operators, Oil and Gas, 41, 240

Design Printing Machine Setters and Set-Up Operators, 173, 404

Design Work Group, 59–61, 268–270

Desktop Publishers, 173, 404–405

Diagnostic Medical Sonographers, 120, 334

Dietetic Technicians, 124, 341

Dietitians and Nutritionists, 124, 341

Digital Equipment Repair Work Group, 147–148, 364

Dining Room and Cafeteria Attendants and Bartender Helpers, 132, 351

Directors, Religious Activities and Education, 140, 358

Directors—Stage, Motion Pictures, Television, and Radio, 62, 270

Directory Assistance Operators, 67, 275–276

Dishwashers, 131, 350

Dispatchers, Except Police, Fire, and Ambulance, 67, 276

Door-To-Door Sales Workers, News and Street Vendors, and Related Workers, 194, 437

Dot Etchers, 173, 405

Dragline Operators, 48, 248

Drama Work Group, 61–62, 270–271

Dredge Operators, 220, 461

Drilling and Boring Machine Tool Setters, Operators, and Tenders, Metal and Plastic, 164, 380

Driver/Sales Workers, 221, 463–464

Drywall Installers, 48, 248–249

Duplicating Machine Operators, 81, 290

E

Economics Teachers, Postsecondary, 88, 300

Economists, 204, 446

Editors, 56, 265

Education Administrators, Elementary and Secondary School, 84, 293

Education Administrators, Postsecondary, 84, 293

Education Administrators, Preschool and Child Care Center/Program, 84, 293

Education and Training Interest Area, 82–92, 292–308

Education Teachers, Postsecondary, 88, 300

Educational Psychologists, 204, 446

Educational, Vocational, and School Counselors, 92, 307–308

Electric Home Appliance and Power Tool Repairers, 179, 416

Electric Meter Installers and Repairers, 50, 256

Electric Motor and Switch Assemblers and Repairers, 179, 416

Electrical and Electronic Equipment Assemblers, 170, 400

Electrical and Electronic Inspectors and Testers, 172, 403

Electrical and Electronic Repair Work Group, 177–179, 415–418

Electrical and Electronics Installers and Repairers, Transportation Equipment, 179, 416

Electrical and Electronics Repairers, Commercial and Industrial Equipment, 179, 416–417

Electrical and Electronics Repairers, Powerhouse, Substation, and Relay, 50, 256

Electrical Drafters, 47, 245–246

Electrical Engineering Technicians, 212, 454

Electrical Engineers, 209, 450

Electrical Parts Reconditioners, 179, 417

Electrical Power-Line Installers and Repairers, 50, 256–257

Electricians, 49, 249

Electro-Mechanical Technicians, 212, 454

Electrolytic Plating and Coating Machine Operators and Tenders, Metal and Plastic, 166, 388–389

Electrolytic Plating and Coating Machine Setters and Set-Up Operators, Metal and Plastic, 165, 380

Electromechanical Equipment Assemblers, 171, 400

Electronic Drafters, 212, 454

Electronic Equipment Installers and Repairers, Motor Vehicles, 179, 417

Electronic Home Entertainment Equipment Installers and Repairers, 179, 417

Electronic Masking System Operators, 173, 405

Electronics Engineering Technicians, 212, 454–455

Electronics Engineers, Except Computer, 209, 450–451

Electrotypers and Stereotypers, 173, 405

Elementary School Teachers, Except Special Education, 86, 294

Elevator Installers and Repairers, 50, 257

Embalmers, 124, 341

Embossing Machine Set-Up Operators, 173, 405–406

Emergency Management Specialists, 151, 366

Emergency Medical Technicians and Paramedics, 158, 372–373

Emergency Responding Work Group, 157–158, 372–373

Employment Interviewers, Private or Public Employment Service, 74, 282

Engine and Other Machine Assemblers, 171, 400

Engineering Managers, 199, 441

Engineering Teachers, Postsecondary, 88, 300–301

Engineering Technology Work Group, 210–212, 453–456

English Language and Literature Teachers, Postsecondary, 88, 301

Engraver Set-Up Operators, 173, 406

Engravers, Hand, 173, 406

Engravers/Carvers, 173, 406

Environmental Compliance Inspectors, 106, 319

Environmental Engineering Technicians, 212, 455

Environmental Engineers, 33, 232

Environmental Science and Protection Technicians, Including Health, 35, 235

Environmental Science Teachers, Postsecondary, 88, 301

Environmental Scientists and Specialists, Including Health, 202, 444

Epidemiologists, 202, 444–445

Equal Opportunity Representatives and Officers, 106, 319–320

Etchers, 173, 406

Etchers, Hand, 173, 406

Excavating and Loading Machine Operators, 41, 240

Executive Secretaries and Administrative Assistants, 76, 282–283

Exhibit Designers, 61, 268

Explosives Workers, Ordnance Handling Experts, and Blasters, 41, 240

Extruding and Drawing Machine Setters, Operators, and Tenders, Metal and Plastic, 164, 380

Extruding and Forming Machine Operators and Tenders, Synthetic or Glass Fibers, 166, 389

Extruding and Forming Machine Setters, Operators, and Tenders, Synthetic and Glass Fibers, 164, 380

Extruding, Forming, Pressing, and Compacting Machine Operators and Tenders, 166, 389

Extruding, Forming, Pressing, and Compacting Machine Setters and Set-Up Operators, 164, 381

F

Fabric and Apparel Patternmakers, 175, 411

Fabric Menders, Except Garment, 177, 414

Fallers, 38, 238

Family and General Practitioners, 113, 327

Farm and Home Management Advisors, 88, 301

Farm Equipment Mechanics, 182, 422–423

Farmers and Ranchers, 31, 228

Farmworkers, Farm and Ranch Animals, 36, 236

Fashion Designers, 61, 268

Fence Erectors, 49, 249

Fiber Product Cutting Machine Setters and Set-Up Operators, 164, 381

Fiberglass Laminators and Fabricators, 181, 423

File Clerks, 80, 287

Film and Video Editors, 66, 273

Film Laboratory Technicians, 173, 406–407

Finance and Insurance Interest Area, 93–100, 309–316

Finance/Insurance Customer Service Work Group, 98–99, 314–315

Finance/Insurance Investigation and Analysis Work Group, 95–96, 310–313

Finance/Insurance Records Processing Work Group, 97–98, 313–314

Finance/Insurance Sales and Support Work Group, 99–100, 315–316

Financial Analysts, 96, 311

Financial Examiners, 106, 320

Financial Managers, Branch or Department, 95, 310

Fire Inspectors, 106, 320

Fire Investigators, 156, 369

Fire-Prevention and Protection Engineers, 210, 452

First-Line Supervisors and Manager/Supervisors—Agricultural Crop Workers, 31, 228–229

First-Line Supervisors and Manager/Supervisors—Animal Care Workers, Except Livestock, 110, 326

First-Line Supervisors and Manager/Supervisors—Animal Husbandry Workers, 31, 229

First-Line Supervisors and Manager/Supervisors—Construction Trades Workers, 44, 244

First-Line Supervisors and Manager/Supervisors—Extractive Workers, 31, 229

First-Line Supervisors and Manager/Supervisors—Fishery Workers, 31, 229

First-Line Supervisors and Manager/Supervisors—Horticultural Workers, 31, 229–230

First-Line Supervisors and Manager/Supervisors—Landscaping Workers, 31, 230

First-Line Supervisors and Manager/Supervisors—Logging Workers, 31, 230

First-Line Supervisors, Administrative Support, 73, 280

First-Line Supervisors, Customer Service, 73, 280–281

First-Line Supervisors/Managers of Air Crew Members, 159, 375

First-Line Supervisors/Managers of Correctional Officers, 151, 366

First-Line Supervisors/Managers of Food Preparation and Serving Workers, 127, 343

First-Line Supervisors/Managers of Helpers, Laborers, and Material Movers, Hand, 163, 378

First-Line Supervisors/Managers of Mechanics, Installers, and Repairers, 163, 378

First-Line Supervisors/Managers of Non-Retail Sales Workers, 189, 432

First-Line Supervisors/Managers of Personal Service Workers, 127, 343

First-Line Supervisors/Managers of Police and Detectives, 151, 366

First-Line Supervisors/Managers of Production and Operating Workers, 163, 378

First-Line Supervisors/Managers of Retail Sales Workers, 189, 432

First-Line Supervisors/Managers of Transportation and Material-Moving Machine and Vehicle Operators, 215, 458

First-Line Supervisors/Managers of Weapons Specialists/Crew Members, 159, 375

Fish and Game Wardens, 106, 320

Fish Hatchery Managers, 31, 230

Fishers and Related Fishing Workers, 39, 239

Fitness Trainers and Aerobics Instructors, 92, 308

Fitters, Structural Metal—Precision, 168, 395

Flight Attendants, 130, 346

Floor Layers, Except Carpet, Wood, and Hard Tiles, 49, 249

Floor Sanders and Finishers, 49, 249

Floral Designers, 60, 269

Food and Beverage Preparation Work Group, 130–131, 348–350

Food and Beverage Service Work Group, 131–132, 350–352

Food and Tobacco Roasting, Baking, and Drying Machine Operators and Tenders, 166, 389

Food Batchmakers, 166, 389

Food Cooking Machine Operators and Tenders, 166, 389–390

Food Preparation Workers, 131, 350

Food Science Technicians, 35, 235

Food Scientists and Technologists, 35, 235

Food Servers, Nonrestaurant, 132, 351

Food Service Managers, 127, 343

Foreign Language and Literature Teachers, Postsecondary, 88, 301–302

Forensic Science Technicians, 156, 369–370

Forest and Conservation Technicians, 38, 238

Forest and Conservation Workers, 38, 238

Forest Fire Fighters, 158, 373

Forest Fire Fighting and Prevention Supervisors, 151, 366

Forest Fire Inspectors and Prevention Specialists, 106, 320

Foresters, 33, 232

Forestry and Conservation Science Teachers, Postsecondary, 88, 302

Forestry and Logging Work Group, 37–38, 238–239

Forging Machine Setters, Operators, and Tenders, Metal and Plastic, 164, 381

Foundry Mold and Coremakers, 169, 397

Frame Wirers, Central Office, 50, 257

Freight Inspectors, 223, 465

Freight, Stock, and Material Movers, Hand, 186, 428–429

Funeral Attendants, 141, 358

© 2006 JIST Works

Funeral Directors, 189, 432–433

Furnace, Kiln, Oven, Drier, and Kettle Operators and Tenders, 166, 390

Furniture Finishers, 176, 413

G

Gaming and Sports Book Writers and Runners, 128, 344

Gaming Change Persons and Booth Cashiers, 196, 439

Gaming Dealers, 128, 345

Gaming Managers, 127, 344

Gaming Supervisors, 127, 343

Gaming Surveillance Officers and Gaming Investigators, 157, 372

Gas Appliance Repairers, 180, 418

Gas Compressor Operators, 184, 425–426

Gas Distribution Plant Operators, 184, 426

Gas Processing Plant Operators, 184, 426

Gas Pumping Station Operators, 184, 426

Gaugers, 184, 426

Gem and Diamond Workers, 171, 400

General and Operations Managers, 71, 279

General Farming Work Group, 36, 236

General Farmworkers, 36, 236

General Sales Work Group, 191–192, 435–436

Geographers, 201, 442

Geography Teachers, Postsecondary, 88, 302

Geological Data Technicians, 35, 235

Geological Sample Test Technicians, 35, 235–236

Geologists, 201, 443

Glass Blowers, Molders, Benders, and Finishers, 175, 411

Glass Cutting Machine Setters and Set-Up Operators, 164, 381

Glaziers, 49, 249

Government and Public Administration Interest Area, 101–107, 317–324

Government Property Inspectors and Investigators, 106, 321

Government Service Executives, 103, 318

Grader, Bulldozer, and Scraper Operators, 49, 249–250

Graders and Sorters, Agricultural Products, 172, 403

Graduate Teaching Assistants, 88, 302

Graphic Arts Production Work Group, 172–173, 404–411

Graphic Designers, 61, 269

Grinding and Polishing Workers, Hand, 175, 411–412

Grinding, Honing, Lapping, and Deburring Machine Set-Up Operators, 164, 381–382

Grips and Set-Up Workers, Motion Picture Sets, Studios, and Stages, 51, 259–260

H

Hairdressers, Hairstylists, and Cosmetologists, 135, 353

Hand and Portable Power Tool Repairers, 180, 418

Hand Compositors and Typesetters, 173, 407

Hands-On Work, Assorted Materials Work Group, 174–175, 411–413

Hazardous Materials Removal Workers, 49, 250

Health Educators, 92, 308

Health Protection and Promotion Work Group, 123–124, 340–341

Health Science Interest Area, 108–124, 325–341

Health Specialties Teachers, Postsecondary, 88, 302–303

Health Specialties Work Group, 114–116, 331–332

Heat Treating, Annealing, and Tempering Machine Operators and Tenders, Metal and Plastic, 166, 390

Heaters, Metal and Plastic, 166, 390

Heating and Air Conditioning Mechanics, 50, 257

Heating Equipment Setters and Set-Up Operators, Metal and Plastic, 165, 382

Helpers—Brickmasons, Blockmasons, Stonemasons, and Tile and Marble Setters, 51, 260

Helpers—Carpenters, 51, 260

Helpers—Electricians, 51, 260

Helpers—Extraction Workers, 41, 240

Helpers—Installation, Maintenance, and Repair Workers, 51, 260

Helpers—Painters, Paperhangers, Plasterers, and Stucco Masons, 52, 260–261

Helpers—Pipelayers, Plumbers, Pipefitters, and Steamfitters, 52, 261

Highway Maintenance Workers, 52, 261

Highway Patrol Pilots, 156, 370

Historians, 204, 446

History Teachers, Postsecondary, 88, 303

Hoist and Winch Operators, 186, 429

Home Appliance Installers, 50, 257–258

Home Economics Teachers, Postsecondary, 88, 303

Home Health Aides, 123, 339

Hospitality and Travel Services Work Group, 129–130, 346–348

Hospitality, Tourism, and Recreation Interest Area, 125–135, 342–353

Hosts and Hostesses, Restaurant, Lounge, and Coffee Shop, 132, 351

Hotel, Motel, and Resort Desk Clerks, 130, 346–347

Housekeeping Supervisors, 73, 281

Human Resources Assistants, Except Payroll and Timekeeping, 80, 287

Human Resources Managers, 71, 279

Human Resources Support Work Group, 73–74, 281–282

Human Service Interest Area, 136–142, 354–359

Hunters and Trappers, 39, 239

Hunting and Fishing Work Group, 38–39, 239

Hydrologists, 201, 443

I–K

Immigration and Customs Inspectors, 106, 321

Industrial and Safety Engineering Work Group, 209–210, 452–453

Industrial Engineering Technicians, 77, 284

Industrial Engineers, 210, 452

Industrial Machinery Mechanics, 180, 418–419

Industrial Production Managers, 163, 378

Industrial Safety and Health Engineers, 210, 452

Industrial Truck and Tractor Operators, 186, 429

Industrial-Organizational Psychologists, 204, 446

Infantry, 159, 375

Infantry Officers, 159, 375

Information Technology Interest Area, 143–148, 360–364

Information Technology Specialties Work Group, 145–147, 361–364

Instructional Coordinators, 84, 293–294

Insulation Workers, Floor, Ceiling, and Wall, 49, 250

Insulation Workers, Mechanical, 49, 250

Insurance Adjusters, Examiners, and Investigators, 96, 311–312

Insurance Appraisers, Auto Damage, 96, 312

Insurance Claims Clerks, 98, 313

Insurance Policy Processing Clerks, 98, 313–314

Insurance Sales Agents, 100, 315

Insurance Underwriters, 96, 312

Interior Designers, 61, 269

Internists, General, 113, 327

Interpreters and Translators, 58, 266

Interviewers, Except Eligibility and Loan, 142, 359

Irradiated-Fuel Handlers, 186, 429

Janitorial Supervisors, 73, 281

Janitors and Cleaners, Except Maids and Housekeeping Cleaners, 130, 347

Jewelers, 171, 400–401

Job Printers, 173, 407

Judges, Magistrate Judges, and Magistrates, 153, 367

Keyboard Instrument Repairers and Tuners, 68, 276

Kindergarten Teachers, Except Special Education, 86, 294

L

Landscape Architects, 45, 244–245

Landscaping and Groundskeeping Workers, 37, 237

Lathe and Turning Machine Tool Setters, Operators, and Tenders, Metal and Plastic, 164, 382

Laundry and Drycleaning Machine Operators and Tenders, Except Pressing, 177, 414

Law and Public Safety Interest Area, 149–159, 365–376

Law Clerks, 154, 368

Law Enforcement and Public Safety Work Group, 154–156, 369–371

Law Teachers, Postsecondary, 88, 303

Lawn Service Managers, 31, 230–231

Lawyers, 153, 367–368

Lay-Out Workers, Metal and Plastic, 169, 397

Legal Practice and Justice Administration Work Group, 151–153, 367–368

Legal Secretaries, 76, 283

Legal Support Work Group, 153–154, 368

Letterpress Setters and Set-Up Operators, 173, 407

Librarians, 89, 306

Library Assistants, Clerical, 89, 306

Library Science Teachers, Postsecondary, 88, 303

Library Services Work Group, 88–89, 306

Library Technicians, 89, 306

License Clerks, 107, 323

Licensed Practical and Licensed Vocational Nurses, 123, 340

Licensing Examiners and Inspectors, 106, 321

Life Sciences Work Group, 201–202, 444–445

Lifeguards, Ski Patrol, and Other Recreational Protective Service Workers, 157, 372

Loading Machine Operators, Underground Mining, 41, 240–241

Loading, Moving, Hoisting, and Conveying Work Group, 185–186, 428–430

Loan Counselors, 96, 312

Loan Interviewers and Clerks, 99, 314

Loan Officers, 96, 312–313

Locker Room, Coatroom, and Dressing Room Attendants, 128, 345

Locksmiths and Safe Repairers, 180, 419

Locomotive Engineers, 219, 460

Locomotive Firers, 219, 460–461

Lodging Managers, 127, 344

Log Graders and Scalers, 38, 238

Logging Tractor Operators, 38, 239

Logisticians, 77, 284

M

Machine Feeders and Offbearers, 186, 429

Machine Setup and Operation Work Group, 163–165, 378–386

Machinery Repair Work Group, 179–180, 418–420

Machinists, 169, 397–398

Maids and Housekeeping Cleaners, 130, 347

Mail Clerks, Except Mail Machine Operators and Postal Service, 80, 287

Mail Machine Operators, Preparation and Handling, 81, 291

Maintenance and Repair Workers, General, 50, 258

Maintenance Workers, Machinery, 180, 419

Makeup Artists, Theatrical and Performance, 62, 270

Management Analysts, 77, 284

Managerial Work in Agriculture and Natural Resources Work Group, 30–31, 228

Managerial Work in Architecture and Construction Work Group, 43–44, 244

Managerial Work in Arts and Communication Work Group, 54–55, 263–264

Managerial Work in Business Detail Work Group, 71–73, 280–281

Managerial Work in Education Work Group, 83–84, 293–294

Managerial Work in Finance and Insurance Work Group, 94–95, 310

Managerial Work in General Business Work Group, 70–71, 279–280

Managerial Work in Government and Public Administration Work Group, 102–103, 324

Managerial Work in Hospitality and Tourism Work Group, 126–127, 343–344

Managerial Work in Information Technology Work Group, 144–145, 361

Managerial Work in Law and Public Safety Work Group, 150–151, 366

Managerial Work in Manufacturing Work Group, 162–163, 378

Managerial Work in Medical and Health Services Work Group, 109–110, 326

Managerial Work in Retail/Wholesale Sales and Service Work Group, 188–189, 432–434

Managerial Work in Scientific Research, Engineering, and Mathematics Work Group, 198–199, 441–442

Managerial Work in Transportation Work Group, 214–215, 458–459

Manicurists and Pedicurists, 135, 353

Manufactured Building and Mobile Home Installers, 49, 250

Manufacturing Interest Area, 160–186, 377–430

Mapping Technicians, 212, 455

Marine Architects, 209, 451

Marine Cargo Inspectors, 106, 321

Marine Engineers, 209, 451

Market Research Analysts, 96, 313

Marketing Managers, 189, 433

Marking and Identification Printing Machine Setters and Set-Up Operators, 173, 407–408

Marking Clerks, 80, 287

Marriage and Family Therapists, 138, 355

Massage Therapists, 121, 337

Materials Engineers, 209, 451

Materials Inspectors, 172, 403

Materials Scientists, 201, 443

Mates—Ship, Boat, and Barge, 220, 462

Mathematical Clerical Support Work Group, 77–78, 285–286

Mathematical Science Teachers, Postsecondary, 88, 303

Mathematical Technicians, 207, 448

Mathematicians, 207, 448–449

Mathematics and Data Analysis Work Group, 205–207, 448–449

Meat, Poultry, and Fish Cutters and Trimmers, 166, 390–391

Mechanical Door Repairers, 180, 419

Mechanical Drafters, 212, 455

Mechanical Engineering Technicians, 212, 455–456

Mechanical Engineers, 209, 451–452

Mechanical Inspectors, 106, 321–322

Media Technology Work Group, 65–66, 272–275

Medical and Clinical Laboratory Technicians, 120, 334–335

Medical and Clinical Laboratory Technologists, 120, 335

Medical and Health Services Managers, 110, 326

Medical and Public Health Social Workers, 138, 355–356

Medical and Technical Equipment Repair Work Group, 182–183, 424–425

Medical Appliance Technicians, 171, 401

Medical Assistants, 112, 327

Medical Equipment Preparers, 119, 335

Medical Equipment Repairers, 183, 424–425

Medical Records and Health Information Technicians, 120, 335

Medical Scientists, Except Epidemiologists, 202, 445

Medical Secretaries, 76, 283

Medical Technology Work Group, 118–120, 334–336

Medical Therapy Work Group, 120–121, 336–339

© 2006 JIST Works

Medical Transcriptionists, 113, 327–328

Medicine and Surgery Work Group, 110–113, 326–330

Meeting and Convention Planners, 73, 281

Mental Health and Substance Abuse Social Workers, 138, 356

Mental Health Counselors, 138, 356

Merchandise Displayers and Window Trimmers, 60, 269

Metal Fabricators, Structural Metal Products, 168, 395

Metal Molding, Coremaking, and Casting Machine Operators and Tenders, 164, 382

Metal Molding, Coremaking, and Casting Machine Setters and Set-Up Operators, 164, 382

Metal-Refining Furnace Operators and Tenders, 166, 391

Meter Mechanics, 50, 258

Meter Readers, Utilities, 80, 287–288

Microbiologists, 202, 445

Middle School Teachers, Except Special and Vocational Education, 86, 294

Military Work Group, 158–159, 373–376

Milling and Planing Machine Setters, Operators, and Tenders, Metal and Plastic, 164, 383

Millwrights, 180, 419

Mine Cutting and Channeling Machine Operators, 41, 241

Mining and Drilling Work Group, 39–41, 239–242

Mining and Geological Engineers, Including Mining Safety Engineers, 33, 233

Mixing and Blending Machine Setters, Operators, and Tenders, 166, 391

Mobile Heavy Equipment Mechanics, Except Engines, 182, 423

Model and Mold Makers, Jewelry, 171, 401

Model Makers, Metal and Plastic, 169, 398

Model Makers, Wood, 176, 413

Models, 194, 437

Mold Makers, Hand, 175, 412

Molding and Casting Workers, 175, 412

Motion Picture Projectionists, 128, 345

Motor Vehicle Inspectors, 106, 322

Motorboat Mechanics, 182, 423

Motorboat Operators, 220, 461

Motorcycle Mechanics, 182, 423

Multi-Media Artists and Animators, 66, 273–274

Multiple Machine Tool Setters, Operators, and Tenders, Metal and Plastic, 165, 383

Municipal Clerks, 107, 323–324

Municipal Fire Fighters, 158, 373

Municipal Fire Fighting and Prevention Supervisors, 151, 366

Museum Technicians and Conservators, 91, 307

Music Arrangers and Orchestrators, 63, 271

Music Directors, 63, 271

Music Work Group, 62–63, 271–272

Musical Instrument Repair Work Group, 67–68, 276–277

Musicians, Instrumental, 63, 271–272

N

Nannies, 141, 358

Natural Sciences Managers, 199, 441–442

Network and Computer Systems Administrators, 145, 361

Network Systems and Data Communications Analysts, 147, 363–364

New Accounts Clerks, 99, 314–315

News, Broadcasting, and Public Relations Work Group, 57–58, 265–267

Nonelectrolytic Plating and Coating Machine Operators and Tenders, Metal and Plastic, 166, 391

Nonelectrolytic Plating and Coating Machine Setters and Set-Up Operators, Metal and Plastic, 165, 383

Nonfarm Animal Caretakers, 118, 333

Nuclear Engineers, 209, 452

Nuclear Equipment Operation Technicians, 205, 447–448

Nuclear Medicine Technologists, 120, 335

Nuclear Monitoring Technicians, 106, 322

Nuclear Power Reactor Operators, 184, 426–427

Numerical Control Machine Tool Operators and Tenders, Metal and Plastic, 169, 398

Numerical Tool and Process Control Programmers, 169, 398

Nursery and Greenhouse Managers, 31, 231

Nursery Workers, 37, 237

Nursery, Groundskeeping, and Pest Control Work Group, 36–37, 237–238

Nursing Aides, Orderlies, and Attendants, 123, 340

Nursing Instructors and Teachers, Postsecondary, 88, 304

O

Obstetricians and Gynecologists, 113, 328

Occupational Health and Safety Specialists, 106, 322

Occupational Therapist Aides, 121, 337

Occupational Therapist Assistants, 121, 337

Occupational Therapists, 121, 337

Office Clerks, General, 80, 288

Office Machine and Cash Register Servicers, 148, 364

Offset Lithographic Press Setters and Set-Up Operators, 173, 408

Operating Engineers, 49, 250–251

Operations Research Analysts, 77, 284

Optical Instrument Assemblers, 171, 401

Opticians, Dispensing, 120, 336

Optometrists, 116, 332

Oral and Maxillofacial Surgeons, 114, 331

Order Clerks, 196, 439

Order Fillers, Wholesale and Retail Sales, 80, 288

Ordinary Seamen and Marine Oilers, 220, 462

Orthodontists, 114, 331

Orthotists and Prosthetists, 120, 336

Other Services Requiring Driving Work Group, 220–222, 463–464

Outdoor Power Equipment and Other Small Engine Mechanics, 181, 423

P–Q

Packaging and Filling Machine Operators and Tenders, 166, 391

Packers and Packagers, Hand, 186, 429–430

Painters and Illustrators, 59, 267

Painters, Construction and Maintenance, 49, 251

Painters, Transportation Equipment, 175, 412

Painting, Coating, and Decorating Workers, 175, 412

Pantograph Engravers, 173, 408

Paper Goods, Machine Setters, Operators, and Tenders, 164, 383

Paperhangers, 49, 251

Paralegals and Legal Assistants, 154, 368

Park Naturalists, 31, 231

Parking Enforcement Workers, 156, 370

Parking Lot Attendants, 221, 464

Parts Salespersons, 192, 435

Paste-Up Workers, 173, 408

Patient Care and Assistance Work Group, 121–123, 339–340

Patternmakers, Metal and Plastic, 169, 398

Patternmakers, Wood, 176, 413

Paving, Surfacing, and Tamping Equipment Operators, 49, 251

Payroll and Timekeeping Clerks, 78, 286

Pediatricians, General, 113, 328

Percussion Instrument Repairers and Tuners, 68, 276–277

Personal and Home Care Aides, 141, 358–359

Personal Financial Advisors, 100, 315–316

Personal Soliciting Work Group, 192–194, 436–437

Personnel Recruiters, 74, 282

Pest Control Workers, 37, 237

Pesticide Handlers, Sprayers, and Applicators, Vegetation, 37, 237

Petroleum Engineers, 33, 233

Petroleum Pump System Operators, 184, 427

Petroleum Refinery and Control Panel Operators, 184, 427

Pewter Casters and Finishers, 171, 401

Pharmacists, 113, 328

Pharmacy Aides, 112, 328

Pharmacy Technicians, 112, 329

Philosophy and Religion Teachers, Postsecondary, 88, 304

Photoengravers, 173, 408

Photoengraving and Lithographing Machine Operators and Tenders, 173, 408–409

Photographers, Scientific, 205, 448

Photographic Hand Developers, 66, 274

Photographic Processing Machine Operators, 173, 409

Photographic Reproduction Technicians, 66, 274

Photographic Retouchers and Restorers, 66, 274

Physical Science Laboratory Technology Work Group, 204–205, 447–448

Physical Sciences Work Group, 199–201, 442–443

Physical Therapist Aides, 121, 337–338

Physical Therapist Assistants, 121, 338

Physical Therapists, 121, 338

Physician Assistants, 113, 329

Physicists, 201, 443

Physics Teachers, Postsecondary, 88, 304

Pile-Driver Operators, 49, 251

Pilots, Ship, 220, 462

Pipe Fitters, 49, 251–252

Pipelayers, 49, 252

Pipelaying Fitters, 49, 252

Plant Scientists, 33, 233

Plasterers and Stucco Masons, 49, 252

Plastic Molding and Casting Machine Operators and Tenders, 166, 391–392

Plastic Molding and Casting Machine Setters and Set-Up Operators, 164, 383

Plate Finishers, 173, 409

Platemakers, 173, 409

Plumbers, 49, 252

Podiatrists, 116, 332

Poets and Lyricists, 56, 265

Police Detectives, 156, 370

Police Identification and Records Officers, 156, 370

Police Patrol Officers, 156, 370–371

Police, Fire, and Ambulance Dispatchers, 67, 276

Political Science Teachers, Postsecondary, 88, 304

Political Scientists, 204, 446

Postal Service Clerks, 80, 288

Postal Service Mail Carriers, 221, 464

Postal Service Mail Sorters, Processors, and Processing Machine Operators, 80, 288

Postmasters and Mail Superintendents, 215, 458

Postsecondary and Adult Teaching and Instructing Work Group, 86–88, 296–306

Potters, 59, 267

Pourers and Casters, Metal, 166, 392

Power Distributors and Dispatchers, 184, 427

Power Generating Plant Operators, Except Auxiliary Equipment Operators, 184, 427

Precision Device Inspectors and Testers, 172, 403–404

Precision Dyers, 177, 414

Precision Etchers and Engravers, Hand or Machine, 173, 409

Precision Lens Grinders and Polishers, 171, 401–402

Precision Mold and Pattern Casters, Except Nonferrous Metals, 171, 402

Precision Pattern and Die Casters, Nonferrous Metals, 171, 402

Precision Printing Workers, 173, 410

Preschool Teachers, Except Special Education, 86, 294–295

Preschool, Elementary, and Secondary Teaching and Instructing Work Group, 84–86, 294–296

Press and Press Brake Machine Setters and Set-Up Operators, Metal and Plastic, 164, 384

Pressers, Delicate Fabrics, 177, 414

Pressers, Hand, 177, 414–415

Pressing Machine Operators and Tenders—Textile, Garment, and Related Materials, 166, 392

Pressure Vessel Inspectors, 106, 322

Printing Press Machine Operators and Tenders, 173, 410

Private Detectives and Investigators, 157, 372

Private Sector Executives, 71, 279–280

Probation Officers and Correctional Treatment Specialists, 138, 356

Procurement Clerks, 80, 288–289

Producers, 55, 263

Product Safety Engineers, 210, 452–453

Production Helpers, 166, 392

Production Inspectors, Testers, Graders, Sorters, Samplers, Weighers, 172, 404

Production Laborers, 166, 392

Production Machining Technology Work Group, 168–169, 397–399

Production Precision Work Work Group, 169–171, 399–403

Production Quality Control Work Group, 171–172, 403–404

Production Work, Assorted Materials Processing Work Group, 165–166, 386–395

Production, Planning, and Expediting Clerks, 80, 289

Professional Photographers, 66, 274

Program Directors, 55, 263

Proofreaders and Copy Markers, 98, 314

Property, Real Estate, and Community Association Managers, 189, 433

Prosthodontists, 114, 331

Psychiatric Aides, 123, 340

Psychiatric Technicians, 123, 340

Psychiatrists, 113, 329

Psychology Teachers, Postsecondary, 88, 304–305

Public Address System and Other Announcers, 62, 270–271

Public Administration Clerical Support Work Group, 106–107, 323–324

Public Planning Work Group, 103–104, 318–319

Public Relations Managers, 55, 264

Public Relations Specialists, 58, 266

Public Transportation Inspectors, 223, 465

Pump Operators, Except Wellhead Pumpers, 186, 430

Punching Machine Setters and Set-Up Operators, Metal and Plastic, 164, 384

Purchasing Agents and Buyers, Farm Products, 31, 231

Purchasing Agents, Except Wholesale, Retail, and Farm Products, 195, 437

Purchasing Managers, 189, 433

Purchasing Work Group, 194–195, 437–438

R

Radar and Sonar Technicians, 159, 375–376

Radiation Therapists, 121, 338

Radio and Television Announcers, 62, 271

Radio Mechanics, 179, 417–418

Radio Operators, 66, 274–275

Radiologic Technicians, 120, 336

Radiologic Technologists, 120, 336

Rail Car Repairers, 182, 424

Rail Vehicle Operation Work Group, 218–219, 460–461

Rail Yard Engineers, Dinkey Operators, and Hostlers, 219, 461

Rail-Track Laying and Maintenance Equipment Operators, 49, 252–253

Railroad Conductors and Yardmasters, 215, 458

Railroad Inspectors, 106, 322–323

Railroad Yard Workers, 223, 465

Range Managers, 33, 233–234

Real Estate Brokers, 192, 435

Real Estate Sales Agents, 192, 435–436

Receptionists and Information Clerks, 196, 439

Records and Materials Processing Work Group, 79–80, 286–290

Recreation and Fitness Studies Teachers, Postsecondary, 88, 305

Recreation Workers, 128, 345

Recreational Services Work Group, 127–128, 344–346

Recreational Therapists, 121, 338–339

Recreational Vehicle Service Technicians, 182, 424

Reed or Wind Instrument Repairers and Tuners, 68, 277

Refractory Materials Repairers, Except Brickmasons, 48, 253

Refrigeration Mechanics, 50, 258

Refuse and Recyclable Material Collectors, 186, 430

Registered Nurses, 113, 329

Regulations Enforcement Work Group, 104–106, 319–323

Rehabilitation Counselors, 138, 356–357

Reinforcing Iron and Rebar Workers, 49, 253

Religious Work Work Group, 138–140, 357–358

Reporters and Correspondents, 58, 266–267

Research and Design Engineering Work Group, 207–209, 449–452

Reservation and Transportation Ticket Agents, 130, 347

Residential Advisors, 138, 357

Resource Science/Engineering for Plants, Animals, and the Environment Work Group, 33, 232–234

Resource Technologies for Plants, Animals, and the Environment Work Group, 33–35, 234–236

Respiratory Therapists, 121, 339

Respiratory Therapy Technicians, 121, 339

Retail and Wholesale Sales and Service Interest Area, 187–196, 431–439

Retail Salespersons, 192, 436

Riggers, 48, 253

Rock Splitters, Quarry, 41, 241

Rolling Machine Setters, Operators, and Tenders, Metal and Plastic, 164, 384

Roof Bolters, Mining, 41, 241

Roofers, 49, 253

Rotary Drill Operators, Oil and Gas, 41, 241

Rough Carpenters, 49, 253–254

Roustabouts, Oil and Gas, 41, 241–242

S

Safety and Security Work Group, 156–157, 371–372

Sales Agents, Financial Services, 100, 316

Sales Agents, Securities and Commodities, 100, 316

Sales Engineers, 191, 434

Sales Managers, 189, 433–434

Sales Representatives, Agricultural, 191, 434

Sales Representatives, Chemical and Pharmaceutical, 191, 434

Sales Representatives, Electrical/Electronic, 191, 434

Sales Representatives, Instruments, 191, 434–435

Sales Representatives, Mechanical Equipment and Supplies, 191, 435

Sales Representatives, Medical, 191, 435

Sales Representatives, Wholesale and Manufacturing, Except Technical and Scientific Products, 192, 436

Sawing Machine Operators and Tenders, 166, 392–393

Sawing Machine Setters and Set-Up Operators, 165, 384

Sawing Machine Tool Setters and Set-Up Operators, Metal and Plastic, 165, 384–385

Scanner Operators, 173, 410

Scientific Research, Engineering, and Mathematics Interest Area, 197–212, 440–456

Screen Printing Machine Setters and Set-Up Operators, 165, 385

Sculptors, 59, 267–268

Secondary School Teachers, Except Special and Vocational Education, 86, 295

Secretarial Support Work Group, 74–76, 282–283

Secretaries, Except Legal, Medical, and Executive, 76, 283

Security and Fire Alarm Systems Installers, 49, 254

Security Guards, 157, 372

Segmental Pavers, 49, 254

Self-Enrichment Education Teachers, 88, 305

Semiconductor Processors, 171, 402

Separating, Filtering, Clarifying, Precipitating, and Still Machine Setters, Operators, and Tenders, 166, 393

Septic Tank Servicers and Sewer Pipe Cleaners, 52, 261

Service Station Attendants, 192, 436

Service Unit Operators, Oil, Gas, and Mining, 41, 242

Set Designers, 61, 269–270

Sewers, Hand, 175, 412–413

Sewing Machine Operators, Garment, 166, 393

Sewing Machine Operators, Non-Garment, 166, 393

Shampooers, 135, 353

Shear and Slitter Machine Setters and Set-Up Operators, Metal and Plastic, 165, 385

Sheet Metal Workers, 49, 254

Sheriffs and Deputy Sheriffs, 156, 371

Ship and Boat Captains, 220, 462–463

Ship Carpenters and Joiners, 49, 254

Ship Engineers, 184, 427–428

Shipping, Receiving, and Traffic Clerks, 80, 289

Shoe and Leather Workers and Repairers, 177, 415

Shoe Machine Operators and Tenders, 166, 393

Shop and Alteration Tailors, 177, 415

Shuttle Car Operators, 41, 242

Signal and Track Switch Repairers, 180, 419–420

Silversmiths, 171, 402

Singers, 63, 272

Sketch Artists, 59, 268

Skin Care Specialists, 135, 353

Slaughterers and Meat Packers, 166, 393–394

Slot Key Persons, 128, 345–346

Social and Community Service Managers, 103, 318

Social and Human Service Assistants, 138, 357

Social Science Research Assistants, 207, 449

Social Sciences Work Group, 202–204, 445–447

Social Work Teachers, Postsecondary, 88, 305

Sociologists, 204, 446

Sociology Teachers, Postsecondary, 88, 305

Soil Conservationists, 33, 234

Soil Scientists, 33, 234

Solderers, 168, 395

Soldering and Brazing Machine Operators and Tenders, 168, 396

Soldering and Brazing Machine Setters and Set-Up Operators, 165, 385

Sound Engineering Technicians, 66, 275

Special Education Teachers, Middle School, 86, 295

Special Education Teachers, Preschool, Kindergarten, and Elementary School, 86, 295–296

Special Education Teachers, Secondary School, 86, 296

Special Forces, 159, 376

Special Forces Officers, 159, 376

Speech-Language Pathologists, 121, 339

Sports Work Group, 132–134, 352

Spotters, Dry Cleaning, 177, 415

Statement Clerks, 78, 286

Station Installers and Repairers, Telephone, 50, 258

Stationary Engineers, 184, 428

Statistical Assistants, 207, 449

Statisticians, 207, 449

Stevedores, Except Equipment Operators, 223, 465–466

Stock Clerks, Sales Floor, 80, 289

Stock Clerks—Stockroom, Warehouse, or Storage Yard, 80, 289–290

Stone Cutters and Carvers, 49, 254

Stone Sawyers, 166, 394

Stonemasons, 49, 255

Storage and Distribution Managers, 215, 458–459

Stringed Instrument Repairers and Tuners, 68, 277

Strippers, 173, 410

Structural Iron and Steel Workers, 49, 255

Studio Art Work Group, 58–59, 267–268

Substance Abuse and Behavioral Disorder Counselors, 138, 357

Subway and Streetcar Operators, 219, 461

Surgeons, 113, 329–330

Surgical Technologists, 112, 330

Survey Researchers, 96, 313

Surveying Technicians, 212, 456

Surveyors, 47, 246

Switchboard Operators, Including Answering Service, 81, 291

Systems and Equipment Installation, Maintenance, and Repair Work Group, 49–50, 256–259

T

Talent Directors, 63, 272

Tank Car, Truck, and Ship Loaders, 186, 430

Tapers, 49, 255

Tax Examiners, Collectors, and Revenue Agents, 106, 323

Tax Preparers, 78, 286

Taxi Drivers and Chauffeurs, 221, 464

Teacher Assistants, 86, 296

Team Assemblers, 166, 394

Technical Directors/Managers, 55, 264

Technical Sales Work Group, 189–191, 434–435

Technical Writers, 56, 265

Telecommunications Facility Examiners, 50, 258–259

Telecommunications Line Installers and Repairers, 50, 259

Telemarketers, 194, 437

Tellers, 99, 315

Terrazzo Workers and Finishers, 49, 255

Textile Bleaching and Dyeing Machine Operators and Tenders, 166, 394

Textile Cutting Machine Setters, Operators, and Tenders, 165, 385–386

Textile Knitting and Weaving Machine Setters, Operators, and Tenders, 165, 386

Textile Winding, Twisting, and Drawing Out Machine Setters, Operators, and Tenders, 165, 386

Tile and Marble Setters, 49, 255

Timing Device Assemblers, Adjusters, and Calibrators, 171, 402–403

Tire Builders, 166, 394

Tire Repairers and Changers, 181, 424

Title Examiners and Abstractors, 154, 368

Title Searchers, 154, 368

Tool and Die Makers, 169, 398–399

Tool Grinders, Filers, and Sharpeners, 169, 399

Tour Guides and Escorts, 130, 347

Tractor-Trailer Truck Drivers, 218, 459–460

Traffic Technicians, 223, 466

Train Crew Members, 223, 466

Training and Development Managers, 71, 280

Training and Development Specialists, 74, 282

Transformer Repairers, 179, 418

Transit and Railroad Police, 156, 371

Transportation Attendants, Except Flight Attendants and Baggage Porters, 130, 348

Transportation Managers, 215, 459

Transportation Support Work Work Group, 222–223, 464–466

Transportation, Distribution, and Logistics Interest Area, 213–224, 457–466

Travel Agents, 130, 348

Travel Clerks, 130, 348

Travel Guides, 130, 348

Treasurers, Controllers, and Chief Financial Officers, 95, 310

Tree Trimmers and Pruners, 37, 237–238

Truck Drivers, Heavy, 218, 460

Truck Drivers, Light or Delivery Services, 218, 460

Truck Driving Work Group, 216–218, 459–460

Typesetting and Composing Machine Operators and Tenders, 173, 410–411

U–V

Umpires, Referees, and Other Sports Officials, 134, 352

Upholsterers, 177, 415

Urban and Regional Planners, 104, 318–319

Ushers, Lobby Attendants, and Ticket Takers, 128, 346

Utility Operation and Energy Distribution Work Group, 183–184, 425–428

Valve and Regulator Repairers, 180, 420

Vehicle and Facility Mechanical Work Work Group, 180–182, 420–424

Veterinarians, 118, 333

Veterinary Assistants and Laboratory Animal Caretakers, 118, 333

Veterinary Technologists and Technicians, 118, 333–334

Vocational Education Teachers, Middle School, 86, 296

Vocational Education Teachers, Postsecondary, 88, 305–306

Vocational Education Teachers, Secondary School, 86, 296

W–Z

Waiters and Waitresses, 132, 351–352

Watch Repairers, 183, 425

Water and Liquid Waste Treatment Plant and System Operators, 184, 428

Water Vehicle Operation Work Group, 219–220, 461–463

Weighers, Measurers, Checkers, and Samplers, Recordkeeping, 80, 290

Welder-Fitters, 168, 396

Welders and Cutters, 168, 396

Welders, Production, 168, 396

Welding Machine Operators and Tenders, 168, 396–397

Welding Machine Setters and Set-Up Operators, 168, 397

Welding, Brazing, and Soldering Work Group, 167–168, 395–397

Welfare Eligibility Workers and Interviewers, 142, 359

Well and Core Drill Operators, 41, 242

Wellhead Pumpers, 41, 242

Wholesale and Retail Buyers, Except Farm Products, 195, 437–438

Woodworking Machine Operators and Tenders, Except Sawing, 166, 394–395

Woodworking Machine Setters and Set-Up Operators, Except Sawing, 165, 386

Woodworking Technology Work Group, 175–176, 413

Word Processors and Typists, 81, 291

Writing and Editing Work Group, 55–56, 264–265

Zoologists and Wildlife Biologists, 33, 234

© 2006 JIST Works

GOSHEN PUBLIC LIBRARY

3 9531 00166 7392

R
331.702   Farr, J. Michael
FAR   New guide for
4th.ed.   occupational
               exploration

FOR REFERENCE

Do Not Take From This Room